The Best of 2600

A Hacker Odyssey

Emmanuel Goldstein

Wiley Publishing, Inc.

The Best of *2600*: A Hacker Odyssey

Published by
Wiley Publishing, Inc.
10475 Crosspoint Boulevard
Indianapolis, IN 46256
www.wiley.com

Published simultaneously in Canada

ISBN: 978-0-470-29419-2

Manufactured in the United States of America

10 9 8 7 6 5 4 3 2 1

Library of Congress Cataloging-in-Publication Data:

Goldstein, Emmanuel, 1959-

The best of 2600 : a hacker odyssey / Emmanuel Goldstein.

p. cm.

Includes bibliographical references and index.

ISBN 978-0-470-29419-2 (cloth)

1. Computer security—History. 2. Computer crimes—History. 3. Computer hackers—History. 4. Telecommunication—Security measures—History. 5. Wiretapping—History. I. 2600. II. Title. III. Title: Best of 2,600.

QA76.9.A25G643 2008

005.8—dc22

2008018567

2

This book, and all of the articles contained herein, is dedicated to anyone who has in any way proclaimed themselves "different from the rest" and has had the courage to stand up against the forces of sameness which pervade our world. You have always been my inspiration.

About the Author

Emmanuel Goldstein (emmanuel@goldste.in) has been publishing *2600 Magazine, The Hacker Quarterly,* since 1984. He traces his hacker roots to his high school days in the late '70s, when he first played with a distant computer over high-speed, 300-baud phone lines. It didn't take long for him to get into trouble by figuring out how to access something he wasn't supposed to access. He continued playing with various machines in his college days at the State University of New York at Stony Brook. This resulted in an FBI raid as he once again gained access to something he really shouldn't have. It was in the midst of all of this excitement that he cofounded *2600 Magazine*, an outlet for hacker stories and tutorials from all over the world. The rapid growth and success of the magazine was both shocking and scary to Goldstein, who to this day has never taken a course in computers. Since 1988, he has also hosted *Off The Hook*, a hacker-themed technology talk show on WBAI 99.5 FM in New York City. In addition to making the hacker documentary *Freedom Downtime*, Goldstein hosts the Hackers On Planet Earth (HOPE) conferences in New York City every two years, drawing thousands of hackers from all over the world.

You can contact *2600* online at www.2600.com or by writing to *2600 Magazine*, P.O. Box 752, Middle Island, NY, 11953.

Credits

Executive Editor
Carol Long

Development Editor
Maureen Spears

Production Editor
Elizabeth Ginns Britten

Copy Editors
Kim Cofer
Mildred Sanchez

Editorial Manager
Mary Beth Wakefield

Production Manager
Tim Tate

Vice President and Executive Group Publisher
Richard Swadley

Vice President and Executive Publisher
Joseph B. Wikert

Project Coordinator, Cover
Lynsey Stanford

Compositor
Chris Gillespie,
Happenstance Type-O-Rama

Proofreader
Sossity Smith

Indexer
Jack Lewis

Cover Image
©Toledano/Stone+/Getty Images

Cover Designer
Michael E. Trent

Acknowledgments

This is far and away the toughest part of the book to write. How do I sum up in words what so many people have meant over so many years? I'll undoubtedly forget someone, they'll notice, words will be exchanged, and new enemies for life will be formed. It's a painful yet necessary part of the process.

From the beginning there have been people who have been there to encourage me in various endeavors, *2600* included. And there have also been those who have actively sought to discourage me and painstakingly point out the many errors of my ways. I would like to thank each of these groups equally. The former gave me the positive reinforcement that helped convince me that this was all worth it and that it would eventually have a beneficial and lasting effect. The latter gave me the obstinacy and unmitigated wrath to prove them wrong. A positive outlook fueled by anger is really all you need to succeed in this world.

On to specifics. First, I must thank three people who helped me wade through well more than 1,000 articles to sort out the ones that would eventually appear here: Tony Fannin, Mike McTeague, and Kevin Reilly. It was a mountain of material, but I managed to scale it successfully thanks to their help. The many people at Wiley who dealt with our rather unconventional way of piecing together a book deserve particular thanks, especially Carol Long and Maureen Spears. The hard work of my agent, Cameron McClure, made this all come together with remarkable speed and clarity.

My cofounder, Dave Ruderman, deserves special gratitude for coming up with the name "2600"—which I initially hated—way back in 1983. Those late nights of plotting and scheming are among my most favorite memories on this planet. My good friend Dave Buchwald defies any sort of description. He's done everything from office management to cover design and is somehow able to come up with new skills overnight like some sort of power computer. We've also been blessed with some truly talented layout artists over the years—Ben Sherman, Scott Skinner, Terrence McGuckin, and Mark Silverberg—all of whom I'm honored to call my friends. And without Mary Nixdorf, our office manager, *2600* would last about a day. Her incredible dedication and attention to detail make the whole enterprise function smoothly—a feat that people to this day tell me is impossible. Our previous office managers (Pete Kang and Fran Westbrook) also got us through some vital periods of our growth. People like Mike Castleman, Carl Shapiro, Mike Kaegler, Ed Cummings, Rob Nixdorf, Nick Jarecki, Kevin Mitnick, and Mark Abene have always been there to offer encouragement, expertise, and words of advice for all sorts of projects over the years, no matter how crazy they may have actually been.

And some of our projects have been pretty bizarre. And, speaking of bizarre, the magazine covers, T-shirt art, web site work, and various designs for the HOPE conferences, put together by such artists as Frederic Guimont, Holly Kaufman Spruch, Kiratoy, Kerry Zero, Tish Valter, and Affra Gibbs, have been nothing short of eye-opening in every regard.

Oh, yes, the HOPE conferences—how could I forget? Since 1994, we've been holding hacker conferences in New York City called Hackers On Planet Earth, which have drawn thousands of people from all over the globe to the historic Hotel Pennsylvania. And this has all been made possible by a phenomenal volunteer effort, which would take many more pages than I have to adequately acknowledge. Nothing symbolizes the power of the hacker community more than seeing hundreds of people come together to pull off a feat like this every couple of years, a feat which is, of course, impossible. Having these conferences is indeed a real motivation to keep doing what we've been doing. It's one thing to sit back and write stuff from some remote location; it's quite another to actually meet the audience and hear their stories and realize that it all actually matters.

And none of this would have ever been possible (for me, at least) without the creative inspiration that I got from working at a magical place called WUSB, the noncommercial radio station at the college I went to: the State University of New York at Stony Brook. My fondest memories of the station include cohosting the eclectic program "The Voice of Long Island" with my good friend Mike Yuhas back in the early '80s. That place (both the college and the station) taught me so much about diversity and imagination. I was able to steer all of the creative energy from there to the various projects that I became involved in after graduation. I can honestly say that none of this would have ever happened were it not for that initial inspiration. This also led to my involvement with another magical place: WBAI-FM in New York City, a full-power noncommercial station that reaches four states, accepts no corporate money and basically exists to challenge the status quo. (Do I even have to point out how impossible this is as well?) They gave us an outlet for the hacker perspective on technology and *Off The Hook* was thus born. That radio show gave hackers a voice and served as a valuable staging ground for everything from the Free Kevin movement to our defense against the Motion Picture Association of America when they decided to sue us. Particular thanks must go to past program director Andrew Phillips, who recognized this need before even I did.

Three of my very best friends in the world—Walter, Naftali, and Huey—have given me the spirit I needed when I needed it the most. Inspiration also came from family, especially Patricia O'Flanagan, who taught me to think for myself, and Monica Clare, who always makes me remember the value of the small things in life. There are many other relatives who I must also thank for just letting me do my thing without trying too hard to stop me.

Thanks must also go to Mike Tsvitis who printed our magazine for decades and truly helped us achieve levels of excellence we had only dreamed about.

The international community of hackers continues to inspire me every day. Nothing is cooler than going to some far off remote land and discovering that there are people there who are asking the same questions, performing the same experiments, and generally engaging in the same level of mischief as those of us back home; it's just further proof that hacking is a distinct part of the human genome.

And of course, none of any of this would have happened were it not for the many people who have written for *2600* over the years. Even if your work doesn't appear in these pages—for that matter, even if your work hasn't been published in the magazine itself—know that your interest, feedback, and willingness to actually put pen to paper and come up with something different and engaging is the driving force for everything that we've been doing since 1984. I cannot thank all of you enough.

And finally of course, a special thank you to God for not striking me down with a bolt of lightning despite the many requests s/he must get on a daily basis. Respect.

Contents

Introduction

The question we get asked more than any other at *2600* is how in the world did we pull this off? Meaning, I suppose, how did we manage to not only put out a magazine for nearly a quarter century that was written by hackers but also to get the mainstream public to take an interest in our subject matter?

Well, it certainly wasn't easy. I guess the first thing to make clear—and probably the one fact that both those who love us and those who hate us can agree upon—is that it was never supposed to get this big. When we first started out in 1984, we never envisioned it going beyond a few dozen people tied together in a closely knit circle of conspiracy and mischief. Those first issues were three sheets of paper with loose leaf holes punched in the sides stuffed into envelopes. In late 1983, we sent messages to a bunch of bulletin board systems (BBSes) that had hacker content on them. In these messages, we invited people to send in self-addressed stamped envelopes and in return they would get a free copy of the premiere edition of our new hacker magazine. I'll never forget the thrill I got from seeing the first responses come in the mail.

As for content, we had grown into an interesting group of storytellers and educators by way of the BBSes. Basically, by logging onto one of these systems, we would be able to find other people who seemed able to string together a sentence or two and either tell an interesting tale of a hacker adventure or explain to someone exactly how a particular computer or phone system worked. This is how the core staff developed. And we always knew there would be more people out there to add to the mix.

For me, this was a natural expression of my various interests fueled by all sorts of inspirations. Computers had fascinated me ever since I first encountered one in my senior year of high school back in 1977. I never was a programmer, and to this day I have never taken any sort of computer course. That would have taken all of the fun out of it. No, for me the computer was the ultimate toy, a device that could spit back all sorts of responses and which had almost endless potential. My main interests, though, were writing and media. I came from a family of writers and my major in college was English, plus I had worked in some capacity on every high school and college publication I encountered. Then there was my involvement in radio. I was lucky enough to stumble upon WUSB at Stony Brook University, a freeform noncommercial radio station where I was encouraged to be creative and alternative in all sorts of different ways. So when you added all of these elements together, the volatile mix that was to become *2600* seemed almost inevitable.

When we mailed that first issue, we didn't know what to expect. Arrest and imprisonment was one possibility that crossed our minds. There was, after all, an investigation underway into some of the people involved in the magazine before we had ever published our first issue—something to do with logging onto computers that didn't belong to them using other people's names. Back then, having a computer was something reserved for very few people. There was no Internet to explore. Apart from the BBSes, the only way to learn about real systems that actually did something was to figure out a way to get connected to them and absorb as much as you could. It was never about being malicious or destructive, although even then we had our hands full fighting that misconception, which was fueled by the mass media. We were a diverse bunch of curious folk, exploring a new universe and sharing our findings with anyone who cared to listen. We were dangerous.

Strange things started to happen after we sent out the first *2600* in mid January of 1984. People started to send in checks for an entire year! Our magazine became the talk of the BBS world and, we would later learn, numerous corporate boardrooms and government agencies. It seemed such a simple idea and yet nobody else was doing it. There had been a newsletter before *2600* known as *TAP*, which had started publishing back in the '70s with the help of Abbie Hoffman and a bunch of Yippies. It was a fun publication but it came out sporadically and eventually stopped altogether in the early '80s. What people saw in *2600* was something previously unheard of in this community: consistency. Every month at the same time we released a new issue. And not only was it consistent, but it actually looked somewhat professional, thanks to my recently acquired job as a typesetter for an unsuspecting local newspaper. It really felt as if everything had come together at just the right time for *2600* to be born.

After the first year, when people started to actually *renew* their subscriptions, we knew we were on to something. The word continued to spread, more writers came out of the woodwork, and the media followed our every move with rapt attention. While technology was booming, it was still very early in the whole computer revolution. We were seen as pioneers, and I quickly became a "computer expert" even though I had never taken a course and wasn't particularly technical. It didn't seem to matter. Any time something happened involving computers or telephones, it was assumed the staff of *2600* knew all about it—that is, if we weren't in fact accused of being responsible for it in the first place!

We expanded from six pages (three double-sided sheets of paper) to eight pages (two really big sheets folded in half) and kept that format until 1987 when we decided to try something new entirely. We became a magazine in the true sense of the word with a color cover and staples and a total of 24 pages. But the workload and expense for this kind of a format quickly began to exceed our resources, so we switched to a quarterly format in 1988 with 48 pages. Shortly after that final format change, we got on the radar of magazine distributors and began to see *2600* show up at newsstands and bookstores! That's when I realized I must have been dreaming, because this was never supposed to happen.

A good deal of the reaction and attention that has surrounded *2600* has occurred because of the almost mystical aura surrounding the world of computer hacking. So why all the fascination with hackers anyway? To understand this you simply have to study the American spirit. Despite what much of the world may think today, Americans cherish individuality and innovation and they simply adore a rebellious spirit. The hacker world could not be defined more accurately than with these words. How many movies have been made where the protagonist breaks the rules and fights a system that doesn't care and doesn't understand? Are we not always cheering for the individual and hoping that they find the truth and blow the whistle? We have only to look at some of our greatest heroes—Benjamin Franklin, Nikola Tesla, Martin Luther King, Jr.—to see that individual thought and a steadfastness of purpose are prized attributes that can often lead to great things. There was a bit of a hacker in all of these great minds.

Of course, Alexander Graham Bell was another of those people that we all look up to, both inside and outside the hacker community. The Bell system was one of the first massive networks to capture the imagination of a type of hacker referred to as a phone phreak. This was what people played with before computers came along, and I have to admit, it's always fascinated me more than most other things. Relatively few people today even know what it used to be like when there was just one telephone network. We were lucky with our timing of *2600* in that it started publishing at the precise time when the Bell system was splitting apart. So we were there to explain how it all worked and also explore all of the new systems that were coming into being at the time. And, as those in charge seemed incapable of designing easy-to-understand methods of making phone calls through alternative companies, we became by default the experts on how to place a simple telephone call and, by extension, how to save money.

This ties in to something else the hacker community has always endorsed: free communications. Back before my time, the early phone phreaks were going around whistling a special frequency into the telephone. The long-distance phone network, upon hearing that particular tone, would then enter a mode where the caller could input all sorts of other tones and route phone calls all over the world. In addition to regular phone numbers, the caller would then be able to access all sorts of internal numbers as well, things that only operators should be able to do. The trick was that the system assumed the caller was an operator, which basically opened an almost unlimited number of doors. This was called blue boxing. Some people used it to avoid expensive long distance charges. Others used it to map out the system and figure out how it all tied together. And the special frequency that started this whole process? Why, 2600 hertz of course!

I actually didn't like the name "2600" at first. I wanted something stupid like "American Technological Journal." I'm forever indebted to those who worked hard to change my mind. "2600" summed it all up. It was all about reaching out and grabbing technology, making it do what you wanted to do, and communicating with people all around the globe. Not to mention the fact that in any alphabetical list of publications, we would always be first. It was a match made in heaven.

Of course, running the magazine itself has been anything *but* heaven. When you deal with material that is—to put it mildly—controversial, you wind up with an impressive number of powerful people who want to see you go down in flames. Our very existence has embarrassed almost every major corporation at some point, resulted in numerous emergency board meetings, and made some people's jobs a bit harder. None of that was our intent, although that's little comfort to those affected. What we've always been primarily interested in doing is simply getting the information out there and watching it grow into something productive. Phone companies have learned not to leave sensitive billing information on computers with default passwords that anyone can access. Credit agencies now actually work to protect all of that data they keep on every one of us. And the people who design secure systems, many of them our readers and sometimes writers, know how to think like hackers, which makes their creations innovative and flexible. I believe we've contributed quite a bit of good to the world of technology and things are better now than they would have been had we never come on the scene. Of course, that doesn't mean there haven't been numerous attempts to put us out of other people's misery. But when someone believes firmly in freedom of speech and full disclosure, it's kind of impossible to shut him up.

What has amazed me the most in the decades that followed is that the interest level has never subsided. Over the years, more and more people have become entranced not only with the technology itself but also with its social implications and overall importance to the future of humanity. It may sound a bit heavy handed but all of this—the development of the Internet, computers being used as printing presses, the prevalence of low-cost or free telecommunications all around the world, the sharing of information and resources—is having a profound impact on the human race in ways that no one from our forefathers to Aristotle could ever have predicted. Somehow we wound up right in the middle of all the turmoil. And just like it felt back in the early days when everything just sort of came together at a particular moment, this feels like the right people are in the right place at the right time to test the system, develop new tools, and keep freedom of speech alive.

The 1980s: In the Beginning

1 Stories and Adventures

One of the true joys of the hacker world is the wealth of firsthand accounts that get shared throughout the community. Everyone has a story and many hackers have a whole treasure trove of them. This is what comes from being an inquisitive bunch with a tendency to probe and explore, all the while asking entirely too many questions. The rest of the world simply wasn't prepared for this sort of thing, a fact that hackers used to their advantage time and again.

In the hacker world, you can have adventures and obtain information on a whole variety of levels, using such methods as social engineering, trashing, or simply communicating and meeting up with each other. All of these methods continue to work to this day. Back in the 1980s, excitement via a keyboard was a fairly new concept but it was catching on pretty fast as personal computers started to become commonplace. It seemed incredible (and still does to me) that you could simply stick your telephone into an acoustic modem, type a few letters on a keyboard, and somehow be communicating with someone in an entirely different part of the country or even another part of the globe. Of course, hackers had already been having all sorts of adventures on telephones for years before this, whether it was through boxing, teleconferencing, or just randomly calling people. And there were also the occasional "real-life" adventures, something hackers were certainly not averse to, contrary to the usual stereotypes of pasty-faced teenagers who feared going outside and interacting with the world. The point is that whenever you got a bunch of bored, curious, and daring individuals together, it didn't really matter what the setting was. On the screen, over the phone, or in real life, there was fun to be had and plenty to be learned in the process.

Tales from the Distant Past

Something that is true in any community of forward thinkers is the desire to learn about the past. In our early years, most of those stories had to do with telephone-related material from years and decades past. The two examples that follow rewind to the middle of the 20th century when phones and communications were radically different than what they had become in the 1980s. While the technology may have become obsolete, the interest in how telephones shaped our world remained strong—regardless of the era.

A Story of Eavesdropping (April, 1986)

Everybody knows an old man who was in the Second World War and has plenty of war stories to tell. Well sometimes it pays to take the time to listen.

We knew that the enemy was monitoring all of our international radiotelephone channels, despite the sophisticated voice-scramblers which "inverted" speech, making high tones into low ones and vice versa. Only authorized persons were permitted to use overseas telephone circuits.

We were equipped with elaborate recorders and switching control boxes which permitted us to cut off either side of a conversation, or to substitute ourselves for either party. A strict set of rules forbade us to permit maritime information, weather reports, cargo information, etc. to pass over the circuits.

Influences in Washington sometimes resulted in orders issued to us to permit use of the overseas telephone circuits, even though we were suspicious of previous conversations because parables and unusual phrases often used, made it difficult to follow what was being said. "How can we monitor carefully, when we can't understand what they're saying?" went unheeded.

We caught one fellow red-handed in South America using weird terms like "birds leaving the nest with a basket of eggs." I finally cut in the circuit and told him I'd forgotten what they meant. He tried a couple of other phrases, which I also couldn't understand. Finally, he lost his patience and blurted out, "Oh hell. I'm talking about those special munition orders which left yesterday for Germany."

By this time, a special telephone speech scrambler had been developed which was small enough to fit and use on a desk. Its availability was extremely limited, but a couple of army officers—one in the U.S. and the other in Panama—had been able to get hold of a pair of them, and between them secretly installed them on their desks, unbeknownst to us of course!

One day I heard the fellow in Panama say, "OK Joe, now over to the scrambler," and their ensuing conversation became unintelligible. We quickly checked the radio telephone circuit equipment and discovered that the technical characteristics of the equipment they were using and our own were identical. As a result, when they inserted their scramblers the speech inversion righted itself and their conversations went out over the radiotelephone circuit in clear language—readable by anyone! That was the end of the use of their private "secret conversation system."

Some of the worst offenders of overseas telephone use security were the top people. I'll have to list Generals Eisenhower and Marshall as two of them—at least sometimes. I can remember one day the circuit between London and Washington happened to be very poor in quality and "understandability" was stretched to the utmost.

General Marshall in Washington had General Eisenhower on the line in London who couldn't understand a word of what Marshall was saying. Marshall repeated several times "Ike, this is GCM—Marshall—GCM—got it?" without results. Finally in frustration Marshall turned to an aide and could be plainly heard to say "What's the code word for my name?"

The next thing we knew, Marshall was slowly and distinctly repeating his code name interspersed with "GCM" and "Marshall." Of course, we had to cut the circuit and notify the code group in Washington to immediately "bust" the code—we couldn't take any chances—revelation of the code word for his name might have been all the enemy intelligence was waiting for to help it "code-break" other communications.

On the other hand, President Roosevelt and Prime Minister Churchill were two of the best and easiest to monitor. Both used references to previously transmitted overheard messages by numbers and most of the conversations were along the lines: "Well Winnie, on number 528, I really don't think we should do that—you know how they are." Nobody could gain any information from listening to their telephone conversations.

I always enjoyed listening to Sir Winston originating a call. The British telephone operators were required on *every* connection to announce in advance of a conversation: "You are warned not to mention the names of vessels, sailing dates or conditions, cargoes, weather, etc., etc., etc., any violation on your part will result in the circuit being cut off and your action being reported to the highest authority. Do you understand?" Sir Winston always dociley replied. "Yes ma'am. I understand."

One enemy group had learned the "language" of speech inversion. For example, listening on the air to a radiotelephone circuit, one might hear a word that sounded exactly like *krinkanope*. That was the word *telephone* after it had passed through the speech inversion system!

The First Atomic Bomb: A True Tale (March, 1984)

This story was originally related by Laura Fermi, widow of the nuclear physicist Enrico Fermi who, along with assorted colleagues, participated in the first test bomb in the desert outside Alamogordo, New Mexico, in the early morning hours of a summer day in July 1945.

When the date had been established for the secret test, staff members from the Manhattan Project (as the secret test was known) were invited to bring their spouses to New Mexico to watch the results of the several years of research. Each staff member had been assigned specific tasks to handle while there. Generally, they acted as observers and were stationed in a circle around the perimeter of the bomb site. Enrico and Laura were stationed in an area about twenty miles to the southwest of the bomb site.

The morning came when the bomb was scheduled to be detonated in the test. Laura told it like this…

Enrico and I woke up at 3:00 a.m., to go to the site. The test was scheduled for 4:30 a.m. that day, which was July 19, 1945. We drove to our post, about twenty miles from the site. It had been arranged that the nearly 100 of us present would be located in a circle about 100 miles in circumference surrounding the bomb site. We were all to be in communication with each other over telephones, all of which were connected through the exchange in Alamogordo.

We arrived at the site at 4:15 a.m. and almost immediately it began to rain, quite a heavy, very typical torrential downpour during the summer. We waited in our car, and at 4:30 a.m. the time came and went, but the bomb did not go off. Enrico and I assumed it might have been postponed due to the rainstorm, but decided to check with the other staff members to see for sure. For some reason, the telephone there at the site did not seem to work; the operator would not respond. *(Note: At that time, nearly all phones in the United States, and certainly in New Mexico, were manual. No dialing of any sort was possible—you had to use the operator for everything.)*

Finally Enrico decided that we would drive into town and try to contact the others and see what went wrong. So we drove back to town, and got there about 5:15 a.m. The only place open at that time of night was a hotel, and we stopped in there to use a pay phone. Strangely enough, the pay phone was not working either, or at least the operator never came on the line to ask what we wanted. Enrico was quite curious about all this and decided to investigate. We went outside the hotel, and Enrico found where the telephone wires came off the pole and down into the building. He decided that we would follow the wires, so we walked down the street looking overhead at the wires on the pole as we went along. Finally, we turned down one street and saw a house. The telephone poles and wires from all directions seemed to come down to this house. There must have been hundreds of wires from telephone poles all coming down onto the side of this house and going in through an opening.

We noticed that there was a front porch light, which was on. The front door was open, but there was a screen door, which was closed. We went up on the front porch and looked into the house. A switchboard was there, and there were a dozen or more lights on the switchboard lit, blinking off and on as people were flashing the switch hooks on their phones trying to raise the operator. The room was just dimly lit, and near the switchboard was a sofa, and a woman was laying on the sofa sound asleep! Enrico pounded very loudly on the screen door, and shouted at the woman. Suddenly she opened her eyes and looked at him, very startled. Then she looked at the switchboard. Immediately she sprang up, dashed over to the board, sat down and began frantically answering the calls.

Without saying any more, Enrico and I left, went back to the hotel where our car was parked, and drove back to our monitoring post twenty miles out into the desert. We had been at our post only about five minutes when the explosion went off, at about

6:30 a.m., which was two hours behind schedule. Later, we talked to the other staff members and found that there had been some confusion because of the rain. None of them had been able to reach the others because the telephone operator had fallen asleep, and the phones were not getting answered/connected…

We on the staff all had a big laugh out of it, but nothing more was ever said or done, and I doubt to this day that that woman is even aware that the first atomic explosion in the world was delayed two hours because of her.

Amazing, but true. Alamogordo was a tiny town back in the '40s, and it's very doubtful that the night operator had ever seen so much traffic in her life as the hundred or so people all on the line at once that early morning. More than likely, the poor dear had had a very rough day the day before, in the miserable summer heat, had been unable to sleep during the day, and had come to work that night thoroughly exhausted. She probably decided that "it won't hurt just to close my eyes for a minute…," and the rest of the story is already told. After all, experience had taught her that in fact she would not usually get a dozen calls all night on her shift, and she felt relatively safe in stretching out "just for a minute."

Numbers That Led to Trouble

Having access to telephones and the increasing variety of new uses for them invariably led to all sorts of fun for the average phone phreak. (It was quite common in the hacker world to append a "ph" to any word with an "f" if it had anything at all to do with phones, such as "phreak," "phriend," or "phraud." Sometimes the exact opposite was true, which resulted in the word "fone" popping up every now and then.) Of course, fun in the hacker world usually translated to trouble in the real world, which pretty much summed up where hackers fit in societywise. Our innocence and adventure was always seen as evil and threatening to the uninitiated who couldn't seem to understand what motivated these strange individuals to go and play with phones for hours on end. As a result of our hard work, we would share whatever strange phone numbers we were able to discover with anyone who was interested in hearing about them. Because there weren't as many methods of communication as there are today and because there were significantly less phone numbers floating around, discoveries like the ones that follow seemed to mean a lot more. And then, of course, there was one of the all-time favorite phone phreak pastimes: running a teleconference. The unparalleled pleasure of hooking several dozen of your closest friends together and going on a telephonic voyage around the world was something so few people could even conceive of in the 1980s. And yet, *everyone* in the hacker community had some sort of encounter with teleconferences back then. Some were even rumored to have spent most of the decade connected to one.

The Scariest Number in the World (December, 1984)

Recently, a telephone fanatic in the northwest made an interesting discovery. He was exploring the 804 area code (Virginia) and found out that the 840 exchange did something strange. In the vast majority of cases, in fact in *all* of the cases except one, he would get a recording as if the exchange didn't exist. However, if he dialed 804-840 and four rather predictable numbers, he got a ring!

After one or two rings, somebody picked up. Being experienced at this kind of thing, he could tell that the call didn't "supervise," that is, no charges were being incurred for calling this number. (Calls that get you to an error message, or a special operator, generally don't supe.) A female voice, with a hint of a southern accent said, "Operator, can I help you?"

"Yes," he said. "What number have I reached?"

"What number did you dial, sir?"

He made up a number that was similar.

"I'm sorry, that's not the number you reached." Click.

He was fascinated. What in the world *was* this? He knew he was going to call back, but before he did, he tried some more experiments. He tried the 840 exchange in several other area codes. In some, it came up as a valid exchange. In others, exactly the same thing happened—the same last four digits, the same southern belle. Oddly enough, he later noticed, the areas it worked in seemed to travel in a beeline from Washington D.C. to Pittsburgh, PA.

He called back from a pay phone. "Operator, can I help you?"

"Yes, this is the phone company. I'm testing this line and we don't seem to have an identification on your circuit. What office is this, please?"

"What number are you trying to reach?"

"I'm not trying to reach *any* number. I'm trying to identify this circuit."

"I'm sorry, I can't help you."

"Ma'am, if I don't get an ID on this line, I'll have to disconnect it. We show no record of it here."

"Hold on a moment, sir."

After about a minute, she came back. "Sir, I can have someone speak to you. Would you give me your number, please?"

He had anticipated this and he had the pay phone number ready. After he gave it, she said, "Mr. XXX will get right back to you."

"Thanks." He hung up the phone. It rang. *Instantly*! "Oh my God," he thought, "They weren't asking for my number; they were *confirming* it!"

"Hello," he said, trying to sound authoritative.

"This is Mr. XXX. Did you just make an inquiry to my office concerning a phone number?"

"Yes. I need an identi—"

"What you need is advice. Don't ever call that number again. Don't even think about calling that number again. Forget you ever knew it."

At this point our friend got so nervous he just hung up. He expected to hear the phone ring again but it didn't.

Over the next few days he racked his brains trying to figure out what the number was. He knew it was something big—that was pretty certain at this point. It was so big that the number was programmed into every central office in the country. He knew this because if he tried to dial any other number in that exchange, he'd get a local error message from his CO, as if the exchange didn't exist.

It finally came to him. He had an uncle who worked in a federal agency. He had a feeling that this was government related and if it was, his uncle could probably find out what it was. He asked the next day and his uncle promised to look into the matter.

The next time he saw his uncle, he noticed a big change in his manner. He was trembling. "Where did you get that number?" he shouted. "Do you know I almost got fired for asking about it?! They kept wanting to know where I got it!"

Our friend couldn't contain his excitement. "What is it?" he pleaded. "What's the number?!"

"It's the President's bomb shelter!"

He never called the number after that. He knew that he could probably cause quite a bit of excitement by calling the number and saying something like, "The weather's not good in Washington. We're coming over for a visit." But our friend was smart. He knew that there were some things that were better off unsaid and undone.

(If you have a phone or computer story, call or write us!)

The Truth Behind Those 9999 Numbers (January, 1984)

By Mark Bluebox

Once upon a time, I was talking to one of my favorite friends, one of the nation's oldest and most experienced telephone enthusiasts—some might refer to him as a phone phreak. In this particular conversation, he mentioned to me that I might want to experiment with a series of 800 numbers: exchanges starting with 9, followed by the suffix 9999 (800-9xx-9999). And so I did, and a whole new world began to open up in front of me.

They were mostly weather and time numbers in various locations throughout the country. And, because these were 800 numbers, there was NO CHARGE! One number in particular was of a great deal of interest to me and to many others. This was 800-957-9999, which hooked up to WWV, the radio station operated by the National Bureau of Standards that does nothing but tell the time and give shortwave reports. This is the most accurate clock in the entire world! You either have to tune WWV in on a shortwave receiver or dial 303-499-7111 in Fort Collins, Colorado. Yet, here I was with an 800 access! Being a bit of a shortwave enthusiast, I don't have to tell you how convenient this was for me. Unfortunately, it got too convenient for too many people.

I guess I made the mistake of giving it to a former president of a large amateur radio club in the Dallas area. He, in turn, printed it in the Amateur Radio News Bulletin where thousands of people probably saw it. Another statewide News Bulletin picked it up and printed it. Through an amateur radio news network, which this bulletin was a part of, the news got as far as California.

One day, I called up the West Link Amateur Radio News Service at 213-768-7333. (This is a service located in West Link, California that broadcasts news over amateur radio, VHF, UHF, etc.) Their latest report had this little item: "Speaking of interesting things, the National Bureau of Standards has got a very convenient time number for those of you that are not constantly at a shortwave receiver. You can dial 1-800-957-9999 for WWV. It's just another good toll-free service for us to use." The avalanche had really begun now.

The West Link report was heard on bulletin stations all around the world and apparently one station in Nashville, Tennessee, broadcast it. From there it fell into the hands of one of the writers for the DX program on Radio South Africa! I happened to be listening to a program where they were talking about pulling in distant time stations, weather stations, etc. He then mentioned, "For those of you that live in the United States, a convenient toll-free 800 number has been provided by the National Bureau of Standards for WWV and that number is 1-800-957-9999." Imagine my surprise! Once again, the number had been broadcast all around the world. People in many, many nations now had that number. Of course, the number only worked inside the United States, but the word was being spread by shortwave listeners and QSL people everywhere.

The number was getting swamped. Needless to say, it was busy much of the time. A government official, who *also* had this number, thinking that it was legitimate, called up WWV and complained. He told them that they needed to add some more lines to their new 800 number. The general manager of the station said, "I don't know *what* you're talking about. I don't know of any 800 number that gets you WWV."

The government official told him what the telephone number was. The general manager called it and heard his own station. Astounded, he contacted the Mountain Bell Telephone Company in Denver, Colorado. They said, "You're not paying for any 800 in-WATS number. We show 303-499-7111 for WWV, but we don't have any 800-957-9999."

Mountain Bell checked it out and sure enough, the number existed but not on *their* records. No one was getting charged for this! Now, of course, you know a monopoly as well as I do—they're *sure* not going to let anyone have a free ride. So they told the

WATS coordinator to find out what happened. He finally made the discovery that some technicians had hooked that number up for transmission testing. (These switching technicians are toll technicians, AT&T Long Lines switching technicians, and carrier systems technicians. In other words, they're the group of people who link switching centers together, from New York to Los Angeles, for example. In this case, the whole escapade was a kind of group effort. The switchmen and the carrier people got together and set up this number for testing, finding noisy carriers, carriers with cross talk on them, etc.)

The WATS coordinator told them they'd better get this number off—too many people knew about it. He told them to erase *every* 800 test line number that was on the system. Not surprisingly, someone also got chewed out very severely.

So, consequently, 800-957-9999 is no longer in existence. But since then, less than two weeks later, several of the 800 test numbers have begun to defiantly reappear. Check around, you'll probably find a few interesting ones. But I doubt if WWV's brief stint as a toll-free service will ever be repeated.

A True Saga of Teleconferencing (April, 1984) *By Electric Moon*

"God, I wish I had a box." David said. "I can see it now. I bump off information in Wisconsin and get an empty WATS line to play with. I keypunch a few multifrequency operator tones, and ta da! It gives me a conference. But I can't do that anyway, because I'm on ESS."

"David," I responded. "I know this sounds stupid, but I don't understand a word of what you just said. Okay, this is what I know from the conference: With a blue box you make tones of certain pitches, so that the phone thinks you're an operator. That way you can make long-distance calls for free or start a conference."

"Very good."

"But what's ESS?"

"Anyway," David said. "It's easier and safer to use an extender to call long distance than to box."

"*But what's ESS?*" I repeated.

"Okay here we go. The famous Smith briefing for beginning phreaks. Fasten your seatbelts, ladies and gentlemen."

"I resent being called a beginner," I said.

"In the history of our great phone system, Ma Bell has undergone many changes in her youth. She was made up of so-called step-by-step systems. These were lovely and easy to circumvent, but noisy and slow. Also, 2600 Hertz disconnects a step system, so you can't box off of one. Most of these were switched by hand by small-town operators. Then someone came up with crossbar switching, and Ma Bell made little clicking noises all day long as she switched almost automatically.

"But, horror of horrors, Ma Bell finally got old. She grew senile and paranoid. In order not to forget things, she wrote them down. Every time a little customer called a number he shouldn't have known, she wrote up a trouble card on him and filed it neatly away. This system was noiseless and easy. Soon Ma came up with better security measures, longer customer records, and tighter filing cabinets. She buried light-fiber cables, and everyone knows you can't splice two light-fiber cables together. She changed her own phone numbers regularly, and computerized everything. Each change came about slowly, but the final product was ESS. So the main phone systems are step, crossbar, and ESS."

"Which one am I on?" I asked.

"I don't know. Some people can tell by listening to the ring or the busy signal, but I can't," he admitted. "If you can get call-waiting, you're on ESS. Call customer service and ask."

We talked on conferences almost every night for two weeks. Napoleon Bonaparte set them up, and we talked to the Hacker, Cracker, Tom Keevis, and Max Wilke.

I learned a few things from conferences, and a lot from David. He told me about the Michigan loops. Apparently, if I called a certain number, some stranger would pick up the other end and we could talk. How stupid. Then David explained that the other person was calling a phone number too, and we'd get connected somehow. A loop around here was 424-9900 and 424-9901. If I called one end and someone else called the other, we'd be connected. This was useful if we didn't want to give out our phone numbers. In Detroit, lots of people—not only phreaks—know about loops. If you call up one end of a Detroit loop, someone else is likely to call within five minutes.

"You never know who you'll get," David said. "Hacker and I call and wait, and sometimes homosexuals get on and say, 'Looking for guys?' or girls get on and say, 'Guess what color underwear I have on?' But you also get other people—car salesmen, teenagers, and college students—lots of college students."

He gave me some Michigan loop numbers and I started calling them through extenders. I talked to a lot of weird people and a lot of normal people. I also called some pay phones in Berkeley and Carnegie-Mellon, and talked to whoever answered.

The Phreak was my idol. He was the idol of most of the phreaks I knew. Lots agreed that he was the best phreak and hacker (okay, little did we know then). He was only fourteen years old, and lived in Boston.

One day I called up a Michigan loop and heard a lot of static and clicking. I also heard some people talking—mainly two boys. One of them had an unmistakable Boston accent. It was Steve the Phreak.

"Hey Phreak," I said. "This is Electric Moon!"

"Hi Electric," he said. Then he asked his friend, "Should we keep her?"

"Yeah, what the heck!" said the anonymous phreak. A beep signaled the departure of the Phreak.

"Where'd Steve go?" I asked.

"Off to look for more loops, the idiot," said the boy. "It's too loud in here already."

"What's your name?" I asked.

"I'm Ivanhoe. I'm a Steve too, but you can call me George."

"What?"

"To differentiate between me and Phreak."

"I'll just call you Ivanhoe," I said. "Where're you located?"

"I'm in California. I'm seventeen. And you?"

"I'm in Ohio. I'm sixteen. Call me Electric." I suddenly realized I was yelling above the din of the loops. The Phreak kept putting on more and more. The loops themselves made clicks and static, but the people on them made it even worse. They couldn't hear us and they couldn't hear the people on the other loops, so they loudly chatted away.

Every time Ivanhoe or I heard the Phreak beep on or off, we screamed at him to stop adding loops, but he pretended not to notice, and continued at a rate of six or so a minute.

Finally I couldn't take the noise, I yelled a loop number to Ivanhoe, and we ducked out.

"Hello?" asked a quiet, low voice.

"Hi," I panted. "Thank God we're out of that mess."

"Yeah. He'll probably have it up for a few days before they figure it out."

"He's crazy!" I said.

"Yeah, but he knows a lot. He still has a long way to go, though. He has to learn to be careful."

"I know." I tried to act experienced. "Boxing a conference from his home is incredibly stupid."

"Have you heard him on AUTOVON, though? He's a riot, but I'd never do what he does!"

"What does he do?" I asked.

"He'll have to show you," Ivanhoe said.

Click! "Emergency break from G.I. Joe. Will you accept?" asked the operator.

"No," we said in unison. I smiled, imagining the shocked operator. She probably thought his mother was dying.

"No?" she asked uncertainly.

"NO!" we yelled, and laughed as she clicked off again.

"Well," Ivanhoe said, "that must be Phreak. He probably wants me to call him. I'll tell him to start another conference."

"Okay," I said. I hung up the phone and walked into the kitchen. I set my notebook and pencil on the kitchen desk and took a cold apple from the refrigerator. The phone rang as I crunched the first bite.

"Hello?"

"Hi. Anyone you want to add?" asked the Phreak.

"Sure. Add Trader Vic."

"Okay," he said. I heard a beep, silence, then people talking.

"Quiet down, everyone!" Ivanhoe said. "The Phreak is going to show off, but what he's going to do is pretty dangerous."

Beep-beep! Beep-beep! The Phreak had brought Trader Vic on.

"Hey dudes, what's going on?" he asked.

"Shh!" we said.

"You can't hang up on them once they're on a conference," said Ivanhoe.

"If someone suspects what we're doing, we'll have to hang up the whole conference."

The Phreak beeped off. He was back in a minute, talking officiously.

"Yes, I have a Flash Override call for location four-zero-two-niner," he said calmly.

"Flash Override? Who is this, suh?" asked a deep southern accent.

"This is General Watt." The Phreak had to make the guy believe he was a Joint Chief of Staff.

A nasal tenor came on the line, heralded by an amazing overture of clicks, beeps, and tones.

"General, for whom are you placing this call?"

"For Ronald Reagan," said the Phreak. I felt like I had been stabbed. What an idiot! But I couldn't hang up, because the operator would hear the beeps. I listened instead.

"Ronald Reagan?" asked the voice disbelievingly. "Sir, what is the code on this call?"

"I'm at the White House right now," said the Phreak coolly. I knew he was stalling for time as he flipped through stolen AUTOVON manuals. "Sergeant, I have the code right here. I'm at location C-one-four-six-two-D, placing a Flash Override for Timberwolf to location four-zero-two-niner. The operation code is zero-five-zero-niner."

"That is correct," the operator said, and I could have hugged the Phreak. "Please hold, sir, and I'll put your call through."

Beep! Beep!...ker-chunk.

"Andrews Air Force Base," said a woman. "General Hodge is out right now. Should I sound his beeper?"

Silence. What now? Two people spoke at once. Trader Vic broke through loudly.

"Yeah, like, this is a conference call, and we just, like, wanted to see how you were doing, you know?"

"Excuse me?" asked the startled woman.

"I'm sorry," I interrupted quietly. The time had come to try and salvage this thing. "I'm the White House internal operator, and we seem to have given the wrong location identifier. Thank you very much."

The General's secretary clicked off and our nasal operator checked on. "What seems to be the problem, General?" he asked.

"I'm sorry," Ivanhoe said. "The President decided not to make the call after all. Thank you, though."

"Yes sir, thank you," the operator said, and checked off. We held our breaths until we heard the final beep-beep.

"Vic, you idiot!" I cried.

"What?" he asked. "I thought it was pretty funny!"

"Funny, my foot," Ivanhoe said angrily. "That was a stupid thing to say. And Steve, why didn't you answer?"

"My mom called me and I had to go take out the trash," said the Phreak.

"Phreak, you're crazy," I said.

"I know," he said in his deepest Boston accent. "But you all love it."

A week later, the Software Pirate called me and said the Phreak had been caught. I called Ivanhoe, who told me that Steve was visited that morning by three FBI and two Bell Security agents. Ten other people were also caught. The FBI woke all the boys up at 6:00 a.m. so they wouldn't have a chance to warn friends.

As soon as school was over, the Phreak called Ivanhoe and told him all this. He waited an hour until it was 4:00 in Utah and called the Software Pirate, who called me.

The news spread among phreaks and pirates so that anyone involved knew about it by dinnertime on the East Coast.

Late that night, the White Knight set up what we thought was the last conference call. Ivanhoe, David, Demon Diode, and the Cracker all expected they would be caught.

We called the Cracker and asked him to talk.

"Why not?" he said dryly. "I'm just sitting here waiting for the FBI. I have nothing better to do."

They got him the next morning.

(The names and locations used in this story have all been changed, so don't even bother.)

Mischief and Ingenuity

While we like to say that hacking is all about education, that's really only partially true. People often got involved in this little world for no other reason than the fact that it was incredibly fun. Apart from simply impressing those around you with your seemingly superhuman abilities by making pay phones ring back or figuring out someone's phone number without their telling you (which actually *was* a big deal back then), you got to meet some really interesting people and explore technologies that most folks didn't even know existed. So invariably anyone who was drawn into the hacker culture wound up learning an awful lot whether they wanted to or not. But it was mostly the fun of playing with some incredible new toys that got them involved in the first place. And in the end, hackers were able to apply their knowledge to all sorts of practical applications such as in our first story below. Or, as in the case of our trashing adventure, they figured out another way to quench their thirst for knowledge, this time by invading an often ignored part of the "real world." And throughout it all, new bits of information and all sorts of theories were constantly making the rounds concerning the latest discoveries.

A Phone Phreak Scores (April, 1985)

This is another story to add to the annals of social engineering, one that we all can learn from...

A few months ago my Mom had some people refinish and blacktop our driveway. So she called some companies in the phone book, and she chose the cheapest one. They came and did most of the work, and Mom paid them, providing they came back soon to finish the blacktopping job. This all sounded fine, but after several weeks of the company calling up and postponing the final work, Mom wanted it done. She decided to visit the company at the address listed in the phone book, because she would always get an answering machine when she called them, but when she got there, she found out that it was just the back room of a storefront and that the company had vacated it a few months earlier. When she tried calling them, their number had been changed. So I did a CNA on their new number for Mom, and she visited the new address that I got. When Mom got to the new address she found a vacant lot. It was at this point that it started to sound pretty fishy to Mom and I. But how could we find out where they were, if they gave a fake address to the phone company?

That's when it occurred to me to call the business office that handles that company's telephone. I called and they answered: "Your number, please." So I gave them the company's number, and I proceeded to tell them how I did not get my last phone bill, and how I wanted to make sure they were sending it to the right address. They told me the real name and address (not the one at CNA or Directory Assistance, which was the one it was listed under; there is a difference, you know), they asked if I was "Mr. So and So," to which I responded "Yes." Then they asked if I wanted to change the mailing address. I said, "No, that's my partner's address. No need to change it. Thank you."

And that was it. I found their address. Mom visited their new location, which happened to be a trailer in the middle of a big field with a telephone and a power cable going into it. When she found the people at the company, they were quite startled, because it seemed that they did not have a license to do the work that they were doing and had several other customers and some government agencies looking for them. Because Mom had the goods on them, they were obliged to finish our driveway, and that's all Mom wanted after all.

Trashing Alaska Style (February, 1985) *By The GCI Guy*

We left that Friday night with no idea that we would end up at our local CO. A group of computer enthusiasts and I usually go cruise and look for trouble in our car properly named The Lead Sled. It is named this because it is an extremely old Monte Carlo that is painted five different shades of gray.

There was nothing happening on the local drag and that is when I remembered something I had seen on a BBS the night before.

"Let's go trashing," I said with hopes of an answer. But all I got was a grumble from the back seat and a question thrown at me from the driver. I explained to them what trashing was and the whole car seemed to like the idea of looking through someone else's garbage, especially our local CO's.

Now the thing that I really hate about our CO is that they have a "mascot" color, baby blue. They paint their repair trucks, representatives, and main building all this same color.

We carefully turned the engine off when we approached the baby blue monster and coasted behind a group of trees. We had to run about a mile to the dumpsters and I think that this was our biggest mistake. But what can you expect from first time trashers?

The CO has a "protective" fence around their lot. So we picked a small, thin phreaker to slide under the gate. He then dived into the dumpster with a look of triumph in his eyes.

We waited for him to emerge with a bag when suddenly a man in baby blue overalls appeared. I yelled for everyone to blow and that's what we did. The skinny phreaker slid under the fence and we were history.

I ran fast, the fastest I think I ever ran. But with the CO's security guards after you, you had to. We ran back to the Sled but found that it was surrounded by men in baby blue overalls. This is where we made another mistake—we split up, hoping that maybe we wouldn't be caught if we weren't a large group.

"They've been caught!" was the only thing that ran through my mind as I ran for an abandoned shopping mall. Me and about two other phreakers hid out there for about two hours until we thought the coast was clear. But we were wrong.

As we were making our way back to the Sled, we were stopped by a security guard who asked us *a lot* of questions. Luckily we were able to B.S. him. But when we got back to the Sled, it was gone.

I panicked. No Sled, no ride, and no trash. Then suddenly I heard a honk and it was the Sled.

Since that unfortunate experience we have made countless trips to the CO and have retrieved bags and bags of trash. Learn by your mistakes.

An American Express Phone Story (March, 1986) *By Chester Holmes*

This story is a memory of hacking a formidable American institution—American Express. No, not AX's internal telecommunications network, but the corporation's toll-free charge card authorization computer. The following can be safely told as our "system" went down a few years ago.

It all started in the summer of 1982. I had been on the lookout for various extenders and other nifty things a phone could link up with. Most were found by scanning and searching 800 number series using the time-honored "hang-up-if-a-human-answers" technique. After a long and fruitless afternoon of such looking, I decided to take a run on down to the local Chinese eatery as my stomach's contents had been depleted several hours earlier. I wasn't wont on dining there, take out would be fine. Well, as Murphy would predict, my fried rice order wasn't ready at the appointed time, so I found myself at the register with a few moments to kill. Murphy struck again: on the register was a sticker with several 800 numbers and the words "American Express Charge Authorization" emblazoned thereon.

The MSG in Chinese food affects people in a variety of ways. Some folks get rambunctious, but I get sleepy. I told my associate about this number and told him my right index finger was worn down from hours of dialing. He understood and made some discoveries while playing with the system all that night.

If I can recall correctly, when one dialed the number (alas time has erased the number in my brain's RAM), the merchant would be prompted to enter the card number amount etc., and the computer would give an approval code. A *# would abort the procedure at any time and disconnect. Merely pressing ## during the call would get an AX operator. This was accomplished by the system obtaining a dial tone and then automatically touch-toning the four-digit extension. We had our fun harassing the operators, for when they hung up, the dial tone would return but would not automatically dial. We were thus free to make local calls within New York City. We soon tired of this game so instead we developed a method of beating the system's demon dialer. Upon dial-tone receipt, we quickly touch-toned 9958. The first 9 would give us an outside line, and the 958 was the Automatic Number Identification code for New York. The four system-generated digits would then come through and be ignored. This trick saved us from continual arousal of credit-operator suspicion, and the dial tone was returned after AN1 did her thing. We also learned how many different phone numbers they used for this system.

You'll note I said we were free to make local calls. We were able to dial 9-0 to get a Bell operator who was most happy to assist in placing our long-distance calls. For some reason however these operators couldn't help with 900 calls (I got the same operator three times in one night while trying to listen to the space shuttle. We developed a kinship by the last call). The AX PBX would give a stern warning if we tried to dial a long-distance call directly ("Class of Service Restriction Class of Service Restriction"), but we soon outsmarted it: it wasn't looking for a 1+NPA etc. but had a timer going and if you dialed more than eight digits (9+ etc.) in a period of about five seconds you'd get that message. So we dialed the first few digits, paused dialed the remainder, and the call went through (even to the space shuttle).

Connections were generally less than optimum (in fact they sucked) but if you and your called party were in quiet rooms, you could talk for hours. Another minor annoyance was crosstalk. I had often heard the familiar 9958 off in the background and once I even faintly heard my buddy. We shouted at one another for a while until one of us hit *#.

I don't think AX was ever quite aware of our exploits on the system since it was on line for several months: a new system was installed when their authorization people moved to Florida. I had had an Amex card all the while but recently gave it up when they raised their annual "membership" to $45, and didn't tell me. It was them pissing me off like that that prompted me to tell this tale. I hope you can carry on this tradition and it's *2600*'s pleasure to inform technology enthusiasts everywhere of your stories.

2 The Last Days of Ma Bell

Sometimes fate has a way of putting you in the right place at precisely the right time. How else could you possibly describe having the opportunity to publish a newsletter on telephones from a hacker perspective right at the exact moment when the phone company as we knew it was coming to an end? It really wasn't planned this way. We just happened to be there and nobody else was doing what we wanted to do. So what we have as a result of this is a unique time capsule that captures not only the technology of the day but the spirit that guided us in our first few years and that more or less defined the tone of the magazine from then on.

First, some history. Divestiture is what they called what was happening to good old Ma Bell. Prior to January 1984, the Bell System encapsulated the whole phone network. Your telephone, the wire connecting it to your wall, the wire connecting it to the telephone pole, the telephone pole itself, the connection all the way back to the central office, the central office itself, and everything long-distance related—all of that was part of one single enormous system. That hugeness and the lack of any real competition was in no small part what fueled the spirit of the early phone phreaks and inspired them to figure the whole thing out and eventually to defeat it. After all, monopolies were always by default the enemies of free-thinking individuals and you couldn't get much more monopolistic than Ma Bell.

So what happened after January of 1984 (which also happened to be the very month of our first issue)? Basically, *everything* started to change—the technology, the equipment, and, most of all, the playing field. For the first time ever, competition to the phone company was introduced nationwide. Granted, it didn't happen overnight and it wasn't exactly a smooth transition. But that's what made it all so very interesting. And as we already had some familiarity with how it all worked, we found that people began to turn to us to get advice on how to make the right decisions. Oh, the irony.

With divestiture came seven new phone companies, each assigned a geographic region. They were called Regional Bell Operating Companies or RBOCs. (We all referred to them as Baby Bells.) Under these companies were the local phone companies, often labeled by state and previously a part of the one massive Bell conglomerate. We were still many years away from seeing competition on the local level. But the long-distance network was another matter entirely. New companies started to materialize and older ones that had only existed in limited areas began to rapidly expand. Names like MCI, Sprint, Allnet, and Skyline started to become well known. Equal access (the ability to choose your own default long-distance company) became available in some parts of the country and, for the rest, these oddities known as 950 numbers and equal access carrier codes became new tools in the long-distance world.

Of course, for people like us it meant that we had a whole new playground to mess around in. For most consumers, it was a total nightmare of confusion and complication. Many longed for the simpler days when one company did it all. But there was obviously no going back. Divestiture changed it all—forever. And we were incredibly lucky to have come in at a time where we could still play with and write about the last days of the original Bell System.

This chapter is divided into two sections, each of which I believe sheds some light on unique and important elements of the Bell System in a distinctly hacker view. First, we look at the "boxing" culture, something that drove the phone company crazy over the course of decades. Then we look at the actual infrastructure of the network, again through the eyes of hackers. So much of it is now gone or radically changed, which to me makes this glimpse all the more fascinating and necessary.

MILESTONES: AHOY! (January, 1984)

(That's how Alexander Graham Bell used to answer his phone. For some reason, it never caught on...)

This is the very first issue of *2600*. We will, on this page, explain our motives and what the goals are which we hope to achieve with this publication.

The idea for *2600* was born in 1983. We saw a tremendous need for some form of communication between those who truly appreciate the concept of communication: technological enthusiasts. Of course, others have different ways of describing such people—these range from words like "hacker" or "phreaker" to stronger terms such as "criminal" or "anarchist." Our purpose is not to pass judgment. *2600* exists to provide information and ideas to individuals who live for both. All of the items contained on these pages are provided for informational purposes only. ***2600* assumes no responsibility for any uses which this information may be put to.**

Of course, a lot has changed since our first days. *War Games* came out. And then the 414 gang got caught. Suddenly everyone was talking about phreakers and hackers. And while there were some that sort of jumped into the limelight, others were a bit more cautious. In fact, some were quite upset. Sure, the publicity was fun. But what would be the cost?

Well, time has passed and the cost has been high. Phreakers and hackers have been forced into virtual isolation. Raids by the FBI have become almost commonplace. The one magazine that was geared towards phone phreaks (*TAP*)

MILESTONES: AHOY! *(continued)*

mysteriously disappeared at the height of the crisis, sparking rumors that they, too, had been raided. However, in November, the magazine resurfaced, with an explanation that a fire had destroyed part of their mailing list. (Incidentally, if your name was one of the ones that was lost, you can claim the issues you are entitled to by sending *TAP* a copy of their mailing label or a cancelled check.)

And then there was the legendary computer bulletin board known as OSUNY. Enthusiasts from all across the country called up this board and left messages ranging from the latest in Sprint codes to how to crash an RSTS system to what to do once you've finally gained access to Autovon. Within a week after being mentioned in *Newsweek*, OSUNY was disconnected. Word has it that they are still in existence somewhere, but by invitation only. A truly smart move, if that is the case.

Many hackers were keeping a low profile even before the October raids. When the FBI confiscated equipment from 15 sites across the country on the 12th and 13th of the month (sponsored by a grant from the folks at GTE), many of our contacts were lost because they feared the consequences of continuing. Two organizations, the Inner Circle and PHALSE, were deeply affected by the raids. The latter group (whose initials signify Phreakers, Hackers, and Laundromat Service Employees) is still in contact with us on occasion and has promised to contribute many articles devoted to just what was really going on.

So it seems that the events of 1983 have conspired to actually strengthen the resolve of hackers and phreakers across the country to put out this monthly newsletter. We hope you will help us continue by subscribing, spreading the word among your friends, and of course contributing articles and information. Since we are non-profit, it really doesn't matter to us if you Xerox your copy and send it to someone else—all we ask is that you let us know so that we can have a rough idea of how many people we're reaching.

Welcome to *2600*. Turn the page and become a part of our unique world.

The World of Boxes

Every phone phreak had at least a passing familiarity with those magical devices known as boxes. They were all color coded, some for historical reasons and some simply to use up an available color. But they each did something different and vital in the phreak world. The blue box was the king as it was the one that could send out those magical multifrequency (MF) tones that could route calls internally on the Bell network. With one of these you were a part of the machine and you could literally reach anywhere in the world including internal operators and forbidden countries. The silver box was little more than a modified touch-tone pad with the extra column of tones activated. (Every touch-tone pad is actually a 4×4 grid, not a 4×3 grid.) Those four extra tones had some magical abilities, both in the Bell System and on the mysterious AUTOVON (the military phone network). Red boxes were at the bottom of the totem pole. All they did was beep a certain frequency a set number of times to mimic a pay phone that had just ingested a coin. Yes, all it took to make a free phone call at a pay phone was a series of repeating beeps.

New boxes were always being invented and there were scores of other points of interest in the phone network. The following represents a mere scratching of the surface.

But How Does It Work? (August, 1984)

How much do you really understand about the way your telephone works? Probably not as much as you should. Considering the amount of time most people spend on the contraptions, this is really quite a disgrace. Ask questions and make an effort to learn and you'll be the exception to the rule, which is basically: "Safety is Stupidity." Read on.

Wiring

Assuming a standard one-line fone, there are usually four wires that lead out of the fone set. These are standardly colored red, green, yellow, and black. The red and green wires are the two that are actually hooked up to your central office (CO). The yellow wire is sometimes used to ring different fones on a party line (i.e., one number, several families—found primarily in rural areas where they pay less for the service and they don't use the fone as much), otherwise the yellow is usually just ignored. On some two-line fones, the red and green wires are used for the first fone number and the yellow and black are used for the second line. In this case there must be an internal or external device that switches between the two lines and provides a hold function (such as Radio Shack's outrageously priced two-line and hold module).

In telephony, the green and red wires are often referred to as tip (T) and ring (R), respectively. The tip is the more positive of the two wires. This naming goes back to the old operator cord boards where one of the wires was the tip of the plug and the other was the ring (of the barrel).

A rotary fone (a.k.a. dial or pulse) will work fine regardless of whether the red (or green) wire is connected to the tip (+) or ring (-). A touch-tone fone is a different story, though. It will not work except if the tip (+) is the green wire. (Some of the more expensive DTMF fones do have a bridge rectifier, which compensates for polarity reversal, however.) This is why under certain (nondigital) switching equipment you can reverse the red and green wires on a touch-tone fone and receive free DTMF service. Even though it won't break dial tone, reversing the wires on a rotary line on a digital switch will cause the tones to be generated.

Voltages, Etc.

When your telefone is on-hook (i.e., hung up) there are approximately 48 volts of DC potential across the tip and ring. When the handset of a fone is lifted, a few switches close, which cause a loop to be connected (known as the "local loop") between your fone and the CO. Once this happens, DC current is able to flow through the fone with less resistance. This causes a relay to energize, which causes other CO equipment to realize that you want service. Eventually, you should end up with a dial tone. This also causes the 48 VDC to drop down into the vicinity of 12 volts. The resistance of the loop also drops below the 2500 ohm level, though FCC licensed telefone equipment must have an off-hook impedance of 600 ohms.

As of now, you are probably saying to yourself that this is all nice and technical but what the hell good is the information. Well, also consider that this drop in impedance is how the CO detects that a fone was taken off hook (picked up). In this way, they know when to start billing the calling number. Now what do you suppose would happen if a device such as a resistor or a Zener diode was placed on the *called* party's line so that the voltage would drop just enough to allow talking but not enough to start billing? First off, the calling party would not be billed for the call but conversation could be pursued. Secondly, the CO equipment would think that the fone just kept on ringing. The Telco calls this a "no-no" (toll fraud to be more specific) while phone phreaks affectionately call this mute a black box.

How These Boxes Are Built

It's really surprisingly easy to build a device such as a black box. If it weren't for the amazingly high morals inherent in today's society, you'd most certainly see more of them in use. Only two parts are needed: an SPST toggle switch and a 10,000-ohm (10 K), ½-watt resistor. Any electronics store should stock these parts.

A person would then cut two pieces of wire (about 6 inches long) and attach one end of each wire to one of the terminals on the switch. Then the K-500 (standard desk fone) would be turned upside down and the cover taken off. A wire would be located and disconnected from its terminal. The switch would then be brought out the rear of the fone and the cover replaced. Labeling the switch usually comes next. A position where one receives a dial tone when picking up is marked "NORMAL." The other side is, naturally, "FREE."

Making Them Work

When phriends call (usually at a prearranged time), the person with the black box quickly lifts and drops the receiver as fast as possible. This stops the ringing (if not it must be done again) without starting the billing. This must be done within less than one second. The phone can then be picked up with the switch in the "FREE" position. Most phone phreaks are wise enough to keep their calls under 15 minutes in length, greatly minimizing the odds of getting caught.

Some interesting points: (1) If someone picks up an extension in the called party's house and that fone is not set for "FREE," then billing will start. (2) An old way of signaling a phriend that you want to call him is to make a collect call to a nonexistent person in the house. Since the phriend will (hopefully) not accept the charges, he will know that you are about to call and, thus, prepare the black box (or vice versa). (3) The phone company can detect black boxes if they suspect one on the line. This is done due to the presence of AC voice signal at the wrong DC level! (4) The black box will not work under ESS or other similar digital switches since ESS does not connect the voice circuits until the fone is picked up (and billing starts). Instead, ESS uses an "artificial" computer generated ring.

Ringing

To inform a subscriber of an incoming call, the Telco sends 90 volts (PK) of pulsing DC down the line (at around 15 to 60 Hz; usually 20 Hz). In most phones this causes a metal armature to be attracted alternately between two electromagnets, thus, striking two bells. Of course, the standard bell (patented in 1878 by Tom A. Watson) can be replaced by a more modern electronic bell or signaling device.

Also, you can have lights and other similar devices in lieu of (or in conjunction with) the bell. A simple neon light (with its corresponding resistor) can simply be connected between the red and green wires (usually L1 and L2 on the network box) so that it lights up on incoming calls.

Be advised that 90 VDC can give quite a shock. Exercise extreme caution if you wish to further pursue these topics.

Also included in the ringing circuit is a capacitor to prevent the DC current from interfering with the bell (a capacitor will pass AC and pulsing DC while it will prevent straight DC from flowing—by storing it).

Another reason that Telcos hate black boxes is because ringing uses a lot of common-control equipment in the CO, which uses a lot of electricity. Thus, the ringing generators are being tied up while a free call is being made. Usually calls that are allowed to "ring" for a long period of time will be construed as suspicious. Some offices may be set up to drop a trouble card for long periods of ringing and then a "no-no" detection device may be placed on the line.

Incidentally, the term "ring trip" refers to the CO process involved to stop the AC ringing signal when the calling fone goes off hook.

It is suggested that you actually dissect fones to help you better understand them (regardless of whether or not you want to build any devices). It will also help you to better understand the concepts here if you actually prove them to yourself. For example, actually take the voltage readings on your fone line (any simple multitester (a must) will do). Phreaking and/or learning is an interactive process, not a passive one!

(Any questions on the above? Write us and we'll try to answer them.)

The Theory of "Blue Boxing:" (February, 1985)

Their history, how they're used, their future

After most neophyte phreaks overcome their fascination with Metrocodes and WATS extenders, they will usually seek to explore other avenues in the vast phone network. Often, they will come across references such as "simply dial KP+2130801050+ST for the Alliance teleconferencing system in LA." Numbers such as the one above were intended to be used with a blue box; this article will explain the fundamental principles of the fine art of blue boxing.

Genesis

In the beginning, all long-distance calls were connected manually by operators who passed on the called number verbally to other operators in series. This is because pulse (aka rotary) digits are created by causing breaks in the DC current. Since long-distance calls require routing through various switching equipment and AC voice amplifiers, pulse dialing cannot be used to send the destination number to the end local office (CO).

Eventually, the demand for faster and more efficient long-distance (LD) service caused Bell to make a multibillion dollar decision. They had to create a signaling system that could be used on the LD network. Basically, they had two options: (1) to send all the signaling and supervisory information (i.e. ON and OFF HOOK) over separate data links. This type of signaling is referred to as out-of-band signaling, or (2) to send all the signaling information along with the conversation using tones to represent digits. This type of signaling is referred to as in-band signaling. Being the cheap bastards that they naturally are, Bell chose the latter (and cheaper) method—in-band signaling. They eventually regretted this, though (heh, heh)...

In-Band Signaling Principles

When a subscriber dials a telephone number, whether in rotary or touchtone (a.k.a. DTMF), the equipment in the CO interprets the digits and looks for a convenient trunk line to send the call on its way. In the case of a local call, it will probably be sent via an interoffice trunk: otherwise, it will be sent to a toll office (class 4 or higher) to be processed.

When trunks are not being used there is a 2600 Hz tone on the line: thus to find a free trunk, the CO equipment simply checks for the presence of 2600 Hz. If it doesn't find a free trunk, the customer will receive a re-order signal (120 1PM busy signal) or the "all circuits are busy..." message. If it does find a free trunk, it "seizes" it—removing the 2600 Hz. It then sends the called number or a special routing code to the other end or toll office.

The tones it uses to send this information are called multifrequency (MF) tones. An MF tone consists of two tones from a set of six master tones, which are combined to produce 12 separate tones. You can sometimes hear these tones in the background when you make a call, but they are usually filtered out so your delicate ears cannot hear them. These are *not* the same as touch tones. To notify the equipment at the far end of the trunk that it is about to receive routing information, the originating end first sends a Key Pulse (KP) tone. At the end of sending the digits, the originating end then sends a STart (ST) tone. Thus to call 914-359-1517, the equipment would send KP+9143591517+ST in MF tones. When the customer hangs up, 2600 Hz is once again sent to signify a disconnect to the distant end.

History

In the November 1960 issue of the *Bell System Technical Journal*, an article entitled "Signaling Systems for Control of Telephone Switching" was published. This journal, which was sent to most university libraries, happened to contain the actual MF tones used in signaling. They appeared as follows:

DIGIT	TONES
1	700 + 900 HZ
2	700 + 1100 HZ
3	900 + 1100 HZ
4	700 + 1300 HZ
5	900 + 1300 HZ
6	1100 + 1300 HZ
7	700 + 1500 HZ
8	900 + 1500 HZ
9	1100 + 1500 HZ
0	1300 + 1500 HZ
KP	1100 + 1700 HZ
ST	1500 + 1700 HZ
11 (*)	700 + 1700 HZ
12 (*)	900 + 1700 HZ
KP2 (*)	1300 + 1700 HZ

(*) Used only on CCITT SYSTEM 5 for special international calling.

Bell caught wind of blue boxing in 1961, when it caught a Washington State College student using one. They originally found out about blue boxes through police raids and informants. In 1964, Bell Labs came up with scanning equipment, which recorded all suspicious calls, to detect blue box usage. These units were installed in CO's where major toll fraud existed. AT&T security would then listen to the tapes to see if any toll fraud was actually committed. Over 200 convictions resulted from the project. Surprisingly enough, blue boxing is not solely limited to the electronics enthusiast; AT&T has caught businessmen, film stars, college students, doctors, lawyers, high school students, and even a millionaire financier (Bernard Cornfield) using the device. AT&T also said that nearly half of those that they catch are businessmen.

To use a blue box, one would usually make a free call to any 800 number or distant directory assistance (NPA-555-1212). This, of course, is legitimate. When the call is answered, one would then swiftly press the button that would send 2600 Hz down the line. This has the effect of making the distant CO equipment think that the call was terminated, and it leaves the trunk hanging. Now, the user has about 10 seconds to enter in the telephone number he wished to dial—in MF, that is. The CO equipment merely assumes that this came from another office and it will happily process the call. Since there are no records (except on toll fraud detection devices!) of these MF tones, the user is not billed for the call. When the user hangs up, the CO equipment simply records that he hung up on a free call.

Detection

Bell has had 20 years to work on detection devices; therefore, in this day and age, they are rather well refined. Basically, the detection device will look for the presence of 2600 Hz where it does not belong. It then records the calling number and all activity after the 2600 Hz. If you happen to be at a fortress fone, though, and you make the call short, your chances of getting caught are significantly reduced. Incidentally, there have been rumors of certain test numbers that hook into trunks thus avoiding the need for 2600 HZ and detection!

Another way that Bell catches boxers is to examine the CAMA (Centralized Automatic Message Accounting) tapes. When you make a call, your number, the called number, and time of day are all recorded. The same thing happens when you hang up. This tape is then processed for billing purposes. Normally, all free calls are ignored. But Bell can program the billing equipment to make note of lengthy calls to directory assistance. They can then put a pen register (aka DNR) on the line or an actual full-blown tap. This detection can be avoided by making short-haul (aka local) calls to box off of.

It is interesting to note that NPA+555-1212 originally did not return answer supervision. Thus, the calls were not recorded on the AMA CAMA tapes. AT&T changed this though for "traffic studies!"

CCIS

Besides detection devices, Bell has begun to gradually redesign the network using out-of-band signaling. This is known as Common Channel Interoffice Signaling (CCIS). Since this signaling method sends all the signaling information over separate data lines, blue boxing is impossible under it.

While being implemented gradually, this multibillion dollar project is still strangling the fine art of blue boxing. Of course, until the project is totally complete, boxing will still be possible. It will become progressively harder to find places to box off of, though. In areas with CCIS, one must find a directory assistance office that doesn't have CCIS yet. Area codes in Canada and predominantly rural states are the best bets. WATS numbers terminating in non-CCIS cities are also good prospects.

Pink Noise

Another way that may help to avoid detection is to add some "pink noise" to the 2600 Hz tone.

Since 2600 Hz tones can be simulated in speech, the detection equipment must be careful not to misinterpret speech as a disconnect signal. Thus, a virtually pure 2600 Hz tone is required for disconnect.

Keeping this in mind, the 2600 Hz detection equipment is also probably looking for pure 2600 Hz, or else it would be triggered every time someone hit that note (highest E on a piano = 2637 Hz). This is also the reason that the 2600 Hz tone must be sent rapidly: sometimes, it won't work when the operator is saying "Hello, hello." It is feasible to send some "pink noise" along with the 2600 Hz. Most of this energy should be above 3000 Hz. The pink noise won't make it into the toll network (where we want our pure 2600 Hz to hit), but it should make it past the local CO and, thus, the fraud detectors.

(Taken from Basic Telecommunications, Part VII, written by BIOC Agent 003.)

An Overview of AUTOVON and Silver Boxes (March, 1986)

AUTOVON (AUTOmatic VOice Network) is a single system within DCS (Defense Communications System). It is presently mostly based on electro-mechanical switches and is a world-wide network for "unsecure" voice communication for the DOD and several related agencies. There is a good deal of basic redesign going on right now, but things don't get changed that fast at the DOD. It works in tandem with AUTODIN (AUTOmatic DIgital Network) and AUTOSEVOCOM (AUTOmatic SEcure VOice COMmunications), and is tied closely to DSCS operation (Defense Satellite Communications System). Just under 200 DCS switching offices around the free world connect about 68,000 government circuits and 73,000 (DOD leased) commercial carrier circuits. Almost all lines in the USA are leased from AT&T, WUI, and GTE.

AUTOVON provides direct interconnect capability to NATO allies and others as well. System service control is entirely hierarchical. Switches respond to fourth column DTMF (1633 Hz mixed with row frequencies—silver box tones—the "missing" row of buttons on your touch-tone phone) to provide a means of prioritizing the switching response, where key A is highest and key D lowest priority.

Much work is being done on updating the digital services of DCS to "DDN" (Defense Data Network) but that doesn't affect AUTOVON; it is still all analog. All these systems are basically run by the DCA (Defense Communications Agency) at the Pentagon. One important office of the DCA is DECCO (DEfense Commercial Communications Office) at Scott Air Force Base in Illinois. This office of the DCA manages acquisition and use of all commercial leased lines worldwide. DCA and DECCO also handle lots of other government telecom stuff, like TACNET, the EBS (Emergency Broadcast System), FAA national air system, and reportedly paid some $1.1 *billion* for their '84 phone bill all together (15 *million* miles of leased lines and service). That's at very heavy discounting, too!

How to Participate

You can easily alter your touch-tone phone to make it have the extra column that utilizes the 1633 Hz tone. Standard Bell phones have two tone generating coils, each of which can generate four tones. This gives you sixteen possibilities of which you only use twelve. This leaves you with access to the four unexplored tones.

A standard way to modify the touch-tone phone is to install a switch to tell it whether to use the silver box tones or not. When the switch is in one position, you will get normal tones, in the other you'll get 1633 Hz tones.

Bell calls these buttons A, B, C, and D, while the army named them, from highest to lowest, Flash Override, Flash, Immediate, and Priority. All other calls are called Routine if no precedence button is pushed.

These are used as varying degrees of priority during wartime and wargame activities. Bell's use of A, B, C, and D is not so clear. However, the last button (D) has an interesting property: on some of the directory assistance lines in the country, it will give you a pulsing dial tone. You can then enter commands to what appears to be a test system for 4A boxes.

How to Use the Silver Box

Call directory assistance using normal tones out of state (NPA-555-1212). Then switch quickly to 1633hz, and press down on the # key (which you've converted to the D key). If you are on an old switchbox (4A), you will get a pulsing dial tone. You will not receive a pulsing tone until the operator actually picks up on the line. If you hear ringing, keep pressing. The tone must be on at the same time the operator gives her "beep." This mainly works with rural information operators.

You can then switch back to normal, and try dialing a 6 and 7. After hearing the pulsing tone and switching to normal tones you can press 6. If another person does the same thing (same area code of course) and presses 7 then you may get a loop-like voice link.

These extra tones are also said to work when using MCI and Sprint and any other long distance services for phreaking. If the service has a six-digit access code then you can simply enter the first three digits and then enter an A tone for the last three digits. This acts as a wildcard tone and eliminates the need to know the last three tones. In this way, one can hack out codes at a thousand per code entered. We'd like to know if anyone has actually done this.

If you have a line on AUTOVON, you call another AUTOVON number by the same process as on the public switched net. To call any DCA office on AUTOVON you dial 22x-xxxx. It breaks down further in hierarchic fashion, so 222-xxxx is DCA directorate. 222-xxxx is also for directors/commanders of major parts of DCA, etc…

Calls into AUTOVON from outside use the area code of the desired AUTOVON location plus public access prefix plus same extension. The exchange gives you the appropriate AUTOVON switch center, then the local extension (usually last 5 digits) is the same as on AUTOVON.

The AUTOVON directory is one of the biggest. Calling the 202 NPA and just hacking numbers on AUTOVON exchanges can be both fun and rewarding for the daring! Remember though, a lot of these people can cause you grief if you get serious about harassing or frivolous calls to the same number, so take care!

(Special thanks to Tiger Paws III.)

Introducing the Clear Box! (July, 1984)

A new device has just been invented. It's called the "clear box." It can be used throughout Canada and through rural United States.

This interesting gadget works on "post-pay" pay phones, in other words, those phones that don't require payment until after the connection has been established. You pick up the phone, get a dial tone, dial your number, and then put in your coins after the person answers. If you don't deposit money, you can't speak to the person at the other end, because your mouthpiece is cut off—but not your earpiece. (Yes, you can make free calls to the weather, etc. from such phones.)

In order to bypass this, all one has to do is visit a nearby electronics store, get a 4-transistor amplifier and a telephone suction cup induction pick-up. The induction pick-up would be hooked up as it normally would to record a conversation, except that it would be plugged into the *output* of the amplifier and a microphone would be hooked to the input. So when the party answers, the caller could speak through the little microphone instead. His voice would then go through the amplifier, out the induction coil, and into the back of the receiver where it would then be broadcast through the phone lines and the other party would be able to hear the caller. The clear box thus "clears" up the problem of not being heard.

The line will not cut off after a certain amount of time—it will wait forever for the coins to drop in.

Many independents are moving toward this kind of stupid pay phone system. For one thing, it's a cheap way of getting DTF (dial tone first) service. It doesn't require any special equipment. That type of pay phone will work on any kind of a phone line. Normally a pay phone line is different, but this is just a regular phone line and it's set up so that the pay phone does all of the charging, not the CO. With the recent deregulation of pay phones, this kind of a system could become very popular.

Hardwiring Your Way In (Winter, 1988–1989) *By Dr. Williams*

One of the most obvious ways of obtaining free telephone service is through "hardwiring"—that is, directly connecting a phone to somebody else's line without their knowledge. This can be accomplished in a few different manners. One technique is just to hook up a phone to the exterior of a house or business. Another way, canning, is a little less blunt. Any dime store phone can be hooked up, and voila! Free telephone service is yours just for the begging.

There are basically two types of exterior phone boxes that are used for homes and small businesses. The older ones are a pukey green color, are square, and have four terminals inside: two for the grounds, and two for the charged wires. These are kept closed by a long bolt. The newer ones are rectangular and have a phone jack inside of them. They are kept closed by a lid. There is only one tool you'll need, and that is a touch-tone phone. The ones where all of the components are contained in the headset are the best for this. Take the cord, cut it in the middle, and strip the wires on both halves. There should be four wires: green, red, black, and yellow. The green and red ones carry the current, and the black and yellow are the grounds. There could be some variations in the colors of the wires, depending on the phone, but there should always be two grounds and two charged wires. After stripping the wires, put an alligator clip on the green and red wire on both halves. Putting one on the grounds is a good idea, too.

Now you have what it takes to connect up to any phone box. On the older ones where there are just four terminal posts, you take the headset and connect up to the terminals via the alligator clips on the headset. You won't need to use the other half of the cord with the phone jack since there is no place to hook it up. You may also have to bring some vise grips to unscrew the bolt, which holds the box closed. Sometimes, the colors of the terminals aren't marked, so it will take some trial and error to find the two live ones. On the newer boxes that have a telephone jack inside of them, you use the other half of your cord containing the jack to plug inside of it. Then you connect the alligator clips together on the headset. This should be no problem to open since they are held down with a plastic lid. Easy, isn't it! One note, though. There may be other variations out there. From my experience, these are the most common types of boxes.

There are some drawbacks; relationships are always two-sided. The good points are that it's easy (it beats hacking out codes to the local extender at the pay phone) and, since most residential areas still use AT&T as their primary carrier, you can call anywhere in the world. Some other long-distance carriers have limited calling areas. The drawbacks are, first, you have to do this at night—like, 3 or 4 a.m., and if you do this, you always run the risk of getting caught. Some neighbor might think you're a prowler. You should therefore dress in dark clothes and not carry any identification with you. There is also a limited amount of things you can do. After all, you can't call up your relatives or too many of your friends at that time of day.

There is a wealth of locations where one can try to hook up. One spot is housing construction—going up and coming down. Sometimes, when houses or apartments are being built, the phones are connected before construction is complete. I've also seen cases where people move out and the phones are not disconnected. Once the people lived in a mobile home and they moved out, leaving a vacant lot with a utility pole. Well, lo and behold, the phone was still connected. The phone company didn't disconnect it until about seven months later, and that was after practically everyone in the neighborhood had crank-called people in Japan and Australia. You can also try rural neighborhoods late at night, although using your own probably isn't a good idea.

Small business clusters or industrial centers are also good spots. These usually have the green boxes clumped together in lots of four. Late at night, no one is around, so it's only a matter of hooking up. I'm talking about those places where a company leases the shop or office space to various companies. Trying to hook up where a 7-11 is located probably wouldn't be too smart.

Canning

A subject I'm going to touch upon is canning. The reason I say I just want to "touch" upon it is because this topic really deserves a whole article by itself, but since you can use the same tools of the trade, I'm going to mention it here. Cans are those ugly green containers that stick out of the ground. Most of the smaller and isolated cans can be easily opened with vise grips. The bigger ones sometimes have locks on them, but nothing a bolt cutter couldn't handle. Most cans that I've come across come in two flavors: ones where there are just masses of individual telephone wires clumped together, and the others that break apart the clumps of wires to help the distribution of the telephone wires. The ones that have just the bundles of wires clumped together I've found to be of little use. I imagine that a guy would have to match up the two wires for each single phone to get a current that will work. But then again, I'm not an expert. Sometimes these do break up a few individual houses in the neighborhood. There might be a metal plate attached to the top of the can with four or five terminals sticking out. Use trial and error again to find a live current. It is usually pretty easy. The other cans, the bigger ones, which are sometimes locked, can be a gold mine. They usually distribute pairs of wires in a horizontal fashion, with a row of metal stubs sticking out. Inside it might look a bit confusing. Around the perimeter, there are wads of wires tangled together and going every which way. Inside the perimeter are rows and rows of square metallic stubs. These stubs are thin, about three eighths of an inch wide, and they stick out about an inch. The telephone wires will connect to both sides of the horizontal rows of these metallic stubs. All you need to do is connect up to two horizontal stubs. Not all of the wires in the can may be live, so you need more than one try. Sometimes these bigger cans have some goodies in them, such as lineman's headsets and papers containing technical data. From what I understand, the purpose of these cans is to help troubleshoot problems by breaking up units (or clusters of wires) into smaller units. I want to emphasize that I am not an expert on these cans. These are just my observations and I'm sure things work differently in different parts of the nation.

The real benefit of hooking up comes when you own a portable computer with a modem. If you find a target computer that you'd like to get to know better, and you're not stupid enough to try to get to it from your home phone, then this might be a good way to go. Portables are going down in price; I've seen some in pawn shops for about $125.

There are a couple of other observations that I'd like to make. I've attended two different high schools and I found their long-distance dialing procedures in the same place. On the principal's desk, there was a bread board that slid out on the left-hand side. The instructions for making long-distance calls were typed on a piece of paper taped to this location. Perhaps this is a common occurrence. I've also lived in a few different dorms, and I've noticed similarities in their setup, too. In each room there was a plated telephone jack. The plate was only held down by two flathead screws. I unscrewed the plate and behind were most of the telephone wires for the whole floor. I could have hooked up to any room on the floor undetected.

Finally, if you find that any of the above works out pretty good for you, don't be too greedy, too stupid, or start taking life for granted. As they say on Wall Street: "Bulls make money, bears make money, pigs get slaughtered."

How Pay Phones Really Work (Spring, 1989) *By The Infidel*

Fortress phones, aka pay phones, are something that every phreak should have had experience with at least once in their career. Such devices as the red box and the green box also make the fortress a great place to phreak from. In this article, I will try to explain how a pay phone works, and how one can (ab)use it.

Basically, pay phones are not too different from normal phones, requiring all the speech and signaling facilities of ordinary telephones, but, in addition, requiring signals to handle the charge for the call with the money inserted. However, the pay phone itself has undergone some changes through the years.

Some Pay Phone History

In most coin telephones, the stations operate on a pre-pay basis, that is, the coins must be deposited before the call can be completed. A few of the older central offices using step-by-step equipment that had only a few public telephones accepted deposits after completion of the call. This form of operation, post-pay coin service, was chosen usually because of the long distance between the local community dial office and the serving toll switchboard, which often resulted in large costs due to the returning of coins on uncompleted calls.

The older versions of pre-pay phones (the ones made famous by David in *War Games*), the A-type set, would produce a dial tone only *after* a coin was deposited. These were also rotary phones. As ESS emerged, with such options as 911 and 411 directory assistance, the need for a dial tone-first phone emerged, the C-type station, which resulted in the dial tone-first rotary phone.

With the advent of touch tone, calling cards, and long-distance carriers, pay phones developed into the touch tone, dial tone-first public telephone. As you may have noticed, the intermediate telephone, the rotary, dial tone-first phone is very hard to come by these days, obviously due to the increasing demand in the many services now offered by Ma Bell and other companies, which take advantage of the touch-tone service.

Up until 1978, signaling for coin deposits was accomplished by a single-frequency tone, sent in pulses, as they are today. As an Automated Coin Toll Service (ACTS) appeared necessary, to automate the routine functions of TSPS (Traffic Service Position System) operators, there developed a need for improvements in the station to prevent simulation of the coin signals, and therefore, toll fraud. As a result, before the introduction of TSPS/ACTS, all coin sets manufactured after 1977 were then equipped with dual-frequency oscillators. These coin boxes produced the current form of coin signaling, the dual-frequency tone. This resulted in the D-type station, which, due to its power requirements and electronic components, rather than mechanical, could only be used in a dial tone-first environment, and is, therefore, what we see today.

Operation Logic

As noted above, the pay phone is, essentially, the same as a customer-owned telephone, with the main difference being, quite obviously, the presence of the coin box.

In the design of the coin box, the following must be considered. The coin box can be very sophisticated, to handle many functions, thus requiring a very simple exchange to just receive all billing information from the phone itself. Or, vice versa, the coin box can be quite simple, and the exchange can be much more complex, to interpret the data from the box needed to place the call and charge a toll for it.

Today's standard Western Electric/AT&T telephone follows the latter, a more simple coin box design. These boxes signal forward to exchange the value of each coin inserted using tone pulses. This technique requires Coin and Fee Check (C and FC) equipment in the exchange, ACTS, to carry out the call accounting necessary between the value of the coins inserted and the rate of charging of the call. This arrangement lets you insert coins into the phone at any time during the call, but its main disadvantage is that the speech transmission must be interrupted while the coin value is signaled to the exchange.

Thus, the property of requesting a coin for a call *is not in the phone*, but in the exchange itself. If you took a pay phone home and hooked it up to your line, it would not request a coin deposit. On the other hand, if you were to tap into a pay phone line and tried to place a call, you would get the familiar coin deposit request message.

What Happens to Your Money?

When you first put your coin in the slot, it is tested for size, weight and material. Size is determined by the size of the slot the coin passes through, as well as the coin chute it slides through in the phone itself. A coin that is too large is not allowed into the phone itself, while one too small just falls through without having accomplished anything. Material is identified by the use of magnetic fields; slugs will be deflected, while coins will not. If the coin is right, it is allowed to hit a sprocket, which when hit by the coin, spins a certain amount of times, determined by its weight. This spinning of the sprocket controls a tone generator within the telephone, which creates the coin deposit tones, which, in turn, the exchange then interprets to determine the amount to credit the customer.

As the pay phone can accept only three different coins, there are three coin signals to identify each one. The signal consists of 1700 Hz and 2200 Hz tones generated together to produce a dual-frequency tone. The dual tone is more efficient, because it cannot be confused with (or simulated by) human speech, since the human voice can only produce one tone at a time, and is also more difficult to simulate electronically, in an effort to prevent fraud. To identify the value of the coin, the tone is sent to the exchange in pulses.

- **Nickel Tone:** One 60 millisecond pulse (1700 Hz + 2200 Hz)
- **Dime Tone:** Two 60 millisecond pulses separated by 60 milliseconds (1700 Hz + 2200 Hz)
- **Quarter Tone:** Five 35 millisecond pulses separated by 35 milliseconds (1700 Hz + 2200 Hz)

As mentioned earlier, the main problem with this design is that the conversation is interrupted by the insertion of coins, which can be quite annoying on long-distance calls placed on peak hours, when the rates are highest. Yet, since the tones do interrupt the speech transmission, a phreak can send, along with the speech transmission, these same tones, generated artificially by a device known as the red box.

After the coins have been accounted for, they are held in a hopper, which is controlled by a single-coil relay. This relay is controlled by the application of negative or positive DC voltage, depending on whether the coins are to be returned or collected. The line reversal can occur by one of two ways. One way the line reversal can be accomplished is at the phone itself, via the switch-hook. In the on-hook position, the hopper will not allow coins to fall through, and so, they must be released by lifting the handset to cause a line reversal and activate the relay. The second way in which a line reversal can occur is by remote, from ACTS. ACTS can signal the station to either collect or return the coins. The signals are also in the form of dual-frequency tone bursts. Three signals ACTS can send to the fortress are the Coin Collect, Coin Return, and Ringback. These tones are also known as green box tones. The frequencies of these tones are as follows:

- **Coin Collect**: 700 Hz + 1100 Hz (900ms)
- **Coin Return**: 1100 Hz + 1700 Hz (900ms)
- **Ringback**: 700 Hz + 1700 Hz (900ms)

The function of the first two should be obvious, but the Ringback may be unclear. When you walk away from a phone after not having deposited money for overtime, the phone rings. That's ACTS. It's not actually "calling" the pay phone, but sending a signal to the station to order it to ring. When you pick up the phone and hear the message, "Please deposit 40 cents," that's also ACTS playing the recording. After you hang up again or don't deposit your change, ACTS signals a TSPS operator, who then breaks in and asks for the money personally, since Telco knows you're definitely not going to put money in a phone just because a machine asks you to. If you've been coerced into handing over your money, it's also ACTS which then thanks you.

Alternate Designs

An alternate telephone design allows for a drastically less complex exchange, while requiring a much more sophisticated coin box.

A pay phone equipped with a "pay at any time" box allows for meter pulse signals to be sent from the exchange to the pay phone, with the coin box performing the call accounting. The meter pulses may be signals at 50 Hz, or tones of 12 kHz or 16 kHz, depending on the network. Therefore, the insertion of coins won't interfere with the conversation. Coins inserted prior to the call being established, and during the call, are held suspended until the control logic within the pay phone (rather than the exchange) determines that they need to be collected. Coins remaining in suspension are returned to the user when the pay phone goes on-hook. When no more coins are held in credit and the next meter pulse is received, the pay phone requests coin insertion and then clears the call after the designated grace period has elapsed. If only part of the value of the credit held in suspension needs to be collected when the phone goes on-hook, the remainder will be lost, unless the phone is equipped with a "follow on call" button to credit the unused portion to a call made immediately afterward. This design, seen in England, is somewhat similar to the privately owned pay phones available here.

Since the local telephone network will only allow their pay phones to be connected to their special ACTS lines, privately owned pay phones cannot use the ACTS to perform call accounting for it. Thus, these phones must be installed on a normal subscriber's line, a drastically less complex exchange, and as a result such phones require a much more sophisticated coin box.

Owning a pay phone, especially in high-traffic areas, can be quite advantageous, since the owner keeps all coins collected, but only in the long run, because he has to pay for the line fee as well as the charge for the call placed. Yet, at 25 cents a call, and the current peak rate being 10.2 cents, the profits can be worthwhile. This profit is, however, substantially diminished by the expensive price tag of these units, costing between $2,000 and $2,500 each.

There are essentially two types of pay phones out that can be purchased. One type is basically a Western Electric/AT&T look-alike. The other is the newer and fancier electronic pay phone, complete with LCD digital display. Such phones offer sophisticated features such as LCD display of number being dialed, amount of money on credit, time allowed for credit, and time elapsed. Both of these telephones cost somewhere in the range of $2,500–$3,500, depending on the manufacturer and dealer. Though they appear quite different, these phones do not differ as much internally.

Both units require billing equipment within the unit itself, since normal customer lines cannot aid the phone in that capacity. As a result, these phones contain a "Rating Module," which includes a database with all inter-LATA rates and site-specific rates, as well as a clock, to determine when to apply off-peak discount rates. As rates change over time, the module can be upgraded or replaced to accommodate them, making these units quite flexible in that respect.

These telephones must also be able to discriminate between slugs and the different denominations of coins, which they do in a manner similar to standard pay phones.

The main difference between the two types of privately owned pay phones is the manner in which each places the call.

On the Telco copies, the billing equipment within the unit receives the number to be dialed from the keypad, compares that number to the number of the line on which it is installed (pre-programmed by the owner/installer), requests the appropriate fee from the caller, and then places the call itself; the keypad does not generate the actual touch tones, which place the call.

The majority of the digital models, however, place calls through a PBX (Private Branch eXchange), often owned by ITT, and the owner in turn pays the company for the calls made and keeps the remaining dividends. The fact that these units utilize

PBX's is not a condition required by the unit, but rather the choice of the manufacturer, seeking increased profits by the use of their own lines to place the calls for which they can then charge a fee.

When you make a call with this telephone, the number you enter with the keypad is shown on the LCD display and is then processed by the billing equipment. After requesting the corresponding fee, the call is placed through the PBX. This results in the rapid sequence of touch tones heard when placing a call with this phone. What the phone does is dial the PBX and then enter an access code used solely by the pay phones. That way, the local network will not bill the owner of the phone for those calls, since the calls are being placed through the PBX, and the PBX has a toll-free dial-up.

However, there are many disadvantages to this setup. Most notably, a local network operator cannot be reached through this arrangement. If you dial "0," the operator will be one selected by the company that owns the PBX used by the telephone. These operators are much more limited than the local network TSPS operators. They cannot perform such tasks as collect call placement, third-party billing of calls, calling card calls, customer identification for person-to-person calls, and busy line verification. Another problem is that calling card calls cannot be made from these phones. This is due to the fact that ACCS (Automated Calling Card Service) and ACTS, which automate basic TSPS functions, are not available from within the PBX and even if they were, the touch tones needed to enter the card number cannot be generated directly from the keypad. This lack of touch-tone access also prohibits calls through other long-distance carriers via the 950 exchange. Directory assistance is also inaccessible and 911 calls cannot be placed. Many bugs in the design can also make the phone inoperable or make it enter a "Maintenance Mode" just by hitting it hard enough, since many of these stations are not very secure, in some cases made from nothing more than plastic. In some units, the touch-tone access is available, yet the telephones are not configured to accept 950 calls as toll-free, again inconveniencing the customer.

The Telco copies are not much better. Operator assistance is limited to that which can be obtained from home lines. Again, calls cannot be completed through long-distance carriers since the station is not configured to accept toll-free 950 calls, although these telephones are usually configured to allow AT&T calling card calls (0+ calls) to be placed through them.

The Cheese Box

There are files circulating about the modem/phreak world regarding a device known as a cheese box. According to the files, when one forwards his number to an Intercept Operator within his prefix, all subsequent outgoing calls made will be prompted for coin insertion, supposedly turning the subscriber's telephone into a pay phone. It should be quite obvious that this is impossible, since not only does the Intercept Operator have nothing to do with pay phones, coin accounting, and ACTS, but it also seems quite impossible that one's line could become interfaced with ACTS simply by forwarding it to an operator. Obviously, these files are bogus.

Phone Abuse

In this last section, I will discuss how you can use the knowledge obtained from above to use to your advantage when dealing with these telephones, I am not going to get into such topics as phone theft and vandalism—I'll leave that up to your imagination.

The main advantage of the pay phone, to the phreak, is that it provides anonymity. This makes the pay phone a perfect location for blue boxing, engineering operators, and other Telco employees, modeming (for the more daring), and general experimentation.

Yet, perhaps the most famous aspect of phreaking regarding the pay phone is the use of the red box. As mentioned above, the red box is used to simulate the tones that signal ACTS that money has been deposited in the phone and ACTS may place the call and begin billing (if service is timed). The red box is used by dialing the desired number first and then, when ACTS asks for the change, using the red box to send the coin signals. In an attempt to stop red boxing, the pay phone checks to see if the first coin is real, by conducting a ground test. To circumvent this, at least one coin must be deposited—a nickel is sufficient. However, the number must be dialed first since ACTS must return your coins before reminding you that you have insufficient credit to place the call. Afterward, any subsequent deposits required can be red boxed successfully, and the duration of the call can be as long as you like.

Red box schematics have proven to be hard to come by and are notoriously a pain to build, not only in the somewhat more complex circuit design than the simple tone generators used in blue, beige, and similar boxes, but also in the fact that they are hard to tune precisely, since not only is a frequency counter needed, but also an oscilloscope, both of which are hard to come by and are very expensive.

However, there are alternatives. One method is to locate a pay phone that produces the coin deposit tones quite loudly when coins are inserted. You can then record the tones with a Walkman (I do not recommend a micro-cassette recorder for this, because they are not stable enough for the precision required by ACTS) and simply play them back into the mouthpiece when you want to place a call just as you would if you had an actual red box. When you record the tones, record mostly quarters, since obviously they are worth the most calling time.

But if you don't have your trusty Walkman with you, there is still another way. Simply find a set of two pay phones (or more) with at least one that generates loud coin deposit tones. This phone will be Phone A. Now dial the desired number in Phone B and when ACTS asks you for the amount required, deposit a nickel in Phone B. Now put the two handsets of the phones together (the wires are long enough to reach across the booths) with the earpiece of Phone A held tight against the mouthpiece of Phone B. It doesn't matter where the other two ends are. The purpose of this is to get the sound of the deposit tones from Phone A's earpiece into the mouthpiece of Phone B. Then simply keep depositing coins in Phone A until ACTS thanks you for using AT&T. If you were smart, you only used quarters in Phone A, so you could get some credit toward overtime. Since a number was never dialed with Phone A, when you hang up, all the change will be returned to you.

Red boxes are very useful but not convenient for local calls, though they will of course work. Another method for placing local calls free of charge is very similar to what David did in *War Games* to the pay phone. The problem with that method is that Telco has now sealed all mouthpieces on the pay phones. However, by puncturing the mouthpiece with a nail, the metal inside it will be exposed. There are two variations on this "nail" or "paper clip trick," depending on the telephone in use.

On the older D-types, by either placing a nail or a paper clip in the hole made in the mouthpiece and then touching the other end to any metal part of the phone, a short circuit will occur, which will render the keypad inoperable. If this is the case, then dial all digits of the number except for the last as you would normally and then short circuit the phone. While doing that, hold down the last digit of the number, disconnect the "jumper" you have made and then release the key. If this doesn't work, try rapidly connecting and disconnecting the jumper while holding down the last digit. The call should then be placed. What happens is the short circuit causes the coin signaler to malfunction and send a coin signal, while also shorting out the station, so that it passes the ground test.

On the newer pay phones, the short circuit will not deactivate the keypad. In this case, simply short circuit the phone throughout the entire dialing procedure and once completed, immediately and rapidly connect and disconnect your "jumper," which, if done properly will allow the call to be placed.

A more direct approach to pay-phone abuse is actually making money from it. To accomplish this, you need access to the line feeding the telephone. This is often easiest in cases when the telephone is in a location that is below ground and the main distribution cable is in the ground above the telephone's location, such as the lower levels of buildings and subways. If you are able to get to the wires, then cut them, or at least one, so that the dial tone has been lost. Wire colors are irrelevant here since I have seen many different colors used, ranging from blue to striped multicolor. By cutting wires, you should have the effect of cutting all power to the phone. When someone walks up to the telephone, he doesn't usually listen for a dial tone and simply deposits his quarter. The quarter then falls into the hopper, and since there is no power to cause a line reversal, the relay will not release the coin. The coins can then be retrieved by reconnecting the wires and flicking the switch hook to initiate a line reversal, which will result in a coin return.

A word of warning: Telco monitors their pay phones and knows when to expect the coin box to be full. Computer-based operations systems aid collection by preparing lists of coin boxes that are candidates for collection, taking into account location and projected activity. The coins collected are counted and entered into the operations system. Discrepancies between actual and expected revenue are reported to Telco security, which investigates them and reports potential security problems. Routine station inspections are also performed during collection, and out-of-service or hazardous conditions are reported immediately for repair.

The privately owned electronic pay phones are just as susceptible to attack, if not more so. Most notably, just by hitting the digital ones hard enough in the area of the coin slot sometimes causes the pay phone to enter a "Maintenance Mode," where the LCD display shows something to the effect of "Not in Service-Maintenance Mode" and then prompts you for a password, which, when entered, places you in a diagnostic/maintenance program.

Another notable weakness lies in the touch tones the digital telephones produce when it places a call through the PBX. If you can record them and identify them, you will have a number and working access code for the PBX used by the telephone. Identification of the tones is difficult, though, since they are sent at durations of 50 ms.

Perhaps even more interesting with these phones is that the operator will not identify the phone number you are calling from. She does, however, appear to have ANI capabilities, since one operator confided that she knew the number, yet was not allowed to release it. There is a reason for this. These telephones can be serviced from remote, being equipped with an internal 300 baud modem. The phones enter the "Maintenance Mode" when they are connected to, and are therefore "Out of Service," as the display shows. Others will enter a "Maintenance Mode" only at a specific time of day, when activity is lowest, and only then can they be reached. From remote, diagnostic functions can be performed, as well as the ability to poll the unit to determine the amount of money in the coin box, plus an accounting of local and long-distance calls, though these functions will, of course, differ from phone to phone.

The "Telco copies" also contain a 300 baud modem. Since ANI is locked out from the keypad, the number can only be obtained through the operator; she is not aware that you are calling from a pay phone, since the station has been installed on a standard customer line. Since 0+ calls are available through this unit, Directory Assistance can be obtained for free by dialing 0-NPA-555-1212. Since the telephone is configured not to charge for calls placed with 0's before them (to allow for calling card calls) the call is free.

Conclusion

I have tried to make this article as informative and accurate as possible, obtaining information from various manuals as well as personal experience. Since pay phones are public, the best way to learn about them is simply to experiment with them on your own. Good luck.

The Phone Company Infrastructure

In order to truly appreciate what the Bell System was, it's essential to have some understanding of how the whole thing was put together. There were so many aspects to the massive operation from pay phones to central offices to the computer systems that ran it all. There was also a lot of diversity in the network since it was right at this time that the conversion from mechanical to electronic was in full swing. Ancient step offices still operated side by side with modern #5 ESS switches. Rings sounded different depending on where you were calling. Some people had incredibly modern service while others barely had a dial tone. Some even managed to avoid the Bell monopoly well before the divestiture by having what was known as an independent phone company to serve them. As you'll read, that didn't always work out for the best.

The Early Phreak Days (November, 1985) *By Jim Wood*

When I decided to get married back in 1962, I traded my DJ and broadcasting odd jobs for one at the phone company; employment which, at that time, was ultimately secure though my take-home pay was about $300 a month.

Assigned to the Palo Alto, California, central office as a Toll Transmission man, my duties included maintenance of toll traffic circuits and related short-haul N and ON carrier equipment. Circuit testing was initiated at a black bakelite Type 17B Toll Testboard. A field of several hundred jacks gave access to as many interoffice trunks, many to the San Jose 4A and Oakland 4M 4-wire switching centers.

Though it was strictly forbidden, one could easily and safely "deadhead" toll calls for one's self, family, or friends from the Testboard. Around Christmastime our office could easily have been confused with the Operator room on the floor below.

The 17B Testboard had a 0-9, DTMF keypad arranged in two rows of 5 buttons wired to the central office "multifreq" supply. A rack of vacuum tube L/C oscillators comprised the MF supply and was buried somewhere in the bowels of the building.

Long days with too much (mostly union) staff and not enough to do precipitated a lot of screwing around on the job. Some of the guys would just daydream out the windows, others would hassle and torment the operators downstairs. One favorite trick was to sneak into the access space behind the bank of 3C switchboards and push the cords slowly up toward the operators. The screams and commotion caused by a tip, ring, and sleeve "snake" was worth the risk of getting chewed out by the old battle-ax who ran the place. Myself, I just played with the Bell System; never with any intent to defraud, merely to increase my understanding of how the whole thing worked.

It was during a singularly dull day that I hit on the idea of "deadheading" calls through one of the local subscriber loop jacks, which rang into the Testboard. Sure enough, I could rotary-dial through the step office to Sacramento (the shortest hop on

L carrier with in-band signaling), "dump" the call in Sacramento with a blast of 2600 from the 19c oscillator mounted overhead, then multifreq out of Sacramento anywhere I wanted to go. Wow! I could hardly wait to demonstrate this potential source of lost revenues to my first-line supervisor. Both he and his boss were mildly impressed, but assigned minimal importance to the event since, in their words, "no one has a multifreq supply at home."

Ma Bell invented the transistor but was among the last to put it into service. One of the few places a transistor was used in our office was in the alarm circuit of the ON carrier system. The 13H was a wretched little "top hat" PNP with just enough beta to work in a bridged-T oscillator configuration. A half-dozen of these, some Olson Radio push buttons, and a handful of resistors and caps made a dandy MF supply.

The next demonstration was from the chief's own desk and did finally raise some concern. I was asked to "donate" the box and told to keep my findings strictly to myself. I have done so for more than 20 years now.

Vital Ingredients (October, 1984)

Switching Centers and Operators

Every switching office in North America (the NPA system) is assigned an office name and class. There are five classes of offices numbered 1 through 5. Your CO is most likely a class 5 or end office. All Long-Distance (Toll) calls are switched by a toll office, which can be a class 4, 3, 2, or 1 office. There is also a 4X office called an intermediate point. The 4X office is a digital one that can have an unattended exchange attached to it (known as a Remote Switching Unit—RSU).

The following chart will list the office number, name, and how many of those offices existed in North America in 1981.

Class	Name	Abb.	# Existing
1	Regional Center	RC	12
2	Sectional Center	SC	67
3	Primary Center	PC	230
4	Toll Center	TC	1,300
4P	Toll Point	TP	
4X	Intermediate Point	IP	
5	End Office	EO	19,000
R	RSU	RSU	

When connecting a call from one party to another, the switching equipment usually tries to find the shortest route between the Class 5 end office of the caller and the Class 5 end office of the called party. If no interoffice trunks exist between the two parties, it will then move up to the next highest office for servicing (Class 4). If the Class 4 office cannot handle the call by sending it to another Class 4 or 5 office, it will be sent to the next office in the hierarchy (3). The switching equipment first uses the high-usage interoffice trunk groups. If they are busy it goes to the final trunk groups on the next highest level. If the call cannot be connected then, you will probably get a reorder [120 IPM (Interruptions Per Minute) signal—also known as a fast busy]. At this time, the guys at Network Operations are probably going berserk trying to avoid the dreaded Network Dreadlock (as seen on TV!).

It is also interesting to note that 9 connections in tandem is called ring-around-the-rosy and it has never occurred in telephone history. This would cause an endless loop connection (an interesting way to really screw up the Network).

The 10 regional centers in the United States and the 2 in Canada are all interconnected. They form the foundation of the entire telephone network. Since there are only 12 of them, they are listed below:

Class 1 Regional Office Location	NPA
Dallas 4 ESS	214
Wayne, PA	215
Denver 4T	303
Regina No. 2 SP1-4W [Canada]	306
St. Louis 4T	314
Rockdale, GA	404
Pittsburgh 4E	412
Montreal No. 1 4 AETS [Canada]	504
Norwich, NY	607
San Bernardino, CA	714
Norway, IL	815
White Plains 4T, NY	914

In the Network, there are three major types of switching equipment. They are known as: step, crossbar, and ESS. Check past and future issues of *2600* for complete details on how these systems work.

Operators

Another vital ingredient of the Network is the telephone operator. There are many different kinds. What follows is a discussion of some of the more common ones.

- **TSPS Operator.** The TSPS [Traffic Service Position System (as opposed to This Shitty Phone Service)] operator is probably the bitch (or bastard for the phemale liberationists) that most of us are used to having to deal with.

  Here are her responsibilities:

  1. Obtaining billing information for Calling Card or 3rd number calls.
  2. Identifying called customer on person-to-person calls.
  3. Obtaining acceptance of charges on collect calls
  4. Identifying calling numbers. This only happens when the calling number is not automatically recorded by CAMA (Centralized Automatic Message Accounting) and forwarded from the local office. This could be caused by equipment failures (ANIF—Automatic Number Identification Failure) or if the office is not equipped for CAMA (ONI—Operator Number Identification).

- (I once had an equipment failure happen to me and the TSPS operator came on and said, "What number are you calling *from?*" Out of curiosity, I gave her the number to my CO, she thanked me, and then I was connected to a conversation that appeared to be between a frameman and his wife. Then it started ringing the party I originally wanted to call and everyone phreaked out (excuse the pun). I immediately dropped this dual line conference!)
- You shouldn't mess with the TSPS operator since she *knows* where you are calling from. Your number will show up on a 10-digit LED read-out (ANI board). She also knows whether or not you are at a fortress phone and she can trace calls quite readily. Out of all of the operators, she is one of the *most dangerous!*
- **INWARD Operator.** This operator assists your local TSPS ("0") operator in connecting calls. She will never question a call as long as the call is within *her service area*. She can only be reached via other operators or by a Blue Box. From a BB, you would dial KP+NPA+121+ST for the INWARD operator that will help you connect any calls within that NPA only.
- **DIRECTORY ASSISTANCE Operator.** This is the operator that you are connected to when you dial 411 or NPA-555-1212. She does not readily know where you are calling from. She does not have access to unlisted numbers, but she does know if an unlisted number exists for a certain listing.

- There is also a directory assistance for deaf people who use Teletypewriters (TTY's). If your modem can transfer BAUDOT (45.5 baud—the Apple Cat can), then you can call him/her up and have an interesting conversation. The number is 800-855-1155. They use the standard Telex abbreviations such as GA for Go Ahead. They tend to be nicer and will talk longer than your regular operators. Also, they are more likely to be persuaded to give more information through the process of "social engineering."
- Unfortunately, they don't have access to much. I once bullshitted with one of these operators and I found out that there are two such DA offices that handle TTY. One is in Philadelphia and the other is in California. They have approximately seven operators each. Most of the TTY operators seem to think their job is boring. They also feel they are underpaid. They actually call up a regular DA # to process your request—no fancy computers here! Other operators have access to their own DA by dialing KP+NPA+131+ST (MF).
- The TTY directory assistance, by the way, is still a free call, unlike normal DA. One might be able to avoid being charged for DA calls by using a computer and modem at 45.5 baud.
- **CN/A Operator.** CN/A operators do exactly the opposite of what directory assistance operators are for. You give them the number, they give you the name and address (Customer Name Address). In my experiences, these operators know more than the DA operators do and they are more susceptible to "social engineering." It is possible to bullshit a CN/A operator for the NON-PUBDA# (i.e., you give them the name and they give you the unlisted number). This is due to the fact that they assume you are a fellow company employee. The divestiture, though, has resulted in the break-up of a few NON-PUB#'s and policy changes in CN/A.
- **INTERCEPT Operator.** The intercept operator is the one that you're connected to when there aren't enough recordings available or the area is not set up to tell you the number has been disconnected or changed. They usually say, "What number did you dial?" This is considered to be the lowest operator life form since they have no power whatsoever and usually know very little.
- **OTHER Operators.** And then there are the: Mobile, Ship-to-Shore, Conference, Marine, Verify, "Leave Word and Call Back," Route and Rate (KP+800+141+121+ST—new number as a result of the breakup), and other special operators who have one purpose or another in the Network.

Problems with an operator? Ask to speak to their supervisor...or better yet, the group chief (who is the highest ranking official in any office), the equivalent of the Madame in a whorehouse (if you will excuse the analogy).

Some CO's, by the way, have bugs in them that allow you to use a 1 or a 0 as the fourth digit when dialing. (This tends to happen mostly in crossbars and it doesn't work consistently.) This enables a caller to call special operators and other internal Telco numbers without having to use a blue box. For example, 415-121-1111 would get you a San Francisco-Oakland INWARD Operator.

(Taken from Basic Telecommunications, Part IV, written by BIOC Agent 003.)

The Simple Pleasures of a Step Office (May, 1984)

There are still more than a few step offices in the United States today. Most of them are in rural areas, but there are still a few cities (mostly in the southern, southwestern, and western areas of the country) that have step. These antiquated telephone systems can best be described as a bunch of relays and wires—clicking and stumbling over themselves.

It's easy to find out if you're in a step office—especially if you're using a rotary dial phone. (In many step areas, that's all you *can* have, particularly on the east coast since they don't have what's known as common control, which allows for touch tones. Some offices have been converted, however, using some sort of tone to pulse converter—every time you hit a tone, you hear it being pulsed out.) With a rotary dial phone, you can hear the actual switching. If, say, you're dialing 675-9112—you'd dial a 6 and you'd hear what's known as the selector kick in (more on that later) with a kind of a clunk. Then you'd dial 7, and hear a second thing kick in with a mild click—that's what's known as the digit absorbing relay. Depending on the office, this relay can kick in on any or none of the numbers. What it does basically is absorb an extra digit which is only needed to make the telephone number seven digits long. So, in this case, the second digit of the number, which is 7, is the extra digit. You would probably be able to substitute any number for the 7 and still have the call go through, since that digit is ignored. Some offices absorb two of their digits, which means that they had five digit phone numbers before uniformity struck. To continue with our demonstration, you'd next dial a 5, and hear another click at the end of your dialing sequence. After dialing 9, you'd hear click, pop, snap—several things kicking in, then the 1, clunk-clink, and then the last two digits, which wouldn't produce any sounds at the end of them. Then it will go into a ring cycle, assuming that's a valid number in the office.

Step offices usually have a very mechanical sounding ring, similar to crossbar. Ring generators, though, can make step sound like ESS. Often you hear what sounds like a busy signal or static in the background as the number rings. An easy way to tell if you're dialing into a step office is to try dialing XXX-1111 and see how long it takes to get a ring or reorder or whatever. Then try calling XXX-0000. If it takes more time to get to the same point, it's a step office because step is the only system that actually pulses out the numbers all over again.

A Phreaker's Delight

It's much safer to blue box and phreak from a step office because they're very basic, crude offices with no safety features (safety for them, that is). And if you're lucky enough to live in a fairly large metropolitan area that's still on step, you might dial up a number that you know is ESS from your step area and flash the switch hook. You'll get what's known as a wink. That's the equivalent of whistling 2600 hertz for about a half second to reset the trunk. You'll hear a click-click. That's your cue to put in various multifrequency tones (KP+number+ST). 2600 hertz is not needed at all, and since that's the tone that usually sets off alarms, this is a very safe way to blue box. (Incidentally, this occurs more through a flaw with ESS and not step.)

If you *really* know what you're doing and you know a few things about step switching, you can, on a touch-tone phone, dial up a number and listen in the background for the switch level. Let's say you're dialing 941-0226. You won't hear it rotary dial *those* numbers, but you *will* hear another number or series of numbers in rotary step pulses. That's the selector we mentioned earlier. Let's say that after you dialed 941-0226, you heard a 5 being pulsed out. What does that mean? The selector is the decision-making part of the phone call. Different prefixes are stored in different levels in each central office. In this particular case, 941 happens to be stored in level 5 in whatever office you're calling from. There's no rhyme or reason to it; the selector level could be anything up to three digits in length. (If it was three digits, you'd hear each individual digit get pulsed out.) The toll center is usually level 1 and the operator is usually level 0. So what can be done with this information? If, after dialing 941-0226, you enter your *own* rotary five, you'll once again hear the click-click, which is your cue for MF tones.

While step offices have no special phone phreak trapping capabilities, they are just as dangerous as any other office as far as being traced. They have what's known as trap and trace. If a certain person (or computer) is being harassed, they'll put a trap plug on that particular line. If you happen to call into that number, you won't be able to hang up until the other party does.

Some More Tricks

In some step areas, local calls are limited to certain exchanges that have the same first digit as yours. For example, the 222 exchange can dial 235 and 263 as local calls. But in order to call the 637 exchange, you must first dial a 1, which makes the call non-local. If you dial a 6, you'll get an immediate reorder. But somewhere between you and the 637 exchange are the 231, 233, 235, and 239 exchanges. There's no 237. So you dial 2. Clunk-clunk. You dial 3. Click. And then you dial 7. Ching-clunk. It goes to the 637 exchange! Similarly, a 281 from the 287 exchange could wind up in 471. Why? Because these numbers are all coming from the same switching center. That just happens to be the way step works (and in some cases crossbar). If you could seize the 222 trunk, you'd enter KP+25500+ST to reach 222-5500. To reach 637-5500, you'd enter KP+75500+ST.

Then there's "step crashing"—if the number you're calling is 675-2888, and it's busy, you can dial 675-2887, and in between the last pulse of your rotary dial and the time it would start to ring, you can flash your switch hook extremely fast. If you time it right, you'll hear an enormous loud click on your end. Then, all of a sudden, you'll cut into your party's conversation. (This works because of step's relay system. One relay has determined that the line you dialed is open. Then, before a second relay sends along the ring pulse, you throw in a 1, which jumps the number you dialed up by one, and fools the system into connecting you to a busy number.) There is one drawback to this, though. You, the party you've crashed in on, and the party they were talking to are all stuck together until you all hang up at the same time.

If you're in a step office where 411 is used for directory assistance, chances are that there are test codes in the format of 11XX. 1191 might be ringback, etc. In such places, dialing 1141 will also get you directory assistance, but at no charge! In some of the newer step offices, 410X is the format for tests. There, you can dial 4101 for free directory assistance. Other test numbers are (usually): 4100—off-the-hook recording, 4102—testboard, 4103—miscellaneous, 4104—ringback, 4105—disconnects your line for about 5 minutes, 4106—various tests, 4107—pulse test, 4108—testboard, and 4109—your telephone number in touch tones.

Different Varieties of Step

There's more than one kind of step office. We've been talking about the most common type, used by both GTE and Western Electric (Bell). It was invented by Automatic Electric early in the century. 214-381 is a typical Bell step office (note the reorder in the background of the ring) while 214-256 is a typical GTE step office (the ring sounds like it's underwater). For both of these, a suffix of 1798 will always provide a busy signal, free of charge.

There is also something known as XY step, which is strange, unusual, and for the most part put together very poorly. It looks similar to a crossbar in appearance. Instead of a round switch, it's tall and rectangular-shaped. To dial a number, it moves up and across a ladder of contacts, as if it was a piece of graph paper, hence the name XY. On these systems, the last digit in the phone number is usually up for grabs. You can accept collect calls on a number with a different last digit from yours. The calls will still reach your number, but it won't show up on your bill. Also, suffixes beginning with 9 and 2 are usually interchangeable. A typical XY step office is 518-789. A suffix of 3299 will get you a standard step test.

Great Britain uses the Strowger system and there is also the all-relay step, which is *very* rare. It was developed presumably to save switches. One such system exists in

Heath Canyon, Texas, with only 36 subscribers at 915-376. A neighboring town that's also all-relay can be found at 915-386.

If you'd like us to tell you something about a particular exchange anywhere, send us the info. We'll investigate and print the results.

How to Get Into a CO (March, 1985) *By The Kid & Co.*

Having spent a lot of time trashing outside the CO, I decided it was time to see what was inside. The first idea that came to mind was to try and make my own informal tour. This was impossible due to the magnetic lock on the door. So my next thought was to arrange a tour legitimately; who would expect a phreak to try that?

A call to the business office started me on my way. They in turn gave me the phone number of the Public Relations people, who told me to send a letter to a primary switching office in my area. I anxiously waited for several weeks. Then one day I received an urgent phone call from the Telco while I was out. Thinking it was Bell Security, I became nervous. I called back but the person who called was out. So I had to wait. Sure enough he called back. I was very relieved when he informed me that he was calling about the tour I had requested. I was also surprised to find that he sounded like a reasonable human being. We worked out some details and set up a date for the tour. I now had to select the group to go with me and prepare some questions.

I could bring up to 10 people on the tour. My obvious first choice was my phriend, The Shadow. The real problem was who else could I bring? I did not want to take a chance on someone saying too much and thus creating a problem. So I chose several others, sticking to people who were just interested in the tour because they wanted to know what the CO was, but weren't smart enough to ask embarrassing questions.

The Shadow and I spent several hours preparing questions to get the maximum benefit from the tour. We found that those few hours we spent preparing ourselves were well worth the time. We started with simple questions to which we already knew the answers. These would lead to the more complex and specific questions, without revealing our true identities as telecommunications hobbyists.

After weeks of waiting, the day of the CO tour arrived. We were ready! Notebooks in hand, ready to record the commentary, we drove the familiar route to the CO. We looked nostalgically at the dumpster and thought, "No. Not now, later." Upon arrival, we were forced to wait outside while our guide, the system manager, was being notified. He finally appeared and greeted us pleasantly. Much to my surprise, he did not look like a standard Telco employee, for he did not wear the obligatory flannel shirt. We entered the building and took the elevator to the switching room. I took control of the situation by BS'ing our guide while The Shadow copied down anything he could find written on the walls, etc. We were shown a # I Crossbar Tandem and the ESS# I A, which were co-residents on the switching floor. We examined the billing tape drives and asked several questions as to the nature of the tape. After 20 minutes or so on the switching floor, he took us to the floor where the wires came in from the outside. While on this floor we also noticed a TSPS machine, of which he had little knowledge, since "that's AT&T." After asking a few more questions and taking more notes, he gave me his number and told us to call him if we had any more questions.

Some Facts

The tour was very informative. We had several misconceptions cleared up. The first—and probably most important—was the mystery of the *billing tape*! Exactly what does it contain? The tape contains records of the following types of calls: 0+, 1+, and 7-digit numbers out of your local calling area. In other words, they only record the numbers that you or someone else will have to pay for (1+800, collect calls as well). The tapes are then sent to the billing office, which handles the billing for both the local Bell and AT&T. According to our guide, the ESS does *not* keep track of every digit dialed. This is not to say that it can't be done, but that it would be impractical. His CO handles well over a million calls a day, and if it were to keep track of all the digits dialed, the storage requirements would be tremendous. Does the ESS print out a list of exceptional 1+800 callers every day? The answer is *no*, the ESS does not! But the billing tape does contain records of 1+800 usage, and that type of processing may be done by the billing department, not the CO.

During the tour, we were introduced to the ESS#1A. Our ESS is running a #7 generic program. The #9 generic program is the revision that identifies the number calling you before you answer. It consisted of two equipment racks, each 6×10 full of printed circuit boards and IC's. All of the boards were push-in, pull-out for easy servicing. One might think from the description of the ESS that we have given that it does not require much space. The ESS processor does not require much space at all, but the equipment that interfaces the local loop with the call processor requires quite a bit more. Unknown to most, the ESS #IA consists of two independent processors that are constantly checking each other. They perform diagnostics if discrepancies do occur. This is a technique similar to the one used by the space shuttle's computers except that it is more reliable. You cannot shut down the ESS and put a whole town out of touch with the world just because the computers don't agree. The ESS is programmed via magnetic tape drives. The ESS stores the information about its configuration and information about your phone line (special features like call waiting, call forwarding, speed calling, touch or rotary dialing) on two massive hard drives.

Fiber optics are in use! As my group discovered, they are being put on poles all over the place. The cabling is called Light Guide and is made by Western Electric. The transmission system used is called SLC-96 (Slick 96). This system carries 96 simultaneous phone conversations on a single optic fiber. Our guide unfortunately did not know more than the name of the system and its capabilities.

How You Can Meet Your CO

You probably would like to know how you can arrange your own CO tour. You've spent all that time staring in, but now you're willing to meet all those nice people inside. The first thing to do is to find a group to go with. The people at the Telco are more likely to let a legit organization visit, rather than just a random group of people. Having just one or two people show up will really make them suspicious. Be sure to take along at least one responsible person to make it look legit. Try groups such as the Boy Scouts, an Explorer Post, a school class, a computer club, or simply come up with a legitimate-sounding name (not the Legion of Doom or the 2600 Club). This group should consist of people who logically have an interest in the phone system—the Audubon Society might seem a little out of the ordinary. The group should be interested in electronics. A bored group will want to move on quickly, despite your interest. Don't take only phreaks, as the Telco may get suspicious. The person who attempts to set up the tour should also have no record with Bell Security, as a routine check might be implemented. Be sure to get a good mix of technical/nontechnical people on the tour.

After finding such a group, you should contact the local telephone company's public relations office. Companies are worried about their image, for people tend to acquire an anti-big-business bias when they receive big bills. They will jump at the opportunity to combat this prejudice, and will do their utmost to ensure a tour, even over the objections of workers. Set up a mutually convenient time for your appointment and let your group know.

Proper planning is the best way to maximize information gathering. Questions should be thought out in advance. The questions should start out nontechnical, gradually progressing toward the technical as the guide lets down his/her guard. Be careful not to make the questions obviously phreak-oriented. Ask about common knowledge and general interest subjects, such as equal access, the AT&T split-up, fiber optics, and just how does my call get where it is going. Remember, the guide thinks he is showing around another group of idiots. Questions relating to phraud should be asked innocently, and with references that you have heard about this terrible, dreadful subject in the popular media. Questions about blue boxing should quote articles about general phreaking and hacking. *Newsweek* articles and "$12,000 calling card bills delivered via UPS" news stories. Remember, you don't want to put him on his guard. For better results, spread your questions around for trustworthy friends to ask. Don't be stingy for you don't want all the attention.

On the actual day of the tour, be sure to bring along notebooks. You will want to record this event for posterity, and for your phriends. If the guide comments on your note taking, just say you are going to write a report for school or an article for your club's newsletter (sounds familiar?). Take down any test or other numbers you see on the wall, but try not to "borrow" or you could be in big trouble. We have heard, third hand, of some phreaks on a CO tour who took whatever they could down their shirts, etc. After the tour, they were taken into a room where they were forced to disgorge all they had phound. It isn't worth the risk to steal.

On the tour, conduct yourself properly; you don't want to stand out. Resist the urge to answer others' stupid questions yourself. Do not show off knowledge. Only gently prod the tour guide on subjects you are interested in. The guide will usually give you his number for further questions; be sure to keep it. Leave a good impression so that fellow telecommunications hobbyists can tour the place in the future.

These basic techniques can be used to get a tour at almost any location. Other places you might consider are local AT&T Bell Research facilities, GE, Northern Telecom manufacturing plants, or any computer center. On a tour you can easily pick up information that is difficult or impossible to find otherwise. At the very least you can get the type of switch your CO uses. For the most accurate information on your telephone system, go right to the source, your local CO!

A Friend in High Places (September, 1984)

Yet Another True Story of Telecommunication Fun

Once upon a time there was a most unusual phone phreak and it was a phone phreak who didn't realize it. Her name was Joanne. She had a very remarkable position in that she was a telephone operator in an extremely small, rural, Midwestern community. A friend of mine, who was a radio D.J., got a job in this small town. One night he had a few drinks after he got off work. He called this operator up and started talking to her for a while. She didn't hang up. In fact, she was quite cordial, quite nice, quite friendly. She said, "Would you like to call Dial-a-Record (in Australia)? Or Dial-the-Time in London? Or any other dial-it services? If there are any phone calls you'd like me to place *for free*, just let me know."

So Joanne proceeded to place a lot of long-distance calls for the guy for free. He introduced me to her and said you can call Joanne for free by dialing a certain out-of-service number. She'd say, "What number did you dial, please?" And then she would quickly forward it to the other intercept operator in the nearby large city where she would tell the operator what number was dialed and then they'd put on the standard out-of-service or number-changed recording. I'd say, "Hey Joanne, it's me, call me back!" And she would. And I'd talk to her all night long because I was a security guard at the time. We'd place long-distance calls, conference calls like you wouldn't believe. One day she said that the switchboard was going to get phased out—a new TSPS switchboard was being installed in the large community and was going to serve all of the small communities in a four or five state area.

But Joanne continued to be a phone phreak and to this day she's working as a secretary for a senator in Washington, DC. She still does some pretty remarkable things, even though she's not an operator.

You might want to call up your local operator, provided you live in a small town, and just say hi sometime. I've done it on occasion and operators are usually fairly friendly, but far from phone phreaks. You might want to try this with directory assistance (they double as operators in smaller locales).

Who knows, you might find another Joanne someplace. One never knows.

The Woes of Having a Small-time Rural Phone Company (May, 1984)

This story is for those of you who hate Ma Bell. In many parts of the country, Bell is not the company that provides you with telephone service. There are lots of tiny telephone companies out there and some of them make Bell (and her children) look pretty terrific. The following is from one of our readers who has to put up with a rural telephone company.

I had a problem with my telephone company. I picked up my line, and there was a dial tone there. I began to make a long-distance call. After the tenth digit went through, I heard: "do weee doo...We're sorry, your call cannot be completed as dialed. Please check the number before dialing again or call your business office for assistance."

So I switched to my good phone, which makes clean crisp tones and dialed the same number again. I got the same message again! I said, "What the hell?!" (It was an 800 number, of course.) So I switched over and dialed a regular "1 plus" number—I started dialing the number direct: the same recording came on!

So I dialed my local business office, which is the repair service. It was a local seven-digit number. Again, all I got was: "do weee doo..." Then I dialed the operator, waited a second or two, and the recording came back on. I had an idea. "I know what they've done; they've made a mistake in the central office and changed my touch-tone rating to rotary!" Doing that would certainly produce the effect I was getting. If you tried to break the dial tone, you couldn't call anything because it's not programmed in. They must have made an error somewhere. I picked up my rotary dial phone and dialed the local repair service again. But it did the exact same thing on the rotary phone!

So I tried calling a local number (local to my exchange) and got the recording. *I dialed my own number!* "Your call cannot be completed as dialed." I tried 411—same thing. I dialed 611, the old centralized repair service that had been phased out in my area but which rings in a distant city served by the same telephone company. An operator said, "Can I have the number you're speaking from?" and I told her, "Thank you," ring, ring, ring, click, "This is telephone repair service. Can I have the number you're reporting, please?" I gave her the number. "Oh sir, I'm sorry, that number is no longer served by our repair service. You'll have to call your local repair service number," which was the one I couldn't get through to. I said, "Operator, I tried calling that and I got a recording saying the number I called cannot be completed as dialed." And she said, "Well, I'm sorry, you'll just have to call and report it to your office." I said, "I cannot! Can you pass this information along to *my* repair service? There's something wrong with the phone line—it only dials you." "I'm sorry, I'm not allowed to do that. I *can't* do that."

So I hung up and called 611 again and the first operator popped on the line again, and I said, "Operator, I'm not going to give you the number I'm calling from—I'm having a very difficult time. I called repair service; they were nasty and hateful and wouldn't respond to getting my phone fixed." I told her I had to call my local repair service, but was physically unable to. I asked if she could call it for me. "Certainly, I'll be glad to. What's your phone number and I'll call you back." I gave her the phone number, waited about 40 seconds and called her back. I asked, "What happened?" She said, "I got a recording when calling your number saying that my call couldn't be completed as dialed." "OK, that's the problem, anybody trying to call my number gets that recording—anything I try to call *gives* me that recording." "Well, let me try to ring repair again."

We ring repair service and get the *same lady* again. "Sir, I told you you're going to have to call your own repair service. Don't bother me with this anymore! I've told you we cannot help you here." I said, "Don't you have a phone there?" "Yeah." "Can't you pick it up and call my local repair service number? It's a seven-digit listed number, can you not call it?" "No, I cannot! It's not my duty; it's not my job. You should be able to do this yourself. You're going to have to go down to the repair service or use a [semi-]convenient pay phone," which is 10 miles away. Hell, the repair center is closer!

I got in the car, red-faced with hysteria, and I drove in and called repair service from inside the telephone building. I went into a door marked "Employees only!" I just picked up the phone; no one was there. A person picked up and said, "Can I have the number you are reporting, please?" I yelled, "NO!" "What are you calling me for?" "I want to talk to somebody in person about my problem. I've got a terrible problem and it cannot be handled over the phone. Please come down the hallway—I'm somewhere in your building."

She came in and I explained to her the rude treatment I got from centralized repair service. "I'm terribly sorry that happened...OK, you're going to have to come into the business office. Just go down the hall. Talk to one of our well-trained service representatives, and they will help you." "Why can't *you* help me—you're the repair service!" "Just take this form and hand it to the lady at the desk."

I went to one of the service reps and went over the whole story again. While I was telling her this, I noticed a 75-year-old senior citizen right next to me talking to *his* rep. He had a very similar problem. He was getting nowhere. And I said to him, "You might as well take your telephone and throw it in the river, because you're not gonna get any service out of these people! They are the sorriest human beings that ever drew a breath. They don't give a damn about you. They certainly don't give a damn about me!" (I'm now yelling at the top of my lungs, by the way.) I said, "These people don't care about anything except collecting their paychecks. You might as well just leave!"

All of the people in the telephone company were looking at me: all the customers, all the business reps. And I told them, any time I report anything there, I get treated like some sort of an asshole. For instance, two weeks earlier I had reported that pay phones in this particular prefix wouldn't dial 800 numbers. If you dialed an 800 number, you got a request to put in a 25 cent deposit. When I reported *that*, they said, "Yes, you must pay for your 800 number, like it was a local call." (You won't get your money back from the phone—they are Northern Telecom phones that don't have a return coin slot, so it can't give you your coin back.) I had told them, "It is a *toll-free* 800 number, hence the word 'toll-free'. You do not have to put in a quarter." All of the representatives said, "No, you've got to put in a quarter. You must pay for a toll-free 800 number."

Well, to make a long story short, the young lady was so upset that I was yelling and screaming at everyone in there, that she took my record, dashed out of the room, came back and said, "I'm terribly sorry to have inconvenienced you. I'm sorry that you're upset—I notice you're red in the face. Your phone will be turned back on before you get home. It was just an error. Someone didn't pay their bill and it was one digit away from your number and it was all a mistake."

The next day, I spoke to the vice president of the phone company and told him about my problem and the 800 incident, as well as a whole collection of other things that shocked and upset him. He said he was very grateful to me, and would consider hiring me as a consultant.

Since that episode, things have gotten better. 800 numbers are now toll-free from pay phones and the repair service is a little bit better. But there are still plenty of problems almost every time you dial.

You might say that it takes a phone phreak to straighten out a phone company. You might also say that Bell never looked so good.

Surveying the COSMOS (February, 1985) *By Firemonger*

COSMOS is Bell's computer for handling information on customer lines, special services on lines, and orders to change line equipment, disconnect lines, etc. COSMOS stands for Computerized System for Mainframe Operations. It is based on the UNIX operating system and, depending upon the COSMOS and upon your access, has some, many, or no UNIX standard commands. COSMOS is powerful, but there is no reason to be afraid of it. This article will give some of the basic, pertinent info on how users get in, account format, and a few other goodies.

Password Identification

To get onto COSMOS you need a dial-up, account, password, and wire center (WC). Wire centers are two letter codes that tell what section of the COSMOS you are in. There are different WC's for different areas and groups of exchanges. Examples are PB,

SR, LK, etc. Sometimes there are accounts that have no password; obviously such accounts are the easiest to hack.

Checking It Out

Let's suppose you have a COSMOS number which you obtained one way or another. The first thing to do would be to make sure it is really a COSMOS system, not some other Bell or AT&T computer. To do this, you would call it and connect your modem, then hit some returns until you got a response. It should say: ';LOGIN:' or 'NAME:' If you enter some garbage here it should say: 'PASSWORD:' . If you hit a return and it says 'WC?' , it is a COSMOS system. If it says something like 'TA%' then you're in business. If it doesn't do any of the above, then it is either some other kind of system, or, if you're not getting anything at all, the dial-up has probably gone bad.

Getting In

COSMOS has certain accounts that are usually on the system, one of which might not have a password. They consist of ROOT (most powerful and almost always on the system), SYS (second most powerful, still many privileges), BIN (a little less power), PREOP (a little less), and COSMOS (hardly any privileges, like a normal user). The way to tell if they have passwords is by entering the accounts at the ';LOGIN:' or 'NAME:' prompt, and if it jumps straight to 'WC?', all you need is a WC to get in. But suppose all of the accounts have passwords? You have two choices. You can try to hack the password and WC to one of the above accounts. I won't deal with this method, as it is self explanatory. Or you can do something I find much easier—call the COSMOS during business hours and hope that someone forgot to log off. Keep calling until when you connect and hit return until you get a 'WC%' prompt. 'WC' is the WC that the account you found is currently in. You are now in!

What to Do While Online

The first thing you want to do is write down the WC you are in. The command 'WCFLDS'(!) should list all WC's. On your first login it is a good idea to print everything or dump everything to a buffer:

- 'WHO' should print everyone currently logged on the system, giving some accounts.
- 'TTY' tells what terminal port you are on.
- 'WHERE' should tell the location of the COSMOS installation.
- 'WHAT' tells what version of COSNIX, COSMOS' operating system it is.
- 'LS *' prints all the files you have access to.
- 'CD /dir' connects you to directory 'dir.'
- 'Cat / filename' prints file 'filename.' Typing the name of a file runs it.
- 'ED filename' edits file 'filename.' 'Q' quits the editor.

If you've got privileges, you can try to print the password file. To do this, type 'CAT /ETC/PASSWD.' If you have access, it will print the password file out. The passwords are almost always encrypted, but you get a list of all the accounts. If you are lucky, one of the lines will have two colons after the account name. This means there is no prompt from the ';LOGIN:' or 'NAME:' prompts when you enter that account. If you can't print out the password file, you're going to have to hack a password for an account or call again until you get in the way described above. To logoff, type CTRL-Y. 'TAT' sometimes prints a little help file. To do a check on some telephone line, type 'ISH' at the COSMOS 'WC%' prompt. Then type 'H TN XXX—XXXX' (Hunt Telephone Number) to tell you about the local number you are interested in. When the system gives you a '—,' you type a '.', and it will type all kinds of info on the phone number you entered (in Bell abbreviations, of course). If it is not a good exchange, it will say something to that effect. You type a period to end the ISH.

If you wish to learn more information about COSMOS, find yourself a COSMOS manual or look at future issues of *2600*. A UNIX manual would also be helpful for standard UNIX commands.

An Interesting Diversion (October, 1985) *By Lord Phreaker*

A *diverter* is a form of call forwarding. The phone phreak calls the customer's office phone number after hours, and the call is "diverted" to the customer's home. This sort of service is set up so the phone subscriber does not miss any important calls. But why would a phreak be interested? Well, often diverters leave a few seconds of the customer's own dial tone as the customer hangs up. The intrepid phreak can use this brief window to dial out on the called party's dial tone, and, unfortunately, it will appear on the diverter subscriber's bill.

How Diverters Are Used

One merely calls the customer's office phone number after hours and waits for him or her to answer. Then he either apologizes for "misdialing a wrong number" or merely remains quiet so as to have the customer think it's merely a crank phone call. When the customer hangs up, he just waits for the few seconds of dial tone and then dials away. This would not be used as a primary means of calling, as it is illegal and as multiple "wrong numbers" can lead to suspicion, plus this method usually only works at night or after office hours. Diverters are mainly used for calls that cannot be made from extenders. International calling or the calling of Alliance Teleconferencing (see *2600*, May 1985) are common possibilities. Another thing to remember is that tracing results in the customer's phone number, so one can call up TRW or that DOD NORAD computer number with less concern about being traced.

Some technical problems arise when using diverters, so a word of warning is in order. Many alternate long-distance services hang up when the called party hangs up, leaving one without a dial tone or even back at the extender's dial tone. This really depends on how the extender interfaces with the local phone network when it comes out of the long haul lines. MCI and ITT are known to do this frequently, but not all the time. Also, hanging on the line until "dial window" appears doesn't work every time.

Now the really paranoid phreaks wonder, "How am I *sure* this is ending up on someone else's phone bill and not mine?" Well, no method is 100 percent sure, but one should try to recognize how a full disconnect sounds on the long-distance service of his choice. The customer's hanging up will generate only one click, because most diversions are local, or relatively local as compared with long distance. Also, the customer hanging up won't result in winks—little beeps or tweeps of 2600 hertz tones heard when an in-band trunk is hung up. The 2600 hertz tone returns to indicate the line is free, and the beginning burst of it is heard as it blows you off the line. Also, if there are different types of switching involved, the dial tones will sound radically different, especially between an ESS and a Cross-Bar (X-Bar) or Step-by-Step, as well as sounding "farther away." These techniques are good for understanding how phone systems work and will be useful for future exploration. The really paranoid should, at first, try to dial the local ANI (Automatic Number Identifier) number for the called area and listen to the number it reads off. Or one merely calls the operator and says, "This is repair service. Could you tell me what pair I'm coming in on?" If she reads off the phreak's own number, he must try again.

How to Find Diverters

And now a phreak must wonder, "How are these beasties found?" The best place to start is the local yellow pages. If one looks up the office numbers for psychiatrists, doctors, real estate agents, plumbers, dentists, or any professional who generally needs to be in constant contact with his customers or would be afraid of losing business while he is at home. Then one merely dials up all these numbers after 6:00 or so, and listens for multiple clicks while the call goes through. Since the call is local, multiple clicks should not be the norm. Then the phreak merely follows through with the procedure above, and waits for the window of vulnerability.

Other Forms of Diverters

There are several other forms of diverters. Phreaks have for years known of recordings that leave a dial tone after "ending." One of the more famous was the DOD Fraud Hotline's after-hours recording, which finally ended, after multiple clicks and disconnects, at an AUTOVON dial tone. One common practice occurs when a company finds its PBX being heavily abused after hours. It puts in a recording that says that the company cannot be reached now. However, it often happens that after multiple disconnects one ends up with a dial tone inside the PBX—thus a code is not needed. Also, when dialing a company and after talking (social engineering) with employees, one merely waits for them to hang up and often a second dial tone is revealed. 976 (dial-it) numbers have been known to do this as well. Answering services also suffer from this lack of security. A good phreak should learn never to hang up on a called party. He can never be sure what he is missing. The best phreaks are always the last ones to hang up a phone, and they will often wait on the line a few minutes until they are sure that it's all over. One item of clarification—the recordings mentioned above are *not* the Telco standard "The number you have dialed..." or the like. However, Telco news lines have been made to suffer from the diverter mis-disconnect.

Dangers of Diverting

So, nothing comes free. What are the dangers of diverting? Well, technically one is committing toll fraud. However, a list of diverter numbers is just that, a list of phone numbers. Tracing is a distinct possibility, but the average diverter victim doesn't have the technical knowledge to identify the problem.

There has been at least one investigation of diverter fraud involving the FBI. However there were no arrests and the case was dropped. It seems that one prospective victim in Connecticut realized that he was being defrauded after receiving multiple phone calls demanding that he put his diverter up now so that a conference call could be made. He then complained to the FBI. However, these aware customers are few and far between, and if a phreak does not go to such radically obnoxious extremes, it is hard to be caught. Unless the same number is used to place many expensive calls.

Competition... It's the Next Best Thing to Being There (Autumn, 1989)

We've just about had it with this NYNEX/New York Telephone strike. Since early August, we in the New York region have been living with substandard service, long delays getting through to information, nonresponsive repair service, a suspension of new orders, 50-minute waits for service reps after interminable busy signals, and pay phones that never seem to work.

Here's an exchange one of us had while trying to reach a service rep. One hour before closing, busy signal. Three phones were set to redial mode, each trying the same number. After half an hour, success! A ring, then a recording. "Due to the work stoppage, there will be a slight delay answering your call. Please hold on, etc." The announcement repeated every minute. Finally, at one minute before closing, a human being came on the line. "Hello, I can't hear you," they said. "What?" we asked incredulously. "I said I can't hear you." Click. We redialed. Sure enough, we were connected to their after-hours recording. Please call back when we're open. Right.

It gets worse. After going through about a dozen pay phones in the streets of New York without a single one working properly, after losing 75 cents trying to make a local call, the New York Telephone operator suggests we place the call using a calling card. "I can't access the billing information because of the strike," she said. "But I do know the surcharge is only 45 cents."

New York Telephone has this incredible habit of fixing their own faults by charging you extra. Another example centers on our fax machine, which, according to our AT&T bill, was calling people in Delaware and staying on for 15 minutes. When we started hearing from people who were trying to send us faxes but were instead getting strange human beings in another location, we realized what had happened. Again. An incompetent repairman had routed our fax line into someone's house. They got our calls and we got their bill. Apparently, the problem was fixed without us ever being notified. New York Telephone says there's no way for us to get credit for the local calls these people must have made or for the service interruption because what happened to us simply wasn't possible. If we wanted more information, though, we could obtain a local usage list for only $1.50.

In 1984, we made reference to the AT&T strike of 1983. The strikers weren't paid, the customers were charged full price for poor service, and the company made lots of unearned money. The same is true today of NYNEX/New York Telephone. With all the confusion that divestiture brought, we now at least have options to AT&T. With New York Telephone, there is no choice. No competition. And it's high time there was.

3 New Toys to Play With

The fact of the matter is that hackers simply love toys. Especially the kind that wind up controlling vast telecommunications networks, the kind that reach across the planet in ways most people could never imagine or appreciate, and the kind that you're really not supposed to be playing with in the first place.

Hackers always had a fascination for that sort of thing, for decades before the 1980s and right up until the present day. It will likely always be the case. But there was something really special about the decade of the '80s with regards to telecommunications toys, something that you had to live through in order to appreciate it fully.

Within those few years, everything exploded. There were suddenly all sorts of new telephone companies to explore and play with. Making a simple phone call became a cross between an ordeal and an adventure. Systems were popping up that were the ancestors of today's voicemail. We even found some early voice recognition systems. Faxes, pagers, teleconferences, cellular phones...in this decade it all came upon us so quickly. And with every discovery that a hacker or phone phreak made, there was an eager audience of readers waiting to figure out what it all meant.

Now obviously the world of computers was also expanding and evolving at an incredible rate. But the world of telephony and the changes it was going through at the time often gets glossed over. To me, both of these worlds along with the various others associated with hacker discoveries and adventures are utterly fascinating and revealing of where we've come as a culture, both hacker and human. But I've always had a soft spot for anything that could be done using a mere telephone because to me, that simple instrument was always the invitation to go and do more, to learn, to explore, to create mischief and mayhem. And it was weirder than anything I had ever witnessed to see the entire world appear to magically become aware of the full potential of these devices over the course of a few short years.

So what were all of these new toys? We can only scratch the surface in this chapter. Some were physical in nature, others were found on our phone lines, still others were merely conceptual in nature, for instance, the idea of being able to route your own phone calls over the long-distance network of your choice. In a nation where only a few years earlier, you couldn't even *own* a phone or put an extension into your house without permission from the phone company (yes, the one and only phone company), this meant all sorts of possibilities and new ways of doing things that hackers naturally played around with more than anyone else. Of course, there was much debate over whether or not we were in better shape as a result of the Bell System breakup and that is something that is also explored in this chapter. I think the growing pains naturally caused a lot of complaining, but almost everyone understood that the technological advances would far outweigh the confusion and chaos, which, to be honest, most of us got a real kick out of anyway. Other toys previously only enjoyed by large corporations (such as cellular phones and teleconferences) could now be accessed by normal everyday people, albeit at a significant price. But I find it intriguing to look back at how new and different it was back then to even *have* the access in the first place and at how incredibly expensive and clumsy that new access looks from our vantage point today.

Wherever there was some kind of a technological advance—and there was a new one practically every day in the telecommunications world of the 1980s—you could count on hackers being there to be the first ones on the block to find a way of playing around with it, mostly in ways not originally intended by those who had created it in the first place. Today, many of those mischief makers who were messing with phone lines, figuring out ways to monitor calls over radio waves, or simply letting the world know through our pages what didn't work and what new services were a rip-off—those people are now the ones making the new systems and creating new toys for the next generation of hackers. The sense of wonder and discovery you'll see here is the thread that unites young and old in the hacker community and it's what makes us who we are.

Alternate Long Distance (March, 1984)

First of a persistent series—how the companies work and a guide to MCI

SWAGIMA. That's the word that National Public Radio uses to describe long-distance services. It stands for SBS (or Skyline), Western Union (or Metrofone), Allnet (or Combined Network Services), GTE Sprint, ITT, MCI, and of course AT&T. And there are many more, each of which will eventually be covered in our pages. Right now though, we would like to give you an idea of what these systems are and how they work.

Except for AT&T, all of the above systems work in a fairly similar manner. (This will be changing very soon and very dramatically under the terms of the Bell divestiture.) Each system has its own series of networks, i.e. landlines, lines leased from AT&T, microwave relays, satellite links, etc. They each have local city access numbers, although some like Allnet and MCI have special ways of using a "travel" service by dialing a special number, while Sprint uses a "travelcode" to access nodes outside the subscriber's city. On others, like Metrofone, you can use the same authorization code from any of their access points.

A long-distance telephone company consists of four major parts: You have your input—that is, a local access number or a toll-free "800" number to access the system.

When you do this, a device called a "switch" answers, giving you the familiar "computer dial tone." When you enter your authorization code and destination number, you are routed over their network. The heart of the system is the controlling system, which includes the "switch." This is the computer that checks the authorization code, has provisions for time-of-day restrictions, travelcodes, accounting codes, and the like. They have a few provisions, which the long-distance services don't appear to use, such as the infamous "speed number" recording, which was a favorite of many phone phreaks (for reasons you'll soon know if you don't already). The system checks to see if the location being dialed is on the network, and acts accordingly. It makes a log of numbers called, the authorization code, and time usage, which is stored on a word processing tape and then read by another system for billing. Some companies charge in one minute increments, although the system has the capability to record time usage in 6-second increments.

There are quite a few different systems in use today. A couple of the most common ones are made by Northern Telecommunications, which is based in Dallas, Texas. Another company that sells similar equipment is Rockwell Wescom. MCI allegedly is in the process of buying new switches from them, and they will be installed by Dynacomp Telecommunications, also based in Dallas.

Microwave Links

Most of the low-cost services, at one point or another, use microwave antennas to transmit calls. Each microwave station is located about 30 miles from each other to make up for the curvature of the earth since microwaves travel in a straight line. Each of these stations has four dishes (at least). One dish is used to receive from a previous station and one is used to transmit to that station. The other two dishes do the same thing to the destination station—one receives and one transmits. So if you make a call 3,000 miles away, you may wind up going through 100 different microwave stations, many of which you can see next to major highways.

This is how the alternate long-distance companies manage to charge less than AT&T; they use their own systems. But this is also why, in many instances, the sound quality is poorer on the alternate services. Remember, a chain of microwave towers is only as strong as its weakest connection.

A Look at MCI

MCI (Microwave Communications Inc.) was the first new kid on the block, way back in 1967 when the idea of an alternate phone service was almost unheard of and practically illegal. MCI was first used solely by businesses who wanted to communicate between the cities of Chicago and Cleveland. That was it. And even with this amazingly limited system, MCI ran into problems with AT&T, who didn't want *anybody* trying to do what they did. Lawsuits followed, with MCI eventually getting a promise of eventual equal access to the AT&T network. In fact, MCI's legal action is largely considered to be one of the motivating factors behind the breakup of the Bell monopoly.

Now MCI is the biggest of the alternate services (they have well over a million subscribers at present, having opened their doors to residential customers a mere five years ago) and also one of the hardest to penetrate. The system has 5-digit codes that are entered before the 10-digit phone number, a total of 15 digits. But these codes only work from one location, making it rather unlikely to find one by guesswork. If you want to use the system from another city, you have to sign up for MCI "credit card" service, which costs an additional $5 a month (on top of an initial $5 a month charge for the regular service). Here you get a list of 48 phone numbers around the country and a 7-digit code, which can be used from any one of them. Most code seekers prefer scanning the "credit card" numbers since more numbers work overall. However, a strong argument can often be heard in favor of the 5-digit numbers that are located in densely populated areas like Los Angeles or New York. Naturally, the odds of finding something increase under those circumstances.

No Proven Method for Finding Codes

MCI, being the oldest of the companies, has learned quite a bit in that time. Therefore, no major bugs are still crawling around on their system. Hackers have many theories on number patterns, of course. For example, numbers like 22222 or 12345 tend *not* to work. In other words, your guess is as good as ours. As far as what they do when they know a code is being abused, MCI seems to be more interested in changing the code rather than laying a trap, as other companies have been known to do. Of course, this doesn't mean that they're incapable of doing such a thing.

MCI Features

The MCI tone sounds like all the others (a hollowish, medium-pitched, steady tone), but it has its own set of recordings, depending on what you do to it. If you enter an invalid code, you'll hear a mechanical female say: "THEE AUTHORIZATION CODE YOU HAVE DIALED IS INVALID TWO ZERO THREE" and then an ESS reorder that trips over itself (listen to it and you'll understand). If you dial someplace you're not supposed to call (for whatever reasons), you'll hear: "THEE NUMBER YOU HAVE DIALED IS NOT ON THE NETWORK TWO ZERO THREE" and the reorder. Each MCI dial-up has its own 3-digit identity code and they tend to be similar the closer together they are.

Many businesses are installing MCI "dedicated lines" in their offices, which takes away the task of having to dial the MCI access number. In addition, you don't have to enter an authorization code and you don't even have to have touch tones. You simply pick up the phone and there's your MCI dial tone! According to MCI, you have to make at least $75 worth of out-of-state calls per month for this system to pay off. Of course, you can't access operators, directory assistance, 800 numbers, and that sort of thing because 1) MCI doesn't support any of those services and 2) they're certainly not going to let you connect to something they can't charge you for. Of course, if you know what you're doing, you can route calls in such a way that numbers that aren't supposed to go through for you will work, and God knows where it finally shows up! This doesn't involve extra codes, blasting the line with tones, or anything overly suspicious. All you need is the right combination of area codes. Now this has been proven to work with MCI dedicated lines; it's rumored to work on dial-ups as well...

Finally, MCI is starting to offer its own phone booths at airports, which we'll report on as soon as we find one. And of course, there's MCI Mail, an electronic overnight mail service started up last fall, which hackers are currently probing.

IBM's Audio Distribution Systems Sure Can Be Fun! (May, 1984)

One day several years ago, a hacker was doing some routine 800 number scanning on his touch-tone telephone. This has become a very popular pastime because it's totally free and not easily defined as illegal in itself. Usually, what somebody does is zero in on a particular 800 exchange and dial many different numbers (often in sequential order), jotting down the interesting ones. That's exactly what this person was doing when he made a most interesting discovery. After hearing literally dozens of modem tones, and "Doo-Dooo-DOOOO! The number you have reached," "Eastern Airlines, can I help you?" and "Special operator, what number did you dial?" messages, he heard a recorded female voice say, "Please keypress your last name." After a millisecond or two, he looked at the letters on his touch-tone buttons (never get a phone without those letters), and started to spell out a name. Another recorded voice read back someone's full name and then the old voice came back and said, "Please keypress your password." He suddenly got an idea and spelled out the person's first name. It worked! He had broken in—to something.

What this person found that day (and what many others have been discovering ever since) was an IBM Audio Distribution System or ADS. Nearly every IBM regional office has at least one of them. Operating out of an IBM Series I computer interfaced with a telephone switchboard, their original purpose was to provide a fast, easy way for IBMer's to contact each other without playing "telephone tag." All a subscriber has to do is call the system, log in, and leave or receive aural messages. Commands are entered using touch-tone keys (*R—record a message, *T—transmit a message, *L—listen to a message, *C—customize certain features, *D—disconnect are the main commands. By pressing a 9 or a #, brief help messages can also be heard.). No computer terminals were needed here. Nearly *anybody* could figure out how to use the system.

Fortunately for hackers, IBM people were both careless and apathetic. Many of them had very easy passwords and others never used the system at all, even though they had been assigned accounts.

So guess what happened? Friendly tech enthusiasts found their way into these systems and grabbed accounts left and right. Many of them set up impromptu networks where they would exchange technical information, phreaking news, stories, anything! (Sort of like a computer bulletin board, except that your voice is your keyboard. This proved very beneficial to those phone phreaks that hadn't integrated themselves into the world of computers—here was a computer that could be played with without the requirement of a terminal and modem, as well as the means to communicate with computer hackers for the first time.) Messages could be as long as 8 minutes or as short as 3 seconds. Users could, by entering commands, adjust volume and speed, classify their messages (personal, confidential, personal *and* confidential, or internal use only), create distribution lists, change their status, etc. In short, the ADS has become a favorite toy of phreaker and hacker alike.

There are hundreds of ADS's all around the world, with more being plugged in every day. IBM is selling the systems to other companies, who then use them for their own employees, or lease accounts out to other people. IBM tells us that the price for a system with a 1,000 user capacity is about $110,000. Financing terms are available, they say.

It is quite reasonable to assume that every ADS that is presently operational has at least a few usurped accounts on it. Even systems in Italy and England are being mercilessly invaded by American crackers. What's particularly funny about all this is that IBM has no way of knowing whether the users of the system are legitimate or not, since the software is written to prevent eavesdropping, even from the system operator's account. It is also impossible to find out what somebody's password is, without being in that person's account. As one IBM executive told us, "As long as they don't do anything outrageous [like send abusive messages to other users] and the legitimate user doesn't tell us that his/her account is being used by someone else, we'll *never* know they're in there."

Needless to say, some high-level administrative meetings dealt with this problem. For IBM, things were starting to get out of control. One group of phreakers had so many different systems under control that they started to color code them. Rumor has it that they ran out of colors and were forced to buy a jumbo box of Crayola Crayons to find out the names of more. On the East Coast, a system was so heavily inundated with unauthorized users that it was commonly believed that there were more of them than legitimate users. And, somewhere in Italy, Midwest accents slowly started to abound on that country's sole system.

IBM began to make some drastic changes. To prevent intrusions from occurring in the first place, many of the systems were programmed to delete an account if it wasn't used within a certain period of time or if the password had not been changed from the system default (the first letter of the last name repeated three times). In an attempt to get rid of those that had already broken in, they started to look at their 800 number user logs, to see which accounts were constantly being logged into on the toll-free line instead of the local number or the IBM internal tie-line number. A company employee wouldn't have to use the 800 number unless he was on the road. But, they reasoned, a phone phreak would.

On this, of course, they were completely wrong. A phone phreak can make a call to anywhere he damn well pleases without spending a cent. A few even managed to access the IBM tie-line! Good phreaks, to avoid suspicion stopped using the toll-free numbers.

IBM reset passwords on suspect accounts and then went in to see what other names were linked by "reading" distribution lists and seeing what other names were being communicated with. The intruders answered this by deleting their distribution lists and erasing all old messages.

This battle of wills is continuous. One system operator in Los Angeles attached a recording that told anyone who failed to log in after three tries that their call had been traced. She later admitted to *2600* that this was simply a scare tactic used out of desperation.

Ironically enough, some of the worst offenders—as far as leaving doors wide open—are the system operators themselves. A few operators have left their privileged accounts' passwords set to the default (three zeroes). This allowed an intruder to come in and use the special "star-zero" command, which allows *system* messages to be changed. (These are the messages that tell the subscriber what to do next, etc.) "Please keypress your last name," could easily become "What the hell do you want?" There are hundreds of messages and oftentimes pranksters would change only the most rarely heard ones, to add to the surprise of the user who wound up hearing it; "Your message has reached the maximum length" was reportedly replaced by "You have spoken for too long and you may not speak again." Any user's password can be reset to the default from the operator account, so entry to all accounts is indirectly possible after cracking the operator account. Brand new accounts, though, are created offline.

If you like keeping in touch, an ADS may be just what you're looking for. With this system, your phriends are always reachable, no matter where they are.

Unless they've left the magical land of touch tones.

The Dark and Tragic Side of the Great Breakup (June, 1984)

I have had it up to here with this divestiture crap! I consider myself to be a very loyal phone phreak who has always hated Ma Bell with a passion. What I wouldn't give to have the good old days back, when Bell was the only game in town!

Now there's this strange entity called AT&T Communications. I *still* don't know where it is they're coming from. They're not my local company. They're my long-distance company that I never asked for. My local company (not AT&T!) decided to tell my long-distance company that I wanted a special service that allowed me to make lots of long-distance calls within my state for a discount. I didn't object at first. But then I saw myself getting charged a minimum fee every month I didn't use it! Who do I complain to? My local company? AT&T? They both blamed each other. Finally, AT&T said they'd fix it, but they never did. Now who do I complain to? The Public Service Commission in my state doesn't handle national telephone companies—only statewide ones. The business office ladies of my local company are very happy to listen to my complaints and are even happier to say, "That's AT&T, not us. We're not the same company anymore."

My local operator, for some reason, seems to be a part of AT&T. If I call to tell her that my house is burning, I fully expect to hear her say that I have to call my local telephone company and please leave AT&T out of it.

We never should have been allowed to get hooked on the Bell System—that's what spoiled us. Equal access from the beginning would have made sense. To have it suddenly start now is one big fat pain!

It's the government that's to blame, really—they're the ones that have screwed things up so badly. No one knows from one minute to the next how they're going to dial a number. First, they say we're going to dial 950-10XX for every long-distance call. Then they say we're going to skip the 950 part and just dial 10XX plus the number. Now they're telling us that we're going to have to subscribe in advance to MCI, Sprint, etc. Meanwhile all of these long-distance companies are popping up out of nowhere with advertising blitzes that make you feel like an idiot for not signing up right away. All it's doing is confusing the hell out of older people and people who aren't too bright as well as those who just aren't phone phreaks. My parents can't keep up from one minute to the next and I'm not much better off, despite my knowledge of the system!

The way I see it, this divestiture is going to cause all the smaller companies to give poorer service and go up on their rates even more. (Soon I won't be able to afford to call people *unless* they're long distance—local rates just keep climbing!) Local companies are letting their exchanges fall apart. They claim they're going to have to raise their rates to pay for maintaining the CO's. Service has gone downhill—even worse than it ever was. The whole thing is a mess.

Think of how easy it used to be. It was you and the phone company. The phone company provided your phone, fixed your phone, gave you local calls, long-distance calls, operators, free directory assistance. If you were a phone phreak, you had to worry about the phone company. Today, a phreak has to worry about so many different companies it'll make his head swim!

The old days will never come back, I guess. But let's try to remember them this way: Things were horribly unfair and dictatorial. But at least everything worked. The phone company took pride in its work instead of shifting the blame to another phone company. It was easy to complain, easy to get repair service to your door, easy to figure out if you could afford to make a call. The instruments lasted forever—in fact, my phones from the forties and fifties are in *much* better shape than the new crap I have!

Today things are fair and equal, or getting there. I, for one, can really see the difference.

MILESTONE: *2600* WRITER INDICTED (JUNE, 1984), 2600 *News Service*

It's been reported here and there that the editor of an underground magazine called *2600* has been charged with wire fraud in connection with the GTE Telemail investigation (see previous issues for details on this case).

One of our coordinating writers is, in fact, involved with this case—however he is not the "editor" of our magazine. *2600* is not handled by a single person, but by different people all over the country who contribute whatever they can, according to their abilities.

We are not an "underground" magazine; we don't break laws or publish items that are illegal to publish. We simply discuss interesting things that can be done with today's technology. There is certainly no reason for us to go underground.

As for the investigation, we are confident that our writer will be vindicated and left alone. He is planning to write a story concerning this "adventure" when it's all over, regardless of how it ends. He has our full support and we hope he has yours as well.

Exploring Caves in Travelnet (November, 1984)

One fine summer day several years ago, a phone phreak discovered yet another interesting telephone number. What was it? A modem? A dial tone? A very special operator? No to all of the above—*this* was something truly amazing and unique. This was TRAVELNET.

Of course, he didn't know at the time what he had dialed into. But this is what he heard. Two rings, a tone that lasted for about half a second (it had about the same pitch of a Sprint tone), and then a voice! Not just a recording, not just a human asking what it was you wanted, but a *recording* asking you what it was you wanted! Sort of like hearing an answering machine for the first time. But this was no answering machine.

"Authorization number, please," a sensual, husky female voice asked. And since he was a rather clever guy, he hit his touch-tone keypad. Every time he entered a tone, he heard a short "booop." like an acknowledgement of some sort. After four of these "booops" the automated lady came back and said "eighteightsevenzero." But, alas, those were not the keys he hit. In semi-desperation, he hit another key. The female voice came back and said, "Please repeat, yes or no?" But what was the question? He quickly realized that she must have been somehow trying to confirm the entry of his numbers. But how do you convey the word "no" on a touch-tone keypad?

He went through the whole process again and wound up getting dumped into a recording that said (in an authoritative female voice), "The Travelnet number you dialed is incorrect; please check the number and dial again."

He called back. Again he tried entering numbers and tried to figure out why they wouldn't correspond. All of a sudden, his baby sister (who had been growing increasingly bored with a rattle in the next room), decided to let out the sort of scream that baby sisters are known for. What's important about this is that after the scream was over, our friend heard quite distinctly over the telephone lines: "booop."

"Wow." he said. "Booop." it repeated. It recognized speech! He called it back and started entering numbers with his voice. It worked! After four numbers were entered, it would repeat them back to him and he had the option of saying either "yes" or "no." If he said "yes" or remained silent, he had the opportunity to enter four more numbers. If he said "no" the machine would make every effort to find out what the number was by asking him twice just what it was he meant to say. There were a few simple rules—he had to enunciate clearly and say the word "zero" instead of "oh."

But what would this lady let him do if he guessed the right eight numbers? And how could he possibly get such a long number anyway. Would he have to call up the lady and slowly and patiently pronounce little words over and over? Since he knew that there were over 100,000,000 possible combinations and that no more than a thousand probably worked, he understood that it would take some thinking to satisfy the mechanical voice. He needed to find some good old-fashioned human incompetence. If the machine had trouble hearing him, or if he remained silent, it would eventually say, "Sorry, we're having difficulties." Then it would connect him to a human. He stuck on the line and when the operator answered, he asked her what number he had dialed. "This is General Motors Travelnet, sir," she replied. "I'm terribly sorry," he said. "I was trying to get the speaking clock." "That's okay," the operator said. "Good-bye."

So it was General Motors! This would be easy. He waited a day and called back. He got connected to another operator, who asked him what he wanted. "This is J.C. Steppleworth from Fort Wayne GMAC," he snarled. "And I've been having trouble using this confounded phone system." "Well, why don't you call the instruction number, sir?" She gave him the number. He called this number and heard a full demonstration on how to use the system. It was used to make phone calls, which he sort of suspected. After you enter your 8-digit code, you enter a 10-digit phone number or, if dialing internally within General Motors, a 7-digit number. The recording even spoke a demo authorization code to get the point across. After hearing this, our friend wondered if he should try the demo code. "No," he decided. "They couldn't possibly be *that* stupid." He tried it anyway and guess what? The moment he confirmed the last number, the lovely voice asked a new question: "Destination code, please?" (In other words, the phone number you're trying to call.)

It was an extender—a long- and short-distance phone service. He proceeded to test it, out, and he found that he could call virtually anywhere in the country for free. But who cares about free calls? He wanted to explore. And explore he did. He tried many things and learned many things. He found that he could avoid the lady's voice if he keypadded in the numbers before she could speak. This way the call would go through normally without any arguments on pronunciation. This allowed him to test many, many codes without much hassle. He found that by mixing up his working code a little, he was able to find many new ones. The simplicity was astounding. In a short time, he had found literally hundreds of codes. After this, he sat down one day and stared at his list of codes. All of a sudden, he realized something. Each group of four added up to either 9, 19, or 29—a sort of base-nine code. He wrote a short program and printed out all possible four-digit combinations that added up to these magic numbers. He was set for life.

He used the system to explore internal offices. If no area code was entered, every exchange put you in a different part of the country. One exchange, 999, simply dumped him into a feed from a Detroit radio station. One day, his Demon-dialer, which is basically a touch-tone generator with a memory, came across a reorder (a fast busy signal) that turned into a dial tone in 20 seconds. The connection wasn't great, but he found that he could make a direct call *anywhere*. He could dial overseas directly. He figured that he was at the switchboard of some office branch far away from where he originally called. He found out what the number was by calling a friend person-to-person collect, who then asked the operator for the number so that the "person" could call back when he returned. When he called up the number he was dialing from, they answered. "GMAC." So it was some distant office that he was making his calls out of, using a Travelnet code and an internal number to get there. It was so roundabout that he knew nobody would figure it out. In fact, several people that he called received calls from that office asking if they knew anybody who worked there that would call them at three in the morning. It was incredible! Even if a friend had *wanted* to frame him, it was doubtful that they would connect him with this distant city from which the call supposedly emanated. And the funny thing was that the company was probably placing a 24-hour armed guard on the building, thinking that someone was breaking in and making calls. Someone was, but in a way they could never figure out.

There's much more to the world of Travelnet, particularly on their internal network. And the same number works to this very day, which, by the way, is toll-free. But we've heard of cases where people have been trapped into paying for what they did and it's quite likely the system is heavily monitored.

A similar system called WIN was used by Westinghouse before they gave up in disgust after their lines were constantly tied up by phreakers and hackers. Honeywell makes the actual system and there are others in use around the country—one, we hear, for the state offices of Illinois, another for Ralston-Purina, the folks who blow up sewers in Louisville, KY.

As usual, nobody at Travelnet understood any of the questions we asked them and no one returned our calls. Maybe the lines were all tied up.

How to Run a Successful Teleconference (May, 1985)

By The Shadow

Alliance Teleconferencing Service is a bridging service offering teleconferencing to businesses. A conference merely is several phone lines tied together allowing people to talk to many locations at once. Alliance is owned by AT&T Communications. They use #4 ESS's (Electronic Switching Systems) to control their conferences. According to Alliance, conferences can be originated and controlled from most locations in the United States. The service started out in area code 202, but has been spreading throughout the country. One thing to remember is that even in the same area code some central offices will allow access, and others may not. Conferees can be from anywhere dialable by AT&T, including international. Alliance can be reached at 800-544-6363 for social-engineering or for setting up conferences in locations that cannot access Alliance directly. Using this, the conference can be billed to a Calling Card or to a third number.

Alliance says the cost of a teleconference is 25 cents a line per minute, as well as the cost of a direct dialed call for each of the locations from the conference site. A monitoring Alliance operator costs an additional $3 an hour. Thus, rumors of $6,000 conference bills seem a little exaggerated. However, conferences can last for several days and can have several international participants, thus running the bill up.

Conference Numbers

Dialing 0-700-456-X00X will result in "This is Alliance Teleconferencing in [location]. You may dial during the announcement for faster setup." The main conference numbers are -100X and -200X. The locations indicated by the X (as given by Alliance and the logon recordings) are 1 being Los Angeles, 2 being Chicago, 3 being White Plains, New York, and 4 being Dallas. 0 gets you the conference site closest to you. The -100X lines only accept up to 21 conferees, and usually don't allow international dialing. The other conference numbers allow up to 59 lines when available as the lines have to be apportioned between the various conferences going at the site, and also allow international dialing. According to Alliance themselves -200X are graphic conferences, -100X allows up to 59 conferees, and both always allow international dialing. However, actual exploration doesn't bear these out.

Alliance doesn't seem to admit that -300X conference (X is from 0 to 2, all located in Chicago, Illinois) numbers even exist. These conferences announce that they are graphic, and they seem to bear this out. They can also be handled as an audio conference. The only difference is that it asks when adding conferees whether the location is graphics (hit 4) or audio (hit 5). It's generally best to choose audio. These tend most often to allow the passing of control, dialing of international calls, and are also less used than the other lines.

Dialing 0-700-456-150X or -250X results in a modem connect sounding tone, followed by "You have reached Bell System Teleconferencing Service's Special Set for testing and measurement. Please enter your service code [3 digits] or wait for instructions." These cannot be reached from most area codes, resulting instead in a "The number you have dialed cannot be reached from your calling area" just as if it were an 800 number not reachable from your calling area. The only one I know that does get through is 201 (Northern New Jersey). The X goes from 0 to 4, just like the normal -100X and -200X conferences. There is no -350X series. I haven't as of yet figured out the "service code." This can be used as a normal conference, except that it requires you to confirm your choice by voice, and each section is separated by those modem connect sounding tones. Rumors are that this is the upcoming new conference system, which is supposed to add features such as the deletion of conferees. However, any keypress I have tried other than 1, 6, or 9 (the normal controls) results in a dire warning telling me "Please wait for an Alliance operator to come to your assistance." I haven't yet stuck around long enough to find out what "assistance" means. Alliance won't admit these exist, and therefore the -150X and -250X warrant much further and deeper investigation.

Alliance can be reached by other means. Blue boxing to 213-080-0123 and other direct routing to the Alliance machines (which used to be the only way to get through) no longer seems to work. However, box routing to 0–700-456-X00X does work. PBX's in conference country are often used to call conferences. Merely dial a PBX's inward access line, enter the access code, dial an outside line, and then either touch tone 0-700-456–X00X yourself, or dial 0 and get the operator to do it for you. Sometimes they insist that the 0-700 SAC doesn't exist, but just remain firm and tell them to try it. Social engineering also works, just call an operator and try to convince her to KP+0–700-456-1000+ST and position release, after getting her to believe you are maintenance/whatever. Getting a direct drop on an inward operator increases the chance of succeeding, such as by dialing 0-959-1211 from a pay phone (BIOC Agent 003's Basic

Telcom VI, discovered by Karl Marx). Another trick suggested by Shooting Shark is to use a white boxable phone (see *2600* page 1-40, July 1984) or even an ATM help line or a hotel phone in an airport (as in the April 1985 *2600*, Page 2-19). Since when arranging a conference you really don't need to speak, just set up a conference normally, and when done call another pay phone nearby, pass control, and continue. The conference will still be charged to the first pay phone.

Several techniques are available to improve the quality of the call. Since the call may be going through up to several extenders to reach a non-800 PBX, and from there to Alliance, the signal quality can get quite poor. A technique that helps to keep Alliance from knowing your number is to call Alliance via a PBX, add in the lower end of a loop, pass control to it, and then call the high end. A variation on this technique is to call your other line or a pay phone next to you, or even, if you have call-waiting, to call yourself again, pass control to yourself (it works), and then hang up the original call. All these techniques may not always work, as sometimes Alliance refuses to pass control, as mentioned above.

Conference Controls

Alliance is extremely user friendly, as it was designed for businessmen. Help messages abound, and all you need to do is to follow their directions, but here is a brief going over of the commands. After the logon recording, choose the number of locations for your conference. Choose below 15 locations, as many people use Alliance, and using more locations than available results in "no conference facilities available now." To change your choice, dial a * or to go onward hit a #. To add a number while in control mode dial 1+ the phone number. To dial international, dial 1 + 011 + the phone number. Passing control can be done by dialing 6 plus the number of the person on the conference you wish to pass control to. Then by hitting a # you rejoin the conference, or by just hanging up you leave. When in the conference dialing a # will return you to control mode.

When conferees hang up, a "dee-doot" will be heard. The controller also hears the phone number of the person who left. Hitting the # immediately calls the departed back. There is no way to drop people from conference other then getting a conference operator to do it or by blowing 2600 hertz down the line. However, this will drop each and every person on a trunk using in-band signaling. Hitting a 0 in control mode summons a conference operator, however, she/he takes control before he/she answers, so only do this when you know what you are doing. Hitting a 9 in control mode requests a "silent attendant listener line." According to the Demon this option allows the controller to hear the tones and phone numbers of people hanging up while he is in control mode. Conference op's claim this function is for secretaries and such to listen to, but not participate in, conferences for note taking purposes.

If these instructions sound confusing, don't worry. Remember, the entire conference is accompanied by extremely user friendly messages. Recently, on weekends or late night, many Telcom hobbyists have had problems with transferring control, instead getting a recording "Not available at this time." Also, similarly, international dialing is sometimes unavailable. Generally, -300X does this less often, then -200X next.

Dangers

One must always be prepared for listeners whenever one conferences. If one is discussing "questionable" matters on a conference, last names and phone numbers should NEVER be given out. One of your fellow Telcom hobbyists might be an FBI agent, or sometimes a conference operator listens in on conferences, which sound "suspicious." They do not do this usually, as Alliance most often carries business calls (you have to remember this folks!) and, thus, doesn't expect fraudulent calls. Sure ways to interest an op is to have either all the conferees but one or only just the controller hang up. When a controller hangs up the conference op takes control and attempts to let the former controller "regain his conference" by calling him at home. Also, controllers who spend long amounts of time in control mode, resulting in everyone else hanging up, arouses the attention of the op. The number, which originally started the conference can hang up though, after passing control, but the conference will still be billed to it.

Dangers of fraudulently started conferences seem to be slight. The only person I knew who got caught was forced to pay for a phone call from Dallas where the conference was started) to his home in California. This is not to say it is safe, but it definitely is sefer than using 950's fraudulently. Even phreaks who set up several conferences a night for months, including the harassment of DA operators, haven't been caught. However, we don't suggest you attempt a fraudulent conference. Even permitting yourself to be added to a fraudulent conference is enough for prosecution, according to AT&T. One thing that prevents a lot of this investigation is that most fraudulent conferences are set up with PBX's, and thus the prosecution lies with the owners of the PBX, and AT&T isn't even involved. For this reason, PBX's often are traced.

Another risk is that all numbers dialed are recorded by Alliance, even misdials. The numbers dialed are all printed out and sent to a vault at the Chicago Bell Test Labs for storage for their records. In addition, conferences are randomly taped and monitored for fraud. It would seem safer to use Alliance to call an extender, and then dial out from there, as although Alliance records all numbers dialed, logically they probably only pay attention to numbers they intend to act on, i.e. add to the conference. The subsequent use of an extender is a matter of investigation by another company, and don't forget AT&T and the extender companies are competitors, and thus they wouldn't always go out of their ways to cooperate.

Stunts

Often when a conference starts to slow down, people start suggesting various stunts to liven things up. One word of warning, most of these techniques would be construed as harassment, and thus are illegal. One of the most commonly used is adding a multitude of Directory Assistance operators. Listening to them ask each other "What city please?" and then arguing about who belongs on the line is extremely humorous. Confusion reigns when you attempt to get them to look up a number. Some DA's have had this done so many times that they realize that this is a conference and will either hang up immediately or will threaten you with taking over your conference. Remember, only the conference operator can take over a conference, so lots of these threats are ineffectual. When any of them give a hard time, just ask to speak to their supervisor, as this usually adds even more confusion. Similar things can be done with business offices, repair service ("Sir, I'm getting all this cross talk on my line" "No, it's my line." ad infinitum) telex ops, and other phone company personnel. Also, computer companies or other corporate bureaucracies have similar chaos potential. One interesting thing to try is to pose as a phone company employee for social engineering purposes. However, most phreaks fail to realize that "TSPS maintenance" or "Bell Security" gets a little too repetitious and suspicion arousing due to their over-heavy use.

Generally, for courtesy's sake, one should call people who generally expect to get weird calls at odd hours, and are often bored at their jobs. Radio station D.J.'s often enjoy this, as do hotel operators and bell boys. Going international often increases the fascination with conferences. Several hotel ops around the world expect and look forward to conferences calling them during the dull early morning hours, and the conferences sometimes place calls for them in appreciation. Military bases are another good site, as are unattended pay phones. Sometimes people at random are called up. It often is impossible to convince people that they *are* getting a conference call, as they twist up some impossible theory to explain 15 chaotic people speaking at once. Even President Reagan (*2600* 1-23 April, 1984) and other "celebrities" have been attempted to be reached by conferences. Often telling their secretaries that this is a conference call can arouse their curiosity enough to come on line. A common statement is, "You damn computer hackers are so smart to have figured this out." Little do they know how simple it is, and it also shows how people and the mass media constantly misidentify anything mildly out of the ordinary as the fault of computer's influence on people. (Sorry about the side digression.)

Remember that when adding recordings or extenders to a conference that they generally will not hang up. Similarly, people added can't be forcibly disconnected without the conference operator's help, and can stay on as long as they want, monitoring or taking notes. Only way to rid a conference of these is to blast 2600 down the line, with the results predicted above. When adding "dangerous" people such as FBI agents or informants the use of three-way calling by one of the conferees is generally more intelligent, as it permits the caller to forcibly drop them.

Many of these stunts mentioned are plain childish, rude, and unthoughtful to others. Many of these definitely would count as harassment. Frequent resortation to these often arouses the suspicious curiosity of Alliance ops. Continual use of these may end up in a general tightening up of security in Alliance, not due to fraudulent calls, but from complaints. Obviously, these utterly senseless acts should be conducted in extreme moderation.

Other Conferences

The old method of conferencing by calling the operator and asking for a conference still works. This however is controlled physically by the operator, as it uses a cord-board. Three-way calling of course is another conferencing option. Multiline loops are rare, but do exist. Sometimes businesses connect several phone lines together to form a conference.

Every once in a while conferences are set up in the old historical phreaking mold on PBX switchboards or on telephone switching equipment by renegade linemen and the like. One of the most historic of these was the "2111" conference," which was arranged through an unused telex test-board trunk in a 4A switching machine in Vancouver, Canada. For several months phone phreaks could MF via a blue box 604 (Vancouver area code) then 2111 (code for telex testing board) to reach phreaks and other Telcom hobbyists around the world. Sometimes conferences set up by this method are accessible via normal phone lines. These conferences, by their very nature of actual adjustment of switching equipment, are rare.

Several companies offer alternate bridging services, otherwise known as conferences. These all claim they have higher quality than Alliance. They control the conference themselves "so you can just get down to business without worrying about details." You can ask them to leave, but then there is no one in control of the conference. Generally, they offer smaller conferences than Alliance's 59 (Market Navigation's limit is 19). They all charge considerably more than AT&T (Market Navigation Inc. quoted a rate as $195 per hour for a 12-person conference plus the cost of the dialed phone calls). You generally have to set up conferences ahead of time. They all will send a bill to your company, and some will allow the use of a credit card instead. Generally, you have to book ahead of time.

Conclusion

Basically, conferencing, even fraudulently, is one of the safest ways to get in contact with other Telcom hobbyists, by its track record of busts. They are very few and far between. Several times Alliance operators have dropped in on conferences and carried on conversations with the participants. Much of the information in this article was picked up from these sources. Often one hears the common comment of many Telcom corporations that "they are using us as a tax write-off." However, how long can they keep taking losses in this post-divestiture age of Telco competition? Expect in the near future to see other Telcom companies such as ITT, MCI, and GTE Sprint get into the act, as conferences are really pretty cheap to set up and aren't that technically exotic. Telcom hobbyists can get together to pick each others brains for info, and starters can learn the ropes in the presence of several more experienced phreaks. Also, just normal socializing with people all over the country is fun, especially when you realize you probably would have never met them otherwise. In order to join in a conference, try calling someone on it who has call-waiting or two phone lines, as he can relay to the controller that you want to be added. Conferencing is all in all an excellent way to communicate with the Telcom community at large, when used in moderation. Use, don't abuse.

Information provided by Alliance Teleconferencing, the Demon, Elric Bloodaxe, Forest Ranger, John Doe, Keymaster, Market Navigation Inc., the Serpent, Shooting Shark, Telcom.ARPA, Joe Turner and the members of the official BBS of *2600* magazine: the Private Sector.

Divestiture: What Happened? (January, 1986)

It's been two years now since they broke up the telephone company, and if you ask around, most people seem to believe it was a bad idea. In the past, you received only one phone bill and you never had to worry about *how* to place your calls. It seemed so much simpler then.

For phone phreaks, though, the last two years have meant an increasing number of toys to play with: new pay phones, new long-distance companies, new ways of doing what could only be done one way before. While many of us miss the days of that single formidable opponent (Ma Bell), we manage to have fun by figuring out all of the jargonese and being looked upon as the only people who still understand how to make a phone call.

This is meant to be a brief guide to just what has happened because of the divestiture and what the ramifications may be. We're not going to compare rates of the many companies like all of the newspapers are doing and we're not going to complain about how difficult it is to cope with phones these days like all of the columnists are doing. In plain English, we'll simply try and figure out what the hell is going on.

The Way It Used to Be

Let's look at the way things were. Except for some independent local companies, your local phone company was a part of the nationwide Bell System. It all tied together nicely—if you wanted to call long distance, you'd place the call through your local company and they would bill you for it, and that was it. What you most likely didn't know (or care about) was that your local company had hooked into the national company and they in turn had hooked into the local company on the other end. As far as we were all concerned, the local company did it all.

Under this system, things worked fairly well. It was simple for customers, all of the companies benefited (the local companies could keep their rates lower because the national company would pay them and the national company got a monopoly on every long-distance call placed), and there were no real problems.

But it wasn't fair. In nearly all countries, the phone company is run by the government and that's it. But here, the phone company was being run by private enterprise, yet there was no competition. It was inevitable that this would be challenged, especially when it started becoming economically feasible for alternative companies to offer similar services.

Signs of Trouble

In the late sixties, MCI became the first company to challenge the Bell monopoly. Slowly the rules were changing. As the years passed, more companies appeared and began to cry foul. Consumer services were offered for the first time. As technology got bigger, it became obvious that one phone company simply shouldn't do it all. And one day, the government agreed.

First off, the nationwide network had to be dismantled. So it was split into seven parts, none of which are supposed to be related to each other (however, we suspect they still see each other socially). They are: Pacific Telesis, U.S. West, Southwestern Bell, Ameritech, BellSouth, Bell Atlantic, and NYNEX. Each of these companies has a fleet of local operating companies under its control, in much the same way as Ma Bell had nearly *all* of the local operating companies under *its* wing—in fact these seven new companies have been dubbed "Baby Bells."

But the nationwide network was not completely eliminated, because AT&T still exists. Instead of tying together all of the local companies, AT&T is now just another long-distance company, with no connection to any of the local companies or the seven regional companies. Of course, having constructed the network in the first place, AT&T has tremendous advantages in the long distance market.

Equal Access

Clearly, the emerging long-distance companies have to be protected against AT&T, so that they can have a fighting chance. If AT&T were to lower its rates, everyone would use them. Because of AT&T's position, it's much easier for them to do this, and re-establish a monopoly. This is prevented by the divestiture agreement, which regulates AT&T more than the other companies. In a weird way, it's kind of like affirmative action.

Another way of protecting the new companies is to give them equal access to the network that AT&T built. What good is it to be allowed to compete for long-distance customers if by the time the customer gets to your dial tone, it sounds like it's on another planet? Not to mention the fact that to use your service, the customer has to use a touch-tone phone and key in a whole lot of extra numbers to identify himself, since your company isn't able to identify him as soon as he picks up the phone, like AT&T can. In all fairness, shouldn't your dial tone come in as loud and clear as AT&T's?

The answer is of course. But how can this be accomplished? There was no easy way, but it had to be done. And so, "equal access" was developed.

In the early stages, the most that could be done under equal access was to provide a clear connection to an alternate long-distance service. In addition, this connection had to be toll-free since quite a few customers were being lost because they had to pay for a phone call to the dial tone of the company they chose, whether or not the call they were making in the first place ever got through. It couldn't be an 800 number because of technical and administrative reasons, not to mention the fact that an extra area code (800) would have to be dialed.

So the 950 exchange was created. This is an exchange which is nearly the same everywhere in the country. It doesn't really exist in any one place; it's a theoretical exchange within local central offices. Calling 950 plus four digits, which are different for each long-distance company, connects you with their dial tone—with no ringing and with a very clear connection. For instance, 950-1022 gets you MCI anywhere in the country, 950-1088 gets you Skyline, etc. There are still drawbacks, though. Primitive local companies sometimes insist on charging for these calls, as do some hotels. Then there is also the matter of still having to input your authorization code and being forced to use a touch-tone phone. But it represents a start.

The next and most significant step towards achieving equal access was to actually make it possible for somebody to pick up their phone and make a long-distance call using whatever company they wanted without dialing any extra numbers. So at last it would be just as simple to make a call using Sprint or Western Union as it was using AT&T. All the customer had to do was tell his local company (when the time came) which long-distance company he/she wanted.

This is the point where something interesting began to happen. Phone companies all around the country started to realize that there are a great number of people who really don't care which long-distance company offers what—they just want to be left alone. Some of these folks never make long-distance calls in the first place and others don't have the time or inclination to try and figure out which company is economically advantageous to them.

But last year a new twist was added. If you don't choose a long-distance company, one will be assigned to you at random! In other words, if you close your ears to all of this divestiture talk, you could find yourself subscribing to a company that charges a $15 monthly minimum, which is a bit of an affront to someone who only makes local calls. Yet, this is what's currently being done.

It's true you will be writing more than one check when it comes time to pay the phone bill. Many long-distance companies still don't go through your local phone company's billing office like AT&T used to (and still does), so they must bill you separately.

Then, you could choose to make some calls with one long-distance company and others with another. Then again, you could make calls using Visa or American Express and get billed *that* way. There are so many different ways to make a telephone call these days, so naturally there will be at least as many ways to be billed. You could also wind up paying AT&T for equipment rental, if you're wary of owning your own phone equipment. So that's another check to write.

Then there are pay phones, which are starting to be deregulated. You may see two totally different phones that charge totally different rates to call the same place. This will be confusing to most people, because they were never trained to *think* about the phones they use. But for phone phreaks, this represents more ways to have fun.

What the Future Holds

In theory, what we have today is the beginning of total equality. Unfortunately, it's also total mayhem, but that will undoubtedly clear up in time, as everyone slowly gets used to the new system. Many mistakes are being made and it's fun to find them. Skyline has a page in their bill that says, "Retain for your records," in much the same fashion as other telephone bills. The difference here is that there is no information on this page at all except your name and the month of the bill. The amount owed appears on another page. Why would someone want to retain this useless data? Then there's U.S. Tel, who supposedly has a new credit card system—you dial a number, then enter your credit card number, which is something like 14 digits long. Miraculously enough, we've been told, any series of numbers at all allows the call to go through!

But mistakes aren't the only thing we'll be seeing. Since Bell Labs is now able to compete openly, we'll see a great number of the projects they've been working on secretly for Ma Bell. This will be of great benefit to us. At the same time, it may get a lot harder for authorities and spies to keep tabs on certain people, since there's no longer a guarantee that a person will use a certain phone or even a certain network. Diversity is good for the individual.

All of this is only the beginning. Many more changes are on the horizon and technological enthusiasts will have quite a time. For the average person who doesn't care, things may be unpleasant, especially if the explanations aren't as plentiful as the changes. Hopefully though, these folks will be comforted by the knowledge that it's all *fair.*

Cellular Telephones—How They Work (December, 1986)

By Bruce Alston

This is a non-technical explanation of the newest in mobile telephone communications, the cellular telephone. For some background let's review the mobile telephone as we knew it prior to late 1983 when cellular systems began operating in Chicago and

Washington/Baltimore. Improved Mobile Telephone Service (IMTS) allows calls to be made from a car to a land telephone or vice-versa. Car-to-car service is also available. Based on radio transmission characteristics any city or town can have a maximum of 12 radio channels in the 150 Mhz band for mobile telephone service. The transmitter power for the base station (telephone company) can go as high as 200 watts Effective Radiated Power (ERP). This may cover an area of 20 to 25 miles depending upon terrain. The mobile radio is limited to 15, 25, possibly 50 watts ERP, keeping in mind the power consumption from the automobile battery. To receive the signal from the mobile radio the telephone company encircles the transmitter with receivers, so wherever the mobile unit might be, it can be heard, as it also must hear the base station transmitter. With IMTS in New York City, Los Angeles, or Madison, Wisconsin, or any city, only 12 mobile telephone conversations can work at one time, assuming the FCC allocated these cities all 12 channels.

The FCC has allocated 666 channels in the 800 Mhz band for cellular telephone service. The maximum power for the base station is 100 watts ERP, for the mobile radio 7 watts ERP (that is not a misprint—7 watts!). Based on transmission characteristics, a cellular radio system can have up to 333 channels in a given geographic area. Each area can have two cellular systems, each with its own 333 channels in a given geographic area. Each area can have two cellular systems, each with its own 333 channels for the total 666. Picture the IMTS system with its receivers encircling one powerful transmitter. Change the receivers to combined transmitter/receiver/control equipment located throughout the geographic area. These are called cell sites. Where the one powerful transmitter base station was located, cellular has an MTSO (Mobile Telephone Switching Office) that channels telephone calls from the land lines to the cell site nearest the mobile radio. The MTSO can also switch mobile-to-mobile calls. As the mobile unit travels from one cell site toward another, where a more powerful signal can be transmitted between mobile radio and cell site, the MTSO switches the connection to the best cell site. It now looks as if a maximum of 333 calls could go on in any one cellular system at any given time. This is not so. Based on topography and radio interference patterns, the same radio channel might be used in two or more cell sites in the same system. These cell sites are probably 10 to 15 miles apart, unless a mountain or hill is in the way. In the United States, various manufacturers are claiming that a properly engineered cellular system can handle up to 75,000 calls at a given time. (The telephone term is 75,000 BHCA - Busy Hour Call Attempts.) No system has been installed that approaches this figure. Notice, though, that this beats the 12 BHCA of IMTS with a heavy stick if cellular is only capable of half its proposed capacity.

Let's suppose your cellular telephone (it can be in a car, on a boat, or carried with you) has the number (516) 555-2600. I'm in Red Lodge, Montana and want to call you. Using my friend's telephone, of course, I dial 5165552600 and wait while the call goes through the regular telephone system. It will end up at the (516) 555 MTSO where it is sent to *all* the (516) 555 cell sites and transmitted. If your mobile telephone is turned on it will recognize the call, inform the MTSO that it is in service, and the MTSO will assign its most powerful cell site a voice channel for the conversation. The MTSO will also transmit information to your radio advising of the channel number on which you will be talking to me. Your radio will ring. I'll hear ringing, when you answer we talk. You push no buttons, turn no knobs. When the call is over, we both hang up. Should you wish to call me, pick up your handset, dial my number, push the SEND button, and wait until you get a busy, I answer, or you have a "ring-don't-answer" condition.

Yes, you can use your modem... But cellular telephony is in its infancy; results may not always be all that you hoped for. Right now, voice communication is the principal commitment of cellular systems.

In review, cellular telephones have opened a whole new area of usage availability. Having an older mobile telephone means that you might receive a call if one of twelve circuits were open, and you might be able to make a call under the same conditions. With cellular systems, when you are in the coverage area and your telephone is turned on, you will receive calls and you can make calls and expect to have the ability to talk until you are finished. The city of Sacramento, California, has seven cell sites. Anywhere you drive in that area you have cellular service. If you drive toward San Francisco, as soon as you get within range of cell sites, service is again available. The mobile radio has a "no service" light that is on when you are not in cellular range. If you have a "transportable" cellular radio, pack it with you into the dentist's office, or bank, or whatever, and use *your* telephone, both to send and receive calls. Cellular telephones can be equipped with every type of regular telephone feature: speed dialing, last number redial, call forwarding, three-way calling, call waiting, and eventually cellular service will be available in every community and along the highway between towns.

Prior to deregulation and divestiture, IMTS service was provided only by the local telephone company, called "wireline" companies. Now, each city or town with cellular service can have two companies, the "wireline" (local telephone company) and "non-wireline," a Radio Common Carrier (RCC). Each company has a total of 333 radio channels in the 800 Mhz range devoted to cellular telephones. Actually, 312 channels in each group are for the voice communications and 21 are used for control data transmission (the information that tells the mobile radio which voice channel to use, for example). Cellular service is already so popular that the FCC is allocating additional channels for the service. Since cellular radio in the rest of the world uses up to 1000 channels, most cellular telephones are designed to cover these channels. For detailed information on cellular radio, consult "EIA Interim Standards, Mobile Station to Land Station, CIS-3-A," available from the Electronic Industries Association.

Cellular communications derives its name from the radiotelephone signal being transmitted by a series of low-powered microwave antennas or cells.

History

First proposed by Bell Laboratories' creative thinkers in the late 1940s, the advanced computer technology to actually make cellular work was developed in the 1960s.

The FCC, after a 13-year discussion, formulated its "final" rules on implementing the technology in 1981. (Other countries, such as Japan, Saudi Arabia, and Scandinavia acted more quickly and began operating cellular systems in 1979 to 1981.) Chicago was chosen as the city for an experimental system in 1979, and a second experiment was built in Washington/Baltimore, going on air in late 1981. Both experiments proved that the cellular systems functioned perfectly and that cellular communications is a valuable service.

The FCC then issued an order licensing cellular systems for the country's 305 largest population centers; to date, the 100 largest markets are either online or soon will be. Each market is served by two cellular companies: a "wireline company," a subsidiary of the local existing phone company after the historic breakup, and a "non-wireline company", one that is not associated with the phone company. Two providers of service, according to the FCC, would prevent a monopolistic marketplace and foster competition.

How a Cellular System Works

The FCC designated the 800 Mhz band for cellular communications. Of the total 999 thirty-Khz-wide channels in the band, 333 channels are reserved for the wireline cellular company, 333 are reserved for the non-wireline company, and the last 333 are held in reserve for future cellular (or other mobile) service.

When a cellular call is initiated, it is received by the closest low-power microwave antenna in the cellular area. From there, the call is routed completely over the microwave system if it is going to another cellular phone, or if it is going to a landline (regular phone), the call is then routed through a highly sophisticated computer switch and connected through to regular landline phones. As a vehicle moves throughout the cellular area (the geographic area in which the cellular company operates), the signal is automatically "handed off" from one cell to the next, so that the signal stays strong and clear. Just as an FM broadcast channel can be used in many cities across the country, a cellular channel can be used in different parts of the coverage area. This geographic sharing permits a cellular system to use radio channels more efficiently than existing mobile phone systems. A number of phone conversations can take place throughout a cellular area, at the same time, on the same channel without interfering with each other.

Cost

Cellular hardware varies according to the area of the country, and features of the model. Generally speaking, perhaps $995 to $1,800 or so for a vehicle-mounted unit, and $2,000 to $3,000 for portable and transportable units. Leasing and rentals are available in some areas. For the usage of the unit, the phone company charges a monthly fee, and a small charge per call.

Phones (January, 1987)

So few of us really see the possibilities when we look at our telephones. But just think of what's really there, especially today.

With a telephone, you can take a trip to anywhere. The average person sees it as an everyday tool, an annoyance, a necessity, nothing to play with, nothing to wonder about, nothing to get excited about. What a pity. But in a way, how much better for folks like us who recognize the beauty of it all.

We pick up the phone and we hear a dial tone. The game is afoot. Where are we going? Who are we going to speak to? What exchanges work near us? What area codes work throughout the country? Can we make international calls? How many different operators can we find and what can we make them do?

On a phone, there is only one way to be judged. Your voice tells the whole story and if you can do things with your voice, there is no limit to what you can do over a telephone. This column, and in many ways this whole publication, is dedicated to those who have made telephone use into an art form.

Ask the average person what they think of the AT&T breakup and you'll hear what a bad idea it was. Ask the average telephone repairman and you'll probably get a 40 minute dissertation. (We should listen to these—they can be very revealing.) Ask an elderly person and you may even see some tears. What does this tell us? Did Judge Greene make a mistake? Will making a phone call ever be a simple process again?

All of a sudden phone calls are being treated differently—as a product instead of a natural right we're all kind of born into. We have to make decisions now where they were made for us before. It's all kind of like racial integration. Some preferred the status quo, but it's obvious the system had to change to even approach being fair. And that means we all have to work a little harder, at least for a while to come. We may not even get it right the first or second time. But it's a change that had to happen. Those of us who understand it all a bit better than others should lend a hand and not assume the answers will show up in the front of the phone book.

While the mood here in the States is negative, over in England it's indifference. British Telecommunications PLC was denationalized in late 1984 and; according to a recent survey, 72 percent of those polled think the quality of telephone service hasn't changed since. Another 12 percent thought service had improved, 10 percent thought it had declined, and 6 percent had no opinion whatsoever.

Meanwhile, British Telecom has launched a new service for the London area called Talkabout. It enables up to ten telephone callers from the same area to be linked together on the phone for a chat.

There are two lines to choose from. Both are available 24 hours a day. One is for adults who dial 0055 0055 to join the service. The other is the service for teenagers up to 18 years, who dial 0055 0033.

Callers to the service first hear a recorded message telling them the cost of the call, informing them that all calls are monitored, and—for the teenage line—advising them to tell their parents that they are calling the service. This message is followed by a tone and customers are then linked in with the other callers. The tone alerts other callers that they have a new member joining their group.

So that callers do not lose track of the time, a buzzer sounds every 10 minutes on the adult line to remind people how long they have been connected, and monitors personally interrupt callers on all lines approximately every 10 minutes to remind them of the cost of using the service.

In addition, callers to the teenage line are automatically cut off after 10 minutes.

We've seen it before; many phone companies in the United States have already given this a try. But the phone phreaks have been doing it the longest, either through teleconferencing or loops.

People and companies try making money in the strangest ways.

Conferencing is only one. Now there's even competition for what you listen to while on hold!

Businesses have begun to program customized advertisements—pitching everything from corporate securities to used trucks—for customers who get put on hold. But Robert D. Horner, president of The Hold Co. Inc. of Fort Washington, Pennsylvania says, "We don't like to call it advertising." Can anyone blame him?

Meanwhile, W. Evan Sloane of San Diego has started a telephone service that offers advice on how to beat drug testing at the workplace. The two-minute, tape-recorded message provides callers with information on the lengths of time that commonly used, illicit drugs stay in the body and suggests ways to doctor urine samples to mask evidence of drug use.

Sloane's a member of a group called Question Authority, which he defines as "an attempt to focus some common sense on what's going on in our lives. The little guy is getting beaten down by this and doesn't know how to defend himself because he assumes these tests are accurate. We believe forcing people to take a urine test to get or keep a job is unwarranted search and is unconstitutional."

Not to mention unpleasant. As is the latest move within the Soviet Union to eliminate unlimited local dialing. It's all part of Gorbachev's drive to reduce government subsidies.

Soviets currently pay the equivalent of a couple of dollars a month for as many local phone calls as they want. But the party is over. All calls will have to be paid for very soon.

The Soviet phone system has its problems. Every call to another city or out of the country must be booked through the operator and it can take hours to get through.

Direct dialing was introduced briefly just before the 1980 Olympics, but was then abruptly terminated.

It's also next to impossible sometimes to get phone numbers since directories aren't available. You can call directory assistance, but the number is almost always busy. And if you need the number of someone with a common name, you'll be turned away.

But things may be looking up for the folks in Yugoslavia. The phone companies of the Slovenian Republic and Ljubljana have ordered the country's first System 12 digital telephone exchange. This will lead to local manufacture of nearly 700,000 lines of System 12 in Yugoslavia over a five-year period.

There's a lot going on down those little telephone wires.

Telecommunications may indeed be a business for some, but for the entire human race it's becoming a vital link, a taste of freedom. We can never let control slip from our fingers.

Telecom Informer (February, 1987) *By Dan Foley*

Cellular Phreaking

The future hinted in the December issue of *2600* is already here. Cellular fraud is becoming a concern of the CPC's (Cellular Phone Companies). Much fraud is from the same old source—the theft of cellular phones or even the entire car, resulting with the new "owner" making calls on the victim's cellular ID (and phone bill). Another form of fraud is from roamers (cellular users using their phones in a different city from where they signed up) who don't bother to let the CPC in the new city know their billing info. Roaming will become more prevalent as more people buy cellular phones and use them while they travel. However, this form of fraud will soon become a thing of the past, as the CPC's are creating a national billing data clearinghouse that will ensure that bills will reach the right user. This clearinghouse will also (further in the future) allow someone to call a cellular telephone, and the call will be correctly routed to wherever in the United States the phone happens to be.

Of more interest to the readers of *2600* is something that is quickly growing and represents the most dangerous threat to CPC's billing. Spoofing another cellular user's ID isn't as hard as it seemed. Some of the more exotic schemes involve reading cellular ID's off of the airwaves as calls are being placed. Most CPC's don't even bother to encrypt the ID signals (and you don't even need to decrypt if the encryption algorithm doesn't include time and date stamping). But there is even a simpler method than using an "ether" box (so called because the box snatches ID's out of the "ether").

The easiest method by far needs the complicity of a cellular phone repair or installation shop. For many brands of phone the cellular ID is not in a ROM like "they" tell you, but instead is programmable. Motorola, for one, is supposed to have easy-to-follow instructions on programming their phone's cellular ID's inside the repair manual. And even if the ID is encoded in a ROM, you can just burn a copy. Rumor has it that cellular ROMs are already available on the black market. Perfect for your local terrorist to call in death threats and be untraceable, as the authorities would accuse the wrong person.

The Largest Cellular Companies

The largest cellular system in the world encompasses almost the entire Gulf of Mexico. On July 15 Coastel (sic) Communications began serving from Brownsville, Texas, to Mobile, Alabama, with a switching office in Lafayette, Louisiana, and cell sites on off-shore platforms out to about 160 miles from the coast. Coastel plans to target the oil business, fishing and other commercial marine operations. Airtime averages $1 a minute; rather expensive, but they do provide a specialized service. Cellular rates average about 60 cents a minute peak.

The largest cellular telephone company is now Southwestern Bell Corp. It bought out Metromedia's nonwireline rights for $1.65 billion. The FCC originally broke the cellular frequencies into three bands, giving one to the local telephone company (the wireline carrier), one to a non-wireline carrier, and saved one for the future. However the distinction has become academic as more RBOCs (Regional Bell Operating Companies) purchase cellular rights in other cities (with our local phone revenues we subsidize their investment in real estate, manufacturing, and all sorts of things having nothing to do with our dial tone). Southwestern Bell now competes against NYNEX in Boston and New York, Bell Atlantic in Philadelphia and Baltimore/Washington, and Ameritech in Chicago and Dallas. It also got about 500,000 paging customers in nineteen cities. U.S. West also competes against a fellow RBOC, PacTel, in San Diego.

800 Number Allocation

It used to be that you could tell the geographical location of an 800-NXX number by the NXX part. XX2's were intrastate, XX7's were in Canada, and every prefix represented an area code. However, about five years ago AT&T introduced "Advanced 800 Service," which permitted any INWATS (Inward Wide Area Telephone Service) call to be routed anywhere in the US, and even to different destinations depending on both the time of day and where the caller placed the call. Thus, 800-DIALITT would reach the nearest ITT billing complaint center during the day, and at night the call could instead reach a main office left open. The company has to pay for the normal 800 INWATS lines and then an extra couple of hundred a month for the "vanity" number and a few cents for each translation of end phone line by time or location.

Until Fall 1986, if your CO was switched over to equal access your 800 call was routed to AT&T no matter what your default carrier. But now your CO must route all 800 calls to MCI, which have any of these "exchanges": 234, 283, 284, 288, 289, 274, 333, 365, 444, 456, 627, 666, 678, 727, 759, 777, 825, 876, 888, 937, 950, 955, and 999. U.S. Sprint gets 728 and WUD Metrofone gets those to 988. The individual BOC's get the XX2 exchanges (as these are filled with intrastate WATS lines). More exchanges will undoubtedly be grabbed by other carriers as they begin to offer 800 service. I don't know what happens if your company's 800 number's exchange gets taken over by Bargin Bob's Telefone Kompany. Hopefully you get to keep the old provider, but this would really make it tough to route. Don't know what happens either if your clever little phone number "word" belongs to Bargin Bob; guess you gotta suffer. If your CO isn't equal access yet, it just kicks the call onto the nearest intra-LATA tandem site for the proper routing.

However, don't bother to remember this. When Bellcore finally finishes the new Advanced 800 service the INWATS buyer can route his or her incoming call through a different carrier depending on the originating point or the time of call, as well as sending it to a different company office. When this happens, all 800 calls will have to be sent to the nearest tandem switch and get routed based on all this info. The local Telco will get the money for providing the routing service.

As far as I know, only AT&T gets your 900 calls, which were never grouped according to geography. Trivia fact number 1: INWATS numbers in England (to the US. International INWATS further confuses the geographical determination) are of the form 0800-XX-XX-XX. Only AT&T provides this. Trivia fact 2: INWATS was not introduced in 1967 as stated in the December *2600*, pages 3–95. The first interstate INWATS lines were in 1967, but intrastate INWATS started in 1966.

Airfone Update

The future of Airfone, the pay telephone for use on airline flights, is in limbo. Airfone's experimental license expires at the end of 1987, and the FCC will not reconsider its January 1985 decision refusing permanent frequencies. Airfone expects to continue with over 300 plane phones and the 65 ground stations even though there is no provision for frequency allocation. Airfone hopes to be allowed to use cellular frequencies.

Getting the Most Out of Equal Access (March, 1987)

By The Hobbit

The axing of good ole Ma Bell has rendered wrong everything you now know about phone companies. The procedure for placing a long-distance call is now above the understanding level of a good proportion of the public, and the various companies are doing very little to educate them. Thus, this attempt to inform the reader what new evil lives at the other end of his pair.

In areas that are now equal access, it is possible to place a long-distance call using any of the carriers who will complete it for you. You do not have to have previously set up an account with the carrier, as in the past. They will complete the call and pass the billing back to your local operating company (LOC), which in turn bills you for the call. So to place the call via the "alternate" carrier, you pick up and dial:

```
10nnn + 1 + area code + number
```

The nnn is magic; it allows you to select a different carrier for that call. There are a zillion little Mom-n-Pop carriers in different areas, but here are some of the major ones whose access codes should be fairly consistent.

220	Western Union	Consistently bad audio 90% of the time
222	MCI	Duplexey lines sometime
288	AT&T	You know the story
333	U.S. Telecom	Reasonably OK
444	Allnet	A major reseller of others' services
488	ITT	Bad audio, useless for modems
777	GTE Sprint	Usually good quality—rivals AT&T

When you complete a call this way, via a carrier who "doesn't know who you are," you are referred to as a "casual caller." Most of the major carriers will complete casual calls. The smaller ones usually want an access code and a preexisting account. Note that all this is perfectly legal and nobody is going to come pound on your door and demand your firstborn for making your calls this way. The fun part starts when one considers that this two-stage billing process involves a lot of red tape and paper shuffling, and the alternate [i.e. not AT&T] carriers often have poorly designed software. This can often lead to as much as a six-month lag time between when you make the call and when you get the bill for it. There is a chance that you won't get billed for some calls at all, especially real short ones. And if you do get billed, the rates will be reasonable. Note that if you don't have an account with a given company, you won't be able to take advantage of any bulk rates they offer for their known customers.

It is likely that for this reason, i.e. all the mess involved in getting the billing properly completed, that the local Bell companies are attempting to *suppress* knowledge of this. Notice that when you get your equal access carrier ballots, nowhere do they mention the fact that you can "tenex" dial, i.e. 10nnn, through other carriers. They want you to pick one and set it up as your 1+ carrier so you don't have to learn anything new. Now, it's already highly likely that the little carriers will fold and get sucked up by AT&T and eventually everything will work right again, but this policy is pushing the process along. The majority of people aren't going to want to deal with shopping around for carriers, are going to choose AT&T because it's what they've come to trust, and their lines are still the best quality anyway. However, the more people become casual callers, the more snarled up the billing process is going to become, and the resulting chaos will have many effects, one of which may be free calls for the customers, and the carriers and LOCs being forced to either straighten up their acts, disable casual calls and lose business, or knuckle under completely.

So where can you get more info about equal access, if not from your local company? You call 800-332-1124, which AT&T will happily complete for you, and talk to the special consumer awareness group dedicated to helping people out with equal access. They will send you, free of charge, a list of all the carriers which serve your area, with their access codes, customer service numbers, billing structure, and lots of other neat info. The LOCs will give out this number, but only under duress. They will *not* give out any information about other carriers, including what ones serve your central office, so you shouldn't even bother trying. It's apparently been made a universal company policy, which is ridiculous, but the case.

Let's get into some of the technical aspects of this. First off, you might ask, why 10nnn? Well, it could have been 11nnn too, but it wasn't. If you think about it, other numbers could be misparsed as the beginnings of area codes. 3-digit carrier codes also leave plenty of room for expansion (haw!). Some of the carriers won't complete casual calls, and may even give recordings to the effect of "invalid access code." Basically when you dial this way, your central office simply passes the entire packet containing your number and the number you want to call to the carrier and lets the carrier deal with it. You'll notice that this process takes longer for some of the carriers. The carriers have differing database structures and hardware, so it takes some time to figure out if it knows who the calling number is, if bulk rates apply, and a few other things. While it's doing this search, you get silence. What's a lot of fun is that in areas that have recently gone equal access, the central offices do this exact same process for public phones. And since the carrier usually has no idea of what a public phone is, it happily completes the call for you as though you dialed it from home. It is unclear who gets the resulting bill from this, but it usually doesn't take them long to fix it. It's conceivable that the carriers can hold numbers to *not* complete calls from in their database, as well as regular customer numbers.

Some carriers also handle 0+ calls. If you dial 10nnn 0+ instead of 1+, the office will hand it off as usual, and you'll be connected to the carrier's switch, which gives you a tone. You are expected to enter your authorization code at this point, and then off the call goes. This is so you can complete equal-access style calls from friends' phones and use your own billing. It also requires that you have an account with the carrier already and an authorization code to use. Some carriers, in places where the public phone bug has been fixed, will handle 1+calls from them this way as well. This mechanism introduces a security hole, because it's real easy to determine the length of a valid authorization code from this since something happens right after the last digit is dialed. Carriers that don't do this will sometimes tell you to dial "operator-assisted calls" by dialing 102880+ the number you want. Already they're admitting that AT&T is better than they are.

And as if this wasn't enough, carriers that do this will also usually connect you straight to the switch if you dial 10nnn#. The LOCs are finally getting around to using the # key as sort of an "end-of-dialing" feature, so you can reach the switch directly without having to dial a local number or 950-something. Being able to get to the carrier's switch is useful, because they often have special sequences you can dial there to get their customer service offices, various test tones, and other things. If you get the switch and then dial # and the tone breaks, you may have one of these. Another # should bring the tone back; if digits have already been dialed then # is a regular cancel or recall. Some carriers use * for this. Anyway, if # breaks the tone, an additional digit may start a call to an office. You can tell if it's working if # has no further effect; you'll eventually either hear ringing or nothing if that digit hasn't been defined. Many of the carriers have magic digit sequences that would otherwise look like authorization codes, but go off immediately upon being dialed and call somewhere.

Call timing and billing is a very hazy issue with the alternates, as one may see from the consumer group sheet. AT&T is still the only one that can return called-end supervision, i.e. the signal that tells your local office that the called party has picked up. The alternates, although they may be planning to install this through agreements with the LOCs and AT&T, have not done so yet, so they use timeouts to determine if billing should be started yet. This is assuming that most people will give up after six or seven. So if you listen to your brother's phone ring 20 times because he went out drinking last night and is now dead to the world, you will get billed for the call whether he wakes up or not. This is sort of a cheapo compromise, but since AT&T is so reluctant to hand them supervision equipment, their hands are sort of tied. But notice that it's likely that you won't get billed for a real short call that is answered quickly, either. With the advent of 9600 baud voice-grade modems, this could have some interesting applications as far as message passing is concerned, and avoids pissing off operators by trying to yell through non-accepted collect calls or long lists of what person-to-person name meant what. But in general, you should keep your own records of what call and what carrier and if it completed or not, so you won't get erroneously billed by a silly timeout.

Carriers often use their own switching equipment; they also often lease lines from AT&T Long Lines for their own use. Allnet, for example, leases equipment and time from other carriers at bulk rates and resells the service to the customer. So if you use Allnet, you can never tell whose equipment you're really talking on, because it's sort of like roulette between satellite, microwave, or landline and who owns it. Some of this latter-generation switching equipment is warmed-over AT&T stuff from a few years ago, and therefore may be employing good old single-frequency trunks, i.e. 2600 Hz will disconnect them. In the early days of carriers before equal access, 2600 would often reset the local switch and return its dial tone. This is less common these days but there's a lot of equipment still out there that responds to it.

When you select your default carrier, there is another valid option that isn't on the ballot. It is called "no-pick," and is not exactly what it sounds like. If you simply don't pick one or return the ballot, you get tossed into a lottery and you will wind up with any random carrier as your default on 1+ dialing. You still won't get bulk rates from this earner unless you call them up and create an account (or you may get a packet of info from them in the mail anyway, because if they got selected for you they will probably want you to sign up). However, no-pick is the condition where you *do not* have a default carrier, so if you pick up and dial 1 + area + number the call will not complete. This is great for confusing people who attempt to make long-distance calls on your phone and don't know about tenex dialing. Probably your best bet as far as saving money goes is to sign up with all the carriers, and examine their billing structures carefully. You can then choose the one that's cheapest for a given call at a given time. You may need a computer to do this, however. It is surprising that nobody has yet tried to market a program that will do this for you.

Post-parse, or 10nnn0+ dialing, is not the only security hole that carriers have to deal with. There are often magic sequences that, when dialed after a trial authorization code, will inform the caller if the code was valid or not without having to dial an entire number. These usually take the form of invalid called area codes, like 111 or 0nn or *nn. Most of the carriers have fixed the problem in which an invalid code plus some sequence would return silence and allow recall, and a valid one would error out. This allowed valid codes to be picked out very quickly. Longer authorization codes and improvements in the software have largely eliminated this as a major problem, but it took a few years for them to get the idea. Note that abuse of other peoples' authorization codes *is* illegal and they will probably come after people who do it. However, it is often interesting to play around with a carrier you are interested in purchasing service from, and see if you can break their security easily. If you can, then it's clear that someone else can, and this carrier is going to have a lot of problems with fraud. Someone may even find your code and then you'll have to deal with bogus billing. So if you find some algorithm that allows you to come up with a 6- to 8-digit valid code, one thing you might do is call the carrier and tell them about it. They'll thank you in the long run and might even offer you a job, a side benefit of which may be unlimited free calling via their equipment.

Telecom Informer (April, 1987) *By Dan Foley*

Cellular Fraud Bust

As some of you may know by now, the first cellular phreaking bust in the U.S. happened last month. On Friday, March 27, the FBI and Secret Service arrested 18 New Yorkers for making cellular phone calls on altered cellular phones. They also arrested seven others for altering and selling these phones. The method that was used is exactly the one described in our February column. A cellular phone transmits two numbers whenever a call is placed. The first is the ESN (Electronic Serial Number). The cellular MTSO (Mobile Telephone Switching Office) then checks whether this number is valid. Then the cellular phone transmits an MIN (Mobile Identification Number), which identifies the party to be billed for the call. By reprogramming the MIN one can make a multitude of calls ending up on the MIN owner's bill (much like using a stolen calling card or extender code). Any cellular repair shop can do the reprogramming on the side, and seven of them in Brooklyn actually did. It makes you wonder how many others are also doing this on the side. According to the FBI, organized crime wasn't involved in this case. Estimates claim that cellular fraud costs the New York cellular companies $40,000 a month, and about $3 million is lost per year to cellular fraud in the U.S. This is the first of a series of ongoing investigations by the FBI and Secret Service, so expect a bust near you soon.

Electronic Communications Privacy Act

With the passage of the Electronic Communications Privacy Act (Public Law 99-508) earlier this year (effective January 19, 1987) there's now a new breed of cellular criminals. Now anyone who listens to the "forbidden frequencies" of cellular telephony is committing a federal crime. The law is questionable in many aspects. The act makes it illegal to manufacture, sell, advertise, or own any device or kit "primarily useful for the surreptitious interception of electronic communications." Nowhere is it stated what "surreptitious" means in this case, and attempts to have this clarified have been ignored. "Surreptitious interception" is *not* limited to electronic communication that is illegal to receive. One could interpret any receiver that monitors between 15 and 30 MHz or between 50 and 500 MHz as illegal, even though they are widely available. One could even go so far as to claim that any radio primarily for indoor use (and, thus, not readily observable from the outside) or AM-FM radios within stuffed animals are "surreptitious receivers."

Another problem is that if one is receiving interference from a source that was illegal to receive, and knew this, then one would be in violation of this act. So if your TV or stereo was getting noise from a cellular phone, and you knew this, you would be a federal criminal, even though your TV or stereo was listening to the proper frequencies. Previously it would have been the fault of the cellular phone company for transmitting such a dirty signal that one could receive on other frequencies not allocated for cellular phones.

The premise behind this law is that cellular phone calls are "not readily accessible to the public" anyway, so why not make it illegal to receive them? However, as many readers of *2600* and scanner users know, this is false. Cellular uses old TV channels, so an old TV set tuned to channels above 80 will receive listenable calls. Also, many videocassette recorders, service monitors, and scanners receive these frequencies, totally unmodified and out of the box. Cellular is in fact more vulnerable to interception than cordless phones, as there are millions of old TV sets in the U.S., and comparatively few radio scanners that receive cordless frequencies. Cellular phone calls are much more modulation-compatible with TV's, and their range is many miles, as opposed to cordless ranges of hundreds of feet.

Instead of dealing with the problem of scanner users listening in to cellular calls by encrypting the calls, the cellular phone companies and suppliers instead decided to legislate away a serious problem. Now cellular users can use their phones in communicating business deals and personal conversations believing that no one is listening. This false sense of security is misleading. Cellular phone companies don't want to deal with the problem logically. And this brings up the final problem, enforceability. This law is totally unenforceable. All it is good for is to tell customers not to worry about the confidentiality of their calls. The FCC was against the bill, along with the Electronic Industries Association and other cellular industry organizations and companies. However, many powerful companies lobbied for this bill, as they saw it as a quick fix to the very serious problem of cellular eavesdropping. The Justice Department at the time of the hearings on this bill clearly stated that they "have no intention of enforcing that part of the bill," referring to the privacy sections of the Electronic Privacy Act. There basically is no way they could attempt to enforce the law, considering that England has outlawed pirate radio, and millions still listen to the offshore stations. The Soviet Union has to jam Western broadcasts that they don't want their citizens to receive.

When AT&T filed a petition asking to merely label cellular phones with a warning sticker saying that calls may be monitored, other cellular phone companies reacted violently. AT&T's petition with the FCC states that "cellular users have an unwarranted sensation of privacy, which a label would help dispel....Customers buy cellular telephone sets with the expectation of privacy. In due course, they learn that they lack the privacy they expected, and may feel that their suppliers have misled them." Instead of dealing with the problem by scrambling cellular signals or even merely placing a warning label, the Cellular Telecommunications Industry Association instead replied that the FCC "should not consider any labeling regulation, which would place the burden on citizens to protect their privacy," and lobbied Congress for the passage of the Cellular Privacy Act. Bell South Mobility went as far as to say that "cellular users can expect a high degree of privacy," despite the fact (which any scanner user knows) that all it takes is to tune in to the 800-890 megahertz band with a scanner (or even an old TV tuned to the UHF channels). "Forbidden frequencies" include those in the February *2600*. A penalty of up to $10,000 would result from merely detecting the signal of one of the protected frequencies, even as much as the hiss from an encrypted transmission. Monitoring by scanner the VHF and UHF bands is illegal in the 153, 161,

450, and 455 MHz bands. Also, receiving radio common carriers in the 153, 158, and 454 MHz band along with FM subcarrier service or voice or message paging services is a crime, and certainly, receiving 800 to 890 MHz (that of cellular telephony) would be a crime. Willful receiving of a cellular telephone call results in up to six months in jail, plus a fine of up to $500. Receiving manual and IMTS car telephone calls could result in up to a $10,000 fine plus up to a year in jail. Cordless phones, amateur radio, CB, and General Mobile Radio Service are not protected.

"Fixing" Your Radio Shack PRO-2004 Scanner

The release of the Radio Shack PRO-2004 scanner was delayed until the passing of the Electronic Communications Privacy Act. Radio Shack is a major marketer of cellular phones, and thus lobbied hard for the passage of the bill so purchasers of their cellular phones could feel that the privacy of calls was secure. Therefore the release of their PRO-2004 scanner was delayed for four months in order to see if the bill would be passed. When the scanner was finally released, the "forbidden" 800 megahertz region was unable to be accessed. All Radio Shack did was connect an extra diode to the circuit board to prevent reception of the "forbidden frequencies." Below are instructions reprinted from page 48 of the March 1987 (Volume 6, Number 3) issue of *Monitoring Times* on how to remedy the situation.

1. Remove the four cabinet screws and the cabinet.
2. Turn the receiver upside down and locate circuit board PC-3.
3. Remove seven screws holding board and plug CN-501.
4. Carefully lift up the board and locate diode soldered in place below the module.
5. Snip one lead of the diode carefully, leaving it suspended by the other lead for later reattachment if desired, such as warranty repair.
6. Reverse first four steps above for reassembly. Radio will now cover 825–845 and 870–890 MHz and search in 30 KHz increments for no-gap 760–1300 MHz reception.

The "Forbidden Frequencies"

Now the more adventurous readers may want to go listen to these forbidden frequencies. Check the February 1987 issue of *2600* for a common breakdown of the cellular channels, which are between 800 and 890 megahertz. Not all cellular networks have this number of channels, but they can be easily figured out by careful listening to a scanner. Most cellular conversations can be listened to in their entirety without losing them due to cell site switching hand off. However, even when this occurs to the call you are listening to, you can easily pick it up again by merely scanning the frequencies again for the next cell. In this way and with a car one can follow a conversation in its entirety. A few words of warning though. This use of a scanner clearly violates the

Electronic Communications Privacy Act. The use of a scanner (or often the mere presence of a scanner) within a car violates laws in many states and localities, so check this out before you let one into your car. Using any information gathered off of the airwaves for personal gain violates federal law. As this activity is clearly illegal, *2600* does not condone or encourage listening to cellular calls.

Paging for Free (June, 1987) *By Bernie S.*

Did you ever want a beeper or paging service but decide against it because of the cost? Well, in many areas the local voice-paging system can be used without charge!

First, a brief description of how a voice-paging system works. Many voice-paging systems work by broadcasting all paging traffic on the same radio frequency in the VHF band around 150 MHz. All pagers on that system are tuned to the same radio frequency but each one has an audio tone decoder tuned to a unique sequence of audio tones. Every subscriber is assigned a different local or toll-free phone number that people should call when they want to reach him through his pager. When that number is dialed, the caller hears a tone, which prompts him to start his verbal message. This is limited to a few seconds, after which another tone cuts him off. This voice message is then temporarily stored in an audio tape buffer or a digital memory subsystem before being routed to the paging transmitter. A unique tone sequence is broadcast just prior to the voice message, which triggers the appropriate paging receiver so the subscriber only hears messages intended for him and not everyone else's on that same frequency. The pager times out after the fixed-length message is over.

A couple of years ago while listening to the local voice-paging channel on my scanner; I figured that anybody could just call any one of those phone numbers and get their message on the air. So after calling some numbers above and below my friend's voice pager number I found that this was true—I heard myself on the scanner. Problem was, you had to listen to everyone else's messages, too. Some kind of selective tone decoder for the scanner was in order—the cheaper the better. Also, some kind of tone-encoding system was needed that anyone had access to, so why not use touch tones? After some experimenting, I found that a touch-tone decoder chip with two 2N2222 transistors and a few resistors and capacitors (about $10 total at Radio Shack) could be used to decode the* (or any other) touch tone from the scanner's audio section and switch the audio on to the speaker. It all fit quite nicely into a matchbox-sized-container taped to the back of my portable scanner, and could be powered by the scanner batteries.

Now, when anyone called *any* of the paging system phone numbers and preceded their voice message with the * touch tone, the scanner speaker would sound off and allow me to hear it. At least a full second of tone was needed to unlock the decoder chip. Whoever was assigned that pager number would also hear the * tone and the message, so it wasn't entirely private, but it was *free* and you could take a "free ride" on any of the several hundred pager phone numbers to help avoid detection. The scheme worked quite well for over a year and it never was found out. Those paging me had to be careful not to give out their regular phone numbers or exact locations over the air, so a simple code was devised to allow a "modified" phone number to be broadcast without giving the intended one away.

If you already own a portable scanner, you already have most of a voice-pager. A programmable unit is needed to find the proper radio-paging frequency, but once you know it, a less expensive crystal unit can be used. The paging system phone numbers can be found by dialing numbers above and below a known pager number (ask somebody who has one or call the paging company and tell them you forgot yours). A schematic for the tone-decoder chip circuit is included if you buy it at Radio Shack, but the hook-up to your scanner's audio section depends on your model. You can usually get a schematic for your scanner by writing the manufacturer, and a friendly hardware hacker can help you with the hookup details if you're not electronically inclined. If you can bear listening to all the other paging traffic while waiting for your messages, you can skip the modification altogether and just tune in.

Scanner World in Albany, New York, probably has the lowest scanner prices around. They sell a crystal-controlled, pocket size, single-channel receiver that's ideal for this application for only $39. Be sure to specify the right frequency before ordering it, though. Since you'll want to leave your unit turned on most of the time, it's cheaper to use rechargeable Ni-Cd batteries. One could get fancy and add a 555 timer IC to the circuit which would automatically time-out and shut the audio off after the message is over, but turning the scanner off and back on again will reset it just the same. Some mobile scanners have enough room in them to mount the extra circuitry right inside, but portables are too tight a squeeze.

You probably don't need to be reminded that theft of telecommunications services is a crime, and that calling the same pager number repeatedly (not very smart, and unnecessary anyway) could be considered harassment. But if one is reasonably careful about what is broadcast, changes the pager number frequently, and places calls from pay phones when possible, the chances of being found are almost zero.

Cellular Phone Fraud and Where It's Headed (July, 1987)

By Bernie S.

The recent FBI/Secret Service cellular sting operation that culminated in the arrests of over 25 people in New York City confirms what many of us have suspected for quite some time: that cellular telephone fraud is widespread. The FBI estimates that cellular phone fraud costs system operators $3 million annually; with the average subscriber's airtime bill about $50 per month for 100 minutes of usage, there could be over 2,500 cellular pirates on the air if a pirate uses twice the normal amount of airtime. The term "pirate" rather than "phreak" is used here because the vast majority of illegitimate CMT users (Cellular Mobile Telephone) are only interested in stealing airtime, while phone phreaks are mainly interested in learning more about the telephone network through its manipulation.

The six-month FBI investigation used "cooperative sources" who named fraudulent installers; then FBI agents posing as customers and installers used standard entrapment techniques to gather evidence against those allegedly involved. The FBI's press release statement that "recent technological advances in computerized telephone switching equipment and billing systems were instrumental in....(their investigation)" is deliberately misleading. New York cellular carrier NYNEX merely supplied the FBI with its billing data to document the use of bogus and stolen ESN's & MIN's (Electronic Serial Numbers and Mobile Identification Numbers) discovered in the investigation. The Secret Service later became involved because the laws relating to the credit fraud being alleged are under their jurisdiction.

Safe Phreaking

In practice, cellular phreaking is very safe if one does their own transceiver modifications, changes ESN's & MIN's regularly, and uses standard phone phreak precautions. Indeed, FBI agent Greg Meecham has stated that fraudulently programmed CMT's are "unattributable, unbillable, untraceable, and untappable." A cellular carrier will become aware of any bogus or stolen ESN's and MIN's used on its system within a month or so after their initial use once the subscriber or carrier who is assigned those codes is billed and notifies them of the error. The home carrier will then change the legitimate subscriber's MIN in the MTSO (Mobile Telephone Switching Office) and arrange for a new NAM (Number Assignment Module, or ROM) to be installed in that subscriber's CMT transceiver. The MTSO maintains a database of all its valid ESN/MIN pairs, as well as a "negative verify" file on all known invalid numbers for the deadbeats and pirates in its area. The carrier may choose to leave certain fraudulent codes active to have any activity monitored, but as long as all parties at the receiving end of any phreaked calls become amnesiac to any inquiries, the phreak's identity will remain secret. If a phreak uses a different ESN & MIN every month, it'll be extremely difficult for the carrier to react in time to gather any information.

As with any landline, in-band signaling (i.e. 2600 Hz, MF tones, etc.) will work but can be easily detected by the ESS controlling that line. Since all cellular systems are in metropolitan areas, it's logical to assume that most cellular lines are on ESS. Although Telco security may be aware of any blue-boxing, the links in their security chain stop at the MTSO. Moreover, since the MTSO selects outgoing landlines from a trunk group, a pen register at the CO would be useless for establishing any toll fraud patterns.

Because of cellular's inherent frequency-hopping nature, it is very difficult to track down a CMT using conventional radio direction-finding (DF) techniques, even if it's stationary. A small directional antenna aimed randomly at surrounding cell-site repeaters with a TV antenna rotor will thoroughly confuse any DF attempts, although keeping calls as short as possible is always a good precaution. Locating a mobile CMT is virtually impossible. I was recently given a tour of an FCC monitoring van in Washington DC, and was surprised to see how lacking in sophistication their onboard DF gear was. The only equipment available to readily locate a CMT transmitter is primarily used by the military and intelligence agencies, which couldn't care less about CMT fraud unless it involved national security.

Equipment

Most CMT's are actually two main pieces of equipment: the transceiver and control head. The transceiver (transmitter/receiver) is usually a nondescript metal box with three external connectors and contains sophisticated circuitry. There are usually two main circuit boards inside: an RF board with all the radio transmitting/receiving circuits, and a logic board with a microprocessor, A/D and D/A circuits, and control logic. The control head is a touch-tone telephone handset with an extended keypad, numeric, or alphanumeric display, and volume and mic mute controls. It often has a separate speaker mounted in the cradle for on-hook dialing and call-progress monitoring. Some CMT's have a speakerphone option that allows you to drive with both hands on the wheel by talking into a small microphone mounted near the vehicle's sun visor, and listening to the cradle loudspeaker. This may seem to be the ultimate in laziness, but remember you could be maneuvering your five-speed through heavy traffic on the expressway when the phone rings! The control head/cradle is usually bolted to the transmission hump by the driver's seat, and the transceiver is usually mounted in the trunk with a power cable connecting it to the car battery and ignition switch. A shielded control cable links this equipment together and allows data and audio to pass between them. Most first-generation CMT's used the AMPS bus, developed by AT&T, which specified a system of 36 parallel wires in a bulky control cable. Some manufacturers later developed their own buses—Novatel's serial bus specifies a thin cable of just a few wires, which is much easier to install in vehicles. For fixed use, a CMT may be powered by any 12-volt regulated DC power supply that can deliver at least 5 amperes.

Any would-be cellular phreak must first obtain a CMT. Used bargains abound in some cities, where many subscribers found they couldn't afford to pay their airtime bills after they bought their phone! First-generation E.F. Johnson transceivers are a good choice because they're easy to work on, use a uniquely effective diversity (dual-antenna) receiver, and use the AMPS control bus, which means that several manufacturers' control heads will work with it. Another good choice is Novatel's Aurora/150 model. It uses a proprietary parallel bus and control head, but costs less, is very rugged, and is also easy to work on. In addition, all Novatel CMT's have built-in diagnostics which allow (among other things) manual scanning of all 666 repeater output frequencies—great entertainment when you're bored!

Antennas

A mobile cellular antenna is usually a short (less than a foot long) piece of stiff wire with a half-dozen or so turns in the middle, like a spring. The "spring" acts as a phasing coil in a 5/8-wave configuration. The antenna is mounted vertically either through a hole in the vehicle's roof or at the top of the rear windshield using silicon adhesive with conductive plates on either side to pass RF energy right through the glass. It's not quite as efficient as a roof mount, but most folks prefer not to drill a hole in their Mercedes. A 50-Ohm coaxial cable such as RG-58/U links the antenna to the transceiver with a male TNC-type UHF connector. A ceramic duplexer allows the transmitter and receiver to share the same antenna simultaneously. Mobile roof-mount antennas are designed to work with the ground plane provided by the vehicle's body, but for fixed use an "extended-feed" or voltage-fed coaxial antenna (which requires no ground plane) can be used if there's no tin roof on your house. A capped PVC pipe makes an ideal rooftop housing for this type of antenna, concealing it and making it weatherproof at the same time. As with any kind of antenna, the higher the better—but unless you're surrounded by tall steel buildings any height will probably do (provided you're within range of a cell-site repeater). It should even work indoors if near a window—remember that cellular systems are designed to work primarily with inefficient antennas at ground-level. Yagi and comer-reflector antennas are available for fixed use and provide very high gain and directivity. Antenna specialists Co. manufactures a broad line of cellular antennas.

Interfacing

Interfacing audio devices such as MF tone-generators to a CMT can be accomplished by coupling the device's output through an audio coupling transformer and capacitor across the control head's microphone wires. If it's available, a schematic diagram will show which CMT bus lines carry the transmit audio; coupling the signal there would be preferable. Acoustic modems can be interfaced acoustically, or by coupling the mic and speaker wires to those on the control head or to the appropriate bus lines. Direct-connect modems, answering machines, regular and cordless telephones, and other devices can be interfaced to a CMT through the AB1X cellular interface manufactured by Morrison & Dempsey Communications. This $300 device is a one-line PBX that connects between the transceiver and control head and provides an RJ-11C jack that accepts *any* direct-connect telephone accessory. It recognizes touch-tone and pulse dialing, provides 1.0B equivalent ringing voltage, and generates dial and busy tones when appropriate.

Access Codes

Every CMT manufactured has a unique ESN, which is a four-byte hexadecimal or 11-digit octal number in a ROM soldered directly to the logic board. It's supposed to be there for life and never removed. Some newer CMTs imbed the ESN in a VLSI chip along with the unit's program code, which makes ESN modifications virtually impossible. The ESN is also imprinted on the receiver ID plate mounted on the outside housing. When converted to octal (11 digits), the first three digits specify the CMT manufacturer, and the other 8 identify the unit. Typical ESN's might be 13500014732 (octal) for a NEC brand CMT, and 8E01A7F6 (hexadecimal) for a Novatel. The other important chip is the NAM, which contains the MIN (NPA-XXX-XXXX), lock code (keeps the kids from using it), and various model-specific and carrier-specific codes. Some newer CMTs have no NAM at all and use an EEPROM, which allows a technician who knows the maintenance code to change NAM data through the control head keypad.

Basically, when one attempts to make a CMT call, the transceiver first automatically transmits its ESN and NAM data to the nearest cell-site repeater by means of the overhead data stream, or ODS. The ODS is a 10 kilobaud data channel that links the CMT's computer to the MTSO computer, which controls the phone's entire operation right down to its channel and RF output power. If the MTSO doesn't recognize the received ESN/MIN pair as valid, it returns a reorder signal and will not process the call. In most cities with cellular systems there are two carriers: the wireline operator (usually Bell or the local telco) and the non-wireline operator, an independent company. Both maintain their own MTSO and network of cell-site repeaters, and occupy separate halves of the cellular radio band. Non-wirelines operate on system A (channels 001 to 333), and wirelines on system B (channels 334 to 666).

Custom-calling features such as call forwarding, call-waiting, and three-way calling are all standard with most cellular carriers, but the procedures for using them differ so it's best to call the carrier for more information.

Obtaining Codes

The most difficult task for cellular phreaks and pirates is obtaining usable ESN's and MIN's. One method involves having an accomplice who is employed at a CMT installation center. They will have a file on every CMT installed at that location, including the ESN's and MIN's assigned to those subscribers. Using several codes from one source could focus attention there, however. Another method involves the help of an inside person at the cellular carrier's customer service or billing department, where many low-paid employees have access to thousands of valid ESN's and MIN's. The most sophisticated method requires interfacing a CMT's A/D circuitry to a personal computer, enabling one to literally pick valid codes out of thin air.

Programming the CMT

Once a valid ESN/MIN pair is obtained, it must be programmed into the CMT's ROM's. Some CMT manufacturers use different devices and memory maps, but most adhere to the AMPS 16-pin, 32×8 bit format. The most common ROM's are Signetics 82S23 (open collector) and 82S123 (tri-state) or equivalents, but it's best to check the part numbers used in your unit. The existing ESN ROM should be carefully removed from the logic board using grounded de-soldering tools and read using a NAM programmer's bit-editor mode. Any PROM programmer that is device-compatible can be used, but dedicated NAM programmers have built-in software which greatly simplifies the process. The ESN printed on the ID plate (if in decimal, convert to hex) should be found in memory and will be immediately followed by an 8-bit checksum determined by the 8 least significant bits of the hex sum of the ESN's four bytes. The old ESN data (now copied into the NAM programmer's RAM) should be replaced with the new ESN and checksum. A new blank ROM of the same type should be inserted into the programmer and "burned." It would be advisable to solder a ZIF (Zero Insertion Force) DIP socket onto the logic board to accommodate the new ESN chip and any future versions.

The NAM chip is usually already ZIF socketed on the logic board for easy replacement. It, too, should be copied into the NAM burner's RAM and the old MIN replaced with the new one. The NAM checksum should also be updated to reflect the new data. Although the carrier's system parameters must also be programmed into the NAM, they can be left the same if the NAM being changed had previously been on the carrier now to be used. All that needs to be changed in this case is the last four MIN digits and checksum (and maybe the exchange if they're using more than one). An excellent write-up on NAM programming is available free of charge from Curtis Electro Devices. Ask for the May '87 reprint from Cellular Business magazine. Bytek Corporation sells a good budget NAM programmer for about $500, and the operations manual (available separately) explains in detail the memory maps, part numbers, and programming techniques for most CMT's on the market. This same unit is also capable of programming many ESN chips using the bit-editor mode. Some carriers and their installation agents will provide NAM system parameters on request, and some CMT service facilities will provide NAM and ESN memory maps and schematics of specific CMT's for a price.

One could eliminate the need for a NAM programmer altogether by programming and interfacing a personal computer to the CMT's ESN and NAM sockets. Another approach is to interface 2 banks of 8 hexadecimal thumbwheel switches to the sockets, although a computer program would still be needed to determine the proper switch settings. Either of these two approaches would allow quick emulation of any CMT at will.

Roaming

Whenever a CMT is used in a cellular system other than the one indicated by the SID (System ID) code in its NAM, it is in the ROAM mode and the ROAM indicator on the control head will turn on. A CMT can roam in any system its home carrier has a roaming agreement with, and most carriers now have roaming agreements with each other. If there is no roaming agreement, the MTSO will transmit a recorded voice message to the CMT user with instructions to call the carrier (the only call the CMT will be able to make) and give his name, MIN, ESN, and American Express Card number. All roamed calls will then be completed by the MTSO and billed to the credit card account. Fortunately, this procedure is becoming less common as more roaming agreements are made.

Usually, a carrier can only determine if a roamer came from a system with which it has a roaming agreement, not the creditworthiness of that roamer. Consequently, many carriers have been abused by roamers who have been denied service on their home system due to nonpayment. Once the home carrier is billed for roaming services provided by the roamed carrier, it will notify same to add that ESN and MIN to their MTSO's "negative verify" file to prevent further abuses from occuring. Several independent companies are establishing system software and data networks to allow Positive Roamer Verification (PRV) which will allow near real-time roamer validation by sharing data between carriers. Because of the many technical, financial, and political details that still need to be resolved, PRV systems will probably not be in place for at least two more years. In the meantime, even fictitious ESN's and MIN's can roam if they follow the standard format, although some carriers are sharing roamer data on a limited basis to prevent this.

To call a roaming CMT, the caller must know which system that unit is in, and call that carrier's roaming number. Roaming numbers vary, but are usually in the format: (NPA) XXX-ROAM, where NPA is the carrier's area code and XXX is the MTSO exchange. Calling that number will return a dial or ready tone, after which the roamed CMT's full MIN should be entered in Touch-Tones. After a few seconds, the mobile unit will ring or the caller will hear a recording stating that the mobile unit is out of range. Telocator Publications publishes a nationwide roaming directory for travelers with cellular phones.

Cellular Telephone technology offers phone phreaks complete safety by allowing miles of physical separation from the wire pair, and by offering thousands of lines to choose from. In addition, all this is possible from just about any location, even from a car, boat, train, or aircraft. It is these characteristics that are attracting a sophisticated new breed of phone phreaks who will enjoy unprecedented convenience and security.

How Phone Phreaks Are Caught (July, 1987) *By No Severance*

Until about four months ago, I worked in a switchroom for a large long-distance company. I was given the pink slip because some guy in my office found out that I did a little hacking and phreaking in my spare time. It seems that most companies just aren't into that anymore. I feel I should do all I can to keep phreaks from getting caught by the IC's (Independent Carriers or Inter-exchange Companies). Remember: A safe phreak is an educated phreak.

When you enter an authorization code to access a long-distance company's network there are a few things that happen. The authorization code number you enter is cross referenced in a list of codes. When an unassigned code is received, the switch will print a report consisting of the authorization code, the date and time, and the incoming trunk number (if known) along with other miscellaneous information.

When an authorization code is found at the end of a billing cycle to have been abused, one of two things is done. Most of the time the code is removed from the database and a new code is assigned. But there are times when the code is flagged "abused" in the switch. This is very dangerous. Your call still goes through, but there is a bad code report printed. (This is similar to an unassigned code report, but it also prints out the number being called.) You have no way to know that this is happening but the IC has plenty of time to have the call traced. This just goes to show that you should switch codes on a regular basis and not use one until it dies.

Access

There are several ways to access an IC's network. Some are safe and some can be deadly.

Feature Group A (FGA). This is a local dial-up to a switch. It is just a regular old telephone number (for example 871-2600). When you dial the number it will ring (briefly) and give you a dial tone telling you to proceed. There are no identifying digits (i.e. your telephone number) sent to the switch. The switch is signaled to give you a dial tone from the ringing voltage alone. The only way you could be caught hacking codes on an FGA number would be if Telco (your local telephone company) were to put an incoming trap on the FGA number. This causes the trunk number your call came over to be printed out. From the trunk number Telco could tell which central office (CO) your call was coming from. From there Telco could put an outgoing trap in your CO which would print the telephone number of the person placing a call to that number—that is provided that you are in an ESS or other electronic switch. This is how a majority of people are caught hacking codes on an FGA access number.

Next down the line we have **Feature Group B (FGB).** There are two FGB signaling formats called FGB-T and FGB-D. All FGB's are 950-XXXX numbers and I have yet to find one that doesn't use FGB-T format.

When you dial an FGB number your call can take two paths: 1) Large CO's have direct trunks going to the different IC's. This is more common in electronic offices. 2) Your call gets routed through a large switch called a tandem, which in turn has trunks to all the IC's.

When you dial an FGB-T number the IC's switch receives:

```
KP + ST
```

This prompts the switch to give you a dial tone. The IC gets no information regarding your telephone number. The only thing that makes it easier to catch you is that with a direct trunk from your central office, when you enter a bad code, the IC knows what office you're coming from. Then it's just a matter of seeing who is calling that 950 number.

On the other hand, when you dial an FGB-D number the switch receives:

```
KP + (950-XXXX) + ST followed by
KP + 0 + NXX-XXXX + ST or KP + 0 + NPA NXX-XXXX + ST
```

The first sequence tells that switch that there is a call coming in, the 950-XXXX (optional) is the same 950 number that you call. The second sequence contains your number (ANI—Automatic Number Identification). If the call comes over a trunk directly from your CO it will not have your NPA (area code). If the call is routed through a tandem it will contain your NPA. FGB-D was originally developed so that when you got the dial tone you could enter just the number you were calling and your call would go through; thus alleviating authorization codes. FGB-D can also be used as FGB-T, where the customer enters a code but the switch knows where the call is coming from. This could be used to detect hackers, but has not been done, at least not in my switch.

FGB-D was the prelude to **Feature Group D (FGD).** FGD is the heart of equal access. Since FGD can only be provided by electronic offices, equal access is only available under ESS (or any other electronic office). FGD is the signaling used for both 1+dialing (when you choose an IC over AT&T) and 10XXX dialing (see equal access guide, *2600*, March 1987). The signaling format for FGD goes as follows:

```
KP + II + 10D(10 digits) + ST followed by
KP + 10D + ST
```

The first sequence is called the identification sequence. This consists of KP, information digits (II), and the calling party's telephone number with NPA (10D ANI) finished up with ST. The second or address sequence has KP, the called number (10D) followed by ST. There is a third FGD sequence not shown here, which has to do with international calling—I may deal with this in a future article. When the IC's switch receives an FGD routing it will check the information digits to see if the call is approved and if so put the call through. Obviously, if the information digits indicate the call is coming from a coin phone, the call will not go through.

This is a list of information digits commonly used by Bell Operating Companies:

Code	Sequence	Meaning
00	Identification	Regular line, no special treatment
01	Identification	ONI (Operator Number Identification) multiparty lines
02	Identification	ANI failure
06	Identification	Hotel or Motel
07	Identification	Coinless, hospital, inmate, etc.
08	Identification	Inter LATA restricted
10	Address	10X test call
13	International	011-plus: direct distance dialed
15	International	01-plus: operator assisted
27	Identification	Coin
68	Identification	Inter LATA-restricted hotel or motel
78	Identification	Inter LATA-restricted hospital, coinless, inmate, etc.
95	Address	959-XXXX test call

There is a provision with FGD so when you dial 10XXX# you will get a switch dial tone as if you dial a 950. Unfortunately, this is not the same as dialing a 950. The IC would receive:

```
KP + II + 10D (ANI) + ST
KP + ST
```

The KP + ST gives you the dial tone, but the IC has your number by then.

800 Numbers

Now that we have the feature groups down pat we will talk about 800 numbers. Invisible to your eyes, there are two types of 800 numbers. There are those owned by AT&T—which sells WATS service. There are also new 800 exchanges owned by the IC's. So far, I believe only MCI, U.S. Sprint, and Western Union have bought their own 800 exchanges. It is very important not to use codes on 800 numbers in an exchange owned by an IC. But first...

When you dial an AT&T 800 number that goes to an IC's switch, the following happens. The AT&T 800 number is translated at the AT&T switch to an equivalent POTS (Plain Old Telephone Service). This number is an FGA number and as stated before does not know where you're calling from. They might know what your general region is since the AT&T 800 numbers can translate to different POTS numbers depending on where you're calling from. This is the beauty of FGA and AT&T WATS but this is also why it's being phased out.

On the other hand, IC-owned 800 numbers are routed as FGD calls—very deadly. The IC receives:

```
KP + II + 10D + ST

KP + 800 NXX XXXX + ST
```

When you call an IC 800 number, which goes to an authorization code-based service, you're taking a great risk. The IC's can find out very easily where you're calling from. If you're in an electronic central office your call can go directly over an FGD trunk. When you dial an IC 800 number from a non-electronic CO your call gets routed through another switch, thus ending up with the same undesirable effect.

MCI is looking into getting an 800 billing service tariffed where a customer's 800 WATS bill shows the number of everyone who has called it. The way the IC's handle their billing, if they wanted to find out who made a call to their 800 number, that information would be available on billing tapes. The trick is not to use codes on an IC-owned 800.

The way to find out who owns an 800 exchange is to call 800-NXX-0000 (NXX being the 800 exchange). If this is owned by AT&T you will get a message saying, "You have reached the AT&T Long Distance network. Thank you for choosing AT&T. This message will not be repeated." When you call an exchange owned by an IC, you will usually get a recording telling you that your call cannot be completed as dialed, or else you will get a recording with the name of the IC. If you call another number in an AT&T 800 exchange (i.e. 800-NXX-0172) the recording you get should always have an area code followed by a number and a letter, for example, "Your call cannot be completed as dialed. Please check the number and dial again. 312 4T." As of last month, most AT&T recordings are done in the same female voice. An MCI recording will tell you to "Call customer service at 800-444-4444" followed by a switch number ("MCI 20G").

Some companies, such as U.S. Sprint, are redesigning their networks. Since the merger of U.S. Telecom and GTE Sprint, U.S. Sprint has had 2 separate networks. The U.S. Telecom side was Network 1 and the GTE side was Network 2. U.S. Sprint will be joining the two, thus forming Network 3. When Network 3 takes effect there will be no more 950-0777 or 10777. All customers will have 14 digit travel cards (referred to as FON cards, or Fiber Optic Network cards) based on their telephone numbers. Customers who don't have equal access will be given seven digit "home codes." These authorization codes may only be used from your home town or city. The access number they will be pushing for travelcode service will be 800-877-8000. This cutover was supposed to have been completed by June 27, but the operation has been pushed back.

One last way to tell if the port you dialed is in an IC's 800 exchange is if it doesn't ring before you get the tone. When you dial an FGA number it will ring shortly but when you dial 10XXX# you get the tone right away.

Telecom Informer (October, 1987) *By Goldstein*

- If you're thinking of stealing a bus in Manhattan, you should know that unless you get around an electronic anti-theft device, you'll have the words "Call Police" flashing in the front where the destination usually is. A couple of months ago, that's exactly what happened. Except nobody noticed the flashing sign, or at least no one thought anything of it. It seems this guy went around picking up people for free and depositing them at their doorsteps. "All my life I've wanted to do this," he said.
- We've seen surprisingly few pirate television transmissions recently. In fact, we haven't seen any. But in Poland, they're becoming rather frequent—and popular. Most recently, a Solidarity radio station broke in on the sound frequency of a TV broadcast to urge Poles to shelter a Soviet army deserter who was in town.
- MasterCard is buying the Cirrus system, which means that Cirrus customers will be able to use MasterCard's telecommunications capabilities and MasterCard will become the world's leading debit card organization. This will link together about 30,000 automatic teller machines starting January 1, 1988.
- CLASS service is being tested in New Jersey with features like Return Call, Call Block, Priority Call, Repeat Call, Select Forward, Call Trace, and Identa Call. These features make it easier to identify incoming calls and to get through to busy numbers. If any of our subscribers have the opportunity to participate in these tests, please contact us. We have a whole series of experiments we'd like to try on these features.
- We may as well get used to it; nationwide beepers are popping up everywhere. At a cost of $30 to $60 a month, it will soon be almost impossible to be out of range.
- U.S. Sprint is going through hell. Combining the telephone networks and accounting systems of United Telecommunications and GTE has proven to be a much greater task than originally anticipated. Already, $76 million has been written off in uncollectible accounts, apparently due to an inability to function efficiently. Currently, there are three different Sprints in existence: the old GTE Sprint, the old U.S. Tel, and the new U.S. Sprint. And introducing the new fiber optic network and FON cards has added to the pressure.
- Sprint is filing a number of civil lawsuits against people who are accused of long-distance fraud. So far, the lawsuits are for $20 million plus penalties and have been filed in Kansas City and Seattle. According to Bernard A. Bianchino, U.S. Sprint vice president and associate general counsel, Sprint is filing lawsuits because criminal prosecutors don't have the resources to pursue all leads in these cases.

- Meanwhile, a really big fraudster has been caught selling Sprint and MCI codes for $100 each. Thomas Alvord of South Shore Electronics in Lake Tahoe, California allegedly used a computer to scan for codes and even advertised his service in the yellow pages. He used the name "General Bell," which showed up right next to Pacific Bell. Customers would obtain their codes by calling a voice mailbox. It's believed that this one person cost the long-distance companies more than two million dollars. As long as they know it's not hacking.
- AT&T is now distributing free copies of a business-to-business Italian yellow page directory. If you have a need for Italian yellow pages, call 800-538-BOOK.
- In the mood for some fun? In Washington, DC, students living in college dorms now can disconnect their telephone service without even talking to a Chesapeake and Potomac Telephone representative. Bell Atlantic is testing a service called "quick termination" or "Q.T." A student uses a touch-tone phone and calls a special number any time of the day or night. Voice prompts guide the caller through the entire process. The system can store a maximum of 300 disconnect requests. So far, we're unable to determine what, if any, security precautions are present here.
- C&P is also experimenting with distinctive ringing. By assigning up to three telephone numbers to the same phone line, each line can produce a different type of ring. Residents will pay about $4 a month for one additional phone number and $6 for two. We hope they don't mislead people into thinking they're getting three separate phone lines that can all be used at the same time.
- The following news item appeared recently in *Network World*. "A Bell Communications Research, Inc. scientist may have found a solution for often-annoying call-waiting tones. Deluxe call-waiting, not currently available, can temporarily suspend the call-waiting feature, quell the tone, and signal the second caller to try later. This solution requires complex software to program computerized switches to execute the multitiered signaling between users; telephone company central offices and those placing the calls on the busy line." Let's cut the crap! This service has already been available, at no charge, in many locations for years. All a caller has to do is dial *70 or 1170 before placing a call or during a call and call-waiting is disabled. The tone is "quelled" and, as far as signaling the second caller to try again—ever hear of a busy signal? That's what they're talking about, although they make it sound so much more complex. So who is this scientist that has found a solution that already exists? Bell Communications Research and *Network World* are doing us all a disservice by announcing an invention that is nothing new. No doubt this is happening so that we'll get used to the idea of paying for it. Deluxe call-waiting, what next?!

- The American Credit Card Telephone Company says it plans to offer a new service that would let customers charge long-distance calls to major credit cards from any public or private touch-tone phone. A customer would dial an 800 number and enter a Visa, American Express, or MasterCard number. The number would be validated and the call processed in seconds. According to *The New York Times*, this new service will compete with calling cards offered by AT&T. They also say that AT&T plans to offer a similar service by 1989. Does this mean AT&T will be competing with themselves? It wouldn't surprise us one bit
- The FBI is installing personal computer networks at remote sites that will be linked via gateways to mainframes at regional data processing centers. The project is known as Intelligent Workstation (IWS) and calls for more than 8,000 terminals, 700 networks, and 640 gateways. Iverson Technology of McLean, VA was awarded the contract
- According to a new government report, computers are now keeping track of more than seven million American workers. They monitor rest breaks and productivity, and even the number of individual keystrokes on a terminal or typewriter. The report was requested by Representative Don Edwards of California and was prepared by the Congressional Office of Technology Assessment. It's called "The Electronic Supervisor: New Technology, New Tensions." "We are becoming a surveillance society," Edwards said. "Every day we are seeing new invasions of the privacy and dignity of workers. We have occupational health and safety laws to protect workers' bodies. Now, Congress needs to respond to technological threats to their dignity and privacy." The report, which describes today's office as "an electronic sweatshop," said most jobs now monitored by computers were clerical data-entry type positions, but the management technique is spreading to other more complicated work. This is leading to a substantial increase in stress level. And it doesn't stop there.

  Computers are installed on the dashboards of trucks to record speed or how long a driver stops for. They can now also be monitored by satellite. Drug tests are popping up all over the place and they can tell a great deal about a person's private life. Telephone logs and video cameras are also on the rise. Today's technology makes it easy and cheap to monitor all kinds of things. In Alexandria, Virginia, there are devices called telecoms. Basically they're telephones with cameras attached used to monitor people on probation and parole. The person calls the corrections officials after his "curfew." The telecom transmits a photograph of the person talking every few seconds. The authorities know that the person is at home and is not using an impersonator. According to the authorities, the subjects don't think of this device as intrusive at all. It will be used more and more in the future, they say.

"Everyday an American wakes up, he or she is less free as far as private information is concerned," says Edwards. "Privacy is being invaded on a wholesale basis." Computerized tracking in this country now begins at age five, when children claimed as dependents must apply for a Social Security number. That number becomes their name. One FBI system is named Big Floyd. It plots relationships between people entered into a crime data bank and draws a graph of those relationships. It then reveals if the suspects seem to have violated labor-racketeering statutes. The IRS is interested in a similar arrangement. Where is it all leading?

- The State University of New York at Buffalo has adopted new computer methods to conceal the identity of reading material its students borrow. In November 1986, the university refused an FBI request for records on material a foreign student borrowed. Later they were forced to surrender the records when served with a subpoena. Stephen Roberts, associate director of libraries for the university, says the new system destroys the link between a person and any books as soon as the books are returned. He says, "We think you ought to be able to read whatever you want without anybody asking questions about it." Amen.

Scanning for Calls (Summer, 1989) *By Mr. Upsetter*

A radio scanner is a fun and useful tool for anyone interested in eavesdropping on phone calls. This article will be primarily concerned with receiving two types of telephone calls: cordless and cellular.

Although some of the old cordless phones operated on 1.6-1.7 MHz, the new ones operate on 46 and 49 MHz. Usually the base transmits both sides of the conversation on 46 MHz and the handset transmits only one side on 49 MHz. There are also phones which operate only on 49 MHz.

The following is a list of corresponding base and handset frequencies:

base (MHz)	handset (MHz)
46.610	49.670
46.630	49.845
46.670	49.860
46.710	49.770

base (MHz)	handset (MHz)
46.730	49.875
46.770	49.830
46.830	49.890
46.870	49.930
46.930	49.990
46.970	49.970

The cordless phone transmissions on these frequencies have a range of about 1,000 to 2,000 feet. That's plenty of range to eavesdrop on all your neighbors. The longest range I've gotten is about 3,000 feet with an indoor telescopic antenna. If you know your neighbor has a cordless phone and you want to find his frequency, program the frequencies I've listed into your scanner, then call your neighbor. When he answers (hopefully on the cordless), scan the frequencies and you should hear your own conversation.

It is obvious that anyone's cordless phone conversation could be received with ease. If you use a cordless phone, you should be concerned about security. It is not unlikely that someone near you has a scanner. Uniden Corporation, a major manufacturer of scanners, reports that there are scanners in over four million American homes. Think twice before you use that cordless phone.

Cellular phone transmissions are also easy to receive. The frequencies allocated to cellular phones are in the 800 MHz band. Scanners that receive the 800 MHz band are much more expensive than other scanners with standard coverage. Some manufacturers also block out cellular phone reception in their scanners. However, in my location (San Diego) I discovered a cellular service that operates between 451 and 459 MHz. These frequencies are covered by virtually all scanners on the market. The company using this system is called Vectorone Cellular. They use the following frequencies:

451.2875	452.7625	454.4375
451.400	452.8625	454.650
451.500	453.2875	454.8625
451.600	453.600	454.9625
451.7125	453.8125	454.175
451.8125	453.9125	455.3875
451.925	454.025	455.4875
452.125	454.050	457.200

452.2375	454.225	457.5125
452.3375	454.275	458.775
452.550	454.325	
452.650	454.3375	

If you own a scanner I would suggest searching the 450 MHz band to see if there is a similar cellular service in your area. Needless to say, I was surprised to find a cellular service operating on this band. I finally found out the name of the company after hearing the transmission of a recorded message which said "the Vectorone user you called is not available," which is played when one mobile user tries to call another unavailable mobile user. A quick check in the phone book verified the company's existence.

While we're on the subject of snooping, I would like to point out another interesting method. Some people use an "electronic babysitter" to keep track of their kids. An "electronic babysitter" is basically a radio (usually FM) transmitter that is placed in the child's room so the mother can hear the kid cry or whatever from another part of the house using the matching receiver. Some of these "electronic babysitters" transmit on 46 and 49 MHz along with cordless phones. One near my house transmits continuously on 49.83 MHz. People in effect bug their own houses by using an "electronic babysitter." I would estimate the range of these units to be short, about 500 to 1,000 feet.

Scanners have many other uses besides eavesdropping on phone calls. If you happen to be a criminal, you can keep track of the police with one. You can also hear air, marine, fire, business, military, and countless other transmissions. Scanners are pretty cheap. A decent one can be bought for about $100. Scanner World in Albany has a good selection and prices.

4 The Early Days of the Net

While the timing of our first issues could not have been more fortuitous with respect to the evolving phone world, the timing was pretty damn good in the computer world as well. In fact, I don't think we could have started at a more pivotal period. Computers had most definitely begun to make real inroads into our everyday lives. And there was little question among the few who cared at that point that various sprawling computer networks had existed for some time. But personal computers were still a rare exception and many years away from being the rule. And something on the order of the Internet remained little more than a dream. However, by the end of the decade, all of that had changed.

War Games had come out less than a year before our first issue and for me it had hit very close to home. To this day it's one of the few films that actually seemed to understand the true hacker spirit. Those magical moments when Matthew Broderick managed to get inside that computer system, or when he figured out how to make the free call from the pay phone, or when he was apprehended by the feds—all of us who found ourselves messing around with phones and computers at the time felt like we were living that story because in many cases we were. That thrill—and that fear—is something that never really leaves you. And those of us who experienced it at that relatively early stage of the game were really quite privileged, even though it sure didn't feel like it at the time.

In a big way, the Internet would be the death knell for the kind of hacking most popular in the 1980s. Back then, the most attractive targets were the big packet switched networks like Telenet and Tymnet. These systems allowed you to connect to computers all over the world once you dialed into a local node. Unlike the Internet, it was geared primarily toward businesses and institutions. So if you wanted to play around with it, you pretty much *had* to break in. We couldn't get accounts as individuals and we sure couldn't quell our curiosity. Nor could we effectively explain this to most people. But as computers got cheaper and access became much easier, this reasoning was harder to justify. The playing field of hacking was about to change in a very dramatic way.

And it wasn't just the hacking that was profoundly altered by the arrival of the Internet. The way people communicated would also be forever changed. In the '80s, most of our electronic communications was done via single-line BBS's, which connected at speeds of 300 or 1200 baud. (Basically, that was slow enough so you could actually read the text as it came across your screen or hardcopy terminal.) If someone else was using the BBS you were calling, you would have to wait—sometimes for many hours—until the busy signal turned into a ring and you could connect. And once you finally got on, it would take forever to read files or e-mail. Oh, and about that e-mail...more times than not it could only be from other users of the same system. You would have to make multiple calls to collect your mail from other places. But with the Internet, it suddenly became possible to get e-mail from people on other systems in all parts of the world. There was no longer a need to wait for busy signals to go away. Communication became orders of magnitude easier. And a whole lot more people got involved. For some that would mean the end of the magic. But for most of us it simply meant the rules had changed. If there's one thing the hacker spirit is known for, it's adapting to an ever-changing environment.

Other Networks and Systems

Today it's all about the Internet. But before that massive wave covered our landscape, we had a number of other toys to play with and their potential alone was inspiring to us. At the magazine, we were most intimately familiar with GTE Telenet, so much so that I actually wound up getting indicted for using it without permission. But that's another story. It meant a lot to us because of the amazing things it allowed us to do, like instantly send e-mail to someone in another part of the country. In the 1980s, that simply wasn't something the average person could do and we thought it was something they *should* have been able to do. It was also very inspirational to be able to find all of these computers that were hooked up to their network without having to scan entire telephone exchanges looking for them. After all, *every* computer was interesting to us in those days. They all represented new worlds and opportunities for learning. And the first thing we learned in most cases was that the security for these systems was laughable. In the early days of *2600*, we spent a good deal of time pointing out the various security flaws in the networks and computer operating systems, the most popular of which were made by Digital Equipment Corporation (DEC) as outlined in our examples below. At times we went beyond that and pointed to something really specific, like the New York City public school grading system, an exposé that was widely covered in the mass media. And apart from all of that, there were massive amounts of new toys to play with as the landscape continued to change. Something as simple as a fax machine or a new consumer service for modem users like PC Pursuit was enough to captivate our attention for huge amounts of time.

Hacking on Telenet (February, 1984)

Telenet. Or, to be more specific, GTE Telenet. A massive network formed by the people and technology that were used to develop packet switching for the Department of Defense. Telenet was purchased by GTE in 1979 and has been growing in size and revenue ever since.

There are quite a few data networks in existence today. Datapac, Autonet, Tymnet, ARPANET, to name some of the better known. A data network is basically a collection of mainframes, specialized minis, and high-speed lines. Through Telenet, you can connect to literally thousands of computers, all over the country, even the world if you know the proper procedures. All this is possible by making a local phone call, in most parts of the country. [Telenet access numbers are made readily available to the public by Telenet and systems on the network, such as the Source, Compuserve, etc.]

Once your modem is connected to Telenet, you have to hit two carriage returns. You'll see:

TELENET
XXX XXX

where the first 3 X's are the area code you're connected to and the rest comprise the Telenet node identifier. You'll then be asked for your terminal identifier. Usually "Dl" works for most terminals, but a simple carriage return is also accepted.

At this point you first receive the @ prompt. It is from here that you get places. And that's what's so unique about Telenet—the *way* in which you get places. You simply type a "C", a space, and the Telenet address. Then you enter the *area code* of the computer you want to connect to, followed by a two or three digit code. That's all there is to it. Telenet tells you whether or not you've found a working computer. If you want to exit from one computer and connect to another, just type an "@."You'll then get the Telenet @ prompt. Before you type the next address, type "D" to disconnect from the computer you're still connected to.

Hackers across the country have for years programmed their computers to scan the system for interesting things. All that has to be done is this: Pick the city you want to scan—let's say Boston. The area code is 617. Have your computer start its search at address 617001. If you get connected to a computer, Telenet will skip a line and print 617 001 CONNECTED. If you don't get connected, there are a variety of messages you could get. 617 001 REJECTING, 617 001 NOT RESPONDING, 617 001 NOT REACHABLE, 617 001 REFUSED COLLECT CONNECTION are a few of them. They all mean basically the same thing—there is no way to hook up to this address.

At this point, several things can be done. Naturally, you'll want to increment the address by one and search for a computer at address 617002. But how do you have your computer recognize when a connection has been made? This is necessary because you can't just keep entering C XXXXXX over and over—once you get connected, you have to enter the "@" to get back to the Telenet prompt, followed by a "D." Of course, you could type C XXXXXX, followed by "@,"followed by "D" for *every* attempt, but that can get rather time consuming. It's better simply to be able to save to disk or output to a printer the addresses of connections. And, fortunately for hackers, Telenet makes that very easy.

You can either search for a string that has the word "CONNECT" in it somewhere—the only time you'd find one would be when you got the CONNECTED message. But, as we mentioned earlier, an extra line is skipped right before the CONNECTED message, for some reason. Why not simply look for that extra line? If you get it, record the address, send the "@" and "D" and increment by 1. If you don't get the extra line, simply increment by 1.

Naturally, you will be collecting Telenet addresses for informational purposes only, to find out which computers are located where, in case you ever have to get onto one in an emergency of some sort. Keep in mind that you are not *entering* any of these computers; you're merely connecting for a brief second or two. And there is no login procedure or identity check for Telenet, so you're not fraudulently using their system either.

Also, the area code system is not the only system that works on Telenet. These are simply set up to be convenient, but an address can actually have any kind of a number in it. For example, addresses beginning with 311 or 909 (the latter being Telenet's own private "area code") also abound, and there are certain to be many more.

Without a doubt, though, it's the existence of the area code system that has helped Telenet become one of the easiest data networks to hack. And until they install some sort of a user identification program, or at least have the system disconnect after it becomes obvious that there's a strange person online, hackers will continue to be one of Telenet's biggest problems.

The Trouble with Telemail (April, 1984)

Last month, two of our reporters took a trip to National Public Radio studios in New York to reveal a very interesting development. It seems that Telemail, the electronic mail service of GTE Telenet was *still* just as easy to access as it was last year, prior to the October raids on computer owners who had allegedly broken into the system.

What had happened was this; a directory containing names of users on the Telemail system was obtained by our reporters—this list can be obtained from virtually any account on the system and, when printed out, is a couple of inches thick. They decided to go through this list and see if there were any accounts that still had the imaginative default password of "A" assigned to them. It had generally been thought, by both the public and press, that this incredibly foolish blunder had been corrected after the raids—in fact, new software *was* installed, which forced a user to change their password from the default when they logged on. All new passwords had to be between 6 and 8 characters in length. But, in a system with many thousands of customers, the reporters reasoned that surely there must be a few who hadn't yet logged on since the policy was implemented.

They decided to start their search with user names that began with "B." They'd enter Telenet through an 800 number, type MAIL, and enter usernames beginning with B that were listed in their directory. For each username, they'd enter "A" as the password, and if it didn't work, they'd go on to the next one.

The first account they tried was named B.ALEXANDER. They entered "A" as the password, and lo and behold, they were in! On the very first attempt! Robert Alexander of BUREC hadn't logged in since last summer. The "invaders" were told by the system to change the password and they complied. Then they decided to have a look around.

While there was no mail to speak of in Mr. Alexander's box, they were able to access bulletin boards that this account was allowed to look at. (Bulletin boards on Telemail are simply long-term storage message bases where messages of general interest to a particular group of people are posted.) All kinds of internal memos from the Department of the Interior were displayed.

In other words, the same old story. Nothing had really changed. Nearly half a year after seizing computers from coast to coast, the Telemail system was just as vulnerable to outsiders as it was before. Were the folks at GTE really interested in securing their system in the first place? Or did they just want to put the fear of the lord into hackers?

At first, when this story was breaking, GTE tried to deny that such a break-in was even possible. It had to be an inside job, they claimed, because nothing is wrong with our system. Then, when it finally started to become clear that this break-in did occur and that it was because of the default passwords once again, GTE took the expected step of blaming the customers. "We're not responsible for maintaining the security of the accounts." they said. "That's up to the subscriber," in this case, the Department of the Interior.

So, our two reporters came up with a plan. What if it hadn't been an outside agency's mailbox, but one belonging to GTE themselves? Who could they blame then?

They went to the letter "D" this time and searched for accounts that were affiliated with GTE. The first one was D.CORCORAN and, once again, they got right in. And Denise Corcoran of GTE had access to literally hundreds and hundreds of bulletin boards with names like PAYROLL, GOVT.AFFAIRS, and JAPAN.

On top of all this, it took GTE nearly a week to close access to these accounts, even after they were exposed on nationwide radio.

What our reporters proved here is that Telemail is either unable or unwilling to protect its customers. Unable? That hardly seems likely. After all, most computer bulletin boards run by high school kids are able to protect their users' accounts from outsiders. Why can't one of the largest and most expensive electronic mail systems do the same?

Apparently, what we have here is a company that has grown too big too soon, and is now unable to overcome the inertia that its size has created.

How to Really Have Fun

Once a hacker manages to get into a Telemail account, he's really set. By typing DIR " at command mode, he can get a listing of everyone that the account is allowed to see—their username, full name, company and division, and user number. He can see *any* user if he figures out their full username or user number. Typing DIR USERNAME or DIR USER NUMBER will give all of the above information about that person, if he exists.

From the huge list that DIR " generates (which takes a couple of hours to print at 300 baud), a hacker can scan for passwords that are defaults, first names, last names, usernames, or company names. Some GTE test accounts, for instance, used to have a password of GEENOGTE.

Telemail allows three logon attempts per access. Telenet allows four accesses per call. So each call to Telenet will yield 12 logon attempts to Telemail. Judging from the huge amount of users on the system, finding an easy password doesn't take all that long.

There are all kinds of neat features within Telemail accounts that seem to be exclusively beneficial to hackers. If the account has access to the SET command, the user can tell the system not to print a welcome banner on logon. The information that's printed on the welcome banner tells the user when his last access was. If a hacker arranges for that information not to be printed, the *real* user won't find out that his account was being used at 3:00 in the morning. And odds are that he won't really notice the absence of the message—if he does, he'll probably blame it on Telemail.

Then there's the UNREAD command. This actually allows a person to read through someone else's undelivered mail, and put it back when they're finished without anyone knowing that it's been read (unless a message was sent with a return receipt, which is rare). Telemail, it seems, practically bends over backwards to accommodate hackers.

What's so great about having a Telemail account? Why should a hacker spend all this time getting one? It's another means of free (or cheap) communications. All one has to do is call Telenet, enter Telemail, and read or send messages that can be *unlimited* in length. He can share one account with someone else (which is the least risky way to work things) or communicate with another usurped account that's allowed to send to and receive from his account. This is naturally a bit more risky since if one account is reclaimed, both may end up being taken down. Transmission of messages on Telemail is instant and there's never a busy signal. More importantly though, Telemail seems to be beckoning the hackers to come back home.

(Shortly after this article was dispatched, we received word that Telemail no longer uses "A" as a default. Whether this is true at all, whether they're now using a default of "B," or whether they're using defaults period, is something that hackers will no doubt find out soon. Drop us a line if you find out anything.)

Interesting Things to Do on a DEC-20 (July, 1985)

By The Knights of Shadow (as seen on the late Sherwood Forest][)

The first thing you want to do when you are receiving carrier from a DEC system is to find out the format of login names. You can do this by looking at who is on the system. {DEC> @ (the 'exec' level prompt) YOU> SY} SY is short for SYSTAT and shows you the system status. You should be able to see the format of login names. A SYSTAT usually comes up in this form: Job, Line, Program, User. The JOB number is not important unless you want to log them off later. Line is a number that is used to communicate with the user. These are both two- or three-digit numbers. Program tells what program they are running under. If it says 'EXEC' they aren't doing anything at all. User is the username they are logged in under. You can copy the format, and hack yourself out a working code. Login format is as such: {DEC> @ YOU> login user–name password}. Username is the username in the format you saw above in the SYSTAT. After you hit the space after your username, the system will stop echoing characters back to your screen. This is the password you are typing in. Remember, people often use their name, their dog's name, the name of a favorite character in a book, or something like this. A few clever people have it set to a key cluster (qwerty or asdfg). PW's can be from 1 to 8 characters long; anything after that is ignored.

Let's assume you got in. It would be nice to have a little help, wouldn't it? Just type a ? or the word HELP, and you'll get a whole list of topics. Some handy characters for you to know would be the control keys. Backspace on a DEC–20 is rub, which is 255 on your ASCII chart. On the DEC–10 it is Ctrl+H. To abort a long listing or a program, Ctrl+C works fine. Use Ctrl+O to stop long output to the terminal. This is handy when playing a game, but you don't want to Ctrl+C out. Ctrl+T gives you the time. Ctrl+U will kill the whole line you are typing at the moment. You may accidentally run a program where the only way out is a Ctrl+X, so keep that in reserve. Ctrl+S to stop listing, Ctrl+Q to continue on both systems.

Is your terminal having trouble? Like it pauses for no reason, or it doesn't backspace right? This is because both systems support many terminals, and you haven't told it what yours is yet. You are using a VT05 (isn't that funny? I thought I had an Apple), so you need to tell it you are one. {DEC> @ YOU> information terminal} "Info ter" also works. This shows you what your terminal is set up as. {DEC> assorted garbage, then the @ YOU> set ter vt05} This sets your terminal type to VT05.

Now let's see what is in the account (hereafter abbreviated acct.) that you have hacked onto. DIR is short for directory; it shows you what the user of the code has saved to the disk. There should be a format like this: xxxxx.ooo. xxxxx is the filename, from 1 to 20 characters long—ooo is the file type, one of: EXE, TXT, DAT, BAS, CMD, and a few others that are system dependant. EXE is a compiled program that can be run (just by typing its name at the @). TXT is a text file, which you can see by typing "type xxxxx.TXT." Do not try "type xxxxx.EXE." This may make your terminal do strange things and will tell you absolutely nothing. DAT is data they have saved. BAS is a basic program, you can have it typed out for you. CMD is a command type file, a little too complicated to go into here. Try "take xxxxx.CMD."

By the way, there are other users out there who may have files you can use (gee, why else am I here?). Type "DIR <*.*> on a DEC–20 or "DIR [*,*]" on a DEC–10. * is a wildcard, and will allow you to access the files on other accounts if the user has it set for public access. If it isn't set for public access, then you won't see it. To run that program: {DEC> @ YOU> username file name}. Username is the directory you saw the file listed under, and file name was what else but the filename?

Remember you said (at the very start) "SY," which showed the other users on the system? Well, you can talk to them, or at least send a message to anyone you see listed in a SYSTAT. You can do this by: {DEC> the user list (from your systat) YOU> talk username (DEC–20) send username (DEC–10)}. Talk allows you and them immediate transmission of whatever you/they type to be sent to the other. Send only allows you one message to be sent, and only after you hit <return>. With send, they will send back to you, with talk you can just keep going. By the way, you may be noticing with the talk command that what you type is still acted upon by the parser (control program). To avoid the constant error messages type either: {YOU> ;your message YOU> rem your message}. The semi-colon tells the parser that what follows is just a comment. Rem is short for "remark" and ignores you from then on until you type a Ctrl+Z or Ctrl+C, at which point it puts you back in the exec mode. To break the connection from a talk command type "break."

If you happen to have privs, you can do all sorts of things. First of all, you have to activate those privs. "Enable" gives you a $ prompt, and allows you to do anything to any other directory that you can do with your own. To create a new account, using your privs, just type "build username." If the username is old, you can edit it. If it is new, you can define it to be whatever you wish. Privacy means nothing to a user with privs. There are various levels of privs: Operator, Wheel, CIA. Wheel is the most powerful, being that he can log in from anywhere and have his powers. Operators have their power because they are at a special terminal allowing them the privs. CIA is short for 'Confidential Information Access', which allows you a low level amount of privs. Not to worry though, since you can read the system log file, which also has the passwords to all the other accounts. To de–activate your privs, type "disable." When you have played your greedy heart out, you can finally leave the system with the command "logout." This logs the job you are using off the system (there may be variations of this such as kjob, of killjob). By the way, you can say (if you have privs) "logout username" and that kills the username's terminal.

There are many more commands, so try them out. Just remember: leave the account in the same state as you found it. This way they may never know that you are playing leech off their acct.

RSTS for Beginners (April, 1986) *By The Marauder*

RSTS/E is an acronym for Resource System Time Sharing Environment. It is an operating system, most commonly found running on Digital Equipment Corporation's (DEC) PDP series of computers (i.e. PDP-11/70 being quite common.). This article describes the basics of identifying, obtaining entry, and some basic things to do once you are in a system running RSTS/E.

System Identification

Upon connection to a RSTS/ E system, it will usually identify itself with a system header similar to:

KRAMER CORP. RSTS/E V7.2 JOB 5 KB32: (DIAL-UP) 18-FEB-84 3:46 PM
User:

So as you can see, an RSTS/E system is quite easily recognized due to the fact that it actually tells you in the system header. It is possible for the system manager to modify the login to not display this information, but very few systems do not print out a standard system header. If it has been changed, it will most likely still display the 'user:' prompt. Note: it's also not entirely uncommon for RSTS systems that prompt for a User number to use the "#" character. In either case once you have reached the user: (or "#") prompt, RSTS/E is now awaiting you to enter a valid user (account) number. Once you enter a valid PPN, RSTS will prompt you with: "Password:" If you enter both a valid account, and its matching password, you're in.

Login/Account/Password Formats

An account on an RSTS system is always two numbers between 0 and 255 (inclusively) separated by a comma. This is normally referred to as the Project-Programmer Number or PPN. The first number is the Project Number, and the second is the Programmer Number. Some examples of valid PPN's are: 200,200; 50,10; 30,30; or 1,7.

Passwords on RSTS/E system are always 1 to 6 characters long and can include: the uppercase letters A–Z, the numbers 0–9, or a combination of both. No lowercase letters, and no special characters are allowed (i.e. !, #, $, %, &, ', etc.). So you can eliminate using these in an attempt to hack a password.

On all RSTS systems there are accounts that *must* be present. Unless *major* software modifications are made, they *will* exist. Here is a list of these accounts and the default passwords that are used when Digital installs a system.

ACCOUNT	DEFAULT PSWDS(S)	COMMENTS
1,2	DEMO, SYSLIB, SYSMGR, DECMAN	SYSTEM LIBRARY/SYSTEM MANAGER ACCOUNT
1,3	DEMO	AUXILIARY LIBRARY
1,4	DEMO	
1,5	DEMO	

Of all the accounts, it is most difficult to remove "1,2" due to software requirements, so if you are hacking a system from scratch, it is suggested that you try to work on a password for this account, also note that "1,2" is the system library, and the default system managers account, so the passwords chosen for it sometimes reflect these facts. Also hacking at this account kills two birds with one stone—not only must it be present, but it also has full privileges, as does any account with a project number of 1 (i.e. 1,XXX). Once obtained, you will have full access to anything on the system.

Basic System Functions

Once in, RSTS/E will prompt you with 'Ready.' You are now in the RSTS/E 'BASIC' monitor, and you could type in a BASIC program, etc. Here are some useful system commands/programs that can be of use.

- HELP: Simply type help. It's available on most systems and fully self-documenting and menu driven. It will give you a complete description of most system commands and functions.
- DIRECTORY (or 'DIR'): Will give you a listing of programs/files that reside in any account you specify. Simply typing 'DIR' will list the files in the account you are in, to obtain a directory of another account, simply use the format: 'DIR (XXX.XXX),' where 'XXX,XXX' is any valid account number. You can also substitute an '*' in place of either, for a 'match all' or 'Wildcard' search.
- SYSTAT(or 'SY'): Will give you a listing of who else is currently on the system, what they are doing or running, and some other information. This command is especially useful for obtaining other valid account numbers (PPN's).
- OLD: Allows you to load a basic program (any file with a '.BAS' extension) into memory. If the program is in the same account as you, simply type 'OLD NAME.EXT,' and if the program resides in another account, use the format 'OLD (XXX,XXX) NAME.EXT,' where NAME.EXT is the name of the basic program and XXX,XXX is the account/PPN that it resides in.
- PIP: Is the Peripheral Interchange Program. It is a fancy name for a basic file utility used to transfer files from one place to another. You can get a full description of its uses by typing 'HELP PIP.'
- BYE: Logs you off the system. Always use this command to log off! If you simply hang up, your account will remain logged on, in a 'DETACHED' state, and this will automatically arouse the suspicion of even the densest Sysop, especially if you've managed to obtain a privileged account.

Some Final Notes

Once on under any account, do a directory of all the (0,*) and (1,*) accounts. You will notice a column in the directory listing that is labeled 'PROTECTION.' This is a program/file protection code. It can be set to various levels (i.e. any account can run/list, certain accounts can run/list, etc.). Look for any programs (files with extensions: .BAC, .BAS, and .TSK), which have a protection of (232) or (252). These are programs that give *anyone* who runs them privileges at the time they are run, so make a note of any programs with extensions of this sort and try running/exploring every one. Many programs have *bugs* that can be used to your advantage. This can be discussed in future articles. There is also a program that will allow you to chat with other users on the system. You can usually run it by typing 'RUN $TALK.' It will ask for a 'terminal to talk to,' and you can obtain active users/terminals by using the 'SYSTAT' command.

In conclusion, RSTS/E is a fairly user friendly system to use/abuse, and one of my personal favorites. You can learn the basics and become fairly proficient in a relatively short time.

Stumbling Into Control on a VMS (January, 1987) *By The Mole*

Once a hacker has gained access to a VMS system, his goal should be to try to get a hold of the most powerful privileges he can. Here are some tips on taking over a VMS system.

There are two routes to take—either through programming or by modifying the User Authorization File. The first method generally requires the CMKRNL privilege. This privilege allows one to modify the data structures used by the operating system. By writing the correct code a hacker can change his, or anyone else's, privileges and quotas. This method requires very detailed knowledge of the operating system and should be left only to the very experienced. If you do not know what you are doing, it's very likely that you will crash the system and if you do there will be an accurate and detailed record of what you did. (You should never take down a system because doing so leaves a trail that the system manager can use to track you down.)

The easier way to gain control of a system is through the User Authorization File or UAF. If you modify the UAF you must log out and then log back on to get any privileges you added to your account. With programming you can make them take effect immediately. The cost you pay is complexity.

First, here are some tips for breaking onto a VAX:

Every VAX that is serviced by DEC has a Site Management Guide. This is a brown loose-leaf binder that the DEC field service personnel use to keep a maintenance log.

Field service people like to write the FIELD password down in this book. If you can get a quick browse at it you may be able to come up with several passwords. If you find the FIELD password, you are all set to take control of the system.

The VT200 series terminals have an answerback feature that allows the terminal to save a character string that can be recalled by pressing CTRL/BREAK. Users often make this character string "username(CR)password(CR)." This allows them to log in by pressing two keys. It also allows you to do the same. The way you can get in is by bringing up the username prompt and by pressing CTRL/BREAK. You won't be able to see the password, though. To get the password, enter "$CREATE PASSWORD.DAT CTRL/BREAK CTRL/Z" then "$TYPE PASSWORD.DAT." This method is more likely to work with a terminal that is in someone's office as opposed to a terminal that is in a common area.

Of course, the simplest way to get in is through a terminal that is left logged on. If you have access to a user area, you probably can find a terminal that has not been logged off.

A list of usernames on a system is often helpful. In my experience, around 50 percent of all passwords are usernames or slight variations on the username. This is especially true of such usernames as GAMES, DEMO, and USER.

Once you are logged on to a system, the very first thing you should do is enter the command "$DELETE/SYMBOL/ALL/GLOBAL." Digital-related trade magazines are filled with articles on how to catch hackers and prevent them from doing things by defining global symbols. If you execute that command you have removed all of those silly little traps.

Now for taking over that VAX. First, the easy way. Once you are logged in use the "$SHOW PROCESS/PRIV" command to see if you have any of the following privileges:

BYPASS
SYSPRV
SETPRV
CMKRNL

If you do have one of these, you already have the system in your hands. If you have BYPASS or SYSPRV you can modify the UAF directly. Just enter the command "$SET DEFAULT SYS$SYSTEM" and then the command "$RUN AUTHORIZE." Then follow Lex Luthor's instructions in the VMS series, the last of which appeared in the March 1986 issue of *2600*. If you have SETPRV you have all privileges available. Just enter the command "$SET PROCESS/PRIV=ALL" and then follow the instruction above. If you have CMKRNL enter the command "$SET UIC [1,4]" and then follow the instructions above.

Also, use the "$SHOW PROCESS" command and see if the first number of your UIC code is 10 (octal) or less. UICs look like [100,4]. If you do, you have SYSPRV automatically even if it is not listed when you SHOW PROCESS/PRIV.

An easy way for a system manager to help keep you off of his system is by not creating any privileged accounts. Fortunately for the hacker, system managers do not follow this rule (often not by personal choice). The only privileged accounts that are needed to run a VMS system are the FIELD and SYSTEM accounts (the FIELD account is not absolutely required). In spite of this, very often executives in computer departments (as well as system managers) keep privileged accounts for themselves (presumably for ego purposes) even though they have nothing to do with maintaining the system. Also, support people often have system privileges when they could get by with group privileges. At colleges, often many of the professors have privileged accounts. The excuse is that they need to read their students' files. The more there are the more targets there are for the hacker. It's harder to get in if five people know the SYSTEM password than if all five people have privileged accounts.

Here's a little story for you. When I was in college the "systems people" created a command called ORACLE so that users could send them mail messages. For some reason they also created an account called ORACLE to read the messages. Guess what the password for the account was? ORACLE, that's right. How did you know? Would you believe that this account had full privilege also? The whole school knew the password to the account.

A smart system manager is also going to use the SYSTEM account only to manage the system and use a personal, non-privileged account to program with and to write memos. Luckily for you, most system managers are lazy. They use their CHKRNL privilege to change their UIC code so that the SYSTEM account temporarily becomes their personal account (but with privileges, of course). The more the SYSTEM account is in use, the more likely it is to be left logged on. In my experience, this is the absolute easiest way to get to take over a system. The SYSTEM account should only be used from a secure area.

When I was in college, I had a reputation for breaking into the computer. Now I am going to reveal The Mole's break-in secret to the world. Every time I got in it was because someone in the computer department had left a terminal logged on to a privileged account. That was the only method I ever used personally (although I did teach other people more sophisticated means). So I never broke in. I just walked right through the front door. As a direct result of my "hacking" (if you can really call it that), the school created all sorts of rules governing computer use when all they really needed was some common sense from their "systems people."

Once you're on a VMS system you should try to get a copy of the program SYS$SYSTEM:AUTHORIZE.EXE. Once you get a copy of this program, bring it back to your microcomputer and save it. The AUTHORIZE program should be protected but often it is not. Once you get it from one system, it is good anywhere.

Now what do you do once you get your own AUTHORIZE program? Create a new UAF, of course. Enter "$RUN AUTHORIZE." That will generate an error saying that there is no UAF and a prompt asking if you want to create one. Of course you do, so you answer yes. Next, enter "UAF) MODIFY SYSTEM/PASS=MANAGER." Now in your own UAF MANAGER is the system password. So what good is having your own UAF when the system is not going to use it? Well, why not make the system use it? At this point you need a privilege called SYSNAM. Many programs, especially scientific ones, require that the user have it so it is not too difficult to find an account with this privilege. When you are logged onto the system, enter "$SET PROCESS/PRIV=ALL" and then "$SHO PROC/PRIV." If you see SYSNAM listed you are in luck. Enter "$SHOW DEFAULT" to get your directory name. Then enter "$DEFINE/ SYSTEM/EXEC SYSUAF dev:[directory]SYSUAF.DAT," where dev and directory are the names you get from the SHOW DEFAULT command. Now log out and log back on to the SYSTEM account using the password you just created.

SYSNAM privilege is also nice if you want to just screw up a system. By redefining such logical names as SYS$SYSROOT, SYS$SYSTEM, SYS$SYSDEVICE you can bring the system to a halt.

If you have not guessed by now, I am a VMS system manager. I am assuming that many of the people who are reading this are other system managers who, like myself, are trying to keep hackers off of their systems. I think the benefit from system managers reading this in a hacker publication is greater than the harm that could come from hackers reading it.

Grade "A" Hacking (Autumn 1989) *By The Plague*

What is UAPC?

UAPC stands for University Applications Processing Center. This is a computing and data processing facility that deals with academic record keeping and processing. One of their jobs is to process student applications for CUNY (City University of New York) schools. Another job, and this is the part that interests us most, is to process student records for the New York City public high schools.

Nearly all New York City public high schools are connected to UAPC. There are 116 public high schools in New York City (with several hundred thousand students). The reasons for interconnection are obvious. If every school had its own student data storage computer, its own proprietary software, and its own staff trained on that particular system, the cost would be too great. Not only that, but data transfer and statistical analysis would be impossible for the school system as a whole. As an example, there would be much paperwork, chaos, and confusion just to transfer a student from one school to another. Computing the drop-out rate and other valuable statistics like standardized test scores would involve every school sending in reports generated by its own computer system, and hence more paperwork, more bureaucrats, and more confusion.

So now you understand why all NYC high schools are linked by modem to this one computer. All grades, attendance, course records, and schedules for every New York City high school student are stored and processed at UAPC.

Where is UAPC?

UAPC is located in Brooklyn at Kingsborough Community College (across from Sheepshead Bay at the far end of Manhattan Beach). The actual computers and personnel are in Building T-1 (or simply building ONE). If you happen to go trashing there sometime, building T-1 is a one-story tan colored aluminum shed. It looks sort of like a gigantic tool shed. Above the entry door is written "ONE" in large black plastic lettering. By the way, you're allowed to go in. Nobody is going to check ID or anything like that. If you look like a student, no problem. The reason for this is that T-1 connects to T-2, another shed (blue in color), which has many classrooms. The actual UAPC office is directly to your right as you enter T-1.

In each New York City high school, there is something called a "program office." This room usually contains terminals and big printers and it's where each school creates class schedules for teachers and students, among other things. The staff that work in these offices are trained at UAPC.

Technical Information about UAPC

Enough background; here's the scoop. UAPC computers run on IBM mainframes (IBM 370 and 3090). The virtual operating system that is used is MVS (which is much like the familiar VM/CMS). On top of MVS runs Wylbur (pronounced will-burr, not while-birr), which is sort of like a command shell plus a batch language plus an editor all rolled into one. On top of Wylbur, run the actual applications (jobs) for processing of grade files.

There are several applications for various tasks (entering grades, entering attendance, class scheduling, generating transcripts, and various other reports). These applications are written in a batch-like language and are stored on disk in source code format. The reason for this is that each school has its own way of doing things (i.e., naming conventions for classes and sections), and the batch programs can be modified by either UAPC or qualified people who work in each high school's program office. These applications are submitted to run on the IBM machines with the JCL code appended at the top of each application.

Each school connects to UAPC via a terminal and modem and each school is allocated its own directory (or library as the batch-heads call them) on the system. This directory contains the applications (jobs) that the school uses each day for various activities. Data files are also contained in these directories. The data files are in a pretty much IBM standard format (although stored in EBCDIC instead of ASCII). Input records for each application are usually fed in using punch cards or scan-tron type readers at the local school. If you've ever gone to a New York City high school you'll know what I mean: The attendance punch cards are brought down each day from each homeroom to the program office. Also, each teacher would fill in attendance forms (used to detect class-cutting) using a number-2 pencil. These forms look like the test forms for the SATs.

Sometimes, however, input is entered manually at the terminal in the program office, usually for query type jobs. For instance, if one student lost his class schedule and wanted a replacement, he would have to go to the program office and ask for one. They would run that application on the terminal, print up a schedule for that student, and give it to him.

How Do You Know if Your School is on UAPC?

If you go to a New York City public high school, then the chances are 95 percent that your school is on UAPC. If you are not sure, look for the telltale signs at your school. Does your homeroom teacher use punch cards? Is your transcript laser-printed on white paper and divided into nice columns grouped by academic subject? Does your school's program office contain terminals and printers? Is your class schedule (aka program card) printed on 5.5"× 7" paper (either heavy-bond white or thin-bond blue)? Is your grade report (aka report card) printed on computer paper, about 5.5" high (regular width) with a blue Board of Ed logo in the middle, with explanation of grades (in blue) on the back? Do you get little yellow or white laser-printed cards in the mail when you play hooky or cut classes? Any of these sound familiar, boys and girls? They should, because almost every New York City public high school fits all these categories. If your school fits any of these (especially the punched cards and terminals in the program office), then you can be sure that your grades are lurking somewhere in the bowels of UAPC.

Logging on to UAPC

To get on, you're going to need a dialup. It's not too much work getting the dialup, if you do a little snooping and trashing around the program office at your school, you should find it written down somewhere. However, I will save you some time and tell you that there are at least 12 dialups for UAPC in the 718-332-51XX number range and several in the 718-332-55XX range. There are many more elsewhere (usually exchanges local to Kingsborough Community College).

You should only connect to UAPC on school days during valid school hours. You can connect to UAPC at either 300 or 1200 baud. However, in an effort to thwart people for finding their dialups, UAPC will not print anything to the screen unless you connect at the right format and hit a few of the right keys. Therefore, you should use the following procedure in order to connect: Call at 300 or 1200 baud, using 7 data bits, even parity and 1 stop bit (7E1), and local echo (or half duplex). Once connected, hit the RUBOUT/DELETE key (ASCII code 127 or 255 [hex $7F or $FF]) three times, and then hit return twice. You will be greeted with the following:

```
UAPC MVS390A LINE - 10-TEN 11:59:02 03/22/89
11:59 Wednesday 89-03-22
You are signed on to U.A.P.C. Have a good day.
TERMINAL?
```

When you are prompted for the terminal, just enter a letter-two-digit combination (A99 works just fine).

You will then be prompted for "USER?" which is your school's login ID. The format for the username is $HSxxn, where xx is a two-letter abbreviation for your school's name, and n is a digit from 1 through 9, indicating the particular account used by the school. N is usually 1, 2, or 3. An example of a user ID is $HSST1 or $HSST2, which are the user ID's for Stuyvesant High School in Manhattan.

You can guess at your school's user ID (it's easy enough, for instance Sheepshead Bay High School would be $HSSB1 or South Shore High School would be $HSSS1, etc.), but a better way is to pick up the trash from the program office. You should find stacks of green and white printer paper that is 132 columns in width. The user ID will be almost everywhere throughout most printouts generated. Remember to look for the $HSxxn format.

After entering a valid user ID, what you will see next depends on several things. Normally you should see the "PASSWORD?" prompt, but on some accounts you may also see a "JOB?" or "KEYWORD?" prompt. This simply depends on the school, however 90 percent of the accounts only ask for the PASSWORD. The JOB and KEYWORD are simply additional passwords. However, every user ID has a PASSWORD on it. Usually only $HSxx1 accounts have JOB or KEYWORD passwords. However most schools have several accounts (usually two or three), and the $HSxx2 and $HSxx3 will usually have only the "PASSWORD?" prompt. There is no difference in access privilege between the various accounts at each school. They are simply there so that more than one terminal at each school can be logged in at the same time.

Getting the Password

Naturally, you're going to need the password if you are serious about doing anything with UAPC. There are several options here. However, one option that I would not recommend is that you attempt to hack the password by brute force. UAPC has a nasty habit of allowing you four attempts at the password before it disables that account and notifies the security dudes at UAPC. If you disable your school's account, your school's program office must call UAPC by voice in order to reactivate it. There is a way around this, if you really want to brute-hack the account. After three password attempts, you should hang up and redial, and then do another three attempts, and so on. This will keep the counter from ever reaching 4 and disabling the account. Although it's a pain in the neck, there isn't much we can do about it. However, if you have no plans of ever getting into UAPC and just want to annoy your school, simply log on as them early each morning and disable their password. This will give them a headache to say the least, having to call up UAPC each day to reactivate their password.

Other ways of getting the password include our old favorite, social engineering. Here there are two options. You can attempt to engineer UAPC by voice, thus saying that you are the school and that you need the password. Conversely, you can attempt to engineer the school by calling the program office by voice and saying that you are from UAPC and that you need them to change their password to a diagnostic password, which you will so kindly provide. If you're going to do social engineering, make sure you get some valid people's names at either UAPC or at your school.

Yet another way to get the password is to do what was done in *War Games*, snooping around the program office. They usually do not have the password written down. But, and this is important, you can get the password if you can somehow manage to look over the shoulder of the terminal operator when he/she is logging in. Remember, they connect to UAPC at half duplex, and thus keys are echoed locally, meaning that you will see the password on the screen as it is typed. I know this for a fact.

If you're hardware inclined, you can tap the line that connects to the modem and terminal. These lines are usually not connected to the schools switchboard, and can even be exposed outside the building itself. Use a tape recorder and a Radio Shack auto-pickup device to tape the transmission (which is usually 300 baud anyway). Play the tape into your own modem (set it on answer) and you'll be able to see the originate data (including the password) on your screen. If you haven't tapped modem lines before, I do not suggest using this method.

Note that UAPC requires each school to change their password once a month, so make sure you get the password right after they change it. This will give you plenty of time to learn how to use UAPC before you attempt any stunts with modifying data.

All About Wylbur

Okay, you're in UAPC; what now? Well, once in you will be dealing with Wylbur. Like I said before, Wylbur is sort of like a command shell plus batch language and editor all built into one. You will know you're in Wylbur when you are given a "COMMAND?" prompt.

There are some misconceptions about Wylbur that I would like to clear up right now. When most New York City hackers talk about the "grades computer" they simply refer to it as Wylbur. This is misleading because they are referring to UAPC. Wylbur is not synonymous with UAPC; the Wylbur shell is used at many different computing sites, which use MVS and IBM mainframes. It's sort of like equating VAX/VMS to the computers at DEC. VMS is an operating system and has very little to do with the machines at DEC headquarters. The same holds true for Wylbur and UAPC.

Wylbur also runs on the other IBM machines at Kingsborough (which have different dialups, separate from UAPC). These machines have no affiliation with the UAPC machines. Therefore students using these other machines at Kingsborough must know Wylbur as well. Lucky for us, you or any student can purchase (no ID required) a Wylbur manual at the Kingsborough bookstore (Building U) for $4. Just ask the nice lady for the "Wylbur User's Guide," written by Ganesh Nankoo, and tell 'em I sent ya. If you do get into UAPC, I strongly suggest that you buy this manual. It is very informative and can keep your ass out of hot water.

Some useful commands under Wylbur:

```
RUN PRINT: run the exec program in your active area and print the output.
RUN FETCH: same as above, but place output in fetch queue.
FETCH*: fetch the last output and place into your active area.
LIST: list current active area to screen.
LIST OFF: list current active area to printer.
LOCATE: locate all jobs submitted.
LOCATE*: locate last job submitted.
LOCATE 056: locate job 056.
PURGE 056: purge job 056 which is on the output queue.
COLLECT: input/enter data into your active area.
CLEAR ACTIVE: clear your active file in memory.
USE #name: load the file "name" from disk into your active area.
SAVE #name: save your active area.
SET PSW: change your password.
SET KEY: change your keyword.
SHOW DIR: show current files in your directory.
SHOW USERS: show current users on UAPC.
```

(Note: Your active file is a buffer used by the editor. You can list it, save it, clear it, load into it, run exec jobs from it, etc.)

You can also get help on UAPC by typing HELP HELP (yes, twice. One HELP will not do the trick).

Applications That Run on UAPC

Once inside UAPC, you may have very little contact with Wylbur itself, and you will see a "WHICH JOB?" prompt instead of the "COMMAND?" prompt. The reason for this is because most of the time the applications are all automated and accessed from menus that are run by batch files, which execute when you log in.

Thus, the system is very friendly. You may see a menu that asks you if you want to view a transcript, view a schedule, admit a student, dismiss a student, transfer a student, add classes, delete classes, etc. You simply choose what you want to do. Via these menus you will be able to do anything that the school administrators can do, including changing grades. Sometimes, however, there are no menus, and you will have to execute commands yourself. A list of these commands can be gotten using one of the HELP menus. Here are some of the jobs you can execute: ABSCOR, ABSINFO, ABSREP, ACADROP, ACAINFO, ACAMSTR, ADDSECT, ADDROP, ADRPLST, BATINFO, ABSINQ, CLASSLST, CODELIST, CUTINFO, CUTDEL, FIXCODES, FIXOFCL, HITRAN, GRDUPDT, LATCOR, LATINQ, MAIL, NGRUPDT, OFCLLIST, PUNRQST, REGISTER, REQADRP, REQINFO, REQUPDTE, SCAN, SCHEDULE, SKED, TRAN, TRANUPDT.

You can drop straight into Wylbur by sending a <BREAK>. This will cause your menu shell program to stop executing. If you happen to leave the menu system and do drop into Wylbur (with its "COMMAND?" prompt) you can get back to the menu system by typing RUN. This will execute the menu shell program that is currently in your active area.

Remember that each time you or your menu program submits a job (i.e., to change a grade), the job will be executed and the output will be placed on the fetch queue. If you don't want to leave a trail, then you must use one of the above Wylbur commands to find and PURGE the output of your completed jobs. If you do not PURGE the output, it has a good chance of being printed out at the program office when they print the output of all the jobs that they submitted.

Changing Grades

Clearly, this thought has crossed your mind in the past few minutes, so let me begin by saying that I do not recommend changing any records on UAPC. You can use UAPC to get all kinds of useful information on people and never get in trouble.

If you do hope to change grades and get away with it, there are several things to consider. You must remember that your guidance counselor has physical backups of all your grades in his/her little notebook. If you've gone to your counselor for advice on which classes to take, you'll recognize the book of which I speak. The grades in this book are not generated by UAPC but instead entered into the books at the end of each grading period by the counselors using a pen or pencil. This physical record is only used as backup in case UAPC gets wiped out or something like that. Comparisons between UAPC transcripts and the physical record are almost never done, unless there is some kind of disagreement between the student and the school regarding the transcript itself. If you do plan to make a clean run, you had better cover all the angles. This means bribing some stupid kid to borrow the book for a little while so that you can make some modifications, give the dude $20, and make sure he doesn't know who you are.

Guinea Pigs

Before modifying either your physical record or your UAPC grades, I would strongly suggest using a guinea pig test subject. What this means is that you should pick some kid, any kid, who goes to your school and that you have never met and never plan to meet, change their grades, purge the output on the fetch queue, sit tight for a few days, and watch what happens. Keep a close eye on your test subject. If you notice the kid getting suspended or federal agents running around your school or something like that, you know that you better not mess with UAPC, at least not in your school anyway. If nothing happens, then you should decide whether to take the risk of changing your own grades.

If you consider the use of innocent human guinea pigs to be distasteful, then you had better be prepared to risk your ass by using yourself instead. I do not consider it to be distasteful, but then again I am devoid of all ethics and morals anyway.

You can still bail out at this point and your life will proceed normally. However, if you do change your grades (both physically and on UAPC) and nothing happens to you for several weeks, you can be almost 100 percent sure that you got away with it. Since both records (physical and UAPC) have been changed, there can be no discrepancies. Only your previous teachers will know what grades they gave you, and by now they will have forgotten who you are. Only your transcript speaks for them now. If you do get away with it, you can start mailing out those applications for Stanford and MIT.

MILESTONE: OUR WISHES FOR '86 AND BEYOND (December, 1985)

Around this time of year, we always get to thinking about how the things around us can improve. So we assembled a few of our writers and had them come up with some suggestions on how technology can better serve everyone. We hope that these ideas will someday be followed and we encourage our readers to come up with additional ones, which we'll gladly print.

Uniform Long Distance Rates

With the many advances in modern communications, one end result is quite obvious. It's gotten easier and cheaper to establish contact in all parts of the country, and in most parts of the world. We want to see an end to rip-off long distance rates that charge you more to call one place when it really costs the company about the same to reach anywhere. Why not have uniform rates to *everywhere*, whether it be long distance or local? Technology is making the entire world fit into our backyard—how about granting us some access to it? Many of us phone phreaks have come to look at phone calls in a different way.

continues

MILESTONE: OUR WISHES FOR '86 AND BEYOND *(continued)*

When you can call *anywhere* you want to, for as long as you want, without worrying about how much it's going to cost you, it all starts to take on new meaning. You begin to realize how offensive it is to be charged for something as basic as talking! Shouldn't we all be able to talk to whoever we want, whenever we want, and for as long as we want? If it were possible (as it someday will be) to have an unlimited amount of people using telephone equipment at the same time without tying it up, wouldn't we be better off with this philosophy? We believe so. The telecommunications giants can still profit handsomely without making communications a luxury.

We're not simply after a free ride; we'd still pay something, though not as much and not as often. We want to see advances in technology shared by all and then perhaps we'll see some of its real potential. Right now, there are many of us that can't afford to call the White House when we want to voice our opinion on something. The ones that can afford it have no problem. And that's the problem here.

The time for change has arrived. After all, how can we call it long distance if it no longer is?

Some Reasonable Prices on "Public" Services

Compuserve, Source, Dow Jones, are you listening? Is it any wonder you're constantly being ripped off with the outrageous prices you charge? A session on one of these services can be a nightmare, as every second costs you, every mistake is money out the window. Come on already; times have changed. Enough with the surcharges and access fees—provide affordable services for people or go join the dinosaurs.

Access to What Is Being Said About Us

One of the most frustrating things is to have to pay to see what TRW is telling people about you. Any wonder why people break in? Shouldn't it be just as easy for us to see our credit record as it is for some schmuck at Sears?

While we're on the subject, how far are we going to let these people go with our credit history? Is it fair to be denied credit because you paid a bill late four years ago? Or because you were tried for a crime and the charges were dropped? Is it fair for companies to analyze your buying tendencies and theorize as to what type of person you are, and to use *that* as a deciding factor?

We feel it's only fair that we be shown, perhaps on an annual basis, what is being said about us and given the opportunity to correct any errors, or at least to question or explain them. We shouldn't have to pay a penny for this "privilege."

MILESTONE: OUR WISHES FOR '86 AND BEYOND *(continued)*

An End to Information Charges

Again we're at a loss to explain why the phone companies charge for something that encourages using their service. If we have to pay sixty cents to find out what someone's phone number is in another state, and *then* pay for a phone call as well, we're sure as hell going to think twice about making the call in the first place! While it's true that some people would use an alternate service to make the call, the losses to AT&T can't be that stupendous. We feel that this is an unjustifiable charge, one that hurts everyone in the end.

Our suggestions include: providing one call to information (at least) for every long-distance call dialed; providing free phone books (originally, charges for information were to encourage people to use the phone books instead); alternate information services for alternate carriers, i.e. a subscriber to Skyline would have the advantage of free access to Skyline information; or an online database where you can find out as many numbers or cross-references as you like via modem. We'd like to hear more suggestions and we hope they get to the right people.

Nationwide Access for All

If there are databases that are so big and extensive that anyone can check our credit history from anywhere in the country, what is stopping us from using our bank card in New York to withdraw money while we are in Los Angeles? When will these systems be integrated so we can all benefit from technology? There is already statewide connection of auto teller banking, and some limited interstate use, but when will a national network be set up?

Hacking PC Pursuit (April, 1987) *By Cheshire Catalyst*

PC Pursuit (PCP) is a service provided by Telenet (a division of U.S. Sprint) for $25 a month for use after business hours weekdays, and all day on weekends. You can use it during the business day for rates that will beat out long-distance voice, but not by much. Some interesting hacks have presented themselves in abusing, that is using, this service.

At the Telenet "@" prompt, a user types "CDIALXXX/12,USERNAME" where XXX is the area code of the modem near your destination, and 12 is the speed (1200 Bits Per Second (BPS)) you want to use at the destination modem. PCP provides you with a Username when you sign up for the service. We'll come back to the data rate later.

After you enter that command line, PCP then asks for a password. You are provided with a password by PCP, and cannot change it. You can have *them* change it, and send you the new password in the mail. After you type in your password, you are either connected to a "Hayes-compatible" modem in the distant city, or you are given the message "XXX BUSY," where XXX is once again the destination area code. As more people try to use the limited number of modems PCP has in what it thinks are major hotbeds of BBS action (Seattle?), more and more "busy signals" are encountered on the Net.

When placing your call to the remote modem, the number after the slash tells Telenet what speed to set up the connection at. Besides "12," "3" is also valid (for 300 BPS). However, "12" is valid even if you are calling into Telenet at 300 BPS, such as from a Tandy Model-100 (don't laugh; I'm preparing this article on a Model-100). Telenet is known as a "value added" network, and this is where it provides its "value added" services. The modem at the other end doesn't know if you are at 300, or 110, or even a synchronous mainframe with Ebenezer Scrooge for a system manager (watch for more "stingy manager" types to take advantage of these low rates).

It must be said, however, that if you download huge ASCII files via a 1200/300 connection, you may overload the network buffer with your transfer. If that happens, you will get an error message of "BUFFER OVERLOAD - SOME DATA HAS BEEN LOST." The thing to do is to send a Ctrl+S once in a while. The stuff will keep coming at you for a while, because of the speed differential, and when the network buffer finally empties, the transmission will stop. Naturally, a Ctrl+Q will start you up again, if your host hasn't logged you off for inactivity in the meantime. Protocol transfers only transfer 128 or so bytes at a time, and will be slow, but will not overflow buffers.

PCP says that the first thing you should do when you hit the modem is type "ATZ" to reset the modem. On the contrary. The first thing to do when Telenet reports "CONNECTED" is to type "A/," the Hayes command to "Repeat last command received." Most people will let their host hang up the connection, and then just hang up on PCP. In such a case, the last command given the modem was an "ATDT" command to place the call. The PCP modems are funny, though. If they have received an "ATZ," and therefore have no command in the command buffer, they will not echo a "/" character. This tells you to immediately go about your own business. When you've finished perusing the computer your PCP predecessor left in the modem, dial up your own machine.

When you're through with your computer, either it will hang up on you, or you must tell the modem to hang up on it. If you have to hang up, type "+++."You have just sent the "Hayes wake-up" command to two modems. Yours (assuming you have a Hayes compatible yourself), and the remote PCP modem in the distant city. Type "ATS2=65" followed by a return. You've just told your modem that it should only wake up when you type "AAA" (three capital A's) instead of "+++." Now type "ATO" to get back on line with PCP.

When we last left our remote modem, it was waiting for your command after receiving "+++" from you. Type "ATH" to hang it up. If you have other machines to dial in the remote city you've dialed, keep dialing (send the next "ATDT" command). If you've called area code 212 and want to reach a Brooklyn BBS, type "ATDT17185393560," since the 718 area code is within the New York City LATA (Local Access and Transport Area). The same for calling Burbank (818) out of the LA area code, 213.

One friend of mine recently had the mistaken impression that PCP no longer went to the 415 area code. Sure, it's busy a lot, but that area's a busy hotbed of activity. To check out his claim, we got up on PCP and got busy message after busy message—at 415/12. We decided to try 415/3 for a 300 BPS modem, and sure enough, we got one. It was slow as expletive, but we got there. Then our BBS in Berkeley was busy, and we were back to square one.

After you've had your fun, *remember!* Now is the time to hit "ATZ," before you hang up on the remote modem. When you're through with all the calls you want to make in the city you've reached, you should type the "ATZ" to your remote modem, and get back to Telenet to set you up with a call to a modem in another city. The best way is to type "@" followed by a carriage return. This will wake up Telenet, and give you an "@" prompt. Type "D" for Disconnect, and it will drop your connection to the modem in the city you had called. At the next "@" prompt, type "C DIALYYY/12,USERNAME" (YYY being the new area code), and begin the whole process again.

Are you in an area with multiple calling rates (such as New York City), with toll rates within the LATA? "Some people" are known to use PCP within their own area code (my modest nature and my constitutional rights preclude me saying any more). A caller in Manhattan can get his or her 25 bucks back quickly just by using PCP to call up BBS's on Long Island. Westchester also has some neat boards in 914 that are easy to hit this way.

So there you have it. Remember to "ATZ" the modem before you leave it. While the next caller can't find out what number is in the buffer, they can certainly get at least one call into whatever you've just hung up on. I've even wound up on Teleconnect Magazine's BBS on an "A/," much to everyone's surprise.

Some of you may recall back in the early days, PC Pursuit had a rather unique system. You dialed a special number and entered all of your personal information—ID code, password, and number you wanted to reach. PC Pursuit would then hang up and call you back at a predetermined number.

That system was limiting because you couldn't use it from more than one location. Some hackers claim to have gotten into their outgoing lines as they were dialing out and gained access in that way.

The way the system is set up now is almost acceptable. PC Pursuit must set up many more modems in many more cities before we sign up again.

It's also possible the way they have it working to tie up the entire system single-handedly. For example, from the Telenet number in New York, we could call the Telenet number in Seattle, enter our ID over there, call the Telenet number in Dallas, and set up a huge nationwide circle.

We saw this done once and the delay between the time a character was typed and the time it showed up on the screen was nearly 30 seconds! Needless to say, there were many busy signals that day.

FAX: A New Hobby (May, 1987) *By Bernie S.*

Occasionally when scanning phone numbers you'll come across what sounds like a computer modem carrier but isn't. What it often turns out to be is a facsimile (FAX) machine. For those unaware of it, a FAX machine lets you send printed info (text, diagrams, or photos) over a phone line or radio link. Like computer modems, they use a carrier tone, but it is a different frequency and unlike "normal" data communications.

A FAX machine scans a printed document using an optical sensor that sweeps over the print detecting light and dark sections of the paper. There are presently three common FAX standards in use: Group I, II, and III. Until fairly recently, most FAX transmissions were of the Group I variety. Group I machines (many of which are still in use) use a rotating drum that the document is clamped to while the sensor traverses the length of the drum slowly. The light and dark sections modulate the carrier tone frequency which is transmitted over the phone line to another FAX machine. At the other end, it works in reverse—the modulated tone is translated back into an image by a hi-voltage stylus, which scans over a blank sheet of electrostaticly-sensitive paper, "burning" the image onto the sheet. (This makes a rank smell; real old machines would fill a room with smoke!) Group I transmissions typically take 6 minutes for an 8½ by 11 inch sheet.

With the advent of cheap digital IC's, Group II and III standards emerged which transmit signals digitally (not unlike computer modems). The fastest group III machines can send a document in less than a minute at 9600 baud, the limit for unconditioned dialup phone lines. A Group IV standard now exists which is much faster but requires Bell DDS or similar dedicated digital lines. The mechanical drum is now obsolete—a sheet is simply "dropped in" a newer FAX machine in which a tight row of phototransistors scans the whole document as it's pulled in between small motor-driven rollers. For output, ink-jet or similar printing technology prints out the received document.

For experimenters with little (or no) money, a lot of companies are getting rid of their older Group I and II machines for cheap—I got an Exxon Quip 1200 Group I FAX from a local newspaper for $50, and they threw in about ten reams of the special paper. This model was very popular about six years ago, and sold for about $1000.

Look around! Most Group II and III machines can be switched into Group I mode for compatibility. Some newer machines double as copiers, though you can cheat and use a tape recorder to "play" a document back into a machine to get a copy in a pinch. Eventually, a FAX machine/laser printer/copier will be invented and will be a standard office machine everywhere. Expensive PC add-on cards exist that convert a PC and printer into a fax that'll store images on disk, but they're almost as expensive as a new FAX machine!

Now we can all send schematics, drawings, and photos over the phone for cheap—just like the big boys do. I may be the first to coin a new term: PHAXing! As an added bonus, if you have a shortwave receiver with a BFO, you can pick up FAX images relayed from weather satellites, wire and press service photos, etc. before everybody else sees them. Some minor modifications are needed to convert the speed since they use nonstandard scan rates, but it's worth the effort.

I hope you're all tuned on to this "new" hobby. Let's see some enthusiasm and support for FAX!

The Beginnings of the Internet

Today we take it all for granted. But in the mid '80s, nobody really knew how, or even if, all of these networks would come together. Just look at the complex and seemingly insane method of addressing an e-mail in the articles explaining the potential. I doubt very many of us would have the talent or patience to do that today. Mail delivery on the networks used to take days and often didn't go through at all. But for me the most interesting revelation here is the definition of abuse of the network: "chain letters, mass mailings, *commercial use of the network....*" On that level at least, it was all so much simpler then.

ARPANET Hopping: America's Newest Pastime (June, 1984)

What is ARPANET?

ARPANET (Advanced Research Projects Agency Network) has been around since the 1960s. Its intentions were to link many computers together in order to share resources. The various research projects on ARPANET involve both major universities and the United States military (the two are closer than either would care to admit).

Up until last year, ARPANET was one big happy family of military and university computers. Then, in view of *War Games*, etc., it was decided that perhaps the military would be better off on their own separate network. And so, MILNET was established.

This proved to be very convenient for hackers, since they now *knew* where all of the military computers were—all it took was access to MILNET in order to play with them.

Since ARPANET can communicate with MILNET and vice versa, all kinds of interesting possibilities exist. Elaborate routing makes it easy for a hacker to cover his trail, in much the same way that a phreak routes calls through three different long distance companies to protect his/her identity.

Where can dialups to ARPANET be found? All over the place. For one thing, many numbers are in circulation among hackers. For another, they're not considered all that much of a secret, since the numbers by themselves don't allow you to log on.

If you know of a major university computer, there's a chance that it's already hooked into the ARPANET. If this is the case, HELP files will be readily available on that system to explain how to access the network.

The network itself is an entire world waiting to be explored. Ironically, many sensitive computers that are "not accessible by phone lines" *are* accessible by ARPANET! There are a lot of lessons that still must be learned, it seems.

So Simple a Child Could Do It

Moving around ARPANET is very easy as almost any hacker that has used it will attest to. It was designed upon the principle that people on one system should have easy access to other systems. "Easy" is the key word here. If a direct ARPANET dialup is being used, there shouldn't be any problem. If a MILNET dialup is being used, you will need a TACID, which is a private authorization code.

The word ARPANET is used to denote all networks. There are many networks (see *2600*, May 1984), but all can be accessed as one through "gateways," which are basically windows into other networks.

How It Works

There are two basic commands that can be used on the ARPANET: "@o" and "@c." "@o" *opens* a connection with a host. (For example, @o 26.0.0.1 will connect you with a host hooked to ARPANET—indicated by the 26.) Finding addresses is really the only hard part. At one time, a few systems had a HOST command that would give you a complete listing of hosts, and their addresses. In fact, this command is still on many systems but what was unique here was the fact that you could run the program *without logging in!!* Apparently, they got wise to hackers, and fixed HOST so that it only works from logged in accounts.

After typing "@o," the network will respond with "Open" or, if the attempt was less than successful, a self-explanatory error message such as "Bad" or "Destination host dead." When you get the "Open" message, that means you are now connected to the host computer and you can do whatever you want, like log in, read help files, etc. Communication with the network is not cut off, however. The network is always there, waiting to be spoken to. Commands to the network must begin with "@." For example, type "@c" when you want to close the connection with whatever computer you hooked into. This will probably take a moment or two, since the network has to close up a few things before it can transfer control back to you. (Incidentally, if you need to send a command to the remote host that contains "@" in it simply type an extra "@" next to the first one and ARPANET will ignore it.)

Some Safety Tips and Interesting Programs

If you can dial up to a host that is connected to ARPANET, and you have an account on it, this is ideal. There is a good chance that the host will support a terminal simulation program, that when supplied the hostname that you wish to communicate with, will connect you to it through ARPANET. It will then seem as if you're on a terminal connected to that remote host. To close the connection, you will have to read the documentation on the host that you dialed up to, since it changes from system to system. Naturally, using a local dialup to access a host instead of going through a MILNET or ARPANET dialup is much "safer," since you are not accessing ARPANET directly.

Another feature of ARPANET is the FINGER command available on most TOPS-20 systems, and many other types as well. The FINGER command will provide you with a listing of people currently logged into the system, with some information on them, such as their full name, where their terminal is located, and what their account is known as. You will also show up on a FINGER, and it will show whether you're on a remote host or not. FINGER followed by a valid account on that system will give you some *very* detailed info on that person. One other very nice feature of FINGER is that you can supply a remote hostname, and get a listing of people on another host, *without connecting to it!!* (For instance, FINGER @SRI-NIC will give you a listing of people logged onto the Network Info Center.) Another program that gives details on users (though not all that much) is SYSTAT. Both can, in many cases, be run *without logging in*, and many HELP files are also accessible without logging in. Certain HELP files give information on login formats or list dialup numbers.

If you have an account on a system, the chances are quite good that that system will support FTP, which is short for File Transfer Protocol. This allows you to take files from one system, and copy them to the system that you're on. The one problem here is that you will need a valid account to use on the system you wish to take the files from. Most (if not all) TOPS-20 systems support file transfers, and consequently have an account set aside for that purpose. The account is called "ANONYMOUS" and it works with any password. Some other hosts use the account "ANONYMOUS" as well, but they are by no means consistent. The way file transfers work is through an FTP on the system that you're presently on. This program communicates through ARPANET with the host you want to take files from. On the remote host, there will be a program running that will take requests from other hosts, and transmit files through the network to them. You can do more than take files, though. You can transmit files from the host you are on to the remote host, or delete or rename files on the remote host, or get a directory of an account on the remote host. It's very handy to get a file from SRI-NIC, which contains all network base addresses, addresses of gateways (ways of getting from one network to another), and addresses of all hosts on all networks.

And, of course, there's the ARPANET mail system, which allows you to communicate with *any* ARPANET user. It works in a similar fashion to FTP and FINGER as far as roaming the network to find a matching username or host ID. It is still said that there is a very active hacker community living in ARPANET mailboxes and it hardly seems surprising when considering how fast and efficiently this mail system works.

The Future

Since ARPANET was designed to be, and is still being, used by people who are not very familiar with computers, it will always be easy to use ARPANET, and "hop" about it. It's very unlikely that they will change it in any way, since it is, for the most part, pretty good at keeping hackers away from things that they're not supposed to be looking at.

Maybe...

Mastering the Networks (November, 1986) *By John Anderson*

The desire to allow computers to talk to each other has given way to a multitude of networks each having their own protocol and characteristics. These diverse networks are all gatewayed to each other such that a user on any one of these networks can communicate with a user on another network. In a sense the networks themselves are networked together. In this article, we will attempt to untangle the wires connecting these networks and examine the ARPANET, BITNET, CSnet, Mailnet, UUCP network, and their gateways.

The ARPANET is perhaps the most well known of all the networks. The ARPANET is funded by the Advance Research Projects Association (Department of Defense) and exists to allow the various research institutions to share both resources and information. All types of machines running every imaginable operating system are on this network. Having an account on a machine which is an ARPANET node is the most desirable position to be in from a networking standpoint. This situation is advantageous because the ARPANET has gateways to all of the networks we will discuss. Because of this and some properties we will discuss later, the ARPAnet has also been termed the InterNet. Physically, ARPANET nodes are connected by dedicated data lines and use the TCP/IP protocol for communications. The TCP/IP protocol is one of the most popular and versatile networking protocols currently available. TCP/IP was made popular by the ARPANET and evolved on it. A node on the ARPANET can remotely login to, send mail to, and transfer files with any other node on the network directly. This is the only network which allows a user to remotely login to all of the nodes on the network. The hacking possibilities for a user on this network are almost unlimited.

The Network Information Center computer that is available to ARPANET users is the ultimate network resource. It provides abundant information about the ARPANET and the various gateway sites. A user on the ARPANET can contact NIC by using the command TELNET to open a connection with SRI-NIC.ARPA.

The BITNET is similar to the ARPANET in that it also uses dedicated lines for communications. The similarities end there because instead of the TCP/IP protocol the BITNET uses the RSCS (Remote Source Control System) protocol. This network was originally composed of IBM mainframes and minicomputers due to its use of the RSCS protocol which is exclusively IBM's. Recently RSCS emulators have become available for machines running VMS and UNIX. Several non-IBM machines have joined the BITNET using these emulators and many shall follow. It is doubtful, however, that the BITNET will ever support all of the features that the ARPANET boasts since the RSCS protocol is very restrictive. The BITNET only supports electronic mail and file transfer between its nodes. It is *not* possible for one node to remotely login to another.

The CSnet or PhoneNet is a network of university computer science departments and other research institutions. The CSnet is radically different from the networks mentioned above in that every node on the network is only connected to the relay node (CSNET-RELAY). The connection to this central node is not via a dedicated line but via dialup phone lines. Periodically (usually once a day) the CSNET-RELAY will call each node on the network to see if there are any messages to be transferred. This type of network architecture gave the CSnet its second name, PhoneNet. The CSnet only supports electronic mail and is not likely to ever support any other network functions if it does not change its method of networking. The CSnet is run by Bolt Beranek and Newman Inc.

A network similar to the CSnet is the Mailnet. Apparently this network only supports the transfer of mail. At this time the type of network structure and machines using this network are unknown to the author. However, it would not be unreasonable to assume that this network uses a structure similar to the CSnet's. Please address any additional information about Mailnet to this magazine.

Perhaps the largest and most loosely structured network is the UUCP network. This network has nodes in Canada, Japan, Europe, Australia, and many other countries. The UUCP network is composed exclusively of machines running the UNIX operating system. The network uses dialup phone lines for the transmission of data and uses the UUCP protocol. UUCP (Unix to Unix Copy Program) is found on every system running UNIX and systems need only establish a connection with one system on the network to become a fully functioning node. The transfer of mail to any node on the network is supported. Remote logins and file transfers are only supported with your direct neighbors.

With so many different networks, a need for inter-network communications arose. Gateways are the bridges that link these networks together. Gateway sites are sites which reside on two or more networks. These gateways allow for the transfer of mail messages from one network to another. They do *not* allow remote login or file transfer. Almost every gateway site is a node on the ARPANET/InterNet. Therefore if a user can send a message from his/her network to the ARPANET, it is possible to communicate with any other network which has a gateway site on the ARPANET. Below is a list of gateways to and from the ARPANET and the mailer syntax required:

Gateways to the ARPANET		
From	ARPANET gateway site	Mailer Syntax
BITNET	WISCVM.BITNET	user%node.ARPA@wiscvm.BITNET
CSnet	CSNET-RELAY.CSNET	user%node.ARPA@csnet-relay.CSNET
MailNet	HARVARD.MAILNET	user%node.ARPA@harvard.MAILNET
UUCP	SEISMO.UUCP	seismo!user%node.ARPA
Gateways from the ARPANET		
To	ARPANET gateway site	Mailer Syntax
BITNET	WISCVM.ARPA	user%node.BITNET@wiscvm.ARPA
CSnet	CSNET-RELAY.ARPA	user%node.CSNET@csnet-relay.ARPA
MailNet	HARVARD.ARPA	user%node.MAILNET@harvard.ARPA
UUCP	SEISMO.ARPA	node!user.UUCP@seismo.ARPA

Example #1: A user on the BITNET wishes to send a message to a user on the CSnet.

```
user%node.CSNET%csnet-relay.ARPA@wiscvm.BITNET
```

(The @ is known as the separator and specifies the username at the node. An address can only have one @ in it. As the message gets closer to its destination, the @ and everything to the right of it will be chopped off. The % that is furthest to the right will then become an @. The % indicates additional directions.)

Example #2: A user on the UUCP network wishes to send mail to a MailNet user.

```
seismo!user%node.MAILNET%harvard.ARPA
```

(The UUCP network syntax is reversed. The ! appears on the left. In this example, Seismo is the machine or gateway the user must go through. There can be more than one! in a line. As the message progresses, the ! furthest to the left and everything to the left of it is chopped off. When the last! is chopped off, the % on the right becomes an @. UUCP is not auto-routing, while the other networks are. This makes the ! feature necessary.)

By following the above examples, a user with a little knowledge of the network he/she resides on can communicate with any node on any network. It is quite possible that a user in Europe and a user in Australia could communicate with each other on a regular basis with a message delivery time of only two days. The uses for the above mail networks are limited only by one's imagination. These networks could be used to unite hackers all over the world at an almost negligible cost.

Worldnet: Getting Closer Every Day (September, 1987)

By Hank@Taunivm.Bitnet

First off, let me say that I am on the other side of the fence. My job is to make sure the system I work for is secure and that there are no hackers or crackers trying to do damage to the system I am employed to defend. In one instance, I assisted the police in collecting all the necessary information to create a court case against a cracker. The kid in question (a high school student) ended up getting a year of civil work. I subscribe to this magazine not to learn how to do something illegal but rather to learn what others are trying to do to me. Knowledge is a tool and by hiding a tool you gain nothing. Therefore, I have decided to explain how international computer networks work, how they are tied together and what services you can hope to receive from them.

There are dozens of computer networks—all of them spawning off the grandfather of all networks: ARPANET. Today, it has grown so large that it is known as The Internet. As more and more networks begin to interconnect, the concept of a Worldnet becomes feasible.

Basic Concepts

All users are known by three variables: userid, nodename, and network. A userid can be the person's initials, or the person's last name, or anything else the person decided upon when he opened his computer account. A nodename is also known as a hostname. It designates the computer the user is using. The network indicates which of the two dozen or so networks the computer is connected to. If you look at my name at the top of this article, you will see that my userid is Hank, my nodename is Taunivm (that is in Israel, in case you were wondering), and my network is called Bitnet. The nodename and network section of a user's "handle" has been undergoing a transformation in the past few years and this will be explained later.

The one common protocol that all networks talk is something called RFC822 standard mail. Within individual networks there are other protocols which will be covered where necessary.

ARPANET

This network is based on a protocol called TCP/IP. (I know there are people out there reading this and saying, "What does TCP/IP stand for?" But I do not think it is important to know what the letters stand for. When it is important, I will explain it.) It allows for three major applications: FTP, SMTP, and Telnet. FTP stands for File Transfer Protocol and allows a user on one machine to extract a file from any other machine on the network (assuming you know the read password) or allows a user to write a file onto any other machine assuming you know the write password for the destination user and machine. SMTP stands for Simple Mail Transfer Protocol and allows users to send electronic mail almost anywhere in the world. Telnet is a remote-login application. It is not Telenet. But it does basically the same thing. You specify the machine you want to log in to, and Telnet makes the connection from your machine to the one you specified.

Most links within ARPANET are 56KB leased lines although there are cases where it may be higher or lower. There are other networks that are modeled after ARPANET: CSnet (Computer Science network), Nsfnet (National Science Foundation Network—which interconnects all supercomputers in the United States), and a few smaller ones. CSnet, up until recently, used primarily X.25 connections via Telenet to establish a connection. They are now switching more and more links over to leased telephone lines. Nsfnet uses primarily T1 lines, which run at 1MB per second. In case you were wondering, ARPANET stands for Advanced Research Projects Agency and is owned by the U.S. government. All of these networks use the TCP/IP protocol and are therefore part of an ever-growing Internet.

Bitnet

This network spans 27 countries (U.S.A., Canada, West Germany, France, Italy, the Netherlands, Finland, Denmark, Spain, Turkey, Israel, Japan, Mexico, Taiwan, to name a few) and has more than 1,800 computers interconnected. It uses a protocol different than ARPANET but the one common language they talk is electronic mail (RFC822). The European segment of the network is called EARN (European Academic Research Network) and the Canadian section is called NetNorth. All links within Bitnet/EARN/-NetNorth are 9600 baud leased lines. Bitnet stands for Because It's There or Because It's Time. It all depends on who you ask. Bitnet is not the largest network by computer hosts, but is the largest by number of connected countries. If you are an academic institution or a research lab, all you need to do is pay a membership fee per year to Bitnet, Inc. (varies between $1,000 and $10,000) and order a leased line from Telco to your nearest neighbor that has a connection to Bitnet.

UUCP

Unix to Unix Copy Program Network is a freewheeling, anarchy-type network. It is unknown how many computers are connected to this network but estimates vary from 4,000 to 10,000. Lately, some organizers are trying to put some order into UUCP. It is a slow and grueling process but one that I hope they will succeed at. It has the worst reputation for mail delivery, where delays can be sometimes a week and it is not infrequent that the system loses the mail.

Others

Here is a brief list of some of the other networks that share RFC822 mail: MFENET: Magnetic Fusion Energy Network; SPAN: Space Physics Analysis Network; JANET: England's National Academic Network; VNET: IBM's corporate internal network; Easynet: DEC's corporate internal network; EUnet: European section of UUCP.

There are many other smaller networks that are starting to get off the ground, but as you will see later on, the world of networking is moving away from the concept of an "xxxxNet" to one that imposes a hierarchical structure on all networks.

When you add up all the networks and all the machines that can exchange RFC822 mail, the number of machines (from a VAX 730 up to a Cray X/MP) approaches 20,000. Some of the larger systems have 50,000 registered users on their systems while more typically it is around 2,000 users. That means that as a rough estimate, there are about 40 million users that are accessible via RFC822 mail. This grows even larger when you consider that there are experimental gateways that allow networks like Dialcom and MCI Mail to pass RFC822 mail into the Internet and vice versa (no, I will not tell you where they are or how to use them). Most of the users are students, professors, academics, researchers, and school administration personnel. The number of corporate users, like IBM's 200,000 Vnet users, only makes up about 10 percent of the network. What makes this Worldnet system so attractive is that for a large part it is free to use. The university or the company pays Telco for a leased line and connects to the network of their choice. The users of the newly connected computer are then given free access to the network (certain universities impose access restrictions on their users). European sites will soon be undergoing a severe hardship. Their PTTs will require volume charging, so each site will have to restrict usage by their users. At present charging by European PTTs is still on a leased line monthly cost.

Since it is a free system, abuse is closely monitored. For example, it is considered bad manners to start a chain letter in the network, since it can quickly grow to saturate the network. Users are caught and in general they understand that disrupting the network will only cause their "free" and genuine mail to be delayed also.

Addresses

Now for a brief tutorial on how to read network addresses. All RFC822 mail addresses are composed of a LHS and a RHS (Left Hand Side and Right Hand Side). You look at the address and scan for an @-sign. This is the separator between the LHS and the RHS. The LHS is considered the local part of the address. Examples:

Hank
John Smith
steve%hbo.HAIRNET
philco!sun!munarri!john

These are all samples of LHS addresses. The first two are simple userids. The third one is a gateway. It says that there is an indirect network called HAIRNET that has a machine on it called hbo and you wish to contact the user named steve. The %-sign is used as a kludge to indicate indirect addressing via a gateway that is not directly addressable from all over the Worldnet. The last example is one of UUCP addressing. It reads from left to right. With standard RFC822 addresses, you do not need to know the path the mail will take to get to its final destination. The system takes care of that. UUCP is dumb in that respect. You need to know the path the mail will take. So example 4 says to send it to a machine called philco, which will send it to a machine called sun, which in turn will send it to a machine called munarri, which has a user called john. You can see why people hate UUCP addressing. This type of "bang" addressing is slowly being phased out for the new style of addressing detailed below. But there are still many UUCP sites that prefer their "old" ways. Then again, there are still a lot of people who like Cobol.

Here are some examples of a RHS address:

taunivm.bitnet
wiscvm.wisc.edu
relay.cs.net
decwrl.dec.com
vax.camb.ac.uk
vm1.tau.ac.il

The first is an example of the old style of addresses—taunivm.bitnet. It is a node-name and a network identifier. The next three are examples of ARPANET addresses. They read from right to left and are tree based. The right-most token represents the higher authority, such as EDU (educational), .NET (network information center), or .COM (commercial). It no longer makes a difference if wiscvm.wisc.edu resides in ARPANET or Bitnet or CSnet. It may indeed be directly connected to all three. The user shouldn't care what network the end user is connected to. Imagine if your friend was connected to Sprint while you used ATT. It shouldn't make a difference in your dialing to know that the end destination is being serviced by Sprint. Just dial the number. That is the concept of "dotted domain names."

As soon as you leave the United States, things get even more organized. Every country has an ISO (International Standards Organization) country code. Within each country, an authority decides what second level domain names to assign—such as .AC (academic), .RD (research and development), .COM (commercial), etc. As you move from the right to left of the RHS address, you move from the macro to the micro. Once again, it is important to note that the concept of what network the user resides on becomes a "thing of the past."

Putting it all together, we end up with addresses that might look like these:

Hank@vm1.tau.ac.il
John Smith@decwrl.dec.com
steve%hbo.HAIRNET@relay.cs.net

In conclusion, the Worldnet supplies electronic mail traffic for free to users with an account on any machine that is connected to one of the networks listed above. The institution ends up picking up the bill for the leased line, while the user only gets charged for the local CPU time and connect time used to create and send the letter. Abuse (chain letters, mass mailings, commercial use of the network, etc.) is frowned upon by the ones who run the networks as well as the hackers who make use of them. If you use the network, don't abuse it.

For further reading: Communications of the ACM, October 1986, Notable Computer Networks, Quartermain and Hoskins.

Morris Found Guilty (Winter, 1989–1990)

Robert T. Morris Jr., the 25-year-old Cornell student responsible for the Internet Worm, was found guilty on January 22 of federal computer tampering charges in Syracuse, NY. He now faces five years in prison and a $250,000 fine. He was the first person to be prosecuted under a portion of the 1986 Computer Fraud and Abuse Act. A hearing is set for February 27 in Albany, NY. Sentencing will probably be scheduled then.

The government argued that Morris intentionally wrote the worm program to break into "federal interest" computers he was not authorized to use, and by doing this prevented their authorized use and caused a minimum of $1,000 in damage.

Several jurors said it was obvious Morris didn't intend to do damage. But they say the damage would never have happened if Morris hadn't put the worm there. None of the jurors owned a home computer.

One juror said of Morris, "I believe his integrity. I did not believe there was any malice intended."

Another said Morris was "not a criminal. I don't think he should go to jail. I don't think jail would do anything for him. To me jail is for criminals, and he's not a criminal. I think somebody should thank him in the end."

In its November 26, 1988 edition shortly after the Internet Worm made its appearance, *The New York Times* described Morris as "fascinated with powerful computers and obsessed with the universe created by interconnected networks of machines."

Last year Senator Patrick Leahy of Vermont said, "We cannot unduly inhibit that inquisitive 13-year-old, who, if left to experiment today, may, tomorrow, develop the telecommunications or computer technology to lead the United States into the 21st century." He also expressed doubts that a computer virus law of any kind would be effective.

There is no doubt that Robert Morris Jr. has a lot of potential. There seems to be no doubt that he's an honest person. Even the prosecution seems to believe this. We all know that he was the person responsible for the Internet Worm. So, with all of this in mind, it seems as if the last few weeks have been a tremendous waste of time for everyone.

Yes, he did it. He admitted doing it. He didn't mean to cause damage, but he made a programming error. The shocking fact is that one programming error could cause so much confusion. Add to that the fact that the holes he made use of were common knowledge to the Internet community. Yet, nothing was done to close the holes until after all of this happened. It seems like someone should answer for this neglect of responsibilities. And let's not forget one other important fact. Morris never logged into another computer system without authorization. There is no proof that he ever planned to. He simply sent out a program to collect data—through normal and legal channels. It was data he never should have had access to, but thanks to the holes in the system, he did.

Morris made a mistake. That's all a part of the learning game, which he's now been banished from. This technology is still in its infancy and, like any system, its limits need to be constantly tested. We're making a very grave error if we choose to simply focus upon the debatable legalities of what he did, rather than learn from what he's taught us.

We're damn lucky it was Morris who did this. Because if a malicious or immature person had done it first, the damage would have been real.

5 Corporate History

Where would we be without the corporate world? I dare say we would have had a fairly short life span were it not for the endless material fed to us from "companies without a clue." Having a magazine like *2600* to tear apart their various products and services must have been corporate America's worst nightmare. But at the same time we got some of our most enthusiastic responses from people within these very same institutions. It was no different than all of our other interactions with the mainstream. Deep down they were cheering us on because everyone wanted to see the individual stand up to the monolithic entities and win. But on the surface everyone also had to follow the rules and pay the rent. This is why from the beginning we found ourselves being fed all sorts of leaked information from behind the corporate (and government) walls. Being thought of as *worthy* of receiving top secret information has always been a real badge of honor for us.

Most of the various examples in this chapter have little to do with insider knowledge. Rather, this was simply a bunch of hackers looking at developments in the world of high tech with a critical eye. And there was much to criticize. For as the world changed around us, all sorts of new products were being introduced. More times than not, the people introducing them had less of an idea of what they were doing than the people in the hacker community. While this in itself was nothing new, for the first time we had the means to spread our message to the general public. And that's what we tried to do in those early years. From what we heard through our various insider sources, this caused quite a stir back at their assorted headquarters.

The phone companies were obviously one of our favorite targets. Since Ma Bell had been broken up, there was a whole flurry of new companies springing up with various offerings to the public. *Equal access* was the term for the altruistic concept of the freedom to choose your long-distance carrier. Of course, it never quite worked out as planned or promised. The new companies oftentimes resorted to sleazy practices to get more customers. We caught several of them doing just that and let the world know. As everyone in the country was going through the shell shock of the Bell breakup, these stories were of great interest to the average person. What's more, it showed how valuable a resource hackers were in telling consumers when and how they were getting ripped off. One of the best examples of this was with our own local phone company, New York Telephone. In ways that nobody else had been able to, we explained how they were charging people (and businesses) for absolutely nothing by imposing a touch-tone fee. In actuality, there was no equipment or service that had to be paid for. Customers were in effect simply paying *not* to have their touch tones disabled by the central office. The icing on the cake was the fact that only the newer switches even had the ability to disable touch tones in the first place; older switches were unable to differentiate the difference, which pretty much proved that it was a standard part of the switch. Of course, our local company wasn't the only one doing this but they had the misfortune of being *our* phone company so we had to start with them. It took years before that battle was eventually won. But we made some powerful enemies along the way.

As mentioned, there were also new companies springing up trying to take advantage of the confusion surrounding the breakup of the Bell System. Alternate Operator Services were a new concept that caused a degree of pandemonium in the telecommunications world. People thought they were giving their calling card number to their normal phone company, but in actuality a totally different company was processing it and charging them many times more than what they were expecting. It was amazing how much they were able to get away with using such a slimy business practice. Not only were we there to expose this sort of thing, but we also were able to provide proof of the symbiotic relationships between these sleazebags and more mainstream companies like MCI.

Oh, the fun we had with MCI. They really made it so easy though. Like when they introduced this new product called MCI Mail. This was *their* vision of electronic communications. For a dollar you could send a letter electronically to one of their subscribers. A dollar! Fortunately, a number of us had already experienced true electronic communication (albeit it without authorization) so we knew this was a load of crap. But it served to show how corporate America envisioned how things should unfold. Charging people for every e-mail sent was their dream, which fortunately never became reality. It's pretty amazing, however, to see how even we were enthused by the prospect of using their service as a "free word processor" or figuring out ways of exchanging messages without incurring a fee. These were the early and clumsy days of email, and nobody really knew how it would all turn out. But our instincts told us that MCI's vision sure wasn't it.

Nor did we have many nice things to say about Pronto, one of the earliest home banking systems run by the old Chemical Bank. To be fair, nobody else had really gotten it right at that stage either. But the mere thought of paying a bill electronically only to have some bank employee somewhere physically write out a check and drop it in the mail as part of that "electronic" process was as hilarious to us then as it is now. Clearly their ideas needed work.

It's fun to look back at these days and see all of the companies that never made it: ICN, Skyline, Allnet, NTS, People Express. They each had business plans and modes of operation that rubbed hackers the wrong way, whether it was because they seemed intent on cheating people or because their systems were just set up so badly. We were pretty ruthless in tearing them to pieces and I doubt any of us feel any lasting guilt over that. After all, imagine where we'd be now if these organizations had been successful in implementing their bad ideas?

MCI Mail: The Adventure Continues (July, 1984)

You really have to hand it to those folks over at MCI. First they tackle Ma Bell and now they're going after the U.S. Postal Service! MCI Mail's slogan, "The Nation's New Postal System," is printed on every bright orange envelope that they send through, you guessed it, U.S. Mail.

On this system, a user is assigned a "mailbox" that he can use to send and receive mail. Sending is done either electronically, that is, to other people with MCI mailboxes or through the post office, which covers everybody else in the world. The first type of letter will cost you $1 for the first three pages while the second type is double the cost. It's also possible to send an overnight letter ($6) or a four-hour letter ($25) to some places.

The purpose of MCI Mail is to stimulate the use of electronic mail by making it more accessible to the average person. For that we must give them credit—anybody can get an account on this system! There is no start-up fee and no monthly fee of any kind. To get an account, all you have to do is call them—either by voice or data. If you call by data (see page 5 of April issue of *2600* for numbers), you'll have to enter REGISTER as the username and REGISTER as the password. The rest is self-explanatory. After a couple of weeks, you'll get in the mail (regular mail, that is) a big orange envelope that has, among other things, your password. With this info, you're now free to log onto the system, look for people you know, send and retrieve messages, read all of their help files, or even hop onto the Dow Jones News Service (watch it though—*that* can get pretty expensive!).

The system is set up on a network of VAXes throughout the country. They've been operating since September 1983 and claim to have over 100,000 subscribers. Many of these are actually subscribers to the Dow Jones service, who are automatically given MCI Mail accounts whether they want them or not.

While the rates aren't overly expensive, they're certainly not cheap. Mailing regular letters is much cheaper and often just as fast since not every MCI Mail user checks their mailbox every day. Apart from that, though, there are many problems with the system as it stands now. For one thing, it can take forever getting on it, particularly through the 800 numbers. When you finally do get a carrier, you should get a message like this after hitting two returns:

```
Port 20.
Please enter your user name:
```

Enter the username you selected and the password they assigned you. It should say, "Connection initiated....Opened." From that point on, you're in.

But the system will often appear to be bogged down. Often you have to hit twenty returns instead of two. Sometimes the system won't let you in because all connections are "busy." Other times it will just drop the carrier. Real mailboxes don't do that.

Another thing that will drive you crazy is the menus. *Every* time you enter a command, you get a whole new menu to choose from. If you're at 300 baud, this can get pretty annoying, especially if you know what all the options are. There are two ways around this: Get the advanced version, which allows you to enter multiword commands and even store some files, at a cost of $10 per month, or simply hit a Ctrl+O.

One part of the system that works fast and is very convenient is the user info. As soon as you type the command CREATE to begin writing a letter, you'll be asked who you want to send it to. Enter either the person's last name, first initial and last name, or username (which is usually one of the first two, but which can be almost anything the user desires). Immediately, you'll get a list of everyone with that name, as well as their city and state, which often don't fit properly on the line. There are no reports of any wildcards that allow you to see *everybody* at once. (The closest thing is *R, which will show all of the usernames that you're sending to.) It's also impossible for a user not to be seen if you get his name or alias right. It's a good free information retrieval system. But there's more.

MCI Mail can also be used as a free word processor of sorts. The system will allow you to enter a letter, or for that matter, a manuscript. You can then hang up and do other things, come back within 24 hours, and your words will still be there. You can conceivably list them out using your own printer on a fresh sheet of paper and send it through the mail all by yourself, thus sparing MCI Mail's laser printer the trouble. You could also share your account with somebody else and constantly leave unsent drafts for each other. Again, they have to be retrieved within 24 hours.

Yet another way of getting "free" service from these people is to obtain many different accounts. There doesn't seem to be any kind of a limit on this and since each account comes with $2 of free messages, a few accounts can get you quite a bit of free service. And, of course, there's no charge for *receiving* messages on any of these accounts.

2600 has learned of several penetrations onto MCI Mail by hackers. This isn't really surprising considering: (a) there are multiple usernames, i.e. John Smith's username would always default to JSMITH, which means that several passwords can work for one username; (b) all passwords seem to follow a similar pattern—8 characters with the odd-numbered characters always being consonants and the even-numbered ones always being vowels—any true hacker would obtain several accounts and look for any correspondence between the random password and the account number everyone is assigned; (c) MCI Mail doesn't hang up after repeated tries—the only thing that will make it disconnect intentionally is inactivity on your part.

But by far the biggest blunder that MCI Mail has made is not found on the system. It lies in their bills. *There is no carry over from month to month!* If you get billed for $8 one month and you don't pay it, then proceed to use the system for $3 more the next month, your next bill will only show the $3! The $8 has vanished! (This is by far the dumbest mistake we have *ever* reported in these pages.)

You'll find quite a few unanswered questions in your travels through MCI Mail, which you can try to solve by reading the HELP files or by sending a *free* message to MCIHELP. It usually takes them a couple of days to respond to you instantly, however.

There are some software lapses as well. The system seems to be patterned largely after GTE Telemail, but it never really reaches that level of clarity. A small example can be seen in the scan tables, which have a heading of From, Subject, Size, etc. On outbound messages, the name of the person you're sending *to* appears under the *From* heading! Pretty silly.

MCI Mail shows every indication of overspending with a passion. Free messages, free accounts, sloppy programming, toll-free dialups, single sheets of paper (like their bills) sent in huge envelopes, etc. Either they're very optimistic out there or they're very naive.

MILESTONE: WRATH OF GOD STRIKES *2600* (November, 1986)

On July 26 of this year, *2600* came very close to being wiped out of existence. While we have taken extraordinary precautions to protect ourselves against any form of harassment from all kinds of authorities, there was one occurrence that we were almost completely unprepared for. We stress the word almost.

On this fateful night, our offices took a direct hit from Mother Nature herself in the form of a lightning bolt. While nobody was injured and no fires were started, nearly every piece of electronic equipment was completely and irrevocably fried.

Computers, modems, printers, tape machines—all totally nonfunctional. We started sending equipment out for repairs the day after this horrible kick of fate, and even now we're still waiting for satisfaction on a number of them. We feel we must point out that two companies in particular—Epson and Zenith—seem very much bewildered as to how to fix their own machines.

continues

MILESTONE: WRATH OF GOD STRIKES *2600* (*continued*)

But there is a bright spot and that should be pointed out as well. Only a few months earlier, we had taken out a policy with Safeware, the computer insurance people. We don't mean for this to come off sounding like an advertisement, but these people were simply incredible. Immediately after we notified them of our problems, they sent us forms to fill out and were ready to answer any questions we had. And in less time than it took for any of our equipment to be fixed, they had a check sent to us for the entire amount, minus the fifty dollar deductible.

We whole-heartedly recommend these folks for all computer users. They protect you against theft, fire, power surges, and in our case, lightning. Most users can be fully protected for well under $100 a year.

Naturally, this incident and its aftermath have set us back a bit. You may have even noticed a slackening off from our usual efficiency. New subscribers were subjected to longer waits for their first issue and back-issue orders were delayed up to a couple of months! Our long-awaited expansion and format change had to be delayed. And all of our uninsured radios and monitoring equipment were destroyed.

It's now November and we're about back to the point that we should have been at in August. Most of our equipment has either been replaced or repaired. We're better prepared for the next lightning hit, although little could have been done to ward off that last dagger of destruction. Our phones are in working order most of the time but occasionally you may get a busy signal, a reorder, or total silence that will last for days. This, according to New York Telephone, is not really happening. We'll see if the Public Service Commission agrees.

We're back on track now. Many thanks to those who lent their time and support during this time of crisis.

Banking from Your Terminal—A Look at PRONTO (July, 1985)

By Orson Buggy

Electronic banking services via personal computer and modem are springing up as various banks try to jump on the information age bandwagon. This month *2600* takes a look at one of the older and more varied services available in the New York City area.

Chemical Bank's PRONTO provides a host of banking services all available for dialing up with your personal computer and modem. After signing on with your account you can make balance inquiries, transfer funds between accounts, use the bank's computer to keep track of your checkbook and budget, pay bills to selected merchants, and send electronic mail to other subscribers. All this costs twelve bucks per month, and you get a checking account and cash machine card thrown in, too.

Naturally, PRONTO includes numerous security features to make sure that only those authorized to do so can play with the accounts. First of all, you can't call up PRONTO with just any dumb terminal. You must be using their special software. This means that you can't even subscribe unless your computer is one of the popular series that they support (Apple II, Atari, Commodore 64, Compaq, and IBM compatible). On top of that, there's your personal password that you have to fork over each time you connect. This sounds good enough to keep the average troublemaking hacker out of their hair, but is by no means bulletproof. If someone eavesdropped on a PRONTO conversation he or she could easily pick up the codes needed to get into that account, since they're probably the same ones for each session (unless, of course, the eavesdroppee has changed the password lately). Of course, this hypothetical intruder would need their own copy of PRONTO software. But that would not be much of an impediment to many hackers.

One bank officer, when presented with this argument, countered with, "But there's really nothing an intruder could do with your account even if they did manage to sign on to it somehow. They could get their jollies transferring money between your accounts, but they can't take any out for themselves." PRONTO allows you to pay bills, but only to a selected list of merchants. This has over 300 companies on it, including other banks where you might want to make loan or credit card payments, all of the area utilities, insurance companies, several clubs, newspapers, and other kinds of businesses that bill you every month. If there's someone you want to pay that's not on the list, you can ask for them to be included. Chemical claims this is a big security advantage over other banks' home services, since you can only send money to someone on their pre-approved lists. Just in case the unthinkable should happen, the customer is liable for the first $50 of a fraudulent electronic banking transaction, just like in the credit card and cash machine services. Except in that case, the customer may be liable for the first $500 (the maximum) if he or she fails to notify the bank within two days of losing the bank card or access code.

Chemical also provides another service called PRONTO Business Banker. Like PRONTO, it has slick promotional material telling the prospective manager how he can get complete control over his company's accounts. The selling style is a little different, but it appears to be basically the same service except with a few minor changes for business customers.

The way the money actually gets transferred when you pay your bills is also interesting—as of March when Chemical received a PRONTO request for a payment somewhere, some clerk in New Jersey would actually write a check out, shove it in an envelope, and mail it off. I don't know whether they've modernized this at all, but they were planning to. Chemical also speaks of future expansions to PRONTO, such as news, home shopping, and stock quotes.

In the bad old days, most bank transactions needed a human being's signature to be processed. Electronic banking services replace the handwritten signature with a digital identification. The security is fairly good when it comes to a handheld bank card, suitable for sticking into cash machines wherever you go, which otherwise stays in your pocket where no one else should have any access. But the home banking services take this one step further—the latest "signature" is merely a computer identification code, which, like a common-carrier access code or credit card number, is only secure while no one else knows about it.

Citibank's recognition of your digital signature is rather disappointing. Their first level of security is the individual copy of the software they give you, which has an embedded identification in it. The next one is the number printed on your bank machine card that they give you (shades of the ATT calling card blunders). The last one is the same "personal identification code" (PIC), a four- to six-digit password, that is magnetically encoded on your banking card and must be typed in whenever you use their cash machines. This puts a lot of strain on the PIC, since its disclosure would compromise both your cash machine and home banking accounts. Citibank warns you in their literature to inform them immediately if, among other things, your banking software is "lost or stolen." Either they don't think copying of that software is a threat, or they have (ha ha) copy protected it.

By the way, one of the other home banking services is called EXCEL from Manufacturers Hanover (aka Manny Hanny). The only one of merit that I know of is PRONTO, and then only because of the electronic mail included in the monthly fee. You would have to be the kind of person who writes a lot of monthly checks or has a difficult time making it out to the nearest cash machine in order to benefit from those services.

[Citibank's bank-by-phone system is called DIRECT ACCESS. We tried out this one using a simulation disk, which we ordered for free through an 800 number. The people there were very happy to send us a demo-floppy for an IBM compatible. This system has several other services including Dow Jones.]

Pursuit for People (September, 1985)

On August 7, GTE Telenet announced a new service that, if handled properly, will usher in a whole new phase of computer communications.

The service is called PC Pursuit and it enables people to connect their computers to other computers for $25 a month (plus a start-up fee of $25). In other words, a hobbyist in New York can connect his computer to a bulletin board in California and not have to pay for a long-distance call. The "computer conversation" goes through GTE Telenet, a packet-switching network for computers, previously used exclusively by large corporations.

"To access the service," GTE's press release explains, "a user calls his PC Pursuit access number and is prompted to enter his home phone number and make a request for a destination phone number in a distant city. If the user's telephone number is not authorized, the phone call is terminated and a record of the call is generated. If the number is authorized, the subscriber is called back and automatically connected to the desired telephone number in the distant city, which could be a specific database or remote PC user. GTE Telenet is able to maintain full accounting of the origin and destination of all calls. Each user session can last a full hour, and users may access the service as many times a month as they wish."

PC Pursuit represents the first time a major corporation has attempted to win over computer hackers rather than intimidate them. J. David Hann, president of GTE Telenet, says, "We hope that we will be providing a safe, positive outlet for computer hobbyists, giving them inexpensive, virtually unlimited access to hundreds of free databases and bulletin boards. By removing the prohibitive cost from recreational data communications, perhaps PC Pursuit will encourage growth and advancement rather than mischief and abuse among hobbyists."

We think it's great. At last we are being encouraged to take advantage of technology without paying ridiculous prices. We look forward to the day when all "long-distance" calls will cost the same as local calls, and free databases will be made available to everyone.

Naturally we are a little concerned that all of this data will be going through GTE Telenet, i.e. just about every hacker bulletin board would at some point be called through it. It wouldn't be too difficult to spy on someone's data from within the system, but we feel that's already the case at present with all communications. As always, we recommend scrambling sensitive or private communications.

It's unlikely that this new system (co-developed by Digital Pathways, Inc. of California) will be victimized by hackers because of the callback feature. Still, if there is a way to defeat this, you can count on it being discovered. Even at this point, though, the most that any one person could cheat the service out of is $25 a month.

Our main complaint with PC Pursuit is that it isn't available in nearly enough places. Only the largest of cities can use it to call other large cities. A list of dial-ups appears in this issue. When GTE finally gets around to implementing nationwide or even worldwide service, they will have a powerful, trend-setting, people-oriented product.

People Express to Be Hacked to Pieces (May, 1985)

By Paul G. Estev

If a business is starting a new, expensive touch-tone interactive phone service, it should assess its real usefulness. New systems should be tested by the real users as well as the system creators. All too often, businesses do not notice that their systems have fatal flaws or are user unfriendly.

People Express, the growing economy airline (economy carrier) has started such a new service that has many of the worst features of any Tone Activated Service (TAS). Other services like this are George Bank by Phone, IBM-Audio Distribution System, and Mobil Credit Check.

The new service is called "Pick Up & Go" and has been described in detail in recent advertising. It is a system where anyone could reserve airplane tickets for any People's flight using a telephone. Originally developed by AT&T, Pick Up & Go should be going soon.

This service is in many ways like other TAS's, but unlike a voicemail system, there is no real reward for exploring this system. With voicemail systems, people acquire accounts that they can use. In Pick Up & Go, there are no free plane tickets to get, because you can only book the flights. The tickets must be picked up at your flight...and paid for then. Yet, it is an example of poor design using this now common technology, which integrates phone systems with data lines—in this case, the reservation computers.

People Express is known for their low prices, which gives them the competitive edge to be known as the fastest growing airline as well as good investment. This also has its drawbacks. Low prices mean low incentive for travel agents to book flights on the airline. In addition, People's is well known for overbooking flights while expecting many of the potential passengers to not show up. People's instituted this service so they could get around the travel agent problem. But it is expected that they will have more of the same problems with the booking of flights, if not more of different problems...

This is how the system works: As with most TAS's, there is a voice that asks for touch-tone input as to what date, time, flight, etc. you wish to take. At first, a female voice asks you for a 7-digit identification number, which you can make up (they suggest that you enter your phone number, so it is easy for you to remember). You tell the people at People Express this number when you pick up the tickets, so they know that it is really you who made the reservation. In effect you are just giving them a password. So you enter your seven-digit code then a '#.' (Remember, you enter a '#' after each command, and numbers can be either one or two digits. You will be prompted by the voice for each entry.) Then you enter the month you wish to travel then a '#;' then the date you wish to travel; then the coding for the airport you wish to leave from; your destination; then the number of tickets you want; then your desired departure hour.

(Follow the hour by an 'a' or a 'p' for a.m. or p.m. After this prompt, the voice will tell you the two closest flights to the hour you indicate. It will also check to see if any seats are available at this point.) Finally, you enter the flight you desire. You are then told the price of the flights you have booked. At this point you are looped back to the beginning, where you can hit a '#' at each prompt and it will 'ditto' your previous entry. You can book up to five seats per code, but you are able to enter a new code when you loop back, in order to book ten, a hundred, or even thousands of flights, if you are patient and devious.

Note again that you do not pay for your tickets until you get to the plane, nor do you even tell them who you are, in fact you cannot if you wished to. In addition, there is no provision to cancel reservations; you cannot do this if you wished to either.

This system will allow anyone to reserve almost any number of tickets on any flight leaving in the next two months or so. You can book a flight anywhere, even to London (code-549). This is the way things should be for travelers, fast and easy, but People Express is just waiting for people, travel agents, and other airlines to take advantage. United Airlines could book whole planes and clog up People Express just by making a phone call.

It is predicted that this system will be gone quite quickly, or the software will be changed but this takes time as we all know. If they do not do away with this system, there should be a commotion about hundreds of people waiting in line for empty flights.

Some airport codes you may need to know are: 397-Newark, 529-Los Angeles, 626-Orlando, 743-St. Pete. The codes correspond to the three-character initials that every airport in the world has.

There are a few more things you can do after you are done booking your flight, like *H#-Help, *B#-discard last entry, *D#-Delete last reservation request, *R#-Review current reservation, *L#-Review all your confirmed reservations. At this last prompt you can use the following commands: D#-Delete, K#-Keep, X#-Exit this function.

The system itself is fairly user friendly, but the female voice should tell you about the help function, you should not have to read about the help function in a newspaper advertisement. The voice should also note that you must enter a '#' after each entry, but it only does this after you make an error. You should also be provided with the list of airport codes. (Actually, some are easy to find yourself: DEN-336-Denver, SYR-797-Syracuse.) If People's really wishes to encourage the system's usage, it should also have a toll-free number. In the end, this service will result in confusion and reduced service, as well as longer lines at the terminals. Those who have taken People Express flights have both regretted and come to depend on overbooking. And there will be overbooking: by people who want to play with the system, by people who make mistakes, by people who do not mind booking a flight just 'in case' they plan to travel, by travel agents who customarily book hundreds of tickets, and by competing airlines who wish to do People Express wrong. This service will do nothing but increase the problem. It is indicative of the lack of human factor in creating these systems. It is surely a pity that big companies do not have real people test their new technology for them. Marketing consultants and programmers just seem to forget that it is people who use the products in the end. It will be people who make mistakes using their new system, and it will be people who will take advantage of this new system.

MCI: The Phone Company with a Lot of Explaining to Do (Winter, 1988-1989)

It all started with what sounded like a friendly phone call in October:

"Hello, this is Patricia from MCI. We noticed that you presently have an account with MCI and we wanted to let you know that we'll be offering 'one plus' service in your area starting December 10. We'd like to verify your address."

The nice lady then read us our address, which was one hundred percent correct. She then said another person would call us to confirm this information. That call came within minutes and was almost identical in content.

A couple of weeks later we got another one of those calls on another of our lines that had an MCI account attached to it. But this time the second call never came.

In early December, equal access came to our phone lines. We decided to check the status of those two lines that had gotten the calls. We dialed 1-700-555-4141, the toll-free number that identifies who your long-distance carrier is. And guess what? They had both been claimed by MCI. Surprised? We weren't. In fact, when those calls come in, we *expected* them to try and pull this scam we'd heard so much about. They made one big mistake though—they tried it on us.

We always listen very carefully when phone companies call us. And we can say very definitely that MCI never asked us if we wanted to choose them as our long-distance carrier. All they asked us to do was to verify our address.

OK, so it was a sloppy representative. Maybe even a corrupt one. How can you condemn an entire company because of the actions of one person? That's quite easy. It happened more than once. Different representatives called different phone numbers and gave the same little speech. And we've found out that other people have gotten the same treatment. This indicates to us that these representatives are reading a script that tells them *not* to ask the customer whether they actually *want* MCI's "one plus" service. Address verification, after all, is a much less controversial issue.

Perhaps MCI feels they're taking a calculated risk here. They only seem to make these calls to people who already use MCI in some form. Maybe they feel these people won't raise a fuss when they discover who their long-distance company is. In fact, they may never even discover that MCI is their carrier since they most likely have been getting

MCI bills in the past. Remember, these are people who have already been using MCI's services.

Regardless of whether or not it pays off, it's distressing to see such dishonest tactics on the part of a major company.

This isn't our only gripe with MCI. We had been using an account on MCI's 950-1986 dialup. In November we paid the bill a few days late (it was under $10). Well, lo and behold, they disconnected our code without *any* warning. When we asked them to reconnect it, they said they would have to handle our payment for 10 days first. Ten days went by and the code was still down. We asked again. This time, they said they were phasing out that service, so they couldn't reconnect us. But they came up with a bright idea. We could use our 14-digit MCI Card code instead of our old 5-digit code. "It's just as easy to remember," they said.

Clearly, they have the right to phase out their services and replace them with less desirable ones. But once again, it's the way in which they did it. MCI jumped at the first opportunity to take away our old code instead of being up front and letting their customers know that as of a certain date this service would be terminated. Being sneaky about it doesn't do anyone any good.

The Real Scam

We've saved the best for last. When we discovered that MCI had selected themselves as our long-distance carriers, we decided to experiment a little. One of our experiments involved trying to make an operator assisted call ("zero plus") on an MCI line. MCI doesn't offer operator assisted services. So we were curious as to what would happen when we tried to do this.

What happened was a big surprise. We got the same little fading dial tone that we got on AT&T—in other words, the prompt to enter our AT&T calling card number. We entered the card number and were astounded to hear a recording say, "Thank you for using NTS."

NTS? Who the hell were *they?!* And what were they doing accepting AT&T calling card numbers on MCI lines?

We'll skip all of the drama and simply tell you what we found out. NTS is an Alternate Operator Service (AOS) company. They handle calls from hotel rooms and privately owned pay phones. Their rates are often double those of AT&T. And it seems that in various parts of the country, MCI has a clandestine relationship with these people. We say clandestine because we're in the habit of reading all of the literature from every phone company that serves our area. And nowhere has this little "service" been mentioned. We have yet to find anyone in MCI who is even aware of this arrangement. On the other hand, NTS (based in Rockville, Maryland) is quite proud of the MCI connection. All of the NTS operators (who can trick anyone into believing they're really from AT&T) are aware that they provide service for MCI "zero plus" customers.

Why does MCI use an AOS? We can't imagine. But we can tell you the effects. If you decide to call someone collect from your phone and MCI happens to be your long-distance carrier, the person who accepts on the other end will wind up with one hell of a surprise when they get the bill. You'll be the one getting the surprise if you forget that MCI doesn't have operators and you attempt to place an operator-assisted or calling card call through them. The most likely scenario, though, would be something like this: You visit a friend and need to make a phone call from his house. Since you don't want to make your friend pay, you dial it "zero plus" and bill it to your calling card. How are you to know that your friend selected MCI as his long-distance carrier and that you've just been swindled by an AOS? Perhaps MCI's new slogan can be: "We bring the thrill of hotel phones right into your own home!"

Now we should point out that this "NTS Connection" doesn't work everywhere. In some areas you get recordings when you try to make "zero plus" calls using MCI. We need to know where it does work. You can find out at no charge by dialing 10222-0 followed by a ten-digit phone number (you can use your own). If you hear a fading dial tone, it means you're about to be connected to NTS. You can stay on and ask a whole lot of questions if you want. Let us know if it works in your area. (You can do the above even if MCI isn't your primary carrier—the 10222 routes the call to MCI. You must have equal access in your area in order to try this.)

There's really not much more to add. We are demanding a public statement from MCI addressing the issues of signing up unsuspecting consumers and billing their own customers exorbitant rates for operator-assisted calls without telling them. We don't expect to ever get such a statement.

Several years ago, we printed a story about MCI's electronic mail system, MCI Mail, which had a policy of terminating accounts that had received mail not to MCI's liking. We called it a flagrant invasion of privacy to peruse the mail of their own paying subscribers. The president of MCI indicated that he couldn't care less.

So all we can say right now is that it would be a very good idea to **boycott MCI** for all of the above reasons. A company that resorts to such devious methods of making money and that treats its customers so shabbily is not worthy of the historical significance its founders achieved.

We would appreciate it if this article was spread around in whatever ways possible.

2600: A Hacking Victim (August, 1985) 2600 *News Service*

When we received our June SBS Skyline bill, we were a bit surprised. More than $600 of it came from calls we never made. But what's really interesting is the way that the Skyline people handled it. In early June, we got a call telling us that their sophisticated equipment detected hackers trying to guess a code by scanning numerically. They said our code would soon be discovered, so they were going to give us a new one, with two extra digits added. They did this and that very day our old code was inactivated. The illegal calls had occurred *before* that day, and we figure Skyline must have known this. Maybe they thought that *2600*, in our corporate clumsiness, would pay a huge bill without investigation. Many big companies would. Gotta give them credit for trying.

When we called up about it, they didn't want to handle it over the phone! "Send the bill through the mail," they said. "Mark the calls you made and deduct the rest." Why are phone companies so afraid to do things over the phone?

As long as Skyline decided to give the "perpetrators" some extra time before the investigation starts, we figure we might as well lend a hand too. Our old code was 880099. We loved that code and are very upset at losing it. Our new eight-digit one is very difficult to remember and nowhere near as fun.

And one last note about those new eight-digit numbers. Phone phreaks have *already* figured out a way around them. If you dial the first six digits of an eight-digit code, then the ten-digit phone number and hit a # key, you'll get your tone back! That means there are only a hundred possible codes since there are only two more digits to figure out and one of them *definitely* works! If you enter six digits that are not part of an eight-digit code, and then a ten-digit phone number, you'll get an error message immediately or that fake carrier tone Skyline loves to send out. That tone, incidentally, is for you hackers with Apples and Commodores that scan all night long looking for the code that will get you through to a number that responds with a carrier tone. In the morning, you see how many carrier detects you got and which codes got them for you. Skyline's idea is that if *every* invalid code gives a hacker a carrier tone, there is no way for a computer to separate the good codes from the bad ones. Come on! How about setting your computer to dial a *non*-carrier and telling it to print out only those codes that *didn't* get a carrier tone? And there are probably a hundred more ways. Big corporations can be *so* much fun.

Allnet: A Horror Story (June, 1987) *By Mike Yuhas*

A feature in April's *2600* noted that Allnet would give customers five bucks credit if they persuaded a friend to sign up for Allnet's equal access service. If you recall, this pyramid scheme was a wee bit deceiving—the friend would need to designate Allnet as their *primary* carrier. April must have surely been a good month for promotional creativity over at Allnet: I ended up with Allnet as my primary carrier, *without my consent!!!*

This tale begins in February, shortly after I had started a new job. Part of my job requirement is to spend some time on the phone talking to clients, etc., in the evenings. Since these calls would be reimbursed by my company, I decided to use another long-distance carrier to make accounting easier. At random, I chose Allnet. This was to be a stopgap measure until I had received my MCI Cards (TM).

(Remember that with equal access, if you want to make calls on a secondary carrier, i.e., not your primary carrier, all you would need do is dial 10XXX (XXX being the identification code of the secondary carrier) plus the number you wish to reach. The local Bell company would then bill you in the event you didn't have an account with this carrier. It's also interesting to note that this billing cycle is often delayed by several months.)

A few weeks after I had made a bunch of Allnet calls, I got a call from someone who claimed she was from Allnet, saying that her records indicated I had been using Allnet, and would I give her my name and address so Allnet would bill me directly, instead of letting my local Bell company bill me. It sounded like a reasonable request—they wanted to get their funds quicker—so I asked her to recite some of the numbers I dialed to prove her affiliation. Thus convinced, I gave her the information she asked for. At no time did she mention anything about setting me up with Allnet as my primary carrier.

But that is precisely what happened.

A few days later, my postman delivered a form letter: "Welcome to Allnet 'Dial-1' Long Distance Service. You now have the benefits....You are a highly valued Allnet customer...." and a load of other diplomatic rubbish from Allnet's Director of Customer Service, Elaine Delves. It listed a toll-free customer service number, 800-982-4422, for questions, changes and "suggestions for improving our service." I felt my blood pressure rise about 50 bizillion points as I read. I wanted Sprint back! Of course, I called their number, and was put on hold for about 20 minutes. The fellow who finally answered said that no one in customer service had switched me over to Allnet, so naturally there was *absolutely nothing* he could do to remedy the situation. He suggested I call my local Allnet office.

Bennett Kolber, who is apparently some sort of big shot in Allnet's Philadelphia office, listened to my story: That Allnet had surreptitiously (and you thought only hackers and the folks in the National Security Council acted surreptitiously) connected me to their network, and I wanted to be reconnected back to Sprint, and that I would not call my local Bell company to make those arrangements due to the principle of the thing, not to mention that they'd charge me five bucks for the change. My plight must have really hit home with him because he said he'd look into the matter and promised—*promised*—that I'd get connected back to Sprint within a couple of days.

Unfortunately, he did not define the term "couple."

I had spoken with him a "couple" of times to try to resolve the affair in an expeditious manner. I got nowhere. I then spoke with Steve Edmonds, who also seemed sincerely disturbed by my situation. I thought my fortunes would change.

My fortunes stayed the same.

Now I was mad. I spoke to a bigger big shot named Bill Love. He was new on the job, he said, but he would rectify my problem *immediately*. After waiting a week, I called again. And again. He finally said something like this: "I'm sorry, okay, that it's taken us, okay, so long, okay, to get this matter resolved. But since I, okay, don't represent Sprint, okay, or your company, okay, there's no way, okay, that we can switch you back, okay, to Sprint." (He really did talk that way.) In short, I would have to call my local Bell company, arrange to be disconnected from Allnet, and deduct the $5 charge from my bill.

There have got to be serious internal problems with a company that asserts that I am "a highly valued customer" but seems to go out of its way to make me feel damn sure that I won't do business with them in this century, if I can help it. It took these clowns over a month to tell me that they were indeed powerless to satisfy me, but my local Bell company had the problem fixed in one 5-minute phone call.

ICN—More Than a Bargain (November, 1986)

By John Freeman and Emmanuel Goldstein

Last month, we printed a story on a company called ICN. This month, we have more details, which may prove useful.

The Independent Communications Network supposedly allows you to make all the calls you want for $100 a month. To sign up for this, you need a sponsor. You can also, if you choose, sponsor other people. If you manage to convince somebody to use this system, you make $25. If that person convinces someone else, they make $25 and you make $5. It goes down six levels, so the maximum you can make is $50 on one sale. But there's no limit to how many sales you can make. That's how that end of the deal works. Some people who sign up for ICN choose the "marketing plan," which is what was just described. Others choose both this and phone service (which is referred to as "partyline service"). And some just choose to use the phone service alone.

We called ICN to ask about signing up. The person at the other end said that if we wanted to sign up, we'd be given an 800 number to call to get our dial tone. Everyone gets the same 800 number. If it's busy or if it rings more than once, the customer must hang up and try again. He said straight out that we probably wouldn't get through the first time. He said on the average you have to redial for about ten minutes to get the dial tone. He said that evenings were very busy and it wasn't a good idea to try then. "What about days?" we asked. "They're busy too," he said.

What ICN is doing is reselling ATT's WATS lines. This in itself isn't illegal. But ICN is estimated to have over 8,000 customers and only 54 lines for their long-distance network. It would be quite a trick to find out how many customers ICN *really* has. All personnel seem to take offense at this question.

ICN was started in Wautoma, Wisconsin, on July 15, 1986. It didn't take long for complaints to roll into the Wisconsin Public Service Commission. In September, ICN relocated in Cody, Wyoming. The representative told us that there is no corporate income tax in Wyoming.

ICN saves a lot by never sending out bills. The $100 is due on the last working day of the month. Presumably, if they don't get paid, your access code is shut off. There is also another method, which is a little frightening. They subscribe to a service known as Checkomatic, which will automatically take $100 out of your checking account every month!

We have yet to find anyone who has successfully completed a call on this system, or even gotten a dial tone. The 800 number we obtained never stops ringing.

And not all the complaints come from irate customers who can't get through. In ICN's first ad campaign, they gave an example of a WATS number. The number was given presumably so customers or sellers could see what a real 800 number looks like. The number they gave, 800-ICN-FREE belonged to the Life Control Institute in New Jersey. LCI was stuck paying for every call that people made to the sample 800 number, thinking they could get free phone calls. Eventually the people from LCI sent ICN a letter requesting that they pay for their share of the WATS bill, but ICN never sent a response.

According to the representative, customers have 30 days to claim a refund. He also told us that once you did get through, there were three possible ways your call could be completed. The first was optic-fiber, which gave the best connection. The second was FX copper, which was fairly good. The third was AT&T WATS, which he said was the worst and that you could barely hear the person on the other end.

The company has some kind of a deal worked out with AT&T in which they get more lines put in as they get more customers. Their codes are six digits long and calls can be made to anywhere in the United States, including Alaska, Hawaii, and the Virgin Islands. Calls can't be made from Alaska or to Canada or Mexico.

We did a little detective work on ICN and this is what we came up with. The General Manager is Larry Hartsough, the President is John Heeg, and the Vice President is Robert Boch. The current address for ICN corporate headquarters is 808 Meadow Drive, Cody, Wyoming, 82414. At this address they have 25 lines allocated as follows: 307-587-4700 to 09 is the customer service department. As of Monday, November 3, there was only a five-line hunt sequence. 4701,6,7,8,9 are being eliminated. They have another ten-line hunt sequence: 307-587-4730 to 39. We suspect this is used for sales people to call in regarding sales that have just been completed. On these lines, the representatives seem much nicer. Some useful info: Larry Hartsough's phone number: 307-527-6812. The WATS resale switch is located at 526 West Main St., Wautoma, Wisconsin, 54928. The WATS service number is 800-367-8672, which translates to 414-765-9027 in Wisconsin. We believe this is the number that is supposed to give you a dial tone. We've tried hundreds of times at all hours with no success. This line has a

54-line hunt sequence. It used to always be busy but now they've "fixed it" by making it ring forever instead.

The offices in Wyoming are in a small office building, formerly the Marathon Oil office building. It's about 25,000 square feet and approximately 55 people work there. They use a Novell Star "state of the art" computer with Epson Equity 1 terminals. They tell us there are other companies like them all over the country, including one called Ideal in Washington state. Ideal supposedly charges $120 per month.

We thought it would be interesting to find out what the rates are for AT&T WATS lines to see if these people are doing well or not. To start with, it costs $123 to install a line and $99 to have someone come out to do it. Rates for "Service Area 6," which enables you to call the entire United States are:

	Day	Eve	Night
First 15 hours	$21.77	$14.15	$9.63
Next 25 hours	$19.37	$12.67	$9.63
Over 40 hours	$16.98	$11.04	$9.63

If ICN has 54 working lines and they are all in use at all times, it would cost them about $8,000 per line per month, close to $430,000 in line charges alone for 54 lines, assuming they pay the lowest rate. Now, 54 customers paying $100 each only bring in $5,400. It doesn't sound very profitable. But consider this. There is a very definite limit on the line charges, high though they are. There are only so many hours in a month. But there is no limit to how many people will send ICN $100. So, if instead of a mere 54, their estimation of 8,000 actually sent them money, they'd bring in $800,000. After paying the phone company and the salespeople, they'd still have over a quarter of a million dollars coming in per month. And if that's not enough, consider this. What if those WATS lines weren't really available 24 hours a day? From the beginning, they tell you how days and evenings are the worst times to call and you should never expect to be connected during those hours. So why bother leaving the lines on in the first place during those times? Nobody is going to expect to get through anyway. This maneuver would bring their costs down to $180,966.96 in total for the WATS lines. They'd only need 1,810 customers to break even. The possibilities are endless in a situation like this, where the customer never really knows what's going on. That's why we feel it pays to stay away.

2600 Exposes New York Telephone (July, 1987)

In late June, we at *2600* got around to doing something we've been meaning to do for a long time. We've mentioned before in these pages how unfair it is that telephone companies charge consumers a monthly fee for using touch tones. They're not providing any additional service or equipment. The only real technological advance they've come up with is a device that can ignore touch tones coming from nonpaying customers. Sounds more like blackmail than a service, doesn't it?

So after having received about 25 calls from New York Telephone virtually begging us to sign up for this "service" by July so we wouldn't have to pay the "installation" fee, we reached the conclusion that enough was enough. On June 26, we mailed a press release to every newspaper, television and radio station in New York State, as well as state senators, state assemblymen, and a whole host of others we thought would be interested. Well, as it turns out, many of them were. Inside of a couple of days we were talking to all kinds of media people and it would not be an exaggeration to say that many thousands of people now know about this. The support has been terrific. Nobody likes the idea of paying a little extra every month for something that's not really there. And businesses, large and small alike, are flabbergasted when confronted with evidence that they're paying over $4 a month per line for this non-service. Take a company with 500 lines and this comes out to $24,000 a year. Not inconsequential.

And more recently, we were confronted with additional evidence of wrongdoing. It seems New York Telephone has taken to sending out undated notices informing the customer that they are about to be charged for touch-tone service since touch tones were detected on their line. Many people disregard this notice because it looks just like all the other pitches they've received to sign up for touch tones. So they wind up being signed up for something they never wanted. Think about that. If touch tones were really a service, wouldn't the phone company punish a "violator" by stopping the service, rather than signing the person up for it?

We must be fair about this, however. New York Telephone is not the only telephone company doing this. But since they're local to us, we felt it only right that we tackle them first. Odds are your local company is up to the same trickery. If they are, it's up to you to make people aware of it. Call your elected officials and explain the situation to them. Keep in mind that most people accept this *simply because* they don't understand what's actually happening. They're thinking precisely the way the phone companies want them to. By letting people know they're being cheated and by getting them to say something about it, we're taking the most important step in reversing an unfair policy.

Telco Response (October, 1987)

After months of trying, we've finally managed to get a response from the telephone company concerning our battle to eliminate the fee for touch-tone service (see [the] July, 1987 issue).

We've received a fair amount of publicity concerning this matter. Consumer-oriented radio stations like WMCA in New York have shown a great interest and devoted time to the growing battle. Several newspapers have reprinted our press release and it was one of those that drew the response which was written by Bruce Reisman, a staff director of media relations for New York Telephone. Since more than a month passed between the printing of the press release and Reisman's reply, we believe that some consultation was involved and that this is pretty much the official view of New York Telephone.

"There is nothing improper here," Reisman states. "This is the practice throughout the United States....It's longstanding public policy." The same words could have been used to describe racial segregation once. The fact that an unfair practice is occurring all over does not make it right or justifiable. And the populace is most definitely waking up to this unfairness.

He goes on to justify the cost, claiming central office equipment that recognizes tones has to be paid for, as well as the labor involved in making the change from pulse to tone. This logic is so flimsy that a child could knock it over. As we said in our press release, touch tone decoding devices are *standard equipment* for practically every central office in existence. Every electronic switch has the capability of allowing touch tones on all of its lines. The only thing preventing this is an "N" instead of a "Y" inside the customer database. Which brings us to the labor question: Just how much should the company rake in for changing an "N" to a "Y" anyway? Reisman says $10.55 is reasonable. We say let's stop kidding the public.

We were accused of misleading when we claimed that customers very often lost the use of their touch tones when an area upgraded to electronic switching. Not so, says the phone company—the customer is always asked to pay before service is disrupted. Well, we don't base our conclusions on mere speculation. We know of many people who have lost the use of their tones the instant their central office cut over to electronic switching. The fact that the phone company claims this never happens is further evidence of their distorted perception.

It's only eight cents a day, they protest. Figure out how many people are paying the phone company eight cents a day for doing absolutely nothing. Take into account that the cost is higher for business customers, a fact they conveniently forgot to mention. This is a very large amount of money.

And finally, the usual mistruth: "Touch-tone service also enables the customer to conveniently bank or shop electronically from home." This is simply not true. As long as you have a touch-tone phone, you can use any of those bank-at-home services. The only thing the phone company can do is prevent you from *placing* a call with tones. Once you're connected, they have no way of deactivating your tones. The tones, after all, are created inside your phone, not inside the phone company. If everyone realized that, their policy would never have survived this long.

But things are changing. There will be an article in the November issue of *Popular Communications* that points out the unfairness of this fee, not just in New York, but nationwide. We are bombarding the New York Public Service Commission with information about this and we expect some kind of a reaction from that entity. We need your continued support. Spread the word. Tell your parents. Tell your children. Tell your elected officials. Write letters to your local papers and send us a copy.

6 Raids

One of the unfortunate realities of the hacker world has been its ongoing brushes with various forms of law enforcement. In fact, at this point it's likely that *all* forms of law enforcement have taken a keen interest in the activities of hackers at one point or another. And while it still seems like overkill to those actually involved in that world, back in the 1980s it was a real surprise to see them pay such close attention—and more than a little scary.

Since it was all so new at the time, nobody really knew what was going on or what was going to happen next. Hackers and phone phreaks were just out playing with the latest toys by either war dialing with their phones to find interesting phone numbers, connecting all sorts of people together through illicitly obtained long-distance codes and teleconferencing systems, or learning the ins and outs of the growing amount of computers that were reachable over the phone lines. It shocked the hell out of them to see the authorities swoop in as if they were some sort of terrorist group. But swoop in they did, time and time again. And, more often than not, they hardly understood what it was they were looking for. Every raid that took place invariably yielded at least one humorous anecdote relating to the investigators' overall cluelessness. Add the mass media into the fray with their misperceptions, misquoting, and hunger for headlines, and the carnival atmosphere was complete.

Our very first issue in January of 1984 had what was probably our biggest bombshell ever with regards to hacker raids and prosecutions. In that debut edition we printed an "interview" with an FBI agent who was discussing an ongoing case against hackers. What he didn't realize was that he was talking to a hacker magazine. Somehow he was under the impression that he was conversing with an IBM system administrator and he was *very* generous with details of the investigation. Our printing his words pretty much derailed the entire case and wound up changing certain people's career paths. Most importantly, it exposed one of our own as an informant responsible for the prosecution of many in the community. We couldn't have asked for a better cover story.

The following year our flagship BBS was targeted by prosecutors in New Jersey who took the Keystone Cops routine to a new level. They accused us of "changing the positions of satellites" by running a hacker-oriented bulletin board system. When the laughing stopped, we began to realize just how serious this ignorance could become if allowed to run unchecked. We convinced the ACLU to take on the case and we got the media to start paying real attention. A few months later, they had no choice but to quietly return our system. But we learned something important through all of that. We realized that it was absolutely vital that the legal rights of computer users be taken as seriously as those in the physical world. Why should electronic speech be any different from non-electronic speech? And so the drive began in earnest to educate lawmakers and those in the legal community so that such overzealousness not be allowed to continue. We had no idea of the many challenges that would lie ahead...

When our BBS was returned, we decided to take a stand right then and there to allow users to say whatever they wanted in private mail and not to hold ourselves accountable for its contents. Up until then system operators were held responsible for *anything* on their BBS, public or private. But what if private really *meant* private? What if even the people running the system couldn't access the private communications of their users? It was an intriguing challenge to the way things had been running and it was a fight that was being undertaken on a growing number of fronts as the potential of the computer revolution became apparent.

Of course, the hacker world and the technological world were far bigger than what we were directly involved with at *2600*. We touched upon the battles happening on other fronts and reported whenever another BBS (invariably run on an Apple IIe or equivalent) was raided by the authorities for one reason or another. We stood with them by occasionally reprinting material that had been taken away by the authorities. The intent was to spread forbidden knowledge even further once it had been suppressed. In one of these excerpts, it's both humorous and revealing to us now to see the author bemoaning the fact that in 1985 things just weren't the same as they used to be in the good old days. At least *that* philosophy never seems to change.

It all got a lot more ominous as the decade drew to a close with the involvement of the Secret Service in hacker cases and the first reports of people actually being imprisoned for their misdeeds on computers. In 1989 we first reported on someone named Kevin Mitnick who seemed to be getting an undue amount of attention and prosecution. (We even managed to repeat some of the Mitnick myths in that initial story.) The level of paranoia among law enforcement and, by extension, the general public, seemed to grow exponentially with the increasing influence of computers and high tech in our everyday lives. While this world was getting more fascinating by the day, it also clearly was getting more dangerous.

RAIDS INVOLVING *2600*

FBI Goes After ADS Hackers (January, 1984)

IBM must press charges before action can be taken—Feds reveal their tactics, blow source

On this page, we had originally planned to run an article entitled: ESS—Orwell's Prophecy. *At the last minute, however, we received this bombshell from an anonymous contributor. It seems that a group of hackers was making use of one of IBM's ADS systems. (Audio Distribution Systems enable users with touch-tone phones to send voice messages back and forth to each other. Look for an in-depth article on them in a future issue.) Unfortunately, as is all too often the case, one of these hackers was really an FBI informant who was taking note of all of the illegitimate users (around 40 or so). Luckily for this particular group, the informant was sloppy and left many telltale clues, which gave them literally months of warning. So, when the informant decided to send a message to the system operator, advising IBM to take action against the hackers and to call the FBI for more information, the hackers were ready. The system operator's account had also been penetrated by them and hence, the message was received by the hackers first! One of them actually followed the instructions in the message and called the FBI! And for some reason, the investigator there thought he was talking to an IBM executive. This is some of what he said.*

One of the individuals that supplies me with information from time to time has uncovered a lot of abuse within the ADS systems, not only here in the United States, but in England and Italy. I talk to this individual on a private bulletin board...

We have no ability to come in as an outside investigative or law enforcement agency and do anything about it because, first off, we don't have a complainant. We don't want to step on anybody's toes, but it's been our policy to monitor bulletin boards and the phone phreaking activity across the country and advise commercial computer systems and corporations if we do discover certain computers along with the passwords and account numbers being published on the board. We do this on a one on one basis.

The GTE Telemail Connection

That was my baby, too! As a matter of fact, that's how we came across the ADS system—through the GTE investigation. [These] people are not just interested in data communications through terminals—they will leave voice messages on an ADS. We have been slowly uncovering more and more on the ADS in the last two months.

The major phase of [the Telemail investigation] was about 20 individuals that we had located and identified and we're looking for indictments on most of them coming down in the next month or two. We're talking about a group of highly organized people that do communicate on a daily basis all the way across the country—from San

Francisco and L.A. to Denver to upstate New York. So we have a core of individuals that we are still looking at that are using your system and then we have this peripheral that we are not as concerned about because they are not part of an out and out conspiracy or an organized network, per se. I know of at least 8 or 10 that are the central figures in this, the carry-over from Telemail. And we keep hearing information of other people who are calling in with junk messages—there's no real substance to their messages. Now the reason I know that is that they have included one of my sources of information onto their system and so he gets messages from the other parties.

The Communist Connection

In a way we're somewhat fortunate that it's 16-year-olds or 26-year-olds as opposed to people from behind the Iron Curtain. It gives us the opportunity to see how these systems work and see if we can plug any loopholes before somebody from a not-friendly nation would try the same thing. I personally fully expect it—I'm surprised it hasn't happened in the past. It may have. We just haven't caught it. But the kids are a little bit sloppier and they're getting caught...I hate to sound paranoid, but we're supposed to be considering the big picture as far as is there anything sensitive in nature. For us within the bureau, sensitive in nature first off means national security and you've got corporate trade secrets and the like that you don't need being distributed.

How the FBI Wins Trust and Gets Info

The subjects have an ego problem and they love to talk to other individuals about what they are capable of doing and bragging about it. They have a tendency to trade information. Everything is negotiable with them. We have never had to barter away access to systems—we do it more on the technical information of phone networks, computer systems, and the like to where it's more of a technical information tradeoff as opposed to an access tradeoff. [An example would be the] login procedure for a PDP-11. You integrate yourself within their confidence and their circle of friends. You feed them a little bit of bait and a lot of times they'll go for it. You enter into a dialogue with them and they end up taking you for a ride.

These people are very hungry for technical avenues through which they can communicate. It used to be the personal computer bulletin boards—public messages that anybody can read. You start finding out that they leave a phone number or an address—and you start finding out who the parties are. There are thousands of these bulletin boards across the country and you narrow in on maybe twenty or so that are the more hardcore bulletin boards that are being used for exchange of illicit information. Then they move from there to an electronic mail service, namely GTE Telemail. They caused fits within Telemail when they decided to get a little bit cocky and see if they could shut down accounts and change passwords of the administrators and things like that. From there they have moved one step further to where they are now the same individuals communicating through the ADS systems and they also set up conference calls through the Bell System, so they're not just attacking one particular system or one individual avenue of communication—they try to hit them all. It's an ego trip for all of them.

Pen Registers

We would put a pen register on the phone line of the individual (suspect) and it would record only the digits dialed on his telephone—we would not use a full-blown wiretap to record his voice. We can only put a pen register on an individual's phone for like, 30 days before we have to go back to a judge and try to get an extension and we try to minimize the use of our electronic surveillance equipment so the public does not think we're the Big Brother of 1984. (laughter) It's coming. Actually, we're already there! (hearty laughter)

We have not utilized any pen registers for the specific purposes of going after abusers of the ADS systems. First off, we have to have an actual case presented to us or a complaint. It's a roundabout way of doing it, but it's the way that we, in the bureau, have to have somebody outside come to us. Otherwise we can carry on the whole investigation without IBM even being aware that we are monitoring activity within their system and we don't want to become that secret police, or anything like that. We want to be above board and work with the corporations in the community.

Just How Much Trouble Are These Hackers In?

On the federal level we can prosecute them for telephone fraud (fraud by wire) if we can determine that the ADS is an ongoing business operation and that you are being denied your just revenues by them sneaking onto your system and abusing your system. The strictest penalty is a $1,000 fine and five years in jail for an actual conviction of fraud by wire violation. Those are always lax—a more common sentence may be for an adult maybe a year in jail, 18 months, or a fine, sometimes they get probation, or agree to pay back any fraudulent money obtained or for services rendered or whatever to the client company—it stays on his record for a year, he's on probation for a year and at the end of that, his record is wiped clean. Rarely do they get the maximum penalty. It just doesn't happen.

Do Me a Favor

Please do not disclose any geographic location because we are kind of unique in that we do not have any other source available in any other part of the country that could supply us with information like this. He may be one of 200 people, but if you identify Michigan you identify between two or three individuals and it may burn the source.

We'd like to make it clear that we don't intend to do this kind of thing very often, since rumors about certain people being informants are very common in this business. But this is no rumor. This, friends, is solid fact—we would not have printed this story if we weren't able to substantiate the claims it makes, and we had no trouble at all doing that. Our intent in making this information known was not to screw up the FBI's fun (they're really not doing all that much out of the ordinary anyway), but rather to expose a very dangerous individual who goes by the name of Cable Pair (some say his real name is John Maxfield). This person has been posing as an extremely friendly hacker who lives in Detroit and is just bubbling over with technical information in exchange for your secrets. He claims to have been one of the nation's first phreaks, which may or may not be true. He gives out his telephone numbers freely, will do anything to communicate with somebody (like place conference calls from his own private PBX system, provided you give him YOUR phone number), and generally will use anything you say to him against you in the future. Our advice is simple: Stay the hell away from this person. Even if you haven't done anything wrong yourself, your life can still be made miserable by him if you're even suspected of having contact with wrongdoers.

This latest turn of events has saddened us—we thought Cable Pair would be a promising contributor to this publication and instead we learned a valuable lesson: Don't trust anybody. Have fun, Cable Pair. Enjoy yourself. Just don't expect to see any of us over at the Chestnut Tree Cafe with you. You're on your own now.

Seized! (August, 1985)

2600 Bulletin Board Is Implicated in Raid on Jersey Hackers

On July 12, 1985, law enforcement officials seized the Private Sector BBS, the official computer bulletin board of *2600* magazine, for "complicity in computer theft," under the newly passed, and yet untested, New Jersey Statute 2C: 20–25. Police had uncovered in April a credit carding ring operated around a Middlesex County electronic bulletin board, and from there investigated other North Jersey bulletin boards. Not understanding subject matter of the Private Sector BBS, police assumed that the Sysop was involved in illegal activities. Six other computers were also seized in this investigation, including those of Store Manager who ran a BBS of his own, Beowolf, Red Barchetta, the Vampire, NJ Hack Shack, Sysop of the NJ Hack Shack BBS, and that of the Sysop of the Treasure Chest BBS.

Immediately after this action, members of *2600* contacted the media, who were completely unaware of any of the raids. They began to bombard the Middlesex County Prosecutor's Office with questions and a press conference was announced for July 16. The system operator of the Private Sector BBS attempted to attend along with reporters from *2600*. They were effectively thrown off the premises. Threats were made to charge them with trespassing and other crimes. An officer who had at first received them civilly was threatened with the loss of his job if he didn't get them removed promptly.

Then the car was chased out of the parking lot. Perhaps prosecutor Alan Rockoff was afraid that the presence of some technically literate reporters would ruin the effect of his press release on the public. As it happens, he didn't need our help.

The next day the details of the press conference were reported to the public by the press. As Rockoff intended, paranoia about hackers ran rampant. Headlines got as ridiculous as hackers ordering tank parts by telephone from TRW and moving satellites with their home computers in order to make free phone calls. These and even more exotic stories were reported by otherwise respectable media sources. The news conference understandably made the front page of most of the major newspapers in the US, and was a major news item as far away as Australia and in the United Kingdom due to the sensationalism of the claims. We will try to explain why these claims may have been made in this issue.

On July 18, the operator of the Private Sector was formally charged with "computer conspiracy" under the above law, and released in the custody of his parents. The next day the American Civil Liberties Union took over his defense. The ACLU commented that it would be very hard for Rockoff to prove a conspiracy just "because the same information, construed by the prosecutor to be illegal, appears on two bulletin boards," especially as Rockoff admitted that "he did not believe any of the defendants knew each other." The ACLU believes that the system operator's rights were violated, as he was assumed to be involved in an illegal activity just because of other people under investigation who happened to have posted messages on his board.

In another statement, which seems to confirm Rockoff's belief in guilt by association, he announced the next day that "630 people were being investigated to determine if any used their computer equipment fraudulently." We believe this is only the user list of the NJ Hack Shack, so the actual list of those to be investigated may turn out to be almost five times that. The sheer overwhelming difficulty of this task may kill this investigation, especially as they find that many hackers simply leave false information. Computer hobbyists all across the country have already been called by the Bound Brook, New Jersey office of the FBI. They reported that the FBI agents used scare tactics in order to force confessions or to provoke them into turning in others. We would like to remind those who get called that there is nothing inherently wrong or illegal in calling *any* BBS, nor in talking about *any* activity. The FBI would not comment on the case as it is an "ongoing investigation" and in the hands of the local prosecutor. They will soon find that many on the Private Sector BBS's user list are data processing managers, telecommunications security people, and others who are interested in the subject matter of the BBS, hardly the underground community of computer criminals depicted at the news conference. The Private Sector BBS was a completely open BBS, and police and security people were even invited on in order to participate. The BBS was far from the "elite" type of underground telecom boards that Rockoff attempted to portray.

Within two days, Rockoff took back almost all of the statements he made at the news conference, as AT&T and the DOD discounted the claims he made. He was understandably unable to find real proof of Private Sector's alleged illegal activity, and was faced with having to return the computer equipment with nothing to show for his effort. Rockoff panicked, and on July 31, the system operator had a new charge against him, "wiring up his computer as a blue box." Apparently this was referring to his Novation Applecat modem, which is capable of generating any hertz tone over the phone line. By this stretch of imagination an Applecat could produce a 2600 hertz tone as well as the MF, which is necessary for "blue boxing." However, each and every other owner of an Applecat or any other modem that can generate its own tones therefore has also "wired up his computer as a blue box" by merely installing the modem. This charge is so ridiculous that Rockoff probably will never bother to press it. However, the wording of *wiring up the computer* gives Rockoff an excuse to continue to hold onto the computer longer in his futile search for illegal activity.

"We have requested that the prosecutors give us more specific information," said Arthur Miller, the lawyer for the Private Sector. "The charges are so vague that we can't really present a case at this point." Miller will appear in court on August 16 to obtain this information. He is also issuing demand for the return of the equipment and, if the prosecutors don't cooperate, will commence court proceedings against them. "They haven't been particularly cooperative," he said.

Rockoff probably will soon reconsider taking Private Sector's case to court, as he will have to admit he just didn't know what he was doing when he seized the BBS. The arrest warrant listed only "computer conspiracy" against Private Sector, which is much more difficult to prosecute than the multitude of charges against some of the other defendants, which include credit card fraud, toll fraud, the unauthorized entry into computers, and numerous others.

Both Rockoff and the ACLU mentioned the Supreme Court in their press releases, but he will assuredly take one of his stronger cases to test the new New Jersey computer crime law. By seizing the BBS just because of supposed activities discussed on it, Rockoff raises constitutional questions. Darrell Paster, a lawyer who centers much of his work on computer crime, says the New Jersey case is "just another example of local law enforcement getting on the bandwagon of crime that has come into vogue to prosecute, and they have proceeded with very little technical understanding, and in the process they have abused many people's constitutional rights. What we have developing is a mini witch hunt, which is analogous to some of the arrests at day care centers, where they sweep in and arrest everybody, ruin reputations, and then find that there is only one or two guilty parties." We feel that law enforcement, not understanding the information on the BBS, decided to strike first and ask questions later.

2600 magazine and the Sysops of the Private Sector BBS stand fully behind the system operator. As soon as the equipment is returned, the BBS will be back up. We ask all our readers to do their utmost to support us in our efforts, and to educate as many of the public as possible that a hacker is not a computer criminal. We are all convinced of our Sysop's innocence, and await Rockoff's dropping of the charges.

[NOTE: Readers will notice that our reporting of the events are quite different than those presented in the media and by the Middlesex County Prosecutor. We can only remind you that we are much closer to the events at hand than the media is, and that we are much more technologically literate than the Middlesex County Prosecutor's Office. The Middlesex Prosecutor has already taken back many of his statements, after his contentions were disproven by AT&T and the DOD. One problem is that the media and the police tend to treat the seven cases as one case, thus the charges against and activities of some of the hackers has been extended to all of the charged. We at *2600* can only speak about the case of Private Sector.]

The Threat to Us All (August, 1985)

We're very used to reporting on this kind of a story. We've done it so many times in our pages that we're tempted to gloss over "raid" stories because they've become so commonplace. But we realize that we cannot ever ignore such events, because we all need to know what is happening out there. It's really not a pretty sight.

Mention the word computer to someone and you'll see a variety of reactions. In our case it would be overwhelming enthusiasm, much like an explorer confronting a new adventure. But to many people, computers are evil and scary. This takes two forms: fear of the computers themselves, and complete ignorance as to what they and their operators are capable of doing. We saw plenty of the latter last month.

We don't care if people refuse to understand computers and how they fit in. What we do object to, however, is when these same people insist on being the ones to pass laws and define abuses concerning computers. In every investigation we have seen, ignorance abounds. True, such ignorance can be amusing—we all got a good laugh when we heard the New Jersey authorities insisting that the hackers were moving satellites "through the blue heavens." But losing the Private Sector isn't at all funny, and whether you were a caller to that bulletin board or not, its loss is a very troubling sign.

What was the Private Sector? Picture a sounding board of ideas, theories, and experiences and you'll have a good idea. The Private Sector was a place to ask questions, talk to experts, and learn a hell of a lot about high technology. It was *never* a place to trade illegal information, such as Sprint codes, credit card numbers, or computer passwords. The system operator took elaborate measures to ensure this, such as going through each and every message, public and private, on a daily basis to make sure nothing shady was transpiring. We don't believe he should have had to do even this. We can't condone censorship of any kind—our feelings were that if people wanted to do illegal things, then *they* would face the consequences, not the people who simply talked to them. But the Sysop had his own policy and he stuck by it and kept the board clean. He wanted two things: a good, interesting bulletin board and no trouble with authorities. At least he managed to obtain one of those goals.

Again we see ignorance and a disregard toward the rights of all of us. They came and took our board, whose only "crime" was being mentioned on another board that had been raided the month before. The Private Sector was completely innocent of any wrongdoing. Yet it is being held at this moment, without bail. See the connection to free speech yet? Many people have trouble seeing this because of that word computer. Yet a computer bulletin board is probably the purest form of free speech that exists today. Anyone can call, anyone can speak. True identity is not required. Why should this be considered a threat in a democracy?

We've been told there is legislation pending in the House of Representatives to "regulate" bulletin boards. What this would mean is a re-definition of BBS's into a sort of public utility. The system operator would have to take full responsibility for everything that was posted. (This means if he went away for a week and didn't censor messages, he could find himself facing charges when he came back!) The system operator would also be *required* to confirm the identities of all users and we wouldn't at all be surprised if part of this involves the paying of some sort of fee for a license. These sound very much like the kind of tactics used by repressive regimes to curb public assemblies and newspaper. Is this in fact what is happening? Aren't bulletin boards a form of public assembly, a kind of electronic publication?

Before all of the computer hobbyists out there start hating the "hackers" for ruining the future of bulletin boards, we'd like for them to view this whole affair as an important and inevitable test. True, some boards today are being used for sleazy things and criminals are involved. One could say the same thing about telephones or even cars. (Think of how much illegal information must be passed within the confines of some people's cars.) The fact is we cannot sacrifice a freedom simply because some bad people are using it.

We see this sort of test frequently. When police pull you over and ask all kinds of questions when you haven't done anything wrong, you probably wind up fairly annoyed. But when they say it's a way of catching drunk drivers—well, now that's different. A little bit of freedom isn't all that important when the public welfare is at stake. What rubbish! And what a perfect way to start eroding our rights as individuals.

We're glad that we were able to convince the American Civil Liberties Union to take the case, which is most likely their introduction to the issues that surround the use of computers. We've found good media like *The New York Times* that actually cares about what is said in their stories and attempts to find out what all the sides are. We've also seen sensationalism at its worst, such as WABC-TV, which took our comments out of context and made us seem like an anti-hacker establishment! Or *The New York Daily News* reporter who asked us after we said the system operator was "surprised" to see his computer taken, "Was he *shocked?*" Most of all, though, we're amazed at the response of hackers and non-hackers alike, who came to the defense of the Private Sector, offering services, equipment, advice. Our phones have been jammed—we've never seen anything like this. Everyone who called the Private Sector knows it was devoid of all the things it's being accused of having. The most important thing anyone can do at this point is to make sure *everyone* knows. The concept of a bulletin board must be understood. The value of the Private Sector must be known. The connection to publications and freedom of speech has to be established so that people understand the threat to *them* whenever a bulletin board is shut down. When we do this, we'll be that much closer to getting the Private Sector back online and making a positive precedent.

What Was Really Going On? (August, 1985)

[When the details of the Middlesex County Prosecutor's Office press conference hit the newspapers the next day, the ridiculous charges made many people knowledgeable about technology and computers very disgusted. Many simple and innocent bits of information had been twisted into "evidence" of illegal activities. With the aid of The Shadow, we have put together a guide to these misinterpretations in the hopes that everyone can see how this investigation has gotten completely out of control.]

One of the more sensationalist of the crimes of the hackers was, as Middlesex County Prosecutor Alan Rockoff said, "changing the positions of satellites up in the blue heavens" and causing communications satellites to "change positions" in order to make free phone calls "possibly disrupting intercontinental communications and making legitimate phone calls impossible." This story was twisted by the media to the extent of dire predictions of hackers causing satellites to crash into the Soviet Union, provoking a nuclear war, as heard on one Wednesday morning radio news program, and the "disruption of telex and telephone transmission between two continents." Very soon afterwards AT&T and Comsat denied that any attempts to re-route satellites had been made. In fact, an AT&T executive on the MacNeil-Lehrer Report stated that the computers that controlled the satellites weren't even connected with the phone lines and that the satellites were constantly monitored for movement, and none had ever been detected.

So how did this fallacy arise? Not having been on the other boards we can only assume that they may have contained information on making illegal international calls, giving the police the idea that there was international phreaking. Many long-distance companies use satellites to transmit their calls. The Private Sector BBS had much information on satellites, fitting in with its purpose as a telecommunications information source. One recurring topic was TASI (Time Assignment Speech Interpolation), a method of transmitting satellite conversations. TASI is only the packet switching of telephone conversations, where the conversation is converted into small packets and sent over satellite and many long-distance circuits effectively simultaneously along with many other conversations. TASI permits several conversations to be sent over one satellite circuit, thus permitting more conversations without sending up more satellites. It is comparable to talking about modem transmission methods. As far as we know there is *no* way to use TASI and similar information fraudulently, and certainly one cannot move satellites using this. Evidently Middlesex County law enforcement saw posted messages on the routing of calls *through* a satellite and jumped, due to paranoia, to the conclusion it was for the *moving* of the satellites.

Another of the more sensationalist charges that the youths had Department of Defense "secret telephone codes" that could enable them to penetrate the Pentagon. Due to the subject matter of the Private Sector BBS (telecommunications), AUTOVON, the DoD's private telephone network, was often brought up because it offers an extremely interesting network architecture quite different than civilian phone systems. Some AUTOVON phone numbers were on the board as examples of the format of the unique numbering plan. These numbers are easy to obtain and have appeared on other boards. These AUTOVON phone numbers can be obtained from a declassified DoD phone book available from the Government Printing Office for a small fee.

One of the more muddled of the charges was reported by media sources variously as hackers "ordering tank parts using stolen credit cards by computer from TRW," breaking into TRW computers for top secret information on tank parts, and other variations. It turns out that TRW does do some defense contracting, but it has nothing at all to do with tank parts, instead making automobile parts for various non-tank military vehicles. TRW does have a credit rating service accessible by computer, but this is in a completely separate division. Somehow the authorities and the press had mangled the different alleged crimes of credit card fraud and the breaking into of a defense contractor's computer system, which happened to have defense department information in it. Since TRW is in both credit ratings *and* defense contracting, it would be an obvious jump in illogic to have the hackers break into TRW computers and order tank parts by credit card.

And just why was the Private Sector discussing TRW in the first place? TRW's credit rating computers were discussed on the Private Sector much as TRW was discussed in *2600* (July 1984). Since people's private credit information is stored under shoddy security, it naturally came up in the discussion of computer security as a particularly bad instance. Such discussions weren't for the purpose of breaking into computer systems, but were conducted by various hackers (*not* computer criminals) and data processing managers who were interested in security methods and computer abuses.

Another possible source of confusion is the fact that many of the messages on the BBS's that were confiscated were written by people 13 years old or younger. People this age may brag and tell stories as young people sometimes do. We're sure that you can imagine a young person telling his friends how he blew up an AT&T computer or knocked a satellite out of orbit, much the same way he might brag about the speed of his father's new sports car. It would be quite irresponsible of authorities to issue the kid's father a ticket based on this just as it was irresponsible of them to announce to the press the list of computer crimes without verifying that actual crimes did occur. The authorities are still unsure what crimes, if any, actually took place.

When all these exotic charges are revealed to be mere flights of fancy, a great lack of knowledge about computers and telephony is uncovered on the part of law enforcement. We feel that law enforcement officials along with telecommunications hobbyists, should start to research the field by looking in their public library, or even better a local college library (under 621 Dewey Decimal). Several magazines also provide good information, such as *Telecom Digest, Communications Age*, as well as *2600* and other telecom industry publications.

With regards to the credit card part of this whole thing, here is a brief guide to how credit card numbers are used fraudulently.

First one obtains a complete credit card number including expiration date. If a driver's license number, social security number, or other information is also obtained, then it is easier to use the credit card number to charge goods and services. Credit and other information are usually found in the form of carbons (actual carbon paper that fits between the credit slip and the receipt) that are often discarded after their use. Carbons contain all of the information from a previous legitimate purchase. If someone is required to include their address or social security number with their credit card number then this will also appear on the carbon, which is found in the daily trash of many retail stores. One can then call up a company that takes charge requests over the phone and order goods using the credit card information that was found with the trash.

But the real hurdle to committing credit card fraud is to have the package delivered and for this one needs a mailing address. This can be obtained a few ways. One is to get a post office box under an assumed name, and another is to have it delivered to a place where it can be picked up before the package is noticed. By using stolen or false identification or by being convincing to a postal clerk, one can obtain a post office box. One can also ask for general post office delivery, where the post office will put your package on the racks behind the counter waiting for you to pick up. By finding a vacant or temporarily empty home one can also have the objects delivered there.

And this is how it is done from start to finish. There may be more effective ways to complete the various stages, but all in all it is that simple. This is mainly because companies make it easy to make a purchase while only supplying a small amount of personal information. Often if a company has been guaranteed that it will be covered for the value of fraudulently charged goods, then the company will make it easier for a person to charge them.

The problem of credit card fraud has a few simple cures: Make it harder to order objects by phone (companies can issue a code that must be verbally communicated in order to complete the purchase—one that *doesn't* appear on the carbon) or discontinue the use of carbons in credit card receipts. There are many other safeguards that can be used to decrease this type of fraud.

This section was not intended to be a guide in how to commit a crime, but an edification of how this crime is *not* committed. Credit card fraud is not high tech crime. No computer is involved or has to be involved; no illegal phone calls are involved; and it is not necessary to break into TRW or other credit bureaus to commit this crime.

Computers may be used as notepads or message boards where individuals might write down the information that they found in the trash. With regards to credit card fraud, computers are only used as a medium for communication. Credit card carbons are so easily found and the process of performing the actual illegal charge has been made so easy that it is not even necessary to discuss the topic with others to be able to commit the crime.

Because of the use of U.S. mail or post office boxes, the post office is involved in investigating this type of crime. The Secret Service was authorized last October to investigate credit card fraud. The FBI has a variety of reasons to investigate. There are already laws everywhere against credit card fraud, and there are already associated penalties. It is nothing new to law enforcement. In addition, much of all credit card fraud is committed by those who steal, manufacture, or find whole credit cards.

We hope that this thorough explanation will help to get rid of those inaccurate stories we've seen abounding. Again we'd like to clarify that law enforcement people should learn a bit about computers and telecommunications and above all try to control their enthusiasm.

We are, of course, only qualified to comment on the specific case of the Private Sector. We feel that Rockoff and his cohorts will have to search a long time for the "special codes that provided illegal access to the information at issue" on the Private Sector, as they just aren't there.

How Can Sysops Protect Themselves? (August, 1985)

A wave of anxiety is sweeping across the nation as BBS operators wonder if they'll be next, and BBS users worry about whether or not their names will show up in raided userlogs. As we've now seen, it makes no difference whether or not you're actually engaged in illegal activity. Any bulletin board anywhere could be next and there's not all that much that can be done to prevent it. Not until we get some laws passed to protect *us*.

In the meantime, however, there are a few suggestions we can pass along to either lessen the odds of a raid or to thwart the invaders before they manage to get into confidential material.

Obviously, if you have a bulletin board that frequently posts codes and passwords, you can almost expect to get visited, even if it's only being done in private mail. What's very important at this stage is the role the system operator is playing with regards to this information. If he/she is an active participant, there will most certainly be an attempt to make an example of them. It's similar to draft registration evaders who publicize their opposition—they are the ones that get prosecuted, not the ones who keep a low profile about it. By running a bulletin board, you are calling attention to yourself, so it stands to reason that you should keep your act clean.

Had this article been written before July 12, we would have advised Sysops to encourage people not to post credit card numbers, passwords, etc. in order not to get hassled. But this is no longer the case. With the Private Sector, authorities moved in *even though* the board was kept spanking clean of the above. So now, the only way we can guarantee that your board won't be snatched from you is if you unplug it and put it in a closet. Using a bulletin board for communication between two or more people can now be considered risky.

Assuming that you still want your board up, there are other precautionary measures. For one thing, the boards that ask the caller whether or not they work for law enforcement really are working against themselves. First off, do they honestly expect all law enforcement types to dutifully say yes and never call back when they're denied access? Do they really think that these people can't get their foot in the door even if it is an "elite" board? Even if there is nothing illegal on such a board, attention is drawn to it by such statements and it will become impossible to persuade the authorities that there simply isn't a higher access level. By the same token, Sysops that run a disclaimer with words to the effect of "the Sysop takes no responsibility for what is said on this board" are kidding themselves if they think this is going to save them from harassment. Those words *should* apply, naturally, but at the moment they don't seem to.

Whether or not you want to censor the messages on your system is up to you. Sometimes it helps to weed out undesirables and sometimes it's an intrusion into someone's privacy. We never liked the practice, although it was done regularly on the Private Sector. It's your board and you have the right to run it your way.

What really needs to be addressed at this point is the concept of protection. Yes, you have the right to protect yourself against thugs that come into your home, no matter who sent them. One way is by scrambled data. There are many scrambling programs around and some of them are quite good; even the NSA would have a time cracking the code. We feel that all userlogs should be scrambled, at the very least. (In some cases, a valid form of protection would be to keep no userlog at all.) System operators should try to figure out a way to scramble everything so that nothing is available to unauthorized parties. When raids become totally fruitless, maybe then they will stop. Of course, now there is the problem of being forced, under penalty of law, to unscramble everything. A vivid imagination can probably find a way around this as well.

The best method of protection is complete destruction of data. Some people hook up their computers so that if the wrong door is opened or a button isn't pressed, a magnet activates and wipes the disk clean. Bookies like to do this with their Apples. Similar systems can be rigged so that if a computer is unplugged, the first thing it does upon revival is a purge (not a directory purge, which comes with simply deleting file names—a complete reformatting of the disk, which erases *all* data). This means, though, that every power failure will have the same effect. It will take some time to make a good system of protection, but this is probably the most constructive project that BBS operators can engage in. It doesn't matter if you have "nothing to hide." The fact is you have everything to protect from intruding eyes. Because when they seize equipment they read everything without concern that the Sysop may be the caretaker of people's personal messages and writings.

We'd like to hear other methods of outsmarting these goons. It's not very hard. For instance, you could have a bulletin board dial-in at one location, which will then call-forward to the real location, or still another dummy location. Each of these requires another phone line, but you'll get plenty of warning, especially if a dummy computer is set up at one of the locations. And this is only the beginning.

We don't enjoy having to suggest these courses of action. We'd like very much to be able to get on with what we're supposed to be doing: discussing telecommunications and computers in our own way. Instead we have to pause again to defend our right to say these things. It's a necessary course of action and, if we hold our heads up, it will be a successful one.

Private Sector Returning (January, 1986)

Back Online Next Month but Many Questions Remain

The Private Sector bulletin board system (the official BBS of *2600* Magazine), seized by New Jersey authorities on July 12, 1985, is in the process of being returned. However, Tom Blich, the system operator, feels he is being forced to plead guilty to a token offense.

When the board was taken, the prosecutors seemed to have little idea as to what it was they were looking for. At a press conference the following week, they claimed that Blich and six others were moving satellites in space with their computers and doing strange things to the nation's defense department. Now, six months later, this, or anything else, has yet to be proven in Tom's case.

On December 6, Judge Mark Epstein gave Assistant Prosecutor Frank Graves one last month to find something in order to prove his conspiracy case, otherwise the case would be thrown out. Graves only came up with a blue box program that was originally discovered on the Private Sector's hard disk back in July. This program was consequently defined as a "burglary tool." "Cat's Meow," the program's title, can be used to generate blue box tones (MF tones), as well as regular touch tones, speech synthesis, and other sound effects. Middlesex County reportedly sent the program, along with Blich's whole computer system to Bell Labs to see if it could produce the nasty MF tones. "Cat's Meow," written by the Tempest, was approved by Bell Labs as a working blue box, as long as it was used with an Applecat modem. Blich said it was given to him by an associate along with other programs and that he found it entertaining because of the noises it made and educational in that it taught him a little bit about the phone network. He claims never to have used the program to make free phone calls or do anything of a fraudulent nature. The program was not accessible to anyone calling the bulletin board, either. According to the authorities, no illegal calls have ever been traced to Blich and there is no evidence of any illegal activity on his part. In New Jersey, though, under a particular statute, it is illegal to possess virtually *anything* that can be used to perpetrate fraud.

Blich was told that if he pleaded guilty to the fourth degree misdemeanor, which would carry no sentence, his equipment would be returned and all other charges against him would be dropped.

But none of this explains how various law enforcement departments could justify searching his home and seizing his equipment, especially if it was based on the possibility that Blich was undermining the security of the United States by disrupting international telecommunications and infiltrating the Defense Department, when absolutely nothing would point anyone with the intelligence of a stone to this conclusion. More specifically, Prosecutor Alan A. Rockoff stated that one charge was that the "young computerniks...threatened this nation's defense" by stealing information on military tank parts manufactured by a Connecticut defense contractor. Now, after no evidence is found, no complaintants are found, and Prosecutor Rockoff's outlandish headlines have worn away, Blich will be on probation for a year because he had a blue box program—and all this to cover up for some fool's overzealousness.

Will somebody please wake us up? Can this really be happening? Almost any computer is capable of producing "illegal" tones. Programs that produce such tones are commonplace, to say the least. Many people possess them just for the sake of seeing what they look like and how they work. Are New Jersey authorities now punishing people for being curious?

What if Blich himself had written this program? Are they now telling us it's illegal to *write* certain things, because they could potentially be used in a bad way? Clearly, there's something fundamentally wrong here.

It's easy to say that someone who has a blue box program is only going to use it for illegal activity. But it's simply not true and it's also a very dangerous assumption. If a program on disk can be construed as a burglary tool, then why did the prosecutor send Blich a printout of the four-page program? Isn't this distribution of a burglary tool?

And what of the programs that appear in the *Information Bureau* section of this issue? Possession of a gun is one thing, because there aren't all that many things you can do with a gun, unless you're a collector. (Of course, possessing a deadly weapon *is* legal, but we won't get into *that.*) With a computer program, however, there are an infinite number of possibilities. Someone could possess it for the sake of having an interesting program, so that they can learn how to make sound effects with their computer, so that they can hear what these magical tones actually sound like, and so on. Yes, there is the *possibility* somebody could use this program for illegal purposes. But it's really just as easy (in fact, much easier) to use a standard touch tone phone to commit fraud these days. How is possession of a touch tone phone any less of a crime than this program? They can both be used for legitimate purposes as well as illegitimate ones. It's not hard to retrace the logic that is used to argue this, but is this logic correct? Or is it potentially a danger to everyone, not just us?

We feel threatened by such actions. How hard would it be to conclude that this magazine itself is a burglary tool? Because we discuss how the various networks work and because we expose the inadequacies and weaknesses, are we not paving the way for criminals? Perhaps we are, but at the same time we're waking up an awful lot of people. People who realize that their secrets aren't safe in a particular computer or people who need to know how their phone system works—we exist for the purpose of education alone. We cannot be held accountable for the potential misbehavior of one of our subscribers—that is an unreasonable expectation.

Fortunately, we're not yet at a stage where such affronts can occur at a magazine. Why? Magazines are tangible, people generally understand them. You can't hold a computer bulletin board in front of you, though. Most people don't understand what a BBS is in the first place. It's so much easier to get away with something if most people don't understand what you're really doing—this is what the authorities have accomplished.

We've made some important progress in this case. We succeeded in getting the prosecutors to reveal their true knowledge of the matter in front of the entire world. And we convinced the American Civil Liberties Union to take up the case of the Private Sector. We expect them to be involved in similar cases in the future. Slowly but surely, we're getting through to people.

We hope to see this kind of thing stop once and for all. Too many innocent people have already been victimized by these little-publicized Gestapo tactics. Sensitive equipment has been damaged by careless law enforcement agents. Valuable time has been lost, voices have been silenced, and people's lives have been adversely affected. Please, folks, wake up those around you *now!* That's our brightest hope.

We apologize about having to devote yet another article to this distressing subject. Until we see some basic changes in attitude and evidence of real protection for all of us, we must continue to speak out. We hope you do the same, in whatever ways possible.

The good news is that at last the Private Sector is returning. At press time, the estimate for having the board up and running is sometime in February. (Extra time is needed to look for any damage and also to see if any "back doors" have been installed while we weren't looking.)

In the interim and as a supplement, *2600* will operate a limited access subscriber bulletin board from our New York office. All subscribers are welcome to call and participate in discussions with other readers on topics such as this. There will also be a facility for uploading articles to us, using XMODEM or ASCII transfer methods. This board will be run on an experimental basis and *only* between the hours of midnight and noon on Saturday and Sunday mornings (also known as Friday and Saturday nights), Eastern Time.

To get onto this board, call our office line between these times. Leave your subscriber code (those funny letters and numbers on the upper right of your mailing label) or your name as it appears on our mailing list, along with a first and last name of your choice and a random password. These will be installed in time for the next day of activity. Don't worry about personal information leaking out—we only need to see it once to verify that you're a subscriber and then it will be destroyed.

If you call that number at any other time, you'll either get a human or machine. If you reach the machine, leave a message so that we can pick up for real if we're within earshot, which is more often than you might think.

We're also planning to have meetings in various cities throughout 1986. If you think a particular city is well-suited for this, let us know and we will take it into account.

We have a lot of fine articles just waiting to be printed and we're always looking for more. Feel free to send us *anything* of interest.

Other Hacker-Related Raids

Sherwood Forest Shut Down by Secret Service (June, 1985)

An All Too Familiar Story

Yes, it's happened yet again. This time, two of the most prestigious computer hacker bulletin boards around, Sherwood Forest II and III, were raided by the government. The by now familiar scene of law enforcement types shutting down a bulletin board system because somebody didn't like what they'd been saying is no longer even newsworthy, judging from the complete lack of media coverage. That is probably the most worrisome ingredient here.

On this occasion, it wasn't the FBI that carried out the raids, but the Secret Service. Why? According to William Corbett in the Washington public affairs office, the Secret

Service became authorized to conduct these investigations after October 1984 under United States Codes 1030 (fraud by wire) and 1092 (credit card fraud). Because it's still an "active investigation," Corbett declined to give out any details on the case.

Bioc Agent 003, a co-sysop on Sherwood Forest II, claims that warnings were posted all over the board concerning the posting of credit card numbers. "The management didn't have enough time to constantly look after the system," he said. He attributes the raids to "schmucks that posted numbers anyway." He also believes that posted information on credit firms (CBI and TRW) led to the seizures.

The Summer Games of '87 (August, 1987)

We've seen this so many times before. Nationwide raids of computer equipment at teenagers' houses. Newspaper headlines about electronic gangsters. Long periods of silence from the investigators and the investigated.

First the facts: At least six homes across the country were raided by the Secret Service in mid-July. They were in Rockville, Maryland; Burlingame, California; Kentfield, California; two in Brooklyn, New York; and one in Bronxville, New York. (At the same time, a number of houses in Pittsburgh were being searched, supposedly for simple credit card fraud and reportedly unrelated to the action that we are concerned with.)

What were these people allegedly up to? Everyone seems to want a piece of this one. Los Alamos National Laboratories, Stanford University, TRW, US Sprint, AT&T, MCI, and local phone companies are the ones we've heard from so far.

Unfortunately, when something like this occurs and very little additional information is given out, imaginations tend to roam wild. Given the overall technological illiteracy of the media and law enforcement coupled with the almost hysterical paranoia of the phone phreaks and computer hackers, it soon becomes abundantly clear that nobody knows what the hell is going on.

That's what's most disturbing here. It's one thing to break into people's homes and go on a confiscating binge if you've got something to say when others ask why. To do otherwise is not too far from arresting someone and holding them without naming a specific crime. Having most of your possessions taken away from you is unsettling enough without having to wait to find out why.

We also have many questions concerning the methods used. A teenager was almost shot by the Secret Service when he reached for a shirt after having been woken up in his room.

Naturally, they assumed he was reaching for a gun—that's what hardened criminals are supposed to do, after all. A member of AT&T security found this out—from the Secret Service themselves. Apparently they thought it was funny.

The Secret Service knocked down at least two front doors with battering rams in their haste to get into these homes. In each case that we heard of, there was substantial damage, much more than what was necessary to get in. That was according to neighbors and eyewitnesses.

And in at least one other instance, the Secret Service disguised themselves as United Parcel Service employees. They had a truck, packages, even the standard UPS clipboard.

We've had other reports of agents who refused to identify themselves, didn't produce search warrants, or acted in a rude fashion.

What in the world is going on here? Are these atrocities to be tolerated? Is the Secret Service attempting to live up to their initials or are they just incredibly unaware of what they're really doing?

These were all teenagers who were involved in the raids. And while they may have been quite intelligent, they most certainly were not about to shoot at police or pose any kind of a threat. There was no need to "trick" them into opening the door. That kind of gimmick is appropriate for mobsters, perhaps, but not for adolescents.

We object to the methods used by the Secret Service. In fact, we question the very use of the Secret Service themselves. Why was a group such as this called in to deal with a matter that virtually any law enforcement entity could have handled?

Regardless of what comes out of this case (if one is ever even presented), the events that transpired are quite inexcusable. Unfortunately, most of those involved have been scared into silence. Scared by the strongarm tactics of the law, scared by the sensationalist media, scared by not knowing what the hell is going on. This is a very scary situation.

If such an occurrence should happen to you or anyone you know, this is what we suggest: Keep an eye on everything that is going on. Remember what is taken, what is handled, what is said. Write it all down when they leave. Do not, under any circumstance, give them an excuse to play rough. Law enforcement types can take lives and they can often get away with it. You don't have to answer any questions without a lawyer present. Get the names of everyone who comes into your house—you are most certainly entitled to know this. And if you do decide to talk to the media, avoid the sensationalist types like the *New York Post*. Go for the newspapers that put a little time into their stories and have been known to uncover things in the past. Make sure they understand what you're saying so there's no misunderstanding. Avoid local TV news—they're mostly after ratings.

Naturally, you should try not to let yourself get into a situation where such unpleasant things can happen to you. But sometimes that isn't enough. In 1985, the Private Sector, a bulletin board run by *2600*, was seized merely because its phone number had been mentioned on another bulletin board system that was being investigated. Clearly, these are precarious times.

On the subject of bulletin boards, we've made some important decisions in the last month. We are going to try and start up some boards as quickly as possible. Each of our boards will have public levels that are open to anyone who calls in. Verification of callers will not be required. Being anonymous is your right. Each caller will also be given a private mailbox, through which he can communicate with other individual callers. What goes on in the private mailboxes will only be seen by the sender and the receiver. The system operator won't even be able to access this information, at least not without resetting the account so the password no longer works. Passwords will also not be accessible by anyone other than the caller.

We feel this will uncloud the issue of what is legal and what is not. On the public levels, illegal information, such as credit card numbers and long-distance codes, won't be permitted and will be removed if spotted. Public levels will be accessible to everyone who calls. Private mail will remain private. It will be analogous to the mail we get from the post office. By making these distinctions, we think it will become much harder for bulletin boards to be "raided" because of supposedly illegal activities.

We've received some calls from folks interested in running bulletin boards. We now need software that can perform the above functions. If you have access to this, please contact us.

If you belong to a company or organization that agrees with what we're saying, you might want to donate or loan computer equipment for this purpose. We'll also be happy to run boards for anyone who wants to sponsor one, but has misgivings about doing it from their home. We have the means to save a little bit of freedom here. We cannot do this alone.

MILESTONE: IMPORTANT NEWS (December, 1987)

A number of circumstances have forced us to make some changes in the way *2600* is published. As of 1988, we will become a quarterly publication instead of a monthly publication.

We've been printing *2600* under the "new" format for a year now. And one thing we can't help but notice is that it's frightfully expensive. We adopted this format so that we could present longer articles and also become a little more visible. And we have succeeded in both of these ambitions. However, if we were to continue at this pace, we would run out of funds entirely. The $15 we charge for an individual subscription is actually less than what it costs to produce one issue for a year. This is why we charge more to those that can afford more, namely corporations and large organizations where the magazine is passed around to many people. And this is why we continue to sell back issues. By providing alternate sources of income, we are able to continue to keep the magazine going at a low cost.

MILESTONE: IMPORTANT NEWS *(continued)*

By raising the price to cover the costs of printing, mailing, and running an office, we could easily put the magazine out of the reach of most of our subscribers. We've seen publications smaller and less informative than ours with annual prices of more than $100! We don't want to take that road.

By reducing the amount of times we publish during the year (at the same time increasing the size of each issue slightly), we can keep the price down, keep ourselves out of financial problems, and hopefully give ourselves more time to make each issue mean a little more.

This brings us to the time factor. We put a great deal of time into putting out the magazine. But *2600* is more than just a magazine. We're constantly trying to educate the populace on the uses and abuses of technology. We're told that as a result of our campaign to abolish the touch tone fee in New York, a bill may be introduced in the state legislature proposing just that. Our growing bulletin board network will do much to ensure freedom of speech for all computer users. And, of course, we want to make sure that people see and hear about this magazine and our organization, either by getting maximum exposure in the media or by getting international distribution. At our current frenzied pace, we just don't have the time to adequately pursue these goals. At a more relaxed pace, we feel we'll be better able to put out a quality publication and make it more memorable overall.

Naturally, we don't expect everyone to agree with our conclusions. If you feel strongly negative about this change or about anything else, we'll certainly give you a refund for the balance of your subscription. We hope, though, that you'll stick it out at least to the first issue of our quarterly format to see if we live up to your expectations.

Our spring issue will be mailed on or around March 15, 1988. Subsequent mailing dates are scheduled for June 15, September 15, and December 15. Your expiration date will be adjusted in the following manner: January, February, and March will end with the spring issue; April, May, and June—summer; July, August, and September—fall; and October, November, and December—winter.

continues

MILESTONE: IMPORTANT NEWS *(continued)*

A number of subscribers have complained about their issues arriving late or sometimes not at all. It appears we must become militant in convincing the post office to do their job. If you do not get an issue within a week of when we send it out, you should call us and call your post office. Usually it is the post office on the receiving end that is at fault.

As always, we welcome your feedback on what we're doing. We hope this change results in a better publication and a stronger *2600*.

Hackers in Jail (Spring, 1989)

Story Number One

By now we've probably all heard about Kevin Mitnick. Late last year, this computer hacker was arrested after being turned in by his friend, who explained it all by saying, "You're a menace to society."

Mitnick has been described in the media as 25, an overweight, bespectacled computer junkie known as a "dark side" hacker for his willingness to use the computer as a weapon. His high school computer hobby was said to have turned into a lasting obsession.

He allegedly used computers at schools and businesses to break into Defense Department computer systems, sabotage business computers, and electronically harass anyone—including a probation officer and FBI agents—who got in his way.

He also learned how to disrupt telephone company operations and disconnected the phones of Hollywood celebrities such as Kristy McNichol, authorities said.

Over the past few months, several federal court judges have refused at separate hearings to set bail for Mitnick, contending there would be no way to protect society from him if he were freed.

Mitnick's family and attorney said prosecutors have no evidence for the accusations and that they are blowing the case out of proportion, either out of fear or misunderstanding of the technology.

Mitnick has an amazing history, to say the least. He and a friend logged into a North American Air Defense Command computer in Colorado Springs in 1979. The friend said they did not interfere with any defense operation. "We just got in, looked around, and got out."

Computer security investigators said that as a teenager Mr. Mitnick belonged to a shadowy Southern California group of computer enthusiasts, the Roscoe Gang, who met in a pizza parlor in the Los Angeles area. The group also stayed in contact through a variety of computer bulletin board systems, including one, 8BBS Santa Clara, California, run by employees of Digital.

In 1981 Mr. Mitnick and three other group members were arrested on charges of stealing technical manuals from the Pacific Telephone Company. Mr. Mitnick was convicted and served six months in a youth detention center.

He was caught again by University of Southern California officials in 1983 trying to break into the school's computers. In another incident, Mr. Mitnick fled to Israel to avoid prosecution after being accused of tampering with a computer storing credit information at TRW.

In December, 1987, he was convicted of stealing software from Microport Systems in Santa Cruz, and was sentenced to 36 months of probation.

What made Mitnick "the best," according to a friend, was his ability to talk people into giving him privileged information. He would call an official with a company he wanted to penetrate and say he was in the maintenance department and needed a computer password. He was so convincing that they would give him the necessary names or numbers.

Mr. Mitnick was supposedly able to avoid being apprehended by tampering with telephone company switching equipment to mask his location. An internal memo of the Pacific Telephone Company indicated that Mitnick had compromised all of that company's switching systems.

Investigators believe that Mitnick may have been the instigator of a false report released by a news service in April 1988 that Security Pacific National Bank lost $400 million in the first quarter of 1988. The report, which was released to the NY Stock Exchange and other wire services, was distributed four days after Mitnick had been turned down for a job at Security Pacific.

The false information could have caused huge losses for the bank had it reached investors, but the hoax was uncovered before that could happen.

The prosecutor said Mitnick also penetrated an NSA computer and obtained telephone billing data for the agency and several of its employees.

As of this writing, Mitnick has been sentenced to a year in jail. They won't even let him use the phone, out of fear of what he might do.

Story Number Two

An 18-year-old telephone phreak from Chicago who electronically broke into U.S. military computers and AT&T computers and copied 55 programs was sentenced to nine months in prison on Tuesday, February 14, in Federal District Court.

Herbert Zinn, Jr. was found guilty of violating the Computer Fraud and Abuse Act of 1986 by Judge Paul E. Plunkett. In addition to a prison term, Zinn must pay a $10,000 fine and serve two and a half years of federal probation when released from prison.

United States Attorney Anton R. Valukas said, "The Zinn case will serve to demonstrate the direction we are going to go with these cases in the future. Our intention is to prosecute aggressively. What we undertook is to address the problem of unauthorized computer intrusion, an all-too-common problem that is difficult to uncover and difficult to prosecute..."

Zinn, a dropout from Mather High School in Chicago, was 16 at the time he committed the intrusions, using his home computer and modem. Using the handle "Shadow Hawk," Zinn broke into a Bell Labs computer in Naperville, Illinois, an AT&T computer in Burlington, North Carolina, and an AT&T computer at Robbins Air Force Base in Georgia. No classified material was obtained, but the government views as "highly sensitive" the programs copied from a computer used by NATO, which is tied into the U.S. missile command. In addition, Zinn gained access to a computer at an IBM facility in Rye, New York, and logged into computers of Illinois Bell Telephone Company and the Rochester Telephone Company.

Assistant United States Attorney William Cook said that Zinn obtained access to the AT&T/Illinois Bell computers from computer bulletin board systems, which he described as "...just high-tech street gangs." During his bench trial in January, Zinn spoke in his own defense, saying that he copied the programs to educate himself and not to sell them or share them with other phreaks. The programs copied included very complex software relating to computer design and artificial intelligence. Also copied was software used by the BOC's (Bell Operating Companies) for billing and accounting on long-distance telephone calls.

The authorities didn't find it difficult to identify Zinn. But rather than move immediately, they decided to give him enough time to make their case stronger. For over two months, all calls from his telephone were carefully audited. His activities on computers throughout the United States were noted, and logs were kept. Security representatives from Sprint made available notes from their investigation of his calls on their network. Finally, the "big day" arrived, and the Zinn residence was raided by FBI agents, AT&T security representatives, and Chicago police detectives. At the time of the raid, three computers, various modems, and other computer peripheral devices were confiscated.

As of this writing, Zinn is still in jail.

Conclusions

This is without a doubt one of the most disturbing articles we've printed since we began publishing in 1984. When people actually start winding up in jail because of playing with computers, it's time to start asking some very serious questions.

Let's start with the Mitnick story. Here we have what appears to be a malicious person who is determined to get those who have crossed him. OK, not very nice. In fact, this could well be a nasty, vindictive human being. And we've already proven that he has a history of trouble with the law. But is this enough to lock him up without bail?

In regular life in almost any democratic society, the answer would be a resounding no. But there are special circumstances here: computers. Doing nasty things with computers has become infinitely worse than doing nasty things without computers. That's why a murderer would get bail so much easier than Kevin Mitnick. Because of computers.

So let's try and pretend that computers don't really exist. Where does that leave us? He would have to have disconnected Kristy McNichol's phone using wire clippers. Vandalism, maybe trespassing. That's good for a fine of maybe $100.

He and a friend walked into the North American Air Defense Command Center one day. They didn't break anything and they soon left. Had they been caught, they would have been thrown off the grounds, maybe arrested for trespassing and held overnight. The person who left the door open would be fired.

Mitnick managed to manipulate central office switches by walking through their doors and adjusting them. Nobody questioned him or tried to stop him. He called up a news service and told them a fake story about a bank, which they almost printed. Again, nobody questioned him.

In our society, such a person would be classified as a mischief maker, at worst a real pain in the ass. Such people currently exist all over the place. But because Mitnick used computers to perform his mischief, he's another John Hinckley.

Society is indeed endangered by what's happening here. But Mitnick has nothing at all to do with it. He is simply demonstrating how vulnerable our information and our way of life has become. If one person can cause such chaos, then clearly the system is falling apart at the seams.

The Zinn case is equally deplorable. A bright kid is languishing in prison because he didn't know when to stop exploring. The authorities admit they did nothing to stop him so that he would get himself in deeper. What would have been wrong with a simple warning? It might have been enough to stop him from logging into any more systems. There would have been no trial and an intelligent 18-year-old would not be locked away.

All of the papers accused Zinn of stealing software. But nothing was taken. All he did was *copy* some programs. If these programs were so valuable, why in hell was he able to download them over the phone lines? To even suggest that this is the same as stealing is a gross distortion. There is not one shred of evidence that this kid meant to sell these programs or benefit in any way except his own knowledge. This isn't surprising—most hackers are primarily interested in learning.

But they say a message had to be sent to stop this kind of thing from happening. The message here is that our nation's brightest kids are being imprisoned for being a little too inquisitive. And that's a frightening thought.

Judges should consider what actually took place and forget about the fact that computers were involved. Would it even be a crime if computers weren't involved? And what about intent? Did the person willfully do something that could be detrimental to an organization? Or was that simply a side-effect of the organization's carelessness?

Much can be learned from what the hackers uncover. While hackers are far from being knights in shining armor, the notion of their being criminals is so far from the truth that it's almost funny. These are kids doing what kids have done for all time. The only difference here is that they've learned how to use a tool that the rest of us have ignored. And unless more of us know how to use this tool, there will be many more abuses. Not just abuses *of* the tool. Abuses *by* the tool. That's where the real danger is.

We take a very hard line on this. Hacking is not wrong. Hacking is healthy. Hacking is *not* the same as stealing. Hacking uncovers design flaws and security deficiencies. Above all else, hacking proves that the ingenuity of a single mind is still the most powerful tool of all.

We are hackers. We always will be. Our spirits will not be crushed by these horrible happenings. Call us co-conspirators, fellow anarchists, whatever you want. We intend to keep learning. To suppress this desire is contrary to everything that is human.

Like the authors who rose to defend Salman Rushdie from the long arm of hysteria, we must rise to defend those endangered by the hacker witch hunts. After all, they can't lock us all up. And unless they do, hacking is here to stay.

7 The Hacker Philosophy

One thing that has to be said about *2600* is that we've always had a rather unique perspective on the world. It doesn't matter if you love us or hate us. There just isn't anyone else out there standing up for the things we believe in—at least, not in the way that we do it.

I've often wondered exactly why that is. It could be that we're just so out of touch with reality that our viewpoints and values are simply flat-out wrong. I know a lot of people are convinced of this and always have been. It could also be that the subject matter is so complex and intimidating to most of the public that nobody else has been compelled to come forward and speak out on something, which they may not fully understand in the first place. There's also the whole propaganda angle—you know, people are sheep following the mass media, we're the voice of the enlightened few, etc., etc. Or the old standby: Maybe nobody really cares what hackers say and think.

Whatever. It doesn't really matter to me *why* we've been on our own in the publishing world from the beginning. What I get out of all this is that we're a voice that is *needed*. That rings true with the massive amounts of feedback we've gotten over the years. When an opinion or a statement evokes such a strong reaction, there's a pretty good chance it's fulfilling a need. History will be the judge as to whether or not that was a good thing.

Looking at the various philosophies we've espoused over the years has proven to be a fascinating history lesson in itself. In our first few years, we tried to share that hacker perspective with the world and met with varying degrees of success. Some people got it right away and others treated us like the second coming of Satan. The important thing is we got their attention and helped to make this whole thing of ours into a conversation piece.

Some of what you'll see here is incredibly dated with references to Reagan, the Soviets, and a BBS culture that has long since faded into obscurity. But I think that makes the whole thing even more relevant. What we believed in, what we stood up for, what we fought against—it transcended the political scene, global events, the technology of the day. We talked about freedom: freedom to explore, to be an individual, to spread information through whatever means were available. And all of that carries on to the present day and will continue into the indefinite future. It's part of who we are, not as hackers but as humans.

Our first opinion pieces were filled with early warnings about such things as surveillance and increased FBI attention to anyone who may have at one time associated with anyone suspicious. I can only wonder what our reaction would have been if we knew then what the world would be like in the 21st century. From a technological view we would of course have been thrilled with all of the advances. But I doubt we would be too overjoyed to see how we've become infatuated with the idea of monitoring each other for suspicious behavior or how we are subjected to all manner of searches or scans when entering everything from offices to schools or how lie detectors and drug tests have become a routine part of so many employment opportunities. This all didn't happen overnight. Such changes need time to develop and take root in a society. I think we saw the warning signs right from the start.

Of course one thing has remained constant throughout: the demonization of hackers by the mass media and government. The fear and suspicion that people were met with when they demonstrated more knowledge of technology than those who were allowed to use it was what convinced us that we were really on to something. It's fascinating to practically see the battle lines being drawn as the various camps started to form.

Back then, mostly everyone in the hacker community knew about the various cases going on, from the 414s to Telemail to the Private Sector. The particular details of those cases aren't important here. Rather, an understanding of the mood of the day is what matters. And that mood was one of anticipation coupled with a degree of fear. We all knew we were on the threshold of some amazing developments that could even alter the future of mankind if we let our imaginations run free for a while. But we also knew that those who wanted us put out of their misery were people with a lot of power. The future could have gone a number of different ways.

One of the really interesting pieces here deals with the self-reflection that inevitably came when someone found themselves at the center of an investigation for doing something unauthorized with a computer. In addition, you get to see how those around such a person dealt with the situation. There's something inspiring here and also something incredibly sad as you realize how many inquisitive minds may have been quashed for no good reason.

There's also a rather controversial bit in here where a writer took a more sensationalist approach to what hackers were all about, invoking such fables as strict organization in the hacker ranks, actual *trials* of people who offended them, and a notion of such unmitigated power amongst us that anyone in their right mind would have no choice but to be mortally afraid of us. It was such nonsense that we felt compelled to preface the piece with our own disassociation from it. We naturally got a ton of responses, one of which we've also included here. Ironically, in dispelling the myth of hackers being super organized, this piece put forth the opinion that most hackers had a very limited amount of intelligence to begin with. This spawned still more outraged responses. Such was the hacker world of the 1980s.

The section ends with tributes to Abbie Hoffman and one of our own writers, both of whom passed well before their time.

The Constitution of a Hacker (March, 1984)

With every generation of humans, there are certain types of individuals that emerge. There are (always have been and always will be) leaders, followers, general nuisances, etc. And then there are folks who like to play with things and figure out how they work.

Before technology came along, there really wasn't all that much for these people to play around with. And certainly there was no way for them to pool their resources except through face-to-face communications.

With telephones, of course, all aspects of human life changed. Here was a toy that *anyone* could play with and get virtually unlimited results. But of course, most people didn't (and don't) see it that way—phones are phones and nothing more. You're not supposed to have fun with them. Yet, certain adventuresome types insisted on having fun with their phones anyway. They did all kinds of things they weren't supposed to do, like figure out the way phones work and interconnect. For the first time, these technological enthusiasts posed a "threat" to technology by reaching out and touching it rather than simply using it without asking any questions.

Today there are lots of people still having fun with their phones and making all kinds of technological advancements of their own. But the real focus at the moment is on the newest "threat," people who like to experiment and have fun with computers. Not the kind of fun they're *supposed* to be having with Pacman and Mr. Do, but *unauthorized* fun with other people's computers.

Why do they do this? What do these people possibly have to gain by breaking into computer systems and seeing things that don't really concern them or that is of no possible use to them? In the great majority of cases, computer hackers don't gain anything material or financial from their exploration. Add to that the high risk of getting caught and it becomes very hard for the average citizen to understand what motivates these people.

Many computer hobbyists, in fact, are resentful of hackers, considering them immature and troublesome. Quite a few computer bulletin boards prohibit certain topics from being discussed, and when they do, hacking is almost always one of them. There is some justification behind this, since the image of all computer users can be adversely affected by what the hackers do.

There are also the legal people who insist on telling everyone that breaking into a computer by phone is just like physically breaking into a home or office. Fortunately, that logic seems to be shared by very few people.

In spite of all of the threats and criticism, though, the hackers are not "cleaning up their act." And public opinion, particularly among the young, seems to be in their favor, mostly as a result of media coverage.

There's even a weekly TV program about hackers called *The Whiz Kids*. Each week, this group of amazing kids has a new adventure. The scripts are a bit moronic but interesting nonetheless. In one episode, the kids (only one of which is a true hacker) find out about an evil person who happens to be stealing Social Security checks. (They discover this by casually logging into his bank account.) To teach him a lesson, they break into another computer and enter his name as being deceased. In each program, these kids break into at least one new computer. But do they ever get into trouble? Of course not. First of all, they're only children. And second, they're entering these computers for good reasons, even if they are unauthorized.

Now what kind of message is this program conveying? Apparently, it's OK to invade other people's privacy if your intentions are ultimately "good." It sounds like something Reagan would get a kick out of.

A genuine hacker breaks into computers for the challenge. He's not out to save the world or to destroy it. He is not out to make a profit out of what he's doing. Therefore, it's not fair to categorize him as a criminal and it's just as wrong to say he's some sort of a savior.

Technological enthusiasts operate with the same motivation that a good mountain climber has. Regardless of what may happen to him, a computer hacker will *always* be interested in playing with computers. It's in his nature. And any laws that are created to "eliminate" hacking simply won't work because of these facts. There will always be people who want to experiment with things and this urge cannot be stifled. Did hacking come to a grinding halt because of the "414" scandal? Or because of the Telemail raids? No. Judging from the proliferation of computer bulletin boards where hacking *is* discussed, it's getting bigger than ever.

The realistic way for the owners of large computer systems to look at this is to regard hackers as *necessary security checks*. That's right. Necessary because if the hackers weren't the ones to break in, who would be? Let's assume that hackers had never even tried to break into the Memorial Sloan-Kettering Cancer Center computer. Someone else would have, because the system was practically wide open. And maybe they would have had a *reason* to get into the system—to do various nasty things. But now, because of what the hackers did, the Sloan-Kettering system is more secure.

One could almost say that a person with hacking abilities has an *obligation* to try and get into as many different systems as he can. Let's get nationalistic for a moment. If you have the number for a top secret government computer in Ft. George G. Meade, MD, odds are that the Albanians have it also. Now, would it be better for them to break into the system and find out all kinds of nice things or for you to break in and be discovered, forcing the system to become more protected? And, if you do break in, don't you deserve a note of thanks for waking them up?

Keep in mind, though, that a computer hacker is under *no* obligation to turn himself in or warn operators that their system is easily penetrable. It's the job of the Sysops to notice when their computers are being tampered with and if they don't detect you, then that's a second security lapse for them.

This is a pragmatic view, however shocking it may seem. In closing, we should point out to the hackers themselves that there is no need to worry or fret if their methods or secrets are eventually discovered. This is only the beginning. Our world is turning into a technological playground.

"Look Out, He's Got a Computer!" (July, 1984)

Fear of computers is one thing. Almost everyone has experienced this to some extent, though some of course are able to handle it far better than others. But *misunderstanding* of computers is a great deal more damaging and far less recognized among the mainstream.

What's the difference? The two are definitely related, there's no denying that. But they are far from identical. One of the most outstanding differences lies in the fact that people who claim to be "afraid" of computers (whether it's because of their efficiency, rapid growth, or whatever) tend to keep away from the things. But people who misunderstand computers are the ones who are running and regulating them.

Last month it was reported that Tom Tcimpidis, who operates a computer bulletin-board system from his home in the Los Angeles area, had his equipment seized by the Los Angeles Police Department. Why? Somebody somewhere had called up his system and left an AT&T credit card number posted. Pacific Telephone found out and decided to flex its muscles. Officials involved in the case insist that the system operator be held responsible but it's impossible to ascertain *why*. The man who approved the search warrant, Superior Court Judge Robert Fratianne, was quoted in *Info World* as saying, "As far as I can see, for someone to commit a computer crime, they have to have the knowledge, the equipment, and the access to an illegal [bulletin] board." Does anyone know what he's talking about? What in the world is an *illegal* board? What kind of equipment is he talking about? The only equipment here is a home computer! In another article, one of the officials claims that he knows all about this kind of thing, because he saw *War Games*, the film where a kid tries to start a nuclear war. Perhaps he didn't see the same film as the rest of the world, but in any event, seeing *War Games*, whether you understand it or not, doesn't make you an automatic expert on anything having to do with computers! This is what is known as aggressive ignorance.

Another fun thing that happened last month was the TRW escapade. The nation was shocked to find out that the TRW computer, which houses credit information on a *large* number of people, *might* have been broken into. Nobody knew what had even happened! Did someone raid the system and destroy or change info? Did the feds bust another BBS for posting "illegal" info? Were real criminals involved this time? Did a large bill get sent to an innocent corporation? According to all of the articles that have been written, not one of the above happened, but they all *could* have happened. So where is the story?! Are they saying that the worst thing that happened here was the posting of this nifty information somewhere? Well, that's not even interesting since any employee that uses the system could tell someone else about it at any moment.

Again, what we are seeing here is a failure to appreciate the full implications of such a thing. There is a story in this whole TRW thing. But it's not in the possibility that some hacker somewhere figured out a password. The story lies in the existence of the TRW database itself. Why was this completely downplayed? Because an article about kids breaking into a computer makes for good, sensationalist reading. It doesn't matter if most of the information is totally wrong; the people will read it. Nobody wants to read about how we're losing whatever freedom we have left, not to a machine, but to the people running the machine. It's depressing to hear about your entire life story being written to disk somewhere and to know that there's not a thing you can do about it. But, like it or not, this is *exactly* what's happening.

It's quite possible that TRW has a file on you that can be checked and appended by people all over the place. It's also entirely possible that some of that information is wrong. And it's a fact that TRW itself claims no responsibility for the accuracy of this info. But even if all of the information *is* right, how do you feel about being categorized?

On the back pages of our issue this month, we've devoted some space to the way TRW operates and the information that can be found. We didn't print this so that everybody could figure out a way to break into their system, although we'll certainly be accused of this by our critics. We're publishing these facts so that as many people as possible can become aware of the wide availability of increasingly personal tidbits and how this can affect us for the rest of our lives. We're doing this so that people can realize how easy it is for items to be altered and for assumptions to be made by people reading this data. Look at the sample printout and see if its thoroughness surprises you. Try to imagine how thorough it could become in 10 years with improvements in technology and continued erosions of personal freedom. The FBI recently came very close to expanding its files on criminals. They wanted to include "known associates of criminals." Next would have come "known associates of known associates," etc. They lost the battle for the moment, but you can count on seeing another drive for this increased surveillance real soon.

What many are not realizing is that this constitutes true "misuse" of computers. What kind of a society are we heading toward that wants to keep close personal data on *everybody*? Regardless of whether or not one is on the right side of the law, nobody wants everything about them to be known. We all have our secrets and more systems like TRW will make those secrets increasingly hard to keep. But according to today's papers, the biggest problem with computers is the hackers.

People who do little more than type some numbers onto a terminal and do a little bit of thinking are referred to alternately as computer geniuses and computer bandits by the media. And nearly every story written about such things is full of astronomical lapses, misinformation, corporate sympathy, and the obligatory Donn Parker quotes. *The Washington Post* recently did a three-part story on "computer crime," which said absolutely nothing new. It could have been manufactured by a computer program!

Meanwhile, legislators are tripping over themselves trying to get laws passed to *control* these computer people before they take over the world. The intensity with which the FBI has chased hackers in the past year or so indicates the power they think those with computers either have or are capable of achieving. And most of this fuss is being made over people simply *accessing* other systems. What in the world is going to be the reaction when people finally start to *use* the computers, to calculate and design?

A new bill has been proposed to outlaw computer crime. Isn't that wonderful? Do you know what they consider a computer crime? Personal use of a computer in the workplace. This means that if an office worker were to open a file and write a note to himself reminding him to stop at the store later on, he'd be committing a felony. Plans are also in the works for bills that would add penalties to crimes that were committed with the help of computers. In other words, stealing is stealing, but stealing with a computer is stealing and a half.

The hysteria continues. The United States government is doing everything in its power to prevent the Soviets from obtaining computers that are practically a dime a dozen here. What good could this possibly achieve in the long run? And why pick on the computer? It's not a weapon in itself, but merely a tool. A *vital* tool, yes, but still a tool.

It's clear that computer people are in for an era of harassment from the authorities, who haven't been this riled up since Prohibition. And everyone else will be getting it from the computer abusers, who insist on tracking everything that moves. We can survive by staying awake. But we'd better start working on it.

Getting Caught: Hacker's View (October, 1984)

Deep down, every hacker wants to get caught. Computer hacking isn't really the same as killing or stealing, after all. You need at least a *little* brains to be able to hop around on the corporations' DEC systems or to know the ARPANET better than your own PC. So if and when you get caught, you wind up getting a little bit of credit for having some brains. Most people exaggerate and call you a genius! Who can resist *this* type of an ego boost?

So when the FBI came knocking at my door early this spring, it seemed like the beginning of an adventure. It was *me* they were after! I had done something to deserve national attention!!

At first I didn't know what it was they wanted. They came to my house before I was awake and showed my mother the search warrant. I'll never forget the tone in her voice when she called me that day. "You'd better come down here right away," she said, sounding very worried and pissed off at the same time. I knew something was up when I heard that.

So then I came downstairs and saw what was happening. I was very calm throughout the whole thing—I even kept my sense of humor. After I figured out which of my many "projects" they were interested in, I showed them where all the good stuff was hidden. "Go tell the world," I said.

I had been hacking for about a year. I seemed to pick up things incredibly fast and before I knew it, I was buried inside the weird world of phones and computers. In this case, I had been running a huge corporation's mainframe for them for a few months. This computer had so much data in it that I could find out (and change) just about anything: paychecks, profit margins, telephone numbers, you name it. I had lots of fun.

My friends used to come over late at night and watch me explore. Nobody they knew had ever been able to do anything like that and it seemed pretty amazing. Then *War Games* came out and I turned into a sort of cult figure in my neighborhood. But it was OK—nobody knew *exactly* what I was doing.

Even my parents didn't seem to mind that much. They'd shake their heads and wonder what kind of mischief I'd get into next. Most people (grown-ups, that is) seemed to act exactly the same. And my friends were all into it as something fun and rebellious.

So now that I was caught, I expected the fun to continue. My parents would be outraged that a mischievous kid was being hounded by the feds while murderers and presidents were roaming free. And of course, my friends would stick by me more than ever. We were pretty tight.

For about a day, that's exactly what happened. My name got in all the papers, I was on a few news shows, and nobody really understood anything. I suddenly became popular at school. Everybody seemed to agree that it wasn't fair for them to come to my house and take away my two computers just like that.

Then, after the initial shock, people's moods started to change. My parents were the first. They suddenly got mad at me. "What a stupid thing to do!" I remember those words. "If you don't care about yourself, at least think about what you're doing to your family," and so on. They also said that I never listened when they told me to knock it off, which was totally false, since they never really seemed to care at all.

But all that didn't upset me. After all, parents are supposed to say those kinds of things. I knew they really cared, so it didn't matter what they said.

It wasn't until a few more weeks that the really bad stuff started happening. The feds began calling my friends and tried to scare them into saying incriminating things about me. They told them they'd be in just as much trouble if they didn't say anything. I could tell something was wrong when all of a sudden no one was talking to me. People I used to hang out with suddenly seemed uneasy when I was around.

Then the feds started calling *me*. And I could tell from the pointed questions they were asking, that someone I trusted had told them a lot. Much more than they had to. It wasn't like they had just cracked and said, yes, he did this and that. They *volunteered* information!

I tried to figure out why someone would do this—no one I knew had any grudges against me. I didn't really have any enemies. They must have thought that telling everything was for my own good. The feds had probably told them that I was really sick and needed help and that only the truth would set me free. Could that have been it?

It might have been. But there was definitely more than that. When the feds started scaring my friends, that was my fault. At least it seemed that way to my friends. A couple of them got so scared that their families hired these big, expensive lawyers. And that was my fault, too, even though I knew they were being ripped off.

So what did I get out of the whole thing? Well, nobody trusts me anymore—people are even afraid to let me use their phone. I've gotten a reputation as someone who doesn't care at all about his friends, otherwise how could I have put them in such a spot? Everyone in town knows that I did something bad to some corporation somewhere, but nobody understands how much of a game the whole thing seemed at the time. The newspapers were never really interested in my side and nobody else seems to be either.

Maybe this is good in a way, because I found out that most people value friendship less than their own safety. As soon as the pressure is applied, they lose all feeling for you. Then they trick themselves into believing that you were always a bad seed from the start. They do this so they won't feel guilty about the way they shafted you. But there were a couple of others who didn't desert me because they knew who I really was. If it wasn't for them, I might have just jumped off a building one night. That's how bad it makes you feel sometimes.

Yes, I'm through hacking. Let the professionals do it—they can't get hurt like I was.

Name withheld by request.

A Time for Reflection (December, 1984)

1984 will not go down in history as the year of the phone phreak or computer hacker. Instead it will most likely be labeled something dumb like the year of the communications revolution or the PC bonanza. That's not surprising at all; those are precisely the things that *appeared* to have occurred this year. But we know better.

The true communications revolution has been going on for quite some time. Many years ago, the first telephone enthusiasts started using their phones to do a little more than just call people they knew. They began to experiment. They sent strange tones down the line, activated distant machines, and traded information among themselves. Not only that, but they took it upon themselves to learn all about the infrastructure of the biggest company on earth, Ma Bell. Now almost everyone knows something about the way the giant phone company used to work and the way the near-giants work today. All you hear now is talk of long-distance services and how great each one is. All you see advertised everywhere are telephones, as if they'd just been invented, which, in a way, they have been—for the average person. Others, though, have been participating in this "revolution" for quite some time.

A similar story holds true for computers. The field is exploding now on Madison Avenue. But all of this talk of floppies, K, megabytes, and Control+C's is old news to hackers (both the programming and the cracking kind). As a rule, they've been into this kind of thing for years.

So what are we saying here? Two things, really. Looking at the past, it's pretty clear that those "mischief-makers" weren't only interested in causing chaos and perpetrating fraud, but also in being among the first to try their hand at the new technology, without being hovered over and told what not to do. Our other point lies with the future. Those phone phreaks and computer hackers of today may still be in a position to shine the light in front of the masses. We had at least one example of that in 1984, when hackers uncovered the wealth of information that is stored in the TRW computers—personal information about almost everyone that can be looked at by almost anyone. A glance at this year's pages of *2600* reveals a disturbing number of Owellian touches in the works—cameras surveying streets for possible crimes, vastly expanded FBI files on innocent people, neat categorization of human beings. Technological enthusiasts aren't the only kind of people that can find these nasty things in their beginning stages. But these days, they can sure be one of the most important. Happy new year.

MILESTONE: THE GALACTIC HACKER PARTY (Autumn, 1989)

The Galactic Hacker Party could very well have been the strangest gathering of computer hackers ever to have assembled. It wasn't just a meeting of silicon-heads who talked binary for three days. It wasn't simply a group of rowdy individuals out to give the authorities a headache and cause general chaos wherever they ventured. Nor was it merely an ensemble of bizarre, crazy, and ultra-paranoid types, like the ones who make it to the *2600* monthly meetings in New York. The Galactic Hacker Party was *all three* of these put together, and a good bit more.

MILESTONE: THE GALACTIC HACKER PARTY *(continued)*

The conference took place at the Paradiso Cultural Center in Amsterdam on August 2, 3, and 4. Hackers and techno-rats from all over the world converged on the scene, some remaining for quite some time afterward. Information about computer systems, phone systems, famous hackers, governmental regulations, privacy abuses, and new toys flowed freely and openly. Since there are no laws against hacking in the Netherlands, there were virtually no restrictions placed on anybody.

Representatives from the Chaos Computer Club (West Germany), Hack-Tic (the Netherlands), and *2600* met for the first time, along with hackers from many other countries. We tried to figure out the best way to pool our resources, to share information, and to support one another's existence. It was most heartening to see other people in strange and distant lands who also had developed an infatuation with knowledge and a strong desire to share it. It was at the same time a bit disconcerting to see this enthusiastic spirit, and to wonder why it would seem so strange back home in America.

Like any good conference, the best things happened behind the scenes. That's where the contacts were made and the methods divulged. Press from all over the world showed up, as did people from all walks of life. It was a curiosity shop, a coming together of inquiring minds.

But enough poetics: What does this all mean? Well, for starters, it's injected us with some new enthusiasm and some brand new knowledge. We tend to forget that there's a world of diversity out there, different lifestyles, alternative ways of accomplishing things.

The Germans taught us the importance of organization. In Hamburg alone, there's at least one meeting of hackers a week. They play with computers, compare magazines (in West Germany there are several magazines that deal with hacking), and figure out their various strategies. Hacking is much more political in West Germany than any other country.

The Dutch showed us how, above all else, having fun is what really matters. Learning about the things that you're really interested in can be the most fun of all. In the Netherlands, what the authorities do or think is less than secondary. The openness of Dutch society helps to foster this healthy attitude.

continues

MILESTONE: THE GALACTIC HACKER PARTY *(continued)*

We, the Americans, shared our beloved and practical hacking traditions, like the art of trashing. Almost as soon as we raided our first trash bin, the anti-authority Dutch figured that the dumpster of a police station would be the best place to get info! We must now live with the knowledge of what we have started.

We also helped to convey the importance of thorough scanning. It's easy to get discouraged in countries that don't have the wealth of services that we've grown accustomed to. But, regardless of how primitive or restrictive a phone system may appear, scanning almost always accomplishes something. There are now people scanning in both East and West Germany, as well as the Netherlands, England, Belgium, and France, discovering strange tones, dialing shortcuts, ringbacks, and other nice things.

In Europe, the hackers are continually expanding their grasps on technology, from pirate radio to voicemail systems to videotex to well-organized computer networks. Here, we seem to be reverting to one-upmanship and conformity when we should be finding new toys of technology to play with and shape to our needs. What happened to the huge conference calls, the hundreds of hacker bulletin boards, the clever pranks, the legendary phone phreaks? Are we afraid? Are we losing our spirit? Or are we just getting comfortably dumb?

A look through these pages will tell you that there are plenty of entities just aching to gain control of technology and in due time, the individual. This magazine is only one voice. We need more.

If you think you can do something, then you can. People all over the world know and understand the spirit of the hackers. It's up to all of us to keep it going.

A Hacker Survey (August, 1987)

At times like these, people begin asking philosophical questions. What is right and what isn't? We thought that would be a good subject to ponder for the hackers of the world and this is what we've managed to come up with so far. Feel free to write in with your own comments, whether you're a hacker or not.

The one thing that most of the hackers we spoke with seem to agree upon is that stealing merchandise with credit card numbers is wrong. Many went on to say that this does not comprise hacking at all. In other words, any moron can get a credit card number and many do.

Why are such people categorized as computer hackers? Probably because some of them use computers to get credit card numbers, said a few. Others believe it's because the public and the media don't understand how anything involving credit card fraud can be accomplished without the help of a computer. It's quite possible to commit credit card fraud simply by picking a credit slip out of the garbage or by standing around an ATM machine until somebody discards a receipt that has their Visa number on it. Since many credit checks don't verify the person's name or the card's expiration date, it's become extraordinarily easy. Which is another reason many hackers dislike it.

What should happen to such people? Many hackers believed they should be dealt with severely, although prison terms weren't mentioned. Almost all believe they should pay back whatever it was they stole.

How about long-distance fraud? Reactions to this were mixed. Some feel that ripping off long-distance companies is exactly like credit card fraud. Others believe it's a few steps above it, particularly if a hacker uses ingenuity and common sense to avoid being caught. A few questioned whether or not there was actually any loss of money to the company involved, particularly the big ones, "Who does AT&T have to pay when they're stuck with a fraudulent phone bill? Do they pay themselves? The smaller companies usually pay AT&T, but who do the bigger companies have to pay? It's not like we'd make a two-hour call across the country if we had to pay for it, so the lost revenue speech is kind of hard to swallow." "It seems to me that the phone lines would still be there whether or not we were on them, the computers would still be running if we weren't on them, either way the cost to the company is almost the same." A few pointed out that the bad publicity surrounding code abuse probably does more harm than the actual phone bills.

Some said that toll fraud was a necessary part of computer hacking, but it wasn't a form of hacking in itself. But nearly all we questioned seemed to agree that when caught, the culprit should be made to pay back what they used, as long as they're presented with evidence that they made the calls.

What kind of hacking is acceptable in the hacker world? Generally, access to systems that a hacker would never gain access to, regardless of how much he was willing to pay. Systems like the phone company computers, credit checks, census bureaus, and private military systems were mentioned most. "By accessing these, we're learning a lot more than we ever could on Compuserve." "We can uncover lots of secrets, like how easy it is to change somebody's credit or how easy it is to find an unlisted phone number. People would never know these things if it weren't for us." These kind of hackers look upon themselves as "technological Louis and Clarks."

What kind of price should a hacker pay if he's caught on a non-public system? A few said a fine of some sort should be imposed. But most seemed to believe that an agreement of some sort could be reached between the various parties, such as the hacker telling the operators how they accessed their system and what bugs were present to allow them to do this. Very few were sympathetic to companies or organizations that allowed hacking to go on for long periods of time. "It's their own fault—who else is there to blame? If we didn't get in there, somebody else would have." "Lots of times we tell them about their bugs, and they either ignore us or just fix it without even saying thanks. I think they deserve what they get, honestly."

Hackers have a distinct definition of what is good hacking and what is bad hacking. Bad hacking would include actions like crashing a system for no particular reason. "Good hacking is entering a system, creating ambiguous accounts, covering your tracks, defeating the accounting, gaining high access, exploring, learning, and leaving. A bad hacker erases files and reads others' mail."

An Interpretation of Computer Hacking (Spring, 1988)

By Captain Zap

The following article is one view of computer hackers. We'd like to say right up front that it is not ours and in fact we take exception to a good many of the facts presented. We would be most interested in hearing what the hackers of the world have to say regarding this perception of them. Please send us your feedback.

The ongoing wave of computer crime that is being reported in the media around the world shows the ease of computer system break-ins that are becoming more and more widespread. Both the technology and the society have changed since the birth of the first computer and the growth of the computer has come to the average household in the U.S.

The speed has increased while the size has shrunk. One simply has to compare the Apple or IBM personal computer to ENIAC, the first computer. ENIAC was very large and needed a small electrical substation to operate while the personal computer today runs on batteries or household electric. The memory in ENIAC was just about 2K compared to today's personal computers, which commonly have 16 Megabytes of RAM.

All of this computing power is now in the hands of everyday persons and the equipment can be carried to anywhere in the world. In addition, these people can gain access to the computer center of any major and a large number of minor computer sites. How? Through the phone lines around the world and the ability of such a vast global network to interface almost anywhere on the face of the planet. Simply put, the phone and the computer are now one and the use of dial-up ports to the computer is becoming standard operating procedure. The reasons are due to the desire for distributed databases and the need for all of the information to flow over the phone networks around the world. We will now look at the issue of information flow over the phone network and how easy it is for someone to gain access to any part of the transmission.

Telecommunications and Fraud

The beginning of the formal underground phone network started in 1971 with the formation of the newsletter entitled "*YIPL*," or *Youth International Party Line*. This newsletter was structured with information on how the phone company equipment would work and ways to defeat it. This was also seen as a protest against the Vietnam War and the Federal tax that was placed on phone service to help pay for the war.

The idea was to be able to place calls to others without paying any form of toll charge. This one form of toll fraud was done with the use of homemade electronic gear known to this day as the "blue box." The "box" was able to simulate the signals of the phone company switches and it could place calls as if one had the same controls as a regular AT&T operator.

Calls were placed over toll-free trunks such as 800 numbers. The phone company, seeing the problem, placed a tone detector on trunks looking for the distinct tone frequency of 2600 hertz. (This tone is the signaling frequency for the long-distance trunks to disconnect but the blue box could still maintain a hold on the trunk and place calls from remote locations.)

One other interesting aspect should be mentioned—the use of a whistle that was found in the boxes of "Captain Crunch" cereal. The name "Captain Crunch" was used by the earliest phone phreak known to the phone system security force. His real name is John Draper and he was the first person who used this whistle from the cereal boxes and discovered that the toy would produce the exact same tone (2600 hertz) that the phone system produced for the seizure of the trunk lines needed to make long-distance phone calls.

Other "boxes" also exist. Here is a brief list:

- **Blue:** Produces all (SF) single frequency tones and (DTMF) dual tone multi-frequency. Able to dial without incurring toll charges.
- **Red:** Able to produce coin identification tones that correspond to coins placed in a pay phone (nickel, dime, or quarter).
- **Green:** Coin return. This allows the caller to return coins instead of the coins dropping into the coin box of the pay phone.
- **Silver:** Able to simulate the DTMF and have the availability of generating 1633 Hz. Tones are used on the AUTOVON voice network (the military phone system).
- **Black:** Does not allow the connection of billing circuits to call. Must be used on called party's line. This is only usable on older switches such as step by step or #2 or #5 Crossbar.
- **Clear:** Allows for calls to be placed from the new private pay phones that block the phone's microphone until a coin is inserted. But by using an impedance tap

type of device the speech of the caller can be electronically placed in the earpiece and the conversation can proceed normally.
- **Cheese:** Allows for a call to be placed to one location and then transferred to another location on a different line than the original number called. Used to hide actual location of the caller from traces by separating and isolating the call from the other line.

There are combinations to these boxes. They can be red-blue, or red-green, or silver-red-blue.

But one of the simplest ways to defeat the phone system would be to use a portable tape recorder. This would allow for the tones to be played into the mouthpiece or to use an induction coupler to enter the tones. This way there is no illegal equipment to be found and the phone phreak can do his work.

Other methods of phone fraud are now taking place due to the use of other long-distance carrier networks. Carriers such as MCI and Sprint have had toll fraud problems for years and now are starting to compare notes about toll fraud and other pertinent information. The carriers have recently formed a group that pools information about suspected code abuse. Such information includes phone numbers dialed, called party name and address, suspected or known toll abusers, and the new problem of multi-carrier abuse.

Most of the known abuse is being directed from the hacker bulletin boards that post port numbers and access codes. Other incidents include employee use after hours or just plain fraud by using another person's code.

We will first discuss the problem of multi-carrier abuse or "weaving" through the different networks. This form of toll abuse gets its name due to the way that calls are placed to the target phone.

In the United States, there are five major long-distance telecommunications carriers: AT&T, U.S. Sprint, MCI, Allnet, and RCI.

If a caller wanted to hide in the different networks, he could start by dialing a local PBX (Private Branch Exchange) and use the PBX as the first point of contact to place the call. Most major PBX's today have the ability to allow outsiders to gain access to the local telephone line through a switch in the PBX.

This switch gives the local dial tone and allows a call to be placed to the first local access port of one of the common carriers. The local port answers and places a carrier or system dial tone across the line and the caller inputs the access code, area code, and number to the next target switch.

The number input is the number of a target switch in another city and allows for the caller to hide in the network of Bell and the first carrier. The second targeted switch then answers and gives a system dial tone and the process is repeated.

This progression will continue until the final target phone line is reached. Such tactics can confuse even the best telephone company attempts to trace a call. So the final product of the call is that the caller could be coming from any major port on any of the carriers. Plus the added problem of being on all carriers at the same time with the different interconnections allows for some very interesting complications to occur.

Such access to the switch is very easy as many persons use these common carriers to make long-distance calls. With the vast amount of persons who use such services, the ability to find working accounting codes is still very easy! Such codes can be found by the use of a modified *War Games* dialer program. This particular program will call the local port of the common carrier and just like its cousin the port scanner, will scan the common carrier port with the ability to generate touch tones and "hack" out a working code that can be used for that switch.

An example of a simple *War Games* program is listed at the end of this article. This program was written for use with an Apple II+ and a Hayes Micromodem.

The operation of the program is very slow but other faster versions of this are available to the system hacker. Other programs have been written for use by the Hayes Smartmodem and the Prometheus ProModem 1200A.

It should be noted that some of the common carriers have changed the programming of their switches to only accept valid codes for the local area—that is, not to accept any other code that might work in other parts of the country. Traveling callers must call a special number and insert an additional four-digit code after the regular authorization code.

Hacker Communications and Bulletin Boards

Some of the ways that the hackers communicate is through the use of conference calls and the underground bulletin boards. Such methods of message traffic go without charge and are able to be done by the vast majority of the hackers. The hackers have the ability to place up to 30 calls to any place in the world and join all of these calls together.

Most of the calls are placed to pass information over to other hackers that can work on a problem and compare results and plan for more tactical attacks to the target system.

The logic behind the thought is that the ability of one person to attack a system is multiplied tenfold by the others working on the same system.

Such attacks have been placed on varied computer and communications systems by the hackers. One such incident took place in Los Angeles, with phone phreaks and hackers attacking the Bell System master control computers and trying to turn off all the phones in the city with the exception of the emergency circuits. This attack was for the most part successful resulting in the loss of phone service for thousands, but not complete in its goal.

But this writer's opinion about the attack is that it was very successful showing the ability of certain persons who were able to shut down some of the phone service in the city. If such actions can be performed by persons who do not have inside information or access to the facilities, then it is a very real situation. Such attacks can be placed to a series of phone lines or just one. Other attacks have involved the reprogramming of Bell System switches, changing the destination of 800 toll-free calls to other locations, or ringing a vast number of phones at the same time.

The phone/computer underground is still growing with the vast amount of personal computers coming into the hands of many different persons who now have a large amount of computing power at their fingertips.

Bulletin-Board Systems

Bulletin boards are, as they sound, a place where persons can place information or requests for information. But in the world of the hackers, the bulletin boards are a way to pass information via computer to other hackers. These boards are set up by individuals in their homes and the users of the board call a phone number that is attached to a modem and the host computer. A bulletin board is nothing more than a place to swap information.

Such information like dialup port numbers, logons, and passwords are common information available to the main hacker population. Other more secret information is passed in confidential messages to each other and through the use of sub-sections of the board where only a select few are able to enter.

The bulletin boards contain a wealth of information if one can gain access to them. One reason that the boards are difficult to enter is because of their security. A good rule to remember is that the hacker bulletin boards have far better security than most large computer systems, and that the hackers check out each user for their real identity. A series of checks is done that include the place of employment, the phone number and the owner of that number, driver's license, health records, and the like. Other security checks require that a prospective user be recommended by another user to gain access, and then the new user is granted a lower status than most users until he proves his worth in the hacker world. The chance of a law enforcement person gaining access is thereby greatly reduced. Other aspects of the security of the boards is that some of them have a clause at the sign-on that states that the board is not responsible for the information posted and that any information placed on the board is for informational purposes only and that the person who is logging onto the system is not a member of any law enforcement agency in any way, shape, or form.

One of the methods used by the hackers to keep control and order in the hacker community is know as Tele-Trial. Tele-Trial is a court that is convened by the hackers to listen to complaints, set laws, and hand down decrees upon suspects. Such decrees can include not granting access to the boards or having someone executed electronically.

Such actions have come to the public's attention with the Tele-Trial of *Newsweek* reporter Richard Sandza. The story with Mr. Sandza is that he wrote an article about the hacker community and the hackers did not approve of the story, so Mr. Sandza had his credit card information posted on a number of bulletin boards and numerous articles delivered to his home.

Other interesting parts of this story include the distribution of his private non-published phone number and a number of death threats. Mr. Sandza then wrote an article entitled "Revenge of the Hackers" and was bombarded with another wave of abuse from the hackers. This writer's opinion is that it is better to make an ally with the hacker rather than to antagonize him, as he can perform your destruction in a matter of seconds and such destruction can happen at any time. And remember, the hacker can be the best prevention for computer security sickness and that a reformed hacker can make for the best data processing security person.

In general, most of the computer bulletin boards are nothing more than a place where persons of general interest are allowed to communicate their ideas and comments about hobbies, art, science, cars, ham radio and electronics, and of course the major reason this article has been prepared—the computer/phone underground. The boards in general have been a major problem in the control of information due to the use of the boards by what some may call "information junkies."

But the problem of the "information junkies" is one that is spanning the computer arena with all types of persons using this form of high-speed communication. And one of the major contributing factors involving the computer abuse is the non-education of the users in ethics.

But the problem is twofold: The user must be held accountable for his actions and the owners must secure their machines with a reasonable amount of security.

Part of the problem with the owners and of course the transmission facilities is that the carriers do not take responsibility for the security of the transmission, only that the transmission will get to the intended destination. Add to that the cost of point-to-point encryption and you get very high costs both in the equipment and in the maintenance of the system.

The bulletin boards contain a vast amount of information at the fingertips of thousands of persons at any time. Some of the boards have the ability to have multiple users on them at one time. And the boards that we will concern ourselves with, the underground or clandestine boards, are the toughest to crack. Information on these systems can range anywhere from how to make free telephone calls to the formulation of crude plastic explosives to a person's credit and personal information. Mostly the boards are a place where the study of telecommunications and computers is placed above all other things. The hackers call it nothing more than "electronic geography." They have nothing more than a good sense of curiosity and they want to learn. So they go exploring and find things that most would consider to be trivial. Information found has been well documented and proven to be embarrassing to the owners. The government has therefore given both the Secret Service and the FBI the job of investigating all computer crimes. This includes the investigation of the underground bulletin boards.

The boards are considered a major nuisance to the phone companies, but are only considered a small threat to the computer owner. But they still produce good copy for the morning paper and evening news. The general public thinks that the hackers are wonder kids able to launch a nuclear missile in any direction who can invade any computer system out there. They hear that a computer that belongs to the U.S. government in a nuclear research facility has been "tapped" by the hackers, or that there is a possibility of the hackers controlling satellites and moving them out of their assigned orbits. Granted, they did not move the bird, but they did gain access to the rotation control for the satellite.

And it was stated that the information needed to do such things was found on an underground bulletin board. That might be true, but information that is far more valuable to people on earth is being posted on the boards. And this information comes from the trash can or from insiders who have become disgruntled or just from plain old research—looking for publicly available sources. Some of these public sources constitute users' manuals and system documentation.

Another interesting fact about the boards is that they contain a group of sub-sections that include subjects on telecommunications, software piracy, and cracking of software protection systems, computer systems overviews and how different systems work, and ways around the system security features. Some bulletin boards also contain page after page of dial-ups to major computers around the country. These include all of the Fortune 500 companies and a large amount of military systems. So to the persons who state that the bulletin boards are not a problem, I believe that they have not been on any of the major underground boards and therefore should not make such rash statements.

As to the overall damage that a bulletin board can cause, the final cost has yet to be determined. The boards allow for the transmission of information to a large group of persons. What the person who gets this information does with it is another story.

```
1 REM "WARGAMES DIALER PROGRAM" FILE MUST BE OPEN FIRST
5 INPUT "NUMBER TO START";N
10 D$=CHR$ (4) : Q$ = CHR$ (17):Z$ = CHR$ (26)
15 FOR I=N TO 9999
20 N$ = "0000" + STR$ (I):N$= "567" + RIGHT$ (N$,4)
25 PRINT D$ "PR#2"
30 PRINT Q$ " " N$
35 IF PEEK (1658) 1/4 128 THEN 1990
40 PRINT D$ " PR#0 "
45 PRINT D$ " APPEND DIALER 567 "
```

```
50 PRINT D$ " WRITE DIALER 567 "
55 PRINT N$
60 PRINT D$ " CLOSE DIALER 567 "
65 PRINT Q$ " CHR$ (26)
70 REM HANG UP AND BE SURE THAT YOU DID
75 PRINT D$ " PR # 0 "
80 PRINT D$ " PR # 2 ":PRINT D$:PRINT Z$
85 FOR J=1 TO 600:A= -1:NEXT
90 NEXT
```

A Reader's Reply to Captain Zap (Summer, 1988)

By The Rancid Grapefruit

Query: "What happens to inept computer criminals who get caught?"
Answer: "They open up 'security' companies and start preaching to an extremely gullible public—usually casting themselves as some kind of 'hacker expert' whereas the only thing they are 'experts' at is getting caught."

The opening comments have absolutely nothing to do with Captain Zap, whose reputation is impeccable, and we most certainly would not want people to misconstrue the comments as a vicious attack on his person. Lord, no...

Obviously, we disagree with Captain Zap's brilliant observations on the state of "Hacking and Phreaking." If we did agree with him, we'd hardly be writing this swell response, eh?

"The ongoing wave of computer crime that is being reported in the media around the world shows" the shallowness of the media's never ending quest for anything that will titillate a technology-ignorant public, and push up the ratings of whatever publication or feed happens to be catering to the public's fear of technology on that particular occasion.

"An Interpretation of Computer Hacking" is just that: Captain Zap's personal *opinion* on the subject. In the first several paragraphs, Zap essentially summarizes the opening chapter of almost any given "Beginner's Introduction to Computers" and somehow manages to pass off observations that have already been made a few hundred times as his own "ideas." The only real mystery to us is why he decides on "16 Megabytes of RAM" as an arbitrary amount of memory that "today's personal computers" are supposedly equipped with.

This leads into the "information is power" spiel, and the inevitable arrival of ISDN wherein phones and computers will become one glorious entity and live happily ever after.

All of this ends up with Zap giving you his opinion on "The Dawn of Phreaking," the usual mention of Draper and blue boxing, followed by a summary of the boxes that matches slang to function, and terminating with a simplified account of toll fraud where Zap babbles about the various OCC's for a while.

Although we were very impressed by the programming ingenuity of the supplied "Wargames dialer" listing, and find ourselves constantly looking to the first section of Zap's article when we feel lost or at a need for guidance, we will regrettably have to let it stand. Since aside from the ill-chosen "highlights of yesteryear" there is nothing there that hasn't been discussed or otherwise summarized too many times in the past. As such it would be a waste of our time to do so yet again.

Hacker Communications! Shhhhh! Secrets being exchanged!

While we don't dispute the fact that people do call each other, sometimes in large groups hooked together on a conference (without paying for it, gasp!), *rarely* is the purpose of a conference to "pass information over to other hackers that can work on a problem and compare results and plan for more tactical attacks to the target system." The usual reason a conference starts is because one kid is bored and wants to talk to a bunch of his peers at the same time. What takes places on almost any given conference is a bunch of screaming kids harassing TSPS operators, calling pizza parlors in Europe, and in general pranking or annoying anyone they can think of at the moment.

"Attacks" placed on Bell System computers are usually the result of one kid—who is *not* some genius; rather he's quite often the friend or relative of somebody who understands the *concepts* involved, not only the commands—who thinks it would be a blast to turn off CAMA on a few switches, or disrupt COSMOS operations. All of this potential damage is made possible by the RBOCs themselves, which provide extremely minimal security that is more of a study in faulty security techniques and shoddy organization than any kind of obstacle to the potential hacker.

While "computing power" is now within reach of a vast number of people, almost all of that "vast number" are ignorant as to their system's potential. In fact, most never get beyond running their spreadsheet or doing taxes on that wonderful PC with "16 MB RAM." And if they ever do sink into the sordid depths of depravity and actually try something awful like making a bit copy of someone else's program and Xeroxing its manual, it's our personal belief that the world will in all probability not come to an end. Of course, we could be wrong.

Almost all potential hackers are little kids with a lot of time on their hands, and most of those kids will never get anywhere because they are not brilliant, or in any way gifted—regardless of what the public might think of them. The vast majority of people that the public views as computer geniuses are quite average teenagers whose only "skill" is calling up boards—with "better security than most large computer systems"—and blindly applying things they see posted on them, *without* understanding what they are doing. Granted this is a "threat," but it's the *only* threat that boards pose. And the only reason it's a problem to begin with is because the "threatened" organizations or companies have ridiculously bad security.

While it is true that more people now own personal computers than at any other time in history, the overall effect of this influx of new hackers is negligible. Instead of one kid annoying his local CO from information he found on some board, there are 10 kids using the same information from the same board to harass the same CO. In short, there is a deluge of "idiot savants" who are capable of doing no more damage than trained chimps.

The Bulletin-Board Systems

Bulletin-board systems (BBSs) pose a possible threat for the simple reason that the more highly skilled users will post potentially dangerous information in a place where the "idiot savants" can read it. The better-versed user's reason for posting it is ego gratification. Regardless of what he claims, the only incentive he has to post this information is an ego boost. He already knows that the "idiot savants" are going to do something stupid with the information, at worst simply making it valueless, at best flexing their muscles and showing their target how vulnerable they are to an outside attack.

Granted, if BBSs didn't exist, much of the trouble various people and companies now experience would vanish along with the "idiot savants." But the only thing the boards really do is provide a forum for the more intelligent users to bask in the adoration of fools. They are not some great organized crime wave of the future; they are simply used by several thousand bored kids, the great majority of them trying to live out some kind of power trip while the remaining minority congregates together because they like being surrounded by those they view as their peers.

In summary, boards are a social medium—not the forefront of some well-orchestrated, nationwide attack on loopholes in "the system." Just about any issue of *Soldier of Fortune* contains all the information you could possibly want about where to obtain books on plastic explosives, nerve gas, special weapons, electronic devices, and anything else that has been dreamed up. You hardly need a BBS in order to have access to that kind of knowledge. In fact most of the information posted on the "death and destruction" subs of boards is a word-for-word copy of some article that originally appeared in one of these books. The only crime taking place is copyright infringement.

Remember... (Summer, 1989)

Why should we remember Abbie Hoffman? What relationship did he have with *2600*?

Abbie was, of course, the founder of the Yippies, and the founder of *YIPL*, which turned into *TAP*. *TAP* was the first publication to look at technology through hacker eyes. It's doubtful *2600* would exist in its present form were it not for the inspiration *TAP* offered.

But apart from that, Abbie Hoffman was, for all intents and purposes, a hacker of the highest order. No, he didn't go around breaking into computers, although we know the subject interested him. Abbie hacked authority, which is what a lot of us unwittingly do whenever we play with phones and computers. Abbie, of course, was much more direct. He stood up to the ultimate computer system known as Society. He was relentless in his attack on the status quo. He fought the Vietnam War, got arrested so many times that nobody could really keep track, and wound up pissing off Richard Nixon to no end. He became a fugitive from the law after being accused of dealing drugs, a charge he vehemently denied to his closest friends right up to the end. And even under a disguise, Abbie accomplished a lot under the name of Barry Freed, leading an environmental group called Save the River in Upstate New York.

Abbie gained a reputation for outsmarting the FBI. It's reported that the FBI gathered more information on Abbie Hoffman than on anyone else in their entire history. That's something to be proud of.

Like a computer hacker, Abbie Hoffman was thought of as a pest by some. His presence was inconvenient and he made people uncomfortable because he wasn't afraid to point out the flaws.

On the personal level, Abbie had a sharp mind and a great sense of humor. He had a terrific enthusiasm for life's little pleasures and his friends compared him to a little kid who loved toys.

We're sorry he never really seemed to reach the younger generation. That upset him quite a bit. But when you consider how Abbie turned the world on its side, a lot of what we do today would probably be done quite differently if he hadn't been around.

So the next time you're playing with a computer somewhere and you feel that little rush of excitement as you realize the endless possibilities, say hello to Abbie. He'll be right there.

On yet another sad note, one of *2600*'s most knowledgeable and articulate writers died on June 4, 1989, at the age of 22.

David Flory was known in these pages as The Shadow and, most recently, as Dan Foley. On bulletin-board systems, David was known as Shadow 2600.

In the days of the Private Sector BBS, Shadow 2600 would always be the person to take charge of a technical discussion and explain things so that everyone could understand. In many ways, the Private Sector was an extension of his ever-present quest to learn and explore. We all benefitted from that.

David was shocked along with the rest of us when the Private Sector was seized by the authorities in July of 1985. He played a major role in publicizing the action and setting up a support network. Throughout this rather trying time, he never lost sight of our ideals: freedom of speech and the quest for knowledge.

Our sadness over David Flory's loss won't disappear soon. We gained much from him and he enjoyed the work he did for *2600*. Like Abbie, we intend to keep his spirit alive.

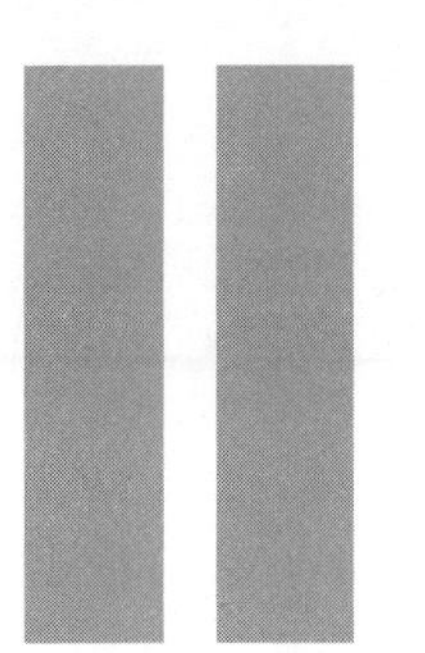

The 1990s: The World Discovers Hackers

8 Pop Culture and the Hacker World

I suppose it was inevitable. A lot of us even saw it coming. From the very beginning, there was this overt fascination with the hacker mindset. We saw it in the eyes of the reporters who wanted to know just what kinds of powers we actually had. The fear that others showed—mostly from afar while they were busy passing laws or implementing draconian policies—was one step removed from actual respect. The intense curiosity coupled with the unbridled panic came together to create yet another example of popular culture. And there was nothing we could do about it.

The 1990s was the decade when hackers were truly discovered in the mainstream. Oh sure, there was a smattering of books and movies in the 1980s, but that was merely a prelude of what was hurtling down Hollywood Boulevard and Madison Avenue. In the course of a couple of years, it was as if a new life form had been discovered, and everyone had to have a piece of the story whether it was to dissect us or to attack us. Being a hacker in the 1990s was like being a member of a British pop band in the 1960s—there was just this crazed aura that surrounded you that you couldn't shake no matter how hard you tried. Not that we tried all *that* hard.

It really was a ton of fun, no denying that. Every couple of months it seemed there would be a new flick or hardcover coming out that either dealt with our world peripherally or was about some of us specifically. What this did to our egos was not a pretty thing. But, cool as the whole mess was, none of us really benefited from any of the publicity. In fact, it's safe to say that all of the attention on the hacker world made things a whole lot harder on us for a couple of reasons. The first being that everyone from congress to parents to corporate tycoons felt it was high time that the "real life" shenanigans being portrayed as entertainment in movie theaters and bookstores be brought to a screeching halt by whatever means necessary. Hackers were out there stealing identities and killing people (*The Net*), terrorizing innocent scientists via modem (*Takedown*), and programming robots to change the programs aired on our beloved television stations (*Hackers*). Clearly these delinquents were out of control, even if none of those things had ever actually happened. Think of the children.

And of course, the second reason why being a hacker turned into a real pain in the ass in the 1990s was due to all of the "wannabes" that came flooding out of the woodwork once they saw the way hackers were portrayed in the mass media. People who could barely turn a computer on were swaggering around their communities proclaiming themselves as hackers and the very same mass media that had helped to create these monsters gave them additional strength by focusing more attention on their half-witted attempts to be cool. But what these unenlightened newbies really wound up doing was feeding into the media definition of hackers by creating their own little cults of personality, mostly being motivated by profit and greed, and making ridiculous claims and boasts.

MTV arguably was the worst offender in 1999, broadcasting a nonsensical tale of "true" hackers without ever bothering to check any of their subjects' claims, nearly all of which were made up on the spot. It didn't matter to them—all they cared about was the demographic. With ominous music playing, they quoted a 19-year-old bragging about how he had "been to the end of the Internet and back—over the course of my years, I've done everything possible" without ever pursuing it any deeper than that! (Where exactly *is* the end of the Internet anyway?) This was almost typical of the type of journalist integrity we were facing. Yes, hacking in the '90s was no picnic for those few who were trying to *avoid* the limelight.

Entertainment

Pain in the ass that all of the attention was, we still felt obligated to take it seriously and even share the thrill of seeing at least part of our world being represented everywhere from the big screen to the boob tube to the pages of bestsellers. We even tried to help them get the story right with varying degrees of success. I had a hand as technical adviser for the movie *Hackers* and it turned out to be a real blast. And, despite the constant crap I got for it, I think overall the film came out pretty well. It was also fun to see so many little elements of what was then a fairly small and tight hacker community in New York City actually getting played out in a major Hollywood release. After all, the writer of the screenplay had been coming to the New York City *2600* meetings and—as we did with almost everyone—we told him stories, showed him cool stuff, and answered his questions. So you wound up seeing things in the movie like the flare gun incident, the meetings on late night subway cars, the weird personalities, even some of the names taken right out of our pages (yes, mine was one of them and I was totally cool with it). We had to at least *try* to help them get it right and capture the spirit. Plus, I'll always be able to say I helped Angelina Jolie learn how to use a Mac.

We also focused on the books that were coming out about the hacker community, dealing with everyone from the Legion of Doom to the Masters of Deception to Kevin Mitnick. In fact, the decade began with a Mitnick story and ended with another completely different one. By then, there were no less than four books out at the same time relating the now famous tale.

But what was most amazing was that we wound up getting steered in a totally different direction when in 1998 we got a hold of an internal copy of the screenplay (don't ask) for a new movie called *Takedown*. To put it mildly, we thought it was treating the hacker community and Mitnick in particular in a very unfair manner. So we decided to speak up about it. And *that* would lead to the making of our own film....

When Hackers Ride Horses: A Review of *Cyberpunk* (Summer, 1991)

Cyberpunk: Outlaws and Hackers on the Computer Frontier
By Katie Hafner and John Markoff

$22.95, Simon and Schuster, 354 pages

Review by The Devil's Advocate

The exploits of Kevin Mitnick, Pengo, and Robert Morris have become legendary both in and out of the hacker mainstream. Until now, however, hackers have had to worship their idols from afar. *Cyberpunk: Outlaws and Hackers on the Computer Frontier* unites hackers in this true-life testimony by presenting an in-depth, up-front view of these "techno-menaces" without the overreactive doomsday prophecies that usually accompany such a work.

Cyberpunk is a fitting sequel to Steven Levy's classic *Hackers*. Whereas Levy's treatise addressed the origins of hacking in its infancy, *Cyberpunk* is the New Testament depicting hacking as it is in the here and now. More than just a synthesis of current trends, however, *Cyberpunk* depicts the hacking lifestyle and cyberpunk culture that has evolved alongside our boundless fascination with computers and information. *Cyberpunk* portrays hackers as they really are: real people with lives not unlike our own. Yes, hackers have emotions, desires, and problems just like we do. No, they're not all computerholics or socially inferior psycho cases withdrawing into the depths of the "matrix" to escape from reality. If anything, *Cyberpunk* will blast away some of the antiquated stereotypes that have persisted throughout the '80s.

In *Cyberpunk*, all the central characters identify closely with their science fiction counterparts. Indeed, the (Inter) "net" is one of the many threads that tie the lives of Mitnick, Pengo, and rtm (Robert Morris) together. The most interesting story by far is that of Pengo, a West Berliner who, more than any other character, epitomizes what it means to be a cyberpunk. Pengo was truly a computer outlaw: aspiring to the likeness of the character Case in William Gibson's *Neuromancer*, traveling the Net in search of data to sell, and owing no allegiance to country or nation. Readers familiar with *The Cuckoo's Egg* will find this section particularly interesting. *Cyberpunk's* account of the West Berlin hackers makes *The Cuckoo's Egg* look like a fledgling fluttering in the quirkiness of Stoll's campy prose. Now readers can see what it was that Stoll himself was trying to vicariously experience through his own terminal. *Cyberpunk* provides the missing pieces and puts Stoll's *Cuckoo* into perspective.

The book confirms what hackers on all coasts have known and preached for years: that a computer system's worst enemy is its users. Nearly every system was hacked by exploiting poorly chosen passwords or bugs in the operating systems. Interestingly, *Cyberpunk* also confirms that the authorities amount to only so many bumbling Keystone computer cops desperately trying to match wits with misfits. The fact is that everyone described here got busted because they either talked too much or were betrayed by close friends. Without such help, the long arm of the law appears to be nothing more than a wet noodle.

Perhaps the central weakness of *Cyberpunk* is its somewhat blatant bias and lack of objectivity. Time and time again, readers will encounter the author's own prejudices slipping through the cracks between the lines. Although no one is innocent in *Cyberpunk*, readers will easily get the impression that Mitnick is the sinner of the three. This is despite the fact that Mitnick's exploits appear equal, if not less damaging, than those of the others. Unfortunately, the bias rears its ugly head in a number of passages, a telltale sign that the authors appear to be more incensed with Mitnick's attitude than with anything else. It is also no coincidence that Mitnick is the only central character that refused to be interviewed for the book.

Despite this weakness, *Cyberpunk* remains a thought-provoking looking glass into the lives of the most interesting people in the Information Age. The true tales of these harbinger hackers will leave readers spellbound while they eagerly await a sequel.

Pure Cyberfiction, Says Mitnick

The following are comments by Kevin Mitnick on the portions of the book that are about him.

I am sad to report that part one of the book *Cyberpunk*, specifically the chapters on "Kevin: The Dark Side Hacker," is 20 percent fabricated and libelous. It seems that the authors acted with malice to cause me harm after my refusal to cooperate. Interestingly enough, I did offer to participate as a factual information source if I was compensated for my time, but the authors refused, claiming it would taint my objectivity. So consequently, I declined to cooperate.

However, my codefendant, Lenny Dicicco, of Data Processing Design, chose to participate probably in the hopes of being recognized as a "hero" who was responsible for bringing me to justice. Lenny seemed to have gained unquestionable credibility when he turned us both into Digital and the U.S. government. Surprisingly, he who "snitches" first is believed to be totally credible by the U.S. government. Case in point: Most of the U.S. government's argument to hold me without bail was based on false information (this was later admitted by the U.S. government). This information, I believe, was mainly from Lenny Dicicco and his cronies (Steven Rhoades of Pasadena, CA). So once Lenny lied to the U.S. government, he couldn't change his story, since he could risk violating his plea agreement or being indicted on federal perjury charges. Unfortunately, this probably resulted in a lot of false material being introduced by Lenny Dicicco, and Katie Hafner printing it as factual information in *Cyberpunk*.

Katie probably wasn't happy with me for refusing to help her, so part one of the book was written with a strong anti-Mitnick, pro-Dicicco bias. This bias rewarded Lenny for his participation but robbed the readers of the real truthful facts! Lenny was described simply as an "errand boy" in our hacking exploits. This is the furthest thing from the truth! Lenny was just as culpable as me; we were hacking partners for over 10 years. What do you believe?

Let's examine some interesting cover-ups Katie Hafner did for Lenny Dicicco:

1) In the galley copy of *Cyberpunk*, Katie Hafner wrote that Lenny Dicicco was going to work for DEC as a computer security consultant in lieu of court ordered restitution ($12,000). Why was the information eliminated from the final printed copy? Probably DEC wouldn't be happy with Lenny—he did provide Katie with enormous detail regarding the DEC break-in. Not to mention the controversial issue regarding DEC hiring the person that penetrated their network.

2) On page 80, Katie wrote that Lenny Dicicco obtained a false identity to obtain a job that required a "clean" driving record. The name Katie printed was "Robert Andrew Bollinger." This is false! The name of the "false" identity was "Russell Anthony Brooking." But why would Katie print this erroneous information? I know why! Lenny was working under the fraudulent identity (Russel Anthony Brooking) while he was collecting unemployment under his real name, thereby defrauding the State of California! Now Katie wouldn't want the "truth" to be know—it might cause Lenny to refuse to participate in possible upcoming interviews and talk shows promoting her book.

I could go on and on, even simple verifiable information. For example, on page 84, Katie describes a scenario where I asked Bonnie out on a date. To paint an unsavory picture, she stated that I was always eating in the computer room when talking with Bonnie. Very interesting, since at the Computer Learning Center of Los Angeles, no food or drinks can *ever* be brought into the computer room. Even though this scenario is pretty insignificant, it demonstrates the introduction of inaccurate and misrepresented facts.

Again, when describing my arrest at USC in 1982, Katie wrote on page 71 that I taunted Mark Brown (USC System Manager) in his investigative techniques. This is truly amazing, since I never spoke with Mark Brown.

There are many, many false statements, misrepresentations, and inaccurate stories in part one of this book. I could only say it is sad that the authors were too cheap to compensate me for my time. Instead they hid under the ruse of "tainted objectivity." This resulted in my refusal to participate.

In summary, *Cyberpunk* is an interesting read-through as long as readers understand this purported nonfiction book is not what it claims to be. Part one of the book is 20 percent inaccurate. I believe the authors acted with malice due to my refusal to participate for free. Katie Hafner's only hope was seeking the cooperation of my convicted codefendant, Lenny Dicicco. She did gain his full cooperation, which resulted in a strong bias and misrepresentation of facts.

Assorted Videos from Commonwealth Films (Summer, 1993)

Review by Emmanuel Goldstein

The corporate world contributes a great deal to the lives of the everyday human. Perhaps the most significant gift they offer, second only to global pollution, is the wonderful art form known as corporate comedy.

We've all seen it in some way. Whether it's a phone company claiming one of their memos is worth $80,000 or a governmental agency saying they believe a raid can actually help a business become profitable, it's all part of the same humor. After all, it is just a big joke, isn't it? An escape from reality into the world of the absurd in order to make life more bearable. Art in its truest form.

Those of you who wish to enjoy the latest in corporate comedy ought to check out three videos recently released by Commonwealth Films. *We Lost Control: Illegal Software Duplication* is easily the funniest. This 16-minute piece is designed to put the fear of the Lord into anyone who's even *thought* of copying software.

The story unfolds through the eyes of Steve Roberts, head of a company that wasn't careful enough. Federal marshals conduct a raid and find that, lo and behold, every piece of software is *not accounted for!* This could spell doom for him and everyone he's ever known, according to his lawyer who can't seem to say a single positive word. Yes, Steve, the Software Piracy Association did their homework—you're not exactly squeaky clean—out of the hundreds of cases SPA has prosecuted, they've only lost one—you're liable for up to $100,000 per unauthorized copy of each program, including the ones you've bought—you'd better hope the media doesn't latch onto this and ruin your life even more....Steve does some serious soul-searching ("I had no idea we were in so deep") and realizes that copying a program is indeed exactly like stealing a computer. "For some reason," he ponders, "it didn't seem serious." At this point, the viewer feels compelled to shake the TV and scream at Steve to come out of his corporate coma. But alas, it just gets worse. In a rather patronizing tone, his lawyer says, "Let's set the basic facts straight and eliminate ignorance." Oh, if only we could.

The "facts" that we are hit with run counter to every instinct a human being could have. The SPA, and anyone who falls for their self-righteous dogma, lives in a fantasy world. They actually expect everyone to not only pay outrageous prices for every bit of software on their machines, but to pay these prices *again* whenever they copy a program to another machine. And for those people who can't afford to pay $500 for a word processor, SPA takes the position that such people simply should not have access. In other words, admission to technology is solely for people with money to spend. It's precisely this philosophy that has inhibited progress in the past and will continue to do so to a far greater degree if left unchallenged. Access to the future is something that needs to be encouraged, not restricted. Software developers should, and will, make tons of money. And when the dust finally settles, it ought to become quite clear that the SPA position articulated in this film was never about fair compensation. It was simply greed.

The other two films, *Virus: Prevention, Detection, Recovery* and *Back in Business: Disaster Recovery/Business Resumption* actually offer some useful suggestions, the most basic being to make backups and keep them offsite. Newsflash.

There are a few good laughs in these offerings as well since everything has to be exaggerated beyond believability in order to drive the point home. For example, we are introduced to a dark hacker who speaks to us from within a shadow with a disguised voice. His sole reason of existence is to make our lives miserable. Remember that.

Although we could find little more than sentence structure to agree with in these offerings, we do recommend them to our readers as a fascinating study of alien culture. As a final example of the utter thoroughness of corporate comedy, the price for these three films (63 minutes total viewing time) is $1,338.75. Happy viewing.

West Side Hacker: *Masters of Deception* (Spring, 1995)

By Michelle Slatalla and Joshua Quittner

$23.00, HarperCollins, 225 pages

Review by Scott Skinner

One of the first things that comes to mind after completing Slatalla and Quittner's *Masters of Deception* is Sergio Leone's classic western *The Good, the Bad, and the Ugly.* Not that the two have much in common, mind you. They don't. Only I couldn't help but recall that the three characters from Leone's film—far from following their titled namesakes—are all downright bad. They all rob, steal, and kill with alarming simplicity and regularity. They all commit crimes. Yet there are, nonetheless, subtle distinctions of badness, which allow the audience to draw markedly different conclusions concerning the morality of each of the characters. So it is that in *Masters* we meet some teenagers, all of whom commit crimes (at least, in the legal sense), all of whom belong to an exclusive hacking group, yet each retaining an individual moral sense in both spirit and action of what the hacker ethic entails. It is in terms of these two realms—that of the individual and that of the group—that *Masters* attempts to deconstruct the story of MOD, sometimes stressing one over the other, sometimes integrating the two, but always implying that both are integral to understanding what has become the most notorious network saga since that of Robert Morris and the Internet worm.

In the same vein as *The Cuckoo's Egg* (1990), *Cyberpunk* (1991), and *The Hacker Crackdown* (1992), *Masters of Deception* is yet another story about yet another group of hackers and the officials who eventually catch up to them. But whereas the subjects of these earlier works seemed content to use phone networks to hack computers on the Internet, the teenagers who comprise MOD go one step further and hack the telephone switches themselves. The implications of this are alluded to from the opening scene, that of the AT&T crash of 1990, which crippled long distance telephone service to millions of customers nationwide. The crash, which is a textbook case of AT&T's technical incompetence, is rather tactlessly used as an example of what MOD could accomplish, inadvertently or otherwise, at the height of their own technical prowess. *Masters* is also a unique work in its class for its portrayal of hackers not merely as individuals but as members of organized gangs with conspiratorial goals and agendas. This is perhaps the most challenging aspect of *Masters,* as any depiction of a group will naturally detract from the individuality of its respective members.

Far from achieving any dialectical synthesis, however, *Masters* accomplishes its portrayal mainly by ignoring the obvious conflicts inherent in such a task. For example, *Masters* is replete with sentences such as, "A group mind had already taken over. Something bigger than all of them had been born," notions that certainly suggest a sacrifice of individual ethics toward that of the group. But how, then, are we to interpret this "group mind" when *Masters* tells us that, "Mark is Mark...Whatever Eli or other MOD members did...they did on their own, without Mark's help or commiseration or even knowledge," and "If Eli called it 'The Mission,' Mark thought of it as 'The Project.' And Paul? He just wanted to know more." Just as real people have an amazing capacity to hold mutually exclusive beliefs, *Masters,* it seems, has an equally impressive capacity to narrate and compartmentalize its own contradictory themes.

Masters is undoubtedly a good read. Ironically, however, it is precisely the ease with which one can surf through its pages that accounts for why so many of its finer points are lost. For example, MOD, we learn, is a gang. The authors like that term. Gang. Quittner even uses it in his articles on the same subject. After all, these hackers are all from the inner city, the spawning ground of gangs. Gangland, as it were. It is unfortunate that Slatalla and Quittner have latched onto this word, given the negative connotations that are now associated with it, and even more unfortunate that many readers will see the word and miss the meaning. What sort of gangs are we talking about here? *Masters* tells us, "Gang members on the electronic frontier don't live in the same states, wouldn't recognize each other if they were standing shoulder to shoulder on the same bus." Gee, that doesn't sound like any gang I know of. Sounds more like some national club. Perhaps that is why *Masters* describes Eli's room as, "...the closest thing to a clubhouse that they'd ever have." OK. So MOD is both a gang (albeit a strange one) and a club. Anything else? The point is that the authors are using the term gang in an extremely broad sense, a fact that is likely to escape the attention of their readers as they rifle through this text. At one point, *Masters* even describes the LOD gang as being "just like any schoolyard pack of boys." Interestingly, *Masters* implies that MOD was somehow more ganglike than LOD despite the fact that MOD had neither the rules nor the parliamentarism of their Texas-based counterparts. In any case, I know of no better way to arouse confusion than to use relatively distinct terms as if they were synonyms. One thing I was hoping to find and never did was the rather innocuous term "friendship." The core of MOD was first and foremost a friendship (and, incidentally, where I come from, when you put friends together in one room, you get a group of friends, not a gang).

While *Masters* is indeed a fine book, it is by no means a great book, if only because it does what so many other hacker books have done before: attempt to explain hackers to an audience that has barely become comfortable with the idea of computers, let alone computer wizards. But this is 1995, and hackers have been around in their present incarnation for some 15 years now. Yet at times, *Masters* appears to have been written in an historical void. Missing are the countless points in history that would provide some context as to what the characters are doing. Missing are the references to the fact that—by the time MOD came into existence—a hacker culture had already existed and flourished around the world. To its credit, *Masters* does tell us that "To be a hacker in the late 1980s was to be a kid with a notebook stuffed with passwords for Unixes and VAXes, switch dialups, and all kinds of university mainframes." And *Masters* does have a token page or two acknowledging Robert Morris, Operation Sundevil, the Steve Jackson case, and other unquestionably important events in hacker history. But you will need a scanner and some OCR software to find these paragraphs because—wouldn't you know it—*Masters* does not have an index, or source notes for that matter. And it is precisely omissions of this nature that make one wonder to what degree this book should be taken seriously. Add to this the factual errors. While addressing these errors is beyond the scope of this review, one thing I found absolutely inexcusable was *Masters'* use of the moronic "house" paradigm to describe being locked out of one's corporate computer. Once again, for the record: Being locked out of one's corporate computer is not like being locked out of one's own home; if anything, it is like being locked out of one's private golf course. Even worse, *Masters* makes this analogy even while drawing attention to other ridiculous analogies that were presented in the now famous *Harper's* forum on computer hacking. *Masters,* then, has a way to go before greatness. The fact is that there are a lot of characters in this story—a whole lot—and they all fit together in a myriad of complex ways. If *Masters* has any weakness, it's in trying to simplify a story that could fill volumes to something under 226 pages (to give you some perspective, Mark's indictment alone could fill volumes). While I certainly respect the magnitude of Slatalla and Quittner's undertaking, I sometimes cringe at the result: a sort of fun-to-read children's story for adults.

This review was written without the use of the following terms: cyberpunk, cyberspace, digital highway, global network, infobahn, infoway, information superhighway, cracker, on-ramp. With a little effort, you can avoid using these terms as well.

The Net (Autumn, 1995)

Starring Sandra Bullock, Jeremy Northam, Dennis Miller
Columbia Pictures

Review by Emmanuel Goldstein

The summer of 1995 will be remembered as the year Hollywood discovered the Internet. And, now more than ever, we need to pray that life will not imitate art. Barring an even more intensive dose of stupidity in the land, it's very unlikely that *The Net* will ever come true.

This is not to say that it's necessarily a bad film. In fact, the first part is nearly flawless, with a growing sense of something about to happen and an unpredictable yet plausible way of the plot unfolding. Toward the middle and especially at the end we see the standard Hollywood clichés coming into play—car chases, incredible luck on the part of the victim, incredible stupidity on the part of the villains, and technological fantasizing that people who have never seen a computer before would have no difficulty picking apart.

You'll feel a rush after seeing *The Net,* as if you had just been through an exhilarating experience—a good sign for any action flick. However, the more you think about it, the more those little tiny things will bother you, to the point where you'll experience frustration and the desire not to think about it anymore. This is all very natural.

You'll wonder how it's possible for a person to lead a somewhat normal life and not have a single person anywhere who can identify them. At least on UPN's *Nowhere Man,* all of Thomas Veil's friends and relatives have been touched or removed in some way. The villains of *The Net* are not nearly as omnipotent. So where the hell is everybody? True, Angela Bennett's mother has Alzheimer's (not a good person to rely on for verification of anything), and her ex-S.O. (Dennis Miller) meets an untimely end. But surely there must be someone *else* on the planet who will recognize Angela (played convincingly by Sandra Bullock, who really shouldn't have gotten off the bus for this part). Nobody surfaces. Conversely, where are all the people who can identify her as Ruth Marx, the person the evil Praetorians have turned her into? They don't exist either yet no doubt is cast on her identity in this case because everyone has blind faith in The Computer. It's oversimplification. As is the pitiful scene where Bullock seizes the wheel of a car driven by a fake (and evil) FBI agent and crashes it into another car that coincidentally happens to have the evil mastermind in it. We can forgive the technical inaccuracies but the unbelievability and dumbing down of the plot cannot go unremarked.

The point is made early but that doesn't stop it from being hammered repeatedly into our heads. Yes, it's not a good idea to live our lives entirely through computers, where we order pizzas, conduct our social lives, and get medical attention entirely through the virtual world. We need to remain human. We've got to go outside and leave the computers and modems behind for a while.

What the average computerphobic viewer will do after seeing this film is vow never to get near one of these monsters at any time in the conceivable future. After all, look at all the harm that can be done with such an instrument. Look at what happens to someone who uses computers frequently—they lose their identity in the real world and nobody will know who they really are. Using one is bad and having one used against you can be deadly.

But the real enemy in *The Net* was never the computer itself but rather the complacent stupidity that gives way to technological ease. Just because technology makes something a hundred times easier to accomplish is no reason to not look upon it with a healthy dose of skepticism. After all, *what if* somebody manages to gain control of the system and make it say what they want it to? Are there any backups? Is there a defense?

The Net does manage to send a very clear message. We *do* need a national health care plan. Insofar as a message that actually pertains to the plot, however, you'll have to dig much deeper.

"Baby...You're Elite": *Hackers* (Autumn, 1995)

Starring Jonny Lee Miller, Angelina Jolie, Fisher Stevens
United Artists

Review by Thee Joker

If you're waiting for me to rip this film to shreds and then burn it, you can just turn the page because that's not going to happen...entirely.

There are going to be obvious comparisons between this film and *The Net,* both because of subject matter and because of the release dates. I would have to say that *Hackers* blows *The Net* out of the water. It is much more accurate and it portrays hackers in a pretty positive light. However it still needs some work.

The problem with making a film about a subculture is that everyone in that culture will find obvious flaws in it, such as the overbearing computer graphics. So we need to skip the fact that there are inaccuracies as far as hackers are concerned and focus on the film as a piece of entertainment.

First off, we should discuss the actors' performance. They did really well, given what they had to work with. Jonny Lee Miller plays Dade (aka Zero Cool and Crash Override) with a kinda cool that makes me think that he's seen too many Tom Cruise movies with the way that he smiles at just the right time. The fact that he is a British actor and speaks with a flawless American accent also heightens my opinion of him. Angelina Jolie is great as Kate Libby (Acid Burn), and strikingly beautiful in the role of the tomboy trying to fit in with the male-dominated world of hackers. Fisher Stevens (yes, the Indian guy from *Short Circuit)* as the antagonist hacker "The Plague" is humorous, pointed, and altogether ferret-like. His hair looks like a wig, though, and he rides an old school Powell Peralta Mike McGill in the film (time for a new deck buddy). He looks like a vampire in a Mel Brooks remake of *Dracula.*

The rest of the supporting cast is played by Jesse Bradford in the role of Joey, a hacker in search of a handle, Matthew Lillard as Cereal Killer whom you may recognize from *Serial Mom,* Laurence Mason as Lord Nikon, due to his photographic memory, who was also in *The Crow* and *True Romance,* and Renoly Santiago as Phantom Phreak, the self-proclaimed "King of NYNEX." Last but not least is Academy Award Nominee Lorraine Bracco in the role of The Plague's girlfriend Margo. All of the supporting actors have been well cast in their respective roles, especially Lillard, whose character's *real* name is Emmanuel Goldstein. (Yes, this was on purpose and the resemblance is frightening.)

From the beginning, the film sports some great, albeit unrealistic, computer graphics provided by Research Arts, The Magic Camera Company, Matte World Digital, The Moving Picture Company, and GSE. The shots of the inside of the Gibson Super Computer look like an ad for Intel Inside though. There is also a video game sequence that was provided by Sony. If you treat them as a glamorous Hollywood money thing they won't bother you so much.

Now for the pros and cons. The film is engaging and the plot moves along steadily up until the ending. Ah yes, the ending... If any of you ever pick up a woman (especially a female hacker) by saying "Baby... you're Elite," I'll give you my first-born. The ending, in a word, sucks. It almost blew the whole movie for me. Almost. Other than the ending I enjoyed the film, although there were times that I was forced to laugh at it rather that having it make me laugh. For one, the way that the word "elite" was tossed around only goes to show that the word has now come to mean nothing except to codes kids on IRC.

The way that Emmanuel's name was used was comical but will be only to hackers, or to anyone who catches the *1984* reference in the film. The use of a red box in this film was great since they showed it being used as well as instructing viewers on how to make a simple one. (In an apparent concession to phone companies, however, real red box tones are not used.) It would have been wild if Radio Shack had a little product placement but thankfully they didn't. However, Apple Computers has product placement all throughout the movie (just like in *The Net),* including the see-through laptop that The Plague gives to Dade, as does Coca-Cola (including one really long shot of Dade in the kitchen of his apartment at the table with a two liter bottle in center frame). Aside from these I didn't see any other blatant product placing.

The makers of this film did a good job of not playing up the recent enlargement of the public's interest in the sport of rollerblading. After I saw the trailer I was sure that all this film was going to be was *Hackers on Blades* but it was never emphasized in any way; they just used them as a means to increase their mobility during the crucial moments, like the chase between the hackers and the Secret Service.

While *Hackers* was not made for the hacker community in particular, it does score some points with me for several reasons. The hackers were portrayed in a positive light for once. The only character in the film that slams hackers at all was Agent Richard Gill from the Secret Service and he not only gets his throughout the film as the subject of a hacking duel between Dade and Kate, but he has egg on his face when the Secret Service finds out they arrested the wrong people.

Most of the terminology was accurate or close to it even if the graphics and operating systems weren't. The word "cyberspace" wasn't used once.

The musical score is pretty cool techno/house albeit commercialized. Urban Dance Squad has a scene where they play live. The costumes are cool, kind of a clubesque sport biker blend, and the hackers are, accurately, a cross-section of people and not one-sided Hollywood cutouts.

The plot moves along rather well and is good up until the aforementioned ending. United Artists did a good job of turning Rafael Moreu's story into a workable script with the exception of a few cheesy lines. The subject matter is also topical given the recent arrests of Bernie S. and Kevin Mitnick for what most people consider to be crimes that were blown way out of proportion. The Secret Service is portrayed accurately too, from what several of my friends who have been raided tell me.

To make a long story short, The Plague gets cured, boy gets girl, hacker gets handle, everyone is acquitted, and the world is safer for democracy.

So, is it worth your $8? I think so...especially given the alternative choices. *Hackers* will probably raise a lot of consciousness as to what we do so, as always, watch your ass.

Cashing in on Mitnick: *The Fugitive Game* (Winter, 1995-1996)

By Jonathan Littman

$23.95; Little, Brown and Company; 384 pages

Review by Scott Skinner

In *The Fugitive Game,* Jonathan Littman has written the most sympathetic account of hackers since Bruce Sterling penned his own investigation in *The Hacker Crackdown.* But Littman's sympathy has very little to do with the hacker lifestyle or its ethic; indeed, he does not seem to condone either. Rather, Littman's brand of compassion is an acute understanding of the abuses of his own craft, that of the media in distorting facts to the point of creating fiction. *Fugitive* is the story of how just such irresponsible journalism turned computer expert Kevin Mitnick into "the most wanted computer hacker in the world."

Readers will remember Mitnick as the spiteful and vindictive teenager featured in Katie Hafner and John Markoff's *Cyberpunk: Computers and Outlaws on the Electronic Frontier.* At the time of its release, *Cyberpunk's* portrayal of Mitnick was thought to be biased, allegedly because Mitnick was the only hacker featured who refused to be interviewed. Biased or not, he was portrayed by the authors as a "Dark Side" hacker, and the antithesis of the hacker ethic. He was considered more evil than Pengo, a West Berlin hacker who sold his knowledge of American systems on the Internet to the Russians for cash. But Mitnick's worse crime, by comparison, seemed only to be a lack of respect for anyone who was not up to his level of computer expertise, and few people were.

In *Fugitive,* Mitnick returns, only this time the reader is left with the distinct impression that something is missing. The question is what? Mitnick, after all, is hacking as usual. He's listening to private phone conversations, reading email, penetrating systems at will. He's also telling jokes, laughing, and expressing his feelings and vulnerabilities in late-night phone calls to his friends and to Littman. Perhaps what is missing, then, is the Dark Side that has stigmatized Mitnick ever since *Cyberpunk* hit the stands. Or perhaps this malicious nature was never really there to begin with? In any case, the Mitnick of *Fugitive* has little in common with the Mitnick of *Cyberpunk,* except, of course, for the hacking. What accounts for this difference seems to be that Littman actually *talks* to Mitnick, something the authors of *Cyberpunk* did not feel was worth the expense. And it is by listening to Mitnick that we begin to understand him, in ways that are far more comprehensive than *Cyberpunk's* Dark Side stigma can convey.

If *Fugitive* was nothing more than a dry transcription of phone conversations between Mitnick and Littman, the book would still rank as the definitive work on this elusive hacker, easily ousting *Cyberpunk* for the coveted honor. But *Fugitive* is much more than this. In *Fugitive,* Littman reminds us that an investigative journalist's most powerful weapon is still to question. Question everything. Question the good guys. Question the bad guys. Question authority. *Fugitive* is replete with questioning, most of which remains unanswered. While loose ends are not usually considered praiseworthy for an investigative work, in this case, the kudos are indeed appropriate because Littman seems to be the only one doing the questioning. Certainly John Markoff, despite *Cyberpunk* and all of his *New York Times* pieces, has never bothered to scratch below the surface of Mitnick or acquire the true facts of his case. Littman spends entire chapters debunking the myths and distortions surrounding Mitnick, most of which originated from these very sources. And Littman's questions have a way of reminding the reader to remain skeptical, that things are never as simple as we would like them to be. We may never know, for example, exactly how it was that Markoff—a reporter—came to be tagging along with computer security expert Tsutomu Shimomura and the FBI on their stakeout of Mitnick's Raleigh residence, but that won't stop Littman from asking. Of course, the use of the rhetorical question is not lost upon Littman either, as when he asks Shimomura, "Are you a hacker?" knowing full well that Shimomura hacks all right—only he hacks for the Feds. Questions, then, in and of themselves, can make a point, and good questions can make for a fine piece of journalistic work.

Fugitive, then, is as much a story about John Markoff as it is about Mitnick. Here we learn that Markoff has been obsessed with Mitnick for years. And Markoff had everything he needed to fulfill this obsession: he had the skills, the experience, the contacts; he had Shimomura and *The New York Times.* There's just one thing that he didn't have, and that was Mitnick. Markoff did not have Mitnick because Littman did, a fact that Littman shamelessly conveys to the reader through his careful balance of ponderosities and conversation. By and large, the power of *Fugitive* comes from the exchange of dialogue between Littman and Mitnick. Littman knows that this is the main attraction, and he does not disappoint. *Fugitive* is full of interesting phone ironies, as when Littman puts a federal prosecutor on hold to take a call from Mitnick, whose whereabouts at that time were still unknown.

Fugitive adds credence to the notion that people are indeed judged by their motives, and not merely by their actions. In *Fugitive,* however, it is not Mitnick's motives that are being questioned, but rather those of Markoff and Shimomura. Together these "business partners" have sowed their involvement with Mitnick into a cash crop estimated at nearly $2 million. With a purported $750,000 book deal signed, along with a $200,000 Miramax movie option, and an estimated $250-500,000 for foreign book rights, Markoff and Shimomura have made more money off of Mitnick than anyone dreamed possible. One wonders just what sort of criminal acts Mitnick could have perpetrated to deserve so much attention. When all the dust settles, one may very well wonder in vain.

Lies (Summer, 1998)

We've gotten pretty used to people getting it wrong. The authorities, the media, the clueless wannabe idiots, who never quite get just what it is that hackers are all about. At times the distance they've achieved between themselves and the truth has been humorous. But mostly it's depressing, because when the dust clears, theirs are the perceptions the populace will accept as gospel.

But how far can this go? In recent weeks, a number of us have had to wonder this. Stories and "facts" so bizarre as to be unbelievable even by those people who believe whatever they're told have been surfacing and circulating. And they have brought us to a turning point. Either things are about to get a whole lot worse or maybe, just maybe, people will finally begin to wake up. We'll know soon enough.

It all started with a rather strange article in a magazine called *Signal*. They bill themselves as the "International Armed Forces Communications & Electronics Association's (AFCEA) premiere, award winning magazine for communications and electronics professionals throughout government and industry." In an article entitled "Make-My-Day Server Throws Gauntlet to Network Hackers," *Signal's* Editor-In-Chief, Clarence A. Robinson, Jr., rambles on at great length about something called the "Blitzkrieg server," which is able to magically "self-organize and self-heal, recognize an infiltration, isolate it, adapt to it, and create a totally different networking route to overcome an invasion." It also supposedly has all kinds of offensive options just waiting to be used. "These options could eventually end in the destruction of an attacker's network resources." Yeah, right, whatever.

According to the article, the server predicted that "a hacker attack would be targeted at specific U.S. corporations and California state government installations" and that the "attack would be from Japanese nationals with the help of U.S. collaborators affiliated with the *2600* international hacker group."

We found that interesting. Especially since this is the first time that a *machine* has slandered us and our intentions. Since we're relatively sure a human was involved at some stage, we haven't determined who is to blame for this just yet, or even whether the entire story was a piece of fiction created by *Signal* to get attention. That kind of thing doesn't happen very often. However...

Mere days after the *Signal* absurdity, another story appeared in a well-respected journal: *The New Republic*. In their "Washington Scene" section was a story entitled "Hack Heaven." It told the tale of Ian Restil, a 15-year-old computer hacker who was terrorizing corporate America. A first-hand account of Restil's demands for large amounts of money from Jukt Micronics grabs the reader's attention as the story opens. As we read on, we see that the company is tripping over itself to give this brat whatever he wants because, quite frankly, they're terrified of what he can do if he hacks into their databases again. And hackers know this. "Indeed, deals like Ian's are becoming common—so common, in fact, that hacker agents now advertise their commissions on web sites. *Computer Insider*, a newsletter for hackers, estimates that about 900 recreational hackers were hired in the last four years by companies they once targeted. Ian's agent, whose business card is emblazoned with the slogan 'super-agent to super-nerds,' claims to represent nearly 300 of them, ages 9 to 68."

The article goes on to point out how such deals make it virtually impossible for the police to arrest or prosecute "most hackers" since corporations are so reluctant to come forward and so afraid of what the hackers will do. It's become such a problem that legislation has been brought forward to criminalize such immunity deals between hackers and corporations. But the all-powerful hackers have their own lobbying group—the National Assembly of Hackers—who are vowing to keep the legislation from passing.

We found that impressive. We had no idea that hackers were this powerful. Somehow we had managed to miss this hacker lobbying group, we didn't know this Ian kid at all, and we had never heard of the *Computer Insider* hacker newsletter. But before we could feel the frustration of our ignorance, the world found out something about the article's author, Stephen Glass.

It seems he was a liar. He had made the whole thing up! There was no Ian Restil, no Jukt Micronics, no *Computer Insider,* and no National Assembly of Hackers. And this time, the deceit actually got some attention. The story of the lying journalist was picked up nationwide and reputations were forever tarnished. But in all of the media coverage, we found one thing to be missing. Nobody seemed to care about how the hacker community had been unfairly portrayed. Yes, we know that truth, integrity, and journalism all suffered a black eye because of this pitiful display, but digging a little deeper would have quickly shown how there were human victims as well. The American public *believes* this kind of trash because this view of hackers is constantly reinforced by all of the stories that stop just *short* of blatant lying. It's not at all uncommon for multinational corporations to be portrayed as helpless victims forever being preyed upon by ruthless hackers. Reality paints a very different picture, as in the case of Kevin Mitnick, a hacker imprisoned for three and a half years with no trial, no bail, and no visitors while his alleged attacks on multinational corporations are questionable at best and, even if proven, trivial and insignificant. Figures given by these corporations on hacker "damages" are believed without question by the authorities while individuals are imprisoned without the opportunity to counter the charges. It may seem incomprehensible that such points are constantly being missed by the media. But, once you do a little digging of your own and see how much of the media these same corporations own, it all becomes painfully clear.

Perhaps you can see now why we find these things so depressing. But all of the above pales in comparison to what we are currently facing.

In early June, it was announced that Dimension Films, in conjunction with Miramax and Millennium, would be making a film version of *Takedown.*

Why is this important? *Takedown* was the first of the Kevin Mitnick books to be released in 1996, less than a year after his capture in North Carolina. It was also the most flawed, not so much because of the writing, although we could certainly go on at length about the self-centered, egotistical prattling of Tsutomu Shimomura. Rather, it was his and co-writer John Markoff's questionable motives in bringing this story to the American public that have made an increasing number of people take notice. Consider the facts. Markoff had co-written a book called *Cyberpunk* a few years back that had a section devoted to Mitnick, even though he had never interviewed him. Markoff, a reporter for *The New York Times,* managed to somehow get a front page story about

Kevin Mitnick published on July 4, 1994. All the story really said was that Mitnick was a fugitive being sought by the FBI. Hardly the kind of thing normally printed on the front page. Even then suspicions were raised. Markoff, in publishing such pieces, was becoming the "Mitnick expert," despite his lack of firsthand knowledge. When Markoff published another front page story in January of 1995 that detailed how the security on Shimomura's computer system had been defeated (again, hardly a front page item), he neglected to mention that the two of them were friends. When Mitnick was captured the following month, Markoff published yet another front page story claiming that he was the prime suspect in the Shimomura incident. Again, an important detail was omitted: Markoff had played an active role in helping Shimomura track down Mitnick in North Carolina. The two had even intercepted telephone traffic between Mitnick and the *2600* offices! And when the book deal was complete less than a week later, Markoff and Shimomura became very wealthy while Mitnick was all but forgotten in prison.

So now there's a movie in the works. Apart from the indignation many of us will feel over the fact that these people will make yet more money off of Mitnick while exploiting a story they practically made up themselves, the real injustice lies in the screenplay itself. While the book was bad and filled with inaccuracies and omissions, the script (written by Howard Rodman), is far worse, a concept admittedly hard to grasp but unfortunately quite true. For in addition to all of the badness of *Takedown*, the film version adds dialogue and situations that are complete fabrications, all in the interests of entertainment.

Only one problem: *Takedown* is supposedly nonfiction. We obtained a copy of the script and can confirm that there is more fantasy in the film version than in the entire *Star Wars* trilogy. And when you consider that this is a film that will be using real people's names and circumstances, the harm it will cause becomes quite apparent.

The anti-Mitnick paranoia is well-established a mere 20 minutes into the film. Shimomura, in a sobering tone, warns his girlfriend: "He could be... reading your mail, listening to you when you talk on the phone, looking at your medical records, what your shrink said when he sent in the forms to the insurance company, what kind of gear you ordered from North Face, whether you like down, or Thinsulate, your college transcript, your credit card statement, how many times you went to the drugstore, and what you charged." It's just like *The Net* except Kevin Mitnick replaces today's society as the primary threat to privacy. As we progress, concern over Mitnick's capabilities grows: "He could be going into medical records, f*cking them up. He could be killing people, and we're just standing here." In fact, as Mitnick suspects he is about to be caught, we see him actually trying to change someone's medical records—which is about the dumbest thing anyone in such a situation could ever do. Then the FBI becomes concerned over Mitnick's ability to wriggle out of the situation. "Every step of what we do will be scrutinized. Did we have the warrant for this? Did we have the right to do that? *He* won't be on trial. *We* will." There is no mention made of the fact that the feds have so far managed to lock him up *without trial* for three and a half years. That's something the makers of this film clearly don't think the American public needs to know.

From the opening scene where Mitnick is shown as a foul-mouthed, cheating 12-year-oid to the end where he gets his just deserts in prison, we see Mitnick lie, steal, and hack his way across America, stopping long enough to unleash racial epithets toward the film's noble hero Shimomura. ("I think that man needs a haircut. I mean, he can cover his ears, but I, for one... well, *I* still remember Pearl Harbor." Or, "I cannot f*cking believe what I hacked out of Japboy.")

Not surprisingly, Markoff's involvement in the search and capture is erased completely. And Shimomura is made into someone with compassion who actually reaches out to Kevin while he's in prison, attempting to make peace and saying he's sorry it had to be like this. In real life, Shimomura has never said a word to him.

Mitnick, who will be played by Skeet Ulrich of *Scream,* is made out to be nothing less than a demon, who doesn't care who he hurts and who will stop at nothing to get what he wants. He equates his life to a video game, if you can believe *that:* "It's like Pacman: There's food, you find it, you eat it, you stay alive. Then there are a couple of ghosts chasing you. They find you, you die. That's it." By the end of the film, you will be so happy he's behind bars that you will start searching for "Free Kevin" stickers to rip down.

Technical inaccuracies abound, like the typical Hollywood perception that modems are always screeching in the background. Or this stage direction: "He takes a long chug of his Big Gulp, wets his lips, licking them thoroughly. Then picks up the phone, waits for the dial tone, and... *whistles*. It's not a tune. It's the tones of the touch-tone system, and Mitnick is whistling in his own code."

Most of the characters who are *not* named Shimomura are seen as bumbling idiots or vindictive assholes who let their personal dislike of our hero get in the way of the investigation. In a real stretch of the truth, the staff of San Francisco's *The Well,* refuse to erase Shimomura's sensitive data that Mitnick supposedly uploaded via a hacked account. They say, "It's the policy of *The Well* not to change, censor, tamper with, or delete the work of our users. It's not ours. It's theirs." Of course, anyone in their right mind would realize that an *unauthorized* user would never be given the same rights as an authorized one! This is clearly not the way it happened at all.

The only real dramatic tension comes from making Shimomura into someone with a secret past who had files that could destroy the world or something—the details are never gone into. And Mitnick is his evil counterpart who intends to spread those files to the world: "Sooner or later, he's gonna upload. The OKI data, the credit cards... my, ah, Los Alamos files." Yeah, right, whatever.

But easily the most bizarre and offensive part of the film comes when Shimomura and Mitnick come face to face in Seattle, an incident *everyone* admits is completely fabricated. "Just as Shimomura relaxes... *THWAACK!* ...he's clubbed on the side of the head. Mitnick, wielding the top of a metal garbage can like a weapon, sees Shimomura drop into the muck. He staggers out of the alleyway. Shimomura, dazed, blood flowing freely from a gash above his ear, raises himself to his elbows...and watches Mitnick disappear, into the night." Mitnick thus graduates from evil, destructive, racist hacker to violent criminal.

There is nothing and nobody to back up any of the absurd allegations in this movie. From the people who know Mitnick to the news reports that did their best to demonize him to the court records that document his repeated failure to be treated fairly, even to the book that this film is based on, there is *no evidence whatsoever* of the kind of despicable criminal behavior portrayed in the script.

So how could such a libelous piece of trash even be attempted? This is the interesting part. Since Mitnick is considered a "public figure," the Hollywood people figure they can get away with bending the truth while using real names. But, as indicated above, the only reason Mitnick is a public figure is because of the antics of John Markoff and Tsutomu Shimomura. Without the two Markoff books and all of those front page articles that wound up feeding hundreds of other newspapers and magazines around the world, how much of a public figure would Mitnick really be? For that matter, would the government have made such a point of keeping him locked away for so long? These are most troubling questions.

But even more troubling is the prospect of such a film being made without the opportunity to set the record straight. Think of what it will mean. For the millions of people who pay to see it, *this* will be the story of Kevin Mitnick. Whenever his name comes up in conversation or in the news, the image from *Takedown* is what people will remember. For that reason alone, action must be taken to stop this.

We have absolutely no problem with bad films being made. And if this were a work of fiction, we'd either trash it when it came out or ignore it completely. But *Takedown* is purported to be documenting a true story and its distortion of the truth will gravely hurt some very real people. How likely is it that Mitnick will be able to get a fair trial (if he's ever allowed to have one at all) once people have seen this film? Oddly enough, his trial has already occurred at the end of the film, which only further confuses the issue. Incidentally, legal experts tell us that the two charges he's convicted of in the film (probation violation and "felony theft of intellectual and real property in violation of Section 6 of the Penal Code" would never get him a sentence approaching the amount of time he's already been in prison. But why confuse the public with facts?

We find this outrageous. And so do a whole lot of other people who have been getting involved in the "Free Kevin" campaign. The movement was already picking up steam when this news hit. Now it's growing faster than we anticipated.

We intend to stop this production in its tracks and—make damn sure everyone involved is aware of the facts. And if we are unable to change this reality-based story into something resembling reality, then we will use it as a vehicle to get our own message out. This will include pickets, boycotts, phone/letter/fax campaigns, whatever it takes. There is a story here, a really good one. And while we may not be able to get someone to tell that story, we *can* do something about the lies. We will either stop them or we will make the world aware of what they really are.

We encourage you to continue showing support by spreading the "Free Kevin" stickers around as much as you can. Remember, the money we raise through the stickers goes straight to Mitnick's defense fund. The more of these we can get in public view, the more people will become aware of the other side of this story.

As always, we thank you for your support. This is going to be one interesting summer.

MILESTONE: THE HACKER VIDEO (Autumn, 1991)

Over the summer, military computer systems in the United States were accessed by Dutch hackers. One of the episodes was captured on videotape by *2600*, portions of which were shown on a recent nationwide television show. Most of it, however, has never been seen. We are releasing this videotape to the public so that more people will witness just how shamefully easy it is to get access to military computers.

The intrusion took place in late-July, 1991. The purpose of this demonstration was to show just how easy it really was. Great care was taken to ensure that no damage or alteration of data occurred on this particular system. No military secrets were taken and no files were saved to a disk by the hackers. What is frightening is that nobody knows who else has access to this information or what their motivations might be. This is a warning that cannot be taken lightly.

Why We Are Exposing This

The hackers responsible for this are not interested in military secrets. But they do recognize the importance and value of the information that is stored on such computers. The fact of the matter is that if these gaping security holes are not openly exposed, they will never get fixed. Ironically, the bug that was used in this particular case is a fairly old one that has been fixed on most systems. Why it still existed on a military system is beyond us. But we do know that this is only one system and only one bug.

continues

MILESTONE: THE HACKER VIDEO *(continued)*

Corporate computer systems also continue to operate with security holes. As hackers, we are concerned with the lack of safeguards that are being placed upon sensitive data. In addition to military data, much information about individual people continues to be sloppily managed. Our credit ratings, telephone records, banking information, and computerized files of all sorts are open to scrutiny for anyone who can gain access.

We should stress that the vast majority of unauthorized access does not involve computer hackers. Since we have no ulterior motives, other than the quest for knowledge, we openly reveal whatever we find out. Unfortunately, this often results in our being blamed for the problem itself—confusing the messenger with the message. In reality, there are countless instances of employees invading the privacy of individuals by accessing credit files or billing information that they have no business seeing. Since this information is so easy for them to get a hold of, there is virtually no way of their being detected. And, even if they were detected, they aren't really breaking any laws.

Add to this the increasing fragility of our modern technology as computers become dependent upon other computers and it becomes evident that serious problems, even catastrophes, lie ahead. The actions of computer hackers are, at worst, an annoyance to some rather powerful people. Were we not to expose the flaws in the system, they would still be there and they would most definitely be abused.

Progress (Autumn, 1998)

The announcement of the *Takedown* movie in our last issue and in other forums produced a strong reaction, the likes of which we have not seen in our entire publishing history. It was bad enough knowing Kevin was still in prison after more than three years of waiting for a trial that never seemed to come. But now, a film that would portray him as a truly evil person and at the same time line the pockets of those who helped put him in the position he now faces? Even people who thought he was guilty of *something* came out strongly opposed to this.

It started in July with a demonstration outside Miramax offices in New York by around two dozen of us. That doesn't sound like much but whenever you can get that many people to stand in front of a building with picket signs in this day and age, it's a very significant statement. Sad but true. And the impact of that demonstration was clearly felt throughout the industry. Even the press took notice, although it took most of them a few weeks to get around to covering it. But in the end, our demonstration achieved everything it set out to do: Raise awareness, begin a truly organized campaign, and show support for someone who was unable to defend themselves against a host of really powerful entities.

Miramax, to their credit, had the script rewritten several times, addressing nearly all of our objections to the original version. The infamous garbage can scene has been scrapped. Kevin is no longer portrayed as a violent racist. And, in a nod to reality, serious questions are raised as to just how involved Kevin actually was in the hacking of Tsutomu Shimomura's machine and, even more importantly, just why the FBI was targeting Kevin in the first place. But we can't say we support the film until Kevin himself feels that he's being treated fairly. As of this printing, that has still not happened.

We found a lot of the cause and effect to be really inspiring, so much so that we decided to do something more. So, for a good part of the summer, a group of *2600* people drove through the entire country (unlimited mileage rental car) searching for answers in the whole Mitnick affair and filming as much of it as possible. We spoke with dozens of people on all levels of involvement in the case and came away with nearly 100 hours of footage. What we do with it now depends on what kind of editing equipment we can get our hands on but, suffice to say, we've got a fascinating story to tell and a most interesting counterpoint to the major motion picture that will be out in a year.

Considering the weakened state *2600* was in at the time we began this project, such an endeavor could best be described as foolhardy. Nevertheless, we knew this was the right time, and the only time, we could cover the story in this way. The "Free Kevin" movement has been growing with every passing month and the news of the *Takedown* movie only served as a catalyst. Again, good has come out of bad and all of us emerge from the darkness with more strength and determination.

We're certainly not the only ones getting the word out. All over the country, kids are handing out leaflets in their schools and malls, spreading awareness and adding to the movement. While we've heard many of them say they were inspired by *2600*, the real truth is that nothing makes all of this seem more worthwhile than hearing what they're doing. People in high schools and colleges are realizing they *can* make a difference, just by standing up for what they believe in. It seems like such a simple thing to do but so few of us actually take the trouble to go and do it. In the end, we believe this will be shown as one of the major reasons why the battle was won.

One of the most dramatic incidents in recent memory was *The New York Times* web page hack. On Sunday, September 13 (an extremely busy news day due to the Clinton scandal), hackers replaced the usual page with a rambling text, the entirety of which may have been hard for some to understand. But one section quite clearly told of the injustices of the Kevin Mitnick case as well as the culpability of *The Times* in his capture and the ensuing cashing in of the story. For many, this was their first exposure to any of this.

The message from Kevin and his attorney was very clear: this kind of thing is bad as it sends the wrong message and somehow makes it appear as if he's responsible for net chaos. However, we have mixed feelings. While doing something destructive in Kevin's name certainly won't help his case, we're not entirely sure that's what happened here. *The Times* is not claiming that there was any destruction to their original page. A glance at the many forums on the subject reveals that most people don't think the hack itself is a serious matter and that *The Times* had it coming, both for their lack of security and their apparent lack of journalistic integrity. And most everyone began to express an interest in the Kevin Mitnick story. On the www.kevinmitnick.com site (which was linked from the hacked site), our counter went from 13,534 hits the day before *The Times* hack to 62,582 hits the day of the hack and 98,116 the day after! Since then it seems to have leveled off between 20,000 and 30,000 a day but it's clear that a lot of interest was generated and many of those new people have been checking in for updated info. Yes, working within the system is preferable. But we cannot control the way everyone spreads the message, nor should we. When the system doesn't respond to continued injustice, people who have any spirit at all will find some way of getting the word out. The net is a far more level playing field than many of us realize. And *The Times* once again missed an opportunity to get it right by merely vowing to prosecute the hackers to the fullest extent of the law instead of looking at themselves to see what might have spurred this.

The Media

The media would continue to demonize hackers throughout the decade so we weren't really surprised by any of the nonsense they printed. But we still felt the need to constantly remind people that this sort of thing needed to be responded to. After all, when stories circulate that imply that there are 250,000 of us trying to break into the Pentagon, it can make life more than a little tense, especially if your friends and family already suspect you of having computer superpowers. And when President Clinton decided to chime in on the subject, we knew we were going to have a tough time ahead. Also included in this section is an instructional article on how to handle the media, which hopefully a lot of people (hacker and non-hacker alike) were able to take advantage of.

Guided Perceptions (Summer, 1996)

If the media is to be believed, 250,000 hackers are out there somewhere trying to get into Defense Department computers. A quarter of a million. They sure do know how to get our attention, don't they?

After reading past the initial screaming headlines, you discover that there is not, in fact, a veritable army of hackers encircling the Pentagon. OK, we can exhale a little bit. When the General Accounting Office released this figure, they *meant* that there were 250,000 *attempts* to access Defense Department computers. Oh, and, by the way, two thirds of those attempts were successful.

Now it becomes interesting.

We have yet to hear a straight answer as to just what is meant by 250,000 "attempts" to break in. Were these login attempts? Telnet sessions? FTP accessing? Perhaps even web hits?

A success rate of 66 percent leads one to believe that we're dealing with incompetency on a phenomenal scale. There are systems out there where users mistype their passwords frequently enough to only have a two-thirds success rate and here we're talking about hackers somehow managing to achieve that rate. Do Defense Department computers use default passwords? Do they use passwords *at all?*

Even more amazing than this weird story of a non-story was the media reaction to it. Even though virtually no specifics were given, the piece was given prominent placement in newspapers, magazines, and on network radio and television. And we started to wonder what this was really leading up to.

It didn't take long to find out.

Mere weeks after these strange figures were released, Senate hearings were held to determine what actions needed to be taken. Some of the conclusions reached are truly frightening.

Senator Sam Nunn (D-Ga.) actually concluded that it was now necessary to turn the attention of the Central Intelligence Agency towards the American public, presumably so these evil hackers could be stopped from doing harm to the nation's defense. (Intelligence agencies like the CIA and the NSA have long been forbidden from focusing on domestic targets.) And Senator Jon Kyl (R-Az.) came up with this gem: "The United States currently has no ability to protect itself from cyberspace attacks." No ability? What exactly is it that would make these senators feel better? Is it not enough that people like Kevin Mitnick and Bernie S. have been forced to endure more inhumane treatment than killers and rapists? If individuals accused of so little can be subjected to so much, it seems hard to believe that real criminals would ever manage to slip through the cracks. If anything, there is *too much* ability and not enough common sense being used when dealing with these issues.

Of course, there's still that nagging little question of just what "real criminals" we're talking about here. Virtually everything we've been hearing seems to be based upon mere speculation. Even the Pentagon admits this, saying that there's no way to know just how many attacks there really were since few of them were noticed and because the ones that are noticed don't have to be reported. Yet they're able to make a number up, throw it to the media, and have it become the gospel truth. Imagine if all of us had *that* power.

To us, it's very simple to see the hypocrisy and the exaggeration but it's not so readily apparent to people who depend upon the mass media as their sole source of news. People want clearly defined villains and overly simplistic and satisfying solutions. Or, at least, that's what those in charge of statistics seem to think. Maybe it's time to start giving people a little more credit and offering some alternative scenarios. We've found with both the Mitnick and Bernie S. cases that non-hackers have developed a genuine mistrust for what they have been told by the media and the government. The appalling actions of the Secret Service in the latter case have opened more eyes than anything else. It's hard to imagine where we will be in a few years if the current disintegration of trust continues. But it's bound to result in some desperate measures on the part of those in charge. What we are seeing in this Pentagon report and the ensuing Senate hearings may be one of the first signs of this frantic effort to regain our confidence.

Attorney General Janet Reno has gone before the nation and made hackers out to be one of the gravest threats facing all of us, again, with no real evidence other than speculative fears to point to. The danger of this witch hunt mentality cannot be overestimated.

But we must also be careful not to over generalize ourselves. We are every bit as guilty if we simply sit back and do nothing when such threats become apparent. The recent overturning of the Communications Decency Act by a three judge panel in Philadelphia is an example of what can be done when people join forces to challenge something that is unjust. And, while congratulations are certainly in order, the utter failure to do anything substantive for those people already locked away because of technophobia and/or malice towards hackers speaks volumes. The two issues *are* most definitely related. It's just more difficult to stand up for a person who some see as a criminal than it is to stand up for freedom and democracy on their own merits. Which is exactly why the former is so important.

Naturally, we hope the striking down of the Communications Decency Act is upheld. But what we really want to see is a more aggressive stance taken in challenging the information that we're being fed. When intelligent people ask intelligent questions, we'll see less nonsense about phantom hackers, less cruel and unusual punishment, and, quite possibly, some sane and well thought out policy.

It's in our hands.

The Big Time (Spring, 1999)

Yes, we've finally hit it big. There's really no other way to describe it when the President of the United States comes right out and makes a speech targeting your kind as a significant part of the future threat facing Western civilization. In a few sentences, he was able to put teenage kids from suburbia in the same class as international terrorists who, we might add, have really worked hard to establish their image. It hardly seems fair.

It didn't take very long for the thrill to wear off. The realization that people that high up in the command structure actually believe things people like Geraldo Rivera and Mike Wallace say is pretty damn scary. But it's nothing compared to some of the things they have planned for us.

That's right. We can look forward to an accelerated erosion of our freedoms and fairly open way of life. And it's all the fault of computer hackers. Oops.

We really do want to express our sincere regret for breaking our democracy and ruining the whole thing for everybody. But before the history books get written, we'd like to examine the facts a bit more closely.

First, let's look at just what was said. The speech in question was given on January 22, 1999, at the National Academy of Sciences in Washington, DC, and was entitled "Keeping America Secure for the 21st Century." A good part of it had to do with the threat of bioterrorism. The rest focused on "cyber attacks" and what must be done to prevent them.

"Revolutions in technology have spread the message and the gifts of freedom but have also given new opportunities to freedom's enemies," Clinton says. "The enemies of peace realize they cannot defeat us with traditional military means. So they are working on...cyber attacks on our critical computer systems....We must be ready—ready if our adversaries try to use computers to disable power grids, banking, communications and transportation networks, police, fire and health services—or military assets.

"More and more, these critical systems are driven by, and linked together with, computers, making them more vulnerable to disruption. Last spring, we saw the enormous impact of a single failed electronic link, when a satellite malfunctioned—disabled pagers, ATMs, credit card systems and television networks all around the world. And we already are seeing the first wave of deliberate cyber attacks—hackers break into government and business computers, stealing and destroying information, raiding bank accounts, running up credit card charges, extorting money by threats to unleash computer viruses."

Clearly, someone's been watching too much television. Even if we do accept the bad science fiction scenarios described above, one has to wonder what kind of genius would allow critical systems to *become* more vulnerable to disruption in the first place. It seems that kind of poor thinking would pose more of a threat than any organized attack.

But, assuming the threat is real, this characterization of hackers is both unfair and completely inaccurate. We expect people without a clue to believe that hackers do this kind of thing. Are we now to believe that this cluelessness extends all the way up to the top? Where is the evidence of hackers "raiding bank accounts," "destroying information," or "extorting money" if their demands aren't met? Fiction doesn't count—

where is the evidence in the *real world?* Such things certainly happen but they are invariably at the hands of insiders, career criminals, or people with a grudge against a certain company. To make the jump that because it involves computers and crime, it can only be hackers is a most unfortunate, and all too typical, assumption. Now that it's come from Clinton himself, more people will believe this and hackers will universally be seen as a negative force.

Too bad, since hackers may be the one hope our nation has of avoiding a prolonged period of technological ignorance and fear, as well as increased manipulation and suppression of individual thought and alternative perspectives. Who else will figure out ways of defeating systems that are impenetrable without keeping the details to themselves or selling their allegiance to the highest bidder? Who else will remember the simple yet vital premise of free access that has shaped much of what today's net community is? And who else will have the guts to use these hopelessly naive ideals against the well-funded agendas of control and influence put forth by corporate and government interests? As perpetual questioners, it's our responsibility to be skeptical and to never accept the obvious answers without thorough scrutiny. Never has that been more important than now, when new technology increasingly affects our lives with every passing day. By demonizing us, our concerns become that much easier to dismiss.

We said it gets worse and it does. In addition to allocating $2.8 billion to fight both "bioterrorism" and "cyberterrorism," Clinton is considering appointing a military commander to oversee these battles, *right here in the United States*. Such military presence in our own country would be unprecedented. According to *The New York Times*, "Such a step would go far beyond the civil defense measures and bomb shelters that marked the cold war, setting up instead a military leadership" right here in the United States to deal with the above-described hackers as well as all the other evil people plotting our nation's destruction.

Obviously, this kind of a thing is raising concern among all kinds of people, not just hackers. But it illustrates why we have to make sure we're not drawn into this little game. It would be so much more convenient if we played along and turned into the cybervillains they so want us to be. Then it would be easy to send in assault teams to flush us out, online or offline. There also is a certain allure to *being* a cybervillain, and this is what we have to be particularly careful about.

Earlier in the year, hackers belonging to the group Legions of the Underground (LoU) held an online press conference to announce a campaign to cripple the infrastructures of China and Iraq, supposedly because of human rights abuses. Led by Germany's Chaos Computer Club, virtually every major hacker organization (*2600* included) condemned this action as counterproductive, against the hacker ethic, and potentially very dangerous. Fortunately, this had an effect, and other members of LoU quickly stepped in and denied any destructive intent.

This incident served to bring up some rather important issues. While hacking an occasional web page is one thing that can even be thought of as an expression of free speech, declarations of war and attempts to cause actual damage are very different indeed. We don't doubt that this is exactly the kind of behavior the authorities have in mind when they come up with plans like the above.

It also plays right into the hands of the Clinton view of hackers by making us into some kind of tool of war that can be used to disrupt infrastructures and destabilize societies. No matter how right the cause seems to be, we must not allow ourselves to be manipulated into this position. In addition to being targeted as enemies of the state, this would also raise the possibility of being used *by* the government to enact their version of "cyberwar" against this week's enemy. It's not inconceivable that such "service" could be held over the head of hackers who get in trouble with the law. Given the choice between recruitment as an agent of electronic warfare and a federal prisoner, which would you choose? Being put in that position is clearly not where we should want to be.

It's truly unfortunate that Clinton has chosen to accept this misinformed view of hackers. But by forcing the issue, perhaps we will have a chance to correct this perception before the troops move in or public hysteria fuels the fire. It would be wise to do whatever we can to make sure the image we project is an accurate one.

Hack the Media (Winter, 1999–2000) *By Jim Nieken*

Much has been said lately about journalists and the media, from their outright disregard for the likes of Kevin Mitnick and others, to MTV's much-criticized foray into the lives of hackers. Few would deny the power and influence of journalists, yet no one seems to like them. They tend to paint hackers and most other "underground" subcultures in a negative light, and there are a number of reasons for this. Among them, deadlines and other time constraints, the betraying nature of the news gathering process, and the necessity to simplify information. But there are ways to turn the idiosyncrasies of journalism to your advantage, and to help reporters present an accurate and positive account. Follow my advice, and you might even find something good written about you in the paper.

First, some background. I have been working for various newspapers for years, both in freelance and staff reporter positions. My byline has graced the pages of papers both big and small, but I grew up working with local papers and tend to prefer them. I haven't done very much work with television, but the news gathering process is mostly interchangeable. Although a writer by trade, I am a geek at heart and must sympathize with the poor treatment my colleagues often give hackers.

This article is intended to explain how print and television journalists investigate and report a story, and what you can do if you are ever asked for an interview.

The Deadline: Your Ticket to Increased Adrenaline Output

Years ago, when I was just getting into the newspaper business, a grizzled old editor took me aside and explained what I was really supposed to be doing there. "My job," he said, "is filling up newspapers. Your job is meeting deadlines." His point was that while journalistic integrity was all well and good, newspapers couldn't print blank pages.

Deadlines are not just a part of the job; they are often the single most important concern. Reporters need to get their work in on time, and that can sometimes mean sacrificing accuracy for haste.

No one wants to print an untruthful story, but the fact is that the less time you spend researching, the less quality information you will get. That information also needs to be analyzed if it is to be conveyed correctly, which also takes time.

Looming deadlines are not the only factor in inaccurate reporting, but if you ever find yourself the subject of a story you should take them into account. If a reporter says that he or she has a day or less to cover a story, be concerned. If they have more than a few days they probably won't totally misrepresent you, and if they have several weeks the deadline is not likely to affect the quality of the reporting at all. This is why local television news reports are often so shoddy. Local TV reporters (carpetbaggers all) often work under deadlines of a few hours or less. They are told to run out to a location, pose in front of a building or a car accident, and rattle off a few facts provided by local law enforcement. They don't have time to actually investigate, which is the curse of all time constraints.

As a subject, there is little you can do about deadlines, but you may want to ask when their story is due. If you want to help yourself and create a better story, try your best to work within the limits of the reporter. If you just did something especially nasty to the local power grid and you would like your side of the story told before they haul you off to a holding cell, try to be available to media sources. You can't get your side out if you won't talk, and newspapers may be forced to print only what they have heard from other sources. Those may be your friends and family, but they could also be the police and other government agencies, or the guy whose life was ruined because he missed the season premiere of *Ally McBeal* when you took out the electric company.

The Interview as Seduction and Betrayal

In college, a journalism professor once told me that there are only two kinds of people in the world, those who are interviewed often and who know how to be interviewed—and those who aren't and don't. As a reporter I get most of my information via the interviewing process, but no other news gathering technique has a greater potential for distorting information. Unlike a school district budget, or the winner of an election, or something equally quantifiable, conversations are more subject to interpretation than most people realize. Your ideas must survive the transfer into your own words, into my head or into my notes, into new words in the final story, past the mercurial tempers of various editors, and finally back into the heads of a hundred thousand readers. It's not at all uncommon for people to complain that they were misquoted or misrepresented when they see their words in print. I hear it all the time.

The distortion extends beyond merely getting the exact wording of a quote wrong. Words are usually taken totally out of context, poorly extrapolated from sloppy notes, or even shamelessly fabricated. It's very uncommon for a reporter to totally fake quotes (we tend to be pretty anal when it comes to what's inside quote marks), but danger lies in how quotes are set up. It all depends on how your comments are explained and what context they are placed in.

You could say something like: "I don't really like people who break into other people's computers just to mess with stuff. I mean, the idiots usually deserve what they get for leaving stuff wide open, but it's really mean and no one should take advantage of people like that."

But a week later, this might be printed in the local paper: "...One hacker said that he feels no sympathy for people whose computers are attacked or vandalized. 'The idiots usually deserve what they get for leaving their stuff wide open,' he said casually."

The quote was reproduced accurately, but the context was totally reversed. Beware of this. Reporters love juicy, callous, or controversial quotes. They spice up a piece of writing like you wouldn't believe. If you're not careful they could even end up right in the headline. If it takes three minutes of set up and hypothetical situations and philosophical justifications before you can say something like, "...so I guess if looked at it that way we should probably just blow up the phone company building," you can be assured they will not print the philosophical justifications and skip right into your admission of a terrorist plot.

As an interviewee, you can help in a number of ways. First, don't say anything that needs a lot of background or buildup. We work with sound bites, and you should never say anything you don't want printed unless you make it clear that it's off the record. All reporters will respect your wishes to not have a quote printed, but always pay attention to what you are saying. Don't say anything too sociopathic. Go slowly. We can only write so fast, and it allows you to choose your words more precisely. If you're ever suspicious, ask the reporter to read your words back to you. Make sure you like what it says, because they may come back to haunt you and this is the only chance you are going to get to change them. Also, always realize that you never have to answer any question asked by a reporter. We're not cops, and we can't force you to do anything. On the other hand, most journalists have large expense accounts and bribes are an extremely common industry practice. You might suggest that you sit down over dinner to talk. Be sure to order a dessert.

Journalists May Be Stupid, but Our Readers Are Even Stupider

My handy Microsoft Word grammar checker tells me that this document is written at or around the 10th grade reading level. This means that if you can read this paper without moving your lips, you are capable of reading at least that level. Most magazines and nearly all newspapers are written at or around the sixth grade level. This is not because this is all the average American can handle. Rather, it keeps Joe Public from choking on his coffee at 7:30 a.m. as he slams into words like "axiological." Put simply—newspapers are mass mediums. They are consumed by the general public, and are written so people don't have to know anything about the subject being reported.

Newspapers are expected to provide only general information and basic facts. You might succeed in explaining the intricacies of exploiting a CGI loophole and stealing root access on a server to a reporter, but the writer still needs to explain that to 500,000 non-technical people. Most journalists are fairly good at assimilating information, but they are still not likely to get technical details correct. Even if they do understand it for some reason, it is likely to get twisted in the translation.

There is little you can do in this regard, other than to try simplifying your language. Assume that the reporter has no clue when it comes to technology, and no intention of printing anything the least bit technical anyway.

Journalism Is a Business: A Lesson in Economic Theory

News reporting organizations are not a public service. They are a business like any other, and they must remain profitable if they want to continue printing or broadcasting. In order to do this, they must run interesting stories about interesting events. If that means slanting an issue or exaggerating a point, it can easily be justified. Most of my journalism classes in college centered on giving otherwise mundane stories enough "sizzle" to make them interesting. But there is a duality at work: "sizzle" versus "responsibility." Most reporters have no desire to print a false story, but most reporters have no desire to print a boring story either. Often the two sides are at least partially in conflict. But it could be worse than that, depending on the particular ethics of the organization doing the news gathering.

The journalistic reputation of the network or newspaper doing the story is typically a good barometer of how concerned they are about responsible reporting. I would trust PBS or *The New York Times* with just about anything, although they make errors like anyone else. I would trust the *Boston Globe* or the *Washington Post* to get most of the story right. I would expect the Associated Press, CNN, ABC, and the average local paper to at least get the basic information correct. I would bet some amount of money that CBS, NBC, MSNBC, Fox News, and most larger city papers retain at least a passing resemblance of reality. As for most Internet news clearinghouses, any local television news station, or the likes of MTV—their efforts are more akin to self-serving propaganda than journalism. I wouldn't trust MTV to report anything accurately, let alone something as delicate as what it means to be a hacker.

Every news-gathering company has a different perspective on sensationalism versus responsibility. It's probably in your best interest to evaluate how much you trust the particular organization before you consent to a story about or involving you. If you don't already trust most or all of what they tell you, don't expect that you and your story will fare any better. One thing you can do to help is to constantly mention how much you distrust the media and how they've let you down considerably in the past. Bring it to the forefront of the reporter's mind that accuracy is more important to you than what is provocative. Make him or her think that they will be betraying you if they misrepresent you in any way. It usually helps a lot.

Conclusion: Reporters Are People, Too

If you ever find yourself the subject of a news story, be aware that the end product will probably not show you the same way you see yourself. Complicated details tend to be simplified, and that can mean a significant change for something as technical as computer hacking.

Like I said, no reporter and no newspaper wants to print an untruthful story. It's not likely that they will totally fabricate facts, but they can be taken out of context and reworked to create a more interesting story. Reporters often go into a story with preconceived ideas, and it can be difficult to change them. Just act natural, be truthful, and explain things as clearly as you can. If the reporter is any good, you may actually like what you read in the paper or see on TV a few days later.

A Critical Eye

One thing that we've always tried to do throughout the history of the magazine is to constantly take a critical look at ourselves and our culture. An important thing to remember is that the perspective that we print in our pages is ours, not necessarily those of others in the hacker community. But we like to think that we share certain common values, such as spreading information freely and not being destructive. So we felt the need to speak up when it appeared the hacker community might be getting overrun by those people who really only wanted to call themselves hackers because they had just seen a cool movie or TV show, or had read about us in a book (the latter not being all too likely based on the mentality of some of these individuals). You don't just become a hacker by saying you're one nor can you just get all of the answers from somebody. Being a hacker is a state of mind and *this* is what the media could never understand. Don't get me wrong though—we had lots of really cool people learn about our world after being exposed to it through some mass appeal outlet and it's gotten us all sorts of friends for life. We've always walked a fine line of expecting a level of intelligence and maturity in the hacker community while at the same time being open to new and possibly somewhat naive and misguided people. Another major threat we faced in the 1990s was shrapnel from the whole dot com boom where suddenly everyone seemed to be making obscene amounts of money. Surprisingly, that's not always a good thing and it certainly took its toll on our unique environment in ways we weren't expecting.

Crime Waves (Spring, 1994)

A decade is a long time to be doing anything. When we first started this project back in the summer of 1983, nobody could have predicted our growth, or even our existence in 1994. It's pretty strange to look back at the early days when we literally snuck around in offices and alleyways to get our first issues printed. And today you can find us in chain stores. Reality has always been weird to us.

Of course, if we had just been doing the same thing for ten years, we would all be abject failures. Fortunately, the hacker world is such that you can spend a long time within it and never feel the kind of boredom that has become such an important part of the average American's life. There is always something happening in this world, always something new to explore and discover, more knowledge to share, more friends to meet for the first time. The last ten years have been tinged with hilarity and fun, but also sadness, fear, anger, and determination. One thing these years have not been is a waste of time.

We know that with every page we turn, there is a risk. The most obvious of these include pissing off the powerful corporations and their law enforcement drones. Each and every time we share knowledge, we engage in a conspiracy of some sort. We risk having our lives disrupted by our accusers, our very means of learning taken from us by large armed men. We risk being chastised by our friends and family for being different and ostracized in school for not asking the proper questions or memorizing the standard answers.

These are the obvious risks of who we are and what we do. Most of us have come to recognize them. But there is a far greater risk facing us and it's one that many of us could fall victim to with little or no warning.

Over the years, we've tried to dispel the myth that hackers are criminals. This has been most difficult. As the tabloid press loves to scream, hackers *can* get into your credit file. But so can anybody else. Hackers *can* make thousands of dollars of long distance calls. Anyone is capable of this unimpressive feat. Hackers *can* break into thousands of sensitive computer systems around the world. And the holes will still be there if we never try.

What the press fails to see is the distinction between hacking for the sake of adventure and using hacker knowledge for personal profit. To them it's all the same. Somebody who sells phone codes is the same person as somebody who manipulates the telephone network in wild and imaginative ways. By defining the two as one and the same, we could actually find ourselves being nudged into criminal behavior because it's what's expected of us.

With this in mind, the massive growth of the hacker community is cause for concern. Many people are being drawn into our fold through these very same media perceptions. People have shown up at our meetings assuming that we're there to sell or buy codes. A disturbing number of people who engage in credit card fraud, that is, the stealing of actual physical, tangible merchandise, are trying to ingratiate themselves into the hacker community. It's not surprising. And they might actually be able to prey on our temptations and suck some hackers into their midst, thereby learning a few new tricks. And by calling *themselves* hackers, they manage to justify what it is they do. Ironically, their technical prowess oftentimes doesn't extend beyond knowing how to operate a red box or punch in a code.

This kind of thing was inevitable, given the growing awareness that the mainstream world, and hence the mainstream criminal world, has developed for hackers. Carrots are being dangled in front of our faces. Our brains are suddenly in demand. You might say that society has finally found a use for us.

Knowing this, the most important thing as individuals is to realize why we do what we do. Is it that we want to find out things and spread knowledge around? Or do we want to get what we feel the world owes us? Are we trying to survive and get access to a locked world? Or are we intent on selling our knowledge to the highest bidder?

Truthful answers to these questions are more valuable than anything else. Once we understand our motivation, we can at least be honest with ourselves. Those who use their hacker knowledge to embark upon a life of crime can at least admit to themselves that they are now criminals, thereby salvaging some self respect. The rest of us will have some sense of where we draw our lines.

But how do we know what constitutes criminal behavior and what does not? Regrettably, the law no longer seems an accurate definer. With many of us, we just *know* when something doesn't feel right. And in such a case, trusting your instincts is always a good idea.

To be a hacker, your primary goal must be to learn for the sake of learning—just to find out what happens if you do a certain thing at a particular time under a specific condition. A good way to know if you're a genuine hacker is to look at the reaction of the non-hackers around you. If most of them think you're wasting your time doing something incomprehensible that only you can appreciate, welcome to the world of hacking. If, however, you find yourself being trailed and hounded by a bunch of drooling wannabes with a list of plots and schemes to make your knowledge "pay off" in a big way, you're probably on the verge of becoming a criminal and leaving the rest of us back in the age of innocence.

Obviously, embarking on such a journey en masse would mean the end of the hacker world. We would play right into the hands of our enemies and criminalize hacking by definition, rather than by legislation. Nothing would be better for the anti-hacker lobbyists. As a curious side note, in more than one instance, people who were found to have been helping the government prosecute hackers have been caught actively encouraging criminal behavior among hackers. We have to wonder.

We hack because we're curious. We spread what we find because segregated knowledge is our common enemy. This means that some opportunists will get a free ride and run the risk of giving the rest of us a bad name. The only surefire way to keep this from happening is for us to behave like the phone companies and restrict knowledge. Not likely.

It's not our job to catch criminals. But it is our moral obligation to keep our noble, if somewhat naive, aspirations from becoming subverted by those who truly don't understand.

The Victor Spoiled (Winter, 1998–1999)

What could possibly threaten the hacker world more than government raids, selective prosecution, Orwellian surveillance, and mass hysteria? The answer will no doubt come as a shock to many. Success.

Success a threat? What kind of insanity is this? Success is what everyone *dreams* about; it's the *goal,* after all.

Well, yes and no. There's a difference between *true* success and *perceived* success. One is a lot easier to come by than the other. And one is a great deal more likely to be obscured.

The unusual problem we face is that much of our curiosity and talent has led to a good deal of marketability. In other words, hackers are now in great demand. This is a rather recent phenomenon. Despite initial misgivings and warnings from people who really never knew what they were talking about, "reformed" hackers are being hired in great numbers by corporate America for everything from system administration to research and development to tiger teaming.

This in itself isn't a bad thing. We've long known that hackers are a great resource and it's certainly a lot better to be hired than thrown into prison. But too often, this allegiance comes at a price that isn't realized until it's been paid.

Hackers tend to be an idealistic lot. Some might even say naive. We believe in freedom of speech, the right to explore and learn by doing, and the tremendous power of the individual. Unfortunately, this doesn't always synch with the corporate world, which oftentimes sees an individual aware of free speech with a desire to explore as their biggest threat.

It may seem like a trivial notion to dismiss this corporate world when it conflicts with your own values. But what happens when you realize you can make a tremendous amount of money because your skills happen to be in demand? Would that be worth... suppressing your ideals a bit? It's very hard to say no. Ideals don't pay the bills and it's not unheard of for high school dropouts to wind up making 100 grand with the talents they've picked up while not attending classes.

Plus, in our money-based society, stature is everything. The more you make, the more of a "success" you are. That is the perception.

But what we define here as true success is so much harder to achieve. To believe in something, to not compromise your ideals, to be at peace with yourself...these are the elements of that success. Yeah, it may sound like a vision left over from Woodstock. But it is an important and an enriching aspect of life. Not very many of us manage to get there and remain there.

The people who have it easy are those who don't have that many ideals to begin with. You'll find them in abundance in politics or the music industry where insincerity and changing what one believes in at the flick of a switch are par for the course. We wish them luck.

Things are so much more complicated in our weird little community where there are people with all kinds of strong beliefs and values. With a combined intelligence and an awareness of where technology is heading, the importance of our perspective cannot be overstated. In the years ahead, we are going to be facing some milestones in human development with regard to free speech, communications, access, and privacy. It will be the equivalent of the civil rights movement, the American Revolution, and the Age of Enlightenment all mixed together. How it pans out will depend in large part on who is around to help steer the course. And that is what's worrisome. Imagine if all of the cypherpunks were whisked away to Microsoft to work on a high-paying project that took all of their skills and all of their time? Who would make encryption safe from the prying eyes of governments? What if hacker organizations like the L0pht, cDc, or the Chaos Computer Club went out of existence because its members feared losing lucrative corporate positions if it were revealed that they were part of a community of hackers? Who would show the public how insecure Microsoft really was?

The result would be obvious and very sad. We would lose a perspective that we need quite badly at a critical turning point in the world's history. And those people would lose touch with something unique that they would be unlikely to find again.

The simple cliché tells us that money isn't everything. In fact, when looked at objectively, it's very little, in some cases even a negative thing. Finding people who share your true beliefs, expanding your mind, learning and exploring—these are the precious things that can be forever wiped away when success becomes a commodity. In the hacker world, this is doubly tragic as we have so much to gain from each other for an almost indefinite period.

In some ways, what we are facing parallels what has been happening to the Internet. Vast commercialization has completely changed the net's tone in recent years. We see the same corporate powers slowly gaining a stranglehold on every element of connectivity, at the same time merging, engaging in takeovers, and gathering strength. The future of the net as a safe haven for individual thought and independent development of new and competing technologies is very much in jeopardy and this is without even introducing the government's efforts to muck things up. By finding yourself in a position where the money is good but the work is a waste of your brain, you're experiencing a variation of the same thing.

It's a good idea to occasionally ask yourself a few questions such as what is really important to you, what is your definition of real success, and where do you want to be in the future? There are a great number of people who can answer all of those questions with a high-paying corporate career and who have always felt that way. And that is just fine. But then there are the others, the ones to whom we are addressing this, who face a conflict at some point. It may seem as if the only logical course to follow is to sacrifice your ideals for the sake of materialism, especially when you're young, impressionable, and watching a lot of television. It's what everyone would do—the path of least resistance. Looking out for number one. And most of all, it's what's encouraged in society because idealists are the ones who cause all the trouble.

But there are alternatives. It's not impossible to get the best of both worlds especially if your skills are truly in demand. You can set conditions and draw lines that you absolutely will not cross. You can use some of the money you make to somehow strengthen the community that helped bring you to this point. And, most importantly, you can remain a part of that community and not lose touch with those heading down different paths. The learning process never ends.

We've deliberately avoided mentioning all but the most general goals since everyone has different priorities. The only real common goal we should all share is keeping our community alive in some form and using our gains to advance the future.

And for those who reject the corporate allure altogether, you have a real opportunity to channel your talents to places and people who need them the most. And to do it entirely your way. Anyone suggesting you're a failure for taking this road deserves nothing more than your pity.

Oddly enough, one can actually draw a comparison between this dilemma and credit card fraud. You're young, you can get virtually anything you want if you play the game, and all you have to do is throw away a few of your values, which you may or may not have in the first place. It can be almost impossible to resist, especially if you feel you're owed something. Most people who bow to the temptation of credit card fraud eventually wake up and realize it's wrong one way or another. Far fewer get such a wake-up call from the all-enveloping corporate mentality.

If nothing else, the spirit of hacking can teach you to hold your head up and maintain your values no matter the cost. If you take this approach into the corporate environment, you might even have a chance to change the system from within and make a real difference.

The thinkers and dreamers of our little niche in society have an interesting ride ahead. There will be all kinds of triumphs and defeats and what comes out of all this will change history. It's entirely up to you where your knowledge and skills take you. Not us. Not the Fortune 100. Not any government. You're at the steering wheel. And we wish you *true* success.

Hacker Conventions

The '90s also brought something entirely new to the American hacker scene: hacker conventions. Today they're quite common and obscenely huge. But back then, the only place where something of that magnitude (1,000 or more hackers in one place) was pulled off was in the Netherlands at either the Galactic Hacker Party in 1989 or Hacking at the End of the Universe in 1993. It was those two events that helped to inspire us to make it happen somehow in the States. And we did. In 1994, as part of the *2600* tenth anniversary, we held the first massive hacker conference in American history with something like 1,500 attendees. Right in the middle of New York City. And so, the HOPE tradition was begun.

Hacking at the End of the Universe (Autumn, 1993)

They did it again. For the second time, the hackers of Holland have thrown a party second to none. It is estimated that up to a thousand hackers from around the globe descended upon a campsite near Amsterdam for three days where they did what has never been done before: Merge high tech with the wilderness. Tents were set up throughout the site and an Ethernet was established to keep the various computers inside the tents connected. This in turn was hooked into the Internet. Yes, it was possible to be hooked into the Internet from a laptop in a tent in the middle of nowhere. And it still is.

Hacking at the End of the Universe was organized by *Hack-Tic,* the Dutch hacker magazine. The spontaneous semi-anarchistic way in which everything fell together made many think of a Hacker Woodstock. It was an event a long time coming, which the hacker world needed. And even though very few Americans attended, we can still benefit from what happened this summer.

Imagine a setting where paranoia is at a minimum, government agents keep their distance, questions are encouraged, and experimentation rewarded. This was the environment the Dutch hackers created. Forums on networks, phone phreaking, social engineering, and hacking techniques were attended by hundreds of enthusiastic people from a wide variety of backgrounds. This, despite the fact that Holland now has laws against computer hacking, proves that the hacker world has a very bright future.

Many times we were asked if such an event would succeed in America. And it became hard to stop thinking of reasons why it wouldn't. After all, we live in one of the most self-censoring, paranoid, mass-media patrolled societies ever to have existed—how could an event like this ever possibly work?

It can, and so can a lot of other things. The trick is to know what we want to accomplish and work together to achieve it. For instance, a large hacker event like the HEU could easily be held in the United States next summer as part of *2600's* tenth anniversary. (That's right, we've been doing this for a decade!) Instead of using a campsite, we could use a large warehouse in the middle of an easily accessible city. One section would be devoted to hooking up a massive network that would tie into the Internet. Another area would be used for forums where all kinds of topics would be addressed by people from all over the world. Another section would be for displays and exhibitions. It would be a 24 hour operation lasting for a week and there would be enough space for people to sleep. Sounds like a fantasy? It is, make no mistake. But we always have the ability to turn our fantasies into reality. It involves working together and using as many connections as we can. This means finding a cheap building to rent for a couple of weeks, getting imaginative and enthusiastic hackers to wire the place, and encouraging as many interesting and diverse people as possible to show up. The result, if successful, will be a radical change in the way hackers are perceived. We can initiate change and do things to technology that nobody has ever done before. Or we can just say we can.

This reality extends way beyond a single event. Hackers can lead the way to technological access. It is our goal to get an incredibly economical Internet and voice mail link up and running in the near future. If you have or know of equipment that can be donated to this cause, please let us know. You could wind up changing history. And this is only the beginning.

There are a lot of powerful idiots out there who want us to live within their close-minded and stagnant parameters. And a number of good people are being hurt because they question the logic. We cannot forget this. But dwelling upon it will only encourage us to come up with more reasons why we can't do all of the things we should be doing. When we drive away the fear and ignore the brain-dead bureaucrats, we stand a chance of actually getting somewhere. And whether it's the wilderness or a warehouse, we'll be the ones creating a network.

Hackers on Planet Earth (Summer, 1994)

It was a little less than a year ago that the idea of a major hacker event in the United States this summer was first expressed. The success of Hacking at the End of the Universe (HEU) in Holland led many people to ask why such an event couldn't occur in the United States. In our autumn 1993 issue, we wondered if such a thing would ever happen here. But it wasn't until a couple of months ago that the enthusiasm here began to spread like an infectious disease. It's been a long time coming and this summer seemed like the perfect time. After all, it's our tenth anniversary and the hacker world is bigger than it's ever been.

And so, Hackers on Planet Earth (HOPE), the first-ever global hacker event to take place in this country, will be held in New York City on August 13 and 14. One way or another, history is liable to be made.

What exactly is a "global hacker event?" It's different from the various hacker conferences that take place in this country—Summercon, Def Con, and HohoCon are all well worth attending and usually take place every year. The annual Hackers Conference that takes place in California might also be worthwhile—we can't seem to find any hackers who have ever been invited to it though. The *2600* meetings in various cities are still more ways for hackers to get together, this time on a monthly basis.

We believe HOPE will have ingredients of all of these events but will also add something to the equation that just hasn't happened here yet. Hackers will work together for two days and nights and celebrate their existence in what has unfortunately become an often hostile environment. The general public will have a chance to see things from our perspective—the conference will take place in the middle of New York City and will be cheap enough for nearly anyone to attend. Seminars, talks, and workshops will take place around the clock in an open atmosphere. The uses and abuses of technology will be discussed—and demonstrated. A giant Ethernet, similar to the one created at last year's HEU, will be constructed here (everyone is encouraged to bring a computer for maximum effect). This, along with our hookup to the Internet, will give many people their first taste of the net. And it will be hackers, not large corporations, leading the way.

An excellent example of what we intend to do was recently demonstrated on New York's WBAI-FM. During a fundraiser for this noncommercial radio station, listeners were offered a year of unrestricted Internet access on escape.com, a new Internet service in New York for a pledge of $100. People in the hacker community have designed this system and are the ones who keep it going. (The normal rates for this system are $16.50 per month with no time limits, probably the cheapest net connection possible.) New Yorkers jumped at the chance to get true access to the net without having to always watch the clock and pay outrageous fees. In two hours, escape.com brought 86 new people onto the net and raised $8600 for a noncommercial radio station. This means something. There are swarms of people in our society who want to listen to what we are saying and who understand our spirit, if not our language. The hacker spirit has manifested itself in many of us but it lies dormant in a far greater number. If we have an opportunity to reach still more people, we should. Some won't understand but those who do could turn out to be very important to the hacker world. Only when the general public begins to see that there is far more to us than what they read in tabloids will their perception of us begin to change. And that could change everything. It's always been in the interests of the phone companies and corporate online services to paint us in as evil a light as possible. Then they can continue to play by their rules, charging consumers as much as they want and not having anyone credible to challenge them. But a growing number of people are realizing that it's not as black and white as these entities want us to believe.

We've seen it happen twice in Holland. The United States is long overdue. But this isn't the only "Hacker Congress" happening this year. On October 7, 8, and 9, the "First International Congress about Viruses, Hacking, and the Computer Underground" will take place in Buenos Aires, Argentina at the Centro Cultural Recoleta, Junin 1930 from 3:00 p.m. to 9:00 p.m. We're happy to learn that there is a thriving hacker culture there as well and we hope many Americans and Argentines attend both events.

According to the organizers, "the congress will be oriented to discuss subjects related to hacking, viruses, and the technology impact in the society of now and in the future. We will also have discussions about cyberpunk, virtual reality, the Internet, the phone system, programming, etc....We expect the congress to be as open as possible, offering freedom to speak to all attendants, being from the "bad" or "good" side of the discussed issues. As we in Argentina don't yet have laws against hacking or virus writing or spreading, we think it is very important to discuss all those items as freely and deeply as possible." Admission to this event is, incredibly enough, totally free.

There are a lot of bad things we can focus on—the Clipper chip, increased surveillance, technological rip-offs, imprisoned hackers, and so much more. But there's also a great deal to be optimistic about. We've got the means to see things in different, non-traditional ways and, most importantly, share these perceptions with each other. This August, we'll have the chance to take that one step further. It may be the only hope we have.

Opening Doors (Autumn, 1994)

You've probably noticed that this issue is coming to you a bit later than it should. We have one thing to say: Blame HOPE.

Never before in this country has such an event occurred. And never again will we be able to say that. Things are different now and it's up to all of us to hold onto the ground that we've gained.

By all estimates, somewhere between 1,000 and 1,500 people descended upon the Hotel Pennsylvania in New York City on August 13 and 14. At some point on the second day we just lost count.

In stark contrast to the commercialized "Son of Woodstock" taking place simultaneously to the north, Hackers On Planet Earth was a grass roots, down to earth labor of love and obsession. People came from all around the world with their computers, radios, music, toys, and expertise. For the first time, hackers in America were able to meet with the Chaos Computer Club of Germany. Other groups from Holland, England, Italy, Canada, Australia, Russia, Israel, and Argentina were also on hand, not to mention the diversity of all the attendees from the United States. Whether they journeyed cross country in a van, crosstown in a subway, or over the ocean in a plane, HOPE attendees came to learn and to share information about hacking and about technology.

It was really everything we could have hoped for. When people from the United States attended Holland's Galactic Hacker Party in 1989 and Hacking at the End of the Universe in 1993, they saw a spirit and an energy that had been largely quelled in this country. By organizing something as large as HOPE, we wanted to try and bring that spirit over here, or rather, nurture the spirit that has always been present. At long last, through the help of those present, we succeeded in doing this.

And for once, the press had something to say about hackers when we weren't being raided, charged, or sentenced to prison. Here we were holding seminars, reviewing our history, playing with new technology, and showing the public how to hook into the Internet. Of course, media stupidity is hard to defeat—one *New York Times* piece made it appear that our only purpose in gathering was to make free phone calls. But such blindness seemed to be the exception rather than the rule.

All of the worries about hackers roaming loose in such an environment proved unfounded. The massive crowd was extremely well behaved by any standard. We found this especially true in the face of our botched registration system, which forced people to wait on line for long periods of time in order to get a photo ID. It was a little taste of Eastern Europe and the patience of the participants was unbelievable. (Eventually we scrapped the system and just gave everyone handwritten numbers.) Our thinking was that having a picture that matched an existing face would be less intrusive than having a name printed on a badge. While that still may be so, the technology just wasn't with us. Maybe next time. (By the way, we had always planned on wiping the pictures out of the computer after HOPE. Through another misfortune, we managed to wipe them before the conference ended.) Attendees will also be pleased to know that all of the registration forms were intentionally destroyed—if this conference ever becomes the focus of some absurd investigation of "hacker conspiracy" in the future, gathering evidence on those present will be tricky at best.

Despite a flaky net connection, mostly because of an uncooperative hotel phone system, the internal network managed to keep going. And, no matter what the topic (social engineering, cellular phones, boxing, lock picking, hackers from overseas), the auditorium always seemed to be filled with an enthusiastic audience. We even managed to get Phiber Optik on the phone live from prison to speak to the crowd. That in itself added a great deal of magic to the event.

We couldn't have come close to making this work without the dedicated help of many dozens of people. We toyed with the idea of trying to list them all by name. Then we realized that inevitably someone would be left out, which might cause bad feelings. Or perhaps somebody who carried a small box from one room to another would be listed right next to someone who got no sleep for three days trying to keep the net up. This might cause resentment. Or maybe a person would be listed who wanted more than anything to remain anonymous. This could result in fear and paranoia. Rather than risk all of that negativity, we decided to keep it on a personal level. Suffice to say, we know who helped change the future of hacking this summer. And we won't forget.

For those of you who weren't able to make it, we will have video transcripts available in the future. We'll announce the details in a future issue.

We have been deluged with requests from people asking if they can help with HOPE 2 next summer. We need to set the record straight. There isn't going to be another one of these next summer. HOPE was a special event and such events don't take place on a regular schedule. This is not to say that there won't be other special events taking place in other parts of the world. But the next HOPE isn't going to happen for a while. One of the main reasons for this is the fact that such an endeavor is very draining. We have bill collectors, subscribers, and close personal friends who are very angry with us for having neglected them. If you're one of those, we apologize for our lapses. For now, our priority will be to continue the work of *2600*. And when it's time for another HOPE-like event, we know we can count on our readers to make it happen again.

9 The Computer Revolution

Intimately tied to the "discovery" of the hacker scene was the almost frightening evolution in the world of computers. The "Net" was still in its infancy as the decade began and by the time those ten years had passed, it was a very different animal indeed. While a significant number of people were connected in 1990, nobody had ever heard of the World Wide Web. By 1999, nobody *hadn't* heard of it, and the amount of connectivity in our everyday lives (e-mail addresses, web sites, high-speed "always-on" connections) was simply staggering. In the early days, you could get any Internet domain you wanted for no cost. An Internet where people bought and sold things, including names of sites, just didn't exist. But it sure didn't last long.

By extension, computers themselves were undergoing rapid transformations. If you had a 286 at the start of the '90s, you were one of the lucky ones. Portable computers weighed a ton. Having a 40-meg hard drive was impressive. Speed, memory, graphic capabilities...you get the picture. Things changed fast and they changed a lot.

This meant a lot of things to the hacker world. There was suddenly so much more to play with. Of course, a lot of the hackers from the '80s were now the programmers or designers of the 1990s. The Net itself, though an offshoot of the military, was largely managed with the hacker ethic—avoidance of any sort of social hierarchy whenever possible, disdain for the profit motive, strict adherence to the principles of free speech in public forums, and an almost religious devotion to UNIX. Had it played out differently—if the mainstream had somehow gotten there first or if the phone companies had been running the show from the start—I think the Net would have resembled one gigantic AOL. So its very existence was seen as something of a triumph for the hackers, as many of them were actively involved in building something truly substantive that would inevitably be discovered by the masses.

General Computing

The Net was of course the major development of the decade. Some might argue that it was the major development of the last few centuries but there's no need to debate that here. Throughout the '90s, if it involved computers in any way, it likely was undergoing rapid change of one sort or another. And hackers were always trying to stay one step ahead, whether by using the latest hardware or figuring out how to defeat the most recent copy protection or security limitations. But now, for the first time, it was possible to do a good amount of hacking without leaving your home, telephonically or otherwise. Unless of course, you wanted to be one of the first to go portable.

On the Road Again: Portable Hacking (Summer, 1992)

By The Masked Avocado

From the beginning, phone phreaks realized that the surest way to avoid being busted was to use pay phones. They called them "phortress phones." Phreaking from a pay phone was not that much harder than doing it from home. However, many found this to be an inconvenient, if not a somewhat overly paranoid, option. Given the technology, ignorance, and lack of law enforcement on the part of the enemy at the time, very few were busted. I remember when people set up their computers to hack 950 codes all night, scan entire 1-800 exchanges, and blast all sorts of illegal tones down their home telephone line without giving it a second thought. Today, this kind of behavior is equivalent to suicide. It has gotten to the point where, if you have a DNR (Dialed Number Recorder) on your line, and you actually have the balls to call your favorite bulletin board or (gasp!) call a Telenet port, you could be raided or have yourself hauled in for questioning. Because of easier tracing, recent examples have shown that you can be raided for calling a board, especially one under investigation, perhaps not even knowing that the board was set up illegally on a hacked UNIX. Big Brother may be eight years late, but he has arrived. Let us take Darwin's advice, and adapt before we become extinct.

Who Should Go Portable?

Everyone, actually. However, novices and explorers should learn as much as they can from others, and try not to do anything overtly dangerous from home. There is much exploration that is completely legal, like public access UNIX machines and the Internet. Those who should go portable right away are experienced hackers, those with a relatively high profile in the hacking community, or those who have many associates in the hacking community. Because of this, they are likely to have a DNR already slapped on their line. Sometimes, all it takes is to have one DNR'ed hacker call another, and the second one has a pretty good chance of getting a DNR of his very own. Enough gloom, let's see what lies ahead.

What You'll Need

Okay, you don't particularly want to get busted by hacking from home, and you want to take your recreation on the road, eh? Well, let us explore the options. Knowing your options and getting the right equipment can make your experience of hacking on the road a less difficult, more comfortable, and more pleasant one. Depending on the hacker, several factors come into play when purchasing equipment, among them price, power, and portability.

Obviously, one does not need a 486-50DX laptop with an active matrix TFT color screen, 64 megs of RAM, 660 meg hard disk, running UNIX V.4 to go hacking. Besides the $13,000 cost, I don't think getting a hernia is anyone's idea of a fun evening. Besides, with a system like that, chances are the laptop you are calling from has twenty times more power than the piece of shit 3B2 with a 40MB hard disk that you're likely to hack into. Similarly, a dinky little pocket computer with a 20×2 flickering LCD screen and a conveniently alphabetized ultra-bouncy membrane chicklet keyboard is not what is needed either.

Important factors in purchasing a laptop or notebook computer are price, weight, screen readability, keyboard, memory, disk storage, and battery life. The price that you can afford should be determined by you. As far as the screen goes, it should be large enough, preferably 80×24 characters, and easy to read. LCD is okay, supertwist LCD even better, EL and PLASMA are even better than that, but if you plan to hack at night or in the dark like most hackers on the road, you should make sure your laptop has a backlit screen. Color LCD screens are useless unless you plan to call Prodigy or download and view GIFs, in which case you should stop reading this article right now and go back to play with your Nintendo.

The keyboard should be a standard full-sized QWERTY keyboard, with full travel plastic keys. You don't need a numeric keypad or function keys or any of that crap. Membrane keyboards or chicklet rubber keys are out of the question. Unless you are utterly retarded, having your keys alphabetized is not an added benefit. Basically, if you can touch type on a keyboard without your fingers missing keys, getting jammed, or slipping around, then it is a good keyboard.

You don't need a lot of memory on your portable either, since you will mostly be using it as a dumb terminal. However you should have enough memory to run your terminal software and be able to buffer most of your online sessions for later analysis. A floppy drive or some kind of permanent storage is also a good idea. If your portable has battery backed RAM, you may get away without using a floppy drive, since you can always transfer any buffers to a larger machine via the serial port.

The last, and perhaps most important factor in determining your choice for a laptop or notebook is battery life, or more precisely, how long you can use the machine (when it's turned on) before needing a recharge or battery change. Unless you plan to find an AC outlet at every location you hack from, battery capacity is a crucial factor. These battery times vary greatly, anywhere from two hours to 20 hours on some notebooks and palmtops. I would recommend a machine with at least four hours of battery life per charge. If you have a floppy disk drive, your battery life will decrease significantly with each disk access, so try to keep any disk access to a minimum. If your terminal software accesses the disk a lot, I would suggest running it from a ram disk.

Having a hard disk on a laptop is pretty useless in relation to hacking, unless your sole purpose in life is to climb a telephone pole so that you can leech all the latest nudie GIFs from Event Horizon's 1-900 number.

The laptop and notebook market has changed more quickly than any other segment of the computer industry. New models are literally coming out every three months. While the new models offer better screens and lighter weight, they are usually far too expensive, especially for use as mere hacking rigs. But, an interesting byproduct of all this change is the fact that the older models are constantly being liquidated at almost rock bottom prices by companies like DAK, Damark, and Underware Electronics, which sell by catalog through mail order or by any number of companies that advertise in *Computer Shopper*. The prices are dropping constantly, and by the time you read this article I'm sure the prices I mention will sound high once you've looked through some of these catalogs. Not long ago a friend of mine purchased a brand new, 4.4-pound, discontinued NEC Ultralight computer with a backlit LCD screen, with a 2MB battery backed silicon disk, and a built-in 2400 modem for just under $500. I've seen a Toshiba 1000 going for $399, Zenith Minisport machines going for $299. If you want, you can pick up a 386SX-20 notebook for under a thousand bucks easily. The point is that the hardware is there, and it's usually far less expensive than any desktop machines.

Modems and Couplers

One does not need a 57,600 baud V.32bis/V.42bis modem to go hacking. Unless you plan to download all of the UNIX System V source code from an AT&T mini in under 5 minutes, a high-speed modem is not required. A 300 baud modem may be too slow for most purposes, and the only times I would recommend 300 baud is if your notebook or palmtop has a small screen where everything would scroll off too quickly or if you're a slow reader.

A 1200 or 2400 baud modem will do fine. If it has error-correction (i.e., MNP), even better. If your laptop doesn't already have one built-in, I would suggest buying a pocket modem. Pocket 1200 baud modems can be found for as low as $29. Most pocket modems are the size of a cigarette pack and run for 15 hours or so off of a 9 volt battery. Other pocket modems, like the Practical Peripherals' Practical Pocket Modem (Model PM2400PPM, price $159 retail, can be found for $79 mail order) or the Novation Parrot, use low-power chips and run off either the power from your RS-232 port or the phone line voltage or both. These modems are not much more expensive than the battery powered ones, and you never have to worry about your modem running out of power. All pocket modems are Hayes AT compatible and some, like the WorldPort 2496 Pocket Fax/Modem, even have G3 fax capability.

If you're going to be hacking from pay phones, you're going to need an acoustic coupler to attach to your modem. Several are available from stores specializing in laptops and laptop accessories. The most popular among hackers is the CP+, available from The Laptop Shop. There's also the Konnexx coupler, which can work with 9600 baud modems and faxes. Look in magazines like Mobile Computing for ads for other models. A coupler will run you around $100 mail order.

Ultimately, it is best to keep your portable hacking system as small as possible and made of the minimum number of parts. A notebook machine such as the Tandy WP-2, Cambridge Z88, NEC Ultralight, and the acoustic coupler/modem mentioned above is probably the best possible combination for a compact and inexpensive portable rig. It's small and light, consists of only two or three pieces, fits in a small briefcase or knapsack, and weighs just less than 5 pounds.

By planning and designing your system from start to finish you can achieve a sleek efficient portable hacking system. Poor planning can result in uncomfortable heavy multi-piece systems that one has to drag around. Before laptops really existed, a friend of mine decided to put together a portable rig from parts he already had, and this did not turn out too well. His system consisted of an Apple IIc, a 12 volt car battery, AC power inverter, 7-inch monochrome monitor, and a full size external Hayes modem. The only things he ended up buying were the inverter and acoustic coupler. However this system was a nightmare of a machine, weighing almost 45 pounds, consisting of seven cumbersome pieces [each] with tangled cables, and capable of completely draining a fully charged car battery in a matter of 30 minutes. He managed to fit the entire system in a large suitcase. It took him almost 15 minutes to set the entire thing up inside a phone booth, leaving very little room for him. If trouble would arise, he would have a very difficult time making a quick getaway. This is an example of what not to do when putting together your portable rig.

Where to Go Hacking

Location is just as important as having a good portable rig. Where you hack from determines how long you can hack, how late you can hack, whether you'll be bothered by interruptions or have to look over your shoulder every minute, and many other factors. Unless you happen to be traveling around the country and staying in hotels every other week, your only options for portable hacking are pay phones, junction boxes, and exposed phone wiring. Finding a great hacking location takes some work, but is well worth the effort. You can save time by surveying locations beforehand, that is, before you actually go hacking. You should find several possible locations that meet your needs. After using one location for a week or so, you should move on. Depending on the sensitivity of the machines you hack, using the same location for an extended amount of time is hazardous to your freedom.

Time of day is also another important factor. It is best to go out late at night to do the majority of your hacking. Besides, 3:00 a.m. is about the only decent time you can cut into people's phone lines to attach your portable without being noticed. However,

3:00 a.m. is also when the local cops like to make their rounds through quiet neighborhoods, so be careful, because it's very hard to explain what you were doing inside a junction box to the police, even if you were wearing a lineman's helmet, because linemen don't work at 3:00 a.m.

If you don't have an acoustic coupler, you can't really use pay phones unless you manage to get access to the wiring. Therefore, you are limited to using whatever telephone lines you can get your wire cutters on. Junction boxes are great, but the ones directly on the street are too dangerous. For all junction boxes, bring along the necessary hex wrench. Almost all junction boxes in suburbia are unlocked and usually very secluded. In the city, however, the best junction boxes are in back of large apartment buildings, or in their basements, or in back of stores and in parking lots. As an added bonus, junction boxes not on the street are not locked. When using a junction box, it is very preferable if you cannot be seen from the street. Junction boxes on poles are also good if you can find them in secluded or remote areas. I found one near me that fits my needs well. It is a huge unlocked box, atop a pole, with a very nice and comfortable seat. What is really great though, is that right next to the pole there's a tree. The branches and leaves of the tree completely engulf the top of the pole, thus I am completely invisible to people passing by on the street. I simply climb the tree to get high enough to start climbing the metal ladder spikes on the pole, and climb up to the seat, unpack my rig, and I'm ready to rock. This is the perfect hacking and phreaking location at 3:00 in the morning. Having access to hundreds of different lines also allows one to use such a location for many hacking sessions before moving on. If you're a college student, dorms are great places to find indoor junction boxes. They are usually in stairwells and in the basement.

If you are not able to use a junction box, all you have to do is find a running line in a secluded location. Again, the backs of apartment buildings and the backs of stores are good places to find wiring. Be sure you know what you are doing, because there is a lot of other wiring that can get in the way, such as cable TV, antenna, and electrical wiring. If you fry yourself on a power cable then you deserve it, because you're too stupid to even go hacking.

If you plan a direct connection (running wiring or junction boxes), other parts you will want to bring along on your hacking trips are a lineman's handset, wire cutters and strippers, and an RJ-11 phone jack with alligator clips.

If you have an acoustic coupler, you have the added option of using pay phones and phone booths. But stay away from COCOTs [Customer Owned Coin Operated Telephones], they are too much of a headache, and the sound quality usually sucks. Good places to find secluded pay phones late at night are parks, playgrounds, beaches, and boardwalks. If you live in New York City, then this does not apply to you unless you enjoy being harassed and urinated upon by homeless people while trying to gain root. Obviously, outdoor hacking becomes much less of an option when it rains or when the weather turns cold. During the day, good places to find secluded pay phones are old public buildings, college buildings, airports, hotels, libraries, and museums. I once found a phone booth in an old secluded hallway at the Museum of Natural History in Manhattan. This phone was rotary and hadn't been used by humans in I don't know how long. The phone books in there were from 1982. The phone booth was recessed in a wall, well lighted, with a door. Needless to say, this was the perfect spot for several hacking sessions during the day.

With pay phones, there is the added problem of the phone constantly wanting money. A red box is very cumbersome, and modem transmissions are immediately killed when the phone wants money every few minutes. Unless your hacking consists entirely of machines with 1-800 dialups, codes or calling cards are a must. Using a phone company with good sound quality, such as AT&T or Sprint, will reduce errors and line noise. Given the acoustic nature of the connection, it becomes necessary to manually flash the switch-hook between calls, and perhaps even manually dialing if your modem cannot autodial. This hassle can be avoided by using a dial-out such as a UNIX with cu, an Internet dial-out, or PC Pursuit.

Unlike on TV and in the movies, cellular phones are not really an option for portable hacking, unless you have the ability to completely reprogram yours at a moment's notice, by changing both the Electronic Serial Number and the Telephone Number to someone else's. This type of phreaking requires some advanced knowledge. Getting the ESNs and TNs is not a problem since they are broadcast digitally over the air, and you can pluck them right off the air if you build a decoder and hook it up to a scanner with 800 MHz capability. This is, however, a topic for another article. Just as an aside, modem transmissions over cellular phones are quite possible with error correcting modems up to 9600 baud. Telebit even makes a very nice cellular modem called the Cellblazer, which can pump data through at 16,000 baud.

Taking to the Road

Another crucial element in successful portable hacking is planning. In light of time constraints and battery life, you should plan as much of your work ahead of time as possible. Any preliminary work should be done before the mission (research, social engineering, etc.). I understand that hacking is somewhat of an unorganized, unplanned activity, but you should at least have some sort of agenda laid out. That's not to say that you can't have any fun or enjoy yourself; you could spend all night calling pirate boards in Europe, for all I care. Nothing is worse than sitting atop a telephone pole at four in the morning trying to think of where to call next.

Be prepared, and bring everything you will need: your rig, handset, notebook, flashlight, food and drink, a list of computers to call, and if you live in New York City, bring along a weapon for self-defense.

When using pay phones, it is also a good idea to have a good excuse ready in case someone asks you what you're doing. A favorite among hackers on the road is, "I'm a freelance writer and I'm transmitting a story to my editor." During the daytime at a pay phone no one is likely to even notice you since so many people have laptops these days. If you're at a junction box or cutting into someone's phone wiring at three in the morning, no excuse is necessary. Just be prepared to shoot to injure, and run like hell.

During your hacking mission, try to have a good idea of where you are, and make a note of any exits that may be needed if you need a quick getaway. And buffer everything for later review.

The Future

The ultimate thrill would be to carry around a notebook machine with a pocket packet radio TNC and a portable HF transceiver. There are places on the packet nets where you can link into TCP/IP gateways and telnet to any place on the Internet. Also rumored to exist on the packet nets are telephone modem dial-outs. With this kind of setup, you could literally be in the middle of the desert outside of Phoenix, and be hacking a machine anywhere in the world. When you're done, you can just move on. I'm sure this scares the shit out of law enforcement, and rightly so. But that may be exactly what we're doing five years from now.

Conclusion

I have been on many portable hacking trips, sometimes alone, and sometimes with friends. All I can really say is that it's a lot of fun, just like regular hacking, but without any of the worries associated with hacking from home. Also, portable hacking is more exciting than just sitting at home in front of your computer. If you find good locations, and bring along a couple of buddies and plenty of good American beer, hacking on the road can be the best thing in the world.

MILESTONE: THINGS THAT HAPPEN (Winter, 1994-1995)

At long last it's going to happen—2600.com will soon be in operation on the Internet. We're in the process of picking out hardware, software, and a Net provider for what we hope will be a useful and historic site. We're open to suggestion at this point and we're also looking for help of any kind, particularly with regards to good deals on hardware.

Killing a File (Autumn, 1999) *By THX1138*

Getting rid of all traces of a file sounds like an incredibly simple thing to do. You get yourself a program that overwrites the file and that's it. Right?

Unfortunately, getting rid of all traces of a file is far more complex than you could have imagined. You'll need to get yourself a program that does more than the DOS, UNIX, or Windows delete file command. These commands merely mark the space on the disk used by the file as available without actually erasing the contents of the file, even if the file is emptied from the Windows recycle bin.

Programs that overwrite the contents of a file are called "secure delete" programs. Scorch is good and it has some interesting options. BCwipe is also good.

Make sure these programs rename the file first with a name of equal or greater length! Inferior programs may erase the file data and then mark the entry in the disk table of contents as deleted without actually overwriting the filename. Or how about a filename that previously existed on a corporate computer and they would like to know how a reference to that file got on your computer (assuming it's been seized). Filenames alone may not be solid evidence against you, but wouldn't it be cleaner not to leave a trace? Several programs will rename the file with X's first, and then erase the actual file contents. But make sure your secure delete program does this. Even if you have done all of the above, the filename and its data can still exist all over the place!

If you're using Win 95 or NT, click Start, then "documents." Is that your filename? Blow away the shortcut in C:\WINDOWS\RECENT using your secure delete program. If you're using Win NT blow away the shortcuts in C:\WINNT\PROFILES\ADMINI~1\RECENT\. This assumes you have the administrator account. There's another directory called C:\WINDOWS\QFNONL\RECENT\ that can contain references to your file.

There may be other software that opens the file and keeps the filename on a list somewhere, such as the "last files opened" list. Use the Windows file explorer to search the software directories in question for a substring (use "contains" field) of the filename. On UNIX, cat all the files through grep and an appropriate substring. Yes, you're going to have to examine each piece of software that opened the file for any traces of it.

In a state of shock yet? It gets worse.

Windows 95, Windows NT, UNIX, and other operating systems use virtual memory files to extend RAM. When a process or program becomes completely inactive, the operating system puts the process with all memory (RAM) contents out on disk in order to conserve memory. This method of extending RAM is called virtual memory. When the program becomes active again its data is copied back into memory, and, yes, the data is left in the virtual memory file until it is overwritten. Your data could stay there for days or even months!

Windows 95 uses the file win386.swp. You can boot into DOS and erase the file, but you'll have to change the permissions first. More robust operating systems will automatically re-create the swap file at boot time if they detect it missing. Some "secure delete" programs (such as Scorch) may have an option to leave the WIN 95 swap file intact but just erase its contents.

Some operating systems like Win 95 and NT 4.0 have swap files that grow and shrink dynamically, using empty disk space as needed. Turn this option off or get enough memory so that you don't need a swap file. Wiping the swap file in its shrunken state could leave parts of your file in what was the swap file in its enlarged state, but in what is now unused disk space. For example your data got swapped out to the last 10 megabytes of the virtual memory file and then later the virtual memory file shrunk leaving your data in what is now marked as unused disk space. If you think this has already happened on your system, wipe the swap file while booted in DOS and then, before exiting DOS, fill up the disk with big null files and erase them all. Use DOS pipes to keep concatenating the null filled files until the entire disk is full. Then simply delete them all.

On UNIX you can switch to an alternate swap file just long enough to erase the original swap file with a secure delete program, then re-create and switch back to the original swap file. Check /etc/fstab for references to your swap partitions.

Windows NT uses a virtual memory file called pagefile.sys. Wipe its contents while booted in DOS. If you have NTFS, you'll have to temporarily get rid of the virtual memory file, fill the disk with null files, then delete them.

If a DOS FAT based file system has problems, you are told to run a program called scandisk. If scandisk finds "lost" pieces of files it puts the pieces in a series of files called FILE0001.CHK, FILE0002.CHK, and so forth. These files could contain data you want erased. If so, blow them away with your secure delete program.

The Windows registry can be littered with references to a file. The registry keeps all kinds of information about a Windows machine. If you are unfamiliar with the registry try browsing through it in read only mode. Use the registry editor (regedit.exe) to find references to recently accessed files that you want eradicated. (Don't use the 32 bit registry editor. The piece of crap doesn't find all strings!)

Most Windows software such as RealPlayer keeps a list of recently accessed files. Use the registry editor to find these old references.

While you're in there you may want to look under Netscape for "URL History" and get rid of the URL references to *Hustler* and *Penthouse*. The boss or coworker might get upset about them. So, you just hit the delete key and those registry values are gone, right? Mistake! Deleting registry values is almost like making a permanent record of them, because the registry marks the entries as deleted without overwriting them. If you run a binary editor (like HEXedit) on the registry, then search for the values, you'll see they're still there! The registry is actually a file called C:\WINDOWS\SYSTEM.DA0 and on NT it's a series of files in C:\WINNT\SYSTEM32\CONFIG. I have successfully erased these "lost" values with a binary editor. (Don't try this on your own.)

The best way to get rid of registry values is to overwrite them. Instead of pressing delete, modify the value and change it to something of equal or greater length. So, using the registry editor, find Netscape's "URL History," change `www.hackFBI.com` to `www.paranoid.com`, or change `www.Hustler.com` to `www.barney.com`.

If you opened any files with Netscape, data could be stored in the Netscape cache. Use your secure delete program to delete these cache files.

One way to simplify the whole business of killing files is to create a "killall" script to do a lot of the deletions and then run it just before shutdown. C2 compliant operating systems have a "secure delete" option that will overwrite a file when you do a regular delete command, but there is no undelete or wastebasket with this type of deletion. I prefer to put most stuff in the wastebasket and Scorch the files I really want to get rid of.

There is a program called Shredder that attempts to kill (in real time) files and references everywhere they may be. It is good but not perfect.

Every piece of software out there could keep some internal record of your file or even its contents, especially software made by Big Brother in Washington State. His software leaves references all over the place. Remember, a moderate dose of paranoia is healthy.

Quantum Hacking (Autumn, 1999) *By skwp*

Many of the articles in *2600* deal with exploring today's computer, telephone, and electronic systems in new ways. I wish to introduce one new system into this list—a quantum computer. Although I will try to introduce the concept in a simple manner, quantum computing is by no means a simple subject. It is recommended that the reader have at least some understanding of physics and chemistry.

Quantum computing is an area that is being very actively researched today as one of the hottest topics in both computer science and physics. Although scientists say that quantum computers won't be physically realized for several decades, the theoretical work that already exists makes it possible to learn about quantum computing through simulation.

Whereas current computers work with bits, i.e., movement of electricity (thousands of electrons) which we interpret to mean one or zero, a quantum computer may operate on only several quantum objects (such as atoms or electrons) and interpret their states (spin of electron or ground/excited state of atom) as a logical one or zero.

Now, without going into the reasons behind the theory, quantum mechanics states that objects can exist in indeterminate states. For example, say we have an atom that has a fifty-fifty chance of decaying within the next half hour. If we do not observe this atom after the half hour, quantum mechanics says it has neither decayed, nor not decayed. Instead, it exists in neither state with equal probability. While the concept may be strange, the theory is sound in that it explains effects observed in experiments. For more information on why this is true, see Young's double slit experiment in your local physics book.

The whole quantum theory has something to do with the behavior of small particles. Basically, it is said that everything in nature has wave and particle characteristics, but small particles are small enough that we can observe their wave characteristics. Thus, light can be said to be both an electromagnetic wave, and a stream of particles that we call photons. Quantum theory also says that these particles exist as "probability waves" and only become real when we observe them.

The reasons for these theories are too complex to be discussed here, but it turns out that this property of objects to exist in indeterminate states can be used to create a new type of computing machine, a quantum computer, that can operate on quantum states.

A quantum computer operates on quantum bits, or "qubits," which are much similar to our bits, except that they can represent a zero, one, or a mix of a zero and one. This mix—known as a superposition of states—collapses into a one or a zero with a certain probability for each outcome when observed. The advantage is that while a three bit classical computer can hold the numbers from zero to seven, a quantum computer of the same size can hold the numbers zero through seven at the same time, in a "coherent superposition."

Classically, it is possible to increase computing power by adding more processors working in parallel, but to increase the power of a machine exponentially we need to add an exponential amount of processors. This is not true in a quantum system. By adding one "bit," the power is increased exponentially because this bit can now be part of the superposition. Quantum computers can use this exponential power to solve problems that were before thought to be unsolvable.

Factoring is one such problem. It is relied on heavily in modern cryptosystems because it is "hard" to factor large numbers into two prime factors. There is no known efficient algorithm (meaning one that runs in polynomial time or less) to factor numbers. However, in 1994, Peter W. Shor proposed an algorithm for quantum computers that would factor numbers in polynomial time, meaning that it would become as easy to factor numbers as it was to multiply them. This means that any current encryption could be broken in a reasonable amount of time.

Thus, quantum computers will be machines that are not just "many times" faster than today's machines, but exponentially faster. They will be able to break any code, factor large numbers, and find items in unsorted lists in an insanely short amount of time. A good way to explore quantum computing, since such machines are not physically in existence as of yet, is to build a simulation.

I have created an Open Source project for Linux to build a quantum computer simulator, known as OpenQubit. There is a ~200 person mailing list consisting of physicists, computer scientists, and anyone who cares to discuss quantum computing and related topics. So far, we have created a working simulator that can run Shor's algorithm and factor numbers. The only problem with simulation of such a system is its exponentiality. Because a classical computer does not operate in the same way as a quantum computer, it must use an exponential amount of memory to work. Thus the largest number I can factor on my system with 32MB of RAM is 63. However, building this simulator gave me great insight into a very interesting technology that will probably become standard during our lifetime. So get ready for the next computer revolution. If you are interested in reading more about quantum computing, search for quantum computing (www.google.com seems particularly nice for this).

Viruses and Trojans

You didn't need the Internet to be able to spread computer viruses. But it definitely helped. Generally, this sort of behavior was looked down upon in hacker circles as being destructive and childish. And yet, there was a certain fascination with figuring out how it all worked as well as coming up with theoretical ways of efficiently spreading a virus or a trojan. Of course, misinformation was abundant and companies that claimed to protect users from viruses benefited more than anyone. We tried to instill common sense into our pages concerning ways to avoid becoming a victim. But it sure was fun to see the mass panic whenever the media announced a new virus, which was scheduled to hit and cause all kinds of mayhem. One of the more fun and creative pieces of mischief ever put out was, of course, Back Orifice, released publicly and brazenly by members of the Cult of the Dead Cow and discussed at length in our pages.

Analysis: Gulf War Printer Virus (Winter, 1991–1992)

By Anonymous

I work closely with the technical aspects of the operating system on IBM mainframes so I followed with some interest the accounts of the "Gulf War Virus." (News organizations in January 1992 reported the story of a computer virus introduced into an Iraqi air defense system via a printer.) My first reaction was one of amazement that the National Security Agency had pulled off such a stunt. But when I thought about it further it began to seem less and less reasonable and more and more likely that the whole thing was a piece of "disinformation."

There are three ways that the printer might have been attached to the mainframe: (1) Channel attached. If it was channel-attached then there is virtually no way that it could initiate an action that would cause the modification of software on the mainframe. A printer is an output device. It can only tell the computer stuff like, "I finished printing a line," "I have a jam," etc. It does this through very simple codes; (2) Attached to a network; or (3) Attached remotely....(2) and (3) are similar in terms of requirements. If it were attached in one of these two ways then it is at least conceivable that, with an enormous effort, it could transform itself from a print server into something capable of initiating input into the mainframe. This would involve a lot of "fooling the system." Once it had transformed itself it would have to fool the mainframe again into considering it a legitimate user who had the proper security to either initiate batch jobs or work interactively. Once it had done that it would have to know the name of the library where the CRT software resided and the name of the module that controlled the CRTs. It would have to convince the security system that it should be allowed to access this library. Once it had done that it could then make the very subtle change indicated in the article that would only go into effect under special circumstances. (A subtle change like that would be more difficult than a gross change that would, for example, simply bring down the entire system.) And, all of this incredible coding would, presumably, be done in the 1k or 2k that is available in a ROM chip!

Now consider what I think is more likely: First you have to ask yourself, "Why would the NSA tell this story? If they could really do something neat like this, why wouldn't they keep it a secret to use again in the future?" I can only imagine two reasons that they might tell such a story: (1) There is an Iraqi computer insider who they are trying to protect (the guy who really did the deed) by diverting attention; (2) The software (like most of the Iraqi equipment) probably came from a Western country. The company that created the CRT software might well have left a "logic bomb" in the software in case Saddam pulled a stunt like he pulled. The company probably does not want it to be known that they leave such bombs in their software, so the NSA wants, again, to protect them and divert attention.

I think that the disinformation theory gains some credibility from the information that is presented in the stories that are circulating. We are told almost nothing about the technical details but we are told everything about the printer. How it came in, where it came from, the approximate timeframe, everything but the serial number. I suspect that when the Iraqis read the story and open up the printer there will probably be color-coded chips there stamped "NSA."

As if mainframe security people don't have enough to worry about, I imagine that for the next 20 years they will have to answer questions about the possibility of introducing a virus into the mainframe from the least likely source: a printer.

Virus Scanners Exposed (Spring, 1992) *By Dr. Delam*

In 1989, virus expert John McAfee reported there being a whopping 52 known computer viruses in existence for the IBM computer. Lacking the most recent figures to date, it could be estimated at well over 300 known to the public, and probably a couple hundred more known to traders and collectors. Projections for the increasing trend are indefinite, but it is evident that the current popular methods of stopping viruses are grossly ineffective.

The following text provides some insight into just a few methods that could be used in a virus that current virus protection wouldn't catch.

When most viruses replicate, they try not to reinfect any programs. A marker will be left behind to signify an infection. One of the easiest places to leave a marker is in the file's directory entry.

Of the marking methods, the 62-second trick is most popular. When a file is saved, it's given a time and date. The time is saved in hours, minutes, and seconds. But the seconds do not appear in directory listings. Because of this fact, and the fact that the second's value may be set to 62, it's a great way for a virus to identify an infection.

Two more areas of interest in directory entries are the attribute byte and the 10 reserved bytes, neither of which have been used by viruses as markers. The attribute byte consists of six used bytes, for read-only, archive, volume label, directory, hidden, and system. The two unused bits cannot be used effectively. If either is set high, the ATTRIB command will not be able to perform changes on that file. The 10 reserved bytes however, can be changed without any adverse effects that I have noticed. They are normally set to zeros.

One other marking method is to leave an identification within the virus, and scan for that before each infection. This is not only time consuming, but it leaves the virus scanners something to detect, and is impossible for use with random encrypting code.

Note: If you are not familiar with the ATTRIB command, type "ATTRIB *.*" to see the current attributes of each file in a directory. For a cheap thrill, go to the local Radio Shack, get into DOS, and use EDLIN to modify AUTOEXEC.BAT. Be creative—if ANSI.SYS is loaded in CONFIG.SYS, you might want to add the line "PROMPT $E[=1hEat ME!." Then type "ATTRIB +R AUTOEXEC.BAT." It's harmless fun, and it will effectively annoy the salespeople because they won't be able to delete or change AUTOEXEC.BAT.

Virus size can become a critical factor in programming. An easy way to reduce size is to place some of the code in a common location and load it in during execution. An overlooked area, again, is the directories.

If the root directory's capacity is 112 entries (number is found in the boot sector), using the 10 reserved bytes would give you 1120 undisturbed bytes in a great location, free from scanners. Subdirectories provide an even better amount of free space...the number of entries for subdirectories is unlimited, and furthermore, a subdirectory doesn't show its size in directory listings. A generous amount of empty entries could be provided to a subdirectory, after which a full virus could reside.

The only other places that would be considered undisturbed, safe hiding spots would be in the DOS directory as a pseudo file like GRAPHICS.SYS, which doesn't really exist, but may be overlooked, or assuming the name of a useless file like 12345.678 file.

The ideas presented were original, and may give a small feel for how insecure computers are and how far behind the times virus researchers using the old scan string technique really are. At the head of the pack for those researchers who are still scanning is McAfee Associates in California.

McAfee Associates use a somewhat desultory method of catching viruses. A new virus infects someone, they then send a copy to McAfee, and McAfee looks for a sequence of bytes common within the virus (the scan string). A few more come out and McAfee puts out the new version of Scan—yippy!

"Hmmmmm, McAfee foils me again; they have a scan string to my virus!" It didn't take much thinking on the part of virus writers and connoisseurs to figure out the solution—just change the scan string in the virus itself, and voilà: the virus is no longer scannable! The obvious was too obvious though—McAfee made sourcing Scan to find the scan strings near impossible. Scan works by encrypting the program it is scanning, and comparing it to an encrypted scan string, like when comparing a dictionary to a DES password file. This was done so Scan wouldn't detect itself. Picking apart Scan seemed to be more bother than what it was worth, as how any security should work.

"Bahahah, they missed something!" is probably something like what Flash Force was thinking when he pioneered the way around the encryption. Flash Force called my board and told me what he was working on. He found that all the scan strings were 10 bytes in length, so he made a program called "Antiscan" to fragment a known virus into hundreds of little 10-byte files. Sure enough, Scan pointed out the 10-byte file containing the scan string.

McAfee caught on that new viruses were coming out that were actually old ones with a few bytes mixed around, just enough to evade Scan. Their response was to make some new scan strings of varying lengths, and allow for a wild card where the strings varied slightly. It's obvious McAfee didn't know what was really going on or they would have checked the length of the program they were scanning, and made a percentage match to warn of near matches.

(It would be fun to see how they would cope with a virus that randomly exposes scan strings of other viruses. You have to wonder if Clean would obliterate the program it was trying to save.)

The problem McAfee posed was easily remedied. I used Flash Force's idea and made a program that forced Scan to look at two files at a time, working much faster than AntiScan. Take the first half of the bytes in the virus and make one file. Take the second half of the bytes and make another. Now shell to Scan and make it look at the files. If Scan finds nothing in either half, the scan string must be broken between the two halves, so center on that section and reduce the resulting file's size, still centering, until Scan can't detect the string. If Scan had found the string in one of the original halves, the program would make two more files from that half, etc. Finally a resulting file that can't be halved or reduced while centered upon is produced. From that point the program fragments like AntiScan and Scan will point out the scan string it looks for, all inside of a couple minutes or less.

I visited with Mark Washburn, writer of the V2P series of research viruses, and of a protection program known as Secure. I found Mark to be a pretty kewl guy, and we got into discussing phreaking, which he had no previous experience with. He wouldn't be labeled a hacker by today's standards, but I think you'll see that much of what he does parallels that of one.

Mark saw a way to circumvent virus scanners altogether. Just write a program that encrypts itself 100 percent and varies the encryption from infection to infection! Most programmers would say, "Yeah, but the part that decrypts the virus would have to be executable, therefore it can't be encrypted, and the scanner would pick that up!" Not if you figure out an algorithm to make thousands of decryptors that all perform identical...which is what he did. In his latest V2P7 virus, only 2 bytes stay constant, the two required to form a loop. How many programs do you suppose have loops in them!? He scares the hell out of McAfee while showing them the fault in their programs. They've never listened.

I had to wonder who Mark gives copies of his research viruses to. He only made two copies of V2P6, and one of them went to McAfee. He didn't believe me when I told him I had a copy of V2P6, so I had to show him. To say the least, he was shocked. Trusting that he only gave a copy to McAfee would mean one of two things: either McAfee has warped staff, or someone gained higher access on McAfee's board (if McAfee was stupid enough to put their copy of V2P6 anywhere near their BBS computer). Either way they lack security.

Though the V2P viruses are unscannable, Mark made sure he had a way to protect against it. His Secure program is a shareware virus protection that watches over reads and writes to executable files, vital sectors, and memory. It effectively stops new and old viruses as well as trojans, bombs, and replicators. Probably the only ways around it are to use direct control of the drives, which is too much bulk for a virus; remove Secure from memory; or have the virus rename the file it is infecting to a filename without an executable extension, and then replace the original name.

To date, no virus uses any of these methods to avoid detection, because not enough people are using Secure to worry about it. McAfee has gained popularity only because it is easy to obtain a recent version via their BBS, and the average computer user isn't smart enough to understand the mechanics of virus protection and the quintessence of hampering all activity resembling a virus before its propagation.

If it weren't for people like Mark, who test the security of computers and the integrity and validity of software, cyberspace might just as well be ruled by the sadistic and vindictive.

Durum et durum non faciunt murum!

Back Orifice Tutorial (Autumn, 1998) *By skwp*

The hacker group known as Cult of the Dead Cow (CdC) recently released a great hacking tool known as Back Orifice, or BO, on August 1, 1998. On August 9, the client code was ported to UNIX. The legitimate purpose of BO is the remote administration of one's machine. BO affects Win95/98 but not NT. The following article explains the uses of BO, how it works, and how to prevent it from attacking you. Much of this information is taken from BO documentation, and resources on the Net.

How It Works

BO consists of two parts, a client and a server. You have to install the server on the machine you wish to gain access to. The server is included in the BO installation as boserver.exe. Once run, it self-installs, and then erases itself. After that the server machine will run BO server every time it starts up. The process is not visible in the processes list (Ctrl+Alt+Del). The server exec itself copies itself to c:\windows\system as ".exe."

The server can be configured using boconfig.exe, which allows you to specify the name of the file (default: " .exe"), description in registry, port (default: 31337), and password (default: no password) among other things.

Once the server is installed, you can use boclient.exe (bounix for the unix versions), or bogui.exe (graphical) to access the server machine. The client sends encrypted UDP (connectionless) packets to the server machine in order to communicate.

How to Get It Installed

Here's where our favorite skill, social engineering, comes in. Make up any kind of bullshit story in order to get the person to run this file. Pretend to be a lamer, say it is a new game, tell them it's a couple of xxx pics in self extracting format. Be original, and don't push them to run the file—this will make people suspicious. When they run it they may say something like, "What the f*ck? It disappeared!" This is when you know that you have full access to their machine.

Using the Client

The client interface has many features. You can read the supplied docs. I will discuss some of the more fun features and their uses.

Once you start the client you can type "help" or "?" for assistance on available commands. First of all to connect to a machine you have BO'ed, use "host <IP>."

Now you can use standard DOS commands (dir, cd, copy, del, etc.) to move around on this person's hard drive. However, this is awkward and takes a long time. Luckily, BO includes a built in http server so that you can download and upload files to the machine. Use "httpon <port>" to activate the http server. Now you can access their machine through a web browser on that port. (I use Netscape; my friend reports weird problems accessing BO'ed machines while using Internet Exploiter.) BO includes a convenient form on the bottom of the page for you to upload files. Fun things to do while browsing: look at person's pr0n, read personal docs, steal warez.

Another fun thing to do, which tends to scare the sh*t out of people, is to display a dialog box on their computer. Use "dialog <text> <title>" to make a dialog box pop up on their machine. I have found that in the windows boclient, the dialogs do not come out right if you use quotes. I'm not sure about the LINUX version as I have not been able to test it. However, using the GUI client for windows this bug does not exist. Be careful using this as it lets people know that their machine is in the process of being owned and they tend to reboot as quickly as possible. If this happens you can use the sweep command to sweep their subnet and find their machine again (in the case of dynamic IPs). You can also use the multimedia "sound" feature to play sounds on their machine. Specify the full path to the sound.

The network commands menu allows you to view their network and share resources. This may prove to be very fun. Share their printer and print out a nice message telling them how to remove BO (discussed later).

You can also have fun with processes. Use "proclist" to list running processes, and "prockill" and "procspawn" to kill and spawn new processes, respectively. This is useful, for example, if you have modified some sort of ini files (like mIRC) and you need them to restart the program. Just kill the program and they will probably restart it, thinking it was just a stupid Windows bug.

One of the more fun features of BO is keystroke logging. This feature will log all keystrokes in a very convenient manner, including the name of the window where they were typed, into a text file on the person's machine. Use the http server to download/view this file. Another convenient way to get passwords is the "passes" command, which lists cached passwords. I have found many unencrypted passwords sitting around in this way, including passwords to Tripod homepages and PPP accounts.

Finally, you can redirect ports and tie console apps to ports. For example, if this person is running a 31337 WaReZ fTP SeRvEr, you may want to redirect all connections to port 21 to pentagon.mil, or whitehouse.gov. I can only think of one example of tying apps to ports which is included in BO, and that is to tie command.com so that you have a DOS shell on their machine. Usually you can just put it on port 23 (default telnet port), which makes it a lot easier. I have found, however, that accessing their machine in this way is extremely slow for some reason.

Other features of BO include modifying the registry, capturing screenshots and movies from attached input devices, and using plug-ins (read included plug-in docs for info on how to write them), locking up the machine, and rebooting it.

BO and plug-ins (buttplugs) can be downloaded at `http://www.cultdeadcow.com/tools/`.

How to Get Rid of It

According to the ISS Security Alert Advisory made on August 6, BO installs itself by entering itself into the registry. To stop BO from starting every time the machine boots, edit the key at HKEY_LOCAL_MACHINE\SOFTWARE\Microsoft\Windows\Current Version\RunServices and look for any suspicious program names. The length of the BO exe is close to 124,928 bytes, give or take 30 bytes. Erase this entry, and erase the file itself. If possible, format your hard drive and reinstall all OS's and software, as the use of BO may be part of a larger security breach. The full text of the ISS Advisory can be found at `http://www.iss.net/xforce/alerts/advise5.html`.

Microsoft's Response

"This is not a tool we should take seriously or our customers should take seriously."
—EDMUND MUTH OF MICROSOFT, as reported by *The New York Times.*

Well, Microsoft was wrong. There have been an estimated 65,000 downloads of the BO software package, and I myself have owned over 15 machines using it (I was bored, wanted to look at other people's pr0n....).

Conclusion

Back Orifice is a fun toy, but you must remember hacker ethics while using this tool. Do not put something like "@echo y | format c:" in autoexec.bat. The purpose of hacking is to learn and create, not to destroy.

SOBERING FACTS (Autumn, 1997)

You may be wondering why this issue is so incredibly late. Depending on who you listen to, you may also be surprised to see it at all. We've basically been hit with a crisis that is part of the risk any publisher takes. We owe it to our readers to explain just what's been going on.

When we send issues to stores, we have to go through a process that involves companies known as distributors. The vast majority of stores will not deal directly with publishers and most publishers don't have the time or staff to deal directly with individual stores. This is where distributors come in. They take care of contacting stores and getting our issues to them. In turn the stores pay them and the distributors pay us. By the time we get paid, it's generally at least half a year since the issue was printed. The distributors keep around half the cover price (some actually want more than this).

SOBERING FACTS *(continued)*

For a number of years a distributor based in Austin, Texas, known as Fine Print has been getting us onto shelves in Barnes and Noble, Borders, Hastings, and a large number of independent stores nationwide. They've done this for all kinds of independent zines for years. But, during those same years, there were all kinds of financial mismanagements taking place there, which we didn't have a hint of until fairly recently. It started with a lot of smaller zines not getting paid at all. Some were eventually forced out of business. Early in 1997, Fine Print filed for Chapter 11 protection, owing us nearly $100,000—printing costs for three issues. The first signs of trouble came this summer when we began to not get paid for the current debts as well. We started to run out of money to pay bills, our web site development had to be frozen, paid staff became unpaid staff, and numerous expansions and new projects had to be indefinitely postponed or canceled. We were advised by numerous professional sorts to consider bankruptcy ourselves.

The biggest nail in the coffin came as a result of Beyond Hope, our second hacker conference that took place this summer. By all accounts, the conference was a terrific learning experience and a huge success. Financially, though, we lost over $10,000 on it, mostly due to last minute greed and deception on the part of the venue and our network provider. Ordinarily, we could have handled this and we would have even considered it a worthy expense for all of the positive things that came out of it. However, coupled with the Fine Print problems, it was enough to practically make our financial wounds fatal.

Practically. Because there's one thing we have that most businesses and corporations lack. That is a spirit and a knack for survival. The people who read *2600* and give us moral support were the main reasons we knew we couldbeat the crap we were facing. And that's exactly what we intend to do. That is why, no matter how bad things get, we won't declare bankruptcy and absolve ourselves of responsibility to our debtors and our readers. We know how that feels and we won't continue the cycle.

But we have come up with a plan where our readers can help and at the same time get stuff back. We've dropped prices on a number of things that we sell that we already have in stock. Since we already have all of this merchandise, we don't have to worry about paying for it. If enough people buy these things, we'll have more money to work with and we'll be able to hopefully pay a larger percentage of our bills if not all of them. Look for details on specifics in various ads in this issue.

continues

SOBERING FACTS *(continued)*

Because of the lateness this has caused, we have suspended putting the season of our issues on the front cover. If the Autumn issue comes out nearer to Winter, a lot of places may pull it off the shelves too soon. We are trying to tighten up our schedule so that, inside of a year, we will be back on track.

The reorganization plan was recently announced by Fine Print and the cash settlement offered to us was a whopping $150. Needless to say, we're now taking the plunge and moving our accounts to other distributors where it will take a while for the sales to reach us. Once that happens, again within the next year, we expect things to start turning around. After all, had we been getting paid all along, we'd be in pretty good shape right now.

We're sorry to put a damper on what should be a positive period. Beyond Hope was an inspiration to a large part of the hacker community and was technically as flawless as we had hoped for. Once we climb out of the hole we will begin planning the next one. We've made tremendous progress getting our weekly radio show out on the Net and now, thanks to bandwidth donations, regular live listeners include people all over the world. It will take a great deal more than financial disaster to stop hacker progress.

We bear no animosity toward Fine Print. Please don't turn off their phones—they have enough problems. They helped to get us into a lot of places we may never have reached. We hope they work out their problems and once again help independent zines reach a greater number of people. There's no question that people are hungry for information and alternative ideas in every region of the country. The most important thing is to make sure the ideas keep on flowing.

The Internet

Having all of these computers linked together on the Internet would, of course, prove to be no end of trouble and mischief. Obtaining global access at increasingly cheap rates made exploring even easier than it was for the privileged few who had packet switched network access back in the '80s. And the growing visibility of the hacker world brought significantly more people into the scene who spent every waking hour trying to figure out ways into all manner of machines. The mere concept of computers belonging to the Pentagon being just as accessible as a public access UNIX system was a bit more than a lot of us could handle. And I'm sure people inside the military had their fair share of culture shock, too. But seeing how the whole thing tied together was indeed fascinating.

Another bit of fun that we all started to become aware of courtesy of the Internet was the phenomenon of spam, which naturally led to all sorts of theories and debates on how to fight it. We also can't forget the emergence of Internet Relay Chat (IRC), which linked people from all over the world together in real time chats, both privately and in massive channels. Many people got addicted to this and remain so to this day. And also included in this section is an article on the early days of Internet radio.

News Items (Summer, 1997)

We may think things are bad here in the United States as far as threats to freedom of speech on the Internet go. But the truth is that there are always places where things are worse. Sometimes much worse.

In China, even meeting in an Internet cafe can be looked upon as a threat. And it's no wonder with enlightened laws that decree things like "Neither organizations nor individuals are allowed to engage in activities at the expense of state security and secrets. They are also forbidden to produce, retrieve, duplicate, or spread information that may hinder public order." Don't expect a flurry of *2600* meetings in China anytime soon.

Germany, however, does have *2600* meetings. And it claims to be part of the Western world. We're beginning to think they may be trying to gain admission into the deep South. The head of Compuserve's German subsidiary was recently indicted for helping to distribute child pornography and violent computer games by not doing enough to block offensive material. An individual was charged more recently with maintaining a link on her web page to a leftist newspaper in Holland. This is a country where people who access "violent" games like Quake are punished. Apparently the German government sees the Internet as a threat to their society. The Internet community is beginning to look upon the German government in the same way.

You can bet that the Exons, Helms, and even Clintons of our nation are looking at the situations in these two countries with great interest. And they're taking lots of notes.

As the Net continues to grow, it was inevitable that existing top level domains would become insufficient. There is talk of expanding them to include things like .firm (for businesses), .store (for places to buy things), .web (for WWW-related activities), .arts (for cultural and entertainment crap), .rec (for recreational activities), .info (for information service providers), and .nom (for individuals). We're surprised we haven't seen .xxx suggested as a potential domain for, gosh, who knows?

But this is only part of the story. The entire structure of the Net is about to change and many people think this is for the better. Whereas there is currently only one registrar for the .com, .net, and .org domains, as of April 1998 there will be a more competitive atmosphere. Anyone who can afford the $10,000 application fee and demonstrate financial stability and Net access can apply to become a registrar and register domain names all around the world. Customers will be able to keep their domain names if they switch registrars. The deadline to apply is October 16, 1997, and the form can be found at www.gtld-mou.org. If you don't have Net access and can't get to that site, why in the world would you want to become a registrar in the first place?

Incidentally, in the sucker of the century department, the domain business.com recently was bought for the cost of $150,000!

Cyber Promotions is undoubtedly one of the most hated organizations on the Internet. Why? Read this little pitch that these sleazebags use to con other sleazebags into sending them $1,000: "Cyber Promotions is now presenting three new technologies that will only work properly if used all together. The first technology can change the message ID before your e-mails leave your computer! The second technology allows you to send over 50,000 e-mails an hour—with a single computer and modem—without stealing other peoples' resources, and the third technology will relay your e-mail messages through Cyber Promotions' own proprietary high-speed relay network, without identifying the domain name or IP address of the origin! The end result is that you will be able to send all the bulk e-mail you wish—at lightning fast speed—from your own local dialup account—without the risk of account termination."

Basically, they are forging e-mail addresses so people can't reply to the sender with dark threats and spectacular Internet justice. But any good hacker can get to the root of the problem one way or another. In May, cyberpromo.com was hit by a relentless mail bomb campaign designed to slow down their harassment campaign, if only for a little while. It worked rather well although Cyber Promo claims it had little effect. In another action, one of the Cyber Promo machines was accessed and a list of customers, i.e., people who themselves are involved in unsolicited mailings on the Net, was widely circulated.

Organizations like Cyber Promotions have practically destroyed the effectiveness of Usenet and now they are clogging up individual users' mailboxes with unsolicited junk. The last thing we need are more laws designed to regulate the Net. So the most effective way of dealing with people like these is to use the power of the Net in a positive way. If someone makes the first strike, you are entitled to do what is necessary to get them to stop. Since, by forging their headers, they have made it impossible to be asked politely to stop, cutting it off at the source is the only action left. In addition, we as individuals can commit ourselves to wasting as much of these losers' time as possible. That means expressing an interest in whatever product they happen to be peddling and getting them to believe that you're really interested. At some point they will become vulnerable to your full wrath. If enough of us do this, this problem will go away once and for all because of the massive amounts of money being lost.

The Consequences of .gov/.mil Hacking (Spring, 1997)

By Chocolate Phoetus

In recent times, the Air Force homepage has been hacked by someone with enough patience to deal with the bloody thing. We've all probably seen the hacked pages now thanks to 2600.com, but how many of you know how the military reacts to such an "attack?" What you're about to read may help you think twice about any ideas you have concerning government sites. I'm not condoning anything, and I'm certainly not telling you how to run your affairs, simply giving you a little advice that's commonly known in the ".mil" and, ".gov" community.

The military does not, as a general rule, leave "sensitive" systems containing classified information open to anyone who wants to "dial in." There are many different ways of preventing access, from closed systems with no dialups, to restricting usage to users with ".gov" or ".mil" addresses. You won't, as a matter of course, find classified information on a government computer that is hooked up to the Net. That's not to say that you won't find material you shouldn't, by law, access. There's plenty of information protected by the Privacy Act floating around out there. But, let's face it, that info is pretty boring unless you are into social engineering, and know how to use the information once you get it. The government world has strange protocols and routines that someone "not in the know" will "tread on" unknowingly. The simple misuse of a bit of jargon or ignorance of an acronym will often raise eyebrows, and get you "looked into." If you are bewildered by that last line, that's a clear indication you don't understand the minds of people who work for these agencies. Beware—your ignorance could get you into trouble.

Mistakes Hackers Make

One of the biggest idiosyncrasies of ".gov" and ".mil" people is the incessant need for immediate damage control. Example: When the Air Force homepage was hacked, a press release was immediately put out, saying that the incident was being investigated, and that hackers had put "pornography" on the site. Anyone who has seen the *2600* posts of these pages knows that a single moving .gif with a couple having sex was on there. The impression by the press release was that there were loads of vile images posted to the poor Air Force homepage. The people who wrote the press release would never consider telling the truth about what happened—that someone made them look foolish by cracking a pathetic security system and posting loads of sarcasm towards the Air Force in general.

Hackers who put "pornography" on their target sites are actually helping these people put "spin control" on these incidents. Many hackers are also blissfully unaware that the Air Force (as well as other branches of government) has a special office that is dedicated to research and arresting so-called computer criminals. By putting links to other pages, you could be getting your friends an unwanted phone call by people in blue suits. You may also be leading right back to yourself, if you frequent these sites.

Sadly, many hackers go right for the throat when they "alter" these web sites. It's clear that the page has been hacked, usually discovered by some retired sergeant with nothing better to do than surf the web, and then rat you out. Subtlety is a desired trait. Instead of changing the entire page, why do hackers not make more subtle alterations? The best pranks are the ones where the mark doesn't realize he's being had, at least not right away. Altering only the links, for example, to go to porn sites would be a hell of a lot more shocking to a ".mil" person surfing the Net than logging into the Air Force homepage and seeing that "somebody hacked it." Many people surf the ".mil" sites at work. They're permitted to do that. But the people who monitor the networks (and yes, they do) are looking for "unauthorized" or "not for official business" surfing and downloading. Imagine the sick feeling the person surfing on their government computer would feel to link to what they think is some other base's site, only to be taken to "www.bigtits.com." These people live in an atmosphere of fear, and seeing that on the government computer would give them apoplectic fits.

I would never encourage anyone to do something as risky and profitless as to hack or to intrude on a government web site. These systems are run on taxpayer dollars, and that means your dollars. But there are some interesting legal stipulations that affect the people who have hacked these sites:

On the front gate of any military installation, a sign can clearly be read stating that access to the installation is permitted only by the commander's authority, and that trespassing is a Federal Offense. Don't think that those warnings apply only to your trying to walk into the installation. The same rule applies to ".mil" sites as well. Even though there is no sensitive information on these systems, you can still be arrested for espionage for trying to hack a government site. The intent is what they're after. Consider this if you're thinking about "becoming a hacker."

When you "modem in" to a military site, you are also entering into a military phone system, which is monitored. Every telephone in every military base has a sticker saying so. This is no joke, and your modem is not immune. Use of the system implies consent, even if you object later. There is legal precedent for this—challenging it will do you no good in court. If a military site is hacked, someone will be assigned to look into it, sometimes in conjunction with the FBI. Hacking is taken very seriously by the government, and they do not give up easily.

I hope this has helped someone rethink hacking a ".gov" or ".mil" site.

Internet Peering (Spring, 1999) *By The Prophet*

As anyone who has a dialup Internet account knows, there are plenty of providers. Everyone wants to sell you a dialup account. Providers use many different backbones—

sometimes multiple ones. And yet, if you dial into any of them and go to `http://www.2600.com`, you're likely to see the *2600* web page load.

How that page loads is really a remarkable event. Many people don't realize that the Internet is not all one network. It is a network of networks, operated by a myriad of providers. Each of these operate a backbone, which consists of high-speed links (usually T-3 and above) between "Points of Presence" (POPs) located in major cities. By far the largest backbone is the legacy MCI.NET, which is now operated by Cable and Wireless and was renamed CW.NET. Cable and Wireless also owns cwix.net, which they are slowly integrating into CW.NET. As of this writing, MCI Worldcom is the second largest backbone operator (though catching up quickly), operating uu.net (formerly alter.net), wcom.net (formerly compuserve.net), and ans.net (previously owned by AOL, and before that ANS CO+RE Systems). And in a distant third place is Sprint. There are a number of smaller backbone providers as well—AGIS, Digex, GlobalCenter, Exodus, CRL, netaxs, and others. Many of these, paradoxically, lease fiber trunk capacity from MCI Worldcom (this has obviously led to friction, as the bandwidth provider of many backbones is also a major competitor).

Of course, not every network extends to every point on the Internet. For instance, ANS handles a great deal of traffic into and out of Albuquerque, since they are one of only a few backbones with POPs there. Some great places to see network maps and POPs for the various ISPs are their web pages, or the *Boardwatch* Directory of Internet Service Providers. In order to solve the problem of moving packets from one point to another, backbones peer with one another.

Peering is, at its essence, the passing of traffic between networks. Let's start with a traceroute, which shows the routers between an origin and a destination:

```
traceroute to www.fbi.gov (32.97.253.60), 30 hops max, 40 byte packets
1 hil-qbu-ptt-vty254.as.wcom.net (206.175.110.254) 245 ms 218 ms 253 ms
2 hil-ppp2-fas2-1.wan.wcom.net (209.154.35.35) 216 ms 209 ms 210 ms
3 hil-core1-fas4-1-0.wan.wcom.net (205.156.214.161) 210 ms 227 ms 226 ms
4 chi-core1-atm5-0-1.wan.wcom.net (209.154.150.5) 434 ms 223 ms 215 ms
5 chi-peer1-fdd0-0.wan.wcom.net (205.156.223.164) 222 ms 1882 ms 1815 ms
6 ameritech-nap.ibm.net (198.32.130.48) 369 ms 222 ms 222 ms
7 165.87.34.199 (165.87.34.199) 231 ms 303 ms 228 ms
8 www.fbi.gov (32.97.253.60) 233 ms 241 ms 242 ms
```

This may look like a bunch of gobbledygook at first glance. However, it is very revealing about how peering works.

You can see that the first stop is a terminal server in wcom.net (formerly compuserve.net), probably located in Columbus, Ohio. The connection bounces from there to an ethernet port, to an ATM router, and over a high-speed link to another ATM router in Chicago. Once in Chicago, it proceeds to the peering point (at Ameritech NAP), is handed off to IBM.NET, hits a router that isn't identified (probably somewhere in the Washington, DC area), and finally ends up at `www.fbi.gov`. Bear in mind that when `www.fbi.gov` sends data back, it does not necessarily follow the same path. The path that is followed is based on route advertisements and other factors, which a good set of TCP/IP texts, like the *TCP/IP Illustrated* series, reviews in detail.

You will notice that Ameritech NAP is the peering point that was used. There are actually four "official" NAPs, set up under the review of the NSF. They are the Ameritech NAP in Chicago, the New York NAP (which is actually in Pennsauken, New Jersey—across the river from Philadelphia), the Sprint NAP (which is in West Orange, New Jersey, near Newark), and the PacBell NAP in the San Francisco area.

This system of NAPs is supplemented by two "unofficial" NAPs known as the MAE's. These are Metropolitan Area Ethernets (hence the acronym) that are operated in the Washington, DC and Silicon Valley areas by MFS (now owned by MCI Worldcom). Additionally, the Federal Government operates two Federal Internet eXchanges (FIX's), one at Moffett Field in California and one in the Washington, DC area. The FIX's handle Internet traffic bound to and originating from .MIL sites and some .GOV sites. Finally, CIX operates a peering point in a Palo Alto, CA WilTel POP. This is mostly a salutatory point and is rarely used nowadays. At one point, all commercial Internet traffic was transited through CIX, but the NAPs were set up in part because of infighting between the competing backbones who could not agree on who was allowed to peer at CIX. Finally, many larger backbones have set up private peering points among themselves. For instance, since Cable and Wireless' acquisition of MCI.NET, they have set up a number of private peering points to exchange traffic with their own CWIX.NET.

Peering is a very controversial area. For one, end-to-end performance of a backbone is positively coordinated with the number and speed of peering points. Therefore, a smaller Internet backbone that cannot afford a number of private peers, or to peer at every MAE and NAP, is likely to have poorer performance. Additionally, backbones often cannot agree with whom they will peer. For instance, bbnplanet.net (now owned by GTE) decided that exodus.net was no longer worthy of peering, even though exodus.net offered to peer with BBN at any place in the country it liked. BBN claimed that exodus.net was leeching their bandwidth—though one must wonder who's really better off in the value equation, since BBN hosts many dialup and corporate users, and Exodus hosts primarily very popular web sites (like Yahoo! and ESPN Sportszone). How useful are the dialup accounts to customers without good performance to popular web sites? This is a question other backbones considering similar actions would be wise to consider.

The controversy is somewhat justified. Peering requires sharing BGP route advertisements, which if used improperly can blackhole large parts of the network (imagine large amounts of CW.NET traffic being routed via a 56K link to Iran—this is conceivably possible with bad BGP). Clearly, larger networks don't want clueless admins from smaller networks creating such episodes. Additionally, larger networks wonder why they should pay to transit traffic cross-country to a MAE for a smaller network that may only haul the traffic across town from the peering point. This is the case with many very small peers at MAE WEST in the San Francisco area. Many backbones at first demanded “hot potato routing,” so as to shift traffic away from their networks onto the network to which packets were bound as soon as possible. However, the opposite demand is often the case with smaller backbones (such as Exodus): They’re told to do “cold potato” routing, meaning that Exodus is expected to deliver traffic bound for UUNet at the nearest UUNet peering point to the IP for which the traffic is bound. Meanwhile, UUNet does “hot potato” routing, shifting Exodus traffic to their network as quickly as possible!

Meanwhile, while all of this is going on, people are buying—and expecting—access to the Internet. This is an important point. My mother is, for her $19.95 per month, not buying access to CW.NET’s network. She wants to use the *Internet* to visit knitting, cooking, and travel web sites. She knows how to send me e-mail, but wouldn’t know what a NAP was if one bit her on the leg. Customers are justifiably angry if they are unable to reach certain points on the Internet, or if the performance is awful. This puts backbones between a rock and a hard place. Those providers who are clued seem the most likely to actively seek multiple peering points with multiple providers, and PSI is a market leader in this regard—they’ll peer with anyone operating a backbone, free of charge. Others, such as UUNet, are demanding that smaller providers purchase circuits from them at regular customer rates until they meet certain criteria (which seems to change frequently). And finally, the MAEs and NAPs are collapsing under their own weight. They handle so much traffic that the majority of “net lag” is introduced at these peering points. Many larger networks are eschewing these peering points altogether in favor of private peering points. The problem with this, of course, is that it makes certain parts of the Internet faster than other parts, which drives traffic away from the smaller backbones, which makes the bigger networks even larger, so they can create more private peers...you get the idea. One backbone threw up their hands and gave up on the idea of public peering. SAVVIS buys transit from most other backbones, routes traffic exclusively through their own data centers, and by keeping more than 80 percent of their traffic away from the NAPs, has consistently performed very well in Keynote Systems network performance tests.

I don’t know where all of this will end. Nobody does. But I’ll pull out my crystal ball anyway. Historically, backbones have been great at creating murky peering arrangements, using convoluted reasoning. This is likely to continue. Chances are that we’ll see the existing small backbones either solidify their positions, become acquired by larger players, or run out of venture capital and disappear. However, it’s pretty unlikely that the Internet will cease to exist. It’s dependent on peering, the backbone operators know this, and while there may be power struggles and political games as exist in any large organization, there are also too many competitors for anyone to try to “steal” the Internet (by cutting off peering). Jack Rickard, editor of *Boardwatch Magazine*, put it best: “Trying to control the Internet is like trying to choke a Jell-O snake in a swimming pool full of Wesson oil.” Wise words, which astute backbones will heed.

Internet Radio Stations (Autumn, 1999) *By -theJestre-*

A new phenomenon is becoming increasingly popular on the Net: Internet radio stations. Some of the benefits to these stations are that they can reach a far broader audience than a traditional FM transmitter (anyone with Internet access can listen), and the FCC isn't regulating them because they don't use radio waves. I would like to give some basic information on these because I haven't seen much documentation and they could be useful to further link the underground hacker culture together.

The main company propelling these stations is Real Networks. They make the Real Player, Real Server, etc. and use streaming media techniques. Their software is very buggy, but there isn't much of an alternative. Because this is a new frontier so to speak, most people, including Real Networks' tech support people, don't fully understand all the details. I am the webmaster for one of these stations and have found that most everyone has a lot of trouble setting them up and making them work.

Right now a majority of the Internet radio stations use one of two main Real servers, the new Real Server G2 or the Real Server 5.x. If you have the Real Player (downloadable from `www.real.com`) you will notice it has a list of presets. All of these presets are required to use the Real Server G2 (even though some of them don't). The Real Server G2 has an interesting feature that the older servers don't: a web-based Java monitor and control center. This control center can usually be accessed by opening the web page:

```
http://realservername.radiomain.com:PORT/admin/index.html
```

Where realservername is the name of the computer the RealServer is on, and radiodomain is the domain of the radio's web site. You can also replace everything in front of :PORT with the IP address. There are a few barriers that one must go through if they want to access the control center, though. First off, you have to know the port number. In the G2 betas the default is usually 8080 but sometimes 9090. The full G2 version, however, picks a (somewhat) random port value during the installation usually in the 6000's like 6336. The port isn't the hardest thing to figure out if you do a portscan from 6000 to around 8000, but the next obstacle is a little trickier. It will ask for a username and password. The default username is "Administrator" and the default password is "letmein." Any competent administrator will change this quickly, but I'm sure someone out there has left the default settings alone. If you can gain access to the server the password is encrypted and stored in a file called "rmserver.pswd" and usually located in Program Files\Real\RealServer\ or a similar directory. Sometimes the password can also be found in the configuration file rmserver.cfg. The config file is written in XML so if the password is there then you don't have to deal with the encrypted file. The Java control center allows you to alter anything to do with the Real server, such as change port settings, restart the server, add/alter usernames and passwords for the Real server, and other fun oddities such as track the listening audience.

A few notes for someone trying to set up their own Internet radio station: The encoder program (which sends out the content to the server) and the server program must be run on separate computers. Unless you have very high speed access to the Internet (like a T1), I would not recommend setting up all the software for a station because the server uses a lot of bandwidth. This shouldn't prevent you from broadcasting, though! You can download a "test version" of the Real Encoder (for 5.x servers or below) or the Real Producer (for G2) at `http://www.real.com` for free. The encoders will not work on an NT platform, just Win 95/98 and some flavors of UNIX. You can then send your encoded stream to a remote server and use their bandwidth! Before you can do this, though, you need to find a server that doesn't have restrictions set on encoders or hack the G2 administrator and change the restrictions. The default is to have no restrictions. It is probably not advisable to "overstay your welcome" on a server because they can track where the stream is coming from. So in other words, do a good job covering your tracks and don't do something stupid like a 24 hour broadcast seven days a week!

Some final notes—if you do a portscan on the RealServer it will usually have ports 554 (for rtsp), 4040 (for the encoder), one port from 6000-8080 (for the administrator), and 8080 (for misc http) open among others. The port 9090 is the default monitoring point and will only be open if a monitor is also open. I recommend scanning in the 9000's before attempting to try anything because the monitor can tell how many monitor connections are open and where they are coming from. If an administrator is casually monitoring the server and suddenly sees an extra monitor pop up he might get a little suspicious.

I hope this information has been useful to at least a few people out there. On a final note, all this information has been gathered using the WIN NT versions. Although the other versions are bound to be similar, I cannot say for certain.

Cryptography

The 1990s brought another issue to the forefront of the hacker world: encryption. Since we were well aware of how fragile and insecure private communications were, we knew it was a damn good idea to be able to encrypt your data so that only you and the people you authorized could read it. The Clinton administration agreed that this was a good idea, so much so that they tried to gain total control over the use of encryption in America with the introduction of the Clipper and Capstone chips. It was considered a big step in the direction of criminalizing non-approved encryption schemes. Plus, the proposed system was classified so it was impossible to examine it for security issues like back doors. This controversy alone probably did more to galvanize the encryption community, much of which was also tied to the hacker community. While a lot of the technical aspects soared over many of our readers' heads, it's somehow very comforting to know that there are people out there keeping an eye on this sort of thing in an open and transparent manner.

Toward More Secrets (Winter, 1996-1997) *By Seraf*

Encrypted data communications is quite possibly the least understood piece of the popular Internet culture's technological backbone. Perhaps this is because cryptology is not trendy technology, but rather a complex science that is only beginning to be well-understood. Since the times before Christ, the study of secret writing, or cryptology, has played an important but largely invisible role in government. In fact, the Caesar Cipher (as in Julius) now appears in nearly every textbook on the subject.

But don't use an ancient code for anything more than slipping cuss words through monitored e-mail. While the Roman Empire's system simply rotates the alphabet three places, turning A's into D's, B's into E's, C's into F's, etc., present-day cryptographic algorithms are much more complex. While pen and paper can break a simple substitution cipher like Caesar's on short notice, cracking most any of the heavy-duty cryptosystems developed over the past twenty years requires more time and more computing power than potential adversaries apparently have.

Cracking modern cryptosystems by brute force—trying every possible key until one "works"—usually takes a huge amount of time and/or money. Many newer symmetric cryptosystems use 128-bit keys, and this key size seems to have become a standard minimum in recent years. Building a machine to guess such a key within a year would presently cost billions of billions of dollars (no kidding) and require quite a feat of engineering. Many symmetric ciphers, though, use a smaller key. The Data Encryption Standard (DES) uses a 56-bit key, and (disregarding the shortcuts available for breaking DES) its messages can be cracked by brute force in a month with equipment costing well under $1 million. It is a fact that the National Security Agency (NSA) has such equipment ready and waiting, as do many other institutions public and private—from American Express to the British Government to CalTech.

What is really at issue here is the value of the potentially obtained information to a privacy-invading party. Uncle Sam will not take a chunk out of the Defense Budget, nor allocate a sizable portion of NSA's computing power, in order to discover the key you're using to send articles to *2600*. But he will—at the very least—put a few hundred thousand dollars worth of computers to work for a month on your e-mail if he thinks you're spending your afternoons meeting with Saddam. These days, cryptosystems with keys of about 56 bits are not trusted to keep data secure for more than a few days or weeks. 64-bit keys are a significant improvement, and may secure data for decades. 128-bit keys are currently rated at 50 years, and slightly longer keys at about 100. (With computing power and resources on the rise, it's good to take these statistics with a grain of salt.)

Of course, all of this depends on the security of the algorithm being used. Cryptanalysis, the Zen of cipher-cracking, has become as much of a science as cryptography itself. DES has had significant holes poked in its weak sides by a number of cryptanalysts over the years, as have numerous other algorithms created by corporations, universities, and brilliant mathematicians alike. The best route is to use a well-respected crypto package. Experimenting with your own ciphers can be fun, but will often lead to disaster if implemented for communications which must be reliably secured.

Right now, the U.S. government holds what may be the best cryptographic technology in existence. Skipjack, the algorithm implemented in Capstone and the much-criticized Clipper Chip, is classified, but is likely to be far ahead of current crypto research in the scientific community. (Note: One of the few civilians allowed to review the algorithm was Dorothy Denning, a slightly overzealous Georgetown University professor who is opposed to all non-government use of crypto.) When the National Security Agency—perhaps the most secretive publicly-known sect of our government—created the Data Encryption Standard in the mid-1970's, it was optimized to be resistant to differential cryptanalysis. It was not until 1990, however, that this method of crypto-cracking was publicly discovered by the notorious Eli Biham and Adi Shamir. This means that not only are today's government cryptosystems designed to resist attacks that won't be in use for twenty years, but that the government is ready to deploy those futuristic attacks against the algorithm you're using today. Does this secret research not defy the scientist's ethic to share knowledge and information?

This is only the beginning of a growing U.S. government cryptomonopoly. New encoding algorithms are being developed in America constantly, and *2600* would be an ideal forum for their review and discussion. However, because of the U.S. Defense Trade Regulations (DTR) and *2600*'s international readership, they cannot be detailed here: Our favorite rag would be busted for trafficking in munitions, "transferring [cryptographic] technical data to a foreign person" (DTR 120.10). See for yourself. The United States Munitions List includes, along with plastique and land mines, the following items: "Speech scramblers, privacy devices, cryptographic devices, and software (encoding and decoding)..." (DTR 121.1). Even documents describing "unapproved" cryptosystems or listing their source codes are munitions.

What is "approved?" RSA's nonthreatening authentication facilities have been deemed exportable, but its unmatched public key encryption remains restricted to domestic use, along with PGP and other RSA-bearing products. Superslick modern systems like RC4 have been given the green light to appear in such globally available products as Netscape, but only after security-reducing modifications. Then there are the algorithms denied export altogether, or that won't even be given a hearing. Such has been the fate of Granddaddy DES, as well as that of many cryptosystems being developed at the undergraduate and graduate levels in American universities.

This is without question a breach of our First Amendment rights. If you design a cryptosystem, you are forbidden by your government to share it with whomever you please. Approval is required. We have had trade restrictions placed on our ideas. Exporting information that is "required for the design...of defense articles" (DTR 120.23) is illegal—so a book such as Phil Zimmerman's "PGP Source Code and

Internals" is by definition banned for export. (If you thought that banned books were a thing of the past, think again.) Even a foreigner on American soil is technically forbidden to examine such a publication at the corner bookstore.

American cryptologists are considered to be the best in the world, and the majority of strong cryptosystems originate in U.S. companies and universities. This technology has brought electronic privacy and freedom to Americans who put it to good use, and could do the same for citizens of other nations if it was not so feared by the powers that be. If we don't act soon, restrictions on the domestic use of cryptographic technologies are just around the corner. Legislation to impose such constraints on the American people has already been introduced on at least one occasion, nearly forcing all available cryptosystems to be made readily crackable by Big Brother.

Simply put, NSA is scared: terrified of Americans enforcing their own privacy with such strength; living in fear of foreign government organizations, businesses and individuals obtaining the same level of security as their American counterparts.

Use crypto anywhere you can—and make sure it's strong. Fight the U.S. government ban on knowledge and its underhanded attempts to thieve the world of digital privacy. U.S. citizens—write to your senators and congressmen and explain how important this technology is to every citizen of the Electronic Age, here and abroad. Foreign citizens—obtain source code to strong European algorithms such as Xuejia Lai and James Massey's IDEA, and make every attempt you can to secure "restricted" algorithms. Raise your voice!

Fortezza: The Next Clipper? (Summer, 1997) *By Seraf*

In recent years, the U.S. Government has pursued a project aimed at secure communications on its new Defense Messaging System (DMS). The requirements have been for a system to serve as the standard for unclassified American military encryption, easily implemented on any system (servers, workstations, mobile units, etc.). The project began in 1991 as the Pre Message Security Protocol, or PMSP. In 1993, the name changed to MOSAIC, and the associated device was introduced as the "Tessera Cryptographic Card."

The most recent incarnation of the project—now managed by the National Security Agency's MISSI (Multilevel Information Systems Security Initiative)—is called Fortezza, and the tiny device that does the dirty work is called the "Fortezza Crypto Card." As we will learn shortly, Fortezza's purpose has grown beyond military encryption, and may pose a threat to our electronic privacy.

Fortezza usually takes the form of a PCMCIA card, compatible with a tremendous installed base of personal computer hardware and viable on most any modern computer. Inside, Fortezza embodies a full suite of cryptographic functions for secure communications. It provides symmetric encryption with Skipjack (of Clipper-chip fame), secure key exchange, digital signature, and secure timestamp functions.

With all its versatility, MISSI has recommended Fortezza for a number of applications. Security for both the storage and transfer of files is an obvious one. Among the others: authentication of remote network hosts, secure communications with remote hosts, unforgeable (signed) directory services, encrypted web browsing, and secure electronic commerce. Fortezza applications have been developed to interface the unit with SMTP and MIME (Internet mail), ITU X.400, ACP-123 (the Allied Communications Protocol, a superset of X.400), ITU X.500, ASN.1 (ITU's Abstract Syntax Notation), and SDNS (the Secure Data Network System, an NSA standard).

Fortezza would blend in with countless other military programs, if it were being used exclusively for government communications. This, however, is not the case. Several companies now manufacture Fortezza cards, and their target is the *mass market.*

Fortezza represents an attempt to implement NSA-breakable cryptographic technology as widely as possible: a strategy we've seen before. The Clipper/Capstone project aimed to make the Clipper chip voluntary, and then to force it as the only option, either by further legislation or market dominance. Fortezza tries to implement this same strategy on an even greater scale. Rather than encrypting only telephone calls with its special brand of so-called security, the NSA is now aiming to dominate cryptography across the public's information frontier. It's rather telling that the heart of Fortezza is the Capstone chip.

Skipjack is an algorithm made to be cracked by the NSA. Like DES, it is a good algorithm for its time, but with weaknesses designed to be exploited by those in-the-know. Without a doubt, the Agency has built machines dedicated to cracking Skipjack. A separate algorithm in Fortezza, the Digital Signature Algorithm (DSA), also has potential weaknesses introduced by and for the NSA. The consequences include a government capability to forge digital signatures with Fortezza. These weaknesses aside, Fortezza's key material is supplied and *escrowed* by something called the Certification Authority (CA), which reports back to the NSA. So, before you even receive your Fortezza card, your key is in a Federal database.

The effect is that, when you use Fortezza, (a) the National Security Agency knows your key; and (b) if for some reason it doesn't, it can crack it with relative ease.

How can we protect ourselves? The answer is simple—stay away from NSA crypto. If we examine the National Security Agency's persistence in introducing tainted cryptosystems and attempting to make them *standard,* we find that this strategy first appeared with DES in the 1970's. The Agency has no interest in standardizing cryptography for the good of the public—only for the good of Big Brother. We should all press for the continued right to make *our own* choices in cryptographic technology, and those choices should be informed ones.

Fortunately, NSA technology is relatively easy to spot. All of the available Fortezza products (so far) have proudly proclaimed their Agency endorsement. There are some cryptologic firms with NSA affiliation that doesn't show on the surface, such as Cylink—but we must *always* be wary of our sources for crypto.

Available Products

The following products relate to the Fortezza project, and are available to the general public. Every hacker interested in this project should consider the purchase of a Fortezza card for experimentation. It is not a crime to reverse-engineer *any* of these devices, or to publish the results, unless you are a government employee or contractor involved with Fortezza or its sponsoring entities.

Mykotronx, Inc. is the NSA's favorite MISSI contractor. The Mykotronx *Capstone MYK-80/82* is the heart of the Fortezza Crypto Card. The IC is a 144-pin TQFP package, with a clock speed of 20MHz. The 32-bit architecture runs at 18 MIPS, and performs Skipjack at up to 20Mb/s. Mykotronx also manufactures the *Fortezza Crypto Card* and *Fortezza ISA Bus Crypto Card*. The enigmatic *Fortezza PLUS Crypto Card* is available as well, and supposedly suitable for classified communications (it is not based on the Capstone chip, but apparently does use Skipjack)—this item may be secret. Mykotronx also makes the *Cawdaptor,* a workstation for central management of Fortezza equipment, and the *Mykotronx Communicator Fortezza Modem*. Group Technologies Corporation and National Semiconductor also manufacture Fortezza cards. Spyrus designed the original Fortezza crypto card and sells its own. They also make the *HYDRA Privacy Card,* which implements key exchange, encryption, hashing, and digital signatures. For these functions, it can use either Fortezza algorithms (KEA, Skipjack, SHA-1, and DSA, respectively) or a less governmental set (RSA, [3]DES, MD-5, and RSA, respectively). If a stronger algorithm were substituted for DES in the latter set, it would provide formidable security—the NSA probably pressured Spyrus into using DES. Information Resource Engineering, Inc. manufactures the *A400S Fortezza Serial Modem*. It is much like a regular 14.4Kbps modem (AT command set, R-232-C interface, etc.), but it offers some Fortezza crypto services.

We Are Still Safe

With all this talk of government intervention in our lives, it's easy to forget that we can still make our own choices. Nobody is *required* to use NSA-sanctioned crypto today (other than our own government), and we can keep it that way if we don't start. Putting the NSA's agenda out in the open will, I hope, also help.

What options, then, do we have for strong cryptographic technology? IDEA, RSA, and MD-5 are what I use for almost everything. I also trust the recommendations of the Public-Key Cryptography Standard (PKCS), which has been adopted by numerous American corporations. (Information on PKCS can be obtained from RSA Data Security Inc.)

The lesson is that there's no shortage of powerful, untainted crypto—make an informed decision when choosing your technology, and we'll all be able to enforce our electronic privacy.

10 Learning to Hack Other Things

I often think it's a bit unfair how the word "computer" has somehow attached itself to the word "hacker" as if the two are vital parts of the same concept. While true on some occasions—perhaps even quite a lot of occasions—I think it's more than a little limiting to always have the two together. I like to tell people I'm a hacker (provided they're not the kind who will freak out and run away or start shouting for a cop) but they usually inject the computer part on their own. And while admittedly I do like to play with computers and have developed a real talent for finding unusual bugs and ways to make things stop working, I hardly consider myself an expert and am constantly astounded at how little I actually know and how little I care about what I don't know. Not that you need to be a computer expert in order to be a computer hacker. My point is that I don't want to limit myself to just one piece of hardware, especially when it's not something I consider my field of expertise.

I think there are a lot of people out there who have no interest at all in computers but are true hackers. The fact of the matter is there are so many things in the world to hack. A lot of it is hardware—digital, electronic, mechanical—and a lot of it is purely conceptual. The important thing is to be able to say you have the mind of a hacker. That means always thinking outside the box, questioning what others assume to be true, trying to do something in another way just to see what happens, not listening to those who tell you to stick to the rules for no reason other than they're the rules, and invariably getting into deep trouble at some point.

There are many contributions in these pages from those "other" hackers known as phone phreaks. I think the only reason we don't use the phrase "phone hacker" is because "phone phreak" looks and sounds so much cooler. But the hacker world involves much more than phones and computers and that's what I'd like to focus on in this section.

While technical knowledge is always an advantage when it comes to hacking, it isn't essential to being a hacker in the first place. The reason so many hackers are technical is because the technical world lends itself to the practice of hacking. An inquisitive person who asks hundreds of questions all in a row to someone is liable to wind up getting ignored or seriously injured. But computers and phones don't lose patience like that. You can keep going until your fingers fall off and these electronic beings won't ever get mad at you, unless of course a human programs them to.

The amount of hackable things out there is virtually unlimited. Any decent explorer has to have a bit of the hacker spirit or else he'd just be doing what everybody else does and not discovering anything new. A good journalist must always doubt what he's told and think of ways around limitations to find a decent story. The hacker spirit is a part of the human spirit and always has been. It's simply become so much more noticeable now due to the explosion of new toys to play with and create using our developing technology, which itself is another byproduct of the hacker mindset.

New Technology of the Day

Since we never wanted to stay focused on the same things for too long, our writers have always been in search of new bits of technology to play with and discover insecurities and vulnerabilities for. Here we have a hodgepodge of items that came into focus in the 1990s and which were attacked with a full dose of hacker zeal. The push button locks that are detailed here were actually around well before this period but had never before been systematically defeated in such a manner. Traffic devices such as E-ZPass and traffic lights that were changeable by certain types of vehicles were new to most people, hence the intense interest expressed in them by our readers. While extremely common today, such items as cable modems and ATMs were fairly new back then and so there was a great amount of curiosity in figuring out exactly how they worked. Also, since there were substantially fewer manufacturers of these new toys, tricks that were printed in our pages would be applicable to a somewhat high percentage of them throughout the world.

Simplex Locks (Autumn, 1991)

By Scott Skinner and Emmanuel Goldstein

No lock is 100-percent secure. As any locksmith will tell you, even the best lock can be opened if one wishes to invest the time and resources. However, a good lock should at least be secure enough to prevent the average person from compromising it. Common sense dictates that a lock that can easily be opened by anyone is simply not a safe lock to use.

While an average person may not have the necessary skills and expertise to use a lock pick or a blowtorch, almost everyone has the ability to count. And the ability to count is all that is necessary to compromise a Unican/Simplex push button lock. In addition, one needn't count very high. Only 1,081 combinations are used, and in most cases this number is reduced considerably.

Anyone can easily open a Simplex lock by merely going through all the possible combinations. As arduous as this may sound, members of 2600 average ten minutes when put to the task. This method becomes even easier if one can find out the "range" of the combination. For instance, if one knows that only three push buttons are being used, then one merely has to go through 135 combinations. In this example, a Simplex lock can be compromised in less than 5 minutes. With some models (particularly the commonly used 900 series), a new combination can then be set without a key. One can literally lock someone out of their own home.

Far worse than the low number of combinations is the illusion of security that surrounds the lock. We called ten locksmiths at random and were told that "thousands," "millions," and in some cases "a virtually unlimited number" of combinations were available. These claims are somewhat misleading considering the actual number of possible combinations. In addition, no locksmith was able to tell us exactly how many combinations were available, nor did any locksmith believe us when we told them.

Simplex advertisements also claim that these "maximum security" locks are "ideal for security-sensitive areas" and that some models meet the requirements of the Department of Defense Security Manual. We contacted Simplex to find out just what these requirements are. According to Thomas Nazziola, Vice President of Marketing, the locks comply with paragraph 36a of the Department of Defense Security Manual (DoD 5220.22-M). Mr. Nazziola refused to quote paragraph 36a of the manual as he felt it was "restricted." However, he summarized the section by claiming that Simplex locks comply with the DoD Security Manual for security-sensitive areas.

2600 was able to obtain a copy of this "restricted" manual just by asking. Upon close examination of paragraph 36a entitled "Automated Access Control Systems," we were unable to find any information concerning mechanical push-button locks. The section that does apply to Simplex locks is paragraph 36b entitled "Electric, Mechanical, or Electromechanical Devices." According to this section, mechanical devices that meet specified criteria may be used "to control admittance to controlled areas *during working hours*." While there is an element of truth in Mr. Nazziola's claim, he did not tell us that according to the DoD Security Manual, Simplex locks may not be used as the only lock source except during "working hours." In addition, it is relatively easy to meet the requirements of the DoD Security Manual. Virtually any combination lock with changeable combinations, and indeed even padlocks, will meet these requirements.

Although Simplex claims that "thousands of combinations are available," in truth only 1,081 combinations are used. Another 1,081 combinations are available in the guise of "high security half-step codes." These are codes that require the user to push one or more buttons only halfway. Because of the extreme difficulty in setting and using these half-step codes, Simplex advises against their use, and in most cases, does not even inform the user that these codes are available. According to one locksmith,

"[Simplex] only suggests it for really high security installations. Government installations. For the average consumer, they don't want anyone to know about it."

We shudder to imagine which high security government installations are using Simplex locks as the only lock source. The "high-security codes" are an example of misleading information being used to sell the locks (in this case, to the U.S. government). Naturally, the addition of 1,081 combinations does not make the lock considerably more secure. (If 2,162 combinations seem like a large number, consider that a $5 Master lock has 64,000.) In addition, we have yet to find one single instance where the half-step codes are used.

We have found that numerous organizations use Simplex locks as the primary lock source. Among the guilty parties in the New York metropolitan area are Federal Express, United Parcel Service (UPS), Citicorp Center, John F. Kennedy International Airport, and the State University of New York at Stony Brook. Others around the nation include General Motors, the State Department, McDonald's, NSA, and the University of Wisconsin.

The biggest offender is Federal Express, which uses Simplex locks on more than 25,000 dropboxes nationally. According to Robert G. Hamilton, Manager of Corporate Identity [sic] for Federal Express, "[Federal Express dropboxes] are extremely secure. As a matter of fact, there's probably double the cost of security built into these boxes than what's necessary. The idea of having somebody put something extremely important and vital—and it's obviously important and vital or they wouldn't ship it Federal Express—in one of these unmanned receptacles was, I mean security was uppermost on people's minds....[The dropboxes] are like vaults."

These "vaults" were accessed by members of 2600 in less than 10 minutes. The dropboxes are particularly insecure because Federal Express uses the same combination for all of their dropboxes in every state on the east coast! So by opening one dropbox, we now have access to thousands.

Members of 2600 also gained access to a UPS dropbox—in one shot. UPS did not even bother to change the default combination, which is set by Simplex. And, just like Federal Express, UPS figures that a single combination is good enough for every dropbox.

Another big offender is the State University of New York at Stony Brook, which uses Simplex locks in both dormitory and academic buildings. According to University Locksmith Gerry Lenox, "I don't consider [the Simplex lock] to be a secure lock. I prefer a deadbolt lock which operates with a key more than I would a Simplex lock.... I think it's more of a convenience lock than it is a security lock." When asked why the university continues to use the lock, Mr. Lenox said, "[The university] did not consider contacting the university locksmith on his expertise. I had originally told them years ago when the Simplex locks were first introduced...not to use [the locks] in the dormitories." Not only are they being used in the dormitories, but the university is considering purchasing 1,500 more for additional rooms.

The illusion of security Simplex is portraying with misleading advertising is that Simplex locks are just as secure, if not more secure, than key locks. The result of this myth is that many businesses, institutions, and homeowners confidently use Simplex locks as the only lock source despite the fact that the locks are inherently insecure. Even when locksmiths are consulted, we have found that they simply perpetuate the illusion of security by claiming that Simplex locks are "top of the line" and "even the Department of Defense uses them." Nowhere is it mentioned that Simplex locks should never be used as the only lock source. Even worse, Simplex is now aggressively pursuing the homeowner market with their new "residential" 6000 series. These new locks employ the same insecure mechanism, and are being marketed as primary locks.

Realistically, Simplex locks are more of a convenience lock than anything else. They are convenient because they do not require keys and the combinations are easily changed. However, this convenience backfires when it comes to security. These locks are so convenient that people tend not to use other locks that may also be present on the door.

For those organizations currently using Simplex locks, we recommend following the guidelines of the *DoD Security Manual*: the locks may be used as the sole lock source *only during working hours*. For home or private use, we strongly advise that consumers use these locks in conjunction with a key lock and never as the sole means of security.

Hacking Simplex Locks

In this issue is a list of all possible combinations for Simplex locks. We have divided the list into four groups according to how many push buttons are used. The numbers listed in parentheses refer to push buttons that must be pressed together. If you find that none of the combinations appear to open the lock, then it may be a rare instance of a half-step code. In this case, only the last number (or numbers if they are in parentheses) should be pressed in *halfway* and held while the knob or latch is turned. Slowly press in the push button(s) until you feel pressure. If you hear a click then you have pushed the buttons in too far. If all of this sounds complicated, then you are beginning to understand why it is that Simplex does not recommend the use of half-step codes, and subsequently why half-step codes are virtually never used.

Simplex locks come in many different shapes, sizes, and colors. However, the two models that you will most likely see are the 900 and the 1000 series. The characteristic features of the 900 series are five black buttons spaced in a circular fashion on a round, metallic cylinder. In addition, the 900 series utilizes a latch instead of a doorknob. The 1000 series is much larger, with five (usually metallic) push buttons spaced vertically on a rectangular metal chassis. Unlike the 900 series, the 1000 has a doorknob.

We suggest that novices attempt their first hack on a Simplex 900 model. If the latch is located below the buttons, then the procedure is as follows: 1) turn the latch counterclockwise to reset the lock; 2) enter a combination from the list; 3) turn the latch clockwise to open. If the latch is located above the buttons, then simply reverse the procedure. Make sure that you reset the lock after each try.

To hack a 1000 model, simply enter a combination from the list and turn the knob clockwise. You will hear clicks as you turn the knob, indicating that the lock has been reset. It is sometimes difficult to tell when you have cracked a 1000 model by simply turning the knob. When you do get the correct code, you will hear a distinctive click and feel less pressure as you turn the knob.

You will find that turning the latch on a 900 model requires less wrist motion and makes much less noise than turning the knob on a 1000 model. These details seem trivial until you realize that you may have to turn the latch or doorknob a few hundred times before you crack the lock.

We cannot stress enough how much easier it is when you know the range. For instance, if you know that only three digits are being used, then you do not have to waste time trying four digits. One way to find out the range is to stand nearby while someone punches in the code. You will hear distinctive clicks, which will give you an idea of the range. If you cannot stand nearby, then try hiding a voice activated tape recorder near the door. The tape recorder will remain off until someone comes up to punch in the code. You can then retrieve the recorder later at your convenience and listen for the telltale clicks. We find that this method only works in quiet areas, such as the inside of a building. Another way to find out the range is to take a pencil eraser and carefully rub off a tiny bit of rubber on each of the push buttons. When someone comes to enter the combination, they will rub off the rubber on all of the push buttons that they use, while leaving telltale traces of rubber on the push buttons that they do not use. This method works particularly well because you eliminate push buttons, which drastically reduces the number of combinations that must be tried.

We find that certain ranges tend to be used more than others. Group B (three push buttons) tends to be used in "low security areas," while Groups C and D tend to be used in areas that seem like they should be more secure. We have never found a lock that uses a combination from Group A. For some reason, we find that the 1000 series mostly uses Group C (four push buttons). In addition, most combinations tend to be "doubles," which require at least two of the push buttons to be pressed together. When you decide on a particular range to start with, try the doubles first. For instance, try "(12) 3 4 5" before you try "1 2 3 4 5." We have never found a lock that uses a triple, quadruple, or all five push buttons pressed at the same time.

Although we are providing a list of all the possible combinations, you may find it useful to invest some time and record these codes onto cassette. This makes it much easier for one person to hack a Simplex lock because he does not have to hold the codes in one hand while hacking, nor cross out the codes to keep his place. A walkman also looks far less conspicuous than sheets of paper filled with numbers. The only drawback to using a walkman is that the person will not be able to hear anyone coming from a distance. We find it easier to hack Simplex locks in small groups, so that each person can take turns, and everyone has their ears open.

Finally, it is always good to take a few lucky shots before you initiate a brute force hack. Always try the default combination "(24) 3" before you try anything else. Above all: *Don't give up!* Even if you do not get the combination in ten minutes, you are still that much closer to figuring it out. We recommend that you do not stress yourself out trying every combination in one shot. A few minutes a day will do just fine, and the thrill of achievement will be well worth the wait.

1081 Possible Combinations Divided into Four Groups

GROUP A: 5 total:				
1	2	3	4	5

GROUP B: 30 total:									
12	13	14	15	21	23	24	25	31	32
34	35	41	42	43	45	51	52	53	54
(12)	(13)	(14)	(15)	(23)	(24)	(25)	(34)	(35)	(45)

GROUP C: 130 total									
123	124	125	132	134	135	142	143	145	152
153	154	213	214	215	231	234	235	241	243
245	251	253	254	312	314	315	321	324	325
341	342	345	351	352	354	412	413	415	421
423	425	431	432	435	451	452	453	512	513
514	521	523	524	531	532	534	541	542	543
(12)3	(12)4	(12)5	(13)2	(13)4	(13)5	(14)2	(14)3	(14)5	(15)2
(15)3	(23)1	(23)4	(23)5	(24)1	(24)3	(24)5	(25)1	(25)3	(15)4
(25)4	(34)1	(34)2	(34)5	(35)1	(35)2	(35)4	(45)1	(45)2	(45)3
3(12)	4(12)	5(12)	2(13)	4(13)	5(13)	2(14)	3(14)	5(14)	2(15)
3(15)	4(15)	1(23)	4(23)	5(23)	1(24)	3(24)	5(24)	1(25)	3(25)
4(25)	1(34)	2(34)	5(34)	1(35)	2(35)	4(35)	1(45)	2(45)	3(45)
(123)	(124)	(125)	(134)	(135)	(145)	(234)	(235)	(245)	(345)

GROUP D: 375 total

1234	1235	1243	1245	1253	1254	1324	1325	1342	1345
1352	1354	1423	1425	1432	1435	1452	1453	1523	1524
1532	1534	1542	1543	2134	2135	2143	2145	2153	2154
2314	2315	2341	2345	2351	2354	2413	2415	2431	2435
2451	2453	2513	2514	2531	2534	2541	2543	3124	3125
3142	3145	3152	3154	3214	3215	3241	3245	3251	3254
3412	3415	3421	3425	3451	3452	3512	3514	3521	3524
3541	3542	4123	4125	4132	4135	4152	4153	4213	4215
4231	4235	4251	4253	4312	4315	4321	4325	4351	4352
4512	4513	4521	4523	4531	4532	5123	5124	5132	5134
5142	5143	5213	5214	5231	5234	5241	5243	5312	5314
5321	5324	5341	5342	5412	5413	5421	5423	5431	5432

(12)34	(12)35	(12)43	(12)45	(12)53	(12)54	(13)24	(13)25	(13)42
(13)45	(13)52	(13)54	(14)23	(14)25	(14)32	(14)35	(14)52	(14)53
(15)23	(15)24	(15)32	(15)34	(15)42	(15)43	(23)14	(23)15	(23)41
(23)45	(23)51	(23)54	(24)13	(24)15	(24)31	(24)35	(24)51	(24)53
(25)13	(25)14	(25)31	(25)34	(25)41	(25)43	(34)12	(34)15	(34)21
(34)25	(34)51	(34)52	(35)12	(35)14	(35)21	(35)24	(35)41	(35)42
(45)12	(45)13	(45)21	(45)23	(45)31	(45)32	3(12)4	3(12)5	4(12)3
4(12)5	5(12)3	5(12)4	2(13)4	2(13)5	4(13)2	4(13)5	5(13)2	5(13)4
2(14)3	2(14)5	3(14)2	3(14)5	5(14)2	5(14)3	2(15)3	2(15)4	3(15)2
3(15)4	4(15)2	4(15)3	1(23)4	1(23)5	4(23)1	4(23)5	5(23)1	5(23)4
1(24)3	1(24)5	3(24)1	3(24)5	5(24)1	5(24)3	1(25)3	1(25)4	3(25)1
3(25)4	4(25)1	4(25)3	1(34)2	1(34)5	2(34)1	2(34)5	5(34)1	5(34)2
1(35)2	1(35)4	2(35)1	2(35)4	4(35)1	4(35)2	1(45)2	1(45)3	2(45)1
2(45)3	3(45)1	3(45)2	34(12)	35(12)	43(12)	45(12)	53(12)	54(12)
24(13)	25(13)	42(13)	45(13)	52(13)	54(13)	23(14)	25(14)	32(14)
35(14)	52(14)	53(14)	23(15)	24(15)	32(15)	34(15)	42(15)	43(15)
14(23)	15(23)	41(23)	45(23)	51(23)	54(23)	13(24)	15(24)	31(24)
35(24)	51(24)	53(24)	13(25)	14(25)	31(25)	34(25)	41(25)	43(25)
12(34)	15(34)	21(34)	25(34)	51(34)	52(34)	12(35)	14(35)	21(35)
24(35)	41(35)	42(35)	12(45)	13(45)	21(45)	23(45)	31(45)	32(45)

(12)(34)	(12)(35)	(12)(45)	(13)(24)	(13)(25)
(13)(45)	(14)(23)	(14)(25)	(14)(35)	(15)(23)

GROUP D: 375 total *(continued)*

(15)(24)	(15)(34)	(23)(14)	(23)(15)	(23)(45)
(24)(13)	(24)(15)	(24)(35)	(25)(13)	(25)(14)
(25)(34)	(34)(12)	(34)(15)	(34)(25)	(35)(12)
(35)(14)	(35)(24)	(45)(12)	(45)(13)	(45)(23)

(123)4	(123)5	(124)3	(124)5	(125)3	(125)4
(134)2	(134)5	(135)2	(135)4	(145)2	(145)3
(234)1	(234)5	(235)1	(235)4	(245)1	(245)3
(345)1	(345)2	4(123)	5(123)	3(124)	5(124)
3(125)	4(125)	2(134)	5(134)	2(135)	4(135)
2(145)	3(145)	1(234)	5(234)	1(245)	4(235)
1(245)	3(245)	1(345)	2(345)		

(1234)	(1235)	(1245)	(1345)	(2345)

GROUP E: 541 total

12345	12354	12435	12453	12534	12543	13245	13254	13425
13452	13524	13542	14235	14253	14325	14352	14523	14532
15234	15243	15324	15342	15423	15432	21345	21354	21435
21453	21534	21543	23145	23154	23415	23451	23514	23541
24135	24153	24315	24351	24513	24531	25134	25143	25314
25341	25413	25431	31245	31254	31425	31452	31524	31542
32145	32154	32415	32451	32514	32541	34125	34152	34215
34251	34512	34521	35124	35142	35214	35241	35412	35421
41235	41253	41325	41352	41523	41532	42135	42153	42315
42351	42513	42531	43125	43152	43215	43251	43512	43521
45123	45132	45213	45231	45312	45321	51234	51243	51324
51342	51423	51432	52134	52143	52314	52341	52413	52431
53124	53142	53214	53241	53412	53421	54123	54132	54213
54231	54312	54321						

(12)345	(12)354	(12)435	(12)453	(12)534	(12)543	(13)245	(13)254
(13)425	(13)452	(13)524	(13)542	(14)235	(14)253	(14)325	(14)352
(14)523	(14)532	(15)234	(15)243	(15)324	(15)342	(15)423	(15)432

continues

GROUP E: 541 total *(continued)*							
(23)145	(23)154	(23)415	(23)451	(23)514	(23)541	(24)135	(24)153
(24)315	(24)351	(24)513	(24)531	(25)134	(25)143	(25)314	(25)341
(25)413	(25)431	(34)125	(34)152	(34)215	(34)251	(34)512	(34)521
(35)124	(35)142	(35)214	(35)241	(35)412	(35)421	(45)123	(45)132
(45)213	(45)231	(45)312	(45)321	3(12)45	3(12)54	4(12)35	4(12)53
5(12)34	5(12)43	2(13)45	2(13)54	4(13)25	4(13)52	5(13)24	5(13)42
2(14)35	2(14)53	3(14)25	3(14)52	5(14)23	5(14)32	2(15)34	2(15)43
3(15)24	3(15)42	4(15)23	4(15)32	1(23)45	1(23)54	4(23)15	4(23)51
5(23)14	5(23)41	1(24)35	1(24)53	3(24)15	3(24)51	5(24)13	5(24)31
1(25)34	1(25)43	3(25)14	3(25)41	4(25)13	4(25)31	1(34)25	1(34)52
2(34)15	2(34)51	5(34)12	5(34)21	1(35)24	1(35)42	2(35)14	2(35)41
4(35)12	4(35)21	1(45)23	1(45)32	2(45)13	2(45)31	3(45)12	3(45)21
34(12)5	35(12)4	43(12)5	45(12)3	53(12)4	54(12)3	24(13)5	25(13)4
42(13)5	45(13)2	52(13)4	54(13)2	23(14)5	25(14)3	32(14)5	35(14)2
52(14)3	53(14)2	23(15)4	24(15)3	32(15)4	34(15)2	42(15)3	43(15)2
14(23)5	15(23)4	41(23)5	45(23)1	51(23)4	54(23)1	13(24)5	15(24)3
31(24)5	35(24)1	51(24)3	53(24)1	13(25)4	14(25)3	31(25)4	34(25)1
41(25)3	43(25)1	12(34)5	15(34)2	21(34)5	25(34)1	51(34)2	52(34)1
12(35)4	14(35)2	21(35)4	24(35)1	41(35)2	42(35)1	13(45)2	12(45)3
21(45)3	23(45)1	31(45)2	32(45)1	345(12)	354(12)	435(12)	453(12)
534(12)	543(12)	245(13)	254(13)	425(13)	452(13)	524(13)	542(13)
235(14)	253(14)	325(14)	352(14)	523(14)	532(14)	234(15)	243(15)
324(15)	342(15)	423(15)	432(15)	145(23)	154(23)	415(23)	451(23)
514(23)	541(23)	135(24)	153(24)	315(24)	351(24)	513(24)	531(24)
134(25)	143(25)	314(25)	341(25)	413(25)	431(25)	125(34)	152(34)
215(34)	251(34)	512(34)	521(34)	124(35)	142(35)	214(35)	241(35)
412(35)	421(35)	123(45)	132(45)	213(45)	231(45)	312(45)	321(45)

(12)(34)5	(12)(35)4	(12)(45)3	(13)(24)5
(13)(25)4	(13)(45)2	(14)(23)5	(14)(25)3
(14)(35)2	(15)(23)4	(15)(24)3	(15)(34)2
(23)(14)5	(23)(15)4	(23)(45)1	(24)(13)5
(24)(15)3	(24)(35)1	(25)(13)4	(25)(14)3
(25)(34)1	(34)(12)5	(34)(15)2	(34)(25)1
(35)(12)4	(35)(14)2	(35)(24)1	(45)(12)3

GROUP E: 541 total *(continued)*							
(45)(13)2	(45)(23)1	(12)5(34)	(12)4(35)				
(12)3(45)	(13)5(24)	(13)4(25)	(13)2(45)				
(14)5(23)	(14)3(25)	(14)2(35)	(15)4(23)				
(15)3(24)	(15)2(34)	(23)5(14)	(23)4(15)				
(23)1(45)	(24)5(13)	(24)3(15)	(24)1(35)				
(25)4(13)	(25)3(14)	(25)1(34)	(34)5(12)				
(34)2(15)	(34)1(25)	(35)4(12)	(35)2(14)				
(35)1(24)	(45)3(12)	(45)2(13)	(45)1(23)				
3(12)(45)	4(12)(35)	5(12)(34)	2(13)(45)				
4(13)(25)	5(13)(24)	2(14)(35)	3(14)(25)				
5(14)(23)	2(15)(34)	3(15)(24)	4(15)(23)				
1(23)(45)	4(23)(15)	5(23)(14)	1(24)(35)				
3(24)(15)	5(24)(13)	1(25)(34)	3(25)(14)				
4(25)(13)	1(34)(25)	2(34)(15)	5(34)(12)				
1(35)(24)	2(35)(14)	4(35)(12)	1(45)(23)				
2(45)(13)	3(45)(12)						
(123)45	(123)54	(124)35	(124)53	(125)34	(125)43	(134)25	(134)52
(135)24	(135)42	(145)23	(145)32	(234)51	(234)15	(235)14	(235)41
(245)13	(245)31	(345)12	(345)21	4(123)5	5(123)4	3(124)5	5(124)3
3(125)4	4(125)3	2(134)5	5(134)2	2(135)4	4(135)2	2(145)3	3(145)2
1(234)5	5(234)1	1(235)4	4(235)1	1(245)3	3(245)1	1(345)2	2(345)1
45(123)	54(123)	35(124)	53(124)	34(125)	43(125)	25(134)	52(134)
24(135)	42(135)	23(145)	32(145)	15(234)	51(234)	14(235)	41(235)
13(245)	31(245)	12(345)	21(345)				
(123)(45)	(124)(35)	(125)(34)	(134)(25)	(135)(24)			
(145)(23)	(234)(15)	(235)(14)	(245)(13)	(345)(12)			
(45)(123)	(35)(124)	(34)(125)	(25)(134)	(24)(135)			
(23)(145)	(15)(234)	(14)(235)	(13)(245)	(12)(345)			
(1234)5	(1235)4	(1245)3	(1345)2	(2345)1			
5(1234)	4(1235)	3(1245)	2(1345)	1(2345)			
(12345)							

The Chrome Box (Spring, 1994) *By Remote Control*

Emergency vehicles in many cities are now using devices called OptoComs. OptoComs are sensors on traffic lights that detect a pattern of flashes from vehicle-mounted strobe lights.

This flash pattern varies from city to city depending on the manufacturer of the equipment used. Often the sensors are installed only at major intersections. Nevertheless, the Chrome Box, which simulates these strobe patterns, can often be used to give your car the same priority as an ambulance, paramedic van, fire truck, or police car.

Because of the varying patterns on different systems, this article will outline a general procedure for making the Chrome Box.

Decoding Flash Patterns

First, you need to observe an emergency vehicle in action. You can wait until you encounter one by chance, running out to see when you hear a siren, or pulling over in your car to let one pass by. You might wait near a fire station for the next emergency to occur. Or, if you are very impatient, you can summon one by calling in a false alarm (not recommended).

If the OptoComs in your area are the kind with a pattern of single flashes at a steady rhythm, you have merely to buy a strobe light at Radio Shack and adjust the flash rate until you can induce a traffic light to change. If the flash pattern is more complex, you can videotape the emergency vehicle and then play back the tape in single-frame mode, counting the number of frames between each flash. Each video frame is 1/30th of a second. Using this, you can calculate the time between flashes in the pattern. Another way is to count the number of flashes (or flash-groups) in one minute and use that to compute the rate. Counting video frames will give you a good idea of the spacing of the flashes in a complex pattern.

For really accurate information, call the fire station and ask them, or write to the manufacturer for a service manual, which will include a schematic diagram that you can use to build one. A good cover story for this is that you are a consultant and one of your clients asked you to evaluate Optocom systems, or you could pose as a freelance journalist writing an article.

Modifying the Strobe Light

You may not have to modify the strobe at all. But if you need a faster flash rate than your strobe allows, open it up and find the large capacitor inside. Capacitors are marked in microfarads, abbreviated as mf, mfd, or ufd. By replacing the capacitor with one of the same voltage rating (usually 250 volts or more) and a *smaller* value in microfarads, you can increase the flash rate. Halving the microfarads doubles the rate. The other component that can be changed is the potentiometer (the speed control device with the knob on it). Using a smaller value (measured in ohms or kohms, abbreviated with the Greek letter "omega" or the letter K) will speed up the strobe. There may also be a resistor (a small cylinder with several colored stripes on it, and wires coming out of each end). Replacing this resistor with one of smaller value will also speed up the strobe.

To generate a complex pattern, you will either have to design and build a triggering circuit using IC chips, or rig up a mechanical device with a multiple-contact rotary switch and a motor. It *has* been done.

To modify the strobe for mobile operation the simplest thing is to get a 110-volt inverter that will run off of a car battery by plugging into the cigarette lighter and running the strobe from that. Or, you can figure out (or find in a hobby electronics magazine) a strobe circuit that will run from batteries. Battery-powered strobes may also be available, either assembled or as kits.

Stealth Technology

Most light sensors and photocells are more sensitive in the infrared area of the light spectrum. Infrared (IR) is invisible to the human eye. Putting an infrared filter over the strobe light may allow the Chrome Box to operate in traffic undetected by police or other observers. IR filters can be obtained from military surplus sniperscope illuminators, or from optical supply houses like Dow-Corning or Edmunds Scientific Co.

Using the Chrome Box

Mounted on your car, the Chrome Box can guarantee you green lights at major intersections in cities that have OptoComs.

Handheld Chrome Boxes may be used to create gridlock by interfering with the normal flow of traffic. If you have access to a window overlooking a traffic light, you can play pranks by switching the signals at inappropriate moments, or you can plug the strobe into an exposed outlet at a laundromat or gas station.

Some Decoded Patterns

- **Torrance, California**: Standard large Radio Shack strobe lights are used. Moderately fast rate.
- **Manhattan Beach, California**: Flash-pairs in a 4:1 ratio, at a rate of two flash-pairs per second.

Hacking LED Signs (Spring, 1997) *By Bernie S.*

We've all seen them—those annoying, attention-getting LED signs with moving, flashing messages. They're in airports, train stations, bus terminals, vending machines, retail establishments, banks, and even government offices. Almost without exception, they're in high-traffic areas where lots of people are subjected to their not-so-interesting messages. This article provides a brief overview of most types of displays out there, how they're programmed, and how you can use them to get your message out to the people. In no way should this article be misconstrued as encouraging unauthorized programming of such signs, for that would be in violation of State and Federal laws and punishable by up to 10 years in prison. No matter how harmless the method may seem, expressing yourself in ways our government doesn't approve of can be hazardous to your health. (Maybe all electronic hardware and software should have government warning labels similar to cigarettes and alcohol.) In any case, be forewarned.

Most LED signs out there are self-contained, microprocessor-based units that are field-programmable by a variety of methods depending on the manufacturer, model, and configuration. These methods include direct RS-232 connection, telephone modem, proprietary or PC keyboard connection, wireless telemetry (via cellular modem, packet radio, ARDIS or RAM radio data networks, FM broadcast via SCA or RDS, or Motorola paging data receiver), and wireless infrared keyboard programming. Older "dumb" LED signs require constant connection to a proprietary or PC-based data source, which stores messaging data in addition to controlling the LED display. All use multiplexed Light Emitting Diode arrays, from tiny one-line units only a few inches long to massive 16×40 foot models.

Large dynamic text displays using arrays of incandescent bulbs or electromechanical flippers painted fluorescent green and illuminated by black light are often placed alongside highways or on overpasses to inform automobile travelers of road and traffic conditions. Portable programmable road signs are often mounted on wheels atop a small trailer (complete with gasoline generator and a dedicated PC or proprietary controller or cellular modem) and towed to road construction sites as needed. Surprisingly, the metal cabinet containing the programming electronics is seldom (or insecurely) locked. Large LED array signs are often used on factory floors to display production run data to assembly-line workers, or in call centers to indicate call volume, ANI data, or other information to operators. These units are usually hardwired via RS-232 interface to a company computer.

If you come across a programmable sign (say, at a garage sale but there is no manual or programming device with it) get the manufacturer's name off the unit and contact them for an operations and programming manual for that model. Often, you can get it free if the company believes you're a previous customer. Also request a catalog of accessories for that model; it will be helpful in determining specifically what additional hardware you'll need to program and power it. There are so many manufacturers, models, and programming interfaces out there that it's not always obvious how to go about it without proper documentation or social-engineering one of the manufacturer's technicians. Once you have the sign plugged in and operating (they're usually powered by an AC adapter, which is filtered and regulated on the sign's main circuit board), you can experiment with programming various messages.

Some models are fairly intelligent and allow for multiple and scheduled messages, and special effects like rotation, scrolling, zooming, bitmapped graphics, and multiple colors (using rapidly switched red and green diodes at various duty cycles). Blue LEDs are still too expensive to use in volume, which is why you don't see any blue or true-color LED signs yet. When blue LEDs are cheap, all primary color requirements will be met and any color in the spectrum will be easy to generate, like the color cathode-ray tubes in TVs and computer monitors do. Eventually, giant full-color LED video billboards will be commonplace.

The author has heard of several humorous situations involving LED signs programmed by unauthorized parties. In one case, a state-owned lottery ticket vending machine with an LED sign mounted on it was located in a drugstore. It had apparently been reprogrammed from the street through the drugstore's main window using an infrared keypad to say, "This machine sells only losing tickets—don't waste your money on another government scam!" When this was called to the store manager's attention, he panicked and began wildly pushing all the vending machine's buttons in a futile effort to delete the message, eventually unplugging the entire machine (preventing it from vending tickets altogether). In another case, an LED sign on a prepaid-phone-card vending machine in a major train station had been reprogrammed to say, "These phone cards are a total rip-off at 50 cents a minute!" The machine didn't indicate the true cost of the cards; a call to the vending company confirmed they were indeed 50 cents a minute, so some hacker arguably provided a valuable consumer advisory service.

A bank's LED sign in their main window soliciting homeowner loans had been reprogrammed to say it was offering a special one-day sale on new hundred-dollar bills for only fifty dollars each (one per customer). There were some rather excited people lining up until a chagrined bank manager unplugged the sign.

An observant reader wrote in to this issue's letters section to say he'd noticed a large LED sign by the escalators at New York's 53rd and Lexington subway station (by Citicorp Center where monthly *2600* hacker gatherings are held) had been reprogrammed to announce the time and dates of the hacker gatherings, inviting everyone to come. Previously, the sign merely advised people to watch their step on the escalator. Tens of thousands of people a day got to read that sign; that's real power. There must be thousands more LED signs out there just begging to be programmed with more interesting messages. Do any come to mind?

The E-ZPass System (Autumn, 1997) *By Big Brother*

I am responding to the comments in the summer 1997 issue about the New York State Thruway's E-ZPass system and its ability to identify a particular vehicle for violation enforcement by using "secret detectors."

These "secret detectors" are probably nothing more than conventional radar units, wired to a central location for recording data. If the "secret detector units" are state of the art, they are video cameras feeding a video unit with software that allows individual vehicle speed determination and recording. The use of E-ZPass to cite speed violators is cumbersome and can only "average" the vehicle's speed over a known distance, as I will explain below. Radar units, RF or laser, or video systems are much easier to use for the actual speed determination.

What is a "toll pass"? There are many types of toll passes in use. E-ZPass is only one. To alleviate the paranoia concerning toll passes, let's understand how the system works and with this understanding come the realization and, perhaps, relief that the "authorities" sometimes really do try and make things easier for the motoring public without always hiding some Big Brother device among the goodies.

Transponders (a.k.a. "toll passes," or "tags") are used to identify the *location* of a particular vehicle. When passing a particular location, a motorist's location, time, and date will be recorded. *Not* the speed. It takes *two* stationary installations to determine a vehicle's speed. The vehicle's average speed is then calculated between these two known locations. There are *many* ways to easily determine a vehicle's speed without trying to adopt the E-ZPass type system to this use but, if they have enough stationary locations, it can certainly be done. This is not rocket science. Let me explain (without, hopefully, writing a booklet). The technical types might find this interesting.

Toll pass systems use microwave frequencies, usually in the 900–928 MHz, or 2.8 GHz, or (soon) 5.8 GHz bands to communicate between the stationary transmitter/receiver and the vehicle transponder. Can you jam these frequencies? Sure. If you do, and the system uses gated access, you will not be granted access. So what good have you done?

Could you cause a signal that would indicate a lower charge than you should be paying to be transponded? Some systems only query the transponder for its unique identifier number. The central computer keeps the rest of the data for the billing occurrence. This would seem to me to be impossible to "hack" at the transponder end. Other systems record the entry time, location, etc. into the transponder. Then, when the transponder is queried upon exiting, both the entry and exit data are sent to the stationary receiver. There is potential here for hacking. It is also federally illegal (two years and $10,000 per occurrence) and not recommended. (Hey guys, there ain't no free ride. Somebody has to pay for the road. Let the users pay or all of you nonusers will wind up paying for the roadway via higher income taxes, fuel taxes, and so forth.)

900–928 MHz is the most common frequency spectrum presently in use. Want to hear what the transmissions *from* the vehicle transponder sound like for a 900 MHz system? Place a cellular telephone near the transponder and depress the SND key. The transponder will usually react to the nearby cellular frequency and think it is being queried, hence causing a transpond. You will hear the transpond as a burst of data in your cellular telephone's handset earpiece. Record this for analysis. It is not encrypted and usually consists of a simple multiple digit code. Depending upon the system being used, this transpond will always contain the transponder's unique identifier code, and it may also include the date, time, location of last time it was queried, and other administrative information.

One commonly used toll pass system uses backscatter modulation to activate vehicle transponders. From a stationary transmitter with the antenna mounted over the roadway, microwaves are caused to impinge upon the vehicle-mounted transponder, causing the transponder to power up, use some of the absorbed microwave energy, and reflect ("backscatter transpond") back to a nearby stationary receiving antenna, on another nearby frequency, with the transponder's identifying code number (usually about eight digits). A central computer records the identification number, location, time and date, and performs the desired action. This is all that is required for entry verification to a parking lot, etc. More normally, this initial information will be the entry point to a controlled access tollway.

Intelligent Vehicle Highway Systems (IVHS) use a second occurrence of the proceeding action, occurring at a second location, usually where the vehicle exits the tollway. The central computer will then access the billed to account and record this data for end-of-month processing into an invoice.

As you may have deduced, backscatter modulation is imperfect as a speed determining medium. Within a distance of many meters there is no relatively accurate method to determine just when the transponding action will occur. As an aside, if the vehicle has one of the metallic impregnated windshields used to reduce ultraviolet ray transmission into the vehicle, the transponder (normally mounted inside the windshield) will have to be mounted on the outside—usually in the area of the front bumper—so it is unshielded. But I digress. Different stationary microwave transmitter/receiver combinations can cause the distance-to-vehicle measurement to vary. Multiple vehicles being almost simultaneously measured are another cause for error. At highway speeds the inaccuracy of the distance determination is enough to potentially flaw any attempt at speed measurement at a given location.

This same argument applies for battery-operated vehicle transponders. However I do believe they would be inherently more accurate than backscatter types, even though I do not believe their accuracy would be sufficient for speed measurements over short distances. A counterpoint can be made that, if the distances between the two stationary transmitter/receivers is great enough—and I am not going to bother with the calculations but a quarter mile or so would certainly do it—the distance inaccuracy in reading the transponder would be rendered inconsequential and speed could be determined with sufficient legal accuracy.

So why not measure speed this way? Each stationary installation will cost *many* thousands of dollars. ($30,000 each is a good estimate.) And it takes two such installations. Why complicate life when it is unnecessary? It is *much* easier and *vastly* less expensive to perform the speed determination with radar and a camera, or with a video system. Especially with a video system. Betcha this is what the New York State Thruway is using!

If you want to join the modern age in speed enforcement you would use a pure video system. Forget the radar; this system is undetectable. There are no emissions and, consequently, nothing to detect.

Fully automatic video enforcement is not yet legal in all states. (Aren't you lucky?!) However, the laws of some states do allow ticketing speed violators via this method. Imagine a scene being photographed with the frame rate of the camera being known. Therefore a vehicle moving between two known points on the video picture can have its speed easily calculated. There are several systems that can do this. You do not even need an actual known point of reference.

Some systems allow you to "draw" two lines on the screen of your video monitor like the sportscasters do during a football game. When the vehicle crosses the first line a clock timer begins. Crossing the second line stops the counter and, bingo, the vehicle's speed can be calculated very accurately. When the calculated speed is above an arbitrarily set threshold a freeze frame will be captured and held. And, just to terrify you more, up to 26 lines can be drawn on one video screen, meaning that up to 13 vehicles can be simultaneously tracked. (You have to have one entry line and one exit line for each "detection block.")

Lines can define detection blocks for each lane located adjacent to each other, or they can be located in the same lane, perhaps a quarter mile apart, subject to the video resolution possible. Different timing thresholds can be set for each detection block. And the camera does not need to be near the site in question, just have a clear field of view. However, since bad weather would limit the system's ability to "see" vehicles, the camera(s) will usually be mounted near the site in question.

Using near infrared technology cameras that are quite inexpensive, and near infrared illuminators, which are really just floodlights operating in the near infrared spectrum, the entire site can be flooded with light for the camera to use, light that your eyes cannot detect; it will look dark to you *and they can still see you!*

With a line drawn for height detection and a side-mounted camera, over-height vehicles, usually trucks, can be detected and someone alerted to stop them. If there are different speed limits for trucks and cars, this is how they can be differentiated.

The resultant freeze frame will be automatically processed to produce a printed picture of your vehicle from the rear, showing your license plate, and then imprint the image with your vehicle's speed, the date, and time. AT&T is above 95 percent accuracy in doing optical character recognition on your license plate and automatically entering the plate number into the computer system. Imagine how easy those European license plates must be for OCR. Now if we could just standardize the print and colors used on U.S. plates....

Not uncommonly, a second camera will simultaneously take a photo of the driver. Look around when you see one camera and see if you can find the second one. It can be mounted more than a block away from the site in question. Again, location is determined by the ability of the camera to take a good picture in adverse weather conditions. All of this results in a citation, including copies of any photographs taken, being mailed to the address shown on the vehicle's registration. Pay up or see you in court.

As another aside, in some states the use of the second camera to photograph the driver has been considered an invasion of privacy and may not be allowed by that particular state, hence they do not know who is driving the vehicle. It is possible that the vehicle's owner may be held liable for the operation of the vehicle. One case comes to mind where the citation, including the driver's photograph and that of the incident passenger next to him, arrived at his house and was opened by the driver's wife. Needless to say, as revealed in the ensuing divorce proceedings, the driver had been thought by his wife to be elsewhere and not in the company of the lady next to him! I believe this case was sufficient to obtain the elimination of the driver's camera in that state and hence prevent future incidents such as this from occurring.

I am somewhat sure, but not absolutely positive, that the New York State Thruway is not issuing speeding citations solely via the use of the E-ZPass system. Perhaps a reader is with that fine agency?

In closing, do not lose the convenience of the E-ZPass system because of paranoia about speeding violation enforcement. If they want you they will get you with much easier and more efficient incontestable methods!

And, no, I do not work for the New York State Thruway. But I would use their E-ZPass system if I lived there.

Descrambling Cable (Spring, 1993) *By Dr. Clayton Phorester*

If you were thinking about opening your cable box, don't! Most cable boxes have a small metal connector in the front right of the box. Once the lid is off, the connection is broken and a little battery inside remembers. I learned this the hard way with a Pioneer converter. Once the connection breaks, the little channel display on the box will go all screwy, and the only button that will work is the power button. If you did open the box, you would now notice that whenever you turn the TV on, it goes to a preset station and can't be changed. This station is usually the one that your box displays when you tune to a premium channel that you don't subscribe to. At any rate, cable companies will fine you around $25 to reactivate your box. And if they think you've tampered with it, that goes up to $1,000 (according to California law). All the cable company has to do is press a few keys on their cheap computers in their cozy little offices to get the box at your house back on line. (And you thought their regular rates were bad!)

If you did open it, maybe you could tell them that it fell on the floor during an earthquake or something. Or, you could do what I did. I told my cable operator that I was throwing away a TV, and was going to return my cable box. Well, I returned the box (after I closed it back up, of course) and about a month later I told my cable company that I got a new TV. I went to the cable office and picked up a new box. Result: I got a perfectly good box, while some dumb Wilson got the old tampered-with one! And, of course, the Wilson won't know what the hell's going on when his box doesn't work, so he'll call the cable company and complain. The cable company (arrogant as they all are) will naturally assume that this person was trying to tamper with it, and they aren't gonna believe anything this guy is gonna tell them. Ha! Ha! Ha! (That's just my sick sense of humor.)

The point is: Don't open the *damn* box! Inside there are a hundred little dials, screws, and thingamabobers, but messing with them won't do you a lot of good if the box won't respond to any commands in the first place!

I just recently downloaded from a local BBS the following instructions to make a cable descrambler. It appears to have been uploaded in 1988 (how's that for Sysop incompetence?) but it's worth a shot anyway. I'm almost certain that it won't work with a handful of cable systems because every one is different in its own little perverse kind of way. In Step 6, the author assumes that you will be using a cable box. I don't think that having a box is a requirement, because I don't have one, and my descrambler works just fine. On my cable system, boxes are an option for old TVs that don't go any higher than Channel 13, and TVs that you want to receive premium channels. So if you have one or not, don't sweat it.

Enough talk! Whip out your wallet, your car keys, your soldering iron, and kick some cable company butt!

HOW TO BUILD A PAY TV DESCRAMBLER: AUTHOR UNKNOWN

Materials Required:

1 Radio Shack mini-box (RS #270-235)
1¼-watt resistor, 2.2k-2.4k ohm (RS #271-1325)
1 75pf-100pf variable capacitor (hard to find)
2 F61a chassis-type coaxial connectors (RS #278-212)
12″ No. 12 solid copper wire
12″ RG59 coaxial cable

Instructions

1. Bare a length of No. 12 gauge solid copper wire and twist around a ⅜-inch nail or rod to form a coil of nine turns. Elongate coil to a length of 1½ inches and form right angle bends on each end.

HOW TO BUILD A PAY TV DESCRAMBLER: AUTHOR UNKNOWN *(continued)*

2. Solder the variable capacitor to the coil. It doesn't matter where you solder it; it still does the same job. The best place for it is in the center with the adjustment screw facing upward. Note: When it comes time to place coil in box, the coil must be grounded. This can be done by crazy-gluing a piece of rubber to the bottom of the box and securing the coil to it.
3. Tap coil at points 2½ turns from ends of coil and solder to coaxial chassis connectors, bringing tap leads through holes in chassis box. Use as little wire as possible.
4. Solder resistor to center of coil and ground other end of resistor to chassis box, using solder lug and small screw.
5. Drill a ½-inch-diameter hole in mini-box cover to permit adjustment of the variable capacitor from the outside.
6. Place device in line with existing cable on either side of the converter box and connect to a television set with the piece of RG59 coaxial cable. Set television to HBO channel.
7. Using a plastic screwdriver (or anything else nonmetallic), adjust the variable capacitor until picture tunes in. Sit back, relax, and enjoy!

Cable Modem Security Holes (Summer, 1997) *By Sciri*

Note: All references to the specific Internet Service Provider affected have been censored and replaced with [ISP] due to the nature of this article.

The advent of cable modems has opened up a wealth of security nightmares for Internet users in this area. Unfortunately, most of these users have never touched a UNIX machine and have no idea how packet transport works over wide area public networks such as the Internet. Because of this, hundreds of new Internet users may be at risk from extremely old security issues.

In the past, virtually all home Internet users connected to their Internet Service Providers (ISPs) or colleges using standard modems and logged into UNIX or VMS shell accounts. Due to the fact that these shell accounts required at least a rudimentary knowledge of computers and networking, most users logging into these accounts had an understanding and respect for the Internet and its limitations. The majority of these users also understood the security issues at hand and took the proper precautions to safeguard their data.

Over the past few years, UNIX and VMS shell accounts have been slowly phased out in favor of SLIP and PPP dialup connections. The advantage of this type of dialup protocol was that the Internet and its resources were now within reach of novice Windows and Macintosh users. The downside of this, however, was that many of these users didn't understand how the Internet worked and were ignorant of the dangers posed by sending confidential and private data over their connections.

The introduction of cable modems and WebTV has created a whole new breed of novice Internet users who no longer need to know how to set up a modem connection and, in a lot of cases, no longer even need to know how to use a computer. This trend is pushing the commercialization of the Internet and most companies and ISPs seem to be more interested in making a profit than making sure a secure and reliable service is being released.

Of all the security issues at hand today, the hottest topic right now seems to be the ability for malicious hackers to take advantage of problems with TCP/IP and sniff network traffic going over the Internet and corporate Intranets. Companies such as Netscape Communications Corporation and Open Market, Inc. are pushing secure commerce servers so conducting transactions over the Internet and corporate Intranets can be safe and secure.

The problem with this approach is that only transactions via SSL equipped WWW browsers can take advantage of this security. Most other forms of connections are left unsecured because not all clients are capable of SSL or encryption. Another problem is that these extreme novice Internet users don't understand what sniffing is and don't know why they should only use SSL equipped WWW browsers to conduct transactions and send confidential data over the Internet.

In the past, the risk of someone sniffing Internet data was relatively low. In order for a sniffer to be successfully set up, a key gateway machine sitting in between the client and server had to be compromised and superuser access had to be attained. Once superuser access was attained, the intruder had to hide their tracks from the system administrators and find a way to silently retrieve sniffer logs from that compromised host. Usually, these gateway machines were UNIX based and vast amounts of knowledge about the UNIX operating system were required to keep oneself hidden.

The routing used by cable modems in this area (Zenith HOME*Works Universal transceivers), however, completely bypasses the need to compromise a gateway machine in order to sniff. Each cable modem network interface (NI) acts as an Ethernet transceiver and directly connects each cable modem user's machine to the Internet via 10BaseT. Because of this, each machine a cable modem user has connected to the Internet is considered a local node on whatever subnet has been assigned to that user's geographical area.

This trend was first noticed when the cable modem NI was installed and powered up at this site. The TX, RX, and NET-ACTIVE status LEDs had immediately lit up and started reporting network traffic even though the cable modem NI had not yet been plugged into the Ethernet card of the firewall/gateway machine. It was then hypothesized that it may be possible for cable modem users to sniff all traffic passing over the same subnet.

Software, such as sniffit and tcpdump, was used to test this hypothesis and, not surprisingly, every other cable modem user on the same subnet could, in fact, be monitored. Due to the fact that this type of major security hole could put the privacy of hundreds of cable modem users at risk and quite possibly destroy the reputation of an ISP, it was decided that [ISP] should be contacted regarding the sniffing issues.

After playing phone tag and being on hold for nearly an hour, I was finally connected to someone within [ISP]'s security group and explained exactly what was being tested and the methods being used. I was then told that the ability for any cable modem user to sniff network traffic on their subnet is a "known bug, and no fix is available at this time."

According to the [ISP]'s security group, the fact that cable modem users can sniff network traffic was not publicized because "this cable modem service is not being sold as a secure service and no such claims are being made in the service agreement." Baffled by this, I posed the question, "since this isn't a secure service, [ISP] has decided upon the policy that it's the sole responsibility of the end user or system administrator to make sure that all connections are secured and encrypted by third party software?" The response was, "Hrm...that's actually a pretty good way of phrasing it."

This is an extreme display of [ISP]'s inability to plan ahead and take steps to keep their networks reasonably secure. Topped off by a seemingly intentional coverup to keep cable modem users from finding out that virtually every single keystroke that goes across their Internet connection could very well be monitored, it's frightening to think that most end users are ignorant of the fact that any problems such as this even exist.

With today's threats of credit card fraud and the widespread value of personal information, [ISP] should have taken all steps possible to make sure that cable modem subscribers were educated and aware of these dangers. With more and more users transmitting confidential and personal information over the Internet and World Wide Web, more security issues need to be addressed and publicized.

The issue of sniffing does not stop here, however. With cable modem technology being pushed as the next "big thing," ISPs and cable companies should take as many precautions as possible to make sure cable modems become a secure and reliable service. If current technology is not updated to reflect these problems, thousands, if not millions, of future users could be at risk.

ATM Tricks (Summer, 1995) *By Helen Gone*

During college I alternated semesters as an electrical engineering co-op student. This was for the pursuit of bucks to stay in school and some experience. One co-op semester, I met a group of about ten computer science students who were pretty much forced to work 50 to 60 hours a week "testing." Testing was looking for errors in third-party PC software. Testing was extremely dull, boring, tedious, monotonous, etc., and it made for a lot of unhappy co-ops who wished they had other co-op jobs. This testing was comprised entirely of doing repetitive keystrokes with the odd batch file now and again. Repetitive keystrokes simply meant they took each menu tree out to its very end, filled out some paperwork, then started at the next branch, and worked it out to the end and so on. One guy had been working on Lotus 123 for his whole co-op. He was the unhappiest of all.

Anyway, this technique seemed relevant to my ATM interests and I soon started some testing of my own. With as many times as I hit the ole money machine, it was pretty easy to work the menus over pretty well for anything that seemed soft. The task led me to begin noticing the obvious differences between the manufacturers of ATMs, then slowly, the subtle differences between different hardware and software revs. I've never documented any of this. I simply started remembering the differences, especially the differences in the similar machines that were owned/leased by different banks.

Number 1

One rev of Diebold machines began to stand out as the one with the most problems. Its most-notable feature and flaw is its cash delivery door. You all have used it. It's the one where the door stays locked until your cash is delivered (and while delivering, it makes that heartwarming chug-chug-chug "oh I got bucks" sound) at which time it starts beeping, saying: "Please lift door and remove cash" and then makes that wonderful "bang!" sound when you crash the door to the top to see your well-earned money laying in a stack inside this clear anodized box. This machine became my central interest because of the door. The designers all (mechanical/electrical/software) made a bad assumption concerning the door. I put the three designing disciplines in that order because that is typically the order the BS slides. Good software can usually save the screw-ups the others make—usually. The other feature/problem, which I found during my testing, was the use of (I'll guess) a watchdog timer to recover from software bombs. If the software did not tickle the watchdog in some allotted time, a hardware reset would occur. The reset typically resulted in the loss of your card. These Diebolds seemed particularly sensitive to the hitting of Cancel during different operations. Some revs would say thank you and spit your card back, while other revs would begin not tickling the watchdog, and of course, reset. I soon learned that trips to different branches of my bank for extra/replacement cards became necessary. My bank was cool in the fact that they could make cards in-house, and I did not have to wait a couple of weeks for the card to come back in the mail, either usable or cut up with an ever-so-sweet letter explaining who I should call should I not understand how to use my ATM card. Also sweet-talking the people at the bank where the card was "captured" the next day sometimes got the card back.

Going back to the main feature/flaw, the designers made the assumption (Assumption #1) that if a cherry switch, located somewhere inside the door mechanism, had made closure then this meant the user, the ATMee, had removed the bucks. We'll guess some pseudo-code might look like (just because I've always wanted some code in *2600*):

```
UnloadBucks(MaxBuck$)
DoorWithFlawIs(UnLocked)
Print "PLEASE OPEN DOOR AND REMOVE CASH"
While We'reWaiting
      EverySoOftenTickle(The WatchDog)
      TellBeeperTo(BEEP)
      If DoorSwitch == CLOSED then
               MaxBuck$ = Removed
               We'veNotWaiting
      endif
EndWhile
etc.
```

And, ta-da! The flaw is simply that the door could be open and cash removed without the switch ever having made closure. The switch can be heard to click (this varies of course) around the first 1/3 motion of the door. A small hand or a Popsicle stick works just fine with an added bonus if the myth holds true that the camera takes your photo once the door is opened. See Assumption #1. For completion several more things must next occur. The first is waiting. With cash in hand and switch never closed, the machine will just loop, beeping and asking you to remove your already removed cash. The second is the Cancel. Most revs spit your card back at you and correctly assume that you magically removed the money. The target rev did not behave this way. At t >= 30 seconds and Cancel key hit, the poles shift over to that imaginary side of the plane and the machine resets. Money in hand, card in machine, but hopefully another card in pocket! The final chapter shows up in your monthly statement.

DATE	AMOUNT	DESCRIPTION
7/11	-350.00	WITHDRAW 7/11 LOC-D 1972/2002 1000 MAIN STREET USABIGBANK
7/11	+350.00	DEPOSIT 7/11 LOC-D 1972/2002 NET RES ERROR 3R3-01312000342-809 TRANS AT LOC-D BIGBANK

Assumption #2: If the machine bombs during a transaction even past the point of delivering money, a transaction error assigns you the cash back. This weekend, the kegger's on me, huh! I've been out of college seven years now and can say that these machines are today quite few and far between due mostly due to the door/switch flaw.

The replacement machines have any number of configurations, most with no doors at all or a totally different door approach. I'm pretty sure the laws concerning tampering with ATMs have also been replaced as well.

Number 2

This one I just saw the other day is pretty much the impetus for writing this whole article. It's not so much of a hack other than observing the plain stupidity of a company providing customers with an ATM-like service. This nameless company provides a card reader/keypad/terminal/printer inside their establishment. At the terminal you swipe your card (no card capture here!), enter your PIN, and then the amount you want. The printer promptly shells out a receipt and informs you to take it to the counter for the bucks. After you sign it, the salesperson then takes the receipt and gives you the amount indicated. Simple, with the single point cash idea, and life is just way easier with this low maintenance machine. My transaction had one slight hang-up, which was pure coincidence. The printer became somewhat jammed and my receipt had no place for me to sign. The receipts are quite similar to those of any credit cards where there is a white copy on top and a yellow one for the customer underneath. At seeing the problem, the salesperson comes over and first opens the bottom up and fixes the jammed printer. A key is needed here. Next, enter the shaky world of high tech computer terminal security: a five-digit code is entered into the terminal. No magic key card swipe then code combination, just a plain old five digit shoulder surfable code. Five digits, press Enter, and the terminal displays "Authorized Reprint—Press Enter for Reprint." Here comes my new receipt and the machine is back in swipe-a-card mode. Looking over my new authorized reprint I do find one small clue to indicate this is not the original. Easily missed, it says "Reprinted" midway down amongst a slew of other bank babble. Sign it, get the cash, and go. Now [nameless] is a large nationwide chain with many locations even within the city; what are the odds that the same code will work at another location? Sure enough. Walk in, five digits, press Enter then enter again, tear off the print out, sign it with some mess, take it to the counter and do the ole "Boy, that Brad Pitt sure is a cutey, huh!" distracter, and ta-da! You just got handed the same amount of money the last person got. Since it was a non-network function, [nameless] is the loser, the reprinted account never knows the difference. As for how do you get the chance to shoulder surf the code? Refeed the copy on to itself? Spill coffee on it? You see it over and over how rules that apply to the user do not for the administrator. The user is required to have a card and code while the administrator needs just a code. The administrator usually means many (salespeople, managers, etc.) and the policy to direct many appears to weigh much heavier than any fear we install.

Special thanx to FlyCac Technologies and iBruiseEasily for some thoughts and memories.

Gadgets

New consumer gadgets were all the rage in the '90s. Back then, having a pager was a real status symbol and was the equivalent of today's cellular phone, although far less people overall had pagers back then. Learning how the network actually worked, comparing and theorizing about features, and figuring out ways to listen in on other pagers was of major interest to so many of us back then. With this knowledge you could grab all sorts of secret information, literally out of thin air. And of course, there were always the random little surprises like the electronic greeting cards that seemed to come out of nowhere and gave the hacker community something else fun to play with and use for purposes other than what they were intended. To the non-hackers of the world, it looked like we were just wasting our time on nothing. And that made it all the more fun.

A Gift from Hallmark (Spring, 1994) *By Bernie S.*

Once again, the mass-market consumer electronics industry has succeeded in bringing down the cost of very sophisticated technology to ridiculous levels. Hallmark, Inc. (the greeting card company) has teamed up with Information Storage Devices, Inc. to produce the Talking Greeting Card.

For a mere $7.95, you can buy a completely assembled digital audio recording device (complete with speaker and microphone) built into a greeting card. The idea is to record your 10-second voice greeting on the card and mail it to the person of your choice. The possibilities abound....

If you take the card apart, you'll find a plastic and cardboard frame inside containing a tiny 1-inch square circuit board, four 1.5-V watch batteries, two switches, a piezoelectric microphone, and a decent 1.5-inch, 16-ohm speaker. This is much smaller and much cheaper than any standard "tone box" kit. And it's all ready to go!

My hacker friends and I have removed these modules and concealed them inside all kinds of unlikely containers: a chewing-tobacco tin, a Zippo lighter, a dental floss dispenser, even a coat collar! The voice-band fidelity is quite good, and it's excellent for recording (and playing back) ACTS coin-deposit tones, Sprint voice FONcard codes, call-progress tones, Telco recordings, etc.

Thank you, Hallmark, for "caring enough to send the very best" in a cheap, accessible, and readily hackable device!

Pager Major (Spring, 1995) *By Danny Burstein*

This article has been put together to answer some of the more common questions about pager systems. It is primarily focused on the U.S. and Canadian arrangements, but other countries are not forgotten.

What Is a Pager Anyway?

As usually described, a pager is a portable unit, generally about half the size of an audio cassette box, which can be signaled to send a one-way message to the pager owner. (There are lots of versions available. For example, Motorola offers up the Sensar, which is shaped like a flattened out pencil. There are also extra thin credit card units, PCM-CIA cards that fit into computers, etc.)

What Types of Messages?

The earliest units, usually called beepers, simply gave a tone alert. This was a signal to the wearer to, for example, call the answering service.

The next step was units, which could display numbers. While the most common use is to send it the phone number you want the person to call, you can, of course, add code numbers to mean anything else you'd want.

For example, the number xxx-yyyy-1 might mean to call the xxx-yyyy number at your leisure. Xxx-yyyy-9 might mean call ASAP.

The most-recent units, called alpha-numerics, display complete written messages. So, for example, the pager could show the message: "Please call home; you have a letter from the IRS."

There are also voice pagers, which will let you actually speak into the phone and have it come out the person's pager. These are pretty rare. Typically these are used within local areas, i.e., in a factory. They are also used, on occasion, by groups such as volunteer fire departments.

How Are Messages Sent to the Pager?

Messages are sent by radio. Actually, it's a bit more complicated than that. Let's take a look at how a pager actually works: The pager is a small sized radio receiver that constantly monitors a specific radio frequency dedicated to pager use. It remains silent until it "hears" a specific ID string that tells it to, in effect, turn on, and then listen up for, and display, the forthcoming message. (Again that could be a numeric or other string.) This ID is called (in the U.S.) a capcode. It has nothing to do with the phone number you call or the ID you give to the page operator (see below). (The ID number you associate with the pager is actually merely "column a" of a lookup table. The pager radio service uses it to get the capcode, which is in "table b," and sends the capcode over the air. These tables can and are modified each time a new pager is added to the database.)

So the key point is that the pager company radio transmitter is constantly sending out pages, and your specific unit will only activate when it hears its ID/CAPCODE over the air.

How Do I Send Out the Message?

This depends on your pager vendor. Let's take the most common examples:

- **Alert tone only (the old style):** You call up a phone number assigned to the pager. You'll hear some ringing, then a signal tone. At that point you hang up. Shortly after, the pager transmitter will send out the individual unit's capcode and it will go off. (Note that earlier models, some of which are still in use with the voice pagers, don't use a capcode, but instead use a simple tone sequence. Since these give a very limited number of choices, they are pretty much phased out except, again, for things like volunteer fire departments.)
- **Touch-tone entry:** You will call a unique phone number dedicated to the specific pager. It will ring, and then you'll hear a signal tone. At that point you punch in, using touch tone, the number you want displayed on the pager. A few seconds later the transmitter will kick out the pager's capcode, followed by the numbers you punched in. Then the pager will give its annoying alert tone, the person will read it, and call you back. (Note that there is a variation on this in which the company uses a single dialup phone number. You call it up, then punch in the pager's ID number, and continue as above. This is often used by nationwide services with an 800 number.)
- **Alpha-numeric:** With this one there are various ways of getting the message to the system.
- **Via an operator:** The pager company will have you dial up their operator. When they answer, you give them the pager ID number and the message. They'll type it into the computer and shortly afterward the transmitter will send out the capcode and the message.
- **Using your computer:** Most pager companies with alphanumeric have a dialup number you can call yourself. Some of these will work with regular comm programs, while others require proprietary software. If you call the tech department chances are they will give it to you. (They'd rather have your computer call their computer than have you call a person.) The most common method is to have your computer dial up the number, then you type in the pager ID, followed by the message. Again, a moment later, the system will transmit it over the air, etc. (There are also various software packages that automate some of this.)
- **Special terminals:** Because of the popularity of this type of system, there are various standalone terminals specifically designed for this purpose. The most common one is the Alphamate (Motorola) and it's preprogrammed with many of the functions. It's basically a half-decent keyboard with a two-line display, and is set up with the phone number of the company, etc.

How Large/Long a Message Can I Send?

This depends on a few key items. This is of most concern with an alpha-numeric, although it has some relevance with numeric ones (i.e., if you're giving a long-distance number, extension, and code...). In no particular order these are:

- **The design of your sending computer or pre-programmed terminal.** For example, if you get an Alphamate, chances are it will be preset to 80 characters. (You can reset it, provided the next two items work out.)
- **The design of the pager transmitter system.** It will place a limit on the maximum length message it will send over the air. This can vary dramatically. Generally (with a BIG YMMV [Your Mileage May Vary]), you'll get at least 15 numbers with a numeric, and at least 80 characters on an alphanumeric. Some systems will allow up to 225 or so alpha characters.
- **The design of the pager.** Especially a problem with alphanumerics. Many of the ones on the market will only hold 80 characters, so anything above that will be lost.

Other Questions

My company has given us pagers, and I notice that I have both an individual ID and a "group" number. When we page out to the group, everyone's unit goes off. How does this work?

Remember that a pager is basically a radio receiver that is constantly monitoring for its capcode. You can get pagers that listen for more than one. In this case (which is quite common) your personal capcode might be yyyy, while your boss's might be yyzz. In addition, both pagers will be listening for the capcode zzzz. When zzzz is detected, all the pagers with that capcode will go off. (Alternatively the pager company's computer may be smart enough to take a group id and translate it into capcodes xxyy, xxya, xxzz, etc., and send out 50 sequential messages. There are some software tricks that reduce overhead here so it doesn't actually send the same message 50 times.)

I keep hearing about sports or news services available by pager. How do they work?

Keep in mind that pagers work by constantly monitoring the radio channel for their capcode. So if you have ten pagers, or a hundred, or a thousand, all with the same capcode, they will all go off at the same time.

The service company will have someone (or perhaps, a smart computer) monitor the news broadcasts/radio channels for something interesting. At that point they'll send out the message to the group ID/capcode subscribing to that information. This way the news company sends out one message and it gets displayed by all subscribers.

(Again, they can also send out the capcodes for the 500 subscribers. It gets into a security/cost/radio time equation as to which method they'll use.)

So if I find one of these sports-news pagers on the sidewalk I can use it for free?

Umm—kind of. As long as the company providing the service keeps using the same group code, your pager will continue to receive the messages. But the individual pager ID will probably be changed immediately so you won't be able to use it for your personal messages. Note also that some pagers do have the ability to be turned into a lump of clay over the air. Very few systems have actually implemented this security feature (which is called "over the air" shutoff), but it is there.

I've found a pager on the sidewalk and would like to use it. What can I do?

Not much. Keep in mind that you need an account with the paging company for them to send out the radio signal. So unless you keep paying them, the pager will soon be a paperweight. You might as well turn it in for the reward.... (On the other hand, if you already have a pager, you may be able to get this new one cloned to your first one, which will allow you to have a duplicate unit. See below.)

Speaking of that pager on the street, it's got all sort of numbers on it. What do they mean?

There will be a lot of items printed, some by the manufacturer, some by the dealer. In no particular order these will include (usually in *very* small print)

- The pager frequency
- The pager's serial number
- The capcode programmed into it

Very frequently, especially with numeric units, there will also be the phone number assigned to it. And, of course, there will be the dealer's name, the local supplier, an "if found here's the reward number," and other housekeeping. Note that often the capcode will not be printed on the unit, but will only be readable via the programmer.

Can I listen in/monitor pager channels?

Kind of. The frequencies are readily known and the data is a digital stream going over the air. There are various vendors of equipment to decode the material and display it or feed it into your computer. Some of these folks advertise in communications magazines such as *Popular Communications*. However:

The federales and the pager companies don't like you doing this. (See the ECPA.)

The volume of traffic is quite high. If you figure a 1200 baud channel in use 75 percent of the time, well, you can work out the math.

By the way, the numeric units do *not* use touch tone over the air. Some did way back when, but I doubt any do these days.

I have a pager for which I'm paying big bucks every month. I miss a lot of pages since I'm in the subway a lot. What can I do about this?

There are several things:

Some of the pager companies will resend messages on request. Basically you call up their phone number, punch in a security code, then go through a menu, which tells them to resend the last, say, five hours worth of messages.

You can get a second pager unit cloned identically to the first. Leave this one at home or in your office. When you get back you can compare its messages to the one on your belt. While the message may be a few hours late, at least you'll be getting it.

Actually, most pager companies will refuse to clone your unit for you. However, there are many third parties that will do it. Check out the ads in technical and communications magazines.

What are the prices/services offered?

These vary dramatically by area and company. Unfortunately there is no central database keeping records on this. Generally the following factors get counted in determining what you'll be paying:

How sleazy the company is.

Which type of pager and service should you get? Again, the most common are numeric (cheaper) and alpha-numeric (more expensive).

Level of usage. You may get, say, 25 free messages a month and then pay $0.25 for each additional.

Whether you own the pager or lease it.

Insurance, etc.

Area of coverage. Smaller area means less expensive.

Speaking of coverage, what's this satellite nationwide paging?

Well, it's not quite what they're telling you. It's not a single satellite covering the nation. Rather, what's done is: You call up the paging company. It then signals transmitters in the top 500 cities to send out your capcode. Shortly afterward you get the message. Note that you are not receiving a satellite transmission.

What's in the pipeline?

Two key features are slowly filtering down.

- **Much more pager memory/longer messages.** Most pagers are severely limited in the amount of material they can hold, with a typical maximum being about 20 messages. Units with much larger memories, or even better, units that are hooked into palmtop or laptop computers, are making it to market.
- **Two-way communications.** In its simplest form this allows the pager to verify reception to the transmitter. Also on the way is complete two-way communication, which would basically be wireless email. These systems are still a bit limited, but are rapidly gaining footholds in industry and should soon be consumer level. Take a look, for example, at what the FedEx folk carry.

An Introduction to Paging Networks (Winter, 1999–2000)

By Black Axe

Pagers are very, very common nowadays. Coverage is widespread and cheap, and the technology is accepted by most. Ever wonder, though, what happens on these paging networks? Ever wonder what kind of traffic comes across those pager frequencies? Ever listen to your scanner on a pager frequency in frustration, hearing the data stream across that you just can't interpret? Want to tap your radio, get a decoding program, and see what you've been missing?

Before I begin, let's cover just exactly how those precious few digits make it from the caller's keypad to the display of the pager in question. Or perhaps your monitor....

Let's entertain a hypothetical situation in which I would like to speak with my friend, Dave. First, I pick up my phone and dial Dave's pager number (555-1234). I hear the message "type in your phone number and hit the pound sign." So I comply, enter 555-4321# and then hang up.

Here's where the fun starts. This is all dependent on the coverage area of the pager. The paging company receives the page when I enter it, and looks up the capcode of the pager it is to be sent to. A capcode is somewhat akin to an ESN [Electronic Serial Number] on a cellphone; it identifies each specific pager on a given frequency. The paging company will then send the data up to a satellite (usually), where it is rebroadcast to all towers that serve that particular paging network. (Remember last year, when everyone's pagers stopped working for a few days? It was just such a satellite that went out of orbit.) The paging towers then transmit the page in all locations that Dave's pager is serviceable in. In this case, let's say that Dave's pager has a coverage area that consists of a chunk of the east coast, going from Boston down to Washington, DC, and out to

Philadelphia. The page intended for him is transmitted all throughout that region. Since a pager is a one-way device, the network has no idea where the pager is, what it's doing, etc., so it just transmits each page all over the coverage area, every time.

"So?" you may say, "What's that do for me?" Well, it means two different things. First, pagers can be cloned with no fear of detection because the network just sends out the pages, and any pager with that capcode on that frequency will beep and receive the data. Second, it means that one can monitor pagers that are not based in their area. Based on the example of Dave's pager, he might have bought it in New York City. He also could live there. However, because the data is transmitted all over the coverage area, monitoring systems in Boston, Washington, DC, and Philadelphia could all intercept his pages in real time. Many paging customers are unaware of their paging coverage areas and usually do not denote the NPA (area code) from which the page is being received. This can cause problems for the monitoring individual, who must always remember that seven digit pages shown on the decoder display are not necessarily for their own NPA.

The Pager Decoding Setup

Maybe you knew this, maybe you didn't...Paging networks aren't encrypted. They all transmit data in the clear, generally in one of two formats. The older format is POCSAG; which stands for Post Office Code Standards Advisory Group. POCSAG is easily identified by two separate tones and then a burst of data. POCSAG is fairly easy to decode. FLEX, on the other hand, is a bit more difficult, but not impossible. FLEX signals have only a single tone preceding the data burst. Here's how to take those annoying signals out of your scanner and onto your monitor. You will need:

1. A scanner or other receiver with a discriminator output. A discriminator output is a direct connection to the output of the discriminator chip on your scanner. This is accomplished by soldering a single wire to the output pin of the NFM [narrow FM] discriminator chip to the inner conductor of a jack installed on the scanner. RCA jacks are commonly used for convenience. For obvious reasons, the larger and more spacious a scanner is internally, the easier the modification is to perform.
2. A computer is actually required to interpret and display the pages. Most pager decoding software runs under Win95. This includes all software that uses the sound card to decode signals. If you have a data slicer, there are a few programs that will run under DOS.
3. You will need a SoundBlaster compatible sound card. This will let you snag POCSAG traffic. Or you can build a data slicer and decode FLEX traffic, too. Or you can be lazy and buy one from Texas 2-Way for about $80 or so. The SoundBlaster method will obviously tie up your computer while decoding

pages. Using the slicer will let you run decoders on an old DOS box and will let you use your better computer for more important stuff.

4. Antennas, cabling, etc. You will need an RCA cable (preferably shielded) to take the discriminator output either into the sound card or into the slicer. If using a slicer, you will also need the cable to connect your slicer to your computer. As far as antennas go, pager signals are very strong, so you won't need much of an antenna. A rubber ducky with a right angle adapter, attached right to the back of the radio, will be more than enough. The signals are so damned strong that you might even be able to get away with a paper clip shoved into the antenna jack. Think of what kind of an antenna your pager has; this should give you a good idea of what the requirements are in the antenna department.

Connect your scanner's discriminator output to either your data slicer or your sound card. If using a sound card, be sure to use the line in connection. If using a data slicer, connect that to the correct port on your computer. Tune yourself a nice, strong (they're all strong, really) paging signal.

Where are they? Well, the vast majority of numeric pagers are crystalled between 929 and 932 MHz. Try there. Or if you want to try decoding some alphanumeric pagers, try the VHF range around 158 MHz. There is also some activity in the 460–470 MHz range.

Now what about software, you say? That is where things start to get somewhat difficult. Motorola developed most paging protocols in use and holds licenses to them. Any software that decodes POCSAG or FLEX is a violation of Motorola's intellectual property rights. So one day, the people at Motorola decided that they didn't want that software floating around. They proceeded to look up everyone who had copies posted on the Web and told them that if they didn't take those specific programs off of the Web, it was court time. The threatened Webmasters removed the offending copies, fearing a lawsuit from Motorola. After this, our good friends from the U.S. Secret Service arrested Bill Cheek and Keith Knipschild for messing around with decoding hardware and software; the SS appeared to want to make data slicers illegal. Of course, these arrests were ridiculous, but nobody wanted to get busted...so the vast majority of resources on American web sites disappeared. Checking around English or German sites may yield some interesting results.

Now you're ready. Fire up the software. Get that receiver on a nice, hot frequency. Look at all of the pages streaming across the network. Give it a few hours... getting bored yet? Yes? Okay... now that you have a functional decoding setup, let's make use of it. Know someone's pager that you want to monitor? Here's how to snag them. First you need the frequency; it's usually inscribed on the back of the pager. Also, you can try to determine what paging company they use, and then social engineer the freq out of the company. `www.perconcorp.com` also has a search function where you can locate all of the paging transmitters (and freqs) in your area, listed by who owns 'em. Not bad. So you have the frequency, now what? Well, wait until you have to actually talk to this person. Get your setup cranking on the frequency that this person's pager is using. Now, page him. Pay close attention to the data coming across the network. See your phone number there? See the capcode that your phone number is addressed to? That's it. Some better decoding programs have provisions to log every single page to a certain capcode to a logfile. This is a good thing. Get a data slicer, set everything up on a dedicated 486, and have fun gathering data.

MILESTONE: DISTRIBUTOR UPDATE (Winter, 1997-1998)

Since our last issue, there have been some rather significant developments. Fine Print (our main distributor located in Austin, TX) changed their status to Chapter 7 protection from Chapter 11 shortly after we stopped using them. We did this after they offered us $150 as a settlement for the $100,000 they owe us. This means that they are now out of business.

According to some rather interesting court documents filed by The Fine Print Distributors, Inc. Official Unsecured Creditors Committee, the United States Trustee's Office, and ANA Interests, Inc., it appears that there were some financial improprieties going on, almost to the very end. According to the documents, "During the last six to eight weeks, the Debtor also began to dispose of its hard assets in sales out of the ordinary course of business without permission of this Court. Many of these items appear to have been sold at below market value." Also, "Upon information received by the Committee beginning on December 2, 1997, the Committee also would show the Court that apparently the salary of Debtor's president was increased from $27,000 to $50,000 post-petition, and that of its Chief Financial Officer from $22,000 to $37,900 during the same period. Additionally, it appears that the Debtor enacted corporate policies post-petition to provide significant vacation and severance packages to employees that were not in existence prior to the pendency of the bankruptcy. The Debtor's bank account appears to have been completely decimated on Friday, December 4, 1997, for the payment of these 'benefits,' even though sizable other debts have arisen post-petition which remain unpaid."

If such allegations are proven to be true, we only hope criminal charges are filed. In our last issue we told you that we bore no animosity toward Fine Print. Perhaps we believed in them more than their own employees did.

Obviously, since you're reading this, we managed to get this issue printed and sent out. If it's still winter by the time you see this, it means we really hauled ass and pulled off a minor miracle. The moral support we have received on this

MILESTONE: DISTRIBUTOR UPDATE *(continued)*

journey is more valuable than anything tangible could ever be. We'll always be indebted to our readers for that.

We'll be facing all kinds of challenges and hurdles in the months and years ahead that hopefully won't be so tied into our very survival. When these happen, we need to be able to stay focused on the issues and not be distracted by the mundane. Because if the present is any indication of what the future will be like, we will need as much strength as we can garner. We hope you're looking forward to it as much as we are.

Audio Mischief

Another major community of hackers lies in the radio world. People who play with radio, learn how to communicate across vast distances, assemble and configure equipment to make it do incredible things; these are all hacker qualities. And of course, so is figuring out how to listen to signals that are coming over the airwaves, despite any restrictions that may be in the way. Radio hackers have a long history of monitoring everyone from law enforcement to ham radio to shortwave to fast food drive-thrus. And, of course, the act of just "listening in" is also of great interest to hackers everywhere. This is why a lot of them turn into really good private eyes.

How to Listen In (Autumn, 1994) *By Q*

This article relates to the field of surveillance. I will not digress into an explanation as to the great importance of surveillance to the serious hacker or phreaker, nor will I attempt to delve into the many legalities regarding this field, as a whole book could be written on this fascinating and important topic. While reading this article, the question might arise as to what surveillance has to do with the field of hacking, phreaking, and computer security. Without getting technical, the answer is simply "everything." As a professional in the surveillance and countermeasures field as well as being an avid telephone phreak and "network traveler," I have found that my professional line of work in surveillance greatly complements my explorations in hacking and phreaking.

The following information is only a partial listing of the many devices that are available to the general public. There are many more advanced methods developed and utilized by federal agencies with one sole purpose, and that is to spy upon innocent Americans.

Long-Range Listening Devices

- **Shotgun Microphones:** A shotgun microphone consists of a long tube either of metal or plastic with a length of 12 to 36 inches. One end of the tube is open while the other end consists of a super-sensitive microphone. The microphone is surrounded by a damper to eliminate vibrations of the tube being picked up. The microphone is connected to a powerful handheld amplifier that usually contains a low pass audio filter to cut out low frequency sounds such as wind and vibrations. The shotgun microphone is extremely directional. A top of the line model can pick up ordinary voices from ¾ of a mile away.
- **Parabolic Microphones:** A parabolic microphone consists of a "dish" composed of metal or plastic with a diameter of 12 to 32 inches. The dish focuses sound waves onto a center focal point an inch above the reflector dish. This sound is picked up by an extremely sensitive microphone and is sent to an amplifier with a low pass audio filter to eliminate wind noise. A top of the line parabolic dish can pick up ordinary voices from over one mile away. As a note, the pattern of pickup is much wider with a parabolic dish so it picks up more background noise than a shotgun microphone would, however the range is considerably greater.
- **Laser Listeners:** This is a truly remarkable and complex device that picks audio by demodulating the interference patterns in a laser or microwave beam. A simple system consists of a 15-milliwatt laser. The laser beam is aimed at a piece of glass such as a window. Whenever someone talks, the audio waves vibrate the window a minute amount. As the glass vibrates, it modulates the laser beam much in the same manner that a transmitter modulates voices onto a radio wave. A collector on the receiving unit captures the reflection from the light bounced off the window and an electronic circuit demodulates the collected light and amplifies the audio producing the voices of the subjects under surveillance. Low-end units have a range of 60 feet, while top-of-the-line units can pick up audio from over 500 feet away. High-end systems utilize multiple laser and/or microwave beams to cancel out noise caused by wind. In addition, mylar reflectors are utilized. These reflectors are an inch wide and allow an increased reception range.

Through-Wall Listening Devices

- **Contact Microphones:** A contact mike is a sensitive microphone utilizing a unique principal that listens for vibrations rather than sound waves. It usually consists of a piece of piezoelectric material that produces an electric current that is modulated by vibrations caused by audio. The contact microphone is coupled to a powerful handheld amplifier either as an integral or separate unit. Contact microphones can clearly pick up a voice through up to 12 inches of concrete or 3 inches of solid wood.

- **Spike Microphones:** A spike microphone consists of a supersensitive crystal or electret microphone, and is coupled to a 2- to 12-inch metal spike. This metal spike is driven into the wall and picks up resonations from the wall very clearly. The audio signal from the microphone is then fed into a powerful handheld amplifier.
- **Tube Microphones:** A tube microphone consists of a small 2- to 12-inch hollow metal tube approximately ⅛th of an inch in diameter. The tube microphone is placed into a hole in the wall or through an air duct, etc. and picks up sounds coming from directly in front of it. The sound resonates inside the small diameter tube and is amplified by resonation. The audio then reaches a sensitive microphone on one end of the tube. The electric signal from the microphone is then amplified by a powerful handheld amplifier.

Hardwired Room Microphones

Occasionally the placement of a transmitter aka "bug" is impossible, impractical, or unnecessary. In certain situations it may only be necessary to use a wired remote microphone. Police often use this technique in hotels when engaged in sting operations. Typically, one hotel room is used as the setup room, and an adjacent room contains the surveillance listening post.

- **Microphone with In-line Amplifier:** This technique simply consists of a miniature microphone hidden about the target's room. This microphone is then wired into the adjacent surveillance room via an air duct or a hole in the wall. When the microphone is to be placed over 50 feet from the listening post, a miniature in-line amplifier is used to boost the audio signal, and increase the microphone's sensitivity.
- **Hidden Wire-Line Microphone:** This is a clever technique similar to the above method, only a pre-existing wire is utilized so as to avoid detection. Usually an electret microphone is hidden inside a splice block, modular phone jack, coaxial cable, intercom wire, or an alarm sensor element, and is connected to a pair of alarm or telephone wires. The listening post simply taps into the wire pair and can monitor all sound within the target room.
- **Fine Wire Laying Kits:** This is an old but very advanced technique of hardwiring a microphone that was extensively used by government agencies. It utilizes ultra-thin coated wires, similar to magnetic winding wire. This wire can

be laid and run throughout a room or house and remain undetected indefinitely. A fine wire-laying tool is used to spool the wire, as it is laid. This wire can be placed into cracks in the floorboard and under carpet, as well as behind moldings. After laying, a small amount of silicone or beeswax is used to hold the fine wires in place. Advanced fine wire kits utilize a three wire system, where two of the wires are intertwined and the third is run alongside. This eliminates any RF emission from the wire, making it extremely difficult to detect.

- **Hookswitch Bypass:** This is an old but very effective technique to monitor room audio by bypassing or shorting out the hang-up switch on a telephone receiver making the phone "hot-on-hook." The room audio can then be monitored by simply tapping into the subject's telephone wire pair.
- **Telephone Line Microphone:** This method is similar to the hidden wire-line technique. Only the telephone equipment is used to hide and transmit the room audio. A simple electret microphone could be placed inside a modular phone jack, or perhaps connected somewhere along the line in the target's room, picking up all of the room sounds, when the telephone is not in use. The listening post then taps into the subject's wire pair. A specialized audio filter is then used to strip off the dial tone.
- **Coaxial Cable Microphone:** This device consists of a microphone placed onto a television coaxial cable. This method is subject to interference, and there are much better methods discussed later in this article.

Transmitters aka "Bugs"

Transmitters, often referred to as "bugs" or, when worn on the body, as "wires," are perhaps the most commonly known form of surveillance. This equipment is also the subject of the most misinformation and exaggeration created by the media and Hollywood. Bugs come in a variety of sizes ranging from the size of a beeper to slightly smaller than your pinky fingernail. The greatest falsity created by Hollywood is that bugs can transmit at a range of miles. This is entirely false; bugs transmit on the order of feet, not miles. Typically, bugs can transmit between 75 and 2,000 feet. Another misconception is that the greater the range, the better. While a greater range is certainly more convenient, it leaves the bugged conversations open to accidental interception. Bugs are often prepackaged in various innocuous household items such as RJ-11 telephone jacks and electrical outlets, and can also be carried on your person concealed in fountain pens, calculators, watches, beepers, lighters, etc.

- **FM Transmitters:** These are the most commonly available bugs that amateurs can obtain and lawfully use. They operate at a frequency range of 88–130 MHz, and have a power output of between 10 and 100 mW. High level amateurs will usually want to transmit on the 109–130 MHz air band because that frequency can only be picked up on a wide band scanner. FM bugs use a circuit called a free-running oscillator for convenience. This allows the bugs to be tuned on a variety of chosen frequencies. The main problem with operating within the FM radio band is the strong background emissions from commercial radio stations. If the signal from the bug is too weak, it will be ignored by the receiver in favor of the stronger commercial signal. FM bugs are also subject to interference from aircraft.

- **VHF Transmitters:** VHF transmitters are occasionally used by law-enforcement personnel and amateurs. They operate at anywhere between 130 MHz and 450 MHz. They either have free running oscillators or are crystal controlled.
- **UHF transmitters:** Almost all professionals or law enforcement personnel use UHF transmitters. These operate at much higher frequencies, between 400 MHz and 3 GHz. UHF units are always crystal controlled and operate on a very narrow bandwidth. As a result of the higher transmission frequencies coupled with a narrow bandwidth, these UHF units are free from interference caused by commercial RF background signals and natural anomalies. The transmission range is typically three to five times further than their free-oscillating counterparts.
- **Wafer Transmitters:** Wafer transmitters are the most exotic devices ever designed. They are extremely small in size and do not even require an internal power source. They are specially designed transmitters that are powered by strong highly directional RF signals, usually in the microwave range. These powerful signals charge up the circuits of the wafer transmitter. The range of these devices is not very far, but they are extremely small, being no larger than the size of your pinky fingernail. There is another unique type of listening device often categorized as a wafer transmitter that operates on a principal similar to a laser listener. A strong highly directional microwave RF signal is aimed at a target's area. This type of bug simply consists of a very small special piece of material that is flexible and will be modulated by voice waves, and is highly reflective to microwave signals. When room audio is present the wafer transmitter will vibrate. This in turn will modulate the microwave signals that are being beamed into the area. The receiver simply demodulates the reflected microwave signals, producing the audio which was present in the target's room. This technique is extremely high-level and was believed to have been invented by the Russians, who developed this type of device and used it to spy on the American Embassy in the USSR.

- **Crystal Controlled vs. Free Oscillating:** Free running oscillators are always used on lower grade bugs. FROs can be tuned through a great range of frequencies for convenience. This type of circuit suffers from three main problems: the first being that the signals are untuned and can produce spurious outputs and harmonics, which allow the frequency to drift, making reception somewhat difficult if the signal is weak. In addition, harmonics allow the signal to be picked up on alternate frequencies by "ghost" images of the signal. The second problem is the weak power output of the circuit. The signal of an FRO is not maximized for any one frequency. As a result, the power output is not as high. And third, an untuned circuit is not as efficient and uses more power, resulting in a shorter operating lifetime and a higher operating current. Crystal controlled units, however, are locked on one particular frequency and, as a result, apply all of their energy to a very narrow bandwidth, making the crystal controlled circuit very efficient. This higher efficiency allows a greater power output per size ratio compared to an FRO. In addition, the highly tuned circuit produces no harmonics, spurious emissions, and no frequency drift, allowing a much greater receiving distance. The power supplies of crystal controlled units typically last 5 to 10 times longer than FROs.
- **Mains vs. Battery Powered:** All transmitters are of two types, the first being battery powered. Typically, a battery powered device will last between one day and three weeks, depending upon the efficiency, the power output, and whether the device is free oscillating or crystal controlled. Mains powered devices are powered by anything but batteries. Mains powered transmitters usually come prepackaged into wall outlets or plug adapters. But a clever surveillance expert can wire a transmitter up to anything that runs on house power producing either AC or DC electricity, such as thermostats, intercom wires, alarm wires, and anything else you can think of.
- **Remote Activation and VOX:** To extend the lifetime of battery powered bugs, the transmitter must have the ability to turn itself off when not in use. This is done in one of two ways: by remote activation or by VOX (a voice actuation circuit). Remote activation utilizes a special receiver on the transmitter. When the signal is given by the listening post, a particular bug will either turn on or off. A better method is to utilize a voice actuation circuit referred to as a VOX. When a voice of sufficient amplitude is present around the bug, the transmitter will automatically turn on. Both of the aforementioned techniques use a very small amount of current to operate the activation circuits. VOX activated transmitters can have a lifetime of up to one month. Aside from conserving power, an actuation circuit serves another purpose and is useful on both mains devices and battery powered devices. That purpose is to prevent detection of

the device. If a transmitter is left running constantly it has a much greater chance of being discovered by various means, including accidental interception on a scanner. A remotely or VOX activated bug is extremely hard to detect except by using advanced countermeasures equipment. If a bug is not activated, then it cannot be detected by conventional transmitter detectors. Specialized devices such as non-linear junction detectors, or a simpler device that feeds an audio source into the room to activate the device, can be used in conjunction with a standard bug detector.

- **Advanced Modulation Techniques:** Very advanced bugs are utilized only by government intelligence agencies. Very high-level bugs operate using odd modulation techniques that cannot be demodulated by an ordinary scanner. These odd modulation transmissions also allow for a greater transmission range due to their very nature.
- **Frequency Hopping Transmitters:** One method developed to prevent accidental interception or discovery of a bug by a countermeasures expert is to rapidly alter the frequency at a preset rate. This makes it nearly impossible to receive the transmission by accident or on purpose. Even if one knew the various frequencies that this bug operated on, it would be impossible to hear any audio. The reason is that the frequency hopper alters the frequency at such a rapid rate that a modern digital wideband receiver would be too slow to lock onto the signal. All that would be heard is a popping sound for a brief fraction of a second. It takes a specialized multi-crystal, multifrequency receiver to receive this type of signal.
- **Scrambled Transmitters:** Scrambled transmitters encrypt the audio signal before it is transmitted, using various methods including the very simple frequency inversion technique, as well as utilizing much more sophisticated methods. If anyone were to intercept a coded signal, the speech would be unintelligible. A special receiver is needed to decrypt the signal.
- **Spread Spectrum Transmitters:** Spread spectrum transmission is a fairly sophisticated method of preventing interception of the signal. The RF signal is transmitted on an extremely wide bandwidth. If anyone were to intercept the bug's signal with a wideband receiver, they would hear only an extremely small portion of the transmitted audio. In order to hear the bug's signal one would need several receivers operating simultaneously, each picking up a separate band of audio. A special ultra-wideband receiver is needed to pick up transmissions from this type of bug.
- **Wideband Transmitters:** Similar in operation to the spread spectrum transmitter, this type of device operates on a slightly smaller bandwidth. The signals from this type of bug can be picked up on high-end scanners, which have a wide band FM (WFM) mode.

- **Narrow Band Transmitters:** Narrow band transmitters have a smaller bandwidth than ordinary RF transmissions. The signal from this type of bug can be picked up on high-end receivers with a narrow band FM (NFM) mode.
- **Sliver Band Transmitters:** This is an advanced form of bug that transmits the signal over an extremely small bandwidth. A special ultra-narrow band receiver is needed to demodulate the audio signal.
- **Subcarrier Transmitters:** Subcarrier transmitters use an advanced transmission technique to prevent accidental reception and detection of the RF signal. A subcarrier is a type of hidden signal that is modulated piggy-back style on a regular radio signal, both operating on the same frequency. One cannot receive a subcarrier signal with a standard receiver. It takes a special receiver or device connected to a receiver to "strip away" the hidden subcarrier signal. This makes the transmission secure from being received by ordinary persons. One of the problems with subcarriers is inefficiency. The subcarrier is only about 10 percent as strong as the main parent signal. Meaning that it requires a great deal of electric power to transmit a signal of sufficient strength. As a result, the batteries on this type of device usually do not last very long. Most subcarrier bugs are "mains" operated, meaning they operate using household A.C. power. Using utility power, the device has an infinite lifetime and can transmit a much stronger signal. An example of a subcarrier signal is elevator music. This music is transmitted by a regular radio station, on their subcarrier signal. Another example is the closed caption for the hearing impaired on television transmissions. You cannot see the closed caption words because it takes a special subcarrier decoder to demodulate them.

Carrier Current Devices

Carrier current devices are a combination of technologies. They are a cross between wired microphones and subcarrier transmitters. The only difference is that the signal is not transmitted via radio waves, but rather through a wire pair. A person cannot accidentally intercept or detect a carrier current signal by simply tapping into a wire like with wired microphones. A carrier current device works by picking up room audio through a microphone. The signal from the microphone is then modulated by a low frequency circuit, which produces a carrier current signal at approximately 100–200 kHz. A common example of carrier current devices are the newer wireless telephones, intercoms, or baby monitor type devices that plug into the electric socket and use the pre-existing wiring rather than having wiring run all over the house. A special circuit, which can demodulate the low frequency signal, is used as the receiver. Carrier current devices require no batteries, as they are powered by the mains. Only a sophisticated receiver with a low frequency probe can detect this sort of device.

- **Powerline Carrier Current Device:** Powerline carrier current devices are usually placed inside of wall outlets and are clipped to the powerline. These types of devices are often pre-packaged inside of wall outlets. All that is necessary is to replace the old wall socket for the "modified" wall socket. The receiver can occasionally be placed at any point along the powerline, but usually it has to be on the same side of the utility company power transformer. This is by far the most common form of carrier current device.
- **Telephone Line Carrier Current Device:** This type of carrier current device is usually prepackaged inside of modular phone jacks, and then you simply swap the old jack for the new one during the installation process. Telco carrier current devices also can be purchased as separate units that are approximately ½ an inch in diameter and are clipped onto the phone line with alligator clips.
- **Piezoelectric Coaxial Microphone:** This is perhaps the most ingenious method ever invented for intercepting room audio. Unlike the hidden wired-line method, which utilizes a microphone to pick up sounds and then transmits the audio down a set of wires, this device consists of a length of coaxial wire 2 to 6 feet in length, which contains a thin layer of piezoelectric shielding that is sensitive to vibrations produced by sounds. When audio vibrations are detected by the piezoelectric material, an electric audio signal is sent down the cable wire. All one has to do is tap into the coax at any point and the target's room audio can be heard. An agent simply replaces the pre-existing wire for the "special" wire. Even though the audio is quite easily intercepted, this method will escape detection by even the greatest TSCM (Technical Surveillance Countermeasures) experts, because very few people know of this method (until now!).

Infinity Transmitters

This is one of the most diverse and useful pieces of surveillance equipment. It is a room audio monitoring device designed to operate on your telephone line. Unlike a bug that can only receive the signal at a finite distance, the infinity transmitter can work at an infinite distance. The design of this device has varied greatly over the years with the advancement of telephones. The device is placed inside of a telephone jack or a telephone itself, and is connected in series to the line. To operate the device, you call the target's house and before the phone rings once, the infinity device answers the phone. You temporarily activate the device using a touch-tone code. This puts the device in a stand-by mode. You then have a brief amount of time to enter an access code consisting of two or three touch-tone digits. If the code is correct the device will be activated and an audio path is established. You will hear all of the sounds within a particular room. Note: If a person does not enter the correct access code then the device will not activate and calls will go through as normal. Infinity transmitters lost a bit of popularity after telephone companies switched to electronic switching systems (ESS). Under crossbar switching systems, telephone lines possessed an audio path between the calling and destination points even if the destination line had not answered the phone.

- **Hook-Switch Bypass:** This is one of the most popular surveillance devices of the past. They are not as useful today, because of the switchover to ESS. The "hot-on-hook" technique involved placing a microphone on the target's telephone line, or shorting out the hang-up switch of a phone so that it picked up room audio even when the phone was hung up, and that room audio would be sent down the line. To activate a hot-on-hook device one would call the target's house and enter a touch-tone code before the first or second ring. That code would activate a circuit, which would stop the ringing, and activate the microphone, which would send the target's room audio down the line. The surveillance technician could listen to the line without ever being charged for the call, because the phone was never actually answered. However this type is defunct, because nowadays, under ESS, a device cannot be activated on the target's line until the target answers. This is because ESS never actually connects the two line pairs together until the destination line is answered. Modern infinity devices have found ways around this limit, mainly by having a circuit that answers the phone by itself. You can create a simple hot-on-hook device by placing a microphone on the phone line and listening at some point down the line with a high impedance telephone tap.
- **Dialup DTMF Activated:** This is similar to the device described above. You can have multiple infinity devices in one house connected to each phone, each using a different activation code. Each device can be switched on at any time during the monitoring process.

Slaves and Loop Extenders

Modular telephone taps, often referred to as a slave unit and loop extenders (LEs) are more advanced models of the infinity transmitters. They utilize various multiple line and dial-out techniques. A slave is generally any device that bridges two lines together by a capacitively coupled circuit.

- **Dual Line Bridge Slave:** A dual line bridge is a simple connection between two wire pairs. The target's line is bridged at some point along the telephone line, such as an entrance bridge, 99 block, junction or splice box, or a cross-connect-cabinet to a pre-existing or leased line specifically ordered for surveillance purposes.

- **Multiline Dial-Out Slave Infinity Device:** This unit is a slightly more advanced type of device that utilizes two phone lines that are bridged across the line pairs at some point. There are two versions of this type of device. The first is a room monitor that is placed within the target's premises and is either built into the telephone or is hidden in a phone jack. The device is actuated by voices through a VOX circuit, which dials out to the listening post on a second line not used or owned by the target. The second is a telephone monitoring device, which can be placed at any point along the telephone line, such as at 99 blocks, entrance bridges, splice boxes, junction boxes, and cross-connect-cabinets. The target's line pair is bridged onto another line usually owned or leased by the surveillance expert. When the target attempts to use his telephone or a call is received, this slave unit automatically dials out on another line to the listening post, which enables the surveillance expert to monitor and record the target's phone calls.
- **Advanced Dial-Out Slave Infinity Device:** A third more advanced type of unit is simply a combination of the above two that incorporates voice infinity and telephone infinity transmission. Units may be a combination of dial out or dial in. Typically the dial out function is for telephone, and the dial in function is for room monitoring.
- **Remote Listening Post Infinity Device:** This is the most advanced and diverse type of slave infinity device that utilizes multiple telephone lines as well as radio receivers, and a built-in tape recording unit, which is all microprocessor controlled. This unit is an all-in-one surveillance infinity monitoring system.
- **Loop Extenders:** These devices are too complex to discuss in detail in this brief article.

Telephone Taps and Transmitters

- **Hardwired Tap:** A hardwire tap, which is commonly referred to as wiretapping, is the easiest and oldest form of monitoring telephone conversations. All that is needed is a pair of mono headphones with the jack cut off and replaced with alligator clips, or a lineman's handset (often referred to as a butt set). A phreak might refer to a lineman's handset as a beige box. An individual can tap into a phone line at virtually any place along the line including entrance bridges, 99 blocks, junction boxes, and cross-connect-cabinets. This type of tap is extremely simple and can be performed by even an amateur. If a permanent tap is left in place by running a wire to the listening post, and is too close to the target's residence or office, it could be detected by physical search or with advanced equipment such as TDRs or phone analyzers, if countermeasures sweeps were performed.

- **Inductive Coupled Line Pick Up:** This is virtually the same type of hardwire tap as above, however no direct connection is actually made to the line. An inductive probe is simply clipped around the telephone wire and the emanations from the wire are picked up by the probe. Since no actual electrical contact is made during the tap, not even the most advanced equipment could detect such devices. As with the hardwire tap, if a permanent induction tap is left in place too close to the target's residence or office, a thorough physical search could find the tap.
- **Series Transmitter:** A series transmitter is a bugging type of device that monitors phone conversations instead of room audio. This type of device is connected in series to the phone line and never requires batteries because it draws its power from the phone line itself. The range is not as great with series transmitters as it is with parallels, however its virtually infinite lifetime is an advantage. The frequency and power output of telephone transmitters is virtually the same as for standard room bugs. Series transmitters occasionally incorporate an automatic activation switch that turns the device on only when a telephone conversation is taking place.
- **Parallel Transmitter:** A parallel transmitter hooks to the phone lines in parallel, which enables the transmitter to be simply clipped on without breaking any connections. The power output of parallel telephone transmitters is a bit higher than with series devices usually by 20 to 50 milliwatts. However, parallel devices must use their own power source, usually a 1.5–12 volt battery. The frequencies are identical to that of series telephone taps and room bugs. The lifetime of these devices is finite and can only operate constantly for two to five days. Higher quality models almost always incorporate an automatic activation circuit, which will turn the device on only when the telephone being monitored is in use. This additional circuit extends the lifetime of the tap from three weeks to a month.
- **Advanced Transmitters:** This advanced type of tap is a combination of series and parallel circuits and bridging. When the phone is not in use the parallel circuit "trickle charges" a rechargeable battery. The device contains an automatic activation circuit and when the phone is being monitored by lifting the handset from the base, the series circuit activates and transmits using the self contained battery. This device yields the higher RF output of a series device while having a virtually unlimited battery lifetime similar to a parallel device.

Super Miniature Tape Recorders

Super miniature tape recorders are extremely useful devices for surveillance purposes. They have many uses: primarily recording conversations pertaining to illegal or civil matters, which can be either used as evidence in a court of law or simply to alert law enforcement personnel. Recording devices vary greatly in size, recording quality, as well as other important features. Top of the line models designed and manufactured specifically for surveillance purposes can cost several thousand dollars.

- **Size Specifications:** Super-miniature recorders designed specifically for surveillance are generally much smaller than tape recorders available for consumer purposes. Many of the features available on consumer recorders are not necessary on covert surveillance recorders. Only the most important features are designed into these super small recorders in order to save space. High-level recorders never have built in speakers, since speakers take up a considerable amount of space and serve no purpose on a recorder. To play back the recorded media, a separate speaker and amplifier playback unit is used.
- **Electronic Shut Off:** Surveillance recorders almost always incorporate electronic shut off. The mechanical shut off buttons are too bulky, and more importantly make too much noise when the tape automatically is shut off. Should a surveillance recorder ever shut off automatically, the loud click of the mechanical button could make the subject being recorded very suspicious.
- **Silenced Motors:** In typical consumer micro-miniature recorders, the tape drive motors can produce a sufficient amount of unwanted noise. Surveillance recorders contain extremely quiet motors that cannot be heard even in the quietest atmosphere.
- **Altered Bias Oscillator Frequency:** This is perhaps the most advanced feature of surveillance recorders. When recording a subject, every precaution must be made to avoid detection and suspicion. If the person under surveillance is an expert in surveillance or if he is particularly suspicious, then the subject could use a counter-surveillance device that detects tape recorders. This antibugging device detects the emanations from the bias-oscillator of a tape recorder within a certain range. These devices can detect a tape recorder from up to several feet away. A true surveillance recorder will alter its bias oscillator frequency so that it cannot be detected by the aforementioned countermeasures device, rendering it undetectable. Tape recorders that alter the bias-oscillator frequency must contain special audio compression circuits to compensate for the effects of the altered circuit.

- **Multitrack Recording:** High-end recorders will usually have several tracks for recording. Two tracks are usually for the stereo signal and the third is for time coding or reference signals.
- **Extended Play:** Surveillance recorders often are required to record for extended periods of time. Rather than using longer tapes, the recording speed is slowed down. This results in a bit of distortion, so extended play recorders incorporate compensation circuitry.

Nagra Magnetic Recorders Inc. is the leader in manufacturing surveillance recorders. Their top of the line model is the Nagra JBR, which contains all of the advanced features described. Its dimensions are 110×62×20 mm and it weighs 143 grams.

The National RNZ 36 is one of the smallest units ever produced, however it does not contain several advanced features necessary in high security situations. This unit has a three-hour extended recording time. Its dimensions are 85×54×14 mm making it nearly as small as a credit card.

Trunking Communications Monitoring (Autumn, 1998)

By TELEgodzilla

The powerful marriage of computers and radio communications created a new child of the twenty-first century: *trunked radio systems*. Trunked radio communications allot multiple users to all available channels/frequencies through a series of user programmed controls. Conventional radios traditionally limit user access to their assigned channel grouping (channel 1 to repeater 1, channel 2 to repeater 2, etc.). Whereas trunking allots full implementation of all available channels' frequencies at any given moment while yet allowing full system programming. Note how the term "trunking" is used: it's from (you guessed it) telephone trunking.

In trunking, "talkgroups" (groups of radios programmed to speak to one another) are the norm. Individual radios are programmed via a typical PC (usually a laptop to allow for ease of portability). Each trunked radio holds a computer chip allowing for a "personality" programming. Groups of radios can be programmed by creating "profiles"—usually in minutes—and rapidly duplicated or, if need be, individually tailored. System users, thus, better employ the number of channel sets their overall system employs. In many instances, a typical trunked system can carry over 3,000 user-specific talkgroups allowing for several hundred radios to be assigned to each individual talkgroup.

Trunked communications employs precision computer control, enhancing system efficiency. Trunking controls to whom and for how long each user can talk as well as the priority each user possesses. "Dumping" or "crowding" is far less likely to occur on a trunked radio system than any other and waiting time is dramatically reduced.

Users are "queued" and stored in memory. Users with higher priorities are enabled to be put on the air quicker than others (based upon how the radios are programmed) while data communications (depending upon the model of the system) functions on background operations.

Trunking also allows a system overseer to turn off a (or several) radio(s), should it/they become lost or stolen. When recovering a trunked radio, enjoy it while you can; it generally doesn't take long for that radio to become a useless paperweight with the flick of a remote switch at the System Controller.

Security is enhanced. Digital trunking systems enable full digital communications, ensuring against eavesdropping. Depending upon the make—Motorola and Ericsson are the two top contenders (E.F. Johnson also makes a conventional trunked system, but they're having problems with their design)—there are different approaches and points to consider.

Motorola: Smartnet and Astro

Motorola's two primary trunked systems—Smartnet and Astro—are worlds apart. Smartnet is junk; a recent State of Hawaii court ruling illustrated that Motorola's Smartnet is not, as so defined by trunked communications requirements, a true trunked system (which goes to show that when buying Motorola, stick with their pagers). Agencies using Smartnet can be readily breached via a typical trunked scanner (also known as trunk trackers). Some recommended models are the Uniden Bearcat BC235XLT (handheld) or BC895XLT base scanner), assuming that the Smartnet system in question is actually functioning. There have been a growing number of localities who've had their Smartnet systems ripped out and replaced.

Astro is a tougher nut, but not too many organizations use this system as Astro is expensive and is non-compartmentalized; in other words, when you buy an Astro, you gotta buy everything at one time. Unless an organization has a couple of million to spend every time it needs to upgrade or expand, this is not an economically viable system to obtain.

Ericsson: EDACS

Ericsson systems are choice; if you want a good, reliable system for a decent price and one that'll keep out the weirdoes, get an Ericsson EDACS system. EDACS (Enhanced Digital Access Communications System) is used by the Secret Service Presidential Bodyguard as well as the U.S. Navy's Carrier Strike Force's ship-to-ship communications backbone, and is currently used by Boris Yeltsin's bodyguards. EDACS has been used in Bosnia by U.S. forces because they truly meet military specs, designed to be tossed out the back of a C-130 (via parachute, of course), and ready to be deployed in minutes. EDACS can also be readily enhanced for specific parts or services; one need not buy an entirely new system when you got EDACS.

Ericsson systems use AEGIS encryption. Forget about trying to crack AEGIS; it's NSA (National Security Agency) rated and unless you got heavy iron with massive power and time on your hands (and I mean *lots* of time), you ain't gonna crack it—period. It's not surprising that the feds are always assigned at least one radio to keep their hand in the action, no matter how small or insignificant the locality's trunked radio system is. Don't waste your time; it's not enough to obtain the algorithm as AEGIS is fully digital and unless you have full physical access to the System Controller, you can't listen in.

Trunked radio systems dedicate one frequency out of their total set for the control channel: this control channel constantly transmits each and every transmitter/receiver's own unique programming, thus locking out anyone from "stepping" on the frequency set. If you do tune into the control channel, all you'll get is a rapid sledgehammer sound effect and quite possibly a busted speaker (and headache) if you have your volume up too loud. Accessing it won't do you any good.

All is not lost, however, as encrypted radios are not cheap. They usually go for about $2,000 apiece; most private and public entities, therefore, use the regular unencrypted communications, allowing listeners to employ trunk trackers with no problem. When monitoring trunked systems, remember that you first need to know the frequency set that the system is using. This can be achieved by contacting the FCC and obtaining a listing of frequencies that are being used; this is, after all, public information. Other frequency resources to consider are the Pocket Guide series of frequency directories for selected portions of the United States. Trunked trackers can be readily purchased for as little as $150 on up, if not cheaper. *Make sure that the frequency set you wish to check out is carried on the tracker of your choice.*

Some systems will defeat the trunk tracker, however, by setting up a "tail"—the end of the communications broadcast—to hang a second or two longer; this confuses the tracker and makes it hard to listen in on the action. Many radio managers don't do this kind of thing as this, however, would involve prescience and intelligence on the part of managing a radio system. As with most hierarchical structures, radio controllers tend to be awarded on the basis of obedience and trust, not necessarily of intelligence and initiative.

Utilities (read: telephone), oil refineries, airports, police, fire, and paranoid private/public security forces are among the primary users of trunked systems. Trunking enables system deployers to request a minimal number of frequencies which, through the enlightened vision of our FCC, often costs a lot of money or requires a tremendous waiting time. There are also conventional trunking systems, which piggyback onto regular radio systems; a typical trunk tracker can, however, handle these with no problem.

Radio communications carry a lot of information and trunked systems are the coming wave!

Fast-Food Phun (Summer, 1997) *By VaxBuster*

Before I start into having Phun with Phast Phood, I want to go over a few basic radio items. This will give you a general idea of the type of equipment involved and what kind of radio features you should look for to maximize your hacking potential.

The first thing you want to look for is a ham radio that is dual-band. Whenever you see this word in various ham radio magazines, they are referring to the fact that the radio supports two bands. These bands most often are the 2-meter band (approximately 140–148 MHz) and the 70-cm band (approximately 440–450 MHz). These are both amateur bands and you will mostly hear a bunch of old farts talking about how ridiculous the no-code tech license is.

The most important feature of the radio you're looking for is one that is easily modifiable. How do you know which are? Check out `www.qrz.com`. See, even with a license, the FCC regulates where you can transmit and receive.

While looking through the mods, find one that you are technically capable of performing and also one that gives you transmit and receive capabilities in the following ranges. Note these ranges are approximate:

- 140–174 MHz TX and RX
- 440–475 MHz TX and RX
- 800–900 MHz RX (cellular)

Now although this might not seem like a big range, it is pretty much all you will need. These ranges are broken down into extremely small channels of only a few kilohertz wide. This will give you access to everything from handheld radios, police, fire, ambulance, fast food, cellular, I could go on forever. Now cordless phones operate on 46/49 MHz, but don't go looking for radios that will transmit on there, or transmit on cellular. In general, ham radio rigs won't support these ranges, even after modification. Trust me, you can have a ton of phun if your radio supports the frequencies I listed above. A couple of other important features to look for are CTCSS [Continuous Tone Coded Squelch] (I'll explain this later), DTMF [Dual Tone Multifrequency—touchtone], lots of memory channels, and alpha tagging.

OK, you've bought your radio. It's modified. It works. Now where do you tune to? I'm not going to reprint the 19 lists that are out there on the net. If you do a web search for "fast food frequencies" you'll get plenty of hits. I'll give you a basic idea on where to look when scanning. Remember, when scanning, that the output side of the repeater is almost always broadcasting, meaning that your scanner will stop and you will hear basically an open customer mic on the output frequency.

- Scan 30.xxxx to 35.xxxx for the output side of repeater
- Scan 151.xxxx for the input (clerk) side

- Scan 154.xxxx for the input (clerk) side
- Scan 157.xxxx for the input (clerk) side
- Scan 170.xxxx to 173.xxxx for the input (clerk) side
- Scan 457.xxxx to 469.xxxx for input/output
  FYI: 469.xxxx for output and 464.xxxx for input are popular.

I realize this last range is pretty broad, and I apologize, but this list would be huge if I broke out each individual range.

A radio repeater is basically a device that repeats a signal from one frequency to another. The repeater's antenna is usually placed high atop a mountain or building. The purpose of this is to get line-of-sight to as many points on the ground as possible. Once a signal is received, it is then transmitted out the output frequency at a high rate of power. The purpose of this device is to allow communication among a bunch of low-power radios. Often, these low-power radios have much smaller antennas as to make them more portable.

Fast food repeaters in general operate in this fashion. There is one frequency in which what the customer says is broadcast as well as what the clerk said is broadcast. You'll see me refer to this as the *output* side of the repeater. If you tuned to that frequency on your radio, what you'd hear is the same as if you were standing right next to the speaker at the drive thru. You would hear the entire conversation. This will be your receive frequency.

Now the input side of the repeater is what you will be transmitting on. This frequency is what the clerk actually transmits on, both to talk to other clerks, *and* to talk to the customer. Now, the determining factor on whether or not the repeater transmits the signal to the customer's speaker is PL [Private Line]. This will be the transmitting frequency. Just FYI, if the repeater is using standard frequency pairing, the input frequency is 5 MHz below the output. This is true in the UHF (4xx MHz) band. So if you find the receive frequency at 469.0125, you know the transmit frequency is probably at 464.0125.

The "security" that exists is designed to keep unwanted noise and parties from interfering with the communications and is pretty basic. It is not at all built to withstand hacker attempts to transmit through the repeaters, as I'll show. CTCSS, continuous tone coded squelch system, or PL, as it's more commonly known, is made up of a sub-audible tone that is transmitted in-band along with the communication (usually voice). These low frequency tones must be received by the repeater at the same time as the communication. If the repeater does not receive the proper PL, it in essence ignores your communication by not repeating the signal to the output side of the repeater. If you do transmit the proper PL with your transmission, it will break the repeater's squelch and it will pass on your voice to the output side of repeater. There are a total of 32 PL tones ranging from 67.0 Hz to 250.3 Hz.

As far as fast food is concerned, the PL tones vary from location to location. Since there is no standard, we need a method to find it. Sometime at dinner time, stop by your local joint, and tune to either the output or input side of the repeater. Once you've tuned there, set your CTCSS squelch to ON. We're telling the radio to *only* receive transmissions with the PL you've told it to receive. Since you can change the PL one at a time, you can go through all the possible PLs until you hear a transmission. To do this, select tone-select (or equivalent). A PL tone should appear. Spin your dial to select different PLs. Do this while they are transmitting of course. As soon as a transmission of theirs breaks the squelch, you'll hear the voice. Bingo, you have the proper PL.

Adjust your transmit shift to the proper frequency. Key up. You are now broadcasting loud and clear out the PA speaker. Your voice will definitely override the clerk's because of the fact that your signal is much stronger. Go capture effect!

From this point, feel free to add 20 burgers to the next order taking place, or curse at the customer. Feel free to use a crossband feature to link a McDonald's drive-thru to a Burger King clerk. The fun here is endless.

Standard disclaimers apply. Don't be stupid and you won't get caught.

Become a Radio Ninja (Winter, 1998–1999) *By Javaman*

Recently many of my ninja hacker friends have been asking me for info on one of my big hobbies: radio, or to be more specific, amateur radio. This article will hopefully dispel some of the myths and shed a bit more light on what amateur radio is all about, from "our" perspective.

Before continuing, I have to say that if you spent more time in front of a keyboard and had no interest in playing with a carburetor, never took a VCR apart, and were just a wuss when it came to getting your hands dirty, this is not for you. Amateur Radio is the art of using and designing equipment for communicating on frequency bands that we, as licensed operators, have been granted (more on this licensing stuff later). Although many never test their technical ability, amateurs are encouraged to design and build their own antennas, pick up soldering irons and whip up devices to help get themselves on the air, and take electric shocks from vacuum tube equipment that needs servicing. Once you have a station together, be it handheld, flowing out of the dashboard of your car, or taking up a corner room in your house, there are several ways to modulate your signals.

As it is today, Amateur Radio operators have developed numerous ways to communicate with each other. The most frequent method seen amongst the script kids of radio (people I consider lame because their lust for knowledge ends at what is superficial) is VHF/UHF FM, which basically means local, high quality voice. Most radio geeks start with this mode as well, as I did myself. After time, different modes of communication grabbed my interest, such as satellite (yes, amateurs have their own satellites), HF [High Frequency] Phone, short-wave worldwide communication, ATV or Amateur Television, and packet, or wireless, digital communications.

You can get as deep into any of these facets as you want. Entry level packet radio allows for 1200 or 9600 bps mobile communications. The input to the interfaces, known as a TNC, is standard RS232, with the output being either audio tones for 1200 bps, or a slightly different modulation scheme that does not take well to the microphone jack. For people who want to spend more time on the digital side of things, TAPR, or Tucson Amateur Packet Radio, is always looking for talented engineers to help on their projects, like a 115 kps spread spectrum 900 MHz transceiver, using TCP/IP as the underlying protocol. Input to the rig is Ethernet and output is an antenna. For me, that concept is cool as sh*t. I am a big fan of HF SSB [High Frequency Single Side Band], or worldwide voice communication. During times of good solar activity, I have been able to talk to the remnants of Yugoslavia with little more RF power than it takes to light up a light bulb. Once again, individuals who are hard core into this facet of the hobby may have talked to one person in every single nation on this planet. Morse Code, which is a requirement for higher class licenses, allows you to communicate with very simple equipment. I have seen some Morse Code-only transceivers being built into Altoids tins. It's all well and good that cell phones are that small, but equipment like this was hand built by another amateur. It takes teams of people to design a cell phone. Message boards (think Usenet groups) are ripping around the earth right now, available on only the amateur frequency bands. These birds are built by amateurs for amateurs, and it takes a great deal of talent and skill to communicate with these systems.

Some of you may be asking, "Why not just buy, like, CB radios, and then we will be cool?!" Well, in Amateur Radio, the opportunity to learn about and build a great deal of electronics presents itself. Unlike CB, or Citizens Band, where you must purchase a pre-approved radio that has only 40 channels and allows 4 watts out (that is 36dBm, for those with RF in the blood), Amateur Radio operators are encouraged to build their own equipment, and are permitted to radiate a maximum of 1500 watts in pursuit of long-distance communication. *Note*: This much power is rarely needed, except in moonbounce. Yes, it is possible to bounce your signals off the Earth's largest satellite.

I seem to be getting off track from my main point. The reason why most of us installed Linux, then further installed a BSD variant or BeOS, was to learn about a new OS. This is a hobby that encourages you to design and construct innovative circuits. To build anything permanent, you will need soldering skills. This is not for the weak of heart, or those who think that coding is good since you can't be hurt. You may inflict pain here. This is all in the spirit of learning and innovation. Innovation brings faster methods of communication. Communication is good.

Now, as I mentioned before, you need a license. I realize that half of you rootshell brats are thinking "Bite me Big Brother, I don't want you to track my 12-year-old hide with a license, yo, cause I'm leet like dat." The test required to get the license is multiple choice and the question pools are published. (*Note*: The manuals are available at Radio Shack. The entry level test does not require Morse Code anymore.) You stand to learn more from studying for your amateur radio tests than from a lot of high school physics classes. Don't get a license and you piss people off. Get a license and you learn something and are able to put a good hobby on your resume. Probably the main reason why I have my job right now is because of the road I started upon when I was 14 and receiving my Tech-No Code license.

I realize that I cannot cover all the material that should be discussed, but hopefully this will provide you with a good starting point.

Fire up your copy of Mosaic or Lynx for these URLs:

- The largest Amateur Radio club, the ARRL, or Amateur Radio Relay League: `www.arrl.org`
- Tucson Amateur Packet Radio (TAPR): `www.tapr.org/`
- If you have a scanner, here are the frequencies that amateurs are allowed to operate on: `www.arrl.org/field/regulations/bands.html`

Hopefully I am going to help open a door for some of you. This is another opportunity to learn, and when I was a young one crackin the sh*t on a C64, that was my only goal.

Miscellaneous Things to Play With

This ought to give you a decent idea of how much stuff there is out there to hack. Whether it's figuring out how credit cards work, looking at an envelope and learning the entire postal system, "unshredding" documents, or just hacking stuff you never really thought could be hacked, it's all a part of the same basic culture. And like any bit of knowledge that gets spread around, it could be used for good or for evil. There are those who believe that the mere *possibility* that some information could be used in a harmful way is reason enough to restrict access to it. This mentality is everything the hacker world is fighting against and this fierce opposition is possibly the one ideal that holds us all together. Look carefully at each of these examples and see how hard you have to struggle to find the good applications that can come from the knowledge contained in each.

An Algorithm for Credit Cards (Autumn, 1990)

By Crazed Luddite & Murdering Thug

K00l/RaD Alliance!

As some of you know, the credit card companies (Visa, MC, and American Express) issue card numbers that conform to a type of checksum algorithm. Every card number will conform to this checksum, but this is not to say that every card number that passes this checksum is valid and can be used, it only means that such a card number can be issued by the credit card company.

Often this checksum test is used by companies that take credit cards for billing. It is often the first step in checking card validity before attempting to bill the card; however, some companies stop here. Some companies only check the first digit and the card number length, others use this very convenient algorithm, while others continue on to check the bank ID portion of the card number with a database to see if it is a valid bank. These tests are designed to weed out customers who simply conjure up a card number. If one were to try to guess at an Amex number by using the right format (starts with 3 and 15 digits long), only about 1 in 100 guesses would pass the checksum algorithm.

Why do companies use the algorithm for verification instead of doing an actual credit check? First, it's much quicker (when it's done by computer). Second, it doesn't cost anything. Some credit card companies and banks charge merchants each time they wish to bill or verify a card number, and if a merchant is in a business where a lot of phony numbers are given for verification, this can become rather costly for them. It is a known fact that most, if not all, online services (i.e, Compuserve, Genie, etc.) use this method when processing new sign-ups. Enough said about this, you take it from there.

The majority of transactions between credit card companies and merchants take place on a monthly, weekly, or bi-weekly basis. Such bulk transactions are much less expensive to the merchants. Often a company will take the card number from a customer, run it through the algorithm for verification, and bill the card at the end of the month. This can be used to your advantage, depending on the situation.

If you trade card numbers with your friends, this is a quick way to verify the numbers without having to call up the credit card company and thus leave a trail. Also, a few 1-800 party line type services use this algorithm exclusively because they don't have a direct link to credit card company computers and need to verify numbers real fast. Since they already have the number you're calling from through ANI, they don't feel it necessary to do a complete credit check. I wonder if they ever heard of pay phones.

Here's how the algorithm works. After the format is checked (correct first digit and correct number of digits), a 21212121...weighing scheme is used to check the whole card number. Here's the English pseudocode:

```
check equals 0
go from first digit to last digit
product equals value of current digit
if digit position from end is odd
then multiply product by 2
if product is 10 or greater
then subtract 9 from product
add product to check
end loop
if check is divisible by 10, then card passed checksum test
```

Here is a program written in C to perform the checksum on a Visa, AMEX, or MC card. This program can be easily implemented in any language, including ACPL, BASIC, COBOL, FORTRAN, PASCAL or PL/I. This program may be modified, with the addition of a simple loop, to generate credit card numbers that pass the algorithm within certain bank prefixes (i.e., Citibank). If you know the right prefixes, you can actually generate valid card numbers (90 percent of the time).

```
/* CC Checksum Verification Program
   by Crazed Luddite and Murdering Thug
   of the K00l/RaD Alliance! (New York, London, Paris, Prague.)
   Permission is given for free distribution.
   "Choose the lesser of two evils.  Vote for Satan in '92"
*/

#include <stdio.h>
main()
{
char cc[20];
int check, len, prod, j;
printf("\nAmex/MC/Visa Checksum Verification Program");
printf("\nby Crazed Luddite & Murdering Thug\n");
for(;;)
{
printf("\nEnter Card Number [w/o spaces or dashes.] (Q to quit)\n:");
scanf("%s",cc);
if ((cc[0]=='Q')||(cc[0]=='q')) break;  /* exit infinite loop, if 'Q' */

/* Verify Card Type */

if ((cc[0]!='3')&&(cc[0]!='4')&&(cc[0]!='5'))
```

```
      {
       printf("\nCard number must begin with a 3, 4, or 5.");
       continue;
      }
    else if ((cc[0]=='5')&&(strien(cc)!=16))
      { printf("\nMastercard must be 16 digits.");
        continue;
      }
    else if ((cc[0]=='4')&&(strien(cc)!=13)&&(strien(cc)!=16))
      { printf("\nVisa numbers must be 13 or 16 digits.");
        continue;
      }
    else if ((cc[0]=='3')&&(strien(cc)!15))
      { printf("\nAmerican Express numbers must be 15 digits.");
        continue;
      }

    /* Perform Checksum - Weighing list 2121212121212121.... */

    check = 0;                          /* reset check to 0 */
    len = strien(cc);
    for (j=1;j<=len;j++)                /* go through entire cc num string */
    {
    prod = cc[j-1]-'0';                 /* convert char to int */
    if ((len-j)%2) prod=prod*2;         /* if odd digit from end, prod=prod*2 */
                                        /* otherwise prod=prod*1 */
    if (prod>=10) prod=prod-9;          /* subtract 9 if prod is >=10 */
    check=check+prod;                   /* add to check */
    }
    if ((check%10)==0)                  /* card good if check divisible by 10 */
    printf("\nCard passed checksum test.");
    else
     printf("\nCard did not pass checksum test.");
    }
   }
```

USPS Hacking (Autumn, 1991) *By The Devil's Advocate*

The U.S. Postal Service (USPS) is just like any other system. It is huge and complicated, with lots of acronyms and technical jargon. It is riddled with inconsistencies, and is prone to human error. Most importantly, it beckons to be explored by that very same bunch who are so fond of creative exploration: Hackers!

POSTNET

The Postal Numeric Encoding Technique (POSTNET) is a bar code system initiated in 1983 to help accelerate the sorting of letter mail by automated equipment. The term "POSTNET" refers to a bar code, which represents either a five digit ZIP code, or a nine digit ZIP+4 code. POSTNET is most often preprinted on business or courtesy reply mail by businesses. POSTNET can also be jet sprayed on envelopes that are processed by an Optical Character Reader (OCR) machine.

POSTNET consists of a combination of 22 long bars and 30 short bars. The 52 bars encode a nine digit ZIP+4 code plus a checksum number. Learning to read POSTNET is easy for anyone familiar with binary. The first and last bars (always long) are guide bars, and play no part in determining the encoded ZIP+4. Each group of five bars after the first guide bar represents one ZIP+4 number. The group consists of a combination of two long bars and three short bars. The position in the group has a corresponding value. The values from left to right are 7-4-2-1-0. A ZIP+4 number is obtained by adding the values of the positions containing the two long bars. The only special case is when the added values equal eleven. In this case, the number represented is zero. POSTNET also includes a checksum number at the end for the purpose of error detection. You can determine what the checksum number should be by adding the numbers of your ZIP+4. The last digit of the resulting sum, when subtracted from 10, will yield the checksum number. For instance, if your ZIP+4 is 11953-0752, then the sum is 1+1+9+5+3+0+7+5+2=33, the last digit of the sum is 3, and the checksum is 10-3=7.

The USPS encourages companies to preprint the ZIP+4 POSTNET on business reply mail by offering reduced postage rates. The advantage of using POSTNET is not only in savings but in speed. Letter mail that uses POSTNET is processed faster and more accurately than mail that does not use POSTNET.

MARK

The MARK facer-canceller serves three purposes:

1. It cancels and postmarks letter mail.
2. It arranges letters so that they all face in the same direction.
3. It separates POSTNET letter mail from mail that does not use POSTNET.

The MARK utilizes fluorescent and phosphorescent detectors that enable it to detect the presence of minute traces of phosphor on stamps, prestamped postcards or envelopes, and meter marks. The MARK is also capable of detecting preprinted Facing Identification Marks (FIM).

FIM

Open any magazine and you will find business reply mail cards inside. Nearly every card will contain a FIM. These six-line bar codes are much taller than POSTNET, but not nearly as wide. They are located at the top of the card, just left of the postage area. The MARK recognizes four types of FIMS:

FIM A	five vertical lines (2,1,2)	Letter uses POSTNET and needs postage. Used for courtesy reply mail.
FIM B	six vertical lines (1,2,2,1)	Letter does not use POSTNET and does not need postage. Used for business reply mail.
FIM C	six vertical lines (2,1,1,2)	Letter uses POSTNET and does not need postage. Used for business reply mail.
FIM D	seven vertical lines (3,1,3)	Letter does not use POSTNET, needs postage, and is OCR readable. Used for courtesy reply window envelopes.

Business reply mail that uses FIM B or FIM C (indicating that no postage is necessary) must also use horizontal bars to indicate that USPS must collect postage from the business to which the mail is addressed. The horizontal bars are located on the right hand side of the cards and allow clerks to easily spot these cards in a tray full of other letters.

The MARK first checks to see that a letter has postage (stamp, meter mark, or FIM). After passing this test, the letter is then canceled, postmarked, and directed to one of eight bins based upon the orientation of the letter and the presence of POSTNET. Four of the eight bins are for POSTNET letter mail, while the other four bins are for mail that does not use POSTNET. Each group of four bins accepts letters according to their orientation. Because letters can enter the machine right side up, upside down, backwards, or forwards, the MARK must have a bin for every possible orientation.

The MARK also utilizes a ninth bin for letters that are rejected by the machine for lack of postage. For example, if a letter does not have postage, and the letter does not have FIM B or FIM C (indicating that no postage is necessary), then the letter will end up in the reject bin. Sometimes letters that do have legitimate postage may end up in the reject bin. If a stamp is not placed in the upper right hand corner of an envelope, then the MARK's sensors may not detect the phosphor, and the letter will be rejected. A clerk manually goes over all of the rejected letters individually to determine why they were not processed.

LSM

The Letter Sorting Machine (LSM) was first used by the USPS in the late 1950s. The huge semiautomatic beast requires a group of operators to sit in front of twelve consoles while letters are zipping by at a rate of one per second. The machine automatically positions a letter in front of an operator, who then has one second to key in the first three digits of the ZIP code. The letter is then whisked away to one of several hundred bins according to the keys that were depressed. If an operator fails to key in anything then the letter will go to a reject bin and will eventually be fed back into the LSM. If an operator happens to key in the wrong code, then a slight possibility exists that the misguided letter will be caught by a clerk before it is shipped. Otherwise, the letter will be delivered to that location, wherever it may be, and will eventually be delivered back again.

LSM places a marker on the back of every letter that is processed. The marker consists of two alphanumeric symbols. The first symbol is always a letter ranging from A to Z. The second symbol is either a letter ranging from A to C, or a number ranging from 1 to 9. The marker can therefore be one of 319 possibilities. The marker may also be one of several different colors, although the color does not indicate any useful information. According to USPS LSM operators, the marker indicates which console processed the letter. However, this information is fairly useless because we still do not know which specific LSM processed the letter. The USPS uses hundreds of LSMs nationwide, and each of those LSMs has twelve consoles. I am uncertain how to translate a specific marker into a specific console, nor do I understand why the marker can be one of 319 possibilities if there are only twelve consoles.

BCS

The Bar Code Sorter (BCS) processes POSTNET letter mail. The BCS is therefore limited to sorting only business reply mail and other high volume mail that incorporates the POSTNET. At a sorting rate of ten letters per second, the BCS is considered slightly faster than your average clerk. The letters must be properly positioned and fed into the machine manually by an operator. This is accomplished by stacking trays of letters received from the MARK onto a feeder unit. The operator does not have to properly position each letter because the letters received from the MARK are already facing the same way.

MLOCR

The Multiline Optical Character Reader (MLOCR) is the latest and most advanced machine in the USPS letter sorting arsenal. This million-dollar monster is capable of reading all of the lines that comprise a letter's address. It then takes this information and compares it against its own internally stored address directory. Finally, an appropriate POSTNET is jet sprayed on the letter so that it can be further processed by a BCS. The purpose of the MLOCR is therefore to spray POSTNET on letters that do not use POSTNET, so that they can be processed by a BCS.

The advantage of the MLOCR is that it can determine an address even if parts of the address are illegible, incorrect, or missing. For instance, if someone forgets to include a ZIP code, or uses the wrong ZIP code by mistake, then the MLOCR can still determine the correct ZIP code by comparing the street, city, and state with its own address directory. It will then spray the letter with the correct ZIP+4 code (the MLOCR will always try to spray the letter with a ZIP+4, even if the letter uses a five digit ZIP code).

Early OCRs could only read type or clearly printed handwriting. In the near future, however, the MLOCR will recognize script as well. The MLOCR is capable of reading the address even if it is skewed (i.e., printed at an angle). The MLOCR does not have the capability of knowing whether or not a letter already has POSTNET, nor can it sort mail according to POSTNET. Therefore, it is possible to receive a letter that has two overlapping POSTNET bar codes.

Like the BCS, the MLOCR only accepts trays of properly positioned machinable letters that must be fed into the machine manually by an operator.

Mail Hacks

There are at least three things that everyone familiar with the USPS would like to do: 1) Mail letters for free; 2) Get their letters delivered quicker; 3) Find out why it takes so long for their letters to arrive.

Free Mail

It is not difficult for someone to mail a letter for free. It is, however, extremely difficult to mail many letters for free. The USPS is always looking out for mail fraud, and has an entire agency devoted to just this task. Even if a good mail hack works once, it is not likely to work if used repeatedly. Therefore, if you are reading this article with the intent of saving money by tricking the USPS and mailing letters for free, then you would do better to give up now before you are busted. Of course, anyone with even the slightest iota of curiosity would want to know some of the methods.

Perhaps one of the oldest scams in the book is to switch the destination address with the return address and mail the letter without postage. The USPS will then return the letter to its "sender" for postage. Of course, the USPS is not that stupid, and this trick rarely works for nonlocal mail.

A much better mail hack would be to use a laser printer to print a FIM B on an envelope. The MARK will then treat this letter like a business reply mail card, and will not reject it for lack of postage. Of course, the problem with this technique is that a mail carrier will almost certainly notice the missing postage before the letter even gets to a MARK. Therefore, you would have to bundle this letter with another letter that has postage, place the letter with postage on top of the illegitimate letter, and use a rubber band to bundle them together. The mail carrier will not disturb this bundle. Eventually, the bundle will reach a General Mail Facility (GMF) where clerks quickly separate bundles on a conveyer belt. It is extremely unlikely that they will notice the illegitimate letter at this point. From the conveyor belt, the letter will journey to the MARK. Once the MARK processes the letter, it is unlikely that anyone will notice the missing postage until the letter reaches its destination. The final obstacle is the mail carrier who will physically deliver the letter to its destination. At this point, the letter is postmarked, so one can only hope that the mail carrier is not too nosy.

Fast Mail

Getting your letters mailed quickly is a much better hack than trying to mail your letters for free. Not only is it legal but the results are guaranteed.

Normally, a letter reaches a MARK where it is processed and sent to an MLOCR. If the address on the envelope is readable by the MLOCR, then it is jet sprayed with a POSTNET and sent to a BCS. Otherwise, the letter is rejected and sent to an LSM. The one thing you really want to avoid is having your letter processed by an LSM. The operators who run these machines are notorious for keying in the wrong code, causing your letter to journey out of its way to strange and exotic parts of the country. Never write the address on your envelope in script unless you want to delay your letter.

One way you can get your letters processed quicker is to have your letters skip some of the steps in the sorting process. The method involves using a laser printer to print a FIM A and a POSTNET on an envelope. The FIM A will instruct the MARK to treat the envelope as courtesy reply mail. The MARK will look for postage, which you have thoughtfully provided, and then send the letter into a bin with all of the other POSTNET mail. This mail will then be placed in a tray and sent directly to a BCS, skipping the MLOCR and completely avoiding the LSM.

By using POSTNET, you are taking advantage of the same multimillion dollar equipment that is used by businesses. Another advantage to using this method is that your letter will be processed entirely by machines. From the moment your letter enters the MARK until the moment it leaves the BCS, no clerk will see your letter. In addition, the USPS will be pleased with your creative use of their multimillion dollar machinery.

Snail Mail

Now that you know what happens to your letter when you mail it, you can use this information to determine why it takes so long for your own mail to arrive. The next time a letter comes in the mail, analyze it for telltale USPS markings that may give you insight into how the letter was processed. If the letter has POSTNET on it, then you know that the letter was processed by an MLOCR and a BCS. You can then read the POSTNET to make sure that it represents your ZIP code. If the POSTNET is incorrect then that would certainly explain why your letter was delayed. You should also flip the letter over and look for LSM markers. You should not see any more than one or two markings. If the back of your letter is covered with them, then you know that your letter probably had quite a journey, whipping back and forth around the country before it reached you. Keep in mind that it is not unusual for a letter to be processed by both a BCS and an LSM. Not all GMFs use the same machinery, and the average clerk can screw up any letter, even if it is processed by machines.

Unshredding the Evidence (Spring, 1996) *By Datum Fluvius*

The key to reconstructing shredded documents is to sort the shreds prior to paste-up. There are so many differences in the angle of each shred, what text each document contained, which color its paper was, and which weight, that the identification of individual documents by their shreds is fairly simple. It is, of course, tedious. It also takes practice. But once the shreds have been properly classified, only a few pages exist in each little group of sorted shreds. These will submit easily to careful paste-up and reconstruction, since only one or two hundred shreds exist in a three-page group of average size. (This article assumes you are not dealing with cross-cut, chipped documents, or ashes, but with "paper spaghetti.") A three-page group only takes an hour or two to completely reconstruct. The key to paste-up, in turn, is proper and systematic comparison of each and every shred against as many others as seem to fit. This has to be done systematically in order to avoid recomparisons, and to identify patterns in the reconstructed portions.

The Procedure

Place the sorted shreds into a "raw" area to one side, and place the first shred on the paste-up board, anywhere. (Tape it down with masking tape, top and bottom. Masking tape pulls back off the board easier than clear tape.) Next, pick up the second shred, and place it alongside the first in the same orientation. Compare it against one side, then the other. If it matches, tape it down, and if it does not, tape it down a little farther away, perhaps an inch or so away, parallel to the first. Repeat, repeat, repeat. Uncrook your back every little while. When you compare the shreds in this manner, you are limiting the number of comparisons to a fixed, predictable number. If you run out of room to paste down new strips, grab a fresh paste-up board and keep it handy or prepare to recycle the "no-match" pile, which will develop opposite the raw pile. But that adds steps, and time, to your task.

Inspect the reconstructed document strips as they grow. Read what develops to guess which shreds match the open edges. The widening strips are compared as if they were shreds, and joined whenever possible. If two matching strips coexist on a paste-up board but remain unjoined, they retard your further comparisons since two of the available edges will not match any free shreds. That also wastes time.

When a few documents have been completed, transparent packing tape can be used to fuse them, or care can be taken to tape only the tops and bottoms of each document with masking tape. That way, when the shreds are cut free of their tape, they are just a bunch of loose shreds again, ready for disposal. Clear contact paper has been used, but it can ruin documents whose shreds will not lay flat anymore due to dampness or lengthy storage. Tape is easier to control than contact paper, but both media will pull shreds up with their static electric charges unless you ground them. Fully taped documents are much easier to store and preserve, if you need the original. If you want the data, invest in photocopies. Press completed documents between plastic (overhead projector) sheets to keep the copier's glass clean and to align the shreds.

One thing to remember is that businesses and governments use forms whenever possible to save cost. These can be road maps to incomplete reconstructed documents, and are invaluable to have prior to beginning a project. If need be, clear plastic can be traced over a completed form to outline just the form boxes. When laid over the partial document, these give a clue to what information is missing, and what shred patterns to look for to complete it.

Obviously there are many uses for such a simple technique, even in this "information age" of the brave new world order. But it isn't foolproof. You may see coffee grounds mixed in with the bag, used cat litter, and even lunch waste mixed with the shreds. The targets who do that are probably well aware of this reconstruction technique, and will expect your forays into their dumpster. Their other main defense, subterfuge and decoy, is even more effective. They simply increase the shred volume to include everything available, and overflow the sorting capacity of the reconstructionist. Or they salt the real shredded information with errors and omissions, even fake derogatory documents, to elicit a revealing admission from the snoop.

Burning is best, but is not legal in many urban areas. Even when it's legal, it's expensive; it requires safety equipment and personnel supervising every moment of the burn. The military, however, prefers fire and flushing to any alternative. When it absolutely, positively has to disappear overnight, fire and water should be your choice, too.

Extra Assignment for the Artful Programmer

Who needs this headache and tedium? Anyone who needs the data would have to give up their job or their social life to have time for reconstruction! Why not let a computer do it?

Of course, feeding the data in is now easy with a flatbed scanner, and can be easier if you have thin sheets of clear, stiff plastic to sandwich/mash the shreds down. A programmer would then want to compare the edges of the images in the computer's memory. The basic idea is to turn the edge of a shred image into a "word" according to its pixel pattern. This word would then be sorted with the other words and the results would indicate which images are matches. Only a small portion of each edge would be compared, since a close match in one area is a good indicator for the whole. A sample size might be three inches in length, starting one inch down from the top of each shred. Reconstruction would be accomplished by drawing in the images in their relative positions and printing the result, or passing the image to an OCR routine for translation into completed ASCII text pages. Have fun, but publish your results!

11 More Hacker Stories and Adventures

If technology had stopped dead in its tracks before the '90s even began, I would still have had a hard time getting the number of interesting hacker tales down to a manageable number. That's one of the biggest joys of being in this unique culture. It's just as much fun to figure out how an ancient phone system works or to break the security on an obsolete mainframe as it is to play around with the most modern equipment.

We all had our hands full during this decade. Learning the intricacies of a particular voicemail system was still a challenge and fun to share amongst your peers but it no longer was a feat that *everyone* was affected by because there would be a totally new system out in a couple of weeks. Now that more and more people had their own computers, a good deal of time was spent figuring out ways to maximize their potential. It was still very much hacking but it had become a bit more insular. This didn't prevent hackers from reaching out, however. With more and more people getting drawn into the hacker world every day thanks to all of the increased media and mass culture attention, there was anything but a shortage of "exploratory missions" into remote systems owned by everyone from universities to banks to governments. We now had the Internet popping up in more and more places and for many the temptation was far too great to resist. Add to that the fact that so many new entities were going online without having done an iota of study on *securing* their systems and—well, it was a hacker's paradise.

This collection of stories has a little bit of everything. We'll hear how hackers get started and how they find the hacker mindset even without an abundance of technology. There are also perspectives from different angles such as the military, the academic community, inside the federal government, and someone who wound up being the target of a hacking attack. A very unfortunate part of the '90s was that more and more hackers were winding up in prison for one offense or another. But that didn't stop them from applying their curiosity and observation to their new and unpleasant environment and sharing the results with us and hence the entire world. This desire to share experiences has always been one of the most valuable contributions hackers have to offer. How else would the rest of us have ever known what it was really like in that kind of a strange and forbidding place? The utter irony of such a punishment instead turning into a source of still more exploration was not lost on us. It was also pretty damn inspiring.

In this section you'll also see some legends from the past along with instructive narratives on how mischief is caused in all sorts of places from the workplace to the phone lines. Getting around barriers and eventually controlling them completely is a recurring theme of hackers, and that is portrayed here quite literally using the actual gates that guard apartment complexes in one of our stories. What you will gain from this collection of tales is the realization that nearly everything under the sun can be interesteing to people with a hacker mindset.

The best thing about hacker stories is that, unlike the technology itself, they never get old. The spirit of adventure, discovery, and rebellion lives on long after the tools have given way to something else.

Birth of a Low-Tech Hacker (Winter, 1991–1992)

By The Roving Eye

I hope by this article that you can see how a hacker is born in a totally different culture than yours.

I was born on the coldest day in North India in 46 years, though I do not think that that was the true birth of the hacker that I call myself. I was born into a poor family and in place of the usual inclination for crime that goes with such a background, I was instead given three things: a permanent dark tan, a curious brain, and a desire to beat the system with that curious brain. It was this combination of the last two that gave me the hacker spirit that I share with you, whereas everything else about me is very different. All my life I have thought of ways to defeat authority and power, but always within the framework of their own system. When I was little, I always found loopholes in my parents' statements and got away with whatever I wanted. At the age of eight I was already experimenting with radios, trying to make magnets and so on. When I was ten, I learned to read circuit diagrams and I started making my own 10-bit binary adding machine using only simple switches, small bulbs, and a battery. My parents were impressed and so I got my first book allowance. For the equivalent of a dollar a month, I could get whatever Soviet books I wanted.

But that was not enough for me. I started my own library with books that my older friends donated, and by twelve I had a cataloged library of four hundred books. I now found that because of my good knowledge of things, I could often get away with all sorts of things. I soon learned to manipulate the water meter so that it would not move at all and, thus, the company would charge us by the flat rate. By experimenting I got the electric meter to run slowly when I stuck a magnet to the side. The technology was so simple that even I could defeat it at the age of thirteen.

But India is a low-tech country. I had not seen a credit card or a touch-tone phone or even been to an airport before I came to the United States. So I had to find other avenues for my talents.

At thirteen, my parents were sick of my tricks and sent me away to boarding school. It was there that I found the real inspiration. First and foremost, I defeated the system to switch the lights out at lights out time. By putting a switch in parallel, I could switch the lights on from inside the dormitory, after the teacher had put them out from outside. My father used to work in research then. Using the excuse of a science project, I got him to get me a photocell. Using this, we put a trip on the main dorm door to warn us when the master came. Finally, we put a power relay to the lights with input from the radio, and we had our own mini disco. Soon I was unstoppable.

One adventure led to another. The school had a few BBC Acorn Electron computers, which we used to "become familiar with computers." Actually, they were no good for this or any purpose. The thing we did use them for was to get to our billing records. The student computer room was separated from the school computer room by only a grill, to save the air conditioning costs. One night two friends and I managed to remove a section of this grill and hook up an IBM keyboard and monitor to the school system. Then we placed this keyboard as that of one of the Acorn Electrons, so no one would suspect anything; even when a teacher walked by, he only commended us on our efforts to educate ourselves.

It was not long before we had used the accountant's daughter's name as the password to break in. We did not change anything, though, but the thrill of being able to was so great. Soon my friend was able to acquire a "keyboard tap." This is a great device that lets you put two keyboards and monitors on a computer, and switch between them by flipping a switch. I am really surprised that in the mass of tangled wires that only the fellow from the company understood; no one ever found the tap device for a full semester.

My friend was rich and had a computer at home, and he did all the work, and my job was merely to be a lookout, keep trying passwords, or something like that. I had no clue as to what my friends were doing most of the time, because they already knew about all this stuff, and they never had time to explain. But I tried to learn the system on my own. Whenever I had time, I would be back at the computer. Not, as I look back now, that it did much good. Without the manuals I just wasted most of my time.

You must understand that in our sort of technological setting, this was quite an achievement for all of us. We looked at our grades, saw other people's reports and so on quite at will, all the time right under the nose of the people. And because of the thrill the whole thing gave me, a true hacker was born.

Since then I managed to tap phones, and even hook up my own homemade intercom to the new internal phone system that the school got when some big alumnus donated us some money. The crowning glory arrived when I came to America. Not fully realizing what the potential of someone with a need and zeal can achieve, the corporations are quite lax in this direction. But I have found that the best answers to beating the system are the simplest. The "phone does not work correctly" method of fooling the operator, especially with my accent, has been the most effective for me. And as for breaking into the systems of our school, anyone with a bit of sweet-talking skills can find out anything. Not to mention the advantages one can reap by being aware of the tremendous amounts of money, things, information, and so on that Uncle Sam and Cousin Big Blue or the Fed are ready to give out for free, when presented with the right story. I cannot lay claim to very great technical knowledge or achievements. "But the spirit is the thing," my mother says. So I guess as a low-tech hacker I have definitely made my mark.

My life has become quite different as a result of seeing my friends access our billing accounts. Being a socially insecure person, I have built a digital wall against society. By being sort of apart from them, I am able to understand people much better. Thus, I am now trying to hack the ultimate machine: the human brain. I have found that most often people are much more vulnerable to manipulation in undesired ways than machines. Though I must admit that toying around with the mega-monsters of this technocratic society is a lot more fun....

The View of a Fed (Summer, 1992) *By The Fed*

Why don't they understand? Why do both sides think they understand?

I never dreamed when I began a journey to obtain my first "hacker magazine," specifically *Phrack*, that my days would end up much like they are today. Let me explain. I am a computer security specialist for a division of the United States Federal government, which will go unnamed. I am not writing this article as a government representative, but as an individual. I had been a computer security analyst for a couple of years before obtaining my first modem. I spent most of my day massaging our mainframe security software to ensure our more than 8,000 users could obtain and maintain their necessary access. I didn't have time to worry about hackers and really didn't understand much about what the press talked about anyway. Hackers seemed to be these super-intelligent, terrifying individuals I couldn't compare with in regards to technical knowledge and I wasn't about to try. It didn't seem to apply to our systems anyway.

After I started calling other computers and interacting with individuals, I decided to try to get a copy of *Phrack*, the magazine that super-hacker Knight Lightning published and was arrested for, mostly for publishing the 911 computer program (well at least that is what I thought at the time, based on things I had read and heard). It was frightening to even decide to pursue this venture. I had read that hackers could break into any computer system and that they were constantly breaking into credit reports and messing up people's lives. I wasn't anxious to become a target of the "underground." What I realize now is that most of the underground could care less about me and my ventures. I was simply flattering myself by believing that I was important enough to become a target...who gives a damn about me? The Fed ego is something else, eh? It's out there though, thick as ever. I see it mostly when I try to introduce folks to "hacker material" such as *2600*. I once told a whole conference room full of security folks about *2600* and the benefits of receiving it. The responses from the audience were things like, "Yeah, but don't use your real name when you subscribe, these are hackers you know." One man even told me he was going to set up a fake name with a P.O. Box before ordering *2600*, to protect himself. I find it amazing that people think a magazine that supports itself from subscriptions is out to destroy its subscription base.

In my travels, I also wasn't sure if I should be honest about my position or assume a hidden identity. I mean, I could call a "hacker BBS" and say, "Hi, my name is... and I am a Fed. Can I have a copy of all your files? I just want to read them. Honest." I wasn't sure that I would get much success from that, but at the same time I was afraid if I did try to hide my real identity, those evil hackers would find out and destroy me. So, I signed on a BBS and said, "Hi, I'm a Fed." You know what, it worked. I found out by being honest and to the point, folks were very helpful. The more I learned from interacting with the underground, the more I realized just how deceptive the government had been in a lot of regards (I don't trust mirrors in hotels anymore!). I was hoping, by being honest, that others would realize that fed was not always equal to deception.

You know what else I found out? There are evil hackers, but they seem to be few and far between (of course these evil ones are the ones that have hacked my account!). Matter of fact, other hackers didn't even seem to accept them. Know what else I found out? The Secret Service really messed up on the *Phrack* case. Knight Lightning was patient enough to explain his side of the story to me and has filled me in on things the press "neglected to mention." Know what else? I realize now how clueless I was in regards to *a lot* of computer security issues. I know I am still clueless in a lot of regards and will always be, but I have learned so much over these past years that I now want to make an effort to educate others in the computer security arena of the benefits of knowing both sides of the story. Believe it or not, I am actually getting a chance to do that. I have been contacted by Federal agencies that have learned of "my contacts in the underground" and wanted to use me as a buffer between them and the hacker community. One agency was interested in hiring some of "my trusted hacker friends" while another was interested in learning about hackers and "getting inside their heads." Additionally, non-government agencies have contacted me for much the same reasons. I'm not sure how the word of my interactions got around (well, I have a pretty good idea), but I actually think it funny in many ways. I see the same naive fear in these folks that I experienced myself when I started my journey to learn "the other side of the story." Now, I interact with as many if not more hackers during the day as I do security professionals and, as a result, my knowledge of the holes that exist in computer systems has increased immensely. I even learned enough to hack into one of our computer systems, expose our security holes, and get them fixed. As a security specialist, that is priceless to me. I was only able to do that because of the training I received from these so called notorious malicious hackers. Hackers helping to improve the security of government computer systems, hmmmmmm, seem suspect to you? Not to me. If I found a security weakness in a computer and wrote articles about it, published and sent it out so that thousands of folks could get it, I would expect the hole to be fixed. If I found that hole still open, I may become just a bit upset or assume it was an open invitation to violate the system. While underground files that explain these techniques have become a routine part of my day, there was a time I didn't even know they existed and certainly didn't know they existed to the extent they do. So part of the issue as to why they don't listen is that most of us have never heard the message.

I have accidentally tripped over holes in systems before and disseminated the information, only to be told that we could not put those controls in place because it would impact the operations of the organization, which it very well may do. It's a judgment call for management. Many security professionals are viewed as having tunnel vision (many of them do) and not understanding the operational end of the business. While many understand the holes that exist and have made every effort to get them fixed, management just won't let them.

One other thing I have learned by interacting with the computer underground is that sometimes we security folks aren't the only ones who are clueless. I have heard from hackers who said to me that they did not understand our side of many of the issues. One view that seems the most prevalent is that a security professional's real job is to keep people out of computer systems. That is a small part of what we do but the largest part of our job is ensuring that authorized users get the access they need to do their daily jobs. The main reason access is controlled on our systems is to ensure the integrity of the data we process. We want to ensure that our data is accurate. This is done by limiting the number of users that have certain access rights to it. Privacy is always an issue with sensitive data but we don't spend our days thinking "keep 'em out, keep 'em out." We are thinking, "Gotta give our users the access they need." Sometimes we just don't have the time to do anything else. That is why we don't always discover security holes in our systems. That is why many of them go unfixed. That is why picking up a magazine, like *Phrack* or *2600*, and learning the holes hackers are using to violate the systems we are trying to protect is so helpful. We may not have known that such holes existed without the underground's help. What is even better than reading it in an underground publication is having an e-mail address of the author so that you can contact them and get further assistance. It has been an amazing tool for me.

I am going to continue to interact with the underground as long as I am able and will continue to lead other security professionals to that same interaction. I think only then does a person really begin understanding the true issues involved in security. I think only through this type of interaction does a person learn the rest of the story. It has made me realize more than anything else that both sides don't understand the factors affecting the others. Usually the main factor involved in preventing this is the ego and arrogance of the individuals on both sides, each of the players saying, "they just don't listen."

Letter from Prison (Winter, 1992–1993)

The following information comes to us from a prisoner in California. We've removed the name and location to protect his or her identity.

I would like to let you know how much I enjoy your magazine. My opportunities to enjoy computer "fun" and phreaking are about zero right now since I am engaged in involuntary solitude. It is with some interest, therefore, that I have followed your reports of rejection by Federal prisons and by the Texas Department of (In)Corrections. As you now know, prison inmates whose First Amendment rights are protected only by Federal law have a tough way to go. The Federal Prison Rulebook allows a warden to reject a publication "if it is determined detrimental to the security, good order, or discipline of the institution or if it might facilitate criminal activity." This rule was held valid under (in spite of?) the Constitution's First Amendment by the U.S. Supreme Court (Thornburgh vs. Abbott (1989) 490 US 401, 104 L Ed 2d 459, 109 S Ct 1874).

Much to my delight (and surprise) it seems that the great state of California is somewhat more liberal about prisoners' rights to read "questionable" literature than the Federal standard. California Penal Code, sections 2600 (!) and 2601 are, together, sometimes called, "The [California] prisoner's bill of rights." The only restriction on reading material is a restriction against printed matter, which depicts the manufacture of weapons, explosives, poisons, or destructive devices, or which depicts sexual assaults against Department of Corrections employees. No other subject matter can be legally excluded.

Lest you think that the First Amendment is completely healthy in California, here are some examples to show that it is not: A friend of mine was recently refused two issues of *Hustler* magazine. One issue had an article on Asian street gangs in the U.S.A. The other had an article about female inmates in the California Youth Authority (convicted delinquent children) being raped by staff members. Both articles were called "a threat to institution security." Sound familiar? Mailroom personnel here have clearly exceeded their authority and the case is headed for court.

Two years ago I was refused a Loompanics book catalog because pages 85–86 were not allowed. I later discovered that the offending pages contained a tongue-in-cheek article on how to use the catalog itself as a weapon.

A friend of mine was denied a book on computer hacking that he ordered from Loompanics. He did not contest the refusal, but should have. I received *Out of the Inner Circle* by Bill Landreth with no problem.

The exclusion of "unsolicited advertising" literature allowed by CCR, sec. 3147(I)(1) is also much abused. I sent in reader service cards to *Byte* and *Popular Communications* magazines requesting 42 different brochures. I received one reply. One year later I sent off again, this time for 44 brochures. I also informed the mailroom in advance that the brochures were coming. It's been six months now with no responses so I guess it's time to sharpen up my pencils and oil up the typewriter. (Electronic typewriters are not allowed here. They are terrified that we will hide something in the 4K RAM and they won't know how to access it.) Still, we at least have a fighting chance to beat the censors. A considerable body of case law exists to support P.C. 2600 and 2601. If I can't play with phones and computers, I might as well learn about the law.

Prison Phreaking

I have not tried phreaking here and probably will not (will not be able to, I mean). All phones have "this phone is subject to being monitored" signs above them. A beep tone sounds at 15 second intervals. Occasionally, the monitor circuit can be heard clicking on. Phones can be turned off and on remotely from a single, central, location. The phones themselves are of a type very common as pay phones. They are approximately 21 inches high by eight inches wide by seven inches deep; black case with blue front plate; no coin deposit slot but does have a coin return slot; a Bell System emblem is on the right side of the blue front plate about halfway up; coin return piece says "Bell System—Made by Western Electric" on it. The local carrier is Pac Bell and the long-distance carrier is MCI, as of about two years ago. Prior to that it was AT&T. Calls are collect only. Alternate carrier access is blocked as is 800 access. 10777### brings a ringing signal and a recorded message saying, "An alternate carrier access number is not needed to complete this call. Please hang up and place your call again." 10333### brings the same. Dialing an 800 number brings a recorded message that says, "This call cannot be completed as dialed."

A normally placed call from here (collect) is placed in the standard way: 0, area code, plus seven-digit number and brings on a live operator identifying him/herself as an MCI operator and asking for the caller's name. They then disappear and check for call acceptance without the caller hearing any conversation with the called party until after the call is accepted. Perhaps I can look forward to automation in the future.

Normal access to local directory assistance (555-1212) is also blocked. A recording informs the caller that the number cannot be reached. I tried 555-1212, 411, plus 555-1212 with my area code, and preceded by 1 and 0. These all bring up prerecorded rejections except for the last (0+), which brings on an MCI operator who sounds perplexed that anyone would try to call collect to directory assistance and says they won't accept collect calls.

Long distance information, anywhere in the U.S.A., is available by dialing (area code) 555-1212, with or without a 1 in front. Best of all it's free. Sometimes local information can also be obtained by dialing information in an adjacent area code. As I said, alternate carrier access is blocked here, but another prison I was in had 10777### and 10333### direct access to alternate carriers. Unfortunately this access was blocked due to "overuse." We switched to an 800 access number until—finally—all 800 access was blocked. The fun lasted about one year. At the time my wife had a legitimate Sprint card (which supplied the 800 access number) and I usually used her legal code number to call home (I was more cautious than most). We discovered that 10777### leaves a calling phone number record, which appears on the bill. Using 800 access causes the bill to say "western wide area access call" in the calling number column of the bill. These cost 75 cents extra over direct access calls.

We also tried having people direct dial to the jail pay phone to avoid operator assistance charges yet still be legal. But the phones were blocked to incoming calls. They did not even have their numbers posted on the phones. We got it off of phone bills. To this day I marvel at the nimble-fingered few who could come up with valid nine digit Sprint codes in 10 to 15 minutes. There is magic there. I could do it in an average of one and a half hours. I would blunder around with a "used up" nine digit code number until I got a valid first seven digits (I made it through code number and 10 digit phone number before getting reject tone) then plodded along through the 100 possible combinations of last two digits (00 to 99) until a "hit" occurred. It was slow, grueling work but God damn it, somebody had to do it after "Nimble Fingers" went home.

Interestingly enough, Sprint seemed to prefer an electronic war rather than working with law enforcement. On occasion jail guards were spotted watching phones (from 50 feet away) with binoculars as guys dialed. On another occasion two guards rushed a guy who had been dialing continuously for over an hour and took his notes away from him (a 00 to 99 grid) but nothing came of it. A lieutenant in the jail even said that they had called Sprint repeatedly with information, in case Sprint wanted to prosecute, but "they didn't seem to care." However, we lost 10777### and 10333### access. Once, at about number 17 while running a 00 to 99 sequence, I had an operator come on the line asking if I was having a problem. I switched to random number choice on the grid and had no more problems. But the code numbers were going dead in shorter and shorter time spans. Before loss of 800 access killed our fun the code numbers were lasting only two or three days. There is a proposed bill that could grant the Director of Corrections the power to choose which long-distance carrier to use in all California prisons. Think of the revenues involved! There is a 15- to 25-million-dollar-per-year payback to the prisons for supplying phone locations (to captive customers with no choice of alternate carrier and no other way to call than "collect"). This money may be up for grabs soon and screw the poor families who are forced to pay the "operator assistance" charge for all calls or else forgo phone calls.

A logical compromise to the high expense vs. phone fraud problem would be to allow use of "Call Me" cards, which can only be used to call the card holder's home number yet avoid operator assistance charges. But it is difficult to establish meaningful communication with minds that ban TV remote controls because "transmitting devices" are forbidden in California prisons, and electronic typewriters are considered a "threat to institution security."

We used to have a large collection of California phone books in our library. They were all locked away when a guard supposedly found his own home address listed in one. This place makes me think of the sign I once saw: "Help, the paranoids are after me."

Growth of a Low-Tech Hacker (Winter, 1992–1993)

By The Roving Eye

About a year ago I wrote an article about the birth of a hacker in a low technology atmosphere. A lot has happened since then. For one thing, I have been able to meet with hackers from the area. For the other, I have been able to gain some hacking experience. These two combined have led me to appreciate a "problem that exists in our community" (pardon the sap). Hence this article.

I find that a lot of newcomers to the field have no idea where to turn, hacking being no product of corporate America, which is blared across our TV screens every five minutes. Thus, if you are a newcomer, read this! You probably will not find much else! Hacking is first and foremost a time-consuming enterprise. It requires tireless devotion as well as relentless perseverance. This is why you will never beat that curious kid next door who started letting his curiosity take him places when he was too young to pay for *2600* out of his allowance. This is also why a newcomer finds it hard to get around in this neighborhood. If you are not serious about hacking and intend to let your "determination" quiver after six months, leave now. Hacking is not a hobby, it is something that stays with you for life. If you are serious, then there are very few gaps that you will not be able to fill in with hard work. But like everything else in life, it is also important to work smart. Here are some pointers that I have come up with from my own experience:

1. **Definitions first**. It will help you a lot if you define to yourself who you are, what you are interested in doing, what your goals and priorities are, what sacrifices you want to make, and what lines you are not willing to cross. In this respect, hacking is a discipline. You will waste a lot of time or feel rotten if you skip this most important step. I personally decided that I support the free

flow of information, but I do not believe in even risking harm to others. I do not believe in following the law, but I do believe in living honestly. I believe in what is right, not what is just.

2. **Stop doling out information now.** Living in this society, almost every minute we announce ourselves to the world. Stop letting out information to the world. Unless absolutely necessary, use a false name. And don't reveal your social security number to every Tom, Dick, and Harry. I usually use two Hindi swear words, and not even Ma Bell had a problem issuing me a calling card. Can there be a more silly point than this to make? Yet this advice went unheeded and a boastful friend of mine is in big trouble. Arrogance is never worth it.
3. **Get others working for you.** This country is full of people waiting to give you stuff for free. Use them, abuse them, and you will even get thanked for it! Call the FCC and get put on their mailing list. And this does not apply only to the electronic frontier. Tourist offices will love to cover your walls with their awesome posters. The Fed would love to tell you everything the *Wall Street Journal* can tell you, and more, for free. You just have to appear to be corporate and know how to ask.
4. **Use the easiest way.** AT&T does not want you to know a lot of things. But for most of these, you need not break into their computer or even think of a great scheme. A little social engineering will do the trick. I called their 800 number and asked about ANI. They kept transferring me from office to office, until I got them to give me the number of the AT&T FIND service, an internal number that employees use to find out technical information. *And they even paid for the calls I made to them.* No blue boxing, nothing illegal.
5. **Play on people's ignorance.** If people weren't stupid, hacking would be nearly impossible. Try simple insecure passwords. Assume insecure networks and sites. I have even managed to get system access to a computer by logging in on Telnet as anonymous! Talk fast to the AT&T operator and tech support, and they will tell you the DTMF codes! Do not assume that these people have any brains at all!
6. **Use all the legitimate resources you can lay your hands on.** Learning UNIX out of a book will not teach you much about hacking, but it will give you the tools to your art. Approaching hacking without some of this kind of formal support is like trying to learn C by reading the comp.lang.c Usenet newsgroup. Learning UNIX security from a text will not only accelerate your progress, it will also make your skills valuable in the outside world.
7. **Get a feel, and then get a plan.** Perhaps I should have put this higher up in the list. But I purposely left it for down here. The above pointers should help you get an idea of our world. But then you must step out and do something

for yourself. Play with an arm tied behind your back. Increase the challenges. But whatever you do, get a plan. I wasted a lot of time because I was doing some serious dabbling in stuff I could not give two hoots about. A plan helps one go right back to the definitions stage...where it all begins.

8. **Work cheap**. My poverty has proven to be my greatest asset. No one can afford Radio Shack, no matter how rich they may be. Not because RS is that expensive, but because the maxim of more money, more hot air holds very true here. The more money you plan to spend, the more bullshit you will be fed. If you buy cheap, you will learn more by doing things yourself. You will value your equipment. And you will have more of it.
9. **Get friends...use the resources.** Before I started reading *2600* and *Phrack*, I had no one to turn to with my problems, no one to guide or encourage me. Reinventing the wheel may have its virtues, but riding a sports car that you built from a kit is a lot more fun!
10. **Review.** If you want to get anything out of this for the long run, review what you have done. A present problem may have been solved in the past. Take account of what you have learned. Know where you stand. And *bash on regardless*.

A Study of Hackers (Spring, 1993) *By Dr. Williams*

In *The Hacker's Handbook* on page 123, Hugo Cornwall discussed an idea of setting up his home computer system to look and act like a mainframe system. He would let hackers attempt to gain access to it while he monitored the results. He wanted his home system to emulate the M15, the most notorious hacking target for British hackers. The hackers would get into the system and attempt to gain privileges, when unknowingly they were really trying to get into his system. Hugo did not carry out the plan, even though he did set up a sophisticated emulation of the M15. About the time he was to carry out his plan, a disgruntled employee left the M15 crew, and went to *The News* hanging out all of the dirty laundry. Hugo thought carrying out the stunt may get him into trouble, or at least give him more publicity than he wanted, so he didn't go through with it.

I just carried out this idea myself, and I thought the results were interesting.

I had just completed a class in operating systems. The class used MINIX as a model to study and modify. MINIX is an operating system compatible with version 7 of UNIX, specifically made to be run on IBM and its clones. It has over 12,000 lines of source code written in C. After finishing the class, I decided to use MINIX because I thought it could best mimic a big computer system under the guise of UNIX.

It took me a while to build an appropriate "pseudo-system," one that I thought was capable of fooling novice users of UNIX into thinking they were indeed on a UNIX system. It would have been beyond the capacities of my machine to do all that was necessary to fool expert users of UNIX though, not to mention the time constraints I had. First, I had to reformat my hard drive for the MINIX operating system. Then I had to write a device driver to run the modem, which took a while to do. I had to change physical appearances: names of files, directories, syntax of items, and emulation style. I added some characteristics—putting in games, files with interesting names, eye catching items, and additional mail facilities. Finally, I wrote the program that did the actual mimicking, which also gathered statistics of the users' activities. Overall, I spent six months worth of free time making a satisfactory system.

The program was made to imitate UNIX in all regards. At various times, it would "show" different users on, different processes being run, disk quota, terminal statistics, free space, printer job status, and so on. It showed different disk packs, had most of the files which UNIX uses for system and administrative functions, and backup schedules.

On the login screen, I was tempted to put something like "Boeing node #2, please log in," or "General Dynamics Site 3, spot 2." However, I thought this could get me more trouble or attention than I wanted, so I settled for a more generic approach:

```
BN Site #2
<current time>
please log in:
```

After login the first screen would show:

```
****************************************************************
There was a crash on /group3 on 6/8/89 at approximately 03:00.
Some files from that location have been deleted. Please inspect
your account for file integrity. Call the operators at ext. 3524
if you need to get any files from backups.
There will be a gathering on 6/24/89 at noon in the cafeteria
during lunch for all employees wishing to form a group of people
interested in remote control cars and planes. Please call Jeff
Smith at ext 2146 for further details.
****************************************************************
```

And the prompt was:

```
June[1]
```

Every time a command was entered, the number in the square brackets was incremented by one.

In the program, I left in some famous UNIX bugs, hoping somebody would try to manipulate the account into getting more privileges. I left in mail bugs, writing commands to the 25th line, and using the same encryption scheme for the password file which UNIX uses, and a few other smaller items. To egg them on, I put in games that could only be executed with privileges, and files with tempting names like CAR.DATA, PRIVATE.DOC, and DOCUM.SECRT, which also could only be read with privileges. Every time the account logged off, I returned most things back to the original setting, including any gains they had made. So if a person logged on more than once, they had to start from scratch every time. I didn't like doing this, but since I thought a lot of people would be using a few accounts, I thought it would look more phony if the account drastically changed every time the person logged onto it. It also helped me make more accurate observations. At this time, I got a friend to agree to give up his dorm room phone for a few months, since he was taking off anyway. So I plugged the computer into there and let 'er rip.

I wanted to put the accounts into three different targets: hackers, hacker wannabes, and the academic community. On the bulletin boards, which I had hacker privileges on, I posted a message telling users to call this "neat" system I discovered. The message went something like:

"I recently discovered an account to a UNIX system at 555-5555.
The account name is 'PAULS,' with password 'dog$car.'
Have fun!"

A day later, I posted the same sort of message on different bulletin boards, those which I had only a normal status on, but where there were more "kiddies" on. I changed the account name and password. Finally, a week later, I told some of my friends by word of mouth in the academic community, but with another different account/password combination.

Something that I predicted would happen is that a lot of the sysops whose system I had posted the message aimed for the "kiddies" erased the message. Over half of them had erased the message in less than a few hours. The other half had the message erased in about a day. It still served my purpose though, because a lot of people had seen the message. I was tempted to tell the sysops whose system I had posted the message on that it was all a hoax—an experiment, but I thought some of them wouldn't keep the lid on that information.

Something that I sort of expected was that a lot of the sysops wrote me mail back, furious that I had posted that message. Most of them thought I was putting them in legal jeopardy (understandably). Others said that their board was not into that type of information, threatened to call the police, warned me to never post that type of message again, and even deleted my account (no loss). None of the messages to the hacker crowd were lost. I posted the message 17 times for the kiddies, five times for the hackers, and told four friends, who I know passed it on to a few other people.

I suppose if somebody would have thought about it, he or she might have concluded that it's pretty hokey to post an account/password combination on a public BBS room where everybody can read it. Either I had to be really arrogant, or had to have ulterior motives.

Within eight hours of posting the message, the system got its first call. I was really hoping that it would be somebody who knew what they were doing. I wanted to see if anyone was going to be able to jump the hoops I set up to gain further privileges. The first person didn't seem to be familiar with the UNIX operating system—they kept on trying MS-DOS commands. They couldn't do a disk directory, or any other basic operations in UNIX. In fairness, if you're not used to UNIX, it is pretty user unfriendly.

The next few callers seemed to know more about what was going on. They were logged on under the hackers' account. They were able to find out the attributes of the account, get a view of what the overall system looked like, and see what the range of the system was. A few of those were able to locate some of the targets of interest I put in, but did not gain access.

Next, the kiddies' account took a big jump in usage. The majority of them were unfamiliar with the UNIX system. Some of them had a cursory knowledge of the basic UNIX commands, but didn't really know how to manipulate the machine.

Finally, a few calls started coming in on the academic account. Most of them didn't spend too long on the account. Since they knew more about what was going on, they took a look to see what was around and split. One or two of them tried using some of the more sophisticated commands that work on UNIX, but not on MINIX.

Over a two month period, I was able to see what the overall attributes of usage were. I don't know how many unique individuals logged into the account, but I did keep track of how many times the account was used. By looking at the log of commands from the kiddie account, about half of its usage came from people unfamiliar with UNIX. Using MS-DOS commands or commands of other PCs, inability to access the help file, and no experience with the UNIX environment were characteristic of these users. Approximately a quarter of the usage came from people who had exposure to UNIX with a basic knowledge. They were able to find out the basic structure of the account and system, wander around a bit, but did not do anything sophisticated. The last quarter had at least competent users; some were quite expert. They were able to discover items of interest, find most items of importance, gain further privileges, and attempt to hide the account that had been used.

From the 50 percent of users who were UNIX competent, only one third of them tried to gain privileges. The other two thirds must have been content where they were at. Of the others, the most popular scheme used to gain privileges was to read the password file (which, like in UNIX, is publicly readable but encrypted). This was not a bit surprising to me, since the Cornell Worm used essentially the same method. Many articles have talked about it, some showing how in a cookbook recipe manner the steps were taken. Users would try to decrypt the password file and gain the root password. The next most common method was written commands to the 25th line of a more privileged account. This wasn't surprising either, since much ado has been made about that. The rest seemed to be evenly spread around on mail bugs, finding bugs in commands that ran shells in privileged modes, or some other method.

From the third of the users left over, 32 percent of them succeeded in raising the account's privileges. Out of that 32 percent, 68 percent of the people were able to get at least operator privileges. Out of that 68 percent, 18 percent (25 people) were able to get root privileges. I didn't know though if that was one person who got root privileges 25 times, or 25 different people. The program I had written really only mimicked the root privilege, and did not allow total control of the machine.

The sophistication of the user was directly related to the amount of "stupid" things the user did. Some of the kiddies did some real stupid things, like creating files saying something like, "Ha. Ha. I'm a hacker and I'm in your system," deleting files, or editing files in an obvious manner. Others romped around the system, checking out every file in every subdirectory. Other items which were not as obvious were using the help files excessively, entering many incorrect commands consecutively, and continually trying to access items for which they had insufficient privileges. The most knowledgeable users tried to hide their presence. Some of them successfully edited the user log without leaving a trace, kept a low profile of activities, and did not play the games at all or for great lengths of time. Out of those who gained privileges, there was only one incidence of someone deleting a file on purpose without cause.

Overall, the kiddie account logged in 2,017 users. The hacker account logged 1,432 users, and the academic account logged 386 users. I have no way of knowing though how many unique people used the accounts. I was disappointed at the low turnout from the academic community. I talked to somebody I had given the account to, and some of the reasons seemed to be that some people just weren't into hacking, had legitimate accounts, were not curious about other systems, and just didn't want to risk getting into trouble.

Overall, the most incompetent users came from the kiddie account. The hacker account seemed to be most familiar with all of the system weaknesses, but lacked an overall understanding of the system. The academic account was just the opposite; they knew how to work the system, but did not know of the security shortcomings of UNIX. However, the best users came from the academic account, where there was probably an elite crust of students who are also hackers.

One side effect came shortly after I posted the original message on BBS's. Soon, other people started posting the kiddie account/password combo, claiming they got it from a friend or had "hacked" it themselves. That's why when the sysops deleted my message, I wasn't worried, because enough people had seen it to spread the word around.

I half expected some law agency to raise an eyebrow and look into the matter. After all, I had done a pretty blunt thing. I did not get any questions about it though, nor did the person who owned the phone number. But then again, maybe somebody did, and I just didn't find out about it.

The Ghost Board (Autumn, 1994) *By Autolycus*

The Evergreen State College in Olympia, Washington is an "alternative" (aka hippie) college that grew out of the academic counterculture of the late 1960s. During the '70s and '80s, Evergreen was the home for a variety of innovative phreaks and proto-hackers (testimony of this can be found in the campus computer center occupying Room 2600 of the Evans Library building—but how we pulled that off is another story).

Some activities of this community are public knowledge due to individuals' entanglements with Telco cops and other powers that be. The busts by the FCC over the campus radio station's (KAOS) bootleg phone switchboard system during the era of Ma Bell's monopoly over such systems was, fortunately, the worst bust we were ever involved in. A number of text files are circulating which document Saladin's conversion of an elevator emergency phone to an active WATS line, as well as his overdubbing the screech used in the Emergency Broadcast System radio tests with 2600 Hz. But nothing has been written about the locally infamous "Ghost Board." In the Pacific Northwest, the Ghost Board is legendary, though much that has been written about it is more mythical than factual (no, the Ghost Board never posted classified dialups for the nearby Bangor Missile Base).

The Ghost Board was a parasitic bulletin board—mostly a message system—which sporadically and temporarily operated covertly in a number of computer dial-up systems *without* the knowledge of the sysop (though more than once the assistance of a co-sysop was used). In the early days, this was accomplished very simply (usually through shared accounts and simple encryption methods), but with time more intricate operational procedures were used. Regardless of the system used, the basic Ghost Board procedure was as follows:

1. Members would call the system in the wee hours of the morning and access non-"advertised" message areas. (This was done in a variety of ways ranging from simply typing an unlisted character at the main menu of a Wildcat system, hitting ALT E, S, C on a LAN system, or using an ANSI bomb to drop to DOS.)
2. A message/database system was available where Ghost Board members could communicate, and a rough date for the next Ghost Board was listed.
3. The system would (ideally) self-delete at a predetermined time and no trace of the system would be left.

The Ghost Board only operated between midnight and 5:00 a.m. It was little more than a floating database system collecting: compiled addresses and phone numbers of every pay phone in the area, test loop numbers, information on local computer systems and security flaws, flaws in local PBX systems, pilfered system passwords and account names, etc.

The original Ghost Board never lasted for more than two or three evenings at a time and only operated every sixty days or so. In the late 1980s, one ghost board member operated an elite local text and phreak-utility based BBS called the Ghost Board, but this was actually a separate entity.

With time, the method of notifying members where and when the Ghost Board was up and operating was changed. The most common method was to use the free lost and found classified ad section of the local newspaper where periodic messages conveyed the needed information (i.e., "LOST—Dalmatian puppy with tag reading ATDT, call 555-7734 before 7/22, ask for Keith"—where "Keith" was the name needed to gain access to the system).

As BBS systems proliferated in the early and mid eighties the Ghost Board began using simple ANSI bombs to gain superuser access to poorly tended systems. From this vantage unused menu keys were assigned to access the hidden sub-board system. At different times, work-study positions and academic "internships" at State agencies were used to burrow out hosts for the Ghost Board. For half a year, I periodically set up a message system on a state agency's computer system and hooked up my own external modem. At a later date the local dialup card catalog for the library was hacked and bogus book entries were used to pass on information.

For a short period of time in the early '90s, one Ghost Board pioneer abandoned an AT (he'd purchased it for $40 at the Goodwill) on the roof of a rural supermarket. The AT was water-protected and hardwired into the store's power grid and the 2400 modem was spliced into the store's phone lines. This system operated for almost five months before it was (apparently) detected and shut down.

At present the Ghost Board is still sporadically operating with the assistance of various UNIX systems and child-operated BBS systems. With any luck, this is the last you will hear of us!

Day of the Hacker (Summer, 1995) *By Mrgalaxy*

I run a BBS in Atlanta, GA. This is a true story of how my BBS was hacked, and how I came to appreciate it.

Several years ago I started a bulletin board in Atlanta, GA. I tried several "test" versions of the available popular bulletin board systems of that time and ended up choosing to run a Wildcat BBS. The software installed quickly, and as the manual said, I was up and running within the hour.

Wow! I was excited! What a neat hobby! Over the months, the BBS grew and grew. First, I added one hard drive and then two. Later, I added one CD-ROM, then another, then another, and even another. Wow! This was neat stuff. People began calling from around the world. I started "meeting" new and exciting people. At the time, I was very security conscious. Each person had 30 days to try the BBS, and then if they didn't subscribe, they would get downgraded to a very low access level. People joined and joined, and all was right with the world.

Then I started having weirdos call. Some would log on without filling out the short questionnaire. Others would fill the questionnaire with false information. I started getting pissed off. I, then, decided to buy a caller ID box. These boxes had just come out, and I was determined to stop these guys. Each night I would carefully compare my activity log against my 40-memory caller ID box. Those entering false information were locked out. A log book was kept of the evildoers. Bam! I'd locked one out. Smack! I'd then lock another out.

Wow, this was fun! What a great time I was having. I was a super SYSOP. I had the power! Don't mess with me! I was getting some folks pissed off. Fake logins increased. Threats increased. I countered with the phone company's phone block feature. *Ha!* Don't mess with me...I'm a super SYSOP!

The BBS continued to grow...I now had a massive system. I was keeping out the evil enemies...and winning! My doomsday was about to begin, yet I wasn't afraid because my software user manual told me that *no one* had ever hacked a correctly set up Wildcat BBS.

I was so proud of myself. I had written my own BBS upload virus-scanning program. I used a massive batch file to scan upload files with two virus scanners and an ANSI bomb detector. *Ha!* Let them try something! They can't beat me!

Well, they tried and tried to beat my super system...Every time they tried, they failed. Again and again they tried. Again and again they failed! *Ha!* I was a super SYSOP. Don't mess with me! I grew more confident...I was invincible! Let them attack! I had the super computer, the super intellect...They were nothing more than insects to me! The laughter in my mind grew in its intensity...

Doomsday Strikes

One night I arrived home later than normal. Boy, I was tired. What a long day...As I was about to fall into bed, I decided to check my e-mail on the BBS. I turned on my monitor and saw a message, which stated I had an "Environment error..." At the time I was using DR DOS 6. I grabbed my DR DOS manual and tried to find out what this meant. After not being able to find any meaningful information about this error, I decided to reboot my computer. After all, I was used to the machine freezing...I had so many TSR's loading in for my four CD-ROMs that freezing was common. I often had to reboot my computer to restart my system after someone had attempted to download from one of my CD-ROMs. I wouldn't say this freezing problem happened every night; in fact, it really only happened once or twice a month, but I was never surprised when it happened. When I came home and saw this error message, I just assumed this was one of my usual "freeze-ups."

I rebooted the computer. The machine whirred and clicked as it started up. As it booted, I noticed that when the computer executed the MSCDEX.EXE program in the AUTOEXEC.BAT file, the file appeared to load, but the indicator lights on the CD-ROMs didn't blink in sequence like they used to do. Damn! I asked myself what was happening. I couldn't figure it out! On a whim, I grabbed my antivirus scanning program and scanned my computer. Bells started to sound. Oh crap! I had the Screaming Fist II virus! How had it gotten there? I began to swear in several languages.

My computer rebooted itself. Damn! This time the machine refused to completely boot up. A cursor sat there in the top right hand corner of my screen, doing nothing! I reset the machine again! Nothing! I was worried. The hard drives in my machine were compressed using SUPERSTOR. In order to boot up my machine from a clean floppy, I not only had to find a clean DR DOS boot-up disk, but I also had to find the correct compression files to run in my new CONFIG.SYS file. After 40 minutes of failed attempts, I was finally able to boot my system. I ran my virus cleaning program, and then rebooted my machine from the hard drive. My machine was running! Yea!

I had won! I was a *god!* Don't mess with me; I'm a super SYSOP! Then, midnight struck. My machine bleeped and reset itself. *Huh!?* What had happened?! My CMOS was erased, gone! My computer now no longer knew what types of hard drives I had or what type of floppies I had. The list went on and on. Oh man, I was furious! I vowed to search the Earth forever for this evil hacker of destruction.

I labored on into the night. Due to the nature of my job, I was experienced with computers, and I was able to recover within a couple of hours. I finally restored my CMOS, cleaned the infected files, rescanned my system with other virus scanners, and got my system working. It was now 4:00 a.m. ...I was exhausted. With a smirk of satisfaction I went to sleep...*after* I had disabled the uploading function.

The next day I scoured the activity log. Ah ha! The guy had called at 2:00 a.m. the previous morning, and I simply had not noticed the problem until late at night later that day. Unfortunately, when the BBS went down, people had called again and again attempting to get on the board. The caller ID had lost the call! So many people had called that I had lost perhaps the most important clue as to my caller's identity. Damn!

At this point I decided to determine what the hacker had done to zap me. As I can best determine from the activity logs, the caller had performed a multi-file batch upload. He had uploaded a file called PKUNZIP.BAT and another file, COMMAND.COM. I began to understand what this guy had done. I was impressed. This guy knew how Wildcat BBS's work!

When a file is uploaded to a Wildcat BBS, the file is often uploaded into a directory called C:\WILDCAT\WCWORK\NODE1. In the Wildcat manual, the SYSOP is given some sample lines of a file called SCANFILE.BAT. SCANFILE.BAT is the batch file that the SYSOP creates to scan files that are uploaded. I had used the sample lines from the manual as a template to create my super SCANFILE.BAT batch program. My attacker had batch uploaded a file called PKUNZIP.BAT and an additional infected COMMAND.COM file. When my SCANFILE.BAT file tried to unzip the files in my C:\WILDCAT\WCWORK\NODE1 directory, the PKUNZIP.BAT file was run rather than my legitimate PKUNZIP.EXE file! The PKUNZIP.BAT file ran the infected COMMAND.COM file, which in turn turned the Screaming Fist II virus loose upon my system before the SCANFILE.BAT batch file ever got to a point where it could scan the uploaded files! What the attacker didn't know and couldn't have known was that I was using DR DOS, not MS-DOS. When the infected COMMAND.COM file was run, the virus loaded itself into memory, but DR DOS didn't appear to like the non DR DOS COMMAND.COM program. I believe at this point DR DOS essentially "puked" giving the now infamous environmental error. It was this error or conflict with DR DOS that actually kept many of my files from being infected. In all, only about 25 files ever became infected. Unfortunately, the files that did become infected governed the drives' compression routines. The great "problem" was restoring these files. I didn't have a ready backup, I didn't have my files where I could easily find them, and I couldn't find my operating system files. The super SYSOP wasn't so super after all.

After several days of analysis of what had happened, I rewrote my SCANFILE.BAT file, turned my upload feature back on, and began the BBS again. I was now very respectful of what this guy had done. In fact, as the weeks passed, I came to appreciate the intellect and cunning of this hacker. I hope that one day I can have a conversation with this special person. If this special person is out there and can figure out who I am, I hope he will call me. I'd love to meet him...

Since the time of my "hacking" I have come to respect my fellows in cyberspace to a much greater degree. I now feel that I am a part of this wonderful infinite world. Have I, the hacked, become a hacker? I suppose it depends on your definition...

War Dialing (Summer, 1995) *By VOM*

Living in small towns most of my life it has been hard to find any information on phreaking and related topics. So most, if not all, of what I have learned has been through trial and error and from a select few of other people I have met who share the same interests as I do—namely computers and phone systems.

Also, the town where I live owns the phone company. It is a rare situation and not many other cities own a Telco. And up until about 1989 they hardly had any computerization at all and were still using very old equipment.

I had one Telco person say there were still some mechanical switches in the CO. I don't know if that was true or not but with Citytel I would not discount it. They completely upgraded their system in 1990 and *everything* is computerized now.

Years ago when I was still in high school I read about a program that would dial numbers sequentially for some mundane purpose. At the time I had just bought a 300 bps modem for an Atari computer I had and was intensely interested in finding computers that I could connect with. Being in a small town in 1983 (under 3000 people), there was no BBS or anything local that I could dial into so everything was long distance. Not knowing a thing about phreaking I figured I could write my own program like the one I read about to dial everything in my prefix area and have it look for computers.

After about a week, I had a program in Basic that worked and did what I wanted. I could only dial at night since it was on my parents' line. In about two days, the program found a number that answered with a modem.

All I got was a prompt ("login>") when I connected to my mystery number. I tried to get in for a few days but I had no clue as to what it was asking for. I was in the local library and looking at some computer books when I saw the same prompt in a book. It was a UNIX machine apparently. Well, after that I started to look for anything that was about UNIX. I finally found an ID that got me in—UUCP I think it was. I must say after that little hack I was hooked. I wandered around that system for a few days and read anything I could on UNIX. Eventually I found that the computer belonged to the local school board. I told a friend in my computer lab at school what I had found and he went and blabbed it around and the next thing I know I was having a little chat with the principal and a few others from the school board. Needless to say the powers that be freaked when they found what I had done. They did a little audit on their system and found that I had logged in quite a few times over a few weeks.

I knew nothing about hacker ethics at the time but all I wanted to do was learn about computers and other systems so I was careful not to damage their system. I can say all the books and mags that I read helped out quite a bit. I tried to explain that to them but they didn't listen and I was given one month's suspension and my parents were shocked that I could even do such a thing. All my computer stuff was carted away in a box and I was not let near it for about two months. Needless to say I was kinda famous when I got back to school.

I moved away to a larger town of about 16,000 when I finished school and I did not really think about doing any hacking again until I read about the famous Clifford Stoll and his hunt for the German hacker. By then, I had an old XT and a 286 and was using a comm program called Qmodem. I wrote a script in Qmodem's script language that did what my old dialer program did for my Atari.

I found lots of computers over a period of about a week. Lots were open systems with absolutely no security at all. I guess no one thought about hackers and how unprotected their systems are. Also I had learned more about computer systems and networks. Some of the UNIX machines I was able to log into and gain root access almost right from the start.

As fate would have it, the first system I found was the local school board and I got system administrator access first try with sysadmin. No password on it at all. I attempted to cover my tracks but did not do a very good job of it and they eventually took the system off line and changed the number. I found it again about a month later and they had upgraded the machine quite a lot. But I didn't do much with it as they were savvy to intruders. But not enough...they still left the system wide open and I got root access almost right away. That really amazed me. After being hacked, they still left the system wide open.

I did find one interesting thing that to this day I don't know what exactly it was for. I found a number that I could connect with and I was trying to get a prompt and suddenly some phone numbers appeared on the screen. I decided to let it run for a while and see what else happened. Over a period of about half an hour new phone numbers would suddenly show up on the screen. One column always had one of four numbers in it and the second column was always a different one. Eventually I figured out that it was something that the phone company had set up that recorded who was calling the police department, fire department, a shelter for battered women, and a small RCMP substation. Nothing spectacular, but interesting nonetheless.

I found a computer that controlled a gas cardlock system where you had to use a punch coded card to pump gas. I wondered how to get into it as the prompt was "Password:". The town is not that big so I drove around until I found the one I figured was the one. I looked over the system where you inserted your card and saw a little plate on the side with a serial number. Seeing that, I wrote down the five numbers and went home and called the system. Not really thinking that the serial number was the password, I entered the five digit serial number at the prompt and bingo! I was in. I think it was mostly a fluke that I got in, but hey...a fluke is better than not getting in at all. I found I could shut the pump down or give myself free gas if I wanted to but was always afraid of getting caught.

After about three months of getting into every computer I could, I found I got kind of bored of it. Also, this time I told only one other person about what I was doing but it was a fellow who approached me with a number that he had found. I thought of telling others but no one would have really understood anyway what motivated me to get into systems. Mostly curiosity about other systems, how they work, and I guess the challenge of just doing it.

Another reason I stopped was the phone company upgraded their switch so people could have caller ID and all the bells and whistles. I'd still like to do it but I don't know how much of an eye the phone company has on lines these days. Before it was almost nil with the mechanical switches but now their switch is pretty good.

However, a few days ago I accidentally dialed a wrong number and got a computer tone. My old hacker curiosity got the better of me and I dialed it again with my modem. To my surprise it was the CityTel switching computer! I got the prompt "Username>" with a banner saying city telephones so I'm assuming it's a VAX but I'm not sure as I hung up fairly quickly and I don't know what they have for security. Too bad...I'd like to see what they've got in there!

I've kind of grown out of it but still think about doing it now and again. But to the point of why I'm mostly writing this. I still have the old Qmodem script that scans prefixes and thought that others might want to use it as they see fit. It's short, but it works well. I don't know how any other scanners work but this is the one I made. The only thing is you have to have Qmodem for it to work but it is available in a test drive version probably on most BBS's.

The script is as follows:

```
;Autodialer Script for Qmodem.

clrscr
assign 1 ATDT
assign 9 0

display 'Autodialer Script for Qmodem.'
writeln ' '
writeln ' '
write 'Enter the three digit prefix: '
getn 2 4
writeln ' '
write 'Now enter the four digit starting number: '
getn 3 4
writeln ' '
write 'Enter filename to save numbers to: '
get 6 20
writeln ' '
write 'Do you want to stop dialing at a certain number? (Y/N): '
inkey 4 1
writeln ' '
if '$4' = 'n' go_dial
writeln ' '
write 'Enter the number you wish to stop at: '
getn 5 4

turnon online

go_dial:
  displayln 'Now dialing $2-$3'
  pause 2000
  send '$1$2$3^M'

pause 25000   ;timing for how many rings.  25000 is for 20 seconds or
about
                          ;three or 4 rings.
if $offline add

gosub save
goto go_dial
```

```
add:
  displayln 'No connection made with $2-$3'
  hangup
  flush
  incr 3
  if '$3' > '$5' bye
goto go_dial

save:
  displayln 'CONNECTED with $2-$3'
  incr 9
  writeln 'Hanging up modem.'
  hangup
  clrscr
  writeln 'Writing number to disk.......'
  pause 3000
  openfile c:\$6 append
  writefile $2$3
  closefile
  writeln 'Done.'
  pause 1000
  clrscr
  flush
  incr 3
return

bye:
  writeln ' '
  writeln 'You connected with $9 computers.'
  writeln ' '
  writeln 'Terminating Program.'
  exit
```

Military Madness (Autumn, 1995)

The true story of my experiences as a paid hacker for the military.

Most people aren't technical wizards, and they don't want to be. Most people are happy to understand the technology they have to use in everyday life, like their VCR's, for example. Some of us live for technological joys and toys, but we're a smaller group. There is an even smaller, rarer third group: new, eager computer users, anxious to be techies, but who aren't there yet. One such individual was a Lt. Colonel I knew during my years with the U.S. Air Force.

Don't get me wrong, no one hated the guy. Far from it; he was friendly and well-liked. He just had too much time on his hands. His retirement was just months away. All his official duties had already been assigned to others. He went from office to office, trying to help people out, while filling his time by playing with their computers. He would give them public domain programs, reorganize their hard drives, whatever struck his fancy. Sometimes he actually helped, sometimes it didn't quite work out that way. As long as he didn't do any real damage, no one had the heart to tell the guy to quit trying to help them. Besides, he was a Colonel; you don't tell Colonels to stay the bleep off your computer!

One day the Colonel "helped" everyone out by reassigning all their function keys—without asking their permission, or even telling them about it. That was the last straw. Colonel or no, something had to be done. Everyone had work to do (usually in a hurry) but no one knew how to anymore; all their accustomed keypresses were no longer valid. The Colonel had standardized keypresses to match his favorite word processor, assuming everyone else knew and loved that word processor. No one else had any experience with it. Being technophobic, they weren't about to learn anything new either!

At first, the poor users just called me, their resident techie, to have me quietly undo what the Colonel had done. They just wanted their computers to work like they used to. One brave (and very ticked off) Sergeant, though, had me install a password program on his computer, specifically to keep certain people from "helping" him anymore. Everyone told him he was crazy and he'd get in trouble. Time went by. When he didn't get in trouble, everyone else wanted password protection too. Until then the standalone, non-networked computers didn't have passwords. Since you had to be physically there, on a guarded military base, to get info from them, no one worried: We didn't anticipate problems from within our own ranks, though!

Suddenly, nearly everyone had password protection. It wasn't super serious protection, but it didn't have to be. It just had to keep honest people honest. Remember, though, that these were non-technical people, who resisted learning anything new.

As strange and foreign as the idea may seem to techies, within two weeks, people had forgotten their passwords. Yes, they had locked themselves out of their own computers! These were simple, obvious passwords, too, made up by the users themselves, not some super hard-to-break computer generated codes.

I was used to being called in to fix other people's computer problems, since I was the official technical whiz in residence. I've seen some pretty strange problems, too, but this one took the cake! I had to break into their computers, find out where the password program was hidden in their computer's hard disk drive, and read its computer codes. All this, just to tell them what their own password was! Unbelievable!

The first time it happened, I mentally wrote it off as someone's hangover. The second time, I was starting to reconsider general stupidity as an option, but I was still in denial and considered it another fluke. Two patterns became clearer as time went on. One, that the users weren't going to learn. Two, that all their computers had enough similarities to make it possible to automate the breaking-in process, which I had been doing by hand.

One afternoon (when the rest of my office left me alone while they went on an extended lunch break—the bastiges!), I took the opportunity and hacked up a better solution. Mostly, I just wanted to see if I could do it. I told no one about it, in case I couldn't make it work. Why shoot your mouth off and be embarrassed later? Besides, I wasn't sure I wouldn't get in trouble for doing this, since I didn't have any sort of permission to do it. So, quietly, secretly, I wrote up a program, testing it on my computer first.

Next, I needed to test it on someone else's computer. I had a whole building to pick from. I wanted a real challenge. I wanted to be extra careful, though. I trusted one coworker, another techie, who I knew would appreciate my sense of humor in all this. I asked him to pick a computer for my test, one that he knew would be difficult to crack. He chose one, and I went to that office, asking to use their computer. Incredible—they waved me into their private computer area, not even getting up or asking why I wanted to use it! I did my little automated cracking routine, saw the password on the screen, and wrote it down by hand on scratch paper. I covered my tracks, thanked them, left, and showed my friend. Once he got over the initial shock, he told me that if it were a "real" program, it would print out the password, using their printer. Smart ass—I knew all along that he had the right sense of humor for this!

I went back to my office, added that feature, then added a few more just in case he upped the stakes on me again. The new version could not only print its output, but could show it three different ways. One was for normal text (easy) passwords, and two were computer-only codes for harder passwords. I guess I had overdone it; instead of being merely impressed and amused, my friend was starting to worry about all this. I was disappointed to hear that. He quit before I got to show him the countermeasures I had devised, to protect my computer from my program, I wanted to show him how my computer would trick my program into displaying a phony password. We both agreed to quit while we were ahead, though, disappointment or not.

One morning, just minutes after I arrived at work, I got a call. Another forgotten password. No big deal; I was prepared. Not taking it too seriously, I grabbed my cracking disk and headed down there. Great! When I arrived, the place was full of big shots, and everyone's stressing out, trying to get this one important computer going. The Colonel himself was there working on it. He saw me come in, and stepped aside to let me try it. Normally, no one cared what I did to fix things. This time, when I least needed it, I had a super-attentive audience.

I'm silently cursing my luck. I reluctantly get out my password busting diskette, insert it in front of everybody, and make the program do its thing. Seconds later, there's the password. The in-joke prompt, asking me if I want a printout of the password, doesn't look so funny right now. "I'm in deep trouble now, for sure," I think, "and I've only been to work for fifteen minutes!" I try to act nonchalant as I get the computer going again, hoping no one thinks to ask where I got that disk. No one asks. I leave and go back to my normal tasks, wondering if I'm going to get called into some big shot's office to explain all this.

He comes to me. The Colonel himself shows up, right at my desk, and waves me out into the hallway. At first I panic. I don't really hear what the Colonel is saying; I'm too busy looking around for the military cops! Slowly, when they fail to show up, I start listening closer. It seems that the Colonel just wants a copy of the program for himself. "Sure, Colonel, all the copies you want! What? Keep the program a secret? No problems there, either!" Talk about relief. I'm probably shaking a little by now, thinking about how many big rocks I almost had to break into little ones, or something.

Life went on pretty much normally after that, except for the funny awed stares I got from time to time. I had the impression that the Colonel had been bragging to some of his high-placed friends about this guy he had working for him. Once I found out that I wasn't in trouble, and that the powers-that-be seemed to like what I had done, I relaxed quite a bit. I was even proud, in a strange sort of way, to have my program all but classified as a government secret. And the Colonel loved his new toy, too! The other computer users weren't exactly thrilled, but I was too safe and happy to care.

Everything was pretty sweet until I came back from lunch one day, and saw the Colonel sitting at my computer desk. Suddenly, I remembered the countermeasures I had put on my computer and then forgot about. Panic time again! I walked up quietly and peeked over his shoulder. Sure enough, my computer's screen was displaying the message; "This computer's password is: 'Try harder, asshole!' Do you want a printout?" I leaned over, quickly typing in the real password for him. Lucky for me the man had a sense of humor!

Confessions of a Beige Boxer (Spring, 1996) *By RedBoxChiliPepper*

Here's what happened when I took beige boxing just a little too far while living in Celina, Ohio (population 8,000). I started out like most people, just finding a Telco box or a neighbor's box on the side of their house, plugging in my phone and dialing away at the 900 numbers and harassing operators. But that got really old after awhile. So I set up sort of a permanent beige box on my next door neighbor's line. I hooked a line into their box, ran it under the siding to make it invisible, down next to a basement window and into the ground. From there I dug a trench in the ground about 3 inches deep from their box to my box and hooked the wire into my box, to the yellow and black wires.

Now I could use their line to call BBSes around the world for free! I decided not to make any direct long-distance calls so they wouldn't start investigating and find the extra line going into the ground. So I only third-number billed and used calling cards from their line and tried as best as I could not to annoy the operators too badly.

So you see, it started out sort of innocently, but then I began to eavesdrop on a lot of my neighbors' conversations. After awhile the conversations got sort of boring so I hooked up my two-line phone to both of the lines and started conferencing total strangers onto their line while they were in the middle of a conversation, which caused quite a bit of confusion, especially when I hooked them up to overseas people. Then to make things worse, I'd pop in and say in a deep voice, "Please deposit 25 cents!"

Pretty soon, my neighbors got to be too boring for me. I mean, they reacted to my pranks on their line the exact same way every time and their conversations without me were totally boring, hardly worth listening to. So I went to my *other* next door neighbor's house one night to check out the possibilities on their line and ended up doing the same thing to their line only running the line in my basement window and upstairs to the spare bedroom where the other two lines were hooked up.

Since I only had one conference phone that didn't work very well to begin with, I decided to build a simple switchboard on top of my desk. It ended up being a piece of sheet metal with five two-position switches on it. Switch 1 was my own phone line, switch 2 was the first neighbor's line, and switch 3 was the other neighbor's line. Also, each switch had a light above it to indicate In-Use. Normally, the switches would be in the "off" position. If I wanted to use a line, I flipped it on and hit the speakerphone button on my desk phone or used my official Bell operator headset. (Actually, one of those cheap headsets that you buy from Radio Shack, but hey—I drew a Bell symbol on it, okay?)

So now with their two lines and my own three-way calling line, I had a total of four phone lines to play with. The new neighbor's calls proved to be much more interesting than the others. They had a son and teen-aged daughter who liked to talk on the phone a lot. And when their conversations *did* get a little boring, I helped them out by patching my Sound Blaster card directly into my switchboard so I could add sound effects, movie clips, and rude noises to their conversation. Lemme tell you, their reaction to this was fantastic. Each kid would blame it on the other and when I did it to either of the parents, they would yell at their kids to quit playing around on the phone.

Now I was happy and had plenty of things to do with my spare time, which I had a lot of. I'd been using various calling cards from both of their lines late at night to call bulletin boards for about a month and a half and still Telco Security hadn't called them up questioning them about anything. I thought maybe they were just trying to build a case against them and were holding out for more fraud. In any case, I decided to keep close tabs on their phone calls in case AT&T called them questioning anything so I'd have advance warning to sneak back over and disconnect their lines. To help with this I bought a few of those cool Radio Shack deals that automatically record all incoming and outgoing calls on your lines so I could keep up with their phone calls while I was at work.

Then something horrible happened. Most of my favorite phone companies around the United States figured out that they were being ripped off big time by people who order calling cards with personalized pin numbers for other people. This security flaw was my major source of calling cards and now they had set it up so if you wanted to do this you needed the victim's social security number. Getting their social security number wasn't a super hard task but it sure was a pain in the ass to have to do that every time I wanted a new calling card. They were making things *hard* for me. I only had about twenty cards left and my cards went dead pretty quick lately because of my extensive international calling. I could third-number bill everything but if you've ever tried to do that for a BBS call you know that it's a pain in the ass to get it right.

That's when I went over to the window and looked across the street. I saw a little shop with a pay phone next to it and a guy in a suit talking on the pay phone. Since car phones weren't a big thing yet in this little town, the few yuppies that there were usually stopped by this phone to make their important phone calls. And of course they preferred credit cards to pocket change. A plan started to form in my head. Of course I couldn't run a phone wire underneath the street because the police probably wouldn't be too happy if I used a jack hammer. So...

That night at 3:00 a.m, I got on my cellular phone and dialed the direct line to the Celina police. I explained to them that I had just seen a few kids jump the fence to the boatyard by my house and break into the office. I listened in on my scanner as the dispatcher sent all available units to the boatyard. (All two of them, eh?) I was ready when I heard that and I ran across the street to the pay phone. I had done this a million times before but usually it was in a secluded area and there wasn't such time pressure.

I pulled out my specially cut Allen wrench and opened the bottom panel of the pay phone. I set the base unit of my cordless phone there in the bottom and clipped the wires into the pay phone line. Then I plugged the AC cord into the receptacle. (Most phones have these in the bottom panel to power the light on top of the phone.) I wrapped a garbage bag around the phone to protect it from water damage and the evil GTE linemen and put the panel back on. The whole thing took less than four minutes. Meanwhile, the brutal Celina police force was crawling around the boatyard with flashlights, looking underneath all the boats for these hardened criminal kids. They never found them, though.

I went back home and picked up my cordless handset. I turned it on and dialed the local Wal-Mart. A recording came on, telling me to deposit twenty-five cents. So I called a number a little further away. I called Mann's Chinese Theater in Hollywood, California and was asked to deposit $2.25. I tried red boxing the coins in but I think the reception was screwing it up. I ended up going through a live operator who put the call through for me.

I decided I'd better get this fixed. I didn't need GTE dropping a trouble card on my pay phone and discovering my cordless base unit in there. So I took the handset apart and hard-wired it into my switchboard. I replaced the rechargeable batteries with an AC line and built a red box on the switchboard that was hooked directly into the cordless phone's microphone. Then I boosted the antenna by hooking it to the old TV antenna on top of my house. This was getting to be pretty fun!

The next morning I had the alarm set for 10:00 a.m. so I could sit at my window and wait for yuppies to use my pay phone. My first customer came at 10:18, a little kid who used a copper slug. Damn him, I should call his parents for this. Anyway, I came on and impersonated the operator, telling him he was in big trouble and if he didn't put in a real fifty cents immediately I would come over there and rip that St. Louis Cardinals hat right off his head and hit him with it. He hung up, looked nervously around and quickly disappeared into the alley.

At 10:57, while I was in the middle of my Frosted Flakes breakfast, the neighborhood mailman stopped by to use the phone. I looked through my binoculars and saw him punch a "zero" first. I was so happy milk came out of my nose. When he tried to enter his calling card number, I interfered by hitting some extra numbers. He tried it again and I messed him up again. Then I heard the AT&T recording, "Please hold for operator assistance." An operator came on and asked for his card number. He read it off as I wrote it down. I was so grateful to him that I didn't even harass him during his call.

I got three calling card numbers that day. The next day I got a little more creative. I got on the pay phone line and dialed a phone company number that just sat there, blank. When a guy picked up the phone, I played a recording of a dial tone into the phone. When he began dialing I stopped the recording and when he finished dialing I played the recording, "AT&T! Please enter your calling card number now..." He began to enter his calling card, and I came on and talked to him in a really annoying nasal voice:

Me: "AT&T, what seems to be the problem?"
Him: "I'm just using my calling card."
Me: "Okay, what's your calling card number?"
Him: [gives me his number]
Me: "That card's not going through here. Do you have another card?"
Him: "Uh...yeah, I have my AT&T calling card."
Me: "Okay, let's try that one."
Him: [gives me his number]
Me: "Okay...yep, that one's okay. Here's your call and fuck you for using AT&T!"

I had no idea what number he had dialed in the first place so I got an old recording of Tina, the phone sex operator and put it on the line. "Hi, this is Tina...Are you ready for a hot time?" The poor guy tried to talk to her and finally realized that it was a recording and hung up. I watched him walk down the street and use the phone booth a few blocks away.

A few days later, I bought one of those touch-tone decoders. It had an LCD display that showed me exactly what digits were being dialed on any line I hooked it up to. I hooked this into my switchboard, and not only was it easier for me to get calling cards, but I could see exactly who my neighbors were calling. I started keeping files on the neighbors and who they called. Oh, did I mention that I have no life? You may have figured that out already.

Two months later not much had changed. I still had the same setup and was working on expanding it. I added ten more switches to it for extra lines and started wandering around my neighbors' yards late at night, looking for new possibilities. I also hooked an old bulky cellular phone into my setup so I could connect neighbors to the cellular roaming network and I added another phone so I could listen in on more than one line at a time without them hearing each other.

The little green Telco box on our block was very well secluded. It sat near some bushes in the alley behind my house, about three houses over. The only problem with it was that it was sitting right underneath a bright street light. I eventually took care of the street light with my pump pellet rifle. It took an hour's worth of patience to finally hit it just right, but I finally turned it off. That being accomplished, I went to the hardware store and bought a cable. This nifty little cable had 50 separate wires inside of it, enough to hook 25 phones to.

When dark finally came, I grabbed my back pack and hiked over to the Telco box. I opened it and started hooking my phone, dialing 1-800-MY-ANI-IS on every set of terminals in there and taking notes of what was what. I was going to go for choice and pick my least favorite neighbors but decided that that would take forever so I hooked up to the first 50 terminals (on the backside, so Telco wouldn't notice) and put the box back together. I hoped I hadn't hooked up one of my neighbor's that I already had hooked to my house 'cause it'd suck to waste a whole line like that.

Now the hard part. I dug a trench a few inches deep from the Telco box, down the alley, into my own back yard, then through the yard and into that little hole underneath my basement window. It took me over three hours to complete all of this but when I was finished there wasn't a trace that anything strange was going on. I had to cut a hole in the floor to get the cable upstairs to my switchboard and found myself hoping that my landlord wouldn't drop by anytime soon. He got testy when I drilled holes in his property. So I got that far and went to bed. I couldn't really do much more 'cause I needed to go to Radio Shack and buy some more switches and a larger piece of sheet metal.

Another month passed. I discovered that I had access to the phones in random houses as far away as two blocks *and* another pay phone. I'd hooked about every sound device I owned into the switchboard, including my computer's SoundBlaster, tape deck, CD player, voice changer, and echo machine. I had the ability to hook 28 lines up to a single phone, creating a monster party line of confused people and my calling card list had reached almost 100 numbers. That's the most I'd ever had all at once.

Then on Friday the power bill arrived. It was an outrageous amount, probably because I had a habit of turning on heaters while opening windows, leaving lights and my computer on all day, etc. It didn't seem fair that I should have to pay so much to them, especially since I stopped going to work as often so I could sit at home and play operator. My neighbors had a receptacle on their deck that they used to plug in the bug lamp and sometimes a radio. I figured if they weren't using it all that much, I'd take advantage of that.

That night I dug down about a foot where the plug was and cut open a section of the plastic pipe to expose their wires. Carefully using rubber gloves and pliers, I managed to splice my orange 100-foot extension cord into their line. I ran that underground to my basement window and start plugging my large appliances in. The refrigerator, space heater, microwave, and electric oven. So I walked over to their power meter and peered in to the glass bubble and noticed the disk was spinning quite rapidly. Oh well. They owned a pool and deck. Obviously they could afford a little more electricity.

I figured that if they were rich, they could probably afford cable TV and I noticed that their cable line was conveniently located next to their phone box. So the day after that I got free cable. A few weeks later, free cable alone just wasn't enough for me. I wanted to be able to control what my neighbors watched. So I hooked up sort of a loop so that their cable line was coming to my house before it got to them. Then I built this little switchboard next to my phone switchboard that consisted of a few TV monitors, a VCR, a video camera, and some video mixing devices.

By the time I was through hooking it all up, I had the power to change their channels, make them watch my home video collection, or wipe their TV show off the air with a variety of 37 different wiping techniques! I also had a monitor set up showing me exactly what they were seeing in their house. By now you're probably wondering what these neighbors did to me to make me want to be so mean-spirited to them. Well, nothing. They just lived at the wrong house at the wrong time.

I tuned in to their phone and TV. The old lady was talking to Gertrude while watching *The Price Is Right* and her husband was out in back, trying to figure out the problems they've been having with their bug zapper light. I left her TV picture on but muted the sound so I could talk over Bob Barker. Using my voice changer, I announce, "Greetings, Earthling Mildred. I am alien visitor Q359-Kriegsmitzelpapshmeer. I come in peace. Take me to your leader, Bob Barker, or I will disintegrate your house. Oh, and I also want a Metallica box CD set and I want to know what a vacuum cleaner is..."

I left them alone completely until Mildred got back from the hospital. While they were gone, I bought some heavy duty wire and tapped into their circuit breaker box, giving me complete control. I also ran their water line through my house so I could leech and control that. When they got home, Mildred got in the shower and Herb sat down to watch Tammy Faye Bakker on TV. I walked over to my "Department of Water" switchboard and turned a valve. This valve released the five gallon tank of washing machine Blue (dye) into their water lines. Then I popped in the porno video "Edward Penishands" and sent that into their living room TV set. Herb was so engrossed in his show that he didn't even hear Mildred screaming something about alien invasions.

A few months passed. I spent the day mowing my neighbor's lawn while they were gone (I mowed the words "WE COME IN PEACE"). It was 2:30 in the morning and I grabbed my backpack and sprinted over to the Celina Power and Light building. I began to dig a trench from their building to my basement window...

Ahem, wait a second. I think I've been using a few too many illegal substances or something. Actually, I made this whole thing up. I was bored, okay? Anyone who believed any of it even for a second needs to have their head checked out. The story is probably full of holes although I really did live in Celina, Ohio alone and bored for a few months and ran up quite a hefty phone bill. It was my own bill, though. I really hope this article is an inspiration to all and hope that the Celina Police will stop looking for those kids in the boatyard after they read this.

Downsizing Insurance (Spring, 1997) *By Hans Gegen*

You can buy insurance for just about anything these days. Some kinds of insurance, however, are better procured at home...or in the office. In an increasingly worker-hostile business environment, it's best to have something on hand in case disaster strikes. I don't recommend doing anything illegal. But your employers should be vaguely aware that if they let you go arbitrarily, there will be consequences. I once watched a co-worker clean out his desk after being let go. He was so angry about what happened he was stuffing pens, calculators, note pads, and staplers in his bag. This was fairly pathetic. In the end, even a few hundred dollars worth of office supplies won't be missed. If you want to be *really* missed, make a "fire kit."

Before I get into specifics, I want to stress that you should begin working on your fire kit long before you're put on the death watch. So *start today.* In fact, start poking around the corners of the company's networks and file cabinets for sensitive material as soon as you're hired. Watch what comes in on the fax machine. If you see the president's assistant photocopying something, distract him or her so that they leave the original in the machine.

This leads me to your second tactic: *plausible deniability.* It's worked for the CIA for 50+ years, and you can make it work for you! Yes, if you're going to be caught nosing around somewhere where you shouldn't be, it's important to have an alibi ready—and a good one at that.

Boss: "Why were you digging around in the file servers?"
You: "What's a file server?"

Boss: "The place where all of our computer files are stored."
You: "Oooh. *That*. I'm sorry, I'm new! I'm still trying to figure out where my predecessor's memos are stored."
Boss: "Oh. Here, let me show you."

(A note on my imagined dialogue: It's important to your credibility to understand how your co-workers perceive your computer savviness. If they know that you can recompile Linux kernels on a unicycle, then you're not going to be believed. So, if you're going to play dumb, *stay dumb* to the outside world. Once caught, be warned that you have already started a trail.)

Approach all of your actions as if you were prepared to explain it to a jury (just hope that it doesn't come to that!). The key is believability, and someone who has a clear and precise recollection of events will be most believable. In short, don't make enemies, *make notes*.

Step One: Collecting Sensitive Information

With these precepts in mind, you should begin your fire kit. What's in a fire kit, you ask? Well, basically anything that will make your company worse off without you than with you. This can translate into actual documents/intelligence that your company would not want you taking with you as you're being escorted to the door on your last day. I work for a building maintenance firm in downtown Philadelphia. Some of the components in my fire kit are:

- Rates charged clients.
- Contracts/proposals.
- Personal contact databases. (ACT! databases, for example, are often networked. If you're careful not to leave a trail, you can get client notes and histories for all of your company's clientele in one fell swoop!)
- Pay records. This makes your boss real nervous.
- Future business plans.
- Lotus Notes archives.
- Potentially embarrassing e-mails authored by your superiors. (For example, your boss confides in an e-mail that they've overcharged a client.)
- Just about anything that your company's competition will drool over.

Step Two: Making Your Successor's Job Impossible

Your fire kit can also consist of nothing more than a systematic effort to make your successor's job impossible. If this is done carefully, your company will genuflect every time your name is mentioned. ("Why did we let go of Hans? He was the only one who could do this job!") If, however, they suspect that you intentionally destroyed data that your co-worker needed, they will curse and spit at any mention of your name. The key is to leave behind a work trail that is organized but extremely idiosyncratic. It doesn't hurt to add a few surprises. Here's what you can do:

- **Encrypt everything**—but "forget" passwords.
- **Lose file layouts for any data dumps**. (My predecessor did this to me!)
- **Create slight, but significant errors in your personal files**. Careful with this. They can be minor—go into your contact manager and change the zip code of the company address of your major client so all of your successor's letters of introduction never arrive. Or they can be major—transpose quoted rates in your notes to indicate that you gave the client a 52 percent discount instead of a 25 percent discount. This will affect only those people who are using your notes to continue a business relationship. Remember to keep track of your "errors" in your fire kit.
- **Organize data into extremely complex directory structures.** Embed directory after directory. Give them mysterious and useless names. Keep the key to these structures in an analog notepad, and put that notepad in your fire kit.

The Big Day

So the day of the merger has arrived and people are being called into the boss's office one by one. Your entire office has been deemed redundant and the pink slips are flying like a tickertape parade. It's time to put your kit into motion. There are a few questions to consider:

What do I turn in on my last day?

Some companies will not process your last bonus checks, expense reports, or even paychecks if you do not turn in certain files in a timely manner. This is largely a response to having salespeople take their rolodexes with them as they leave the company. I won't get into the legal aspects of who owns this information. You'll probably end up giving them the information. So what? The important thing is that you give your company the wrong information. Keep a "shadow" rolodex complete with incorrect rate quotes, inaccurate notes, and not-so-glaring omissions. You want the Rolodex/address book to be considered the real thing until those last checks come through.

You will have no choice but to turn in your computer, of course. If the company is smart (which is not a sound assumption), they will be primarily interested in what's sitting on your hard drive—the value of the computer itself will evaporate in two fiscals.

So keep your hard disk lean. Keep the applications on the disk, but keep the data with you. Don't put data on the company network if possible, because networks are usually backed up on a regular basis. If you keep files on floppies (or better yet, a 100MB ZIP disk) you're ready to roll. And always remember, intentionally destroying data is illegal.

Before you give up your computer, however, make sure to do one thing. If you take nothing else away from this article, take this: wipe out the slack and unused space on your hard drive. For those of you who don't understand the mechanics of disk drives too well, let me briefly explain. When you delete a file, you are not necessarily wiping the files off of your hard disk. Rather, you are wiping the location of the file from the FAT (file allocation table), so the disk operating system does not know where to look for the file. The one's and zeroes that make up the file are still on the hard disk. Utilities such as Norton's UnErase can do a pretty fair job of recovering "deleted" files. Therefore, those embarrassing e-mails, resume drafts, and otherwise sensitive data that you thought went down the bit bucket are still there. There are utilities such as COVERUP.COM that will actually write random garbage over the disk, making full recovery of erased data nearly impossible. (I've read that it is extremely difficult to completely obliterate a file from a hard disk. There are companies out there that do nothing but recover such "irretrievable" data—their techniques are jealously guarded trade secrets.) Unless you're working for the DoD, however, COVERUP should do a pretty good job of wiping data from your hard disk.

Where do I keep this stuff?

Keep your kit on floppies and keep the floppies with you. Use PKZIP to crunch down the file sizes. It's best to use the encryption flag on PKZIP when doing so. Also, don't do something dumb like name these files SECRETS.ZIP. If you are taking hard copies with you, don't wait until your last day. You may not have the opportunity to get anything out of the office. Also, have a system-formatted disk with COVERUP and virus-creating software on hand.

What do I do with this stuff once I've been fired?

This, of course, is the question to answer. My only concrete advice is to be careful. If you lead a trail back to yourself, you may have more than a career in the toilet, you could be facing criminal charges. It's important to remember that when you leak information, the first thing your company will want to do is figure out who is leaking. If you were recently let go, guess whose door they will knock on first. That's why it's important to set this up long before you are put on the death watch. For instance, what if some sensitive files mysteriously disappear when you are still in good graces with the company, but John Doe has been recently let go? If that material leaks, it's plausible that the material was leaked by John Doe. Take advantage of any strange opportunities. If you're willing to take the risk of exposing yourself, here are some ideas:

- Send your company's main competitor an anonymous "care package" chock-full of your company's secrets.
- Better yet, if you include an anonymous cover letter in the care package, cc your boss! (If you do this, you don't even have to send the actual package! Your company will go into freefall mode regardless! Imagine your boss talking to his competitive peer, trying to figure out what he knows!)
- Hold onto it so you can have leverage over your old company in case you're hired by the competition.
- Destroy it. If you're the only source of this info, then their cost-cutting maneuver of downsizing you will end up costing them lots! Rule of thumb—destroy/wipe anything that they don't know exists. Don't destroy files that they know you filed every week for three years.
- If the information is embarrassing, blow the whistle. (You should probably do this anyway.) Drop your local muckraking news team that bit of sensitive e-mail that came your way (please use an anonymous remailer). The material may not even be that bad—let the news team decide. If you have hard proof, they will be interested. In my company, engineers have been falsifying reports to the city for years. "Someone" in my company right now has the ability to let the city know tomorrow if the need arises!

Whatever you do, *don't* post information to the Internet. In some ways, it's easier to have something done on the Net traced back to you than by analog means. Besides, it's probably better if we didn't make the Net vulnerable to misguided media attacks for a while.

Conclusion

The goal of your fire kit is to make your company regret its decision to let you go. But it's important to keep your company from realizing that you are the cause of any "irregularities" that occur after your departure. Let them think they fired a hard-working saint. If enough of us do this, employers will have to reconsider our country's legendary "workplace flexibility."

So start building your fire kit today. Be on the lookout for any sensitive material early. Make notes of any events or comments that will be potentially damaging to your employers. Stay believable. Keep your documents on media that you take with you on the day of reckoning. Make your successor's job impossible. Last, if you're going to be vindictive, be careful. Don't let the indignity of being downsized make your actions sloppy.

Adventures with Neighborhood Gates (Summer, 1999)

By jaundice

This article will attempt to enlighten you a little on those security gates found on gated communities, office buildings, etc.

The way most of these gates are set up is that there are two lanes: one for residents, and another for visitors. The residents have either a magnetic entrance card of some sort, or a numeric code. The visitors must either have a default entrance code (not likely), or must dial the house of the person whom they wish to visit. The dial box varies with different models—most will give a list of last names with corresponding three or four digit codes. When you find the name of the person you wish to visit, you dial pound followed by the three or four digit code in most cases. The box then calls that house and you have a time limited two-way conversation with that person. They may allow you entrance by pushing a number on the keypad, which opens the gate (the number nine in this case). Most gates have a default entrance code. I've heard "911" works on most gates. There is also a default code for postal workers, delivery people, emergency vehicles, etc.

While visiting friends who live in a gated community, they told me that they had picked up the phone number for the front entrance gate on their Caller ID. This model also had a great feature on it: video access. There was a camera no bigger than a dime built into the call box. We could actually tune a television set into channel 18 and have a visual on who was at the gate. I was curious about the number that the box used to call out with. When we called it back we got a carrier, but when dialed with any terminal program, it would send back indecipherable gibberish. After a few minutes of playing with the number, we found that it would do something strange. When a visitor at the gate would dial the three digit code to call out and we dialed the box at the same time, it connected! The line was somehow patched through to that person, and we would have two way voice contact, with a visual on our end. Of course, you can use your imagination as to what you could do to a person who is waiting at a gate for entrance, and you have total control as to whether or not they get in.

There was one problem though. The time was limited, and unless we were very quick on the redial, we didn't have a very good chance of connecting at that magic moment when both we and they dialed. The number would ring twice, and on the third ring the carrier would pick up. At this time we were intent on controlling the gate completely. We took a walk out to take a look at the call box, and in addition to the names list, the name of the company who manufactures the system. With the quest for gate programming software in mind, we hit the Net. Of course this company had a web site, and some downloads. Though they didn't have the programming software for the dial-up connection, they had a pretty useful FAQ. This FAQ had codes to establish two way voice connections with the person every time (hit pound when the carrier picks up). It also had a code to lengthen the connection time. With the video option you had the chance to view the expressions of the people at the gate. Let's just say that we had total control over who was or was not going to visit the complex.

We were curious as to what kind of password protection it had, and if there was a backdoor. According to that FAQ, the box had a six-digit code in order to edit the names list on it. It would allow three tries, followed by a three minute delay. It said that if you forget your password, all you need is the serial number of the box. You call them and tell them the serial number, and presto, there's the password! We didn't go as far as to pry the cover off the box to find a serial number, but hey, if you're willing to do that...

To make a long story short, we abused the video call box for four days straight. They eventually just shut off the video channel, which took a lot of the fun out of messing with people. The box, however, is all hardwired so they can't deny you access to it without some work. These things won't work on all gate systems, but I can assure you that they aren't that different from model to model. Have fun!

12 The Changing of the Telephone

The world of phones continued its radical transformation throughout this period as was foretold by divestiture. What we wound up with was a real playground of brand-new telephony-related devices, each of which was itself transforming before our eyes. Cell phones, for instance, had become more prevalent but their days suddenly became numbered with the advent of digital cellular. As pay phones became deregulated, it was now possible to have different long-distance companies handling your calls. But then came those monsters known as Customer Owned Coin Operated Telephones (COCOTs), which got a lot of people angry and confused due to their astronomical and sneakily imposed charges. And as overall phone rates continued to decline and cell phone use of one sort of another increased, the major phone companies started to realize that pay phones just weren't the money makers they used to be.

Meanwhile the technology involved in actually *making* calls was rapidly changing as well. Digital switching became the norm as the last of the electromechanical phone switches was retired. That to me was the saddest part of the whole transformation. No more would we hear those deep baritone rings or be able to tell what equipment was being used just by the sounds we heard on the line. It all started to sound exactly the same, whether you were calling New York City or Nome, Alaska. I had hoped that with all of the supposed competition in the telephone arena that there would be a huge variety of sounds and features. But alas, standardization dictated that it all be uniform. Sane I suppose, but not nearly as much fun as the chaos I was hoping for.

Features like Caller ID slowly began to take over our telephonic experiences. It may seem strange today but there were real privacy concerns when we first started to hear of the possibility of called parties actually knowing who was calling them. I'll bet most people today can't fathom what it was like to never know who was on the line until they answered the phone. For me, that was all part of the fun. You see, telephones simply didn't ring as much as they do today. Calls cost more and you didn't always have a phone within reach in order to constantly update people on your every waking thought. So when the phone in your house rang (and in the '90s there was still a good chance that it was an old-fashioned Bell telephone with a mechanical ringer, perhaps even a rotary dial as well), it somehow meant much more than it does today. It was an event. You ran to answer it, not knowing who it was until you heard the voice on the other end. And, if they hung up before you got there, it could really cast a shadow on your entire day because there was *no way* of knowing who it was. Naturally, this system made it a whole lot easier to make prank calls as well. Once the first Caller ID boxes and *69 features were implemented, it really changed the entire tone of the phone culture. And it was only through the efforts of various consumer groups that the ability to still make anonymous calls was somewhat preserved through the *67 or "all call block" feature. The phone companies nearly succeeded in making it impossible to dial anonymously. From their point of view it would make little sense for a consumer to pay all this money for a Caller ID box plus the monthly service fee if people didn't send their numbers in the first place. Plus, in those early days, Caller ID only worked in very small regions and the idea of it working interstate or even nationwide seemed very remote. We all know how quickly *that* changed once it started to catch on.

While most phone phreaks would probably resist the temptation to refer to the '90s as the decade that boxing died, it's really hard to argue that it wasn't the decade where boxing was given a terminal disease. Quite simply, digital switching used out-of-band signaling, which meant that all of those magical tones that blue boxes could make were no longer sent by the phone company on the same audio path as your voice. Therefore, there was nothing to be accomplished by generating them. Other boxing techniques like silver and black also had their days numbered by the advancing technology. Red boxing, on the other hand, continued to thrive for a bit longer as phone companies were slow to change the absurdly simple method for collecting coins at pay phones. But even with the inevitable death of the boxing culture, hackers continued to be interested in how it all worked.

Wireless Communications

The 1990s was the decade where wireless communications really took off. As our first article demonstrates, people had been using mobile phones of one sort or another for quite some time and the security was truly laughable. In this example the phone calls were being transmitted over a VHF marine frequency. But the security was equally amusing with cordless phones used inside one's home or analog cellular phones, which broadcast conversations in the clear on the 800-megahertz frequency spectrum. The cellular industry and federal government, rather than mandate effective security for such calls, had instead chosen to simply make scanners that could tune into the cellular frequencies illegal. It was seen as the typical manner in which the clueless and greedy dealt with security issues, not by addressing the technical aspects but by covering their asses with meaningless legislation. But it was all a moot point; the days of analog cell service would start to become numbered by the end of the decade. The new GSM standard (new for the States at least) used encryption while transmitting so eavesdropping was nowhere near as simple. Other types of monitoring, however, were in the process of being developed....

Listening In (Spring, 1990) *By Mr. Upsetter*

Every now and then, those of us who take the time to be observant stumble across something remarkable. Let me relate to you one of those experiences. It was an all too lazy sunny afternoon in Southern California. I was bored, and I decided to listen to my Realistic PRO-2004 scanner. I flipped it on and scanned through the usual federal government, military aviation, and cordless phone frequencies, but there was no good action to be found. I happened across some scrambled DEA transmissions and a droning cordless phone conversation by some neighbors I could not identify. So for a change I scanned through the marine radio channels.

The scanner stopped on marine radio channel 26, which is used for ship-to-shore telephone calls. A man was reading off his calling card number to the operator, who gladly accepted and connected his call. Calling card numbers over the airwaves! I was shocked—astonished that such a lack of security could not only exist, but be accepted practice. I began monitoring marine telephone to find out more, and it turns out that using a calling card for billing is commonplace on VHF marine radiotelephone.

People use calling cards for billing all the time. That's what they are for. But is it that big of a deal? You bet it is. Marine telephone uses two frequencies, one for the ship and one for the shore station. The shore station transmits both sides of the conversation at considerable power, enough to offer reliable communications up to 50 miles offshore. Anyone with a standard police type scanner, costing as little as $100, can listen in. People using marine radiotelephone can be broadcasting their calling card number to a potential audience of thousands. And that just shouldn't be happening.

But it is. And there is no doubt that calling card fraud is occurring because of this lack of security. From the phone company's (many Bell and non-Bell companies provide marine telephone service) point of view it must be a tradeoff for customer convenience. You see, there just aren't that many ways to bill a ship-to-shore call. Most calls are collect, a few are billed to the ship if they have an account, and a few go to third-party numbers or other special accounts.

Sometimes the operators have trouble verifying billing information. I monitored one man who, after racking up $40 worth of AT&T charges, was informed that they couldn't accept his international account number. The operator finally coaxed him into giving an address for billing. Calls are often billed to third-party numbers without verification. But calling cards make billing easy for both the customer and the phone company involved.

It would also be tricky for a company to not allow calling card use. Doing so would be an inconvenience to customers and would force them to admit a lack of communications security. Of course, people using marine radio should already realize that their conversations aren't private, but announcing the fact wouldn't help the phone company at all. In fact, people may place fewer calls.

The convenience offered by calling cards makes them an easy target for fraud. They can be used by anyone from any phone and with a variety of different long-distance carriers via 10XXX numbers. No red or blue box hardware necessary here, just 14 digits. But of course, the number won't be valid for long after all those strange charges start showing up on someone's bill. It should be noted that when a calling card is used, the number called, time and date of call, and location (and often, the number) from which the call was placed are printed on the bill. A fraudulent user could be caught via that information if they were careless. Also, some long-distance companies may contact the owner of the card if they notice an unusually high number of charges on the card.

Long-distance companies bear the brunt of the bills caused by calling card fraud. However, if you read the fine print, the cards offered by many companies have a certain minimum amount that the customer must pay, say $25 or $50. *(Editor's note: We have yet to hear of a case where a phone company got away with charging a customer when the only thing stolen was a number and not the card itself.)*

So what's the moral of the story? Simple. *Be damn careful what you say over any radio,* and that includes cordless and cellular telephones. If you are using a calling card, enter it with touch tones. If you happen to make VHF marine radiotelephone calls, bill collect or charge to your phone number as you would to a third-party number, without the last four calling card digits. For the most part, radio communications are easy to intercept, and keeping them secure is up to you.

For those of you with scanners who would like to check out marine telephone, here are the frequencies allocated by the FCC. Monitoring marine telephone is a good way to get an inside look at telephone company operations. If you live near the east or west coast, the Mississippi River, or the Great Lakes, there will be marine radio activity. During daylight hours you may hear transmissions from hundreds of miles away due to tropospheric ducting propagation.

VHF Marine Radiotelephone Frequencies

Channel	Ship	Shore
24	157.200	161.800
84	157.225	161.825
25	157.250	161.850
85*	157.275	161.875
26	157.300	161.900
86	157.325	161.925
27	157.350	161.950
87	157.375	161.975
28	157.400	162.000
88*	157.425	162.025

* These frequencies are allocated for uses other than marine radiotelephone in certain areas.

Cellular Phone Biopsy (Winter, 1993–1994) *By Kingpin*

Cellular phones have been a popular topic discussed by media and the underground for the past couple of months. With the rumors about cellular phones causing cancer, cellular scanning laws, the large flow of articles describing cell phones, and the recent news clips on cellular fraud, people of all kinds have become interested and aware of cellular technology. Many articles have been written on the technical aspect of cellular phones, but there is a lot of information dealing with the cellular phone itself that is not usually shared publicly with the entire community. As stated in the first issue of *Wired Magazine,* cellular phones have many hidden functions and abilities that the normal user does not know about.

Since owning my cellular phones, I have been constantly experimenting to uncover unknown functions. Like many people, I feel that obtaining free phone calls is not the only reason to reprogram and reconfigure a cellular phone. Going inside your cellular phone seems to be the truest form of hacking. Exploring somewhere where people don't want you to be, gaining knowledge that most people don't have, and having the ability to do things that most people cannot.

Starting at the beginning, getting an owner's manual for your phone will help explain some of the user-available functions. You should also try to get a hold of a service/technician's manual. These manuals usually contain the more technical side of the phone, including schematics and sometimes reprogramming and reconfiguration codes to use from the keypad of the handset.

When you open up your phone, you should observe all of the components. The first one you should find is the EPROM (Erasable Programmable Read-Only-Memory. This chip is easily found, because it has a little glass window and a number, usually 27xxx, somewhere on it. This 24-, 28-, or 40-pin chip contains the cellular phone's software, and other information, which is "cast in stone." The data stored in this chip is unchangeable, unless you read the chip, change the code, and rewrite it.

Disassembling the code is a laborious task, but should definitely be done. The microprocessor in the phone is often a custom-made applications processor based on a specific instruction set. Z80, 8051, and 8085 microprocessors are all very common in cellular phones, but are not limited to these types. Be prepared to spend many hours exploring the code to find out how the phone operates and what kind of functions are available. Most EPROMs in phones have more capacity for data than actually needed, and sometimes there is plenty of room for customization.

Another key component is the EEPROM (Electronically Erasable Programmable Read Only Memory). Usually just battery-backed RAM, this chip can be programmed and configured to your liking from the keypad of your phone. In my own phones, the following (and plenty more) can be accessed and changed by using reprogramming codes:

Electronic Serial Number (ESN)	Horn Alert On/Off (HAL CLR)	Long-Distance Call Restriction (LU SET)
Initializing the repertory memory (INIT REP)	Online Diagnostics (ONL CLR)	SID "black list" (INVLD ID)
Changing/Setting the Lock Code (LOCKCODE)	System ID Enable/Disable (MAN)	System Selection (IRI CLR)
Allow Quick Recall (QRC SET)	Mobile Identification Number (MIN)	Signal Strength indicator (SSD CLR)
Allow Quick Store (QST SET)	Service Providers ID (SIDH)	Audio Receive On/Off
Turn the Wake-Up tone on/off (WUT SET)	Initial Paging Channel (IPCH)	Transmit Audio On/Off
Mobile to Land Hold (MLH CLR)	Extended Address On/Off (EX SET)	Supervisory Audio Tone On/Off (SAT)
Land to Mobile Hold (LMH CLR)	IPCH Scan Start — Bank A (IDCCA)	Channel Number
Call Round-Up (CRU CLR)	IPCH Scan Start — Bank B (IDCCB)	Volume Control
Extended DTMF (EE SET)	Access overload class (ACCOLC)	Power Control
No Land to Mobile (NLM CLR)	Group ID (GROUP ID)	Hands-Free On/Off

As you can see, there is plenty of opportunity for configuration. Some phones require special codes to let you change the settings, and other phones require a special handset, cable, or dongle-key proprietary to the specific manufacturer. If your phone requires such a device, it is possible to modify an existing handset or build your own cable.

Anything that is stored in the EEPROM can be changed one way or another. The EEPROM can be read in most standard EPROM programmers. The RAM usually emulates a 2716 or 2764 EPROM, but try to get specifications on the particular chip before you plug it into your programmer. Many manufacturers store the information on the EEPROM in plain text, as to not complicate it for the technicians who are performing tests on the phone.

Some companies are aware that their phones can easily be manipulated, so in order to increase security, a few steps are taken. Some phones contain LCC EPROMs instead of the standard DIP EPROMs. These EPROMs are about 1cm by 1cm, the size of the window on a standard EPROM. They perform just like standard EPROMs, except they are surface mounted, harder to erase (although they still use UV light), and because of the size, more difficult to desolder and/or clip onto. In some cases, instead of using an EEPROM or RAM to store the ESN, a NOVRAM chip is used. This chip *cannot* be read by an EPROM programmer, thus making it extremely difficult to do without chip-specific hardware.

Security for changing the ESN is also incorporated into most of today's phones. Due to increasing problems with call-sell operators, drug dealers, and other people using "cloning" techniques, security has increased greatly. An example follows: The software in one phone provides access to change the ESN three times from the keypad. This is done so the phone can be sold to another user, and be reprogrammed. Every time the ESN is changed, a counter, stored in the NOVRAM of the CPU, keeps track. Once the ESN is reprogrammed three times, a flag is set in the EEPROM and the NOVRAM, preventing any more access to the ESN from the keypad. It *is* possible to get rid of the flag in the EEPROM, but since the NOVRAM is located in the CPU, and extremely difficult to read and program without special equipment, it cannot be changed and, in order to be able to use the phone again, it must be sent back to the manufacturer for a replacement EEPROM and a clearing of the CPU NOVRAM. The only way to get around this security is to change the ESN by "hand," directly reading the EEPROM, changing the ESN, and reprogramming. I am sure there are ways around this type of security. There always are.

There are many things that can be done by reconfiguring a cellular phone. For example, by setting the Service Provider's ID (SIDH) to 0000 (and sometimes the Group ID), the phone will be placed in "roaming mode." This mode basically means that you are not confined to the service of one cellular carrier, and can choose carriers depending on your location. I will not go into the advantages and disadvantages of roaming, which can be found in other articles.

Configuring the phone so it is able to receive cellular phone conversations is particularly fun. Since a cellular phone is able to receive much of the 800 MHz band, by setting the audio receive mode to constantly be active, you will be able to hear any audio transmitted on that particular channel. By changing channels, you can scan through the cellular frequencies, receiving other people's transmissions.

Another interesting trick that can be done is to transmit on a channel which is occupied. To do so, first set the transmit audio selection to constantly be active, and after finding a channel you want to interrupt, trigger the SAT (Supervisory Audio Tone). This will drop the person from the current call, and then you can transmit through the cell site for about five seconds. I do not know exactly how this works, but I assume that you would have a higher priority for use of the channel, which would drop the other call.

This article should be used as a starting block, and was written to inform people of the vast possibilities of cell phones. You should experiment with your own phones to see what else can be done.

GSM Comes to North America (Summer, 1997) *By Phiber Optik*

In this article, I will describe various aspects of GSM, the newly implemented Global System for Mobile communications. Groovy? Then let's begin!

Just what is this GSM, anyway?

GSM started out in Europe as Groupe Special Mobile in 1982. Established by the European Conference of Post and Telecommunication Administrators (CEPT), it was to be the new standard for digital cellular. A newer, better network for mobile communications was needed. In comparison to the many nations' incompatible cellular systems, GSM would provide a standard for easy roaming, efficient use of available bandwidth, and privacy through encryption. By the mid-1980s, well over a dozen countries were committed to GSM, and in 1989, responsibility for GSM was transferred to the European Telecommunications Standards Institute (ETSI). In the early 1990s, the first public GSM network was put into place. As you can probably imagine, it wasn't easy getting everyone to agree on the encryption aspect, specifically the encryption used to deter eavesdropping. While the French and British spook agencies wanted "adequate" encryption, the Germans argued for something much stronger, being that they bordered what was, at the time, the Eastern Bloc. A compromise was arrived at, the result being the "secret" A5 encryption algorithm. Two versions were drafted, A5/1 for Europe, specifically the members of CEPT, and A5/2 for export. (If you were a particularly nasty nation, the encryption would be totally disabled.) Anyway, we'll get into the security features of GSM later in this article, so remain calm.

GSM comes to America

In the '90s, the industry began buzzing about Personal Communications Services, or PCS. PCS boasted, among other things, small communications gadgets crammed with neato-keen features to do all sorts of things. Or that's what they hoped. The FCC allocated the 1900 MHz band of the EM spectrum for PCS, and auctioned off frequencies. (I often wondered if I could purchase that part of the EM spectrum known as "blue," or maybe "green;" think of the royalties.) Anyway, certain members of the telecommunications industry recognized GSM as a great technology with which to build upon the PCS idea. The first GSM-based PCS networks were designed, implemented, and tested in the mid-'90s, and by 1995 the first taste of GSM was available to the American public. Or at least, to those who lived in the larger cities where GSM was first being implemented. Now, one obvious problem arose that has yet to be resolved. GSM abroad uses the 900 MHz band. Europe's version of PCS, known as DCS1800 or PCN, uses the 1800 MHz band. Due to the FCC's forward thinking, our GSM/PCS network is totally incompatible with the rest of the world's, simply because of the frequency. GSM phone manufacturers are scrambling to create hybrid phones that work both here and abroad, but are wrestling with the problem of combining all the needed circuitry while keeping the size and cost of the phone at a minimum. So, for the time being, we are restricted to SIM card "roaming," which is using your SIM in a foreign phone, one of the neat features of GSM. So let's get into the technology, shall we?

SIM sala bim!

At the core of GSM's security model is the SIM card, which is the Subscriber Identity Module. The SIM card can be found as either a full, credit-card-size smartcard, or a smaller card no bigger than the actual IC carrier. The former slides and stays in a slit in the handset, the latter in a small latched socket under the battery of the handset. The smaller SIMs can be popped into a credit card-sized "carrier," so it can be used with handsets that take the larger size SIMs. The idea is that a subscriber could insert his/her SIM card into anyone's GSM phone, and use the network, subject to the criterion stored on the SIM card itself. What's on the SIM card that makes it so special? The SIM card is actually a small "tamper-proof" microcontroller that is capable of performing one or two one-way-hash functions. It stores the subscriber's unique secret key (Ki) and IMSI (International Mobile Subscriber Identity) number, the subscriber's MSISDN (Mobile Station Integrated Services Digital Network number, which in English, is the subscriber's phone number), has some EEPROM for storing a PIN to lock the SIM, the preferred language for the handset's menus, a speed dialing directory, station-to-station (SMS) text messages, etc. The IMSI, like the secret key (Ki), is unique; its purpose is to identify the subscriber to the network. It has the following format: MCC-MNC-MSIN, where MCC is the 2- or 3-digit Mobile Country Code (typically the same as land-line country code), MNC is the 2-digit Mobile Network Code, indicating your home GSM provider, and MSIN is the Mobile Station Identification Number, often the same as the MSISDN number. The MCC-MNC together are called the network code, and uniquely identify a GSM provider. Some examples are 310-16 for Omnipoint, 310-15 for BellSouth Mobility, etc. (Why did we get 310 as our country code and not 001? That's probably payback for having country code 1 on the wired telephone network!) You may notice the ISDN acronym in MSISDN; as you'll see, some of GSM's internal protocols were based on ISDN standards. It's hoped that GSM will be gatewayed to land-line ISDN, but I digress.

Provided the SIM was ever used on its home GSM network, a temporary IMSI known as the TMSI is issued by the switch and stored on the SIM. Whenever the SIM is interrogated by the network as to "who" it is, it uses the TMSI instead of its IMSI to protect the identity of the owner over the air. A TMSI can be reissued at some interval, decided by the GSM provider. The secret key (Ki) is considered a shared secret; it's locked away in the SIM, only to be used by the hashing functions. Not you, and not even your phone knows what this number is. The mobile switch that authenticates you and completes your call knows what it is. It has a database containing all the valid Kis, called the AUC, the AUthentication Center database. The AUC also contains some other things, but we'll get to that shortly. The two hashing functions in the SIM are implementation specific, and are called A3 and A8, the authentication algorithm and the ciphering key generating algorithm, respectively. Oftentimes, the recommended "official" A3/A8 COMP128 algorithms are used, which are approved by the GSM Standardizations Group. (Just to satisfy your curiosity, the aforementioned A5 algorithm is implemented in the handset's firmware, and not on the SIM card.) The PIN is only used to lock the SIM, so when placed in a phone and powered up, the user must enter the correct PIN in order to make or receive calls. If the PIN is entered incorrectly some predetermined number of times, the SIM is blocked from use, and only the Personal Unblocking Key (PUK, available from the GSM provider) can unblock the SIM and restore it to usefulness. If the PUK is incorrectly entered too many times, the SIM card is rendered useless. Understand, all billing stems from the SIM, the handset is simply an extension of the medium, nothing more.

OK, so what about this handset?

A GSM phone typically has all the normal touch-tone keys, and in addition, some mechanism to navigate a simple menu of options to configure the phone and use its features. Arrow keys for scrolling, YES and NO buttons for making choices, etc. The menu is viewed on a small, multiline, LCD display. There are commonly undocumented keypad sequences for displaying information about the phone's firmware revision, and IMEI, among other things. The IMEI, or International Mobile Equipment Identity, is a unique ID for your phone. It has the following format: TAC-FAC-SN-X. The TAC is a 6-digit Type Approval Code, the FAC is a 2-digit Final Assembly Code, the SN is a 6-digit Serial Number, and X is a reserved "supplementary" digit. IMEIs are stored in the EIR (Equipment Identity Register) database. The IMEI is to the handset what the IMSI is to the SIM card. In this manner, someone attempting to use the network can be revoked by having an invalid SIM card, or an unregistered or stolen phone, or both. It should be noted that many GSM phones have neat features like firmware debuggers and call progress dumpers built in, accessible with a computer and a specially built serial cable.

Enough, Phiber, now tell me about the switch!

OK, OK. The two most common GSM switches are the Ericsson AXE MSC, based on the AXE 10, and the Nortel DMS-MSC, based on the DMS SuperNode. MSC stands for Mobile Switching Center, which is what the switch is called in GSM lingo. The MSC is part of the network subsystem, and accesses four main databases: the Home Location Register (HLR), the Visitor Location Register (VLR), the Equipment Identity Register (EIR), and the Authentication Center (AUC). The VLR is commonly integrated with the MSC (e.g. the DMS-MSC), leaving the HLR, AUC, and EIR as a separate physical entity (e.g. the DMS-HLR). There is at least one HLR on every GSM network, and commonly multiple MSCs. The MSCs talk to other nodes on the GSM network using Signaling System No. 7 (SS7). Smaller GSM networks, which only serve a particular metropolitan area, may only have a couple of MSCs, which would talk directly to the PSTN (e.g. NYNEX, Bell Atlantic) using SS7. Larger GSM networks, which serve entire countries, make use of Gateway MSCs, or GMSCs, which may need to gain access to other parts of the GSM network over an SS7 capable PSTN, because it would be impractical to have the entire GSM network directly and privately interconnected. The MSC/VLR and HLR together handle roaming and call routing; the HLR also stores all valid IMSIs and MSISDNs, while the EIR stores all the valid IMEIs. This leaves the AUC, which stores all the valid Kis, generates pseudo-random numbers, and performs the A3 and A8 hashes for the network subsystem.

What's up with those flat, funky new antennas on the fronts of buildings?

Your handset and SIM make up the "mobile station." It talks to these antennas, which are hooked up to a Base Transceiver Station (BTS) commonly located either on the roof or in the basements of these buildings. BTSs are analogous to "cells," and are grouped together into "location areas," which are given location area identifiers (LAIs). These clusters of BTSs are linked to Base Station Controllers (BSCs), typically located in yet other buildings. The BSCs talk directly to the switch (MSC) over leased lines.

Coding and multiplexing in brief: from the handset back to the switch

So now we have your phone sampling your voice at 13 kbps using the GSM protocol, the samples get packetized using a modified LAPD (a la ISDN) protocol known as LAPDm (Link Access Protocol for the D-channel, modified), and these packets are multiplexed into time slots (known as "burst periods"), eight of which make up a TDMA (Time Division Multiple Access) frame. The TDMA frames are bundled together into 26-frame multiframes, which are then modulated onto one of 124 carrier frequencies using GMSK (Gaussian-filtered Minimum Shift Keying). These 124 carriers, spaced 200 kHz apart, are the result of dividing up either 30 MHz or 10 MHz of bandwidth using FDMA (Frequency Division Multiple Access) in the 1,900 MHz PCS band. The bandwidth sizes are granted by the FCC based on the service area requirements of the GSM company (i.e., metropolitan versus suburban, etc.), and are lettered A through F, largest to smallest. A, B, and C-blocks are 30 MHz, and D, E, and F-blocks are 10 MHz. One or more carrier frequencies are assigned to each BTS. The wireless path between your phone and the nearest BTS is referred to as a Um link. Your phone converses with BTSs using FDMA/TDMA over this link. The BSCs talk to the BTSs they control over what is termed an Abis link, and talk to the switch (MSC) over an A link using the same Message Transfer Part (MTP) packets as defined by SS7. The highest layer of an SS7 MTP (akin to the "Application" layer in the OSI model) is known as the TCAP, for Transaction Capabilities Application Part. In GSM nomenclature, the TCAP contains the MAP, for Mobile Application Part, which can be rather complex. The MAPs contain the actual messages sent between the BSC and the MSC, and between the MSC and all other entities of the network subsystem.

Authentication and Encryption

The part you've been waiting for! Here's how it all works. The identity of a subscriber is authenticated to use the network using a challenge-response procedure, based on the security of a shared secret. As mentioned earlier, the shared secret is the subscriber's unique Ki, which is stored in the SIM card on the subscriber side, and in the AUC on the switch side. The AUC starts by choosing a 128-bit pseudo-random number (RAND) and hashes it with the subscriber's Ki, using the A3 algorithm, to form SRES ("signed response"), a 32-bit digital signature of Ki. Next, it uses the same RAND and hashes Ki using the A8 algorithm to form Kc, a 64-bit digital signature of Ki used as the ciphering key for A5. The process of generating RAND, SRES, and Kc is called "generating a triplet." This triplet is then cached by the HLR, and can be regenerated at some interval determined by the GSM provider. When a subscriber needs to be authenticated, his SIM tells the local MSC/VLR his TMSI, which the MSC/VLR uses to locate his HLR, which communicates back the subscriber's triplet, which is cached by the MSC/VLR. The RAND is sent to the subscriber's SIM by the MSC/VLR, and the SIM computes SRES and Kc. SRES is sent by the SIM to the MSC/VLR, which compares it to the SRES it has cached. If they match, the subscriber is authenticated! Now that the subscriber is authenticated, communication over the GSM network can begin. But first, a brief description of A5 is in order.... A5 is a stream cipher consisting of three clock-controlled linear feedback shift registers (LFSRs). Kc is used to initialize the three LFSRs, then the 22-bit TDMA frame number is fed into A5, whatever the frame number happened to be at that moment. The output is two 114-bit values, one for the transmit channel, and one for the receive channel. Each "channel," frozen in time (burst period), consists of two significant sets of 57-bit data, for a total of 114-bits. The 114-bit transmit burst period is exclusive ORed (XORed) with one of the two outputs of A5, and the 114-bit receive burst period is XORed with the other output of A5. OK, so now, provided that all over-the-air communications between the subscriber and the BTS (cell) are to be encrypted, a "start ciphering" message is sent to both the BTS and the handset. This message also indicates whether to use A5/1 or A5/2. The Kc that the MSC/VLR got from the subscriber's HLR is passed to the BTS, which feeds it into its A5 engine, and the Kc generated by the SIM is used to initialize the handset's A5 engine. Since the authentication stage was successful, the BTS's Kc and the SIM's Kc would be identical. Encryption proceeds as I laid out in the A5 description. In this manner, all voice and data traffic in the form of TDMA frames is encrypted between the handset and the BTS. How often Kc is rechosen is implementation specific. It could be multiple times during the lifetime of a call, or only once during call setup, or for every *n*th call. In addition to the initial A3 authentication, the subscriber's handset could also be subjected to a test. The handset's IMEI is looked up in the EIR database, and would either be permitted or denied from using the GSM network, e.g., if the phone was reported stolen.

Handoffs and Roaming

As you may well know, the links used for a call are not static for the duration of that call. Handoffs (also called "handovers") typically occur for load balancing during idle points of conversation, or because the mobile user is in transit. Internally, the handoff would be between time slots in the same cell (BTS), between BTSs connected to the same BSC, between BSCs connected to the same switch (MSC), or between BTSs ultimately controlled by different switches.

Roaming, or "location updating," is accomplished by the MSC/VLR and HLR. Location updating is a function of the GSM network that is performed for both home subscribers as well as subscribers from other GSM networks who are roaming partners. When a phone is turned on or is moved to a new location area, it registers its location information (LAI) and TMSI with the local MSC/VLR. The MSC/VLR deduces the subscriber's HLR from the TMSI, and sends it the subscriber's current LAI and TMSI, along with its own SS7 address. If this TMSI checks out with the HLR, the HLR sends some subscriber information that would be needed for call control (such as the triplet) to this new MSC/VLR. It also notifies any previously registered MSC/VLR to cancel its registration of the subscriber, who has relocated.

Call routing

I'll describe call routing using an incoming call from the PSTN as an example. On a large national GSM network, the first hop into a GSM network is the GMSC (Gateway Mobile Switching Center). The GMSC receives the terminating subscriber's phone number (MSISDN) from the neighboring PSTN switch over SS7. The GMSC has a table which contains the SS7 address (point code) of the HLRs for all MSISDNs on the network. The GMSC queries the proper HLR for a Mobile Station Roaming Number

(MSRN). The HLR looks up the SS7 address of the MSC/VLR that the terminating subscriber is currently local to and, using the SS7 capable PSTN to bridge the distance, asks this MSC/VLR to give it a temporary MSRN. This MSRN is allocated from a pool of reserved, valid PSTN phone numbers which are used by the GSM network to "alias" MSISDNs to. This aliasing is only valid for the duration of the call. The MSRN is returned, via the HLR, to the GMSC, which can now use this temporary MSRN phone number to route over the PSTN to the proper MSC/VLR and ultimately to the terminating mobile subscriber. On a smaller GSM network, the process is much simpler. An MSC/VLR is often the first and only hop between the PSTN and the mobile subscriber. The MSC/VLR simply asks the HLR for the IMSI that corresponds to the incoming MSISDN, matches the IMSI to its TMSI, and uses it to ring the proper subscriber's handset.

And there you have it. Consider it a primer on GSM. I know—a little technical for a primer. Well, what did you expect? This should prove ample information to satisfy your neurons for a while. If this article is well received and if I have time in the future, I may cover other topics such as custom calling features, billing, and assorted stuff. If you're looking for the GSM provider in your area, or even if there is one, look no further than the web sites of Omnipoint, Sprint Spectrum, Bell South Mobility, and Pacific Bell Mobile, to name a few. See ya!

News Items (Spring, 1998)

According to the *SonntagsZeitung* newspaper in Switzerland, Swiss police have been secretly tracking the whereabouts of GSM phone users using a telephone company computer that records billions of movements going back more than six months. Officials at Swisscom (the government-run phone company) confirmed this but swear they only used the information in court orders.

According to the paper, "Swisscom has stored data on the movements of more than a million mobile phone users. It can call up the location of all its mobile subscribers down to a few hundred meters and going back at least half a year."

There are 3,000 base stations across the country that are used to track the location of mobile phones as soon as they're switched on. Many people think this only works when they're actually having conversations.

In this country, we do no such thing naturally. However, by October 1, 2001, it will be mandatory for users of these phones to be trackable to within 410 feet.

And on a GSM-related note, that uncrackable encryption scheme that all of the GSM companies use? Cracked in April by the Smartcard Developer Association. According to Marc Briceno, director of the organization of researcher/hackers, the scheme would have been a lot more secure if it hadn't been kept so secret. "As shown so many times in the past"" he said, "a design process conducted in secret and without public review will invariably lead to an insecure system. Here we have yet another example of how security by obscurity is no security at all." In addition, evidence of possible deliberate weakening of the encryption scheme was uncovered. George Schmitt, president of Omnipoint, the New York area GSM company said, "My hat goes off to these guys, they did some great work. I'll give them credit, but we're not at any risk of fraud." The next day Omnipoint announced that it was changing its mathematical formulas for identifying phones.

Here's a story we knew was coming. William McCray of East Palo Alto, California has been sentenced to 28 years to *life* in prison for stealing and reprogramming cellular phones. That's right, life for reprogramming cellular phones! California has this thing called the three strikes law, which enables prosecutors to get extremely stiff penalties against criminals with two prior felony convictions. While this guy had a couple of violent convictions in the past, this one wasn't. And the law doesn't say that violence is a prerequisite. It doesn't take a psychic to see where this is heading.

An Overview of Cellemetry (Autumn, 1999) *By Jinx*

- **Telemetry**: A method of remotely controlling a device, gathering data, taking a measurement, or providing information using a short message burst and not requiring the physical presence of a person.
- **Cellemetry**: A wireless telemetry technology designed to monitor, control, and track anything that is worth being monitored, controlled, and tracked. In other words, just another toy to keep Big Brother watching us, and to help more companies become Big Brothers as well.

Cellemetry was developed and patented by Bell South Wireless Inc., although it is actually a joint venture by Bell South and NumereX Corp. It was specifically designed for transmitting small amounts of data to and from remote devices. Vehicle tracking, alarm monitoring, asset tracking, remote control operations, and utility meter monitoring are just the tip of the iceberg. With this technology, vending machine operators would actually be able to remotely check your office snack machine to see if it needs restocking. If they were too lazy to call the machine, they could have the machine automatically page them when more Twinkies were needed. Or say you forgot to pay your electric bill for two months. It would be possible for the electric company to send a little message causing your service to be disconnected. Meter readers would be obsolete too as this information would be automatically sent to the electric company every billing cycle. Not only that, but a tech could shut down an entire power grid from his PC if an emergency should arise.

Cellemetry devices can not only monitor the status of equipment and perform remote functions, but they can also track all types of mobile equipment and assets using GPS (Global Positioning Systems). This includes automobiles, armored trucks, railroad cars, planes, bulldozers, forklifts, trailers, barges, television camera equipment, cash machines, you get the picture. Cellemetry applications work with GPS to let you know exactly where your sh*t is at any given time.

Cellemetry needs three items to serve its function. A Cellemetry radio or CRAD for short, a Cellemetry gateway connected to a cellular switch, and a computer host to receive and process information sent by Cellemetry. The CRADs are manufactured by Standard Communications and Ericsson and cost about $100 apiece. A Cellemetry customer must have the proprietary software to access their data from the CRADS. Specific software/hardware packages are manufactured by different companies depending on individual needs. Current application packages include: Highway Master (used for tracking commercial trailers), Telemetrac (allows remote monitoring for photocopying machines), OmniMetrix (used to monitor emergency power systems in case of grid failure), Aercom (all types of asset tracking), Orion (for monitoring cable TV outages or to perform maintenance without a site visit), and several other applications, which are either available or being developed. The customer uses this software to call the gateway and once connected, will have several options to have their CRAD paged. Once paged, the CRAD will register at the nearest cellular provider and will trigger a registration notification, which is sent back to the gateway via the network. The gateway receives the registration, removes the data, and issues a registration cancellation back to the cell provider via the network. So now that the data is at the gateway, it either stays there until the customer receives it, or it is sent to the customer's host computer immediately. You cellular wizards will recognize this process as "roaming registration."

Cellemetry service operates just like a roaming phone operates in the cellular system. A roaming phone sends its MIN and ESN via a control channel back to the home system to validate service. The only difference between a roaming phone and a CRAD is that the CRAD's MINs are specially assigned so that the MIN and ESN are routed directly to the Cellemetry Service Bureau (CSB). The MIN identifies the radio to the bureau and the ESN holds the message (up to 32 bits). The CSB processes the data and stores it or reroutes it depending on customer needs.

So now you know how Cellemetry works, but how is it used? A Cellemetry device can operate under one of two modes: modem mode and meter mode. In modem mode, the CRAD acts only as a modem, passing information in both directions. The CRAD is connected to an external controller that would decide if there is a real need to act on the information it received. If it feels there is a need for response, it will relay a message back to the Cellemetry system. The message will be contained in the ESN of course.

In meter mode, the CRAD already has the required onboard intelligence to act independently so no external controller is required. Meter mode operation could be handled in two different ways. The CRAD could collect bits of information that could indicate data such as meter reads, copy machine count, number of snacks in a vending machine, etc. This mode of operation would be used anywhere a count needed to be monitored. Messages would only be sent when paged by the Cellemetry system. In the second subset of operation under meter mode, the CRAD is set to send the message automatically at a certain specified time. The gateway would collect information and report it to the customer at the customer's designated time (next business day, end of month, etc.). This mode is what utility companies would use to monitor your usage. If an immediate meter read was needed, a MIN page would be sent out corresponding to the MIN of the meter that info is needed on. There could also be another function assigned to the CRAD which, when activated remotely, could deliver a pulse to a certain device in the meter that could cause your service to be cut off.

So how well will Cellemetry function in the real world? For one, you're talking about a wireless form of communication and no matter how far cellular technology has come, it is nothing to marvel at. The design of my apartment building makes cellular service practically impossible from within the complex and the electric meters are in a basement-like area. I'd like to see a CRAD operate down there. However, Cellemetry Data Services boasts of its "Cellemetry Network Surveillance Center," which will basically make sure all your messages get through and if one message fails, a redundant system will try another way to get it through. They even offer you access to their gateway using a variety of protocols including TCP/IP, UUCP, or CDMP. Access to your Cellemetry system can be done right through your laptop. And believe it or not, the Bureau even has its own fail-safe software (not fail-proof, but fail-safe). Cellemetry never uses regular cellular voice control channels to transmit info. Instead, it uses any excess capacity in the AMPS analog control channel to send a message between the gateway and remote devices. There are 832 channels in the AMPS system and they're split up between the two competing cell carriers in each market. Twenty-one of these channels are used as control channels. Cellemetry data actually yields priority to regular cellular traffic, meaning that if there is too much cell traffic, no message will be sent, or rather, it will be sent later.

You're probably thinking, what if all these CRADS decide to send their data all at once causing an enormous data collision? From what I've gathered, the CRADS are programmed to respond randomly so you can rest assured that this month's meter read will get through and your electric bill will be right on time. And despite its real and theoretical drawbacks, you can bet your ass that corporations and agencies abroad already have an eye on this technology and are probably signing contracts as you are reading this article. Look for utility companies to implement this first, followed by cable companies, trucking fleet managers tracking their trailers, farming and agricultural folks looking to monitor crops, and I'm sure police and government agencies will find a use for it eventually (if they haven't already).

Some of you may choose to see the dark side of all this, and I can see it too, but I'm one of those guys that can see holes like Swiss cheese in this concept. Since the Cellemetry device is basically a modified cell phone that remotely controls a device, with access available by computer, you can just imagine what the future of hacking looks like. For those of you clueless people, think gateway, think connecting using TCP/IP, think remote access to public utilities and cable networks using a cellular channel, think about seizing a power grid in Florida from your laptop in California (no, don't think about that, bad hacker). Or if you choose to see the glass as half empty, then think about the eye in the sky watching us, think remote monitoring, think control and loss of freedom. Although it's one step closer to 1984, I can't help but think of all the possibilities we may have to hack our future. Big Brother may be watching, but he's just a peeping tom. We can either try to shut the blinds tighter or chase him down the street with a butcher knife in our hands. All meter readers take heed, for the end is near.

Boxes of the World

While boxing was indeed in its dying days in the 1990s, it was by no means dead. For those who really knew what they were doing, it was possible to find distant locations where certain magic tones would still have an effect. For that and historical reasons, our tutorial on boxes was among the more popular articles we've printed. But without a doubt one of the most significant articles that has *ever* graced our pages has got to be the tutorial on how to convert a Radio Shack tone dialer into a red box. This one piece may have caused more overall mayhem than anything else we've printed, spreading by word of mouth well beyond the confines of our readership. Basically, the conversion allowed a common piece of hardware to be converted into a device that easily allowed free phone calls at pay phones all over the country. It was a combination of coincidence and incredible technical agility that made this conversion possible. And it drove all of the phone companies bonkers because there was absolutely nothing they could do about it, other than to change the entire method with which they collected coins. Stopgap measures were introduced, such as imposing limits on how many "coins" could be deposited for a phone call (not really the best idea for a phone company). Some Radio Shacks even began to interrogate any kid who tried to buy a tone dialer, demanding to know what they were *really* going to use it for. As the decade came to an end, red boxing too was finally on the way out. But what a fun ride it was.

Converting a Tone Dialer into a Red Box (Autumn, 1990)

By Noah Clayton

A very simple modification to Radio Shack pocket tone dialer part #43-146 ($24.95) can make it into a red box. The modification consists of changing the crystal frequency used to generate the microprocessor's timing. To make this modification you will need a Phillips screwdriver, a flat bladed screwdriver, a soldering iron, a pair of long nose pliers, a pair of wire cutters, and a 6.5536 MHz (megahertz) crystal.

Orient the dialer with the keypad down and the speaker at the top. Remove the battery compartment cover (and any batteries) to expose two screws. Remove these two screws and the two on the top of the dialer near the speaker. There are four plastic clips that are now holding the two halves of the dialer together. Push on the two bottom clips near the battery compartment and pull up to separate the bottom part. Now slide a flat screwdriver into the seam on the left starting from the bottom and moving toward the top. (You may have to do this on the right side as well.)

When the two halves separate, slide the speaker half underneath the other half while being careful not to break the wires connecting the two. Locate the cylindrical metallic can (it's about half an inch long and an eighth of an inch in diameter) and pull it away from the circuit board to break the glue that holds it in place. Unsolder this can, which is a 3.579545 MHz crystal, from the circuit board.

The hard part of this modification is getting the new crystal to fit properly. Bend the three disk capacitors over so that there will be room for the new crystal. Also remove the screw that is there. Since the 6.5536 MHz crystal you have is probably much bigger than the crystal you are replacing, you will need to bend the leads on the new crystal so that they will match up with the pads on the circuit board. Place the new crystal on the circuit board by soldering it in place. As an added touch you might peel the QC sticker off of the PC board and place it on top of the crystal. Now carefully snap the two halves back together while checking to make sure that none of the wires are getting pinched or are in the way of the screw holes. Put the case screws back in and insert three AAA batteries into the battery compartment.

Your dialer is now ready to test. Switch the unit on. The LED on the dial pad side should be lit. Set the lower slide switch to STORE mode. Press the MEMORY button on the dial pad. Press the * key five times. Press the MEMORY key again and then press the P1 key. A beep tone should be heard when any key is pressed and a long beep should sound after the P1 key has been pressed to indicate that the programming sequence was performed correctly.

Switch the unit into DIAL mode. Press the P1 key, and five tone pulses that sound remarkably like coin tones should come out of the speaker. I usually program P1 to be four quarters (insert one or two PAUSEs between each set of five tones), P2 to be two quarters, and P3 as one quarter. Of course, you can no longer use the unit to generate touch tones.

History and Theory

A friend of mine and I were sitting around his house one day trying to come up with a way to build a reasonable red box. I had built one with analog sine wave generators in the past, but it was difficult to adjust the frequency of the outputs and keep them accurate over time and with changes in temperature. The electronic project box I had assembled it in was bulky, hard to conceal, and definitely suspicious looking.

My friend was playing with his calculator while I was wishing that we had the money and time to design a microprocessor-controlled device with its own custom PC board. After a while, he announced that he had an idea. He had been looking at a data sheet for a DTMF (Dual Tone MultiFrequency, a.k.a. touch tone) generator chip. He calculated the ratio of the coin tone frequencies of 1700 Hz and 2200 Hz to be 0.7727. He then went through all of the tone pairs used for DTMF, calculating each of their ratios. He discovered that the ratio of the tone pair used for * was very close to the ratio for the coin tone frequencies. This ratio, 941/1209=0.7783, differed from the coin tone ratio by less than one percent.

What this meant was that since the tones generated by such a chip are digitally synthesized from a divider chain off of a reference crystal, if one changed the reference crystal to the "right" frequency, the coin tones would be generated instead of the DTMF *. Most DTMF chips use a TV color-burst crystal with a frequency of 3.579545 MHz. To determine the crystal frequency that would generate the coin tones, one would compute 3,579,545 / 941 * 1700 = 6,466,766; 3,579,545 / 1209 * 2200 = 6,513,647; (6,466,766 + 6,513,647) /2 = 6,490,206 MHz.

Unfortunately, this is not a standard crystal value and getting custom crystals made is a real pain for the hobbyist. The closest standard frequency I could find was 6.5536 MHz. I tried a crystal of this value and it worked.

(The actual frequencies produced by a DTMF generator chip depend on the particular manufacturer's design. The color-burst crystal's frequency is divided down to the DTMF tones by an integer divider chain. Because the color-burst crystal's frequency is not an integer multiple of the DTMF tones there will be a small difference in the frequencies produced from the standard.)

When we first tried this, we were using one of Radio Shack's earliest tone dialers. It consisted of a DTMF generator chip only, and as such could not produce a sequence of tones automatically. Tones were generated as long and as fast as one could press the buttons. We were able to simulate nickels using this device but doing so was fairly slow and tedious. Because our manual timing was so far off of the mark, our attempts at producing dime or quarter signals were a miserable failure. A live operator would be instantly connected to the line whenever we tried it.

The Shack's next model had a microprocessor and a tone generator in it, each with separate crystals controlling their respective timing. It was just a matter of changing the micro's crystal to get the right on-off timing for a quarter's tone sequence as well as the tone generator's crystal to get the proper coin frequencies.

Later Radio Shack came out with the model used in this project. I promptly bought one because it was lower cost and more compact than their older model. I put some batteries in it and tried it out. It generated DTMF sequences with very long on and off times but, other than that, seemed like a nice unit. Upon disassembling it though, I became unhappy. There was only one crystal. It controlled the timing for a microprocessor that was specifically designed to synthesize DTMF. There was no way to independently adjust the output frequency of the tones from their on-off timing. I was just about to say, "Oh well, yet another tone dialer for my collection" when it hit me. Why not try the higher frequency crystal? The timing might come out close enough to simulate either a quarter or a dime. I made the mod and tested it out. It worked!

Thank you Radio Shack, for giving us a convenient to use, easily concealable, and non-suspicious-looking red box.

References

Coin frequencies: 1,700 Hz and 2,200 Hz +- 1.5%.

Timing: 5 cents, one tone burst for 66 ms (milliseconds) +- 6 ms; 10 cents, two tone bursts each 66 ms, with a 66 ms silent period between tones; 25 cents, five tone bursts each 33 ms +- 3 ms with a 33 ms silent period between tones.

True Colors (Autumn, 1993) *By Billsf*

There still seems to be much confusion on the color coding scheme of various "Toll Fraud Devices" (TFDs). The mainstream media has confused colors, made many up, and most important of all, usually failed to properly describe their operation. There have been many papers posted by "phreaks," which might be considered the same kind of unintentional (?) disinformation the mainstream has put out for years. Many of the world's best phreaks are a generation younger than the "originals" and may simply not know the operation or history or even the color that was generally agreed upon for a particular device.

The real list of colors is quite short, and their operation may come as a surprise to many. To set the record straight, here they are:

Black Box

While in electronics it refers to an often complicated subsystem that somebody else made and whose internal operation is of little concern to the system designer. To the phone, it is simply a means to reduce the loop current to the point where it appears the phone is back on the hook. The construction was one of the easiest ever. Many variations existed, in fact a field phone or old crank unit with internal battery could be modified to *eliminate* the loop current, reducing greatly the chance of being caught! (This is the real "black box.") A resistor of a value between about 2.2k to 10k was placed in series with the phone loop. This resistor supplied enough current to power the talk circuit of a non-electronic phone. A capacitor of about 330nF or so was often placed in parallel with the resistor to cancel the increase of impedance caused by the resistor, resulting in increased audio level. In parallel also was a small toggle switch, labeled "free" (open) and "normal" (closed). In principle this was all that was really needed! (To allow ordinary people like the parents of the student in a distant city to use it, some way to very briefly seize the line was provided: a pushbutton switch, Zener diode, etc.).

Operation was simple—phone would ring and be picked up with the above circuit in. The switch (in the basic device) would be briefly placed to "normal" and back to "free." This would be long enough to trip the ring off, yet within the "grace period" of the caller's CO's billing system, then two to five seconds. Operation of this was possible in North America because administrative billing requires a "grace period." Older switches had the voice path present during the ringing, so the caller would hear the "fart ring" and finally North America had no timeout then on long-distance calls! While possible on some older switches today, reduced "grace periods" and ring timeouts make it rather impractical. It is interesting to note that there was a timeout on local call ringing then in the U.S.A., so "normal" was usually used. A caller could have the recipient use the device for a quick pay phone call and get his dime back. Operator assisted calls, for obvious reasons, were out of the question!

Red Box

This is a device to simulate the coin signals at pay phones in North America, in some parts of Australia, and perhaps a few other places. In other places details vary from the following description of the North American system. COCOTs may also use this system, but it is unlikely. In the first practical pay phones, a series of bell sounds were used. $0.05 was a single, high-pitched "ding," a dime two, and a quarter a lower-pitched "gong" sound. In later models a contact mic in the phone was switched in to allow the operator to hear the money pass through the phone. This system was *much* more secure than today's! Clever tricks were, however, developed to beat it. A recording of the whole process, a toy xylophone, and even bringing the horn in an adjacent booth were all used, among others. Carefully scratching the outside of the phone with a coin or key made a very convincing "coin dropping through" sound. When the "fortress phones" were introduced in 1970, all this was replaced by a simple 2200 Hz beep. (The original internal tone generating device, a simple one transistor L/C oscillator based on the early DTMF generator, was housed in a pinkish red plastic case, probably giving rise to the name "red box.") The correct timings are one 55-65 mS beep for a nickel, two beeps separated by 55-65 mS silence for a dime, and five 35-40 mS with equal length separations for a quarter. Only the quarter signal is needed, as "some money" should be put in to activate the ground function — two 1k resistors to A and B, with the other sides connected to ground. Later a second tone, 1700 Hz was added to allow automatic coin collection (ACTS) and later still the option to change the second tone to 1500 Hz (IPTS) was added, but is rarely used. Selection of this tone can take place at coin box collection intervals, alternated between callers, or controlled by the ACTS machine (see green box). Use of the above parameters in a real red box is probably the safest method of phreaking, since it forces you to use a coin phone. Use of the modified dialer with the 6.5536 MHz crystal, now very popular in the States, is anything but safe! Do not use!

Yellow Box

Earlier signaling systems use a continuous tone in either direction to indicate supervision states. Examples are R1, C3, and 1vf systems. A trunk idle has the tone (2600 Hz in R1) coming from both ends of the circuit. Upon seizing, the forward tone is removed and the backward tone is removed briefly and put back on to acknowledge. This tone then remains on until the called phone is answered. Removal is referred to as "supervision on" or just "suped." The tone is put back on (in the proper direction) when either end hangs up. The end that stays on hears a very short beep ("pliek") since a filter cuts in in a matter of a few milliseconds, so a disturbing loud, high pitched tone is not heard by the customer. A "yellow box" simply generates the tone (2600 for R1) and provides a filter so the user (the person receiving the call) does not hear the tone. Operation is identical to the "black box," except a tone is used instead of dropping the loop current. Advantages of this one are DC parameters of the subscriber loop are normal and it works on modern exchanges and PBXs! Use today is limited for the same reasons of the "black box" and also because most of today's signaling systems don't use this method. This same device was sometimes used to "shine a trunk" and intercept other people's calls. The victim was at the mercy of the phreak as far as billing went. He could talk to the person with the tone on or, if the person got huffy, take the tone off and charge him for the call. Of course the caller was billed for the number dialed (not the phreak's number)! Taking the tone off and leaving the line silent or playing a recording of a ring signal could rack a several minute charge for the victim caller! Another form is worth mentioning because of historical reasons, and because it can still work today! This is the C5 version. An 800 mS burst of 2400 Hz means supervision on and an 800 mS burst of 2600 means hang-up. Playing 2600 Hz while picking up the phone on an international call will, in effect, produce the same result of the black box! Since the tone need be only a few hundred milliseconds or so (not at all critical) no filter is needed and anybody can quickly learn how to whistle it! The Cap'n

Crunch whistle is the most famous example and this is by far the simplest TFD! Calls placed from the U.S.A. on C5 circuits (say 80 percent of all IDDD countries) will still work for at least a three and a half minute chat (assuming cooperation of the called party) and some will allow you much longer to unlimited time. Calls from countries where there is *no* "grace period" (due to message unit billing) will not work and the ticker will keep on running! Again, as with the "black box," operator assistance is out of the question!

Green Box

This is included on the "blue box" for modern systems. These are the signals the ACTS or operator uses to control a coin phone, if the link does not supply a complete DC path, and almost none do today! Earlier systems used the lower "call progress" frequencies: 350, 440, 480, and 620 Hz for this purpose. This system varies from location to location in North America, so, if in numbering zone one, have someone call, long distance from a pay phone (from a *real* pay phone, not a COCOT) and put in at least one real coin. You then play long bursts of each of the 15 tones. At some point the coin will be returned or collected. Take note of the digit. Have the caller call again and continue on to find the other signal. In some (many?) cases the coin can only be returned when the ACTS machine comes on to "collect" overtime. You just have to beat it out by getting your return signal in *before* it sends the collect signal! *Note:* in some cases this system includes IPTS control, where available. Also note for the caller: the code 15 ("ST," 1500+1700 Hz) signal does interesting things! It can push off the ACTS machine and get your call through without "coin deposit" (and not return!) and push off the calling card validation system and/or operator and get your call through! The exact right time to make this one second signal is important. COCOTs and some pay phones in countries outside numbering zone one may use similar or completely different methods. Listen to what you hear while using a phone and be ready to use the programmable modes of your Demon Dialer! One final note: I've known people who have recorded these control tones on their answering machine OGM to give callers their coins back and allow message retrieval at no cost! The above information is phreaking in the here and now!

Blue Box

Also "phreaking in the here and now." This is perhaps hacking's trickiest art today! A blue box is any device that produces two-tone multifrequency signals other than customer dialing signals. MFC (C5 and R1, for example) and R2 forward are blue box "address signals." In band supervisory signals ("pliek menu") are probably included and are often, but not always, needed. Information on international and national signaling standards is available in most university technical libraries. Full details on this device are far beyond the scope of this article.

Silver Box

The predecessor to the blue box. For signaling systems C2, C3, and 1vf and 2vf systems, etc. Early versions were a single tone oscillator (C3, 1vf) and a salvaged rotary telephone dial. It was possible just after the war, first in Sweden, and later throughout Europe and then to the rest of the world. There are convincing rumors that phreaking got its start in Sweden in the forties with this kind of box that used a *vacuum tube valve!* A slight variation for 2vf and C2 required switching a resistor or a capacitor for frequency shift pulse dialing. C4 and some national 2vf used a binary coded signal for faster working. A somewhat different switching and timing method was required, which could be mechanical, electromechanical, or electronic on both the part of the operating company and foon phreak. C4 required the generating of two separate tones in compound for line signaling in the call buildup process. Two separate oscillators could be used, but some elegant single tube or transistor L/C oscillators were developed by Bell Labs for this purpose in the early days. It is unknown if early phreaks used them! These old systems are still used in underdeveloped and/or remote areas of the world. Some old PBXs also use this for "tie-line" (leased line) working.

There are a few boxes the young generation has brought us. The following are likely to be adopted in Telco/phreak parlance and are therefore presented here:

Silver Box (!)

This is just a 16-button DTMF dialer and has nothing to do with the first real phreak toy! Available legally at better telephone shops. The A, B, C, and D buttons are intended to have special control functions for user devices. However, phone companies use them very secretively to access special tests.

White Box

Just a 12-key dialer box, available everywhere.

Beige Box

Nothing more than a lineman's test set. The original Bell System standard issue was a color that could be called beige.

And finally, the newest of them all:

Rainbow Box

(Known to the old-timer as the mythical "mighty Wurlitzer.") As the name implies, it is capable of doing it all in the inband arena. Can be implemented properly by the use of a modern DSP (modem) like the Zyxzel and proper software. Can also be properly implemented on a digital music synthesizer, like the Yamaha DX series. Personal computers and most "sound cards" can only do a not too convincing job. All of these are just theoretical possibilities for thought. The first and still only "true rainbow box" is the Hack-tic Technologies "Demon Dialer."

Why Redboxing Doesn't Work (Winter, 1999–2000)

By The Prophet

To understand why redboxing doesn't work, it is important to understand why it did at one point work (and still does in some areas), and to understand the various types of pay phones and toll collecting systems.

There are two major types of pay phones. Standard fortress pay phones utilize a ground start and ACTS toll collection mechanism, and are usually operated by the incumbent local exchange carrier (ILEC) in any given area. Examples of ILECs are USWest, GTE, Pacific Bell, etc. Such phones are usually manufactured by Western Electric or GTE, although in Alaska and Canada you still find some old brown post-pay Northern Telecom pay phones. COCOTs (Customer Owned Coin Operated Telephones) are operated primarily by private pay phone owners. However, ILECs operate COCOT-ized pay phones of this type. BellSouth's operations in southern Florida are an excellent example of this. The primary difference between a "standard" pay phone and a COCOT-type pay phone is that with a "standard" phone, toll collection and verification is based in the central office. With a COCOT-type phone, it is handled by the telephone itself. This is a very important distinction, which you will appreciate later. There is another type of fortress phone, which is post-pay. You see these only rarely used, in some parts of Canada, remote areas of the U.S., and in Alaska. I won't go into how post-pay phones work since they're so rarely seen.

Let's briefly consider how a standard fortress pay phone works. To make a local call on a standard pay phone, you insert the amount of money required. In this area, it's 35 cents. After you deposit 35 cents, the pay phone grounds itself. This "ground start" indicates to the central office that the proper amount of money has been paid and the central office lets the call go through. If you didn't put in the correct amount of money, then you'll be routed to a recording instructing you to deposit 35 cents before making your call. Because the ground start mechanism is not dependent on any tones, you cannot redbox local calls, unless you route them through a long-distance carrier. Sometimes this is possible; try dialing a carrier access code before your local call. As an interesting side note, residential phones don't have a ground start mechanism, which can create very amusing results if their line class is inadvertently changed to that of a pay phone.

Long-distance calls are a little more complicated. It costs less money to call Portland, OR (503) from Seattle than it does to call Gander, Newfoundland (709) from Seattle. About $3 less for the first three minutes, in fact. Additionally, toll rates are not flat, and they vary by time of day. Clearly, a ground start mechanism isn't a good way to bill such calls. You can only set one fixed amount for ground start calls, and you can't easily limit the time, either. Recognizing this, pay phones are equipped with a tone generator which plays an appropriate pulse to indicate the type and quantity of coin you've dropped in.

It used to be that when you placed a long-distance call, an operator would come on, inform you of the charge, and then would listen to and write down every coin that you dropped into the phone. (There is one pulse for a nickel, two pulses for a dime, and five pulses for a quarter which is how the operator could tell what you were depositing.) She would proceed to connect your call upon your deposit of the correct amount, and would either collect the balance at the end of the call, or would break in every few minutes to get you to deposit more money. But with the golden age of layoffs and computerization, ACTS was born. ACTS stands for Automated Coin Toll System. It does the job of an operator by listening to the tones generated by the pay phone when you deposit coins and tallying them appropriately. However, it's a computer and is not as smart as an operator. This is where red boxes come into play.

A red box is, quite simply, a device that generates the same coin deposit tones — and loosely the same timing — as a pay phone. Contrary to popular belief, it's not necessary to modify a Radio Shack tone dialer with a 6.5536 MHz crystal to create a red box. (6.49 MHz is a far better frequency anyway.) You can record the tones directly from a pay phone to a voice mailbox and record them to a Hallmark greeting card or a microcassette recorder, and that will work.

Whichever method you use to create a red box (I won't belabor the point of how to manufacture one, there are plenty of instructions elsewhere), its purpose is simply to fool ACTS into thinking you're putting money into the phone.

ACTS has rapidly disappeared over the past few years. The primary reason for this is the FCC. With the 1996 telecommunications bill, the FCC ruled that ILECs may not offer any services to their own pay phone divisions that they do not also offer to independent operators of COCOTs. This made offering ACTS and ground start billing problematic, since ACTS would have to be upgraded to charge different rates based on each COCOT operator's criteria. Additionally, it would have been necessary for ILECs to handle separations and settlements for the COCOT owners. This was a bigger job than ILECs wanted, especially to maintain a system that was increasingly plagued by toll fraud.

As a result, many ILECs began replacing their phones with Northern Telecom Millenniums, or COCOT-izing their Western Electric pay phones (such as what BellSouth did). Because the billing is all done in the phone itself, rather than via ACTS, there is no need to fool ACTS any longer. Therefore, you can play tones at a COCOT or a COCOT-ized ILEC phone all day and it won't work. Also, some ILECs who kept ACTS (usually by offering it to COCOT owners but making the fees so high that nobody took advantage) such as Pacific Bell have installed filter chips in their fortress phones. These filters block the handset microphone until the call supervises, which does an effective job of blocking redboxing.

Redboxing does still work in some places. However, it's eventually going away. What really should go with redboxing are access charges, since long distance ought not be billed by the minute anyway. But I digress....

Evolution of the Network

The phone network of 1999 was quite different from the one of 1990. Digital switching predominated. Services like Caller ID were in full swing after initial mixed reviews. Devices known as COCOTs continued to sweep the land and replace the familiar pay phones of the Bell companies. As witnessed in the COCOT tutorial, there was quite a bit of outrage at some of their practices early in the decade. This brings up an interesting point concerning the hacker perspective. As I've pointed out throughout our existence, the values we put forth in *2600* represent but one interpretation. We don't pretend to speak for everyone in the hacker world. We certainly had a lot of issues with some of the suggestions put forth in that article, such as physically destroying or stealing pay phones. But we still felt it was an informative piece and we hoped that those reading it would apply their own set of values to what they learned from it and that hopefully those values would be similar to the ones we espoused. There would be more harm in suppressing the dialog just because we didn't approve of elements of it.

Phone companies continued to experience growing pains and implement stupid policies, and we were there to point out as many as we could, both in our pages and on our new radio program on WBAI (*Off The Hook*, which still airs on that station to this day). We also tried to explain as much as possible just how it all tied together, why things worked the way they did, how they used to work, and what the future might hold.

An Introduction to COCOTs (Summer, 1990) *By The Plague*

The COCOT, more precisely, the Customer Owned Coin Operated Telephone: good or evil? To the COCOT owner it's a godsend, a virtual legal slot machine for leeching the public, freeing the owner from the monopolies of the phone company. To the public it's a nightmare, a money-stealing machine providing poor service and insanely high rates, a virtual hotel-style phone in the guise of an innocent looking pay phone.

To the telephone enthusiast, a COCOT is something else entirely. A treasure trove of tasty parts, perhaps, including microprocessors, coin identification mechanisms, tone dialers, tone and call progress detectors, a modem for remote connections, speech synthesis and recognition equipment, magnetic strip readers for credit cards, and other parts to be explored and tinkered with. For other phreaks, the COCOT represents an unrestricted phone line, which can be used for exploration of the phone system. Still, for others, COCOTs can represent a storage house of long-distance access codes and procedures. Others may see the neighborhood COCOT as a bunch of imprisoned coins and a future wall phone for their room. Many more treasures are to be found in a single COCOT, as you shall soon see.

COCOT Basics

To those of you unfamiliar with the COCOT, let me quickly fill you in on the basics. Firstly, most if not all, COCOTs operate on regular business or residential (depending on the greed of the owner) phone lines. There are exceptions to this rule in a few major cities where private pay phone lines are available directly from the local phone company; these allow the use of regular operators who are aware of the status of the line as being COCOT based. However, few, if any, COCOTs use this type of line, even when it is available.

Almost all COCOTs are microprocessor-based devices, thereby making them smarter than your average phone company pay phone. A major function of the COCOT is to independently collect coins in return for time during a call. While the real pay phone uses the ACTS system on a remote phone company computer for coin request and collection functions, the COCOT performs these functions locally in its small computer. Naturally, red boxes do not work with COCOTs. However, since their coin detection mechanisms are not as advanced as those in real pay phones, it is much easier to trick them with slugs.

The dial tone you hear when you pick up the handset to a COCOT is usually not the actual dial tone, but a synthesized one (more on the dial tone later). As you press the numbers on the keypad, the COCOT stores each number in memory. The keypad may or may not be DTMF, depending on the phone. Most COCOTs do not allow for incoming calls, since their primary purpose is to generate revenue, and incoming calls simply waste time, which could be used by paying COCOT customers (from the owner's point of view). If you obtain a number to a COCOT, it will usually pick up after several rings in remote mode (more on that later).

After the COCOT has enough digits to dial your call, it will ask for the amount of money to deposit on an LCD screen or in a synthesized voice, unless you have placed the call collect or used a calling card, or if the call is toll free. It will then obtain an actual dial tone from the phone line, and dial your call through whichever method it is designed to use. During this time it may or may not mute out the handset earpiece and/or the mouthpiece. For local calls, it will usually dial the call directly, but for long-distance, calling card, and collect calls, it will usually use an independent hotel-style phone company or PBX. This is done so that you (or the called party in a collect call situation) will be charged up the wazoo for your call. If it detects a busy, reorder, or other progress tone other than a ring, it will refund your money and not charge you for the call, in theory. In actuality a lot of COCOTs will rip you off and charge you anyway, hence their reputation. Unless the call was placed collect or with a calling card or toll free, the phone will periodically ask you to deposit money. Since the small and sleazy long-distance companies used by most COCOTs are chosen on the basis of rates, rather than quality, you can be sure that most calls placed on COCOTs have an extremely large amount of static and bizarre echoing effects.

Identifying COCOTs

A lot of people (non-phreaks) seem to have trouble telling COCOTs from phone company pay phones. I can spot a COCOT a hundred yards away, but to the average person, it's pretty tough because they are made to look so much like the real thing. Actually, it's quite simple. Just look for your RBOC's (New York Telephone, Southwestern Bell, etc.) name and logo on the phone to be sure it's the real thing. Ninety-nine times out of a hundred, it's a real pay phone. The rare exceptions occur when it's a COCOT made and/or owned by your local phone company (in which case, not to worry, these won't rip you off as badly as the sleazy small-company made phones), or when it is in fact a sleazy small-company made phone, disguised by its owner, through the theft and reapplication of actual pay phone signs and markings, to be indistinguishable from the real thing. The latter case is illegal in most parts of the country, but it does happen. Nonetheless, a phreak will know a COCOT as soon as he dials a number, regardless of the outer appearance. The absence of the true ACTS always means you're using a COCOT.

COCOT Varieties

Let us discuss the various varieties of COCOTs. To be frank, there are actually too many different COCOT devices to discuss them individually, and their similarity in appearance to one another makes for difficult identification even to the advanced COCOT (ab)user. They range from simple Western Electric look-alikes to more advanced varieties, which may include LCD or CRT displays, credit card readers, and voice recognition dialing. The range is very wide with perhaps 1000 different pay phones in between.

In reality, you should approach each new COCOT with no predispositions, and no expectations. Experiment with it, play around with it, see what kind of COCOT security measures (more on that later) it implements, attempt to gain an unrestricted dial tone, see how well the beast is fastened to its place of inhabitance, attempt to decipher its long-distance access methods, and so on. In general, just play with it.

Getting the Dial Tone

I started research for this article with the intent of explaining which techniques for obtaining actual unrestricted dial tones work with what phones. In my exploration, I have learned many tricks for achieving this, but have also found that there are too many different COCOTs out there, and devoting an article to defeating a dozen or so brands that can be found in the NYC area would be a waste of my time and yours.

Instead, I have focused on general techniques and methods that can be applied to any new, unknown, or future variety of COCOT.

I have decided to break this down into the various COCOT security measures used by COCOTs and how to defeat each one. In actuality, each COCOT seldom uses more than one of these COCOT security measures. When a single COCOT security (anti-phreaking) measure is used, it is quite easy for the phone phreak to obtain a dial tone. In more secure COCOTs, you should experiment with various combinations of these techniques, and attempt to come up with some techniques of your own.

To begin with, the most basic attempt to get a real dial tone requires you to dial a toll free or 1-800 number, wait for them to hang up, and wait for the real dial tone to come back. At which time, you would dial your free call on an unrestricted line, or better yet, dial 0 for an actual operator and have her place the call for you. The following are methods used by COCOTs in order to stop you from doing this. Like I said, it is rare for any specific COCOT to implement more than one of these.

COCOT Security Measures and How to Defeat Them

1. **Locking Out the Keypad:** If the keypad is DTMF, the COCOT will lock it out after your original call is placed. This can be defeated with the use of a portable DTMF dialer provided that other measures are not in place to prevent this (muting, DTMF detection, and automatic reset).
2. **The Use of a Non-DTMF Keypad:** Here, again, the purpose is the same, to prevent further dialing after the call is completed. Again, this can be defeated with a portable dialer, provided other measures are not in place. Most COCOTs dial out using DTMF anyway, and hence DTMF dialing should be enabled for that line.
3. **DTMF Detection and Automatic Reset:** Here, a different approach is taken to prevent unauthorized dialing. The phone will reset (hang up and give you back the fake dial tone) when it detects DTMF tones on the line after the COCOT dials your call. Most COCOTs do not implement this measure because it interferes with legitimate applications (beeper calls, VMB calls, etc.). To defeat this measure, modify your portable dialer to use shorter tones (less than 50 ms). Since the central office (CO) can usually detect very short tones, whereas the COCOT may be sensitive only to longer tones, you should be able to dial out. Another way to defeat this is to mask your tones in synthetic static generated by blowing a "shhhhhhh" sound into the mouthpiece as you dial the first digit on the unrestricted dial tone. This should throw off most DTMF detection circuits used in COCOTs, and tones should be received quite fine at the CO because their circuits are more advanced and provide greater sensitivity and/or noise suppression.

4. **Dial Tone Detection and Automatic Reset:** This measure is similar to the above measure, except resetting will take place if a dial tone (the unrestricted dial tone) is detected by the COCOT during the call. Since most COCOTs do not use the "hang-up pulse" from the CO to detect the other party hanging up, they rely heavily on detecting the dial tone that comes afterward, in order to detect when the other party hung up. This is a clever measure that is easily defeated by blowing a "shhhhhhh" sound (synthetic static) into the mouthpiece during the time at which you expect the real dial tone to come back. As you keep "shhhh"ing, you will hear the dial tone come back, then dial the 1st digit (usually a 1), the dial tone will be gone, and you dial the rest of the number. If the keypad is locked out, use your portable dialer.
5. **Number Restriction:** Most COCOTs will restrict the user from dialing certain numbers, area codes, and exchanges. Usually these include 0 for obvious reasons, 976- and 1-900-type numbers, ANAC (number identification), and others. On rare occasions, COCOTs will restrict you from dialing 1-800 numbers. Although this is illegal in most parts, it is done nonetheless, because most COCOT owners don't like people using their phone without paying them. In practice this brings in more revenue, because the phone is available to more paying users. Your best bet here is to call any toll free number that the phone will accept instead of the 800 number. These may include 411, 911, 611, 211, or the repair or customer service number for the company that handles that COCOT. (This is usually toll free and is printed somewhere on the phone.)
6. **Muting the Mouthpiece:** This is not really a measure in itself, but is sometimes used in combination with other measures to prevent dialing out. Muting is usually done when the COCOT itself is dialing out, which prevents you from grabbing the dial tone before it does. This is a rather lame and futile technique since we typically obtain the unrestricted dial tone after the call is completed. Thus, there is no need to defeat this. I suppose the designers of the COCOT were really paranoid about security during the start of the call, but completely ignored dial tone penetration attempts after the call was dialed and connected. Just goes to show you what happens with those guys who wear pocket protectors and graduate with a 4.0 average. In theory their designs are perfect; in reality they never match up to the abuse which we subject them to.
7. **Other Measures:** Although I have discussed all measures currently known to me, in defeating new measures or measures not discussed here my best advice would be to use a combination of techniques mentioned above to obtain an unrestricted dial tone or a "real operator" (local, AT&T, or any operator that can complete a call for you and thinks you are calling from a regular line, not a COCOT).

Secret Numbers

Actually, there's not much to say about secret numbers. Most COCOTs have secret numbers that the owner can punch into the COCOT keypad in order to activate administrative functions or menus locally. These functions provide information regarding the status of the unit, the money in the coin box, the owner's approximate phone bill, and various diagnostic and test functions. They also allow a certain amount of reprogramming, usually limited to changing rates and restricted numbers. For more information about these, I would suggest obtaining the engineering, design, or owner's manuals for the unit. Since engineering and design manuals are closely guarded company secrets, mostly to prevent the competition from cloning, it would be very difficult to obtain them. Owner's manuals can be obtained rather easily with a minimal amount of social engineering, but they are sadly lacking in information and primarily written for the average COCOT owner.

Remote Connections

Remote connections provide the same functions as described in the previous section, except they can be accessed remotely by calling the COCOT. Remote connections are usually reserved for authorized users (the company in charge of maintaining the proper operation of the COCOT). Thus, the COCOT can be diagnosed remotely, even before a person is sent down to repair it.

A typical COCOT will pick up in remote mode after someone calls it and lets it ring for a while (between 4 and 10 rings usually). At that time it will communicate with the remote site using whatever method it was designed to use. This is usually a 300 baud mode, or a DTMF/synthesized voice connection. An access code is usually required, which may be a 3- or 4-digit number in the DTMF connection, or anything for a password in the modem connection. Some DTMF based COCOTs are simply activated with a single silver box tone (see Winter 1989-90 issue of *2600*). I've run into a couple of these.

To play around with the remote functions of a COCOT, if they exist in the particular model, it is necessary to obtain the phone number of the unit. See the next section on that. Once you have the number, simply call it and experiment from then on. If you have trouble hacking the formats for the remote mode, it may be necessary to call the makers of the COCOT and social engineer them for the information.

Getting the COCOT's Number

This is incredibly trivial, but is included here because it is such an important function in the exploration/abuse of any COCOT, and because advanced COCOT exploration/abuse techniques will require you to have this information. It is also included here for the novice reader.

There are several ways to obtain the phone number, the simplest being dialing your local ANAC number, plus dummy digits if necessary. A lot of COCOTs will restrict this, so you should get an unrestricted dial tone and then dial ANAC. Some COCOTs will not restrict you, but will ask for money in order to do this. Here in NYC, dropping $.25 and dialing 958-1111 will get you the ANAC readout on this type of COCOT. A small price to pay for such valuable information. Another way to obtain the number is to get it from the operator. Any operator that has it will have no problem releasing it to you; just say you're calling from a pay phone and you need someone to call you back, but there is no phone number written on the pay phone. Yet another choice is to call one of the various ANI Demo 800 numbers, which will read back your number. This choice is particularly useful for people who don't have or don't know the ANAC for their area. If in desperation, social engineer the information out of the COCOT owner, call him up as the phone company, and take it from there.

Hijacking the Bastard

Besides using the COCOT to make calls, the typical phone phreak will usually want a COCOT for himself. Granted, this is stealing, but so is not paying for calls. And while we're at it, stealing for experimentation and the pursuit of knowledge is not the same as stealing for money. Oh well, I won't get into morals here, it's up to you to decide. Personally, I'm devoid of all ethics and morals anyway, so I'd steal one if the opportunity was there. What the heck, it can't be any worse than exercising your freedom of speech and being dragged off to jail by the fascist stooges of the imperialistic American police state. Ahem, sorry about that, I got a little carried away, but I just had to comment on events of the past several months.

Anyway, the reasons for abducting a COCOT range from simple experimentation ("I'd like to see what is in there,") to purely materialistic reasons ("Hmmm, I bet that coin box holds at least $10.") Whatever the reason, a COCOT is a good thing to have. Their retail value ranges from $900 to $2500, but since you can't really resell it, I wouldn't suggest taking one for purely materialistic reasons.

Abducting a COCOT is usually much easier than trying to do the same to a real pay phone. Physical security can range widely and depends largely on the owner. I've seen security ranging from a couple of nails fastening the COCOT to a sheet of plywood, to double-cemented bolted down steel encasements. However, a crowbar will do the trick for about 50 percent of the COCOTs in my area. Expect the same wherever you are.

Once obtained, your options vary. You could take it apart, you could hang it on your bedroom wall, you could hold it for ransom; it's up to you. Most people simply connect it up to their line, or hang it up as a trophy above the mantle. As you can tell from the introduction, dissecting the COCOT will yield you a plethora of interesting devices to keep you busy for a long time to come. If you do connect a COCOT to your line, be sure to tape up the coin slot, as placing money in the COCOT without an ability to remove the coin box will eventually choke the unit. Don't use it as a primary phone, since it demands money; it's neat to have it as an extension.

Destruction

If you can't steal it, and you can't (ab)use it, destroy it.... That's my motto with regard to COCOTs. These evil beasts have been ripping off the public for a long time, and they deserve to pay the price. Destruction can range from breaking off plastic forks in the coin slot, to removing the handset (for display as a trophy of course), to completely demolishing the unit with explosives, to squeezing off a few shotgun blasts at the COCOT. Since repair and/or refund is hard to come by and expensive when it comes to COCOTs (but is free for real pay phones), the COCOT owner will think twice before purchasing another COCOT.

The Phone Line

As mentioned earlier, the phone line used by the COCOT is just a regular line. It is usually exposed near the COCOT itself. For those of you with a lineman's handset, need I say more? For those without, let me just quickly say, get your hands on one.

Advanced Techniques

The next three sections are for the more experienced phone phreak, but most of this can be done by just about anyone. There are many more advanced techniques; the boundaries are limitless.

Code Theft

As mentioned earlier, most COCOTs use various small and sleazy long-distance companies and operator assistance services (ITI, Telesphere, Redneck Telecom, etc.) for long distance, collect, third party, and calling card calls. Many times these are accessed by the COCOT through a 1-800, 950, or 10XXX number. The COCOT dials the access number, its identification number or code; plus other information in order to use the service. The service then bills the COCOT owner (or the middleman reseller of COCOT services) for the services provided but not yet paid for. In the case of calling card calls or collect calls, the service bills the proper party through equal access billing and credits the COCOT owner's account a cut of the action.

Needless to say, all the DTMF tones required to access the service can be taped and decoded (see the DTMF decoder article in the Spring 1990 issue of *2600*), and used for our own purposes. Sometimes, you can tape the tones right from the handset earpiece. Other times, the handset is muted, and it is required for you to either access the wiring itself, or trick the phone into thinking that your called party hung up, and you're making another call, while having the party on the other end give a bogus dial tone to the COCOT and tape the forthcoming tones. Surprisingly the codes obtained from this type of activity last a very long time (usually 3 to 4 months). This is because, once the charge gets all the way down the chain, through the various middlemen and resellers to the COCOT owner, and by the time the COCOT owner realizes that the coins collected don't match the calls placed, and by the time he has to convince all the middlemen above him of possible fraud...well, you get the picture. Suffice to say, these codes last. Used in moderation, they can last for a long time, because the COCOT owner is raking in so much profit, he'll easily ignore the extra calls.

Calling Card Verification

With regard to messing around with calling card verification, I could write a whole separate article on this, but space does not allow it at this time. So, I'll just give you the basics.

Much of the calling card verification that's being done by sleazy long distance and AOS services is very shabby. Since access to AT&T's calling card database for verification is expensive for these companies, they try to do without. Much of the time, they don't verify the card at all; they make sure it looks valid (a valid area code and exchange), and simply throw out the PIN, thus assuming the card is valid. A valid assumption, given that more than 95% percent of the calling cards being punched into COCOTs are valid, it's a worthwhile risk to take. However, the sh*t hits the fan when someone receives his bill and sees that he has a bunch of calling card calls on his bill, and he doesn't even have a calling card! Fraud is reported, the bureaucracy churns, until finally, the sleazy long-distance company ends up paying for the call. Given enough of these calls, these companies get hell from AT&T and the RBOCs for not properly verifying calling card numbers. The FCC gets into the act, and the company pays fines up the wazoo. A pretty good thing, if you ask me, and you get a free call out of it as well. Not a bad transaction, not bad at all....

Other long-distance companies and AOS services steal verification services from AT&T by dialing a 0+ call on another line to a busy number, using the calling card number you punched in. If it receives a busy signal, the card is good, otherwise it is not. In either case, the long-distance company eludes the charge for accessing the database. When it comes to slinging sleaze, these companies deserve an award. And that's why I urge all out there to abuse the crap out of them.

Call Forwarding

This is another of the many interesting things that can be done with your neighborhood COCOT. Simply put, you get the phone number to the COCOT, call up your local phone company, order call forwarding for that line, then go to the COCOT and forward it to your number. A lineman's handset may be required here if you can't get your hands on an unrestricted dial tone. Pulling a CN/A or doing some research may be required if your local phone company asks a lot of information before processing such requests as call forwarding. In most cases they don't, and in some areas there are automated facilities for processing such requests.

Presto! You now have an alternate number you can use for whatever purpose you have in mind. It could be used for anything from getting verified on a BBS to selling drugs. Again, your ethics are your own; this is simply a tool for those who need it. Anyway, it's practically untraceable to you as far as conventional means are concerned (CN/A, criss-cross directory, etc.), and you should use it to your advantage. This is especially a good tool for people afraid to give out their home numbers.

At any time, you can go to the COCOT and deactivate the call forwarding to your number. Since no one ever calls the COCOT (except for using the remote mode, and this is rare and mostly used when the phone is broken), you should have few if any calls intended for the COCOT. If you do get a call from a COCOT service bureau, simply say "wrong number," go to the COCOT, and deactivate call forwarding for a few days just to be safe. In any case, your real number cannot be obtained through any conventional means by those calling the COCOT, or even by those standing at the COCOT itself. However, if they really wanted to nail you, they could examine the memory at the COCOT's switch and pull your number out of its call forwarding memory. However, I have never heard of this being done, and it's very unlikely that they would do this. But I wouldn't recommend using the alternate number for anything more than an alternate number for yourself. If you sell drugs or card stuff or something like that, don't use such an alternate number for more than a few days.

The Future of the COCOT

We're definitely going to see many more COCOTs in the future. They will begin to saturate suburban and rural areas where they can rarely be found at this time. More COCOTs mean more headaches for the public, but it also means more of us will get a chance to experiment with them.

Security, both physical and anti-phreak, will get better, especially after COCOT manufacturers read this article. But it will be a long time before we will see completely secure COCOTs. Which is not so bad really, because then they will actually be worth stealing.

In the meantime, we can decrease their proliferation by destroying any COCOTs that rip people off. Having COCOTs around is a bittersweet proposition. In a way, they are an interesting use of technology and another frontier of exploration for the phone phreak. On the other hand, they are cybernetic money-leeching abuses of technology, which steal from and abuse the public they are meant to serve. Like 'em or not, they're here to stay.

Getting More Info

For those of you who wish to find out more about COCOTs, I would recommend hands-on exploration. I would also recommend getting some of the COCOT industry publications, and various telephone industry publications. You could also request more information from COCOT manufacturers themselves, Intellicall being one of the largest. Also, check out government and FCC regulations with regard to equal access and COCOTs.

Fighting the Bastards

Much of the stuff being perpetrated by COCOTs today is against the law, and the sleazy companies that handle calls for COCOTs are violating many laws. Unfortunately, few of these laws are being enforced. When you see such a violation of consumer rights, please report it to all relevant agencies. You'll know you're being taken advantage of when someone calls you collect from a COCOT and you get charged up the wazoo for the 10-minute local call. And they call us criminals. Give me a break....

The only way to control these cybernetic leeches is to do something about them. Also, if you have a grudge against a COCOT or a sleazy company, by all means take the law into your own hands. But also, write to your legislators, complaining of the abuses being perpetrated by COCOTs and the sleazy telephone companies. Also, it is important to educate the public about COCOTs and how to recognize and avoid them. Whenever possible try to inform your non-phreak friends about the dangers of using COCOTs. I am also in favor of strict regulation when it comes to the subject of COCOTs. If they must charge insane rates, these rates should be stated clearly, and they must provide quality service, clear connections, and free operator assistance. Anything less than this is unacceptable.

In closing, I would just like to say that this article is as complete as my knowledge enables it to be. It by no means explains all there is to know about COCOTs, nor do I claim to know all there is to know. If you have any other information on COCOTs or any particularly tasty COCOT stories, please write to *2600* and tell us more.

Caller ID: The Facts (Autumn, 1990) *By Jake "The Snake"*

You've probably either heard of it, seen it in the media, or maybe you even own one of these little "buggers." There's been a lot of talk, fighting, and discussions in court over the Caller*ID box. Currently existing only in New Jersey, this device is basically a tracer. And, yes, it is legally available to the public.

In case you aren't aware of such a hacker's dream, let me fill you in on the details. The device itself is a small stand-alone unit, about 6 inches by 4 inches, weighing about 8 to 10 ounces, with a 32-character (5-by-48-pixel), two-line display and a few buttons on the front. In size it resembles a simple desktop calculator from a couple of decades ago. It can run on a 9 volt or AC adapter and has two RJ-11 jacks on the back, both identical, for attachment to wall and phone.

Caller*ID is offered along with many other "sister" services that I will explain later. Because of the AT&T divestiture a few years back, the local companies aren't authorized to sell the device itself but can only offer the service (at a cost of $21 for installation and a whopping $6.50 a month) to its customers. The box can be ordered from a few different distributors for anywhere between $60 and $300.

Let's say you purchased a Caller*ID (known as "ICLID" in the industry, which is an acronym for Incoming Call Line Identification Device) and hooked it up to your phone. This is how it would work: After your phone rings once, you'll see some information flash on the little LCD display. Models vary, but you'll definitely see the caller's phone number and current time and date. Most models store the numbers in memory for recall at any time. So, if you're not around to answer the call, you can be sure that anywhere from 14 to 70 numbers will be saved for your convenience. (It's great to be able to come home and see X number of messages on your answering machine and see X+4 callers on your ICLID. With a little matching up, you can figure out who didn't leave a message.)

Of course, there are drawbacks to our little "mirror box." What are the limitations to its tracing ability? First of all, it won't work without the local company providing the service. Only after the first ring does the information come storming down the line to be decoded by your little friend. (I have two lines in my house, and sometimes there's a bit of crosstalk between them. When the phone rings, if I listen carefully enough I can actually hear the coded ICLID information being sent.) Also, only areas that offer this service (and other "CLASS" Calling Services) to their customers will be traceable areas. But this area is growing.

If someone calls from out of state or from the boonies a message like "Out of Area" will be displayed instead of the number. That's the real bummer. But, all of the latest models of Caller*ID devices are area code compatible and show your area code where other NPAs will be in the near future. Many states have been slow to pick up the technology mainly because of political and legal reasons. Many privacy issues have been suggested and debated over, but we won't go into those here. As I understand it, New Jersey Bell contends that if a person has your number and calls you, you should have their number as well; when a connection is made, both ends should know who they're talking to. So, hopefully other states will get in gear.

The option to block particular calls is being juggled around, too. Telephone companies are thinking of offering a service whereby the customer would dial a couple of digits before the seven digit number and the receiver would get an "Out of Area" or similar message on their ICLID display. This would definitely suck, unless you are the caller. But this service is already available now thanks to a small loophole. I'll explain later.

New Jersey Bell started CLASS Calling Services around December of 1987. They were test marketed in Hudson County until December 1988 and then began to spread. Other services include Priority*Call, Call*Block (a personal favorite), Repeat*Call, Select*Forward, Return*Call, Call*Trace, Tone*Block, and others. Many of these are based upon the instant tracing ability of CLASS.

Priority*Call will send you a distinctively different sounding ring when certain people call you. You program a "queue" of phone numbers that, when called from, will sound different than the standard phone ringing.

Call*Block is lots of fun. Again, you can program a queue of people into your phone (really, the phone company's computer). When they call your line, they get a recorded message along the lines of, "I'm sorry. The party you have reached is not accepting calls from your telephone number." Nice and rude.

Call*Trace is a service that is available to everyone on a pay-per-trace basis. If you receive a prank, etc. you hang up, pick up, and immediately dial *57. A recording lets you know if the trace was good or bad, and you get charged $1.00 accordingly. Unfortunately you have to call the phone company to get the phone number. This service is for serious complaining and is meant for people who get pranked a lot and want to file charges.

All of the above features can be generally replaced with ICLID. As a substitute for Call*Block I can simply not answer the phone if I don't want to speak to someone, since my ICLID lets me know who it is. Of course, that prerecorded message adds a nice touch. Call*Trace is pretty much useless with ICLID unless you want to bring in the Gestapo. But, then again, Call*Trace is open for anyone to use and isn't ordered monthly like the other services.

A woman from New Jersey Bell told me, though, some technical legalities regarding Call*Trace and Caller*ID. If someone pranks me, and I return their call (having read their number from my "mirror box") and prank them in return, they can *57 me and sue me for phone harassment. Even though I have their number on my ICLID, if I don't *57 him before I call him back, I get *my* ass kicked in. So, the moral of the story is that ICLID can't be used as evidence of a prank.

Select*Forward is used in connection with Call Forwarding and simply forwards only calls coming from numbers that you choose.

Repeat*Call doesn't have much to do with identifying the caller, but will simply redial a number until you get through, and then call you back when the line is free, allowing you to use the phone for other reasons. Sounds cool, eh? Now you can get through to any radio station you like, right? Wrong. It really isn't as great as it sounds. First of all, it only "redials" for 30 minutes. Also, it really doesn't *dial* the number, but only checks to see if the line is free (and it checks only every 45 seconds). So, it is possible, and happens to me occasionally, that you pick up the phone when the computer calls you back to inform you that the line is free, and you find that it's busy again!)

Return*Call is made for people who just make it out of the shower and to the phone a second after the caller hung up. Boo hoo. In a few keystrokes the call is returned, and the wet, naked person still has no idea what number (s)he returned.

And finally, Tone*Block turns off call-waiting for individual calls. Pick up the phone, dial *70 and then the number. Voila! No interruptions. But let's say someone calls you. You cannot turn off your call-waiting in this case, unless of course you also have 3-Way Calling. If you do, you may switch over to the other line and *70 yourself and you'll be fine for the call.

With instant tracing ability soon to sweep the nation, what's the nightmare? Well, basically the hacker's dream is not only for the hacker but for anyone who's got the cash and happens to live in a CLASS infested area. With the public being offered these services, imagine what business customers, or even Sprint/MCI/AT&T are being offered? When ICLID capabilities spread to more states, LCD displays will be showing more and more area codes. Eventually, long-distance companies will integrate themselves, and for every telephone connection made, there will be two numbers involved and available to each end.

When I first got Caller*ID (the service was actually enabled on my line before I received the box) I wanted to learn as much about it as I could. So I played around with it and took it apart. The model that I have (which is relatively old, but there are more ancient ones, too) has a main board inside with some chips and components on it. By ribbon cable it is hooked to an LCD board with LSI chips. There are two buttons (Review and Delete) up front and a battery clip in the back. When the 30th call comes through, it scrolls old ones off to make way for the newest. (This has happened only once to me when I was away for an extended weekend.) What I like about my model is that it will store every call separately. On many models these days, if a call comes through more than once in a row (from the same number), the series of calls will appear under just one entry with a small "RPT" indicator for "repeated call." Personally, I like to know that a certain person called twice a minute for five minutes to get a hold of me, rather than just "Repeat." But that's a personal preference. The flip side is that the extra calls take up space in memory.

The main distributor for ICLIDs is Bell Atlantic Office Supplies. They sell a few different models. Sears has also been allowed to sell ICLIDs through AT&T (who has yet another company making them). Any Sears in New Jersey will sell you one for around $89.95. Radio Shack expects to be offering one soon. That's about it for being able to order them. But there are of course the manufacturers that build these things. Sometimes you can order directly....

Currently, there are only four manufacturers around that I know of. In Irvine, CA is Sanbar, Inc. Sanbar works jointly with another company called Resdel Communications, Inc. I was able to acquire some helpful information through Sanbar and their technical support. Colonial Data Technologies is located somewhere in the depths of

Connecticut and makes most of the ICLIDs that Bell Atlantic and Sears/AT&T sell. They aren't too helpful when it comes to questions about Caller*ID. RDI in New Rochelle, NY recently created a smaller company, CIDCO, to produce ICLIDs, as the etymology of the name might suggest. (I spoke with a fellow there named Bob Diamond. I was pretty embarrassed when, after a few conversations with him, I curiously asked what RDI stood for and found out it meant "Robert Diamond, Inc.") The other manufacturer is a major telephone equipment supplier. Northern Telecom has a massive set of complexes in the southern United States. They make a standalone ICLID as well as the only living telephone with a Caller*ID display built in. It's known as the Maestro and can be ordered through Bell Atlantic. It's a simple thing with your basic features such as one-touch dialing, redial, hold, mute, etc.

One thing I aspired to do with my tracer was to try and interface it with my computer. If I could just get the information on the LCD to the serial or joystick port, I could write lots of fun programs. You're sleeping in bed and the phone rings. Unfortunately you're too tired to get up, turn on the light, and see who's calling. (Actually, CIDCO makes an ICLID with a backlit LCD display.) But you left your computer running and within a few milliseconds it announces the person's name, and a Super VGA digitized picture flashes on the screen. Now you know who it is.

And the imagination can run wild with things to do with the computer integrated ICLID: auto-validating BBSs, database management, and so on. So I called Sanbar (the manufacturer of mine) and talked to one of the head engineers. I asked him if there was any way to leech information from the unit. He said that piping it off the LCD was the best bet, but it might be easier to build a whole ICLID from scratch. After speaking with many people from many different companies, I finally worked on outputting from an LCD. Sanbar used a Sharp LM16255. From Sharp (who was very friendly and helpful) I received literature and specifications. Unfortunately I didn't get too far. Apparently the information is sent in nibbles to the LCD board in parallel format. One must know a bit about electronics and parallel port communications to wire it up.

But fortunately, now there is at least one box available that sends the information via a serial port. (Ah! Such ease.) CIDCO is selling a "business model" that sends the information at 1200,N,8,1 through a serial port in the back. The price? $300. Too much for me. Other companies said they will have similar items, which I expect to be much cheaper.

As far as I know, there aren't many tricks or secrets about using your ICLID at home. When someone calls, either you get their number or you don't; I don't think any electrical modifications will be able to trace untraceable numbers. I hope I am wrong. When I first read the instruction "manual" (leaflet is more like it) I saw that Bell Atlantic had put a piece of tape over a part of the page. I guess they didn't have time to edit the paragraph out. It was in the section of text showing all the different messages that my box could produce. (It can either show a) a phone number; b) "Out of

Area,"; or c) a junk number with a few question marks, indicating that there was static on the line or the phone was picked up during the information transmission after the first ring.) Looking at it through the light I saw that another possible message it could produce (and doesn't anymore) was "Private No." I thought that was great! After speaking with New Jersey Bell, I found out that unlisted numbers are traced along with everything else! Pretty awesome; New Jersey Bell doesn't skimp.

If you have call-waiting, you'll hear the tone, but unfortunately the ICLID won't trace the number. It needs that first ring to "wake it up," so the phone company doesn't bother to send any info. They tell you this in their brochures, but they don't tell you how you can still trace the number of the person who calls you (without going through *57, the main office, and a law enforcement agent). Here is how to do it: When you hear your call-waiting, tell your friend that you'll call her back and hang up the phone. They will be disconnected and the phone will begin to ring for the person who originally clicked in. Call-waiting leaflets tell you this will happen, but no one tells you what happens next, after that first ring. Voila! Your ICLID will light up and will translate the data that was sent after the first ring. You've traced a call-waiting!

As I mentioned earlier, the idea of a per-call block is being thrown around in courts and behind telephone company doors. Supposedly, soon you will be able to make "Private No." show up on your adversary's LCD display when you call. But, it's quite possible now. If you want to call someone and not have your number traced, all you need is a bit of plastic. No "boxes" or equipment. By going through your Sprint/MCI/AT&T calling card, the received will see an "Out of Area" message. That's what the phone company displays when the incoming call originates through a calling card. Voila! A blocked call. The only drawback is that small surcharge for using the card.

Recently, New Jersey Bell corrected a small computer bug that a bunch of friends and I were having a lot of fun with. When someone called my house collect, the number of their pay phone would show up, so I could reject the call and return it, paying nothing for the connection (assuming the pay phone was a local call). That didn't last for long, and now a collect call brings with it the anonymity of an "Out of Area" message. It was fun while it lasted.

Tidbits (Autumn, 1991)

You would think after all of the commotion about privacy invasion and lack of security that big corporations would begin to learn something. MCI can therefore be defined as learning disabled.

You may have seen the ads for their Friends and Family Circle gimmick. Basically, you get your friends and family to sign up for MCI. Then, whenever you call them (assuming you too have MCI), you can save on the regular rates. In a way, MCI has gotten their customers to do their selling for them. That part is actually rather clever. In fact, we've even heard of families putting the guilt trip on relatives who refuse to sign up with MCI.

But where MCI really messed up is with their 800-FRIENDS update service. This number exists so that customers can check the status of their calling circle—find out who's currently on it, who's been dropped, etc. The touch tone service would ask you to key in your telephone number and then, to verify that it was really you, your ZIP code! Obviously, when you know somebody's phone number, figuring out their ZIP code isn't all that difficult. Yet this was the only bit of security standing in the way of *anyone* having access to customers' frequently dialed numbers. It made no difference if these numbers were unlisted. If they showed up on your calling circle, anybody could get them. And, not only that, but the relationship of the people in your circle was also announced. Example: "Your wife at 516-751-2600, your brother-in-law at 202-456-1414" and so on. One could get quite a bit of information on MCI customers rather quickly.

We had a bit of fun with this on WBAI's *Off The Hook*, the weekly telecommunications radio program in New York. We demonstrated the absurd security live on the air and told everybody to call MCI to complain. Apparently they did because the system was quickly changed. Now you need the last three digits of your account number for verification.

U.S. Phone Companies Face Built-In Privacy Hole (Winter, 1991–1992)

Phone companies across the nation are cracking down on hacker explorations in the world of Busy Line Verification (BLV). By exploiting a weakness, it's possible to remotely listen in on phone conversations at a selected telephone number. While the phone companies can do this any time they want, this recently discovered self-serve monitoring feature has created a Telco crisis of sorts.

According to an internal Bellcore memo from 1991 and Bell Operating Company documents, a "significant and sophisticated vulnerability" exists that could affect the security and privacy of BLV. In addition, networks using a DMS-TOPS architecture are affected.

According to this and other documents circulating within the Bell Operating Companies, an intruder who gains access to an OA&M port in an office that has a BLV trunk group and who is able to bypass port security and get "access to the switch at a craft shell level" would be able to exploit this vulnerability.

The intruder can listen in on phone calls by following these four steps:

1. Query the switch to determine the Routing Class Code assigned to the BLV trunk group.
2. Find a vacant telephone number served by that switch.
3. Via recent change, assign the Routing Class Code of the BLV trunks to the Chart Column value of the DN (directory number) of the vacant telephone number.
4. Add call forwarding to the vacant telephone number. (Remote Call Forwarding would allow remote definition of the target telephone number, while Call Forwarding Fixed would only allow the specification of one target per recent change message or vacant line.)

By calling the vacant phone number, the intruder would get routed to the BLV trunk group and would then be connected on a "no-test vertical" to the target phone line in a bridged connection.

According to one of the documents, there is no proof that the hacker community knows about the vulnerability. The authors did express great concern over the publication of an article entitled "Central Office Operations—The End Office Environment," which appeared in the electronic newsletter *Legion of Doom/Hackers Technical Journal*. In this article, reference is made to the "No Test Trunk."

The article says, "All of these testing systems have one thing in common: they access the line through a No Test Trunk. This is a switch which can drop in on a specific path or line and connect it to the testing device. It depends on the device connected to the trunk, but there is usually a noticeable click heard on the tested line when the No Test Trunk drops in. Also, the testing devices I have mentioned here will seize the line, busying it out. This will present problems when trying to monitor calls, as you would have to drop in during the call. The No Test Trunk is also the method in which operator consoles perform verifications and interrupts."

In order to track down people who might be abusing this security hole, phone companies across the nation are being advised to perform the following four steps:

1. Refer to Chart Columns (or equivalent feature tables) and validate their integrity by checking against the corresponding office records.
2. Execute an appropriate command to extract the directory numbers to which features such as BLV and Call Forwarding have been assigned.
3. Extract the information on the directory number(s) from where the codes relating to BLV and Call Forwarding were assigned to vacant directory numbers.
4. Take appropriate action including on-line evidence gathering, if warranted.

Since there are different vendors (OSPS from AT&T, TOPS from NTI, etc.) as well as different phone companies, each with their own architecture, the problem cannot go away overnight.

And even if hackers are denied access to this "feature," BLV networks will still have the capability of being used to monitor phone lines. Who will be monitored and who will be listening are two forever unanswered questions.

Phreaking in the '90s (Summer, 1992) *By Billsf*

In this article I will try to introduce you to the most complex machine on earth: the phone system. It's a guide to having fun with the technology, and I hope it will help you on your travels through the network. It is by no means a definitive manual: if you really want to get into this, there are lots of additional things you must learn and read.

This article assumes you know a little bit about the history of phreaking. It is meant as an update for the sometimes very outdated documents that can be downloaded from BBSs. In here I'll tell you which of the old tricks might still work today, and what new tricks you may discover as you become a phone phreak.

As you learn to phreak you will (hopefully) find ways to make calls that you could not make in any other way: calls to test numbers that you cannot reach from the normal network, calls to ships (unaffordable otherwise), and much more. As you tell others about the hidden world you have discovered, you will run into people who have been brainwashed into thinking that all exploration into the inner workings of the phone system is theft or fraud. Convincing these people of your right to explore is probably a waste of time, and does not advance your technical knowledge.

Phreaking is like magic in more than one way. Those people who are really good share their tricks with each other, but usually don't give out these tricks to anyone walking by. This will be somewhat annoying at first, but once you're really good you'll understand that it's very unpleasant if the trick you just discovered is wasted the very next day. I could tell you at least twenty new tricks in this article but I prefer to teach you how to find your own.

Having said this, the best way to get into phreaking is to hook up with other phreaks. Unlike any other subculture, phreaks are not bound by any geographical restrictions. You can find other phreaks by looking for hacker/phreak BBSs in your region. Having made contact there you may encounter these same people in teleconferences that are regularly set up. These conferences usually have people from all over the planet. Most phreaks from countries outside the United States speak English, so language is not as much of a barrier as you might think.

If you live in a currently repressed area, such as the United States, you should beware that even the things that you consider "harmless exploring" could get you into lots of trouble (confiscation of computer, fines, probation, jail, loss of job, etc.). Use your own judgment and find your protection.

Getting Started

The human voice contains components as low as 70 Hz, and as high as 8000 Hz. Most energy, however, is between 700 and 900 Hz. If you cut off the part below 200 and above 3000, all useful information is still there. This is exactly what phone companies do on long-distance circuits.

If you think all you have to do is blow 2600 Hz and use a set of twelve MF combinations, you have a lot of catching up to do. One of the first multifrequency systems used was R1 with 2600 Hz as the line signaling frequency, but for obvious reasons it is rarely used anymore, except for some very small remote communities. In this case its use is restricted, meaning it will not give you access to all the world in most cases.

To begin with, all experimenting starts at home. As you use your phone, take careful note as to what it does on a variety of calls. Do you hear "dialing" in the background of certain calls as they are set up? Do you hear any high pitched beeps while a call is setting up, as it's answered or at hang-up of the called party?

Can you make your CO fail to complete a call either by playing with the switchhook or dialing strange numbers? If you are in the United States, did you ever do something that will produce a recording: "We're sorry, your call did not go through..." after about 15 seconds of nothing?

If you can do the last item, you are "in" for sure! Any beeps on answer or hang-up of the called party also means a sure way in. Hearing the actual MF tones produced by the Telco may also be your way in. While it would be nice to find this behavior on a toll-free circuit, you may consider using a national toll circuit to get an overseas call or even a local circuit for a bigger discount. Every phone in the world has a way in. All you have to do is find one!

An Overview of Systems

First we must start with numbering plans. The world is divided up into eight separate zones. Zone 1 is the United States, Canada, and some Caribbean nations having NPA 809. Zone 2 is Africa. Greenland (299) and Faroe Islands (298) do not like their Zone 2 assignment, but Zones 3 and 4 (Europe) are all taken up. Since the DDR is now unified with BRD (Germany) the code 37 is up for grabs and will probably be subdivided into ten new country codes to allow the new nations of Europe, including the Baltics, to have their own codes. Greenland and the Faroe Islands should each get a 37x country code. Zone 5 is Latin America, including Mexico (52) and Cuba (53). Zone 6 is the South Pacific and includes Australia (61), New Zealand (64), and Malaysia (60). Zone 7 is now called the CIS (formerly the Soviet Union), but may become a third European code. Zone 8 is Asia and includes Japan (81), Korea (82), Vietnam (84), China (86), and many others. Zone 9 is the sub-continent of India (91) and surrounding regions. A special sub-zone is 87, which is the maritime satellite service (Inmarsat). Country code 99 is reserved as a test code for international and national purposes and may contain many interesting numbers.

In Zone 1, a 10-digit number follows with a fixed format, severely limiting the total number of phones. NPAs like 310 and 510 attest to that. The new plan (beginning in 1995) will allow the middle digit to be other than 1 or 0, allowing up to five times more phones. This is predicted to last into the 21st century. After that Zone 1 must move to the fully extensible system used in the rest of the world.

The "rest of the world" uses a system where "0" precedes the area code for numbers dialed within the country code. France and Denmark are notable exceptions, where there are no area codes or just one as in France (1 for Paris and just eight digits for the rest). This system has proven to be a total mess—worse than the Zone 1 plan!

In the usual numbering system, the area code can be of any length, but at this time between one and five digits are used. The phone number can be any length, too, the only requirement being that the whole number, including the country code but not the zero before the area code, must not exceed fourteen digits. Second dial tones are used in some systems to tell customers they are connected to the area they are calling and are to proceed with the number. With step-by-step, you would literally connect to the distant city and then actually signal it with your pulses. Today, if second dial tones are used it's only because they were used in the past. They have no meaning today, much like the second dial tones in the custom calling features common in the United States. The advantage of the above "linked" system is that it allows expansion where needed without affecting other numbers. Very small villages may only have a three digit number while big cities may have eight digit numbers. Variations of this basic theme are common. In Germany, a large company in Hamburg may have a basic five-digit number for the reception and eight-digit numbers for the employee extensions. In another case in this same town, analog lines have seven digits and ISDN lines have eight digits. In many places it is common to have different length numbers coming to the same place. As confusing as it sounds, it really is easier to deal with than the fixed number plan!

International Signaling Systems

CCITT number four (C4) is an early system that linked Europe together and connected to other systems for overseas calls. C4 uses two tones: 2040 and 2400. Both are played together for 150mS (P) to get the attention of the distant end, followed by a "long" (XX or YY = 350mS) or a "short" (X or Y = 100mS) of either 2040 (x or X) or 2400 (y or Y) to indicate status of the call buildup. Address data (x=1 or y=0, 35 ms) is sent in bursts of four bits as hex digits, allowing 16 different codes. One hundred milliseconds of silence was placed between each digit in automatic working. Each digit therefore took 240mS to send. This silence interval was non-critical and often had no timeout, allowing for manual working. C4 is no longer in wide use, but it was, due to its extreme simplicity, a phreak favorite.

CCITT number five (C5) is still the world's number one overseas signaling method; over 80 percent of all overseas trunks use it. The "plieks" and tones on Pink Floyd's "The Wall" are C5, but the producer edited it, revealing an incomplete number with the old code for London. He also botched the cadence of the address signaling very badly, yet it really sounds OK to the ear as perhaps the only example most Americans have of what an overseas call sounds like!

In actual overseas working, one-half second of 2400 and 2600 Hz, compound, is sent (clear forward) followed by just the 2400 Hz (seize), which readies the trunk for the address signaling. All address signals are preceded with KP1 (code 13) for terminal traffic, plus a discriminating digit for the class of call and the number. The last digit is ST (code 15) to tell the system signaling is over. For international transit working, KP2 (code 14) is used to tell the system a country code follows, after which the procedure is identical to the terminal procedure.

CCITT six and seven (C6 and C7) are not directly accessible from the customer's line, yet many "in-band" systems interface to both of these. C6 is also called Common Channel Interoffice Signaling (CCIS) and as its name implies, a dedicated line carries all the setup information for a group of trunks. Modems (usually 1200 bps) are used at each end of the circuit. CCIS is cheaper, and as an added benefit, killed all the child's play blue boxing that was common in the states in the '60s and early '70s. In the early '80s, fiber and other digital transmission became commonplace, and a new signaling standard was required. C7 places all line, address, and result (backward) signaling on a Time Division Multiplexed Circuit (TDM or TDMC) along with everything else like data and voice. All ISDN systems require the use of SS7 to communicate on all levels from local to worldwide.

The ITU/CCITT has developed a signaling system for very wide and general use. Once called "the European System," R2 has become a very widespread international system used on all continents. R2 is the most versatile end-to-end system ever developed. It is a two-way system like C7 and comes in two forms, analog and digital, both fully compatible with each other. R2 has completely replaced C4, with the possible exception of a few very remote areas where it works into R2 using registers. Two groups of fifteen and two of six MF tones are used for each direction, the high-frequency group forward and the low group backward. Line signaling can be digital with two channels or out-of-band at 3825 Hz, DC, or in cases of limited bandwidth on trunks, can use the C4 line signals, just the 2040 + 2400 Hz or 3000 Hz or even backward signals sent in a forward direction. The signals can be digitally quantized using the A-law or u-law codec standards, resulting in compatible signals for analog lines. In international working, only a small part of the standard is mandatory with a massive number of options available. For national working, an ample number of MF combinations are "reserved for national use," providing an expandable system with virtually limitless capabilities. R2 is the "system of the nineties" and mastering this, for the first time, allows the phone phreak "to hold the whole world in his hands" in a manner that the person who coined this phrase could have only dreamed of in the early seventies!

With the exception of bilateral agreements between neighboring countries to make each other's national systems compatible, especially in border regions, all international systems in use are: C5, C6, C7, and R2. R2 is limited to a single numbering region by policy and must use one of the three remaining systems for overseas working. There are few technical limitations to prevent R2 from working with satellites, TASI, or other analog/digital underseas cables. The spec is flexible enough to allow overseas working, but is not done at the present time. R2 is likely to displace C5 on the remaining analog trunks in the near future.

National Signaling Systems

CCITT 1, 2, and 3 are early international standards for signaling the distant end. C1 is just a 500 Hz line signaling tone, and was used to alert the operator at a distant switchboard that there was traffic and no DC path, due to amplifiers or repeaters on a relatively long circuit. C1 has only one line signaling function (forward transfer) and no address signaling. It is probably used nowhere.

CCITT 2 was the first international standard that used address signaling, allowing automatic completion of calls. Two frequencies, 600 Hz and 750 Hz, were used for line signaling and by pulsing between the two frequencies, representing make and break, of the loop current at the distant end during signaling, calls were automatically pulse dialable. You may actually find this system in limited use in very remote parts of Australia or South Africa. Fairly high signaling levels are required and may very well make customer signaling impossible, unless you are right there. Travel to both the above countries should be fascinating however, for both phone play and cultural experience!

CCITT 3 is an improved pulse system. On-hook is represented by the presence of 2280 Hz and off-hook by the absence of 2280 Hz. This exact system is still used in a surprising number of places. Pulse-dial PBXs often use C3 to signal distant branches of a company over leased lines. Signaling for this system is generally at a much lower level than C2: the tones will propagate over any phone line.

A system from the early 50s is called R1. Many people remember R1 as the blue boxes of the 60s and 70s. R1 is still in wide use in the United States, Canada, and Japan. The use of 2600 Hz for line signaling is quite rare in the 90s, but can be found in all of the above countries. Address signaling uses the MFC standard, which is a combination of two of six tones between 700 Hz and 1700 Hz as in CCITT 5. Almost all R1 used either "out of band" signaling at 3825 Hz or 3350 Hz or some form of digital or DC line signaling. To use this system from home, one must find an indirect method of using the "out of band" signaling. In North America, most signaling from your central office to your long-distance carrier is R1, as is most OSPS/TSPS/TOPS operator traffic.

Pulse systems like CCITT 2 and 3 are still used in national systems. In North America, the C3 standard using 2600 Hz in place of 2280 for national working was commonplace through the 70s and still has limited end-to-end use today. "End-to-end" use refers to sending just the last few digits (usually five) to complete the call at the distant end. The only use this may have to the phreak would be to make several calls to a single locality on one quarter. It may be possible that a certain code would drop you into an R1, but you just have to experiment! This type of system is referred to as 1VF, meaning "one voice frequency." The other standard frequency, for use outside North America, is 2400 Hz. A national system using two voice frequencies (2VF) may still be used in remote areas of Sweden and Norway. The two frequencies are 2400 Hz and 2600 Hz. Playing these two systems in Europe predates the cracking of the R1 and C5 systems in the late '50s and early '60s, respectively. The first phone phreak was probably in Sweden!

Common Channel Interoffice Signaling (CCIS) is CCITT 6 developed for national use and employing features that are of interest to national administrations. R1 often plays into a gateway being converted to CCIS and CCIS will play into a gateway that converts to C5, C6, or C7 for international working. The bulk of the ATT net is CCIS in North America, while R1 is often used by your CO talk to it and the lesser networks. CCITT 7 is the digital system and is the same nationally as internationally. C7 allows the greatest efficiency of all systems and will in time be the world system. C7 has much more speed and versatility than R2, but is a digital only system. All fiber optic systems employ SS7 (C7).

No discussion of systems is complete without mentioning Socotel. Socotel is a general system developed by the French. It is a hodgepodge of many systems, using MFC, pulse tone, pulse AC, and pulse DC system. Most (all?) line signaling tones can be used. An in-band system can use 2500 Hz as a clear forward and 1700 or 1900 Hz for seize or, in Socotel terms, "confirm." Most line signaling today is "out of band," but unlike normal outband signaling, it is below band: DC, 50 Hz or 100 Hz. It is a "brute force" system using 100 V levels, ensuring no customer has a chance of getting it directly! Call setup on the AC systems often has a very characteristic sound of short bursts of 50 Hz or 100 Hz buzz, followed by the characteristic French series of 500 Hz beeps to alert the customer that the call has been received from the Socotel by the end office and is now being (pulse) dialed. Calls often don't make it through all the gateways of a Socotel system, sometimes giving the French phreak a surprise access where it stuck!

On a national level there are even more systems and some are very bizarre. Some use backward R2 tones in the forward direction for line signaling, giving analog lines the versatility of digital line signaling. There have been some interlocal trunks that actually used DTMF in place of MF! The "Silicon Valley" was once served by DTMF trunks for instance. When I visited my local toll office and was told this and pressed for an answer as to why, I was told, "We had extra (expensive then) DTMF receivers and used them!" As a phreak, be ready for anything as you travel the world.

Stuff to Read

Signaling in Telecommunications Networks, S. Welch, 1979; ISBN 0906048044. The Institution of Electrical Engineers, London & New York

CCITT Red Book, Blue Book, Green Book and whatever other colors of books they have. Concentrate on the Q norms.

Telecommunications Engineering, Roger L. Freeman.

Voicemail Hacking (Summer, 1992) *By Night Ranger*

I decided to write this article because I received numerous requests for voice mailboxes (VMBs) from people. VMBs are quite easy to hack, but if one doesn't know where to start it can be hard. To the best of my knowledge, this is the most complete text on hacking VMB systems.

VMBs have become a very popular way for hackers to get in touch with each other and share information. Probably the main reason for this is their simplicity and availability. Anyone can call a VMB regardless of their location or computer type. VMBs are easily accessible because most are toll-free numbers, unlike bulletin boards. Along with their advantages, they do have their disadvantages. Since they are easily accessible this means not only hackers and phreaks can get information from them, but feds and narcs as well. Often they do not last longer than a week when used improperly. After reading this article and practicing the methods described, you should be able to hack voicemail systems with ease. With these thoughts in mind, let's get started.

Finding a VMB System

The first thing you need to do is find a *virgin* (unhacked) VMB system. If you hack on a system that already has hackers on it, your chance of finding a box is considerably less and it increases the chance that the system administrator will find the hacked boxes. To find a virgin system, you need to *scan* some 800 numbers until you find a VMB. A good idea is to take the number of a voicemail system you know, and scan the same exchange but not close to the number you have.

Finding Valid Boxes on the System

If you get a high quality recording (not an answering machine), then it is probably a VMB system. Try entering the number 100. The recording should stop. If it does not, you may have to enter a special key (such as "*", "#", "8", or "9") to enter the voicemail system. After entering 100 it should either connect you to something or do nothing. If it does nothing, keep entering 0s until it does something. Count the number of digits you entered and this will tell you how many digits the boxes on the system are. You should note that many systems can have more than one box length depending on the first number you enter. Example: Boxes starting with a six can be five digits while boxes starting with a seven can only be four. For this article we will assume you have found a four digit system, which is pretty common. It should do one of the following things:

1. Give you an error message, like "Mailbox xxxx is invalid."
2. Ring the extension and possibly connect you to a mailbox if there's no answer.
3. Connect you to mailbox xxxx.

If you don't get a valid mailbox then try some more numbers. Extensions usually have a VMB for when people are not at their extension. If you get an extension, move on. Where you find one box you will probably find more surrounding it. Sometimes a system will try to be sneaky and put one valid VMB per 10 numbers. Example: boxes would be at 105, 116, 121, etc. with none in between. Some systems start boxes at either 10 after a round number or 100 after, depending on whether it is a three or four box system. For example, if you do not find any around 100, try 110, and if you do not find any around 1,000 try 1,100. The only way to be sure is to try *every* possible box number. This takes time but can be worth it.

Once you find a valid box (even if you do not know the passcode), there is a simple trick to use when scanning for boxes outside of a VMB so that it does not disconnect you after three invalid attempts. What you do is try two box numbers, and then the third time, enter a box number you know is valid. Then abort (usually by pressing * or #) and it will start over again. From there you can keep repeating this until you find a box you can hack on.

Finding the Login Sequence

Different VMB systems have different login sequences (the way the VMB owner gets into his box). The most common way is to hit the pound (#) key from the main menu. This pound method works on most systems, including ASPENs (more on specific systems later). It should respond with something like "Enter your mailbox" and then "Enter your passcode." Some systems have the asterisk (*) key perform this function. Another login method is hitting a special key during the greeting (opening message) of the VMB. On a CINDY or Q VOICEMAIL system you hit the zero (0) key during the greeting and since you've already entered your mailbox number it will respond with "Enter your passcode." If (0) doesn't do anything try # or *. These previous two methods of logging in are the most common, but it is possible some systems will not respond to these commands. If this should happen, keep playing around with it and try different keys. If for some reason you cannot find the login sequence, then save this system for later and move on.

Getting In

This is where the basic hacking skills become useful. When a system administrator creates a box for someone, they use what's called a default passcode. This same code is used for all of the new boxes on the system, and often on other systems too. Once the legitimate owner logs into his new VMB, they are usually prompted to change the passcode, but not everyone realizes that someone will be trying to get into their mailbox and quite a few people leave their box with the default passcode or no passcode at all. You should try *all* the defaults that are listed in the chart before giving up on a system. If none of the defaults work, try anything you think may be their passcode. Also remember that just because the system can have a four digit passcode the VMB owner does not have to have used all four digits. If you still cannot get into the box, either the box owner has a good passcode or the system uses a different default. In either case, move on to another box. If you seem to be having no luck, then come back to this system later. There are so many VMB systems that you should not spend too much time on one hard system.

If there's one thing I hate, it's an article that says "Hack into the system. Once you get in...." But unlike computer systems, VMB systems really are easy to get into. If you didn't get in, don't give up! Try another system and soon you will be in. I would say that 90 percent of all voicemail systems have a default listed in the chart. All you have to do is find a box with one of the defaults.

Once You're In

The first thing you should do is listen to the messages in the box, if there are any. Take note of the dates the messages were left. If they are more than four weeks old, then it is pretty safe to assume the owner is not using his box. If there are any recent messages on it, you can assume he is currently using his box. *Never* take a box in use. It will be deleted soon, and will alert the system administrator that people are hacking the system. This is the main reason VMB systems either go down or tighten security. If you take a box that is not being used, it's probable no one will notice for quite a while.

Scanning Boxes from the Inside

From the main menu, see if there is an option to either send a message to another user or check receipt of a message. If there is you can search for *virgin* (unused) boxes) without being disconnected like you would from outside of a box. Virgin boxes have a "generic" greeting and name: "Mailbox xxx" or "Please leave your message for mailbox xxx...." Write down any boxes you find with a generic greeting or name, because they will probably have the default passcode. Another sign of a virgin box is a name or greeting like "This mailbox is for ..." or a woman's voice saying a man's name and vice versa, which is the system administrator's voice. If the box does not have this feature, simply use the previous method of scanning boxes from the outside. For an example of interior scanning, when inside an ASPEN box, choose 3 from the main menu to check for receipt. It will respond with "Enter box number." It is a good idea to start at a location you know there are boxes present and scan consecutively, noting any boxes with a "generic" greeting. If you enter an invalid box it will alert you and allow you to enter another. You can enter invalid box numbers forever, instead of the usual three incorrect attempts from outside of a box.

Taking a Box

Now you need to find a box you can take over. *Never* take a box in use; it simply won't last. Deserted boxes (with messages from months ago) are the best and last the longest. Take these first. New boxes have a chance of lasting, but if the person for whom the box was created tries to login, you'll probably lose it. If you find a box with the system administrator's voice saying either the greeting or name (quite common), keeping it that way will prolong the box life, especially the name.

This is the most important step in taking over a box! Once you pick a box to take over, watch it for at least three days *before* changing anything! Once you think it's not in use, change only the passcode — nothing else! Then login frequently for two to three days to monitor the box and make sure no one is leaving messages in it. Once you are pretty sure it is deserted, change your greeting to something like "Sorry, I'm not in right now, please leave your name and number and I'll get back to you." *Do not* say "This is Night Ranger dudes...." because if someone hears that it's as good as gone. Keep your generic greeting for one week. After that week, if there are no messages from legitimate people, you can make your greeting say whatever you want. The whole process of getting a good VMB (that will last) takes about 7 to 10 days, the more time you take the better chance you have of keeping it for a long time. If you take it over as soon as you get in, it'll probably last you less than a week. If you follow these instructions, chances are it will last for months. When you take some boxes, do not take too many at one time. You may need some to scan from later. Plus listening to the messages of the legitimate users can supply you with needed information, such as the company's name, type of company, security measures, etc.

System Identification

After you have become familiar with various systems, you will recognize them by their characteristic female (or male) voice and will know what defaults are most common and what tricks you can use. The following is a list of a few popular VMB systems.

- **ASPEN** (Automated SPeech Exchange Network) is one of the best VMB systems with the most features. Many of them will allow you to have two greetings (a regular and an extended absence greeting), guest accounts, urgent or regular messages, and numerous other features. ASPENs are easy to recognize because the female voice is very annoying and often identifies herself as ASPEN. When you dial up an ASPEN system, sometimes you have to enter a * to get into the VMB system. Once you're in, you hit # to login. The system will respond with "Mailbox number please?" If you enter an invalid mailbox the first time it will say, "Mailbox xxx is invalid...." and the second time it will say, "You dialed xxx, there is no such number...." After a third incorrect entry it will hang up. If you enter a valid box, it will say the box owner's name and "Please enter your passcode." The most common default for ASPENs is either box number or box number plus 0. You only get three attempts to enter a correct box number and then three attempts to enter a correct passcode before it will disconnect you. From the main menu of an ASPEN box you can enter 3 to scan for other boxes so you won't be hung up like you would be from outside the box.

- **CINDY** is another popular system. The system will start by saying "Good Morning/Afternoon/Evening. Please enter the mailbox number you wish..." and is easy to identify. After three invalid box entries the system will say "Good Day/Evening!" and hang up. To login, enter the box number and during the greeting press 0, then your passcode. The default for *all* CINDY systems is 0. From the main menu you can enter 6 to scan for other boxes so you won't be hung up on. CINDY voicemail systems also have a guest feature, like ASPENs. You can make a guest account for someone, and give them a password, and leave them messages. To access their guest account, they just login as you would except they enter their guest passcode. CINDY systems also have a feature where you can have it call a particular number and deliver a recorded message. However, I have yet to get this feature to work on any CINDY boxes that I have.
- **MESSAGE CENTER** is also very popular, especially with direct dials. To log in on a MESSAGE CENTER, hit the * key during the greeting and the system will respond with "Hello <name>. Please enter your passcode." These VMBs are very tricky with their passcode methods. The first trick is when you enter an invalid passcode, it will stop you one digit *after* the maximum passcode length. Example: If you enter 1-2-3-4-5 and it gives you an error message after you enter the fifth digit, it means the system uses a four-digit passcode, which is most common on MESSAGE CENTERs. The second trick is that if you enter an invalid code the first time, no matter what you enter as the second passcode it will give you an error message and ask again. Then, if you entered the correct passcode the second and third time it will let you login. Also, most MESSAGE CENTERs do not have a default. Instead, the new boxes are "open" and when you hit * it will let you in. After hitting * the first time to login to a

box you can hit * again and it will say, "Welcome to the MESSAGE CENTER" and from there you can dial other extensions. This last feature can be useful for scanning outside a box. To find a new box, just keep entering box numbers and hitting * to login. If it doesn't say something to the effect of "Welcome to your new mailbox" then just hit * again and it will send you back to the main system so you can enter another box. This way you will not be disconnected. Once you find a box, you can enter 6 to record a message to send to another box. After hitting 6 it will ask for a mailbox number. You can keep entering mailbox numbers until you find a generic one. Then you can cancel your message and go hack it out.

- **Q VOICEMAIL** is a rather nice system but not as common. It identifies itself with, "Welcome to Q VOICEMAIL Paging," so there is no question about what system it is. The box numbers are usually five digits and to login you enter 0 like a CINDY system. From the main menu you can enter 3 to scan other boxes.

There are many more systems I recognize but do not know the name for. You will become familiar with these systems, too.

Conclusion

You can use someone else's VMB system to practice the methods outlined above, but if you want a box that will last, you need to scan out a virgin system. If you did everything above and could not get a VMB, try again on another system. If you follow everything correctly, I guarantee you will have more VMBs than you know what to do with.

Common Defaults

- **Box number** (example: box number is 3234, passcode is 3234)
- **Box number backward** (example: box number is 2351, passcode is 1532)
- **Box number plus zero** (example: box number is 323, passcode is 3230)

Some additional defaults in order of most to least common are:

4d	5d	6d
0000	00000	000000
9999	99999	999999
1111	11111	111111
1234	12345	123456
4321	54321	654321

continues

6789	56789	456789
9876	98765	987654
2222	22222	222222
3333	33333	333333
4444	44444	444444
5555	55555	555555
6666	66666	666666
7777	77777	777777
8888	88888	888888

Toll Fraud: What the Big Boys Are Nervous About (Autumn, 1992) *By Count Zero*

Toll fraud is a serious problem that plagues the telecommunications industry. Recently I have acquired a collection of trashed documents detailing what AT&T and Bellcore are doing to stop these "thefts." I found these papers very enlightening and occasionally humorous. A few insights into what's bugging the Telco.

Toll Fraud Prevention Committee (TFPC):

This is an industry-wide "forum" committee set up in conjunction with Bellcore that deals with, guess what, toll fraud. The TFPC has "super elite" meetings every once in awhile. All participants are required to sign nondisclosure agreements. Fortunately, the participants frequently toss their notes in the POTC (Plain Old Trash Can—see, I can make stupid acronyms just like Bellcore!). As far as I'm concerned, once it's in the POTC, it's PD (public domain)!

The "open issues" concerning the TFPC currently are Third Number Billing Fraud, International Incoming Collect Calls to Pay phones, and Incoming Collect Calls to Cellular. Apparently, they have noticed a marked increase in third number billing fraud in California. To quote a memo, "The most prevalent fraud scams include originating from coin/copt (aka COCOTs) phones as well as business and residence service that is fraudulently established." Third-party billing from COCOTs is an old trick. Another type of COCOT abuse discussed was "10XXX" fraud. By dialing 10XXX (where XXX is the code for a certain LD carrier), the caller on the COCOT gets to choose their LD carrier. However, in some cases the LEC (Local Exchange Carrier) strips off the 10XXX and then sends the call to the IXC (Inter-Exchange Carrier, the guys that place the LD call) as a 1 + directly dialed call. So, when you dial 10XXX+011+international number, the LEC strips the 10XXX and the IXC sees the call as directly dialed international and assumes the call has been paid for by coin into the COCOT. Dialing 10XXX+1+ACN also sometimes works for LD calls within the United States. Anyway, COCOT providers are wigging out a bit because, while they *must* provide 10XXX+0 service, they want to block the 10XXX+1 and 10XXX+011 loopholes, but LECs have chosen to provide COCOTs with a standard business line that is *not capable* of distinguishing between these different situations, which is why central offices have been typically programmed to block *all* types of 10XXX calls from COCOTs. Thanks to the FCC, they can't do that anymore; it's *breaking the law!* So COs have been reprogrammed into accepting these 10XXX calls from all COCOTs, and the burden of selectively blocking the 10XXX+1 and 10XXX+011 loopholes often falls upon the COCOT manufacturer. They gotta build it into the COCOT hardware itself!

Well, many early COCOTs cannot selectively unblock 10XXX+0, so their owners face a grim choice between ignoring the unblocking law (thereby facing legal problems), unblocking *all* 10XXX calls (thereby opening themselves up to massive fraud), or replacing their COCOTs with expensive, more sophisticated models. Other LECs have begun offering call screening and other methods to stop this type of fraud, but the whole situation is still pretty messy.

Incoming International Collect to Cellular:

According to the notes "when a cellular phone is turned on, it 'checks in' with the local cellular office. When this happens, a device that 'reads' radio waves can capture the identification of the cellular phone. A tremendous volume of 'cloned' fraudulent cellular calls are going to Lebanon." Same old trick, grabbing the cell phone's ESN/MIN as it's broadcast. The only twist is that you call someone's cellular phone *collect* in order to get them to pick up and broadcast their ESN/MIN (they will probably refuse the call, but they will have broadcast their ESN/MIN nevertheless!). But why *Lebanon?*

The American Public Communications Council mentioned, "a desire for the TFPC to be involved in the resolution of clip-on fraud." Maybe you guys should try *better shielding* of the *phone line* coming out the *back* of the COCOT?? Apparently, clip-on fraud has really taken off with the recent flux of new COCOTs. COCOTs operate off a plain old customer loop, so clipping onto the ring and tip outside the body of the COCOT works nicely. That is, assuming you can get at the cables and get through the insulation.

Incoming International Collect

This is a *big* issue. A person from overseas calls a pay phone *collect* in the United States. His/her buddy answers the pay phone and says, "Sure, I accept the charges." Believe it or not, this trick works many times! Here's why. In the United States, databases containing all public telephone numbers provide a reasonable measure of control over domestic collect abuse and are available to all carriers for a per-use charge. These databases are offered and maintained by the *local* telephone companies (LTC). Domestic collect-to-coin calling works well, because most operator services systems in the United States query this database on each domestic collect call. Most Local Exchange Carriers in the United States also offer this database service to owners of COCOTs (for those *few* that accept incoming calls).

However, *international* operators across the world do *not* share access to this database, just as United States international operators do not have database access overseas! The CCITT, the international consortium of telecommunications carriers, recognized this serious problem many years ago with its strong recommendation to utilize a standardized coin phone recognition tone (commonly called the cuckoo tone) on *every* public telephone line number. Such a tone would be easily recognized by operators worldwide, and is currently in use by many foreign Telcos.

The United States decided to ignore this logically sound recommendation, having already employed a numbering strategy for public telephones which, together with a reference document called the "Route Bulletin," alerted foreign operators that the called number should be checked for coin with the United States inward operator. This simple procedure greatly reduced the number of times that the foreign operator had to check with the United States operator, yet was effective at controlling abuse. Everyone slept soundly.

But after the bust-up of AT&T in 1984, the local telephone companies, operating independently and under pressure to offer new services (cellular, pagers, etc.), *abandoned* the public phone fixed numbering strategy! In addition, in June of 1984 the FCC decided to allow the birth of private pay phones (COCOTs). And, up until 1989, *nothing* was done to replace the fraud prevention system. Can you say "open season?"

In 1989, the TFPC began seeking a solution to the growing volume of fraudulent collect calls resulting from this void in the fraud prevention architecture. Numerous solutions were explored. A primary solution was chosen.

Validation database! Yes, the TFPC chose to support 100 percent the LEC database solution, with the cuckoo pay phone recognition tone as one of a number of *secondary* solutions. This decision caused problems, problems, problems, since it was evaluated that a great number of foreign Telcos would be unable to implement this database-checking routine (for a variety of technical reasons). Furthermore, because this TFPC "solution" to the United States' problem is not in conformance with international requirements, the foreign Telcos view it with strong opposition as an unacceptable solution due to the additional worktime that would be incurred and the blatant unwillingness on the part of the United States to follow an effective and longstanding international standard. (We balked at using *metrics;* why not this too?)

To this day, the TFPC is still bouncing around ideas for this. And the susceptibility of United States pay phones to international incoming collect calls remains *wide open.* Various phone companies are currently fighting the cuckoo tone system, because they are *cheap mothers* and don't want to spend the estimated $500 to $700 per pay phone to install the cuckoo tone technology. If the cuckoo tone were implemented, it would virtually *eliminate* the problem of international incoming collect calls. But it hasn't been....

Other *brilliant* "secondary" solutions recommended by the TFPC are:

1. Eliminate the ringer on the pay phone.
2. Route all such calls through a United States operator.
3. Eliminate incoming service to pay phones altogether.

And so on. As you can see, this is a *fascinating* story, and the latest TFPC meeting ended with the note, "The issue was discussed at some length with the end result of it becoming a new issue." Truly the work of geniuses.

In closing, I want to share with you a quote from an article I dug out from a pile of coffee grinds. It's from *Pay phone Exchange Magazine.*

> *"The fewer the number of people aware of a primary line of defense coming down, the better. Any qualified person reading the hacker and underground publications knows that many of their articles are written by current LTC and IXC employees [or people like me who go through their garbage!]. Loose lips sink ships. Unrestricted distribution of sensitive information permits fraud. Both cost dearly. Let's stop them both today."*

All I can say is...screw that!

News Items (Summer, 1997)

In New Delhi, GSM phones are turning out to be as open to abuse as their more primitive cousins. This scary excerpt comes from the *New Delhi Statesman:*

> *"In a gross invasion of the law and the citizen's right to privacy, the government is forcing private cellular telephone companies to provide the infrastructure to tap cellular phones.*
>
> *Cellular phone owners, confident that their phones have the latest automatically encrypted GSM technology, are blissfully unaware of the tapping.*
>
> *The cellular phone operator is also forced to maintain confidentiality of the names given to it by the authorities.*
>
> *Since the conversation is automatically encrypted, normal monitoring is not possible. Calls cannot be intercepted except after they have been decrypted at the switching centre. [Law enforcement] takes a line from*

the switching centre and then with the help of cables the call is taken to the nearest Mahanagar Telephone Nigam Limited exchange after which it goes to the secret central monitoring station in North Block.

Another method to short circuit the process involves a junior level official being sent to the switching centre with a tape recorder and a list of names to be monitored. He then simply tapes the calls. Most private companies are too scared to object and do not even ask for the mandatory authorization.

According to a Supreme Court order on the telephone tapping issue, phones can only be tapped on the specific authorization of the Union home secretary. In this case the Department of Telecom, in blatant disregard of the law laid down by the court, has forced the operators to agree to carry out tapping on the authorization of any government official."

The lesson to be learned here is simple. We can put in all the encryption we want but as long as government has the potential to work around that, this is exactly what will happen. There's no reason to believe anything will be any different here.

It now seems almost certain that Bell Atlantic will be replacing NYNEX as the local phone company in the Northeast. This comes as the merger between the two telecommunications giants somehow won approval from all of the regulatory bodies who really should have known better. Earlier, two other Baby Bells also merged: SWB and Pacific Telesis. And for a brief while, there was talk of *that* huge entity merging with none other than AT&T! That insanity was mercifully short-lived but don't be surprised to see more mega-mergers.

It seems almost as if the great breakup of 1984 was little more than a trial separation. If we can stretch the analogy to make Telco customers the children of this marriage, we had better start looking for a foster home.

Congratulations are in order for the city of San Francisco. They've managed to scare away drug dealers by ingeniously removing pay phones! "It looks like it could become a very important tool," says Chief Assistant District Attorney Richard Iglehart. The concern was for the safety of people trying to make phone calls while all the drug dealers were milling about. Now they will have to walk to another street where all of the drug dealers have moved.

NYNEX has also made some changes to their pay phones, specifically those annoying yellow pre-paid card phones that didn't take coins or incoming calls and had a ten minute limit on all calls. In short, they're history. The NYNEX Change Cards, modeled after European phone systems, just never caught on. Restrictive phones are always a pain and we're glad to see these yellow things off the streets. But the new silver phones that are replacing them and the remaining coin phones are hardly much better. These "smart" phones cut off your touch tones shortly after connecting you to a number! Just like a COCOT! An annoying synthesized voice comes on after a total of around 20 digits are dialed and says, "No additional dialing allowed." Why this is needed is beyond us. Has NYNEX never heard of remote answering machines or voicemail? It doesn't matter if you dial direct, use a calling card, or call an 800 number. NYNEX will cut you off just the same. Apart from making people use NYNEX phones a lot less, this stupidity will get many people to journey to Radio Shack and buy more tone dialers.

One of Clinton's latest ideas is to have a three digit number for non-emergency police calls. That number will be 311, according to the Federal Communications Commission, in honor of the Chief Executive's favorite band. Meanwhile NYNEX has replaced its easy to remember 611 repair service with 890-6611 allegedly because of local competition; having a three digit number constitutes an unfair advantage in the marketplace.

Those of you who think you're safe by dialing *67 to block your number had better think again. Omnipoint, a new GSM provider in the New York area as well as other parts of the country, has an undocumented way of getting around those pesky Caller ID restrictions. If you call someone with an Omnipoint phone, your Caller ID data will be displayed on their phone. If you have blocking enabled, they won't see your number. *But,* if the person doesn't answer and the call goes to their voicemail, ANI is recorded onto the time/date stamp. In other words, calling Omnipoint can be just like calling an 800, 888, or 900 number. Except you may not know when you're calling an Omnipoint phone. In New York City, they have bought the 917-770, 917-774, 917-815, and 917-945 exchanges. Since all cellular/GSM phones go through the 917 area code in New York City, you can just add 917 to the area codes not to call if you want to keep your privacy. But other parts of the country are a different story. In 516, for instance, if you don't know that the 516-312 exchange is Omnipoint, you could be in for a surprise.

In a revelation that startled a lot of people, AT&T has been offering customers a dime a minute rate around the clock. The weird thing is that they haven't been telling anyone about this rate, which is designed to compete with Sprint's dime-a-minute plan on nights and weekends. They only give it to those customers smart enough to ask for it. AT&T has gone on record as saying the best deals go to those who haggle best. We hear rumors of a nickel a minute deal....

There's hardly a day that goes by where we aren't subjected to some new phone company offering astronomically low rates for phone calls if we only use their carrier access code before dialing. They almost never want us to sign up as customers; they just want us to dial the five digit code first. We've been asked many times if these companies are rip-offs. We've looked into a few of them and invariably there's a catch of some sort that makes the offer not as good as it sounds.

10502 is Talk Cents and they offer an "unlimited 9 cents per minute" rate. But there's a $4.95 charge, which may catch some people by surprise. Even if you only make one phone call on Talk Cents and stay on for one minute, that call will cost you $5.04. If you are always making calls on this system, it could pay off, even with the fee. But undoubtedly this fee from everyone who dials the code is helping this company stay afloat.

10297 is the Long Distance Wholesale Club. There are no fees or minimum number of calls. It looks pretty good on the surface. But the one thing they don't tell you is how much you're actually paying. All they keep saying is that you will save 15 to 50 percent on every call. That's a pretty wide range and it's bound to change radically depending on the calling plan you happen to be on. The truth is there's no guarantee you'll save anything and it's awfully hard to know for sure when the numbers just aren't there.

10811 is the Dime Line. Only 10 cents a minute, anytime. This is one of the worst ones around. Not only do they charge you $5.00 a month, but all calls have a three minute minimum! That means you will never spend just 10 cents on the Dime Line. It will always be at least 30 cents, even if you only stay on for three seconds. That's far worse than most companies.

Finally, 10457 is Dial & Save. This one is almost exactly the same as the Long Distance Wholesale Club. Except they'll only save you 25 percent. And again, no mention of the actual rates.

Every one of these companies sent us stickers to put on all our phones. The stickers never said anything about extra charges, minimums, or vague rates. We suspect many people are just dialing without thinking. And phone companies love that.

Naming Exchanges (Spring, 1998) *By Jeff Vorzimmer*

I recently came across a web site for which the sole purpose was to preserve and catalog old telephone exchange names. Such Quixotic ventures are not uncommon these days on the World Wide Web, so I wasn't that surprised by it. But the author of the site, Robert Crowe, seems committed to cataloging every exchange ever used in every large city in the U.S. What makes this task so daunting is the simple fact that named exchanges haven't been used in the United States in over 35 years.

In fact, many readers probably don't even know what I'm talking about. Let me explain. Back in the dark ages of telephony, before 1921, before phones even had dials on them, one had to pick up the receiver and tap on the switch hook a few times to get the operator's attention. When she got on the line you would give her the number you wanted to call, such as Spring 3456 or Pennsylvania 5000, and she would connect you.

Once dials started appearing on phones, a caller could dial the number himself by first dialing the first three letters of the exchange and then the number. For example the caller would dial the S-P-R in Spring and then the 3456 or the P-E-N in Pennsylvania 5000. In those days phone numbers were written with the dialed letters capitalized such as SPRing 3456 and PENnsylvania 5000.

By the 1930s, large cities were dropping the third letter from the dialing routine and replacing it with a number, to increase the available numbers for each exchange. So numbers such as SPRing 3456 would become SPring 7-3456 and PENnsylvania 5000 would become PEnnsylvania 6-5000. This simple change added 80,000 new numbers to existing exchanges.

For 40 years, Americans used named exchanges when making calls, but eventually Bell Telephone began phasing out the names in the late '50s and early '60s for various reasons, such as the fact that the names could be confusing or difficult to spell and for the fact that European phones didn't have letters on them, so it would make direct dialing from there difficult, if not impossible.

On his Web page, Robert Crowe explains his venture, entitled, aptly enough, The Telephone Exchange Name Project (`http://ourwebhome.com/TENP/TENproject.html`). He explains that his purpose is to catalog these exchanges, to actually use them and to elicit contributions, presumably from those old enough to know what he's talking about. One section of his manifesto reads, "Why do we care?" Good question. He explains, "Partly because we want to resist the increasing trend toward digitizing our lives." Aha! Luddites! "They're also a link to our more analog past which is fast slipping away," he goes on to say.

I'm not sure how the use of letters for the first two digits of my phone number puts me in touch with my analog past. I don't feel any more or less analog when I dial 1-800-GOOD LAWYER. I just have to hunt and peck at the telephone keypad as if it were a typewriter.

One aspect of the project that can't be overlooked, though, is the attempt at historical documentation of telephone exchanges that played such a big part in the daily lives of Americans for so many years. I also have to admit I found the site quite interesting when I started exploring it. He has Bell Telephone's 1955 list of recommended exchange names, which only had been posted at the TELECOM Digest site. He has also carefully documented the comments of those people who contributed exchanges to the catalog.

He has a matrix of all the possible two digit combinations with which an exchange can start. You just press the link that corresponds to the first two digits of your number and, voila, you have a list of hundreds of exchange names that were actually used at one time, as well as a list of cities where each was used. All the New York City and Brooklyn exchanges I knew about were listed and I realized my current exchange was the old Coney Island exchange, ESplanade. Maybe I'll use it on my business card for that retro look.

As I became nostalgic for an era I never knew, I put on a Glenn Miller album (vinyl of course) and moved the arm to PEnnsylvania 6-5000, the 1940 song that featured the number of the Hotel Pennsylvania, across the street from Penn Station in New York City. It was the number to call to make reservations at the Cafe Rouge, located in the hotel, where Miller and his band often played.

Someone had told me not too long ago that it was still the number of the Hotel Pennsylvania. I decided to give it a call—the old fashioned way. I picked up the phone and dialed "0."

"Operator, get me PEnnsylvania 6-5000 in New York City, please."

"Excuse me?"

"I would like to be connected to the number PEnnsylvania 6-5000 in New York City."

Silence.

"Operator?"

"You would like me to connect you?"

"Yes."

"To P-E-6-5000 in New York?"

"Yes, that's right."

"You understand there will be an additional charge for an operator-assisted call?"

"That's fine," I said, wondering how much of an additional charge.

"Please hold for your party, sir."

The number rang and an automated voice announced that I had indeed reached the Hotel Pennsylvania and gave me various menu choices. I turned down my stereo to be able to better hear the music playing in the background behind the automated voice, which ran down the menu options. It was PEnnsylvania 6-5000!

Robert Crowe might be pleased to know at least that operators are backwardly compatible with what he calls the old analog system, although the operator I got seemed old enough to have been working since the 50s. I guess it's good to know that we still have defenders of lost causes, like Don Quixote.

News Items (Spring, 1998)

New York City's new area codes are on hold until a resolution is worked out with the FCC on what appears to be a really stupid rule. This rule requires *all* residents of an area with an overlay code (that is, an area code that coexists with another area code in the exact same area) to dial eleven digits (1+area code+number) *even when the number is in the same area code.* Supposedly this has something to do with fairness although nobody we could find was able to figure out how deliberately adding an inconvenience makes anything fair. But then, we have trouble figuring out anything the FCC is involved in. Incidentally, New York's new area codes will be 646 (an overlay with 212) and 347 (an overlay with 718).

It's really starting to get pretty ridiculous. The newest alternative carrier came to us in a letter from the Binary Brothers (1 and 0, don't ask) announcing the "Dime Line" — 10 cent a minute calls *anytime*. Of course, the call has to be a minimum of three minutes, which means a five second call will cost you 30 cents. And, of course, you have to pay them $5 a month for the privilege. And, just to add a little confusion, every *other* call is half price, as long as it doesn't go over 10 minutes. We have no idea what happens if it does. But the real milestone here is the carrier access code itself — it's one of the new seven digit ones. VarTec Telecom says, in all seriousness, "Just dial 1010-811+1+area code+the number you wish to call." 18 digits to make a phone call. But the thing that is guaranteed is that if you pick up your phone just *once* this month and dial those 18 digits and stay on the line for a single second, it will cost you $5.30. Plus tax.

The FCC, in an alliance with sheer greed, has agreed to charge 28.4 cents to owners of toll-free numbers for every call made to them from a pay phone. Now let's think about this. Toll-free numbers? Aren't they supposed to be, well, toll-free? The cost of the call is already being paid for by the person who owns the number, right? So what exactly is this extra fee for? Well, it seems some sleazoid pay phone owners are getting all pissed off because people use their phones to call toll-free numbers. They've already managed to disable incoming calls because they can't charge people for those. Now they've figured out a way to charge people for something they have no business making money from. After all, there is no wear and tear on the phone from dialing a toll-free call. The local phone company certainly doesn't charge them anything for making such a call. So the only thing they can gripe about is the fact that while someone is making a toll-free call, someone else *isn't* making a toll call. Great, but when was the last time you ever saw a line at a COCOT? People *avoid* these things because they're so overpriced! OK, not *all* of them, but enough to tarnish the entire industry. And this kind of a move does nothing to fix their reputation. Now companies are *blocking* pay phones from accessing their toll-free lines. Calling card and collect rates have gone up to cover this new charge. People are using pay phones less now. And confusion reigns. One thing that has become clearer is the fact that the FCC doesn't really care.

Where Long-Distance Charges Come From (Summer, 1998)

By The Prophet

Most people when calling long distance pay little regard to how charges are calculated. They simply pick up the phone, dial 1+NPA+7, and pay the bill when it arrives. In fact, more than half of AT&T's customers pay so little attention to long-distance charges that they pay the AT&T "basic rate," which is the highest price charged by the "Big Three" in America! Literally every AT&T customer would benefit from a savings plan, yet people are lazy and do not make the one phone call that would be required to sign up. So AT&T and others make millions of extra dollars a year as a result.

Most people also do not question why long distance costs money. They simply accept that if they call out of their flat-rate area (if a flat-rate area is even available), the call will cost them a certain amount per minute.

But why is there a per-minute charge for a call between Seattle and Portland, when one can use Internet services between the two cities for free? The answer is a Byzantine system of tolls mandated by the FCC known as "access charges."

Access Charges

The system of "access charges" is at the heart of per-minute charges for voice bandwidth. Every area has an area known as "local toll calling." For instance, the Seattle LATA covers western Washington State with a northern boundary of the Canadian border, the eastern boundary of NPA 509, and the southern boundary of roughly a line from the Columbia River at Longview west to the Pacific coast and east to NPA 509. Calls that are placed between points within the LATA are known as intra-LATA calls, and are routed and priced on a monopoly basis by the LEC (in the Seattle area, predominantly USWest). Calls that cross LATAs, such as a call from Seattle to Portland, are carried by an IXC, such as MCI, which you may choose.

IXCs are where access charges begin. Suppose you place a call from downtown Seattle to downtown Portland. The call is routed from your local switch — anywhere within the LATA — to the access tandem. From there, the call is handed off to your IXC. Your IXC carries the call to the access tandem in Portland, where it hands the call back to USWest along with SS7 routing data. Your friend's phone in Portland rings, and when he answers the circuit is completed. And the billing starts; USWest charges the IXC an "access charge" set by the FCC on both the Seattle and Portland sides. These access charges usually add up to about half of the per-minute charge you pay to the IXC.

If the access charges were to be eliminated, the need to bill by the minute would also be eliminated; there would no longer be an artificial "cost per minute." This would result in the elimination of a great deal of overhead in billing, collections, and customer service. Without access charges, flat-rate long distance would probably be as common as flat-rate local phone service.

LECs Incur Expenses

In general, LECs like access charges. Access charges subsidize the cost of providing residential service in many areas. They also provide a very healthy revenue stream. But they also provide an incentive for people not to spend too long on the phone. With flat rate long distance, people will probably make more phone calls and stay on longer.

This is likely to be problematic. Switches are intentionally "under-engineered." Just like ISPs assume every subscriber won't be online at once, phone companies assume that not everyone is going to be using the phone at once. So switches are generally engineered with the "1/7th rule," which holds that on average, only 1/7th (or less) of subscribers will be using the phone at any given time. This works fine when people make short phone calls, but doesn't work nearly as well when a flat-rate unlimited plan is available. The recent explosion in Internet usage has required many LECs to undergo expensive upgrades to local tandems and switches.

In fact, LECs like access charges so much that they think that ISPs should pay them, too. When they began to make expensive upgrades, many LECs petitioned the FCC to force ISPs into the access charge system. ISPs are classified as "enhanced service providers," and are exempt — so far — from per-minute fees, despite the fact that they, like IXCs, carry traffic across LATAs. Pacific Bell was particularly vocal in its criticism of the lack of an access charge revenue stream from ISPs, but became strangely quiet when asked about its explosion in revenue from "second lines," its advertising of "second lines" specifically for Internet use, and in particular its profitable ISP business, pacbell.net.

Thus far, the FCC has ruled against billing ISPs access charges. However, the recent popularity of VOIP has raised interesting concerns. Both the FCC and the telephone industry wonder why a circuit-switched voice call is subject to access charges, but a packet-switched voice call is not. This argument is likely to be resolved soon. The FCC does read all public comments, and posts regular updates on regulatory issues at its web site: `www.fcc.gov`.

Bandwidth

One compelling argument in favor of expansion in data services is bandwidth. Domestic bandwidth is at an amazing surplus. In 1992, Sprint's available bandwidth alone could carry every long-distance voice call made in the United States on a typical business day. It is unlikely that this has changed in the past five years. Sprint has continued to upgrade its existing fiber and lay new fiber. Now, Sprint, MCI, AT&T, LDDS Worldcom/WilTel, Allnet/Frontier, LCI, and numerous other long-distance companies have state-of-the-art digital fiber-optic networks, many with similar amounts of bandwidth to Sprint. North America is literally awash in fiber; some fiber is laid and available, but optoelectronics have not yet been installed to put it into use because there aren't any customers for the bandwidth. (This fiber is known as "dark fiber.") International bandwidth is more at a premium, but expanding rapidly. Bandwidth is wasted if not used at a given moment in time. Consider then, all of the bandwidth that could be put to good use that is currently unused. The figure is even more staggering when you consider how much bandwidth is wasted in circuit-switched technology. Every voice call occupies a 64k channel, although VOIP users know that good voice quality can be obtained over a 28.8 connection. Circuit switching is inefficient.

Where Do We Go From Here?

According to Department of Commerce statistics, Internet use has grown from three million subscribers in 1994 to over 64 million subscribers today. Clearly the Internet is very popular, and its astounding popularity is likely the result of its low cost and ready accessibility. The FCC is well aware of the Internet's tremendous potential, and has created a $2.4 billion Schools and Libraries fund, to help bring universal Internet access. The status quo is likely to be maintained with respect to the Internet as we now know it. However, the future of enhanced services, such as VOIP and videoconferencing, is very much in doubt. If you think that full use of bandwidth is more efficient than access charges, it is important that the FCC know what you think. Through the "enhanced services" provision, they created the Internet and with the stroke of a pen, at the behest of a telecommunications lobby, they can destroy it. Be sure that your ISP (or you, if you are an ISP) is well informed of access charge issues; what the FCC does is important to *you!*

Glossary of Terminology

- **LEC**: Local Exchange Carrier, or the local telephone company (USWest, GTE, etc.)
- **IXC**: IntereXchange Carrier, or the long-distance company, carries calls between LATAs (Sprint, MCI, etc.)
- **LATA**: Local Access Transport Area
- **Tandem**: Connects the IXC and LEC's networks, also interconnects LEC networks within a LATA
- **POP**: Point of Presence
- **CO**: The LEC's Central Office, connects your telephone to its network. This is where your dial tone comes from.
- **Switch**: The heart of a CO, switches calls within or between COs.
- **ISP**: Internet Service Provider (uunet, concentric, netcom, etc.)
- **VOIP**: Voice Over IP (Internet)

13 Hackers and the Law

Apart from all of the gatherings, growth, and awareness by the masses of the world of hackers, there was a much more serious and truly historic aspect to it all. That involved actual individuals who were being targeted by the authorities with unprecedented vigor. This in turn would lead to a reaction against this sort of thing and more of an awareness of the threat facing everyone.

The BBS raids of the 1980s had evolved along with the technology and had become more sophisticated and far-reaching in scope. Now it was about more than a few computers tying together kids in a loosely organized group. With the Internet came the perception of a true global threat at the hands of hackers and the authorities reacted accordingly. Massive sweeps of the nation affected hacker and non-hacker alike. People began to see the parallels between what was happening in the hacker world and what was going on in the real world. The growing perception was that those in charge simply wanted any excuse to get a foot in the door and chip away at our remaining rights. Some of it was sheer paranoia but much was firmly rooted in reality and past experience of what the authorities were capable of. Here, on the threshold of a technological and communications revolution, the rules were clearly on the verge of changing. And that could either be a great thing for the individual or the beginning of the end.

I don't think any of us really knew how chaotic a decade it was going to be. We expected more of the same but what we got instead was a real intensifying of the effort to stamp out the kinds of people who were at the heart of *2600's* existence. Clearly, it didn't work. But the price that was paid by those targeted was almost too high to be imagined. And those cases that we found ourselves close to would serve to strengthen our resolve and belief that these were the last people on earth who should be treated like criminals.

We were lucky. We had a voice and could let the world know when something unfair was happening. And I think that's what may have made the biggest difference of all. Had we not been able to let people know about the Mitnick case, or what was happening to Bernie S., or the facts about Operation Sun Devil while it was all still unfolding, the people running these investigations would have had virtual carte blanche in determining how they would all end. We certainly couldn't count on the mass media to do this for us so we did it ourselves—in the form of our magazine, through our increasingly popular radio show, and by eventually making a documentary about some of the injustices that were going on.

While printing articles about computers and phones is at the very heart of what we do, I think what is documented in this section may be proof of our overall importance in the bigger picture. That was manifested in our reaching out to the non-hacker world and helping them to see things from our perspective. I've been in enough organizations and movements over the years to have learned that you don't get very far from only speaking to the people who already are part of what you're doing. By getting *2600* onto mainstream bookstands and broadcasting our show at 50,000 watts out of New York City, we were reaching people who normally would never have heard of us. And *that* changed history.

Operation Sun Devil and the EFF

One of the biggest and most far-reaching investigations into the hacker world became public in early 1990. Initially, Operation Sun Devil seemed like just another massive raid on hackers, perhaps with a bit more enthusiasm and sound bites from those running it. The seriousness of what was actually happening soon became painfully clear. An electronic newsletter was targeted, private email was being spied upon, wild allegations were made and later disproved, and innocent people paid a heavy price. The chilling effect this had on the hacker community has remained to the present day. Because even when it was proven that the government had overstepped its boundaries and victimized people, it didn't seem to matter. Massive amounts of debt were incurred by those who had to defend themselves, despite the fact that the charges were found to have no merit. Others would be imprisoned, despite the fact that the allegations against them had been proven false in a related case.

But this time something a little different happened. In their enthusiasm, the Secret Service had really overstepped the boundary and harassed a completely innocent (and well known) game designer named Steve Jackson. This part of the story managed to hit home with a lot of people and, before you knew it, we were organizing and communicating online in an effective manner. Through a public UNIX system in California known as *The Well*, we helped spread the story to even more people. The mass media actually picked up on it. I think that's when I first saw the power of the Net in action. Emails came pouring in, scores of people wanted to know what they could do, and the word spread throughout the globe. Among those who expressed a desire to help were Lotus founder Mitch Kapor and former Grateful Dead lyricist John Perry Barlow. They saw these events as a reason to start a new group that would help protect people from this kind of injustice. And so, the seeds for the Electronic Frontier Foundation were planted.

For Your Protection (Spring, 1990)

A year ago, we told the stories of Kevin Mitnick and Herbert Zinn, two hackers who had been sent to prison. It was then, and still is today, a very disturbing chain of events: mischief makers and explorers imprisoned for playing with the wrong toys and for asking too many questions. We said at the time that it was important for all hackers to stand up to such gross injustices. After all, they couldn't lock us all up.

It now appears that such an endeavor may indeed be on the agendas of some very powerful U.S. governmental agencies. And even more frightening is the realization that these agencies don't particularly care who or what gets swept up along with the hackers, as long as all of the hackers get swept up. Apparently, we're considered even more of a threat than we had previously supposed.

In retrospect, this doesn't come as a great deal of a surprise. In fact, it now seems to make all too much sense. You no longer have to be paranoid or of a particular political mindset to point to the many parallels that we've all been witnesses to. Censorship, clampdowns, "voluntary" urine tests, lie detectors, handwriting analysis, surveillance cameras, exaggerated crises that invariably lead to curtailed freedoms.... All of this together with the overall view that if you're innocent, you've got nothing to hide. And all made so much more effective through the magic of high tech. Who would you target as the biggest potential roadblock if not the people who *understand* the technology at work? It appears the biggest threats to the system are those capable of manipulating it.

What we're about to tell you is frightening, plain and simple. You don't have to be a hacker to understand this. The words and ideas are easily translatable to any time and any culture.

Crackdown

"We can now expect a crackdown... I just hope that I can pull through this one and that my friends can also. This is the time to watch yourself. No matter what you are into.... Apparently the government has seen the last straw in their point of view.... I think they are going after all the 'teachers'... and so that is where their energies will be put: to stop *all* hackers, and stop people *before* they can become threats."

This was one of the reactions on a computer bulletin board to a series of raids on hackers, raids that had started in 1989 and spread rapidly into early 1990. Atlanta, St. Louis, and New York were major targets in what was then an undetermined investigation.

This in itself wouldn't have been especially alarming, since raids on hackers can almost be defined as commonplace. But this one was different. For the very first time, a hacker newsletter had also been shut down.

Phrack was an electronic newsletter published out of St. Louis and distributed worldwide. It dealt with hacker and phone phreak matters and could be found on nearly all hacker bulletin boards. While dealing with sensitive material, the editors were very careful not to publish anything illegal (credit card numbers, passwords,

Sprint codes, etc.). We described "Phrack World News" (a regular column of *Phrack*) in our Summer 1989 edition as "a must-read for many hackers." In many ways *Phrack* resembled *2600*, with the exception of being sent via electronic mail instead of U.S. Mail. That distinction would prove to be *Phrack's* undoing.

It now turns out that all incoming and outgoing electronic mail used by *Phrack* was being monitored by the authorities. Every piece of mail going in and every piece of mail coming out. These were not pirated mailboxes that were being used by a couple of hackers. These had been obtained legally through the school the two *Phrack* editors were attending. Privacy on such mailboxes, though not guaranteed, could always be assumed. Never again.

It's fairly obvious that none of this would have happened, none of this *could* have happened had *Phrack* been a non-electronic magazine. A printed magazine would not be intimidated into giving up its mailing list as *Phrack* was. Had a printed magazine been shut down in this fashion after having all of their mail opened and read, even the most thick-headed sensationalist media types would have caught on: hey, isn't that a violation of the First Amendment?

Those media people who understood what was happening and saw the implications were very quickly drowned out in the hysteria that followed. Indictments were being handed out. Publisher/editor Craig Neidorf, known in the hacker world as Knight Lightning, was hit with a seven-count indictment accusing him of participating in a scheme to steal information about the enhanced 911 system run by Bell South. Quickly, headlines screamed that hackers had broken into the 911 system and were interfering with emergency telephone calls to the police. One newspaper report said there were no indications that anyone had died or been injured as a result of the intrusions. What a relief. Too bad it wasn't true.

In actuality there have been very grievous injuries suffered as a result of these intrusions. The intrusions we're referring to are those of the government and the media. The injuries have been suffered by the defendants who will have great difficulty resuming normal lives even if all of this is forgotten tomorrow.

And if it's not forgotten, Craig Neidorf could go to jail for more than 30 years and be fined $122,000. And for what? Let's look at the indictment:

"It was... part of the scheme that defendant Neidorf, utilizing a computer at the University of Missouri in Columbia, Missouri would and did receive a copy of the stolen E911 text file from defendant [Robert J.] Riggs [located in Atlanta and known in the hacker world as Prophet] through the Lockport [Illinois] computer bulletin board system through the use of an interstate computer data network.

It was further part of the scheme that defendant Neidorf would and did edit and retype the E911 Practice text file at the request of the defendant Riggs in order to conceal the source of the E911 Practice text file and to prepare it for publication in a computer hacker newsletter.

It was further part of the scheme that defendant Neidorf would and did transfer the stolen E911 Practice text file through the use of an interstate computer bulletin board system used by defendant Riggs in Lockport, Illinois.

It was further part of the scheme that the defendants Riggs and Neidorf would publish information to other computer hackers which could be used to gain unauthorized access to emergency 911 computer systems in the United States and thereby disrupt or halt 911 service in portions of the United States."

Basically, Neidorf is being charged with receiving a stolen document. There is nothing anywhere in the indictment that even suggests he entered any computer illegally. So his crimes are receiving, editing, and transmitting.

Now what is contained in this document? Information about how to gain unauthorized access to, disrupt, or halt 911 service? Hardly. The document (erroneously referred to as "911 software" by the media, which caused all kinds of misunderstandings) is quoted in *Phrack*, Volume 2, Number 24, and makes for one of the dullest articles ever to appear in the newsletter. According to the indictment, the value of this 20k document is $79,449.

Shortly after the indictments were handed down, a member of the Legion of Doom known as Erik Bloodaxe issued a public statement. "[A group of three hackers] ended up pulling files off [a Southern Bell system] for them to look at. This is usually standard procedure: you get on a system, look around for interesting text, buffer it, and maybe print it out for posterity. No member of LOD has ever (to my knowledge) broken into another system and used any information gained from it for personal gain of any kind... with the exception of maybe a big boost in his reputation around the underground. [A hacker] took the documentation to the system and wrote a file about it. There are actually two files, one is an overview, the other is a glossary. The information is hardly something anyone could possibly gain anything from except knowledge about how a certain aspect of the telephone company works."

He went on to say that Neidorf would have had no way of knowing whether or not the file contained proprietary information.

Prosecutors refused to say how hackers could benefit from the information, nor would they cite a motive or reveal any actual damage. In addition, it's widely speculated that much of this information is readily available as reference material.

In all of the indictments, the Legion of Doom is defined as, *"a closely knit group of computer hackers involved in: a) disrupting telecommunications by entering computerized telephone switches and changing the routing on the circuits of the computerized switches; b) stealing proprietary computer source code and information from companies and individuals that owned the code and information; c) stealing and modifying credit information on individuals maintained in credit bureau computers; d) fraudulently obtaining money and property from companies by altering the computerized information used by the companies; e) disseminating information with respect to their methods of attacking computers to other computer hackers in an effort to avoid the focus of law enforcement agencies and telecommunication security experts."*

Ironically, since the Legion of Doom isn't a closely knit group, it's unlikely that anyone will be able to defend the group's name against these charges; any defendants will naturally be preoccupied with their own defenses. (Incidentally, Neidorf was not a part of the Legion of Doom, nor was *Phrack* a publication of LOD, as has been reported.)

The Hunt Intensifies

After learning of the *Phrack* electronic mail surveillance, one of the system operators of *The Phoenix Project*, a computer bulletin board in Austin, Texas, decided to take action to protect the privacy of his users, "I will be adding a secure encryption routine into the e-mail in the next 2 weeks—I haven't decided exactly how to implement it, but it'll let two people exchange mail encrypted by a password only known to the two of them.... Anyway, I do not think I am due to be busted... I don't do anything but run a board. Still, there is that possibility. I assume that my lines are all tapped until proven otherwise. There is some question to the wisdom of leaving the board up at all, but I have personally phoned several government investigators and invited them to join us here on the board. If I begin to feel that the board is putting me in any kind of danger, I'll pull it down with no notice. I hope everyone understands. It looks like it's sweeps-time again for the feds. Let's hope all of us are still around in 6 months to talk about it."

The new security was never implemented. *The Phoenix Project* was seized within days.

And the clampdown intensified still further. On March 1, the offices of Steve Jackson Games, a publishing company in Austin, were raided by the Secret Service. According to the Associated Press, the home of the managing editor was also searched. The police and Secret Service seized books, manuals, computers, technical equipment, and other documents. Agents also seized the final draft of a science fiction game written by the company. According to the *Austin American-Statesman*, the authorities were trying to determine whether the game was being used as a handbook for computer crime.

Callers to the *Illuminati* bulletin board (run by Steve Jackson Games), received the following message: "Before the start of work on March 1, Steve Jackson Games was visited by agents of the United States Secret Service. They searched the building thoroughly, tore open several boxes in the warehouse, broke a few locks, and damaged a couple of filing cabinets (which we would gladly have let them examine, had they let us into the building), answered the phone discourteously at best, and confiscated some computer equipment, including the computer that the BBS was running on at the time.

So far we have not received a clear explanation of what the Secret Service was looking for, what they expected to find, or much of anything else. We are fairly certain that Steve Jackson Games is not the target of whatever investigation is being conducted; in any case, we have done nothing illegal and have nothing whatsoever to hide. However, the equipment that was seized is apparently considered to be evidence in whatever they're investigating, so we aren't likely to get it back any time soon. It could be a month, it could be never.

To minimize the possibility that this system will be confiscated as well, we have set it up to display this bulletin, and that's all. There is no message base at present. We apologize for the inconvenience, and we wish we dared do more than this."

Apparently, one of the system operators of *The Phoenix Project* was also affiliated with Steve Jackson Games. And that was all the authorities needed.

Raids continued throughout the country with reports of more than a dozen bulletin boards being shut down. In Atlanta, the papers reported that three local LOD hackers faced 40 years in prison and a $2 million fine.

Another statement from a Legion of Doom member (The Mentor, also a system operator of *The Phoenix Project*) attempted to explain the situation:

"LOD was formed to bring together the best minds from the computer underground—not to do any damage or for personal profit, but to share experiences and discuss computing. The group has *always* maintained the highest ethical standards.... On many occasions, we have acted to prevent abuse of systems.... I have known the people involved in this 911 case for many years, and there was *absolutely* no intent to interfere with or molest the 911 system in any manner. While we have occasionally entered a computer that we weren't supposed to be in, it is grounds for expulsion from the group and social ostracism to do any damage to a system or to attempt to commit fraud for personal profit.

The biggest crime that has been committed is that of curiosity.... We have been instrumental in closing many security holes in the past, and had hoped to continue to do so in the future. The list of computer security people who count us as allies is long, but must remain anonymous. If any of them choose to identify themselves, we would appreciate the support."

And the Plot Thickens

Meanwhile, in Lockport, Illinois, a strange tale was unfolding. The public UNIX system known as *Jolnet* that had been used to transmit the 911 files had also been seized. What's particularly odd here is that, according to the electronic newsletter *Telecom Digest*, the system operator, Rich Andrews, had been cooperating with federal authorities for over a year. Andrews found the files on his system nearly two years ago, forwarded them to AT&T, and was subsequently contacted by the authorities. He cooperated fully. Why, then, was his system seized as well? Andrews claimed it was all part of the investigation, but added, "One way to get [hackers] is by shutting down the sites they use to distribute stuff."

The *Jolnet* raid caused outrage in the bulletin board world, particularly among administrators and users of public UNIX systems.

Cliff Figallo, system administrator for *The Well*, a public UNIX system in California, voiced his concern, "The assumption that federal agents can seize a system owner's equipment as evidence in spite of the owner's lack of proven involvement in the alleged illegal activities (and regardless of the possibility that the system is part of the owner's livelihood) is scary to me and should be to anyone responsible for running a system such as this."

Here is a sampling of some of the comments seen around the country after the *Jolnet* seizure:

- "As administrator for *Zygot*, should I start reading my users' mail to make sure they aren't saying anything naughty? Should I snoop through all the files to make sure everyone is being good? This whole affair is rather chilling."
- "From what I have noted with respect to *Jolnet*, there was a serious crime committed there—by the [Federal authorities]. If they busted a system with email on it, the Electronic Communication Privacy Act comes into play. Everyone who had email dated less than 180 days old on the system is entitled to sue each of the people involved in the seizure for at least $1,000 plus legal fees and court costs. Unless, of course, the [authorities] did it by the book, and got warrants to interfere with the email of all who had accounts on the systems. If they did, there are strict limits on how long they have to inform the users."
- "Intimidation, threats, disruption of work and school, "hit lists," and serious legal charges are *all* part of the tactics being used in this "witch-hunt." That ought to indicate that perhaps the use of pseudonyms wasn't such a bad idea after all."
- "There are civil rights and civil liberties issues here that have yet to be addressed. And they probably won't even be raised so long as everyone acts on the assumption that all hackers are criminals and vandals and need to be squashed, at whatever cost.... I am disturbed, on principle, at the conduct of at least some of the federal investigations now going on. I know several people who've taken their systems out of public access just because they can't risk the seizure of their equipment (as evidence or for any other reason). If you're a Usenet site, you may receive megabytes of new data every day, but you have no common carrier protection in the event that someone puts illegal information onto the Net and thence into your system."

Increased Restrictions

But despite the outpourings of concern for what had happened, many system administrators and bulletin board operators felt compelled to tighten the control of their systems and to make free speech a little more difficult, for their own protection.

Bill Kuykendall, system administrator for *The Point*, a public UNIX system in Chicago, made the following announcement to the users of his system:

"Today, there is no law or precedent which affords me... the same legal rights that other common carriers have against prosecution should some other party (you) use my property *(The Point)* for illegal activities. That worries me....

I fully intend to explore the legal questions raised here. In my opinion, the rights to free assembly and free speech would be threatened if the owners of public meeting places were charged with the responsibility of policing all conversations held in the hallways and lavatories of their facilities for references to illegal activities.

Under such laws, all privately owned meeting places would be forced out of existence, and the right to meet and speak freely would vanish with them. The common sense of this reasoning has not yet been applied to electronic meeting places by the legislature. This issue must be forced, or electronic bulletin boards will cease to exist.

In the meantime, I intend to continue to operate *The Point* with as little risk to myself as possible. Therefore, I am implementing a few new policies:

No user will be allowed to post any message, public or private, until his name and address has been adequately verified. Most users in the metropolitan Chicago area have already been validated through the telephone number directory service provided by Illinois Bell. Those of you who received validation notices stating that your information had not been checked due to a lack of time on my part will now have to wait until I get time before being allowed to post.

Out of state addresses cannot be validated in the manner above.... The short term solution for users outside the Chicago area is to find a system closer to home than *The Point*.

Some of the planned enhancements to *The Point* are simply not going to happen until the legal issues are resolved. There will be no shell access and no file upload/download facility for now.

My apologies to all who feel inconvenienced by these policies, but under the circumstances, I think your complaints would be most effective if made to your state and federal legislators. Please do so!"

These restrictions were echoed on other large systems, while a number of smaller hacker bulletin boards disappeared altogether. We've been told by some in the hacker world that this is only a phase, that the hacker boards will be back and that users will once again be able to speak without having their words and identities "registered." But there's also a nagging suspicion, the feeling that something is very different now. A publication has been shut down. Hundreds, if not thousands, of names have been seized from mailing lists and will, no doubt, be investigated. The facts in the 911 story have been twisted and misrepresented beyond recognition, thanks to ignorance and sensationalism. People and organizations that have had contact with any of the suspects are open to investigation themselves. And, around the country, computer operators and users are becoming more paranoid and less willing to allow free speech. In the face of all of this, the belief that democracy will triumph in the end seems hopelessly naive. Yet, it's something we dare not stop believing in. Mere faith in the system, however, is not enough.

We hope that someday we'll be able to laugh at the absurdities of today. But, for now, let's concentrate on the facts and make sure they stay in the forefront.

- Were there break-ins involving the E911 system? If so, the entire story must be revealed. How did the hackers get in? What did they have access to? What could they have done? What did they actually do? Any security holes that were revealed should already have been closed. If there are more, why do they still exist? Could the original holes have been closed earlier and, if so, why weren't they? Any hacker who caused damage to the system should be held accountable. Period. Almost every hacker around seems to agree with this. So what is the problem? The glaring fact that there doesn't appear to have been *any* actual damage. Just the usual assortment of gaping security holes that never seems to get fixed. Shoddiness in design is something that shouldn't be overlooked in a system as important as E911. Yet that aspect of the case is being side-stepped. Putting the blame on the hackers for finding the flaws is another way of saying the flaws should remain undetected.
- Under no circumstance should the *Phrack* newsletter or any of its editors be held as criminals for printing material leaked to them. Every publication of any value has had documents given to them that were not originally intended for public consumption. That's how news stories are made. Shutting down *Phrack* sends a very ominous message to publishers and editors across the nation.
- Finally, the privacy of computer users must be respected by the government. It's ironic that hackers are portrayed as the ones who break into systems, read private mail, and screw up innocent people. Yet it's the federal authorities who seem to have carte blanche in that department. Just what did the Secret Service do on these computer systems? What did they gain access to? Whose mail did they read? And what allowed them to do this?

Take Exception

It's very easy to throw up your hands and say it's all too much. But the facts indicate to us that we've come face to face with a very critical moment in history. What comes out of this could be a trend-setting precedent, not only for computer users, but for the free press and every citizen of the United States. Complacency at this stage will be most detrimental.

We also realize that one of the quickest ways of losing credibility is to be shrill and conspiracy-minded. We hope we're not coming across in this way because we truly believe there is a significant threat here. If *Phrack* is successfully shut down and its editors sent to prison for writing an article, *2600* could easily be next. And so could scores of other publications whose existence ruffles some feathers. We *cannot* allow this to happen.

In the past, we've called for people to spread the word on various issues. More times than not, the results have been felt. Never has it been more important than now. To be silent at this stage is to accept a very grim and dark future.

A Bittersweet Victory (Summer, 1990)

By now, a good many of you have probably heard the news about the Phrack case we talked about in the last issue. In case you haven't, the charges were officially dropped when it became clear that Bell South had provided false information to the prosecution. The document they claimed to be worth nearly $80,000 turned out to be obtainable from them for a mere $13. In an unprecedented move, the superiors of the prosecutor involved demanded that he drop the case immediately. Good news, right?

Well, sort of. It's great that one of the publishers of *Phrack* won't be going to jail for putting out a newsletter. But we won't soon be seeing another issue of *Phrack*. As Craig Neidorf told us, the risks of running *Phrack* at this stage are far too great. Plus he's got a lot of recovering to do. Legal fees of over $100,000 plus the emotional stress of facing many years in prison for being a publisher.... It's a bit much for anyone. So the government managed to shut down *Phrack* and give the publisher a hefty penalty. Not bad, considering they lost the case.

Add to this the fact that there are many other cases pending, cases that are disturbing even to those who know nothing about hacking. Raids are commonplace, as is the misguided zeal of federal prosecutors who seek to imprison teenagers, hold them at gunpoint, confiscate all kinds of equipment, and put their families through a living hell.

We have a lot of education ahead of us. Much of it will involve getting through to non-hackers to point out the serious dangers of a legal system gone mad. A good part of this issue is devoted to those matters and, as a result, many articles we were planning on running were bumped to the autumn issue. It would be nice if there was substantially less of this to report for our next issue.

What is the EFF? (Summer, 1990)

One of the results of our public outcry over the hacker raids this spring has been the formation of the Electronic Frontier Foundation (EFF). Founded by computer industry giants Mitch Kapor and Steve Wozniak along with writer John Barlow, the EFF sought to put an end to raids on publishers, bulletin board operators, and all of the others that have been caught up in recent events. The EFF founders, prior to the organization's actual birth this summer, had said they would provide financial support to those affected by unjust Secret Service raids. This led to the characterization of the group as a "hacker defense fund" by mainstream media and their condemnation in much of the computer industry.

As a result, when the EFF was formally announced, the organizers took great pains to distance themselves from computer hackers. They denied being any kind of a defense fund and made a nearly $300,000 donation to Computer Professionals for Social Responsibility (CPSR).

"We are helping educate policy makers and the general public," a recent EFF statement said. "To this end we have funded a significant two-year project on computing and civil liberties to be managed by CPSR. With it, we aim to acquaint policy makers and law enforcement officials of the civil liberties issues which may lie hidden in the brambles of telecommunications policy.

"Members of the EFF are speaking at computer and government conferences and meetings throughout the country to raise awareness about the important civil liberties issues.

"We are in the process of forming alliances with other public interest organizations concerned with the development of a digital national information infrastructure.

"The EFF is in the early stages of software design and development of programs for personal computers which provide simplified and enhanced access to network services such as mail and netnews.

"Because our resources are already fully committed to these projects, we are not at this time considering additional grant proposals."

The merits of the EFF are indisputable and we're certainly glad that they're around. But we find it sad that they've redirected their energies away from the hackers because that is one area that is in sore need of outside intervention. There have been an unprecedented number of Secret Service raids this summer with many people coming under investigation simply for having called a bulletin board. And in at least one instance, guns were again pulled on a 14-year-old. This time coming out of the shower. Our point is that someone has to speak out against these actions, and speak *loudly.*

It's also important that what the EFF is actually doing be made clear. Many people are under the mistaken assumption that Craig Neidorf's case was funded by the EFF and that they were largely responsible for getting the case dropped. The EFF itself has not made the facts clear. Mainstream media has given the impression that all hackers are being helped by this organization. The facts are these: The EFF filed two briefs in support of Neidorf, neither of which was successful. They mentioned his case quite a bit in their press releases, which helped to get the word out. They were called by someone who had information about the 911 system who was then referred to Neidorf's lawyer. (This is very different from their claims of having *located* an expert witness.) Not one penny has been given to Neidorf by the EFF. At press time, his defense fund stands at $25. And, though helpful, their legal intervention actually drove Neidorf's legal fees far higher than they would have been ordinarily.

So while the EFF's presence is a good thing, we cannot think of them as the solution to the problem. They are but one step. Let's hope for many more.

If you want to get involved with the EFF, we do encourage it. Your participation and input can help to move them in the right direction.

Negative Feedback (Summer, 1990)

Bringing the *Phrack* story to the attention of the public was no easy task. But it would have been a lot harder were it not for the very thing that the whole case revolved around: the electronic transfer of text. By utilizing this technology, we were able to help the *Phrack* case become widely known and one of the more talked about subjects in conferences, electronic newsletters, and BBSs. As with anything controversial, not everyone agreed. We thought it would be interesting to print some of the pieces of mail (electronic and paper) from people who *didn't* like what we were doing. Keep in mind that (as far as we know) these people are not *2600* subscribers and, in all likelihood, have never even seen a copy. (Our replies appear in italics.)

"I suppose you've had this discussion an infinite number of times. Nevertheless....

That old analogy of breaking into somebody's house and rummaging around is quite apt. Nowadays, there are virtually no computers on line that are not protected by password access. Doesn't that put you in the position of a person with knowledge of picking locks? Such knowledge is virtually useless to anybody but a thief; it rarely is of use even to the small community of locksmiths. While I agree that 30 years in the federal slams isn't a just punishment for picking a lock, I suspect that most people found guilty of breaking and entering get lighter sentences, which are probably equally justifiable for computer burglary or whatever criminal label you'd wish to assign to password hacking.

Do hackers do a service? I don't see why. Any mechanical lock can be picked. Probably any electronic scheme can be defeated as well. Yet nobody argues that teenagers should set themselves up as freelance security analysts picking everybody's lock to see if it can be done. If hackers didn't already know they could probably get in, what would be the point?

I see password hacking as a modestly criminal activity somewhere between vandalism, window peeping, and breaking and entering in seriousness, with deliberate destruction or screwing with information as a potentially serious offense depending on the type of information or system screwed with.

Is it necessary to hack passwords in order to learn about computers? Hardly. The country is full of personal computers on which many valuable things may be learned. The cities are full of community colleges, night schools, and vo-tech institutes all clamoring to offer computer courses at reasonable rates. There are even federal assistance programs so the very poor have access to this knowledge. This means that it is unnecessary to commit socially irresponsible acts to obtain an education in computers. The subjects you learn when password hacking are not of use to professional computer people. None of the people I work with have to hack a password, and we are otherwise quite sophisticated.

Privacy is a right held dear in the United States; it's wired into the Bill of Rights (search and seizure, due process, etc.) and into the common law. You will find that you can never convince people that hacking is harmless simply because it violates people's perceived privacy rights. It is one of the few computer crimes for which a clear real-world analogy can be made, and which juries understand in a personal way. That's why the balance has begun to tilt toward heavier and heavier sentences for hackers. They haven't heard society telling them to stop yet, so society is raising its voice. When the average hacker gets the same jail term as, say, the average second degree burglary or breaking and entering, and every hacker looks forward to that prospect, I suspect the incidence will taper off and hackers will find different windows to peep into."

There is a common misconception here that hackers are logging into individuals' computers, hence the walking through the front door analogy. You'll see it in the letters that follow as well. In actuality, hackers are not interested in violating privacy or stealing things of value, as someone who walks through your front door would be. Hackers are generally explorers who wander into huge organizations wondering just what is going on. They wander using the computers of these huge organizations, computers that often store large amounts of personal data on people without their knowledge. The data can be legally looked at by any of the hundreds or thousands of people with access to this computer. If there's a violation of privacy here, we don't think it's the hackers who are creating it.

This letter raised an interesting point about the "right" way to learn, something many hackers have a real problem with. Learning by the book is okay for people with no imaginations. But most intelligent people will want to explore at some point, figuring things out as they go. Ironically, classrooms and textbooks often discourage people from learning because of their strict limitations. And it's common knowledge that the best programmers are those who are self-taught.

As to the poor having easy access to high technology, this is simply not true. In this country, education is a commodity. And if you don't have the money, you're really out of luck. This is becoming increasingly true for the "middle class" as well.

"Using the term 'hacker' to refer to people who break into systems owned by others, steal documents, computer time, and network bandwidth, and are 'very careful not to publish anything illegal (credit card numbers, passwords, Sprint codes)' is derogatory and insulting to the broad hacker community, which is working to make the world a better place for everyone."

There has been an ongoing move afoot by older hackers to distance themselves from what they perceive to be the "evil hackers." Their way of doing this has been to refer to all of the "evil hackers" as crackers. While it's a fine tradition to create new labels for people, we think it's a big waste of time here. There is a well-defined line between hacking and criminal activity. Hackers explore without being malicious or seeking a profit. Criminals steal, vandalize, and do nasty things to innocent people. We do not defend people who use other people's credit card numbers to order huge amounts of merchandise. Why should we? What has that got to do with hacking? While we may find interest in their methods, we would be most turned off by their motivation. There seems to be a general set of values held by hackers of all ages.

"I recently read a post to the Usenet (comp.risks) describing recent events related to the crackdown on hackers. While I feel strongly that federal agencies should be scrutinized and held accountable for their activities, the above mentioned post gave me reason for concern that I thought you should be made aware of.

It seemed to me a great irony that the poster was concerned about the invasion of the privacy of BBS operators and users, and yet seemed willing to defend the (albeit non-destructive) invasion of privacy committed by hackers.

I am a graduate student who recognizes the immense importance of inter-network telecommunications. Institutions such as Usenet are becoming vital for the expansion, dissemination, and utilization of creative thought. Any activity which breaches security in such networks, unless by organized design, is destabilizing and disruptive to the productive growth of these networks.

My point is this: I am Joe grad student/scientist, one of the (as yet) few that is "net aware." I do not want Federal agencies reading my mail, but neither do I want curious hackers reading my mail. (Nor do I want anyone reading company XYZ's private text files. Privacy is privacy.) I agree that the time for lengthy discussion of such matters is past due, but please understand that I have little sympathy for anyone who commits or supports invasion of privacy."

"I just finished reading your call to arms, originally published in the Spring 1990 edition. I was royally disgusted by the tone: you defend the actions of computer criminals, for which you misuse and sully the honorable term "hacker" by applying it to them, and wrap it all in the First Amendment in much the same way as George Bush wraps himself in the American flag.

Bleech.

Whatever the motivations of the cyberpunks (I like Clifford Stoll's term for them), their actions are unacceptable: they are breaking into computers where they're not wanted or normally allowed, and spreading the information around to their buddies. Their actions cause great damage to the trust that networks such as Usenet are built upon. They have caused innocent systems to be shut down because of their actions. In rare cases, they may do actual, physical damage without knowing it. Their excuse that "the only crime is curiosity" just doesn't cut it.

It is unacceptable for a burglar to break into a house by opening an unlocked door. It should be just as unacceptable for a cyberpunk to break into a system by exploiting a security hole. Do you give burglars the same support you give cyberpunks?

The effort to stamp out cyberpunks and their break-ins is justified, and will have my unqualified support.

I call upon your journal to 1) disavow any effort to enter a computer system without authorization, whatever the reason, and 2) stop misusing the term "hacker" to describe those who perpetrate such electronic burglary."

We respectfully decline to do either.

"I just received the *2600* article on the raid of Steve Jackson Games, which was posted to the GMAST mailing list. It's worrying that the authorities in the U.S. can do this sort of thing—I don't know what the laws on evidence are, but surely there's a case for theft? Taking someone's property without their permission, when they haven't committed a crime?

My only quibble is that the 911 hackers are not innocent. Yes, they may well be innocent of computer vandalism, forgery, etc. (the only consistent truth about newspapers is that they couldn't get facts straight to save their lives) but they have still entered a system and looked at a private document (assuming I understood your article correctly—apologies if I'm wrong). People should have a right to privacy, whether those people are ordinary users, hackers, or large companies, and it should not be abused by either hackers or the authorities. Consider the non-computer analogy: if someone broke into my house and started going through my things, I would be severely unhappy with them—and I would not appreciate a suggestion that they had a right to do so because they happened to have a key that fit my door!"

"What does the entire 911/Steve Jackson Games escapade tell us? Well, it's not all that new that the government (like most such things) requires careful watching, and I'm not too happy about how the last I'd heard, an agent had told SJ Games they wouldn't get all of their hardware back, even though no charges had been filed. (Can you say legalized thievery boys and girls? I knew you could.)

But the main thing that moves me to write this missive is the indication from the published article that the authors, and thus quite likely also the party responsible for copying that document and circulating it still do not quite understand what the individual responsible did. Accordingly, and in the hopes that if this circulates widely enough he or she will see it, the following message:

OK—all you did was get into Bell South's computer system (mostly proving that their security sucks rocks) to prove what a hotshot hacker you were, then made a copy of something harmless to prove it. Sheer innocence; nothing to get upset about, right?

Want to know what you did wrong? Well, for starters, you scared the U.S. government and pointed it in the direction of computer hobbyists. There are enough control freaks in the government casting wary eyes on free enterprises like BBS systems without you having to give them ammunition like that. Bad move, friend, bad move. You see, the fact that you didn't damage anything, and only took a file that would do no harm to Bell South or the 911 system if it were spread all over the country is beside the point. What really counts is what you *could* have done. You know that you only took one file; Bell South only knows that one file from their system turned up all over the place. What else might have been taken from the same system, without their happening to see it? You know that you didn't damage their system (you *think* that you didn't damage their system); all Bell South knows is that somebody got into the system to swipe that file, and could have done any number of much nastier things. Result—the entire computer you took that file from and its contents are compromised, and possibly anything else that was connected with that computer (we know it can be dialed into from another computer—that's how you got on, after all!) is also compromised. And all of it has now got to be checked. Even if it's just a batch of text files never used on the 911 system itself, they all have to be investigated for modifications or deletions. Heck—just bringing it down and reloading from backup from before you got in (if they know when you got in) even if no new things were added since would take a lot of time. If this is the sort of thing that $79,449 referred to, I think they were underestimating.

You cost somebody a lot of time/money, you almost cost Steve Jackson Games their existence, you got several folks arrested for receiving stolen goods (in essence), you endangered a lot of bulletin boards and maybe even BBS nets in general. Please find some other way to prove how great you are, OK?"

In other words, ignorance is bliss? Don't show the world how fragile and vulnerable all of this information is and somehow everything will work out in the end? We have a lot of trouble with that outlook. Incompetence and poor design are things that should be sought and uncovered, not protected.

"I've just read the rather long article describing the investigations of BBS systems in the U.S. While the actions taken by the investigators sometimes seemed extreme, I would ask you to consider the following simple analogy:

If you see the front door of someone's house standing open, do you feel it's appropriate to go inside?

See, it's still a crime to be somewhere you're not supposed to be, whether damage is done or not. Wouldn't you be upset if you found a stranger lurking about your house? It's a violation of privacy, pure and simple.

As to the argument that people are doing corporations a "service" by finding security loopholes, rubbish. Again, would you appreciate a person who attempts to break into your house, checking to see if you've locked your windows, etc.? I think not.

The whole issue is very easily summarized: it's not your property, so don't go near it."

"I have not sent along my phone number since there are a few people out there who would try to retaliate against my computer for what I am going to say.

"I have not read such unmitigated BS since the last promises of Daniel Ortega.

You object to the "coming through my front door and rummaging through my drawers" analogy by mentioning leaving the front door open. In the first place, by what right do you enter my house uninvited for any reason? That can be burglary, even if all you take is a used sanitary napkin. (By the way, in Texas, burglary of a habitation (house) is a first-degree felony 5 to 99 or life.) Burglary is defined as the entry of a building with the intent to commit a felony or *theft*. Entry of or remaining on property or in a building of another without the effective consent of the owner is criminal trespass and can get you up to a year in the county jail. When you go into someone's property, even electronically, you are asking for and *deserving* of punishment if you get caught.

Is the nosy 14-year-old going to be any less dead if the householder sees him in the house at 3:00 am and puts both barrels of a 12-gauge shotgun through him? (Not knowing that the late 14-year-old was only there "to learn".) As to storming into a suspect's house with guns, etc., what the hell are they supposed to do? Take the chance that the individual is armed with an assault rifle?

As to the *Phrack* case, I have read the indictments, and if the DOJ can prove its case, these individuals (one called by his own counsel "a 20-year-old nebbish") deserve what they get. Neidorf had to know the material he published was private property, and the codefendant who cracked the Bell South files had to know he had no right to do so. The fact that much of the information was publicly available from other sources is both immaterial and irrelevant. Is it any less theft if you steal my encyclopedia rather than my silverware?

But breaking into a computer is not walking through an unlocked door. Access by unauthorized people is only through an act which is illegal in itself. Whether the motive for the act is good, evil, or indifferent is of no consequence. *You have no right to enter my computer without my authority than you do to enter my house!* You seem to have the idea that if the entry is for experiment or fun and not for profit, then it is OK. BS and you know it.

You say you've been hacked yourself—and *you* blame the people who sold you the product or service, not the hacker. You would blame the Jews in the 40s, not the SS?

Also, if someone breaks into my office and only reads the files of my clients—doesn't take anything—has he harmed them by seeing information that is none of his business?

What we've got is one more expression of the "spoiled brat syndrome." "I can do it, so I may do it and don't you dare punish me if I get caught." Children, I have news for you! I catch you in my house at 3:00 am, I'll fill your behind so full of buckshot you'll walk like a duck for the rest of your life. I catch you in my computer, I'll have the Secret Service on you like ugly on an ape.

A corporation has the same right to privacy as an individual. Due to business necessity, they may have to leave their computers on 24 hours a day. Where is it written that any asshole who can figure his way into the company's computer can do so with impunity? More fittingly, if he is caught, he should be publicly flogged, as I do not like the idea of supplying him with three hots and a cot for five to life.

I might add that in Texas, any unauthorized entry to a computer is a crime and can be anything from a Class B misdemeanor to a third degree felony depending on the circumstances—that works out to anything from one day to ten years in jail. Some fun and games."

Facts and Rumors (Autumn, 1990)

Over the past year there has been a great deal of publicity concerning the actions of computer hackers. Since we began publishing in 1984 we've pointed out cases of hackers being unfairly prosecuted and victimized. We wish we could say things were getting better but we cannot. Events of recent months have made it painfully clear that the authorities, above all else, want to "send a message." That message of course being that hacking is not good. And there seems to be no limit as to how far they will go to send that message.

And so we come to the latest chapter in this saga: the sentencing of three hackers in Atlanta, Georgia on November 16. The three, Robert Riggs (The Prophet), Frank Darden, Jr. (The Leftist), and Adam Grant (The Urville) were members of the Legion of Doom, one of the country's leading hacker "groups." Members of LOD were spread all over the world but there was no real organization, just a desire to learn and share information. Hardly a gang of terrorists, as the authorities set out to prove.

The three Atlanta hackers had pleaded guilty to various charges of hacking, particularly concerning SBDN (the Southern Bell Data Network, operated by Bell South). Supposedly Riggs had accessed SBDN and sent the now famous 911 document to Craig Neidorf for publication in *Phrack*. Earlier this year, Bell South valued the document at nearly $80,000. However, during Neidorf's trial, it was revealed that the document was really worth $13. That was enough to convince the government to drop the case.

But Riggs, Darden, and Grant had already pleaded guilty to accessing Bell South's computer. Even though the facts in the Neidorf case showed the world how absurd Bell

South's accusations were, the "Atlanta Three" were sentenced as if every word had been true. Which explains why each of them received substantial prison time, 21 months for Riggs, 14 months for the others. We're told they could have gotten even more.

This kind of a sentence sends a message all right. The message is that the legal system has no idea how to handle computer hacking. Here we have a case where some curious people logged into a phone company's computer system. No cases of damage to the system were ever attributed to them. They shared information that we now know was practically worthless. And they never profited in any way, except to gain knowledge. Yet they are being treated as if they were guilty of rape or manslaughter. Why is this?

In addition to going to prison, the three must pay $233,000 in restitution. Again, it's a complete mystery as to how this staggering figure was arrived at. Bell South claimed that approximate figure in "stolen logins/passwords," which we have a great deal of trouble understanding. Nobody can tell us exactly what that means. And there's more. Bell South claims to have spent $1.5 million tracking down these individuals. That's right, one and a half million dollars for the phone company to trace three people! And then they had to go and spend $3 million in additional security. Perhaps if they had sprung for security in the first place, this would never have happened. But, of course, then they would have never gotten to send the message to all the hackers and potential hackers out there.

We think it's time concerned people sent a message of their own. Three young people are going to prison because a large company left its doors wide open and doesn't want to take any responsibility. That in itself is a criminal act.

We've always believed that if people cause damage or create a nuisance, they should pay the price. In fact, the LOD believed this too. So do most hackers. And so does the legal system. By blowing things way out of proportion because computers were involved, the government is telling us they really don't know what's going on or how to handle it. And that is a scary situation.

If the media had been on top of this story and had been able to grasp its meaning, things might have been very different indeed. And if Bell South's gross exaggerations had been taken into account at the sentencing, this injustice couldn't have occurred. Consider this: if Riggs' sentence were as much of an exaggeration as Bell South's stated value of their $13 document, he would be able to serve it in full in just more than two hours. And the $233,000 in restitution would be under $40. So how much damage are we really talking about? Don't look to Bell South for answers.

In early 1991, the three are to begin their sentences. Before that happens, we need to reach as many people as possible with this message. We don't know if it will make a difference in this particular case if the general public, government officials, and the media hear this side of the story. But we do know it would be criminal not to try.

EFF Lawsuit (Spring, 1991)

On May 1, 1991, the Electronic Frontier Foundation filed a civil suit against the United States Secret Service and others involved in the Steve Jackson Games raid of last spring. According to EFF Staff Counsel Mike Godwin, Jackson was "an absolutely innocent man to whom a grave injustice has been done." Jackson's business was nearly driven to bankruptcy, a manuscript and several computers were taken, and private electronic mail was gone through.

When asked how important it was that Jackson not be considered a hacker, Godwin replied, "First, the rights we argue in this case apply to hackers and non-hackers alike, so it's not as if we were seeking special treatment under the law for hackers. Everybody uses computers now, so the rights issues raised by computer searches and seizures affects everyone. Second, the facts of Steve's case show how muddy the government's distinctions between hacker and non-hacker, and between criminal and non-criminal, have been. Steve Jackson was never the target of a criminal investigation, yet at least one Secret Service agent told him that his *GURPS Cyberpunk* book was a handbook for computer crime."

Godwin said the interests that Jackson and the EFF want to protect "derive directly from well-understood Constitutional principles."

We're glad to see groups like the EFF emerge and start fighting back. We encourage support for their efforts. It's going to take a lot of awareness and vigilance on everyone's part to keep these injustices from occurring again and again.

News Update (Summer, 1993)

Those of you who get *2600* on newsstands did not receive the special insert that came with the last issue. In it, we announced the good news that Steve Jackson had won his lawsuit against the United States Secret Service. More than $50,000 in damages will be awarded to Steve Jackson Games for violations of the Privacy Protection Act of 1980 and for lost profits as a result of the raid by the Secret Service in March 1990. Jackson's legal fees, which could amount to several hundred thousand dollars, must also be paid by the government. Each plaintiff in the case was also awarded $1,000 under the Electronic Communications Privacy Act of 1986. The Secret Service violated this act when they seized private mail on the Illuminati Bulletin Board System. Every user of the board could have been awarded $1,000 if they had also filed suit. This is obviously a very positive turning point and it wouldn't have been possible without Steve Jackson, the hacker community that stood by him, and the Electronic Frontier Foundation for providing the expertise and financing. We should probably also thank the United States Secret Service.

The Secret Service and *2600* Meetings

In 1992, a truly bizarre incident occurred at our monthly Washington D.C. public gathering. In short, the United States Secret Service orchestrated an illegal search and seizure episode against our attendees who were doing nothing other than hanging out in a food court. They tried to cover this up by having mall security do their dirty work but it didn't take long for *that* house of cards to fall apart. Again, using the power of the Net and our other methods of communication, we were able to get lots of attention on this incident, including a front page *Washington Post* story and the support of Computer Professionals for Social Responsibility, who helped us pursue charges against the Secret Service. But the problem with going after a major government entity that has virtually unlimited power is the intimidation factor. Basically, we had a bunch of innocent kids who had their bags searched and their names taken down by government agents without cause. And, while a good number of them wanted justice, the pressures of family and friends plus the desire to get on with your life without further heartache takes the wind out of your sails. Plus, let's face it—a few of these kids were involved in things that could come back to haunt them. Just a bit of mischief involving computers or phones, nothing really major. But enough to really get slammed if the wrong people got pissed off. And the Secret Service were definitely the wrong people to piss off, as we would learn a few years later. I'm happy we were at least able to tell the story, if not ultimately achieve justice for those unfairly targeted. It turned out to be a really important part of our history.

Hackers in a World of Malls: Secret Service Behind Harassment of *2600* Meeting (Winter, 1992-1993)

It just hasn't been a good year for malls.

First there was the incident in June at a hacker gathering in St. Louis called Summercon. Mall cops at the Northwest Plaza told the hackers they weren't allowed to wear baseball caps backwards. The hackers, in their innocent naivete, questioned authority.

It happened again, this time at the Pentagon City Mall during the November 6th Washington D.C. *2600* meeting. But clothing wasn't the issue in this incident. Instead, the mall police didn't like the hackers' very existence. Or so it seemed.

It started like most other *2600* meetings—people gather at tables in a food court and start talking to each other. Remarkably similar to what real people do. But these were no ordinary people. These were hackers and the mall cops had plans for them.

Eyewitness Accounts

"At about 5:15 someone noticed two people on the second story taking pictures of the group with a camera. Most of the members saw the two people walk away with a camera in hand and we started looking around for more people. [One hacker] noted that he didn't like the guys standing up on the 'fed perch' on the second level and that they looked like feds.... At about 5:30... a mall security guard stopped me and told me to sit down because I was to be detained for questioning or some shit like that. I complied and waited. Now about eight guards were there surrounding the meeting. One guard approached the group and said that he saw someone with a 'stun gun' of some sort and would like to search the person's bag.... The stun gun turned out to be a Whisper 2000 listening device. Also the guard took possession of [a hacker's] handcuffs and asked what he needed them for and so on. At this point the guard asked for IDs from everyone. Most all people refused to comply with this order. At this time the guard called in to their dispatcher and their boss got on the radio and said that he was coming down to see what the 'hell is going on' with us. About two minutes later a gentleman in a suit arrived. Apparently he was the boss and he ordered the guards to get IDs.

"The guards used very coercive tactics to obtain IDs from threatening to call people's parents to calling the Arlington County police and having them force us to produce ID. They got IDs from most people, but some still refused to produce IDs. At this time a guard approached another person at the meeting and asked to search his bag too. This person gave consent to search the bag and the guard discovered a [legal] credit card verification machine. At this point the guards radioed in to call the Arlington County police. About 10 minutes later the police arrived, demanded, and got IDs from the remaining holdouts and the mall security quickly wrote down all pertinent information from telephone numbers to Social Security numbers to date of births and addresses.

"The guards at no time disclosed what would be done with the information and responded that it was 'none of your business' when I inquired about it. When I asked about the illegal searches they were conducting they stated that they were within their rights because it was private property and they could do 'whatever we want, and you'll play by our rules or we'll arrest you.' Arrest me for what I haven't a clue. I asked why they seized the papers and electronic equipment from the bags and they said that it was 'evidence' and could be retrieved when they want us to get it. A wireless telephone bug was seized from my person.... I told them that it was a wireless intercom modification for a phone. When they said that they would keep it until Monday I pressed the issue that they were not entitled to it and I would take it now whether they liked it or not. At this time the guy in the suit said, 'Bring it here and let me look at it.' In his infinite electronics wisdom [he] concluded that it would be OK for me to have it.

"During the entire episode a rather large crowd had gathered in the mall, including several people who other hackers identified as Secret Service agents. I cannot confirm this however.

Most of the hackers who arrived late were not allowed into the scene but many observed the officers with cameras and some had their film taken and were handled in a very belligerent manner by the mall cops."

What It Was All About

The actions of the mall police were outrageous in the eyes of most. Condemnation was swift and plentiful. But if this were simply another entry in a list of stupid things that mall cops have done, it wouldn't really have much significance. And, as many of us already know, this was indeed a most significant event.

Bright and early on Monday, November 9th, Brock Meeks, a reporter for *Communications Daily*, called the mall police and spoke with Al Johnson, director of Security for the Pentagon City Mall. They had the following conversation:

Meeks: "I'd like to ask you a few questions about an incident where some of your security guards broke up a meeting of some hackers on Friday (Nov. 6)."
Al Johnson: "They broke up some meeting of hackers?"
Meeks: "Yes."
Johnson: "I don't know about breaking any meeting up. Who... first of all I can't talk to you on the phone, if you want to come in, I don't talk to the press on the phone."
Meeks: "OK."
Johnson: "Ahh... maybe you oughta call the Secret Service, they're handling this whole thing. We, we were just here."
Meeks: "The Secret Service was part of this?"
Johnson: "Well, FBI, Secret Service, everybody was here, so you might want to call their office and talk to them. There's not much I can really tell you here."
Meeks: "OK."
Johnson: "Our involvement was minimum, you know, minimal."
Meeks: "I see, but your folks were acting on...."
Johnson: "We didn't break anything... I... we didn't... as far as I know, well I can't say much on the phone. But I, well, somebody's awfully paranoid apparently. Where'd you get this information from?"
Meeks: "Umm.... from computer bulletin boards."
Johnson: "Bulletin boards?"
Meeks: "Yep."
Johnson: "When did you get it?"
Meeks: "I got it, ah, Sunday night."
Johnson: "Sunday night?"
Meeks: "Yep."
Johnson: [small laugh] "Ah, yeah, you gotta call the FBI and the Secret Service. There's not much I can do for you here."
Meeks: "OK. Al, if I come down there will you talk to me down there?"

Johnson: "No. I can't talk to you at all. Fact is, there's nothing to talk about. Our involvement in anything was minimal, I don't know where this information came from as far as bulletin boards, and breaking meetings up and you know...."
Meeks: "Well, the Arlington police were down there too. I mean I've talked to several of the kids that were involved."
Johnson: "Um-hmmm."
Meeks: "They said, that ah, members of your, of the mall security forces, ah, or security staff, searched them, confiscated some material and didn't give it back. Did any of this happen?"
Johnson: "Like I said, I'm not, I'm not able to talk to you... we have a policy that we don't talk to the press about anything like that. You can call the Secret Service, call the FBI, they're the ones that ramrodded this whole thing, and you talk to them, we're out of this basically, you know, as far as I'm concerned here."
Meeks: "OK. Is there a contact person over there that you can...."
Johnson: "Ah... you know, I don't have a contact person. These people were working on their own, undercover, we never got any names, but they definitely, we saw identification, they were here."
Meeks: "They were there. So it was all the Secret Service and none of your men?"
Johnson: "Ah, nah, that's not what I said. But they're the ones you want to talk to."

Fallout

At the meeting, several attendees had overheard mention of Secret Service involvement by both the mall police and the Arlington police. Here, though, was clear cut indisputable evidence. And it was even captured on tape!

Calls by other reporters yielded a different response by Johnson, who started saying that there was no Secret Service involvement and that he had never said there was. He was unaware at the time that a tape recording of his comments existed. When this fact became clear, Al Johnson faded away from the public spotlight. The obvious conclusion to draw is that reporter Meeks got to Johnson before the Secret Service was able to. In fact, a couple of weeks later at a hacker court appearance in New York, a Secret Service agent would be overheard commenting on how badly they had screwed up in D.C.

Very few people failed to see the significance of this latest Secret Service action. Outrage was expressed in many different forums, over the Internet, on radio programs, over the phone, through the mail, and in independent media outlets. Mainstream media (as usual) missed the boat on this one. While the story did manage to make the front page of the *Washington Post* (November 13), the issue of Secret Service involvement in illegal searches and intimidation tactics wasn't gone into nearly enough. There was no mention of the person who had film ripped out of their camera for trying to document what was happening. Nor was there mention of the person who tried to write down the names of the cops and wound up having the list seized by them and torn up. Rather, this seemed to be accepted as standard practice and what was unusual, and even cause for concern, was the fact that hackers actually mingle with the rest of America in shopping malls. It's probably not necessary for us to point out the dangers of accepting what the Secret Service did to us. Most of our readers know that accepting one atrocity is the best way of ensuring another. If we allow a small piece of our freedom to be taken away, the hunger pangs for another piece will be even stronger. That is why we will not tolerate such activities and that is why we have begun to fight back.

Our Plans

While a mall can technically be considered private property, in reality it is an area where the public gathers. In a large part of our country, malls have replaced town squares as places to meet and see your friends. We have trouble with, and don't intend to passively accept, policies which allow people to be removed from malls simply because of who they are. This is especially repugnant when the people are mall customers who aren't even being accused of anything!

We intend to continue to meet in such areas and will only stop when it becomes illegal for anybody to meet in such a place. Since we have meetings all over the country and have been meeting in New York for more than five years without incident, we don't really anticipate this to be a problem. In fact, we doubt we ever would have had a problem at the Pentagon City mall if the Secret Service hadn't "ramrodded" their way through.

At the December meeting, hackers from New York came to the Pentagon City mall to show support. A total of about 75 people came to this meeting, ranging from 12-year-old kids to people who read about it in the *Washington Post*. The mall cops stayed away and there were no incidents (except that they threw out Brock Meeks for asking too many questions and for trying to track down Al Johnson). We don't anticipate any problems at future meetings here. The Pentagon City Mall is a great place to get together and we intend to continue meeting there. We also estimate that our little group spent about $1,000 in the food court alone.

We have a little saying at *2600* that seems to hold true for each time we get hassled or challenged. Every time we're attacked, we only get stronger. This latest incident is no exception. We've had more people from various parts of the country contact us wanting to start meetings in their cities. Attendance at the existing meetings has gone up. And people "outside the loop" are finally beginning to see that hackers are not criminals. After all, do criminals meet openly and welcome outsiders?

In addition, there is now the question of legality. Every legal expert we've spoken with tells us that the Secret Service and Pentagon City Mall actions are clearly outside the boundaries of due process. Those responsible may only now be realizing the potential legal trouble they're in. It's very likely they thought that the hackers would be intimidated and wouldn't tell anybody what happened. Perhaps this train of thought works when the intimidated parties are criminals with something to hide. In this case, the hackers immediately got in touch with the New York *2600* meeting, the *Washington Post*, the Electronic Frontier Foundation, Computer Professionals for Social Responsibility, and the American Civil Liberties Union. Word of the harassment swept across the nation within minutes. The authorities were not prepared for this. There just wasn't enough time for a cover-up and this is what did them in.

Freedom of Information Act requests (FOIAs) have already been filed with the Secret Service. This is the first of many legal steps that are now being contemplated. It's time we put a stop to this abuse of power and it's also time for the Secret Service to stop sneaking around shopping malls spying on teenagers and start getting back to something important.

For those of you interested in starting up meetings in your city, we ask that you contact us. We don't have a whole lot of guidelines but we do ask that you use common sense. Pick an open setting with plenty of space and access to payphones. It's far preferable if the payphones can accept incoming calls. Unfortunately, you must be prepared for the kind of unpleasantness that took place in Washington D.C. The mature and professional reaction of the D.C. hackers is what really made the difference in this case.

As far as what actually goes on at a *2600* meeting, there are no rules. Obviously, it's best if you don't cause any problems and don't do anything illegal. New people should be welcomed, regardless of their views or your suspicions. All kinds of information should be shared without fear. But most of all, meetings are for the purpose of getting hackers openly involved with the rest of the world so they can see for themselves what we're all about. Since it's obvious the media won't soon dispel the myths, it's really up to us now.

Lawsuit Filed Against Secret Service: Action is Taken on Behalf of D.C. *2600* Meeting (Spring, 1993)

The Secret Service may have thought that harassing a motley crew of hackers in a shopping mall would have resulted in nothing more than the intended goal of sending them scurrying back to their underground hideouts, fearfully awaiting a knock at the door. But when the Washington D.C. *2600* meeting was detained, searched, and ejected from Pentagon City mall by mall security officials, seemingly acting on behalf of the Secret Service, we knew exactly where to go: to the press and the lawyers.

Since the incident, articles have appeared in the trade journal *Communications Daily*, the *Washington City Paper*, even a front-page story in the *Washington Post*. This is in addition to an uncountable number of pieces throughout the Internet and over bulletin boards. This was certainly more attention than anyone at the Secret Service could have anticipated.

Unfortunately for them, they were not even allowed to slink away, red-faced at their botched job. Computer Professionals for Social Responsibility, whose membership applications were seized at the November meeting, were the first to express interest in our predicament. The Electronic Frontier Foundation and the American Civil Liberties Union would soon follow in offering their legal counsel.

CPSR filed two Freedom of Information Act requests with the Secret Service on behalf of several meeting-goers who were interested in possible legal action against the perpetrators of the "raid." The Secret Service returned the requests, saying that they had no information on any of the meeting-goers. This immediately raised suspicion, as the mall security personnel collected everyone's name and phone number at the November meeting. Presumably this information was on file somewhere. Also, one of the meeting-goers had been visited by the Secret Service about two years ago, completely unrelated to anything computer-oriented. Presumably a file was created on him at that time, and yet the Secret Service said they had no information on anyone involved. Thirdly, one of the meeting-goers was visited by the Secret Service subsequent to the meeting. During this visit, one of the agents made reference to his name being on "the mall list." It seems highly unlikely that the Secret Service had absolutely no information on any of the people on whose behalf CPSR filed FOIA requests.

Acting on these strong suspicions, on February 4th, CPSR filed suit against the Secret Service for failing to provide information requested under the Freedom of Information Act. The SS has thirty days to respond.

All of this is mainly a preliminary game of legal hide-and-seek to establish what role, if any, the Secret Service and other government agencies might have played in the November *2600* raid. Once everyone involved stops contradicting each other and a clearer image forms of who was behind the harassment, we can begin to consider other possible legal avenues to send the Powers That Be a strong message about what to expect when trying to intimidate a group of hackers.

Stay tuned.

Meeting Mania (Autumn, 1993)

Here's the latest in the ongoing Pentagon City Mall/Secret Service scandal that involved attendees of the Washington D.C. *2600* meeting in November 1992:

The Secret Service has admitted possessing six previously unacknowledged documents relating to the breakup of the meeting. In conjunction with that admission, the agency filed an affidavit that provides the most information received so far as to just what was going on.

According to the affidavit, "the Secret Service received information from a business indicating that that business' PBX had been manipulated," and that the business provided the agency with "certain information concerning the individual(s) who had entered the system." Computer Professionals for Social Responsibility, the Washington-based organization that has been relentlessly filing Freedom of Information Act requests since this sordid affair started, translated the available data into the following possible scenario: 1) the "victim business" had some reason to believe that the individual involved had some relationship to *2600*; 2) the business passed this information on to the Secret Service; 3) the Secret Service knew that people associated with *2600* met at the mall on a regular basis; and 4) the Secret Service recruited the mall security personnel to identify the individuals attending the monthly meetings.

Also of interest is the admission by the Secret Service that "the records which are at issue in this case were provided to the Secret Service by a confidential source and were compiled by the Secret Service...."

Towards the end of the summer, the Secret Service took the unusual step of filing an "in camera" deposition. The contents of this deposition are sealed and the only information we've been able to glean from it is that it's at least 56 paragraphs long. CPSR is filing papers to reveal the contents of this deposition. Its existence is considered highly unusual in FOIA cases, but fairly standard in cases of national security. The plot thickens.

More Meeting Fun

2600 meetings continue to spring up around the planet. There are almost always strange people watching the hackers but in most cases nothing comes of it. At the July Seattle meeting, however, security guards at the Convention Center and Seattle police officers harassed and even arrested an attendee who wouldn't show identification. He was released almost immediately, clearly showing that the whole thing was an attempt to intimidate the attendees. It didn't work and subsequent meetings have occurred there without incident.

Sometimes the funniest people show up. In one city, an intoxicated MCI employee came by and said he was going to bomb all of the hackers' computers by using the system batteries. Among his other memorable quotes was, "We didn't have time for this kind of stuff in Vietnam."

More Meeting Advice (Winter, 1993-1994) *By The Judicator of D.C.*

> *"Congress shall make no law respecting an establishment of religion, or prohibiting the free exercise thereof; or abridging the freedom of speech, or of the press; or the right of the people peaceably to assemble, and to petition the government for a redress of grievances."*

> *"All persons born or naturalized in the United States, and subject to the jurisdiction thereof, are citizens of the United States and of the State wherein they reside. No State shall make or enforce any law which shall abridge the privileges or immunities of citizens of the United States; nor shall any State deprive any person of life, liberty, or property, without due process of law; nor deny to any person within its jurisdiction the equal protection of the laws."*

These two paragraphs are the First and Fourteenth Amendments to the Constitution. The First says that as a citizen you have a legal right to peaceably assemble and the *federal* government cannot take that right away from you. It does not say that a State has to allow you to assemble. This was the case until June 9, 1868. The Fourteenth Amendment applied the Constitution and its protections to the States. Before this, each individual state could prohibit the free assembly of persons.

Presently, we can gather on public space and discuss whatever subject comes to mind. There are exceptions to this, however. You cannot stand on the corner of Broadway and discuss the violent overthrow of the government. Nor can you discuss the intimate details of your love life.

So what have we learned? The First and Fourteenth Amendments allow us to gather for meetings anywhere we want, and no one can stop us. Right? Wrong! The Constitution applies to governments and is limited in its application of powers to private industry. For example, in Washington, D.C. there is a law called Unlawful Entry. It states that any person who willfully remains on any property after being asked to leave by the rightful owner or person then in charge is guilty of a misdemeanor and subject to arrest. The constitutionality of this law has been tested and affirmed. Your local jurisdiction may have a law similar to this under different names (Criminal Trespass or Trespassing). The easiest way to find out is to pick up a (pay) phone and call your local police department. Ask them. Don't be afraid. You cannot get in trouble for being a concerned citizen.

What is the basis for these laws? Consider this: You own a beautiful piece of property that overlooks a great seascape. People are using your property for religious gatherings and artistic inspiration without your permission. If the Constitution applied to private property you couldn't stop these people. But since it does not, you can have them removed or arrested, if your local law allows.

Of the 20 *2600* meetings that take place throughout the United States, 13 take place in malls, five in other private places, and two are unknown to this writer. Citicorp Center and Amtrak are private institutions. It sounds like the Galleria on South University and Union Station are also private but I cannot tell by their names. Malls are almost exclusively privately owned. I cannot recall seeing a government owned mall lately. Being privately owned, the rightful owner or the person then in charge can ask you to leave (depending on your local law). The sad thing is that you will have to follow his directions and then follow up with a civil suit. What you base that suit on is another problem. It would not fall under a racial bias, nor a gender bias. If you do not leave at their request, you leave yourself vulnerable to arrest. What does this mean to us dedicated 2600ers?

When you are attending a *2600* meeting, be sure to know the law in your area. If you are hosting a party or attending a party at a mall or on other private property, be informed. When approached by a security officer, police, or the management, don't go on blabbering how the First Amendment allows you to gather any place you like. It *doesn't*. Instead, do the following:

1. If the area you are meeting in has stores, purchase some merchandise that is sold in these establishments *prior* to your meeting. When approached by the charging person, explain that you have just made purchases from the establishments. Does he/she really want to throw out a buying customer?
2. Explain to the charging person your intentions of the gathering. Don't forget these points: You chose this area because of a) its successful reputation, b) its great location, c) the fine merchants, d) all of the above. This sounds like a bunch of crap (which it is), but it will strengthen any court case you bring about in the future.
3. As a last resort, inform them of your research into the local laws and ordinances of trespassing. If possible, give them a copy of the law. Ask them to have the police respond. When an officer arrives, explain that this security officer is unlawfully asking you to leave when you wish to stay. But, if a police officer asks you to leave, *do so!* Do not ask for his name and badge number; you can see that. If you can't, find his car and write down the ID number. Then call the station he is from and ask to speak to a supervisor. Inform the supervisor of the squad car number, the description of the officer, and what happened. Make a written complaint if possible.

You must remember to be *calm* and *rational* during these proceedings. If not, you could be placed under arrest for disorderly conduct or some such. Although not what you were originally bothered with, the security officer has succeeded in his task to get rid of you.

2600 meetings are great ideas for the free exchange of ideas and are, in theory, what this country was founded upon. *But*, they are not worth getting arrested for if you are wrong. There are plenty of legal places to hold meetings. Try a public park or parking area. Call your local seat of government and ask to use their meeting room. How about that for irony! Using a government establishment to hold a *2600* meeting! Under the

First Amendment, they cannot deny you. Look at the court record of such groups as the KKK. They meet and march on any *public* space they like with the proper permits. 2600ers can do the same.

In writing this, a few friends have raised valid questions, which I am sure other 2600ers will ask. What about conspiring to commit a crime? Isn't meeting to discuss committing crimes illegal? Yes and no.

Conspiracy is defined as an agreement to perform an illegal act. Most states, in defining the acts that constitute conspiracy, require an overt act. The best definition would be an example itself. John and Bill are eating dinner while discussing robbing a bank. They talk about the getaway car, what type of gun to use, and the best time to commit the robbery. Both finish dinner and go their separate ways until they meet at work the next day. John tells Bill he bought the gun and obtained the getaway car. As of this moment, John and Bill can be arrested for conspiring to commit a bank robbery.

The First Amendment protects our freedom of speech to a degree. If John and Bill had not done anything else but talk about the bank robbery, no harm could have come to either of them. Since John purchased the gun and getaway car, he showed his intentions to follow through with their plan. This was the overt act. This was what got them into trouble. Both can be arrested, but the case of innocence for Bill is very strong. It must be proven in court, requiring the expense of thousands of dollars for an attorney. A court-appointed attorney can be assigned, depending on financial need, with his/her cost coming out of taxpayer money.

One can see the parallels of this story to that of *2600* meetings. Yes, 2600ers gather in places to discuss illegal acts. Are they conspiring to commit these offenses? Maybe. It depends upon each individual person. Let's say a conversation was entered dealing with the sale, not possession, of proprietary information. No one from the discussion group does anything to forward the idea of the sale. Is this legal? Yes, under the First Amendment. What if one of the members contacts an underground fence offering the document for sale based on information he discussed at the meeting? Is this conspiracy? I'm sure Law Enforcement could substantiate enough evidence to bring about the arrests of the discussion group, but would they have enough evidence to prove "beyond a reasonable doubt" their case in court? Maybe not. However, they have succeeded in harassing the group and costing both the taxpayers and the group members several thousands of dollars in court and attorney's fees. Do you have any means of redress? You could try to sue for damages incurred due to the inconvenience of the arrest, but if the Law Enforcement agency did its job correctly, you will not win.

I cannot speak for all states but the basis for most laws are the same. As mentioned earlier, call your local police or the nearest state police office. You cannot get in trouble for asking. Also ask for examples and a written reply.

The writer is "heavily involved" with the law enforcement community.

Major Crackdowns

If there could be said to be a period in our existence where the shit really hit the fan, well, look no further than here. No fewer than three cases which made international headlines and affected people very close to us played out in the space of a couple of years in the mid 1990s.

We saw the first use of wiretapping in a hacker case involving *2600* writer and *Off The Hook* cohost Phiber Optik. It was further indication of the increasing treatment of hackers like organized crime figures. In fact, at one point Phiber shared a courtroom with the World Trade Center bombers. His prison term was one of the saddest periods we ever went through but we managed to keep him in touch with the rest of the community through the magazine and our radio show where he would often call in live from behind bars.

Then there was the infamous Kevin Mitnick case, which played out in several stages from living on the run to capture to the incarceration that lasted five whole years. It was this case that really gave us the spirit to get angry and speak louder than we ever did before. The Free Kevin movement was started, protests were held worldwide, web pages got hacked "for justice," and we found ourselves in the movie making business all of a sudden. We devoted a lot of time and coverage to this which annoyed some of our readers, but we really had no choice. Despite the fact that Kevin had violated security restrictions on a number of occasions, I never really thought that was enough to condemn him to whatever penalty the prosecution decided to dole out. The fact remained he had never caused damage to anything other than egos and despite having had ample opportunity, he never once profited as a result of his incursions. From our very first issue, we've taken the stand that prison time is a ridiculous way of addressing the issue of hackers. I think Kevin's case proved that more than any other. The system literally didn't know how to handle him so they wound up doing stupid things like sticking him in solitary confinement for eight months because they were afraid of what he could do from a prison phone, denying him a bail *hearing*—let alone bail itself, and of course the whole deal with holding him without trial for over four years.

And as if all that wasn't enough, another one of our writers who went by the name of Bernie S. was imprisoned simply for having common electronic parts and gadgets that theoretically *could* have been used to commit a crime. This was enough to get him locked up *twice* by the Secret Service and have him held with some of the most dangerous people in prison. And, as it turned out, it was all because of a vendetta the Secret Service had against him because he had embarrassed them on television.

So the '90s were a very busy time in the Getting Outraged Department. But I want to think that we did some good by being around and by not shutting up about the injustices we were made aware of. After all, in order for history to be remembered, somebody has to write it down.

Here We Go Again (Summer, 1992)

The United States Department of Justice along with the Federal Bureau of Investigation and the Secret Service announced another round of hacker indictments at a press conference in New York City on July 8. Five hackers were charged with such crimes as conspiracy, computer tampering, illegal wiretapping, computer fraud, and wire fraud.

The five are most commonly known in hacker circles as Phiber Optik, Acid Phreak, Scorpion, Outlaw, and Corrupt. Each entered pleas of not guilty in federal court on July 16.

And for the first time ever, the government has admitted using wiretaps in a hacker investigation as a method of obtaining evidence.

Repercussions

This case is troublesome for many reasons. Wiretapping alone ought to be enough to send shivers down the spine of the hacker world, indeed the world in general. By justifying such an act, the government is now saying that hackers are in a league with the most notorious of criminals—mobsters, terrorists, and politicians. If this action goes unchallenged, this is the way hackers will be perceived in all future dealings. We feel the government wishes to convey this image simply to make it easier to subjugate those it perceives as a threat.

By tapping into phone lines, the government will claim that vital evidence was obtained. Translation: they will do it again. And what assurance do we have that this method will stop at hackers? None. Wiretapping is certain to become increasingly easy in the future, especially if the FBI is successful in its bid for a mandatory surveillance system on all digital phone systems. (They're already claiming that this case proves how badly they need such a system; we have trouble following their logic.)

With the wiretapping comes the realization that *2600* is also under tightening scrutiny. Since we have been in contact with these hackers for years, since some of them have been at our office, and since they all make appearances at the monthly New York *2600* meetings, we could easily be considered "known associates" of major criminals, possibly even co-conspirators. This means that it wouldn't be very hard for the authorities to justify monitoring our every movement, tapping all of our phone lines, monitoring our data traffic, and doing whatever else they deemed necessary for the likes of us, major criminals that we are. And the same for all of *our* associates.

Despite all of our warnings and protestations over the years, the image of hackers has been portrayed in increasingly ominous tones by the government and the media, despite the lack of substantial evidence that hackers are anything more than over-exuberant teenagers and young adults, playing with toys that have never before existed.

If our assessment is correct, then we will not be the last in this chain of suspects. Everyone who has ever expressed interest in the "wrong things" or talked to people in the "wrong crowd" will be subject to surveillance of an increasingly comprehensive nature. And silence is the best way to ensure this.

Fallout

Equally troublesome is the reaction of some members of the hacker community to these recent happenings. There are some that have openly expressed happiness at recent events, simply because they didn't like the hackers involved. A combination of unhealthy rivalry and gross generalization has helped to create an environment perfectly suited to carrying out the government's agenda. Hacker versus hacker.

Over the years, various hacker "groups" have existed in one form or another. PHALSE was formed in the early eighties. Its name meant "Phreakers, Hackers, And Laundromat Service Employees." The FBI regarded them as a closely knit conspiracy. In actuality, few of the members had ever even met each other and spent most of their time trying to figure out how to communicate so they could trade fragments of information. We're told the "laundry connection" was thoroughly investigated by the government even though the words were only included in order to form the PHALSE name. So much for conspiracies. Next was the Legion Of Doom, commonly known as LOD. In 1990, headlines screamed that these techno-anarchists had the potential to disrupt our lives by possessing the E911 "program," which they could no doubt use to manipulate emergency calls everywhere. Sure, it turned out that it wasn't really a program they had but merely a ten page administrative document. And it wasn't really worth $80,000 like Bell South claimed, but a mere $13. It was still enough to send three hackers to prison and plunge the then-publisher of *Phrack* into near-bankruptcy to defend his First Amendment rights. More recently, MOD has been portrayed as the group of potential terrorists that the government needs and the media wants. MOD (nobody really knows what the letters stand for) has developed a reputation of being "evil" hackers. The difference here is that this reputation actually exists *within* the hacker community.

How did this happen? The same naïveté that has so firmly gripped prosecutors and hacker haters over the years has made a direct hit upon parts of the hacker community. MOD was no better organized than PHALSE or LOD, either collectively or individually. Nobody knows how many "members" there were. In fact, it's been said that anyone who wanted to be a part of the group merely had to add the letters MOD after their name because nobody could stop them from doing it. Hardly a well organized group, if you ask us. Yet they were perceived as a threat by some, and thus became all the more dangerous.

We certainly don't mean to minimize any damage or harassment that may have occurred. If proven, such actions should be punished, but within reason. So should any acts that involve tangible theft or selling of unauthorized access. This has always been our position. But to blame the actions of a few (possibly even one) on an entire group, real or perceived, is dangerous. This is something history should teach us, if common sense doesn't.

We've taken a lot of heat for our position on this but we must stand firm. Innocent people are being prosecuted for things they did not do. We know this to be true. And we intend to stand up for them. We cannot judge each other on anything less than individual actions.

If we turn against each other, whatever community we have established will unravel completely. It is in the interests of some to have this happen and we don't doubt that they are encouraging acts of disunity. We have to be smart enough to see through this.

A year ago we warned of the dangers of hacker "gangs" and "elite" hackers. "Egos and machismo tend to cloud the reason we got involved in the first place," we said. They also prove to be fatal if we are trying to justify our existence to the authorities. It doesn't take a genius to figure this out.

By creating the appearance of warring factions, we give the media permission to turn it into reality. Once they do this, it no longer matters whether or not it was ever true to begin with. It becomes the truth.

While we have no doubt that there was childish mischief going on at some point, to claim that it was part of a carefully coordinated conspiracy is a gross distortion. Sure, such a claim will get attention and will probably result in all kinds of charges being filed. Lives will be scarred, headlines will be written, and a lot of time and money will be wasted. Is this the only response we're capable of coming up with when people act like idiots? If so, then we've just made the government's job a lot easier.

Hackers in Jail, Part Two (Winter, 1993-1994)

Yet again, we must pay sad tribute to a hacker who has been imprisoned. Last issue we mentioned that two New York hackers, Acid Phreak and Scorpion, had been sent to prison for six months for "crimes" that nobody was ever able to define in clear terms. Before them were the three Atlanta hackers, who served time for reading a worthless Bell South document on a password-free computer. And Kevin Mitnick, locked up in solitary confinement because the authorities were afraid of what he could do if he got near a phone. Not to mention Shadowhawk and Len Rose, who downloaded programs that some huge company didn't want them to have and were sent away for it. They weren't the only ones but they were the ones you might remember by reading *2600* over the years. And now, there's one more.

What was unique about the Phiber Optik case was the attention it got. Here was a hacker who was not afraid to go public and show people exactly what it was he was talking about. It's precisely this kind of openness that we here at *2600* have been trying to get across for nearly ten years. After all, standing behind voice synthesizers and digital distortion tends to convey the image of somebody with something to hide. Phiber Optik was one of the first hackers to shed this mask and come forward with information. His tutorials went well beyond hacking—anything concerning high technology was a topic worth pursuing. Over the past couple of years, he guest lectured for various college courses on the subject of technology and the general public, made numerous appearances at panel discussions and conferences, was a frequent guest on WBAI's *Off The Hook* radio program in New York where he would answer numerous telephone and computer related questions from listeners, and helped design three separate public access UNIX systems in New York City, the most recent one being Echo (`echonyc.com`), which introduced hundreds, if not thousands, of people to the Internet. Not exactly the life of a criminal, one has to admit. As people who have come to know Phiber well over the years, we've seen what his driving force has been: the ability to answer questions and figure things out. In the eyes of the U.S. Department of Justice, it was subversive.

On November 3, Phiber Optik was sentenced to a year and a day in federal prison. The charges dated back several years and were sufficiently vague to convince Phiber to plead guilty this past July. After all, a hacker can always be convicted for something and the mystery of not knowing what it is they're going to come after you for is enough to convince many people to plead guilty. (Read a little Kafka if you doubt this.) The penalty for being found guilty after pleading innocent can be much more severe. And there is also the financial consideration; legal costs can be crippling, as in the case of Craig Neidorf, even after the government dropped its case against him. In Phiber's case, the charges were conspiracy and access to a federal interest computer. Conspiracy is very difficult to disprove, especially when you're friends with other hackers and you believe in sharing information. It also doesn't help when the government fears hackers as much as any national enemy. As for accessing computers, this was never something that Phiber denied doing. But it happened years ago, it happened because of bad security, no damage was ever alleged to have been done, and Phiber always was willing to talk about security problems with anyone willing to listen. The government didn't want to hear it.

Judge Stanton, in sentencing him, said, "Invasion of computers is seductive to the young both because of the intellectual challenge and the risk. A message must be sent that it is serious.... The defendant stands as a symbol because of his own efforts; therefore, he stands as a symbol here today." In other words, because he has come to represent so much to so many, what better target for severe punishment? The total sentence was for a year and a day in prison, 600 hours of community service, and three years of supervised probation. The judge imposed no restitution because there was no evidence of any damage.

Assistant U.S. Attorney Geoffrey Berman was positively ecstatic with the decision. He said, "The sentence is important because it sends a message that it is a crime to intrude in public data networks. MOD was one of the biggest hacking organizations in the country. The case was very significant." MOD was the name of the group that Phiber and a few others were in at one point. Hearing it referred to as an "organization" only confirms how clueless the prosecutors were in this case. Basically, they succeeded in sending a few friends to prison for trespassing. Forgive us if we forego the champagne.

So what do *we* get out of this, we being the people on the receiving end of this message? Well, we've got another prisoner to take care of at a cost equivalent to four years in college. What we *don't* have is somebody who can help us hook into the Internet for the first time. We don't have the opportunity to hear another side of the story when the next technological innovation is heralded. We don't have someone to explain what might have gone wrong the next time the phone system crashes. What we've got is a warning—a warning not to stray from the safe curriculum, ask too many questions, expose embarrassing truths, or try to find answers through unconventional means.

Sending hackers to prison is a mockery of justice and one day will be recognized as such. Until that day comes, we can only hope that their lives will not be irreversibly harmed and that those of us on the outside won't push each other into a pit of paranoia as we desperately struggle to remain innocent.

On a personal level, we all feel a deep sadness here at *2600* for what has happened. We don't mean to diminish all of the other cases that have taken place and those that unfortunately will occur in the future. But this one hit rather close to home. It's going to be very difficult to go to a *2600* meeting, analyze the latest *Star Trek*, argue over UNIX, or hang out in our favorite Ukrainian restaurant without thinking of the familiar voices that have been locked out.

The World vs. Kevin Mitnick (Spring, 1995)

By this time, you would have to have been living in isolation not to have heard about the Kevin Mitnick story. Front page headlines and TV newscasts around the world announced the fugitive hacker's capture on February 15 in Raleigh, North Carolina.

If you read the opening paragraph of the *New York Times* on February 16, you would see Mitnick described as a "computer expert accused of a long crime spree that includes the theft of thousands of data files and at least 20,000 credit card numbers from computer systems around the nation." That portrayal is rather damning, to say the least. But let's look a little closer.

To the average person, the "theft of thousands of data files" would imply that somebody *took away* specific and valuable items as part of an elaborate plot. In reality, copying thousands of computer files is easy, quick, and, in most cases, relatively harmless. When put into this context, even if the files were of a sensitive nature, we can see how it's not necessarily part of an evil plot if someone comes along and copies them.

With regards to the credit card numbers, this is far more misleading. For one thing, only one computer system (Netcom) had its credit card numbers accessed, not "computer systems around the nation." And this compromise was not even news—the Autumn, 1994, issue of *2600* reported it nearly half a year ago. Apparently, Netcom did nothing to secure the credit card numbers of its subscribers and, despite multiple warnings and basic common sense, kept this sensitive information online. And, as an ironic twist, Netcom claimed responsibility for helping to catch this most dangerous criminal in a letter to its subscribers entitled, "Netcom Helps Protect The Internet."

Nearly every story ever written about Kevin Mitnick can be traced to one source: *New York Times* reporter John Markoff. Markoff was also the co-author of 1991's *Cyberpunk*, a book that focused on Kevin Mitnick (among others) and which was described by Mitnick (*2600*, Summer, 1991) as having "many, many false statements, misrepresentations, and inaccurate stories." Mitnick believed Markoff and his wife (co-author Katie Hafner) were miffed at him for not helping with the book. And, as the years went by, it became clear that Markoff was still fixated on the Mitnick saga. In the summer of 1994 he penned a front page article in the *New York Times*, complete with Mitnick's picture, which announced to the world that he was a fugitive. The only substantive "crime" Mitnick was accused of was probation violation yet the *The Times* saw fit to make this a front page story.

One week before his capture, Mitnick contacted us to express concern over information he had received indicating that Markoff was actively aiding law enforcement to help track him down. It seemed bizarre at the time but as events unfolded, it appeared that this is exactly what was going on. Markoff had been working with a friend of his (Tsutomu Shimomura) whose computer site had been compromised on December 25, resulting in another puzzling front page story that just didn't seem newsworthy enough to be on the front page. When Shimomura concluded that the intruder was "probably Mr. Mitnick," the hunt was on. Shimomura had all the help he needed—he programmed for the NSA and the FBI was almost as interested as Markoff. Using cellular tracking, it wasn't too difficult to track down Mitnick. Less than a week later, Markoff and Shimomura signed a $750,000 book deal, no doubt to be called something like *Cybersleuth*, pitting good hacker against evil hacker.

But how much do we actually know? Obviously, enough for a classic cat-and-mouse bestseller. But what will happen to those facts that don't fit in quite so neatly? Will the awkward questions ever be answered?

What was Mitnick wanted for in the first place, besides the nebulous "probation violation"? Markoff reported that Mitnick was suspected of wiretapping the FBI while a fugitive. But we never hear how such a conclusion is reached beyond pure speculation. The recent charges appear to be nothing more than a smokescreen, designed to demonize Mitnick and make him appear to be a threat to everyone's privacy. Little mention is made of the fact that not one of the 20,000 credit card numbers lying around on Netcom was ever used by Mitnick, nor was he ever suspected of benefiting financially or causing any damage. Mitnick was also accused of leaving taunting messages on Shimomura's voice mail. Upon closer examination, it's fairly obvious that Mitnick was not at all involved in this—for one thing a new message appeared *after* he was apprehended! As for the "sensitive" files, Mitnick was certainly not the only one who had access to them. In fact, serious doubt can be cast as to whether he was the one who figured it out in the first place. The fact that we were able to track down a copy of the directory he was supposedly using tells us that many people already had access. Does this suggest a closely knit conspiracy? Hardly. In classic hacker fashion, word of one person's discovery got out and spread throughout the Net. After all, who could keep quiet about a password sniffer designed for the NSA that could run on virtually any machine? So far, the press has.

A 23 count indictment handed down on March 9 charges Mitnick with possessing device-making equipment, possessing unauthorized access devices, and 21 counts of using a counterfeited access device. We assume this to mean reprogramming a cellular phone in order to remain hidden. The government says that this indictment only covers a period of several days before Mitnick's arrest, the implication being that there will be many, many more charges added to cover the years that he was on the run. This is a spiteful and vindictive approach—these "crimes" came about *because* of Mitnick's fugitive status; it's simply not possible to be a fugitive and live one's entire life on the books. Any damage or outright theft should naturally be followed up on but in this case such actions seem practically nonexistent. It's becoming clear that the government intends to punish Mitnick over and over again for getting away. And we may never find out why he was running in the first place.

How long Mitnick will be imprisoned for is really anybody's guess. Judging from the way some influential people are talking, it could be a very long time. We have to get the facts so that we can judge for ourselves what "real world" crimes we're talking about. The potential to learn from this still exists but the desire to punish and make an example threatens to thwart that.

MILESTONE: OUR FINANCIAL STATE (Spring, 1998)

We are nearly out of the woods in what has been a real disaster thanks to our bankrupt distributor. We've managed to get back into all of the stores we were cut off from when Fine Print went under. But recently we started to face troubles of a different sort when huge numbers of the Autumn issue wound up being destroyed *before* being put on the stands.

There were a number of theories as to why this happened. One rather disturbing possibility was that the stores (primarily B. Dalton and Barnes and Noble, both owned by the same company) were dumping the issues because they contained letters that revealed some details about their computer system. This has been flatly denied by their corporate office, despite our hearing from

MILESTONE: OUR FINANCIAL STATE *(continued)*

two separate employees we had called randomly that there was a memo circulating that advised stores to take the issues off the stands. Another possible reason given for this unfortunate event was a mix-up between the old distributor and the new one. Some stores may have thought the Autumn issue had been sent out by the bankrupt Fine Print and therefore cleared it off the shelves in error.

Whatever the reason, it screws us over again at the worst possible time. More than 10,000 copies were lost because of this—and we take 100 percent of the loss, plus the cost of delivery to the distributor plus the cost of delivery to the stores. Even though it would be a catastrophic screw up of unprecedented proportions, which was completely not our fault and totally our loss, that would be preferable to the possibility that this was content-related. We support Barnes and Noble/B. Dalton as they increase their distribution of independent zines and alternative voices. We back them completely in their fights against neighborhood censors who try to shut them down because they don't like the pictures in a book or the ideas in a magazine. And we want our readers to support them as well, not just for our sake, but because any semblance of literacy and thought that manages to pop up in our shopping malls *deserves* to prosper. But it is vital that those of us fighting for this kind of thing not take on the tactics of our enemies when the subject matter hits close to home. It's not hard to see the hypocrisy in such a move. Which is why we have two more letters in this issue concerning the same subject. Maybe we will be hurt severely by doing this. But if we refrained from printing them because we thought it might adversely affect us, we'd be just as hypocritical as anyone who removed it from the shelves.

We are, always have been, and hopefully always will be, about freedom of information and satisfying our curiosity. In the fights for freedom and justice that we always seem to be in the midst of, we must never forget who we are and what we stand for. The second we do, we've lost the battle.

The Bernie S. Saga (Summer, 1995)

It's almost a given that the first few pages of *2600* will be devoted to the latest travesty of justice, the most recent in the long string of harassment against computer hackers. Regretfully, this issue will not be an exception. In fact, this time what we're talking about could have such profound effects on the rest of us that nothing will ever seem the same. It may sound a bit over-dramatized but we feel the facts have no trouble supporting our cynical conclusions.

Bernie S. (Ed Cummings) was involved in *2600* for most of our existence. If anyone could answer a question on scanners, surveillance, or the technical workings of a certain piece of machinery, he could. His presence at the Hackers On Planet Earth conference last year provided many informative lectures to a fascinated audience. Like most good hackers, Bernie S. believed in sharing the information he was able to obtain or figure out.

At the time of this writing, Bernie S. sits in federal prison, held without bail and without any prospect of a trial in the near future. The more we find out about this case, the more we believe that nobody really knows why he's been imprisoned.

It started outside a 7-11 in Pennsylvania when Haverford Township police came upon what they believed was a drug deal in progress. They were wrong. What they were witnessing was a transaction involving crystals, which could be used to modify Radio Shack tone dialers into red boxes. The key word here is "could" since crystals themselves can be found in a multitude of sources and their possession or sale is far from illegal. Bernie S. believed in making technology accessible to the public and providing something as basic as a crystal was one way of achieving this. However, the police did not understand this and thought they were onto some really big nefarious scheme to do something really bad. So they searched the vehicles of Bernie S. and the people he had met there. They confiscated all of the crystals as well as "suspicious" reading material such as *The Whole Spy Catalog*, a must for any serious hacker. They said everything would be returned if nothing illegal was found to be going on.

Then the U.S. Secret Service was contacted. Special Agent Thomas Varney informed the local police that there was no other use for a red box (and hence, the crystals in question) but to commit fraud. The Secret Service even went so far as to go to a payphone with the Haverford police to demonstrate how an illegal red box call is made. Based upon this, Bernie S. was forcefully arrested at gunpoint by numerous law enforcement personnel and thrown into state prison. All of his books, manuals, copies of *2600*, and anything electronic were seized. The charges were possession of a red box (a non-working Radio Shack dialer that someone had asked him to look at) and unauthorized access to a phone company computer. Apparently the thought behind the latter charge was that if Bernie S. had used a red box, he would have had to have signaled a computer with the red box tones simply by playing them. And so, unauthorized access.

The judge refused to indict him on this charge because it was so far-fetched and because there was no indication that Bernie S. had ever even used a red box, let alone a phone company computer. Ironically, the Secret Service and the Haverford police had already done both, in their eagerness to capture Bernie S. No doubt with all of this in mind, the judge set bail for the remaining charge of possession of a red box: $100,000.

The fact that such a bogus charge and exorbitant bail were allowed to stand shocked many. And shock turned to disbelief when a student questioning this on the Internet found himself threatened with a libel lawsuit by the Haverford police. This was truly turning into a spectacle of the bizarre. Bernie S., meanwhile, endured week after week of squalor and inhuman treatment in a state prison.

Then, one day, the Haverford police announced they were dropping all charges in the case after Bernie S. spent more than a month in prison with rapists and murderers. It almost appeared as if they had realized how flimsy their case actually was and how unfair it was to penalize someone so severely who hadn't even been accused of doing something fraudulent. But this was not to be. The local police had made an arrangement with the federal government that substituted the old red box charge with new federal charges accusing Bernie S. of possession of hardware and software that could be used to modify cellular phones. Was this really the best they could do? Bernie S. had openly advertised this software, which had been used legitimately by many to create extensions of their cellular phones. Many hackers learned about this technology at the HOPE conference. But because this software could also be used by criminals, the government decided to charge Bernie S. as if he were one of those criminals. And for this, the government has declined to set any bail.

To give you an idea of the intellect we're dealing with, here's a quote from Special Agent Thomas Varney's affidavit:

> *"During my review of the items seized pursuant to the state search warrant, I determined that Cummings had in his residence the following items that could be used for the cloning of cellular telephones:*
>
> *a. Three cellular telephone cloning computer disks.*
>
> *b. A laptop computer that had a cloning software program on the hard drive which I confirmed by observation.*
>
> *c. A computer cable that would allow for cloning of Motorola brand cellular telephones.*
>
> *d. Several cellular telephones some of which had broken plastic surrounding the electrical connectors to the battery pack. The breakage of the plastic is a required step before cellular telephones can be connected to a computer for cloning.*
>
> *e. A book titled,* Cellular Hacker's Bible.
>
> *f. Photographs depicting Cummings selling cellular telephone cloning software at an unknown event."*

We congratulate Varney on being the first person to grasp the concept of photographs being used to clone cellular phones. However, until the scientific evidence is in, perhaps we'd just better strike item (f).

Items (a) and (b) are the same—(a) is a disk with a computer program and (b) is a computer with the same computer program. With a little more effort, the next item could have been a house with a computer program in it, but the Secret Service probably felt that a laptop computer would be of more use around the office. (A large number, if not most, of computer hacker cases never see owners reunited with their computer equipment.) So if we follow the logic here, it's possible that Bernie S. got himself thrown into prison without bail because he figured out how to make an extension of a cellular phone and wrote a computer program to do this. Way back before the Bell breakup, people were afraid of getting into trouble for plugging in extra phones without letting the phone company know. We realize now how absurd such thinking was. Yet we're reliving history, only this time the penalties are much more severe.

Item (c) is a cable. Let's just leave it at that.

Item (d) consists of cellular telephones, none of which were illegitimately obtained or used for fraudulent purposes. If any of our readers are interested in how a cellular phone works, we encourage them to take it apart and experiment with it. Any evidence that Bernie S. was doing any more than this has yet to surface.

Finally, the *Cellular Hacker's Bible* is a book anyone interested in electronics and the phone system would want to read. The federal government has managed to outlaw radio frequencies but they have yet to outlaw books. With agencies like the Secret Service doing their dirty work, it's only a matter of time.

So what do we have here? Apart from an inept, backwoods police department specializing in intimidation tactics and a federal agency bent on keeping a vice grip on technology, not a whole hell of a lot. Nothing listed above constitutes a crime, at least not in a democratic society. In a suspicious and fearful regime, however... books, ideas, technical ability—these could all be considered threats. And by permitting this to go unanswered, either through encouragement or through silence, we move steadily down that dark road.

This whole series of events and their consequences is a disgrace to our judicial system and it's essential that we fight back. Every organization that claims to have an interest in justice should know about this. Hopefully, the majority will take a strong stand against what has happened here. The alternative is practically unthinkable; imagine a world where reading, experimentation, and software are the only ingredients needed to put a person in prison indefinitely. There would be very few people looking at these words who would be safe.

News Items (Summer, 1995)

It's official. The trial of Kevin Mitnick begins July 10 in Raleigh, North Carolina. He will be facing a 23-count indictment, allegedly for making cellular phone calls on a cloned phone. Each of the federal counts carries a sentence of 20 years. Assuming

Mitnick doesn't receive a 460-year sentence, the feds have indicated that they will bring him up on charges in other locations as well (San Francisco, San Diego, Denver, and Seattle). Every single one of these charges is directly related to the fact that Mitnick was trying not to be captured. So why was he running in the first place? We may finally have an answer. In 1992, Mitnick was employed by Teltec Investigations, a company that was being investigated by Pacific Bell. According to a source, when the company was contacted, they agreed to testify against Mitnick in exchange for leniency. The focal point of the entire investigation was the unauthorized accessing of Pacific Bell voice mail. Since Mitnick was on probation at the time and since any probation violation could easily result in prison time, he chose to leave. And that's really the whole reason why this wild chase happened in the first place. Either he accessed a voice mail system without permission or someone else in the company did and decided to make him the fall guy. Either way, the punishment far outweighs the crime, if, in fact, there ever was a crime. And in Mitnick's case, the punishment has already been handed down; he lived a fugitive's life for years, never knowing when or if his freedom would suddenly expire. We can only hope this side of the story is told at the trial.

No More Secrets (Autumn, 1995)

The Secret Service is portrayed in the movie *Hackers* as a bunch of dimwitted, overzealous law enforcers. Many will undoubtedly feel that this is an unfair generalization. But recent events have led us to believe that the film didn't go nearly far enough with their unflattering depiction. For example, they didn't even touch upon the vindictiveness and sheer malice that appears to dictate much of this agency's policies. Add to this the fear factor that a large, heavily armed group of people generates and all of a sudden our democratic society is going down the same road so many other countries have traveled.

We told you about the Bernie S. story in our last issue—how the Secret Service helped imprison him without bail because he possessed hardware and software that *could* be used for fraudulent purposes. Nobody has ever accused him of using this technology in such a way and no evidence appears to exist to even suggest this. So how has the Secret Service managed to keep Bernie S. (hereafter referred to by his real name, Ed Cummings) locked away for over six months with no bail for something so trivial as possession of a red box? Through shameful deception and blatant intimidation. By exaggerating the significance of the technology in his possession, the Secret Service was able to probe Cummings with all the fervor that a presidential assassin would receive. People from around the country were visited and asked to reveal what Cummings' political beliefs were as well as anything else that might help to label him a threat to the government. Books from Loompanix, numerous publications (including *2600*), and other widely available printed works were seized from his home and used as further evidence of Cummings' danger to society. The fact that Cummings had a list of Secret Service radio frequencies was used to virtually lock up his image as a potential terrorist. (We've printed such lists in these pages.) The Secret Service also did their best to have Cummings removed from the airwaves of WBAI's *Off The Hook* where he has been keeping listeners updated on his case. At least this attempt at media manipulation failed.

"I never heard Cummings say anything about any political figures except once," Charles Rappa, Sr., his ex-landlord said in a statement for the Secret Service. "One time Cummings made a comment about Clinton not doing a good job, but nothing other than a simple passing comment." This from someone the Secret Service intended to use as a witness *against* Cummings. In fact, Rappa also made a statement that the Secret Service then used to justify holding Cummings without bail. He said that Cummings had called him from jail and said, "If I get out of here, no one will be able to find me, they won't be able to see my dust." Considering Rappa and Cummings were embroiled in a painful landlord/tenant separation at the time, it seemed questionable at best that Cummings would make such a claim to a person he considered an enemy. When the phone records from the jail didn't support Rappa's claim, the Secret Service quietly moved away from having Rappa testify. Yet they still didn't move a finger to allow bail.

The only other person the Secret Service was able to get to testify against Cummings was Paul Bergsman, who had been involved in various projects with Cummings, and who had been present at last year's HOPE conference where he gave a seminar on lock picking. "About one year ago, we entered into a verbal agreement to sell speed dialers at a Hackers Convention in New York City. This convention was called the 'Hope Convention,' held at the Pennsylvania Hotel in New York City, sponsored by the *2600 Magazine*. Ed Cummings and I agreed to buy about 300 of these speed dialers and Cummings separately purchased crystals. These crystals were also sold by Cummings through the *2600 Magazine*. The crystals were 6.5 or 6.49 Megahertz. We went to the convention some time during the late summer of 1994. Cummings and I set up a table at the convention and sold the speed dialers and crystals. None of the speed dialers had been altered and merely emitted the sound of 5 touch tone stars, which is the way we ordered them from the distributor.... We did not provide written or oral instructions on how to convert the dialer to a red box, nor were any crystals installed into the speed dialers." Pretty damning evidence, isn't it? It gets better. "I never saw Cummings clone a cellular telephone or use his computer for cloning. Cummings did have a cellular phone of his own and I saw him use it several times and talked to him on his cellular phone. I understood that he had an account with a local carrier.... I have never known Cummings to use or have illegal, stolen or counterfeit credit cards in his possession. However, I did see him charge items before. I never knew any of the cards to be stolen or counterfeit....Cummings never said anything to me about hacking into computers, though I know he attended the *2600* computer hacker club.... I never knew Cummings to be interested in the U.S. Secret Service or any political figures, past or present.

Cummings never spoke about his political concerns or philosophy. He never spoke about his dissatisfaction with any political figures or the U.S. government. I never heard him say anything that could be interpreted as a threat to anyone."

If the government's two lead witnesses can't find a crime to accuse Cummings of and if the evidence consists of nothing other than electronic devices and books, none of which has ever been linked to a crime, why has this case dragged on for so long and why has the Secret Service devoted so much attention to it? The answer may lie in the one thing that really seems to have pissed off the Secret Service more than anything and which could explain why they've tried so hard to ruin this person's life. Cummings had pictures of Secret Service agents on the lookout for hackers. And by showing these pictures at a *2600* meeting and sharing them with the media, Cummings himself may have become a target. It's a well known fact that undercover agents hate having their own tactics used against them. But by acting against him in this way, the Secret Service has drawn a great deal of attention to their practices. It is becoming clear that this is an agency out of control that threatens to hurt not only hackers but anyone who values free speech in this country.

On September 7, Cummings, in his words, "was forced to make a deal with the devil." He pleaded guilty to possession of technology that could be used in a fraudulent manner. Under the current law (Title 18 U.S.C. Section 1029), which snuck through legislation last October, mere possession is equal to fraudulent use. "Whoever... knowingly and with intent to defraud... possesses a telecommunications instrument that has been modified or altered to obtain unauthorized use of telecommunications services; or... a scanning receiver; or... hardware or software used for altering or modifying telecommunications instruments to obtain unauthorized access to telecommunications services... [as well as anyone] selling information regarding or an application to obtain an access device" is guilty under this section and subject to ten years in prison for each charge. This is a very ominous turn for all of us; virtually anyone even interested in computer hacking or the telephone system can now be sent to prison. Where were all of the "civil liberties" groups when this legislation was being passed? We haven't heard a word from the Electronic Frontier Foundation, the American Civil Liberties Union, Computer Professionals for Social Responsibility, or the Electronic Privacy Information Center on this case and we have been getting the word out to them. This is a case that certainly should have raised their ire and, regretfully, their silence on this matter is equivalent to complicity.

Cummings pleaded guilty because he really had no choice. Even though the law is wrong, he would have been found guilty under it and sentenced to a long prison term. The government also expressed its intention to accuse him of cellular phone fraud in California. Their evidence? Telephone numbers that showed up on a commercial software disk in Cummings' possession—in other words, a disk that he had nothing to do with and that people all over the world also possessed. Cummings realized that the

Secret Service could probably get a non-technical jury to believe this and, again, he would face a long prison term. By pleading guilty under what is known as a Zudic Plea, Cummings can challenge the constitutionality of the law over the next few months. It is also likely that the sentencing guidelines will call for no more than what Cummings has already served. In other words, he will be freed.

Of course, there is a big down side to this. The government will interpret this as a victory and will see a green light to lock up anyone in possession of simple electronic and/or computer tools if they so choose. And, as has been so aptly demonstrated by this case, if they choose to treat the suspect as a terrorist and lock him/her up for six months with no bail, they won't have much difficulty finding a judge willing to do this. Until some sweeping changes take effect, we are all in serious danger.

The Secret Service has lost whatever credibility it once had by its actions over the last few months. (At press time, a series of new raids involving the Secret Service centered around people accused of nothing more than selling electronic devices that had been purchased through a catalog. It now also appears that a "documentary" being filmed at this year's Summercon was actually a Secret Service operation to collect faces.) It is becoming clear that if we are to survive as a democratic society, we must make it a priority to eliminate the Secret Service as a watchdog over American citizens.

In the other major hacker case that we have been following, Kevin Mitnick pleaded guilty in July to one count out of the 23 he was charged with. Under this agreement, Mitnick will only have to serve eight months, although it is unclear if he will be charged with additional counts in California.

Caught in the Web (Spring, 1996)

How do mere individuals stand up to modern day injustices? What can we do to get the word out when the system has failed us and the most important thing is to find others in a similar situation who may be able to help out?

Throughout history, this kind of a challenge has been insurmountable to most. But the times are changing very rapidly. And the one thing individuals have over bloated bureaucracies and huge corporations is the ability to adapt—quickly.

We've learned over the past few years that the Internet is probably the most effective means of worldwide communication in the history of humanity. When word of something needs to be gotten out, all that is required is access and the world can know within seconds. Now, with the growing popularity of the World Wide Web, anyone with the necessary access has the ability to become their own information disseminator, where people from around the world actually come to *you* for information of any sort. And with the growing number and abilities of search engines, people anywhere can find you based on the information you provide.

This kind of power is unprecedented in the hands of solitary citizens. It's precisely because of the hacker mentality responsible for creating this medium that the authorities are in such a panic. This explains the rush to control everything from content to accessibility. But the power mongers are far too late this time. The box is open and the rules forever changed. It no longer matters what those who don't realize this choose to do. They are doomed to failure. What *is* important, though, is for the rest of us to maximize the potential of this technology while it is still in relative infancy.

As consumers, we no longer have to wait for someone to speak on our behalf. With the Net, we can speak for ourselves and be guaranteed an audience and, ultimately, a reaction of some sort. In our last issue, we mentioned a problem we were having with an Internet Service provider (PSI) who had promised us the ability to use 56k data over voice over an ISDN line. When it was finally realized that they didn't offer this service, the contracts had already been signed. Since it was a verbal agreement, there was little recourse and more than a few people (including PSI) believed that we would be held to the contract. Several years ago, that's probably what would have happened. However, by posting our account of the story on our web site (as well as Usenet newsgroups and other Internet forums), we were able to make contact with scores of other people who had had similar run-ins. We used these contacts to pool our resources. When we went one step further and posted *sound files* of telephone conversations where PSI reps were clearly heard saying they supported the service we wanted, there was no way the issue could be avoided. PSI reacted, at first by threatening to sue us. That proved to be an even bigger mistake since individuals on the Net are particularly averse to legal threats by large corporations. Now newspapers were actually starting to take an interest in the case. PSI really had no choice. Shortly afterwards and without fanfare, they sent us a full refund. We believe they learned a valuable lesson and we have no hard feelings towards them. What happened *was* an honest mistake. It was their reaction that made them look bad and pressure from so many people that ultimately made them give in. We didn't have to sue them or waste an inordinate amount of time. All we had to do was speak up.

The same kind of power in a different kind of way was felt with the Ed Cummings (Bernie S.) case, which we have been involved in for over a year now. In January of this year, the United States Secret Service managed to have Cummings locked up yet again for last year's charge of possessing technology that *could be* used to commit fraud.

By being arrested last year, Cummings technically violated probation for an offense committed several years ago in a small Pennsylvania town. Because it was such a minor incident—equal in seriousness to "insulting the flag"—nobody could ever have been expected to go to prison for it. However, the Secret Service made it their business to portray Cummings as a major threat to society. The judge, along with the probation officer and prosecutor who had previously said the case was of little significance, were heavily influenced by having the Secret Service come to their small town. Based on this image, he was put back in prison with murderers, rapists, and death row inmates. He was considered especially dangerous because the judge had set such a high bail—$250,000. This, despite the fact that he was obviously not a flight risk, having shown up for numerous hearings where he could have been imprisoned on the spot. After several weeks, the judge conceded that the bail was too high and had it lowered—to $100,000. In early March, the judge sentenced Cummings to 6 to 24 months, double the sentence of someone convicted of attempted murder in the same district. Under the law, he should be released on May 30, but the Secret Service may attempt to impose even more suffering on him by seeking to have that extended.

Throughout this entire escapade, the Secret Service has said in every court appearance that some of the most disturbing evidence they found in Cummings' possession was information on the Secret Service themselves—frequencies, addresses, codenames, and pictures that had been on a television show. Special Agent Thomas Varney has said under oath that any reasonable person would view this evidence as proof that Cummings was a threat to society. And this assumption was accepted by law enforcement, the legal system, the media, and, ultimately, the public.

We decided to check into this. We found that all of this information was completely legal and available to the public. And, to emphasize the point, *we* made all of it (and more) available on our web page. The reaction was phenomenal; an average of around 1,000 visitors a day. And the irony was delightful; because the Secret Service overreacted at *one* person's possession of this material, *millions* of people around the world now had easy access to it. It may not have been enough to get Cummings freed, but it was enough to get his story into newspapers around the world and have the real issues of the case discussed at long last. We hope this new publicity will cause some heads to roll at the Secret Service and prevent this kind of thing from happening again to more of us. Regardless, Cummings has gained thousands of friends who will be with him in spirit until this ordeal ends.

What we've done with the Net is what the Net has been designed for—freedom of speech and instant access to relevant material. Being an already existing magazine gives us an advantage, but not a tremendous one. Any person could have done what we did with basic connectivity and strength of convictions. Individuals will continue to use the Net to outmaneuver bulky corporations, speak out against bureaucratic and repressive regimes, and take over where the mainstream media has failed us. And those who underestimate this power are in for a very rude awakening.

Fallout (Autumn, 1996)

Some nightmares never seem to end.

This has certainly seemed the case with the ongoing saga of Ed Cummings (Bernie S.). We've devoted many pages to this bizarre tale since it began in March, 1995. And we've learned so very much.

To summarize what we've already told you, Cummings, a *2600* writer for years, was arrested for possession of telecommunications devices that *could* be used for fraudulent purposes. He was never accused of committing any fraud however. The United States Secret Service managed to have him imprisoned for seven months on a charge that virtually any technically adept person could be guilty of. (It was widely believed that the Secret Service had been embarrassed by Cummings' disclosure to a Fox news crew of unflattering pictures of them—pictures that had been given to him by a friend and which we have since made available on our web site.)

On Friday, October 13, 1995, the nightmare ended. Ed Cummings was released from a federal prison where he had spent time with murderers and other "non-technology-oriented" criminals.

He quickly put his life together again, securing a job with a phone company and speaking of his ordeal at various conferences.

But then the Secret Service came back. It seems that a couple of years earlier, Cummings had had a little run-in with a local police department when he parked his car illegally and had it searched by a local cop who didn't understand some of the technical papers and apparatus within. The cop took Cummings and his two friends to the station and proceeded to question them. They were never placed under arrest and, when the police left the room, one of Cummings' friends took the sheets of paper the cop had been interested in and also removed the batteries from a tone dialer, presumably to erase private phone numbers. (For some reason they had been left alone with these bits of "evidence.") The cop discovered this shortly after the three of them left. He managed to find them again and, since nobody was willing to say who had done the tampering, the cop charged Cummings since the car belonged to him and he was considered the one "in charge." And Cummings never saw the need to set the record straight, since it was a ridiculously minor, almost funny, accusation. He was sentenced to probation. Now, after being arrested by the Secret Service, he was in violation of that probation.

In January, 1996, with considerable pressure from Secret Service agent Tom Varney, Cummings was put back in prison with an insanely high bail of $250,000 while he awaited sentencing. And, because of his high bail, he was kept with the most violent and dangerous offenders. When he was finally sentenced in March to 6 to 24 months, it almost seemed like a relief because an end to the ordeal was at last in sight. And, while technically he could be held for two years, it was virtually unheard of for prisoners not to get parole after their minimum time was up, unless they had disciplinary problems. One thing Cummings had going for him was an impeccable behavior record in prison.

It was no secret, however, that the authorities within the prison system and the Secret Service were quite upset with Cummings' outspokenness on his case. His weekly updates on WBAI's *Off The Hook* and the coverage in *2600* as well as the smattering of press coverage in the mainstream media was a real thorn in their side.

June came and went with no parole hearing. And when the hearing finally took place, on July 2nd, Cummings was told that processing only took place on the first of the month, so nobody would even touch his case until August. Such senseless logic appears to be the norm in America's prisons. But in this case, prison authorities seemed intent on making Cummings' life as miserable as possible.

One of the best examples of this occurred in July when he was finally moved to a minimum security facility and allowed to participate in a "voluntary" community service program. (If you don't volunteer, you get sent back to the maximum security prison.) During this brief period, he was contacted by Rob Bernstein, a reporter for *Internet Underground*, who wanted to write an article on his case. Bernstein called the prison, asked for, and received, the fax number at the facility where Cummings was working. His intention was to forward a copy of the article to Cummings before it was finalized so that any mistakes could be corrected. At the time, it seemed logical and in the real world it would have been.

But this was not the real world. When it was discovered that a fax had been sent to Cummings (without his knowledge or consent), prison officials immediately threw him back into the maximum security prison at Bucks County. They claimed he had misused the telephone system by receiving the fax and that, as a result, his time in prison could be increased by nine months.

Cummings appealed this ridiculous judgment as any semi-rational person would. They kept him in maximum for 19 days, nine days more than they were supposed to. His appeal was denied and, at the same time, he was suddenly subjected to shakedowns and was being written up for infractions like having too much reading material or one too many bottles of shampoo. Each of these had the potential for getting his parole denied. All of a sudden his impeccable behavior record had been tarnished.

Believing he was being harassed, Cummings filed a grievance. Right after it was denied, he found himself being transferred from minimum to another maximum security facility in Lehigh County. The reason for this action was "protective custody." It was obvious to everyone that the real reason was to get rid of him.

Then things got much worse. Within a day, Cummings was viciously attacked by a violent inmate. He had his jaw kicked in and his arm shattered by the time the guards got around to stopping it. His jaw wired shut, he was then thrown into the infectious diseases ward at Lehigh County where his medical care was virtually nonexistent. They even refused to give him painkillers. And strangely enough, all of the phone numbers Cummings had called in the past were blocked. If ever anyone was being given a hint to keep their mouth shut, this was it.

But despite all of this, Cummings refused to be silenced. The story of what was happening to him got out and this time it got people so angry that there was nothing left to do but take action. In an unprecedented move, visitors to the *2600* web site, listeners of WBAI's *Off The Hook*, and hackers around the planet joined forces to end the nightmare once and for all. A mailing list, which quickly got hundreds of subscribers, was started. A voice mail hotline was set up at *2600*. Volunteers worked around the clock. People who had never been part of the hacker world began to get involved. It was clear that this was no longer a hacker issue but rather a very significant human rights case. Even members of the mainstream media began to take an interest. (Sadly, the Electronic Frontier Foundation and the American Civil Liberties Union *still* didn't get involved.)

Within a few days, a demonstration outside the Northampton County prison and courthouse (where Cummings had now been transferred) had been organized. After nearly two years, the Bernie S. case had finally become a blatant example of miscarriage of justice to nearly everyone who heard about it.

The strain on the authorities must have been tremendous. The number of phone calls, letters, faxes, and emails to Pennsylvania prison and governmental offices, as well as the Secret Service and congressional offices, was unprecedented.

And suddenly, on Friday, September 13, 1996, the nightmare ended. Ed Cummings was released effective immediately. And, while still subject to parole regulations, it was apparent that the Secret Service was fresh out of the power to put him back in prison. Here was a clear example of people power.

It was a definite victory but not the kind that makes you feel good for very long. Things never should have been allowed to get to this point in the first place. Much work remains to be done. The aftereffects of this torment won't soon go away. Apart from facing permanent disfigurement, Cummings has had his life almost completely destroyed by these actions. There are many pieces to pick up. And, for the rest of us, there are many people we must hold accountable for this travesty.

These questions demand immediate answers: Why was the Secret Service (particularly Special Agent Tom Varney of the Philadelphia office) so intent on imprisoning Ed Cummings? Why were they allowed to have such an undue influence on court proceedings? Why did Judge Jack Panella (Northampton County, PA) set bail at such high levels for such a trivial nonviolent offense? Why did the Bucks County Correctional Facility have Cummings transferred into a prison for violent offenders and what exactly did they mean by "protective custody"? And, finally, how did we ever allow the federal government to pass a law that can put someone in prison for possession of electronic components without any evidence of their being used to commit a crime (Title 18, U.S.C. 1029)?

While we look for answers, we will also need to keep track of the injustices facing all the others in prison, now and, regrettably, in the future.

We can hope that this tragic case and the tremendous response to it will be enough to teach the authorities an unforgettable lesson and keep it from happening again.

Somehow, we doubt it.

Enough is Enough (Spring, 1997)

The question we're asked most often is whether or not we're making any progress in the fight against ignorance and fear. And it's the question that we can never answer the same way twice. There are days when we really seem to be getting somewhere and then there are times when we wonder if we're actually moving backwards.

Looking at the Kevin Mitnick case makes the question really hard to answer. We've managed to reach a whole lot of people and we know that our concerns are shared all over the world. But, as in the early days of the Bernie S. nightmare, mere concern doesn't really amount to much. In the end, only true outrage gets results and, even for us, that can take a while.

It's now been over two years since Mitnick was caught in North Carolina. At the time we asked for a summation of his "crimes" so we would know just what this was really all about. A lot has happened since those early days. At least four books have been written about the Mitnick chase and capture and all of their authors have cashed their checks and moved on to other projects. But our initial question has yet to be answered since Mitnick *still* hasn't gone to trial. How can this be allowed to happen?

The sad truth is that once you're a prisoner, anything can happen to you and not many in the American public will care. The media will latch onto whatever they're fed and more often than not will simply take the word of authority figures without question. Examples? In March the government began its appeal to the Supreme Court of last year's striking down of the Communications Decency Act. Most of us know that the CDA is blatantly unconstitutional and would stifle free speech on the Net. But the media, who should value the concept of free speech, defines this battle as "the fight against pornography on the Net." Ratings over content once again. And we all suffer because of it. The same blindness to the facts and unwillingness to do some real investigative work led to the more recent belief that Dutch hackers had gotten into military computer systems during the Gulf War and had offered secret information to Saddam Hussein, information that could have won the war for Iraq. There was no evidence. There were no facts. Just a crackpot with an authoritative air and the media's desire to get another sensationalist story. Done enough times, this kind of garbage eventually turns into reality and the inevitable reaction against the "crisis" is accepted as necessary. We all know this yet somehow it continues time and again.

If ever there has been a human victim of this constant disregard for the truth, that victim is Kevin Mitnick. While we've been reading the books about him and getting on with our lives, Mitnick's life has been frozen since February, 1995—much longer if you consider the time he spent living the life of a fugitive trying to avoid his current fate. It seems clear that Mitnick knew how the authorities would treat him, which is why he went on the run. After all, these are the same authorities who put him in *solitary confinement* for eight months in 1989! That torture came from the authorities' fear of

Mitnick's phone abilities. After this kind of abuse, anyone who would simply turn themselves in after being declared a fugitive would have to be crazy.

As for what he did to make them want to imprison him for so long, all we know is that it didn't involve theft, personal profit, or damage to any computer system. Everyone seems to agree on this. Whatever it is they finally do come up with, we doubt it can justify locking someone away for as long as they already have, let alone for as long as they seem to want to.

Recently Mitnick was again thrown into solitary confinement for reasons that are still somewhat unclear. *Wired Magazine* said it was because he had too many cans of tuna in his cell and proceeded to make light of the whole thing, choosing to ignore the permanent trauma of Mitnick's 1989 experience in solitary. This absurdity was most definitely *not* the reason. Mitnick was considered a "threat" to the institution because prison authorities somehow reached the conclusion that he was going to modify a walkman, turn it into an FM transmitter, and then proceed to bug the prison offices. (Nobody can explain how Mitnick was supposed to gain access to these offices being a prisoner and all.) These facts come from the administrative detention order, prison guards, and legal people who were privy to the facts of the case. We realize pursuing these facts was too difficult a task for the media people whose real concerns are ratings points and newsstand sales.

Many of Mitnick's legal papers were taken from his cell during his time in solitary and never returned. Issues of *2600* and *Phrack* as well as mail forwarded to Mitnick from his Internet mail account simply disappeared. Much of this material had information pertaining to other cases that Mitnick was hoping to use in his defense. Other returned items appear to have been read.

Prosecutor David Schindler has taken it upon himself to keep Mitnick in prison for as long as possible. Schindler wants Mitnick to sign a plea agreement that would keep him imprisoned for 32 months before he's even charged with anything in California. Not exactly a good deal in our opinion. Schindler has said that if Mitnick refuses to go along with this, he will drag him across the country to face charges in other jurisdictions. That's the beauty of being charged with crimes over the Internet and the phone system; you can be indicted in places you've never even been to! In doing this, Schindler and the government basically get to keep rolling the dice until they find a judge someplace who will sentence Mitnick for however long they want. This kind of tactic is often used on the most dangerous of criminals to ensure that they wind up in prison somehow. To see it used here is frightening and a dangerous affront to the intent of our justice system.

When this story first broke two years ago, there were some people who thought Mitnick was a criminal of *some* sort and that he should be punished for whatever it was he did even though nobody really knew what that was for sure. Now, even those people seem to think that this has gone on long enough. Even if Mitnick *had* committed some very real and recognizable crimes, the time he's spent suffering in prison is more than sufficient punishment. But Mitnick has never even been charged with any recognizable crime and we doubt that he ever will be. If and when this case ever gets to court, we're sure Schindler and his cronies will try to make it seem as if Mitnick stole millions of dollars by copying files and making a few phone calls. And the media, by not probing and asking questions, will swallow the whole thing once more and the American public will somehow believe that justice was served.

It doesn't have to be this way. Those of us who understand the technology involved in this case are able to see when the truth is not being told or when people are being misled. We can't let this go unanswered any longer. Education is the key to stopping this injustice and many of us have the ability to make a real difference. But do we have the guts to turn that ability into action?

We're working on many different approaches. We've started a mailing list that exists for the sole purpose of discussing the Mitnick case and what we can do to help. At the Beyond Hope conference in August (by which time we really hope Mitnick is free) we will be having panels on this case and how to use the power we have to make changes. We welcome skeptics as always.

In the meantime, we ask that you not forget about Mitnick and the many others who are imprisoned unjustly for actions that are hard to consider crimes. We wish we had the staff and resources to adequately pursue all of them. By focusing on this case, we hope to be able to spread whatever change we make to these and future cases.

Mitnick Update (Winter, 1998-1999)

At press time, the trial of Kevin Mitnick had been moved from January 19, 1999 to April 20, 1999 to allow him time to look at the evidence, which the government had failed to provide by the agreed upon deadline. Oddly, the prosecution was not chastised by the judge for this violation, yet Mitnick's lawyer was scolded for requesting a delay. In addition, it was found that an FBI informant may have had access to the offices of Mitnick's previous attorney with the full knowledge of the government. This action also has not been addressed by the court. What *was* addressed was the fact that a *2600* staffer had requested the financial disclosure documents of Judge Mariana Pfaelzer, something entirely within our rights and a routine method of looking for conflicts of interest among judges. Pfaelzer's reaction, however, was anything but routine, demanding to know from Mitnick who was behind this and implying that something nefarious was going on. No doubt she believes that Mitnick will mastermind the destruction of her financial records by whistling touch tones into a walkman. It's become rather difficult to believe in the impartiality of this court.

A Culmination of Efforts (Summer, 1999)

A great deal has happened since we last spoke of the Mitnick case and, more than likely, even more has happened between the time this was written and the time you are reading it. Easily the longest and most complicated of all the cases we've become involved in, the story of Kevin Mitnick is now in the crescendo stage and continues to shock and amaze those who have been following it.

Let's catch up. In April, Kevin was forced to make a deal with the government. We say forced because it's the most accurate word we could find. Most of us are led to believe that when someone pleads guilty to a crime that they are in fact guilty. But it's not really that simple.

The first thing you have to keep in mind is that the federal government wins over 95 percent of its cases. Is this because they have an unerring instinctive ability to track down criminals? Or because the prosecution does such a magnificent job of presenting its case? Possible... but not very likely. The real reason why these numbers are so staggered in the government's favor is because they have tremendous advantages in virtually every case they take on. The Mitnick case demonstrated this time and again; Kevin's court-appointed lawyer had a tightly capped budget that made it close to impossible to hire expert witnesses, take the time to go through the mountains of evidence, or otherwise mount an adequate defense. The prosecution, on the other hand, had an unlimited budget and was able to hire as many people as they needed. The taxpayers covered the whole thing. And a mere look at the court transcripts shows a judge heavily biased in favor of the prosecutors.

The inability of Kevin's legal team to adequately prepare for the case meant that there was a very real possibility of a guilty verdict in a trial. It's not hard at all to get such a verdict when evidence is deliberately confused, missing, or misleading. And, regrettably, this seems to be the way the game is played.

Since Kevin could have faced an additional decade in prison if he were to be found guilty in this manner, it made very little sense to take such a risk. By accepting a plea before trial, Kevin would be guaranteed at most another year in confinement. After more than four years of his life lost to this, not counting the years spent trying to elude this form of "justice" and the 1989 nightmare of being locked in solitary for eight months, it provided a sense of closure to at least know when the nightmare would end. We've seen this before countless times. The Phiber Optik and Bernie S. cases are two historic examples where the defendants were forced to accept a plea when what they wanted above all else was to fight the injustice. Real life isn't like an episode of *Perry Mason*, where all sides of the story are heard and justice always prevails.

When details of this plea agreement were mysteriously leaked (this was never investigated but it would have been an incredibly stupid move for a member of the defense team to leak this as it could jeopardize the entire agreement), many people made the mistake of thinking it was all over.

Far from it.

While Kevin may have had no choice but to accept this agreement, he is a long way from freedom. And, it would appear, there are those who want the suffering to continue and even intensify.

First off, let's consider the actual charges to which Kevin pleaded guilty:

1. Making a phone call to Novell on January 4, 1994, and pretending he was "Gabe Nault."
2. Making a phone call to Motorola on February 19, 1994, and pretending he was "Earl Roberts."
3. Making a phone call to Fujitsu on April 15, 1994, and pretending he was "Chris Stephenson."
4. Making a phone call to Nokia on April 21, 1994, and pretending he was "Adam Gould."
5. Altering data in a computer belonging to the University of Southern California between June, 1993, and June, 1994.
6. Sniffing passwords on `netcom.com`.
7. Improperly accessing `well.com`.

We all know that lying on the telephone to perfect strangers is wrong. And taking advantage of shoddy security to capture unencrypted passwords isn't ethical. And it's always a bad idea to log into a computer system using someone else's account. And as for altering data, no real details on that have ever been released—it could be something as simple as showing up in a log file—thus altering data. If it were anything more, such as erasing a single file, we probably would have heard all about it.

Assuming that Kevin was guilty of all of these charges, how can anyone justify the amount of prison time he has served? Especially when there were no allegations of damage to any system (other than the very vague hint above), profiting in any way, or doing anything that could be considered malicious. The above offenses are, by any reasonable standard, *minor* ones. What aren't they telling us?

It's no secret that Kevin pissed off some pretty big companies when he tricked them into showing him their source code for cellular phones (long since outdated, incidentally). In fact, in letters obtained by *2600* that were put up on our web site, NEC, Novell, Nokia, Fujitsu, and Sun Microsystems all claim direct or implied losses that total several hundred *million* dollars. All of the letters appear to have been solicited by the FBI shortly after Mitnick was arrested in 1995.

This is where things get interesting. If such losses were actually suffered by these companies, it is *illegal* for them not to report this to their stockholders. The Securities and

Exchange Commission is quite clear on this. Yet, not a single one of these companies reported any such loss. In fact, Sun Microsystems implied a loss of around $80 million due to Kevin being able to look at the source code to Solaris. But if one wanders around their web pages, an interesting quotation can be found: "Sun firmly believes that students and teachers need access to source code to enhance their technology learning experience." Even if you don't meet their qualifications for this, you can still get the Solaris source code for $100! That's quite a depreciation in a mere four years, isn't it? If we were to apply this level of exaggeration to the other claims, Kevin's total amount of damages would be somewhere in the neighborhood of $350.

It gets even better. When the government found out that we had obtained these documents and were making them public, they went ballistic. At press time, they had filed a motion to have Kevin's lawyer *held in contempt of court* because they believed he was the source of the documents. (Meanwhile nothing was ever said about the leaking of the plea agreement earlier in the year.) Judge Mariana Pfaelzer has given every indication that she will seriously consider this motion and has already agreed to keep any future evidence to be used against Mitnick at his sentencing a secret. In other words, any other damaging documents that could reveal what a sham this entire case has been will be kept hidden from the public.

At best this is an abuse of power; at worst, a cover-up of massive proportions. Public reaction has become increasingly vocal in this case and we know now that this has had an effect. The government's way of acknowledging this is both irrational and unjust and it cannot go unchallenged.

By the time you read this, nationwide demonstrations in front of federal courthouses all over the country will have taken place on June 4. We are seeing an unprecedented amount of activism in the hacker community and the reason is simple. This is just too much to tolerate. We cannot permit this suffering to continue. And those who stand by silently are as guilty as those cheering on this kind of abuse.

We won't have to look far for the sequels. As we go to press, a new case involving "prohibited electronic communication intercepting devices" is beginning to play out. Radio enthusiast Bill Cheek of California was arrested by federal authorities and accused of violating the law simply because he dared to distribute devices that allow people to monitor police broadcasts, as people have done now for decades. Apparently, such communications, along with cellular and pager traffic, are now to be considered "off limits" to average people.

Fortunately, this case has started to attract attention in its early stages. That is likely to make all the difference in the world. But we have to wonder how many more people will be subjected to cruel and unusual punishment because they dared to explore something that powerful entities wanted to keep secret.

We don't know how many there will be but we do know there will be more. And what happens to those people in the years ahead will be directly affected by what we do here in the present. If we stand idly by, there will be no end of Mitnick and Cheek cases. But for every person who stands up and objects to this kind of treatment, a small bit of the armor will be chipped away. It's a proven fact that we have this power. What has yet to be determined is how much we will use it.

New Legal Threats

We learned a lot more about the law than we ever wanted to in the 1990s. The Clinton administration and Congress seemed to declare war on hackers, who clearly didn't fit into their neat little plan of how technology and communications should be regulated. The Digital Telephony Bill (known to us now as CALEA) set the stage for increased monitoring and selective prosecution. Shockingly, it was helped along by the caving to intense pressure of a trusted civil liberties group. Then there was the Clipper and Capstone chip initiative, which almost killed encryption in this country. It was easy to lose track of all of the bad legislation coming down the pike, most of which would be detrimental to free thinkers and dissidents in one way or another. Some battles were won and some were lost. We did our best to keep track of them all but, not being lawyers or civil libertarians, we know there's a lot we missed. We printed a number of articles focusing on legal issues and reasons why we should all be concerned. Many in the hacker community chose to close their eyes to all of this, hoping that they just wouldn't be affected by the negativity if they didn't know about it. As the decade came to an end, we noticed a change in the way people were starting to deal with these and other issues. More and more were bypassing the traditional channels of communication and simply putting their message out there on their own terms. Blogs, web sites, audio, video—the power of the Net was finally translating into a sense of empowerment for those people who didn't have a voice in the mainstream. People were speaking and more people were listening. The independent media movement was on the Internet as the world approached a new millennium.

Congress Takes a Holiday (Autumn, 1993)

When the congressional aide called the *2600* offices and asked Emmanuel Goldstein to offer testimony before the House Subcommittee on Telecommunications and Finance on June 9, we knew it sounded too good to be true. In our never-ending optimism, however, we decided to grant their request and submit a statement. At the time, it seemed like a good idea with great potential for all sorts of dialogue. After all, it marked the first time that Congress had actually asked for the opinion of hackers in implementing policy. But what we failed to anticipate was the possibility that the whole thing was nothing more than a big publicity stunt designed to generate anti-hacker sound bites rather than any technological inspiration. Quicker than you could say "Geraldo," Congressmen Markey (D-Massachusetts) and Fields (R-Texas) began hacker-bashing. Markey held up a copy of *2600* and called it a manual for computer crime. In a very patronizing tone, he lectured Goldstein on the definition of a criminal. He compared printing articles in *2600* to telling people how to break into specific houses on Maple Street. Fields was no better, accusing *2600* of printing "codes" to listen in on phone calls. When Goldstein attempted to explain that these "codes" were unencrypted frequencies that anyone with a scanner could listen to, Fields dismissed him by saying he was very disturbed that this publication and the people involved in it were allowed to exist.

While Markey and Fields were the only members of the subcommittee who chose to attend the hearing, their ignorance and unwillingness to listen echo throughout the fantasy world of elected officials. What is very unfortunate for us is that these politicians, whose depth of understanding seems unable to surpass that of *A Current Affair*, are very powerful people who pass laws based on their misperceptions. We can hardly wait to see what they come up with next.

What follows is some of what they *didn't* read:

"The next few years will almost certainly go down in history as those in which the most change took place in the least amount of time. The computer and telecommunications revolution that we are now in the midst of is moving full speed ahead into unknown territory. The potential for amazing advances in individual thought and creativity is very real. But so is the potential for oppression and mistrust the likes of which we have never before seen. One way or the other, we will be making history."

I think we can imagine it best if we think of ourselves speeding down a potentially dangerous highway. Perhaps the road will become slick with ice or fraught with sharp curves. It's a road that nobody has gone down before. And the question we have to ask ourselves is what kind of a vehicle would we prefer to be in if things should start getting out of control: our own automobile where we would have at least some chance of controlling the vehicle and bringing it down to a safe speed or a bus where we, along with many others, must put all of our trust behind a total stranger to prevent a disaster. The answer is obviously different depending on the circumstances. There are those of us who do not want the responsibility of driving and others who have proven themselves unworthy of it. What's important is that we all have the opportunity at some point to choose which way we want to go.

Rapidly changing technology can also be very dangerous if we don't look where we're going or if too many of us close our eyes and let someone else do the driving. This is a ride we all must stay awake for.

I am not saying we should be overly suspicious of every form of technology. I believe we are on the verge of something very positive. But the members of this committee should be aware of the dangers of an uninformed populace. These dangers will manifest themselves in the form of suspicion towards authority, overall fear of technology, and an unhealthy feeling of helplessness.

The recent FBI proposal to have wiretap capabilities built into digital telephone systems got most of its publicity because American taxpayers were expected to foot the bill. But to many of the non-technical people I talked to, it was just another example of Big Brother edging one step closer. It is commonly believed that the National Security Agency monitors all traffic on the Internet, not to mention all international telephone calls. Between Caller ID, TRW credit reports, video cameras, room monitors, and computer categorizations of our personalities, the average American feels as if life no longer has many private moments. Our Social Security numbers, which once were for Social Security, are now used for everything from video rentals to driver's licenses. These numbers can easily be used to track a person's location, expenses, and habits—all without any consent. If you know a person's name, you can get their telephone number. If you have their phone number, you can get their address. Getting their Social Security number is not even a challenge anymore. With this information, you can not only get every bit of information about this person that exists on any computer from Blockbuster Video to the local library to the phone company to the FBI, but you can begin to do things in this poor person's name. It's possible we may want a society like this, where we will be accountable for our every movement and where only criminals will pursue privacy. The American public needs to be asked. But first, they need to understand.

In Germany, there is a fairly new computerized system of identity cards. Every citizen must carry one of these cards. The information includes their name, address, date of birth, and nationality, in other words, the country they were originally born in. Such a system of national identity can be quite useful, but in the wrong hands it can be extremely scary. For example, if a neo-Nazi group were to somehow get their hands on the database, they could instantly find out where everyone of Turkish nationality lived. A malevolent government could do the same and, since not carrying the card would be a crime, it would be very hard to avoid its wrath.

Before introducing a new technology that is all-encompassing, all of its potential side-effects and disadvantages should be discussed and addressed. Opportunities must exist for everyone to ask questions. In our own country, nobody was ever asked if they wanted a credit file opened on them, if they wanted to have their phone numbers given to the people and companies they called through the use of Caller ID and ANI, or if they wanted to be categorized in any manner on numerous lists and databases. Yet all of this has now become standard practice.

This implementation of new rules has resulted in a degree of cynicism in many of us, as well as a sense of foreboding and dread. We all know that these new inventions will be abused and used to somebody's advantage at some point. There are those who would have us believe that the only people capable of such misdeeds are computer hackers and their ilk. But it just isn't that simple.

So where is the boundary between the hacker world and the criminal world? To me, it has always been in the same place. We know that it's wrong to steal tangible objects. We know that it's wrong to vandalize. We know that it's wrong to invade somebody's privacy. Not one of these elements is part of the hacker world.

A hacker can certainly turn into a criminal and take advantage of the weaknesses in our telephone and computer systems. But this is rare. What is more likely is that a hacker will share knowledge with people, one of whom will decide to use that knowledge for criminal purposes. This does not make the hacker a criminal for figuring it out. And it certainly doesn't make the criminal into a hacker.

It is easy to see this when we are talking about crimes that we understand as crimes. But then there are the more nebulous crimes; the ones where we have to ask ourselves: "Is this really a crime?" Copying software is one example. We all know that copying a computer program and then selling it is a crime. It's stealing, plain and simple. But copying a program from a friend to try it out on your home computer—is this the same kind of crime? It seems obvious to me that it is not, the reason being that you must make a leap of logic to turn such an action into a crime. Imagine if we were to charge a licensing fee every time somebody browsed through a magazine at the local bookshop, every time material was borrowed from a library, or every time a phone number was jotted down from the yellow pages. Yet, organizations like the Software Publishers Association have gone on record as saying that it is illegal to use the same computer program on more than one computer in your house. They claim that you must purchase it again or face the threat of federal marshals kicking in your door. That is a leap of logic.

It is a leap of logic to assume that because a word processor costs $500, a college student will not try to make a free copy in order to write and become a little more computer literate. Do we punish this student for breaking a rule? Do we charge him with stealing $500? To the hacker culture on whose behalf I am speaking today, the only sensible answer is to make it as easy as possible for that college student to use the software he needs. And while we're at it, we should be happy that he's interested in the first place.

Of course, this represents a fundamental change in our society's outlook. Technology is a way of life, not just another way to make money. After all, we encourage people to read books even if they can't pay for them because to our society literacy is a very important goal. I believe technological literacy is becoming increasingly important. But you cannot have literacy of any kind without having access.

If we continue to make access to technology difficult, bureaucratic, and illogical, then there will also be more computer crime; the reason being that if you treat someone like a criminal, they will begin to act like one. If we succeed in convincing people that copying a file is the same as physically stealing something, we can hardly be surprised when the broad-based definition results in more overall crime. Blurring the distinction between a virtual infraction and a real-life crime is a mistake.

New laws are not needed because there is not a single crime that can be committed with a computer that is not already defined as a crime without a computer. But let us not be loose with that definition. Is mere unauthorized access to a computer worthy of federal indictments, lengthy court battles, confiscation of equipment, huge fines, and years of prison time? Or is it closer to a case of trespassing, which in the real world is usually punished by a simple warning? "Of course not," some will say, since accessing a computer is far more sensitive than walking into an unlocked office building." If that is the case, why is it still so easy to do? If it's possible for somebody to easily gain unauthorized access to a computer that has information about me, I would like to know about it. But somehow I don't think the company or agency running the system would tell me that they have gaping security holes. Hackers, on the other hand, are very open about what they discover, which is why large corporations hate them so much. Through legislation, we can turn what the hackers do into a crime and there just might be a slim chance that we can stop them. But that won't fix poorly designed systems whose very existence is a violation of our privacy.

The future holds such enormous potential. It is vital that we not succumb to our fears and allow our democratic ideals and privacy values to be shattered. In many ways, the world of cyberspace is more real than the real world itself. I say this because it is only within the virtual world that people are really free to be themselves: to speak without fear of reprisal, to be anonymous if they so choose, to participate in a dialogue where one is judged by the merits of their words, not the color of their skin or the timbre of their voice. Contrast this to our existing "real" world where we often have people sized up before they even utter a word. The Internet has evolved, on its own volition, to become a true bastion of worldwide democracy. It is the obligation of this committee, and of governments throughout the world, not to stand in its way.

This does not mean we should stand back and do nothing. Quite the contrary, there is much we have to do if accessibility and equality are our goals. Over-regulation and commercialization are two ways to quickly kill these goals. A way to realize them is to have a network access point in every house. Currently, network access is restricted to students or professors at participating schools, scientists, commercial establishments, and those who have access to, and can afford, local services that link into the Internet. Yes, a lot of people have access today. But a far greater number do not and it is to these people that we must speak. The bigger the Internet gets, the better it gets. As it exists today, cultures from around the globe are represented; information of all kinds is exchanged. People are writing, reading, thinking. It's potentially the greatest educational tool we have. Therefore, it is essential that we not allow it to become a commodity that only certain people in society will be able to afford. With today's technology, we face the danger of widening the gap between the haves and the have-nots to a monumental level. Or we can open the door and discover that people really do have a lot to learn from each other, given the opportunity.

Not Much Good News Here (Spring, 1994)

A trip to the library can reveal all sorts of fascinating items.

A publication called *Prosecutor's Brief*, described as the "newsjournal of the California District Attorneys Association" had some rather shocking advice in its Summer, 1989, edition. (Too bad we didn't catch this one sooner.)

In the lead story, author Jerry P. Coleman proclaims, "Prosecutions of phone 'hackers' are not overly complicated, may be even fun, and can certainly assist your office's strained budget by providing a ready source of computer hardware."

According to California Penal Code section 502.7(g), "An instrument, apparatus, device, plans, instructions or written publication... may be seized under warrant or incident to a lawful arrest, and, upon the conviction of a person for a violation of subdivision (a), (b), or (c), the instrument [etc.] may be... turned over to the person providing telephone or telegraph service in the territory in which the same was seized."

But, according to the article, most of these companies will donate the equipment "right back to law enforcement." What a cozy arrangement.

Concerning monitoring, some of the revelations are pretty scary. It seems that pen registers operated by Pacific Bell double as partial wiretaps, and it's perfectly legal for them to record conversations without a warrant if it's part of a phone company investigation! The article states, "In the case of Pacific Bell, but not necessarily all other companies, the first 90 to 120 seconds of each call made from the trapped line is taped for the purpose of identifying the person(s) using the illegally hacked codes."

The article goes on to describe the ideal scenario: "If you are fortunate enough to receive the case before the search warrant has alerted the hacker to the investigation, your most important decision may well be the length of time the DNR stays on the targeted line. Weighing in favor of greater DNR time are the desires for obtaining at least a $400 felony loss, and identifying with certainty the hacker. Those considerations must be balanced against the risk that the DNR and its attendant call content taping will be suppressed as being an unreasonable privacy infringement, and the moral consideration of continued losses to the common carrier."

The "recorded salutations" on the tape are considered a key bit of evidence since they identify the defendant. In addition, "any notebooks containing handwritten authorization codes, phone numbers called, etc., can be compared to the known handwriting of the defendant (from booking slip and/or court-ordered exemplars). Don't neglect the seized computer's own memory banks—either its internal hard disk or any floppy disks may contain programs or files identifying the computer's user as the defendant."

District attorneys are also urged to look through the evidence for any "contacts among the hacker community" or BBS numbers.

Another "particularly fun" way of prosecuting a hacker is to look through his computer programs for games that have a listing of the top 10 scorers. "If your defendant's name appears close to the top of the list (or exclusively), it is quite reasonable to argue that, having had the most time to play the game this successfully, the defendant must own the computer."

Another absurdity concerns the justification for seizing telephones, described as "entirely appropriate within the statute, and serves to drive home rather graphically to the hacker just how serious this matter of criminal prosecution is."

It's pretty obvious how serious computer crime is to district attorneys in California. Here is our first solid piece of evidence that they consider hacker cases to be fun and easy ways of getting other people's computer equipment for themselves. A true mockery of justice.

The Clinton administration is becoming obsessed with monitoring citizens. On February 4, the administration rejected all of the criticism it has received on the Clipper Chip proposal and announced plans to move full speed ahead with its implementation—on a "voluntary" basis. The Clipper Chip would allow law enforcement to eavesdrop on phone calls that use the government standard of encryption. Civil liberties groups have strongly condemned Clipper and its companion Capstone (for data encryption) because of the potential for abuse and widespread monitoring of citizens. This technology is being developed with the help of the NSA, an organization that's *supposed* to keep its monitoring activities outside our borders. And that's not all. More recently, the administration reintroduced a digital telephony proposal that would require phone companies to provide real-time traffic analysis to all law enforcement agencies. Unlike a pen register, this is an ability that will always be there, one which simply has to be turned on. The data would then be sent to a remote monitoring post. According to the Electronic Frontier Foundation, such information amounts to more than just the numbers we dial: As we all come to use electronic communications for more and more purposes," a recent press release says. "This simple call setup information could also reveal what movies we've ordered, which online information services we've connected to, which political bulletin boards we've dialed, etc. With increasing use of telecommunications, this simple transactional information reveals almost as much about our private lives as would be learned if someone literally followed us around on the street, watching our every move."

Inspiration (Winter, 1994-1995)

The hacker world is constantly weaving from one extreme to the next; one day you may witness something that will be awe-inspiring and filled with a purpose, and the next you might see utter stupidity of one sort or another that shouldn't even be dignified with an acknowledgment. Elite versus lame.

It's all part of the beauty of our strange community where we can stay anonymous or shout our existence out to anyone who's listening—sometimes even to those who don't want to listen. We are a microcosm of democracy and we have to constantly fight with those who want to control the freedom we've built. At the same time, we have to be on the alert for destructiveness from within that could unravel our accomplishments with far more effectiveness than any outside enemy.

In early October, 1994, hackers of Argentina held their very first international conference. While communication between North American and European hackers has been growing steadily, not many of us had ever seen the hacker world of South America. Just as we were pleasantly surprised by what we found in Holland in 1989, we see tremendous promise and inspiration in Buenos Aires.

The hackers there are very hungry for information of any sort—cellular technology, international phreaking, access to the Internet—the list goes on and on. The eagerness with which any new idea or theory is embraced really puts a lot of what we do into perspective. Just being able to experiment and come up with new ways of doing things, new toys to play with, methods of linking the world together, that's where the real driving force of hacking is. It jumps all language and cultural barriers. And it's this that we really need to embrace.

For the people of Argentina, freedom is something that is not taken lightly. It wasn't long ago when young people who spoke up against the government or who did something deemed unacceptable by the junta would simply disappear and never be heard from again. People who understand technology and are willing to shape it to further individual liberty will always be near the top of the enemy list of a repressive regime. We can never close our eyes to this fact and we can never fool ourselves into thinking that we are safe from those malignant forces.

One of the most important goals for the hackers of Argentina is to get connected to the Internet. This remarkable crossroad will enable all of us to share their experiences and trade information of all sorts. We've almost become used to it here. But Net access is not a given in much of the world; in fact, quite a few people in power are nervous about the effect such access will have on the masses. It's rather difficult to keep people in check when they can easily assemble electronically or instantly communicate with people on the other side of the globe. And perhaps that's the whole point: Net access may be the tool that society has built in order to keep *governments* in check.

The bottom line is simply that once people get access to something as open and democratic as the Net, they won't be willing to let it go. That's why it's up to all of us who have the power to bring as many others into it as we can—at home and abroad.

As the world becomes more electronically integrated, it's up to those of us with the ability to constantly test and question. An excellent example of the importance of this came out of the United Kingdom over the summer when a Scottish hacker managed to get into British Telecom databases. By so doing, he gained access to thousands of pages of highly confidential records—the details of which were subsequently splattered across the pages of all of London's newspapers. Unlisted phone numbers for the Prime Minister and the Royal Family, secret Ministry of Defence installations, home addresses of senior military personnel, information on nuclear war bunkers, even the location of undercover intelligence service buildings in London.

The terrorist implications of such information should be obvious. If this information was so easy for one person to get, it should pose no problem for an organization. In this particular case, the hacker managed to infiltrate the system by getting a temporary job with British Telecom. No special screening was done and it was fantastically easy to get full access. This knowledge, coupled with the number of people who work for the phone company, made the course of action quite obvious: a full disclosure of all the data.

This caused a scandal of unimagined proportions. No computer intrusion had *ever* resulted in this many secrets getting out. But what choice was there? To remain silent and hope that nobody else would discover the gaping hole? To tell the authorities and hope that nobody else had already discovered the gaping hole and also hope that the authorities didn't immediately have you killed? Sometimes the only way to make a system secure is to call the vulnerabilities to *everybody's* attention. This is what the hacker did and now everybody has a pretty good idea of how secure British Telecom computers are as well as how much secret information is kept on them. We don't expect British Telecom to be happy but they have no one to blame but themselves.

An interesting sidenote to this is the computer system itself (the Customer Services System) was designed by Cincinnati Bell. Another interesting sidenote is the fact that this significant event has gone virtually unmentioned in American media.

So with all of this positive, inspirational stuff going on, what is it that we have to be on the lookout for? As we said, there are always forces that want to control freedom and, oftentimes, reverse it. And there are those within our own community who will, through carelessness, boredom, or even self-destructiveness give those outside forces exactly what they want.

Now would seem a perfect time for an activist group to sprout in order to keep the Net from becoming subverted by commercialization and overregulation. The manifesto of a group called the Internet Liberation Front gives the impression of pointed, and arrogant, idealism. Which is exactly what we needed. However, instead of attacking the real enemy of independent thought, this anonymous group chose to go after the author of a book! Josh Quittner, whose book on hackers, *Masters of Deception*, is due out in January, had his Internet mailbox flooded with ILF manifestoes. In addition, his phone line was forwarded to an obscene message. Typical hacker pranks, which probably never would have been taken seriously, except that this time it was done by a group with a manifesto. That's really all it takes to make headlines these days.

We hope to see a group come along one of these days that recognizes the importance of free speech and individual power. A group that isn't funded by phone companies like certain "civil liberties" organizations—a group that doesn't see the work of one author as a threat to the community. Ideas, even when they are dead wrong, are a doorway to discussion. Actions, however, carry the real threat.

Something we should all be aware of is the recent conviction of BBS operators Robert and Carleen Thomas in Memphis, Tennessee. The Amateur Action BBS was an adult-oriented board located in San Jose, California. One part of the board contained pictures similar to those found in x-rated magazines. A law enforcement official in Memphis called the board, downloaded some pictures, and actually managed to have the couple brought to Tennessee to face charges of distributing pornographic images via computer. Even though the board was in California, they were charged under the community standards of Tennessee which are significantly more conservative. A jury found them guilty and the couple was sentenced to approximately three years in prison with no hope of early release.

This happened right here in the United States in 1994, yet there was little press coverage and, consequently, little public outcry.

Obviously, these people must be freed and soon. That trial should never have even happened; if the moral standards of Tennessee are imposed upon the rest of the nation, rapidly spiraling de-evolution will become a fact of life for us all. And there will be virtually no limit on future targets. Apart from raising consciousness and spreading the word, those of us concerned with freedom of speech in the digital age should actively fight back against such atrocities. A good step would be to open a dozen boards to replace the one they shut down. Perhaps that will get the message across that electronic freedom is not to be trifled with. The Net and the digital age won't come anywhere near their potential unless courage is the key operating component.

Digital Telephony Passes (Winter, 1994-1995) *By Anonymous*

In the waning minutes of the 103rd Congress—10:30 p.m. on a Friday night, on the day before they went out of session, Congress approved the law enforcement takeover of the nation's (and the world's, really) phone system to make surveillance easier for themselves. Welcome to the future of communications and don't forget to smile when you bend over, otherwise Big Brother may paddle you also.

So What's the Bill All About?

If you liked Clipper, you'll love this new law. It requires that all telecommunications providers—big and small phone companies and anyone else who wants to provide phone service—redesign their old and new phone services with a built-in capability for Big Brother to have remote surveillance capability. To do this, it requires that all the telecom standards-setting bodies set their standards based on the U.S. Department of Justice's requirements. If the bodies don't do it to the liking of the FBI and NSA, the Federal Communications Commission can step in and set the standards themselves. In exchange, the telephone companies got a whopping $500 million in taxpayer money (yours and mine) to play with.

Another section of the bill requires that the phone companies buy as much equipment as requested by the FBI to ensure that they will have enough ports to jack into so they can tap in. New York's figures ought to be interesting.

There are several provisions that you hackers and phreaks should be interested in. As a "privacy protection" section, it is now illegal to listen in with a scanner on cordless telephones.

A "technical amendment" to the Electronic Communications Privacy Act now makes it perfectly legal for system operators to listen in on all electronic communications. No more worrying about those annoying disclaimers that if you logon to a particular computer, you are waiving your right to be left in private.

And finally, for you cellular hackers out there, beware: new amendments to 18 USC 1029 (that's the access control fraud law for you uninitiated out there) make it illegal to possess intending to use, sell, or give a cell phone that has been modified to make free calls or to traffic serial numbers, PINs, or the like.

What About the "Great Privacy Provisions" in the Bill?

In exchange for the most draconian provisions since the 1798 Alien and Sedition Act or the 1940 Smith Act, the DOJ was kind enough to give us a few trivial privacy provisions. Unlike the glowing statements of certain self-interested Trojan horse public interest groups, these really do very little for privacy.

There are limits of accessing of transaction records for online services, however, most of the material is available via a subpoena that any government bureaucrat can ask for. For the text of communications, a warrant is required but it is not a standard warrant.

Now it's also illegal to listen in on cordless telephones without a warrant. Does anyone really believe that with more than 100 million scanners out there that this provides any meaningful privacy protection? As long as the government tries to prevent the dissemination of cryptography, we cannot really expect meaningful communications privacy over wireless systems.

Why Did It Pass?

To put it bluntly, we were sold down the river. The FBI, with additional support from the CIA, the NSA, the Naval Intelligence, lobbied heavily for the bill. FBI Director Freeh even met personally with almost every member of Congress. When the final votes were taken, no recorded votes were tallied so there are no fingerprints for angry constituents.

The phone companies took the half billion and rolled over without a whimper. Oh, sure they carped a bit about how much more it would cost but they were really setting the stage to get more money from the public tit in three years when the first money dried up.

The Electronic Frontier Foundation, once a proud, principled group dedicated to civil liberties, is now funded completely by corporations such as AT&T, Bell Atlantic, MCI, and IBM. They followed the wishes of their corporate masters and cut a deal, then claimed victory for trivial privacy protections. At the last minute, EFF cofounder John Perry Barlow called Senator Malcolm Wallop, who was planning to kill the bill, and asked him to allow the bill to pass. Barlow said in comments on *The Well* that he wasn't proud of what he did but that it "was the price of growing up." As if selling one's soul to Satan was a sign of maturity. The FBI told senators' aides who were concerned about the bill after the public campaign organized by EPIC and Voters Telecom Watch, that "EFF supported the bill so there are no privacy concerns." Many people are still wondering if the lead content in the water fountains at their fancy new downtown offices had been checked lately.

What to Look Forward to Now?

Even before this bill passed, FBI Director Louis Freeh suggested that if the Clipper Chip didn't become as widely successful as the NSA and FBI would like, he would come back to Congress and ask for a ban of all cryptography that they don't keep the keys for. Already a bill was introduced last month that would give the NSA and FBI significant roles in setting all new crypto standards.

It doesn't seem terribly unlikely that next year, maybe the year following, we'll see another push on the hill by the FBI in the guise of a "technical amendment" to extend this bill to all online services. After all, we all know that there are a lot of nasty, dirty, dangerous people using Usenet, IRC, and gopher and shouldn't they be tapped like everyone else.

Anyway, don't just take my word or anyone else's for it, read the bill yourself. You can get a copy via `ftp/wais/gopher/www from cpsr.org /cpsr/privacy/communications/wiretap/hr4922_final.txt`.

News Items (Summer, 1995)

You don't need encryption to blow up a bomb. That's the lesson the Clinton administration seems to be having trouble learning. Almost immediately after the Oklahoma City bombing, there were cries on Capitol Hill for "broad new powers" to combat terrorism. According to FBI Director Louis Freeh, one of the biggest problems facing us today is that of criminals communicating on the Internet using encryption. "This problem must be resolved," they say. According to White House aides, Clinton will seek new FBI powers to monitor phone lines of suspected terrorists as well as more access to credit and travel records. Under the proposal, authorities will be able to do this without evidence of a criminal act underway or in the planning stages. Under the current situation, a lot of people are supporting this kind of a move without considering the consequences. Once such measures are undertaken, they have a history of being abused. In a land where tabloid television describes hackers as "computer terrorists," we wonder if the government is that far behind. After all, our own Bernie S. was denied bail, at least in part because he owned books that explained how explosives worked. With this kind of hysteria dictating enforcement, we shudder at the results of these proposals. In the case of Oklahoma City, one fact remains very clear. None of this would have helped. The suspects weren't significant enough to be noticed. And they didn't use encryption or the Net at all. And yet, the tabloids are screaming about the shocking speech that can be found on the Internet and how something has to be done to stop it. But curtailing speech and liberty never advances the cause of freedom and once begun is very difficult to reverse. Considering that it had no difficulty speaking out against the recent Communications Decency Act, which seeks to outlaw objectionable material over computer networks, the Clinton administration really should know better.

The Neverending Story (Summer, 1997)

Sometimes it seems as if the true driving force behind progress is sheer stupidity. Almost without fail, whenever something truly promising comes along, its true potential is either never realized or hopelessly crippled by fear, ignorance, or overregulation.

Anyone involved in the Internet will recognize this. Here we have something unprecedented in human history—the ability to communicate around the planet with people of all different varieties; to share knowledge in a way that has never been done before. It seems pretty apparent to us that this is a *good* thing. But fear and suspicion soon took control as the focus turned away from the amazing possibilities and instead centered on all of the worst-case scenarios we were able to conjure up in our minds. What if terrorists figured out how to send email? What if pedophiles communicated with children? What if copyrights became meaningless? What if we didn't know what the hackers were up to?

Just tune into your local evening TV news to get a taste of the fear mongering that takes place. If you find it funny and absurd, that's good. You recognize the mass media for what it is. But that's only the first step. Ridiculous as it may appear, the hysterical braying that surrounds us is actually believed by a great many people, including those people with the power to change things.

The Clinton administration, for one. Here we have the first administration in the history of our country that actually had a handle on what high technology was all about. They used the Net. They understood the potential of encryption. They quickly outgrew the antiquated communications systems that existed in Washington before their arrival. And then they tried to control it. They wanted encryption to be regulated and controlled by the government. They wanted digital phone systems to have monitoring capabilities built into them. They seemed to focus more on the potential misuses of the Net and how to punish offenders rather than recognize it as the single most powerful tool of communication and free speech that has ever been known to humanity. The lesson here is that power and awareness don't always add up to fairness. Regardless of what kind of political system is in place, such advances for the common people are almost always looked upon as a threat to those in power.

Of course we have people like Senator Exon, who managed to get the Communications Decency Act passed into law by people in power too scared to stand up to this flagrant violation of the First Amendment. Everyone knew that this legislation went against the Constitution. But who in the government had the guts to stand up and say that indecency was protected speech? Only the Supreme Court, which threw the CDA out earlier this summer. Not the House, not the Senate, not the President. And certainly not the media. They were willing to throw it all away just to avoid being associated with something controversial.

This was a hollow victory because so much time and effort had to be wasted to fight something that was so obviously wrong in the first place. Meanwhile people like Robert Thomas, Bernie S., and Kevin Mitnick are persecuted with little attention because civil liberties groups have their hands tied with stupidity like the CDA and because the public has been conditioned not to care.

But the facts remain. Robert Thomas and his wife were taken away from their family and put in prison for three years because their adult bulletin board in California offended someone in Memphis who called it on their own volition. It could have happened to literally anyone. Those reading *2600* regularly should be quite familiar with the Bernie S. story, where the Secret Service managed to imprison Bernie for nearly two years for possession of electronic parts that almost any hacker would have and which could be used for all sorts of perfectly legitimate things. And, of course, Kevin

Mitnick's continuing plight seems to have no end in sight: indefinite prison time not so much for anything he's done (more than two years later this has yet to be clearly defined) but for what the rest of us are afraid he *could* do.

Nothing we say can illustrate this as well as Mitnick's conditions of supervised release, which will go into effect for a number of years *after* he's released from prison which, it would seem, the government believes should be never. Pay close attention to these restrictions because you will undoubtedly see more of them:

> *"The defendant shall not possess or use for any purpose the following:*
>
> *any computer hardware equipment; any computer software programs; any modems; any computer related peripherals or support equipment; any portable laptop computers; personal information assistants and derivatives; any cellular phone; any television; any instruments of communications equipped with online Internet, world wide web, or other computer network access; any other electronic equipment presently available or new technology that becomes available that can be converted to or has as its function the ability to act as a computer system or to access a computer system, computer network, or telecommunications network, except defendant may possess a landline telephone;*
>
> *The defendant shall not be employed or perform services for any entity engaged in the computer, computer software, or telecommunications business and shall not be employed in any capacity where he will have access to computers or computer related equipment or software;*
>
> *The defendant shall not access computers, computer networks, or other forms of wireless communications himself or through third parties;*
>
> *The defendant shall not act as a consultant or advisor to individuals or groups engaged in any computer related activity;*
>
> *The defendant shall not acquire or possess any computer codes including computer passwords, cellular phone access codes or other access devices that enable the defendant to use, acquire, exchange, or alter information in a computer or telecommunications database system;*
>
> *The defendant shall not use or possess any data encryption device, program, or technique for computers or any other purpose;*
>
> *The defendant shall not alter or possess any altered telephone, telephone equipment, or any other communications related equipment;*
>
> *The defendant shall not use any telephone or telephone related equipment for purposes other than to speak directly to another person;*
>
> *The defendant shall only use his true name and not use any alias or other false identity."*

Again, if you find this funny and absurd, that's good. But this is also scary as hell and something that should not be ignored by anyone. This is by no means an isolated case. Other people are being faced with these kinds of restrictions at an alarming rate. It tells us that the authorities are very wary of almost *any* form of technology (even a television set!) and are prepared to restrict access whenever possible. We find the item about not being allowed to use encryption especially telling. It's no longer enough to confine someone to a certain space and to restrict their movements. Now, *anything* that can be used to achieve privacy is seen as a threat and something to be restricted. Even speech is being regulated: Mitnick isn't allowed to advise people on the subject that he knows best. And, according to this, it would be a violation for him to use voice mail since he wouldn't be using a telephone "to speak directly to another person." We wonder just what it is they expect Mitnick to do when he gets out. It seems that life in our society will be nearly impossible for him.

These conditions demonstrate an utter lack of understanding of technology and would seem to prove quite conclusively that the motivating factor behind them is fear. If you believe that someone like Mitnick is capable of doing anything in the world with a telephone or an electronic device, then these words start to make a little more sense. But judges aren't supposed to think simplistically and in tabloid style like two-bit Hollywood directors out to make a quick buck by creating cheap fantasy. They should be attempting to grasp the basic concepts of the technology that now affects them, rather than letting their emotions and fears dictate their rulings. And we should be watching over them prepared to speak out when things like this occur. Because, eventually, one way or another, the rulings, shortsightedness, and fear will have a profound effect on our lives.

MILESTONE: PROGRESS (Autumn, 1998)

The summer of '98 was one of the most productive times we've seen in a while. And from the looks of it, it's just the start of yet another phase in whatever evolution we're going through.

We've said often that every time we get hit with something, whether it be word of a chilling raid somewhere, a moronic law that has no basis in reality, or something a lot closer to home, we wind up actually *gaining* strength when the dust clears.

Well, the dust is far from clearing but it's pretty obvious that we're heading someplace with renewed vigor. The hacker spirit is self-invigorating and it's surprising how many people either never realize this or forget it rather quickly as they move on in life.

MILESTONE: PROGRESS *(continued)*

Let's start with the close to home stuff. It was a year ago that we first told you about our crippling financial problems, caused primarily by our main distributors going bankrupt and taking a year's worth of our sales with them. We knew we weren't going to let this destroy all we've accomplished over the years but we felt we needed to explain why things might get sort of frozen and unhappy in the months ahead.

To the surprise of many, we didn't stagnate at all. Against the advice of everyone with a modicum of sense, we went forward with new issues, new projects, and new campaigns. We are eternally grateful to those of you who stuck with us in this difficult period, which, we are happy to say, is now behind us. Thanks to strong sales at the newsstands, we've been able to pay just about all of our printing debts and, by the time you read this, we should be entirely caught up. We lost a number of subscribers and we can certainly understand why. If there was even a remote possibility of our going under, who would want to lose their subscription payment? Now that we're back in force, we hope to see the subscription numbers go back up. The advantages to subscribing: you'll get your issues on time every quarter, you'll be able to take out marketplace ads for free, and you'll occasionally get extra things like the "Free Kevin" stickers we threw in with the Spring issue. We're not trying to discourage people from picking us up at the bookstores and newsstands but we feel it's important to also have a strong subscriber base in case we run into another distributor/bookstore catastrophe down the road.

While we lost a year financially, we were able to minimize our setbacks when it came to the truly important things. Since launching the "Free Kevin" campaign earlier this year, we've managed to raise nearly $3,000 for Kevin Mitnick's defense fund through the sale of our bumper stickers. By revamping the `www.kevinmitnick.com` and `www.2600.com` sites, we were able to get many more people interested, and hence involved, in something that really mattered.

Violence, Vandals, Victims (Winter, 1999-2000)

As the '90s fade into history, it's not likely the unhealthy trends of our society will do the same anytime soon. In many ways we've become practically enslaved to the corporate agenda, to the great detriment of the individual.

The signs have been around for a while. You've seen them repeatedly in these pages. People interested in technology who ask too many questions or probe too deeply or thoroughly are seen as a threat because they might adversely affect profits or embarrass those in authority. The Net has steadily been transforming from a place where freedom of speech is paramount to one where it all revolves around the needs of business.

Now there's nothing wrong with commerce, people making a profit, or even people who just don't care about the things others value. After all, there's room for all types in the world as well as on the Net. But that's not how it's panning out. Increasingly, the needs of the individual are being sacrificed for the needs of big business. Corporate mentality is replacing our sense of individual liberty. And it's pointing us down a very dark road.

Consider things that have happened in the very recent past.

A teenage hacker named Zyklon from Washington State pleaded guilty to hacking several prominent government web sites, including the White House and the United States Information Agency. Despite there being no damage caused to any of the sites (apart from embarrassment and having the `index.html` file renamed), the government felt that 15 months in prison and a $40,000 fine was appropriate. Reports say he *could have gotten* 15 years and a $250,000 fine.

Later that same month, coincidentally in the same state, police fired tear gas and shot rubber bullets at a crowd of peaceful demonstrators who were protesting the World Trade Organization's meeting in Seattle. Many said it was the worst civil unrest since Vietnam.

At first glance, you might not think these stories have very much to do with one another. But when you analyze them a little more closely, it's not difficult to see that they are both symptoms of the same disease.

Much of the unprovoked brutality inflicted by the Seattle police went unreported, despite the abundance of sound and picture images. But every major network dutifully ran a story about the "violent anarchists" who started all the trouble. In the end, whenever the word "violence" was mentioned, one thought only of those people.

Zyklon caused no damage to any of the systems he got into. Yet the mass media painted him as someone dangerous. He renamed a file. But all reports say that he shut down the USIA for eight days. This is how long it took them to *install* decent security, something they had never bothered to do in the first place. He didn't take away their security; they never had it to begin with. But this fact wasn't seen as relevant in any of the stories that ran. And what about the act of taking a young person away from his friends and family for more than a year and forcing him to live with potentially dangerous criminals? Well... *that's* justice.

In both cases that which is most precious to our society—the individual—was made to suffer because their actions and form of expression caused humiliation of some greater power. We've seen this before in the hacker world with Bernie S. and Kevin Mitnick (who is at last scheduled for release on January 21, 2000). People who go to forbidden places, utter forbidden speech, or are just seen as an inconvenience are stepped on, abused, even tortured.

Why punish such relatively harmless individuals, whether they be hackers or demonstrators, with such passionate vengeance? Could it be that their very existence constitutes a real threat that the authorities have no idea how to handle?

In Seattle, the disparities between what happened and what was reported were almost comical—vandalism of commercial property being reported as violence whereas violence against individuals was mostly glossed over, with the exception of certain foreign and alternative media. What kind of a society are we turning into when commercial losses are more important than the human injuries? How could the good people of Time/Warner (CNN) have missed this? Or Microsoft and General Electric (MSNBC)? Or even Disney (ABC)? Why would such bastions of journalism ignore the real story? Were they maybe more concerned with whether the WTO would continue to look out for them and their interests?

We may indeed have developed a horribly cynical outlook on society. It's hard not to when things like this are so often tolerated. But the flipside is that our view of the individual has only strengthened. If there's one thing we've learned from recent events, it's that people aren't as brain dead as we were led to believe. People *do* care, they *are* paying attention, and they see the ominous tones of the future. Few persons seem to trust the government anymore, big business is increasingly seen as a threat to our freedom, and individual troublemakers are filling our expanding prison system.

It's not very difficult to see how we got to this sorry state. All of the mergers and consolidation of power have carried a heavy and inevitable price. The real question is how do we regain control of our destinies?

The answer has been staring us in the face for some time. And Seattle was the first opportunity to apply it on a somewhat massive scale.

The technology that has been developing over the years is unquestionably of great benefit to whoever decides to make use of it. The relatively open architecture of the Internet lends itself to a great variety of applications, not just for those with the most power. That is its magnetic allure and it's also the reason everyone in authority is scared to death of it. The Net represents the true potential of the individual and individuals are the most formidable enemy of any oppressive regime.

As the crowds were gassed and shot at, the mass media looked elsewhere. They found a small group who, in the mayhem, had taken to vandalism, smashing windows and torching cars. This became the only "violence" most Americans saw on their televisions. Businesses were the victim, individuals the cause. Newspaper chains ran editorials condemning this "violence" against property, ignoring the assault on the people, and endorsing the continued existence of the WTO. Anyone who was surprised by this simply hadn't been paying attention. When you look at how power has been consolidating in recent years, this kind of coverage makes perfect sense.

But then there was the Net. The same Net that is encroached upon daily by those in power. The one that governments around the world continue to try to regulate. It was the Internet that finally broke through the manipulation and allowed the world to see, firsthand, what was actually happening.

Strategically placed webcams showed everyone what was really going on in the streets. Mailing lists and newsgroups allowed anyone to instantly write their experiences and get them out to the rest of the world. Any person with a tape recorder was able to go out and get sound, then encode it so that people from anywhere could listen. Almost as many people managed to do the same thing with video. Within hours, dozens of these independent media pieces were traversing the planet, all without control or censorship. And, in one of the most shining examples of free speech we've witnessed in a long time, a "pirate" radio station broadcasting live from the streets of Seattle was able to get its signal streamed onto the Net so that people anywhere could listen to its weak but captivating signal. (We put quotes around the word "pirate" because it seems ironic that such free speech on the public airwaves would be illegal while it's perfectly acceptable for one single corporation to control close to a thousand far more powerful stations.)

You probably didn't hear about any of this in the mainstream media for the same reason you didn't hear about what Kevin Mitnick actually did to warrant being locked away for five years. Why dwell on the psychological and physical torture that Bernie S. endured, all because the Secret Service was mad at him? Wouldn't more ad space be sold if Zyklon were shown as an electronic terrorist rather than a simple juvenile delinquent? It's far easier to portray events with the smoke and mirrors we saw in a recent MTV slander piece on hackers as well as so many other corporate media fiascoes. The facts only serve to complicate matters and muddy the message. And people are stupid, after all. All they want is to be entertained and nothing stands in the way of that more than the truth. Right?

The tide has turned. It may take some time, but it seems obvious to us that not everyone is buying into the propaganda. We'll see many more individuals whose punishment far outweighs their crime and we'll see the media distort the facts time and time again. But one thing we know we have now that may be the biggest comfort of all—awareness. That, combined with the technology that we must never let them take away, will be enough to start reaching others.

Part III: 2000 and Beyond: A Changing Landscape

14 The Lawsuits

I used to think that chapter divisions were artificial and that they detracted somewhat from the flow when telling a story. But fate dictated otherwise with regards to the tale of *2600*. Not only did a brand new adventure begin literally on the day that an old one ended, but the dividing line of the year 2000, Y2K, and the conclusion of the Mitnick saga really added a symmetry that I would have thoroughly disbelieved—had I not been there when it all happened.

The year 2000 was indeed the Year of the Lawsuit on the Hacker Calendar. It was like nothing I had ever seen before. Sure, we had gotten our share of lawsuit *threats* in the past. Actually, we got a bit *more* than our share but that was perfectly OK. We *lived* for this kind of a thing. Whenever we had gotten a letter from some angry attorney threatening us with all sorts of unspecified harm if we didn't immediately comply with whatever demands they felt like making, we usually diffused the situation in our own unique style by printing the entire diatribe in the magazine, letterhead and all. The ensuing bad publicity nearly always resulted in nothing else ever being heard on the subject. But we always learned a bit more with each instance. We found out that people *were* in fact reading our magazine and that sometimes our words really pissed off some pretty powerful entities. Cool.

Many people have told us over the years that the way we dealt with these situations was the way they always wished *they* could have. (And some of these folks were actually inside the very same companies that were threatening us!) Obviously, a mere individual had little chance of getting the same level of attention that we could get by challenging these threats. In spite of all the talk of the communications revolution and the digitization of speech, there was still something special about printing ink on paper. The threats, the reactions, the resolutions, it all seemed to somehow count for more when it was in a physical form. And I think that's why we always seemed to wind up front and center in these battles.

What happened in 2000 went beyond what we had grown accustomed to. It really shocked the hell out of us because it wasn't the sort of thing anyone at *2600* figured would be what finally got us hauled in front of a judge. We printed *so many* controversial articles over the years, after all. When we posted the code on our web site to a computer program that was simply designed to allow DVDs to be played on Linux machines, it honestly didn't seem *that* exciting. Oh, but it most definitely was.

The Motion Picture Association of America and all of the major studios that they represented saw the release of this code as a threat to their future control of the DVD industry. To explain briefly, in order for a standard commercial DVD to be played, it first has to be decrypted. Only "licensed" DVD players were supposedly allowed to do this. Unfortunately (for the MPAA and friends), the encryption key (CSS) that was supposed to be kept secret wasn't very well protected. Its release allowed programs (such as DeCSS) to successfully perform the decryption. And in so doing, it became possible to play a DVD on *any* machine, in any part of the world (bypassing the artificial region codes that prevented discs from one country from playing in the machines of a different country), and in a manner chosen by the consumer (such as being able to skip over normally "locked" advertisements that viewers had been forced to play in full). None of this ever had anything to do with *copying* DVDs, despite that misconception constantly being reported during our trial. The simple fact is that you don't even *need* to decrypt a DVD in order to copy it. The ultimate proof that this case wasn't really about piracy came outside the federal courthouse in New York City where, during our trial, street vendors were openly selling illegal copies of movies a block away! No, this was a case about controlling the technology itself and not allowing consumers the ability to manipulate things in a way that suited them. This is what really bothered the industry.

We were literally hand-picked out of the thousands of other web sites that had mirrored the DeCSS code. By taking a hacker magazine to court, the MPAA figured the decision would already be made in the judge's eyes. It was an astute move on their part. And, though we lost the case and ultimately the appeal, we felt we had opened up a lot of eyes in the process. The Digital Millennium Copyright Act (DMCA), which made this court case possible, was now on the radar of everyone concerned with consumer rights and free speech. There would certainly be more cases. (We had planned on appealing all the way to the Supreme Court but it became rather clear that they would not have ruled in our favor and such a precedent-setting decision could have been harmful to the overall cause.)

Suing *2600* seemed to be in vogue as this new chapter in the hacker world continued to unfold. We literally seemed to be getting threatening letters every few weeks. In one instance we noticed that Verizon had registered all sorts of sites that contained critical statements towards them (`verizonsucks.com`, `verizonblows.com`, etc.) so we thought it would be funny to register one that they had missed—`verizonREALLYsucks.com`. We quickly got a threatening letter from them, which we naturally published, then we went and registered `VerizonShouldSpendMoreTimeFixingItsNetworkAndLessMoneyOnLawyers.com` (taking full advantage of the recently increased domain length limit). This got all sorts of publicity and an eventual public statement from Verizon saying that they recognized the free speech aspect of this and would pursue no action against us. It was heartening, to say the least.

We also found ourselves in court in Detroit at the request of the Ford Motor Company who took umbrage at our registering a web site that poked fun at General Motors and then redirected itself over to Ford. It was as if corporate America had decided to save paper and skip over the threatening letters entirely. They simply sued us with no warning. This case was really absurd because the entire nature of the Internet allows for sites to be pointed at all sorts of other places. Not only was it ridiculous to claim damages when someone you didn't like redirected a web site to you, but it was also a trivial manner to disable this at the receiving end. We beat Ford on this one and hopefully sent a message to anyone else planning on wasting time in court. Free speech would be defended on all levels.

In short, this was a very interesting period in history. Litigation was flying all over the place, not just with us but with all sorts of people and companies as everyone tried to figure out where the digital world was going. There were other DMCA cases, the Recording Industry of America was taking on Napster, and words like "BitTorrent" and "peer to peer" became front page news almost overnight. Meanwhile there were all kinds of other battles going on in the free speech arena that seemed pretty earth shattering in nature. In the end, I think we wound up stronger as a result and with a whole lot more resolve. For that, I must sincerely thank our detractors.

Here then is a sampling of some of the fun as it unfolded, including one of many alternative ways we tried to spread the DeCSS code: in actual English language words.

The Next Chapter (Spring, 2000)

It's over. And yet, it's just beginning.

We've always known that the Kevin Mitnick saga was about so much more than one man's fight against injustice or even the future of the hacker world. With increasing intensity, events of the past five years have given us reflections of where our society is going—and what we are losing along the way.

Five years is a very long time. Consider where you were and what you were doing on February 15, 1995, the day Mitnick's ordeal behind bars began. So much has changed, especially in the world of technology. But five years doesn't even begin to tell the story. You would have to go back to 1992 if you wanted to include the years Mitnick spent on the run trying to avoid capture and as far as 1988 to include the case, which supposedly cast him in such a fearful light as to warrant eight months of solitary confinement—obviously a motivating factor in later fleeing the authorities even when the alleged violation was trivial. When you add up the confinement and the supervised release, Mitnick has not had a truly free day since 1988 and won't again until 2003. That's *15 years* of a life. And all for someone who never stole, caused damage, or made a profit through his crimes.

What a tremendous waste of time this ordeal has been. And what a waste of talent when you consider what Mitnick could have contributed to our world over all these years. And still, there is a very definite case to be made for the significance of it all. Never before have we seen such awareness and education on the part of the hacker community. Word of Mitnick's case spread to schools all around the world, people protested outside federal buildings and embassies, and a major motion picture exploiting the Mitnick story was exposed and prevented from spreading most of its blatant lies. While this didn't alleviate the suffering and may not have shortened Mitnick's time behind bars, it at least focused attention on the unfairness rather than on the tabloid headlines. And it made us all the more wary of what the authorities were planning for the future.

In our case, we didn't have to wait long.

In fact, it was with the precision of a soap opera that one crisis was immediately succeeded by the next. On the very day before Kevin Mitnick's release, we at *2600* became the latest targets of a world gone mad with litigation and incarceration.

It was only days earlier that a massive lawsuit had been filed against us by the Motion Picture Association of America. That's right, those people who give ratings to movies. Apparently, that's not all they do. Representing some of the most powerful entities in the world (Columbia/Tristar, Universal City, Paramount, Disney, Twentieth Century Fox, MGM, and Time Warner), the MPAA targeted *2600* and a handful of others, claiming that we were somehow responsible for threatening the entire DVD industry and the future of motion pictures.

What were they smoking? Good question. We still don't know. But this is the truth of the matter: In November, some enterprising hackers were able to figure out how to play the DVDs they had already purchased on their Linux machines. By doing this, they were able to bypass the access control that the DVD industry put on the technology, a draconian control, which had never been implemented in other consumer devices like CD players, VCRs, or walkmans. And it was this control that had made it impossible for computers not running an "approved" operating system (such as Windows or Mac OS) to play DVDs. By defeating this control, the hackers got around this absurd restriction. To the industry however, they had created doubt as to who was in control and, as we saw with the Mitnick case and so many others, people with power who fear losing control of it behave irrationally and will spare no effort or expense to neutralize the perceived threat.

When the DVD encryption was defeated, hackers, as is their instinct, told the world and made the source code available. This resulted in threats being made against them for daring to figure it out. As a show of support, we posted the source code on our web site, as did many others. We actually thought reason would prevail—until one day in late December `webmaster@2600.com` was served (via email) with legal papers from the DVD Copy Control Association. We thought it was pretty funny that a lawsuit could be emailed and even funnier still that they actually believed they could prevail in such a manner. We don't even have a working DVD player and here they were accusing us of piracy. Not to mention the fact that we weren't even involved in figuring it out in the first place.

They sent out legal threats against all kinds of people all around the world using whatever bizarre alias the web sites might have been registered under. But there were also lots of people whose real names were used. We saw it as an incredible waste of money and effort on the part of the DVD CCA, which nobody took very seriously. For one thing, the court they filed the lawsuit with had no jurisdiction outside of California.

But the humor was soon to wear off. On January 14, the MPAA stepped into the fray with guns blazing. Lawsuits were filed against four *individuals* including the editor of *2600* and the owner of an Internet Service Provider who wasn't even aware of the existence of the code that was on one of his customer's web pages. We saw this as a clear intimidation tactic—after all, is Bill Gates summoned to court every time Microsoft is sued?

But intimidation was only the first part. We were about to learn a lesson about corporate manipulation of federal courts.

The first clumsy attempt to serve us with papers was made after 6:00 p.m. on a Friday afternoon. (They never actually succeeded in serving the papers but apparently dropping them on the ground is good enough these days.) A second attempt was made to serve our post office box for reasons we'll never know. Perhaps they thought our offices were within the post office somewhere.

Despite this non-serving of legal documents and despite the fact that the following Monday was a holiday, all of the defendants were ordered to have their entire defense submitted to the court by 7:00 a.m. Wednesday, leaving exactly one day to prepare. Even with the Electronic Frontier Foundation stepping in to help us, this was simply an impossible and extremely unreasonable feat for all of the defendants.

On the following Thursday, January 20, a preliminary injunction was summarily granted against us which pretty much forced us to take the offending material off of our web site or face immediate imprisonment for "contempt of court." Hard as this was for us to accept, we complied, believing that we could fight the battle a lot more effectively without being locked away. Since then many hundreds of sites have mirrored the offending material in a demonstration of electronic civil disobedience. We have in turn put links on our site to these other locations.

Methodically, the MPAA has threatened each and every one of the owners of these sites, which has led to even more new sites going up. While the court order against us does not prohibit our publishing links, we fear that, given the mood of the court, it will be expanded to include this in the future. If that happens, we will convert our links to a list. If *that* gets banned, we will mention the other sites in a paragraph of English text. In other words, we will stand against this kind of restriction until either they back down or we are stripped of our right to speak at all. That is how important this is.

The MPAA is coming at us using a very scary piece of law that civil libertarians have been wanting to challenge since its inception. It's called the Digital Millennium Copyright Act and it basically makes it illegal to reverse engineer technology. This means you're not allowed to take things apart and figure out how they work if the corporate entities involved don't want you to. With today's technology, you are not actually *buying* things like DVDs; you are merely buying a *license* to use them under their conditions. So, under the DMCA, it *is* illegal to play your DVD on your computer if your computer isn't licensed for it. It's illegal for you to figure out a way to play a European DVD on your TV set. And if you rent a DVD from your local video store, figuring out a way to bypass the commercials in the beginning could land you in court or even prison.

It sounds absurd because it *is* absurd. And that is precisely why we're not going to back down on this and why others should take up the fight before things get any worse. The world the MPAA and the megacorporations want us to live in is a living hell. They are motivated by one factor alone and that is greed. If they can make you buy the same thing multiple times, they will. If they can control the hardware as well as the software, they will. If they can prevent equal access to technology by entities not under their umbrella, they will. And you can bet that if they have to lie, cheat, and deceive to accomplish this, they most definitely will.

Let's take a look at what the MPAA has been saying publicly. When the injunction was granted against us, they called it a victory for artists and a strike against piracy. The newspapers and media outlets—most of them owned by the same companies that are suing us—dutifully reported just that. But anyone who does even the smallest amount of research can quickly surmise that this case has got nothing at all to do with piracy. It has *always* been possible to copy DVDs and there are massive warehouses in other parts of the world that do just that. But that apparently isn't as much of a threat as people *understanding* how the technology works. Sound familiar? It's the same logic that the feds have used to imprison those hackers who *explain* things to other people while not even prosecuting the individuals who do actual damage. The real threat, in their eyes, is people like us, who believe in spreading information and understanding technology. By painting us as evil villains out to rip off DVDs and ruin things for everyone, they are deceiving the public in a way that we've become all too familiar with.

Those of us who have been watching the ominous trends in this country might have been able to predict this battle. It was less than a year ago that *Satellite Watch News* was put out of business by General Motors' DirecTV because they didn't like the specific information they printed about the workings of satellite technology. We knew it was only a matter of time before one of these fantastically powerful corporations turned their eye on us. And now we have no less than eight of them lined up against us in a court where we are by default the bad guys.

We've learned a lot over the last few years, much of it from the hacker cases we've been close to. From Phiber Optik to Bernie S. to Kevin Mitnick, we've seen how justice is manipulated and the heavy cost that is borne by individuals. And we've also learned how to respond to it.

The demonstration against Miramax helped stop a truly unjust film from being made, at least in its original form. The Free Kevin movement focused attention on someone who might otherwise have been lost in the system. And we shudder to think what might have happened had people not rallied against the barbaric treatment of Bernie S. in the prison system. What we learned is that we *do* make a difference when we believe in our cause.

In more than 100 cities on February 4, people affiliated with the monthly *2600* meetings and people in countless other towns and cities worldwide took part in a massive leafleting campaign to spread the word about the MPAA. Judging by the many accounts we received, it was extremely effective and successful. Once again we are in the position of getting the word out to the people who the mass media ignore.

That is where we have to focus our efforts and not only because of the MPAA threat. Some of the things being planned are incredibly frightening and *will* have a profound impact on our community, not to mention what it will do to society. It would be a big mistake to assume that the battle has ended with Mitnick's release. Complacency will destroy us and freethinkers everywhere.

On March 7, voters in California overwhelmingly approved Proposition 21, which allows *prosecutors* to decide which youthful offenders are to be tried as adults. In other words, judges will now be entirely bypassed. While the measure was called the Gang Violence and Juvenile Crime Prevention Act Initiative, its effects will extend well beyond that. A kid hacking a web site would be tried and sentenced as an adult if the prosecution decides to go that route. That means we can look forward to more cases of hackers being put into prisons with dangerous offenders. Only now age won't matter. Combine this with California's "Three Strikes" law and it's entirely possible that the next Kevin Mitnick will be put away for life. That's the kind of sick society we're turning into.

We see similar scenarios unfolding all over the country. In New York, Senator Charles Schumer has proposed a bill that would allow teenage hackers to be tried as adults and would eliminate the need to prove *any* damage was caused before the FBI steps in.

Much of this hysteria has been caused by the recent Denial of Service attacks against some major corporate web sites. While this kind of thing has existed on the Net since Day One, when it started affecting the biggest moneymakers on the Web it suddenly became a major crisis. And, not surprisingly, hackers were targeted as the cause even when it became quickly apparent that there was virtually no way to track down the culprits. It also was pretty clear that this kind of thing is relatively easy to do. But the media didn't focus on that nor on the obvious fact that if hackers were so bent on destroying the Net then this sort of thing would constantly be happening on a massive scale. That simply wasn't the story they wanted to report. What *was* reported? Almost word for word: "This was a very easy thing to do. Anybody could have done it. We may never find out who was behind it. But *hackers are responsible*."

In a response that was suspiciously quick and well-prepared, the Clinton administration came up with all kinds of new legislation and budget requests to crack down on hackers. *2600* and others began getting hate mail from people incensed that we would do such a horrible thing to the Internet. Once again, hackers had become the enemy without lifting a finger.

In a somewhat bizarre twist, the government that helped lock Kevin Mitnick away then sought out his advice on the whole matter of hackers by inviting him to testify before the Senate. While no doubt struggling with the temptation to tell these lawmakers where they could go after the horrible way he was treated, Mitnick chose to take the high road and attempt to educate the senators. His subsequent visit to Capitol Hill seemed to have a real positive effect, as the senators saw someone who wasn't a dark and evil cyberterrorist but rather a warm and open individual with nothing to hide. It called into question not only his imprisonment but the absurd conditions of his supervised release, which forbid him from lifting up a cellular phone or having any kind of contact with a computer.

Maybe it had an effect on them and maybe it didn't. What's important is that Mitnick didn't give up hope that things could be changed for the better if communication was allowed. And if anyone has earned the right to give up on the system, he has.

We have what appears to be a long and difficult road ahead. Judging from the sheer size and determination of our adversaries combined with the indisputable significance of the upcoming trial, this may be the opportunity to put us out of corporate America's misery once and for all.

The Mitnick case may have taught us what we need to know to fight this battle. That knowledge combined with the optimism that Mitnick himself personifies, is the best shot we have at getting through this.

Madness (Summer, 2000)

While many are deeply distressed, who among us can say they're surprised at the unfolding events of this year? Anyone who can needs to start paying closer attention.

Corporate America has gone mad with litigation and its obsession with the Net. Meanwhile, governments the world over are doing everything possible to close the Pandora's Box of freedom the Net has created. It's getting pretty ugly out there.

Our troubles are only a small part of the story. Sure, we've never faced this kind of corporate venom before. But when things like the Telecommunications Act of 1996, Digital Telephony, the Digital Millennium Copyright Act (DMCA), and "anti-cybersquatting" bills win easy passage, it's inevitable. The Internet, once the shining beacon of free speech, cultural exchange, and open expression is fast becoming the exclusive property of big business and oppressive regimes. At least, this is how it appears in their minds. We cannot let our own perceptions be corrupted by this invalid premise.

How else would it be possible to claim that a piece of email (the "ILOVEYOU virus") could cause $10 *billion* in damage and that, once again, hackers are responsible? How would it be possible to completely gloss over the fact that, once again, all of the problems were because of a gaping weakness in a program called Microsoft Outlook and that this is a lesson that should have been learned from the Melissa virus a year earlier? Very few in the hacker world have been affected by any of these demonstrations of stupidity and it's because we know not to blindly trust programs (particularly ones from Microsoft) when it comes to security issues. The corporate media misses this vital point and instead looks at hackers as the cause of the problem, when anybody in the world could have done this simply by sending email.

The way the media covers things is only a small symptom of a problem that continues to get worse. Several years ago it would have been almost unheard of for a corporation to bully someone into submission on the Net using nothing but its might. Today we seem to hear of a new case every day.

No doubt a lot of what's happening is bolstered by court developments such as those that are proceeding against us. And if we were to back down and agree that it was acceptable to deny people the right to know how technology works, a dangerous precedent would be set and then you would see a hundred more lawsuits filed for "offenses" ranging from writing source code to writing articles *about* source code.

It's safe to say that new developments in technology are scaring the corporate world to death. What milestones like Napster represent to them is a potential loss of the control they've held for so long. Whereas before, record companies (yes, most of the major ones are owned by the same corporations suing us under the DMCA) made the decision as to what music would become popular, now the potential exists for *people* to do this on their own and completely bypass the traditional means of distribution. There's little debate that this could erode some of the massive profits these companies currently enjoy. But it's far less clear that artists themselves would be adversely affected. Many, particularly those who aren't already in bed with the record companies, have come out in full support of Napster and the increased ability for the consumer to choose. Naturally, the music industry has distorted the issues in this case in much the same way the motion picture industry has distorted the ones in ours. For one thing, all Napster does is point people to sites that have the music they're interested in. One could even consider that to be a service to anyone wanting to shut those sites down. Another issue is that the record companies seem to believe they have the right to make money every time someone hears a song they own. This is the same mentality that has made it *illegal* for Girl Scouts to sing "Happy Birthday" around a campfire. The truth is, they *don't* have this inalienable right to get paid each and every time someone plays their music. Unless we give it to them. The Net is merely a new medium, the modern day equivalent of trading cassettes with friends. In fact, CD sales have been *increasing* over the past year. The record companies' reaction? They would have increased even *more* were it not for MP3s and things like Napster. Right. Eventually, they will lose this battle but not before wasting a lot of time and money trying to stifle the development of technology.

A wise man once wrote, "That ideas should freely spread from one to another over the globe, for the moral and mutual instruction of man, and improvement of his condition, seems to have been peculiarly and benevolently designed by nature, when she made them, like fire, expansible over all space, without lessening their density at any point, and like the air in which we breathe, move, and have our physical being, incapable of confinement or exclusive appropriation. Inventions then cannot, in nature, be a subject of property."

That wise man was Thomas Jefferson.

We don't favor piracy in any way. People who *sell* CDs that they have burned are clearly making a profit off of someone else's work. But sharing music over the Net is just not the same thing. In all likelihood, more people will be exposed to new artists as a result, meaning the record companies will no longer be the only way they can reach the public. This obviously works much better with artists who are *looking* for exposure on the Net. Those who don't want their material spread in this way should make their wishes known, but we cannot see how, short of banning anonymity altogether, it would be at all possible to prevent people from trading music.

Such thoughts are not at all far from the controversy. In recent remarks at a conference, Edgar Bronfman, chairman of Seagram, which owns Universal, which, yes, is suing us under the DMCA, came up with this gem: "Anonymity... means being able to get away with stealing, or hacking, or disseminating illegal material on the Internet—and presuming the right that nobody should know who you are. There is no such right. This is nothing more than the digital equivalent of putting on a ski mask when you rob a bank." Make no mistake, anonymity is as much a perceived threat to corporate America as encryption has been to the Clinton administration. In both instances, the very fabric that defines the Net is being remodeled by people who have no right at all to do this. Unless we let them.

And then there's speech. Free speech has always been the enemy of those seeking to exert massive control. Now that legislation has made it possible for this control to be extended to the Net, we can look forward to increasing attacks on mere speech. For instance, if you intend to register a domain name that is critical of a corporation, watch out!

It used to be that you could criticize whoever you wanted and, as long as you weren't libelous, your rights were respected. That's all changing. George W. Bush said it best when he tried to shut down `www.gwbush.com` for being critical of him: "There ought to be limits to freedom." Fortunately, he failed. But many others are continuing to attack speech nonetheless.

In addition to some parody political sites of our own, we thought it would be fun to register a few four-letter word domains as well—this became possible within the last year as Network Solutions stopped being the only Internet registrar in this country. For years, they had prevented the use of certain words because they considered them offensive. Now, thanks to competition, you can find a registrar who will give you the site you want. And that's how `www.fucknbc.com` was born. We didn't even get around to publicizing the site or, for that matter, *making* a site. We simply pointed it to NBC until we could figure out what to do with it. Somehow, the folks at NBC found our domain name and threatened us with legal action if we didn't stop engaging in "trademark infringement." They either honestly believed that by having NBC anywhere within the web site's name that we were somehow violating their rights or they think they have the right to tell us not to point our sites at them. Neither of these assumptions is true although we have started to see challenges on many fronts recently concerning linking from one site to another. The MPAA has tried to get us to remove our links to other sites that still have the DeCSS files by filing even *more* court papers against us. This time, major media *not* owned by the corporations suing us such as *The New York Times* made a point of linking to our links to show their opposition to this motion.

The fun continues with a company that technically doesn't even exist yet. You may have seen some advertisements for Verizon Wireless, who have somehow managed to co-opt the peace sign as their corporate logo. That's just the beginning—a *really* big company will be named simply Verizon and it is set to encompass all that is currently Bell Atlantic and GTE. In an effort to stave off those free speech advocates, at least 706 domains were registered, including all variations of verizonsucks, verizonblows, verizonshits, you name it. Apparently, their new logic leads them to conclude that if they simply *take* all of the critical names, nobody will be able to criticize them. So we decided to take `www.verizonREALLYsucks.com`, knowing that we would one day find a use for it. It didn't take long. This time the legal threat said we were violating the new anti-cybersquatting law and that we were required to immediately hand over the domain to them for free. While some of the goals behind the anti-cybersquatting act were worthwhile (people who take a company name for the sole purpose of selling it to them at a huge profit are rather sleazy, after all), we knew it would be quickly abused. There is nothing even remotely related to cybersquatting in what we have done. Verizon obviously has all of the sites it wanted to register. We simply thought of a new one that criticizes them. Since *they* already took sites that criticize them and obviously have no intention of using them for that purpose, they are a lot closer to cybersquatting than we are. While we're pleased that we may be Verizon's very first lawsuit, we're annoyed at the utter waste of time these huge entities continue to cause.

We have a distinct advantage as we're able to tell the world when things like the above happen. But there are countless other cases going on right now where individuals are being targeted because some corporation with a huge legal team doesn't like something about someone's site. How likely is it that an individual will be able to stand up to this? Not very, if we don't stand up for each other.

Our trial has been scheduled for Monday, July 17 (the day after the H2K conference ends), at the Federal Courthouse in New York. We hope to see many of you there. Check `www.2600.com` *for updates and any changes.*

DeCSS in Words (Autumn, 2000) *By CSS*

The decryption of data on a DVD encoded through the CSS algorithm can be broken down into three steps. The first is the decryption of the disk key, the second is the decryption of the title key, and the third is the decryption of the encrypted DVD disk sectors.

Each decryption step in software requires the simulation of a 17 bit Linear Feedback Shift Register (LFSR) and a 25 bit LFSR, both of whose outputs are summed eight bits at a time (along with any carry bits from the previous addition) to produce the decrypted output.

There are any number of ways in which the two LFSRs can be simulated in software. The 17 bit LFSR is often implemented using a single machine word where the feedback is computed through cascaded right shifts and XORs. On the other hand, the 25 bit LFSR's output is frequently determined through lookups into byte vectors.

The contents of the low bits in one such lookup table are:

0x00, 0x01, 0x02, 0x03, 0x04, 0x05, 0x06, 0x07, 0x09, 0x08, 0x0b, 0x0a, 0x0d, 0x0c, 0x0f, 0x0e, 0x12, 0x13, 0x10, 0x11, 0x16, 0x17, 0x14, 0x15, 0x1b, 0x1a, 0x19, 0x18, 0x1f, 0x1e, 0x1d, 0x1c, 0x24, 0x25, 0x26, 0x27, 0x20, 0x21, 0x22, 0x23, 0x2d, 0x2c, 0x2f, 0x2e, 0x29, 0x28, 0x2b, 0x2a, 0x36, 0x37, 0x34, 0x35, 0x32, 0x33, 0x30, 0x31, 0x3f, 0x3e, 0x3d, 0x3c, 0x3b, 0x3a, 0x39, 0x38, 0x49, 0x48, 0x4b, 0x4a, 0x4d, 0x4c, 0x4f, 0x4e, 0x40, 0x41, 0x42, 0x43, 0x44, 0x45, 0x46, 0x47, 0x5b, 0x5a, 0x59,

0x58, 0x5f, 0x5e, 0x5d, 0x5c, 0x52, 0x53, 0x50, 0x51, 0x56, 0x57, 0x54, 0x55, 0x6d, 0x6c, 0x6f, 0x6e, 0x69, 0x68, 0x6b, 0x6a, 0x64, 0x65, 0x66, 0x67, 0x60, 0x61, 0x62, 0x63, 0x7f, 0x7e, 0x7d, 0x7c, 0x7b, 0x7a, 0x79, 0x78, 0x76, 0x77, 0x74, 0x75, 0x72, 0x73, 0x70, 0x71, 0x92, 0x93, 0x90, 0x91, 0x96, 0x97, 0x94, 0x95, 0x9b, 0x9a, 0x99, 0x98, 0x9f, 0x9e, 0x9d, 0x9c, 0x80, 0x81, 0x82, 0x83, 0x84, 0x85, 0x86, 0x87, 0x89, 0x88, 0x8b, 0x8a, 0x8d, 0x8c, 0x8f, 0x8e, 0xb6, 0xb7, 0xb4, 0xb5, 0xb2, 0xb3, 0xb0, 0xb1, 0xbf, 0xbe, 0xbd, 0xbc, 0xbb, 0xba, 0xb9, 0xb8, 0xa4, 0xa5, 0xa6, 0xa7, 0xa0, 0xa1, 0xa2, 0xa3, 0xad, 0xac, 0xaf, 0xae, 0xa9, 0xa8, 0xab, 0xaa, 0xdb, 0xda, 0xd9, 0xd8, 0xdf, 0xde, 0xdd, 0xdc, 0xd2, 0xd3, 0xd0, 0xd1, 0xd6, 0xd7, 0xd4, 0xd5, 0xc9, 0xc8, 0xcb, 0xca, 0xcd, 0xcc, 0xcf, 0xce, 0xc0, 0xc1, 0xc2, 0xc3, 0xc4, 0xc5, 0xc6, 0xc7, 0xff, 0xfe, 0xfd, 0xfc, 0xfb, 0xfa, 0xf9, 0xf8, 0xf6, 0xf7, 0xf4, 0xf5, 0xf2, 0xf3, 0xf0, 0xf1, 0xed, 0xec, 0xef, 0xee, 0xe9, 0xe8, 0xeb, 0xea, 0xe4, 0xe5, 0xe6, 0xe7, 0xe0, 0xe1, 0xe2, and 0xe3.

The contents of the high bits lookup table are composed of the following values repeated 32 times:

0x00, 0x24, 0x49, 0x6d, 0x92, 0xb6, 0xdb, 0xff, 0x00, 0x24, 0x49, 0x6d, 0x92, 0xb6, 0xdb, and 0xff.

Using this method, one determines the 25 bit LFSR output by using the least significant 16 bits of the LFSR as two eight bit offsets into the above tables, and using the XOR of these values.

The plain text is obtained by summing eight bits of output from both LFSRs plus any carry bits from a previous addition. If an inversion is required, simply XOR the 17 bit LFSR with the inversion mask before summing with the 25 bit LFSR.

Each player is preprogrammed with a small set of player keys. To determine the correct decrypted disk key we must attempt to decrypt the disk key with each of the machine's player keys. The search ends once a decrypted key hashes to the same 40-bit value as the decrypted disk key hash stored on disk. In order to start decrypting keys we must first set up our simulated shift registers. Seed the 17 bit LFSR with the first 16 bits of a player key and set the MSB to 1 to avoid null cycling. Seed the 25 bit LFSR is with the next 24 bits (specifically, bits 16 to 39) of the player key. All bits except the three LSBs are shifted up a bit. Bit 4 is set to 1 to avoid null cycling. A table lookup with the LFSR state is used to obtain the next state of the LFSR. A bit inversion of the output is performed with a four state inverter in position 1 for this round of encryption.

Using the same process that decrypted the disk key, we will now use the disk key to decrypt the title key. The title key is used for the decryption of the encrypted sectors of the DVD disk. The final bit inversion in this round of decryption is performed with the inverter in State 2. Using the title key as input to the shift registers we can now read each sector off the disk and easily decrypt the data blocks using the aforementioned process with the inverter in State 3.

MILESTONE: A TASTE OF FREEDOM (Spring, 2000) *By Kevin Mitnick*

What a difference 44 days make. Just about seven weeks ago, I was dressed in prison-issued khakis, a prisoner at the U.S. federal correctional institution in Lompoc, California. Last Thursday, March 2, I presented my written and verbal testimony to the United States Senate Governmental Affairs Committee that described how to increase information security within government agencies. Wow.

On The Inside

"Doing time" is a strange thing. When you're on the inside, you can't look out—you have to pretend as though the outside doesn't even exist. Letters are a welcome break to the routine, but as soon as I read them, I'd have to focus and get back into my rhythm of pretending there were no cars outside my window, that there were no people living their lives. During my five years inside, I looked at the sky only to see the weather, and I rarely looked at the cars or the people.

I spent most of my waking hours working on my case, or corresponding with supporters and attorneys who were helping me with legal research. I took the energy I used to spend on hacking and I basically trained myself in law. This took a great deal of time and energy, since I've never had any formal training in law. Many of the attorneys who donated their time and expertise were especially helpful in guiding my legal research, and to them I am particularly grateful.

Conditional Freedom

I spend much of the time available to me when I'm not caring for my father figuring out how to earn a living in light of the overly broad, unreasonable restrictions imposed by Judge Pfaelzer. While I was at the World Trade Center in New York with a friend recently, I saw an iMac used to select gifts from the shop—technically, if I used that iMac I would violate the terms of my supervised release. If I even used a computer to purchase a Metrocard to ride the New York subway system I would also violate the probationary conditions of supervised release.

Those conditions also restrict my First Amendment rights to the extent it prohibits me from acting as an advisor to anyone who is engaged in computer-related activity. My recent Senate talk could be violative, as could a talk to a car mechanic. The conditions are so vague and overly broad that I don't know what I need to do or not do to stay out of jail. It's up to a government official to decide whether or not I go back to jail, and it's not based on my intent—it's completely arbitrary.

MILESTONE: A TASTE OF FREEDOM *(continued)*

Without the support of *2600* and you all, my case would likely have ended up differently. The support of each and every one of you positively influenced media treatment of my case, which gave me the energy to fight the charges against me, which in turn influenced the government's treatment of me—see the `freekevin.com` web site for more details about this. I greatly appreciate the support of each person in my fight against injustice. Last, and definitely not least, Emmanuel hasn't given up—he has dedicated time and resources and has organized extraordinary events to focus the spotlight on injustices in my case involving the federal government and the media. His support has been crucial, and without it, things wouldn't have ended up as positively as they have. Emmanuel took up my case more than five years ago, and has used his radio show and space in *2600* to publicize the government's dramatic manipulation of my case for the self-interest of a pair of misguided, egotistical prosecutors.

I owe him—and all of you—a great deal. I am very, very lucky to have had friends like you.

A Summer of Trials (Autumn, 2000)

One thing the summer of 2000 will not be remembered for is dullness. We've never had so many different things come together at more or less the same time. Yet all of these different things were somehow related and extremely relevant to where we are headed.

Many see it as a bad thing that the DeCSS trial dominated our time as much as it did. Unfortunately, there was never a choice. Like a dangerous disease, it had to be fought with every ounce of our strength. Thanks to the support of the EFF and a terrific legal defense team, we had the best chance possible of getting our side out.

It seemed obvious from the beginning that the court was sympathetic to the case of the MPAA and this was certainly borne out in the decision. But the reaction of the many thousands who have been following this case one way or another around the globe only confirmed that we succeeded in making the points we needed to make. Anyone with a degree of knowledge in either technical issues or the value of freedom of speech seems to get it right away. Why then did our court system fail to?

We can analyze it forever. But it basically comes down to perception. The judge bought into the notion that hackers are evil and only interested in causing problems, pirating films, and bringing down corporate America. Ironically, decisions such as this do more to foster such hostility than anything else and we've seen a very definite change in tone within several communities—hackers, open source, independent artists, activists—it's rapidly turning into an us versus them scenario. And it's all but assured that someone is going to fall into the mass graves that corporate America is digging.

For those without access to the Net and who may have missed it in the media, the MPAA was granted a permanent injunction against our posting the DeCSS code that allows DVDs to be played on alternative platforms such as Linux. The main thrust of the MPAA's argument was that this would also allow people to copy unencrypted DVD files and then transfer them over the Net. It was demonstrated time and again that such activity would take massive time and bandwidth and that it would ultimately prove pointless since encrypted files could still be copied and read through any existing DVD player and since the cost of DVDs was low enough to make piracy a money losing venture. But this case was never about piracy. It all centered around the MPAA wanting control over how people play digital media. They want to be able to dictate how, when, and where you can access content. We're already seeing the results of this in the form of region coding (preventing the viewing of DVDs from one geographical region to another), the elimination of "fair use," which has always allowed for consumers to make personal copies of the material they've purchased, and the ability to force consumers to sit through commercials and FBI warnings without the ability to skip through them. And don't for a moment think it will stop there. You will soon see the same kind of controls introduced on audio recordings. And, with the advent of HDTV, don't be surprised when you have to pay a fee to record your favorite program and another fee for every time you want to view it. All of this is not only possible under the Digital Millennium Copyright Act (the 1998 legislation that made this lawsuit and the many that will follow possible), but increasingly likely to be only the tip of the iceberg. If the rest of the DMCA goes into effect as scheduled in late October, it will be illegal to even *figure out on your own* ways of circumventing these many controls and restrictions.

It's not too late to make the DMCA into a political issue. There are no voting records on its passage other than Clinton's signing it into law. Both the House and the Senate used voice votes to assure its passage. That means it's as good as unanimous. Every single elected official needs to be targeted aggressively so that they realize what a bad mistake the DMCA is. It's extremely likely many of them didn't get the full story when they were considering it. It's up to us to see that they understand it now. And if they refuse to, to replace them with someone who does.

The MPAA has gotten an immense amount of bad publicity because of this case. People who weren't even aware of who the MPAA was now think of them in a negative way. Their victory will be more costly than our loss. And ultimately they cannot hope to hold consumers hostage for very much longer. We find that once consumers become aware of what this is really about, they understand the importance of the case very quickly. That's why getting the word out to as many people as possible—leafleting, demonstrations, web pages, public forums—is so vital at this stage.

What we've seen over the last few months as a direct result of this is the tremendous growth of activism in our community. The Free Kevin movement started us in this direction and the DeCSS case gave us a real push. This in turn has gotten many more people involved and helped to solidify ties between communities that have always been fighting for the same things in different ways. Since we cannot count on the media (most of them are owned by companies who are part of the lawsuit against us) we have to do it ourselves. As Jello Biafra put it during his keynote address at H2K, we must "become the media."

All of us have that ability and the Net is what makes it possible. But the Net is also in danger of becoming co-opted by the same entities who are trying to shut us down. This can happen in several ways. Our best and brightest can be lured away into corporate settings where the values they once held dear are cashed in for stock options. More regulations by nervous governments can reduce the free potential of the global Net to mere folklore. By portraying those in our community as criminals by focusing on absurdities like mail viruses and "potential" crimes, public opinion can be easily swayed to turn us into the enemy, which makes control all the more necessary in the eyes of the masses.

One thing that seemed to come out of this summer's H2K conference was the sentiment that the time to sit back and take it is over. If we want to preserve our existing freedoms and restore those that we've already lost, the only way to accomplish this is to get involved. While it's easy to just sit back and let life happen, joining forces and working towards a goal is what makes for significant change. And it also happens to feel great.

That's precisely why this year's conference had more of an activist slant to it. While the world of hackers is ultimately about playing with technology, figuring things out, and sharing information, powerful entities have decided that these things are not to be tolerated. We find our very existence—and that of free thinkers of all sorts—threatened in ways even we find ourselves surprised by. While it's relatively simple to close one's eyes and play ball, the results would be nothing short of catastrophic. We have to take a stand and we have to be willing to pay the price.

We've seen this sentiment echoed several times this year. Three issues ago we told the story of Seattle and how for the first time independent media people used the Net in a major way to report a story that the mainstream had ignored. As we suspected, it was the beginning of a trend. This summer, history repeated itself in Philadelphia and Los Angeles at the two major political conventions. Crowds were attacked in the streets by police firing rubber bullets (a practice introduced in Seattle last November), peaceful protests were made illegal, and the mainstream media dutifully went along for the ride. Suspected "leaders," including a *2600* staff person, were hunted down and arrested, in some cases just for walking down a street with a cell phone (later defined by authorities as an implement of crime). Bail was set at up to a million dollars and people were thrown into prisons with utterly horrendous and barbaric conditions.

If you watched the news and read the papers, you probably heard the exact same words repeated over and over that would lead you to believe that these actions were somehow justified. For those who were there and for those who participated over the Net, a very different story than what was being reported on the mainstream media soon revealed itself. Thanks to a new and long overdue brand of media not controlled by corporate interests and a belligerent government, firsthand accounts got out to the world in the form of video, audio, and the written word. Most of this was limited to the Internet but at least one brand new satellite channel—Free Speech TV—managed to bring this material into millions of living rooms nationwide. And, just like you would expect to see in those "uncivilized" foreign nations, the authorities came down hard on these independent media types, harassing them at every opportunity, denying them access, and even going so far as to disrupt their legitimate work. One unbelievable incident took place at the Democratic Convention in Los Angeles as the people at Free Speech TV were preparing a live broadcast. Police came in and shut down the facility because of a "bomb threat." But no bomb squad ever showed up and the relaxed attitude of the police made it abundantly clear that there was no threat. The police let the facility reopen ten minutes after the window for the satellite transmission had closed. This was far from an isolated event. In Philadelphia, police repeatedly "inspected" the headquarters of the Independent Media Center during the Republican Convention looking for the most minor of violations in order to shut it down. In addition, helmeted riot cops would surround the building for no particular reason except to intimidate the inhabitants. These exact tactics had been used on Radio B92 in Yugoslavia when they broadcast non-government reports, ironically also using the Internet as their main channel to the world.

On the mainstream networks, none of this was reported. All you saw there were the same boring non-issues. This is what journalism in the United States has been reduced to.

The inspiration of these events along with the tremendous sharing of information and resources that took place at H2K, not to mention all of the crap that's happened to us, has made it clear that we have to work together if we want to have any chance at all of making a difference. That's why we've decided to join with the Independent Media Center to form a base in New York where those who have been shut out and are interested in making a difference can come together, using the Net and some imagination to reach the public. You can get more information at `www.indymedia.org`. No matter where you are in the world, you can participate by opening people's eyes to the issues that have been ignored. Never stop educating yourself on the threats to freedom that keep hitting us day after day. It's about reading, exploring, and communicating.

So now the question remains: what's next for us? It's hard to say. A lot has happened in the past few months. Our documentary *Freedom Downtime* has finally been finished and is now slowly making the hacker convention/film festival circuit. The film, which focuses on the Free Kevin movement and the hacker culture, will be made available on VHS and, yes, DVD in the near future. Our next conference will take place in 2002, a year earlier than normal owing to the great success of H2K and the overall *need* for this kind of thing. Next year we encourage people to attend HAL 2001 in the Netherlands, which we believe will be similar in style to a HOPE conference. More details will be published in upcoming issues.

As for how the result of the trial will affect things, we intend to keep doing what we do for as long as that remains possible. We have complied with the injunctions against us but we doubt that will be enough to satisfy the MPAA or future cases that involve the DMCA. At press time, we have removed all links to sites that contain the DeCSS code as per the judge's incredibly misguided ruling. However, we have not removed a listing of those sites. Listing is not the same as linking and if we're ordered to remove a list, then that's one less thing we're allowed to do. We want the restrictions against us to be crystal clear and not open to any misinterpretation.

We don't yet know what the financial ramifications for all of this will be. We encourage people to make sizable donations to the Electronic Frontier Foundation, who have made this fight possible and have expressed the intention to take the appeal all the way to the Supreme Court. Please help make that happen and visit `www.eff.org`.

We're not the only victims in this fight—even people who make t-shirts with source code printed on them are being sued now—but if we ultimately lose or if the DMCA is allowed to stand as is, you can bet on an uncountable number of legal battles on the horizon. Support and awareness, for this and all related causes, are the only hope we have for averting this catastrophe.

Signs of Hope (Spring, 2001)

As our appeal of last year's DeCSS case draws closer (at press time it was set to be heard by the Second Circuit Court of Appeals in early May), we realize how much we've accomplished since this whole ordeal started and how much other people with half a clue have gotten done too. That's not to say that a lot of bad stuff hasn't happened; we know too well about all of that. New bad laws, new threats, more stifling of technology and speech throughout the world. But despite all that, we're going into this with a real feeling of optimism.

As time passes, more people seem to realize the true motives of groups like the Motion Picture Association of America and the Recording Industry Association of America. They're not about protecting the rights of struggling artists, bolstering creativity, or giving consumers a fair deal. They're about maximizing profit—plain and simple. And as things continue to go their way thanks to laws like the Digital Millennium Copyright Act, people slowly start waking up to the reality that maybe their best interests have been completely ignored.

Perhaps the most dramatic display of this overdue realization came in remarks made by Rep. Rick Boucher (D-VA) in early March before a Consumer Electronics Association Conference where he seemed to actually realize the true dangers of the DMCA:

> *"The time, in my opinion, has come for the Congress to reaffirm the Fair Use Doctrine and to bolster specific fair use rights, which are now at risk. In 1998, responding to the concerns of copyright owners, Congress passed the Digital Millennium Copyright Act. The announced purpose was to protect from piracy copyrighted material in an environment which poses special concerns for copyright owners. They made the point that with digital technology, a copy of a copy of a copy has the same clarity and perfection as the original of the work. They also made the point that in the networked environment, with the single click of a mouse, thousands of those perfect copies can be sent to people throughout the nation and the world.*
>
> *"The DMCA is the result of the effort by Congress to respond to those realities. There are some today who believe that the legislation went too far. For example, it creates, in Section 1201(a), a new crime of circumventing a technological protection measure that guards access to a copyrighted work. Under Section 1201, the purpose of the circumvention is immaterial. It is a crime to circumvent the password or other gateway, even for the purpose of exercising fair use rights. There is no requirement that the circumvention be for the purpose of infringing the copyrights. Any act of circumvention, without the consent of the copyright owner, is made criminal under Section 1201.*
>
> *"Some now foresee a time when virtually all new material will be sent to libraries on CD ROMs, with the material encrypted or guarded by passwords. In exchange for a fee for each viewing, the password may then be used. And so it is predicted that under Section 1201, what is available today on the library shelves for free will be available on a pay per use basis only. The student who wants even the most basic access to material to write his term paper will have to pay for each item that he uses.*
>
> *"Several of us made an effort in 1998 to limit the new crime under Section 1201 to circumvention for the purpose of infringement. But in the momentum to enact the measure, essentially unamended, we were not able to have that change adopted. With the growing realization on the part of the education community and supporters of libraries of the threat to fair use rights which Section 1201 poses, perhaps the time will soon come for a Congressional reexamination of this provision.*
>
> *"Perhaps the only conduct that should be declared criminal is circumvention for the purpose of infringement. Perhaps a more limited amendment could be crafted to ensure the continued exercise of fair use rights of libraries and in scholastic settings, notwithstanding the provisions of Section 1201.*

> *"And I think there are other challenges. I am concerned by the apparent attempt of some in the content community to seek to protect their copyright interests in material contained in television programs by insisting that the TV signal quality be degraded, or by insisting on the use of set-top box technology which prohibits all copying. The reasonable expectations of television viewers to be able to make copies of programs for time shifting and other historically accepted purposes must be honored and must be fulfilled."*

We suspect that there are many others in Congress who feel the same unease but are hesitant to speak out against such powerful lobbies as the MPAA and the RIAA. We must encourage them to listen to the people who elected them, not the special interest groups who use intimidation and money to get what they want.

In another very public display in early March, cartoonist Aaron McGruder devoted his popular comic strip *Boondocks* to the DeCSS controversy. For three days, characters struggled to understand the baffling ruling of Judge Kaplan this past August, which forced *2600* to keep the source code off of our site and even banned our linking to other sites that contained this material. "Why is it perfectly legal to post a diagram of how to build a bomb on the Net, but you can't post a code that descrambles DVDs?" a character asks a teacher. The rest of the strip is blacked out with the words "CENSORED. We just don't like where he's going with this."

On a different day, the entire strip was replaced with the words: "CENSORED. This comic contains numerous references to the DeCSS code used to bypass the Content Scrambling System of DVDs, which, by order of Judge Lewis Kaplan, is illegal to reproduce in any way. We apologize for the inconvenience, but speech that damages the profits of our corporate friends is NOT protected by the First Amendment. Thank you."

This biting political commentary accomplished in two sentences what virtually every major editorial page has so far failed to do. The sobering consequences of the ruling against us were laid out concisely for all to see. Note that the author *understood* that the code was not designed for copying, a fact that virtually every news report on the subject got wrong.

What this illustrates is that we have allies in places we never even thought of. This one comic strip reached millions of people who now have some understanding of what this case has been, and continues to be, about. There are probably a good many more ways of reaching the public that have yet to be utilized. We need to come up with more ideas and those people who can help get the word out need to come forward.

And of course, technological rebellion continues. We've seen people come up with shorter and more creative methods of bypassing CSS—everything from a DeCSS haiku to a 434 byte C program to a seven line Perl script. There's even a prime number that is identical to the gzip data (in decimal) of the original C source code minus tables. T-shirts, bumper stickers, even tattoos with such "illegal" code are popping up everywhere. And it all serves to illustrate the absurdity of the whole thing.

It's imperative that we keep our sense of humor throughout, no matter how it all turns out. There are many levels on which we could ultimately lose; the court case is only one of them. The spirit of the hacker community is what is vital to this and all future fights. It's an inspiration to many more outside the scene who can only dream of taking on the fights we do. Destiny has put us in this position at this time in history and we have to continue to stand up for those things we believe in: free speech, free communication, free access to knowledge, and the ability to control and shape technology to suit our individual needs.

We're very lucky to be where we are, despite the risks. And we're fortunate beyond words to have such an amazing support network that is still growing and developing. Because no matter how the DeCSS appeal turns out, you can bet there will be more fights in our future. If they open half as many eyes as this case has, they will be worth the trouble.

2001-2002 (Winter, 2001-2002)

2001 has been a most difficult year in so many ways. History has been forever changed by world events and the effects will continue to trickle down on our individual lives for a very long time. Despite this, we must look to the battles we've chosen to embark upon with our complete attention, despite the dramatic changes in society that may overshadow them. Otherwise we run the risk of giving up the battle before we even begin to fight it.

We know that freedom of speech—even freedom in general—is considered by an increasing number to be subject to restrictive conditions in the interests of "security." Never mind that total security is completely elusive. There will always be someone claiming we can do better by closing off yet another avenue of activity, beliefs, or speech. And simpletons, fueled by mass media hysterics, will continue to believe it.

That's why it's never been more important to get involved in preserving your rights before they get signed away. Anyone who tells you that this is somehow in opposition to the interests of our nation has an agenda we find frighteningly disturbing. The fact that many of these people are extremely powerful is certainly cause for concern. But the real battle won't be lost until the rest of us actually start to accept this garbage.

We continue to fight legal battles for the absurdly simple reason that they need to be fought. To choose not to do this would grant a default victory to those challenging what we believe to be our rights. If we wait for someone else to come along and fight the battle in place of us (either because they have more resources or even because they may look more respectable than the likes of us), we risk their not standing behind the issues as much as we want them to. And we also risk such people never coming along in the first place.

In some ways, it's an honor to be sued. We're basically being told to put up or shut up, to prove our points, to actually stand up for what we believe in. Too many times we as individuals grow complacent. We say what we believe but completely crumble when someone challenges those beliefs, either by giving in or by not defending ourselves as well as we could. But when we are actually sued and faced with the prospect of losing a great deal because of what we say and do, then we are forced to look inside ourselves and see if we really do believe as much as we say we do. We're happy to have gone through that and to have come out of it knowing that our beliefs are strong and ready to undergo these tests. And in so doing, we have found many others who feel the same.

Although we recently lost the Second Circuit Court of Appeals decision in the DeCSS case, our legal team made the most compelling argument possible. We still strongly believe that computer source code is speech and is entitled to all the protections that speech is normally afforded. We still believe that the Digital Millennium Copyright Act is a gross violator of not only free speech but of the concept of fair use and that it sends a chilling signal throughout our society. We've seen professors intimidated into not releasing their research because a powerful group of corporations threatened to prosecute them under the DMCA. Imagine being prosecuted for doing research! We've seen computer users thrown off of commercial systems and banned from school networks for merely being *accused* of possessing information that the DMCA defines as a potential threat, information that would have scarcely raised an eyebrow a few years ago. And we've seen a growing realization among our readers and others that the DMCA is well on the road to making publications like ours illegal to print, possess, or read.

Our loss in this fight does not signal the end. Far from it. We intend to take this case to the Supreme Court so that our entire court system can be given the opportunity to correct this grievous wrong. Failing that, other cases will be fought, among them the Dmitry Sklyarov case, which will go to trial sometime in 2002. Although it took far too long, basic humanity finally managed to prevail in this case. After an unconscionable period of being forcibly detained in the United States for his part in writing a computer program in Russia, Sklyarov was finally allowed to return home in late December, on the condition that he return to give testimony in the trial, which will now focus on his company (Elcomsoft). The authorities are trying to spin this to make it seem as if Sklyarov is no longer affiliated with his company and will be testifying against them. In actuality he is still very much with them and is looking forward to telling his story at the trial. When this happens, the world will bear witness to the absurdity of this law and how it's damaging researchers and developers all around the world. Nothing will make technological innovation grind to a halt faster than the continued existence of the DMCA and similar laws in other parts of the world.

Even if it takes a hundred cases of people challenging the DMCA, we are confident that there is no shortage of individuals who will proudly step forward to defend the rights they believe in. As our leaders are so fond of saying, we are in a war and we must all do our part and make sacrifices. Some of those sacrifices may be very costly. But who among us ever really believed that the cost of defending free speech would be cheap?

Not all the news is bad. On December 20, a federal court ruled in our favor in the Ford case. If you recall, this was the lawsuit that sought to prevent us from forwarding a controversial domain (`www.fuckgeneralmotors.com`) to the web page of Ford (General Motors' competitor) as a form of Net humor. Regardless of whether or not people were offended by this, we felt it was absolutely imperative to protect the right of Internet users to point their domains wherever they pleased. Ford felt otherwise, claiming that what we did was somehow trademark infringement. They firmly believed (as did much of corporate America who had their eyes on this case) that *nobody* had the right to link or forward to their site without their explicit permission. Had we opted not to embark upon this fight, a very bad precedent would have been set and one more right of speech would have been lost because nobody cared enough to fight for it. We are fortunate that the judge saw the fallacy of Ford's arguments. It's proof that significant victory *can* be achieved within the system. Lately it's seemed as if such victories are very few and far between. All the more reason for us to fight even harder for them.

Of course, you won't see much in the way of mass media coverage of *this* story. Had we lost, it most likely would have been all over the papers as another example of hackers getting their just desserts and society being made more secure. But the fact that you probably didn't read about our victory in all the mainstream places doesn't make the story any less important. It merely underlines the growing insignificance of the mass media itself and how replacing their self-serving agenda is paramount to winning such battles and ultimately preserving our endangered freedoms.

It's likely to become even more difficult to challenge the injustices that lie ahead in the coming months and years. We willll certainly see a good deal of reprehensible opportunism on the part of the powers that be as they try to tie their anti-individual agendas to the fight against terrorism. However, we must not allow them to legitimize their dubious positions in this manner. And we must do our best to reach those who might not otherwise see how they are being taken advantage of. This will be our biggest challenge for 2002.

Positivity (Winter, 2002-2003)

In the fast paced culture that we seem to find ourselves caught in the middle of, it's very easy to get stuck in a default mood of euphoria or despair. Lately it seems that we've been despairing quite a bit. We're certainly not alone.

While it's very important to not lose sight of the bad and ominous things that are happening in the world of technology and what it could do to people like us, nothing is gained if we lose our overall positive outlook. We certainly couldn't have kept on publishing for nearly twenty years if we didn't feel a strong sense of hope for the future.

There will never be a shortage of negative issues to focus upon. Let's take a brief moment to look at the positive developments.

By the time you read this (and hopefully barring any last minute unfortunate circumstances), the excruciatingly long ordeal of Kevin Mitnick will have finally reached an end. January 20, 2003 was the date that Mitnick's supervised release came to an end—three years after his release from prison. That means that he will once again be able to use the Internet, travel without having to ask permission, and talk to anyone he wishes to without having to check to see if they've ever been convicted of a crime. Most of us take these freedoms for granted so it's hard to even imagine what life must be like without them.

In these past three years, Mitnick has become a model for someone who can overcome adversity and triumph in the end. Despite five years of isolation and the aforementioned restrictive conditions upon his release, he refused to let the system defeat him. The authorities made it almost impossible for him to earn a living, insisting that he not be allowed anywhere near a computer and at one point suggesting that he pursue a career in fast food. Instead Mitnick landed a job at a major talk radio station and answered listener questions about technology. He had kept himself educated on all the technological advances, despite being incarcerated and forbidden from experimenting with them upon his release. More recently he had a book published on the intricacies of social engineering and went on a government-approved speaking tour to promote it. Throughout this, Mitnick found time to testify before a Senate subcommittee on the dangers of bad technology and uninformed people. He also provided key evidence in a case against Sprint who had the audacity to claim that their switches were unhackable.

It would have been easy to dwell on the negative in this case, and there certainly was no shortage of negativity. After all, Mitnick hadn't actually had a real day of freedom since 1988 meaning that when all is said and done, fifteen years will have gone by since this all started. And in all that time, there was never a charge filed against Mitnick of anything more substantial than making free phone calls and looking at source code that didn't belong to him. It was all an incredible waste of time. But we get nowhere by letting our bitterness dictate how we live. We have everything to gain by continuing forward in our spirit of curiosity, education, and rebellion against conformity.

There's always a price to pay in order to take those steps and sometimes it's a heavy price. Dmitry Sklyarov spent time in an American prison and was unable to return to his native Russia for nearly six months, simply because he wrote a program that could be used in a way that violated the absurd Digital Millennium Copyright Act. It made no difference that he wrote the program in another country. Even Adobe, the company that originally pressed charges against Sklyarov, realized how ridiculous the whole thing was and tried to drop it. But it was too late and the American justice system went to work, eventually putting Sklyarov's company (Elcomsoft) on trial instead in exchange for his testimony. The authorities didn't count on the defendants putting on a strong fight and they didn't count on the massive show of support for Sklyarov.

There's a reason so few cases ever make it to a jury. People are rightfully terrified of the system and what it can do to them. It's ironic that it took someone from outside our country to stand up to the system and refuse to be intimidated. The trial took place in December and it only took the jury one day to rule in Sklyarov's and Elcomsoft's favor.

Part of the DMCA stipulates that there has to be intent and this was something the jury was unable to find in this case. It doesn't address the overall stupidity of the law itself, which means there will be more such cases. But it's a good start and a significant step towards fixing the numerous problems caused by this horrible legislation. And most importantly, it's proof that determination and standing by one's convictions *can* ultimately lead to victory.

We have to also remember that there's a big world out there, one that doesn't always initially grasp the importance of the issues we value. It's easy to dismiss the general public as ignorant and pawns of the mass media. But, as in all things, the truth is never quite that simple. The general public *can* get it, they *do* tend to value the things that we do, and they are most definitely *not* the enemy. The jury in the Elcomsoft case is living proof of this. The key is getting the message out.

Over the past year or so we've reported (along with many others) some of the really bad ideas that have been passed down from Capitol Hill as a "response" to terrorism—things like the Patriot Act, the Homeland Security color scheme, Operation TIPS, Total Information Awareness, etc. And while many of these things are still around, public awareness and public criticism has soared and it has most definitely made a difference.

People are taking more time to think these things through and more of them seem to be realizing that diminishing our freedoms really isn't going to accomplish a whole lot—other than diminishing our freedoms. We've seen less talk of the alert status color coding system as it becomes mocked more than it's used.

The TIPS system was heavily criticized for its Stasi-like system of informing on one's neighbors and having untrained civilians prowling around looking for potential thought crime. And in true Orwellian style, all mention of TIPS was removed from the `citizencorps.gov` web site where it had been prominently featured. It never happened.

The Total Information Awareness initiative is still very much with us. In their own words, TIA is meant to be a "total reinvention of technologies for storing and accessing information... although database size will no longer be measured in the traditional sense, the amounts of data that will need to be stored and accessed will be unprecedented, measured in petabytes." All of this will supposedly identify terrorists by having *every* conceivable bit of data easily available—from medical records to credit card purchases to Internet activity. It doesn't take much to figure out that since they don't know who the terrorists are they will have to scrutinize all of us using these yet to be invented tools. It's clearly a sensitive topic for the folks at Defense Advanced Research Projects Agency (DARPA) who won't even reveal how much money is being allocated for this. While public pressure has yet to kill this beast, it's probably one of the few things that can. Public ridicule has already put an end to the TIA logo—a pyramid with an all seeing eye within it, apparently looking out over the globe. That also never happened.

As we go to press, yet another monitoring plan is being announced—this time one that makes Carnivore look friendly. It's part of a report entitled "The National Strategy to Secure Cyberspace" and it would require Internet Service providers to participate in a centralized system that would theoretically allow the entire Internet to be monitored along with its users. The apparent frustration the government is feeling is summed up in this statement by one of the plan's coordinators: "We don't have anybody that is able to look at the entire picture. When something is happening, we don't know it's happening until it's too late." That is why the plan will fail. What they want is not only impossible but it flies in the face of everything the Net represents. It would be the equivalent of wiretapping *everyone* at all times and we suspect most people just aren't going to go for that. Expect a backlash on this like nothing we've ever seen—if this scheme even makes it to spring.

Absurd and ridiculous as some of these plans may be, it's no excuse for not remaining vigilant and fighting those who endanger our freedom. Our victories may appear to be few and far between but they are quite significant. As is the fact that none of them could have been accomplished without a degree of organization and activism. Whether the cause is ending the suffering of a single person, overturning a really bad law, or preserving everyone's right to privacy, reaching out to like-minded individuals and helping to make it a major issue is critical. It's gotten us this far and it will continue to be our strongest weapon.

15 Still More Hacker Stories

As more forms of technology come into being, the sheer number of tales having to do with their exploitation rises exponentially. Tying them all together is that sense of rebellion and inquisitiveness that continues to live in every hacker. We've seen a lot of change in the last quarter century but the hacker spirit today is essentially the same as it was in the early years.

In this particular compilation, certain common themes tended to stand out. I wouldn't be at all surprised if we could fill a book just by throwing together all of the stories having to do with schools. Think about it. Most hackers are young and attending some sort of an educational institution, ranging from grade school to grad school. In those places, the people running things are very keen on maintaining control of everything from the curriculum to discipline. You introduce someone with a hacker mentality into such a scenario and you can well imagine the antics that result. As computers have gone from the exception to the rule in every classroom, those people with the ability to manipulate them have gained a particular foothold in the hierarchy of threats to good order. So many tales of paranoia have come our way from schools around the world where students are threatened with expulsion for something as innocent as figuring out how to send a message from one computer to another. You could literally try to burn the school down and not be seen in as threatening a light as if you were a suspected hacker. People in power react in very irrational ways when they see that power being threatened by something they don't understand.

But a place of education is just one of many arenas for good hacker material. For some, the military is an extension of school but with a lot more yelling and running. Inside this institution can be found a number of hackers also sending us stories. They range from figuring out creative methods of getting *out* of the military to discovering ways around some of the same computer restrictions found in the classroom. We always find it inspirational to see an individual emerging from any institution where such individuality is frowned upon, looked at with suspicion, or punished severely.

I can only await with anticipation the arrival of stories of technologies that have yet to be invented. One day we'll be publishing tales of robot hacking and space-based exploits. While the technology will be almost unrecognizable in the decades ahead, the mischief and analytical thoroughness of the hacker mind will be as familiar as it's ever been.

Schools

Most of the school stories we're sharing here are of the instructional variety rather than the experiences of persecution. (Most of the latter steadily flow into our letters department whereas the focus here is on the more thorough articles.) Suffice to say that the people who figured these things out were likely subjected to a good deal of persecution as a result (or would have been if they had been found out).

There are generally one of two themes found in a typical school narrative. Either the story is about figuring out ways of getting around an obnoxious restriction, such as a filter to the Internet or the blocking of a useful program, or it's about a fantastically stupid policy on the part of the school that winds up hurting the students. The latter case is documented in several of our stories with regards to the safeguarding of student privacy, something schools could certainly use a lesson on from the hackers of the world.

Examining Student Databases (Winter, 2001-2002)

By Screamer Chaotix

For the longest time I've been obsessing over an issue that is of the utmost importance to me: privacy. People should have the right to decide what sort of information about them is given out and what is not. For example, if you don't want your number in the phone book you must pay to keep it out (unless you go through the hassle of putting in a false name). But at least there you have a choice. What about your personal records? How many times, and to how many people, have those been given out just so they could "build a demographic" and make more money? If you think about it long enough, it's quite sickening, especially when you consider how many people feel hackers are the ones invading privacy.

With this in mind, I felt it was important to point out something I noticed while visiting a friend of mine at his university. And while naming the school may be a great help to getting the problem solved, it would also imply that this happens exclusively at this school alone. Rather, I'd like to explain the problem and let the world do with the information what it will.

You've probably seen them if you attend a large university. They're called "email stations" and are commonly lower end machines that are meant to be used exclusively for, you guessed it, email. In this case they were iMacs and, given my inexperience with Macs (and all Apple machines for that matter), I was a little uneasy about using them. Nonetheless, I was going to obey the large sign above the machines and use them for their intended purpose. But after doing so, I noticed something that caught my eye and raised my interest. It was a small icon that read "xxxxx Mainframe" (where xxxxx is the school name). As a hacker I was blown away by such an icon, but also knew not to expect too much from something that could have been nothing more than an image file under a different name. Upon clicking on it, I was taken aback by what occurred.

I was immediately presented with a warning, stating the usual "Unauthorized access is strictly prohibited blah blah blah." But rather than take me to a login prompt, it dumped me right into the middle of what appeared to be a specially designed system. A machine with a purpose if you will, and not your common UNIX shell. The machine liked to call itself the "Student Database" and had several options that any user (including a person who didn't go to the school) could use. I chose the student records and was presented with a new screen asking for a student or faculty name. Out of pure curiosity I entered in my friend's name and voilà: I was presented with a screen that listed his name, email address, an ID number (which I believe to be a type of student ID, although I may be mistaken), and, perhaps the most noticeable entry, his address. Right there, clear as day I could see ID information, his email address, and even the place where he currently resided.

Like the good little hacker/citizen I am, I showed this to him, much to his disgust. Having seen one too many hacker movies he automatically assumed I had "hacked into" the school's database, but after walking over to his machine and doing the same thing he was shocked beyond belief. Both of us started throwing around possibilities, such as how anyone could use his ID to obtain his grades, send him emails (even if he didn't want someone in particular to have his email address), and worst of all... come visit him at his home on campus.

Technologically there was little to it, which is what makes it so frightening. Typically when we see sensitive information out in the open it's found by a hacker who had to use some sort of skill to obtain it. But this could have very easily been obtained by anyone! And if you think you need some form of ID to use the machines, or even get into the building, you're sadly mistaken. Student IDs are only required for the cafeteria and to purchase books. Anyone, including your worst enemy, could go onto one of these machines and find out where you live, what your email address is, and perhaps even use your ID for malicious purposes. And all of this is made available without your permission.

Upon closing the terminal connection I was able to view the location of the database on the Internet. When I got back home the first thing I did was telnet to the location, but fortunately there was a login screen that wouldn't let me in. The purpose of this article is not how you can get in from home however. It's how anyone can get in just by walking into a public building and using a computer. To suggest that this information would be difficult to get from the outside would be ridiculous however, especially considering the login screen gives you tips on how to log in.

Hopefully this article has given the reader some idea of just how insecure their private information is, and how anyone can walk up to any machine and open up a connection into the mainframe. If your school, or anyplace that stores your information for that matter, uses these techniques, I strongly suggest you write to the people in charge and tell them how uncomfortable you are. Or maybe you could even use one of the terminals to obtain their home address and send them a letter. I'm sure they'll be quite surprised.

Shout outs to Panther for letting me test out my theories using his private information, and to Dash Interrupt for his constant support.

CampusWide Wide Open (Spring, 2002) *By Acidus*

CampusWide is the mostly widely used card access system in America today. It sadly is the least secure. CampusWide is an ID card solution originally created by AT&T and now owned by Blackboard. It is an ID card that can be used to purchase things from vending/laundry machines or the college bookstore just like a debt card. It's used to check out books from libraries, open computer labs and buildings at night, gain access to parking decks, and even get you into sporting events. The CampusWide system gives everyone a card that lets them access both unattended and attended card readers and Points of Sale. All these actions and transactions are sent to a central server, which stores all the information in a database. A confirm or deny signal is sent back to the card reader.

Back in the day (last ten years), there were two major card systems available to colleges: AT&T's CampusWide system (also known as Optim9000) and Icollege's Envision. Envision was one of the first card systems ever made. The seeds of the current Envision system go all the way back to 1984 with a company called Special Teams. The original engineers from Special Teams went through several companies, each one being bought by another company every year for several years, before they came to Icollege. AT&T saw the market for card systems and jumped into the mix as well, stealing some of the ideas behind the system by hiring developers of Envision away from Icollege. They released a system known as CampusWide. It is commonly called Optim9000 or OneCard; however I will continue to call it by its most well known name, CampusWide. So why do you need to know all this history? Because the core of all modern card systems is based entirely on 1984 technology! The original engineers from Special Teams and people trained in their ideas have been the only people in the country designing and building these things. That means that the weaknesses in the reader/server infrastructure that I point out here are found in every card system made in the United States in the last 15 years! By the mid to late '90s CampusWide held the largest market share. Then in November 2000, a newly formed company called Blackboard purchased both Envision and CampusWide. It sells both systems under the names Envision and Optim9000. Blackboard's first order of business was to upgrade the two systems to use newer technology, only to learn that they couldn't! Too many colleges and even businesses had the older equipment and Blackboard couldn't afford to drop compatibility! They have tried to merge older and newer technology in an attempt to improve security (with the addition of IP converters), but in truth, they have weakened an already frail system.

The CampusWide system is the most prevalent, and easy to spot. The readers are black metal or plastic, almost all have an LCD screen, and they have no writing on them except for the AT&T logo with the word "AT&T" under it. The newer Blackboard ones work exactly the same as the AT&T ones, only they have Blackboard written on them. Information on the CampusWide system was very hard to find. I started looking right after AT&T sold it when they were clearing out their old web pages and Blackboard was still creating their web pages. Needless to say, AT&T had much better documentation of the specs of the system than Blackboard does. Sadly, all of it is off AT&T's page now and you'll have to hurry to still find it cached on Google. Luckily I saved everything, and should post it up soon.

The Server

The CampusWide system is recommended to run on HP9000 machines, though any RISC processor will do. It only runs on HP-UX. (Blackboard currently installs ver 11.x.) The AT&T system had a list of specs that the end users had to have to support the software. These included the above, but also a four gig capacity Digital Audio Tape and a UPS that could keep the system up for 20 minutes. (Blackboard's newer specs suggest a Best Ferrups 1.8 KVA battery that can go for 45 minutes.) More interestingly, the CampusWide system is required to have a 9600 bps modem for remote diagnostics. The system itself consists of two parts: The Application Processor (AP) and the Network Processor (NP). The Application Processor is the back end of CampusWide, the part the users never see. It manages the database where all the information is stored and provides an interface for human operators to look at logs and run reports, as well as change configuration/privileges and transactions/account maintenance. The NP is the gateway from the infrastructure to the AP. It takes in the requests from readers around campus, converts the mode of communications into commands the AP can understand, and then passes it along. AT&T CampusWide could support up to 60 communication lines and 1000 card readers. The new Blackboard system allows up to 3072 readers.

The Database

All the information about a student or employee isn't stored on the card for security reasons. It's stored in the database. (The card simply has an account number that is used to organize the data in the database.) The database used by the current Blackboard system is dbVista. The database for the AT&T version was never advertised by AT&T but was believed to be Informix. However, based on the modular design of CampusWide, I believe any SQL queried relational database should work. The database is most likely not encrypted or protected in any way other than by isolation. The only way to get to it is either at the console of the AP or by the commands sent from card readers that have already passed through the NP. Blackboard's assumption that these two ways of reaching the AP are secure is one of the system's downfalls. The database can store up to 9,999 different accounts, each account having many different fields. The balance the person has and the doors he can open are included in the system. The balance will be a floating point number, and the doors the person can open will most likely be a string of characters, with the bits being used to tell which doors he can or can't open. The doors are most likely grouped into zones, so that the five doors into a building have one bit instead of five separate bits saying whether the person can open those doors or not. This idea is upheld by the fact that Blackboard says the users are given plans and they can be updated regarding their access to buildings. These plans grant different levels of security access to a building. Lower levels can get into the building through all the exits; the next level can access labs on a certain floor, etc. Without direct inspection of the database, only educated guesses can be made about its structure. (I have totally left out any provisions for checking out books and other things the card can do.)

The Workstations

The AP was interfaced originally by the AT&T system only at the server console, or through dumb terminals connected to 19,200 bps serial lines. Toward the end of the AT&T days and now with Blackboard, changes to someone's security privileges can be made from any workstation on campus. I watched this process several times. A certain software package was used to connect through TCP/IP to the AP. (I saw the name once, briefly, and for some reason I thought it was Osiris. Checking on this name has turned up no results. Perhaps this is a proprietary piece of software specific to my college, or simply a closely guarded software package from Blackboard.) A GUI was used to select my name from a list of students. A summary of my security privileges then came up, and the ability to add and remove these was there as well. This GUI was *incredibly* user friendly, as the man using it had nil computer knowledge. I only got to watch a few people having new security privileges activated, and never got to use it myself, so I have no way of knowing if the debt balance can be accessed/changed from this GUI.

The Card

The ID cards that are used are your standard ANSI CR-80 mag stripe cards. They are made of PVC and are 2.125 by 3.375 inches. They are made on site at the college's "card station," and normally have a photo ID on them. A 300-dpi photo printer is used and the company recommended by Blackboard is Polaroid (just like the printers at the DMV). The magnetic stripe on the card is a Standard American Banker Association (ABA) Track 2. Any card reader/capture tool can read these cards. The cards are encoded on high Coercivity stripes (known as HiCo), which are very resistant to wear and tear. These cards only use Track 2 of the card, which is read only. It is interesting that they don't use Track 3, which is read/write. Track 2's information breakdown is as follows:

Start Sentinel	1 character
Primary Account Number	up to 19 characters
Separator	1 character
Country Code	3 characters
Expiration Date or Separator	1 or 4 characters
Junk data	fills the card up to 40 characters
LRC (Longitudinal Redundancy Check	1 character

As you can see, most of this applies to banks. However, the account number I have stamped on my CampusWide card is 16 characters long, so the Primary Account number field is known to be used. CampusWide also allows for lost cards. If a card is lost, an entry is made in that person's table in the database, the last digit of the account number is increased by one. (This is called the check digit, so of the 16 digit account number I have, the first 15 digits are my number; the 16th digit is the check digit.) The old card that uses the old check digit is deactivated and a new card is printed.

The Infrastructure

The infrastructure is a "security through obscurity" ploy of the system. Originally the system was designed to run over several RS-485 drop lines. (These are the 60 communication lines mentioned before.) RS-485 is a very robust means of transmitting data. (The whole CampusWide system is designed to take a beating.) Unlike RS-232, which has a protocol built into the standard that says how devices must talk to each other (stop bits, baud, handshaking, etc.), RS-485 has none of that. It is a way for a master device that sits at the end of a communication line to talk to slave devices that are daisy chained on the line. The CampusWide system uses the full duplex version of RS-485 where slaves can speak to the master before the master polls them for data. (CampusWide needs this to have the sub-seconds times they advertise. However, the NP still polls all the readers on a regular basis and can be interrupted by a reader when a transaction comes in.) The data lines are very robust against noise and interference. RS-485 has two lines in each direction, called A and B. Data is sent by having a difference in the voltage of A and B of more than five volts. This mean that if you have a signal being sent and A is at 10 volts, B is at 15, and a power spike comes along, the spike will boost *both* voltages by the power of the spike. However, the difference between the higher power A and B will still be five volts and the data is not corrupted. Over short distances, speeds of 10Mbit can be achieved. However, the longer the cable is, the lower the speed. All CampusWide card readers operate at 9600 bps, thus making the maximum distance of the RS-485 drop line 4100 feet at that speed. This can be extended through the use of repeaters and boosters on the line. RS-485 is very common in the industry, but "secure" at a college since it is unlikely anyone would have a means of interfacing to it. Commercial RS-485 to RS-232 converters are available and prices range from $50 to a few hundred. VHDL designs of these converts can be found on the Internet, and thus an FPGA could be configured to decode RS-485 signals. While researching I came across a post from someone claiming to be a field tech for some company. He said that you could make an RS-485 to RS-232 converter very easily by wiring:

- RS-232 Xmit = RS-485 RX
- RS-232 Rvcd = RS-485 TX

No one posted after him to say he was wrong. I don't know if it would work, since the second wire of the pair of RS-485 data lines isn't even mentioned, and it's the difference between these two lines that sends the data. Also, the possibility of high voltage on an RS-485 line could easily damage a serial port on a computer, if not fry the motherboard. Also, this assumes the data scheme used to transmit data on the 485 line is identical to RS-232. This doesn't have to be true, since the way data is represented (in packets, streams, stop bits, parity, etc.) is not defined by RS-485. If you could get to the data streams, you have no idea what the scheme used to represent it is, and thus how to decode it. This last problem however, is moot, as you will read in the Exploits section.

AT&T would recommend that these lines be used (indeed all the readers can only transmit their data in RS-485 mode), however the data can travel over any facility from telephone lines to radio waves, provided that full duplex 9600 bps asynchronous communication can occur on them. The NP is the part of the system that would sort all this out. AT&T did however specifically say that using an existing Ethernet or computer network was not a good idea, as it sent the data out into the wild, and would slow down both the CampusWide system and the existing computer network. However, Blackboard now offers an IP converter. This device is a simple computer (it has a Pentium class processor and a standard off the shelf NIC Card) that takes in 16 different RS-485 devices, converts all their communications into TCP/IP packets, and encrypts them to send over the network. The NP then has a converter at its end that converts the packet back to RS-485 format. The IP converter is assigned an IP address, which is most likely a static address. The IP converter also most likely has a daemon on it you can telnet into to look at the status and perhaps change configuration info. Blackboard says the data from these boxes is encrypted and the box certainly has the power to crunch some numbers. However, I have found that if encryption is good, then companies will brag about the key length, etc. The only data Blackboard gives about the encryption is that the keys can be changed automatically at any interval from the AP.

For the longest time at my college if an off-campus food joint wanted to have the student be able to use their school cards to pay for food, they had to pay for an expensive leased line that connected them to the school. It's my guess that this was the RS-485 line or something similar. Recently (in the last six months) my college offered cheap (less than $300) boxes to nearby pizza joints that would allow for payment with a school card. These boxes were simply card readers with modems installed, much like a credit card validator. These modems are dialing the NP directly! Major security risk!

The infrastructure ends up like this. All the devices in a building send their lines into one place in the building. This is where multiplexers exist that split the main RS-485 drop line up into slices for each reader. These multiplexers also can boost the power of the main drop line, letting it travel longer distances. They can be stored in a locked networking closet or in these big metal cabinets on the wall of a room. AT&T called these MW/MHWMENC—Wall Mount Enclosures. This metal box has a handle and a lock, but the front of the handle and lock assembly has four flathead screws. I used a cheap metal knife and opened this locked box. Inside I found the LCM (Laundry Center Multiplexes) that controlled the laundry room I was in. Everything had "AT&T CampusWide Access Solution" written on it, as well as lots of Motorola chips. Sadly, this was early in my investigation, and I haven't gone back to look again.

The drop lines coming to the building can be traced back all the way to the building that houses the NP. There the NP interfaces with the AP to approve or deny transactions.

The Readers

Every reader imaginable is available to a college from Blackboard. Laundry readers, vending machine readers, Point of Sale (POS) terminals in the campus bookstore, door readers, elevators, copiers, football game attendance, everything!!! All of the readers communicate using RS-485 lines, and if any other medium is used between the reader and the NP (such as TCP/IP networking by way of the IP converter), it must be converted back to RS-485 at the NP, since all CampusWide uses that standard. Everything is backwards compatible. The majority of my college campus has AT&T readers on them, though a few new Blackboard readers are showing up.

Readers can be broken into three categories: security, self vending, and POS.

Security readers are made of high density plastic and consist of a vertical swipe slot and two LEDs. They are green when they are not locked and red when they are. When you swipe a card to open a door you are cleared for, the light will change to green for around 10 seconds. If the door has not been opened in that time, it locks again. To allow for handicapped people who may not be able to get to the door in time, a proximity sensor is available to receive signals from a key source to open the door. Information about what frequencies are used to control the door are obviously not published by either AT&T or Blackboard. There is also a model of door reader with both a swipe and a 0-9 keypad for codes. I have encountered no such model and have no idea how it works. Advanced forms of these three security readers that have the ability to have a local database of 4,000 (expandable to 16,000) account numbers stored in NV-RAM are available. This way if for some reason the card reader can't reach the NP to confirm someone's identity, then the reader can check its local records. The tricky bastards also built the readers so there is no visible difference between a reader that can't reach the NP and one that can.

The self vending machines are the most colorful group. They are the best to hack because they are unattended and work 24/7. They vary in size and shape, but all have several fundamental features. They all have an LCD screen of some kind, the most common being 2x16 characters. Most are mounted to walls and the power/data lines are protected by metal conduit. Coke readers are mounted on a Coke machine where the dollar bill acceptor would go. Of this group one stands out: the Value Transfer Station! Unlike the GUI at the workstations, this reader can directly query about the account balance of the cardholder and add money to it as well (by feeding in dollar bills like a change machine). In addition, it dispenses temporary PVC cards that can be credited, so people can do laundry, etc. if they forget their card. This means that this station can tell the AP to create a new account and give it x number of dollars!

Finally there are the POS devices. A student would never get to use these. They are used in cafeterias and bookstores. They allow for payment by the student ID card and several other options.

All these readers have inherent similarities. Most are made from high impact plastic or metal. If it is wall mounted, there will be metal conduit running out of the top that holds the power and data lines. All have their program code on ROM/NV-RAM chips. I once managed to power down a card reader for a copier. When I turned it back on, it ran through several self tests in the span of a few seconds. I saw messages on the LCD that said things like "ROM ver" and "CRC check complete." AT&T and now Blackboard say all the readers, including POS, will power up to full operating status without any user input in a maximum of 20 seconds. All of these readers can store swipes of cards and transactions in their local NV-RAM until it can reach the NP, and through it, the AP to confirm the transaction. While disconnected from the NP, the readers show no warning lights or anything like that. Some readers, such as the security readers, can be wired to a UPS to keep areas secure even when the power goes out.

A Simple Transaction

Let's run through a simple transaction. I am at a laundry reader. I tell the reader with a key pad which washer I want to use. Let's say I choose C4. I then swipe my card. The reader sends a signal that contains the account number (and the amount of my purchase and most likely nothing more) to the NP through some medium. (Most likely it's a straight RS-485 line, but an IP converter could be installed by the university.) The NP decodes the data out of the RS-485 line and parses it into commands the AP can understand. The AP uses the account number to pull up my account and checks the balance against the amount requested. It then either deducts the money from my account and tells the NP to send an OK signal, or to send a deny signal along with the new balance of my account. The NP forwards the reply back to the reader, and the reader (if it got an OK signal) sends an electronic pulse to the coin tester inside the washer C4 and tells it that $.50 was received. The washer is retarded; for all it knows I put $.50 in it with coins, and it gives me a load.

The Exploits

Did you see the problem with the above scenarios? There are several ways to cheat the system. If I can record the "it's OK to sell it to him" signal from the NP to the reader and play it to the reader again, I will get another load of wash. Also, if I could get to the wires that go from the Coke reader to inside the Coke machine that send the coin pulses, I can make the Coke machine think money has been paid. I have looked at Coke machines with these Coke readers. Out the back of them they have an RJ11 jack (though it will have RS-485 signals on it). All I need is a converter and a laptop and I can trap the signals back and forth between the reader and the NP. You don't even need to know what the data scheme used on the RS-485 line is, just send to the reader what you intercepted from the NP, and it will work. It is even easier if the traffic takes place over a TCP/IP network. If I learn the IP address of the IP converter, I can simply send packets to it from anywhere in the world (provided I can telnet into the college's TCP/IP network) that contain the RS-485 code to spit out a Coke! You can fool door readers as well if you can get to the wires that go from the reader to the magnet holding the door shut. Just send the correct pulses. This system is horribly insecure because you can completely bypass the CampusWide interface! The Value Transfer Stations are even worse. They have the ability to make the AP create a new account and set a starting balance of any amount. Just gain access to the RS-485 lines, record the traffic to and from the NP while you are getting a temporary card, and you have the system to create and alter debt accounts.

With a system like this, you would think that the RS-485 lines would be protected with massive security. They aren't. Metal conduit protecting the lines commonly stops at the hanging ceiling. Value Transfer Stations routinely have their backs accessible from janitor or utility closets, which are rarely locked. The 485 line literally comes out of the back of a Coke machine unprotected. The flexible piping that carries the coin wires from the laundry reader to the washer are secured to the back of the washer with flathead screws. It is pathetically unprotected. The phone numbers the modems dial from off campus eateries are easily socially engineered out of the minimum wage workers there, and they let you dial directly to the NP. Or you could simply find the range of telephone numbers of the building that the card system is housed in and wardial it. The AP is required by Blackboard to have a modem for diagnostics. You could steal a copy of the GUI of a computer and then edit people's privileges to your heart's content. And even worse, the Envision system is exactly the same as CampusWide, except it uses a Windows NT/2000 machine using Oracle as its database. Every flaw I mentioned will work against Envision as well. Hell, both systems even use the same readers! And there is no fear of having any of your actions logged. Once you trap the RS-485 signals from the NP to the reader, just play it back to the reader whenever. The AP never knows you are doing anything and thus doesn't log it, and the reader assumes that any data it gets *must* be secure. Now tell me this. The next time you swipe a CampusWide card to get into a football game, how do you know someone isn't trapping the data and creating a copy of your account onto a card from a hacked Value Transfer Station? Hopefully this article will force Blackboard to change to a more secure system.

Thanks to Jim at Blackboard for all the technical info, and various web sites like `rs485.com`, `google.com`'s *cached web pages, and* `howstuffworks.com`.

The University of Insecurity (Summer, 2005) *By chiLL p3ngu1n*

I work for a well known university that recently stopped using Social Security Numbers for identification purposes because of security risks. Instead, we now use a unique, nine-digit, Social-like number. However, the first three digits are all the same: 555. So it's more like a six digit number. Each student is given this school ID number when they register for classes the first time. They are issued incrementally, the first number (555-000-001) going to the person who has been at the university the longest that still owes us money.

Problems

Months before going live with the new system, I had several concerns with it. First off, Socials were more random, so if digits were transposed there was little chance it would pull anyone up. However, with an incremented number system, 555-276-012 and 555-267-012 both bring people up. So the odds of posting payments to the wrong account are increased dramatically. When bringing this up, I was told to "just be careful." I also mentioned that even if we're not using Socials locally (in our office), people still have to use them in order to enroll in our payment plans and for Financial Aid. So I was unclear as to why we needed a full on change in the system. They told me that this decreased the probability of stolen identities.

More Problems

Since the program has gone live, not much has changed. Really, the only place you are required to use your new ID number is our online site, CatNet, where you can register for classes, look up your schedule, review which Financial Aid you've been awarded, change your local and permanent addresses, and so on. In fact, if someone were to walk into our offices and not know their new ID numbers, we've been instructed to look them up by name.

A few months ago, I realized that there was a huge security issue in our new system and reported it immediately. Nothing changed and the hole remained. I reported it a few more times, but all I got was a response that basically said to stop sending them letters and that they weren't going to fix it for whatever reason. I think the basic consensus was that it would probably never happen because people don't understand the system and that they would worry about it if it ever happened.

Ironic

It's almost funny how this new system is much more vulnerable to identity theft than the original one.

Since the numbers are incremented, walking up to an office and saying 555 before six random numbers will pull someone up. You can get a lot of information this way: how much they owe, their addresses, what classes they're in, etc. Mostly unimportant stuff.

But let's say you walk up to the Billings Office and give them someone's name (let's say your roommate's). They will look you up by name, and then you can ask some BS question like "Do I still owe anything?" In any case, before you leave, ask them for your ID number because you "keep forgetting it but you want to remember it real bad." Hell, they'll even write it down for you. Now comes the fun part.

CatNet is, by default, set up to use your ID number as the username and the last six digits of your Social as your password, which can be changed at any time. Unless you have no Social on file, in which case it becomes the last six digits of your school ID. Now, the odds of you just randomly finding someone who has no Social on file are pretty slim; I've only run into a handful of them myself. But if you go to the Registrar's Office you can fill out these neat things called Confidentiality Request Forms. These bad boys keep anyone but a few real-high-ups from looking at things on your account. It makes certain things like phone numbers, addresses, and Social Security Numbers disappear. They don't actually disappear, but access to them is highly limited. They are usually used in cases of stalkers or parents who are trying to steal the student's residual checks.

So here's the trick: now you have the 555 number of the person, which is all that passes as proof-of-identity nowadays. So go to the Registrar's Office and fill out one of those Confidentiality forms. Next, call up CatNet support and complain that you lost your password, or that it's just not letting you in or whatever. I'm not sure how their office works because I've never been there, but either they just have a RESET PASSWORD button or they actually check to see if you have a Social on file and manually change it to that. Either way, just give them your 555 number and magically the password is the last six digits of it because your Social is not accessible to them.

Now you have unfettered access to all of their information, including phone numbers, local and permanent addresses, their Financial Aid, plus the ability to charge books straight onto the account, add or drop their classes, or even withdraw them from the university altogether. But most importantly, you get their Social Security Number. And what can you do with their Social Security Number, phone number, and permanent address? Apply for a credit card! I fail to see how this system is more secure, or secure at all.

Seriously kids, don't try this at home. Identity theft is a major crime. I only wrote about this because it's such a large hole and the administrators here refuse to fix it. If I were attending this university I would hope that there were people looking out for me, which is the point here. Hopefully, someone else will show this to someone higher up and this problem will be corrected very soon. Since most people don't know or understand how the system works, they fail to understand how much they are at risk.

Knowledge is Power.

Fun With School ID Numbers (Summer, 2005) *By gLoBuS*

I attend a medium sized high school with about one thousand students and a few hundred faculty members. Our district has several elementary, junior, and senior high schools. Every student and faculty member has a unique ID number for many uses that I will get into later. Although I may show you ways to circumvent a certain school's security, please insert the standard disclaimer here and don't do anything stupid.

The Discovery

An art student at my school was working on a project one afternoon when I came into the art room. This student had used the barcode generator from `barcodesinc.com` to generate a random code for artistic expression in her project. Anyways, I was passing through on my way to lunch when I noticed this. With wallet in hand and eyes on my student ID card, the light bulb flashed. I should see if I can recreate my own barcode online. So for the fun of it I tried. Using the proper symbols (which I guessed), I was able to make a JPEG file of my ID card's barcode. Well this is all good, but what use is this to me if it's my own number? So I found a friend who willingly gave me his number and I got to work.

The Application

Using plain old MS-Word, I was able to print up the proper sized barcode to fit on the back of my card. Using my friend's ID number on my card, we went up to the lunch line. Lunch was almost over so it was fairly quiet. I had the lunch lady check the balance on the account and, sure enough, my friend's name showed up on the screen. She reminded me that I only had $5 left in my account and we happily returned back to the art room. Once we got there I got to thinking.

The Possibilities

This ID is used for not only lunch accounts, but also computer logins, book checkouts, and teachers have many other uses for them. I brought my findings to my computer class teacher. He was shocked and amazed that the account numbers are as accessible and reproducible as they are. He had me copy his ID for him and it was a carbon copy of his. Being that he is on staff and that he was once a computer repairman for the district he reminded me of the access that his card granted him. His barcode, along with other teachers, could be read and used to gain access to the school. If activated his card would give him the right to go to the main district server room. Going to my next class, I remembered that I was able to access my grade's mass listing of student ID numbers. By going up a few levels from my user account on our network, I was able to see all the ID numbers for every student in alphabetical order.

Conclusion

I asked my computer class teacher to bring this to the attention of the right people and not implicate me on the way. He did and we're waiting for the change to take place. Until then, I plan on paying for my lunch with cash.

FirstClass Hacking (Winter, 2006-2007) *By Cristian*

The idea to write this article came from reading this magazine for a while. I noticed that lots of people were writing in about the (in)security of the place they were studying. Having read all these articles/letters very thoroughly, I decided to look into the security in the place I go to study. I go to an English CEGEP, which is basically a hybrid of year 12 in school and the first couple of years of university. When you first enroll into the CEGEP you are given a student ID card, which has a magnetic strip, your picture, and your student ID number. The magnetic strip contains the SID number too, as well as a "charge" of $4.00 CDN in order to be able to print in certain computer labs throughout the campus. Using a combination of methods, we will obtain both the SID number and the corresponding password, thereby showing how vulnerable this system really is. This of course should be taken as an educational guide and not to be used for your own gain.

The Student ID Number

The student ID number is used to log into your FirstClass (www.firstclass.com) account, which is the piece of software used all over the campus for pretty much any class related tasks. We use FirstClass for everything, from viewing our assessments to communicating with the teachers. Teachers, on the other hand, use it to actually put our grades into the system, calculate class averages, etc. We also use this SID to log into our "For Students Only" section where it shows us all our grade history, our current schedule for the semester, our CRC score (a sort of GPA), and a couple of other features. It is also used for the OmniVox service. We use this web-based service to view our grades with more details (class averages, graphs, etc.), pay our student fees for the semester, get a tax receipt for being a student, or change our home address and phone number. Lastly, we use the SID to be able to make our schedules a couple of weeks prior to the semester starting. The system is phone based, so you simply call and follow the instructions given to log in.

Vulnerabilities

The Birthdate

There are various vulnerabilities in the system, so I will go in the order I discovered them. Upon your first entry to the college, they tell you that your PIN (to be used in FirstClass, "For Students Only," OmniVox, and course registration system) is your birthday, in the form of DDMMYY, including the 0s if the day or month has it. Social engineering, anyone? If you are able to engage a conversation with someone, it should be quite easy to obtain their date of birth. Even worse, the CEGEP I attend is chock full of people who use the infamous MySpace.com web site, so even if they don't tell you their date of birth, asking them for their MySpace page is another option. Simply looking at their description may reveal this bit of information or, if not, look at the comments other people leave. There might be messages wishing a happy birthday and then you can deduce the date of birth of the person.

The Student ID Number

Knowing the birth date is only half the information we need since the SID number is the next important part. The SID number is seven digits and has the format YYXXXXX, where YY is the year you first enrolled into the CEGEP and the remaining Xs are generated at random (to my knowledge). Finding this number is quite easy and there are actually various ways to find it.

For one thing, everyone must carry their SID card inside the campus or they will be kicked out by the security guards as well as fined $50 CDN. Again, social engineering can be applied here and simply asking someone you know to show you their ID card to see how goofy they look in their picture will give you full access to the SID, so memorizing it shouldn't be that big of a problem.

Another way to find it is by looking in the recycling bins. The students over here print like crazy, and in all essays/lab reports, etc. you must provide your name and SID number so the teacher can then input the grade into the FirstClass system. Usually you can find old lab reports or pages that have mistakes in them with the student's name and SID number fully viewable in the page's header.

The third way to find it is directly via the FirstClass system. Upon logging into the system, you will be greeted by the "Desktop" of your FirstClass account, which has links to your mailbox, address book, calendar, current semester registration process, conferences, uploaded files, help, news, and student body forum. To your left you have the FirstClass menu system, which has links to logout, who's online in the system at the time, instant message menu, preferences, and, more importantly, the directory.

The directory is a search engine that takes in a name (or part of a name) and searches matches across the student body and the faculty/teachers. Now if you search for someone (let's say Smith), it will return anyone with the surname Smith in it (both student and teacher). Once the matches appear, it will provide links to their FirstClass shared files folders. For teachers, this is quite useful since they can provide class notes, PowerPoint presentations, etc. for everyone to download. For students, well, I haven't met anyone that actually uses that service yet. The important part here is the list of links that is provided when a match is found. If the person is a teacher (let's say we found a teacher named John Smith), then pointing to the link will provide an address such as the following in the status bar of your browser:

```
http://firstclass.COLLEGENAMEHERE.qc.ca/Login/~SMITHJ/
```

There isn't very much to work with in that link, right? Well, now let's say that the list of matches is greater than a single result and that at least one of the matches is a student. If you point to that link, the status bar will display the following address:

```
http://firstclass.COLLEGENAMEHERE.qc.ca/~YYXXXXX/
```

Recognize something there? Lo and behold, the link provides the SID number of the student we searched for, without even knowing the student in real life.

It is also worth noting that when you change your password for the "For Students Only" page, it only applies to that individual system. Your birth date will still be the password for the OmniVox, FirstClass, and phone registration systems. Even worse, in order to actually change these passwords, you cannot do it via the actual system. You must physically go to the IT Administrator's office (which very few students know how to find) with two pieces of ID in order to change them. Making it this hard to change a password is very unreasonable. Students are lazy and they have work to do. They aren't going to go through the trouble of finding out where the office is just to change their password. They'd rather just keep it as it is and just forget about the potential consequences that could happen.

Combining these two pieces of information gives us literally access to anything related to that particular student. You are able to change their address, their phone number, and once schedule-making time comes, you can easily delete all his/her courses and have him/her be charged $50 CDN for registering late, as well as leaving an empty spot in the classes he/she took (which, if you need that course, can be taken by you).

It's very surprising that they have such an elaborate system for managing your stay at the CEGEP, but it can be very easily bypassed with a few simple clicks and a little bit of social engineering. Even worse is the terrible method that they have to perform a simple task like changing a password. If you ask me, it's a very small price to pay for your privacy.

Military and War Zones

Our readership spans the globe as well as all levels of society. We constantly get mail from people in the military and not just the U.S. military. Curiosity exists anywhere there are bright and observant people. And, perhaps surprisingly, there is a fair degree of rebelliousness in the military environment. We also hear from people in war-torn parts of the world who share our desire and passion for technology. One such story is reproduced here, in tribute to its author who sadly has since passed away.

A Hacker Goes to Iraq (Spring, 2003) *By Chris McKinstry*

On the face of it, it seems rather odd. Why on earth would a hacker go to live in Iraq, the most isolated country in the world? Internet connections certainly must be hard to come by in a country where there are no ISPs and the sole provider of Internet services is the Ministry of Culture and Information. In fact, until halfway through the year 2000 the Ministry restricted Internet use to the government itself. In July of 2000, according to CNN and the BBC, there was at least one Internet cafe in the center of Baghdad, but today I can find no evidence of this; `backpackers.com` lists zero as the count of Internet cafes in Iraq and Google turns up zilch as well. Antarctica has better connectivity.

How can a modern hacker live without an Internet connection? And why would I go anyway?

The key to the answer to the first question is the word "modern" and the key to the answer of the second question is more complex but can be summarized with the words "teach" and "protest."

I am a modern hacker, but I've been interested in computers since I was a child in the early 1970s when "hack" meant "create" and not the current media corruption, which essentially translates to "destroy."

This was a time when there were no visible computers and the government still decided who had ARPANET access. Around then, the first ads started appearing for Steve Jobs' and Steve Wozniak's Apple II—a useful configuration cost the same as taking a family to Europe (or the United States if you're European).

A real physical computer like the ones I saw in the magazines that taught me to program were simply out of the question. My only computer was imaginary. It existed only as a simulation in my head and in my notebook—the old fashioned paper kind.

My computer programs were just lists of commands and parameters on paper, much like those programs of the first hacker Alan Turing, who hand simulated the world's first chess program in the 1940s before the computers he fathered existed. Of course I gleaned my commands and parameters from magazines and trash cans while Turing seems to have gotten them from God.

The situation is much the same for Iraqi children today as it was for me in the 1970s, except the children of Iraq have no computer magazines to teach them to program and U.N./U.S. sanctions are killing them at the rate of 5,000 to 6,000 per month.

My plan of teaching and protest begins with a flight to Amman, Jordan sometime early in 2003, from where I will drive overland to Iraq even if bombs are falling. I will take no electronics. No computer. Not even a camera. Just pen and paper and my 1976 copy of David Ahl's *The Best of Creative Computing*. I will go from town to town and school to school teaching about programming and Alan Turing's imaginary computer and how to teach the same. If there is war, I will stand by my fellow pacifists at hospitals and water treatment plants, willing to die with Iraq's innocent citizens. If I live through a day's bombing, I will write to the world about it at night.

In a land where medicine and toys are blocked by U.N./U.S. sanctions and those who take it upon themselves to bring them in either risk 12 years in prison, a $1,000,000 fine, and a $250,000 administrative fine, I think even an imaginary computer will make a difference.

It is simply true that one day Iraq will return to the world, and if we do nothing now, an entire generation will be completely dysfunctional in this computer dominated world. As an individual person, I can't possibly smuggle in enough medicine or toys to make but the tiniest of difference. But as a hacker, I can smuggle in an idea—the idea of Alan Turing's imaginary computer—and try to infect a people's children with skill and hope.

Getting Busted—Military Style (Spring, 2003) *By TC*

In light of Agent Steal's article on getting busted by the feds that was published in *2600* in the late '90s, I thought I would write an article for the military audience and for those thinking of joining the military.

First, a little background information on military law. Those in the military are all covered under the Uniform Code of Military Justice (U.C.M.J.), which follows Title 10 of U.S. code. The U.C.M.J. became effective in 1951. Before that time, military personnel were covered under the Articles of War. The Articles of War was different, and one of those differences was that it did not allow persons under military jurisdiction to be subject to civilian law. You could say that is where the term "join the Army or go to jail" came from. Congress gave the executive branch control of this as it is the branch that controls the military, even though they have been known to stick their noses in it and make their own changes. This means the President can make changes to the U.C.M.J. at his discretion. The U.C.M.J. is also a separate legal entity so you cannot appeal your case to any federal civilian court except the Supreme Court.

Each branch of the military has its own law enforcement agencies. The Army has the Criminal Investigation Division (CID), Military Police Investigations (MPI), and Military Police (MP). The Air Force has Office of Special Investigations (OSI—not like on the *Six Million Dollar Man* TV series), and Security Police (SP). The Navy and Marines have Naval Investigative Service (NIS) and Shore Patrol (SP). These agencies have authority over government property, military installations, and military personnel throughout the world. The investigation agencies serve to investigate criminal activities that concern the military and its personnel. They are also known to work with federal and local law enforcement agencies, especially when it concerns military personnel or military property. Like every other policing agency, they also have their own undercover agents. Each branch even has its own customs agents overseas. They usually handle black marketing. Congress also has a directive or law that instructs that the military installation is to enforce state laws that the post is in. In fact, I will mention one incident that happened at Fort Sill, Oklahoma in January 1995. The state has a law that prohibits distributing certain kinds of pornographic materials. You may have heard about one case in Oklahoma City in the mid 1990s concerning a couple who ran a BBS there. They got busted for selling the stuff on it. It was the same stuff that you can get from all those x-rated producers in California. Oklahoma, being in the "Bible Belt," decided to ban hard-core porn. In the Fort Sill and Lawton area, local law and the CID got together and busted a couple of people that had BBSs on Fort Sill with some porn on their systems that people could download. One of them decided to become a snitch in order to get out of trouble and they only ended up with a Bad Conduct Discharge.

These investigative agencies are known to use coercion tactics to get people to talk. Coercion is difficult to prove so I would suggest to anyone that they not say anything to them at all, no matter what they say to you. Of course, if you do ever get yourself into a situation where they want to interrogate you, ask for an attorney. They are provided free of charge and you do not need an appointment to see one. The biggest thing that gets people convicted is their own mouth.

Even if you just *think* you are under investigation, go see a military attorney at once at your nearest Trial Defense Service on post. The only problem with these free attorneys is that they do not have a big legal staff to assist them, so they do all the casework themselves. That makes presenting your case difficult.

I should cover some of the rights of military personnel—or lack of rights. Like everyone else, members of the military have the same basic rights. There are a few differences though. One right that is unavailable is the Fifth Amendment right to a grand jury indictment. The Fifth Amendment states, "No person shall be held to answer for a capital, or otherwise infamous crime, unless on a presentment or indictment of a grand jury, except in cases arising in the land or naval forces, or in the militia, when in actual service in time of war or public danger...." This issue has been before the Supreme Court and they have decided that military personnel do not have a right to a grand jury indictment. You of course get something similar, which I shall explain later.

The military also has loopholes when it comes to unreasonable searches and seizures. Any time a person comes onto a military installation it is considered a border crossing by law and all persons and vehicles are subject to a search. Personnel living in the barracks do have rights against unreasonable searches, but on the other hand commanders have the right to do a health and welfare inspection of everything that is under their command. That includes bringing drug sniffing dogs through and having selected individuals search through your stuff to find contraband that may affect the health and welfare of everyone there. Even if you collect knives, they are not supposed to be there and will be taken. Married people who live in family housing on post do have a lot more privacy, but it still is not too hard to get in there either. Your best bet for total privacy from the military is to get a place off post. Try not to get in trouble with your chain of command as they can direct where you can live if you are troublesome to them.

Once an investigation of you has been completed, the case is turned over to your chain of command for decision as to what should be done next. It could be nothing all the way to a general court-martial. So if the commander of that post decides he wants you court-martialed, it would be in the best interest of the other commanders in your chain to go along with his decision, if they value their careers.

There are many types of military justice to recommend against you. First, there is a general court-martial. A general court-martial may try any case and may impose any prescribed punishment, including the death sentence. Then there is a special court-martial. It may try offenses involving non-capital offenses made punishable to code. Next up is a summary court-martial. It can try and sentence persons guilty of more minor offenses. Last is non-judicial punishment. It is known as an Article 15, or in the case of the Navy and Marines, captain's mass. There are also three levels to this. First is field grade. Next is company grade. Last is a type of company grade, but it doesn't count against you. The most you can get from an Article 15 is reduction of rank, forfeiture of pay, extra duty, and restriction.

If you have been recommended for general court-martial, you will next get your charges read to you by your commander. He will read each individual charge to you. I have heard from people who have had something like 200 charges who kept falling asleep during the boring ordeal. Note that you may have many Article 134 charges on your charge sheet. This article is known as the "catchall" article. If there is no other article under the U.C.M.J. to cover what you did, then the catchall will get you.

As soon as the charges have been read to you, the military has 120 days to bring you to trial, but with a catch. As soon as you are indicted, it is considered that you are brought to trial. At that time though you can immediately demand that you go to trial. This may be good if the military is not ready to proceed. Soon after the charges are read to you, you will have an Article 32 hearing. This is somewhat like a grand jury. It's like a mini trial, which you are present for. The purpose of the Article 32 is to determine if there is enough evidence to proceed with a court-martial. The problem with this is it is run by a selected officer who knows nothing about law or procedure. Since this person does not know what they are doing, they will certainly just come to the conclusion that the court-martial must go ahead. They do not want to go against that general who wants the court-martial to proceed (good career move).

After the Article 32, you now get ready for trial. During this time, the same general who wants you court-martialed also gets to select who will be on your jury! Do you smell setup or what? The military calls its jury a panel that consists of six members who are at least the rank of colonel down to major. If you are enlisted, you can have one third of the panel enlisted. They also start at high-ranking sergeant majors and go down. So if you are a lowly ranking enlisted person, you will not have a jury of peers, but supervisors! Here you have a trial with a panel of members selected by the commanding general and you believe they aren't thinking about their future and retirement? Most of the panel members will have a mentality of "He must be guilty or he would not be on trial." (You do have the option of having a trial by judge only. They are sometimes brought in from other commands and tend to be a bit more neutral.) Despite the drama you may have seen on TV, a two thirds vote is what is required for guilty or not guilty. There are no hung juries. I will also note that according to compiled statistics from military organizational groups, the acquittal rate for a military court-martial is about two percent. If you are offered a plea agreement, you should seriously consider it. If you don't take a plea agreement, you look at more time in the long run if found guilty. It has also been noted that a court-martial tends to be more cautious of what it does when the media is paying attention. A good example is the trial of former Sergeant Major of the Army Gene McKinney. His best defense in his case was contact with the media. If you think you are getting snowballed by the military, contact the media and tell them of the military's conduct.

The military justice system despite its flaws is very efficient and swift. On average a trial is about two to three days and you are sentenced and put in jail as soon as it is over. On the other hand, sentencing is not like the feds with their sentencing guidelines. This can be bad or good depending on your crime, personality, demeanor, remorse, and taking responsibility for your guilt (if found guilty). So if you know you are going to get slammed, you might as well put on a good show for them. Tell them how sorry you are, show sadness, cry, anything to get that time down as low as possible.

After sentencing, it's time for appeals. The military judge or panel can only recommend your punishment. Your case now goes to the commanding general for review. He gets together with his advisors to discuss what to do with your case. He can either go with the recommended punishment or reduce it, but not give any more than the recommendation calls for. Once he signs off on it, it goes to the next level for review. This process with the general usually takes about six to eight months. During this time—if your time in the military has not expired—you will continue to get paid until the general takes action on your case. At that time, if you have received forfeiture of your pay, your pay will stop when the general signs off on your case. If you have not received forfeiture, your pay will continue until your end of service date.

The next stage of the automatic appeal of your case goes to the service branch Court of Criminal Appeals. If you are Army, your case would go to the Army Court of Criminal Appeals. At this time you also get a new attorney who will handle your appeal from now until it's done, unless he changes duty stations. The chances of getting any relief from this court are very slim, as it is also run by folks in uniform. How long this process could take is really different for everyone. Some take months, some take years.

The next step of your appeal is to the United States Court of Appeals for the Armed Forces. There is not an automatic review from this court. The court decides if it will review your case. If it does not, your appeals are over and you cannot have the Supreme Court review it.

If you had a plea agreement, it usually takes about one year for your case to go through the appeals review. If you pleaded not guilty and are continuing to fight your case, it is not uncommon for a person to be released before their case has been through an appeals review.

After you have been sentenced it is off to jail. The Army, Navy, and Marines have their own prisons. The Air Force does not have confinement facilities and they send their own personnel to the nearest base. Those who receive a sentence of five years or less will be sent to a regional facility that is closest to their base. These facilities are like basic training and are very boring places. Expect much kitchen duty and filling of sand bags. Everyone else who gets more than five years is sent to the United States Disciplinary Barracks at Fort Leavenworth, Kansas. This is the first and oldest federal prison in the United States. The original building was constructed in the early 1900s. The original site dates back to 1875. The "castle" as they call it is currently in a state of massive decay. People have been injured by the falling matter coming from the very high ceiling. The place has a capacity of about 1500, but there were just around 890 people when I was there in the late 90s. It is closed now as a newer prison has taken its place with a capacity of about 515. Inmates were being transferred to the Federal Bureau of Prisons in order to transition over to the new facility because of its smaller size. Compared to the F.B.O.P., the U.S.D.B. is really not that bad of a place to be.

The U.S.D.B. has five different security levels it handles. Because of this, the old facility had a 40 foot wall around the entire place. The security levels are Maximum, Medium, Minimum Inside Only, Minimum, and Trustee. Once you get to Minimum you can live in a dorm and have a TV and stereo with cassette player, CD player, and of course a typewriter or word processor without disk drive. At one time computers were allowed, but not anymore. They got rid of them through attrition. I know of one person who had to hide a hard drive in his computer, as they were not permitted. He would turn it on and off in the system BIOS. The size of their manpower has shrunk along with the rest of the military and they claim they cannot maintain security of computers with the amount of personnel they have.

You can also leave the wall and work outside as a Minimum with the supervision of a guard. As a Trustee, you live about a half mile from the prison. It's comparable to the Federal Prison Camp of the F.B.O.P. They at one time could get a job in town, but that was taken away. Now you are just able to work around Fort Leavenworth. You can also have a video game machine, go shopping every two weeks at the exchange on post, and receive packages from home. The other custody levels there are not worth mentioning.

Military corrections is controlled by a Department of Defense directive and supplemented by each service's own regulations. Its system is set up quite similar to the feds' "old law." Up front an inmate gets an amount of good time based on their sentence length. A person with ten or more years of a sentence length gets a rate of ten days per month. Less than ten but more than five gets a rate of eight days per month. That amount of time keeps going down as you have less time. There is also extra good time one will receive for working on an assigned detail in the prison. The rate starts at one day per month for the first five months. It continues up the scale until you get to five days per month, which takes nearly two years to achieve. Those who become trustees will get up to seven days per month as long as they remain out there. And that is not the end of it. For special projects and such, it is possible to earn an additional five days per month. But nowadays it is very difficult to get any of those days due to the "lock 'em up and throw away the key" attitude. Those with life or on death row cannot receive any good time.

Military inmates are also eligible for parole after serving one-third of their sentence for those with up to thirty years. Those with more than thirty or life are eligible after ten years. Death row inmates are not eligible for parole. Those who are granted parole must remain on parole until the expiration of their maximum sentence length and they are under the supervision of a U.S. Parole Officer. The problem with parole though is that the conditions could be changed and there is nothing you can do about it, except maybe violate parole.

Military inmates also get a yearly clemency review for a time reduction, restoration to duty, and upgrade of their discharge (DD 214) that is reviewed by a local board and their respective branch secretary. Restoration to active duty is exactly what it sounds like. Individuals are returned to active duty for the remainder of their sentence at the rank they were demoted to. When they successfully complete their time in service, they will receive an honorable discharge. The problem with this clemency review is that no one gets any sort of clemency from them anymore. The process is still on the books and still must be conducted. Nor has anyone been returned to duty in years either. If you are transferred to the F.B.O.P., you are still considered for clemency and restoration to duty, but now the U.S. Parole Commission will determine your release on parole. Unlike the feds, once the military releases you after your expiration of sentence, you are scot-free, even if transferred to the F.B.O.P. If you are released from the military confinement, you are given a release gratuity of $25, your property is mailed home free, you are given some cheap clothes (or you can have your own sent in), and you are given the cheapest transportation home. This usually means bus, but sometimes a plane is cheaper for them.

I hope this article has been informative to you all and if you end up at Fort Leavenworth, in or out of prison, do enjoy the many historic sites they have to offer as well as the scenic views all around the post, with plentiful fruit and nut trees to enjoy.

MILESTONE: CONSEQUENCES (Autumn, 2001)

It takes an event of great magnitude to really put things into perspective, to make us realize how insignificant our daily concerns can be. At the same time, such an occurrence can trigger a chain of events that wind up magnifying these concerns.

It's hard to imagine anyone who hasn't felt the horrible weight of September 11. There, before our eyes, was all the confirmation we needed to see how uncivilized the human race could be and how vulnerable we, as individuals and a society, really are to those who value neither.

We feel the outrage along with everyone else. Anyone responsible for such heinous acts, whether directly or by helping to organize them, deserves no mercy from any court in the world.

continues

MILESTONE: CONSEQUENCES *(continued)*

Rage, however, often makes us lose sight of some of the important things that we're supposed to be defending in the first place. And we have to be extremely careful not to add additional loss of freedom to the loss of life that is the legacy of terrorism.

What perhaps is most disturbing is the *speed* with which things began to change after the attacks. It was as if members of Congress and lawmakers were poised to spring into action the moment public opinion began to turn and before common sense had a chance of regaining its dominance. Within hours of the horrific events, new restrictions on everything from encryption to anonymity along with broad new powers allowing much easier wiretapping and monitoring of Internet traffic were being proposed—all with initial overwhelming support from the terrified public.

We find it absolutely unconscionable that anyone would use such a tragedy to further their own agenda—whether it be by selling a product or enacting a wish list of legislation. We've witnessed a good amount of both recently and it's all pretty repugnant. Almost every new law that's been proposed is something we've already seen in the past—and rejected. And there is very little contained within them that would have been helpful in preventing the terrorist attacks in the first place.

Our concerns can best be summed up by this quote: "Maybe the Senate wants to just go ahead and adopt new abilities to wiretap our citizens. Maybe they want to adopt new abilities to go into people's computers. Maybe that will make us feel safer. Maybe. And maybe what the terrorists have done made us a little bit less safe. Maybe they have increased Big Brother in this country. If that is what the Senate wants, we can vote for it. But do we really show respect to the American people by slapping something together, something that nobody on the floor can explain, and say we are changing the duties of the Attorney General, the Director of the CIA, the U.S. attorneys, we are going to change your rights as Americans, your rights to privacy? We are going to do it with no hearings, no debate. We are going to do it with numbers on a page that nobody can understand."

Those remarks came from Senator Patrick Leahy of Vermont, one of the few who seem to actually comprehend the serious risks we're facing. And when a *senator* expresses these kinds of fears, it's a good idea to pay attention. The consequences of not thinking this through are so great that they're difficult to even grasp.

MILESTONE: CONSEQUENCES *(continued)*

Before any of the really bad stuff started to happen, we were already asking ourselves if things could possibly get any worse. It almost seems as if there is no limit as to how bad it can get.

We lost some architectural pillars and a whole lot of innocent lives on September 11. Now the pillars of freedom and justice which remain must be saved from destruction as well.

Backdoor Exits from the U.S. Military (Spring, 2005) *By Bac*

This article in no way supports using these methods and is only written for informative purposes. If you sign up, you should stick it out like a good serviceperson.

These observations were done when I was exiting the USAF during my Basic Military Training segment. From what I can tell the system is set up to bounce back people who are questionable once they enter into the service.

So you are going into the military. Be sure to have long talks with your recruiter, ask lots of questions, and make sure you can quote questionable remarks or what may be blatant lies verbatim. That is the first thing you can do to protect yourself from what could possibly happen.

In fact, everyone who leaves within the first 180 days of service is granted an "Entry Level Separation," be it for good reason, bad reason, or ugly reason. So the scare tactics they use to keep you in line are in fact not quite as valid as stated. (You know the good ole UCMJ.) That does not fully apply until after your first 180 days of training.

Most of the way the exit process works is very compartmentalized. Each person at a desk knows little to nothing about the other links—from the people in your own wing, to the BAS, to the processing folk, to the docs and other assorted people. Some are enlisted, some are civilians, and some are officers. Not one person has all the answers. All of this I had to learn from experience with all the various people involved in this process.

The intent of all the processes is to deter people from leaving. The military is having major issues with retention so every effort is made to return recruits to training.

Also, some of the information that I received is rumor. Here is my attempt to separate fact from fiction on the subject of exiting.

1. Your recruiter cannot lie to a superior in regards to direct questioning about a statement.
2. The service will do whatever it can to stick you with the bill and not pay you, such as if you come clean about a medical history issue, even if your recruiter

told you to lie. (This is where being able to quote questionable remarks verbatim is important.) They will most likely stick you with the bill and send you home with some of your gear, and may in fact charge you.

3. They will send you back to your point of entry or your home of record.
4. They will spend about two weeks processing your file in regards to exit. Once you try to leave it's not all easy. It is still military protocol and even if you have a complete breakdown, it's no walk in the park. They may lock you up in the mental ward at the hospital.
5. If you try and get hurt or don't drink enough water (heatstroke), they will just send you to get patched up and returned to training.
6. The easiest way to get isolated from your group of recruits and speed up the exit process is to claim self harm or a desire to harm others. Homosexuality has to be attempted in practice, not statement, in order to get removed from basic. Also, if you harm others I know nothing of the process that they would use to isolate you, but I presume they would keep you heavily medicated.
7. Your medical history that you suppressed at MEPS (Military Entry Processing Station) will probably come back to haunt you if you try to use that to leave. Simply put, the blame will be placed upon you and your pay will be revoked, or they will say you are claiming false diseases and return you to training.
8. This one is quite surprising. Going AWOL (absent without leave) from BMT may only get you an orange vest if you return willingly, along with a required service of 40 days with the rest of the rejects, and forfeiture of pay. But you still get an "Entry Level Separation."
9. If you use illegal drugs, even if you pass the test at MEPS, they will test you for traces and kick you out when they have the results back, even if you are a week from graduation from basic.
10. You can exit cleanly if you keep your ears open and realize that the system is not as stacked against you as you might think, and that the exit routine is easy to access.

This is entirely for informative purposes only. It's intended for use in case the draft is reinstated, or if you really make a major mistake by joining.

Circumventing the DoD's SmartFilter (Winter, 2006-2007)

By Comspec—Sigma Nu

I'm a 22-year-old network security engineer for the Department of Defense and have been for a little over four months now. I've been operating in some fashion in the information industry since I was 14. I guess you could say my job is pretty interesting. I work normal hours: 8:00 a.m. to 5:00 p.m., Monday through Friday. I'm a Sigma Nu and I live at Old Dominion University in their crappy semi-new development the University Village. ODU isn't all that bad.

On my first day on the job I noticed the DoD had implemented a proxy that continuously grows in its filtering capabilities based on policies written in by contracted individuals here in my office. It's called SmartFilter. What a pain in the ass this thing is. If you want to write on restrictions of information, this is one hell of a big one. Of course it's a government network and that makes all the difference from a legal standpoint. Personally, I'm all for allowing certain things to be run on my network within limited means. It is widely known that streaming audio is a bandwidth killer in some instances. Well, due to limited funding here at NEXCOM this was said to be a big problem. Until they added it to the proxy list as a big no-no. Oh well....

The chief security guy sits in the office next me. He's continuously trying to get our organization up-to-date with the security standards set forth by Visa and other organizations for transactions but he lacks in just about everything else. For Christ's sake we don't even have any of the necessary security patches for XP yet.

The following is a set of guidelines to go by to circumvent their current system. By no means should this information be used to break any laws. Don't blame me if your supervisor runs in and confronts you about this. I just thought it would be an interesting read. I would appreciate some comments back from those individuals who are able to attempt this in their own departments. If you would like to know any more information pertaining to this network hit me up. I think you'll find it to be a pretty interesting but a crappy international setup. Anyways, back to the real meat....

Let's say your job sucks and you want to pass the day a little faster. So you decide to surf a little and see if you can't find a good radio station that has the magical ability to make you *not* sleep at work. Well, you soon realize that this is nearly impossible with all the filtration going on. I admit this is pretty cheesy but an interesting way to get around it. I'm going to use the example for DI.fm. That seems to be the only music that can keep me awake at work while I am updating network diagrams or fielding phone calls from shitty outposts in Japan or some other remote location around the world.

1. Go to `Archive.org`. (Everyone knows this place well, or should. Read more on them on their site.)
2. Once you're there in the top middle portion of your screen you should see the way-back machine input text area. For this example I used www.di.fm. That's Digitally Imported Radio. Click "Take Me Back."
3. The next page that comes up will list the dates that `Archive.org` crawled across the site and archived its contents. You'll want to look for the most up-to-date one. Out of habit I usually choose those that have a *. That denotes that the

site was recently updated. The last entry that was showing when I performed this was April 1, 2005. Click on the link.

4. Once the Digitally Imported site comes up you can scroll down to the music of your choice. From this point you have two options. Try them both and see which works for you.
    1. Using Winamp, scroll down to whatever music you choose. Click on one of the links listed under Listen Now. Your media player should automatically navigate though `Archive.org` and begin to buffer the stream from DI.fm.
    2. Still using Winamp, right-click one of the links listed under Listen Now and copy the shortcut. Then open up Winamp and under the file menu choose to input the URL. Copy and paste the URL there and click OK.

Like I said before when work has got you down this is always an option. Please continue to experiment with the internal network. Enjoy the information and you all keep up the thirst for information and good work.

Miscellaneous

We could have a whole lot of other categories of various hacker stories but I think you can get a good sense of what's out there by simply glancing at a handful or two of some of the more interesting ones we've received since 2000. Whether it's finding an exploit in an online gambling site, noticing a problem with a televised lottery drawing, witnessing the shocking lack of support at a typical help desk, or feeling the effects of the latest online virus, there are firsthand accounts here that will stick with you for some time. In this collection we also have a look at some memories of the past and fears of a possible future. There are stories of pain as well, specifically of infidelity uncovered by accident on a computer and, as seen in our first tale, what the effects of being caught can be when doing something bad.

The Making of a Pseudo-Felon (Autumn, 2000) *By Brent Ranney*

"I'm bored and depressed. I think I'll hack extenders for seven days, 24 hours a day. It's relatively harmless isn't it?"

At the age of 19, home from college, around the time of Thanksgiving 1993, I used a 386 computer, a special computer program, and a 2400bps modem to conduct hacking activity on Midwest-based LDDS Metromedia Communications—to obtain phone access codes through its service. In other words, I tried to cheat the telephone company.

In the middle of the night, I took a printout of access numbers the computer program generated and strolled over to a pay phone. I tested every access code. They all failed to work despite the computer program logging them as valid with a carrier signal.

When I returned to school, everything appeared normal. I was oblivious to the fact that a federal search warrant had been obtained to search my dorm room.

My friend and I were unaware of anything amiss when we entered our dorm building on an early winter evening. An anonymous student had tipped me off earlier in the parking lot that the school was considering me as a suspect for internal PBX abuse. I was not involved and knew nothing about it.

Before we entered the elevator to reach our floor, a student bellowed, "There are FBI agents running around on the third floor!"

"That's our floor," I thought. "It must be drugs or something." I felt bad for whoever was getting arrested. Though feeling uneasy, I garnered some comfort in thinking it probably had nothing to do with me.

A pudgy man, his face almost blushing, was standing in front of my door conspicuously. The guy greeting me outside my dorm room happened to be the area manager of security for the local telephone company.

"Are you Brent?" he queried.

"Yesss," I said.

The phone cop turned around to face the door. He knocked two or three times. Immediately the door flew open and the barrels of small hand guns were pointed at me, wielded by men dressed in what you might call "land warrior nerd" attire. They were wearing telemarketer headsets and I heard the cracking of walkie-talkies.

I don't remember the specifics. All I know is that I was facing the other way, my hands against the wall up above my head. "What is this?" I asked.

They frisked me and my friend. "Do you have any weapons? Any knives? Guns?"

"No," I said, flabbergasted. On cue, an agent flashed his ID. It wasn't the FBI after all. It was the Secret Service.

I was shocked. Everything seemed to go in slow motion. I didn't feel like it was really happening. I was so nervous.

I asked for a lawyer. A couple of hours later, I found myself in an empty holding cell, after submitting to fingerprints, pictures, and idle chit-chat.

I had a friend whose father was on duty as a cop the night when I came into the police station. "He looked like a stereotypical hacker," his father later told him. Apparently the man had seen a lot of hackers coming through the station (small as the town was) and he could spot them immediately.

Before I was left alone in the cell to lament my sins, another cop stayed behind and eyeballed me for a long minute. His look shot the message, "You're going to get it bad boy, and you are a bad boy, no matter what you think."

I signed a waiver for release, relinquishing some of my rights. I was released from police custody and returned to my dorm, a new man, stripped of all my electronic possessions. They had taken every computer-related article I had, every disk, every issue of *2600*. A year later, after my conviction, everything was returned, mostly broken. I just wish they hadn't destroyed the computer artwork I painstakingly created.

I withdrew from the school. "I hope you get away with it," my political science professor told me as I bid him farewell. "I hate the phone company," he added.

I met with the Secret Service agent again at a later date. Whenever I met the agent, the phone cop was with him—always present, under some shadowy pretense, like cancerman from *The X Files*. I was encouraged, implicitly pressured, to reveal information on other people who committed crimes. I told them about real criminals I was aware of—people who were profiting from fraud.

In these closed door sessions, I admitted illegally obtaining the access codes and divulged every detail about the crime. Prior to my actual arrest, the area manager of security for the local telephone company contacted my mother and promised I would not be arrested or prosecuted, with the understanding that they just wanted me to stop. He told her I was responsible for $100,000 in damages. Unfortunately, she believed his white lie. He told her that if she didn't cooperate by disclosing my whereabouts, she would be an accessory to the crime.

Regardless of what was promised, I openly confessed to involvement unknowing of the unscrupulous tactics employed on my mother. A year later, I plead guilty to "possession of access codes with intent to defraud." I was sentenced to three years probation, fined $500, and ordered to participate in a halfway house program for two months. Throughout my probation, I was tested for drugs. I had no drug history. What I did possess was long hair and a penchant for black clothing.

My offense is a felony for one reason and one reason only: the access codes could be used to call out to any state. Because of this interstate characteristic it is federal and therefore a felony charge. No losses were reported by any of the respective long distance companies I had tampered with, although the local company claimed a loss of about $17 to $30 in administrative fees. The judge and prosecution rationalized that taxpayers are indirectly victimized because of the cost related to investigations and prosecution of "major" cases such as mine.

I don't envy Kevin Mitnick for the ordeal he's endured with the government. I think of myself as lucky to have never spent a day in jail. If I had, I don't think I would have emerged a survivor. Quite honestly, I probably wouldn't be here today.

I don't think this mark on my record, this felony, reflects with much accuracy what kind of person I am, or what kind of employee I am. Many youths do stupid things that aren't necessarily injurious to anyone. Before Steve Wozniak and Steve Jobs co-founded Apple Computer, they "cheated" the phone company with a device called a "blue box" while in college at Berkeley, CA. Didn't they turn into quasi-responsible multimillionaires?

"They didn't get caught," a landlord said to me, whose rental operation routinely turned away convicted felons per police sponsored programs. Is this to be the scale in which we judge the severity of a crime? Simply speaking: "Don't get caught"?

There's no distinction today between a crime of violence and a recreational hacker. I don't expect there ever will be. How do you explain the proverbial Scarlet Letter to the uninformed public who thinks hackers like Kevin Mitnick are diabolic monsters?

Seven years later, I don't justify what I did back in '93. But society shouldn't exaggerate the impact of it either. The interests of the multimillion dollar corporations have been protected, rest assured. Kevin Mitnick was silenced and before him so were many lesser-known hackers.

The branding is done, it's over. No appeals, no expunging. I am a convicted felon for life.

Are we to be made as examples, to sway public fear and distrust? Is this the result of manufactured propaganda to serve corporate interest? Should the minor aggravation of a corporation result in a lifetime felony conviction for a college kid?

I'm not hiding anything and I accept responsibility for something I should have never done for the sake of curiosity to make a few free phone calls.

Kevin Mitnick is, dare I say, an astute genius, but not a criminal mastermind. I was psychologically evaluated by the government and labeled off-the-record as not having "criminal thinking patterns." I've always considered myself an ethical person despite Ma Bell groupies who consider one guy with a few access codes to be of critical importance to the subversion of a nation.

Not abiding contemporary law has disproportionate consequences depending on whether or not the violation of the law involves life and limb or involves property. If you are thinking about tinkering with the phone company or other mega-corporations, think twice. Then consider beating your wife instead. By example of length of sentences served, this act is more acceptable to our society.

But, God forbid, "Don't get caught" beating your wife while in possession of a red box.

Afterthoughts

Since my conviction in the early '90s, I've ceased participating in any hacking activity—anything that might be construed as illegal. Frankly, I absolutely shudder at the thought. I don't keep myself privy to the latest hacking tools. I flee from gray areas of computer activity. I am 100 percent dedicated to a philosophy of anti-hacking. Call it fear, call it cowardice, but I capitulate with tyranny when it threatens my well-being. Paranoia is now a part of my everyday life.

I wasn't always that way. I use to stand up for myself. But the futility of raising arms against a million to one odds is not my cup of tea. But there are others, more courageous than me, who face these odds every day. You may know them: Bernie S., Kevin Mitnick, the staff of *2600*, and nameless others in America and in third world countries.

By writing this article, authoring it with my real name, I fear I'm jeopardizing my well-being. Without any prodding of our imagination, we can assume the Secret Service peruses *2600*. And if the SS thinks I've somehow resurfaced as a threat, they might conceivably pay me a visit. Like Bernie S., they might want to check my wiring.

I don't have a vendetta. I'm just telling a story and offering an opinion. I haven't voiced my disapproval in a domain name like *2600*. But I wonder, how is writing an opinionated article any different?

To the credit of law enforcement and in particular the probation department, I was treated humanely. I'm not going to judge these people. They generally respected me and I respect them. I do think they're part of a larger problem—a preoccupation with power, an aristocracy that pulls the government strings to protect Corporate America. (That's where these laws directed at hackers come from.) Perhaps this threatens our rights of freedom more than any hacker.

A Word of Warning from a Caught Uncapper (Autumn, 2002)

By Kris Olson

Bored during my summer, I thought I would take this project on. I began my research on June 26, before *2600* published the article on uncapping. Through various methods (mainly IRC) I talked to several people and finally figured out how to uncap my modem. Well, it wasn't as easy as it seems.

I went to a lot of trouble that in the end left me without cable and nearly in jail.

My ISP, like many, uses a system called QoS, or Quality of Service. This means a few things.

1. You can't connect without a config that the ISP doesn't already have (i.e., you can't create a config file with a 10mbit/10mbit line if the cable company only offers 400/200 800/400 and 1.5/512). This means in order to uncap, you can only uncap to a better service plan (i.e., going from 400/200 to 1.5/512).
2. To uncap to a better service plan you must get the config for that service plan, as making one with those caps often will not work. Take note, this config file has a different name than the one sent to your modem, and since TFTP protocol doesn't allow directory listing, you must either have once used the faster service and seen the config file, or you have to know someone who has it who can help you out. Should you manage to get this config file, your problems are still not over.
3. The QoS then checks your modem's MAC address every 10 to 50 minutes (depending on the size of your node) to make sure that the parameters set in your modem are the ones that you pay for. Note: the MAC cannot be changed

because you have to register your MAC with the ISP, so they inevitably know who you are. To get around the QoS resetting your modem, one may think "Well hey, let's just change the SNMP ports so they can't send the reboot command to me!" Hah! That pisses them off like nothing else and *yes*, they can track that. All it takes is about a day to find your port. The default SNMP ports are 161 and 162. I changed mine to 9999999941 and 9999999942. In two days they were once again resetting via SNMP.

4. So you figure, "Well, that means I have one or two days of uncapped modem, right?" Wrong. There is another way they can reset you that you can do *nothing* about. In order for your modem to stay connected to the server it must "ping" the server and get responses back. I say "ping" in quotations since it is not your normal 52 byte packet ping. It is a special CMTS type ping. What the ISP can do, should they notice that you are indeed using a faster config, is "suspend" the "pings," meaning that they are lost, and none come back to the modem. This will force an "HFC: Async Error Range Failed" error on your modem's log, which will be followed by "HFC: Shutting Upstream Down," and then "BOOTING: (firmware version)."

So now, this doesn't seem that bad. You may be thinking, "Why is this guy even writing this stuff; if there is a will there is a way." That is true, but my purpose is to show you that if your ISP does use QoS (examples of some that do are: Blueyonder, ATTBI, Cableone, Charter, Comcast, and NTL), then if you *ever* attempt to uncap, they *will* notice and they *will* call you.

I received my first call the morning after I requested tech support to come out and fix the signal strength of my line. (It was way out of spec and kept resetting my modem.) Well, as protocol they watch your line to see what they can diagnose before the tech arrives at your house. Well that morning (the 10th of July) I uncapped and within ten minutes I had a call from the headquarters of my ISP, some 600 miles away. This was a "tap on the wrist" type conversation. They said basically, we see that you are uncapping, and that violates our Terms of Service agreement. Don't do it again. So I didn't—for a while.

A couple of weeks went by and I used Ethereal, a common network "sniffer" to determine whether or not my ISP was watching my MAC address. Later I learned that they were on the entire time and when they saw me "sniffing" for info, they simply hid themselves behind the IP address 255.255.255.254. Not knowing that information, I decided it was safe to uncap again. And so I did and continued to be reset with HFC errors. I tried various methods to get around it: installed hacked firmware, sent various SNMP commands, even attempted to fake a CMTP server so that the CM would send the "pings" to a computer on my LAN, all to no avail. So when my modem would go back to normal, I would send it a new config, and the process went on and on and on like that for two weeks or so.

I left early on Friday morning for a little weekend getaway. While I was out of town, I didn't even think about the status of my cable. No, I did not leave it uncapped when I left the house, but the damage had already been done. My ISP had all the evidence they needed to shut my cable off, and press misdemeanor charges, mainly based on cyber theft.

I returned to find a message on my answering machine from an "Internet Engineer" at the ISP's headquarters. He was *not* very pleased. The message was over 15 minutes long and contained a great deal of threats and comments obviously designed to scare an uncapper. It worked. I was terrified. After hearing the message, I went out to check the mail. In there was an envelope from my ISP containing a "Declaration of Termination of Service." In this letter were several items, including possible criminal charges to be pressed, two pages detailing *every* time I uncapped from July 10 to the present, and a long, *long* list on how I violated the Terms of Service with my ISP. Sure enough, when I went to contact the Internet Engineer by email, (the only contact information that was listed), my Internet service did not work. As a routing check, I looked at my modem's log file only to find this disturbing message:

```
7-Information D509.0 Retrieved TFTP Config TRMNT.cm SUCCESS.
```

It was clear. My service had been terminated. But my problems were not over yet.

The following day (August 5) I received another call from him, telling me that the ISP wanted to press charges. As soon as I was off the phone I immediately called my lawyer and told him the entire situation. My lawyer spent the rest of the day on the phone with my ISP and came to an agreement that for the two months that I uncapped, I would have to pay for the better service.

In the end, uncapping got me these final results:

Pros:

- 200+ KBps downloads (needing to be reconfigured every 35 minutes).
- 100+ KBps uploads (needing to be reconfigured every 35 minutes).

Cons:

- No more cable Internet.
- Almost got charges pressed.
- Ended up wasting about 150 hours of my life to no avail.
- Had to deal with really pissed off nerds with power.

The choice is up to you. This was just my experience.

Infidelity in the Information Age: How I Caught My Cheating Girlfriend (Autumn, 2003) *By atoma*

On a recent Chicago evening, while my live-in girlfriend of three and a half years was at work, I performed some routine maintenance on my home/office DSL/LAN computer network (three PCs {2W98SE 1 XP Pro}, one laptop {XP Pro}, one Xbox, one shared printer, and other PCs and Macs as business dictates). I am a computer repair technician and during the previous week I serviced three computers for virus-related troubles. They were each plugged into my home network after I disinfected them. All of them were error-free after I finished working on them, but I am very protective of my network. I spent many hours building it, and many more making sure no one corrupts it.

After completing repairs on the three PCs, I was checking the created and modified dates on files on each of my workstations. I gave my girlfriend an old computer of mine a year and a half ago (a P2 400 W98SE); I set it up for her, kept it running lean and clean, and never once found any anomalies in my routine network maintenance. However, on this night, her computer displayed a modified file date of 2037 on her `sent items.dbx` file. Since emails are a notorious, tried and true path for virus infection, I immediately grew curious. Her email client (Outlook Express 6) was password protected, and I wanted to see if any suspect email attachments existed in that dbx file.

I copied the suspect dbx file: `(\WINDOWS\ApplicationData\Identities\{AC228580-7D44-11D6-8CF5-D78FCE200233}\Microsoft\OutlookExpress\Sent Items.dbx)` to my PC.

(For those of you who don't know, this is where OE stores your emails, in files *.dbx, one dbx file for each folder you create in your respective identit(y) or (ies).)

I opened it with a disassembly program (W32Dasm V8.93) and I didn't find any suspect attachments. However, amidst the gibberish of random characters, I saw an email that my girl sent earlier that day to a name I immediately recognized as trouble. It was an ex-boyfriend. The message was very concise, six words to be exact. She asked him, "Are we still on for tomorrow?"

This freaked me out, because the tomorrow she spoke of was just hours away. I was supposed to go out on a service call for the day and she was planning to spend it with an ex-boyfriend. I extracted all of the emails from that file with (DBXtract V 3.50) and was absolutely floored. Before my eyes, in forensic black and white, was the outline of 18 months of betrayal. Times, dates, graphic reflections on the sex acts she committed, outpourings of emotion to men I was assured were "just friends." All of it was in front of me, taunting me, sickening me, destroying me. In the midst of making sure her computer was running at its best, so concerned with the performance of the computer I gave her, working into the wee morning hours so that she can painlessly experience the joys of computing, I got violated to such a degree I still struggle to describe it.

I copied all of the dbx files from her identity folder to my PC (oh yes, that OE password protection was so helpful to her huh?). I set up a new "dummy" identity in OE6 on my PC and imported all of her emails into it. I took all of the emails and put them into one folder. I sorted the whole stinking mess chronologically and gave myself a timeline to look at. I went down the list and read all of the emails (about 400) and took notes on the dates and times that stuck out in my mind, some dates where I was out of town, other dates where she convinced me she was working late or going out with her "girlfriends." Can you say, "Deleted Items; wow they're still there! Thank you, Microsoft!"?

I started searching the cookies on her PC within the parameters of the dates and times I was able to map out from reading the emails, and I found even more evidence of her infidelities. The cookies from MapQuest and Google were especially revealing. By simply opening these cookies in Notepad, I had before me addresses that she got directions to, searches for restaurants and nightclubs, movie showtimes, even lingerie browsing at Fredericks.com! All of it beautifully time-stamped, frozen tracks of her lies and deceit.

I tell you it was enough to make me crazy with rage. But I wasn't through yet. At this point, with everything I was thus far able to uncover, I felt it was all up for grabs. Privacy? Fuck her, she had total freedom and look what she did with it. I found enough in the digital world. Now it was time to go "analog."

I went into her cell phone records. She meticulously filed each monthly bill away in a folder. I, in a manner quite similar to her precise filing, painstakingly entered all of these phone calls into a spreadsheet in Excel (almost two years' worth). When I finished, I sorted these by phone number. Boom, an easy to read detail of who she called and when. I took these telephone numbers and typed them into Google. Voilà! The address of record on these "unknown" phone numbers corresponded to the address searches from the MapQuest cookies.

How about her bank statements? In the same file cabinet, not far from her cell phone folder, was the BankOne file folder. I cross-referenced the suspected rendezvous dates against this folder of info and again, voilà! Black and white records of ATM transactions at ATMs very close in proximity to the addresses I found in the cookies from MapQuest and Google. These also fit right into the cell phone records' timeline, some phone calls were made to these other men within minutes of using the ATM! Talk about being busted!

A bomb burst in my chest that night. I medicated myself with 13 beers and a pile of cocaine while I reread the comprehensive, chronological, revolting realities of the double life my woman led. It was sickening, like it was two different people. Confronting her with this evidence has been the most difficult task of my adult life. At times I wish I never knew anything about what she did behind my back.

I've always been an advocate of total privacy for the individual, privacy free from the prying eyes of those with higher powers. Being able to find out so much detail about my girlfriend from her PC gave me a wake-up call. The things she did were indeed terrible; they managed to hurt me immensely. But look at how easily I was able to construct a virtual "play-by-play" of 18 months of her life. This is what shocks me even more than the awful things she did.

As "hackers," we all need to be aware of the digital "footprints" we leave behind while we traverse the world we call "cyberspace." It is a place full of so much information, a world full of the knowledge we love to collect pieces of. It is also a place of danger, for the trails we leave behind us can be collected and analyzed. These trails can be used against us, by powers much larger than any one of us. As the years march forward, we will have to evade, in order to survive.

Strange Love: Or How I Learned to Stop Worrying and Love the Anna Kournikova Virus (Spring, 2001) *By 6M AL*

It's odd the people you keep in your address book. As a reader of *2600* for the past eight years, you learn a lot about what people will and won't find offensive. You learn that people will complain about things that affect them, and won't complain if it hasn't affected them yet.

When I received the Anna Virus, I knew it for what it was: a program created by some hacker that had been sent to me unwittingly by another individual. I guessed it might be a worm that would be sent out to another user after an inadvertent reading or clicking of the email message containing it.

I clicked.

Within minutes I was receiving phone calls and emails, some laughing and joking, others solemn and angry, from all the people in my address book. Some were asking what I had sent. One man even wanted help opening the attachment. "I'm sure she's hot," he replied. "But my mail program won't open the picture."

I had sent email to people who owed me money, to people I am in litigation with, to women I haven't called after an affair went sour, to men I had admired, to persons I had feared.

Worst of all, I hadn't just sent an email. I had sent them the virus.

It took a few hours to sink in—the potential impact of what had happened—and you can imagine that I could have been angry. I could have been dismayed. But I had made the choice to try the virus anyway. I had been in good company. CNN carried news of the virus well into the next few days. I was elated and disgusted at the same time. I had burned bridges and made others laugh at my actions. I felt happy I had made no mistake. I had run the virus on purpose.

Now the most important question many would ask is why create such an ugly virus? "Why do hackers have to waste so much time and money on destructive forces?" they demand to know. My response is simple. If the virus I received had short-circuited my copy of Windows, if it had sent instructions to my hard drive to reach for a sector that didn't exist, gouging a new hole in my storage space, the Anna Virus would have been wrong and sickly twisted, something I could hate.

But it didn't. It taught me, and many of you, a lesson. It taught us to guard against such threats and to be ever wary of what we see and open. It took nothing from me, nothing but a little pride, which I could make do without. And the Anna Virus introduced me to people I haven't spoken to in a long, long, time.

Their emails may begin with "I think you have a virus...." But they all end with "So how are you doing these days? How is life?"

A Look Back (Summer, 2002) *By dufu*

As I read *2600*, I realize just how old I am, or maybe just how young all the new experts and pseudo-experts are. After all, my first computers were a TRS-80 Model I and a Commodore 64. Boy... programming was never so easy as back then.

Every time I get a hold of the newest *2600*, I swear that I'm going to write in and comment on how everyone seems to have gotten so much smarter than me. After all, browsing MCIMail with someone else's account was a big thing back when I was a kid. Getting others' credit card numbers has actually become easier although back then, you could find a list of a hundred or more on any given BBS. 64k? Wow. That would have taken a few months of programming—even in Basic—to fill up. Who would ever need more than that?!? Real time chatting? Some folks did it. But it was more like IRC and I could read at 300 baud so it was easier. Networking? Hmm. Isn't that what they used mainframes for? After all, the 286's weren't even out yet. Color monitors came only in amber or green for the most part unless you had a lot of money.

I remember picking up two, 12-meg hard drives at a local computer flea market for free. The largest hard drives on the market at the time were five megs and I thought we had hit the jackpot. Until I found out I couldn't get them to work on my C64.... Boy. Tossing those 40-pound monsters into the trash must have made the garbage men happy....

Then came my first IBM—a real IBM. Weight was twice as much as any clone. So was the electric bill for using it if I remember correctly. Man. It had multiple megabytes of drive space, semi-color output—although not as good as the sprite driven C64! It could go to the same BBS systems I used to visit and fit more on the screen! Wow. Too bad I couldn't read at 1200 baud. Hacking SuperWilbr—some school's remote word processing system or something. Any old-timers actually know what it was?

Someone came out with 2400 baud. Next computer flea market netted me a few 4800/9600 modems. Too bad they were nowhere near compatible with anything I used or owned. Their big blue boxes looked just like the magnetic bone healers the guy was selling in the booth next to mine. Oh, did I mention I started getting a seller's booth at the shows to make dropping off my find easier? Yeah, I started selling junk from the last year's shows too. Helped finance my life.

Doom, Doom II, Quake, and Heretic were all played on a 386 with no sound card. And beat. I either got lucky a lot, saved a lot, or used the cheat codes a lot. Regardless, I won.

Then came phone phreaking. I never really took part, but I played enough to build my own advanced Rock Box without the aid of others. Loved to blast the random telemarketer who called. Seems they call much more now. I remember that 1-800-424-9096 and 9098 were the White House Press Line and the Department of Defense hotline. One still works. You play to figure out which. I memorized the touch tones so that I could tell you what number or numbers you dialed. That always seemed to freak people out.

I'm drifting from the real purpose of this article. Let me jump back to the present time. I now work for a large accounting firm that has recently been taken down by the DOJ because of the actions of a few dozen people. Their leader has pled guilty to the charges pressed against the firm that fired him for the exact transgressions that got both of them into trouble. We've lost more people and more money than Enron even though they get most of the press. I work with technology all day, every day: Lucent digital phone systems that can be crashed by playing too much, networks that are full of great information—all of which is now useless, drones—aka employees running around with either W95 or W2K but nothing in-between. I even remember my first week when I performed a basic defrag on a PC and almost got fired for "hacking" because they "caught" me doing it. They have since become some of my best friends and beloved coworkers. They come to me for technical advice and guidance in many cases. I push the limits of our in-house technical support folks' knowledge base regularly enough that they have given me the direct number to their dedicated MicroScoff advanced support center, along with the access code. It's even more fun to stump those guys....

I could go on and on about how Lotus Notes and eFax don't mix, W2K and our network keep me from accessing sites, etc. However, it was simply therapeutic to write this. What is the bottom line, you ask? In a few years, you'll be just like me, wondering where all the newbies learned their tricks and how they can possibly have enough free time to use them all.

Keep hacking. Keep it moral. Teach others. Become a leader of the ignorant, not their enemy.

A Glimpse at the Future of Computing (Spring, 2003)

By Phocks

Imagine a world, if you will, plagued by terrorists and evildoers, whose weapon is the personal computer. It has powerful encryption used to block anyone from reading plans of how to destroy structures vital to a country's survival. It contains a slew of programs designed solely for destroying security and rendering the world helpless to attacks. And anonymously connecting to a terrorist network consisting of tens of thousands of systems just like it, bringing together all who oppose a country to share information and formulate plans of attack. Welcome to the government's view of the Internet. An innumerable array of systems that have direct access to any one another at any given time, able to share data with a grade of encryption higher than their own military standards.

Something must be done to contain the threat for the good of the world. These systems, which are run without regulation of any kind, controlled and even built by those who operate them, must be stopped, for there is no telling what they are doing. It has even been proven that millions of these systems can come together to shatter the encryption that holds this country's secrets (`distributed.net`). Something must be done to let all activities be controlled, to bring all this terrorism to a halt, to shut down the Internet.

A scheme that sounds so improbable, nay, impossible, is easily completed. All that must be done is pass a new bill (or hide an appendage to an existing one) that will force the ISPs of the country to obey new government standards, to all connect to a central server array that is tightly controlled by the government, and shut off all access to foreign servers.

Simply put, dismantle the Internet in the United States (or any other country that wants to implement such a system) and rebuild it the "right" way, the way that can be constantly monitored for suspicious, terroristic activity.

Personal computers will also become completely incompatible with the new standard. In exchange for turning in your computer to the local recycling center, you will be given a voucher for a free USNet (the new, patriotic "Internet" name) terminal. The terminal will consist of a flat panel monitor, a moderate processor (450 MHz), a mediocre sound card, 32meg of ram, a mouse, a keyboard, and a USNet connection card (proprietary) ISDN-based modem for both speed and compatibility. No hard drive, no networking card, no CD drive, no floppy drive, no external or internal media at all allowed. The USNet terminal will cost no more than $150 (less than $100 for manufacturers to build), and will be greatly appreciated by the manufacturers because of the extremely high profit made from selling millions of machines to anyone who wants a computer.

How it works without a hard drive is simple. The operating system is stored on preburnt ROM and is checked by the USNet servers every three minutes to make sure it's working properly. All web servers are run on the government's super cluster of servers, and a second cluster (or rather, section of the super cluster) is designated for the personal systems. Every user is allotted one gigabyte of storage on the USNet system, which is more than enough.

Everyone wins on this system, for downloads take mere seconds since the personal data section is directly linked with the servers. All programs are run remotely, and only the data that is entered to them (such as typed words in a word processor) is stored in RAM until sent out. No trace of the program is allowed on the USNet terminal, for fear of terrorists editing the RAM and taking control of the programs.

It even works out for software designers like Microsoft. Office tools will not need to be sold, only paid for on a per-use basis. That way everyone wins; the customer doesn't pay for anything that they don't use and the corporations get paid for every use.

Only programs carefully scrutinized by the government are allowed to be run and no amateur programming at all is allowed, for programs should be left to the corporations; that is what they are for. There is no need for a user to program anything. The corporations will take care of everything necessary, even special USNet games that are finally family-friendly. Even the censors will be happy.

Since USNet covers anything a computer should be used for in a free, but secure, society, all other computers will become illegal to own. Why would you have one for any other reason than keeping secrets from the government? Everything will be taken. But you will get money back because the government knows what an investment all that technology must have been. Desktop computers will be exchanged for $150, enough to buy a USNet terminal, and everything from laptops to PDAs will be confiscated on sight, but a voucher will be issued by the officer stating what model and condition it is, and will be cashed at a fair value (not to exceed $200).

All data that enters and exits the USNet clusters will be scanned thoroughly for anything that may be suspicious, such as terrorist-like texts that defame the country. All transactions between servers and personal areas will be logged, and personal data sections cannot send files to one another, lest there be music or movie piracy. In such a system, everyone will be happy because they can chat and play games and run office programs, and the government gets to carefully watch all activity for anything suspicious and keep a tight control of USNet to let it be safe for children to browse, since only their servers can communicate data. That way even the schools and parents can let young children browse the USNet without a single worry, for there will be no more pornography or online stalkers (because all communications are watched by specialized computers to look for any suspicious activity) and all activist pages like those that share information on the Secret Service to terrorist networks and those that actually help evil software pirates and hackers will be shut down forever.

Shoutouts to psyk0mantis, Vie, Twilyght, Arwynn, everyone from SPR and Taps, and anyone who stands by my side, physically or digitally (too many to name personally). I'd like to point out the obvious—that the general happy and positive attitude is not my own. It merely fits the article.

ParadisePoker.com Blackjack Cracked (Summer, 2005)

By JackAceHole

In March, `ParadisePoker.com` added blackjack to their software so players could, "...enjoy a few hands of blackjack as [they're] playing poker!" A few days later, my brother called me to tell me about it. I immediately dismissed the game as being a losing venture. Internet casinos do not typically offer favorable conditions for blackjack players—even skilled card counters. Internet casinos usually deal from an eight deck shoe (the more decks, the worse the advantage for the player) and they shuffle after every hand. This makes card counting impossible and renders the game unbeatable. My brother insisted that the game was good because he was fairly certain that there was an exploitable bug. "I don't know if this makes the game beatable or not, but every time the dealer has an Ace showing, it takes them an extra long time to ask me for insurance when they have a ten in the hole. When they don't have the blackjack, the insurance prompt comes up immediately." I shook my head in disbelief and quickly started formulating how much money I could transfer from my other poker accounts into my Paradise account. I knew that this would be a huge money maker if it were true.

The Edge

The insurance bet is a side bet that the casino offers when the dealer has an Ace as his initial up card. If you take the insurance bet and the dealer has a ten-valued card in the hole, you win one bet. If you take the insurance bet and the dealer does not have a ten-valued card in the hole, you lose half of one bet. So if you initially bet $100, you are given the opportunity to prevent yourself from losing $100 if the dealer has a winning blackjack. (You will win $100 on the insurance bet but lose $100 on the initial bet.) It doesn't sound like much, but you will essentially have $100 more than if you didn't know about the exploit.

Given the rules of the game, the house edge was 0.56 percent, assuming that you play perfect "Basic Strategy." Basic Strategy is the best way to play your hand when all you know is what you have and what the dealer has showing. When the dealer has an Ace exposed, Basic Strategy tells you that you should *never* take insurance. It is an unprofitable bet in the long run.

The dealer will have an Ace as his up card approximately once every 13 hands. Four out of 13 times, the dealer will also have a 10 in the hole. This means that you would get to exploit this bug approximately four times every 169 hands (1/13 x 4/13). This translates to a 2.366 percent more favorable situation for the player. Without the exploit, you would expect to lose 56 cents for every $100 bet. So with the exploit, this translates to a 1.778 percent player advantage (or $1.78 for every $100 bet) over the house without card counting. The table limit for the Internet game was $300 per hand. Playing quickly, a person can play four hands per minute (240 hands per hour). This means that this exploit was worth over $1,280 per hour for the well-funded player ($300 x 240 hands/hour x 0.01778 edge)!

The Attack

I logged into Paradise Poker and started playing blackjack. I was betting ten cents per hand (the table minimum) until I confirmed the bug. Every time the dealer had a ten in the hole, I would have to wait one or two seconds for the insurance prompt to show up. When he didn't have the ten, it would come up immediately. After making perfect insurance bets eight out of eight times, I decided my brother was right. I got down to business and started making $20 bets. As my bankroll grew, so did my bet size.

Pretty soon, my $400 turned into $800. $800 turned into $2,000. $2,000 turned into well over $6,000 and there was no sign of stopping! I finally stopped after seven hours because my eyes were shot and I just couldn't stay awake anymore. I decided to take a 12 hour break to sleep (it was four in the morning), check in at work, and see whether my actions triggered any red flags in Paradise Poker's monitoring system.

The End of the Line

The next morning I went to work and told my boss that I was going to take a few days off. I made over one month's salary in less than seven hours so I was not going to let a pesky thing like work get in my way. While I was there, I got another call from my brother, "I've been playing for about an hour and it looks like they fixed the bug." I rushed home in disbelief. After a few minutes, I confirmed my brother's bad news. I tried to find other exploits for several more hours, but my efforts were fruitless.

After I was sure the bug no longer existed, I withdrew the majority of my winnings from my account. I was afraid that they might think I was cheating, so I wanted to make sure the money was out of their system before they froze my account. Technically, neither my brother nor I did anything wrong. We didn't decrypt network packets and we didn't hack their servers. We were just very observant and relied on nothing but our sense of timing.

When finding an exploit like this, it is difficult to determine how far to push the envelope. An opportunity like this only comes once every few years. The flaw was very noticeable and I was surprised to see it up for as long as it was. (I assume that it was up since the blackjack feature launched six days earlier.) I am sure that all casinos (both Internet and brick and mortar casinos) have monitoring checks in place when someone is winning big. It is impossible to know what these thresholds are without working for the company. In the U.S., casinos are required to fill out a Cash Transaction Report (CTR) if a player makes more than $10,000 in cash transactions in a 24-hour period. Even though Paradise Poker is not U.S. based, I was not sure whether they would issue the CTR. I decided to stop a little shy of this limit in hopes of staying under Paradise's radar. Apparently, I did not manage to stay in the clear.

I know that some people will be upset with my actions. There were probably a few people out there who knew about the exploit but were content in winning a few hundred dollars a day. It is possible that I could have won more by stretching out my winnings over time instead of going for the throat, but I highly doubt it. This bug was just too easy to stumble across and I knew that they would fix it in a few days for one reason or another. I feel I chose the path that maximized my winnings and I am more than happy with the results.

Observing the Lottery (Winter, 2005-2006) *By CeeJay*

I have a friend (I'll call him Rob) who supplements his regular income with money made from the lottery. He does this in two ways: he publishes a newsletter that contains tips and "hot" numbers, and he is a long-term net winner in playing the lottery himself. He does this by tracking the winning numbers and coming up with a "hot" list—numbers that are coming up more frequently than others. As anyone with any aptitude for math or odds certainly knows, this is bunk, as you cannot predict future random outcomes by looking at past results. But as anyone with any sense can figure out, ping pong balls are not manufactured with great precision. There are slight variations in weight and shape, along with minor imperfections. How these differences can lead to predictable patterns is well documented in several books that tell of roulette wheels in Las Vegas that were not manufactured to precise tolerances and the MIT students who made yearly pilgrimages each summer to finance their educations. I witnessed this firsthand a few years ago when I used to do volunteer work for a local civic organization, working at their nightly bingo games. We had two sets of bingo balls that we would rotate every so often. One set apparently had a few balls that were markedly different from the other balls and, as a result, would be drawn much less frequently than the other balls. It was noticeable enough that the old ladies who played every night would complain to us after three or four days to switch the balls. They were also allowed to hand pick their own cards, and the more astute ones would search for cards without the "dead" numbers on them, just in case we were using that set of balls that night.

Anyway, around 12 years ago, Rob commissioned me to write a simple tracking program so he could load the winning number history for any lottery and have the program determine not only the "hot" numbers, but hot sets of numbers (for example, if two or more numbers are likely to be drawn together). The lottery has a huge odds advantage in that the payoff ratio is far lower than the actual odds. This is the "house edge" that allows them to make money. To give some perspective, most roulette wheels in Vegas have 37 numbers (1 to 35, 0, and 00) and pay off 35 to one on a single number. Thus for every $37 that you bet you can expect to earn back only $35, or about $945 for every $1,000 wagered. The lottery works a little differently; it is a pari-mutuel pool where a certain amount is set aside for paying off winning numbers and the payout for any particular number depends on how many people selected that number. Many lottery players try to determine which numbers no one else likes and play those instead of playing their "lucky" numbers. Regardless, the typical payout for a Pick-3-type lottery is $200 to $300. With three digits there are 1,000 numbers so the odds are 1,000 to 1 against you. For every $1,000 you wager in a Pick-3 lottery, you can expect a return of $200 to $300 back, certainly much worse than Vegas. With those odds against you, it is easy to see why a little numeric edge in selecting numbers has not allowed Rob to take an early retirement.

But that is not the hack. The hack was far simpler than that and is how Rob got started writing and selling lottery newsletters. Rob has been an avid lottery player for a number of years. Rob is also the type of person who is always looking for an edge, an advantage, or some type of information that the average person does *not* have (who isn't?). He played his state Pick-6 lottery regularly. Back then, the Pick-6 had you select six numbers from 1 to 36 and paid for four, five, or six correct picks, six of course being the jackpot. The drawing was televised and always started the same way. The balls were arranged in a rack with the numbers displayed so you could see that they started with all 36 balls. They switched on the machine that started the mixer, released the balls, and one by one the six winning numbers were selected. The rack held six rows of six balls each. Rob noticed that they were arranged in numerical order in each row but that they would rotate the rows with each drawing in a predictable manner. They would start with balls 1 to 6 in the first row, 7 to 12 in the second, 13 to 18, 19 to 24, 25 to 30, and 31 to 36 in the third, fourth, fifth, and sixth rows respectively. In the next drawing they would move the first row to the end and slide all the other rows up, so the rows now were 7 to 12, 13 to 18, 19 to 24, 25 to 30, 31 to 36, and 1 to 6. Each week they would take the front row and move it to the back in the same predictable manner, never deviating from the pattern. Rob made a note of this. It was also about this time that he started keeping track of the winning numbers to see if there was a pattern. After a while he discovered that the first number in the first row came up quite often—almost 50 percent of the time. Because of the way the machine was designed, when they released the balls, this first ball must have fallen directly into the area where the balls were drawn from.

Armed with this information and knowing which ball was sure to be in this spot each week, he started selecting his numbers very differently. He devised a "wheel" system with the one number he knew was likely to come out and "wheeling" the other numbers to play many different combinations containing this number. (This was the basis for his later system of using "hot" numbers.) Now obviously, being about 50 percent certain of what one number is going to be isn't going to make you rich overnight. But he started hitting four out of six enough that it became pretty profitable, enough to come out a little ahead over time. Then he hit five out of six with a payout of several thousand dollars, which put him way ahead of the game.

He went on like this for several months, then decided there was more money to be made with this information. He decided to share this information with others by selling it. Readers of *2600*, interested in the free exchange of information and ideas, might frown upon his approach to sharing, but Rob had a family to support and two kids approaching college age. Besides, he felt he was providing legitimate information that others could use to make money so why not charge for it? He took out a small ad in the back of a tabloid, "Lottery Secrets Revealed—send $5 for more information." He figured he could make a few bucks, that's all. Surprisingly enough, the money came in by the hundreds—$5 bills arriving in envelopes each day, courtesy of the USPS.

One day a different type of envelope arrived. This one was from the State Lottery Commission and instead of a $5 bill it contained a Cease and Desist order. (An interesting note—Rob was not profiting at the expense of the Lottery Commission since the payout is a fixed percentage of all money take in. He (and his customers) were profiting at the expense of *other* lottery players by reducing the winning payout amount.) A Cease and Desist order was a scary thing to Rob so he showed the letter to his attorney. His attorney assured him that he was doing nothing illegal, simply sharing information based on his observance (and also advised him to make sure he was keeping track of, and paying proper tax on, all income from this information). The attorney sent a reply back to the Commission telling them in polite legalese to F*ck off! He received several other threatening letters over the next few months, but nothing ever came of it. Then one day he tuned into the nightly lottery drawing and lo and behold! There was a *new* lottery machine in place and the balls, while all being displayed as before, were in no predictable order. The commission had gotten smart and took the path of least resistance. The least they could have done was thank him or perhaps pay him a "consultant" fee for fixing their faulty system.

So watch your local televised lottery drawings carefully. You may not find a "bug" like Rob did, but who knows? Remember, although the machines themselves have gotten more sophisticated, most of them still use the good old low-tech ping pong ball.

An ISP Story (Summer, 2007) *By Witchlight*

I thought I'd share with you all a little story about a script kiddie, a real nice victim of said kiddie, and an ISP.

I work tech support for a large ISP in a state that will remain nameless. (You should be able to figure it out.) One night I got a call from a rather nice customer requesting a password reset. His name was Mr. O'Reilly. As I pulled up his account to do this for him he told me how he had been "hacked." Now you have to know that we took this with a grain of salt at tech support. In the four years I've been doing tech support I can honestly say that I've only talked to maybe three people who have actually been abused by a "hacker."

Once I got his account up, however, I immediately believed him. See, Mr. O'Reilly's account came up now as registered to one "Assbag O'Reilly."

Some script kiddie had gotten access to his account and reset all the personal information for the account as well as other things. So now whenever the customer sent an email it would say it was from Assbag O'Reilly. I went over with him on how to change it back and advised him to change the secret question for his account as well since it was likely the kiddie had changed this too and would be able to reset the password and we'd be right back where we started in a day.

Now here's where we ran into a dead end. We knew that he had been victimized. What could I do as a representative of a major ISP? Not a thing. Nothing. There was no security team that I could escalate the customer to. There was no phone number for any such department listed in the numbers of approved contacts that I could call or refer the customer to. The only thing I could do was get the customer to email `abuse@hotmail.com` and hope for the best.

How could this be? Well, as we are outsourced support we are given very few tools and absolutely no access to departments that could do anything about this. We follow the call center mantra of the almighty talk time and all issues have to be resolved in an average of 15 minutes or there's the door. It makes for a support culture of saying anything—even if it's total crap—just to get rid of the customer so you can get your metrics met to get your bonus for being the best punter around.

Agents are not hired for their tech ability. They rely on the customer being even more ignorant in order to make them a "tech." About two of every ten people in the center are technically inclined and we pick up the punts and fix what the first person should have been able to do. Rant over.

Having done what the client wanted and recommending a few things to O'Reilly to try and help him, I ended the call. Two days later he called back again with the password issue. The kiddie had used the flavor of the month MSN exploit again, recracked his account, and made himself a subaccount. A friend of mine had the call this time and talked to me about it since he saw my name from the last ticket.

No response to Mr. O'Reilly from the abuse department and nothing done. What was different this time was the kiddie had gotten some balls and was using O'Reilly's MSN account to instant message him. We were watching this happen via our remote assistance tool. Now we had something to track the kiddie! One of our tools for those who know where to look would show us the IP of the last successful login and we found it was not from our ISP. One lookup later and we traced it to an SBC user.

Choosing to ignore the 15-minute rule because Mr. O'Reilly was a nice guy (this goes a long way) we decided to call SBC on his behalf and track the kiddie at the source of his connection. We got a representative from SBC and explained that one of their users was "hacking" our customer as we spoke and that we had proof. Here we learned that SBC operates exactly like our ISP and didn't have any way of doing anything about it. So we got a supervisor instead. You would think a supervisor could do something...Nope. Their job is *not* tech. They are there to make sure there are butts in chairs taking calls and making money for whatever outsourced company is hired by the ISP. They said that there's nothing they can do and don't even have an email address for the abuse/security team. We pressed the point and they actually told us that what their user was doing was perfectly acceptable use of their service!

I'd love to know what the SBC legal team would have said about that one. But it makes my point and shows you the reality of what the average victim of script kiddie mayhem has to go through. We did all we could but until this kiddie grows up and leaves him alone, O'Reilly is stuck (unless he takes legal action). We did more than we were supposed to and got nowhere because outsourced support and the ISPs who use them just don't give a crap.

I wouldn't say it's open season or that you won't get your service pulled for hacking or worse. But the system is actually stacked slightly against the average user and in favor of the script kiddie.

The tally: Kiddie 1, O'Reilly 0, ISP... rich.

Shouts to Gilda, Harrybalz, ZX, and jedi262.

16 A New Era of Telephony

I don't think anyone could have thought in their wildest dreams that the telephonic landscape would look the way it does now, a quarter century after the Bell breakup. Well, maybe *some* of us in our dreams might have. But I doubt the phone phreaks of the '80s actually thought the day would come so soon when making free and legal phone calls all around the world would be a reality. And yet, here we are in the twenty-first century where it's never been easier.

Would there have even been a phone phreak culture if affordable phone calls were this easy from the beginning? Absolutely. Because while making the phone calls was a big part of it, understanding how the vast network tied together was always what it was really about. The communication angle was a fringe benefit of understanding the system. It was that knowledge and the passion that went with it which inspired so much in the way of new designs and alternate ways of utilizing telephony.

Telephones have always meant something special to me. Ever since I was a kid, the mere thought of a phone was something so intriguing to me that I knew I'd never rest until I thoroughly examined and experimented with the system behind it. Even then, people seemed to take the whole thing for granted. And even today, I cannot. The very idea of this form of communication actually being possible seems unbelievable at times, even with a rudimentary knowledge of how voices get passed down wires and through the sky for great distances. I think that sense of wonder is what keeps phone phreaks involved. When it becomes just another tool, there's no reason or desire to want to know more about it.

So much has changed with regard to how we deal with phone calls. In those early days for me, that sound of the ringing phone was a really big deal. Calls were expensive so it didn't happen all that frequently. And you never knew who was on the other end before picking up. The mere notion of Caller ID hadn't been introduced at that point. Plus you couldn't own your own phone and very few people had more than one in their house. Touch tone phones were a rarity; everyone used the circular rotary dials, each one of which seemed to have its own unique sound when rotating. Not to mention the actual rings, which came from a real bell in the phone. When you heard that sound, you dropped everything to find out who was calling. A phone could ring forever if the calling party didn't hang up. There were virtually no answering machines for consumers so a ringing phone had to be dealt with one way or another. Wireless phones of any sort were unheard of. The instruments were rugged; you could literally drop them out of a window and they would still be usable. The telephone landscape was about as unlike the present as it could possibly be.

Yes, it's gotten a whole lot different today. Phones of all shapes and sizes are everywhere. Making phone calls has gotten both overly easy and absurdly complicated at the same time. Sure, you can place calls from anywhere to anywhere with relative ease. But what company do you want as your regional carrier? Do you want to use your local cable company for local calls? Perhaps a VoIP solution for long distance? It's all great fun for those of us who like to play with configurations. For those who don't, it's nonstop confusion. And that doesn't even take into account those people who can't afford the initial investment of a phone line or computer. For them, ironically enough, the cost of using cash in a payphone hasn't come down at all.

The inequities remain and have widened in many areas. I can only hope that the rapid technological advancements in this field will soon be used to help close that gap. There is a certain magic in being able to communicate globally with our fellow humans. That ability can do much towards realizing our common goals, fostering peace, and all that nice stuff that seems to fly in the face of the status quo. Overall, the changes we're seeing now have been positive and it's great to see the abilities that once were only in the hands of a few phone phreaks (without authorization to boot) making its way to the general public in the form of complex phone systems, alternate call routing, and new and creative uses of telephony. It's almost as if the phone phreak bug has spread everywhere through the wires.

History and Background

As always, to understand how the system works, you need to develop knowledge and appreciation for the history and implementation in other environments. We've printed so many articles that cover various aspects of each of these. Obviously, as soon as they get published, something changes to make at least some of the information out of date. But despite this, I find myself going back to such articles for purposes of reference and perspective. Here we can see for ourselves how those *really* old payphones once worked. Seeing how the phone system was put together in a place like Afghanistan gave us valuable insight, as did seeing all of the things that didn't work quite right inside our own system.

Hacking the Three Holed Payphone (Summer, 2000)

By Munzenfernsprechermann

Once upon a time there were no computers to decipher, no electronic voice mail systems, no cable TV, and no Internet. There was one giant phone company and they built, owned, and operated all the payphones. These payphones were standardized. They came in one color (black) and in one basic style. Think about it. For almost forty years, phone hackers in the U.S. and Canada were all tampering with the same piece of equipment. Over time, unauthorized people gleaned a substantial body of information on the mechanics and manipulation of these phones.

Although most of this information is now arcane, it may be of interest to present day phone phreaks or veterans who want to reminisce. The basic characteristic of this unit was the three different sized holes on top for inserting nickels, dimes, or quarters. Each coin generated a specific sound when dropped into the slot. A single ding for a nickel, a double ding for a dime, and a hearty gong for a quarter. Through these audible chimes, the operator could "hear" how much money had been deposited. These phones were invariably rotary dial, although some were retrofitted to tone dialing in later years. There was usually a coin return plunger in the upper right and a return slot or hopper on the lower left. The body of the phone was divided into two separate locked compartments. The upper part was accessible to repair personnel and relatively insecure. The bottom section was heavy steel and held the coin box. It required a separate key. The handset was connected with an unarmored cord and hung in a cradle on the left, which activated the unit when it was lifted. The whole thing was mounted on a cast metal plate that held the phone securely and sealed off the back and sides.

The basic game was to try and get a free or cut-rate phone call out of this ubiquitous black beast. Strategies consisted of various coin manipulations, messing with the wiring, or befuddling the operator (software?) to achieve this goal. A free long distance call was far more difficult and prestigious than a local one.

Coin Hacks

These phones required a coin to activate the dial tone. For the most part, you needed a dime or two nickels just to see if the phone was working. This characteristic led to beaucoup lost coins if a phone was out of order. Lost money was a common occurrence and undoubtedly began the adversarial relationship between the phoning public and the public phone. The least finessed method to get a dial tone was to use a slug to simulate the nickel or dime. Various foreign coins worked flawlessly, my personal favorite being the Trinidadian penny. Drop one in; ding ding, hummmmmm, you were good to go. Aside from genuine slugs made in high school metal shop, a favorite was the #10 large pattern brass washer. Available by the pound, they were the perfect width and diameter of a dime, but usually required a little tape over the hole or some spit to slow them down. They were not reliable enough for a long distance call (please deposit nine washers) but would usually generate a dial tone by the third try.

A rather elegant coin trick involved a nickel and some excellent timing. You dropped a nickel in the slot and if you slammed the coin return plunger at just the right time, you got your double ding and a dial tone. Of course, it was only a 50 percent discount and it hurt like hell, but it was handy if you were short on change. There were people who claimed they could use a coin on a string and pull it out but this was a myth since diameter, magnetic characteristics, and rolling weight were key in getting a coin accepted.

Hardware Hacks

Although not quite the fortress of solitude, this basic phone was fairly well guarded. The handset was unscrewable, which was a boon to vandals but yielded little hacking opportunity. On certain models you could place a wire (paper clip, bobby pin, etc.) through the mouthpiece and then ground the other end to a conductive part (usually the coin return) of the phone. If done properly, it yielded a dial tone. I'd like to know how somebody stumbled across that one. Another similar stunt was to edge a piece of gum wrapper foil under the back right seam and slide it slowly up and down until you shorted out some essential wires, yielding a dial tone. I do recall getting a rather nasty shock while performing this maneuver on a rainy day.

A great deal of effort went into securing the phone itself but the wiring was often exposed. I believe it was a three pair line, but I don't know how many wires were essential. One pair carried a fairly high voltage to operate a coin drop solenoid in the bottom of the phone. Your cash was held in limbo above the coin box. If your call was completed the money was dumped into the box or diverted to the coin return if the call was incomplete. I once witnessed a lineman shorting two posts at the junction box and yielding a load of change from a clogged chute. He told me he was often sent out to repair a phone that simply had a full coin box. He also said the company security guys sometimes planted UV dyed coins in the upper end of the phone to try and catch their repair personnel stealing. I was never able to repeat his performance and yet I once again got a memorable electric shock for my efforts.

Some talented folks were able to momentarily short two of the wires to get a free local call. A bar in my neighborhood had a doorbell rigged to the line for that purpose. They maintained a Bell System employee who hung out there had installed it. It was rumored you could achieve the same effect by piercing the insulation with a pin.

The phones were hardened against attack, but they were often easily pried from their moorings. If one was stolen, however, it took a serious effort to get it open, which discouraged your average impatient thief. People were known to clog the coin return and return later to unstuff it and reap their reward. This led to the retrofit of a coin return hopper that was not so readily plugged up.

The blue and red boxes opened up a world of possibilities for payphone aficionados. There was a much simpler device that predates them and was pretty good at yielding a free connection for the caller. Sometimes referred to as the "brown box," it was a capacitor/resistor combination placed across the receiving end phone line. By absorbing the voltage surge when the phone was answered, the payphone believed the connection was never completed and returned the money when you hung up. Not as facile as a tone box, it was still a cool trick if you were calling someone with one of these devices. A phone installer found one in my house and he just confiscated it, along with half a dozen extension phones that were stamped "Property of the Bell System." Never heard another thing about it.

Software Hacks

Technically, these old electromechanical devices ran without software, but there were some decidedly non-hardware methods to outsmarting the payphone system. The most obvious was simply calling the operator and telling them the phone ate your dime. Sometimes they would mail you a dime but more often than not they'd put through a local call for free. For long distance calls, the operator would come on the line and ask you to deposit the cost of the first three minutes. By adding up the bongs and dings s/he would verify you entered the correct amount. If there was a dispute, they would simply return the change and have you reenter it. Some enterprising soul recorded these sounds and played them back but was foiled when the recorder deposited too much money. The operator activated the return solenoid, but when there was no handy recording of coins spilling into the return slot, the ploy was ruined.

Long distance calls were easily made with bogus or real credit card numbers. The system was pathetically easy to crack, but then it had to be readily understood by thousands of long distance operators. Essentially, the calling card number was the billing phone number plus some extra meaningless digits and a letter. The letter corresponded with one of the specific digits in the billing number. So, say the third digit was the key one. The letter at the end had to match the assigned value of that digit. If you had a list of the ten letters for a given year and the location of the key digit, you could make your own fictitious accounts. There were no high speed computers to verify your number and it would work for quite a while until it hit the hot sheets. As mentioned, the codes changed annually, but if you had a friend who was an operator, or perhaps a night watchman in a big office building, you could come up with enough numbers to puzzle it out by early January. Phone security would invariably call the receiver of a bogus card call and ask if they knew who had called them from the originating city. Not a good system if you lived with your parents.

Abbie Hoffman published a lot of this stuff in *Steal This Book*, and after *Esquire* magazine wrote their seminal "Phone Freak" article, a lot of it came to an end. Eventually the single hole "Urban Fortress" phones phased out the three-hole phone and we all had to improve our skills to stay ahead of the curve. The rest, of course, is history.

Idiocy in the Telcos (Spring, 2002) *By The Cheshire Catalyst*

The people running telephone companies (Telcos) are such idiots. Sorry, I really should explain which idiots I'm talking about since there are so many entities known as "phone companies" out there these days. In this diatribe I'm referring to the LECs, or Local Exchange Carriers—those phone companies that handle "the last mile" from the Telco's central office to your home. LECs are broken up into ILECs and CLECs (Incumbent Local Exchange Carriers and Competitive Local Exchange Carriers). The "Incumbents" are the guys who were around since before the breakup of AT&T, while the "Competitives" are the new guys on the block who are supposed to help keep the old guys "honest" and force them to keep rates competitive. The guys who carry your conversations as a long distance call are IXCs (IntereXchange Carriers).

As an old "phone phreak," it's almost embarrassing that I should have to admit that my "day job" is that of a Directory Assistance (DA) operator for a major Long Distance Carrier (IXC). It doesn't matter which one because I don't really work for them anyway. In these modern days of deregulation, I work for a third-party outfit that is hired to provide the DA service cheaper than they can do the job in-house. That's because I live in one of the numerous "Right-To-Work" states in the nation's sun-belt, and get paid pittance.

One of the major embarrassments of my job happens when someone calls for the local phone company—not just in a small town, but even in major cities! The phone company never puts itself in the directory so it can be found! And of course, I only handle White Pages. If the caller doesn't know the name of the Telco, I'm not allowed (by FCC tariff, I'm told) to provide a "Yellow Pages" search. I keep threatening to take some vacation time to visit the reading room of the FCC in Washington some time and look this stuff up, but I really can't afford the trip (see comment on "Right-To-Work" state above).

Since I cover a number of states in my job, I get to look at the listings of a number of major LECs. Verizon will have "Verizon Wireless" listings for every hamlet and burg in the nation, but try to find a number for residential land-line service that an out-of-state caller can ring up to see about the problem with Aunt Minnie's account back home, and I'm up against the tariff asking "Do you know the name of the phone company in that area?" Even when I break down and suggest that Verizon is the primary local carrier in Boston, or Ameritech in Chicago (hoping that this isn't one of the calls being "monitored for Quality Assurance"), just what number am I supposed to supply? Deregulation began in 1986 with the Modified Final Judgment. Here I am in the next century wondering what I'm supposed to tell a customer who's on their third call to directory assistance looking to get a phone account squared away!

People call in with the most compelling stories about how their elderly aunt back home in Chicago or Boston can't deal with their phone company any more, and they need to call and take care of the charges. Or somebody in the Rust Belt up north is trying to reach the Telco of their winter home in the South to deal with a problem on their bill. It isn't that I've got the time to stop and listen to their stories, it's that I can't shut them up while trying to search the many recurrences of the Directory Sales Office numbers while trying to find a listing for an out-of-state caller to call.

The trick here is that the phone companies have all their information about contacting them packed in the front pages of their local telephone directories. In over 15 years of deregulation, it hasn't occurred to most of them to advertise in their own Yellow Pages under "Telephone Companies" or to put in as big a listing in the White Pages as their Electric Company utility brethren—the ones they keep passing in the halls of the Public Service Commission offices but never need to talk to. Keep in mind that the telephone book publishing arm of those same phone companies has been "spun-off" so the right hand really doesn't know what the left hand is doing, because it isn't its own left hand any more!

The other problem is when callers call out-of-state DA at NPA-555-1212 (NPA is "Numbering Plan Area," the Telcos' in-house term for "Area Codes"), the White Pages listings are never clear as to where an out-of-state caller should call about discussing a bill. Actually, I should compliment BellSouth here. They actually do have a specific number for out-of-state callers to dial. Let me tell you why.

The number in most BellSouth states to reach the Telco for residential customers is 780-2355 (780-BELL). It's always a local number wherever you call from, and if you live in an area that has 10-digit dialing, you have to use your area code in front of that number to get there. The number is never good from out of state, but most of my "colleagues" in the call center don't know this and give it out, causing much frustration when the caller calls back to complain and get a good number. It's a toll-free number and clearly marked "out-of-state," but most callers don't want the "Toll-Free Number Runaround." They want a "direct number," then get the recording that the number in the 780 exchange is not valid.

So how does a Telco go about changing the listings in the directory database that I (and my 600 friends in my call center) use every day? Do what we tell people who call wondering why their number isn't in our directory: "Call your Local Phone Company, and make sure they have your listing correct. Our information is updated from the information that they provide to us."

So there it is. Get with it, you Telcos! Get your act together and pretend you're "just another American company." Even *you* need to check your company's telephone book listings once in a while. Make sure your customers can find you when they call directory assistance, whether they're in town or across the country—just like every other company has to. Otherwise, your customers will go to that CLEC across town. Usually, they can be found in the phone book!

The Afghan Phone System (Summer, 2002) *By Iconoclast*

If you are a curious phreak like me, the telecommunications infrastructure of Afghanistan immediately comes to mind as something that deserves exploration and understanding. Alas, the lack of said infrastructure leads me to say that it is quite possibly the worst place to try to make a phone call from on the entire planet.

We take our precious lovely dial tone for granted, but there you will be hard pressed to even find a working telephone. To begin with, let's take a look at the numbering formats for the country. Country codes are assigned by the International Telecommunications Union (ITU) (www.itu.int). The International Country Code (ICC) for Afghanistan is 93. The "9" signifies it is in geographical region 9 of the world. The United States has an ICC of 1.

From within Afghanistan, to place an international call you would dial the International Direct Dial (IDD) code, which is 00. To place a call within the country you would prefix it with the National Direct Dial (NDD) code, which is simply 0. There are no city codes or area codes in the country on the old electromechanical exchanges. Numbers within the various cities are five digits long. An excellent directory of people to call in Afghanistan was listed by the Afghan Wireless Communications Company (AWCC) but was recently removed. Hopefully, they will restore this information.

Telephone usage is actually dropping, since in 1996 there were 29,000 lines available and in 1998 there were only 21,000 lines. Of course, Taliban bans on Internet use didn't exactly spur telecom growth. My sources in the CIA have stated that "in 1997, telecommunications links were established between Mazar-e Sharif, Herat, Kandahar, Jalalabad, and Kabul through satellite and microwave systems" (www.cia.gov/cia/publications/factbook/index.html).

Two telecommunications companies from China, Zhongxing Telecom and Huawei Technologies, were attempting to install a switching network that could handle 130,000 lines in the capital city of Kabul. The status of this project is unknown at the current time.

Most of the existing exchanges are based on electromechanical switches that are 40 years old. These old exchanges are using Siemens Strowger switches. Completing calls on these exchanges is very difficult. New equipment using digital switches is being installed. In order to place calls to the older switches, one must have the operator service in Kabul complete the call for you. You can reach the operator service by dialing +93-2-290090. Then give them a five digit phone number and the call may have a slight chance of being completed.

Parts of the country have digital exchanges, which can be dialed directly without the operator. The various city codes are: 02 Kabul, 03 Kandahar, 04 Herat, 05 Mazar-i-Sherif, 06 Kunduz, 07 Jalalabad, and 08 AWCC Mobile Telephone Network.

Regarding international telecommunications links, this is primarily done through satellite communications. A company called Telephone Systems International S.A. provides international connectivity. According to Afghan Wireless, there are satellite earth stations—one Intelsat (Indian Ocean) linked only to Iran and one Intersputnik (Atlantic Ocean region), as well as a commercial satellite telephone center in Ghazni.

This New York City based company unveiled a brand new GSM phone network in Afghanistan in May, 2002. Chairman Hamid Karzai was the first person to place a telephone call over it. This has actually been the fastest GSM installation in a developing country.

There are two different kinds of phone cards planned for sale. One is called a "Fixed Line Phone Card," the other is a "Mobile Top Up." To use the Fixed Line Phone Card, one would dial 81 from within the country, listen to the instructions, and then enter the PIN as printed on the back of the card. The destination party number is then dialed. If a mistake in dialing is made or one wants to make an additional call, then "##" is entered followed by the number. The Mobile Top Up card adds funds to a GSM account. The number 171 is dialed from within the country, the PIN is entered as printed on the back of the card, and the account is automatically credited.

Of course, by now you probably just want to "reach out and touch someone" over there in Afghanistan. Why not give Osama a call? He uses an INMARSAT satellite phone, although lately has not been picking up when I call him for some reason (I wonder why?!). To call Osama Bin Laden just dial +873-682-505-331. Have phun!

Phreaking

From our very first days, we've been told by various "experts" that phreaking is dead. But it's never true. Sure, some forms of phreaking become outdated and no longer work. I think I can probably say with assurance that red boxing has finally breathed its last. (No doubt, I will soon hear of exceptions after this is published.) Like the phone network itself, phreaking adapts and changes. The concept of backspoofing described here certainly demonstrates this, along with the various methods of manipulating features like ANI and Caller ID. And of course, the explosion of the telecommunications world has brought forth a plethora of new companies offering all sorts of different services. Back in the early days, there was little more than the Bell System. So with every new company and new technology, there are more possibilities for exploitation and exploration. In that sense, phreaking has never been more of a force than it is today.

Basics On Answering Machine Hacking (Winter, 2001-2002)

By horrid

Before you all start complaining, I know that in the '80s and early '90s, about a million texts were being spread around BBSs about VMB (voice mailbox) and answering machine hacking. This article is, of course, more recent and contains more information about certain brands of answering machines to aid you in getting into an answering machine (provided you know what brand of machine it is). Also, it focuses more on three-digit passcodes as well as two-digit ones. If you don't know what brand the machine is, this article will also contain a generic overview of gaining remote access to answering machines.

Why would you want to hack an answering machine? There are a number of reasons such as spying on people (such as your girlfriend/boyfriend/wife/husband) or just for fun and games (pranking or changing the outgoing message or OGM). Once you are into an answering machine you can listen/delete messages and/or change the OGM to say whatever you want it to. You decide for yourself why you would want to hack an answering machine.

Most answering machines require you to enter the password while the OGM is being played. However, some require you to hit a certain key (such as "0," "*," or "#") after which it will say "please enter your password" or perform a series of beeps. A few answering machines require the password after the OGM has finished and the long beep has been played. Some answering machines will disconnect you after you enter a certain number of digits (in which case, you'll need to call back and start again). Case in point, the Panasonics made in the early '90s (and maybe afterwards?) require a two-digit passcode during the OGM and will disconnect you after six digits have been entered—if they don't contain the password sequence. If you think you are dealing with an old answering machine that uses a two-digit passcode (such as fairly old Panasonic or AT&T answering machines), there is an easy way to break into it or *any* two-digit machine that is simply listening for the correct sequence of numbers. Simply call it and then enter this number during the OGM (or after you hit the initialization key to get the machine to listen for a passcode):

001020304050607080911213141516171819223242526272829334353637383944 5464748 4955657585966768697787988990

The above number works on every two-digit passcode (provided it is like most answering machines that don't read the digits in groups of two or three but rather just listen for the right sequence). It works because it contains every possible two-digit passcode. This is *very* effective. If you get cut off or don't get it all entered during the OGM, call back and start with the number you got cut off on.

However, in this day and age, most answering machines use three-digit passcodes. Despite the digit increase, these passcodes are usually as easy (if not easier) to break. The reason for this is because the company wants the customer to be able to remember his/her passcode so it will be easier for them to access their messages away from home without remembering some random three-digit number the company came up with. These default passcodes are supposed to only be temporary. (The customer is supposed to change it shortly after they purchase the machine.) This is not usually the case, however, because most answering machine owners:

- Don't even know it's possible to remotely access their answering machine.
- Don't think they are vulnerable to attack.
- Are too lazy to change their passcode.

Also, after a power outage, most machines reset to the default passcode and answering machine owners will usually forget to change their passcode back or get ticked off and just leave the default passcode enabled. For this reason, you may have better luck right after a power outage. Most default three-digit passcodes are either the same number three times in a row ("000," "111"—to name some common ones) or three digits in numerical order ("123," "456," "789"). BellSouth's answering machines use the same digit three times in a row (usually "888").

"Is there one big number I can enter that will cover all three-digit possibilities, like the number for the two-digit passcodes?" The answer is yes. However, it is a lot larger. It's 1005 digits long and covers every possible three-digit combination. (Three passcodes are in the number twice, 988 889 898.) I couldn't stop those three codes from being repeated without screwing up the entire number. If someone comes up with a better number that contains all three-digit possibilities without repeating a three-digit sequence throughout, submit it:

0001002003004005006007008009011012013014015016017018019021022023024025026027028029031032033034035036037038039041042043044045046047048049051052053054055056057058059061062063064065066067068069071072073074075076077078079081082083084085086087088089091092093094095096097098099111211311411511611711811912212312412512612712812913213313413513613713813914214314414514614714814915215315415515615715815916216316416516616716816917217317417517617717817918218318418518618718818919219319419519619719819922232242252262272282292332342352362372382392432442452462472482492532542552562572582592632642652662672682692732742752762772782792832842852862872882892932942952962972982993334335336337338339344345346347348349354355356357358359364365366367368369374375376377378379384385386387388389394395396397398399444544644744844945545645745845946546646746846947547647747847948548648748848949549649749849955565575585595665675685695765775785795865875885895965975985996667668669677678679687688689697698699777877978878979879988898988999900

The number may be intimidating at first, but think of it this way:

1. You would normally have to enter 1,000 passcodes to cover all possible combinations. A combination is three digits long, so that is 3,000 digits. This number cuts the number of digits you would normally have to enter by almost two thirds.
2. You only need to use this number as a last resort if the answering machine doesn't accept the normal default passcodes mentioned above. (I would venture to say at least 80 to 90 percent do.)
3. You will most likely come across the three-digit combination before you have entered all 1,005 digits.

Some BellSouth answering machines beep after every digit that is entered. In this case you must slow down so that you get one beep per number and the answering machine doesn't miss any. Also, if you get cut off while entering this number, just call back and start one number before the last one you entered.

Once you have gotten into the machine, BellSouth machines, along with most others, have a recording that tells you what numbers perform certain commands. Another way you can get the passcode to BellSouth machines (and others) is if you are at that person's house (such as your friend or girlfriend); simply press the "code" button when no one is looking. The LCD screen that usually displays the number of messages recorded on the machine will flash the three-digit passcode for that machine. Another good way to get into answering machines (if you know what brand/model they use) is to go to a place like Wal-Mart or Radio Shack and ask to see a user's manual on them. This works only if they have the model in stock. You might also want to tell them you bought the machine and lost your user manual. The vulnerabilities mentioned in this article should not be confined to individual's machines. Company answering machines (we'll let you decide what kind of company) are just as vulnerable.

Greets: Necro, Vega, Jizz, Telepathy, and Seek.

MILESTONE: FEEDING THE FRENZY (Autumn, 2003)

This summer has seen a virtual plethora of nonsensical threats on the net. It's easy from our perspective to laugh at the utter stupidity of so much of it. But oftentimes in our holier than thou smugness, we fail to realize that the absurdity has become the reality.

Such change always occurs gradually. Were it to happen all at once, it would be a lot easier to see the faults. When people have a chance to get used to changes and, more importantly, when people begin to forget what it was like before the changes, the reality landscape change is complete. It's essential to recognize this, even if it seems to be impossible to change it.

What happens online frequently mirrors events in "real life." And on the Internet, we're being encouraged to become paranoid about our safety, hostile to outsiders, and dependent on things we really don't need to survive. And if we're not careful, we'll soon forget just how ridiculous this is.

The Summer of 2003 will be remembered as the summer of worms and viruses, where names like "LoveSan" and "Blaster" became synonymous with online terrorism. The net became clogged, commerce was affected (the claims of billions of lost dollars quickly became accepted as undisputed fact), and our very way of life was once again being threatened.

MILESTONE: FEEDING THE FRENZY *(continued)*

So instead of dealing with the fact that we've become hooked on operating systems with large security holes that any idiot with a basic knowledge of programming can exploit, we handle it as if it were some sort of "cyberwar" complete with enemy combatants, spies, and a terrified populace. It's a not-so-distant cousin of the Y2K hysteria when many became convinced that the world would be plunged into anarchy when the calendar changed. In such cases we need to remember some rational thoughts: Don't become entirely dependent on any single system because failures and flaws are inevitable; Keep regular backups; Put the whole picture into perspective and realize that an occasional glitch in your e-mail or a temporary outage for amazon.com is simply one of the growing pains of the net, not the end of the world; Always have a different way of achieving the same ends so that if a piece of software or hardware becomes unreliable, you won't be completely stuck. This latter point can apply to individual applications or entire networks—even the concept of bypassing computers and networks altogether should that become necessary.

When a massive power outage hit some major cities in the United States in August, speculation quickly pointed to hackers possibly being somehow responsible. The mere suggestion that computers involved in keeping the nation's electrical grid online could be affected by an errant piece of e-mail on the public Internet seems, once again, absurd. Yet it seems to be growing ever closer to reality. This gap in logic is possibly the easiest way to achieve this world of eternal crisis that so many in the media, government, and populace seem to crave.

But before we get to the stage where a denial of service attack by some idiot somewhere causes the lights to go out in a major city or a surge of pornographic spam clogs the life support systems in hospitals, we ought to change our way of dealing with these issues. If a critical system is vulnerable, covering up that fact is every bit as bad as attacking it. We don't advocate the crippling of any system or network, critical or non. We're certainly not in favor of imprisoning people who do something stupid and simple without thinking—as if they did something requiring detailed planning with a clear intent of malice. What we do support is the full disclosure of any wide open security holes that could result in either a royal pain in the ass for people trying to surf the web or something a bit more life threatening. Such disclosure needs to be encouraged and even rewarded. It's clear there's a lot we're not being told—and that there are many in power who would like to keep it that way.

ANI and Caller ID Spoofing (Spring, 2003) *By Lucky225*

This article will explain many methods of Caller ID and ANI spoofing that can still be used as of today. I have also included a brief FAQ for those of you who may not be familiar with the terminology, which should help you understand this article more. I hope that this article will make many of you aware that Caller ID and ANI, although often great tools, can also be a waste of your time and money.

Please don't confuse this article with past ones I've written. While I mention techniques I have used in the past, I also include up-to-date accurate information. This is meant to be a reference article on how Caller ID and ANI can be spoofed, as well as on how they've been spoofed in the past. All of those Telco techs out there who claim it can't be done will find definite proof that it has been. Enjoy.

FAQ

So, just what is ANI? ANI stands for Automatic Number Identification. ANI is a service feature that transmits a directory number or Billing Telephone Number (BTN) to be obtained automatically. In other words, your number is sent directly to wherever you are calling automatically. Unlike with Caller ID you cannot block this feature.

What is flex ANI? Flexible ANI provides "II" (Identification Indicator) digits that identify the class of service of the phone you are calling from. Flex ANI is transmitted as II digits + BTN.

What are ANI "II" digits? Identification Indicator digits describe the class of service of the telephone. Some examples are:

- 00 "POTS" (plain old telephone service) or home phone
- 07 Restricted line
- 27 ACTS payphone
- 29 Prison phone
- 62 Cellular phone
- 70 COCOT payphone

What is an ANAC? ANAC stands for Automatic Number Announcement Circuit. This is a phone number you can call that will ring into a circuit that announces the ANI number you are calling from. When you call these numbers you will get an ARU (Audio Response Unit). This is the circuit that announces your ANI. The ARU will say the following: "The ARU ID is [id], your line number is [trunk number], the DNIS is [DNIS number], the ANI is [II digits followed by ANI]."

- **ARU ID**: Audio Response Unit ID number. This identifies which ARU in a group of ARUs you reached.
- **Line number**: The trunk you came in on.

- **DNIS:** Dialed Number Identification Service—tells you which number you called (i.e., 800-555-1140 is 03122, 800-555-1180 is 03125).
- **ANI:** II digits followed by ANI.

What is a BTN? BTN is the Billing Telephone Number, a phone number charges are to be billed to. It is not necessarily the phone number of the line you are calling from.

What is Pseudo ANI? Pseudo ANI or PANI is a unique non-dialable number used to route cellular calls. PANI is used by 911 operators to find the cell site and sector from which the cell phone is calling.

What is an ANI-fail? An ANI-fail is when no ANI is sent. Usually the area code of the tandem office completing the call will be sent. (For instance, if the tandem office is in 213 the ANI will be sent as II digits+213.)

How do ANI-fails occur? ANI-fails can occur when the tandem office completing a call didn't receive ANI from the central office originating the call. ANI-fails can also be caused when ANI is intentionally not sent. This can happen by using a method called op diverting. Another way you can cause ANI-fails is through the use of the AT&T long distance network. Simply dial 10-10-288-0 or dial 0 and ask your operator for AT&T. When AT&T comes on the line simply touch tone in a toll-free number and the call will be completed with no ANI. Note however that this method is dependent upon the AT&T center you reach. Some AT&T centers still forward ANI, others send an AT&T BTN as ANI. But most AT&T centers currently don't forward ANI.

What is op diverting? Op diverting is a term that describes the process of intentionally causing an ANI-fail by having your local operator dial the number you wish to reach. Most operator centers are not equipped to forward ANI and so they complete the call with no ANI.

What's the difference between ANI and Caller ID? ANI is the BTN associated with the telephone and is the direct number where you are calling from. Caller ID is usually the BTN but occasionally can be incorrect, i.e., the main number of a business instead of the actual number being called from. Another difference in ANI is that it shows the class of service of the phone number while Caller ID just shows the name and number.

Now that you have an idea of what ANI is and how it differs from Caller ID I will explain some methods for spoofing both of them.

Spoofing Caller ID

Method #1: Using a PRI line. Major companies that have a PBX with many hundreds of lines hooked up to a Primary Rate ISDN (PRI) line can spoof Caller ID by setting the Caller ID number to whatever number they want for a given extension on that PBX by typing a simple command on the PBX's terminal.

Some telephone switches also use whatever Caller ID is sent from the PBX as ANI—a major hole in the telephone network that I hope will someday be fixed since the spoofed ANI can be billed for long distance calls! Telephone company billing records should be inadmissible for this reason. I hope the Telcos have switch logs for backup!

Method #2: Orangeboxing. Orangeboxing is Caller ID signal emulation through the use of a Bell 202 modem, sound card software, or a recording of a Caller ID transmission. Orangeboxing is not very effective because you have to send the signal *after* the caller has answered their phone. However, through the magic of social engineering you could have one friend call a number and pretend he has reached a wrong number while sending a call waiting Caller ID signal fooling the victim into believing he is receiving another incoming call from the name and number spoofed and when the victim "flashes over" have your friend hand you the phone and continue with your social engineering.

Method #3: Calling cards. I learned this method from some phone phreaks on a party line a long time ago. I can't recall the name of the calling card company but all one has to do is provide a credit card as a method of payment to obtain a PIN. Once you have the PIN you just op divert or cause an ANI-fail to the 800 number for the calling card and it will ask you to please enter the number you are calling from. You touch tone in *any* number you want, then it asks for your PIN and then what number you want to call. The person you call will see the number you touch toned in as the Caller ID for that call. If the number is in the same area as the caller, it will also show the name associated with the phone number.

Spoofing ANI

Spoofing ANI is a little more difficult than spoofing Caller ID unless you have access to a central office switch.

A few years ago when Verizon was still GTE here in California, the local "0" operator center was located close to me and they had the ability to send ANI without ANI-fails. However, I found a test number on a DMS-100 switch in Ontario that would give me a local "0" operator—only she'd see an ANI-fail and have to ask me what number I was calling from. Any number I gave her would be used as ANI for any call I had her place. A while ago AT&T used to send ANI when you placed calls to toll-free numbers through the AT&T network and you could only call 800 numbers that were hosted by AT&T. After *2600* published my article on how to spoof ANI by op diverting to 800-CALL-ATT, AT&T had their network changed within a month. Their new network, however, just made it easier to cause ANI-fails to toll-free numbers. On the new network you could call any toll-free number, not just AT&T hosted numbers, and there would be no ANI on the call, unless you were calling 800-CALL-ATT or a few other numbers that are internal numbers hosted by the call center itself. All you have to do to cause ANI-fails to toll-free numbers now is dial 10-10-288-0 and touch tone in the 800 number when AT&T comes on the line. This method of causing ANI-fails is great because you don't have to speak to a live operator and you can even have your modem wardial 800 numbers without fear of your ANI being logged.

However there are some AT&T call centers that still forward ANI, and you may be able to reach them even if the call centers aren't in your area. Try op diverting to an AT&T language assistance operator. Since it is not likely that your call center will have a Tagalog speaking operator, you will get routed to a different AT&T center that does, possibly an AT&T center that still forwards ANI. If you get an AT&T center that still forwards ANI, you can spoof ANI by simply giving the operator the number you want to spoof as the number you are calling from and social engineering her into placing a call to the toll-free number you wish to call.

The best method for spoofing ANI and Caller ID is social engineering a Telus operator to do it for you. I stumbled upon this method when I was testing out a theory. In my previous *2600* article about spoofing ANI through AT&T I mentioned something known as the 710 trick. This was a method of making collect calls that the called party wouldn't be billed for. The way the 710 trick worked in the past was you'd op divert to 800-CALL-ATT and give the operator a 710 number as the number you were calling from and have her place a collect call to the number you want to call. The called party would never get a bill because 710 is a "non-existent" area code. AT&T does its billing rates by where the call is being placed from and to and because you used a 710 number, there were undetermined rates. I was testing to see if the 710 trick also worked with a Canadian phone company called Telus. After testing it out, my friend in Canada dialed *69 and it read back the 710 number I gave the operator. This is how I discovered Caller ID spoofing was possible through Telus and I began to come up with a social engineering method to get them to place a call for me without selecting a billing method. I now know that it is also possible to spoof ANI through Telus.

Telus' toll-free "dial-around" is 1-800-646-0000. By simply calling this number with an ANI-fail you can give the operator any number as the one you are calling from. As of January 2003, Telus can now place calls to many toll-free numbers and the ANI will show up as whatever number you say you're calling from. So by simply causing an ANI-fail to Telus' dial-around service you can spoof Caller ID *and* ANI to anyone you want to call. Not only that but if the person you are calling is in the same area as the number you are spoofing, the *name* and number show up on the Caller ID display. To cause an ANI-fail to Telus all you have to do is op divert to 1-800-646-0000 or dial 10-10-288-0 and touch tone 800-646-0000 when AT&T comes on the line.

You can social engineer the Telus operator to place a "test call" for you which is a free call with no billing. You simply tell the Telus operator at the beginning of the call that you are a "Telus technician" calling from [number to spoof] and need her to place a "Test call" to [number to call]. It goes something like this:

You pick up the phone and dial 10102880.

AT&T Automated Operator: "AT&T, to place a call..."

Touch tone 800-646-0000.

AT&T Automated Operator: "Thank you for using AT&T."
Ring.
Telus: "This is the Telus operator, Lisa speaking." (Or, "This is the Telus operator, what number are you calling from?")
You: "Hi Lisa, this is the Telus technician. You should see an ANI failure on your screen. I'm calling from [number to spoof]. I need you to place a test call to [number to call]."
Telus: "Thank you from Telus."

What just happened was AT&T sent an ANI-fail to Telus, you told the operator to key in your new number, Telus then placed the call and used the number you gave as both ANI and Caller ID!

Note about spoofing ANI to toll-free numbers: Not all U.S. toll-free numbers are accessible from Canadian trunks. So even though you are spoofing a U.S. number the call may not be able to be routed through Telus.

Of course, the social engineering method will probably become ineffective soon, although I've demonstrated this at H2K2 in July 2002 and it's now 2003 and it's still working. The spoofed Caller ID also shows up on collect calls (though I think you can only call people in Canada collect with this service), third-party billing (would you accept a third-party bill call if the Caller ID said your girlfriend's number and the op said she was the one placing the call?), and calling card calls, so you could even legitimately spoof Caller ID if you had a Telus calling card. The rates are pretty expensive though. But you can get one if you have Telus as your local phone company. If you live outside Canada you can pay with a credit card. (You need a Canadian billing address though!)

The sad thing is that ANI spoofing and Caller ID spoofing are so easy, yet many companies use ANI and Caller ID as a security feature; Kevin Mitnick even stated in his book *The Art of Deception* that Caller ID was easy to spoof with ISDN PRI lines but that you can't spoof ANI (even though on certain switches it *will* spoof ANI). Here you can spoof Caller ID and ANI using simple social engineering that is very effective. T-Mobile and Sprint PCS allow you to check your voice mail without entering your password if the Caller ID shows your cell phone number. Credit card companies allow you to activate credit cards simply by calling their toll-free number with the ANI of the "home phone" number you put on their application. Some calling card companies allow you to access your calling card by simply calling from "your number." Some utility companies (including the phone company) allow you to set up online billing using only a call to one of their toll-free numbers that use ANI to verify that you are calling from the phone number listed on the account. They activate your online billing with no further verification.

ANI and Caller ID can be nice tools for verification, but you should also verify other identifying information such as a Social Security number or PIN before letting just anyone calling from a certain number access your services.

Verizon's Call Intercept (Winter, 2003-2004) *By decoder*

Call Intercept is a service offered by Verizon that prevents callers that do not send any Caller ID information from directly ringing your line. Instead, callers hear a recorded announcement informing them that you subscribe to this service, then they are prompted to record their name for identification. If the caller does not record their name, then your phone does not ring. If they choose to record their name, your phone rings with a distinctive pattern, and you have the choice of either accepting or denying the call through an automated menu. The monthly charge for this service is $6.00, although it is included in some of Verizon's premium plans.

While this service does have some flaws, I feel that it is better than Anonymous Call Rejection (ACR) for certain types of annoyance calls. For instance, telemarketers can still get through to a line equipped with ACR without sending any Caller ID information. There are also some PICCs (Pre-subscribed Interexchange Carrier Codes, commonly referred to as 10-10 numbers) that can be used to bypass ACR. The reason for this is that ACR is meant to reject callers who block their number by using *67. However if an ANI-fail occurs the Caller ID information is missing, and the call goes through just fine. The display will show "out of area" and no phone number will appear. Keep in mind that *67 sends a Caller ID signal of its own, while a flex-ANI-fail will cause the absence of any Caller ID information, due to the fact that Caller ID information is derived from the flex-ANI. Call Intercept will not let *any* calls directly ring your line unless a number appears on the Caller ID display. ACR is designed to reject certain types of calls and let everything else through. Call Intercept is designed to accept only certain types of calls, and reject everything else.

How It Works

When Call Intercept is activated, anonymous callers trying to reach you will hear an announcement explaining what Call Intercept is. Then they will be prompted to record their name. They can also enter a four-digit override code to bypass Call Intercept (more on this later). At this point your phone will ring with a distinctive pattern and your Caller ID display will notify you that it is a Call Intercept call. During this time, and until you decide how to handle the call, the caller will hear hold music. When you pick up the phone you will hear, "Someone is waiting to speak with you. For more information, press 1." You will then hear the caller's name as they have recorded it and you will have the options of accepting the call, denying the call, playing a "sales call refusal" to the caller, or sending the call to your Home Voice Mail, if you subscribe to it. The "sales call refusal" is pretty useful. If the caller is stupid enough to identify that they are a telemarketer, you can have this announcement played to them. It will inform the caller that you do not accept telephone solicitations and wish to be placed on their Do Not Call list. I have never had a telemarketer attempt to ring my line through Call Intercept, although with the new National Do Not Call List, some of these phone solicitors may become desperate.

I should note that Call Intercept may not interact well with certain Verizon services as well as some types of phone calls. You cannot have Anonymous Call Rejection active on your line with Call Intercept. I suppose the reason for this is that ACR would override Call Intercept, and all anonymous calls would get sent to the ACR intercept message. ("We're sorry, the person you are calling does not wish to speak with callers that block delivery of their telephone number" or something like that depending on where you live.) Also, you cannot use *57 to trace calls that came in through Call Intercept. Remember, *57 is a customer originated trace, and when you receive a call through Call Intercept, it is effectively a call transfer. International cellular calls as well as collect calls made without the assistance of a live operator may also be unable to reach your line.

My Experiences

When I first subscribed to Call Intercept, I was asked to choose a four-digit bypass code while on the phone with the customer service representative. This is the code that you would give to anyone you wished to have the ability to bypass your Call Intercept service. Upon hearing the Call Intercept greeting, an authorized caller would enter the code, and then would be able to directly ring your line, without sending any Caller ID transmission. The Caller ID display would read "Priority Caller," accompanied by the distinctive ring.

According to the Verizon Residence Services User Guide, in former GTE states the subscriber would be able to access their Call Intercept service by calling a toll-free number. Instead of choosing a bypass code while on the phone with the customer service representative, as is done in former Bell Atlantic states, such as my home state of New York, customers in the former GTE regions would have their bypass code defaulted to the last four digits of their home telephone number. When they called the toll-free number, they would be able to change the bypass code, as well as turn Call Intercept on and off. This number was not published in the User Guide.

In the past, when someone would try to ring my line through Call Intercept, my Caller ID display would read "Call Intercept" in the name field and the phone number would come up as my area code followed by all ones. This was the case until recently, when the display began showing a toll-free number. It now displayed 800-527-7070 as the Call Intercept number. This is the number used in former GTE states for a service known as Call Gate. Basically, Call Gate lets you control your phone line in various ways. You can "blacklist" and "whitelist" certain incoming and outgoing numbers. You can block or unblock international calls and calls to premium (900) numbers. You can even block *all* incoming or outgoing calls. It pretty much gives you complete control of your dial tone. These features, along with Call Intercept, are what Verizon refers to as "Advanced Services."

When you call 1-800-527-7070, it informs you that you have reached Verizon's Advanced Services, and you are asked to enter your home telephone number. I recall attempting to call this number in the past, but it wouldn't accept my phone number because this service isn't available in my state. After seeing this number appear on my Caller ID display as the Call Intercept number, I tried calling again. When I entered my home telephone number this time, it accepted it. I was asked for my PIN which is, of course by default, the last four digits of my phone number. From here I was able to hear or change my bypass code, as well as turn Call Intercept on or off. Verizon never informed me that I was able to use this service, and when I first signed up with Verizon, it wouldn't work for me. Apparently this number is now being used in the former Bell Atlantic states to control the Call Intercept feature.

Hacking It

This is where the security issue comes into play. You can call this toll-free number and enter in anyone's phone number in New York State who subscribes to Call Intercept. The PIN will be the default every time. The reason no one has changed their PIN is because Verizon has yet to inform anyone of this service. Anyone who subscribes to Call Intercept in New York is vulnerable. You simply dial 1-800-527-7070, and when prompted, enter the telephone number of someone in New York who subscribes to Call Intercept. When it asks for the PIN, enter the last four digits of their telephone number and you're in. From this menu you could listen to their bypass code, change it, change the PIN for the toll-free number, or turn off Call Intercept altogether. The service that they think is protecting them from unwanted and annoyance calls can actually facilitate these types of calls because of a security hole.

There is an easy solution to this security hole. Require ANI verification in order to initialize the service. It is a common practice for other services such as remote call forwarding. As a matter of fact, Verizon does require that the initialization be done from the line that subscribes to Call Intercept in every other former Bell Atlantic state except New York. If you were to call the toll-free number and enter a Call Intercept subscriber's phone number in Vermont, Massachusetts, New Jersey, etc., you will be informed that the service must be initialized from the telephone number that subscribes to the service. Once the initialization is complete, you may access your services from any telephone. It is quite obvious that Verizon's customers in those states are also unaware of the toll-free number to control their service because they haven't initialized it yet. Fortunately, ANI verification is used so they are not left vulnerable. Why New

York does not require ANI verification is unknown to me, but what I do know is that *anyone* was able to administrate my Call Intercept, and I would have never known.

Conclusion

Hopefully, Verizon will rectify this situation because it simply does not make sense to require ANI verification everywhere except New York. You could always spoof the ANI, or beige box from the customer's line if you are determined to access someone's Call Intercept, but in New York, you simply need to call a toll-free number from anywhere you wish and enter a default PIN code. Now you have control over their acceptance of anonymous calls.

Other than being a large security issue in New York, Call Intercept is a great service. By subscribing to it, you will receive close to zero telemarketing calls. Having your anonymous callers hear hold music while you decide how to handle the call is pretty nifty as well. I have honestly enjoyed having this service and would highly recommend it to all Verizon customers. Just remember, if you are considering subscribing to Call Intercept, or if you already have it, call 1-800-527-7070 and change your PIN! Especially if you live in New York, unless I already have!

Shouts: Lucky225, accident, Licutis, NotTheory, w1nt3rmut3, ic0n, Captain B, Majestic, Scott, doug, phractal, Scr00, WhiteSword, RijilV, Eta, parano|a, dual_parallel, bland_inquisitor at Radio Freek America, Slipmode at `www.slipnet.org`, *and StankDawg at* `www.binrev.com`.

Backspoofing 101 (Spring, 2007) *By Natas*

What exactly is backspoofing? Most people reading this article probably have never heard of the term "backspoofing" before and don't know that the term was coined somewhat recently by a fellow phone phreak named NotTheory. Backspoofing is a very simple, but useful technique. Essentially, it is just calling yourself with spoofed Caller ID for the purpose of getting the CNAM (Caller ID Name) associated with a particular number. The number you spoof as your Caller ID is the number that you want to receive Caller ID name information for. I believe that this will work with almost any 10-digit number within North America. To do this properly you usually need to be calling a POTS line, because POTS lines are the only kind of lines that offer Caller ID With Name, not just Caller ID Number. However, some VoIP providers these days are now offering Caller ID Name service to compete with all the features available on traditional POTS lines. It should also be noted that cell phones do not provide Caller ID With Name on incoming calls and probably never will, as the name always tends to be retrieved from the local database on the phone.

How does backspoofing work? How is the CNAM retrieved from a number? Well, when you spoof your Caller ID to a telephone line with Caller ID Name, what happens is the receiving telephone switch does a lookup in what is known as a CNAM database via the SS7 (Signaling System 7) protocol. This receiving switch dips in and retrieves the name associated with the particular number from the CNAM database and displays it on your little Caller ID box. Now you might be asking why this is the least bit interesting or how it's useful. Well, it's extremely useful because it allows you to see information that may otherwise be private. The telephone companies figure that even if you're some big shot movie star or even if you have an unlisted number, the person receiving your calls should still be able to see the name and the number of the person calling. After all, that's why they're paying for Caller ID. So the Telco puts your name and number in their enormous database that's constantly being updated. Even unlisted numbers will typically come back with a first and last name if it can all fit into the 15-character space designed for the Caller ID Name. This all works because you're tricking the Caller ID service into looking up the CNAM information associated with the telephone number of your choosing. I like to think of these CNAM databases as a private reverse lookup directory!

At first backspoofing may not seem like the best thing in the world, but there are lots of applicable uses for something like this, especially if you're a phone phreak! Ever find a local "elevator number"? The ones that connect you to the phone inside an elevator, allowing you to listen in on the elevator or speak to the people inside? Well... by backspoofing an elevator number you can see what the name comes back as. Usually this is the name of the company whose PBX the elevator number is on or the company that occupies the building that the elevator is in. Now all you would have to do is look up the company's address and find out where the building is and you can find out exactly what elevator you're listening to! This actually came in extremely handy for me. For about five years now, I've had elevator numbers that were supposedly at Brown University but I was never really sure. By simply backspoofing the number I was able to confirm this within a few seconds.

Telco test numbers are some of the greatest things to backspoof, because even test numbers have CNAM entries most of the time. When I first started backspoofing, I assumed test numbers would have discreet listings, but oftentimes they list the Telco's name or even a little description about the number! Someone even showed me a modem that came back as "NET 5-ESS," which is a telephone switch made by Lucent. So it was pretty obvious what turned out to be connected to that modem! If you're doing a scan and you're not sure who a particular modem belongs to, backspoofing comes in very handy! I always like to see what milliwatt numbers, and other numbers around the milliwatt number, come back as. Maybe you have some numbers to your Telco and you're wondering exactly what bureau the number belongs to? Backspoofing can sometimes tell you if you've reached RCMAC, the switch room, MLAC, Information, or the code for a particular wire center.

Also, you can see just how lazy Telcos are and how long some test numbers have been the same, because I've found entries with old telephone company names that are long gone! When was the last time you saw "NYNEX" or "NEW ENGLAND TEL" calling you?! These companies ditched those names years ago, but there are still plenty of CNAM entries out there with those names.

Cell phone numbers are no exceptions to rules of backspoofing either! T-Mobile currently enters their customers' names into CNAM databases. I believe Sprint is now starting to do the same. So if you're looking for a famous celebrity's cell phone number and you know they've got a T-Mobile account, backspoofing can come in very handy. Try backspoofing an entire T-Mobile exchange served out of the Hollywood Hills and see how many famous names you recognize!

Beware that all CNAM providers are not equal! There are lots of different CNAM databases in use, and while most of the information is the same, some databases have conflicting information. It may just be that some databases are not updated as frequently or it may just be that a certain one sucks and contains lots of outdated entries. I've found CNAM entries that were different, depending on the carrier who provided my Caller ID name service. I would get one result with Verizon and another with AT&T. There really is a lot of funky stuff that goes on in the world of CNAM.

To close the article, I want to show you just how cool backspoofing is. I've put together a list of some of the most interesting examples I've found through backspoofing. Keep in mind that phone numbers do change quite often, so unfortunately some of these examples may be gone by the time this article comes out.

- "BROWN UNIVERSIT" <4018637127>
- "USG-FBI" <3104776565>
- "U S GOVERNMENT" <5013246241>
- "CIA,INTERNATION" <5087982693>
- "FAA-ONTARIO ATC" <9093909953>
- "BOOZE" <9099750050>
- "NEW CENTURY TIT" <9099370020>
- "UNITED,NUDE -TE" <2122749998>
- "SPRINT PAYPHONE" <7027319900>
- "28881" <3109265101>
- "A,T &T" <6172271067>
- "BELL ATLANTIC A" <5703870000>
- "OFC# 897 TEST L" <8028979912>
- "ROCH TEL" <5852259902>
- "PACIFIC BELL" <3108580000>
- "VERIZON RC C9" <9093900008>
- "GTC RC WCH3 BC" <9093900006>

- "GTC RC E140 BC" <9093900037>
- "GTE WC XXXX" <9099740010>
- "PYRAMID,TELECOM" <5087989920>
- "VERIZON,INFORMA" <5087989974>
- "VERIZON,GNI" <5087569913>
- "VERIZON" <6316689906>
- "NYNEX" <5087980081>
- "NEW,ENGLAND TEL" <5087989987>
- "BELLSOUTH" <7066679923>
- "T-MOBILE" <7066679994>
- "SWBT" <3142350475>
- "SWB" <3149661736>
- "QWEST MESSAGING" <5072859216>
- "VACANT" <9784468972>
- "UNCLAIMED MONEY" <4104641276>

Shouts: The DDP, NotTheory, Nick84, Decoder, Lucky225, Doug, Majestic, IcOn, GreyArea, Mitnick, Agent Steal, Poulsen, StankDawg, Dual, Cessna, Vox, Strom Carlson, IBall, & Av1d. The revolution will be digitized!

Getting More From T-Mobile (Summer, 2005) *By Psycho*

I am a former employee of a T-Mobile retail store where I was primarily responsible for activating new accounts for customers. The main system we used was called Watson. Watson is a Web-based portal that allowed the user to run a credit check for a customer, activate prepaid phones, access customers' accounts, access the POS, run store reports, and the like. Retail employees of T-Mobile use this system for every transaction that is done throughout the day. The tasty pearl of all of this is that the Watson portal is accessible from an outside IP address. That means that you can do most of these functions from anywhere outside of a retail store. Now before I get into specifics, the standard disclaimer applies: This is for educational purposes only. Any actions that you take within this system are probably tracked. I am not responsible for anything you do with this information. And while the following explains possible ways to activate service through T-Mobile, doing so in this system from outside of a retail store is probably illegal. And as such, I have not actually completed an activation from outside of a retail store. So I have not verified if these processes are even fully possible. If you get stopped by Watson, too bad.

Now, like I said, Watson is accessible from outside the T-Mobile intranet. You can get to it by going to `http://watson3.voicestream.com`. Click login to get to the login page.

Here it asks you for a username and password. These are the usernames and passwords of each retail employee that needs to get in. At the retail store, the username and password have to be entered before every transaction, so most employees make this something very simple that can be typed in quickly. At the store where I worked, most of the people there used their username as the password. So, if your name was John Thomas, your username might be jthomas and you might set your password to jthomas. The password could be set to anything, but most people just use the username. The best way to get some usernames is to do some social engineering at your local store. Since the username is usually the first letter of the first name and the first six letters of the last name, you can get someone's business card and simply take the name off of that. Keep in mind that if the person's last name is shorter than six letters, there is usually a number at the end. For example, John Smith might be jsmith2. So these might be harder to get.

Once logged in you are presented with the same screen that the employees get in the store. You have the following options:

- **New Personal Account:** Where you would run credit and activate a new personal account.
- **New Business Account:** Where you would activate a new business account.
- **Add to Existing Account:** Used to add a line onto an existing account.
- **Work in Progress:** Used to resume an activation that was interrupted. Asks for the SSN to continue.
- **View an Existing Service Agreement:** Where you can access a service agreement (asks for SSN).
- **Number Eligibility Query:** Used to see if another provider's number can be ported to T-Mobile.
- **Prepaid Menu:** Where you can activate prepaid phones.
- **POS Menu:** Access the POS (does not seem to be accessible from outside the intranet).
- **Customer Account Management (or CAM):** Used to access the information on existing accounts (does not seem to be accessible from outside the intranet).
- **SAP Retail Store:** I am not sure what this is for. We never used it in the retail store. Does not seem to be accessible from outside the intranet.
- **Change Password:** duh.
- **Log Off:** duh.

Of all of these, only the POS, CAM, and SAP Retail Store seem to be blocked from outside IPs. Only CAM would be useful for our purposes, but we can live without it. Now, the fun comes when you realize just what you can do from here. Have you ever wanted to activate a new account for someone? Have you ever wanted to activate a prepaid phone for free? Have you ever needed to add a line onto some unsuspecting person's account? Well, here is how some of that can be done.

Activating Prepaid (the easy way to go)

Do you have an old T-Mobile phone that you want on prepaid without paying for the activation? Then head to the Prepaid Menu in Watson. All you need is the SIM card number, the IMEI number of the phone, and a prepaid airtime card. You can put in a bogus name and birthday (which is all that is required) and input the rest. You have to use a virgin SIM so just do some social engineering at a retail store to score one. And you can purchase a $10 prepaid airtime card from the store to use for the activation. You see, when you activate a prepaid phone in the store, the activation is done separately from ringing up the sale. So you can activate it yourself in Watson, and then just not pay anything.

Activating Postpaid (the harder way to go)

If you head to New Personal Account, you are asked for a bunch of personal info. This is information that is taken from a driver's license in order to run a credit check. After putting all this in, the credit result will give you a choice of rate plans that you are eligible for. After picking that, the system asks for the SIM card number, the IMEI number from the phone, which city you want your phone number in, and so on. You have to use a virgin SIM so just score one from a retail store with some social engineering. If it all worked correctly, the contract will pop up and you will be activated.

Add to Existing Account

Using this area, it is possible to add a line onto someone's account using only their SSN. After you put in a customer's SSN, you can add on a line—a process similar to creating a new account. What you can add depends on that person's credit. I do not recommend actually doing this because that person will definitely find out about it when they get their next bill. So this is only good for short-term phone usage.

Another great flaw in T-Mobile's system is their Customer Care department. These guys normally handle most customer issues over the phone, but because of the inefficiencies in the Retail system, it is often necessary for employees to call Customer Care. An employee would have to call in to do credit checks or to activate phones if Watson won't let them. They also call in to change rate plans and to extend someone's contract.

Getting Customer Care to think you are an employee is painfully simple. Every time an employee calls Customer Care, they ask for that employee's first name, first letter of the last name, and a dealer code. All you have to do to get a set of these is to hang around in a retail store long enough for one of the employees to call Customer Care for someone. When they are on the phone, you will hear them give the name and dealer code to the representative. Another way is to get a receipt that the particular employee rang up. On each receipt is an area called Employee ID, or the like, which has the dealer code listed there. Each employee has a unique dealer code that is looked up to make sure it matches the name given. So a typical conversation would go like this:

> **Customer Care:** "Thank you for calling T-Mobile. To better assist you, may I have your cell phone number starting with the area code?"
> **Employee:** "Hi, my name is John and I am a direct dealer for T-Mobile."
> **Customer Care:** "OK. May I have the first letter of your last name and your dealer code?"
> **Employee:** "First letter is T as in Tom and my dealer code is 0045678."

The dealer codes are usually always seven digits long, but it doesn't always start with 00. Another thing is to specify that you are a direct dealer when you identify yourself. These are people who work for direct T-Mobile stores as opposed to authorized agents of T-Mobile. After you give them the info, the rep asks for the customer's phone number and name to verify the account. Sometimes they also ask for the last four digits of the customer's SSN, but most of the time they trust you as a dealer and do what you want to the account. Nine times out of ten, they do what you want without ever wanting to actually speak to the customer. With this total access to the account, you can change almost anything. As long as the name and dealer code match in the system, they are yours to command. And it doesn't matter which department you speak to. They all ask for the same info. So you could talk to Customer Care, Consumer Credit, or Activations, and as long as the name and dealer code match, you are golden.

When you call Activations, you could activate phones manually through them without entering the store. First you would talk to Consumer Credit to do a credit check, then you would go to Activations. At Activations, they ask you for the SSN of the customer or Onyx reference number (which you get after the credit check). From there, they verify the name and address info that you ran the credit with. After that, they ask which city you want your phone number in and which rate plan you want. Then they ask for the SIM card number and the IMEI number from the phone. Remember that it has to be a virgin SIM so score one from a retail store. Now, activating a phone with a rep is not going to do you much good unless you do it under someone else's name. If you did it under your name, you would still be subject to the activation fee and to the annual contract.

Many of these huge security flaws could be easily corrected by blocking access to Watson from outside IP addresses. Changes also need to be made to the verification process that Customer Care goes through to ensure that they are actually speaking to a dealer. Employee ID numbers should not be printed on anything that is given to the customer. With these simple changes, T-Mobile could take active steps in sealing these gaping holes.

So there you go, kids. Have fun, but don't do anything stupid. Now you can truly Get More from T-Mobile.

Shout outs to Amanda, Req, and the rest of the crew at the TPG.

How to Track Any U.K. GSM Mobile Phone (Without the User's Consent) (Winter, 2005-2006) *By Jonathan Pamplin*

As a result of improvements in mobile phone cell technology, U.K. mobile-phone companies have for the past two years been able to sell transmitter data to online mobile phone location services that enable them to triangulate to within 100 yards the location of a given mobile GSM phone. This technology was in the news recently when the police tracked one of the London Bombers across Europe to his brother's house in Italy where he was arrested.

To be able to track a mobile phone and comply with the Data Protection Laws, mobile location services have to prove that the phone owner has given their consent to be tracked. They do this by sending an SMS to the phone's telephone number requesting a reply to the effect that you agree for the phone to be tracked. The majority of the phone location services only do this once to register the phone and then it can be tracked at any time without further SMS alerts to the phone.

This is all very well if you have access to the mobile phone to reply to the SMS agreeing to be tracked but that's no use if the phone is in the hands of someone else. Anyway it's not much fun tracking your own phone.

What I am about to describe is a way around this system that will allow you to track any U.K. GSM phone without the owner's consent on the following U.K. networks: T-Mobile, Orange, 02, and Vodaphone.

To begin with you need to set up an account with one of the mobile phone location services. I have chosen for this article `http://www.fleetonline.net` simply because it offers a pay as you go service and does not charge you extra to add different phones as many of the others companies do.

I would suggest as a username you use something silly like "sexygirls4u," or, "time2buyanewphone" as the target phone will receive an SMS with your username in the beginning and if it's daft they will just assume it's just another junk SMS. You will also need to credit the account with 10 British pounds.

Now set up an account with one of the many fake SMS sites I've used (`http://www.sharpmail.co.uk` is one) to enable you to send SMS messages from a fake number.

Now you're ready to register your target's mobile phone with FleetOnline. Login to your FleetOnline account, go to admin, and add a new member. Enter any name and the mobile phone number you want to track.

The recipient will get a message like this. You can see the message in the sent messages folder within FleetOnline.

"BuyANewPhone 07354654323345 wants to locate your mobile from now on using FleetOnline. Text 'T2Y' to 00447950081259 to agree."

The important thing here is the reply telephone number 00447950081259 and the text "T2Y."

The reply number is always the same but occasionally the text changes to "T2YXDT." You can tell if this is the case as you will see "******" instead of "T2Y" in the sent messages folder of FleetOnline.

Now go to your SharpMail account and send a fake SMS from the phone number you want to track to 00447950081259 with the text "T2Y."

Within a few minutes your FleetOnline account will have registered that phone number and you will be able to track it to within 100 yards superimposed onto a detailed street map using FleetOnline, all without the mobile phone user's consent.

If you have problems with the "T2Y" or "T2YXDT" just attempt to register a random telephone number first. Then register the one you want to track and the reply code should always be "T2Y." There is no charge for adding new numbers using FleetOnline so feel free to experiment.

This will work with many of the other mobile phone location services and fake SMS services. Just use Google to find an alternative if these let you down.

If you're concerned about being tracked using this method, use a Virgin SIM card as this is the only U.K. network not to provide tracking information to the mobile location services at present. Although the current 3G services don't do it either, the fact that their handsets contain GPS suggests that they will be doing it soon!

Shouts to Nemma, Lynxtec, ServiceTec, and 4Mat.

New Tech

Where we are today is most certainly a fascinating place in history. But it's sure not going to stay the way it is for very long. Things change so fast in the telecommunications world that we could probably add on new chapters every few months and still have plenty to talk about. I guess that's why it's good that we have a magazine in order to do precisely that. In this section we focus on some of what is today considered new and will no doubt soon be thought of as ancient. As always, our writers try to consider the potential risks in the development of any technology. The potential for surveillance and the lack of real security in certain Voice over IP technologies are both addressed here in addition to yet another way of making phone calls in future years.

The Future of Enhanced 911 (Winter, 2001-2002)

By Wumpus Hunter

By 2005, if you carry a cell phone your wireless carrier will have the ability to track your location with an accuracy of about 50 meters. No, this isn't some dystopian fantasy. This isn't science fiction. It's real, federally mandated, and all in the name of safety.

It's known as Enhanced 911, commonly referred to as E911, and it's an FCC mandate that started in 1996. It's probably not as bad as it sounds (although some conspiracy theorists would disagree with me). But by the same token, it raises some important issues that must be addressed over the next few years. As E911 will affect every wireless subscriber in the country, it is extremely important that we all understand how it works, how it will be implemented, and what the potential privacy concerns are.

How It Works

While law enforcement has been able to track cell phone users' locations to some extent for a long time, the new E911 standard will greatly increase that ability. The backbone of this new location tracking ability is known as Automatic Location Identification (ALI). When E911 is fully implemented, all wireless carriers will provide ALI to the appropriate Public Safety Answering Point (PSAP). This can be done in one of two ways: Handset-Based ALI or Network-Based ALI.

Network-Based ALI was the original method proposed by the FCC when they first drafted the E911 requirements. At the time, it was the best location method available that could be reasonably implemented. This method provides the caller's location within 100 to 300 meters by using triangulation and the measurement of the signal travel time from the handset to the receiver. If the handset is within range of only one cell site, this method fails completely, giving only which cell the user is in and the approximate distance from the cell site. If there are only two cell sites available, rather than three, the system tends to fail and give two different possible user locations.

Handset-Based ALI requires that the cell phone handset include technology such as GPS to provide location information to the PSAP. Although exact figures are hard to come by at this point, some analysts predict that the inclusion of GPS in cell phones will add an additional $50 to the total cost of the phone. The benefit for wireless companies is that it doesn't require the substantial changes to their network that using Network-Based ALI would mandate. Using GPS for ALI gives this method accuracy within 50 to 150 meters.

Although it is tempting to engage in a debate as to whether Network-Based ALI or Handset-Based ALI is the best option for wireless carriers, it would seem that the best solution is to use a mixture of both technologies. Handset-Based ALI (using GPS) could be rendered useless in the steel and concrete buildings of a large city, while

Network-Based ALI would fail in rural areas with limited cell tower coverage. Therefore, it would appear that Handset-Based ALI is the choice for rural settings while Network-Based ALI would be the best solution for urban users. In addition, some companies may deploy hybrid systems that use both GPS and network-based technologies.

Implementation

The FCC has set two implementation phases for E911 service roll-out. Phase I, which began in April, 1998, required that wireless carriers provide the 911 caller's phone number and cell site to the local PSAP. Phase II went into effect in October, requiring that all carriers begin selling E911 capable phones starting October 1, 2001. Also, as of October 1, 2001, or within six months of a request from a PSAP, wireless carriers must be able to locate 67 percent of handset-based callers within 50 meters and 95 percent of callers within 150 meters. At the same time, they must be able to locate 67 percent of network-based callers within 100 meters and 95 percent within 300 meters.

Sprint was the only company to actually meet any of the requirements with their Sprint PCS SPH-N300 (made by Samsung). And with more deadlines coming up, it appears unlikely that wireless carriers will actually meet them on time. Of all new handsets being activated, 25 percent are supposed to be ALI capable by December 31, 2001, 50 percent by June 30, 2002, and 100 percent by December 31, 2002. The FCC expects to have 95 percent of all cell users using ALI capable handsets by the end of 2005.

Privacy Issues and Concerns

E911 services are coming whether we like them or not, so privacy and security issues must be considered and made public. Originally, the FBI wanted to have ALI services be "always on" for law enforcement purposes. The thought of federal agencies having the ability to track anyone carrying a cell phone at any time caused enough public opposition that the original proposals were changed. Now ALI services can be shut off by the user at all times except during a 911 call. This approach seems to be a decent compromise and reduces some of the chances for government abuse. Even companies seem to have heard the public cry for privacy, with Qualcomm announcing that their Handset-Based ALI technology will only broadcast a user's location when they press an "I am here" button.

However, despite these assurances, some wireless carriers are planning to offer "location based services" for their users (local movie times, McDonald's locations, etc.). The threat of privacy abuse by corporations thus becomes a major concern. Even if users have the ability to turn off their ALI services, we all know that most will just leave them on all the time. This will allow companies to track users and develop demographics and marketing information based on where they go, how long they stay there, and other personal habits. It is then only a matter of time before advertising companies use this information to send location targeted ads straight to your phone. Most disturbingly, even if the government isn't directly tracking your location, local and federal law enforcement are only a warrant away from seizing any of your wireless carrier's location information.

Conclusion

In the end, it would seem that the most distasteful parts of the E911 plans have been dropped, leaving a program of enhanced emergency services that currently don't seem that bad. In that respect, E911 has so far been a success for all parties involved. However, the price of freedom is eternal vigilance and while some privacy issues have been averted, other ones have taken their place. Whether it be by government agencies or corporations, abuses of location based information can erode our privacy just the same.

Now you know the basics of E911—how it works and what to look out for. It is up to all of us to keep a watchful eye on how it is implemented over the next few years.

A New Era of Telecommunications Surveillance: America in the 21st Century (Summer, 2002) *By The Prophet*

As the satellite republics of the Soviet Union fell at the end of the twentieth century, the Western world was shocked at the surveillance societies erected by their authoritarian governments. From a population of 17 million in East Germany, the dreaded Stasi secret police employed 34,000 officers, including 2,100 agents reading mail and 6,000 operatives listening to private telephone conversations. Additionally, over 150,000 active informers and up to two million part-time informers were on the payroll. Files were maintained by the Stasi on more than one out of three East Germans, comprising over a billion pages of information.

While centralized domestic surveillance in the United States has probably not yet reached the levels seen in East Germany, the picture is very different when government databases are linked and especially when government databases are linked with commercial ones. To help it fight the insane "war on [some] drugs," the federal government has already connected the databases of the Customs Service, the Drug Enforcement Agency, the IRS, the Federal Reserve, and the State Department. These are accessible via FinCEN and other law enforcement networks (and probably via classified intelligence networks as well—but sorry, that's classified). Additionally, the United States has relatively few data protection laws (particularly concerning the collection of data for commercial purposes), meaning the extensive use of computer matching has led to a "virtual" national data bank. With only a few computer searches, and without obtaining a search warrant, law enforcement can gather a comprehensive file on virtually any U.S. citizen in a matter of minutes.

Telecommunications, unlike paper and electronic records, enjoyed much stronger privacy protections—until September 11. Americans have the egregious wiretapping abuses of J. Edgar Hoover's FBI to thank for this. However, long before September 11, the FBI was laying the groundwork to turn the U.S. telecommunications system into a surveillance infrastructure. This began in 1994 when, at the strong urging of former FBI Director Louis Freeh, Congress passed the Communications Assistance for Law Enforcement Act (CALEA, pronounced "Kuh-LEE-uh," for short).

The legal reasoning behind CALEA is fairly recent and, to fully understand it, it should be considered in light of the failed Clipper Chip key escrow initiatives of the early 1990s. During the consideration of key escrow legislation (which ultimately failed) and CALEA (which was ultimately successful), the FBI nearly convinced Congress that Americans have no legal or moral right to keep any secrets from the government. Fortunately, Congress was not fooled; they decided that while Americans should be subject to surveillance of all of their communications, citizens could still keep secrets from the government. How magnanimous of them! The stated purpose of CALEA is to preserve, despite advances in technology, the surveillance capabilities law enforcement agencies possessed in 1994. The actual implementation of CALEA, predictably, has been much broader than Congress originally contemplated.

Technically, the FCC is tasked with determining the surveillance capabilities telecommunications carriers are required to provide. Because surveillance is not the core competency of the FCC, they have deferred to the FBI's expertise, and serve as a "rubber stamp" for the technical requirements the FBI requests. Privacy groups have widely criticized the resultant 11-point "punch list," with which telecommunications carriers must comply, as a dramatic expansion of the capabilities originally contemplated by CALEA. For example, mobile telephones containing GPS locators have recently appeared on the market. Touted as a safety feature, GPS is also a surveillance feature mandated by CALEA. If you carry such a phone, the FBI knows exactly where you are at all times. (Of course, J. Edgar Hoover's FBI will only use that capability against criminals and terrorists, right?)

Other technical requirements on the "punch list" include the capability to intercept all packet-switched communications, which includes Internet traffic. The FBI presents this in seemingly reasonable terms; they just want to tap Voice over IP (VoIP) and other packet-mode voice communications like any other telephone call. Of course, to those familiar with TCP/IP, this is very frightening indeed; the only way to intercept the "bad guy's" data is to look at everyone's data. On the Internet, this is accomplished with DCS1000 (formerly Carnivore) and other proprietary surveillance devices. The FBI really likes to keep secrets, so they won't reveal a complete list of the surveillance devices they use, won't reveal the manufacturers, and won't release a full list of surveillance capabilities. In the face of intense Congressional pressure, the FBI reluctantly allowed one "independent technical review" of the nearly obsolete Carnivore system.

However, this was conducted on such restrictive terms that MIT, Purdue, Dartmouth, and UCSD refused to participate on the grounds the study was rigged. Jeffery Schiller, when explaining MIT's refusal to CNN, said, "In essence, the Justice Department is looking to borrow our reputation, and we're not for sale that way."

Eventually a research team at the obscure Illinois Institute of Technology Research Institute was selected to perform the study. While the FBI intended to keep the identities of the "independent researchers" a secret, they accidentally leaked the researchers' names on an incorrectly formatted Adobe PDF document. So much for secrets. As it turned out, three of the supposedly "independent" team members possessed active security clearances (including top-secret NSA and IRS clearance—go figure), and two others had close ties to the White House. With the deck so carefully stacked in the FBI's favor, it is surprising (and telling) the IITRI study warned Carnivore "does not provide protections, especially audit functions, commensurate with the level of the risks," and was vulnerable to "physical attacks, software bugs, or power failures." The ACLU offered to perform its own review of Carnivore, but the FBI not-so-politely declined. In the interim, the next release of Carnivore, called DCS1000, is now in operation. As with Carnivore, the capabilities of DCS1000 are not fully disclosed. Mysteriously, many Internet Service providers (ISPs), including Comcast and Sprint, have implemented so-called "transparent proxy" servers, possessing extensive logging capabilities. Comcast, in a widely publicized incident that even drew the ire of U.S. Representative (and hacker foe) Ed Markey, was caught associating the web browsing habits of its customers with their IP addresses. While Comcast claims they no longer collect this information, it is likely that other ISPs have implemented similar technology and equally likely that Comcast could resume logging at the FBI's request.

While telecommunications providers are wary of providing the FBI with direct access to their infrastructure, most do not object out of privacy considerations. Instead, they are primarily concerned that the FBI's activities do not cause disruptions in service. Telecommunications carriers are particularly indignant at court rulings requiring they provide the FBI with direct access to telephone switches, and grant them the ability to install their own software upon the switches. Lucent implemented this capability on the 5ESS switch in the 5E14 software revision, which nearly every 5ESS in the country now runs. Surveillance capabilities have also been present for some time on the Nortel DMS100 platform. While the capabilities of the FBI's switch software are, like DCS1000, presently unknown, the 5E14 software revision incorporates a number of useful surveillance features on its own. For example, when a surveillance target makes a phone call, the switch can silently conference in a preprogrammed telephone number. Because the FBI also keeps secrets from telecommunications providers, even refusing to share basic architectural information, providers are skeptical of the FBI's assurances that no potential for disruption exists. Additionally, because most surveillance capabilities are provided by the FBI's own software, telecommunications providers cannot audit court-ordered wiretaps. (Of course, J. Edgar Hoover's FBI is trustworthy, so checks and balances are not necessary.)

The cost of implementing surveillance capabilities is also of major concern to telecommunications providers. In exchange for retrofitting the nation's telecommunications infrastructure with a surveillance architecture of which Stalin could only dream (at one point in the CALEA legislative process, the FBI proposed implementing the capability to simultaneously intercept and record one out of every 100 telephone conversations taking place in each central office), the federal government promised $500 million to telecommunications carriers. However, implementing all of the requirements on the CALEA "punch card" is estimated to cost the cash-strapped telecommunications industry as much as $607 million. With the additional "roving wiretap" capabilities granted to the FBI after September 11 in the obliquely named U.S.A Patriot Act, the cost of implementation is likely to soar even higher.

Americans face a new, and potentially dangerous, era of surveillance. History has proven through the nuclear arms race, the Nixon administration, and other similar craziness that things that are possible are not necessarily a good idea. Surveillance societies have appeared in the not so recent past, and they were frightening indeed. Stalin's Russia. Ceausescu's Romania. Hoenecker's East Germany. Perhaps the United States can avoid the mistakes made by the surveillance societies of the twentieth century. And perhaps J. Edgar Hoover's FBI is also completely honest, professional, and incorruptible—just like Robert Hanssen.

Vonage Broadband Security Risk (Spring, 2004)

By Kevin T. Blakley

As a 15-year security professional and Vonage phone-service user over the past six months, I have uncovered some serious security problems with its use and solutions to possible security risks for both business and home users. This broadband phone service, which saves the end user hundreds or even thousands of dollars a year on local toll and long distance charges, can pose certain vulnerabilities to your network. The service, which uses Cisco's VOIP ATA-186 telephone adapter, opens several holes in network security.

Vonage offers little help with serious technical or security issues and in fact several technical representatives stated to me that I should simply allow all traffic on the following ports (UDP: 53 (domain), 69 (tftp), 123 (sip), 5060, 5061, and 10000–20000) into my secured local network for any source IP. There are many exploits for all of these ports that include exploits for tftp on port 69, computer management on port 10000, and others. Vonage refuses to provide their source IPs for the VoIP connections. Given this information one could easily set up firewall rules that would allow traffic only from Vonage's VoIP server addresses to the voice unit. Service redirection, which is known to most seasoned firewall users, allows the firewall to map user-defined ports to a predefined local or private IP address. This, while not suggested by Vonage, would suffice in securing the local private network and also provide security to the ATA unit. What was suggested by Vonage was the placement of the ATA-186 into a DMZ firewall zone. While this offers some logging ability for attempted attacks, it opens up the ATA unit itself to possible attacks via the open service ports mentioned above, specifically tftp, and a service that is normally turned off: http (port 80). Since broadband Internet service is today almost as common as a television and with broadband phone service providers such as Vonage gaining popularity, it is the responsibility of security professionals such as myself to provide information to the general public relating to security threats.

Personal firewalls, such as the one provided in Windows XP and the many variants on the market, protect the computer on which they are installed from various attacks. However, they do not protect any other device that is on the same network connected through a broadband router. Many of the most popular broadband router/firewalls on the market today do offer some packet filtering but most do not inspect UDP traffic, which is what the ATA-186 voice unit uses to communicate VoIP traffic.

For those home or business users who do not employ a firewall on the front end of their network, I would suggest doing so and employing stateful packet inspection of all traffic relating to the use of any VoIP device. Such small office and home products are available from many manufacturers such as Check Point, Watchguard, Netgear, and Linksys.

In no way am I discounting the value of broadband phone service providers. However, it is my opinion that these same providers should be a little more security conscious.

VoIP Cell Phones: The Call of the Future (Summer, 2007)

By Toni-Sama

I was talking to a tech buddy of mine during a visit home when the subject of VoIP-enabled cell phones came up. He was insistent that the technology would never come to pass because it simply wouldn't be profitable. I argued, saying it was the next logical step, and to prove him wrong I've done a bit of homework. Now I don't think the technology is widely available (or hacker-friendly) yet, but with a host of manufacturers (Nextel, Sprint, Qualcomm, and Motorola) planning and developing VoIP-friendly handsets, I think we should prepare for this technology jump.

What is VoIP?

VoIP is simply "Voice over Internet Protocol," a stem of the Network Voice Protocol from the days of ARPANET. It's a fairly neat little thing, utilizing an IP-connected computer and a POTS (Plain Old Telephone Service) line. The computer connects to a web site, which receives the POTS number from the computer, then connects to the POTS line through the PBX (Private Branch eXchange). The connection can also be through a dedicated system (or adapter), or even through a built-in converter. VoIP has been widely utilized by existing phone networks for the transfer of data, which has given way to the "unlimited local calling plans" of the major telephone companies.

Now, obviously, cell phones don't have a built-in IP connection, so the connection comes from one of two sources: Unlicensed Mobile Access or Session Initiation Protocol.

UMA is the "easy" choice because it utilizes Bluetooth technology to connect to the PBX. UMA works very well with Global System for Mobile communications (GSM) operators, and can also switch between VoIP and cellular networks easily. Unfortunately, as a downside of this ease, it's also a bit pricier and it's currently only available on phones with Bluetooth technology, a la Motorola RAZR V3 and the V560. BT Group, out of Great Britain, offers packages that utilize VoIP when the customer is at home. In return for using VoIP, the price is lower when the network is used. The prices can get as low as 55 [British] pence for an entire hour of use.

SIP is the other choice, although it's certainly less popular. SIP utilizes a Wi-Fi router to connect to the Internet, which then utilizes Real-Time Transport Protocol (RTP) to communicate with a SIP router. The SIP router interacts with the Public Switched Telephone Network (PSTN) and the communication runs from there. The benefit of this technology is that it connects to the PSTN via a software standard, not requiring a home router. Unfortunately, you can currently only call other utilizers of the technology because of the G.711 standard. Likewise, only certain phones can use the software (Nokia E60, E61, and E70).

The State of the Technology

To my knowledge, only two companies offer VoIP cellular service. The first is the aforementioned BT Group, which offers service in Great Britain. It utilizes a home service plan and for the price of roughly U.S. $120 you get a phone, modem, and a calling plan. BT's phones use UMA. The other company offering this is Truphone, a company offering a beta test of the SIP for the Nokia E-Series phones, with downloads coming soon for the N-Series (N80, N91, N92, and N93) and Windows Mobile compatible phones. The technology isn't going to be limited for long, though. Phillips Semiconductors is manufacturing UMA chips for cell phones, Texas Instruments is coming out with WiLink 4.0, Ericsson is manufacturing UMA phones, and Qualcomm, Nortel, Verizon, and Sprint are all using a protocol called "EV-DO Revision A." Motorola, through Skype, is planning releases this spring, and this technology is soon to be popular. At present, the more popular option is to run over a managed network, versus an unmanaged network (i.e., the Internet) due to voice quality concerns.

Uses and Abuses

Now if you're a hacker, you understand the great potential behind this. Cellular technology is going to be cheaper and possibly even free (to begin with, since VoIP isn't currently regulated). Of course, you'll still have to contend with quality, and international calls are going to be funky (as per usual), but with the benefit of cellular service you won't have to worry about finding an active connection should you really need to make a call, perhaps in an emergency situation. Also, because of the modern technology of these phones (Truphone programs their software in C++ on Symbian), these things could possibly be tweaked, allowing data transfers as well as digital voice communication. In the future, you might watch more than TV on your cell phones, perhaps acquiring audio/video communication. Think instant global video, with real-time audio. You could communicate with your boss in China as you organize your meeting in New York. You could chat with your international exchange student in Germany from your home in Canada. Soldiers could talk to their families and loved ones face-to-face. Hell, organize a conference with your guild buddies on WoW. See concerts live from other countries. The possibilities are limitless.

However, there are some negatives to it at this time. If you live outside of the United States or Great Britain, you face some difficulties. In Ethiopia, VoIP is illegal. In India, you can't make a VoIP gateway. Likewise, many Latin American and Caribbean countries have imposed restrictions on VoIP due to government-owned phone companies. Also, at this time location registration for VoIP isn't mandatory and can't easily be determined from the calling phone. As a result, Caller ID will seldom work if it works at all. It could also easily be spoofed from a VoIP "land line," so presumably it could be spoofed from a cell phone. In addition, most consumer VoIP networks don't support encryption, so phone calls could be intercepted and even changed. This should be legislated soon, since government is extremely interested in regulating this new form of communication.

Know what I'd love to see? Articles giving more detail on the actual processes of communication over VoIP and POTS, and some really detailed tech specs on VoIP-ready phones. So, all you phreaks out there, get crackin'.

Thanks to Google, O'Reilly, Truphone, BT Group, Wikipedia, and Anthony, who inspired this work. Shout-outs to Jessika, Billy, Bean, Gendo, and Troy.

17 Retail Hacking

One style of article that really exploded in the past few years focuses on various retail outlets. Many people ask why this is. Simply put, everyone uses computers now. Everyone. It used to be just stores like Radio Shack that were technology based. But now they are *all* online in one capacity or another. In this section you'll see how the mind of a hacker works in everyday situations. Whether it's a department store, a grocery store, a video store, or a hotel, you can rest assured that whoever is in charge knows less about how their systems work than a typical *2600* reader who walks in off the street.

We always tread a fine line on this kind of subject matter. It's one thing to understand how to exploit a late-fee system that allows you to never return videos, or how to find an easy way into a major retailer that stores its customers' credit card info online, or how to use a store terminal to access secret stuff behind the corporate firewall. But it's another thing entirely to use this knowledge for personal gain or to screw anyone over. There are many who can't see the difference. After all, why would we even print the information in the first place if we weren't giving our tacit endorsement of following through with the actual act?

This gets to the point of what *2600* is about and has always been about. We exist to publish information and to encourage curiosity and exploration. Now, granted, information can be used for good or for evil. This is true of a lot of things. If I actually were to lay awake at night worrying about each and every article we printed and how it might possibly be used to cause harm or damage, it's fairly obvious we would never print much of anything at all. That simply cannot be a part of the equation, not if we want to fulfill the mission of spreading information and knowledge.

It may not be as apparent but information of all sorts can be used for both good and evil. If a newspaper prints the upcoming schedule of the President, they are performing a public service but also providing valuable information for a potential assassin. Exposing a cover-up, such as Watergate or Iran/Contra, might make for very interesting reading but it could also be very bad for the morale of the country. We can even convince ourselves that printing pictures of bridges or locations of government buildings might serve as tools for terrorists. But the fact remains that the people who are really intent on getting the information for nefarious purposes are likely to find a means of getting it. The ones who lose when journalists are overly cautious are, without exception, the general public.

Now, what possible advantage is there to the populace in seeing articles like the ones that follow in the first place? It varies by individual and there are likely quite a few who would garner no benefit at all. But for those who are interested in maintaining their own privacy, knowing that a particular chain store has little to no security when it comes to safeguarding customer data may be enough to get them to go somewhere else instead and keep their private info private. For a consumer seeking help from one of these companies, it's always nice to know when you're being lied to and such information from an insider could wind up saving them lots of time and aggravation. And of course, we cannot discount the value of the retailers themselves being held up to analysis and critique and hopefully actually *learning* something about how to do a better job in the future.

But just as we don't print the information with the intent of causing people harm, neither do we print it in order to help make things more secure. The only agenda here is to gather the info and see what's out there. Where it goes from there isn't really up to us. We certainly promote responsible behavior and we condemn instances of maliciousness. But if we ever start to hold back on releasing information because it's *too* hot or sensitive, I think we will have lost our way.

With all that said, here's a look at just some of the chaos we've exposed in the post-2000 world of retail.

Best Buy Insecurities (Spring, 2003) *By W1nt3rmut3*

Note: The following material should be considered educational *only*. Attempting anything in this article might result in punishment from Best Buy. No prior knowledge of the Best Buy network was used in my personal exploration.

As with most consumer electronic retailers, Best Buy offers computers, DVDs, CDs, stereos, etc., at decent prices. But did you know that Best Buy also offers insight into their business, right from inside their store? I'll bet you didn't. Let's take a trip to our local Best Buy....

Garnering Access

A few computers in every Best Buy offer Internet access. They can come in the form of a "Build Your Own Computer" terminal or a "Try Out Broadband" terminal. I have found the "Build Your Own Computer" terminals to be most accessible, since they aren't as "locked down" as their "Broadband" counterparts. Both types include a printer, which is useful. They both have access to "Internet," but this is limited to `bestbuy.com`, `microsoft.com`, and some of Best Buy's partners. Normally, some type of interactive demo or fixed browser window protects the units that do allow Internet access. Most keyboard shortcuts (Alt+F4, <Windows key>+R, and the ilk) have been deactivated. One that hasn't been is F1, or Windows Help. To be able to use this keyboard shortcut, you are going to have to get to a pop-up window, or sometimes, it is possible right from the interactive demo itself. Anyways, in Windows Help, you have two options. The first is a drop-down menu in the upper-left-hand corner. Here is your standard close, minimize, etc., but also here is the Go to URL choice. This allows anyone, as long as certain privileges haven't been set, to access local disk drives by going to the URL `"c:/"` or any drive letter for that matter, and of course any Web link too. The other option is the Web Help button on the top bar, which can get you an Internet Explorer window. From there, you can explore to your heart's content.

Exploration—Local Domain

But now you say, "mut3, this doesn't get me anything." I say, "You're a hacker, figure something out!" Well, that's what I did. Cruising around the machine, I discovered that most were running some form of NT and even XP. The one that I was using had a functional printer, which will be useful later. An interesting application to run is Explorer. This allows you to connect to Access Network Drives, under the Tools menu. What you find here is extremely interesting, and extremely insecure. All of the NT domains for each store are accessible. Each domain is labeled with STOR, and the four-digit store number. Inside, there are multiple machines, with the following prefixes: SK, SR, SS, SV, and SW.

The terminal that I use most frequently, which is a "Make Your Own Computer" terminal, had the hostname SK01xxxx, the xxxx being the store number. All of the hostnames follow the pattern of a prefix, some sequential number, and the store number. Machines within your local domain are accessible, but ones outside of your domain should require a login/password pair. But there are many goodies found within the store. By doing a NETSTAT, some connections piqued my interest. When network browsing those computers, a lot of information was accessible, but the greater percentage were just logs related to computers on the premises. Nothing spectacular, but still interesting. More exploration into the local domain is required.

Exploration—Intranet

After thoroughly abusing one Best Buy, I moved onto another, which gave me even more insight into the network of Best Buy. While executing the Windows Help vulnerability on a new machine, I was not allowed to view the C: drive and, for that matter, any local drive. But, by using the second option described previously I was on my way. Because of privileges, we can't see any drives, but we do have access to the "Internet," which, as mentioned before, isn't really much. The real gold comes from history. Some Best Buy employee browsed intranet computers, and left the addresses in history. The hostnames I found were:

- toolkit: 168.94.67.20
- tagzone: 168.94.67.11
- msizone: 168.94.3.46
- cf: 168.94.9.17

toolkit, from my experience, isn't viewable from a floor computer at least. tagzone is a corporate home page, giving you the latest news on the company and the market. msizone is some type of retailer information center, which requires a login/password pair. cf is either customer fulfillment or computer fulfillment—I'm not sure since it's called both on the site. tagzone and cf are the two coolest sites to browse. tagzone, as was mentioned, is a corporate home page. But as you explore it, more than just news is available. I was able to get instructions on how to log on to the company's VPN, how to hire and fire employees, and how the company is structured. Let us assume for a second that Best Buy didn't want the public to see this. Then who the hell didn't think that maybe putting floor machines behind the corporate firewall is a bad idea? But I digress....

cf is a site that allows employees to order items not in store to be shipped from the mysterious "Warehouse 87." I ordered a nice flat panel monitor and had it shipped to the store I was at. Little did I know that for it to be shipped, it must be scanned and paid for at checkout. Well, all is not lost, since from cf you can view warehouse inventory. Now you can see how many box sets of the TV show *24* they *really* have.

If you have access to a printer, go ahead and print. PDFs and documents are available, along with FAQs for employees. Some machines, if you are sneaky, have floppy access. So offloading PDFs is just a matter of time. Don't forget, bringing in programs is also possible, so have fun.

As for the situation with the "Internet," as I said, it's bleak. Every computer passes its traffic though a proxy, called "sproxy," with an IP address of 168.94.3.19. From multiple trace routes, it looks like it is blocking pages right from the proxy, but I might be wrong. I did find configuration files locally that specified what sites you are allowed access to, but I think those must be loaded when you first install the Best Buy demo software on the machine. It might be possible to do something through the registry. Another thing is that other open proxies don't work right off the bat, but I am still fiddling with it.

Conclusion

Best Buy made a *big* mistake in allowing publicly accessible models behind the company's firewall. Best Buy must patch this up soon. It could be as simple as putting a PIN number before entering any intranet site. If not, then they could be headed for a world of trouble.

Shouts: Stankdawg, for getting me going on this whole project, dual for his constant support, the crews of DDP, Hackermind, and Radio Freek America, and most importantly, Sarah and Ashley.

Outsmarting Blockbuster (Autumn, 2002) *By Maniac_Dan*

I used to work at Blockbuster, so I am very familiar with their policies and practices involving late fees. I'm not going to discuss how stupid the policies are, and I'm sure that there are people who would argue with me no matter what I say, but if there comes a time when your car breaks down and the guy behind the counter just won't believe you and you get charged $25 for 15 minutes, then you can use this method to have your fee removed. They try to make you pay your fees whenever they can, and the stores get a daily report of all fees outstanding on any and all accounts worldwide. Pretty much what that means is if you return a movie late to any Blockbuster and don't pay your fees, your account can be suspended in every Blockbuster around the world. The outstanding fees can be paid at any Blockbuster though (for your convenience in giving Viacom more money) but herein lies the weakness in the system: If your account is disabled due to a fee at another store, then the store you are trying to rent at has to call the store where you have a fee. The store with the fee on record must delete the fee and verify that a fee has been added to the account at the store you are trying to rent at. All customer accounts are stored locally, and the only information that is passed between stores is outstanding late fees. You have fees at one store (store #1 from now on) and you need to call that store and pretend to be from another store (store #2) and make the employees at store #1 remove the fees from your account, thinking you're paying at store #2. Now to do this you need a store number from store #2 and your own account number, which can be found on your receipts or membership card. Store #2 must be far enough from store #1 so that the employees don't know each other. There are a number of ways to get this store number. One of the easiest ways is to go to the store you want and buy something—the store number is on the receipt. Another way is to call them and say to whoever picks up, "I'm filling out a job application. What's your store number?" Also, if you have a friend with an account at that store, the store number is digits 2-6 on his customer number on the back of his card. For instance, if your customer number is 26732116547 then the number is broken down like this: 2 designates that the number refers to a customer account, 67321 is the store number, and 16547 is your customer number. Customer numbers are assigned chronologically. This system allows the stores to function independently of each other without two stores assigning different people the same number. Anyway, now that you have a store number, you need to decide on a fake name (or call the store and use the name of whoever picks up; employees are required to identify themselves when they answer the phone, though most rarely do). Now that you have a valid store number and a fake employee to play, it's time to call and get your fees taken care of. Call up store #1, and your conversation should go something like this:

Viacom Slave: "Thank you for calling the Blockbuster in [your town]. My name is Viacom Slave, what can I do for you."
You: "Yes, this is [fake name] from store number [#2's store number] in [#2's town]. I have a customer here who says he has fees at your store he would like to pay before it becomes a problem." (Alternately, you could say "I have a hold on an account from your store," but only do this if your fee is more than a month or two old to make sure your account has actually been frozen or else they will become suspicious.)
Viacom Slave: "OK, can I get the account number?"
You: [your account number from the back of your card]
Viacom Slave: "The account is for [your name] and the fee is [fee amount]."
You: [repeat the fee to your wall, ask if the wall would like to pay it at "this store"] [pause] "OK, he'll pay it over here."
Viacom Slave: "What's your store number again?"
You: *sigh* [store #2's number]
Viacom Slave: "OK thanks, bye."

And there you have it: Fees are removed. If the Viacom slave at store #1 asks you to do anything else, tell him that you're new and that you'll have the manager call them back when she gets out of the bathroom.

Home Depot's Lousy Security (Summer, 2005) *By Glutton*

Next Christmas, if you give out Home Depot gift cards, you may be giving the gift of nothing.

Look at one of their cards and you'll see that there is no mag stripe. It has a barcode on the back, printed right on the plastic. This sort of barcode is called a "codabar" and is a commonplace configuration typically used by retailers for internal organization. It doesn't have a fixed length nor does it use a check digit, although sometimes users will create their own check digit structure. When the customer or cashier flashes the card over the store's reader, a database is checked to see if the card has been activated and how much money remains in the account.

Unfortunately, The Home Depot doesn't use some proprietary or unusual bar code for their cards. It is easily duplicated by evildoers. All they have to know is how to make a codabar.

Now imagine an evildoer downloads Bar Code Pro or a similar product from a file sharing network and cranks out a barcode. How could he use it to pilfer money? For starters, he could peek at other barcodes in the store. Unactivated cards are typically hung in racks for people to buy. How hard would it be to grab one and look at the number? Scanning the code with a reader confirms that the number beneath the code is faithfully represented (which in itself is a security flaw). Then the evildoer prints out the code and tapes it to the back of the card. All he has to do is wait for the code to be activated by another customer.

Another trick might be to figure out what the code represents. Which segment of the code is the store number? Well, that's easy enough to figure out since the store number is printed on the receipt. Analyzing a number of cards could reveal if there's a check digit structure. Which numbers change? Which do not? Once he had it figured out, the evildoer could create random barcodes and see if they are activated.

So the evildoer goes to the store clutching a forged card. What next? Surely any cashier with half a brain cell could tell that there is a new piece of paper taped over the bar code. Fortunately for our villain, The Home Depot decided to hire fewer cashiers and has set up self-check-out stations in a lot of their stores. The evildoer scans his forged card, and if there is money in the account he waltzes out with his ill-gained loot. If he did something wrong and the attendant comes over to help, he palms the fake card and shows him a real card. The attendant "shows him how to do it" and the thief escapes to plot once again.

The security on the system is awful and relies only on criminals not knowing how to make codabars. With self-check-out lanes, a potential thief can experiment all he wants until he figures out how to rob his fellow customers.

So next Christmas, are you going to give someone a card with nothing on it?

Secrets of Dell (Summer, 2000) *By Deamtime*

I work as tech support for Dell computers. Because of Dell's reputation and tradition for reliability and technical excellence, we recently became the biggest OEM, both domestically and internationally. Because of this fact I thought a brief article about this brand of computer might be in order.

Same Computer, Different Support

The first thing you ought to know about Dell tech support is its divisions. All accounts fall into one of three categories: HSB (home and small business), PAI (public and international), and Relationship (large company accounts). Different divisions have different support policies and boundaries. Most computers are in the HSB category. Computers in this category have a "magic 30 day" window from their ship date. PAI accounts are mostly government and education accounts. I haven't had any experience with the Relationship accounts so I won't talk about them.

General Dell Info

All Dell BIOS chips are branded with the computer's service tag. Service tags are five-digit (some new computers have seven-digit tags) alphanumeric identifiers of the specific computer. The database lists all of the information about the components and software that the computer shipped with. It also lists most of the owner's information, including the credit card info. This database is a simple SQL database with laughable security. It also, until recently, has been run off of Compaq Tandem servers. Go figure. The service tag is imprinted into the BIOS for the purpose of identification in the case that the computer is stolen. It can also be found on a sticker on the case.

Dell, like most major OEMs, purchases special versions of most system components. If you see, for instance, an advertisement for an SB Live! card and order one for your Dell the features are likely to be different. Also, many of the cards now have an EPROM chip on them that records the last time diags were run and the results. I don't know how much storage is on the chips or what else they may record, but it isn't unlikely that they store information about the operating system, configuration, or any of a host of other "diagnostic" information types.

The "Magic 30 days"

After HSB computers ship, they are under a "total satisfaction" warranty the first 30 days after. My advice is that anything you are likely to do with the computer, do within the first 30 days. If you are going to install Linux on the box, do it then so that if you are unable to tune any specific driver to your liking (or even if you end up damaging components with "risky" code) you can get a replacement for that component or even for the full system. During this time you can also get upgrades to most components at cost. (This means "really cheap.")

After this 30-day period most computers are covered by a year's worth of "onsite" warranty (although you can also purchase two additional years of this warranty). If you don't want some stranger coming over to your house and fiddling around in your system (not a bad choice, from what I've seen of their work), you have the option of replacing the part yourself. If you take this option you will be asked for "collateral information," which is generally your credit card info. If you refuse to give it to the tech, they will have to get manager approval to send out the part anyway. (Generally, this is pretty easy to do.) The reason for the collateral info is that Dell almost always wants the defective part to be shipped back to them. This aids in issue tracking and also allows for refurbishing. Almost all parts sent out in this manner will be refurbished. You can request that new parts be sent to you. (This also requires an approval, which will almost never be granted if there is no collateral info.) I've seen this become an issue most often with monitors, which go through almost no testing before being reissued.

The next two years generally are "parts only" service. This service follows along the lines of the above requested self-install.

Classified Drives

PAI accounts differ from HSB accounts in several ways. First off, PAI customers do not have to troubleshoot over the phone. They also have the option of "classified drives." A classified hard drive is one that is suspected to contain sensitive information. These drives are most often in the Department of Defense, although any PAI customer may claim one. There is no record on the service tag of which computers have classified drives. These drives, when defective, are destroyed on site and are not returned to Dell. You have to inform the technician that you have a classified drive, as they will not ask.

ZZTop

All Dimension computers come with a compressed drive image on a hidden partition. The only certain way of absolutely getting rid of this partition is a low level format. This "hidden" partition isn't a partition at all. The image is written at the end of the drive. The executable program "ZZTop" finds, expands, and writes this information to the drive, much like Norton's "Ghost" program. Many images are coming out of the factory corrupt these days (see the "Dell Today" section below). If this is the case and it is discovered within the first 30 days, you have the option for an STM CD. This CD contains the same information. If you decide to use the STM as a system maintenance utility, make backups of both the CD and the floppy that comes with it. If either one fails past the first use, you will not only get no sympathy, but no replacement.

support.dell.com

All technical information, from pin-outs to jumper settings, white papers to driver files, on all Dell components ever shipped (including 8086s—seriously) can be found at the support web site. The search function is a little sketchy but with a bit of persistence you can find any information that you might need.

SE Tech Support

"Acts of God" are not covered under the HSB warranty. If a lightning storm took out your modem, for the love of all that is good *don't* tell the technician. As soon as that is entered into your log, that part cannot be replaced by any technician. All phone techs have a badge number to identify them. Make certain you get that number and use it whenever referring to the tech in your communications with Dell. All branches of support have five-digit extensions to their queue. Get that number and watch your call times plummet. Don't mention that you are taping a call; you will be hung up on immediately. Don't threaten legal action. Your tech support will be suspended completely until the legal department reopens it. (Only method of contact with legal? Surface mail, naturally.) Also, don't just stop making payments on your computer expecting that Dell will repossess it. Instead, they will take you to court, usually filing in a federal court (interstate commerce) in North Dakota, or Hawaii on a Wednesday. They give minimum notice, usually down to the minute and almost always win. I have heard that they are able to garnish wages and totally destroy credit for years.

Dell Today

Redhat has started shipping on some Dimension desktops. Support is by Linux Care.

The Dimension line seems to be plagued by unreliable modems. *Do not* under any circumstances order any Conexiant modem on a Dimension. Dell has terminated its contract with Conexiant and will stop shipping their POS when they run out of stock. I have seen examples where a customer ordered a USR hardware modem and got a Conexiant instead. Read your invoice carefully. If this happens to you, call customer service. Because of the increase in sales, the computers are not being burned in any longer at the factory. I have seen instances that make me doubt that they have even been turned on. Loose or unseated cards are not uncommon (sometimes even processor or RAM). Neither are unconnected power or data cables. Misinstallations of software and poor backup images are also common issues. Burn in your computer when you first get it.

This article didn't mention anything about laptop or server support. I don't know much about those divisions. All I can guess is that they are much the same as we are. Have fun with your Dell and, hey, have fun with Dell too!

Fun with 802.11b at Kroger's (Spring, 2003) *By Kairi Nakatsuki*

This guide assumes you already have a working wardriving setup on a *nix machine. This isn't necessarily meant to be a guide to hacking your friendly neighborhood Kroger's location. Though I do hope that this information will be of use in case you stumble upon a Kroger's location where an 802.11b network is present. Remember, don't be evil children!

Info

The particular Kroger's I did most of my dirty work at didn't have a terribly great security model, as you might expect. Evidently, management doesn't care much about their data being broadcast in clear text over the airwaves for 100 feet in every direction, though they seem to think that cloaking their ESSID would suffice. Since Kroger's wifi network(s) are mainly set up to allow their POS terminals to telnet into a SCO OpenServer machine, it is expected that these machines will have to be rebooted from time to time; so if the ESSID is not "kroger/barney" at your Kroger's, then it would be easy to obtain within short order.

This particular network resides on 30.112.16.0. Despite the fact that all of 30.0.0.0 is owned by the DoD, none of the addresses within that network are Internet routable (I confirmed this personally). So, I'm guessing that their address assignment scheme is purely coincidence.

There was a DHCP server that gladly gave me an IP address. I was able to resolve names that are on the Internet, though I wasn't able to get a default route anywhere.

Tools Used

- Kismet 2.8.1
- Ethereal 0.9.9
- Paketto Keiretsu 1.0
- AirSnort
- Linux laptop and a backpack

(Disclaimer: I don't know what you would have to do to use Kismet under Windows, though you can use Ethereal on Windows to read packet dumps from Kismet just fine.)

I used Kismet 2.8.1 to initially discover the networks. After confirming that there were only three or so networks, I made Kismet only scan on the channels those networks resided on, doing something like this:

```
# killall kismet_hopper
# kismet_hopper -s 2,4,6
# assuming that channels 2, 4, 6 are where the
# networks reside; do this while kismet_server is
# running
```

Setting `kismet_hopper` to hop only those channels increases the amount of packets you receive. Be sure to scan from lowest channel to highest channel, as to avoid the pitfalls of overlapping frequencies.

Start `kismet_server` in its own terminal so you can see what IP addresses are found, in real time. I used scanrand from Paketto Keiretsu to stealthily do a portscan on the nodes I found. Mostly Windows boxes with open SMB shares.

Going In

After you have played around a little and have confirmed that your Kroger's has a wireless network, it's time to get down to business. You can associate with their network and use Ethereal to do a packet capture in promiscuous mode, if you feel like using an Ethereal capture filter. This isn't as effective as using Kismet to channel hop and sniff in rfmon mode, however.

Now put your laptop in your backpack. Go up real close; walk back and forth across the storefront. Hell, pretend to fumble through your change pocket and buy your favorite soft drink from a vending machine. I don't suggest going in, however, since people wearing backpacks in a store is kind of frowned upon.

Back at Base

After you feel you've gotten your fill of captured packets, it's time to open the Kismet packet dumps with Ethereal. Use the display filter `telnet`; expand the `Telnet` tree. Scroll through the packets; a lot of them will be `"\033"`, but you'll eventually find the good shit.

This is a mere sample of what I found:

```
SCO OpenServer(TM) Release 5 (xxx.xxx.kroger.com) (ttyp3)
```

You can telnet into the machine that this prompt came from to see how many cash registers are in use; just use the ttypx as a clue. It counts from ttyp0 up.

The POS terminals at Kroger's are used for a lot of things, from the obvious cash register functions, to ordering shelf labels, to entering UPC codes and item names. I don't suggest that you log in if you capture username/password combinations; resist the urge!

Miscellaneous

I did find a single WEP-encrypted network. I wasn't able to stay close enough to the signal, though. If you're brave enough, you can let your car sit in the parking lot long enough to capture enough packets to crack this, if you have a good antenna. You can continue to use Kismet to keep the packets flowing, but I suggest using AirSnort to do the packet capture on a single channel, so you'll be able to see how far you're coming along.

Here's a recap, findings may be different:

```
ESSID: "kroger/barney" (Barney Kroger owns the chain)
Class C subnet: 30.112.16.0
Servers: 30.112.16.1, 30.112.16.2; running SCO OpenServer
```

If anybody can share information on the actual terminal interface used, let us know; I would be more than glad to write a follow-up article.

Obligatory Disclaimer

Have fun with this information. And remember, go to school, don't do drugs, and stay out of trouble! I can't take responsibility for your actions. It's your choice to follow my example, after all.

Fun at Circuit City (Spring, 2000) *By ccsucks*

I was a manager at Circuit City. Unfortunately, Circuit City and I parted ways (their decision), so I decided to write the following article for my friends at *2600* ... enjoy!

Price Tags

If it ends in .99, it is "In Program." (In other words, if it's not in stock, the associate can "special order" it from the main warehouse.)

If it ends in .98, it is a sale price or "CTC" (Challenge the Competitor)—competitor has it on sale.

If it ends in .97, it is "Open Box." As a rule, avoid open box buys at Circuit City like the plague unless you get the chance to see the unit working for yourself. Sales counselors usually don't test units that come back as Open Box, even though they're supposed to. And never believe the story that "it just came off display."

If it ends in .96, it is "Out of Program (OOP)." (In other words, if it's not in stock, the associate will not be able to order more of these.) This is a display that you may be able to purchase if there are none in stock at that store. Same caveat emptor for Open Box, above, though!

If you see an Open Box with a .96 price on it, it was not reviewed by a sales manager and was "auto-priced" by the system. You will *definitely* be able to get money off this price.

If it ends in .95, it is "Going out of Program (GOOP)." (In other words, the associate *may* be able to order from the main warehouse, but probably not.)

This covers 99 percent of the price tags for store merchandise, but does not include pricing for any music software (CDs, tapes, DVD, etc.) or major appliance sales like "10% off," etc.

Telephone Fun

Pick up any phone on the floor. Dial 9 to get an outside line. Long distance lines are blocked, but you can social engineer the 4- to 6-digit code from a floor manager if you say you need to call your wife before you buy that big screen TV. "But it's long distance!" you'll exclaim. The sales manager, not wanting to lose a big screen TV sale, will gladly dial your wife's phone number and, after waiting for the tone, dial in the long distance code. Each store has its own long distance code, but I can't tell you the number of times I've been able to stand in one part of the store while *no one* is standing around watching.

- 0 Front counter (They will see extension you're calling from.)
- 0 PA system on floor and in warehouse
- 150 PA system in warehouse only (wait for beep)
- 5510 First North American National Bank (FNANB): Circuit City card
- 5560 Circuit City Headquarters
- 5570 FNANB Customer Service
- 5580 Help Desk. Social engineer a sales manager's name

The help desk is generally a little more understanding with sales managers because they have not gone through as much computer system training as the operations staff. The store number (4 digits) prints on the receipt or you can get it from the web site.

If you tell the help desk that DPS is down, they will ask you if you're by the CC130. Say "yes." Tell them that there are no lights on the CC130 at all.

If you're not the adventurous type, you can just hit 50, go over the PA system, and say "DPS is down." That'll get the Ops staff running toward the CC130 and calling the help desk themselves!

A Little Computer System Glossary

- **DPS:** Distributed Processing System (the "computer system")
- **CC130:** Main board in the general office behind the counter
- **Wedge:** The main board under the register into which everything (monitor, thermal printer, scanner, check reader, etc.) is plugged

Want to call any Circuit City across the country? Dial 1-800-475-9515 and, after the tone, dial 333 and the four-digit store number.

Fun with Radio Shack (Winter, 2001-2002) *By Cunning Linguist*

In the tradition of writing articles about wreaking havoc at corporations, I've come up with another corporation upon which to raise hell: Radio Shack.

Let me begin by stating that I am writing this article from Canada and most of this article comes from my experience with Radio Shack stores in Toronto (in the Eaton Centre and Fairview Mall) and Montreal (at the Cavendish Mall). There are some parallels to United States Radio Shack stores (I've had experience with them in Beverly Hills and various locations in Los Angeles and New York), and they will be drawn in this article.

Canada's Radio Shack Kiosk

Canada's Radio Shack stores have a special program running on their Windows 2000 machines that disallows use of the Desktop or Start Menu, and in some cases the right-click function on the mouse. (We'll cover that soon.) The program, called "Kiosk vX.X," where X is the version number (I've seen from Kiosk v5.0 to Kiosk v6.0, including Kiosk v5.2.2), is Canada's Radio Shack web site: `www.radioshack.ca`. The Kiosk program doesn't allow a user to surf the Internet freely (even though at all the Radio Shacks I visited in Toronto they were all online via dedicated line and were open for a customer to use). It limits itself to Radio Shack's Canada web site. We can easily bypass this by conducting a little detective work.

Surfing Freely

On the home page of the Kiosk program on the upper-right corner, there is an icon for a shopping cart program. We've all seen them: they allow you to store items you wish to purchase until the "checkout," where you enter all the credit card information and give away your life to a computer. The icon is titled View Cart Checkout. If you click on it, it will lead you to a "secure" page. You know it's secure because you see the little yellow locked padlock on the bottom right-hand corner of the screen. It's secure. Don't question the security. Don't. Anyway, if right-clicking was disabled before, it should be enabled now (it was for me). If you right-click anywhere on the page and scroll down to Properties, another window will pop up. You can click on Certificates, and then, on the third window that pops up, Certification Path. Here you'll see three things: The issuer of the certificate that says the site is secure (most likely VeriSign), VeriSign's web site, and Radio Shack's web site. What you can do now is double-click on VeriSign's web site, and an Internet Explorer browser should pop up, allowing you to surf the Web freely. (If this doesn't work, because I've encountered places where it hasn't, do the following: right-click on the page, go to Certificates > General > Issuer Statement > More Info. VeriSign's web site should pop up in an IE browser.)

United States Kiosks

I haven't seen a Kiosk program, per se, in the United States. If they do have a `www.radioshack.com` kiosk program, you can find ways of spawning IE browsers by playing around on their web site from home. What I have seen at U.S. Radio Shacks are programs that come bundled with the computers on display. In all my experiences (which may be limited in comparison with your experiences, so forgive me) the desktop is accessible, but certain items have been removed (the IE icon, for example). You can use the oldest trick in the book for this one: If they've got the My Computer icon enabled, simply double-click and use that window to type in your URL. Or you may just want to view the contents of the computer. You can do this with pretty much any icon on the desktop that isn't an executable.

Breaking Free from the Kiosk

This pertains to the Canadian Radio Shacks. Breaking completely out of the Kiosk is possible with the following easy steps. (As a side note, I just want to say that none of these tricks apply to the Montreal Radio Shack in the Cavendish Mall because the Kiosk is disconnected from the Internet and only accessible if you ask for help, and if you're younger than the person helping you, you're under strict observation.)

1. Go back to the home page of the Kiosk program. (There are nifty little icons that can help you do this on the upper left-hand corner of the screen.)
2. Click on the Computers tab. (There are numerous tabs on the home page that allow you to access different parts of the site. The Computers tab is the second from the left.)
3. Scroll down and watch the left hand side for "Microsoft" in bold type.
4. Click on Microsoft.

This is where the inconsistency steps in. On Kiosk v5.0 and Kiosk v6.0 I've seen what I'm about to describe, but not on Kiosk v5.2.2.

On the window that pops up when you click the word Microsoft, there will be a File tab on the upper right-hand corner of the pop-up screen. If you click it, there are two choices in the drop-down menu: Exit and Exit All. Exit simply exits the new screen, whereas Exit All exits the entire Kiosk program. Again, this has worked for me inconsistently, so be aware that if you try it might not work.

Other Nifty Things

Screen saver passwords are big deals at Radio Shack. Usually many or all of the computers on display will be screen saver password protected. I've noticed a couple of things: If you come in and ask for assistance with buying a computer, the screen saver password comes off immediately. Just say you're going to browse around, see how good the system is and all that, and the computer is yours. If you happen to catch a glimpse of what the person was typing, all the better for you, seeing as 99 percent of the time the screen saver passwords are the same. Or you can ask for assistance, have them take the screen saver password off, insert the disk you've craftily brought from home, and harvest the passwords on the machine.

If the computer is on, and there is no screen saver password apparent or if there's no screen saver enabled and the desktop is staring you in the face but you still can't seem to get the mouse or keyboard shortcuts to work, it's because the mouse and keyboard aren't plugged in. So reach around the back and plug them in.

Hellos: vel3r, Skrooyoo, Petty Larceny, SpunOut, and the rest of the LA 2600 crew; Real Vonce, PainFull (Ke2nel), SuNsCrEeN460, YEFROhundo. And a very special thanks to Team Hush who helped fix my email account.

MILESTONE: PARANOIA VS. SANITY (Winter, 2003-2004)

Today, nearly 20 years to the day after *2600* printed its first issue, we live in a very different world. The things we took for granted in 1984 (ironically enough) simply don't hold true now. We currently live in a society of barriers. Our leaders have to be kept away from the people because of what we could potentially do to them. Great barricades must be erected in front of buildings we once entered freely because they could be considered "targets" of an elusive and faceless foe. We know little of who they are and how they will strike so the fear becomes all the stronger. Familiar? Of course, because these strategies have been used countless times before.

MILESTONE: PARANOIA VS. SANITY *(continued)*

So shouldn't it be easy to see the threat and to take the necessary measures to keep it from destroying us? Only if we take a couple of steps back and see where we're going without being enveloped in the fear and paranoia that seem to have taken over all elements of our society in recent years.

The danger lies in accepting what we're told without question along with the perception that anyone who stands up to the system is somehow a threat to all of us. There are many people reading *2600* now who weren't even born when we started publishing. They have never experienced what so many others have. And this trend will continue. If nothing changes, the children of tomorrow will only know a nation of orange alerts, hostility to foreigners, endless warfare against an unseen enemy, curtailment of civil liberties to anyone considered an enemy of the state, and fear that never goes away.

Why would anyone want a society like this? Control is like an addiction. Those in control want desperately to cling to it and to be able to strike out at those they don't understand or see as some sort of potential threat.

But hackers have had the opportunity to gain a unique perspective. We understand both the good and the bad in technology. We're not afraid to bend the rules to learn how something works, despite the increasingly severe penalties suffered by those who dare. We can apply this knowledge over society and see the inherent risks involved in the latest ideas put forth by the Homeland Security people to weed out the "evildoers" among us. The fact that many of us understand how technology is being used here adds valuable insight. And it also makes us even more of a threat to those addicted to control.

This clearly won't be a journey for the faint of heart.

As we close the door on our second decade, it's important to note that we have a great deal of optimism for the future, despite all of the gloom and doom around us. Why is this? For the simple reason that we believe the right people are gathering in the right place at the right time. We were happy to learn that a Norwegian appeals court recently upheld a decision clearing the author of the DeCSS program of any charges, despite the wishes of the MPAA and the proponents of the DMCA in this country. In the last couple of years, we've had more people than ever express genuine interest in the workings of technology and in knowing all of the ways it can be used against them by malevolent powers, as well as ways it can be used for something positive. We've seen tremendous attention paid to this at the HOPE conferences and we expect to see even

continues

MILESTONE: PARANOIA VS. SANITY *(continued)*

more this July as we do it again. The alertness of our readers, listeners to our radio broadcasts, and attendees of our meetings and conferences has been a tremendous inspiration to us and to so many others. This is what can change things and move us all into a less confining world. We've seen people better their living conditions and improve the societies they live in once it became evident that the old way was not the right way. There's no reason to believe that the road we're going down won't eventually result in that very same realization. And we'll get there by keeping our eyes open and finding friends in the least expected places. That's what's gotten us this far.

Target: For Credit Card Fraud (Autumn, 2007) *By Anonymous*

I have debated whether or not to write this article for over a month since it has the potential to cause so much damage. I decided that exposing Target's utter lack of network security would bring about change and, in the end, do more good than harm.

During my brief employment at Target, I spent most of my free time exploring their internal network. It did not take me long to realize that there was an absence of any security. All of the computers used by employees are on the same subnet in the network. These computers include registers, employment kiosks, managers' computers, and backroom computers.

In addition, Target installed Cisco Aironet 802.11b routers to support their handheld scanners used for printing labels and storing items in the back room. These routers do use WEP, but that is not a major hurdle to keep computers outside the store from hopping on the internal network and taking advantage of the network flaws to be outlined.

Those responsible for rolling out the network clearly gave no thought to security. The networks are identical from store to store, so the flaws were not isolated to my particular Target location. Every computer except the registers has telnet set up. You can control any computer with the username Target and either a blank password or Target as the password. Every computer, including the registers, has SMB shares set up that allow a user to mount the root directory with no password required. All computers also have ftp set up, and with the username Target and password Target, you get full access to the root directory.

This setup allows any user to retrieve employee records and confidential documents from the computers belonging to the stores' managers. The most dangerous security oversight though, relates to the ability to connect to the stores' registers.

Every register has a share named cpos (common point of sale) that keeps logs for every credit card and debit card transaction for a week. Included in these logs is not only the credit card number and cardholder name for every transaction, but also a raw dump of the card's entire magnetic strip—for reasons unknown. The exact location of these logs on the share is `\app\ej_backup\`. All registers follow the naming convention TxxxxREGyyyy—where *x* is the store number and *y* is the register number. This convention is used company wide, and any workstation can connect to any register at any store.

I do not have much experience writing DOS batch files, but I managed to put together a simple batch file that connects to a register, passed as an argument, grabs all of the credit/debit logs, and strips out the account number and customer name.

```
net use z:\ \\%1\cpos
copy z:\app\ej_backup\*.* .
net use z: /delete

type *.pos | find /n "VISA CHARGE" >> temp
type *.pos | find /n "MASTERCARD CHARGE" >> temp
type *.pos | find /n "AMEX CHARGE" >> temp
type *.pos | find /n "DISCOVER CHARGE" >> temp

type *.pos | find /n "ACCT# (M)" >> temp
type *.pos | find /n "CARD HOLDER:" >> temp
sort /+1 temp >> stripped.log
erase temp
erase *.pos
```

Using this batch file, one could easily grab the transaction logs from every register at every store overnight. Over a month, I imagine somebody could grab tens of thousands of credit card numbers.

I did not work at Target nearly long enough to explore their entire network, but one can only imagine what kind of confidential information could be obtained from their massive network.

Please do not use this information for malicious purposes. I only wrote this article in the hopes that Target will be forced to change its lax security policies.

Hacking Retail Hardware (Autumn, 2001) *By dual_parallel*

These hacks deal with retail systems: customer-operated and point-of-sale (POS) hardware. Actually, these hacks are the beginnings of hacks; all key presses and codes were discovered one time through a line.

The first piece of POS hardware is the VeriFone PinPad 1000. The PinPad utilizes derived unique key per transaction (DUKPT) or Master/Session key management. This simple hack deals with the Master/Session management technique. A master key resides in the pad and a session key is generated for each transaction, ensuring accuracy. To access the master key, press the four corner buttons simultaneously—1, 3, CLEAR, and ENTER. "WHICH MKEY?" appears. Enter any number and "ENTER OLD MKEY" appears. The next step in PinPad exploration would be social engineering the number of digits in the Mkey or the Mkey itself, either from the establishment or a VeriFone vendor. Brute force would be pretty difficult without knowing how many digits comprised an Mkey.

The next piece of POS hardware is the pin pad at every register of your favorite store, Wal-Mart. (These pin pads see a lot of action with a Wal-Mart opening every two business days.) Access the not-to-be-seen screens by pressing the top left arrow button and bottom right ENTER button simultaneously. You'll get:

```
CM2001I
256k V1.40
SM V5.4
```

and then:

```
Enter password...
```

The ever-popular `1234` begets:

```
Validating app...
```

then:

```
EFT prog: 0028
EFT parm: 0032
```

Hitting the red CANCEL button after the password prompt shows the following info:

```
Program          Release
WALUSA1          1.42
```

The pad resets quickly, so the order of the data might not be correct. In fact, I don't know what any of this data means.

The final hack is akin to owning a Create-A-Card machine. At your local Sears Watch Service, you might find a touch screen terminal called Quick-Scribe, by Axxess Technologies. This is a consumer-operated terminal that personalizes, by engraving, trinkets and gifts. Upon first inspection, you'll notice the telltale signs of Microsoft: a grayed-out scrollbar and the bottom of a Windows title bar. So with a little time, you're sure to own this box.

Start by grabbing the screen with both hands, thumbs at each top corner. Now press the top corners simultaneously, quickly, and repeatedly. (Hey, it worked for me.) You should get a white screen with four 0-9 numeric keypads, begging for you to enter the four-digit pass code. With 10^4 possibilities, start with the obvious. "1234" didn't work, but "1111" did. This brought up the best screen of all—a white screen appeared with "PRIVILEGED ACTIVITIES" across the top. Sounds good. The commands under it were:

- View Log Files (Details)
- View Log Files (Summary)

- Engraver Utilities
- Change Stock
- Change Peripheral Configuration (future)
- Modify Site Specific Data (future)
- Run Diagnostics (future)
- Complete Problem Report (future)
- Capture Data
- Merchant Summary Report
- Restart Application

The last command will get you what you want—the NT desktop. Touch Restart Application and the desktop will appear. Quickly pop up the Start menu and it should persist as the Quick-Scribe app restarts. From here you can do as you please.

(Axxess Technologies has another line of engraving machines called Quick-Tag, targeted at the pet owner market.)

(Thank you, Luscious.)

Fun Facts About Wal-Mart (Winter, 2001-2002) *By A.W.M.*

This is just a follow-up to the article entitled "Hacking Retail Hardware." It provides a little more detail on the technical aspects of Wal-Mart.

Customer Activated Terminal

Wal-Mart refers to the debit pin pads/mag strip reader as a CAT—Customer Activated Terminal. Pressing the top-left button and Enter will only restart the CAT. Restarting the CAT can also be accomplished by removing the Enter button and making metal contact with the silicon chip below in the right-bottom corner. As far as the "Enter Password" prompt goes, many a password have I tried (1234, the store number, WALMART using the equivalent number keys, WALUSA1, etc.). After an incorrect password has been entered, it just finishes the rebooting process. I'm assuming the password will give you access to some kind of administrator menu.

Also, the software stored in the CAT can be reinstalled through the register by using a key-flick and entering "18" and pressing the action code button. However, a valid operator needs to be signed on (read below). This also updates the register configuration.

Other action codes:

- 1—complete transaction void
- 2—department sales statistics
- 3—operator/terminal statistics
- 4—department totals

- 6—price inquiry mode
- 9—training mode
- 10—operator productivity
- 14—memory usage
- 18—register config update
- 55—reload AT&T prepaid card
- 60—print electronic journal data for previous transaction
- 61—reprint previous receipt
- 69—online cashier training
- 91—transaction code lookup

Wal-Mart Registers

There is a universal sign-on for *all* Wal-Mart stores. However, I am reluctant to release that information. The user and password are the same for that operator. This operator number gives you access to the register (including permissions to perform overrides with the IBM 9952 or MM42 key or signing on to the register and performing a transaction to open the drawer). It also gives you access to the POS controller stored in the back room, which lets you do many, many interesting things: printing detailed confidential sales reports, changing the store name that appears on the top of the receipt, the trailer message on the bottom of receipts, layaway events (jewelry, firearms, optical, Christmas), and much more!

Also—some interesting things about the registers:

- There are USB ports on the back.
- They use standard Ethernet cards in their registers; very often there are cables located in the lawn and garden and on the sidewalk for portable registers. They may use TCP/IP or something more proprietary; this needs more investigation. Unplugging Ethernet cable from a register activates "OFFLINE" mode. ("*OFF" will be in the corner of the screen.) All operator numbers are accepted with a key-flick and all supervisor numbers are accepted with a key-flick.
- There are two interesting keys on the keyboard you can use when not signed in: S1 and S2. Pressing S1 and entering a number from 1-9 and then S2 will perform a function. I don't know all the numbers. There are ones that will give you messages about hardware problems, system diagnostics, terminal number, etc.

SMART System

There is also a universal login to the SMART (Smart Merchandising through Applied Retail Technology) system with user name "MANAGER" but I don't know the password. The SMART system gives you access to Perpetual Inventory, Keep It Stocked, Be A Merchant, etc. You can do price changes, scheduling, ordering, electronic journal (every transaction in the store in the last month (!), full details including *whole* credit card numbers), etc. This is a very *powerful* system. Users only have access to options granted to them by the store manager or co-manager. However, management tends to leave themselves signed on at various locations....

You can access the SMART system through the service desk using a computer running Windows 3.1. It gives you a menu: "WARRANTY, REPAIR, SMART SYSTEM." After clicking SMART SYSTEM, it opens a telnet session. It logs in as a user called "return." Pressing Ctrl+C after the login but before the system loads the SMART system executable will drop you to a $ prompt. `uname` reveals NCR and the version number. You can read `/etc/passwd`, which will give you root and other system users' encrypted passwords. You may also want to try and `su` a user called `ptc` with password `ptc`. The SMART system can also be used at the console located in the invoicing office, or at various dumb terminals in the back.

The SMART system can also be accessed through the use of portable devices known as "Telxons" or "960s" depending on who you ask. (`www.telxon.com` has lots of details, but few technical specifics.) They run DOS... and you can access a DOS prompt. You get a menu like this when nobody is logged on:

```
SMART
PHARMACY
CONFIG
```

If someone is logged on, even better. You can explore! The ALPHA button lets you type in letters. When it's off it gives you access to function keys.

- F1—help
- F2—available commands
- F3—exit
- F4—accept
- F7—previous screen
- F8—forward
- F10—finalize
- F12—cancel

Arrow keys control selection of menu, enter accesses (duh!).

Press F3 several times and you'll get back to the main (SMART, PHARMACY, CONFIG) menu. Select SMART, press Ctrl+C a few times (ALPHA key on, CTRL is in the corner), and it will ask "Terminate Batch Job? (Y/N)." Press Y. You are now at a DOS prompt. There should be an A: and a B: drive. You can key in almost any character using a combination of Function/Shift/Ctrl/Alt keys. Now, to get back to the main menu, hold Function, Enter, and the ON button. Press the ON button several times when holding Function and Enter. This is, I guess, the equivalent of Ctrl+Alt+Delete. You can probably do an "exit" as well, but I haven't tried.

Pharmacy Computers

The pharmacy uses an RS/6000 running AIX or INFORMIX. However, at the login prompt entering "smart" (no password) gives you access to the SMART system. The pharmacy RS/6000 has a modem for prescription downloading(?) or something else, thus, remote access to the SMART system. How about marking down that Playstation 2 you've been wanting? Or ordering 100 pallets of M&Ms? Oh, the possibilities!

Sensormatic Handheld Deactivator

This is what the door greeters use when the EAS (Electronic Article Surveillance) system detects an activated source tag. Theoretically, after an item is rung over the scanner, it should go by the deactivator and deactivate. But this is often not the case. The deactivator looks like a metal detector type thing. When locked into its base usually found at the service desk, the password is 1234 or the store number (found on the top of a receipt with the ST: prefix; e.g. 0347). Enter 5 to enable Manual Deactivate; press the gray button over a tag and it deactivates it. 6 is search mode—doesn't deactivate, only searches. 3 is admin mode—1234 or store number is the password. This device completely stops working after two hours of being disconnected from the base to protect against someone stealing it. The base is usually screwed into the wall or service desk counter.

Retail Hardware Revisited (Spring, 2002) *By dual_parallel*

In this article I'll discuss some variations in a common pin pad, a couple of hacks at a large retailer, and finally a disturbing trend.

In my last article I discussed the VeriFone PinPad 1000 and the button presses (all simultaneous) needed to access the Master Key, or Mkey. Variations exist. Some pads are set to access the Mkey by pressing the bottom-right and top-right buttons. But the vast majority is set to access the Mkey by pressing the bottom-right and top-left buttons.

The last article discussed Wal-Mart. This article will discuss its failing competitor, Kmart. The pin pads at every Kmart register are Checkmate model CM 2120s, OS 1.07, version 2.1. One can gain access to the pin pad by pressing the four small buttons by the LCD screen, and the two bottom-most buttons, green Enter and red Cancel, simultaneously (think Vulcan mind meld). After an incorrect password, the pad will cycle, verifying the applications that the user has authorized access to.

Now, from pin pads to PCs. Walking into Kmart, at the Customer Service counter, one will immediately see one of two public computers running `BlueLight.com`, Kmart's online shopping application. These computers, the other residing in Electronics or sometimes Sporting Goods, run NT 4, have LCD monitors, a keyboard, and an enclosed trackball where the right button is trapped under plastic. The `BlueLight.com` application starts automatically, so logging off or shutting down just brings the application right back up.

`BlueLight.com` (v 1.0.55) is an e-commerce application that features products and a shopping cart, running on publicly available NT computers in many Kmarts across the nation. The application is a browser, accessing the Internet to transmit selections from the local Kmart to Kmart.com's servers (`kih.kmart.com`). BlueLight takes over the machine, running in the foreground. So the first thing to do is to log off by pressing Ctrl+Alt+Delete and clicking Logoff. The machine will cycle quickly, bringing up the NT desktop and then the BlueLight app. Now, do anything to stop the machine from running the BlueLight app. I was lucky; there was a printer configuration problem that popped up an error window and stopped BlueLight.

I left the printer error window alone and started poking around the desktop. I saw that anything significant that could be accessed from the Start button was missing. Function keys and Task Manager were disabled. The only thing in the system tray was anti-virus and... the clock. I doubled-clicked the clock and the time was correct. Not for long. Windows applications and temporal anomalies do not mix. So I set the year to 1980, clicked Apply, and OK. Dr. Watson promptly crashed.

What can I leverage here? One of the buttons in the Dr. Watson error window was Help. Clicking Help brought up your favorite Contents-Index-Search. I messed around in Help until I had the option to search for Windows Help files. This gave me an Open File dialog box.

Should I search the C drive, `C:\WINNT`? No, I went to Network Neighborhood. And there, with little perusing, I saw vast networks like kmnorthamerica, kminternational, kih.kmart.com—way more than I could write down without being noticed.

I believe Kmart is counting on securing unwanted access from the BlueLight computers (which probably have trusted access) to these large nets by locking down these NT boxes. As you can see this isn't the case.

Finally, I want to discuss, not a hack, but what I can only call negligence. Throughout my explorations I examined quite a few pin pads. And underneath many I would find a sticker with an 800 number and a client number. The 800 numbers belong to either banks or transaction handling companies, and the client number is the only authentication needed to access sales, deposit, and checking account information for a given vendor. Having dealt with small businesses and having found these stickers at such, I know that this information is held closely. It is a shame that someone needs only a remote interest to access this private information.

Hacking the Hilton (Spring, 2004) *By Estragon*

Many hotels are offering high-speed Internet access to people who stay there. Mostly this is via Ethernet cables, though some hotels also offer wireless. This article addresses one particular setup that we will probably be seeing a lot more of, which I got to use and experiment with at a Hilton hotel (at the Schiphol airport in Amsterdam, when my flight was canceled and I was forced to stay an extra day).

I think we'll be seeing a lot more of this type of integrated hotel system because it is very sophisticated and capable. It's not clear whether Hilton is using a standard vendor system or has merged several different types of systems, but the outcome is full integration of television (including games and pay per view), TV-based Internet (similar to WebTV), the hotel's information system (TV-based, to check out and see bill status), telephone, and of course high-speed Internet.

You can guess which one is of interest to the folks who are reading this: high-speed Internet. I will give a rundown of the system and some tips on how to get some time on the system without paying for it. The details of the fully integrated system, which Hilton claims it will be rolling out to all hotels in the future, are probably different than most other hotels with high-speed Internet. But the Internet portion is pretty standard, and the workarounds are similar to what I've encountered at some other places.

OK, so here's the drill: You set up your laptop or whatever and plug in the standard Ethernet cable supplied on the hotel room's desk. You might need to reboot or otherwise tweak your system for it to recognize there is a new connection available.

In other hotels, what happens next is that you open your Web browser and try to visit a page, and instead are redirected to a Web page by the Internet company (for example, STSN, which is found in many hotels such as the Sheraton chain).

But in the Hilton, once I plugged in, the TV came on and beeped annoyingly (the same beep they use for a wake-up call. It got my attention!). It said that I was trying to access the Internet and to enter a room number or PIN using the TV's remote control.

This is actually a good security feature to make sure you didn't somehow get to the patch panel or some other open connection. You can't enter someone else's room number (I tried) because your Cisco unit's address (below) is linked to your room. So you enter your room number.

Next, it steps you through the process of rebooting your computer (obviously, intended for Microsoft users), then says to try to access the Internet.

This is where the free access begins. At this point your computer is (hopefully) connected and has received its IP address via DHCP. However, you did not yet confirm with the TV that you're accessing the Internet and have not loaded any Web pages.

The trick is that standard ports other than 80 are now open. I was able to ssh (port 22) to another computer on the Internet with the -x option (to tunnel X Window connections). I could then start Mozilla or whatever app remotely and have it show up on my computer in the hotel room. (Of course, you need to login via an xterm or similar and have an X server on your computer.)

Unfortunately this bliss only lasted for ten minutes or so. (You might get a little extra time by using the "Back" on the remote control and otherwise trying to reset any timers that are running.) Eventually the TV beeps again and you're back at step one but your ssh session gets blocked.

The good news is you can start over again and get another ten minutes of connectivity. But I was unable to continue my ssh session (even though the DHCP IP address was the same) and needed to reconnect.

Why bother trying to get ten minutes? Well, in this hotel (and probably all those with the same setup) charges for access are by the *hour*, not the day. I was paying ten euros per hour (about $12) once I gave up screwing around and tried to get some work done in segments longer than ten minutes, so I appreciated the extra "free" time. I checked the next day and also kept track of my time (the TV beeps after an hour to let you know your time is almost up), and confirmed that the extra 30 minutes or so I got in ten-minute increments were not charged.

Later, I saw that for about $40 a day you could get a package with unlimited Internet plus unlimited pay per view movies and other perks. Well, maybe that's worth it if you've got the need and the bucks.

Here's a little more information about the configuration. They are using Cisco 575 LRE Customer Premise Equipment (CPE) units in each hotel room. These were attached to the back of a digital TV and have two network connections, two power connections, and what looks like an active security monitoring device. (So be careful if you try to move it around much.)

The Cisco 575 LRE product sheet says it needs to connect to a Catalyst 2900 LRE XL switch, which is probably where the smarts are. The integration with the TV and billing system was not clear, but my guess is that the TV got its commands via the 575. These commands were probably from a separate computer in the building that also was doing the monitoring and billing for pay per view, security, etc.

I did all of the above with my portable Mac running OS X. Unfortunately, I didn't have nscan or other tools to try to probe the network further or sniff the network, and I didn't have enough time to grab them and experiment. Obviously if you could see their server for billing, etc. there would be opportunities to either try to fool the server or get access to it. If Hilton is smart, there would be very limited access from the server to the rest of the hotel infrastructure. (Otherwise, for example, access to non-critical services like in-room Internet and pay-per-view could yield access to critical services like door key-card encoding.)

In closing, the system I used was definitely very cool, but had an easy and obvious way of bypassing the charging system for some free Internet. Even though it costs a lot of money to stay in a Hilton and pay (by the hour!) for Internet service, my guess is that these types of integrated systems (TV, Internet, games...) will be a lot more common in the future.

Cracked Security at the Clarion Hotel (Winter, 2007-2008)

By Gauss VanSant

I recently stayed at the Clarion Hotel in Albany, which offers free high-speed Internet to its guests. During my stay, I decided to poke around on the hotel's network. I had heard horror stories about hotel networks and wanted to see if they were accurate.

The hotel contained three different wireless networks that I could identify. The first network used the SSID "ClarionInn." It was unsecured and broadcasting its SSID. I connected to the network and was immediately disappointed with the network speed; if this was the hotel's "high-speed Internet," then the advertisers deserved to be drawn and quartered.

I ran the standard Linksys router security test: browse to 192.168.1.1, and entered the default passwords for the router. I can't be bothered to look the default up, don't have it memorized, and happen to be lousy at guessing. I tried username: admin, password: admin. The connection failed without displaying a password prompt, so I assumed that the router had been set up to disable wireless administrative access, but just to be sure I checked my computer's IP configuration. Surprise surprise, 192.168.1.1 was not my default gateway, and as it turned out, whatever I had connected to was not even using a private IP address. In retrospect, the device was probably a wireless modem/router combination, but after a nine-hour drive, this didn't occur to me, so I simply retried the "Linksys for Dummies" test, watched it fail, and passed out.

The next morning, I wandered over to the hotel's public computer lab. This consisted of two computers, one running Windows XP, the other running Windows Vista. I sat down at the XP box, which was already logged in, and did a bit of idle Web browsing. Only a bit, though; I quickly discovered that HTTPS was being blocked, although straight HTTP worked fine. At first, I thought that this might be an overly paranoid firewall configuration, but the neighboring Vista box worked perfectly well.

I looked around the installed programs list, thinking I might find some sort of childproofing filter installed, but instead I found good reasons for the hotel to lock down network ports. One thing Vista has right, and the thing which probably saved that box, is that it requires a password to install any significant software. On the XP machine, I found World of Warcraft, Second Life, and, my oh my, Family Key Logger. Well, that can't be good, can it?

I started up the keystroke logger and saw it pull up an icon in the Quick Launch bar, which included an option to view the keystroke log. Well, what would you do? In addition to some test text I entered to see if the program was working, I discovered some lengthy chat transcripts from a program listed as Mail.ru, which turned out to be a Russian language chat client. I also found a username and password for a Citibank Australia account, and some email transcripts from the same user. Oh, hell.

Putting aside that moral dilemma (vacation in Honolulu, anyone?), I looked around to see why the hotel computers seemed to get such a fast network speed while mine was so lousy. As it turned out, the hotel's second wireless network was not broadcasting its SSID, "QUALITY," though it otherwise appeared to be just as unsecured as the ClarionInn network. I headed back to my room to log in.

High-speed Internet, right? No. I couldn't connect to QUALITY and couldn't figure out why, so I decided that the hotel had set up MAC filtering on the router. This may not seem logical at first glance; after all, the hotel clearly hadn't bothered with any other security. But it did make some sense when I discovered a note that hotel customers could come to the front desk to pick up a wireless card for the hotel network.

Here's how not to hand out a $60 piece of computer equipment: Do not ask for identification. Do not ask the person what room he or she is staying in. Do not ask the person to sign his or her name. Do not write down any identifying information about the device. In fact, do not do anything that would prevent anyone from walking out of the lobby and pawning off half of your network infrastructure.

So I picked up a card and tried it out. Now I could connect to the QUALITY network, but my signal strength was miserable: 1% at best, and none at all if I moved in the wrong direction. Since the ClarionInn network had a much stronger signal, I guessed that the card was a dud and spoofed its MAC address on my own wireless device. Still no joy. Eventually, I tried connecting from the hotel's computer room, which, it turned out, worked even without the MAC spoofing.

Go figure: I'd given the hotel credit for implementing a basic security measure when, in fact, they simply didn't have proper signal coverage for their high-speed network. I would understand if it were intended to be used by the hotel systems only, but the desk person who gave me (er, let me borrow) the wireless card specifically told me to connect to the QUALITY network. So, if guests were supposed to be using it, why wasn't it broadcasting an SSID?

I believe I mentioned finding three wireless networks earlier. The third was a near-exact copy of the ClarionInn network, ClarionInn1 or something like that. Its signal was so weak that I never bothered to play with it; presumably, it was covering the other end of the hotel. At this point, I decided that the hotel networks weren't worth poking at, short of locating the hardware and plugging in an Ethernet cable, and I wasn't about to do that without a spotter.

I headed back to the hotel computers and checked in on the XP machine. By this point, someone had logged out of the guest account, killing the keystroke logger, which raises the question of what point there is in a keystroke logger that a five-year-old who understands the concept of right-click could disable. But I digress. I logged back into the account and got this pleasant message for my troubles:

Dear Hotel,

Your security is awful. You're just lucky I was too lazy to break into your admin account.

I'm paraphrasing, but honestly it wasn't much more intelligent than that, popping up in a DOS window on login. The amusing part was that when I sat down at the computer, the administrator account had been left logged in, and pretty much anyone with a finger could have simply clicked their way into it. Presumably the "l33t hax0r" had actually broken into the box over the network. Yet another reason to avoid the box like the plague, but the box was turning into an onion for me: tasty and lots of layers, but peeling them back made me want to cry.

Viewing hidden files and folders turned up a Remote Desktop program in the Documents folder; if this wasn't a back door that the script kiddie had set up, then it probably was the thing that let him into the system. I also turned up another key logging program, Perfect Keylogger. This one was a bit stealthier than the other one, in that it didn't pop in the All Programs menu wagging its tail and smiling. I suppose I could have looked for some logs for this program as well, but at that point the box's virus scanner pinged me about a new piece of malware that was busy installing itself, and I felt a strong urge for an antiseptic and some sleep.

The next morning was checkout time, and it was only with a great effort of will that I didn't grab passing staff by the collar and start screaming about least privilege. Returning the wireless card involved no more checking than acquiring the thing had; in fact, I still have a driver disc for it that I really ought to think about mailing back.

The moral of the story? Don't touch a hotel computer. If you must touch a hotel computer, and you have the option, pick Vista over XP, because a blind stab at security is better than nothing. And, no matter how important you think it is, do not log into anything of value. SSL is no defense against a keystroke logger, and for all I know that poor Australian's bank account is still out in the open.

Electronic Application Insecurity (Spring, 2005) *By clorox*

I'm sure most people searching for a job have filled out an electronic application at a business on one of their machines. I know about four months ago my friend was looking for a job and I figured I'd help him find one. No one was hiring so he decided to try a store in the mall. The store was JC Penney. We were brought into a room with two computers. He sat down and started to fill out his application and I, being the curious one I am, snooped around.

The application itself was an HTML file that was being shown in IE in full screen mode. Ctrl+Alt+Delete did no good so I control escaped and it brought up the taskbar with the Start button and the task tray. The Start menu was bare, no way for me to execute an application there, just a shutdown button. But in the task tray they had McAfee Antivirus running. I'm not sure if it was a corporate enterprise version, but I double-clicked it to try to find a way I could access the hard drive. There was a field with a Browse button next to it where you could change your virus database and it let me view the hard drive as well as the networked drives. I opened a Notepad file just so I could see txt files easier in the browser. I was snooping around when I came upon a folder in the C drive called apps.

The text files in this folder were titled by a nine digit number. I opened one of the text files and it was Amie Laster's application. Formatted in this way:

ssn-ssns-snn | Amie Laster | 00001010101010110101011

The others were exactly like this so anyone could just sit down here, access everyone's applications, and pretty much exploit the person using this data. I sent an anonymous letter to the district office. I'm not sure if it's been fixed or not but I thought that people who are entering in critical information on a computer need to know where it is going and who has access to it.

Shoutz: z3r0, shady, lucas, mayo, and josh.

Hacking Soda Machines (Autumn, 2004) *By MeGaBiTe1*

After reading a letter in 21:1 on vending machines, I decided to do some research into this topic. Soda machines, to be specific. What really goes on behind the six foot tall picture of a Mello Yello bottle?

First of all, I'd like to say that this has been tested by myself and others in the U.S. I don't know how much soda machines in other countries differ from those in the States.

Most aspects of these machines can only be accessed from the inside by the refill guy, but any passerby with the right knowledge can look through a DEBUG menu that is present on any Coke machine with an LCD display.

To get into this menu, you must enter the button sequence 4-2-3-1. On machines where the buttons are aligned vertically, the first button in the column is 1, second is 2, etc. Doing this should display some text on the LCD (sometimes "EROR," sometimes "CASH").

Once in the menu, there are multiple options you can select. To navigate within the DEBUG menu, use these buttons:

- 1—Back
- 2—Up
- 3—Down
- 4—Select

Now on to the nitty gritty of each option.

- **CASH**—This option lets you see how much money is in the machine. You can also scroll through it to see how much money has been spent on each type of soda, ordered by their button number.
- **EROR**—May be some sort of area to log errors. In my personal experience, every machine has displayed the text NONE when I selected EROR.
- **RTN**—An option used to return or exit the DEBUG menu. It is not found on newer machines.
- **VER**—Probably used to display the OS version.
- **SALE**—Displays the number of sodas sold. This option can be navigated in the same fashion as CASH.

Well that's about it for now. If you're wondering, "Can I get free sodas from this menu?" the answer is no. It would be plain stupid for Coke to design their machines to dispense free sodas with a combination of publicly available buttons. There is probably a lot more to find out about these aluminum spitting beasts, so have fun. Also, check to see what model machine you're using. (It should say on the back.) A quick Google search may reveal some manuals or info.

Shouts to Xeon, Spency, CyberHigh, Harlequin, Dave, and all the people at `scriptriders.org` *and* `jinxhackwear.com`.

Hacking on Vacation (Autumn, 2002) *By Eric*

I'll start with Disney World. Both WDW (Walt Disney World) and Universal Studios/ Islands of Adventure have a "Fast Pass" system (Universal calls it "Universal Express") that allows you to get a ticket for a certain time slot (usually anywhere from ten minutes to an hour ahead). When the time slot comes around, you can go to the head of the line (actually, get into a separate, shorter, Fast Pass line). Now, the WDW and US/IOA tickets are only checked by an attendant—no electronic verification is used. And the attendant looks at two things: the color/background of the ticket that indicates the ride for which it is valid, and the black, thermally printed text that indicates what time slot it is for. Universal Express tickets are printed on card stock and have preprinted generic backs (not ride particular) and have low-resolution (thermally?) printed fronts that have the time slot (in Comic Sans MS font) and ride logo. Since the Fast Pass/Universal Express tickets are free and easy to get, a dishonest person would have rather little difficulty reproducing them.

The WDW Fast Pass system uses a simple client/server topology; where the dispenser boxes read the magnetic stripe on the park pass (the one you paid $50+ for), and send it to the central server using "Black Box" short haul modems. (Black Box is the name of the modem model or manufacturer; I was not able to find out which.) They're secured by a lock on the back that needs to be unlocked before the half-moon handle can be turned to unlock the cover of the clients; the lock appears to be a standard pin- or disc-tumbler type. I know that Disney offers $200, 6-hour behind-the-scenes tours of the utility tunnel system and stuff like that for people over 16, photo ID required at the gate. (If it's fake and they find out, you're out $200.) If any reader goes on one of these tours, please write in!

An interesting fact; some of the LED signs in US/IOA have DB9 and PS/2-type connectors hanging off the back. I wonder....

At some of the more expensive themed restaurants in the area (NBA City in the Universal Studios shopping area just outside the park, for example) the "your table is ready" notification system uses things called TouchPaks. What is really cool about these is that they are literally just Compaq iPaqs with the "double the weight and thickness" PCMCIA adapter, an Orinoco WLAN card, a special system extension that is customized to the restaurant—in this case, a basketball theme that allows the user to play trivia games and watch movies—in a special "tamper-proof" case. ***cough*** The trick is with the snaps on the back. They are damn near impossible to open by hand or even by screwdriver unless you know the trick, possibly because of the punched dot on their backs. So anyway, what you do is take out your handy flathead screwdriver (on your SwissTool or whatever) and slide the blade under the snap, between the female and male parts. Stick it opposite the punched dot, but not *exactly* opposite. Some experimentation is needed. I think the trick is to get the corner of the screwdriver's head opposite the dot, but I am not sure. Twist the screwdriver. If you did it right, the snap should lever off with a small amount of force; if you didn't get it right then it won't do anything (except break, if you twist *too* hard).

To put the snaps back on, you need to find the small black tab on the inside rim of the female half of the snap. It's that tab that makes them tough to put back on, so just tilt the snap so the black tab is closest to the male snap-half and push the female down so the black tab hooks under the rim of the male and then you can push the rest of the female down and she'll snap right back in.

Why would one want to access the hardware? The reset button of course! You see, the WinCE UI is protected from "hacking" by the fact that the extension ("overlay" UI) runs at boot and intercepts all button presses. However, if the battery reaches ten percent, the custom UI will drop the user into a "Low battery, please see the hostess" screen, *with the start menu in the upper-left corner!* To get the battery down that low, you can either wait a while, or play some movies. (NBACity's custom UI lets you watch short basketball movies, and the MPEG decoder makes the CPU suck juice like you would not believe.) Incidentally, while you're looking around in the WinCE UI, the overlay UI might not be able to receive signals from the base, so you may want to do the hacking on a busy night when you know it'll be quite a while until your table is ready. Reset the unit to restore it to its original state.

The custom software receives the "table ready" signal using a standard 802.11b network (NBACity's SSID is "NBA") that is not WEP encoded. However, the range apparently does not extend very far outside the restaurant, at least without a directional antenna. Regardless, I doubt the network is Internet-connected, so all one could do would be to sniff and reverse-engineer the protocol. Which would be interesting.... (If you do R-E it, please write!)

The base station in the restaurant is an Intermec "Handheld PC" mini-laptop (in NBA City, located just inside the second entrance doors on a small table) running custom software and using a Cisco Aironet card. Apparently, although there is a "custom message" button in the software, the feature is not yet implemented. Perhaps in the future, or with a bit of sniffing of the message protocol, one could figure out how to send "All Your Tables Are Belong To Us."

Orlando is not the only place you can fiddle around. In many European tourist spots where you can take a self-guided audio tour, you get a squarish black box manufactured by "AntennAudio." It has a row of numbered buttons at the top of the faceplate, and on either side of the LCD display, you have the red stop button, a back button, up and down buttons, and the green play button. The back plate of the unit holds two gold-plated nubs, some recessed contacts to charge the battery, and the on/off slide switch. (Do not turn the unit off unless you speak the local language, as turning it off resets the language. I found out the hard way.) The side panel has a headphone jack and a PS/2-type connector, used to program the unit. When the unit boots up, you can pause the boot sequence by holding down the stop button (it continues when you let go), which is pretty useless, and it displays some rudimentary version information, also pretty useless except for the fact that it tells you that there's some kind of internal memory and processing capability.

As you might guess from the noises it makes when you type in a location code to hear the prerecorded description of what you are looking at, it is just a glorified portable CD player. What you might not guess is that the only thing holding it shut is four or five medium-small Phillips head screws that a handy SwissTool will take care of. If you undo the screws on the "AntennAudio" sticker side and open the cover (being careful not to lose the screws!) you get access to the CD. I did not have time to stick it into my laptop, so I am not sure if the sound files are stored as CD tracks or as data (MP3?). Presumably, the CD would also be able to carry firmware (as it seems to be updatable, since there's a date and version number in the boot screen), so I suspect the latter.

With a bit of hacking, I imagine one would be able to burn a replacement CD; quite handy for those long boring tours. As long as you remember to replace the original when you're done! Note I do *not* advocate changing the tour CD and leaving it in there, regardless of how incorrect or boring the current CD is.

There's another type of audio guide that looks like a really long, skinny remote control and has a remarkably cell-phone-like screen (used at a Roman theatre in southern France) and can take up to four digits for the "commentary code" where typing in 9999 will let you change the language. But that's all I could find.

Something to remember if you go into a French post office: the iMac-based Internet terminals (with a card reader for some kind of credit card) run a pre-OSX variant and use AtEase for protection; pressing Apple-Power (the power key is hidden under a metal strip at the top right of the keyboard, accessible by paperclip or SwissTool-small-flathead screwdriver) will bring up the rudimentary debugger, typing G FINDER should get you to the finder. (PC users: the finder is the equivalent of EXPLORER.EXE; try terminating it in the Close Programs dialog box, or Processes dialog in Win2k/XP, to see what it does.) From there you should be able to find Netscape or whatever. Rebooting will restore it to its original state. Similar but simpler, PC@EASY terminals in airports have the Ethernet cable accessible at the bottom-right corner of the monitor, just behind the bezel. Plugging in a laptop and getting a DHCP address works, but is unethical....

Have fun! And remember, leave no trace.

PayPal Hurts (Winter, 2007-2008) *By Estragon*

This article is about how PayPal transaction reversals can cost recipients a lot of dough. I'm writing from the perspective of a hacker who sees how the shortcomings of the PayPal system could be used to take money out of the pocket of someone else.

The techniques described in this article could be used against anyone with a PayPal account, in amounts from a few pennies to thousands of dollars. With a mass protest against, say, a disfavored political candidate, company, or individual, many people working together could rapidly cause trouble—including plenty of money lost—for their target.

My biggest concern is the "Donate Now!" button linking to PayPal that we see on the web sites of so many charities and open source software development projects. I was inspired to write this article when I received a chargeback, and later a transaction reversal, from PayPal. I run a charity that operates an open source project, and receive donations via PayPal. Getting donations via PayPal is quite nice, and it's a major way we sustain our project.

The basic situation is that on PayPal it costs a recipient extra money when a transaction is disputed by the sender. While this isn't that different from the way banks and credit card companies operate, many individuals and small charities use PayPal because they can't afford the infrastructure, don't have the volume, or haven't got the right type of corporate structure to accept credit cards directly. In other words, this technique can be more hurtful with PayPal against small charities or similar organizations than against bricks-and-mortar stores.

For money that was paid and received by PayPal (from one PayPal user to another), PayPal handles disputes internally. So, if funds were sent to you from someone else's PayPal account, and the transaction is disputed, PayPal has a process to evaluate the claim. You can find their resolution process online, with lots of details. It is very much geared towards the selling of goods.

Here's the rundown of an actual disputed transaction I received recently. Someone made a $2 donation to my organization, then filed a dispute.

For a $2 purchase or donation sent via PayPal with a PayPal account, $0.38 was charged as a fee to accept the payment, then $0.38 was charged to reverse the transaction.

PayPal walked away with 38 cents (19 percent of the original transaction), and my PayPal account was 38 cents lighter as a result of the transaction. The $1.72 netted originally from the $2 donation was removed, but then an additional 38 cents were removed.

PayPal also accepts payments via credit card. If a credit card transaction is disputed, the credit card company interacts with PayPal. PayPal interacts with the PayPal account holder.

If the transaction is reversed (in this case, it's called a chargeback), a chargeback settlement fee may be charged if the credit card company charges PayPal. That is, PayPal passes the fee on to the account holder. In what became an actual chargeback, I received a donation of $100, which was disputed about 10 weeks later and subsequently reversed.

For a $100 purchase or donation sent via PayPal with a credit card, $3.20 is charged as a fee to accept the payment, then $3.20 was charged to reverse the payment, then $10 was charged as a chargeback fee.

PayPal walked away with $13.20 (13.2 percent of the original transaction), and this time my PayPal account was $13.20 lighter as a result of the chargeback. The $100 donation via credit card costs lots more than the $2 donation via PayPal account if there is a dispute and chargeback.

PayPal charges fees as a percentage of the transaction. Normally, this is 30 cents per transaction, plus 2.9% of the transaction. There are variations in different countries, for different currencies, and for different types of transactions.

Doing the math, if ten people worked together to each make a $100 donation, then made a claim against me, I would be out $132, rather than receiving $968. Below, I'll give some ideas about how such mass action could happen with relative impunity.

To sum up, the chargeback (involving someone who made a donation to my organization via PayPal) had these costs. First, the amount of the original donation was removed from my account. Second, PayPal collected their usual fee (described below) on the transaction amount, even though they had already removed it off the top from the donation amount. Third, there was a chargeback fee of $10 from the credit card company.

In my research, I found that PayPal lists different chargeback fees for different countries. (They're all about $10 to $20 U.S.) Some banks list their credit card chargeback fees, which are comparable and sometimes even higher.

How can you work around losing money through disputed PayPal payments? If you're actually selling items via PayPal, follow the terms of their Seller Protection Policy. Read the fine print: protection stops for many purchases at $250.

Protection does not extend to anything other than goods. PayPal's seller protection plan states that "Only physical goods are covered by the Seller Protection Policy. Intangible goods, such as services or items delivered electronically (e.g., software, MP3s, eBooks), are not covered." In other words, there is no seller protection plan for accepting donations, taking payment for work performed, or other non-tangibles.

There don't seem to be dollar limits for seller protection, and I have made and received payments of up to $10,000. But for buyer protection, transactions are only covered up to $2,000 under certain circumstances, $250 otherwise.

During the time of a dispute (which can take weeks or months, but is more typically just a few days), the payment amount is frozen.

PayPal has a policy that they do not reverse PayPal transactions unless they are taking money from the seller. In other words, it's not like U.S. banks' FDIC insurance. Imagine that someone scams you for $1,000 from your PayPal account, then withdraws the money from their PayPal account, leaving it empty. PayPal will not give you your $1,000 back unless the other account has that money. This opens up a whole lot of possibilities, but it's basically all just fraud: take the money and run. There are many stories about this happening on eBay (which owns PayPal). From reading PayPal's policies, it sounds like it doesn't matter whether their "buyer protection plan" applies or not.

Compare this to credit card protection, where you will get your money back regardless of whether the credit card company got their money back, or whether any goods involved were returned. Your mileage may vary, and things might be different outside of the U.S. My few experiences with credit card fraud were that the credit card companies just didn't care: they would hold a transaction during "investigation" and do essentially nothing. At the end, if the merchant fights, the customer loses. But if the customer wins, the credit card company will return the money.

On the two occasions where my credit card was stolen (once physically, once electronically), I provided proof (a police report number) and the charges were reversed. The legitimate stores that were stolen from (with my credit card) were not given their money for the transactions, and did not get their goods back. One of them was assessed a chargeback fee by the credit card company, indicating that the PayPal technique described here can be effective with credit cards, too.

By the way, if this hasn't convinced you to never use your debit card for these types of purchases, you need to read your debit card agreement. Most banks offer very little protection for debit card transactions, even if the debit card holds a major credit card seal.

Let's work through some exploits. First, imagine a hypothetical candidate running for national office. The candidate accepts PayPal as a method of donation on his or her web site. If ten people each make donations of $1,000 to the candidate, using their credit card, the candidate will have $10,000 minus PayPal fees of $293.

If those ten people then call their ten different credit card companies, saying the charge was unauthorized ("my teenager borrowed my card," "I think the Starbucks store I go to every day might have copied my card number," etc.), the candidate will lose the $10,000, plus another $293, plus another $100. Ten people together cost the candidate about $393 from his or her own account.

Would the credit card companies catch on? Probably not, for two reasons: the excuses given are not big enough to warrant serious investigation, and there is not a lot of sharing and reporting of credit card fraud. Will PayPal catch on that the ten people are working together? Maybe, but what if they all had a common excuse like, "we all go to that Starbucks"?

Second, let's look at a larger scale with smaller donations. What if a fraudster has hundreds or thousands of stolen credit card numbers, and a vendetta against a particular open source software project's charity? Assuming the criminal had plenty of time on his or her hands (since it's intentionally hard to automate payments and account creation on PayPal), she could run a few transactions of less than $10 per day to the targeted charity. Then, let the legitimate credit card holder dispute the transaction.

At $10 per chargeback plus fees, any donation of under about $11 is a net loss for the targeted charity of the chargeback fee, in addition to the cost of the reversed transaction.

Finally, let's think of an even larger-scale scam. How about an urban legend sent via tons of spam? Message one: "This charity is doing wonderful work, but is about to have its charitable organization status reversed by the IRS. In order to meet the IRS requirements [insert valid hyperlink here], they need to receive several hundred small donations ($2 to $10). By donating with your PayPal account or credit card, the charity will be able to provide clear proof to the IRS that the charity is legitimate."

Link to the real organization and its real PayPal link. Wait for people to donate. Assume a very small (less than .1 percent) response on the spam but a large campaign of millions of spams. There are clearly a lot of idiots who respond to spam, and you only need a small proportion.

Then, a week or two later send spam message #2, "You might have heard recently about a charity that made a plea to maintain its status with the IRS. If you donated any money, be informed that you are a victim of fraud. The charity's IRS status is not up for renewal, and there is no effort to remove its 501(c)(3) status under IRS regulations [insert another valid hyperlink here]. If you donated with PayPal, protest your donation and reverse it, follow this link [link to PayPal dispute center]. If you donated with your credit card, be sure to file a dispute claim with your bank."

Would your spam campaign bring in more money to the target than was reversed later? Again, let's do some math. Assume 200 donations are made with an average of $5 each, and 50 percent of donations are made via PayPal accounts, while the others are made using PayPal with a credit card. The net gain is 200 x $5, minus 45 cents per transaction for PayPal's fees: $911.

If 100 out of 200 donors file a successful claim with PayPal or their credit card company, and half used their credit card, $500 would be removed from the charity via PayPal. Chargeback fees would net a further $500 ($10 each for 50 credit cards). Further PayPal fees of $48.50 would be assessed as the $500 were removed. Total removed is 500+500+48.50=1,048.50. The charity would get to keep the proceeds from the 100 donors who didn't protest, about $455.50 (half of $911). Net loss to the charity is 455.50 - 548.50 or $93.10, plus lots of aggravation.

PayPal does have a lot of protections in place, but far fewer when no goods are being sold, and far fewer at larger dollar amounts. Just a few reversed transactions can make a charity or other recipient have a bad day. In this article, I have laid out some of the basics, and also worked through some hypothetical scenarios where a larger number of reversed transactions can be truly damaging.

Lots of people have worked on anonymous payment systems, non-repudiation of payments, and escrow systems for delivering goods. For examples, read some articles on e-gold. PayPal does not implement the hard parts of such a system, which require a trusted intermediary (not one who profits from every type of transaction, including illegitimate ones, as PayPal does), and strong cryptographic methods of ensuring identity while maintaining anonymity. PayPal is ubiquitous, but has flaws. Let the buyer, and the seller, beware.

Hacking Answers by Gateway (Summer, 2007) *By Franz Kafka*

I used to work as a technical support representative for Answers by Gateway and would serve as a corporate guardian to ensure that people calling in about pirated software or to help crack passwords were not helped. I have parted ways because my colleagues have a different mentality about hacking than I do. Most people who work as technicians (with some exceptions) can't program in any language, not even in Visual Basic.

But there are some ways the people who call in to Answers by Gateway can get help. Lie to the technician. There is no way that we can verify over the phone that the copy of Microsoft Office or your OS is pirated unless you tell the technician, so don't tell the technician that it is an illegal copy. Remember if you are calling in for support on an OEM copy of Windows to tell the technician that it came with the machine. (We won't tell you this, but all copies of Windows that are a full version OS and not an image disc will work on any machine as long as you have the product key. The trick is to 1) lead us to believe that the disc came with the machine, or 2) lead us into thinking that you bought a new copy of Windows to install on your machine.)

Some of the technicians are anal retentive and may want you to describe what your Windows CD looks like. Use Google Images and describe the image of the CD that you see. Again, we can't tell if you're lying to us over the phone because you are calling a support technician and not a psychic. Use this fact to your advantage.

Getting us to help with passwords is a bit trickier. Sometimes if there is a password for Windows XP, you can boot into Safe Mode and login as the administrator and get in without a password. If you can't get into Safe Mode without a password, we won't be able to help you. What you need to do is this: Tell us that something is preventing you from starting Windows normally and you need help backing up your data in Safe Mode. Tell us you can't get into Windows normally because of a virus, a power surge, your kid tried to install his PS2 game in Windows and hosed the system, or you opened that picture of Britney Spears that your boss sent to you. Whatever you do don't mention that there is a problem with your password. Better yet don't even mention the word password. A lot of technicians at Gateway will refuse to help you if they suspect that you are calling in about a password issue.

If you need to reset your BIOS password, ask us to help you replace the battery on your motherboard. Replacing this battery will reset your password without you even needing to mention the password issue to the technician.

Another part of our job is selling you things that you don't need. Most of the security software that we sell is worse than programs such as AVG and Ad-Aware that you can download for free. Some employees are salesmen posing as technicians and will try to sell you a new system when all you need to do is reload your operating system.

When you call you are really playing the lottery. You are gambling that you will reach a good knowledgeable technician that knows what he is doing. Most of the time you will lose.

Be careful when you call for support on your computer. I can only comment about how Gateway operates, but I suspect that most other companies' support centers would be about the same.

18 Toys of the 21st Century

In the end, it's all about having fun. That's the ultimate driving force behind just about everything we've covered in these pages. I've defended the practice of hacking on ideological grounds for many years but the real reason the majority of hackers get involved in the first place is simply because it's a total thrill. Most people get this. Some don't.

We live in a world full of toys. The boundaries between reality and fantasy have been blurred quite a bit lately so that we don't always see where the fun stops and the crime begins. It may be OK to play a game on your own computer but you could get expelled for doing it at school. Or you can run a program over a network but if you use it on your own machine you could be in violation of some new law. Corporations tell us we're not allowed to figure out how things work even after we've bought them and they have the Digital Millennium Copyright Act to back them up. Ownership of every one and zero in every bit of data in computer software, music, and video is jealously guarded by those companies who want to make it all accountable—at precisely the time when the rest of the world is discovering how *shareable* everything actually is. I can't say I'm completely without sympathy. People deserve to be paid for the work they do. And I believe most consumers see this. But the old rules just aren't working anymore. This isn't a fight that can be won without embracing the technology that's making all of the changes. And that is what the powers that be have yet to understand.

The most fundamental change I think we can all strive for is to realize that playing with toys and having a blast while doing it are *good* things. How often are we told exactly the opposite, whether it's by our parents, our teachers, our bosses, or our legislators? The mentality is that playing with things is a waste of time, not at all constructive, and potentially even damaging. Nothing could be further from the truth. A stimulated mind is a productive mind and the people who spend time doing things they enjoy are likely to become far more creative and imaginative. I can't count the number of times I've seen this unfold in the hacker world. Brilliance that nobody else can understand or appreciate, kids dropping out of school because they're not getting anywhere and are even being punished for the ways they express themselves, people winding up in prison without ever having harmed anyone simply because society can't comprehend how they might be able to fit in. I often hear it said that we're "a nation of laws" whatever the hell *that* means. To me, it says that we're so caught up in our petty rules and regulations that we lose sight of the actual *individuals* who are the vital ingredient of a worthy nation.

So many people want to get involved in the hacker world for the simple reason that it's the kind of world everyone feels a need to be a part of, whether on the surface or way deep down. We all yearn for adventure and challenges, all the while flirting with danger. But here's a secret. It's not always fun and games. In fact, once you actually realize you're a part of the hacker community, you're struck by the fact that there aren't a whole lot of car chases and rollerblade activity. Instead, figure on a lot of nights spent poring over anything from computer code to hardware to manuals to, quite literally, garbage. This is the part of the hacker experience that doesn't draw so many people. But it's what distinguishes the real deal from the wannabes. You see, anyone can have fun and play games. And as I said, that's not a bad thing. But you always need to be doing more and, as far as hackers go, that means figuring out new ways to exploit systems, find bugs, notice the security holes, think outside the box. Most people who want to "become a hacker" aren't really all that into the cerebral stuff. They just want the payoff. It's understandable, particularly when they've just gotten out of the latest action adventure that had a hacker in it and they want to become that character. But it's not reality. What we always have to tell people is that you can't just "become a hacker" by having a mentor or getting someone to vouch for you. It has to be inside of you from the start. I'm not talking about technical expertise or the ability to memorize things. Quite simply, it's the spirit that you need to have. The spirit that will make you question everything, try all sorts of possibilities, and do what almost everyone else considers to be a waste of time—for no other reason than to satisfy your curiosity. In so doing, you will be the person best equipped to figure out how to find the next really cool piece of equipment to play with—or even design.

Wireless

One thing which has really taken off in the 21st century is wireless technology. Of course, we've had wireless devices for many decades. But the playing field is constantly changing. Wireless Internet, for instance, simply wasn't possible a mere decade ago. And now it's everywhere, along with all of the controversy, security issues, and benefits that go with it. All of these are explored here, along with an extensive guide written by the author of Kismet, the most powerful and versatile program designed to find and interpret wireless data signals. But of course, wireless technology also encompasses cellular phones, RFID, satellite technology, and even pirate radio. There are so many interesting things going through the airwaves at any given time in any part of the world. This section will give you a small taste of some of the newer examples.

The Comprehensive Guide to 802.11b Wireless Networks (Summer, 2002) *By Dragorn*

Wireless networking has been around for decades (fixed microwave links, laser links, ham packet radio), but Wireless Ethernet, aka WiFi (short for "wireless fidelity"), aka 802.11b has recently exploded in popularity for home and office use. As is too often the case with any new, widely adopted technology, the average consumer has little understanding of the impact of the little box with antennas that they just hooked up to their cable modem or that their office manager just told them to install on the network.

802.11b Background and Basics

802.11b is part of the 802.11 wireless family (which includes 802.11a and 802.11g, however neither are as widely used as 802.11b). Operating in the 2.4GHz unlicensed radio band, 802.11b is designed to offer up to 11mbit (closer to 6mbit usable) over short distances (typically less than 1,500 feet) but with custom antennas and a clear line of sight, links of several miles are possible. Because it operates in the unlicensed band, no single corporation controls the airwaves. But unfortunately, this means there is also a lot of garbage floating in the 2.4GHz range of the spectrum along with the wireless data. Many cordless phones operate in the same frequency and household microwaves leak significant noise into the 2.4GHz range. Some wireless camera equipment (X10) uses the 2.4GHz range as well. WLANs also recently faced the threat of severely restricted transmission power due to a petition by Sirius satellite radio; however the complaint was recently withdrawn by the company.

802.11b operates in two modes: infrastructure, where dedicated access points (APs) act as the central points for a large number of clients, and ad-hoc, where each client talks directly to other clients. In infrastructure mode, each client needs only to be able to see the AP (or another AP in the same distribution system). Two clients need not see each other directly because the AP will relay traffic. In ad-hoc, every client must be in range of every other client. In either operational mode, it is, by definition, a shared media network; everyone can see all the traffic in the air or, at least, all the traffic in the air that they are in range of.

Each 802.11b network is given a Service Set Identifier, or SSID. This is the name of the network, which all clients use to identify which network they are communicating with. Networks operate on one of 12 (in the U.S.) or 14 (international) channels. Most wireless setups will automatically select the best signal out of all the network points sharing the same SSID.

802.11b has link-layer encryption called Wired Equivalence Protection, or WEP. WEP uses RC4 in 40, 64, 128, or on some recent cards, 256-bit encryption. While never designed to provide a tremendous amount of security (wired equivalence implying "as secure as a shared media wired network," which, as anyone running a sniffer on a wired shared media network can tell you, isn't very secure), additional flaws have been found in WEP that allow key attacks against data encrypted by many manufacturers. More on this later.

802.11b Packet Types

The most common types of 802.11b packets are:

- **Beacon packets:** Typically, access points continually transmit beacon packets containing their SSID, maximum transfer rate, and MAC address of the access point. Most APs send between six and ten beacon packets a second continually.
- **Probe packets:** When a client tries to join a network it sends a probe request packet containing the SSID of the network it wishes to join. If an access point allows the client to associate with the network, it responds with a probe response, also containing the SSID.
- **Data packets:** Typically, these are just TCP/IP encapsulated in the 802.11 frames.
- **Ad-hoc packets:** These are no different than data packets, except they are sent card to card instead of through an access point.

Detecting 802.11b Networks

There are two primary methods for detecting wireless networks, utilized by different programs:

- Active detection, where the client transmits probe requests and looks for networks that respond to them.
  - **Positive:** Sometimes able to detect cloaked networks, does not require a card or driver capable of RF Monitor support.
  - **Negative:** Requires the client to be within transmit range of the access point for it to be detected, generates traffic on the target network which can be traced, and lies on questionable legal ground so far as actively joining a network is concerned.
  - **Used by:** NetStumbler (`www.netstumbler.com`, Windows).
- Passive detection, where the client listens to all wireless traffic in the air and extracts information from the packets found.
  - **Positive:** Client needs only to be within receive range to detect a network, no traffic is generated which can be observed. Passive sniffers are also capable of recording data packets for additional dissection.

- **Negative:** Requires a card and driver capable of RF Monitor support, which enables raw packet detection. Cannot detect a nonbeaconing network with no data traffic.
- **Used by:** Kismet (`www.kismetwireless.net`, Linux/BSD), Wellenreiter (`www.remote-exploit.org`, Linux), Airsnort (`airsnort.shmoo.com`, Linux), and others.

Using passive sniffing it is essentially impossible to detect someone monitoring your network. No traffic is generated by the sniffer and, even in "secure" environments, a handheld such as the Ipaq or Zaurus are more than capable of capturing traffic and can easily be kept in a jacket pocket or bag.

Passive monitoring of wireless data opens many advantages for tracking and analyzing networks. The level of monitoring varies depending on the type of card used. Cisco cards use a very fast hardware channel hopping method, which allows them to scan all of the channels transparently. Prism2 cards must do channel hopping to detect all the 802.11b channels, spending a small amount of time on each channel; most wireless sniffers include this capability either internally or as a helper application. (Kismet uses "prism2_hopper" to hop three channels per second.)

The most simplistic information is in the 802.11b headers—the MAC of the source, destination, and access point systems, the direction of communication, the channel, SSID, WEP, and supported transfer rates. Cisco access points even include an extra status field that often contains information about the function of the equipment, and sometimes even the location of the wireless access point.

Far more information can be gathered by dissecting the data packets of unencrypted networks; FTP, telnet, HTTP, POP, and IMAP traffic are all as vulnerable to observation as they would be in an unswitched Ethernet network. ARP, UDP, and especially DHCP can be used to detect the IP ranges used by the network.

Basic sniffing can be done with almost any wireless card, but some are better than others. Most consumer wireless cards are underpowered, capable of detecting only strong signals, and don't support external antennas. Orinoco cards are more powerful than most, and support antennas, however it is not always possible to do full RFMon mode, which is required for passive monitoring. (There are patches to the Linux Orinoco drivers but they only work on some firmware versions.) While not perfect, one of the best cards for general sniffing is the Cisco AIR-LMC350, which has dual antenna jacks, 100mW transmit, and -95dBM sensitivity (compared to 20 to 30mW transmit for most prism2 cards and -80dBM sensitivity). As mentioned before, the Cisco chipset uses a very fast internal channel hopping scheme, which can sometimes result in missed packets if a single channel is saturated, but overall the performance of the card is excellent. It can be obtained through online retailers for approximately $110 U.S.

Equally important is a proper antenna. Remember that a car is just a big metal box, and metal boxes are not good for radio signals. A car-mounted antenna, while not absolutely necessary, will often triple the amount of data received. 5dB gain magnetic-mount antennas can usually be found for $60 U.S.

The Myth (and Truth) of WEP, SSID Cloaking, and Non-Beaconing

WEP is alternately touted as the only protection you'll ever need, and so weak it's not worth enabling. The truth lies, as always, somewhere in the middle; all, or nearly all, modern chipsets include workarounds for the flaws in WEP key generation. However all it takes is a single older system on your network (access point *or* client) to expose the key.

WEP only encrypts data packets; link layer packets such as joining, beaconing, probes, etc., are left unencrypted. Actually cracking the WEP key depends on the key length, the number of flawed systems generating traffic, and the traffic levels on the network. If there are no systems generating data traffic, you will never have the opportunity to capture weak keys. The most important factor is time. Typically only one or two in thousands of packets contains a weak key, and current key attacks require thousands of weak keys to extract the full key.

Various dictionary-based brute force attacks are under development, but will of course have the same weakness of any brute force attack. Beyond the expected range of likely keys it becomes time-consuming number crunching.

WEP has the additional flaw of being a shared private-key encryption method. Once your key is cracked (or otherwise compromised by system being cracked, insecure means of giving the key to personnel or other network users, an employee leaving, or even an employee losing a wireless-enabled handheld), all systems must be updated with a new WEP key, which has the same weaknesses and vulnerabilities as the previous one.

Coupled with additional security (as discussed later), WEP can be a useful deterrent, however it is by no means sufficient as the only line of defense. While it may foil the casual sniffer, a determined attacker with the right tools stands a good chance of breaching your network.

In a further attempt to make consumer hardware more secure, or to at least appear more secure, many manufacturers include SSID "cloaking," where the SSID is blanked from the beacon packets. Unless a client knows the correct SSID, it cannot join the network. Unfortunately, this "protection" is completely transparent. Once a client joins the network, the SSID is sent by the client and the AP in clear text, even if WEP is enabled. (Remember, WEP encrypts only data packets, not link packets.) Kismet automatically detects this exchange and fills in the network SSID. If you have users on your network, your SSID will be exposed.

Several physical attacks (of varying legality) are possible to force a cloaked network to disclose the SSID. When a card gets a weak signal or loses the signal, it attempts to rejoin the network, disclosing the SSID. Any 2.4GHz RF interference strong enough to disrupt the network and cause systems to rejoin will, in addition to being against all FCC regulations, happily cause a disclosure of the SSID.

The second common trick favored by manufacturers to try to protect APs is to disable beaconing entirely. While not completely in accordance with the 802.11b specifications, this doesn't cause major problems for normal operation. However this, like SSID cloaking, does not provide any significant protection. Any data traveling over the network can still be seen, and the SSID is disclosed in the same fashion as the cloaked SSID by users joining the network.

Securing Wireless Networks

After all of the above doom and gloom, how does one secure a wireless network? There are two primary methods that can be used, and are most effective when used in conjunction:

- **Application or network-layer encryption:** This can be as simple as SSH (or an SSH-tunneled PPP virtual network) or as complex as IPSEC.
- **Proper authentication:** MAC addresses can be easily spoofed. Some APs offer enhanced login authentication (Cisco LEAP). For APs that don't (most consumer equipment), solutions like NoCat (`www.nocat.net`) can provide secure authentication methods to protect the rest of your network from the wireless segment.
- **Properly tuned equipment:** Don't assume stronger is better! Always use the minimum power possible for your network and select your antennas appropriately. Not only is it good for security, this will help reduce the congestion in the 2.4-GHz band.

Community Wireless Networks

Wireless networks provide a phenomenal level of networking possibilities. Most urban areas have at least one wireless users' group aimed at building a free, community wireless network. Often called a wireless mesh or a parasitic grid, community networks aim at blanketing a city (or parts of a city) with free broadband access. Groups such as NYCWireless (`www.nycwireless.net`, New York City, NY), BAWIA, Boston, MA) and PersonalTelco (`www.personaltelco.net`) have already made significant inroads into providing wireless public networks.

Community wireless networks offer an alternative to "big business" broadband, can often get broadband to areas unreachable by conventional means, and can provide a completely independent means of transport for free information without relying on any corporate services or resources. After September 11, the NYCWireless group was involved in bringing back connectivity to areas left without links that the large providers had not been able to restore.

While uncommon, sometimes companies (knowingly) share their wireless networks. Akamai in Boston allows public use of their wireless network equipment, which covers most of Cambridge, with minimal filtering of outgoing traffic (SSH and HTTP both work fine).

In most cases, donating a node to a community network is as simple as putting an access point on a broadband connection (cable, DSL, or other) with a public SSID and registering it with the group of your choice. The web site for a wireless group in your area should contain all the information you need to join.

Threats to 802.11b

802.11b in general and community networks specifically face several hurdles in the near future. Broadband companies are beginning to crack down on the sharing of access and on users who utilize the full bandwidth allocated to them. Connection sharing is already against the acceptable use agreements of most broadband providers, and not far away for most others, and should providers begin charging per megabyte over an arbitrary quota (as Time Warner/RoadRunner is considering), free public broadband could quickly become a thing of the past.

Also, in many urban areas (and even less urban areas) the airspace available for wireless networks is becoming saturated. Just like collisions in shared-media Ethernet, as more wireless networks with overlapping signals are in an area, less bandwidth is available for each. Non-802.11b devices like phones, microwaves, cameras, and even a planned microwave-based lighting system all leak noise into the air that further degrades 802.11b signals.

Finally, while the current 802.11b equipment is well understood and supported with open source drivers, manufacturers are aggressively discouraging community-developed drivers for 802.11a hardware, and in fact as of the time of this writing it is completely unsupported in Linux.

Practical Examples

To gather the data for the cover of the Summer 2002 issue of *2600*, we used a Cisco card, magmount antenna on the roof, a Garmin GPS, and Kismet. In an hour and a half, we found 448 networks. In the center of Manhattan, an area which arguably should be more security aware than anywhere else, only 26 percent of the networks had encryption enabled. At least 75 of the access points were factory configurations, with all the default access granted.

Plain-text data included searches on `outpost.com`, an individual with 129 email messages (every single one of them porn spam), books purchased at Barnes and Noble, IRC sessions, instant messenger conversations, browsing at the Fry's web site, Windows Network Neighborhood file transfers, data from globix.net, uPNP services looking for drivers, and more.

Vulnerable networks ranged from personal systems in apartments, law firms, book stores, and news companies. At the very least they exposed all of the data handled by the company, and at the worst presented an easy entrance into the corporate network. Wireless demo units are often plugged in behind the corporate firewalls of retail stores. (Office Depot for months ran a default Linksys demo unit plugged into the corporate network behind the firewall.)

Getting to Know Your Neighbors (Autumn, 2003)

By Shiv Polarity

Note: In most places, connecting to your neighbor's network without their permission is illegal. Additionally, you can be prosecuted by your neighbor's Internet provider for theft of services if you access the Internet through their network. These instructions are purely for informational purposes and are intended to help you learn how to secure your own wireless network by learning the tactics of potential attackers. Do not invade the privacy of your neighbors; it is rude. Do not steal Internet access; it is wrong.

The use of devices such as 802.11b network cards in schools, coffee shops, and the workplace is becoming more and more common every day. In a setting such as an apartment complex, it is common to have one or more neighbors who have laptops or computers equipped with such a device. If you have a wireless network in your home, you should know how a motivated WiFi user might try to gain access to your network. To adequately protect your network from invaders, you should understand what tools and tactics could be used against you.

The first thing you would need to explore a neighbor's network is a computer with a correctly configured 802.11 network card. I use a laptop with a Compaq WL100 PCMCIA card. The drivers I have found most useful are the linux-wlan-ng drivers from `http://www.linux-wlan.com/linux-wlan`. For the purposes of this article, the use of these drivers will be assumed. Other cards may require other drivers, though almost any Prism2-based card should be fine with linux-wlan-ng. Download the source and follow the instructions to compile for your specific configuration.

Phase 1: Discovery

The first step toward exploration is discovery. By default, your network card will try to connect to the strongest available signal it finds. This is good for accessing the Internet from coffee shops or school, but for our purposes we need a little bit more information. This is where a little app named Kismet comes into play.

Kismet is an "802.11 wireless network sniffer," available from `http://www.kismetwireless.net`. Once it has been downloaded and configured you can use it to scan the surrounding airwaves for wireless networks.

To start Kismet you must first use the root account to start the Kismet server by running `kismet_monitor`. This will put your card into scan mode, which will disconnect you from any previous networks you may have been connected to. The `kismet_monitor` command starts up the Kismet server application. Once that has been started, open a different console and run the command `kismet`. In your `kimset.conf` file, you should have configured Kismet for a default user. This is the only user that can start the application, so be sure you run the `kismet` command as that user.

The graphical interface presented by Kismet can be confusing at first. I suggest you read the documentation at the Kismet web site and get to know what all the symbols and sounds mean. Personally, I find the sounds irritating and usually turn them off by pressing the "m" key. Kismet offers a great deal of information, providing statistics and details for all detected wireless signals. For our purposes, all we are interested in is the list of available access points.

The perfect access point will be unencrypted (access points named "default" are particularly delicious). Kismet will tell you whether or not a given access point is using WEP (Wireless Encryption Protocol). If all of the listed access points for your location are encrypted, you will not be able to proceed. WEP can be broken, but it is a time-consuming process and is beyond the scope of this article (a little too invasive for my taste). Though I will suggest you visit `http://airsnort.shmoo.com` if it is not beyond the scope of your personal ethics.

Once you have identified an unencrypted access point, write down its SSID (name) as well as the channel the signal is using and quit Kismet. Once you have closed the Kismet application, run the `kismet_unmonitor` command as root. This stops the Kismet server and puts your WiFi card back into its normal mode of operation, though it doesn't hurt to also run `/etc/init.d/pcmcia restart` just for good measure, assuming you are using a laptop.

Phase 2: Connectivity

The next step is actually connecting to the access point you have identified. The steps involved in connecting to an access point will differ from one 802.11 driver to the next. These instructions apply to linux-wlan-ng drivers only. If you use different drivers, consult the instructions for those drivers.

Edit `/etc/wlan/wlan.conf` and look for the line beginning with `SSID_wlan0`. The value for that key should be the SSID of the access point you wish to connect with.

Next, look in `/etc/wlan` for a file named `wlancfg-DEFAULT`. That file is your template config file. Do not edit it or overwrite it. Instead, use the `cp` command to create a copy of it. The name of the copy is important and is determined by the SSID of the access point you are trying to connect with. For example, if your target access point is named `myAccessPoint` you would use the following command:

```
cp wlancfg-DEFAULT wlancfg-MyAccessPoint
```

This will create a new file named `/etc/wlan/wlancfg-MyAccessPoint`. For access points named `default` create the file `/etc/wlan/wlancfg-default`. Remember, this is Linux so `wlancfg-DEFAULT` and `wlancfg-default` are totally different files. The linux-wlan-ng drivers will use this new file the next time your wireless connection is initialized.

After you have the new config file, edit it. The contents of the file should be pretty easy to understand. Enter the channel in the appropriate place, as well as the WEP key if needed (if you used Airsnort to acquire one). Most of this file can probably be left as is.

Once all of your values are entered correctly into the new config file, restart your wireless connection. Personally, I use `"/etc/init.d/pcmcia restart"` to do this, though you may have a different means. If everything is correct, you will connect to your target access point. My card gives me two high-pitched beeps to indicate a good connection. One high-pitched beep followed by a low-pitch beep indicates failure.

There are several reasons your connection attempt might fail. If the access point uses MAC address filtering, you will probably not be able to connect to the access point. In this case you are probably up against a fairly savvy access point and you're better off seeking lower-hanging fruit. You may also have made a mistake in your `wlancfg` file. Double-check it. Restart Kismet if you need to make sure you got everything right to begin with. Also double-check to make sure the access point isn't using encryption. Another reason for connection failure could be poor signal strength. Again, check Kismet to make sure there is a reliable signal getting to you. If not, try walking around (assuming you have a mobile computer) and see if you can get a better signal somewhere else. Sometimes just a few feet in the right direction can make a huge difference. If all else fails, check `/var/log/syslog` or one of your other error logs.

Phase 3: Exploration

Now you're connected to your neighbor's access point. Congratulations, you outlaw. Before proceeding, be aware that your connection has been logged on your neighbor's access point or wireless router. Of course, if your neighbor has left his access point wide open, they probably don't even know what the log means and probably never check it. But you should be aware. They have a log of your MAC address, what time you connected, what IP you were assigned, and, depending on the access point, they may be logging everything you do on their network.

So What Now?

Well, my first thing would probably be to see what IP I have been assigned. It is usually 192.168.0.x where x is some number greater then 1. Also, pinging 192.168.0.1

usually works because that is probably the IP to the access point or wireless router. Try opening a Web browser and entering in `http://192.168.0.1`. If prompted for a username/password, try typing in "admin" as the username and leave the password blank. If they are truly using the out-of-the-box configuration, this will usually let you into the configuration page. If you can get into the configuration page, you now have full control of the access point and/or router. One good idea might be to clear the activity log. But hey, this is your gig. Do what you like.

Another interesting venture could be to look at any port-forwarding rules. Finding out which ports are forwarded is a good way to determine what sorts of things go on over this network. Is there a Web server somewhere? An SSH server? Does anyone play video games? If so, what IP do these services run on? This is all very interesting stuff.

If you can't find the access point right away, try using a tool known as nmap (`http://www.insecure.org/nmap/`). As root, run the command `xnmap` to get a nice graphical interface for this incredible tool. You have several options you can perform with nmap. One of my favorites is an IP scan using operating system detection. If you tell it to scan 192.168.0.*, it will scan every possible IP on that segment and return to you a list of all active IP addresses, along with which operating systems they are using. The IP for the access point will have an operating system such as "D-Link DWL 900AP+" or something along those lines. It should be obvious.

So now you know where the access point is. You also know what model the access point is. Try a Google search for that model number. You can sometimes find interesting bugs or vulnerabilities on Web forums for specific models. At the absolute least you should be able to download the PDF manual for the access point to learn how it works along with a confirmation of the default username and password.

You also know how many clients are using the access point, and you know their IP addresses. So now it's time to be neighborly. Go grab an application called LinNeighborhood. This program gives you a graphical interface to your local network, much like Microsoft's famous Network Neighborhood.

Once you've started LinNeighborhood you probably will only see your computer listed in the main window. Since it is highly unlikely that you're on the same workgroup as your neighbor's computers, you will have to do a little work to find them. Click the button at the top labeled Add. This will bring up a dialog asking for a name, group, IP, etc. Enter an IP from the list given to you by nmap, then click Query. LinNeighborhood will fill in the rest of the values for the Add dialog. Once the rest of the values have been filled in, click OK. The new computer should now show up in LinNeighborhood. Do this for each of the computers found by nmap.

Clicking on the computers listed in LinNeighborhood will show you any shared folders they have. You will need to know the usernames and passwords to access them, unless they have been shared publicly. But at this point, why would you suspect your neighbor of not sharing his files publicly? LinNeighborhood will mount the shares to your local file system, and you can look around and see what is there. My personal suggestion would be to not look at the files, and (assuming you can get write access) politely leave a conspicuous text file explaining how to properly secure a wireless network, suggesting WEP encryption, MAC filtering, and setting new passwords and IP addresses for everything. If you do this, most definitely be sure to clear the activity logs in the access point or router.

At the absolute least you should be able to learn the names, groups, and IP addresses of your neighbor's computers. You can use the port forwarding rules from the router to determine what roles the network clients perform and you'll be able to access the Internet, albeit illegally.

Of course, the smartest thing to do would be to not try any of this stuff yourself and instead double-check your own access point or wireless router configuration to be sure they are secure. Also, be sure to change your WEP keys from time to time and keep an eye on your logs. You never know who lives nearby. It could be another *2600* reader.

Hacking the "Captivate" Network (Winter, 2003-2004) *by Darlok*

No doubt many of you have seen those fancy computer screens mounted in elevators in office buildings in major cities like New York, Chicago, and Boston. They provide news, sports, weather, advertising, and other information to the occupants as they enjoy the ride. Well, I was recently able to do some poking around with the Captivate network in my building. Once I figured out that they were actually wireless devices residing on an 802.11b network I broke out my wireless hacking tools and went to work.

In my case, the wireless network did not have Wired Equivalent Privacy (WEP) enabled, so it was open. However, I couldn't obtain an IP address, so I figured either DHCP wasn't running or the network was configured to disallow new clients from associating with an access point and getting on the network. It turned out that the latter was true. How did I know? After using Kismet to capture IP and MAC addresses, I did some MAC spoofing. Once on, I typed the IP addresses of one of the APs into my browser and got the administration page for a Cisco Aironet 4800E. To my (mild) surprise, it was not password protected, so I was able to basically do whatever I wanted.

The main thing I wanted to do was configure it to allow my machine to associate. I accomplished this by navigating to the Association page and changing the "Allow automatic table additions" option from off to on. I was now able to freely associate with this access point without having to spoof a MAC addy. I then performed some network discovery and OS fingerprinting to see what I could see.

I discovered that the screens mounted in the elevators are actually wireless PDA-type devices running WindowsCE and that they have Telnet open. I also found a lone Windows 2000 server which, according to my packet sniffer, was broadcasting the images to the elevator screens every few seconds. As much as I wanted to, I suppressed the urge to attempt to inject my own images. And yes, I also set the "Allow automatic table additions" option back to off. Anyhow, I hope this proves interesting for some of you wireless hackers out there.

An Old Trick for a New Dog—WiFi and MITM (Winter, 2004-2005) *by uberpenguin*

If you are reading this magazine, it is probably safe to assume you are familiar with the concept of a man-in-the-middle attack (which from here will be referred to as MITM for brevity) as it pertains to networking resources. In this article I hope to point out how this old and well known concept can be applied to an 802.11 WiFi network. I will use a case study of a fairly large wireless network I have access to in order to illustrate a possible scenario of a WiFi MITM attack.

The Network

First, let's establish that gaining access to the network is not going to be discussed here. In my case study I already had legitimate access to the network and formulated my scenario from the point of view of one of the numerous persons who also have access to this wireless network. I will not talk about the mundane technical details of the software setup; that is out of the scope and interest of this article. A general description of the wireless network setup follows.

The network in question consists of numerous access points placed throughout a large area that includes both indoor and outdoor coverage. Each access point is "dumb." That is, it simply acts as a bridge between a wired and wireless network and nothing else. The wireless APs are set up with all the reasonable precautions: ESSID broadcasting turned off and WEP. The wired network that all the APs connect to is separate from the rest of the facility's networks. A single gateway is the bridge between the wireless system (including the wired network of all the APs as well as the wireless clients that connect to them) and the rest of the network resources. This gateway also acts as the DHCP server for all the wireless clients. The gateway uses a common MAC-based authentication method that requires you to log in using your user ID and password before it will allow access to the rest of the network. This login form is secured using 256-bit AES encryption that is signed by a large CA. (As we shall see later, this proves to be the most foolproof part of the system.) As you can see, the network is set up with every sensible measure that can be implemented with a non-homogeneous network (hardware, OS, or otherwise). However there are still problems.

The Scenario

The basic concept that this scenario considers is that of DHCP operation. For those of you not familiar, a DHCP client sends a broadcast packet to the network requesting DHCP service. It will then wait for the first DHCP server that responds to the request with configuration information; resending the DHCP broadcast if necessary. Here is where we zero in on the key phrase "first DHCP server." The DHCP client will use whatever information it first receives and ignore all subsequent DHCP responses. Thus we have the basis for our scenario. In our hypothetical setup, we have four important components: a firewall that can perform routing functions, a DNS server, a DHCP server, and an HTTP server (and a WiFi card that works with whatever 802.11 standard is being used obviously). All of these components are readily available for most Free *nix systems.

The idea is to set up a clone of the "real" gateway that bridges the wireless system to everything else. Depending on where a person is physically located in relation to clients, the clone DHCP server may be able to send a response to a given DHCP request more quickly than the real gateway can. To affect a larger number of wireless users, one would merely need to change their physical location. After a client has received the alternate DHCP information and attempts to access a network resource (in this case, an HTTP resource), the normal behavior of the real gateway is mimicked. Specifically, this entails redirecting the user to a secure login page hosted on the gateway. Herein is the largest flaw in this attack, one whose effects will be discussed shortly. There is no good way to forge a secure certificate. We can replicate the normal behavior of the real gateway in every way, down to its domain name thanks to our DNS server. But the false login page will have to be insecure, unlike the real one. Here we must have faith in the ignorance of Joe WiFi User. Even a security-conscious person such as myself can neglect checking the authenticity of a host that is supposed to be secure. In a rush to do other things, one can just quickly log in to the gateway not giving a moment's thought to the security risk they just took. That fact is what makes all of this possible; otherwise the secure login would be a show-stopper.

By now I am sure the reader has ascertained where this scenario is headed. Presented with a familiar login form, Joe WiFi User enters his userID and password and presses Submit. Of course our faux gateway will log him into the real gateway, passing along the values to the real HTTP server for processing and observing the result. However, upon recognizing a successful authentication routine, the script will log this userID and password combo. MITM attack successful.

The Conclusion of the Matter

Let's briefly consider the "flaws" in this scenario. Obviously this setup will not go undetected for long. Upon realizing that the login page being presented is insecure, any savvy user will immediately realize something is wrong and (hopefully) report it to whomever is responsible for maintaining the wireless system. The administrators will quickly be able to spot an unauthorized DHCP server and the traffic it generates. Most cards allow overriding of their built-in MAC address, so tracking the offender may not be easy. However, the network admins will at least be able to figure out general physical location of the fake gateway by determining which access point it is using for its own network connectivity. By changing location and hardware addresses, however, one could likely keep up this routine for a while without being caught.

As mentioned in the network description, the wireless APs in my case study do not perform any network functions other than bridging the wired and the wireless. If these APs were given some packet forwarding and firewall functionality, they would be able to enforce rules on allowable DHCP packets and possibly eliminate the MITM problem described in this article. Another possibility for eliminating this sort of vulnerability is a bit of password trickery using RSA's SecurID system. Obviously this requires a fair monetary investment, but it is a valuable one for any large-scale wireless network. Yet another suggestion I have heard is using Windows' Active Directory policies to disallow DHCP configuration from any hosts that are not specified in a trusted list. Of course, this is only an option in a homogeneous (Microsoft) OS environment where the desktop software can be somewhat controlled. This is not the case in the network I have been describing, but it could be in other cases. Perhaps the best tradeoff that can be used to minimize the vulnerability is enforcing a strict password policy for the gateway. In my case study network setup, the userID and password used to authenticate with the gateway is the same one that is used for most other computing services. This account is meant to protect quite a bit of sensitive data, including and not limited to financial and administration information.

The conclusion we are forced to make, therefore, is that our wireless network is to be treated as wholly insecure. The case study does take that stance for the most part, but a crucial detail was overlooked when important user accounts were allowed to be used for WiFi authentication. Ideally users would use a totally different userID and password to log into the gateway, or at least a different password. Doubtlessly, the users would be unhappy, but that is a small price to pay for the added security. These accounts would no longer be so useful that someone might want to go through all the trouble of collecting them. All they do is give you access to the network itself rather than all the resources on the network.

Above all else, I believe this article demonstrates the extreme necessity of emphasizing to end users the importance of verifying that they are connected securely to the gateway before attempting to log in. Remember that this entire scenario relies on most users not realizing what is happening. While it cannot be reasonably expected for every WiFi user to become network competent, a little bit of knowledge can go a long way in improving your wireless security.

Many thanks go to aydiosmio and openfly for their help in exploring the possibilities of this idea.

Unlocking the Power of WAP (Spring, 2005) *By Josh D*

Let me just say out right that some of the ideas described in this article may *not* be perfectly legal; this article is meant to be educational, and if you attempt to execute any of the ideas presented here, I will take absolutely no responsibility for extra cellular charges you may incur or for any trouble you may get into with your cellular provider.

What Is WAP?

WAP is an acronym that stands for Wireless Access Protocol, which is (on a very basic level) the technology that a cellular phone uses to connect to the Internet. There are several WAP browsers and the one that will be described today is called Openwave, which comes preinstalled on a bunch of cell phones. I have personally seen Openwave in use on LG and Kyocera phones, but I'm sure these aren't the only phone brands that use Openwave.

Openwave is generally not that hard to tweak. Once the browser is running on a cell phone, one just has to press and hold down the zero button (or menu button depending on the phone manufacturer) on their phone until they are greeted with a menu full of everyday browser features, such as Reload and Bookmarks. The last item on the menu is "Advanced," which is where the configuration of your WAP setup will eventually end. If you're following along on your own cell phone and you're seeing what I'm describing, you most likely have a cell phone manufactured by LG or Kyocera and your cell phone company (if you live in the United States) is probably Verizon.

You'll notice that in the Advanced menu, there is an option called Set WAP Proxy. Keep this function in mind. A WAP Proxy is just an IP and a port that points to what's called a WAP gateway, a program running on a computer that acts as a gateway (hence the name) allowing a cell phone to connect to the wireless Internet. It's fairly easy to set up your own gateway, using your own computer's Internet connection. I use a gateway called WAP3GX, available at `http://www.wap3gx.com`.

A detailed explanation of configuration of a WAP gateway is beyond the scope of this article, but just know that the gateway (at least this is true for WAP3GX) listens on UDP ports 9200 and 9201 and that you'll need to configure your router and/or firewall accordingly to forward these ports to your computer. If you're too lazy or don't want to attempt to set up your own WAP gateway, you can just use a free, public WAP gateway found on the Net. For now, let's just assume you have acquired an IP and a port of an active WAP gateway. The next problem is just getting all of this information into your cell phone.

My main areas of expertise include cell phones made by LG and Kyocera, so I'll briefly describe how to get into the service menu of cell phones made by those respective companies. On the newer LG phones with color screens, when you hit the menu button from the home screen you'll notice there are nine menu choices from 1 to 9. Ever wondered why they didn't start at zero? Try hitting the zero button. You'll be asked to enter in a six-digit service code, which is usually all zeros. Now you're in the service menu of the phone, and I wouldn't touch anything you don't feel confident in messing around with, because it's pretty easy to render a phone unusable by entering in incorrect settings. You'll want to select WAP Setting from the service menu and then IP Setting. Select Link3-IP1. Write down what you see on a piece of paper in case something goes wrong (so that you can "reset" the phone to its default settings if you need to) and then replace the listed IP with the IP of your WAP gateway. (Don't enter the port.) Hit OK and then hit CLR. Select Port Setting from the menu, then select Link3-Port1, then again write down what you see, then enter in the port of your WAP gateway. Hit OK and then END. I have tested this method with LG VX4400 and VX6000 cell phones but it will work for other LG phones, although accessing the service menu might be a little different; you might have to press menu and zero at the same time, or press and hold menu and then press zero, or vice versa.

On the other hand, if you have a Kyocera phone, go to the home screen and enter in the number 111-111 like you were going to call that number. You'll see a menu option pop up on the bottom of the phone. Scroll until you see a menu item called Options, select it, and find another menu item called Browser Setup. This is basically the same as the LG setup from here, except instead of Links, there are Uplinks, and there are only two of them. Change the information in Uplink B to that of your WAP gateway.

The service menu is the trickiest part of this operation, and if you're having trouble entering settings or if you find my instructions inadequate or have a phone manufactured by a company other than LG or Kyocera, there is plenty of information about all this on the Internet. (`http://www.howardforums.com` is a good place to start.) Just search for "WAP."

The hardest part is now out of the way. Try reopening your WAP Web browser and change the active WAP Proxy (as described in the beginning of this article) to Proxy 3 if you have an LG phone or Proxy B if you have a Kyocera phone. If you see a page asking you to enable security features, it means that you haven't properly configured the browser to connect to your WAP gateway; you're still connecting to your cellular provider's gateway. If everything went according to plan, the phone should connect to your gateway and prompt for a default home page to display. Note that most of the WAP-enabled phones can browse through and display only WML (Wireless Markup Language) pages as opposed to HTML pages, so you'll need to go hunting for WML pages. Google's wireless WML page is located at `http://wap.google.com`, which is nifty for finding other WML sites. Wireless MapQuest is located at `http://wireless.mapquest.com/aolmq_wml`, and wireless Superpages is located at `http://wap.superpages.com/cgi/cs_client.cgi`, to name a few sites. All of these links would be entered into your cell phone at the prompt.

Browsing isn't the only thing you can do with WAP, however. If you use Cerulean Studio's multinetwork chat program, Trillian Pro (available at `http://www.trillian.cc/`), you can download a plug-in for Trillian called I.M. Everywhere, which is available at `http://www.iknow.ca/imeverywhere/`. This program is a miniature HTTP server (*not* a WAP gateway) that will let you IM anyone that is on your Trillian buddy list from your phone. Trillian supports ICQ, AIM, MSN Messenger, and Yahoo Messenger, which means that you will be able to IM all of your buddies on your phone without paying for text messages. I.M. Everywhere broadcasts in both WML and HTML so you would enter your own IP into the default home page prompt on your phone to get this working, or you could enter your IP into any Internet browser on a computer and use I.M. Everywhere to control Trillian remotely.

One very important thing to note is that WAP requires cellular airtime. You will be charged, in minutes of time spent on the wireless Web, for data transfer on your phone bill. There is no extra charge for wireless Internet (like there normally would be), only regular airtime "talking" minutes (at least with Verizon), which means that you will most likely have free WAP nights and weekends; instead of seeing a dialed number on your phone bill, you would just see "DATA TRANSFER." Your cellular provider will almost definitely not support doing what is outlined here; so if you're going to try any of this on your own, try it with caution. Again, I take absolutely no responsibility for extra cellular charges you may incur or for any trouble you may get into with your cellular provider if and when you try all of this. That said, have fun and I hope you learned something!

RFID: Radio Freak-Me-Out Identification (Spring, 2007)

By Kn1ghtl0rd

RFID has become something of a hot topic in the hacking world. There have been multiple presentations on security and privacy of RFID and also the technology behind it. This article is designed to be a what-if type scenario on what RFID is potentially capable of and where the technology is heading.

RFID stands for Radio Frequency Identification, which obviously means identifying objects using radio frequency. Current implementations include asset management, inventory control, inventory tracking, access control, and entity identification. The first three are usually implemented in a business environment to track inventory from one location to another or to monitor asset activity to isolate theft situations and problem areas. These implementations of RFID are very efficient and perform a valuable task for a business. The fourth example is not so good. RFID is being changed into a new type of ID for people and animals to be used instead of a hard-copy form of identification. This may seem convenient for people and they don't see why this is bad. There are many possibilities for this technology to turn our world upside down and allow for Big Brother to truly manifest itself.

Currently a human being can receive an implanted RFID chip that stores an identification number that associates them with information in a database. This can be anything from personal data such as name, address, and birth date to medical history, financial information, family information, etc. The cost of storage space now is so cheap that it wouldn't be out of the question to store just about every type of information on any one person so that any organization can utilize the technology imbedded in said person. If you don't get where I am going with this, then think a massive database with information on every person who has an implanted tag. Now you may say what is the big deal? There are already databases out there with our information. Why should one more be any different? Well the problem is this. Any database that contains that vast amount of information has to be controlled by someone. More than likely that someone will be the government. This may not seem so scary either. But wait, there is more.

RFID in its current implementations has been proven to be a reliable solution for tracking inventory. Change the word inventory to humans and you see the problem. The technology does not change from one implementation to the other. The data on the tag may change somewhat, but the fundamentals do not. So what is stopping the government from placing readers on every government owned piece of property and monitoring the activities of everyone with an implanted tag? Not a whole lot. Right now the cost for a reader is about $40 to $120 for a LF (low frequency) module. The government, being its omnipresent self, can get these devices for less or manufacture them for less and tailor the technology to act as it wishes. The cost for an implant is around $20 for the tag and the cost of implantation, which can vary from one doctor to another. There is not a whole lot stopping the government from doing this.

The possibilities are then endless for the data and scenarios that the government can observe. Not only can the government observe this information but so can anyone else who can figure out how to get the data off the tags. Since our country is basically run by huge retail outlets it is not too far of a stretch to see product marketing analysis based on human purchase activity that is all based on RFID technology. Picture walking into Wal-Mart and having the racks scan your RFID tags and create some kind of notice to you to point on items that you prefer based on past purchase history. You regularly buy black cotton t-shirts in size large so the rack will recognize this data and highlight the rack with the black cotton t-shirts with little lights attached to all the hangers that flash as you approach. The same can be said about shoes. You wear a size 13 so it shows you only the size 13 shoes in stock. Now take it one step further and say you purchase one of those pairs of shoes. The shoes themselves have an RFID tag imbedded in them so now not only can we see where you are going based on the implanted RFID tag, but we can also see that you bought your shoes from Wal-Mart and produce Wal-Mart advertising on interactive billboards as you pass by.

When you walk into a coffee shop they will already start making your favorite coffee because they got that information from your tag. This may seem cool, but then they ask you how your mother is doing because they saw on the report that she had come down with an illness and had to go to the hospital the day before and they now have her taking penicillin for an infection. That thought in itself is pretty scary. You don't want your local coffee house to know everything about you, do you? How can you even make a small decision like whether you want cream or not if they already know based on trends they have analyzed on your activity for the last fiscal year?

When everyone becomes a number we will see the true possibilities of this technology. A wealth of knowledge is attached to you and that information is accessible by way too many people for it not to be a little scary. There are good things that can come out of this, but is convenience better than privacy or free will? I think not.

MILESTONE: CHALLENGES (Spring, 2007)

Please believe us when we say that we don't intentionally set out to cause trouble and mayhem; they somehow seem to always find us.

We started a hacker magazine because it was a subject that was of interest to a number of us and there was a void to be filled. We didn't expect the fascination, fear, obsession, and demonization that followed us, courtesy of everyone from the media to the government, from the Fortune 500 to high school teachers and principals. It just sort of happened that way.

We didn't ask to be thrown into the front lines of the motion picture industry's copyright battles back in 2000. That also just happened because of who we were and what we believed in. There were many thousands that the Motion Picture Association of America could have taken to court for hosting the DeCSS code on their web sites. But we somehow epitomized everything the MPAA was against and this made us the perfect target for them. Merely existing apparently was enough.

And by simply being present at various pivotal moments in hacker history where there was nothing for us to do but speak out against various injustices, we again found ourselves being propelled into a position of advocacy and leadership, when really all we were doing was continuing to make the same points on what hacking was and what it was not. Locking people in prison for being overly curious or experimenting on the wrong bits of technology was just wrong, plain and simple. It was a point we had started our very first issue with. And since so few others were saying this out loud, it became our fight once more.

continues

MILESTONE: CHALLENGES *(continued)*

This kind of thing never seems to end. Also in the year 2000 while all eyes were on the Republican National Convention in Philadelphia, it was our own layout artist who was grabbed off the streets and locked up on $500,000 bail, charged with being a chief ringleader of opposition. The only evidence against him was surveillance footage that showed him walking down a street talking on a cell phone. Needless to say, it didn't stick and, in fact, a lawsuit against the city for this nonsense was quite successful. But even that wasn't the final chapter of the story. Four years later in New York, our editor was also taken off the streets while the Republican National Convention was in that city. This time it seemed to be a random sweep of people who just happened to be standing on a particular block. Again, it provoked widespread outrage and condemnation, as well as all charges being dropped and a lawsuit which continues to be argued in court to this day. But there's still more. Recently a judge ordered the New York Police Department (NYPD) to release internal documents on these events, which they had been trying to keep to themselves. These documents started to see the light of day in February of this year. And among the first to be revealed so far is a memo that outlines what one of their biggest fears was. Yes, that's right. Us again. Apparently the NYPD was concerned because not only was our layout artist rumored to be in town (possibly prepared to use his phone again) but he had spoken at a conference directly across the street from where the Republican Convention was to be held. And he had spoken on potential ways of causing mischief and mayhem! So once again we were catapulted to front and center, just for discussing the things that are of interest to us. Even the location of our conferences, held in the same place since 1994, was called into question as being provocative because they were so close to the site of the Republican Convention.

It all almost reads like a bad TV script, where the same characters keep getting launched into the center of attention week after week. In that kind of a setting, this happens because there are only a certain number of characters and the story lines have to be kept interesting and active. In real life, this only serves to demonstrate the threat of actually reaching people who may share your interests and goals. Not only can you change the course of history in accomplishing this but the fear you instill along the way among the powers-that-be might itself also have a profound effect on the outcome. Scary stuff indeed.

MILESTONE: CHALLENGES *(continued)*

But now we find ourselves yet again in a position where we have no choice but to take a stand and help start something that could have a profound effect on a lot of people. And this time it goes well beyond the hacker community. We learned earlier this year that the site of our conferences mentioned above—New York's historic Hotel Pennsylvania—is set to be demolished. As of this writing, the only opposition to this has been a whole lot of voices in the wilderness with no apparent unity. So once more it appears that our community will have to step up and hopefully make a difference.

Why should we care? Simple. Ever since starting the Hackers On Planet Earth conferences back in 1994, the Hotel Pennsylvania has been our home (with the exception of Beyond HOPE in 1997). It has three major factors going for it: 1) Location—the hotel is directly across the street from the busiest train station in North America and also centrally located in Manhattan; 2) History—the hotel is a fascinating connection to the past, both architecturally and in the many events and people who have been linked together over the decades in its vast hallways; and 3) Cost—the relative cheapness of the hotel is what makes it possible for us to continue to have the conferences in New York City as well as for our attendees from out of town to be able to stay there.

There was one thing that was drummed into our heads over and over again when we were looking to start a major hacker conference in the United States, especially in response to our desire to have it in New York: It was impossible. And to this day it remains impossible that we could hold an event of this size in a city like New York and manage to keep it affordable. But we do it anyway. It's because of a combination of magical ideas, the magical people who come and build it every two years, and the magical place that makes it all possible. This is all most definitely worth preserving.

XM—The Flawed Future of Radio (Spring, 2003) *By Acidus*

When people talk about XM Radio, they tend to talk about things like its compression and encryption algorithms, its quality, its content, and how to get it all for free. But everyone is missing the big picture: XM isn't important because of its technology or the exploitation thereof. XM is important because it is the dominant player in a brand new industry. Only two companies have licenses for satellite radio and both use approximately the same infrastructure. This means the dominant company's architecture will be the platform for future services transmitted to cars. While taking advantage of existing flaws to save $10 a month is trivial now, the insecurities inherent in the platform could cause some serious problems down the road. Streaming pay-per-view movies to video systems, local traffic reports with GPS, email and limited Web browsing, and Voice over IP are all coming to cars in the next decade. The flaws in XM's infrastructure need to be addressed and fixed now before security is sacrificed later on for profits and backwards compatibility.

XM Overview

There are a lot of myths about XM, so let's clear them up. XM radios are exactly like normal radios in that they receive electromagnetic waves and translate them into information. XM receives its signal from two satellites and, in heavily populated areas, ground-based broadcasters. Normal radio simply has ground-based broadcasters. The info in a normal radio signal is analog and encoded using AM or FM. The info in XM is in digital form, compressed to allow better quality in less space, and the signal is encoded using a proprietary encryption scheme. Just like normal radios, XM has an antenna that receives the signal. You must have an antenna capable of receiving the signal to even get it. You tune to different frequencies to hear different stations on normal radio; all of the XM channels are on one range of frequencies. Think of XM as simply one radio station with lots of programs. Your XM radio then takes the entire stream of channels and extracts the one channel you want to listen to and decodes/decompresses it.

Signal Transmission

XM is broadcast from two Boeing satellites, aptly named "Rock" and "Roll." From 22,000 miles up, they pump out 70 megawatts of signal, painting nearly all of North America. While it is offered only in the U.S. (due to licensing) the signal can be received in most of Canada, Mexico, the Caribbean, and even parts of Alaska. There is no way for the radios to transmit any data to either the satellites or the ground repeaters. This one-way approach offers several fundamental problems with the system:

- All XM signals are received by all XM radios. There are currently no means of "spot beaming" signals to only local areas (as DirecTV does to offer local channels). This means there can be no generic activation signal, etc. It must be personalized to your radio ID (on the bottom of the radio). This eats up more bandwidth.
- Since all radios receive the same signal, all radios use the same decryption keys. From the other end, you could say that based on the limited bandwidth XM has (which we will discuss later), they can't transmit the same channel at

the same time with two different encryption keys. Thus there is only one encrypted signal sent, and all radios must decode it.

- Since none of the radios can transmit, control over them can only be one way. They have no way of knowing if the activation signal, deactivation signal, or decryption keys have been received by your unit. The only way XM will know of any problems is if you call them.

The Signal

This is the bottleneck for XM. The FCC licensed only 12.5MHz to XM, from 2332.5MHz to 2345.0MHz. They have 100 channels (well 101, which I'll get to later), which means that they only have 125KHz of bandwidth for each channel. In contrast, FM radio stations have 200KHz. XM advertises that they have "near CD quality sound." While I don't want to get into how that's an impossible statement, it does mean that they need to take an audio signal of significantly higher quality than an FM radio signal and make it fit into 125KHz. In fact, when you count in the artist/song name/album info displayed for every channel, as well as control signals being sent from the satellite, each channel has even less bandwidth.

The signal contains two types of information, which I call broadcast info and personalized info. Broadcast info is a signal that all radios are supposed to get and act on (such as the channels). Personalized info is information that they intended for only one radio, and thus all personalized info is tagged with your Radio ID. Examples are activation signals and deactivation signals. Don't get confused by this. All radios receive the entire signal and the radios use the broadcast in any personalized info if it's tagged with that radio's ID. If not, the data is ignored, just like IP packets on a network. If/when the type of content is expanded, this could be a way to packet sniff XM, though it would require lots of knowledge of the hardware. If someone attempts to implement a software decoder, this could be easy.

The signal is incredibly redundant. Error checking between the two signals from the two satellites is done to try and determine what is noise. (Ground-based repeater signals are also analyzed if present.) The signal itself uses dual Reed-Solomon codes and Viterbi codes. These are powerful error checking systems commonly used in satellite transmissions. They both work only on blocks of data, which seems to imply that the encryption algorithm is block based instead of stream based.

According to an XM engineer, due to the overhead caused by encryption, the signal is sometimes compressed after it is encrypted. ST Microelectronics makes the chipsets for XM radios. The STA400 channel decoder handles all the nastiness of converting the satellite signal into digital form, checking it for errors, and decrypting it. The STA450 source decoder decompresses the audio and handles volume and tone control. The fact that the decryption circuits are in the chip that receives the signal first seems to imply that the signal is almost always encrypted after it has been compressed.

Compression

The number of theories of the compression schemes that XM uses is around the number of Grassy Knoll theories. MP2, MP3, AMBE, AAC, the list goes on and on. A few things are known. XM Radio had a contract with Digital Voice Systems Inc. to use their AMBE (Advanced Multi-Band Excitation) speech compression algorithm. The XM Radio customer agreement states that the AMBE technology in their product is copyrighted and licensed for their use. That makes it safe to say that AMBE is used at least in part to compress the speech-only channels. Since the STA450 has a built-in EPAC decoder, it is safe to assume that at least a bulk of the music is encoded with this algorithm. This conforms to a claim made by an XM engineer that their compression technology is similar to Mpeg-4.

Encryption

The only really complex part of XM is the encryption. Nothing is known about the encryption algorithm. It is supposedly proprietary, but even its key length isn't published. It is implemented in hardware and works on blocks instead of streams. The keys are dynamic, and new keys are sent to the radio through control signals from the satellites. Your radio must be on to receive any signal including the new keys (based on the fact that you must have your radio on and be able to hear the preview channel to activate your radio). Assuming Flaw 2 is correct, XM needs to be damn sure everyone has the new keys before they switch the signal. They could be broadcasting the new keys for a long time before they implement them (perhaps even a month or two early). These could be sent as broadcast information and all radios would store them. If you didn't have your radio on for several months and reported the loss of signal to XM customer service, they could simply upload a request to the satellite to transmit personalized data to you containing the new key. Perhaps new keys are only broadcast once or twice a year and an aging algorithm in the radio changes it at set intervals until the new codes are transmitted. Further testing with an XM radio would help answer these questions.

However the keys are transmitted, they are stored on what an XM engineer called an "SS Decoder" (Source Secure? Sound Secure? Something like that). He stated this was tamper-resistant RAM in the radio. It was not removable like a flash card, which he said "is where DirecTV screwed up." Supposedly the SS Decoder will erase/destroy itself if someone attempts to remove it.

Activation

Let's step through the activation of an XM radio.

1. You buy the radio and turn it on. The radio checks itself and sees that it has not received an activation signal from the satellite, and thus only lets you listen to the preview channel (Channel 1).
2. You call XM customer service or use their web site and submit the radio ID on the bottom of your XM radio. The XM system tells the two satellites (and perhaps even all the ground-based transmitters since they don't know what city you're in) to transmit an activation signal for your radio.
3. Since the signal is going to be received by every XM radio in the U.S., it is personalized with your radio ID. This activation signal is broadcast every ten minutes for the next 60 hours.
4. You turn on your radio and await the signal. Once it gets the signal, your radio can receive all of XM's channels.

Examining the amount of bandwidth they have and the amount of content they deliver, we can conclude that XM has very little left over to send commands to the radio (such as new decryption keys, control signals, etc.). Indeed, the fact that they only transmit the activation signal every ten minutes for 60 hours supports this. If you never get this signal, you call XM and they will broadcast it again.

Exploitation

So what happens when you cancel your service? Well, basically the same thing. XM broadcasts a cancellation signal, which tells your radio to stop receiving the full XM content. Again this signal must be personalized to your radio ID. But what if your radio never gets the cancellation signal? Bingo. While I have no XM radio to test this with, the sheer overhead in having to transmit personalized cancellation signals for every radio that has canceled service on a regular basis is simply too great a task for the limited bandwidth they have. Granted, they probably transmit a cancellation signal less often over a longer number of hours (such as once an hour for 360 hours), but it's simply too much overhead to keep it up for long. XM's security could be defeated by something as simple as turning the radio off for a month.

Further Strain

XM is now offering premium channels, currently only the Playboy Channel. It doesn't replace an existing channel. So now the limited bandwidth must be divided up even more finely to allow for another station. This doesn't even include the added overhead of all the personalized signals telling radios all over the country to allow access to the premium channels. This will sadly lower quality on all the channels for all the users, even those who aren't paying for the additional channel. They can only push so much through the pipe they have. Now XM doesn't have to allocate the same space to talk stations as music stations, and indeed an online debate rages on how XM assigns the bandwidth to channels: dynamic or static. Regardless of how they do it, adding the Playboy Channel will produce much more overhead on this already strained system. This may force XM to reduce the length of time it will transmit control data. For customer service reasons, they won't cut the time activation signals are broadcast, so deactivation signals would be the first to go, making the system easier to exploit.

XM's Future

XM's stock is one-sixth its IPO. While it is meeting its customer goals (currently around 300,000 subscribers), it is still losing money. They have a big contract with GM and several 2003 models come with XM standard or as an option. The big bad wolf of the radio biz Clear Channel has a good deal invested in XM. Even if it tanks, the expensive part—the infrastructure of the system—is already in place. The system would be purchased for pennies on the dollar and the services restarted. Satellite-delivered content for cars isn't going away.

If you want to use my article to cheat XM out of $10 a month, you missed the point. If you want to use the info to try and open source a decoder, that would be a pretty cool graduate thesis. (An XM antenna would be necessary, along with some interface equipment from Gnu Radio Project, and some spare time.) XM needs to make sure the next generation of its services has some form of two-way communication. I envision using G3 cell phones for upstream and the satellite for downstream, just like satellite modems. XM's delivery system needs to change as more services are going to be delivered to cars, and chances are it will contain much more important information than Rick Dees and the Weekly Top 40.

Final Words

Thanks to all the folks who I got to hang out with and who listened to me talk at Interz0ne and Phreaknic, especially rockit, JohnnyX, Virgil, Strick, psyioded, James Dean, JaneLane, Optyx, specwhore, SD, and Freqout.

Harnessing the Airwaves—A Pirate Radio Primer (Winter, 2001-2002) *By Mark12085*

This article is in no way condoning the practice of illegal radio broadcasting. Read on at your own risk....

Let me start off by letting you know that this article alone will not get you on your merry way to the airwaves. Radio, especially unlicensed low-power transmitting, is a complicated subject. Please do some research and plan wisely. The airwaves are for everyone to use, so don't abuse them.

Arr Ye Matey

The phrase "pirate radio" seems to strike fear in the public. Seems like pirate radio has always had a connotation of brute guerillas seizing national airwaves and replacing it with propaganda. That couldn't be any further from the truth. Pirate radio is simply transmitting radio frequency energy through the air at low power—minuscule compared to the licensed stations spewing kilowatts of power from antenna towers. Unfortunately the Federal Communications Commission seems to believe that they own our air, therefore anyone who does not have a spare $10,000 floating around to go through the licensing process must be raided. Too bad for them, because air is free.

A Heart of Gold

The heart of any station is the transmitter. FM oscillator, broadcaster, exciter—they are all the same thing, just different names. Basically, there are two types of transmitters available: VCO and PLL. VCO, voltage controller oscillator, is just that: an RF oscillator controlled by the voltage. While cheaper (around $50 for one-watt models), it will drift off the frequency it is set to transmit on as voltages, temperature, and settings change. That means if you set it to broadcast at 100.0MHz, you may find it transmitting at 101.2 an hour later. PLL (phase-locked loop) transmitters, while a bit more costly (roughly $40 more than VCO), are a much better deal. They are controlled via microcontrollers, which means they will never drift off frequency.

Most transmitters come in two types: mono or stereo. While a stereo transmitter is slightly more expensive, it is still more economical and space-saving than adding a stereo encoder to a mono setup. Think before you buy about which setup would be right for you.

While great for broadcasting around the house, simple transistor or BA1404 chip based transmitters are *not* sufficient for professional grade radio. They were designed specifically for short-distance broadcasting, so let them do their appropriate job.

Transmitters can be purchased ready-built or in kit form. Kits usually include the PCB, parts, and instructions. Do not attempt a kit unless you are *truly* experienced with soldering SMD parts and RF emitting devices. PCS Electronics and NRG Kitz both carry high-quality transmitters of varied outputs.

Power to the People

A transmitter would be useless if it had nothing to run on. Most transmitters require a power source. PCS Electronics makes a computer card transmitter that plugs into a free ISA or PCI slot, so that would be an exception. A plug-in "wallwart" transformer is *not* a sufficient power source. Remember, the quality of the power determines the quality of the transmission. You will need a well-regulated, well-filtered power supply, like the ones designed for CB and ham radios. (RadioSlack sells one for about $30.) A 12-volt car battery will also work. Just be sure to keep it maintained.

Spread the Love

Although it may not seem like it, the antenna is the most vital part of a station. A 1-watt station with a well-built antenna can easily supersede a 25-watt station with a crap-tenna. The easiest and most common antenna is the dipole, which is basically two wires going out in opposite directions cut according to the frequency you are transmitting on. There are loads of other great antennas that are easy to build, such as the ground plane, J-pole, slim jim, and on and on. I will not go into detail about building the perfect antenna because there are tons of sites devoted only to antennas (check out the list later on) and books on the same subject.

Most antennas are either omnidirectional or directional. Omnidirectional antennas, such as the dipole and 5/8 ground plane, transmit in all directions. Directional antennas on the other hand spew RF in one direction.

While we're on the topic of antennas, don't forget to invest in a good SWR (standing wave ratio) meter. The SWR measurement is probably the single most important factor in determining the effectiveness of your antenna. Although cheap SWR meters made for CB radios will work for our setup, they will be far from accurate. Try to aim for an SWR of 2:1 or lower. An SWR reading of 1.5:1 would be theoretically perfect, but realistically impossible.

Putting It All Together

Connecting everything together is not quite as simple as a length of RadioShrek coax. Firstly, the impedance of the coax has to match the parts you are connecting them to, usually either 50 ohm or 75 ohm. Secondly, cheap coax results in cheap connections—line loss. Line loss is literally losing your transmitter energy out of the cable as heat. Line loss increases as the length of the coax increases. Therefore, use as short of a length of coax as you can. Also, use high-quality, well-shielded cable, such as Belden cable.

Staying Low

You don't have to be a genius to figure out the fact that unlicensed radio broadcasting at more than about 10 milliwatts is illegal. And yes, they *can* pinpoint your location while you are transmitting. Prevention is the key. *Use your head.* Ninety percent of all the pirates busted were caught because they were transmitting crap in other frequencies due to a shoddy setup. Don't forget, the aircraft band is directly above the FM band. Filters (bought or built) are strongly recommended to block out harmonics you may be transmitting. *Stop* transmitting if the FCC contacts you or if you see any suspicious cars circling the neighborhood. If your budget allows, look into a microwave link for your station. A microwave link allows you to operate your transmitter from a distance varying from a couple of hundred yards to miles. Now it is up to you to do your own research on what would be best for your setup. The sites listed below not only sell high-quality transmitters but contain loads of free information on your setup. You might also want to check out some books from the American Radio Relay League (ARRL). Be smart, and happy transmitting.

Reference

ARRL Handbook for Radio Amateurs

ARRL Antenna Handbook

`http://www.nrgkitz.com`—Lots of useful info, transmitters, amps, etc.

`http://www.ramseyelectronics.com`—High-quality products if you have a fat wallet....

Greetz to: TCRams, Zero, FooGoo, ILFs, Ferntheil, APCm, and 2600.

Scanning the Skies (Winter, 2007-2008) *By GutBomb*

The pursuit of knowledge and understanding of the way things work doesn't need to be limited to computers and telephones. We are being bombarded on a constant basis by microwaves from mobile phone towers, radio transmitters, television broadcast towers, and even from satellites thousands of miles above the earth's equator. These satellites are the focus of this article.

Using a system that only costs about $300, you can explore the exciting world of satellite TV broadcasts from the comfort of your own couch (and the roof of your house from time to time). Sports backhauls, news feeds, syndication uplinks, foreign programming, unbiased news, government propaganda, weather reports, Internet access, totally free (free as in beer *and* as in speech) programming, and most importantly, a greater understanding of how the broadcast world works are already being blasted towards you every minute of every day, so why not have some fun?

The Clarke Belt

Television satellites are all lined up along the equator of the Earth. When seen from the Earth's surface, they form an arc across the southern sky known as the Clarke Belt, after science fiction pioneer Arthur C. Clarke. The arc contains more than 80 satellites that usually have a name identifying them and a number that corresponds with the longitude meridian they are on. For example, the main Dish Network satellite is known as Echostar 6/8 and it sits in a geosynchronous orbit over the 110 degrees West longitude line. It is often referred to as 110w (read, "one-ten-west").

Broadcast Bands

There are three broadcast bands commonly used for satellite television distribution. The Ku-band is the most common method of satellite broadcasting in the country. It is used by both major direct-to-home satellite services (DirecTV and Dish Network) as well as by independent satellite bandwidth providers. Ka-band is a newer technology that has been used for years to distribute satellite Internet access and satellite radio but has recently started making inroads to video distribution. Finally, there is classic C-band, which the major networks use for distributing their channel feeds to other satellite providers and cable companies. C-band requires very large dishes, the smallest of which are nearly 6 feet across. Ku- and Ka-band signals can be pulled in with much smaller dishes, approximately 30 inches across, which are easily mounted on a roof or wall.

Video Standards

Much of the available video up there is now digital. Over the past ten years, most analog video has disappeared on the Ku-band, but you can still find a bit available on C-band. In the case of video distribution, digital does not always mean better. A good standard definition feed on C-band will almost always be better than a digital feed of the same channel because it is the master feed. By the time it reaches your cable or direct-to-home satellite system, it has been encoded digitally, compressed, and bit-starved to the point of looking like a pixelated mess. Analog, however, is a huge bandwidth hog, and prone to interference, so along the way, things progressed more to providing digital feeds. An analog channel takes the same space as up to 20 digital channels, and when satellite providers can provide more bandwidth for channel distribution, they get more money from channel producers. Analog programs are just regular NTSC feeds in North America, and can be picked up by cheap analog receivers.

In the digital realm, the possibilities of what you can find expand greatly. So do the difficulties in initially finding the signal and the expense in getting proper equipment. The main digital standard used for satellite TV in North America is called DVB-S. Most of the world uses DVB variants for their digital television distribution, such as DVB-S for satellite, DVB-T for terrestrial, and DVB-C for cable. In North America we use ATSC for digital terrestrial, and QAM for digital cable.

Equipment

The bare minimum setup you would need to get started is a satellite dish, a TV, and a satellite receiver. The dish is usually a parabolic dish that sits on a mast, with an arm shooting out from the bottom, which holds the eye pointing back at the dish. This eye is called a LNB (Low Noise Block). There are a few types of LNBs available. A DirecTV/Dish Network dish contains a circular LNB. Circular refers to the shape of the microwaves being beamed towards it. Circular LNBs pick up spiral-shaped beams.

These are beamed out at very high power, so the dish itself doesn't need to be very big to pull in the signal. Unfortunately, these LNBs aren't suited to picking up the really cool stuff out there, and the dishes they are attached to are a bit too small, usually between 18 and 20 inches.

For the cool stuff, you will need a linear LNB. The term linear, like circular, refers to the type of beam it takes in. Linear beams are less powerful and more prone to weather interference, so they require larger dishes. A certain type of linear LNB that can attain frequencies slightly lower than a regular linear LNB is called a universal LNB. The disadvantage to universal LNBs is that not all switches are compatible with them. There are plenty of newer switches, however, that work perfectly, and if you have a single dish system, then you most likely won't need switches anyway.

If you have more than one LNB that you want to connect to your receiver, then you will need to obtain a switch. The best switches to use are called DISEqC switches. (I have no idea how to pronounce this out loud. I say "diz-e-q-c," but I am probably wrong.) You can hook four LNBs into the switch, and then just run a single cable down to the receiver.

The LNB I prefer is called the Invacom QPH-031 and you can pick it up for about $80 at any of a number of shops on the Internet. It can pick up both circular and universal beams and has two outputs for each. An LNB this fancy is not necessary, however; a cheap $15 universal LNB would be fine for a beginner just getting started.

The dish is an important consideration. A small 18-inch dish won't really do for us, because there are only a few channels available to us legitimately without subscribing to or decrypting an encrypted signal. (This is possible, but not the focus of this article.) Ideally, the best dish to get started with would be 30 inches or larger. I opted for a Fortec FC90P 90cm (36-inch) dish. The dish will come with a mast that you can mount on your roof or on a wall, the reflecting dish, and the LNB arm, but you will have to supply the LNB yourself. This dish will set you back about $100, including shipping.

The receiver is where stuff gets really fun, at least for me. I personally have two receivers. The first is a digital DVB receiver, and then I loop out from it to an old analog receiver. For digital, you have many choices, and unfortunately the market is a bit saturated right now, because these digital receivers can also be used for not-so-legitimate purposes. If you only want to be legit, I recommend the Pansat 2500A receiver. Though it is now discontinued, there are tons of them available on eBay for about $50 to $70. It has a very reliable blind-scan feature, which is essential for finding wild feeds.

If you are looking for analog, you may have a much harder time finding a receiver, because they are old and rare. I recently found an analog satellite receiver from the '80s with which you can just dial up the entire map of frequencies for only $32 shipped. I didn't have a C-band setup so there wasn't very much to find, but the things I did find were pretty interesting: some soccer, college basketball, an outdoor ice hockey game played on a pond, and an FBI training video. Any analog satellite receiver from the Uniden Supra line is highly recommended.

Finally, the last piece of equipment you really won't want to live without is a dish motor. This motor will tilt and pan your dish automatically, so you don't have to go up on the roof every time you want to look at a different satellite. A motor can be found online for about $100. You put your dish on the motor, put the motor on the mast, and point the entire assembly to the satellite closest to true south from your current position. Once you peak your signal there, you can use a feature of the Pansat called USALS that will automatically track the other satellites across the Clarke Belt based on that initial true south positioning. It's amazing to see it in action. My motor of choice is the Stab HH90.

Let's Scan the Skies

Here is where the magic happens. You've got your system all set up, your dish is pointed to true south, you've got your USALS all set up, and you've got your remote in hand. The fun in this is figuring it out, so this won't be a how-to. To point you in the right direction of satellite positions, I recommend `http://www.lyngsat.com`, a listing of satellites around the world and the channels that they contain. Using your receiver, you will tell your dish to point at a specific satellite based on its position (such as 97 degrees West) and blind-scan it. "Blind-scan" will find all channels on the satellite, including full-time channels, data feeds, radio channels, and Wildfeeds. Wildfeeds are on-the-spot news reports that are being sent back to the network, which include times when the reporter is "off the air" while their hair is being fixed, they practice their lines, or have candid conversations with the camera crew. You may also find training videos that are broadcast to government agencies and schools around the country. If you're a sports fan, you'll love the sports Wildfeeds, which are direct from the stadium broadcasts before they go back to the network. You'll sometimes find these without graphics, commercials, and, more rarely, even without the annoying commentators!

News feeds show up a lot on SBS6 (74w), NASA TV is available on 119w with a circular LNB, and PBS has some network feeds on AMC3 (87w). Aside from Wildfeeds, among the other programming available on these satellites (especially 97w) is a ton of foreign programming. You can get an international perspective on news, hit Bollywood movies, sports that aren't normally aired in this region, and just a huge dose of international culture. The real fun is exploring, so I'll leave you to it!

Conclusion

There are tons of things waiting for you to find them up there. Finding something strange and interesting gives me an awesome feeling, and I feel better knowing that I've explored the system enough to gain a greater understanding of the satellite world as a whole. For more information on the topic, check out these great links:

Lyngsat Satellite Index:

`www.lyngsat.com`

Satelliteguys FTA/MPEG Forum:

`www.satelliteguys.us/free-air-fta-discussion/`

Shout outs: sxtxixtxcxh, trollsb, my lovely wife Hypher, and JemsTV who helped me out with this article.

Real-World Stuff

Most of the world tends to think of hackers as people who spend all of their time at home staring at computer screens. Granted, there is a lot of that. But it would be wrong to assume there's not a good deal more. Basically, when you get into the hacker mindset, the potential exists to hack just about *anything*. Here we have a few examples ranging from ATMs to electronic signs to automobiles to locks. In fact, lock picking has been around forever and is probably the best example of "real-world" hacking that's out there. It looks glamorous but requires a lot of patience, skill, and time. As with any hack, those who possess the desire and invest the time are the ones who ultimately achieve their goals.

NCR ATMs (Summer, 2002)

Aurum Ex Machina By Acidus

So I was out at a mall and I needed some cash and I walked up to an ATM at Lenox Mall. It was a PNC Bank ATM, and I couldn't help but wonder why a bank from Pittsburgh had ATMs in a mall in Georgia. Anyway, something was wrong with it, and it appeared that a repairman must have been working on it because the screen showed some kind of configuration program. It looked a lot like the BIOS config screen on any PC.

The screen had something like eight options, things like change system time, change system data, change drive settings, print config, and reboot. These options were printed along the sides of the screen next to the buttons. I pushed the button next to "print config" (or something like that), and instead of taking me to a screen to configure the thermal printer, the ATM hummed for a second, and out of the receipt printer came a printout of the current configuration of the machine. Here is the printout word for word:

```
                PNC BANK

***** 01/01/07 12:19:19 *****

SETUP

DATE (YY/MM/DD)    07/01/01
TIME (HH:MM:SS)    12:19:20
FLEX DRIVE A       1.44MB
FLEX DRIVE B       NONE
DRIVE 1 TYPE       127
DRIVE 2 TYPE       NONE
TOTAL MEMORY (KB) 16000
COPROCESSOR        YES
```

Other than the "Flex" thing, this looked just like the specs of a simple computer. I didn't want to change the date or anything, and I couldn't do much at this screen. I knew I didn't have much time, and the "reboot" option looked really good. So I hit it and the machine went blank. And nothing happened. Then it whirled to life, and in the top-left counter I saw numbers: 4096, 8192, all the way up to 16000. Hello *post!* Then what should my wondrous eyes see but "Phoenix BIOS Ver 4.something or other." The machine then did some kind of check on its Flex drives and then a big IBM logo came up. In the bottom on the screen it said "IBM OS/2 Version 3. Government" There was something after "Government," but the screen was smeared with something so god awful, I sure as hell wasn't going to touch it. The screen cleared and then the words "Load 40" came up, at which point the screen went to 40 columns. At this point I started attracting serious attention and decided I should go. As I left I saw the machine default into the setup program again.

I had always thought ATMs had specialized hardware and crazy stuff like that, not a PC running OS/2 of all things. The more I researched the weirder it was. ATMs are quite a complex blend of software and hardware, and a comprehensive study of them is beyond the scope of this article. However, information on ATMs and their specifics is (for obvious reasons) very hard to come by. This should clear some of the mystery up.

Hardware

The standard computer equipment available on an NCR ATM is: a Pentium processor (speeds from 100 to 166), RAM (16MB to 32MB), a 1.2-gig IDE hard drive, one 1.44MB flex drive (it's just a floppy), a 10-inch VGA color or monochrome monitor (notice VGA, not SVGA, so it's only doing 320x200x256), and RS-232 port. Optional parts include a sound card (to play digitized speech), an IDE CD-ROM to store the speech (speeds range from 6x to 24x), a second Flex drive, and other banking-specific hardware (a better thermal printer for receipts, currency cassettes, etc.).

I found the RS-232 interface a great thing to hack. It is there to allow remote video card systems to be controlled by the ATM. However, this is a rarely used option. RS-232 is extremely well documented but sadly slow. On the other hand, ATMs have really weird connectivity. The NCR ATMs I researched (Personas and 5xxx series) didn't support TCP/IP. They had weird protocols like NCR/ISO Async, IBM 3275 Bisync, and a lot of other very obscure stuff. RS-232 is the only guaranteed way to move lots of data on and off the system.

There is a lot of banking-specific hardware in these things. I don't want to fill this article with specs of currency cassettes or mag card canisters. If you are interested, check my references. The only thing of interest is a DES Hardware encryption system.

Software

The operating system running on the ATMs is OS/2 Version 3. (I have since seen versions of OS/2 Warp for sale for ATMs as well.) I know next to nothing about OS/2, so study on your own if you want. I do know however that OS/2 is used for its multitasking abilities.

The main NCR programming running is something called the Self Service System Software (S4). This keeps a log on the hard drive of "all significant customer and supervisor activity." It also manages all the applications such as the communications software and the graphical display. S4 has an API programmers can use called ADI. ADI handles things like memory allocation and access to the file system. However, programmers can call OS/2's API directly. These machines use FAT as their file system and, since it's IBM, it is most likely still FAT16. Other software running on these ATMs is NCR Direct Connect, which seems to be the interface to the communications. (It handles the protocols, and can convert between them or emulate other ATMs.)

The software running on the ATMs could be pretty old. I mean, the diagnostics asked if I had a coprocessor to enable. Math coprocessors have been standard inside processors since 386DXs and 486DXs. Also, NCR offers a book for Pascal programmers to develop applications for the ATM.

ATM software is developed on standard PCs, and since they use Intel x86 Pentium class processors with a standard DOS-based operating system, anything that doesn't use Windows API calls should work. In fact, a lot of Windows 3.x programs work in OS/2. A good rule of thumb: if it works in DOS, it will work in OS/2.

Communication

Communication in the ATM is conducted through leased lines, though some ATMs in less high traffic areas may still use dial-up. By federal law all information traveling on these lines must be encrypted. The NCR ATMs use DES.

Alarms

Alarms on the ATM mainly protect against a physical attack. These are the mechanical and thermal alarms, and they make sure you don't take a crowbar or a blowtorch to the money door. However, NCR does have an enhanced alarm system, which protects the Flex disk drive door. This enhanced version also has seismic sensors. However, unplugging the ATM or rebooting it a lot shouldn't mess anything up.

Conclusions

There is a lot more info about ATMs and you can check my references. I have no desire to try and steal money from them so I never really looked at the data lines or ways to intercept key presses inside the machine. However, my research shows that the computer part of the ATM, since it uses standard PC parts, is vulnerable. I rebooted it for god's sake. I wish I knew the OS/2 equivalent of <F5>, which would have let me interrupt the boot and get to a command prompt. The machines most hackable are in malls and other public places. These have much less armor plating and other countermeasures and instead rely on their exposure to protect them. If you look like you know what you are doing, no one will question you. Who would like to put anti-virus software on an ATM? With a little research about OS/2 and how it loads, you could easily drop out of the boot-up and get to a command prompt. Using the floppy and the RS-232 port (or better yet a CD-ROM if it's there), you could install your own software. How cool would it be to have an ATM running Doom?

References

NCR PersonaS 88 ATM System Description: Got the bulk of my info from this. Found it after a ton of searching on a cached Google page of NCR's Russian web site. I don't think they wanted this out in the public, but I got it and moved it to my site.

The Banker's Exchange: They sell ATM parts and accessories. Used them to check on parts: `http://www.bankersx.com/`

The idiots at Lenox: for leaving the ATM in diagnostic mode.

Hacking Electronic Message Centers (Autumn, 2002)

By Mr. Glenn Frog

One type of electronic sign that has been around for a while and is gaining popularity is the "electronic message center." These can be found damn near anywhere but are particularly common with schools and other government buildings. The type of message center that is the subject of this article is made by Electronic Display Systems (`www.eds.chiefind.com`) and is the most common, at least here in Detroit. The best way to find out whether or not they supply signs to your area is to check the list of resellers that they provide on their site. Resellers will also be more than happy to provide a list of their signs in operation to an "interested customer," which should provide you with plenty of test subjects.

The Setup

Each of these signs is controlled by a V4 box. These are small beige boxes that hold the messages for the sign in RAM and send the appropriate messages to the sign when they are needed. The sign controllers are contacted by a computer for configuration through either a direct serial connection, radio modem, or dialup modem. The V4 box is generally either located inside the sign or in the same building as the PC used for configuration. There can also be any number of extender boxes located between the actual PC and sign controller. It's not at all uncommon to have communications routed through a mix of direct connect and radio modems. This setup is incredibly insecure as absolutely no authentication takes place within the sign controller. The only time any authentication is required is within the configuration software. This means that if you manage to get a copy of the software and get a connection to the sign, you're in.

The Software

The computers used to configure the sign run EDS's SystemOne software. This can be run on either MS-DOS or Windows and can easily be obtained by social engineering it out of EDS or one of their resellers. It's also likely that you can find it over the giFT or Kazaa p2p networks. The software comes with an installation CD and a configuration floppy. The software will run without the configuration floppy; however, it will be running in a demo mode that only allows for creating schedules and message files, not communicating with signs.

The software requires a password to open and requires yet another password to establish communications with the sign. These are both set to "m2000" by default, which as far as I know stands for Message Center 2000. Once inside the software you can configure it to communicate with your type of sign, create messages, create schedules, and finally upload them to the sign controller. I won't go in depth with the process of creating message files and creating schedules as both of these should be fairly easy for the computer savvy individual to pick up on. Now let's go on to all the different ways to establish communication with the sign.

Radio Modem

The easiest signs to spot and communicate with are radio signs. These can all be identified by either small black curly omnidirectional antennas or the even more conspicuous directional antenna. All you need to communicate with these is a copy of the configuration software and your own radio modem. The radio modem distributed by EDS is a 2.4GHz Hopnet 500, though I don't doubt that any 2.4GHz radio modem would do just fine. Once you've spotted your antenna, simply pick a spot with line of sight to the antenna (adjusting your position if the antenna is directional) and fire up your SystemOne software. From here select Software Configuration from the options menu. Select Radio Modem from the Sign Communication combo box and accept the default initialization string—wn0, wp0—which means address 0, signal power normal. Feel free to set the power to wp1 if you want to be able to communicate with the sign from a longer distance, though in most cases wp0 should be just fine. Next, check to see that you have the correct COM port selected to communicate with your radio modem. At this point OK your configuration changes and select communications from the options menu. Don't worry if the first attempt to connect fails, these connections can sometimes be unstable and are prone to interference. If the first address fails, simply change the address string to wn1 and try again. Keep repeating this process up to wn8 and you should eventually establish a connection and have full control over the sign. When you finally establish communication you're most likely to get an error saying that your row and column settings are wrong and it will give you the correct information. Go back into the software configuration dialog and set these accordingly.

Remote Modem (Dialup)

These are harder to spot than radio modems and you'll actually have to get up close to the sign to spot it and you may or may not have to actually open up the sign. Signs that are likely to be run off of dialup are generally signs that are located very far away from the configuration PC, such as a sign owned by the city set in the middle of a park. If you suspect that a sign is being controlled remotely, inspect for any visible RJ-11 around the base of the sign. Failing this, you can actually remove the panel and light display and look for the sign controller box in the sign. The panels that house the sign controllers will usually be labeled for the convenience of the sign technicians. Upon finding any bare RJ-11 or finding the sign controller, simply patch yourself into the line and call your favorite ANI or ANAC. You'll then get the number of the sign controller. The easier and much less conspicuous way to go about this would be to simply war dial the owner's exchange until you find it. Once you have the sign's number, start your SystemOne software, open up the software configuration, and set the connection type to remote. Now open the Communications dialog and Connect.

Direct Connect

Sign controllers that are hooked directly to the user's PC are generally hard to touch. These are connected by serial cable to the sign controller and then fiber optic cable is run from the sign controller all the way out to the sign. The only practical way to connect to these is to have physical access to the sign controller or the computer which configures the sign controller.

TCP/IP via COM Port Redirector

This setup is becoming popular amongst organizations that own multiple message centers, especially local governments. A COM port redirector is essentially a small box that is placed on a network and connects directly to a sign controller or radio modem allowing an administrator to control the sign from any location on their WAN or LAN. With the poor authentication scheme unfortunately, this means anyone with the software and access to the network can control the sign. The redirector currently shipped and supported by EDS is the Lantronix MSS100. These boxes are configured via telnet, and come with the default administrator password "system." They also come with some utilities that need no password to access such as a ping and a traceroute. The best way to spot these boxes is to download a fast IP scanner (I prefer Angry IP Scanner—`http://ipscan.sourceforge.net`) and scan the network for boxes listening on port 3001. If you've discovered any, the next step is to telnet to that box on port 3001. This is where we determine whether or not the redirector is connected to a radio modem, or if it is directly connected to the sign controller. If you telnet in and receive a standard readable ASCII banner, then chances are you have a radio modem. If you instead receive a bunch of garbled and unreadable ASCII, then the box is probably directly connected. Now that we know where our redirector box is, and what it's connected to, you need to get a copy of the Lantronix Redirector software. This is currently not available off of Lantronix's site due to legal issues involving competitors' software. It can however be easily requested from our friends at EDS and may be available over giFT or Kazaa. Once you've downloaded and installed the Lantronix software, you'll need to set it up to forward an unused COM port on your computer to the location of the MSS100 on port 3001. This software is pretty straightforward and easy to configure so I won't elaborate much here, except for the fact that it is absolutely necessary to have version 2.1.1 of the software for anything greater than Windows 98 and you need version 1.2.6 for Windows 95. Once you've set up the Lantronix software, open up SystemOne, configure it to use your newly emulated COM port, and set the communications for either radio or direct based on your earlier findings. You should now be able to communicate with this sign.

Conclusion

The last thing I should mention is that sometimes you may have to change the software configuration to work with a color sign instead of a black and white standard sign. This option is normally disabled in the configuration but it can be modified with a few keystrokes. First open up the EDS software and type F4, F4, F5. Then open up Software Configuration dialog, hold down Shift, and click on the SystemOne icon in the top left (not the window icon). If you did this right you'll get a window that enables you to change these super secret settings to whatever you need.

Use common sense when modifying a sign. Please don't modify signs that are displaying important information. The system, being so lax on security, is of course made without any type of logging system. So overall, you can strike without fear. Just use your head and have fun announcing fake giveaways at businesses and displaying animated stick-figure porn at your school.

Hacking a Mercedes Benz with a Universal Remote (Spring, 2004) *by TOneZ2600*

This article is intended as an educational reference. In no way should it be used to gain unlawful access. This includes breaking and entering as well as grand theft.

As we all see and know, Mercedes Benz makes the most common luxury vehicles. Prices for these cars go from (new) $24,000 to approximately $250,000. After 1991 Mercedes Benz changed locking systems throughout their cars, from a steel key that had to be "laser" cut to a steel key with an infrared sensor attached to it and recently to just an IR remote. (No more steel key.) The infrared sensor controller is attached to the key and aids in the keyless entry system. Older Mercedes Benz vehicles ('91 to '99) have actual IR sensors for door locks and trunk release mechanisms. Currently Saab, Volkswagen, and other (semi) luxury vehicles have incorporated this new IR system for their vehicles.

When buying new IR keys for your vehicle, the key has to be "trained" to your car. This process takes anywhere from five minutes to five hours depending on the IR coding complexity. Once the key is trained, that's it.

So what does that do for me? Well, let's just say you left something in your car and you lost your key. How do you make an archive key from a Universal Remote? Simple.

First, you are going to have to obtain a remote that has a "learning" function. There are several remotes on the market with this feature. If you have a PDA that is IR equipped, I think the program "TV Remote Controller 5.5" will be suitable.

Now grab your original IR key. The only thing that is left to do is to train the Unlock, Lock, and Trunk Release on your remote. This is done by selecting the button that you want to train and emitting an IR source from the original key. It's that easy and that stupid to own an $80,000 car.

Remote Secrets Revealed (Summer, 2005) *By The AntiLuddite*

I somehow reached my mid 30s without buying a new car, and I had no desire to buy one when I accompanied my girlfriend to a nearby Toyota dealership. I merely wanted to help her find a replacement for her 1991 Camry. After test driving a number of cars, haggling with the salesman, a tearful scene as the old car was driven away, and a couple of hours in the tentacled embrace of the finance department, we fell back out of the rabbit hole and discovered that I was the legal owner of a 2005 RAV4.

And this is where my story begins.

About two weeks after the purchase, my girlfriend threw her security remote against the garage door. I'll omit the details of her feud with the car and get to the point: her remote no longer armed or disarmed the security system.

An LED still flashed at the tip of the banana-shaped remote when I pushed the red button or either of the smaller black and green buttons, so I knew some life yet remained. I suspected the blow caused it to lose synchronization with the vehicle. A yellow sticker on the back read:

> *"If you press the red button on your transmitter and the red light turns on but your vehicle does not respond, press and release the red button two times within one second."*

Simple enough. I pressed and released, pressed and released the button within one second. The remote still didn't work. There was a suggestion that timing was important. For five minutes I clicked, slowly, then slower, then gradually increasing the frequency of my clicks as I tried to hit just the right interval. I finally decided to consult the owner's manual like a good little consumer.

The booklet said nothing about this particular device; the figures weren't correct and the text described an entirely different remote. I did manage to find a small plastic packet with a yellow card though. It read like a trade show blurb:

> *"Each time you press a button on the transmitter, a new code number is sent to the vehicle and the vehicle will no longer respond to an older code number. This eliminates the possibility of a thief reading your code as you disarm your system, then re-sending that code later to gain access to your vehicle. Some high tech thieves use an electronic device known as a 'code grabber' to do just that!"*

The remainder of the card was an elaboration of the instructions on the back of the remote itself. The bulk of the text had an annoying number of exclamation points, as if it had been written to be read to children during story time at the local public library.

I know some devices get wonky when their power supplies run low so I decided to replace the batteries. The case only had a single screw. The interior was sparse; the most interesting feature was a lone chip marked NTK03T. The battery was a generic 12-volt MN21/23 that I replaced with a Duracell. This is a battery that had aspirations to become a AAA but failed halfway; it's a small, unusual battery most commonly used in garage-door openers and security remotes.

I went back outside to the car. The LED winked as brightly as before, but the car refused to acknowledge my thumbing. I was desperate, so I tempted madness by double-clicking the red button again expecting a different result. I put the key in the ignition and turned it on, still clicking the remote. The device lay in my hand like a broken toy.

I remember the ubiquitous HP calculators from my college days and how they could program each other through their infrared ports. I had another, working, remote, so for a few minutes I tried to program the mute with its twin but I was still denied.

I was getting nowhere with my investigation. I decided to let the dealer take care of it. This was my first visit to the dealer's service center since the purchase and I was optimistically expectant, fool that I was.

I found a disinterested clerk who said that he would try to find someone to examine my remote but that, "It might take some time." After waiting an hour and a half (I'm not exaggerating), a technician walked over and verified that the remote was indeed out of synch with the car. He told me I could wait in the customer lounge while he fixed it, so I followed him outside.

I didn't have a good vantage point but I could see the tech was pressing the valet switch under the dash. This was curious. None of the documentation mentioned that the valet switch was used to program the remote.

For those with cars that lack one, the valet switch is a small, push-button toggle with an LED, usually located on the driver's side but sometimes under the seat or in the glove box, that temporarily disables the security system so you don't have to hand your remote to a car attendant. It's often used to disable the alarm when it's accidentally triggered.

As the guy began fingering the dash, the car started honking and blinking its headlights, seemingly in distress, like a large animal being violated by a veterinarian. I realized the chatter was some kind of feedback. The tech hopped out, said it was fixed and started to walk away. I went after him for an explanation. After five minutes of his reassurances that if it ever faulted again he would be happy to take care of it, I realized that I wasn't going to get the data I needed without pinning him to the ground and holding my keys to his throat. At least he didn't charge me.

I drove back to my townhouse and discovered that the green button on the remote still didn't work. This is the button that turns on the headlights for thirty seconds. It's a nice feature to have when you've lost your car in a parking lot so well that you can't hear the horn. Okay, so it wasn't essential but it still meant I had a device with a non-working function. I couldn't sleep until I fixed it.

I began to experiment with various combinations of valet-switch presses and remote-button clicks. The car began bleating loudly again and flashing its lights. I succeeded in programming the green button with the functions of the red button and pissing off my neighbors who stared at me through their windows. The designers obviously intended the programming to be noisy; it was almost as bad as the alarm. At least no one can reprogram the system without the owner's knowledge. Since I wanted to keep living here—and keep living period—I decided to find an empty parking lot to continue my experimentation.

But first I decided to consult the Internet for programming information using two clues from the remote's shell: a white label—TDS—and an FCC ID of ELVAT5G. I felt like kicking myself for not running a search earlier.

Toyota's web site had absolutely nothing to offer. I was able to identify the remote using a remote wholesaler's web site, but they only offered programming instructions with a purchase from their site. Another site offered the instructions separately but for an inflated fee, and with a stated disclaimer that they made no refunds or guarantees that the information was even valid. A seller on eBay auctioned car remote instructions (though not my model), and I was struck by the unfairness of the whole situation.

I had two choices: I could pay an additional fee to acquire operational information for a device I'd already paid for, or I could resign myself to returning the car to the dealer whenever the remote needed to be reprogrammed and just accept the hour and a half wait for something I could do myself in less than a minute. Some dealers even charged for this service. I was not happy.

I discovered that my device was closely related to another remote known by the FCC ID of APS95BT3. It operated at 434MHz. It was manufactured by a company known as Prestige, which appeared to be a subsidiary of Audiovox. Audiovox had wisely and graciously included a manual on their web site rather than charge for it. The manual didn't describe an exact procedure for my remote, but the documentation was very close and helped immensely.

Below I've paraphrased the programming instructions in the manual and added some clarifying information that wasn't in the guide, as well as some personal experiences. Those wanting the information straight from the source should point their browsers to `http://www.audiovox.com` and select the Find a Product > MOBILE > Car Security and Remote Start Systems.

How to Program a Prestige/ TDS/Audiovox (APS95BT3/ELVAT5G) Remote

The remote is a three-button, seven-channel transmitter. Most car security systems only have three or four channel receivers; theoretically, the higher channels in the remote can be programmed for an additional car, but I did not test this. Below is a table outlining the channels:

Transmitter		Receiver	
Channel	**Buttons**	**Channel**	**Function**
1	1	1	Remote arm and disarm Remote emergency panic Remote door lock/unlock
2	2	2	Pulsed output for accessories (lock/unlock w/o alarm on my car)
3	3	3	Switched output for accessories (nothing on my car)
4	2, 3	4	Switched output for accessories (Headlights on my car)
5	1, 2	-	-
6	1, 3	-	-
7	1, 2, 3		

The following procedure will program a new remote or reprogram an unsynchronized remote. Any discrepancies or clarifications are in parentheses.

Note: Each step must be performed within 15 seconds of the previous step or the system will exit programming mode.

1. Turn the ignition key to the "ON" position. (You do not need to start the engine.)
2. Flip the valet switch on-off, on-off, on-off. (My valet switch is on when pushed in and the light is off. Conversely, it is off when popped out and the light is on. Whatever your configuration, the switch needs to be cycled three times.)
3. The valet LED flashes once (it repeats a single flash pattern) and the siren (horn) chirps once to indicate the system is ready to program channel 1.
4. Press and hold transmitter button 1 (or whatever button you want to program on the remote) until the siren sounds a long chirp (horn blast), indicating the signal has been stored into memory.
5. Flip the valet switch on then off (one cycle).

Here, the process repeats for transmitter channels 2 to 4:

6. The valet LED flashes twice (a repeating double flash) and the siren chirps twice to indicate the system is ready to program channel 2.

7. Press and hold transmitter button 2 until the siren sounds a long chirp, indicating the signal has been stored into memory.
8. Flip the valet switch on then off.
9. The valet LED flashes three times (a repeating triple flash) and the siren chirps three times to indicate the system is ready to program channel 3.
10. Press and hold transmitter button 3 until the siren sounds a long chirp, indicating the signal has been stored into memory. (Important: I could not program transmitter channel 3 [button 3] for receiver channel 3. I do not know what receiver channel 3 is used for in my car's security system, or if it's even there. This is why the Toyota tech couldn't get the green button to work. I had to skip step 10 and continue with step 11, and program transmitter channel 3 [button 3] for receiver channel 4. This restored the remote headlight function to my green button.)
11. Flip the valet switch on then off.
12. The valet LED flashes four times (a repeating quadruple flash) and the siren chirps once to indicate the system is ready to program channel 4.
13. Press and hold transmitter button 4 until the siren sounds a long chirp, indicating the signal has been stored into memory.

End the process:

14. Turn the ignition key off. The siren will sound one short chirp followed by one long chirp to signal the system has left program mode.

I hope that someone finds this information useful and it spares them the frustration and loss of time that I experienced attempting to use what is otherwise a great product. I think it's worth noting that none of the security system documentation from Toyota that was included with this brand new car was even "remotely" helpful.

Impromptu Lock Picks (Summer, 2004) *By L. Gallion*

This article assumes you are familiar with lockpicking and lockpicking tools. If you are completely new to the subject, I suggest you Google for the *MIT Guide to Lockpicking* and read it before continuing.

To pick a lock, you need two things: a pick and a tension wrench. The pick is used to press on or rake across the pins inside a lock while the tension wrench applies a turning force to the lock's cylinder. The trouble is it isn't always practical (or even legal, depending on local ordinances) to carry professional lockpicking tools. Fortunately most homes and offices come stocked with all of the materials necessary to make your own basic tools.

For example, here are some items I rounded up in just a few minutes:

- Fingernail clippers (the kind with a built-in nail file and a little hole at one end)
- A couple of bobby pins
- An old credit card (or any plastic card of similar thickness)
- A couple of small paper clips
- A large safety pin
- A "Prong Fastener" (Acco #70022, used to hold large printouts together)
- A good pair of steel scissors
- A plastic cable tie (used to secure cables and wires together)
- A round-head brass fastener

Using just these items and a little imagination, we can create several different lock-picking tools.

Let's get started with the most limited of our resources, the paper clips. Professional picks and wrenches are often made from hardened, flat spring steel, while paper clips are round, soft, and bendable. This means that paper clip picks are useful only against locks with weak pin springs and paper clip wrenches only work with easily turned cylinders.

To make a paper clip pick, straighten out one end of the paper clip (leave the other end curled as a handle) and then bend the very end of the straight section into a small, sharp "hill" sticking up. (This is the classic half diamond pick shape.) The easiest way to do this is to clamp (don't press too hard) about a quarter inch of the paper clip in the jaws of the fingernail clippers and use the clippers to bend the paper clip. Do this again about one eighth of an inch in from the end to finish forming the hill shape. The end of the paper clip should look roughly like this:

______/\

While too soft to work as an actual pin pick, a paper clip can be used to rake simple locks, like the disk tumblers you will find in most Steelcase and Hon filing cabinets, desks, and overhead bins.

To make a paper clip tension wrench, unfold the paper clip as before (leaving one curled end as a handle) and then bend about a half inch of the straightened portion back onto itself. You will want to make the actual bend as small as possible, so use a hard object to press on the bend and "close" it as much as you can. (The scissor handles work well here.) Finally, bend the "handle" so the paper clip now has an "L" shape.

The bend at the end of the paper clip will usually fit into the bottom of the keyhole of most medium-size locks. However, a paper clip tension wrench is very weak and I have only used it successfully on smooth working deadbolts.

Now let's move on to a much better tool: the safety pin pick. Steven Hampton, author of *Secrets of Lockpicking*, says he got started using just a safety pin pick and a bent screwdriver as a tension wrench. Now you too can make just such a pick in seconds. First, carefully open up the safety pin and use the clipper's nail file to dull the point (so you won't poke yourself). Next, insert the pin through the hole at the rear of the fingernail clippers. The pin should just barely be sticking out of the far side of the hole. Then, by rotating the entire clippers up or down, you can pinch and bend the portion of the pin sticking through the hole. Stop bending once the pin has a nice, gentle curve of about 45 degrees. Finally, open the safety pin up a little wider so it stays in a permanent "L" shape.

Being strong and made of flexible steel, your new-and-improved safety pin can be used as a hook pick on a variety of locks. I have successfully used it to pick five-disk tumblers, four-pin padlocks, and six-pin deadbolts.

Next let's tackle another strong performer, the bobby pin. Bobby pins can be made into a good hook pick or a small tension wrench very quickly. First, remove the little plastic tips that come on most bobby pins and spread it apart so it forms an "L" shape. Next, insert the straight leg (not the wavy one) of the bobby pin through the hole in the fingernail clippers so that about a quarter inch sticks out on the other side. The tricky part of the bobby pin pick is that we want to put a bend along the thin edge (not the flat sides). To do this, tightly pinch the flat sides of the bobby pin about a half inch back from the fingernail clipper's hole. Then move the fingernail clipper up or down to carefully bend the bobby pin. If it starts to twist, stop and carefully straighten the twist out and then continue bending again. Stop bending the bobby pin when you have about a 45-degree angle. You have the proper shape when you lay your metal "L" down flat on a table and the end of one of the legs sticks up. The bobby pin tension wrench is a lot simpler. Just open up the bobby pin and spread it apart until it permanently forms an "L" shape. Although a great tension wrench, the width of the bobby pin is often too small to be used on a lot of locks. If the bobby pin wrench is too small, try using the nail file of your fingernail clippers. Just extend the nail file out to a 90-degree angle. The nail file tip will fit into the keyhole of some medium-size locks and the body of the clippers acts as the handle.

Credit card picks are easy to make but are only strong enough for one or two picking sessions. First, cut the credit card into about half inch strips. Next, use a straightened paper clip to measure the depth of the lock (push it in until you hit the back wall). Using this depth, trim down one end of the credit card strip so it is small enough to enter the top of the keyway. As you trim the end of the card down, shape the tip in either a half diamond or half round pick style. (See the *MIT Guide* if you are not familiar with these shapes.) Don't forget, credit card plastic is relatively soft, so try to use your fingers to support the thin shaft as you move it around within the lock.

Our final group of impromptu lockpicking tools is a set of rakes. Rakes are pulled back and forth and up and down against the pins of a lock in the hopes of opening it.

While raking won't have much of an effect against most high-security locks, it works very well against desks, filing cabinets, and cheap padlocks.

Our rakes will be made out of the round-head brass fastener, prong fastener, and the cable tie. Start by straightening out one of the thin metal legs on the brass and prong fasteners. Then use your scissors to carefully cut a series of "V" shaped notches or smooth "hills" at the end of each object (just on one side). Make certain the end is either pointed or sloped so that it can enter the keyway easily. You may also need to trim down the flat bottom portion of the rake to get it to fit into the lock.

Of these three rakes, I have gotten the best results with the cable tie. Its tough, flexible nylon construction allows it to move smoothly in and out of most locks. However, don't think that any of these makeshift tools are going to easily crack that high-security Medeco in your office. Advanced lockpicking takes a combination of skill, practice, luck, and the proper tools. But the next time you lock your boss's big presentation in a filing cabinet and lose the key, don't panic! Just use your lockpicking ability and a few office supplies.

Institutions

In addition to the actual devices that exist in the real world, there are also much bigger entities known as institutions. Basically, we're talking about hacking an entire idea or way of life for many. These are things that people are taught not to question, like elections or censorship or Google. They have become synonymous with normalcy and it could threaten the perceived natural order of things if too many questions were asked or too many experiments performed. Of course, this is of great interest to hackers, which is why you'll see those subjects covered here. We also have a very in-depth analysis of a major metropolitan transportation system drawn entirely from observation through hacker eyes as well as a detailed explanation of how lotteries actually work, which is certainly not something the people in charge were too keen on having spread around.

How to Hack the Lottery (Autumn, 2004) *By StankDawg*

So you want to win the lottery....

Overview

Most states have a lottery these days. Even though gambling is illegal in most states, somehow the lottery is different. I won't go into explaining the hypocrisy in that scenario, as that is not the point of this article. It should suffice to say that the money is supposed to go to the state governments, which justifies the exclusion from the rules.

Regardless of that debate, I would like to shed some light on how the lottery works and settle the question of why (or why not) to play the lottery. I will use some formulas and mathematical functions to explain the logic, but hopefully the text of this article will teach you how to analyze your specific lottery and not rely on the specific examples that I used. I think the point will still be understood.

Logistics

Let's talk about how the lottery works. First of all, it is important to know that each state's rules may vary, but they usually have some physical procedures in common. Most states use different sets of ping pong balls that they rotate in and out of use. This is to avoid the possibility that a set may have something wrong with it that could skew the odds. They could have a ball that is lighter than the others, has a hole in it, or that could be dirty. Along the same lines, the machines that pick the balls are usually rotated in and out of use and calibrated regularly as well. This prevents the machines from malfunctioning and ensures that they haven't been tampered with. Finally, to make sure that the controlled environment stays controlled, an independent auditing firm verifies that all of the equipment, the environment, and the people involved are checked to avoid foul play. The bottom line is that this is a controlled environment! You have to accept that to continue.

Each state varies, but let's pick some arbitrary examples. Let's say you have to match six numbers, in any order, out of balls numbered 1 through 50. You pick six numbers hoping to match all six of the balls pulled from the tumbler. When the first ball is pulled, you have a 6 in 50 chance of being correct with one of your numbers. That is pretty clear common sense thinking, right? OK, so you actually get lucky and one of the numbers you had is pulled from the tumbler! Lucky you! Now on to ball two.

So the first ball has been drawn and now there are 49 balls left. You still have five numbers to match. Your chances of getting the next pick are even better now that there are only 49 balls left, right? Not exactly... as a matter of fact, not even close.

Statistics

Let's preface by saying that all numbers are rounded for the sake of readability. Now the specific area of statistics we are discussing here is probability. What are the chances that an event will happen? You have given information to begin with and a mathematical basis upon which to calculate. The most helpful concept is that of a factorial.

A factorial is notated using a "!" after the number. It usually is located on your scientific calculator as "n!". 3! is a factorial of 3, which simply means (3 * 2 * 1), which is 6. That one is easy to do in your head, but what is 50! without using a calculator?

Now don't go and get all bent out of shape. It is a long process with lots of numbers but it isn't as difficult as it sounds. You can calculate the probability of each individual pick and then multiply them all together to get the final probability. Note that the order of the numbers is unimportant. It doesn't matter if your picks are in the same order as the drawing. If they were, it changes everything and the odds skyrocket astronomically.

Luckily, there are formulas that we can use to apply the factorial notation to the problem at hand. But before we go into that, let's solve this the old fashioned way.

Procedure

Let n = the number of balls in the lottery and therefore the highest possible number that you can choose.

Let x = the number of picks that must be made correctly to win.

Since you have chosen six numbers, the chances of getting one of your six numbers correct out of 50 is:

(n/x) = (50/6) = 6 in 50 (or 1 in 8.333)

Now let's take a step up to see the chances of getting two of the six picks correct. The odds of getting the first pick do not change. You still have that same chance, but the odds of getting two numbers right increases quite a bit. To figure out the chances of getting the second number, you have to consider that you now have one less ball and one less pick left to match. You now have a 5 in 49 chance of getting that second pick alone (1 in 9.8). Unfortunately, that is very much related to your previous pick. It is not a simple matter of getting each pick independently of one another. Statistically, the chances are multiplied for each pick that must be made because you have to get *both* of the numbers.

(50/6) * (49/5) = (8.333 * 9.8) = 1 in 81.666

Those odds are a little bit tougher now, aren't they? Logically, you may see the progression as the odds for each pick become higher and higher individually. Your odds of picking the final ball are 1 in 45. (Remember that you started at 1 in 8.333 for the first ball.) Take each individual chance of a correct pick and multiply it by each one of the others. This, combined with the odds of getting *all* of the picks correct generates the following calculation:

(50/6) * (49/5) * (48/4) * (47/3) * (46/2) * (45/1) = 1 in 15,890,700

So if your state increases in population and/or you have people winning too often, then you may notice that they add an extra ball to the lottery. Redo the calculations above and notice the difference that adding one ball to the lottery can have on the overall odds of winning. Keep in mind that every entry is another dollar taken in by the state.

This is why some states also have a powerball lottery that is shared with other states. Since the population is higher when combining the potential audience of multiple states, the powerball allows some control over the probability. The calculation is based on the same principal, but instead of your final pick being a 1 in 45 chance (still using the example earlier) it is now a 1 in 50 chance (assuming the powerball goes up to 50). Since you are only picking five balls from the original pool, you also only get a 5 in 50 probability to start with (which is 1 in 10 for your first pick compared to the 1 in 8.33 in the previous example). When you multiply that new equation out, you see the following:

$$(50/5) * (49/4) * (48/3) * (47/2) * (46/1) * (50/1) = 1 \text{ in } 105{,}938{,}000$$

By adjusting how high the powerball can be, the probability can be predicted much better. Recalculate the odds with a powerball of only 30 and notice the difference.

Application

Earlier I mentioned the term "factorial." I also mentioned that the order of the picks was unimportant. Because of this, there is a special rule that can be used to calculate the probability using factorials. This lets you use a calculator and save a lot of time. This is a special case called a binomial coefficient. A binomial coefficient has a special formula and notation that can be used to calculate the same probability. It is as follows:

$$nCx = \frac{n!}{(n-x)!x!}$$

Again, the same assumptions earlier are in force. "n" is still the number of balls and "x" is the number of picks. Our friend the factorial helps us out here. In our case:

$$50C6 = \frac{50!}{(50-6)!6!} \text{ can be reduced to: } \frac{50!}{44!6!}$$

Now, you may have to look at this closely, but remember the definition of a factorial and you can reduce this formula even further based on the logic and understanding of what a factorial is. 50! means 50 * 49 * 48 etc. and 44! means 44 * 43 * 42 etc., correct? Well, 50 is obviously larger than 44. Once you get to ...44 * 43 * 42... you are going to be overlapping numbers in the denominator, or bottom of the equation! Since basic algebra tells you that a 44 in the numerator will cancel out a 44 in the denominator, the same holds true for factorials. In the following equation, the 44! in the numerator and the 44! in the denominator can be canceled out:

$$\frac{50 * 49 * 48 * 47 * 46 * 45 * 44!}{44! * 6!} \text{ leaving } \frac{50 * 49 * 48 * 47 * 46 * 45}{6 * 5 * 4 * 3 * 2 * 1}$$

44! is the same as writing out all of the numbers on the bottom and crossing them out with all of the numbers on the top. We recognized ahead of time that this would happen and saved ourselves some time and space. You can write them out if you feel more comfortable visualizing the whole thing, but you will be using a lot of paper.

Now you find yourself looking at a simple multiplication and division problem. Calculate the equation the rest of the way out and what number do you get? I'll bet that it is 15,890,700. And you can easily calculate the factorial portion of these equations on your trusty scientific calculator. The really good ones include the binomial coefficient formula built in and you simply enter the "n" followed by the key and then the "x" and magically your answer appears! It is not magic, it is mathematics.

Myths

OK, so you want to try and "trick" the system and increase your odds. Unfortunately, you can't trick statistics and you can't trick mathematics. One of the more common tactics that I see people trying is to combine their money together as a group, usually at their job, to increase their chances of winning. On the surface it looks like you are increasing your odds of winning by having 20 chances to win instead of just one. Technically, it is a true statement. Unfortunately, it is a negligible amount of an increase compared to the loss you would get by splitting the money with your coworkers.

Method of number choice is another point of question. Does it help to pick your birthday and the birthdays of your family? What about autopicks from the register. Are those more likely to win? Or less likely to win because the machine is "fixed"? Should you stay away from patterns like 1,2,3,4,5,6 and scatter your numbers across the board? The answer is simple. Since history has no effect on picks, and since logistically the machines, balls, and people are verified by an independent accounting firm, the picks cannot be "rigged." All numbers have an equal chance of coming up at any given time.

Some people think there are patterns that emerge in the lottery picks. They think that some balls simply have a tendency to occur more than others. This is simply not true. Individual numbers picked during the lottery change, but the chances of numbers over the career of the lottery will remain constant. Many lottery sites post historical picks for people to look for patterns or analyze the hell out of the numbers. This is all smoke and mirrors. They are perfectly happy to provide these numbers because they know that there is no pattern. If it convinces people to play more using their "pattern conspiracy theories," they will happily allow you to mislead yourself.

Did you really think you were the first to think of the old "play every combination" trick? Let me remind you that you would need almost $16 million to play every combination! Even if you could somehow convince a bank or someone to back you on that bet, I pose two questions: Why would they need you when they could do it themselves? And what if someone else actually gets lucky and you have to split it with someone else? Oops! Don't forget about the government and the tax people!

Summary

The lottery, like most casino games, is fixed. I do not mean to say fixed as in "they are cheating," but fixed statistically. Statistics are analyzed long before it is ever introduced. They know the odds, and they know how often they will win and how much they will make compared to how much they will have to pay out. The lottery will always, in the long run, benefit the states. They cannot lose. I know that is not what you expected to hear.

So how do you hack the lottery? I can sum up the answer to this question in two words. "Don't play." The only time the lottery was "hacked" was in 1980 in Pennsylvania and it involved tampering with the mechanics of the game, something that is now very controlled. If you are still interested in this story, you can look it up on the Internet quite easily. Keep your hard earned money in your pocket and don't let them take it from you through some false dreams of winning. If you play the lottery, they actually hacked *you*.

Shoutz: my statistics professors, all DDP members, everyone who has any part in the Binary Revolution at `binrev.com`.

New York City's MTA Exposed! (Spring, 2005) *By Redbird*

In this article, I will explain many of the inner workings of the New York City Transit Authority fare collection system and expose the content of MetroCards. I will start off with a description of the various devices of the fare collection system, proceeding into the details of how to decode the MetroCard's magnetic stripe. This article is the result of many hours of experimentation, plenty of cash spent on MetroCards (you're welcome, MTA), and lots of help from several people. I'd like to thank everyone at *2600*, *Off The Hook*, and all those who have mailed in cards and various other information.

Becoming familiar with how magnetic stripe technology works will help you understand much of what is discussed in the sections describing how to decode MetroCards.

Terms

These terms will be used throughout the article:

- **FSK: Frequency Shift Keying:** A type of frequency modulation in which the signal's frequency is shifted between two discrete values.
- **MVM: MetroCard Vending Machine:** MVMs can be found in every subway station. They are the large vending machines which accept cash in addition to credit and debit.
- **MEM: MetroCard Express Machine:** MEMs are vending machines that accept only credit and debit. They are often located beside a batch of MVMs.
- **MTA: Metropolitan Transportation Authority:** A public benefit corporation of the State of New York responsible for implementing a unified mass transportation policy for New York City and counties within the "Transportation District."
- **NYCTA: New York City Transit Authority:** Under the control of the MTA, the NYCTA is a public benefit corporation responsible for operating buses and subway trains in New York City.
- **RFM: Reduced-Fare MetroCard:** RFMs are available to the elderly or people with qualifying disabilities. Typical RFM fare is half or less than half of the standard fare.
- **Common MetroCard:** This term will refer to any MetroCard available to the public without special requirements. Examples include standard pay-per-ride cards, standard unlimited cards, and single-ride cards.

- **Special MetroCard:** This term will refer to any MetroCard not available to the general public. Examples include reduced-fare cards, student cards, and employee cards.
- **Single-Track MetroCard:** This term will refer to any MetroCard that has a one-track magnetic stripe (although there is no visible difference between the stripes of these cards and the stripes of two-track cards). The following types of cards are single-track: Single-Ride and Bus Transfer MetroCards.
- **Dual-Track MetroCard:** This term will refer to all MetroCards with the exception of the Single-Track MetroCards mentioned above. The following types of cards are some examples of dual-track cards: pay-per-ride, pre-valued, unlimited, and reduced-fare.
- **Passback Period:** This term will refer to the time period before an access device will allow you to use an unlimited card again after swiping it. During this period, the devices generally respond with the message "JUST USED."
- **Standard Cards and Standard Readers:** These terms will refer to cards containing a magnetic stripe (credit, banking, etc.) or readers of these cards that conform to the standards set forth in any or all of the following ISO specifications: 7810, 7811, 7813, and 4909.

Cubic Transportation Systems

The fare collection system the MTA uses was developed by Cubic Transportation Systems, a subsidiary of Cubic Corporation. The patents I found to be related to the current New York City system filed by Cubic Corporation are as follows:

- 4,877,179: Farebox Security Device
- 5,056,261: Turnstile System
- 5,072,543: Turnstile Mechanism
- 5,191,195: Fare Card Read-Writer Which Overwrites Oldest or Invalid Data
- 5,215,383: Ticket Stock and Ticket Dispenser
- 5,298,726: Fare Card Read-Writer Which Overwrites Oldest or Invalid Data
- 5,333,410: Controllable Barrier System For Preventing Unpaid Admission to a Fee-Paid Area
- 5,574,441: Mass Transit Inductive Data Communication System
- 5,612,684: Mass Transit Inductive Data Communication System
- 6,595,416: System For Rapidly Dispensing and Adding Value to Fare Cards
- 6,655,587: Customer Administered Autoload
- 6,789,736: Distributed Architecture For Magnetic Fare Card Processing

Servicing, apart from routine collection of fares, on MTA equipment seems to be done by Cubic employees, not the MTA.

The MetroCard System

At the core of the MTA fare collection system is the MetroCard. Preceded by a token-based system, the MetroCard is now used for every aspect of fare collection and allows for fare options that would never have been previously possible (e.g., Employee, Reduced-Fare, and Student MetroCards). MetroCards can currently be purchased at MVMs, MEMs, token booths, and various merchants throughout the New York City area. I will categorize the MetroCard access devices into two types: reading devices and fare collection devices. Both of these devices are networked in a complex system that allows the MTA, within minutes, to have up-to-date information on every card that has been issued. This also allows them to disable any card at will. The hierarchy of the network is shown below (as described in patent 6,789,736).

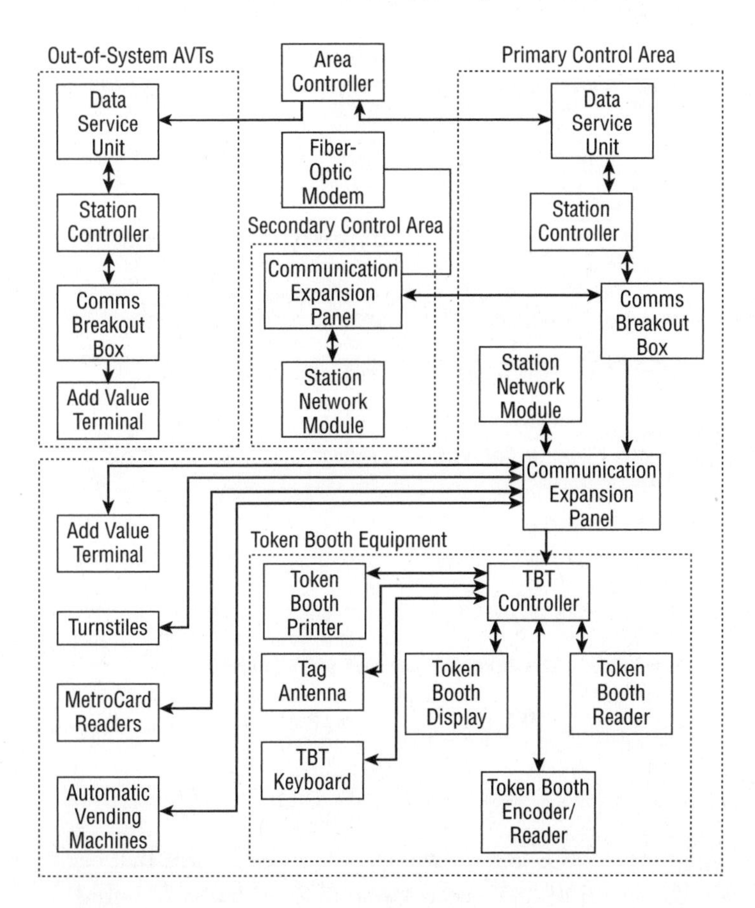

The physical characteristics of MetroCards follow those of standard cards (see Terms) almost exactly, but are one third the thickness. They have a diagonal notch cut out in the upper right-hand corner $3\frac{1}{8}$" from the left and $\frac{5}{16}$" from the top of the card. Additionally, they have a $\frac{1}{8}$" diameter hole, with its center $\frac{1}{4}$" from the left and $\frac{5}{16}$" from the top of the card, which is used to aid machines that suck your card in (bus fare boxes, MEMs/MVMs, handicapped entry/exit machines, etc.).

Vending Machines

MEMs and MVMs are located throughout the subway system. They allow you to purchase or refill various common MetroCards with either cash or a credit card. RFMs can't be purchased at machines but can be refilled. On the front of the MEM or MVM is a tag with the machine's unique ID number.

Receipts

Receipts can be obtained from MEM and MVM machines by answering "yes" when prompted. They possess a lot of information about the MEM/MVM, subway station, and card. You can match a receipt to a card by comparing the serial numbers. Let's take a look at some samples:

```
      MVM RECEIPT                   MVM RECEIPT                   MEM RECEIPT

MTA NYC TRANSIT              MTA NYC TRANSIT              MTA NYC TRANSIT
ASTOR PLACE                  NASSAU AV & MANHATTAN AV     14TH STREET & 6TH AVENUE
NEW YORK CITY NY             NEW YORK CITY NY             NEW YORK CITY NY

MVM #: 0545(R219  0701)      MVM #: 1738(N408A  0500)     MEM #: 5383(N513 0400)

Sun 14 Nov 04 21:28          Mon 04 Oct 04 14:22          Wed 17 Nov 04 12:14

Trans: Sale OK               Trans: Sale OK               Trans: Add Time OK
Payment Mode: Cash           Payment Mode: Credit         Amount:            $ 10.50
Amount:          $  7.00     Amount:           $ 21.00    Initial Type:030
Card Value:      $  0.00     Card Value:       $  0.00      7-DAY RFM UNLIMITED
Change Due:      $  3.00                                  Time Added:   030
                             Credit Card #: XX5346          7-DAY RFM UNLIMITED
Serial #:1059909877          Auth#: 000008
Type: 023                    Ref #: 060615762129          ATM Card #: XX0952
   1-DAY UNLIMITED                                        Auth#: 760346
                             Serial #:1027066848          Ref #: 029089559668
      Questions?             Type: 024
Call (212) METROCARD            7-DAY UNLIMITED           Serial #:0987218036

                                   Questions?                 Questions?
                             Call (212) METROCARD         Call (212) METROCARD
```

Most of the information on the receipt is fairly obvious, but notice the line that begins with "MEM #" or "MVM #". The first four digits correspond to the actual MEM or MVM

ID number as found on the machine. The next letter and following three digits inside the parentheses correspond to the closest token booth. This ID can also be found on the booth itself. The meaning of the next four digits is currently unknown. However, they are unique to each machine that has the same booth ID, but are not unique among machines with different booth IDs. They seem to simply be a unique ID for each MEM/MVM in the station, possibly grouped by location. See "MEM/MVMs" for a table.

Now look to the bottom of the receipt. The line that begins with "Type:" (or "Initial Type:" if an RFM is being refilled) gives the numerical card subtype value followed by a description of the type on the following line.

Receipts purchased with a credit card contain additional fields that allow the MTA to verify the credit card holder in the case that he/she decides to lose the MetroCard.

Turnstiles

The use of a turnstile is the most common way to enter the subway. Entry is granted by swiping a valid MetroCard through the reader/writer located on the outside of each turnstile. Once swiped, the LCD display on the turnstile will display a message. Some common messages:

- **GO:** Message displayed for Unlimited MetroCards.
- **GO. 1 RIDE LEFT:** Message displayed for Student MetroCards, where "1" is the number of rides left for the day.
- **JUST USED:** The passback period for the unlimited MetroCard is not up.
- **GO. 1 XFER OK:** Message displayed when transferring from a bus.

Above the LCD there are a series of round indicators. Of these, one has an arrow pointing in the direction of the turnstile in which you would enter after paying your fare, and another reads "No" and a do-not-enter bar which, when lit, indicates that the turnstile is not active. After paying your fare, another indicator below the green arrow lights to indicate that you may proceed through the turnstile without smashing your groin into the arm.

Above those, there are three horizontal bar indicators contained within a rectangular cutout. When a Reduced-Fare MetroCard is swiped, the top indicator (red) will light. When a Student MetroCard is swiped, the middle indicator (yellow) will light. When an Employee MetroCard is swiped, the bottom indicator (the color of which I'm unsure) will light. These indicators are present on both sides of the turnstiles and they allow transit cops, many of whom are undercover, to monitor the types of cards being used by riders. This helps detect, for example, when Student MetroCards are being used at times when school is not in session or when an obvious misuse of an Employee or Reduced-Fare MetroCard occurs.

Reading MetroCards

MetroCards are relatively difficult to read. You will not be able to read them with off-the-shelf magnetic stripe readers, so please don't waste your money. The reason for this is not that the format is different; MetroCards use Aiken Biphase (also known as frequency shift keying [FSK]) just like standard cards. However, the hardware that ships with these readers is designed for a completely different (and well-documented) specification. They require many "clocking bits," which consist of a string of zero-bits at the beginning of the stripe to aid in setting a reference frequency for decoding. Additionally, most readers also look for a standard start and end sentinel that exists on standard cards to denote the start of a particular track. On top of that, characters on these cards are defined as either four- or six-bit blocks (depending on the track) and contain a longitudinal redundancy check (LRC) character after the end sentinel to verify data integrity. Needless to say, MetroCards don't have any of these properties and contain fields of arbitrary length; thus, another method of reading and decoding is required.

Fortunately, magnetic heads are everywhere (e.g., cassette tape players) and the output from magnetic heads when passed over a magnetic stripe consists of voltage spikes in the audible frequency range. Since sound cards are excellent A/D converters for this range of input and are readily available and very cheap, we can use the microphone input interfaced to a magnetic head for the purpose of creating our own reader (for a lot less than the MTA is paying, I'm sure!).

For the same reason that reading was initially difficult, writing to MetroCards is extremely difficult, and is still a work-in-progress that will not be discussed in this article. A technique similar to that of the decoder (in reverse) can be used to write to cards, although it is much more difficult to implement and obviously requires more equipment than just a sound card and a magnetic head. For those of you who realize how this can be done and have the ability to build the equipment, kudos, but keep in mind the ramifications of being caught using a card you wrote to yourself. Modifying the data on cards does work. But the MetroCard system is very complex and allows for the surveillance of this sort of activity. The goal of this project is to learn how the system works, how it can be theoretically defeated, but certainly not to get stuck in prison.

Apart from these difficulties, MetroCard tracks are defined as follows: Dual-Track MetroCards have two tracks—one track being twice the width of the other—and will be referred to as track 1-2 and track 3; Paper MetroCards have one track that will be referred to as track 1-2. These track names (as I refer to them) correspond to the same track fields that have been established by ISO 7811.

Decoding Dual-Track MetroCards—Track 3

Track 3 on Dual-Track MetroCards contains static data. It is written when the card is produced and the serial number is printed on the back, and is not written to thereafter by any machine. Some data found on this track can also be found by looking at the information printed on the back of the card. The track format is as follows:

```
      Track 3 Content  Offset  Length
      ---------------  ------  -------
   1: Start Sentinel      0       15
   2: Card Type          15        4
   3: Unknown            19        4
   4: Expiration Date    23       12
   5: Unknown            35        4
   6: Constant           39        8
   7: Unknown            47        8
   8: Serial Number      55       80
   9: Unused            135       16
  10: Unknown           151       16
  11: End Sentinel      167       93
```

Decoding track 3 is accomplished as follows:

1. Constant: 000000011000111
2. Convert binary to decimal

Note: See "Card Types" for a lookup table.

3. Use is not yet known
4. To determine the expiration date for common MetroCards:

   Convert binary to decimal

   Divide the decimal value by 2, round up

   Convert the decimal value to year / month format as follows:
   Year: Integer value of the decimal value divided by 12
   Month: Value of the modulus of the decimal value and 12

   Add 1992 to the year

   The expiration date is the last day of the previous month

Note: Non-common MetroCards seem to have different date offsets.
Note: This expiration date is the date the physical card can no longer be used and is considered invalid. See the track 1-2 expiration date field for more information.

5. Use is not yet known
6. Constant: 00001101

7. Use is not yet known
8. Convert binary to decimal
9. Unused field
10. Use is not yet known
11. Constant:

    00100101001100100110100101100101010011001010010
    10011001101010100110100101010011010010101101 01

Decoding Dual-Track MetroCards—Track 1-2

Track 1-2 on Dual-Track MetroCards contains variable data. It is written to by every machine used for fare collection, reading devices excluded. Interestingly enough, track 1-2 does not only contain information pertaining to the last use, but also to the use before that. These two records are separated by a strange set of field separating bits, which contains in it a bit that seems to be half of the one-bit frequency (which is a non-standard use of FSK). The most reliable way to find the second track is to search for a second start sentinel, both of which are identical for each record. The track format is as follows:

```
     Content               Offset  Length
     --------------------  ------  -------
 1:  Start Sentinel             0       10
 2:  Time                      10        2
 3:  Card Sub-Type             12        6
 4:  Time                      18        6
 5:  Date                      24       10
 6:  Times Used                34        6
 7:  Expiration Date           40       10
 8:  Transfer Bit              50        1
 9:  Last Used ID              51       15
10:  Card Value                66       16
11:  Purchase ID               82       16
12:  Unknown                   98       20
```

Decoding track 1-2 is accomplished as follows:

1. Constant: 0011010111
2. See 4
3. Convert binary to decimal

    The card sub-type corresponds to the sub-type as indicated on the receipt if one was obtained from an MEM/MVM.

Note: See "Card Types" for a lookup table.

4. To deal with the limited storage space on the MetroCard stripe, each bit in this field and field (2) represents 6 minutes. To determine the last time used for common MetroCards:

   Concatenate the binary from (2) with the binary from this field

   Convert to decimal

   Multiply decimal value by 6

   Result is the number of minutes since 01:00 that the card was last used

5. Convert binary to decimal

   This field contains the last usage date, which can be determined by calculating an offset based on a card of the same type with a last usage on a known date. However, since this field only has 10 bits, dates will most likely roll over after 1024 (2^10) days and a new offset will have to be determined. Offsets also seem to differ with different types of MetroCards.

6. Convert binary to decimal

   The times used field is incremented every time you use the card to pay a fare except during a transfer. In that case, the transfer bit is set and the times used field remains the same.

7. Convert binary to decimal

   Determine offset based on the description in 5 to determine the exact expiration date of a card. Alternatively, subtract the date field from this field to determine how many days after the last usage the card expires.

   Do not confuse this field with the expiration date field on track 3; it is only used on cards which expire a set number of days after you first use them (e.g., unlimited cards) and will not be set for cards such as pay-per-ride, which do not have an expiration date.

8. Bit is 1 if the last use was for a transfer, 0 otherwise

9. Convert binary to decimal

   This field seems to have a completely separate lookup table that is used internally by the fare collection system.

Note: See "Last Used IDs" for a lookup table.

10. Convert binary to decimal

    The result is the value remaining on the card in cents.

11. Convert binary to decimal

    This field seems to have a completely separate lookup table that is used internally by the fare collection system to match the value of this field with an MVM ID number (such as those you can find on receipts).

Card Types (partial):

Type	Subtype	Description
0	0	FULL FARE
0	10	PRE-VALUED
0	12	PRE-VALUED ($10.00)
0	13	PRE-VALUED ($2.00)
0	14	Long Island Rail Road
0	19	PRE-VALUED ($4.00)
0	23	1-DAY UNLIMITED ($2.00 fare)
0	24	7-DAY UNLIMITED ($2.00 fare)
0	25	7-day Express Bus Unlimited ($4.00 fare)
0	26	30-DAY UNLIMITED ($2.00 fare)
0	29	AIRTRAIN
0	30	7-DAY RFM UNLIMITED ($2.00 fare)
0	43	TransitChek
0	46	TransitChek
0	47	TransitChek
0	48	TransitChek 30-DAY UNLIMITED
0	56	1-DAY UNLIMITED ($1.50 fare)
0	57	7-DAY UNLIMITED ($1.50 fare)
0	59	30-DAY UNLIMITED ($1.50 fare)
0	62	SingleRide ($1.50 fare)
0	87	SingleRide ($2.00 fare)
4	2	Two-Trip Special Program Pass
4	5	Grades 7-12
4	13	1/2 Fare - Grades K-12

Last Used IDs (partial):

ID	Location
1513	14th St/Union Sq
1519	8th St/Broadway (A39)
1880	Lexington Ave (N601)
1942	ASTOR PLACE (R219)
2157	34th St/6th Ave (N506)
2204	42nd St/Grand Central
2278	9th Street PATH

Conclusion

As you may have noticed, I haven't provided a way to decode the Single-Track MetroCards yet. Bus Transfer MetroCards are collected after use and the magnetic stripe of Single-Ride MetroCards is written with bogus data after use. We simply haven't received enough unused samples to be able to reverse-engineer all the information contained on these cards. New things are being discovered and more data is being collected every day, so consider this article a "snapshot" of a work in progress.

Hacking Google AdWords (Summer, 2005) *By StankDawg*

Like many others, I have been a huge fan of Google over the past few years. I have spoken very highly of it on my weekly radio show *Binary Revolution Radio* discussing hacking techniques, interpreting finds, discussing new features, and lots of other things Google-related. Unfortunately, over the years I have started to find that I was beginning to question some of Google's practices. Whether it was the toolbar, the mysterious "pagerank" system, their spidering engine, GMail privacy concerns, their purchase of the USENET archives, or any number of other features, I was starting to think that maybe they are not quite as wholesome as they first appeared.

I liked the fact that they were making advances and pushing the envelope in terms of search engine results. I did not necessarily have a problem with the individual features themselves, but I began to question the way that they went about the features and their relationships with each other. Putting ads in the GMail accounts? Not such a big thing, except that Google allegedly tracks every IP address and associates it with every search request and therefore, every email. They can claim that no human reads personal email, but I am not willing to take their word for it anymore. And what if some law enforcement agency subpoenas that information? That pretty much trumps any privacy statement from Google. If they didn't track such intrusive information then there wouldn't be a problem. But I digress.

There was still one Google product that I had no experience in and I thought it was time to take the dive. I decided that my next area of study would be the Google AdWords program.

Google AdWords, as you might have guessed from the name, is an advertising program offered by "the big G." This program is what puts those ads on the right hand side of the page containing your search results. These results also go in your GMail, groups, or anywhere else that Google has authorized to use the AdWords ads. They also have some partnered sites that use these ads on their pages as well. These locations seem to change frequently and their documented list of clients is no longer correct. Most of the ones that I tried to follow up on have switched over to the Google AdWords competitor, Overture, which is used by both Yahoo! and MSN. In fact, Overture is actually owned by Yahoo! now.

I don't really think that advertising my site(s) in Google is worthwhile, but I figured it would be an interesting experiment and research assignment. It may even be an opportunity for some "investigative reporting," if you will, so I took the plunge. The plunge consisted of heading over to `adwords.google.com` and reading the available documentation and then dropping 20 bones to get an account started. Your $20 is basically a debit from which your fees are pulled and it is the minimum required (at the time of this writing) to create an account. They pull five bucks for a setup fee from that deposit in the first month. There are a few settings that you create when you set up the account, which will come into play later.

Now that you have an account, you need to create a "campaign." Campaigns are logical divisions of different topics that you want to advertise under the same account and bill to the same place. Most small users like me will only need one campaign. If you have sites that cover several different topics, you might want to separate your ads based on the topics that you want to advertise. Perhaps you are a Web developer or a hosting company and you need to advertise for a pet store, a hobby store, and a car dealership. Each one of these will have different keywords for different audiences and you would not want to mix these sites and topics together. This is only for organizational purposes and not very interesting to hackers.

While campaigns are logical divisions for content type, "ad groups" are subdivisions of campaigns. Campaigns are based on topics, but ad groups generally are based on individual sites. Each ad group has one ad that lends to being used one per site. For the example of a car site, you might have a different ad group for new cars and a different ad group for used cars. The reason is because there will be different keywords that fit each site better. In my case, I made a different ad group for different subdomains and projects on our site. For example: We have an ad group for *Binary Revolution Radio* and a different ad group for *Binary Revolution Magazine*. I also have a few other ad groups that I use to do some "testing" but basically you will want to create a different ad group for each different ad that you want to make.

At this point, you should still have $15 left to spend on advertising. The way that the system works is very similar to an online auction process. Instead of bidding on items, however, you are bidding on "keywords." You have to decide what keywords will provide you with the highest number of clicks. Obviously, if you are a car dealer, you would use keywords for different car models or other related search terms. You could also put phrases like "free porn," which may generate many hits but no one will buy anything once they get to your site. You paid for their click but they didn't give you anything in return. They didn't want your car site, they wanted free porn! Choosing appropriate and manageable keywords is one factor, but the other factor is that you are not the only person who wants those particular keywords and there is only so much screen space to dish out. This is where the bidding comes in.

Certain words are worth more than others. Obviously there are many car dealerships out there and they all want the same terms, such as "new car dealer." The way Google handles this conflict is that they sell to the highest bidder. The more you bid on the keywords that you want, the higher on the page your ad will appear. This bidding war is a perfect design for pay-per-click advertising. You only get charged your bid amount when someone actually clicks though your ad. Every time it is shown on the page, it is counted as an "impression" and every time someone actually clicks on your ad, it is counted as a "click-through." You must maintain a certain CTR (click-through-ratio) that generally needs to be at least 0.5 percent (one click-through out of every 200 impressions) but this percentage fluctuates based on other factors like the size of the campaign and the frequency of the keywords. If you do not stay above your CTR, your account will be slowed and/or canceled. An interesting bit of trivia is that the most expensive keywords are usually those related to lawsuits and lawyers who are looking for the big payout. This includes words and phrases like "class action" and "slip and fall" with the idea that it only takes one big payoff from a class action lawsuit to make them millions of dollars and justify the cost of the ads. Insert an obligatory lawyer joke of your choice here.

So this brings you to the keywords section, which is where you will do a lot of hacking to get good keywords and find some interesting things about the system. You choose keywords that you think are relevant and will generate hits on your ads. AdWords will estimate the number of hits and the CTR using some magical formula that is not publicly available. This tool may work fine for larger or medium-sized campaigns, but for small campaigns it was woefully skewed even to the point that I had ads that were being slowed or canceled within a day of creating them. The AdWords system expects more clicks than a very unique keyword can provide and it just gives up far too easily. If your keywords fail too often (there are levels of failure that are unimportant in this context) your account will be "slowed" and your ads will not show as often, or so they claim. I found that my keywords, being very detailed and obscure to the nonhacking world, were still being shown when I tested for the same keywords. I guess you cannot slow something down or lower it in the results when it is so unique that there are no other ads to put in front of it. If you want to reactivate your account to full speed, you have two grace reactivations and then to reactivate it a third time, you must pay a $5 dollar reactivation fee (which is ridiculously unjustifiable for an automated system). My account was "slowed" a mere 48 hours after its initial creation. This created a paranoid existence where I was scared that if I did not check the account daily, they would kill it again. I was suddenly demoted from a Webmaster to a babysitter.

When it comes to the keyword system itself, one of the things that I found interesting was the keyword tool that tries to help you come up with better keywords to add to your campaign. Once you put in a few keywords to get started, the keyword tool will then try to suggest similar keywords or phrases that are related to your original keywords. You will find some interesting results this way. I started with only a few keywords and found myself with many more based on the keyword tool. But this was where more problems started to occur. I found that my keywords were being canceled way too easily and were not given a fair chance to perform. Like I said earlier, if the campaign was on a larger scale, then this statistics model may hold true. But for smaller campaigns it simply was more of a hassle. It also led to another problem that I found slightly ironic, which is that the keyword tool suggested words and phrases to me that I was later denied due to their ToS (Terms of Service) anyway. Why recommend them if you are not going to allow me to use them? This is pretty much when my experience became totally negative with AdWords.

I also admit up front that I knew that their ToS had a rule against "hacking and cracking" sites. I knew this ahead of time, but I know that my site is a hacking site and does not promote cracking. Because of this, I thought that maybe Google would "do no evil" and be liberal with their policy and understand that my site does *not* promote illegal activity and explicitly states that in numerous places. Apparently, Google did not share this viewpoint as I found out later. In the beginning, however, when you create a keyword in your ad group it gets put into the rotation *immediately*! That is important to note. My ad group stayed in rotation for about four or five days before I got the ToS notice that my ads were suspended. I emailed the customer service person and explained to them that my site *did not* contain any reference to "cracking" and I even went so far as to show them the Google link to "define:hacker," which explained the definition of hacker right from their own site. I also pointed out that Google even offers a "hacker translator" service at `http://www.google.com/intl/xx-hacker/`, which seemed quite hypocritical to me. I also gave links to several prominent sites that clearly define and delineate the difference between hackers and crackers. None of this did any good.

That was the motivation for this article. If Google doesn't want to be reasonable and wants to keep forcing their rules on me, then maybe I should point out the flaws in their system for the entire world to see. First, let me point out again that your ads *do not* get checked upon initial creation before they get added, which is very useful if you want to be a *spammer* or promote your pr0n site for a few days on Google (although some words are explicitly banned from being in an ad at all). You will pretty much have your ad out there for a few hours or days before they will catch and ban it. Overture checks your ads before they are made available. They also banned my ads from Overture, but at least they weren't hypocritical about it. Google was banning my ads for having the word "hacking" in them but Amazon and eBay were *both* using that keyword in their ads. I guess they have bigger wallets than I do.

The next big flaw is that when Google "disables" your account, they simply remove it from the rotation until you correct the problem. They have to err on the side of caution and give you a chance to fix the item in question. To do this, you go into your ad and change it based on their explanation of the problem. In my case, they didn't like the words "hacking magazine" so I simply changed it to "security magazine" and it was immediately put back into the rotation. It took them another four or five days before they disabled my account again, this time for the same reason. I again tried to reason with them that the ad did not have the word "hacker" in it and that it was simply a site about computer security but they weren't hearing it. I got the same cut and paste response of the same "no hacking or cracking" rules every time I contacted them like I was some sort of moron. Fine, if they wanted to play that way, I certainly wasn't going down without a fight. And I also wasn't going down without using up my $15 credit that I still had left!

This is the most hilarious part of the story. Due to the method by which they check and verify ads, I simply went back into my ad and changed it again thinking that it would probably go back into rotation immediately. I removed the word "security" this time and simply left "magazine." The ad was instantly reactivated. Well, I began to wonder whether they kept any sort of database or history of ads that were banned to stop me from going back to them again. I edited my ad again and decided that I was damn well going to put my ad back out there. I put the word "hacking" back in front of "magazine" and voila! I was back in business! It was that simple! I can play this cat and mouse game for a long time if they are not going to block my previous ads and even if they tried I will apply some of the tactics from my "31337sp34k" article to make tiny changes and bypass just about any filter they want to throw at me. And so it went for about a month until they tried something different.

When they decided to ban my ad this time, they also added in a little extra twist. This time they went into every single one of my ad groups and banned *all* of my ads (some of which had "security," some had "hacking," etc.) but even better than this, they also went in and banned every individual keyword that I was using. This included "security magazine," "hacking magazine," "phreaking magazine," and included the ones that *they themselves* recommended earlier with their own keyword tool! I decided to push back a little bit and complain that they were banning keywords that were suggested by their *own system* but they still continued to cut and paste the same response to me over and over. Well, now I had to handle this problem as well.

As if it wasn't funny the first time (two paragraphs ago), let me repeat it. I went in and edited my ads again just as I had been doing and they were, once again, instantly reactivated. This time, however, they were not responding to my search terms. Obviously this is because even though the ad groups themselves were back in rotation, the individual keywords were still banned. Well, I figured that since it worked for the ad itself, maybe I could also modify the keywords just as easily and reactivate them as well. I cut my list of keywords out to a text file and saved the ad group with no keywords in it. I then clicked on "add keywords" and pasted those bad boys right back in. I think you can already guess what happened. I was back up and running with all keywords intact. They do not seem to check ads with any regularity.

But this was just the story of the big loopholes that I found in the fundamental aspect of their system. I also have some general advice for people who actually do want to use Google AdWords. One of the controversies with this type of advertising is that you can use just about any keywords that you want. This includes proper names and copyrighted titles of companies. Coke can use the keyword "Pepsi," Honda can use "Toyota," and similar related products can try to capitalize on their competitor's name and, unless someone complains, it will be right there. Now the big guns like the ones just mentioned will put a Cease and Desist on that activity with a quickness, but for smaller sites, you have some more flexibility. I use keywords of some other popular hacking magazines in my ads (*cough*) and some security trade magazines as well to try to let people know that we exist.

Another similar tip is to use misspelled versions of your keywords. This is a huge place to get a leg up on your competition. Google will come up with a suggestion if it notices a user's search terms are misspelled, but in the meantime the user has scanned the page and seen your ad—increasing your visibility. You may get them to click on your ad without even correcting their spelling and running the correct search. I think this is a great example of social engineering where you have to understand how people think and see where that intersects with technology.

One of the more evil things you can do is based on the "daily spending limit," which is one of the items I mentioned earlier that is set up when you first make the account. You can tell AdWords what you want your maximum daily spending limit to be. When you reach that limit, based on enough click-throughs to hit that amount, your ads will be removed from the rotation until the next day. This is meant to be a safety measure for smaller sites who don't want to get overwhelmed with so many hits or orders that they cannot keep up. If you really wanted to be a jerk to your competitor, or just to a random stranger (like me), you could just click their ads as much as possible and they will pay their bid amount for each click-through. Now, I don't believe it is so simple as to allow you to just sit and click over and over. It looks to me like they use session variables to limit how many clicks can come from one person. This may also be used in conjunction with IP resolution to only give one click per customer. I think we all know that a little scripting and a list of proxy servers can overcome both of these obstacles. And since the ads disappear after the daily limit is reached, this attack also doubles as a DoS attack by removing the ads for 24 hours, which might be an interesting move for a competitor to make. I wouldn't recommend that you do this because it is pretty rude and it will cost someone money, which is not a good thing. Don't bother trying this on my campaign because I set my daily limit very low so that it would take you months (literally) to use up my $15 of credit. Those lawyers who pay big money for the expensive keywords have a little more to worry about than I do.

Finally, the funniest hack of all is my last slap in the face to Google. I created an ad group (which will not be working by the time you read this). I immediately took it down, for fear of getting canceled outright, but it is here for posterity. The ad group produced results when searching for the string "Google really sucks." I am sure that my account will be shut down when this article is publicly released, but while I am waiting, I would like to continue to explore. Because of this, I am not leaving this keyword string up and running since they will probably shut me down if they saw it so if you try it as you read this, it will not be working (at least not from me). This is the new way to protest and is reminiscent of the fordreallysucks.com saga a few years back.

You can not only put in company protests, but personal messages to people triggered by keywords. Perhaps you have issues with a certain person and you want their name and a nice message to appear when you search for them. It could be used for almost anything. Theoretically, you could use this trick to send hidden messages to someone by sending them only a very long (80 character maximum) and unique key phrase. The gibberish phrase would not generate any hits, but the ad is still delivered (this is verified). You would contact the receiver and give them the phrase and they would know to look for it on Google and then click on the resulting ad, which would take them to a secret site or message (which you would have encrypted, of course), or the ad itself would contain a key to another message. The applications are endless.

So this research has been going on now for a couple of months as of this writing. I only want to get my $20 back out of it and then I will cancel the account. While I was waiting I thought I would share some of these loopholes with people so that they too could enjoy the Google AdWords program as much as I have. I also shared a few real tips on how to run a successful campaign in general. Tutorials are available on the Internet that contain probably even less information than I have provided in this article, yet people charge hundreds of dollars for them. You should probably save your money and just send them a link to this instead.

I loved Google for the longest time. But about a year ago that all started to change. They began making questionable business decisions that were obviously financially motivated. Google went public on August 19, 2004, and started answering to stockholders whose bottom line is profit. This has been the downfall of many companies. Bias (in the form of financial pressure) has been introduced. Your expectations for privacy should be nonexistent and they are probably too late now anyway. Google is the new Big Brother... and he is definitely watching.

"The Revolution Will Be Digitized!"

Shoutz: Alternative search engines, my fellow passengers on the flight back from interz0ne 4 who formed a circle around me listening to me teach Google hacking, Acidus, Decius, Rattle, romanpoet, Elonka, the listeners of "Binary Revolution Radio," and of course, the DDP.

The Not-So-Great Firewall of China (Winter, 2006-2007)

By Tokachu

When most people think of Internet censorship, they tend to think about China the most. While many other countries have some sort of state-controlled Internet policy, most people would refer to China because of the sheer size of the population and government. Ironically enough, the country with one of the largest Internet populations seemed to go for the lowest bidder when it came to Internet censorship devices, replacing quality control with frantic developers pressed for time.

No matter how strange that may be, it still does not justify a government that wants to keep full control over all media. Which is why I'll tell you, and hopefully a Chinese friend, how the "Great" firewall works and how to keep it from ruining your Internet.

How It Works

Unlike most other countries that simply block all TCP traffic or utilize a filtering HTTP proxy, China relies almost solely on special routers designed to censor based on raw TCP data instead of HTTP requests. The government of China relies on two main methods of censorship: flooding fake DNS requests and forging TCP connection resets.

DNS Poisoning

Very few domain names are actually "blocked" using this method. For a DNS poison to take place, there must be a request for a very, very, very naughty web site (like minghui.org) placed. This keeps anyone from figuring out how to connect to, let alone download content from, a forbidden host.

Here's what an uncensored DNS request would look like in China:

```
0.000000 192.168.1.2 -> 220.194.59.17 DNS Standard query A baidu.com 0.289817
220.194.59.17 -> 192.168.1.2 DNS Standard query response A 202.108.22.33 A
220.181.18.114
```

And here's how it would look if a domain were censored:

```
0.000000 192.168.1.2 -> 220.194.59.17 DNS Standard query A minghui.org 0.288963
220.194.59.17 -> 192.168.1.2 DNS Standard query response A 203.105.1.21 0.289482
220.194.59.17 -> 192.168.1.2 DNS Standard query response A 203.105.1.21 0.289838
220.194.59.17 -> 192.168.1.2 DNS Standard query response A 203.105.1.21 0.290374
220.194.59.17 -> 192.168.1.2 DNS Standard query response A 203.105.1.21 0.290732
220.194.59.17 -> 192.168.1.2 DNS Standard query response A 203.105.1.21 0.290757
192.168.1.2 -> 220.194.59.17 ICMP Destination unreachable (Port unreachable)
0.291311 220.194.59.17 -> 192.168.1.2 DNS Standard query response A 169.132.13.103
0.291337 192.168.1.2 -> 220.194.59.17 ICMP Destination unreachable (Port unreachable)
```

The real reply never gets through because the router forges nearly a half dozen fake DNS replies, along with a few random ICMP messages, to whoever requests a "forbidden" web site. This filter only works on UDP port 53 (DNS), which would theoretically make uncensored DNS requests possible if a sufficient number of DNS servers running on ports other than 53 existed.

You can tell if your packets are going through a Chinese router by one simple test. Try performing a DNS query to a remote machine in China. If it doesn't go through, try performing a DNS query for "minghui.org" on the same machine. If you get seemingly random responses, you're routing through China. If you want to determine which router is responsible for the censorship, run a traceroute and perform DNS requests on each hop, starting at the closest. When you get the fake DNS replies, you've found the offending router.

Forging TCP Resets

If a TCP connection is made from or to a computer in China, the packet data is checked for any "forbidden" words. If the data contains any of those words, the router forges a TCP RST (reset connection) packet. This also triggers a temporary block on TCP connections between those two specific computers. This makes it appear that the server has gone down temporarily.

The list of words not permitted to be used is encoded in GB2312 format, which ensures that businesses with web sites in China will not be able to send any illegal content to computers in China (since GB2312 is a character set required to be supported by all applications in China). The filter works thusly:

- If the word can be written in pure ASCII, look for the word in any mixture of lowercase and uppercase ASCII letters.
- If the word must be written in any combination of CJK ideographs, look for the byte sequence in either raw or URL-encoded GB2312. Hexadecimal strings are also case-insensitive.

Problems

Nearly all the problems of China's firewalls stem from one problem with the routers: they all perform stateless packet inspection. It doesn't matter what protocol the packets are using, nor what computer a packet comes from. All the router is concerned with is finding packets and forging responses, not dropping content.

Unfortunately, that flaw puts the router owners and admins at an extreme disadvantage. Anybody can do a Google search for packet-forging software or libraries (such as libpcap) and whip up a script to flood Chinese routers with fake packets, and the routers will respond, no matter what. It wouldn't be difficult to set up a botnet with DNS request forgers that can send billions of fake DNS requests to various routers, and in return have the victim think China is attacking his or her server! It's also possible to forge a TCP data packet with fake source and destination addresses, which means that if you happened to know the IP addresses of two important diplomats, you could easily cut off their ability to communicate. Popular Chinese web sites are just as vulnerable too; email systems could be cut off for hours at a time. The possibilities are endless. The TCP RST timer may be fairly short, but keep in mind that it only takes one fake packet to close a connection.

Getting Around It

The TCP Stack

One way to tell fake RST packets from real RST packets is to look at the time-to-live (TTL) parameter. Forged packets will always have higher TTLs than the real ones.

Getting around this, however, would require that both parties have a stateful TTL comparison filter at the kernel level. That's no good.

You could, however, rewrite a TCP-based application to send "forbidden" words by using the TCP urgent flag (URG). This only requires that both parties have a modified application—no kernel tweaking necessary. A great example of a program that sends data like that is a proof-of-concept C program called "covertsession" (search for it on Packet Storm Security). It can bypass most stateful packet inspectors, so it easily gets around the stateless inspectors in China. This is probably the best way to modify instant messaging (such as QQ) and IRC applications, assuming one couldn't just use encryption on both ends.

HTTP Traffic

There's nothing really special about how the firewall treats HTTP traffic. Mind you that it only looks for certain strings, no matter where they are. But notice how I said it only uses the GB2312 character set: there's nothing stopping us from simply using UTF-8 instead. You can "switch" your web sites from GB2312 to UTF-8 by simply running them through iconv. It's impossible for any UTF-8 sequence to match a GB2312 sequence, even by accident, so you're partially assured good exposure (for a period of time).

Most China-based web hosts, such as Baidu and Yahoo! China, rely on the firewalls to block some content for them. Google China, however, is the one huge exception. Google's Chinese servers are located in the United States and their censorship is done entirely in-house. What does that mean? For one, we don't need to worry about text being sent in GB2312 format (Google insists on using UTF-8). We can also exploit a "feature" in Google's text engine that was overlooked during the Google China development.

Google doesn't compare strings in their text engine like most of us do. Instead of simply comparing bytes, Google considers some words and characters equal to other words and characters that wouldn't match with a byte comparison algorithm. The character equality is what we want to look at here: mainly, how Google considers "fullwidth" ASCII characters (wide, fixed-width characters mostly used in Japanese character sets) equal to their ASCII counterparts. If you were to search for "computers" using fullwidth characters, you'd get the same results as you would with a simple ASCII search (although some ads might not show up).

Now here's where the hack comes in: Google's censors don't look for those fullwidth characters. So, if we were to search Google China for "tiananmen square" using fullwidth characters, the results wouldn't be filtered (the connection may be reset from what Google sends). Luckily, this trick works for Google Images, meaning that it isn't too hard to get Google's cache of images normally unfindable in China!

Here's some sample code to generate fullwidth characters in a shell in Perl (assuming you've got Unicode support in your terminal):

```
#!/usr/bin/perl -w
# fw.pl - make text W-I-D-E (convert ascii to fullwidth)
use encoding "UTF-8";
$input = $ARGV[0] or die("need one argument for text");
foreach (split //, $input) { print chr(0xFEE0 + ord($_)); }
## end script
```

Just type whatever search term you want, plug in the output to Google, and watch once-censored search results just show up!

Conclusion

Censorship isn't a profitable business. If China were to release an honest budget (and if people and corporations found out a huge percentage of their GDP was going towards censorship and propaganda instead of food and health care), China's economy would collapse in a matter of hours. Sadly, it isn't just Chinese citizens who believe the lies: corporations like Cisco and Google actually believe you can make money by keeping information from people. The sooner the Chinese people and their government realize this, the better.

(There are far too many people to thank—you know who you are.)

Hacking an Election (Autumn, 2007) *By Dagfari*

Working in Elections Manitoba has given me time to think—after all, it's Government work, eh?

Manitoba's election system is designed to provide secure paper voting with easy computer enumeration and vote counting and a thick paper trail. There are, however, multiple possible ways for a candidate to rig an election—at least for him. I'll be showing you one of them.

In case you aren't familiar with how provincial elections work in Canada, here's how. Each party fields a candidate to each electoral division. Thirty-three days before the actual election, the current legislative assembly issues a writ. Then, for two weeks, enumeration takes place, with people going door-to-door collecting names of eligible voters and marking them down. The names are entered into the database and handled with computers from this point on. Each returning office serves one electoral division, and each division is further broken down into various voting areas of about equal population. For example, the "Fort Whyte" division is broken down into a total of 65 voting areas. Each area consists of between 200 and 350 voters; each area has its own voting place where the actual voting occurs.

A week before elections take place advance polls begin, and the next week, Election Day. But a certain candidate, Mr. Theoretically Corrupt, has already guaranteed himself a seat in the next legislative assembly! (oh noes)

Technology

The enumeration software here for Elections Manitoba is called VES, the Voter Enumeration System. It's a Microsoft Access program, secured for multiple users with passwords. If you have access to the Master computer for the returning office serving that division, you have direct access to that database which, if you can edit directly, you can add voters to with no security check.

I'm sure we all know the old adage about "when an unauthorized user has physical access, you lose all security." The bonus is this: at least in my RO, the Master was routinely used as an extra data entry terminal. However, this sort of direct access is entirely unnecessary for a candidate to steal the election, as we'll see....

The Snatch

When the writ is signed, the Corrupt Candidate's goons get jobs as enumerators for his division. As enumerators, they are given everything they need—a badge, a pen, and a carbon copy pad of forms to fill out with each person's address, name, phone number, and other information.

There are no checks on whether the information filled out by each enumerator is necessarily true, and so it becomes a numbers game; 65 goons (one for each voting area) fill out an extra 20 names each. For some bonus, one could add names to vacant houses or add people in such a way that will not be detected with a casual observation of the list, like matching last names with people still at the address, or looking up names of dead relatives.

That's an extra 1,300 votes for the candidate, and that is likely enough to turn the election towards whoever is willing to do it. On voting day, those goons step into the lines at three separate voting places and work their way through each voting area.

Of course, this only gains the party the candidate is a part of one seat in the assembly, hardly enough to form a government or wrest power away from a majority. However, if the corrupt candidate was running against someone important—the premier of the province, for instance—or if all candidates from one party were this corrupt, then it could cause a lot of hassle/panic/disaster.

Conclusion

Thankfully, Canadian Elections' decentralized structure makes this sort of election-rigging hard and costly to do by itself, and there is always the risk that the voters' count would be noticed. It's possible for the candidate's goons to fill in names for those houses that don't have any people living in them, or houses that are under construction, but that may take away from the total number of bonus votes.

As it is though, once a name is enumerated, the voter is considered to be "in the system" and identified. All each goon needs to identify himself is something that has both his fake name and the fake-or-not address on it. Drivers' licenses are good, but for election-stealing purposes mail is better and easier to forge.

But of course, this is all for informational and analytical purposes only. Any use of this information or any other information available in an illegal or dishonest manner is no fault of mine and not something I condone as the writer. Please, do not steal Manitoba's Elections, money, software, or anything else. Thanks.

Using Hacker Skills to Change History (Winter, 2007-2008)

By Rop Gonggrijp

My most recent confrontation with what it means to be a hacker started in March of 2006, after I went to vote for the local council of Amsterdam. At the polling station, I had to use a brand new electronic voting machine that the city was renting from a company called Sdu. In fact, Amsterdam had contracted the entire election as a turnkey service. Sdu was even training the poll-workers. This "voting machine" was in fact a computer with a touch screen running Windows. To make matters worse, inside each computer was a GPRS wireless modem that sent the election results to Sdu, which in turn told the city. I had not been blind to the problems of electronic voting before, but now I was having my face rubbed in it. And it hurt.

I was angry because I felt my election had been stolen. There was no way to observe a count; one just had to believe that this wireless-equipped black-box Windows machine was counting honestly. I knew a little bit too much about the risks associated with computer technology to go along with that. I wasn't the only one who was angry. My longtime friend Barry came home from that March, 2006, election with the exact same story that I had come home with: trying to reason with poll-workers who clearly felt that only the medically paranoid would distrust such a wonderful shiny box. When we met later that day, we vowed to not only get mad but to do something about it.

But that wasn't going to be all that easy. By the time Amsterdam had gotten electronic voting, it was pretty late in the game: Amsterdam, with a population of approximately 750,000, was the last city in the Netherlands (with a population of around 16.5 million) to get electronic voting. Some cities were renting the same system that Amsterdam now had, but the vast majority was using an older system made by a company called Nedap. While I studied the legal requirements for electronic voting, I became even more convinced that all of these "machines" (that were all in fact computers) needed to go if we were to have transparent and verifiable elections. The regulations treated these systems as if they were indeed mere "machines." They worried about the amounts of humidity and vibration they could withstand and they made sure nobody would get shocked from touching one. Computer security wasn't even mentioned. But the biggest problem wasn't the lack of security; it was the lack of transparency. We got together a small group of like-minded people and started planning a campaign.

There had been previous attempts to raise the question of trustworthiness in relation to voting machines, but the Ministry of the Interior was used to painting the opponents of electronic voting as technophobe Luddites. Given that half of our group consisted of hi-tech-loving hackers, this was an approach that wasn't going to work this time. During the next year and a half we managed to get the attention of the media. We claimed that the Nedap "machines" were computers and not "dedicated hardware" (as the manufacturer claimed) and that they could just as easily be taught to play chess or lie about election results. The person selling these computers in the Netherlands wrote wonderful long rants on his web site, and in reaction to our claim he said he did not believe his "machines" could play chess.

So we caused a true media frenzy when we got hold of a Nedap voting computer and made it play chess. (We also made it lie about election results.) There was a debate in Parliament, during which the responsible minister promised to appoint two committees. That next election, an international election observation mission studied the problems with electronic voting in the country, which until then had always been the example country for uncontroversial e-Voting. In their report, they advised that these types of voting computers "should be phased out" and the two committees also wrote very harsh reports about how these "machines" came about and how they should not be used in the future. A lot more happened. We threatened to take the government to court on several occasions, and we even won a case in which the Nedap approval was nullified. But by then the ministry had already decided to throw in the towel, retracting the legislation that allowed electronic voting. The next elections in the Netherlands will be held using pencils and paper (which is really quite OK because over here we've only got one race per election, so counting by hand isn't all that hard).

One of the things that struck me about this campaign was that to win, we've needed almost every hacker skill imaginable. Imagine all the stuff you can learn from this magazine, or from going to (or helping organize) a hacker convention. From general skills such as dealing with the media or writing press releases to social engineering (getting hold of the system to experiment with it), lockpicking (showing that the mechanical locks were bogus as the same one Euro key was used all over the country), reverse engineering (modifying their 68000 code without access to source), and system administration (web site).

Having published a hacker magazine in the Netherlands (*Hack-Tic*) and co-founded a major Internet Service provider (XS4ALL), I was no stranger to conflict. At XS4ALL we had had serious issues with the infamous "church" of Scientology as well as with the German government. Also, the international contacts I got from growing up in the hacker community paid off. The hack was very much a Dutch-German project, and we're still working together tightly to also get rid of these same "machines" in Germany.

At certain moments I had the funny feeling that somehow this was the project that I had been in training for all these years.

So I guess what I'm saying is that if you are a hacker, if you're going to hacker conventions, if you like figuring stuff out, or if you are building your own projects, please realize that, possibly by accident, you may also possess some truly powerful skills that can help bring about political change, and that these skills will become more and more important as technology becomes a bigger part of ever more political debates. So if you don't like the news, go out and make some of your own!

Open Your Mind

As we come to our last section, it's only appropriate that it encompass subject matter that really defies a single categorization. Here we have everything from hacking the human genome to the creation of a new hacker language (God help us). Brain implants, biometrics, and, of course, hacking people themselves through the fine art of social engineering. You can apply the concept of hacking just about anywhere and over the years at *2600* we've seen so many new and imaginative applications. Why do I get the feeling that this is only the beginning?

A Brief Intro to Biometrics (Summer, 2000) *By Cxi ~*

A new area of physical security that has become increasingly popular, and will become exponentially popular as its uses are more easily implemented and its need is more clearly seen, is Biometrics or Bio-access. Access to what? Biometrics is not just to be used for access to buildings or computers, but will soon be used for access to your bank account, your credit cards, or even to make a phone call. Biometric systems grant access based on personal identification, which is based on a preprogrammed pattern of recognition, providing not only identification but also verification. In order for this to work, we must keep in mind the theory that physiological traits are unique for everyone. I will give you a quick synopsis of what occurs when you use a biometric system.

The process for identification begins with a request for recognition by a person who submits certain biological information. This is then compared to an existing database. The speed of this process all depends on the size of the database, size of the usually large file, and processing speed of the computers. New compression technology is shrinking the file size of this "bio 411," allowing for a larger capacity to process large amounts of comparison data.

For the most part, biometrics requires contact with body parts. Because of the chances of disease transmission, video and laser scanning are being implemented in many applications to eliminate the need for anyone to touch anything. With the constant use of computers today, securing access and information is no longer a business matter, but something that people have to be concerned about in their private lives as well.

There are seven common biometric categories being used today. Fingerprint, hand geometry, retina scan, iris scan, facial geometry, voice verification, and signature verification are all considered a part of biometric security. Fingerprint analysis is the oldest and most commonly known form. But this has evolved from the old ink and paper system. Current systems take video images of the fingerprint and break it down into various components. The ridges on the fingerprint are converted into mathematical keys so that each fingerprint is really a series of mathematical equations. Also, the more fingers used for identification means a more accurate verification process. But, this also means doubling, tripling, or even quadrupling the storage size needed. Higher resolution of the systems allows for more of these equations, which in turn results in greater accuracy. Initial reading and storage can take anywhere from five to ten seconds and verification only about one or two seconds. Hand geometry is very similar to fingerprint systems and is actually just an extension of them. It creates mathematical equations usually based on the height, width, and length of the hand. This could lead to a possible problem with very identical twins who have the same hand size. Retinal scans require the examination of the eye at a close range (about one to two inches). This is very intrusive and long and therefore has only been implemented in places with very high security requirements. An iris scan makes a mathematical map of the iris (area around the pupil). With an estimated 200 points within the iris, it is fairly easy to do so and can be very discriminating depending on how many points are processed. Since eye color is not the issue, black and white cameras (which translates to cheaper systems) can be used to capture the image, which will be stored and compared to a live scan during the next verification process. This is much more accurate than hand geometry because even members of the same family, including those very identical twins, will have different iris scans. Face geometry is the result of hand and finger recognition. It takes a video image and selects facial points in order to make a decision to grant access. The most common use determines the distance between two points on the face. Another use involves measuring heat spots with an infrared camera (which translates to more expensive systems). This avoids problems created by objects that may cover the face. Voice verification has also become increasingly popular. It analyzes voice pitch, speed, and pattern and forms it into a personal digital signature. Many systems have been made more accurate by requiring a standard word pattern to be used for reference identification and confirmation. This is also a system that avoids disease transmission because it requires absolutely no physical contact. Signature verification divides a person's signature characteristics into two parts: those that remain constant and those that change. This usually requires using an integrated writing tablet system and can be very costly.

There have also been many different implementations of these kinds of bio-access. Many require some form of card access that is verified by one of the previously described methods. This makes the verification process much quicker since the computer merely compares the live data to the data matching the owner of the card as opposed to searching the entire database for a match (or to not find a match). Future technology will use smart cards to hold the comparison data themselves and therefore eliminate the need for larger, quicker databases to store and process these large bio-information files. But can you just imagine what would happen if someone (and you *know* they will) figured out how to hack one of those smart cards? People would be able to create their own identities pretty easily and gain access to restricted places without much effort on their part, since the computer let them in. And computers never lie, kid (sorry... lame ass *Hackers* quotation. I know... but it had to be done). Also, compatibility is an issue. Many manufacturers of these systems use different protocols and therefore you can't have a "universal file" to be used on all security systems everywhere... yet. But obviously this is something the government (Department of Defense) would want and supports not only with words but also with funding supplied by the National Registry. With the possibility to keep every person's unique characteristics on file (not to mention what else would be possible) and maybe not even need to store the file on your own computer with the new smart cards, wouldn't you prefer to do this? A committee known as Bio-API has been formed to look into creating standards for the industry. Another standard developed by many industrial developers, the government, and even MIT is the Speaker Verification-API (SVAPI). There is a free software developer's kit online, which I suggest you download if you're a Windoze person (95 and NT).

Biometrics itself is such an intrusive and invading procedure that many have said it needs its own form of security. However, as of yet there is no law or regulation governing the sale or transfer of biometric information that is legally acquired. This means that if you apply for a job and are required to submit to a biometric scan, the controlling agency provides absolutely no protection for your private information. There is a pending California bill, AB50, which is attempting to stop the copying of biometric information. Another issue for concern is the efficiency of such systems. Are they really needed? Are people going to stop using ATMs or banks because they can't stand to wait for that damn iris scan only to learn that they can't get their money because of some system bug? Well, the National Biometrics Test Center has developed testing standards for evaluating the performance of biometric access equipment, previously only performed by the manufacturers. The best chance for standardization has come from the National Computer Security Association, which has created a certification program for systems and system components such as scanners that will set error rates based on a standardized testing method.

Now, we can look at this new technology any way we choose. If it's left in the hands of the private and business sectors, and used in ways that doesn't discriminate or eliminate people's options for doing things, this can be a great thing and an added level of security for people in their homes, and for businesses fearing corporate espionage or whatever paranoia they may have. However, if placed in the hands of the government, we could be giving them one more power that would enable them to control and monitor our lives. Depending on where these systems are made, the government could be able to watch when we come and go from our houses, log on to our computers, take money from an ATM, or even see what pay-per-view movies we buy. That my friends, is a very scary thought and something I hope I never have to think of as a reality.

Shouts: ASleep, glock, minus, LordViram, and the rest of the ct2600 crew!

Poor Man's 3D (Spring, 2002) *by diabolik*

This article will explain how to take those cheap "3D glasses" you get in cereal boxes and comic books and use them with Winamp's AVS studio to create very realistic 3D spectrum analyzer effects and trip for days. It's pretty simple and amazing. When it works, you can get effects reaching about a foot to two feet out of your screen toward you. Very trippy. The trick to achieving a 3D effect from your monitor is a pair of those old "3D glasses" you'd get as a kid to turn red and blue lines into a crummy purple picture that was sort of, but not quite, 3D.

Disclaimer: You can hurt your eyes doing this. The day after I figured it out, I woke up with a pretty bad headache. You can experience anything from nausea to tiredness and just a plain bad headache. If those "Magic Eye" things weren't for you, don't attempt this. Use at your own risk; it's not my fault. Don't blame me.

What You Will Need

- **A computer:** (Actually, although it's not that intense graphically, you should have a pretty good video card. The higher the frame rate, the nicer this effect looks. More importantly, a low resolution will force the spectrum analyzers to cancel each other out more often and will result in distorted pictures.)
- **A pair of 3D glasses:** (These are the ones with a piece of red cellophane on one eye and blue cellophane on the other. The ones I'm using have red over the left eye and blue over the right. If yours aren't the same, wear them backwards or mod my code.)
- **WinAMP with AVS Studio:** (These are what I wrote the "3D mod" presets in.) You'll want to be fullscreening these effects at 640x480, although yesterday I was ICQing while I had a portion of my monitor displaying the AVS and the effect was noticeable—it hurt a lot more, too.
- **Booming techno** always helps. Aphex Twin, Clint Mansell...whatever floats your boat.

How to Make the Presets

I strongly suggest writing your own. The AVS presets I wrote are simple spectrum analyzers, a blue analyzer with a red analyzer offset to the right of the blue. The more the two are offset, the closer to your eyes they appear. In Winamp's AVS Studio, the x and y coordinates of the screen begin at -1 and end at 1, no matter what the resolution is. In order to make the analyzers appear to be bulging out of the screen, the offset between the red and blue analyzers (I'll just refer to this as the offset from now on) must vary. A good value for the offset I found was c*cos(2*y)+0.05 for vertical slopes and c*cos(2*x)+0.05 for horizontal slopes, where c is a value of from 0.05 to 0.2. (Note: these values work well for a 14-inch monitor at about two feet away. You may have to modify this range in order to suit your setup.) Since the scopes are offset horizontally, it is easier to see a vertical scope in 3D because the two scopes will cancel each other out less; this is where a higher resolution comes into play. The higher the detail of the scopes, the less one scope will overwrite its companion's position, and the better looking the result.

To make a throbbing vertical scope, try the following:

1. Open the AVS Studio. (Start the visualization and double-click in the window.) Make a new preset.
2. Add a trans/fade (+ -> trans -> fadeout). Set it to be fast enough; you can slow it later if you like the effect. Personally I just click on Main and check off Clear Every Frame so the effect is as clean as possible.
3. Add a Superscope (+ -> render -> Superscope) with the following settings:
   - **Init:** n=40; t=0; tv=0.1;dt=1;
   - **Per Frame:** t=t*0.9+tv*0.1;
   - **Per Point:** x=t+v*(pow(sin(i*3.14159),1)/2)+(0.03*cos(2*y)); y=i*2-1.0; x=x*1.5-0.09
4. Check off Waveform, Center, and Lines. Although you can modify those as you wish, that's just what I suggest. This will be the blue scope. To accurately choose your color, see "Calibrating Your Preset" below.
5. Click the x2 button to copy this Superscope. Modify this one to have the following settings:
   - **Init:** n=40; t=0; tv=0.1;dt=1;
   - **On Beat:** c=((rand(100)/100)*0.08)+0.07;
   - **Per Frame:** t=t*0.9+tv*0.1;c=c*.9;
   - **Per Point:** x=t+v*(pow(sin(i*3.14159),1)/2)+(c*cos(2*y))+0.05; y=i*2-1.0; x=x*1.5-0.09;

This is only slightly more complex than a flat surfaced (in 3-space) scope. When the OnBeat function is run, the offset between the two scopes is randomized between 0.07 and 0.15. Every frame, the offset is reduced to 90 percent of its previous value (the scope appears to shrink back towards the screen). Although Winamp's beat detection isn't that great, during good house music or anything with good bass, you will definitely "see" the effect. You can get another neat effect by making two sets of scopes—one vertical, one horizontal—and have them come out of the screen OnBeat random amounts, with or without decay. To make a 3D horizontal scope, I use the following settings for each scope:

Blue Scope:

- **Init:** n=40; t=0; tv=0.1;dt=1;
- **Per Frame:** t=t*0.9+tv*0.1
- **Per Point:** y=t+v*(pow(sin(i*3.14159),1)/2); x=i*2-1.0+(0.03*cos(2*x)); y=y*1.5;

Red Scope:

- **Init:** n=40; t=0; tv=0.1;dt=1;
- **On Beat:** c=((rand(100)/100)*0.07)+0.08;
- **Per Frame:** t=t*0.9+tv*0.1;c=c*.9; (this would be to decay the scope back to the screen, otherwise remove the latter equation)
- **Per Point:** y=t+v*(pow(sin(i*3.14159),1)/2); x=i*2-1.0+(c*cos(2*x))+0.05; y=y*1.5;

Another interesting effect you could try would be to change cos(2*x) to abs(cos(4*3.14159*x)). This would make two 3D ripples in the analyzer. Instead of just coming out once, it would come out, go back in, out, and in again.

What Can't I Do to the Presets?

I strongly recommend you make your own; mine are just working guides. You probably can do a lot better if you've ever made Winamp AVS settings before; until this project I never tried. However, don't think that you will throw some crazy blur effect into the mix and it will be even more trippy. For this effect to work, the blue pixel must be immediately offset to the left of the red pixel for your eyes to combine them into a single 3D point. I've found to get the most effective 3D effect, keep your presets clean. Whatever effects you do attempt to add, keep in mind, if the red and blue lines cross (this is a reference to a vertical scope—in a horizontal scope, they will cross all the time), you will lose the 3D effect immediately.

It would be really interesting to get a dot-plane working with this effect, but unfortunately I've found that there are far too many dots at most angles to not have one dot plane overlap a large portion of the other. You could do this by writing an AVS plugin in C++, but that is outside the scope of this article.

What Can I Do with the Presets?

Noting the limitations above, you can have some damn cool effects. The most noticeable thing you can do is modify "c" in the formula dynamically. Winamp's AVS Studio contains the ability to do "OnBeat" modifications to your variables.

Calibrating Your Preset

To get the best 3D effect, you want the brightest color of red that still appears dark to the eye seeing through the blue cellophane, and vice versa. To find the right shade of blue, double-click on the blue bar near the bottom-right of the window. Put on your glasses. Close your right eye. Choose a shade of blue that appears dark to your left eye. You should now be looking at the light-to-dark blue vertical gradient near the bottom right of the color selector through the red cellophane. Move the brightness selector upwards as high as it goes while it still appears black, or near black. This will make the color as noticeable as possible to your right eye while still appearing as nothing to your left eye. Click OK, and calibrate the second "Render/Superscope" color by doing the opposite of what you did for the first. If when looking at the presets through the glasses you can see what almost looks like shadows of the scopes on the screen itself, try darkening the chosen shades of blue and red.

Other Ideas with the Glasses

Obviously, Winamp AVS modules are just one idea for these glasses. With basic VB skillz one could write 3D wireframing modules or a starfield generator in pseudo-3D. Of course, you're limited to the color of purple, but considering you've paid about a dollar or less for these you shouldn't really complain. One suggestion I've had from a friend was to make an hour-long mix tape, export the whole thing to VHS, and bring the tape, 20 pairs of the glasses, and a lot of booze/weed/cough syrup/whatever to a party and have a nice massive trip.

Conclusion

Well, when it works, it works well. If you can't get your crazy ass preset to work on the first try, attempt to simplify it; I've found it's a lot easier to see two scopes than one, but three or more need a warm up of simpler effects. Other things you can try are shifting your head from side to side; this helps you really see the effect I've found. If you have too many scopes (four instead of two), try changing the distance or angle you're viewing. Just experiment; half the fun's just seeing what you can come up with. Then again a good chunk of it is staying up 'til 4:00 a.m. coaxing some cough syrup listening to Aphex Twin in headphones.

Greetz: HackCanada, argv, clox, the other members of Priapism, JaidenKnight, all my local friends—you know who you are.

A History of "31337SP34K" (Autumn, 2002) *By StankDawg*

First of all, I am not going to write the entire article in "elite speak." It defeats the purpose and is annoying beyond belief in this context. What I am going to do is enlighten the new generation of hakkerz into what "elite speak" is, where it came from, and when (and if) to use it. It has become commonplace in the hakker community, but I think everyone should understand its origins.

Long before Internet Explorer was even thought of and when Netscape was still a wet dream, the Internet existed. Most people reading this article know that the Internet is not the same as the World Wide Web, but for the novices, it's imperative to point this out. Back then, we used to communicate through earlier aspects of the Internet, some of which still exist today. Some of the most prominent were email, newsgroups, and Internet Relay Chat (IRC).

Let's start with email. It is the most obvious and widespread in use. Its use has exploded since back in the day. Back then, we used emoticons to convey emotions, not to decorate our email with pretty pictures. We didn't come up with the word "emoticons." That was some media label made up to be cute. We used them for effectiveness. Using emoticons could convey in a couple of keystrokes what might take several sentences. Keep in mind that back then, we had to keep our messages short and sweet. I used a 300 baud modem (the coupler kind that you had to put the headset into) to get dialup access. Broadband was never heard of in this low bandwidth world, so messages had to be brief. Think of how telegrams work today, where there is an incentive to be brief (telegrams charge per word). To that end, we would simply use the letter "Y" instead of typing the entire word "Why." We used "R U" to shorten the phrase "are you." These are only a few examples. The drawback to this was that people who weren't used to it may have gotten confused and wondered if "Y" meant "why" or "yes." It could have referred to either of these. It was only after practice and reading for context did people become accustomed to using this new "shorthand" to communicate. But this was only the beginning of the language.

"Elite speak" really took off with the onset of newsgroups. The Net was growing, bandwidth was increasing (I was now up to a 1200 baud modem), and newsgroups were becoming more popular. Newsgroups allowed people with common interests to have a central area to communicate with one another. In this medium, the same shorthand used in email was continued and expanded. But an additional problem arose. Some server administrators felt the need to control the content and censor speech that they found "questionable." They would regularly filter the database to delete posts containing "objectionable material" just like the content filtering software of today.

What this meant was that you either got your message deleted by the administrators or you found loopholes to outsmart the filters. That is what hakkerz do. I get a lot of flak from n00bs who don't understand why I say "hakkerz" instead of "hackers." The reason is simple. Since "hacking" fell under the "objectionable material" category, we had to intentionally misspell the word to avoid getting kill-filed. OK, so they added "hakker" to their filter. But what about "H4ck3r," "H4kk3r," "Hax0r," and so on? We kept adapting the language (and don't think this is any less of a language than Ebonics) until the censors finally gave up. We could make every word adapt and change to avoid being blocked. It got to the point where we started intentionally misspelling words that didn't even have the potential to be kill-filed. Words like "Kool" and "rokk" began to be added and it fit with the pattern of our other words while stilling maintaining meaning. Eventually, they realized that it was impossible to block a polymorphic language, and they gave up.

The final transformation of the language was built purely on ego. That's right, there is an aspect of simple ego involved in trying to look "kool" and it came about mostly on IRC. Those of us who have been online for the genesis of the language communicated like we always had, using the methods mentioned above. It was mostly out of sheer habit. This led to inevitable questions from n00bie Hax0rs and non-hakkerz alike asking why we "can't spell" and asking what we were trying to say. Nubies picked up on the language, but they began to pervert it. Because we used words like "h4kk3r," which used both letters and numbers in it, it made the word appear to be in mIXeD CasE (because using a fixed font, numbers are generally bigger than letters). This caused many people to start using "mIx3d c4Se" just for the sake of making words look like the traditional "elite speak." Quite frankly, it did look kind of kool when not used to excess!

So with all of these things creating and modifying the language, you can see why we have such a beast. It grew out of necessity. The new generations of hakkerz pick up and learn the language as it is today, but they don't always understand and appreciate its roots. Hopefully now they understand the history and the beauty of the language.

Where does it go from here? This is an ever-evolving language! It is, by no means, set in stone. Currently, it is accounting for multiple languages (Spanish, "Spanglish," Portuguese, etc.), adding current slang speaking terms ("wasssssup," "pissed," etc.), and remnants from many other languages. The most complex addition is the integration of actual source code and symbolism into the language. In the beginning of this article I said that the World Wide Web is not the same as the Internet. More than likely, had we been talking online, I would have said "WWW != Internet" just like I always say that "Hakkerz != Criminals." Hopefully, with all of this newfound history, you will not only understand the language, but you will also appreciate it, and use your new power wisely. Use it with other hakkerz, but don't annoy people who don't or can't understand it. 0n1y t#en '//!ll j00 +ruly b '1337!

Honeypots: Building the Better Hacker (Winter, 2002-2003)

By Bland Inquisitor

Honeypots are usually programs that emulate services on a designated port, but once successfully cracked, offer no real power to the attacker. The honeypot program will then alert the admin that an attack is in progress, and will allow the admin to track the attacker's every move. Honeypots will also show the methods the attacker is using to gain entry, and what methods are being used to cover his or her tracks. In this article, I will show how honeypots work, why honeypots are not generally practical for most security situations, and how honeypots are breeding both smarter attackers and dumber admins.

How Honeypots Work

Honeypots are designed to operate on many levels. They increase the time an attacker will spend because the honeypot makes it unclear which attacks work and which ones don't. They let the admin know what method an attacker is using before they succeed, such as port scanning, brute forcing a password, or a Sendmail attack. Once honeypots are widely implemented, the attacker will be forced to spend more time in a system that may be closely watched, and will eventually be scared off. Also, once xy63r n1nja the script kiddie stops going anywhere near the system, admins can focus all their attention on fending off people with actual skill.

In one of the honeypot advertisements I read, port 365 was being used as the honeypot port. This means that a scan that returns port 365 as active will make the would-be attacker turn and run off, and that systems that are not running the honeypot can use port 365 as a bluff, so that when xy36r n1nja the script kiddie sees it and the system looks sexy, he will be less inclined to go in because he thinks that the vulnerabilities he sees are a deception. According to SecTech systems administrator Dan Adams, honeypots are "like opening a fake store, loading it with cool stuff, and sitting back hoping someone will break into it."

Honeypots are catching a lot of pretty serious heat from the legal and ethical community. Some critics are calling honeypots entrapment. Let me clear this up for you. Entrapment occurs when a person is coerced to commit a crime that they would not under normal circumstances engage in. It's going to be next to impossible for poor xy63r n1nja to use an entrapment defense in court, because by the time po po shows up, it will be obvious he was lame-assing around of his own accord. However, if a crafty admin goes on IRC and tells everyone that his honeypot is actually the fabled government computer that holds the truth about the Kennedy assassination, Area 51, and ancient methods of dolphin flogging and people hack him, then an entrapment defense would stand a chance. The reason is that the admin could never prove that xy63r n1nja and his crew were going to hack his system without being enticed. Other critics say that honeypots are akin to electronic wiretapping. This I can agree with. Since there is not much legal regulation of honeypot technology, and the closest legal procedures are loose at best, some very scary things could happen.

Other companies could expand the basic thrust of the technology, perhaps into the p2p networks. At that point it would be us, the hacker community, that stands up and tells the world that this is a gross invasion of privacy. Then, pretty much just like the MPAA did to us, all they would conceivably have to say is: "Consider the source, your honor. *Hackers* want this technology stopped. Hackers are criminals. You don't want to side with criminals, do you? We are here to protect the American people from hackers, and we need you to be brave and give us the power to shut these nasty people down." Then in all likelihood, the corporations would roll right over us again. I don't think it takes a major leap of logic to see that this is where honeypot technology, or more specifically, technology that clearly violates people's rights under the guise of protection, could be headed. Also, I don't trust the "good guys" any farther than I can throw them. We need to put a handle on the situation before the "security community" gets any ideas on how to further expand their powers past our rights on the backs of the hacker community they demonize to get their way.

Why Honeypots Are Not Practical for Everyone

The good news is that honeypots are not a true "solution." The best application for a honeypot is to track an intruder who has already made a home in the system. The most noteworthy case of this happening was documented by Clifford Stoll in his book *The Cuckoo's Egg*. Stoll was an admin at Berkeley when he found an intruder using his system to steal secrets. But only an admin who has been around the block a few times and watches his system often can make full use of honeypots. Apart from that, over 90 percent of attacks against a system come from inside, and there is nothing a honeypot can do to stop someone who has internal access from running amok. For the average company, the extent of a honeypot's effectiveness is to keep xy63r n1nja and the rest of the script kiddies away, and to show that there is a real threat of people breaking into the system. It is almost unheard of that a honeypot traps someone with real skill because it is designed to keep the kiddies at bay.

In the digital arms race, tightening the existing security holes will only force the attackers to get better while the admins get complacent. Most admins are only slightly better than good ole xy63r n1nja in the first place; they get the latest and greatest piece of ready-made software and call themselves experts. What is bound to happen in the majority of the situations is that a company sets up a honeypot and never bothers to spend the time it takes to maximize its effectiveness. Of course, the true answer is for admins and software programmers to actually take a little pride in their work and do their jobs properly. Also, it would help if software companies would take some responsibility when they find security holes in their product and update accordingly. System admins should also feel obligated to keep their software current, and make sure nobody within their company is given more access than they need.

Shout outs: stankdawg, grifter, debug, project honeynet. And an apology if anybody actually uses the name xy63r n1nja.

Hacking the Genome (Winter, 2003-2004) *By Professor L*

The creation of genetically modified organisms (GMOs) is now within the ability of a knowledgeable and dedicated hacker. The most common genetic modification is the insertion of genes from one organism into another. The recipient is called a "transgenic organism" and this article will give you enough information so that anyone who could pass a high school biology lab can create one.

The usual *2600* article starts off with a disclaimer about how the article is for informational purposes only, and should the reader do anything illegal or dangerous, that's the reader's fault. The disclaimer in this article has to be stronger. Creating transgenic organisms has the potential to do great, possibly even catastrophic harm to the entire biosphere. Although the specific manipulations I describe in this article are safe (and often done in biology teaching labs), knowledge of the methods of genetic engineering have the potential to unleash enormous forces for good or for evil.

The most likely harmful consequence of hackers making a mistake with genetic engineering is for the hackers to get sick or to make the people around them sick. Maybe really, really sick. If you are going to try these techniques, learn about safe laboratory practices and follow them. The consequences of screwing up with genetic engineering are much worse than a mere jail sentence, so treat it seriously. No kidding.

If these techniques are so dangerous, why on earth would I want to tell hackers how to use them? I've thought about this long and hard before writing this article, and I have three reasons for writing. First, none of the information in this article is all that hard to find these days. Good high school biology classes teach the ideas (although they often figure out how to make it seem boring), and pretty much every community college will have a molecular biology lab class that teaches all of this information and good lab technique, too. If you think this article is cool, I would strongly encourage you to take a real lab mol bio course and get at the good stuff.

My second reason is that I believe in the hacker mentality. When as a teenager I got tired of stacking tandems with my 8038-based blue box, I built an Imsai 8008, one of the first computer kits. Twenty-five years later, looking at my lab and all the scientific publications and prizes I have, even the straight world would have to admit that some hackers have made positive contributions to society. The hackers in the Homebrew Computer Club in the '70s spawned much of what would become Silicon Valley. The technologies that fascinate us have the power to create a radically different world; that is, they have the potential to be used for both awesome creation and awesome destruction. Hackers, who these days I think of as kids with a thirst for knowledge and the urge to try things for themselves, can be the ones with the powerfully creative ideas about how to use new technologies.

And my third reason for writing is that corporate powers are already using these technologies very broadly, and in ways that I don't feel are doing justice to their potential. With this article, I hope to inspire people to learn about what genetic engineering can do, and to come up with superior alternatives to the profit-seeking corporate approach. How do corporations use genetically modified organisms? Chances are, you are eating them! Pretty much all processed food in America contains GMOs. Monsanto's Roundup Ready crops dominate worldwide commercial agriculture, including soybeans, corn, cotton, canola oil, and sugar. The particular genetic modification in these foods makes it possible to dump the weedkiller Roundup on the crops without killing them. It's convenient for industrial farmers and it helps keep Monsanto the world's largest seller of herbicides. Surely there must be a better use for transgenic organisms than that! I hope someone reading this article will one day invent it.

Now that I have convinced you to be safety conscious and to strive to use this power for good (I did convince you, didn't I?), let's get started on the methods of how new genes are inserted into organisms. First, you will need to know a little bit of terminology. The base organism that we will be adding the genes to is called the "host." The host, like just about all organisms, can be thought of as a machine for turning environmentally available material and energy (food) into copies of itself. One of the key components of any organism is its genome, that is, its complete collection of genes. The genome contains all of the instructions for making the chemicals (mostly proteins) that do the work of transforming food into offspring. We are going to add a new gene, called the "transgene," to the host.

Every organism is made up of cells (adult humans have about one trillion cells; many kinds of organisms consist of only a single cell), and each cell has its own copy of the organism's genome. Both the genome and the transgene are DNA molecules. DNA is a very long polymer, which means it is a molecule made up of a string of repeating components. In the case of DNA, the components are called nucleotides, and referred to by their one-letter abbreviations, A, C, T, and G. The human genome has about three billion nucleotides. The transgene we are going to insert is only a few thousand nucleotides. However, we are not going to learn how to insert new genes into human beings. Not only is that potentially very dangerous (and highly regulated), but inserting genes into all the cells of a multicellular organism like a mammal requires better laboratory technique than a first-time genetic engineer is going to be able to achieve. In this article, I will teach you how to put the firefly genes that are responsible for the firefly's glow into Escherichia coli (E. coli for short), the bacterium that lives in your gut. You're going to make intestinal bacteria that glow in the dark.

So, in this article, the host will be E. coli and the transgenes will be the gene from fireflies that make them glow. This gene is called Luciferase. (Who says scientists don't have a sense of humor?) In order to do your genetic engineering, you will first have to learn how to grow controlled populations of bacteria. Growing bacteria is a lot like keeping any other kind of pet. You need a source of them to start with, you need a home for them that keeps them safe (mostly from other creatures or contaminants), and you need to make sure they have the right kind of food, the right temperature, and so on.

Because cells are too small to see, it helps to have a microscope for this work, although it's not strictly necessary. Bacteria reproduce very quickly and when enough of them grow together (called a colony), they are visible to the naked eye. In order to get started, you need to get some E. coli, some agar-coated petri dishes (their food and home), and loop (a simple thin piece of metal for transporting cells from the source to the dish). You also will need to learn a little about sterile lab procedures so that you don't contaminate your cells. In the "Sources" section at the end of this article, I recommend a kit that you can buy pretty cheaply that has all the materials you need. Eventually, you'll know enough to be able to scrounge all kinds of cool materials for genetic engineering that cost little or nothing, but I'd recommend starting with the kit.

The key task is getting the transgene into the genome of the E. coli. Hosts, of course, have various methods for resisting the addition of foreign DNA. The most basic of these is the cell membrane, which acts like skin for cells. It's the job of the membrane to keep the insides in and the outsides out. However, membranes have to let in food and let out wastes, so they are permeable. In order to get the transgene inside the cell, we have to manipulate it so that it will take up the new genes. For bacteria, figuring out this problem is really the main task in creating a transgenic organism, and it's pretty easy. For higher organisms, there is more structure (the genome stays in an internal structure called the nucleus of the cell) and better defenses against foreign DNA, making the insertion of transgenes more difficult. However, inserting transgenes into higher organisms (including mammals, like mice or monkeys) is routine laboratory procedure these days.

In addition to making the E. coli take in the foreign DNA, we have to make sure that the DNA is treated as if it were the organism's own. In bacteria, this is also fairly easy. Bacteria often exchange small pieces of DNA, called plasmids, with each other. These plasmids are separate from the organism's main DNA and allow bacteria to exchange beneficial genetic material with each other, even though they don't replicate sexually. (Sex is nature's best way of exchanging genetic material between organisms.) Vector is the name that biologists use for something that can introduce foreign DNA into a cell. Plasmids are good vectors for bacterial hosts. Other vectors that work better for more complex hosts include viruses that have had transgenic payloads grafted into them, or even tiny gold beads coated with DNA that can be shot into a cell with a "gene gun."

The creation of plasmids (or other vectors) with transgenic payloads is made possible by the existence of DNA splicing enzymes. Simple laboratory techniques allow the extraction of naturally occurring plasmids from bacteria and splicing the DNA for the new gene into them. The hardest part is figuring out which combination of genes to insert into a host in order to get a desired effect. However, those techniques are beyond the scope of this introductory article. For our purposes, we can just buy plasmids with our desired genes from a scientific supply house. An E. coli plasmid with the Luciferase gene in it is called pUC18-luxR, and can be purchased from many places (see "Sources" section, below).

Once you have successfully grown some E. coli colonies and purchased your Luciferase plasmid, the process of creating glow-in-the-dark bacteria is pig-easy. You make the bacterial membrane permeable to the plasmid by treating it with a solution of calcium chloride. At this point, the cells are said to be "competent" for transformation and the plasmids can be added. Then let the cells grow at body temperature (37C) for 12 to 24 hours. Turn out the lights and look at your petri dish; you should be able to see colonies that quite clearly glow in the dark. Congratulations! You've just created your first transgenic organism! The recommended kit has detailed instructions (called a protocol in molecular biology). The protocol can also be downloaded from the Net without buying the kit.

Now if this feels too much like the script kiddy version of genetic engineering, then there are lots of other projects you might take on. You can design and construct your own plasmids, perhaps with multiple transgenes. In order to breed pure populations of transgenic bacteria, one often includes an antibiotic resistance gene in the plasmid, and then applies the antibiotic to the petri dishes. Only the bacteria that took up the plasmid will survive, and the evolutionary selective pressure will ensure that the bacteria won't lose the transgenes. In considering which genes to add, you might learn to use GenBank and LocusLink, two important Web-accessible databases of genes. Start by looking up green fluorescent protein (GFP). Or buy a GFP transgenic fish from GloFish.

Hacking the genome is the future. You can be there now....

Sources

A complete kit with everything you need to do this experiment is available from Modern Biology, Inc. for less than $75. It is part number IND-9 and you can order it on the Web. Visit `http://www.modernbio.com/ind-9.htm` to see what's in the kit and how to order it.

Modern Biology has all kinds of really cool kits that don't require fancy labs or a lot of experience to use. Check out their whole catalog at `http://www.modernbio.com/TableOContents.htm`. A different $80 kit allows you to extract DNA from any organism (including yourself), which, with some DNA splicing enzymes and some additional knowledge of how to recombine bits of DNA, you could then use for creating new plasmids. It's available from the Discovery Channel store. This kit includes an inexpensive centrifuge, which you are going to need if you want to continue your genetic engineering experimentation. You can get good scientific microscopes on eBay or maybe you have one in a basement somewhere. If you're going to work with GFP, you probably want a microscope for fluorescence work; it will have a filter set and high power illumination.

If you would like proof that many of the foods you eat contain genetically modified organisms, you might be interested in the kits available from Investigen, which uses a similar technology for easy detection of many genetically modified organisms. See `http://www.investigen.com/products.html` for the details.

If you want to look up interesting genes that you might want to add to your bacteria, try using GenBank or LocusLink from `http://ncbi.nlm.nih.gov`. Once you get good at transforming bacteria and want to start thinking about more ambitious transgenic organisms, you should take a look at the offerings from Clontech, Qiagen, and Qbiogene. Or you can just buy a GFP zebrafish from `http://www.glofish.com`.

And before you start working on your plan for creating a Luciferase transgenic puppy by doing genetic engineering on your dog, you should probably learn real molecular biology laboratory techniques by taking a class. Who knows, maybe I'll be your teacher...

Shoutouts: DMcS for taking it seriously and finding the GloFish and the Discovery kit, and to AG Monster for reminding me that although I am old now, I was a hacker once, too.

The Real Electronic Brain Implantation Enhancement (Winter, 2005-2006) *By Shawn Frederick*

I am not a medical doctor, nor does my background in science reflect much neurology. I am, however, a scientist, and currently work for two different laboratories. This article will offer information on the factual and idealistic concept of electronic implants working for or alongside the biological nervous system and brain of man. To keep the attention of my audience I will do this with as minimal biological workings (no more than high school biology) as possible. The theories are my own.

The Human Brain

Computers only rely on the laws of Boolean mathematics while the biological makeup of man's brain follows the laws of physics. There are more chemicals in the human brain that modern medicine does not understand or know of than there are those which are understood. These chemicals can be responsible for such things as anger, happiness, and even thirst; they also are responsible for invoking long- and short-term memory. The human brain is extremely complex, but what if it were broken down into a more simplistic system that resembled computer functionality?

- Human memory (database)
- Cerebellum or thymus (the browser/search engine)
- Human awareness (artificial intelligence)

The Database

There are a few different theories on how the brain's memory (database) works. For the purposes of a short article we will focus on the more popular theories. Short-term memory is described as the mind holding a thought via an electrical circuit. As long as the circuit is continued the memory can be held. If it is continuously stimulated the short-term memory may then transform to permanent memory where the human brain physically changes its shape. It is believed that the brain stores information on the cellular level. With all the different theories there are about how the brain actually works, the truth is that no one knows for sure how it really functions. Medicine has a general idea of the mind's mysterious mechanics, but still is closer to uniting quantum physics with Einstein's classic physics (this is a joke).

The Browser Offers Info to Human Awareness (AI)

Whereas science has a grasp on how the brain essentially works, we are still in the dark as far as understanding human consciousness. For example: 2+2=4. Yes, a computer can tell you this and yes, it reacts a certain way based on an answered value. For humans however it's more than just Boolean. How does one understand and manipulate the meaning of a number or creatively envision and paint a picture? This article is not asking the age-old question "what does it all mean" but merely acknowledging that in all its obviousness human awareness will play a large role in the times of brain implantation.

Broken down as simply as possible, the cells of one's brain hold information. The cerebellum is the command center and let's say it's believed to retrieve the needed information your brain cells (database) are holding. It then browses using a type of "search engine" and, with the information found, offers it up to the human consciousness (AI). Humans are still very primitive; some are running Internet Explorer and Netscape while others are using Firefox or Lynx. The truth of the matter is that from the most superior geniuses at NASA to the mentally impaired, the difference is almost none when looking at the vast picture. Kim Peek is a prime example of this.

At this moment and time it's impossible to scientifically explain human awareness, but some refer to it as the soul. It is linked to creativity and free will. Human awareness is only as good as the "database" and "browser" one has.

The analogy of quantum physics meets Einstein's classic physics was used once already in this article and seems fitting to use again talking about the "browser" of the human brain offering information up to human awareness. There are a few good theories on the medical explanation of human awareness but I recommend Francis Crick's *Astonishing Hypothesis: The Scientific Search for the Soul* if interested.

Humans Interact with the Mattered Universe

The most advanced brain-driven mechanical instruments we have are a few robots and electroencephalogram machines. I also have read that the military has VR that imprints images directly on one's retina (different subject). As cool as the brain-driven robots and EEG machines are, these technologies have little room for advancement and are really no better than a mood ring. The technology reacts to human electrical stimulation. What is really needed is to be able to think a thought or a number and have it appear on a computer screen, enhancing one's intellect by physically jacking into or wirelessly jumping onto the Internet. Unfortunately the "code" of the human mind must be cracked before we can truly see any brain implants or VR worth obtaining.

How I Believe It Will Come to Pass

How do we as humans feel the soft touch of a woman or interact with the surrounding world of matter that we live in? In order to react and comprehend the matter of the universe, we have electrical impulses and chemicals that flood our brain at any given time. But broken down it looks like this:

- Peripheral Nervous System
- Central Nervous System
- Brain

The peripheral nervous system connects the CNS and the brain. Their working together is the only way humans understand textures of the world in which we live. When programming a computer one feels the keys because a chemical is released, read by receptors, and electrical impulses passed from node to node to the spinal cord. The message is then sent and encoded just before or in the brain. I use the word encoded because the spinal cord doesn't tell the brain that the PNS is feeling a rough or coarse textured surface. From my understanding it is all sent via an electronic biochemical reaction that travels nodule to nodule on the axons. The message must be coded until the brain gets the info and can explain or "decode" what is electronically being sent. I will add to this that the electrical mode of transmitted information is actually biochemical. The electrical impulses (the jumping from node to node) are stable until reacted upon. An impulse is produced chemically from an inverse reaction of naturally charged atoms of Potassium (K) and Magnesium (Mg), which are cat ions (positively charged) with a few anions (negatively charged) Chloride (Cl) and bicarbonate (HCO^3). The electrical charge is significant to the audience of this article.

Brain + human awareness + nervous + muscular and skeletal system = action upon matter. Anything else reacted upon or observed in our universe is photonic (nothing more than light photons bouncing off matter) or sound waves. (m=Matter is only understood to the brain when it's told electronically.) Human awareness, soul, AI, consciousness, whatever you will call it is needed for understanding the processed/decoded information—that a picture on the wall is a picture and not just a bunch of bouncing photons.

The Day of Brain Implantation

If humanity does not destroy itself first there will be a day that electronic implantation will be as natural as human sexuality. But the most brilliant of hackers couldn't develop an implant with the great potentials that have been discussed. A programmed implant interacting simultaneously with the nervous system and mind would be a true feat, done by a team of doctors, research scientists, and programmers. When brain implants come to pass they will need to be implanted where the spinal cord meets the brain (foramen magnum). This is believed to be true based on knowledge that information is electronically sent and possibly interpreted in that general area.

Obviously any implant created could not be plug and play. Every individual is unique in the way his or her brain works, both biochemically and electrically. The future implant will not only have to sometimes share or piggyback off the electrical impulses that are being sent via the spinal cord. It would either have to manipulate the spinal cord or use it analogically like a USB 2 cord. The future may allow advancement to bypass the spinal cord completely, sending its electrical messages directly to the "decoder" (possibly thymus) of the brain, then on to the "browser." The implant would need to do this while three other parts of the implanted device simultaneously worked on the brain. One part would be located deep in the brain, another would sit in the center of the spinal cord, and a third would spider around the dark and light matter of the brain sensing and identifying the chemical changes happening there. The first implant would only be able to hook up to an external computer with a specially developed browser and search engine. When a person is asked a question the implant would scan the brain cells for an answer, displaying it on the screen.

Technology then would advance so that if one didn't have the information stored somewhere within the brain cells it would search an online database for the correct response. The Internet would be better protected than just SSL. And if not the Internet, then an Internet type of system where people's brains would be linked from birth in groups of hundreds for their entire lives. After all, hundreds of brains working together are better than one. In time a computer screen would be absolute. A part of the retina would be dedicated to computer info. (Soon there will be a contact lens that displays the time and date for the individual wearing it, which should do away with watches.)

Problems with Brain Implants

As most testing goes, it will start out in a laboratory on some animal, more than likely chimps. It's scary because we are a primitive species. There is no doubt that no sooner will we discover how to create such a device than someone will use it for the worst possible thing imaginable.

It will be advertised as a harmless monitored environment. But how can anyone be sure that he or she isn't being used or manipulated? Evolution is responsible for enhancing man's mind and controlling it chemically and electronically. Implants will be commonly used unfortunately. There will be no need for memory or for us to use our biochemical minds as nature intended. The human species will have taken the role of half biological half robotic while our brains evolve to mush, totally useless, and completely reliant on implants.

I hope it doesn't happen like this. But in addition, there is the prospect of genetic enhancements in mankind's evolutionary future. That is a whole different article but offers the same wonders and terrors.

Social Engineering and Pretexts (Autumn, 2007) *By Poacher*

I worked for a while as a store detective and the man that hired me gave me a piece of advice: "Son, this could be the dullest, most-depressing job you will ever have in your life. Ten hours walking around a store will make you quit in two days. But this job is what you make of it. If you get creative it can be the most fun you'll ever have."

He was right on both counts. My first two days were hell on earth. Then at the end of the second day I sat down and decided that rather than give up I would figure out a way to be good at it. Two years later when I eventually quit over a dispute over wages, I was loving every second of the job.

I took that same attitude with me when I started out working as a private detective. To some people, spending 18 hours at a stretch sitting in a car desperate to take a leak may not sound fun. But it was the challenge, the seeking for hidden knowledge. Spending a week following someone's every movement and at the end of it they don't even know you exist, yet you knew everything about them.

Sounds familiar? It's the "hacker high"—that feeling you get from acquiring knowledge that they don't want you to have and getting it without them ever knowing.

Anyway, back to the topic in hand. As a private eye I was good at the covert surveillance stuff. Sitting in cars and following people eventually became second nature. But early on I started meeting guys who never needed to do that. They could knock on a door and get the information in five minutes that I could spend a week of sitting in a car to get. In short I was jealous. This was something that I just couldn't do. I had spent my entire short career striving to stay in the shadows and the idea of actually knocking on the door and speaking to our subject freaked me out.

Then during one long job in the North I happened to be browsing through a bookshop and came across a copy of Kevin Mitnick's *The Art of Deception*. I devoured that book then read it again immediately. My respect goes to Kevin for what is an excellent book.

However, nothing changed. I still couldn't knock on doors. But the seeds had been sown.

Social engineering is a very personal skill. I believe anybody can do it. In fact I know now that anyone can because we're all doing it all the time. It's done unconsciously a lot of the time and deliberately some of the time. Every time we negotiate a lift in a friend's car or try to minimize the damage from forgetting a birthday we are using social engineering.

Realizing this changed things for me. I reasoned that I had to find methods that fitted my personality. There would be no point in my pretending to be an extroverted character if I wasn't one deep down. I would just be creating another opportunity to get caught out.

Working as a private detective in England is, I suspect, a lot different from doing the same job in many states of the U.S. We have no license, no ID, no authority, no weapons, and, most importantly, no access (legally anyway) to a lot of sources of information. For example, we have no reverse phone directory, no access to criminal records, and what information is public is often locally based and so very difficult to find. So in order to earn our dinner we have to be very creative.

One vital skill is being able to find out who is staying at an address or who has stayed there. I tried many approaches over the years until I hit upon a method that worked for me.

I analyzed my interactions with people and realized that with the right pretext, people would tell you anything. I decided to play upon two fundamental human motivators: the desire to be helpful and the fear of something unpleasant happening. If one wouldn't get them the other one would.

In conjunction with that, the pretext I used would have to be one that I was comfortable with and could be believable in.

The first thing I did was go to a business card machine in a shopping center and make up a few cards with a false name, proclaiming I was a field representative of a finance company. Then I started dressing for work. Rather than wearing what was comfortable I would wear a jacket and tie.

Now if I had to go to an address and find out if, for example, John Doe was living there and if he wasn't, find out where he now was and not alert anyone that a PI was looking for Mr. Doe, what I would do is arm myself with my business cards (later I would add a fake ID), a clipboard, or a document case with a few random printouts, and knock on the door. Then I would pick a name at random.

Resident: "Hello."
Me: "Hi, can I speak to Alfred James."
Resident: "I think you've got the wrong house."
Me: (frowning and scratching my head) "This is 221b Baker Street."
Resident: (now looking confused) "Yes it is."
Me: "OK, ah, you see I'm Harry Belmont from Axis Credit. What happens is if someone applies for a large loan, sometimes we send people out to check the address exists. So you're sure there's no one called Alfred James staying here?"
Resident: (looking alarmed) "No, I've never heard of anyone called that."
Me: "I see, I think someone's given us a false address then. Look don't worry, a few minutes of our time and we can straighten this out and I can get your address removed from our system and you can forget about this. OK, I'll need a few details...."

And that's it. From that point on, the resident will give me almost any information I could possibly want to ask for and as a bonus at the end they'll be thanking me.

So far I've found this method to work for me almost 100 percent of the time. But it's not foolproof and its suitability depends upon what information you're trying to obtain. Nevertheless for a quick cold call at a door it's a pretty good method of getting information that a resident would not otherwise give a stranger.

The golden rules of using a pretext as I see them:

1. Choose one you are comfortable with. This will make you believable. Don't pretend to be a telephone engineer if you know nothing about the business. Don't turn up dressed like a bin man while pretending to be a businessman.
2. Tailor your pretext to the information you want to obtain.
3. Utilize the social motivators like the desire to help or fear of the unknown. People will often volunteer all the information you need.
4. Be confident.

I found that with each success my confidence grew and as that happened I found I could push the limits and try for more each time. But start small. There's always another way to obtain information, but if you make someone suspicious your job will get exponentially harder.

My work kit now includes a few rudimentary props that have proved worth the space they take up in my car. A hard hat and a reflective vest are often all that you need to walk confidently onto a construction site or even into an office building. Carry a small case and some technical looking tools as well and no one will question if they see you poking around computers or telecom equipment. A modest amount of money and half an hour at a business card printing machine can equip you with a range of cards in various names to cover most scenarios.

Even my Thermos proved a useful prop. On one job I had to access a very large, very well secured private housing estate. During my surveillance of the entrance I noticed lots of gardeners' trucks arriving in the mornings to tend the grounds of the idle rich. Quickly improvising with what I had I took my shirt off and tied it round my waist, picked up my Thermos, and strolled round the grounds like I was a gardener on his break. If anyone had stopped me I had a story ready that I had missed my pickup that morning and was trying to find my boss and the work van. As it turned out, despite more CCTV than I could count and uniformed guards at every gate, I managed to stroll around the estate at will for two days.

People are easier to fool than computers and "hacking" a person can be a lot more fun. All you need is a little imagination and ability to think on your feet. Start out by spending a little time each day just observing people and their interactions. Often the very people employed to stop you getting in somewhere can be the most helpful. Think security guard. They are most often bored and underpaid and all too willing to talk to someone if offered the right pretext. Making friends with the security is more useful than a set of keys.

I hope this inspires people to go out and pay a little more attention to their interactions with others. Have fun doing it and always remember to treat everyone with respect.

Conclusion

The More Things Change... (Winter, 2007-2008)

As we move towards our 25th year of publishing, we find that so much has changed in the world we write about. Yet somehow, a surprising amount of things are almost exactly the same.

Let's look at where technology has taken us. Obviously, nothing has stood still in the hardware and software universe. In 1984, ten megabytes of storage was still more than what most people had access to. Those few who even *had* their own computers would, more often than not, wind up shuffling five and a quarter inch floppies before they would invest in an expensive piece of hardware like a hard disk. And speed was a mere fraction of a fraction of what it is today. If you could communicate at 300 baud, it was considered lightning fast to most people. Of course, there were those who were always pushing to go faster and get more. It was this incessant need for expansion and improvement that got us where we are today.

Perhaps not as dramatic in scale but certainly as wrenching in feeling has been the change to our society and the world around us. In the current day, we are security-obsessed without having gotten any better at being secure. We seem to have lost any semblance of the trust that once guided us as human beings. Instead, we live in a state of perpetual alertness, suspicion, and fear. Some would say that this is reality and that this state of mind is the only way to survive in a hostile world. We would say that it's a *sad* reality and one that needs to be analyzed and hopefully altered. Were we to have started publishing in 2008 rather than in 1984, we likely would have been quickly branded as potential terrorists before ever being able to establish a foothold in our culture that enabled us to be seen as a revealing and even necessary voice.

Today we continue to exist in no small part because we *have* existed for nearly a quarter century. It is that history which strengthens us and one we should all try and learn as much as we can from.

So what has managed to stay the same over the years? A number of things actually, some good and some bad.

For one, the spirit of inquisitiveness that drives much of what the hacker world consists of is very much alive and in relatively the same state it's been in for so long. If anything were to sum up what every single one of our articles has had in common over all these years, it's that desire to find out just a little bit more, to modify the parameters in a unique way, to be the first to figure out how to achieve a completely different result. Whether we're talking about getting around a barrier put in place to prevent you from accessing a distant phone number or a restricted computer system, or cracking the security of some bit of software so that you can modify it to perform functions never dreamed of by its inventors, or revealing some corporate secrets about how things *really* work in the world of networks and security—it's all about finding out something and sharing it with anyone interested enough to listen and learn. These are the very foundations upon which *2600* was founded and those values are as strong today as they were back in our early days. In many ways they have actually strengthened. The Internet is an interesting example of this. While its predecessor, the ARPANET of the '60s and '70s, was developed under the authority of the military, what has evolved since then is a veritable bastion of free speech and empowerment of individuals. Of course, it's not all so idealistic. Not everyone cares and there's a constant struggle with those who want the Net to be nothing more than a shopping mall and those who seek to control every aspect of it. But who can deny that literally *any* point of view can be found somewhere on today's Net? And a surprising amount of people will defend that concept regardless of their own personal opinions. Almost without fail, if someone is told that they may not put forth a certain viewpoint or spread information on a particular subject, then the community of the Net will respond and make sure the information is spread more than it ever would have been had there not been an attempt made to squash it in the first place. Nobody has yet been able to put the top back on the bottle and prevent this kind of a reaction since never before in the history of humanity has such a tool been so widely accessible. There obviously is still a long way to go and a good many battles to fight in order to keep free speech alive on the Net. But this is at least encouraging and indicative of how hacker values have easily meshed with more mainstream ones.

But something else which hasn't changed over the years is the malignment of hackers and what we stand for. The irony is that most people understand perfectly well what we're all about when presented with the facts. The mainstream media, however, never has and probably never will. It's simply not in their interests to portray us as anything but the kind of threat that will help them sell newspapers and get high ratings. Fear sells—that is the unfortunate truth. And fear of the unknown sells even better because so little evidence is needed to start the ball rolling.

In the media, as in politics, enemies are needed in order to set forth an agenda. From the beginning, hackers have fit the qualifications to be that enemy. They know too much, insist on questioning the rules, and won't stop talking and communicating with themselves and others. These types of people have always been a problem in controlled environments like dictatorships and public schools. It's not too difficult to see why they're viewed with such hostility by people who want to hold onto whatever power they happen to have. A true individual is no friend to autocrats.

If you read a newspaper or watch virtually any newscast, you won't have to wait too long for a story to appear with details on how the private records of thousands (or sometimes millions) of people have been compromised while in the care of some huge entity. We could be talking about a phone company, credit card provider, bank, university, or government. And the information that was lost might include anything from people's names, addresses, unlisted phone numbers, Social Security and/or credit card numbers, a list of purchases, health records, you name it: data that was entrusted to the company, agency, or bureaucracy for safekeeping, which has been compromised because someone did something foolish, like somehow post confidential hospital files to a public web page, or copy customer information to a laptop, which was subsequently lost or stolen. Yet in virtually every instance of such a profound gap in common sense, you will find that hackers are the ones getting blamed. It makes no difference that hackers had nothing to do with letting the information out in the first place. The media and the authorities see them as the people who will do virtually anything to get private data of individuals and make their lives miserable.

This misdirection of blame serves two purposes—as it always has. The first is to absolve those really responsible of any true blame or prosecution. The second is to create an enemy who can be blamed whenever anything goes wrong. Of course, the irony is that if hackers were the ones running and designing these systems, the sensitive data would actually be protected far better than it is now. There simply is no excuse for allowing people's private information to be copied onto insecure machines with no encryption or other safeguards. The fact that it keeps happening tells us that dealing with this isn't very high on the priority list. Perhaps if those organizations that don't have sufficient security practices were held accountable rather than being allowed to blame invisible demons, we might actually move forward in this arena. But one must ask what would be in it for them? The answer is not a whole lot.

These battles and conflicts will no doubt continue regardless of what direction our society takes us. While we have indeed been frustrated with the seeming lack of progress on so many levels, we can't help but be fascinated with where we will wind up next—both in the technological and political spectrum. The combination of the two may very well seal our future for quite a long time to come.

The one thing that will keep us going (and that has made it so worthwhile for all of these years) is the spirit of curiosity that our readers and writers continue to proudly exhibit. It's a very simple trait, and perhaps one that's an unerasable ingredient of our humanity. It will survive no matter how our technology advances, regardless of any law or decree put forth to stifle it, and in spite of misperceptions and overall cluelessness. If we keep asking questions and thinking outside the box, there will always be something good to look forward to.

Index

Symbols and Numbers

B

C

F

G

H

J

K

M

O

P

Q

R

S

T

U

V